MCSA
Windows® 10
Complete Study Guide
Exams 70-698 and Exam 70-697

William Panek

SYBEX®
A Wiley Brand

Senior Acquisitions Editor: Kenyon Brown
Development Editors: David Clark, Kathryn Duggan
Technical Editors: Rodney R. Fournier, Doug Bassett
Production Editor: Dassi Zeidel
Copy Editors: Judy Flynn, Linda Recktenwald
Editorial Manager: Mary Beth Wakefield
Production Manager: Kathleen Wisor
Executive Editor: Jim Minatel
Book Designers: Judy Fung and Bill Gibson
Proofreaders: Rebecca Rider, Kim Wimpsett
Indexer: Jack Lewis
Project Coordinator, Cover: Brent Savage
Cover Designer: Wiley
Cover Image: © Getty Images Inc./Jeremy Woodhouse

This book is dedicated to the three ladies of my life: Crystal, Alexandria, and Paige.

Acknowledgments

I would like to thank my wife and best friend, Crystal. She is always the light at the end of my tunnel. I want to thank my two daughters, Alexandria and Paige, for all of their love and support during the writing of all my books. The three of them are my support system, and I couldn't do any of this without them.

I want to thank my family, especially my brothers, Rick, Gary, and Rob. They have always been there for me. I want to thank my father, Richard, who helped me become the man I am today, and my mother, Maggie, for all of her love and support.

I would like to thank all of my friends and co-workers at StormWind Studios. I want to especially thank the team I work with on a daily basis, and that includes Tom W, Dan Y, Corey F, Ronda, Dan J, Jessica, Dave, Tiffany, Tara, Ashley, Brittany, Doug, Mike, Vince, Desiree, Ryan, Ralph, Dan G, Tyler, Jeff B, Shayne, Patrick, Noemi, Michelle, Zachary, Colin, and the man who makes it all possible, Tom Graunke. Thanks to all of you for everything that you do. I would not have been able to complete this book without all of your help and support.

I want to thank everyone on my Sybex team, especially my development editor David Clark, who helped me make this the best book possible, and Rodney R. Fournier, who is the technical editor of many of my books. It's always good to have the very best technical guy backing you up. I want to thank Dassi Zeidel, who was my production editor, and Judy Flynn and Linda Recktenwald for copyediting the book.

I want to also thank Doug Bassett, who is my technical proofreader. Special thanks to my acquisitions editor, Kenyon Brown, who was the lead for the entire book. Finally, I want to thank everyone else behind the scenes who helped make this book possible. It's truly an amazing thing to have so many people work on my books to help make them the very best. I can't thank you all enough for your hard work.

About the Author

William Panek holds the following certifications: MCP, MCP+I, MCSA, MCSA+ Security and Messaging, MCSE-NT (3.51 and 4.0), MCSE (2000, 2003, 2012/2012 R2), MCSE+Security and Messaging, MCDBA, MCT, MCTS, MCITP, CCNA, CCDA, and CHFI. Will is also a four-time and current Microsoft MVP winner.

After many successful years in the computer industry, Will decided that he could better use his talents and his personality as an instructor. He began teaching for schools such as Boston University and the University of Maryland, just to name a few. He has done consulting and training for some of the biggest government and corporate companies in the world, including the United States Secret Service, Cisco, United States Air Force, and United States Army.

In 2015, Will became a Sr. Microsoft Instructor for StormWind Studios (www .stormwindstudios.com). He currently lives in New Hampshire with his wife and two daughters. Will was also a Representative in the New Hampshire House of Representatives from 2010 to 2012. In his spare time, he likes to do blacksmithing, shooting (trap and skeet), snowmobiling, playing racquetball, and riding his Harley.

Will is also a commercially rated helicopter pilot.

Contents at a Glance

Introduction   *xxix*

Assessment Test   *xlvi*

Part I   **Exam 70-698, Installing and Configuring**
                  Windows 10   **1**

Chapter 1   Windows 10 Installation   3

Chapter 2   Installing in an Enterprise Environment   49

Chapter 3   Configuring Devices and Drivers   81

Chapter 4   Configuring Storage   119

Chapter 5   Configuring the Windows 10 Environment   175

Chapter 6   Configuring Data Security   237

Chapter 7   Windows 10 Networking   271

Chapter 8   Installing Applications   333

Chapter 9   Managing Authorization and Authentication   375

Chapter 10   Configuring Monitoring and Recovery   457

Part II   **Exam 70-697, Configuring Windows Devices**   **503**

Chapter 11   Installing Windows 10   505

Chapter 12   Automated Windows 10 Deployments   553

Chapter 13   Configuring Storage and Security   599

Chapter 14   Managing Data Access   661

Chapter 15   Managing the Windows 10 Environment   701

Chapter 16   Planning and Managing Microsoft Intune   763

Chapter 17   Configuring Applications   803

Chapter 18   Managing Identity and Authorization   845

Chapter 19   Configuring Network Connectivity   909

Chapter 20   Configuring Recovery   971

Appendixes   **997**

Appendix A   Answers to Review Questions   997

Appendix B   Windows 10 PowerShell Commands   1017

Index   *1025*

Contents

Introduction   *xxix*

Assessment Test   *xlvi*

Part I   **Exam 70-698, Installing and
                  Configuring Windows 10**   **1**

Chapter 1   **Windows 10 Installation**   **3**

                  Understanding the Basics   4
                      Windows 10 Features   8
                      Windows Feature Deprecation   10
                  Windows 10 Architecture   10
                  Preparing to Install Windows 10   11
                      Windows 10 Home   12
                      Windows 10 Professional   12
                      Windows 10 Enterprise   13
                      New Install or Upgrade?   17
                      Disk Partitioning   20
                      Language and Locale   21
                  Installing Windows 10   22
                      Performing a Clean Install of Windows 10   22
                      Performing an Upgrade to Windows 10   30
                      Troubleshooting Installation Problems   35
                      Supporting Multiple-Boot Options   37
                      Using Windows Activation   38
                  Windows Update   39
                      The Update Process   39
                      Using Windows Update   41
                      Installing Windows Service Packs   42
                      Installing Windows Store Updates   43
                  Summary   44
                  Video Resources   44
                  Exam Essentials   44
                  Review Questions   46

Chapter 2   **Installing in an Enterprise Environment**   **49**

                  Understanding Imaging   50
                      An Overview of the System Preparation Tool
                          and Disk Imaging   50
                      Overview of the Windows Assessment
                          and Deployment Kit   55

Using the Deployment Image Servicing and Management Tool	58
Understanding Hyper-V	60
What Is Virtualization?	60
Installing the Hyper-V Role	61
Configuring Virtual Machines	66
Activating Machines in the Enterprise	75
Networking Basics	76
Active Directory–Based Activation	76
Summary	77
Video Resources	78
Exam Essentials	78
Review Questions	79

Chapter 3	**Configuring Devices and Drivers**	**81**
	Configuring Hardware	82
	Understanding Device Stage	82
	Using Device Manager	84
	Installing and Updating Device Drivers	88
	Driver Signing	97
	Managing I/O Devices	98
	Configuring Removable Storage Devices	98
	Managing Printers	101
	Summary	114
	Video Resources	115
	Exam Essentials	115
	Review Questions	116

Chapter 4	**Configuring Storage**	**119**
	Understanding File Systems	120
	File System Selection	121
	File System Conversion	123
	Configuring NTFS	124
	Configuring Disk Storage	127
	Basic Storage	127
	Dynamic Storage	128
	GUID Partition Table	130
	Cloud-Based Storage	131
	Using the Disk Management Utility	135
	Using the Microsoft Management Console	136
	Understanding the Disk Management Utility	140
	Managing Storage	155
	Managing Dynamic Storage	155

Troubleshooting Disk Management   158
    Understanding Disk Management Status Codes   158
    Troubleshooting Disks That Fail to Initialize   159
Managing Data Compression   159
    Using the Compact Command-Line Utility   161
    Using Compressed (Zipped) Folders   161
Understanding RAID   162
    RAID Levels   162
    Storage Spaces   163
Using Disk-Maintenance Tools   165
    Using the Disk Optimization Utility   166
    Using the Disk Cleanup Utility   166
    Using the Check Disk Utility   168
PowerShell Disk Commands   169
Summary   171
Video Resources   171
Exam Essentials   172
Review Questions   173

Chapter   5   Configuring the Windows 10 Environment   175

Managing Windows   176
    Manipulating the Desktop Environment   177
    Configuring Personalization   186
    Using Control Panel   191
    Using the Microsoft Management Console   202
    Using the System Icon   203
    Understanding the Settings Window   206
    Using PowerShell   207
Configuring Mobility Options   209
    Configuring Offline Files and Synchronization   209
    Configuring Power Policies   211
    Configuring Windows To Go   217
Managing Windows 10 Services   219
Configuring Internet Browsers   222
    Cortana   222
    Browser Controls   223
    Pinning Sites to the Taskbar   223
    Searchable Address Bar   224
    Security and Privacy Enhancements   224
    Using the Browser's Compatibility View   225
    Using Protected Mode for IE11   226
    Using InPrivate Browsing and InPrivate Filtering   227
    Configuring Windows Internet Explorer 11 Options   228

		Summary	232
		Video Resources	232
		Exam Essentials	233
		Review Questions	235

Chapter	**6**	**Configuring Data Security**	**237**
		Configuring Network Resources	238
		Configuring HomeGroups in Windows 10	239
		Configuring Folders	244
		Understanding Dynamic Access Control	249
		Securing Access to Files and Folders	249
		Determining and Viewing Effective Permissions for NTFS	254
		Determining NTFS Permissions for Copied or Moved Files	256
		Managing Network Access	256
		Creating and Managing Shared Folders	257
		Configuring Share Permissions	258
		NTFS vs. Share Permissions	260
		Configuring OneDrive	260
		Summary	265
		Video Resources	265
		Exam Essentials	265
		Review Questions	266

Chapter	**7**	**Windows 10 Networking**	**271**
		Understanding the Basics	272
		Peer-to-Peer Networks	272
		Onsite Active Directory Networks	274
		Cloud-Based Azure Active Directory	276
		Other Microsoft Networking Terms and Roles	277
		Configuring NIC Devices	279
		Configuring a Network Adapter	280
		Troubleshooting a Network Adapter	286
		Configuring Wireless NIC Devices	287
		Configuring Wi-Fi Direct	295
		Understanding TCP/IP	297
		Benefits and Features of TCP/IP	298
		Basics of IP Addressing and Configuration	300
		Using IPv6 Addresses	304
		Configuring TCP/IP on Windows 10	315
		Testing Your IP Configuration	317
		Configuring Windows 10 on a Network	319
		Configuring Windows Firewall	324

	Understanding the Windows Firewall Basics	324
	Windows Firewall with Advanced Security	324
	Summary	329
	Video Resources	330
	Exam Essentials	330
	Review Questions	331

Chapter 8	**Installing Applications**	**333**
	Understanding Deployment Options	334
	Understanding System Center	334
	Using the Windows 10 Application Deployment Tool	336
	Deploying Software with the Windows Assessment and Deployment Kit (ADK)	337
	Understanding GPO Deployments	341
	Installing Applications	342
	Using the Upgrade Analytics Tool	343
	Windows Features	345
	Configuring Startup Options	345
	Using Hyper-V for Desktop Applications	345
	Configuring User Experience Virtualization (UE-V)	350
	Understanding AppLocker	352
	Understanding Azure	353
	Using Azure RemoteApp	357
	Understanding App-V	362
	Supporting the Windows Store	363
	Installing and Managing Software by Using Microsoft Office 365 and Windows Store Apps	364
	Sideloading Apps into Online and Offline Images	366
	Integrating Microsoft Accounts Including Personalization Settings	367
	Summary	369
	Video Resources	370
	Exam Essentials	370
	Review Questions	371

Chapter 9	**Managing Authorization and Authentication**	**375**
	Understanding User Accounts	376
	Account Types	377
	Built-In Accounts	379
	Local and Domain User Accounts	379
	Working with User Accounts	380
	Using the Local Users and Groups Utility	380
	Using the User Accounts Option in Control Panel	382

Creating New Users   382
Disabling User Accounts   388
Deleting User Accounts   389
Renaming User Accounts   391
Changing a User's Password   392
Using a Microsoft Passport, Pictures, and Biometrics   392
Using Device Guard   393
Understanding Credential Guard   396
Configuring Device Health Attestation   397
Managing User Properties   398
Managing User Group Membership   399
Setting Up User Profiles, Logon Scripts,
  and Home Folders   401
Troubleshooting User Account Authentication   406
Managing and Creating Groups   407
Using Built-In Groups   408
Creating Groups   412
Managing Group Membership   413
Deleting Groups   415
Managing Security Using GPOs and LGPOs   415
Understanding the GPO and LGPO Basics   415
Using the Group Policy Result Tool   417
Managing and Applying LGPOs   418
Configuring Local Security Policies   420
Using Account Policies   421
Using Local Policies   427
Configuring User Account Control   435
Privilege Elevation   435
Registry and File Virtualization   437
Understanding Smart Cards   437
Configuring Remote Management   439
Remote Assistance   440
Remote Desktop   444
Configuring a VPN Connection   447
Transparent Caching   449
Broadband Tethering   449
Summary   451
Video Resources   452
Exam Essentials   452
Review Questions   453

Chapter   10   Configuring Monitoring and Recovery   457

Understanding Recovery   459
Knowing the Advanced Boot Options   460

Starting in Safe Mode   461
Enabling Boot Logging   464
Using Other Startup Setting Options   465
Understanding System Restore   466
Using the System Image Recovery   467
Using the Startup Repair Tool   469
Maintaining Windows 10 with Backup and Restore   469
Creating a Backup   470
Restoring Files from a Backup   471
Recovering Files from OneDrive   472
Using the Wbadmin Command Utility   473
Using Advanced Backup Options   474
Using System Protection   476
Creating Restore Points   476
Restoring Restore Points   477
Cleaning Up Old Restore Points   478
Using the Recycle Bin   478
Monitoring Windows   479
Introducing Performance Monitor   479
Using Other Performance-Monitoring Tools   488
Summary   498
Video Resources   498
Exam Essentials   498
Review Questions   500

Part II   **Exam 70-697, Configuring Windows**
                   Devices   **503**

Chapter 11   **Installing Windows 10**   **505**

Introducing Windows 10   506
Windows 10 Features   510
Windows Feature Deprecation   512
Windows 10 Architecture   512
Preparing to Install Windows 10   513
Windows 10 Home   514
Windows 10 Professional   514
Windows 10 Enterprise   515
New Install or Upgrade?   519
Disk Partitioning   523
Language and Locale   524
Installing Windows 10   524
Performing a Clean Install of Windows 10   524
Performing an Upgrade to Windows 10   532

Troubleshooting Installation Problems 537
Migrating Files and Settings 538
Supporting Multiple-Boot Options 542
Using Windows Activation 544
Using Windows Update 544
Using Command-Line Options 546
Installing Windows Service Packs 547
Summary 547
Video Resources 548
Exam Essentials 548
Review Questions 549

Chapter 12   **Automated Windows 10 Deployments**   **553**

Understanding Automated Deployment Options 554
An Overview of the Microsoft Deployment Toolkit 2013 555
An Overview of Unattended Installation 561
An Overview of Windows Deployment Services 563
An Overview of the System Preparation
Tool and Disk Imaging 565
Overview of the Windows Assessment and
Deployment Kit 569
Windows Imaging and Configuration Designer 570
Summary of Windows 10 Deployment Options 571
Deploying Unattended Installations 572
Using the System Preparation Tool to Prepare an
Installation for Imaging 573
Using Windows Imaging and Configuration Designer
(Windows ICD) to Create a Disk Image 575
Installing from a Disk Image 577
Using the Deployment Image Servicing and
Management Tool 578
Using Windows System Image Manager to Create
Answer Files 579
Understanding Hyper-V 580
What Is Virtualization? 581
Installing the Hyper-V Role 582
Configuring Virtual Machines 588
Summary 593
Video Resources 594
Exam Essentials 594
Review Questions 595

Chapter	**13**	**Configuring Storage and Security**	**599**
		Understanding File Systems	600
		File System Selection	601
		File System Conversion	603
		Configuring NTFS	604
		Configuring Disk Storage	607
		Basic Storage	607
		Dynamic Storage	608
		GUID Partition Table	610
		Cloud-Based Storage	611
		Using the Disk Management Utility	615
		Using the Microsoft Management Console	616
		Understanding the Disk Management Utility	620
		Managing Storage	635
		Managing Dynamic Storage	635
		Troubleshooting Disk Management	637
		Understanding Disk Management Status Codes	638
		Troubleshooting Disks That Fail to Initialize	639
		Managing Data Compression	639
		Using the Compact Command-Line Utility	641
		Using Compressed (Zipped) Folders	642
		Understanding Distributed File System	642
		Advantages of DFS	642
		Types of DFS	643
		Managing Data Encryption with EFS	643
		Encrypting and Decrypting Folders and Files	644
		Managing EFS File Sharing	645
		Recovering Encrypted Files	646
		Understanding RAID	649
		RAID Levels	649
		Storage Spaces	650
		Using Disk-Maintenance Tools	652
		Using the Disk Optimization Utility	653
		Using the Disk Cleanup Utility	654
		Using the Check Disk Utility	655
		Summary	656
		Video Resources	656
		Exam Essentials	656
		Review Questions	658
Chapter	**14**	**Managing Data Access**	**661**
		Managing File and Folder Security	662
		Folder Options	663

Understanding Dynamic Access Control	667
Securing Access to Files and Folders	668
Determining and Viewing Effective Permissions for NTFS	672
Determining NTFS Permissions for Copied or Moved Files	674
Managing Network Access	675
Creating and Managing Shared Folders	675
Configuring Share Permissions	676
Configuring OneDrive	678
Joining and Sharing HomeGroups in Windows 10	682
Understanding Hardware Security	687
Using BitLocker Drive Encryption	687
Features of BitLocker	689
Windows 7 and 2008 R2 vs. Windows 10 and 2012 R2	691
Using the BitLocker Administration and Monitoring Utility	693
Understanding Smart Cards	694
Summary	695
Video Resources	695
Exam Essentials	695
Review Questions	697

Chapter 15	**Managing the Windows 10 Environment**	**701**
	Configuring the Windows 10 Operating System	702
	Configuring the Desktop Environment	703
	Configuring Personalization	711
	Using Control Panel	717
	Understanding the System Icon	727
	Understanding the Settings Window	730
	Understanding Mobility Options	732
	Configuring Offline Files and Synchronization	732
	Configuring Power Policies	734
	Configuring Windows To Go	740
	Configuring Wi-Fi Direct	742
	Using the Registry Editor	743
	Configuring Remote Connections	744
	Remote Assistance	745
	Remote Desktop	749
	Configuring a VPN Connection	752
	Transparent Caching	754
	Broadband Tethering	754
	Managing Windows 10 Services	756
	Summary	758
	Video Resources	759
	Exam Essentials	759
	Review Questions	760

Chapter   16   Planning and Managing Microsoft Intune   763

Managing Devices with Microsoft Intune   764
  Understanding Microsoft Intune Benefits   766
  Configuring Intune Subscriptions   767
  Provisioning User Accounts   769
Supporting Applications   785
  Deploying Applications Using Intune   785
  Supporting Broadband Connectivity   789
  Understanding Data Synchronization   790
Understanding Updates   792
  Deploying Software Updates Using Intune   792
  Using the Intune Reports   796
Summary   798
Video Resources   799
Exam Essentials   799
Review Questions   800

Chapter   17   Configuring Applications   803

Supporting Desktop Applications   804
  Using the Application Compatibility Toolkit (ACT)   804
  Using Hyper-V for Desktop Applications   806
  Configuring User Experience Virtualization (UE-V)   811
  Understanding AppLocker   813
Understanding Azure   814
  Using Azure RemoteApp   818
  Understanding App-V   824
Supporting the Windows Store   825
  Installing and Managing Software by Using
    Microsoft Office 365 and Windows Store Apps   825
  Sideloading Apps into Online and Offline Images   826
  Integrating Microsoft Accounts Including
    Personalization Settings   827
Understanding Web Browsers   830
  Browser Controls   830
  Working with Web Slices   831
  Using the Browser Compatibility View   832
  Using Protected Mode for IE11   833
  Using InPrivate Browsing and InPrivate Filtering   833
  Configuring Windows Internet Explorer 11 Options   834
Summary   839
Video Resources   839
Exam Essentials   840
Review Questions   841

Chapter   18   Managing Identity and Authorization   845

Overview of Windows 10 User Accounts   846
   Account Types   847
   Built-In Accounts   847
   Local and Domain User Accounts   849
Working with User Accounts   850
   Using the Local Users and Groups Utility   850
   Using the User Accounts Option in Control Panel   852
   Creating New Users   853
   Disabling User Accounts   858
   Deleting User Accounts   859
   Renaming User Accounts   861
   Changing a User's Password   862
   Using a Microsoft Passport, Pictures, and Biometrics   863
Managing User Properties   863
   Managing User Group Membership   864
   Setting Up User Profiles, Logon Scripts,
      and Home Folders   866
Troubleshooting User Account Authentication   871
Managing and Creating Groups   872
   Using Built-In Groups   873
   Creating Groups   877
   Managing Group Membership   878
   Deleting Groups   880
Managing Security Using GPOs and LGPOs   880
   Understanding the GPO and LGPO Basics   880
   Using the Group Policy Result Tool   882
   Managing and Applying LGPOs   883
   Configuring Local Security Policies   885
   Using Account Policies   886
   Using Local Policies   892
Configuring User Account Control   899
   Privilege Elevation   900
   Registry and File Virtualization   902
Understanding Smart Cards   902
Summary   904
Video Resources   905
Exam Essentials   905
Review Questions   906

Chapter   19   Configuring Network Connectivity   909

Understanding Networking   910
   Windows Peer-to-Peer Network   910
   Windows Server 2012 R2 Active Directory Network   912

Cloud-Based Azure Active Directory 914
Other Microsoft Networking Terms and Roles 915
Configuring Windows 10 NIC Devices 918
Configuring a Network Adapter 918
Troubleshooting a Network Adapter 925
Configuring Wireless NIC Devices 925
Understanding TCP/IP 935
Benefits and Features of TCP/IP 935
Basics of IP Addressing and Configuration 937
Using IPv6 Addresses 941
Configuring TCP/IP on Windows 10 952
Testing Your IP Configuration 954
Configuring Windows 10 on a Network 956
Configuring Windows Firewall 961
Summary 966
Video Resources 967
Exam Essentials 967
Review Questions 968

Chapter   20   **Configuring Recovery** **971**

Safeguarding and Recovery Basics 972
Using Advanced Boot Options 973
Starting in Safe Mode 974
Enabling Boot Logging 977
Using Other Startup Setting Options 978
Understanding System Restore 979
Using the System Image Recovery 981
Using the Startup Repair Tool 982
Maintaining Windows 10 with Backup and Restore 982
Creating a Backup 982
Restoring Files from a Backup 985
Recovering Files from OneDrive 985
Using the Wbadmin Command Utility 986
Using Advanced Backup Options 987
Using System Protection 989
Creating Restore Points 990
Restoring Restore Points 990
Cleaning Up Old Restore Points 991
Using the Recycle Bin 991
Summary 992
Video Resources 993
Exam Essentials 993
Review Questions 994

Appendixes   **997**

Appendix   A   Answers to Review Questions   **997**

Chapter 1: Windows 10 Installation   998
Chapter 2: Installing in an Enterprise Environment   999
Chapter 3: Configuring Devices and Drivers   999
Chapter 4: Configuring Storage   1000
Chapter 5: Configuring the Windows 10 Environment   1001
Chapter 6: Configuring Data Security   1002
Chapter 7: Windows 10 Networking   1003
Chapter 8: Installing Applications   1004
Chapter 9: Managing Authorization and Authentication   1004
Chapter 10: Configuring Monitoring and Recovery   1005
Chapter 11: Installing Windows 10   1006
Chapter 12: Automated Windows 10 Deployments   1007
Chapter 13: Configuring Storage and Security   1008
Chapter 14: Managing Data Access   1009
Chapter 15: Managing the Windows 10 Environment   1010
Chapter 16: Planning and Managing Microsoft Intune   1011
Chapter 17: Configuring Applications   1012
Chapter 18: Managing Identity and Authorization   1013
Chapter 19: Configuring Network Connectivity   1014
Chapter 20: Configuring Recovery   1015

Appendix   B   Windows 10 PowerShell Commands   **1017**

Index   *1025*

Table of Exercises

Exercise	**1.1**	Performing a Clean Install of Windows 10	23
Exercise	**1.2**	Upgrading Windows 8.1 to Windows 10	31
Exercise	**1.3**	Configuring Locales	34
Exercise	**1.4**	Troubleshooting Failed Installations with Setup Logs	36
Exercise	**2.1**	Prepare a System for Imaging by Using the System Preparation Tool	54
Exercise	**2.2**	Installing Windows 10 from a Disk Image	58
Exercise	**2.3**	Installing Hyper-V in Windows Server 2012 R2	61
Exercise	**2.4**	Installing Hyper-V on Windows 10	62
Exercise	**2.5**	Creating a New Virtual Machine	67
Exercise	**2.6**	Installing Hyper-V Integration Components	68
Exercise	**2.7**	Creating a Checkpoint of a Virtual Machine	69
Exercise	**2.8**	Applying a Checkpoint	70
Exercise	**3.1**	Opening Devices And Printers to View Device Stage–Supported Devices	84
Exercise	**3.2**	Viewing Device Manager	85
Exercise	**3.3**	Configuring Network Adapter Advanced Properties	87
Exercise	**3.4**	Viewing Driver Details	90
Exercise	**3.5**	Updating a Driver	91
Exercise	**3.6**	Rolling Back a Driver	91
Exercise	**3.7**	Disabling and Enabling a Device in Device Manager	92
Exercise	**3.8**	Uninstalling and Reinstalling a Device Driver	93
Exercise	**3.9**	Verifying Signed Drivers	98
Exercise	**3.10**	Configuring an Input/Output Device	99
Exercise	**3.11**	Installing a Printer	104
Exercise	**3.12**	Installing a Shared Network Print Device	105
Exercise	**3.13**	Managing Documents in the Local Queue	110
Exercise	**3.14**	Removing a Printer from Devices And Printers	112
Exercise	**3.15**	Using the Print Management Tools	113
Exercise	**4.1**	Converting a FAT32 Partition to NTFS	124
Exercise	**4.2**	Configuring Disk Quotas	127
Exercise	**4.3**	Configuring OneDrive	133
Exercise	**4.4**	Adding an MMC Snap-In	138

Exercise 4.5   Creating a New Volume 150

Exercise 4.6   Converting a Basic Disk to a GPT Disk 152

Exercise 4.7   Converting a Basic Disk to a Dynamic Disk 153

Exercise 4.8   Editing a Drive Letter 154

Exercise 4.9   Deleting a Partition 155

Exercise 4.10   Creating an Extended Volume 156

Exercise 4.11   Compressing and Uncompressing Folders 160

Exercise 4.12   Running the Disk Cleanup Utility 167

Exercise 4.13   Using the Check Disk Utility 168

Exercise 5.1   Configuring Windows 10 Desktop Options 190

Exercise 5.2   Installing New Features 198

Exercise 5.3   Changing the Computer Name 205

Exercise 5.4   Changing the System's Virtual Memory 205

Exercise 5.5   Configuring a Power Plan 214

Exercise 5.6   Configuring the Power Button to Allow the System to Go into the
                     Hibernate Mode 215

Exercise 5.7   Configuring Services 221

Exercise 6.1   Managing NTFS Permissions 252

Exercise 6.2   Logging into OneDrive 262

Exercise 7.1   Viewing the Network Connection Details 289

Exercise 7.2   Viewing Wireless Network Connection Properties 291

Exercise 7.3   Accessing the Windows 10 Wireless Properties 292

Exercise 7.4   Configuring a Static TCP/IP Address 315

Exercise 7.5   Using DHCP 316

Exercise 7.6   Connecting a Windows 10 Machine to the Domain 320

Exercise 7.7   Adding Windows 10 to the Domain via Active Directory 321

Exercise 7.8   Creating a New Inbound Rule 328

Exercise 8.1   Installing Hyper-V 349

Exercise 8.2   Creating a Collection 357

Exercise 8.3   Sharing the Collection 359

Exercise 8.4   Setting the Microsoft Account 367

Exercise 9.1   Adding the Local Users and Groups Snap-in 381

Exercise 9.2   Accessing Local Users and Groups via the Computer
                     Management Utility 382

Exercise 9.3   Creating New Users via the MMC 387

Exercise	**9.4**	Disabling User Accounts	389
Exercise	**9.5**	Deleting a User Account	390
Exercise	**9.6**	Renaming a User Account	391
Exercise	**9.7**	Changing a User's Password	392
Exercise	**9.8**	Adding a User to an Existing Group	400
Exercise	**9.9**	Setting Up User Profiles	402
Exercise	**9.10**	Assigning Home Folders	405
Exercise	**9.11**	Creating Local Groups	413
Exercise	**9.12**	Adding Accounts to Groups	414
Exercise	**9.13**	Adding the Local Computer Policy Snap-in	419
Exercise	**9.14**	Accessing an LGPO	420
Exercise	**9.15**	Configuring Password Policy	424
Exercise	**9.16**	Configuring Account-Lockout Policies	426
Exercise	**9.17**	Configuring Audit Policies	430
Exercise	**9.18**	Applying a User-Rights Policy	434
Exercise	**9.19**	Seeing How UAC Affects Accounts	436
Exercise	**9.20**	Enabling Remote Desktop	447
Exercise	**9.21**	Setting Up a VPN Connection	448
Exercise	**10.1**	Booting Your Computer to Safe Mode	462
Exercise	**10.2**	Using Boot Logging	464
Exercise	**10.3**	Backing Up Files	471
Exercise	**10.4**	Restoring Files	472
Exercise	**10.5**	Configuring OneDrive	473
Exercise	**10.6**	Creating a System Image	474
Exercise	**10.7**	Creating a Restore Point	477
Exercise	**10.8**	Restoring a Restore Point	477
Exercise	**10.9**	Using the Recycle Bin	479
Exercise	**11.1**	Performing a Clean Install of Windows 10	526
Exercise	**11.2**	Upgrading Windows 8.1 to Windows 10	533
Exercise	**11.3**	Troubleshooting Failed Installations with Setup Logs	538
Exercise	**12.1**	Downloading and Installing MDT 2013	557
Exercise	**12.2**	Configuring MDT 2013	559
Exercise	**12.3**	Preparing a System for Imaging by Using the System Preparation Tool	575
Exercise	**12.4**	Installing Windows 10 from a Disk Image	578

Exercise   **12.5**   Installing Hyper-V in Windows Server 2012 R2.....................582

Exercise   **12.6**   Installing Hyper-V on Windows 10 583

Exercise   **12.7**   Creating a Differencing Hard Disk 587

Exercise   **12.8**   Creating a New Virtual Machine................................588

Exercise   **12.9**   Installing Hyper-V Integration Components 590

Exercise   **12.10**   Creating a Checkpoint of a Virtual Machine 591

Exercise   **12.11**   Applying a Checkpoint..592

Exercise   **13.1**   Converting a FAT32 Partition to NTFS 604

Exercise   **13.2**   Configuring Disk Quotas 607

Exercise   **13.3**   Configuring OneDrive 613

Exercise   **13.4**   Adding an MMC Snap-In 618

Exercise   **13.5**   Creating a New Volume 629

Exercise   **13.6**   Converting a Basic Disk to a GPT Disk.........................632

Exercise   **13.7**   Converting a Basic Disk to a Dynamic Disk.....................633

Exercise   **13.8**   Editing a Drive Letter 634

Exercise   **13.9**   Deleting a Partition..634

Exercise   **13.10**   Creating an Extended Volume..................................636

Exercise   **13.11**   Compressing and Uncompressing Folders........................640

Exercise   **13.12**   Encrypting a Folder 644

Exercise   **13.13**   Implem+enting EFS File Sharing...............................645

Exercise   **13.14**   Using the Local Security Policy..............................646

Exercise   **13.15**   Using the Cipher Utility 649

Exercise   **13.16**   Running the Disk Cleanup Utility 654

Exercise   **13.17**   Using the Check Disk Utility 655

Exercise   **14.1**   Managing NTFS Permissions 671

Exercise   **14.2**   Logging into OneDrive..679

Exercise   **14.3**   Using BitLocker in Windows 10................................692

Exercise   **15.1**   Configuring Windows 10 Desktop Options 716

Exercise   **15.2**   Installing Features 724

Exercise   **15.3**   Changing the Computer Name 729

Exercise   **15.4**   Changing the System's Virtual Memory 729

Exercise   **15.5**   Configuring a Power Plan 737

Exercise   **15.6**   Configuring the Power Button to the Switch User Option..........738

Exercise   **15.7**   Enabling Remote Desktop 752

Exercise   **15.8**   Setting Up a VPN Connection 753

Exercise **15.9** Configuring Services 757

Exercise **16.1** Setting Up a Microsoft Intune Account 768

Exercise **16.2** Adding Users into Microsoft Intune 772

Exercise **16.3** Creating a Device Group 774

Exercise **16.4** Creating a Security User Group 776

Exercise **16.5** Creating an Intune Policy 777

Exercise **16.6** Enrolling a Device in Intune 780

Exercise **17.1** Installing Hyper-V 810

Exercise **17.2** Creating a Collection 819

Exercise **17.3** Sharing the Collection 820

Exercise **17.4** Setting the Microsoft Account 828

Exercise **18.1** Adding the Local Users and Groups Snap-in 851

Exercise **18.2** Accessing Local Users and Groups via the Computer
Management Utility 852

Exercise **18.3** Creating New Users via the MMC. 857

Exercise **18.4** Disabling User Accounts 858

Exercise **18.5** Deleting a User Account 861

Exercise **18.6** Renaming a User Account 861

Exercise **18.7** Changing a User's Password 862

Exercise **18.8** Adding a User to an Existing Group 865

Exercise **18.9** Setting Up User Profiles 867

Exercise **18.10** Assigning Home Folders 870

Exercise **18.11** Creating Local Groups 878

Exercise **18.12** Adding Accounts to Groups 879

Exercise **18.13** Adding the Local Computer Policy Snap-In. 884

Exercise **18.14** Accessing an LGPO. 885

Exercise **18.15** Configuring Password Policy 889

Exercise **18.16** Configuring Account-Lockout Policies. 891

Exercise **18.17** Configuring Audit Policies. 894

Exercise **18.18** Applying a User-Rights Policy. 899

Exercise **18.19** Seeing How UAC Affects Accounts 901

Exercise **19.1** Viewing the Network Connection Details 928

Exercise **19.2** Viewing Wireless Network Connection Properties 929

Exercise **19.3** Accessing the Windows 10 Wireless Properties. 931

Exercise **19.4** Configuring a Static TCP/IP Address 952

Exercise   **19.5**   Using DHCP 953

Exercise   **19.6**   Connecting a Windows 10 Machine to the Domain 957

Exercise   **19.7**   Adding Windows 10 to the Domain via Active Directory. 958

Exercise   **19.8**   Creating a New Inbound Rule 965

Exercise   **20.1**   Booting Your Computer to Safe Mode 976

Exercise   **20.2**   Using Boot Logging 978

Exercise   **20.3**   Backing Up Files 984

Exercise   **20.4**   Restoring Files 985

Exercise   **20.5**   Configuring OneDrive 986

Exercise   **20.6**   Creating a System Image 988

Exercise   **20.7**   Creating a Restore Point 990

Exercise   **20.8**   Restoring a Restore Point 991

Exercise   **20.9**   Using the Recycle Bin. 992

Introduction

This book was written from more than 25 years of IT experience. I have taken that experience and translated it into a Windows 10 book that will help you not only prepare for the MCSA: Windows 10 Solutions Associate exams but also to develop a clear understanding of how to install and configure Windows 10 while avoiding all the possible configuration pitfalls.

Many Microsoft books just explain the Windows operating system, but with *MCSA Windows 10 Complete Study Guide: Exam 70-698 and Exam 70-697*, I go a step further, providing many in-depth, step-by-step procedures to support my explanations of how the operating system performs at its best.

Microsoft Windows 10 is the newest version of Microsoft's client operating system software. Microsoft has taken the best of Windows 7 and Windows 8 and combined them into the latest creation, Windows 10.

Windows 10 eliminates many of the problems that plagued the previous versions of Windows clients, and it includes a much faster boot time and shutdown. It is also easier to install and configure, and it barely stops to ask the user any questions during installation. In this book, I will show you what features are installed during the automated installation and where you can make changes if you need to be more in charge of your operating system and its features.

This book takes you through all the ins and outs of Windows 10, including installation, configuration, online Microsoft subscriptions, auditing, backups, and so much more.

Windows 10 has improved on Microsoft's desktop environment, made networking easier, enhanced search ability, improved performance—and that's only scratching the surface.

When all is said and done, this is a technical book for IT professionals who want to take Windows 10 to the next step and get certified. With this book, you will not only learn Windows 10 and hopefully pass the exams, you will also become a Windows 10 expert.

The Microsoft Certification Program

Since the inception of its certification program, Microsoft has certified more than two million people. As the computer network industry continues to increase in both size and complexity, this number is sure to grow—and the need for proven ability will also increase. Certifications can help companies verify the skills of prospective employees and contractors.

The Microsoft certification tracks for Windows 10 include the following certifications:

MCSA: Windows 10   The MCSA is now the highest-level certification you can achieve with Microsoft in relation to Windows 10. It requires passing Exam 70-698 (first) and Exam 70-697 (second). This book assists in your preparation for both exams.

Microsoft Certified Technology Associate (MTA)   This is Microsoft's newest certification program. This certification targets those new to the IT field and tests candidates on the core competencies necessary to become an IT professional.

Microsoft Certified Technology Specialist (MCTS)   The MCTS certification program targets specific technologies instead of specific job roles. You must take and pass one to three exams.

MCSE: Server Infrastructure or MCSE: Desktop Infrastructure   The MCSE certifications, in relation to Windows Server 2012 R2, require that you become a Windows Server MCSA first and then pass two additional exams. The additional exams will vary depending on which of the two MCSE tracks you choose. For more information, visit Microsoft's website at www.microsoft.com/learning.

How Do You Become Certified on Windows 10?

Attaining Microsoft certification has always been a challenge. In the past, students have been able to acquire detailed exam information—even most of the exam questions—from online "brain dumps" and third-party "cram" books or software products. For the new generation of exams, this is simply not the case.

Microsoft has taken strong steps to protect the security and integrity of its new certification tracks. Now prospective candidates must complete a course of study that develops detailed knowledge about a wide range of topics. It supplies them with the true skills needed, derived from working with the technology being tested.

The new generations of Microsoft certification programs are heavily weighted toward hands-on skills and experience. It is recommended that candidates have troubleshooting skills acquired through hands-on experience and working knowledge.

Fortunately, if you are willing to dedicate the time and effort to learn Windows 10, you can prepare yourself well for the exam by using the proper tools. By working through this book, you can successfully meet the requirements to pass the Windows 10 exams.

MCSA Exam Requirements

Candidates for MCSA certification on Windows 10 must pass two Windows 10 MCSA tests:

- 70-698: Installing and Configuring Windows 10
- 70-697: Configuring Windows Devices

 Microsoft released the two required exams out of order, which is the reason they're listed with Exam 70-698 first and Exam 70-697 second. Ideally, you should take 70-698 before you take 70-697.

Microsoft provides exam objectives to give you a general overview of possible areas of coverage on the Microsoft exams. Keep in mind, however, that exam objectives are subject to change at any time without prior notice and at Microsoft's sole discretion. Please visit the Microsoft Learning website (www.microsoft.com/learning) for the most current listing of exam objectives. The published objectives and how they map to this book are listed later in this introduction.

For a more detailed description of the Microsoft certification programs, including a list of all the exams, visit the Microsoft Learning website at www.microsoft.com/learning.

Types of Exam Questions

In an effort to both refine the testing process and protect the quality of its certifications, Microsoft has focused its latest certification exams on real experience and hands-on proficiency. There is a greater emphasis on your past working environments and responsibilities and less emphasis on how well you can memorize. In fact, Microsoft says that certification candidates should have hands-on experience before attempting to pass any certification exams.

 Microsoft will accomplish its goal of protecting the exams' integrity by regularly adding and removing exam questions, limiting the number of questions that any individual sees in a beta exam, limiting the number of questions delivered to an individual by using adaptive testing, and adding new exam elements.

Exam questions may be in a variety of formats: Depending on which exam you take, you'll see multiple-choice questions as well as select-and-place and prioritize-a-list questions. Simulations and case study–based formats are included as well. Let's take a look at the types of exam questions, so you'll be prepared for all of the possibilities.

Multiple-Choice Questions

Multiple-choice questions come in two main forms. One is a straightforward question followed by several possible answers, of which one or more is correct. The other type of multiple-choice question is more complex and based on a specific scenario. The scenario may focus on several areas or objectives.

Select-and-Place Questions

Select-and-place exam questions involve graphical elements that you must manipulate to successfully answer the question. For example, you might see a diagram of a computer network. A typical diagram will show computers and other components next to boxes that contain the text "Place here." The labels for the boxes represent various computer roles on a network, such as a print server and a file server. Based on information given for each computer, you are asked to select each label and place it in the correct box. You need to place *all* of the labels correctly. No credit is given for the question if you correctly label only some of the boxes.

In another select-and-place problem, you might be asked to put a series of steps in order by dragging items from boxes on the left to boxes on the right and placing them in the correct order. One other type requires that you drag an item from the left and place it under an item in a column on the right.

NOTE For more information on the various exam question types, go to www.microsoft.com/learning/mcpexams/policies/innovations.asp.

Simulations

Simulations are the kinds of questions that most closely represent actual situations and test the skills you use while working with Microsoft software interfaces. These exam questions include a mock interface on which you are asked to perform certain actions according to a given scenario. The simulated interfaces look nearly identical to what you see in the actual product.

Because of the number of possible errors that can be made on simulations, be sure to consider the following recommendations from Microsoft:

- Do not change any simulation settings that don't pertain to the solution directly.
- When related information has not been provided, assume that the default settings are used.
- Make sure that your entries are spelled correctly.
- Close all the simulation application windows after completing the set of tasks in the simulation.

The best way to prepare for simulation questions is to spend time working with the graphical interface of the product on which you will be tested.

Case Study–Based Questions

Case study–based questions first appeared in the MCSD program. These questions present a scenario with a range of requirements. Based on the information provided, you answer a series of multiple-choice and select-and-place questions. The interface for case study–based questions has a number of tabs, each of which contains information about the scenario. At present, this type of question appears only in most of the Design exams.

Tips for Taking the Windows 10 Exams

Here are some general tips for achieving success on your certification exam:

- Arrive early at the exam center so that you can relax and review your study materials. During this final review, you can look over tables and lists of exam-related information.
- Read the questions carefully. Do not be tempted to jump to an early conclusion. Make sure that you know *exactly* what the question is asking.
- Answer all questions. If you are unsure about a question, mark it for review and come back to it at a later time.

- On simulations, do not change settings that are not directly related to the question. Also, assume default settings if the question does not specify or imply which settings are used.

- For questions that you're not sure about, use a process of elimination to get rid of the obviously incorrect answers first. This improves your odds of selecting the correct answer when you need to make an educated guess.

Exam Registration

At the time this book was released, Microsoft exams are given using more than 1,000 Authorized VUE Testing Centers around the world. For the location of a testing center near you, go to VUE's website at www.vue.com. If you are outside of the United States and Canada, contact your local VUE registration center.

Find out the number of the exam you want to take and then register with the VUE registration center nearest to you. At this point, you will be asked for advance payment for the exam. The exams are $165 each, and you must take them within one year of payment. You can schedule exams up to six weeks in advance or as late as one working day prior to the date of the exam. You can cancel or reschedule your exam if you contact the center at least two working days prior to the exam. Same-day registration is available in some locations, subject to space availability. Where same-day registration is available, you must register a minimum of two hours before test time.

When you schedule the exam, you will be provided with instructions regarding appointment and cancellation procedures, ID requirements, and information about the testing center location. In addition, you will receive a registration and payment confirmation letter from Prometric.

Microsoft requires certification candidates to accept the terms of a nondisclosure agreement before taking certification exams.

Who Should Read This Book?

This book is intended for individuals who want to earn their MCSA: Windows 10 certification.

Not only will this book help anyone who is looking to pass the Microsoft exams, it will also help anyone who wants to learn the real ins and outs of the Windows 10 operating system.

What's Inside?

Here is a glance at what's in each chapter:

Part I: Exam 70-698, Installing and Configuring Windows 10 In Part I, I cover the Exam 70-698 objectives.

Chapter 1: Windows 10 Installation In the first chapter, I explain the requirements and steps to install and configure Windows 10. I will also show you the different versions of Windows 10.

Chapter 2: Installing in an Enterprise Environment   This chapter shows you how to configure automated installation of Windows 10. I will talk about using the Windows Imaging and Configuration Designer (ICD) too, using Active Directory–based activation and implementing volume activation using a Key Management Service (KMS). I will also explain Hyper-V and how imaging works. I will also show you how to configure mobility options.

Chapter 3: Configuring Devices and Drivers   In this chapter, I will talk about installing, updating, disabling, and rolling back drivers. I will also show you how to resolve driver issues and how to configure driver settings. I will talk about using signed and unsigned drivers and also how to manage driver packages.

Chapter 4: Configuring Storage   I show you how to configure disks, volumes, and file system options using Disk Management and Windows PowerShell. I will also discuss how to configure removable devices and how to create and configure storage spaces. I will finally show you how to troubleshoot storage and removable devices issues.

Chapter 5: Configuring the Windows 10 Environment   This chapter takes you through the different ways to configure the Windows 10 environment, including remote connections, mobile computing, and power options.

Chapter 6: Configuring Data Security   You will see how to manage and configure file and printer sharing and how to configure a HomeGroup connection. I will also teach you how to configure folder shares, public folders, and OneDrive. Finally, we will look at configuring file and folder permissions.

Chapter 7: Windows 10 Networking   This chapter will show you how to implement and configure Windows networking, including Workgroups and Domains. I will also talk about HomeGroups and how to configure TCP/IP.

Chapter 8: Installing Applications   This chapter shows you how to configure desktop applications, startup options, and Windows features. I will also show you how to configure the Windows Store and how to implement Windows Store applications.

Chapter 9: Managing Authorization and Authentication   This chapter will show you how to configure authentication methods, including Microsoft Passport, picture passwords, and biometrics. I will show you how to configure Windows Hello, Device Guard, Credential Guard, Device Health Attestation, and UAC behavior.

Chapter 10: Configuring Monitoring and Recovery   This chapter will explain to you how to implement and configure Windows backups and recovery points. I will show you how to use cloud-based backups and how to recover the Windows 10 system using advanced boot options.

Part II: Exam 70-697, Configuring Windows Devices   In Part II, I cover Exam 70-697 objectives.

Chapter 11: Installing Windows 10   In the first chapter, I explain the requirements and steps to install and configure Windows 10. I also show you the different versions of Windows 10.

Chapter 12: Automated Windows 10 Deployments   This chapter shows you how to configure automated installation of Windows 10. I also explain Hyper-V and how imaging works. I also show you how to configure mobility options.

Chapter 13: Configuring Storage and Security   I take you through the advantages and benefits of using NTFS over FAT32. I also show you how to configure and install hard drives and volumes.

Chapter 14: Managing Data Access   I show you how to configure shares and NTFS security. I also take you through the advantages of using BitLocker and BitLocker To Go.

Chapter 15: Managing the Windows 10 Environment   This chapter takes you through the different ways to configure the Windows 10 environment including remote connections, mobile computing, and power options.

Chapter 16: Planning and Managing Microsoft Intune   You will see how to manage and configure Microsoft Intune. I show you how to enroll devices into Intune and how to manage software using Intune.

Chapter 17: Configuring Applications   I show you how to manage and configure Windows applications including using virtual applications. I also demonstrate how to configure cloud-based applications.

Chapter 18: Managing Identity and Authorization   This chapter shows you how to configure users and groups. I teach you the different user and group types and how to create and manage those objects.

Chapter 19: Configuring Network Connectivity   This chapter shows you how to implement and configure Windows networking including workgroups and domains. I also talk about HomeGroups and how to configure TCP/IP.

Chapter 20: Configuring Recovery   This chapter explains how to implement and configure Windows backups and recovery points. I show you how to use cloud-based backups and how to recover the Windows 10 system using advanced boot options.

What's Included with the Book

There are many helpful items intended to prepare you for the MCSA: Windows 10 certification included in this book:

Assessment Test   There is an Assessment Test at the conclusion of the introduction that can be used to quickly evaluate your level of knowledge of Windows 10. This test should be taken prior to beginning your work in this book and should help you identify areas in which you are either strong or need to improve. Note that these questions are purposely more simple than the types of questions you may see on the exams.

Opening List of Objectives   Each chapter includes a list of the exam objectives that are covered in that chapter.

Helpful Exercises   Throughout the book, I have included step-by-step exercises of some of the more important tasks you should be able to perform. Some of these exercises have corresponding videos that can be downloaded from the book's website. Also, later in this introduction you'll find a recommended home lab setup that will be helpful in completing these tasks.

Video Resources   After each chapter summary, if the chapter includes exercises with corresponding videos, a list or description of the exercises with video resources will be provided. The videos can be accessed at http://www.wiley.com/go/Sybextestprep.

Exam Essentials   The end of each chapter also includes a listing of exam essentials. These are essentially repeats of the objectives, but remember that any objective on the exam blueprint could show up on the exam.

Chapter Review Questions   Each chapter includes review questions. These are used to assess your understanding of the chapter and are taken directly from the chapter. These questions are based on of the exam objectives and are similar in difficulty to items you might actually receive on the MCSA: Windows 10 exams.

> The Sybex Interactive Online Test Bank, flashcards, videos, and glossary can be accessed at http://www.wiley.com/go/Sybextestprep.

Interactive Online Learning Environment and Test Bank

The interactive online learning environment that accompanies *MCSA Windows 10 Complete Study Guide: Exam 70-698 and Exam 70-697* provides a test bank with study tools to help you prepare for the certification exams and increase your chances of passing them the first time! The test bank includes the following elements:

Sample Tests   All of the questions in this book are provided, including the assessment test, which you'll find at the end of this introduction, and the chapter tests that include the review questions at the end of each chapter. In addition, there are four practice exams. Use these questions to test your knowledge of the study guide material. The online test bank runs on multiple devices.

Electronic Flashcards   The flashcards are included for quick reference and are great tools for learning quick facts. You can even consider these as additional simple practice questions, which is essentially what they are.

Videos   Some of the exercises include corresponding videos. These videos show you how I do the exercises. There is also a video that shows you how to set up virtualization so that you can complete the exercises within a virtualized environment. I also have videos to help you on the Microsoft exams at www.youtube.com/c/williampanek.

PDF of Glossary of Terms   There is a glossary included that covers the key terms used in this book.

Recommended Home Lab Setup

To get the most out of this book, you will want to make sure that you complete the exercises throughout the chapters. To complete the exercises, you will need one of two setups. First, you can set up a machine with Windows 10 and complete the labs using a regular Windows 10 machine.

The second way to set up Windows 10 is by using virtualization. I set up Windows 10 as a virtual hard disk (VHD), and I did all the labs this way. The advantages of using virtualization are that you can always just wipe out the system and start over without losing a real server. Plus, you can set up multiple virtual servers and create a full lab environment on one machine.

I created a video for this book showing you how to set up a virtual machine and how to install Windows 10 onto that virtual machine. This video can be seen at www.youtube .com/c/williampanek.

How to Contact Sybex or the Author

Sybex strives to keep you supplied with the latest tools and information you need for your work. Please check the website at http://www.wiley.com/go/Sybextestprep, where I'll post additional content and updates that supplement this book should the need arise.

You can contact Will Panek by going to his website at www.willpanek.com. Will Panek also has videos and test prep information located at www.youtube.com/c/williampanek. Will also has a Windows 10 Facebook page and a Twitter account @AuthorWillPanek.

MCSA Microsoft Windows 10: Exam 70-698 Objectives Map

The following table provides a breakdown of this book's coverage of Exam 70-698 topics, listing the chapter where each objective and its subobjectives are covered:

Implement Windows

Objectives	Chapter(s)
Prepare for installation requirements	
Determine hardware requirements and compatibility; choose between an upgrade and a clean installation; determine appropriate editions according to device type; determine requirements for particular features, such as Hyper-V, Cortana, Miracast, Virtual Smart Cards, and Secure Boot; determine and create appropriate installation media	Chapter 1, Chapter 2

Install Windows

Perform clean installations, upgrade using Windows Update, upgrade using installation media, configure native boot scenarios, migrate from previous versions of Windows, install to virtual hard disk (VHD), boot from VHD, install on bootable USB, install additional Windows features, configure Windows for additional regional and language support

Chapter 1, Chapter 2

Configure devices and device drivers

Install, update, disable, and roll back drivers; resolve driver issues; configure driver settings, including signed and unsigned drivers; manage driver packages; download and import driver packages; use the Deployment Image and Service Management (DISM) tool to add packages

Chapter 2, Chapter 3

Perform post-installation configuration

Configure and customize start menu, desktop, taskbar, and notification settings, according to device type; configure accessibility options; configure Cortana; configure Microsoft Edge; configure Internet Explorer; configure Hyper-V; configure power settings

Chapter 2, Chapter 5

Implement Windows in an enterprise environment

Provision with the Windows Imaging and Configuration Designer (ICD) tool; implement Active Directory–based activation; implement volume activation using a Key Management Service (KMS); query and configure activation states using the command line; configure Active Directory, including Group Policies; configure and optimize user account control (UAC)

Chapter 2, Chapter 7

Configure and Support Core Services

Objectives	Chapter(s)

Configure networking

Configure and support IPv4 and IPv6 network settings; configure name resolution; connect to a network; configure network locations; configure Windows Firewall; configure Windows Firewall with Advanced Security; configure network discovery; configure Wi-Fi settings; configure Wi-Fi Direct; troubleshoot network issues; configure VPN, such as app-triggered VPN, traffic filters, and lockdown VPN; configure IPsec; configure Direct Access

Chapter 7

Configure storage

Configure disks, volumes, and file system options using Disk Management and Windows PowerShell; create and configure VHDs; configure removable devices; create and configure storage spaces; troubleshoot storage and removable devices issues

Chapter 2, Chapter 4

Configure data access and usage

Configure file and printer sharing and HomeGroup connections; configure folder shares, public folders, and OneDrive; configure file system permissions; configure OneDrive usage; troubleshoot data access and usage
Chapter 6

Implement apps

Configure desktop apps, configure startup options, configure Windows features, configure Windows Store, implement Windows Store apps, implement Windows Store for Business, provision packages, create packages, use deployment tools, use the Windows Assessment and Deployment Kit (ADK)
Chapter 8

Configure remote management

Choose the appropriate remote management tools; configure remote management settings; modify settings remotely by using the Microsoft Management Console (MMC) or Windows PowerShell; configure Remote Assistance, including Easy Connect; configure Remote Desktop; configure remote PowerShell
Chapter 9

Manage and Maintain Windows

Objectives	Chapter(s)

Configure updates

Configure Windows Update options; implement Insider Preview, Current Branch (CB), Current Branch for Business (CBB), and Long Term Servicing Branch (LTSB) scenarios; manage update history; roll back updates; update Windows Store apps
Chapter 1

Monitor Windows

Configure and analyze Event Viewer logs, configure event subscriptions, monitor performance using Task Manager, monitor performance using Resource Monitor, monitor performance using Performance Monitor and Data Collector Sets, monitor system resources, monitor and manage printers, configure indexing options, manage client security by using Windows Defender, evaluate system stability using Reliability Monitor, troubleshoot performance issues
Chapter 10

Configure system and data recovery

Configure a recovery drive, configure a system restore, perform a refresh or recycle, perform a driver rollback, configure restore points, resolve hardware and device issues, interpret data from Device Manager, restore previous versions of files and folders, configure File History, recover files from OneDrive, use Windows Backup and Restore, perform a backup and restore with WBAdmin, perform recovery operations using Windows Recovery
Chapter 10

Configure authorization and authentication

Configure Microsoft Passport, configure picture passwords and biometrics,   Chapter 9
configure workgroups, configure domain settings, configure HomeGroup
settings, configure Credential Manager, configure local accounts, configure
Microsoft accounts, configure Device Registration, configure Windows Hello,
configure Device Guard, configure Credential Guard, configure Device Health
Attestation, configure UAC behavior

Configure advanced management tools

Configure services, configure Device Manager, configure and use the MMC,   Chapter 5
configure Task Scheduler, configure automation of management tasks using
Windows PowerShell

MCSA Microsoft Windows 10: Exam 70-697 Objectives Map

The following table provides a breakdown of this book's coverage of Exam 70-697 topics,
listing the chapter where each objective and its subobjectives are covered:

Manage identity

Objectives	Chapter(s)
Support Windows Store and cloud apps	Chapter 6, Chapter 7
Install and manage software by using Microsoft Office 365 and Windows Store apps	
Sideload apps by using Microsoft Intune	
Sideload apps into online and offline images	
Deeplink apps by using Microsoft Intune	
Integrate Microsoft account including personalization settings	
Support authentication and authorization	Chapter 8
Identifying and resolving issues related to the following: Multi-factor authentication including certificates, Microsoft Passport, virtual smart cards, picture passwords, and biometrics; workgroup vs. domain, Homegroup, computer and user authentication including secure channel, account policies, credential caching, and Credential Manager; local account vs. Microsoft account; Workplace Join; Configuring Windows Hello	

Plan desktop and device deployment

Objectives	Chapter(s)
Migrate and configure user data	**Chapter 1**
Migrate user profiles	
Configure folder location	
Configure profiles including profile version, local, roaming, and mandatory	
Configure Hyper-V	**Chapter 2**
Create and configure virtual machines including integration services	
Create and manage checkpoints	
Create and configure virtual switches	
Create and configure virtual disks	
Move a virtual machine's storage	
Configure mobility options	**Chapter 5**
Configure offline file policies	
Configure power policies	
Configure Windows To Go	
Configure sync options	
Configure Wi-Fi direct, files, powercfg, Sync Center	
Configure security for mobile devices	**Chapter 4**
Configure BitLocker	
Configure startup key storage	

Plan and Implement a Microsoft Intune Device Management Solution

Objectives	Chapter(s)
Support mobile devices	**Chapter 6**
Support mobile device policies including security policies, remote access, and remote wipe	
Support mobile access and data synchronization including Work Folders and Sync Center	
Support broadband connectivity including broadband tethering and metered networks	
Support Mobile Device Management by using Microsoft Intune, including Windows Phone, iOS, and Android	

Deploy software updates by using Microsoft Intune   Chapter 6

Use reports and In-Console Monitoring to identify required updates, approve
or decline updates, configure automatic approval settings, configure deadlines for update installations, deploy third-party updates

Manage devices with Microsoft Intune   Chapter 6

Provision user accounts

Enroll devices

View and manage all managed devices

Configure the Microsoft Intune subscriptions

Configure the Microsoft Intune connector site system role

Manage user and computer groups

Configure monitoring and alerts

Manage policies

Manage remote computers

Configure Networking

Objectives	Chapter(s)
Configure IP settings	Chapter 9
Configure name resolution	
Connect to a network	
Configure network locations	
Configure networking settings	Chapter 9
Connect to a wireless network	
Manage preferred wireless networks	
Configure network adapters	
Configure location-aware printing	
Configure and maintain network security	Chapter 9
Configure Windows Firewall	
Configure Windows Firewall with Advanced Security	
Configure connection security rules (IPsec)	
Configure authenticated exceptions	
Configure network discovery	

Configure Storage

Objectives	Chapter(s)
Support data storage	**Chapter 3**
Identifying and resolving issues related to the following: DFS client including caching settings, storage spaces including capacity and fault tolerance, OneDrive	
Support data security	**Chapter 3, Chapter 4**
Identifying and resolving issues related to the following: Permissions including share, NTFS, and Dynamic Access Control (DAC)	
Encrypting File System (EFS) including Data Recovery Agent	
Access to removable media	
BitLocker and BitLocker To Go including Data Recovery Agent and Microsoft BitLocker Administration and Monitoring (MBAM)	

Manage Data Access and Protection

Objectives	Chapter(s)
Configure shared resources	**Chapter 4**
Configure shared folder permissions	
Configure HomeGroup settings	
Configure libraries	
Configure shared printers	
Configure OneDrive	
Configure file and folder access	**Chapter 3**
Encrypt files and folders by using EFS	
Configure NTFS permissions	
Configure disk quotas	
Configure file access auditing	
Configure authentication and authorization	

Manage Remote Access

Objectives	Chapter(s)
Configure remote connections	**Chapter 5**
Configure remote authentication	
Configure Remote Desktop settings	
Configure VPN connections and authentication	
Enable VPN reconnect	
Configure broadband tethering	
Configure mobility options	**Chapter 5**
Configure offline file policies	
Configure power policies	
Configure Windows To Go	
Configure sync options	
Configure Wi-Fi direct, files, powercfg, Sync Center	

Manage APPS

Objectives	Chapter(s)
Deploy and manage Azure RemoteApp	**Chapter 7**
Configure RemoteApp and Desktop Connections settings	
Configure Group Policy Objects (GPOs) for signed packages	
Subscribe to the Azure RemoteApp and Desktop Connections feeds	
Export and import Azure RemoteApp configurations	
Support iOS and Android	
Configure remote desktop web access for Azure RemoteApp distribution	
Support desktop apps	**Chapter 6, Chapter 7**
The following support considerations including: Desktop app compatibility using Application Compatibility Toolkit (ACT) including shims and compatibility database; desktop application co-existence using Hyper-V, Azure RemoteApp, and App-V; installation and configuration of User Experience Virtualization (UE-V); deploy desktop apps by using Microsoft Intune	

Manage Updates and Recovery

Objectives	Chapter(s)
Configure system recovery	**Chapter 10**
Configure a recovery drive	
Configure system restore	
Perform a refresh or recycle	
Perform a driver rollback	
Configure restore points	
Configure file recovery	**Chapter 10**
Restore previous versions of files and folders	
Configure File History	
Recover files from OneDrive	
Configure and manage updates	**Chapter 1**
Configure update settings	
Configure Windows Update policies	
Manage update history	
Roll back updates	
Update Windows Store apps	

Exam domains and objectives are subject to change at any time without prior notice and at Microsoft's sole discretion. Please visit their website at https://www.microsoft.com/en-us/learning/exam-70-698.aspx for Exam 70-698 and https://www.microsoft.com/en-us/learning/exam-70-697.aspx for Exam 70-697 for the most current information.

Assessment Test

The Assessment Test covers *MCSA Windows 10 Complete Study Guide*, Part I: Exam 70-698, Installing and Configuring Windows 10, and Part II: Exam 70-697, Configuring Windows Devices. Take the test to quickly evaluate your level of knowledge of Windows 10. This test should be taken prior to beginning your work in this book and should help you identify areas in which you are either strong or need to improve. Note that these questions are purposely more simple than the types of questions you may see on the exams.

Part I: Exam 70-698, Installing and Configuring Windows 10

1. You want to create roaming profiles for users in the Sales department. They frequently log on at computers in a central area. The profiles should be configured as mandatory and roaming profiles. Which users are able to manage mandatory profiles on Windows 10 computers?

    A. The user who uses the profile

    B. Server operators

    C. Power users

    D. Administrators

2. What filename extension is applied by default to custom consoles that are created for the MMC?

    A. .mmc

    B. .msc

    C. .con

    D. .mcn

3. You are the IT administrator for a large computer-training company that uses laptops for all its employees. Currently the users have to connect to the wireless network through the wireless network adapter. Windows 10 now includes this built in as which feature?

    A. Available Network Finder (ANF)

    B. View Networks (VN)

    C. Network Availability Viewer (NAV)

    D. View Available Networks (VAN)

4. If you wanted to require that a user enter an Administrator password to perform administrative tasks, what type of user account should you create for the user?

    A. Administrator user account

    B. Standard user account

    C. Power user account

    D. Authenticated user account

5. You have installed a clean installation of Windows 10 on your computer. You want to create an image of the new installation to use as a basis for remote installs. What Windows 10 utility should you use to accomplish this?

   A. WDS

   B. Windows SIM

   C. DISM

   D. Sysprep

6. You are the administrator in charge of a computer that runs both Windows 7 and Windows 10. Windows 10 is installed on a different partition from Windows 7. You have to make sure that the computer always starts Windows 7 by default. What action should you perform?

   A. Run Bcdedit.exe and the /default parameter.

   B. Run Bcdedit.exe and the /bootcd parameter.

   C. Create a Boot.ini file in the root of the Windows 10 partition.

   D. Create a Boot.ini file in the root of the Windows 7 partition.

7. You have a user with limited vision. Which accessibility utility is used to read aloud screen text, such as the text in dialog boxes, menus, and buttons?

   A. Read-Aloud

   B. Orator

   C. Dialog Manager

   D. Narrator

8. You have just purchased a new computer that has Windows 10 preinstalled. You want to migrate existing users from a previous computer that was running Windows XP Professional. Which two files would you use to manage this process through the User State Migration Tool? (Choose two.)

   A. usmt.exe

   B. ScanState.exe

   C. LoadState.exe

   D. Windows7Migrate.exe

9. You are using Windows 10 Home and you want to update your video drivers. How do you accomplish this?

   A. Install new drivers using Driver Manager.

   B. Upgrade the drivers using Device Manager.

   C. Upgrade the drivers using Driver Manager.

   D. Install new drivers using Device Manager.

10. You are the network administrator for a large organization. You have a Windows 10 machine that is working fine, but you downloaded and installed a newer version of the network adapter driver. After you load the driver, the network device stops working properly. Which tool should you use to help you fix the problem?

    A. Driver rollback

    B. Driver Repair utility

    C. Reverse Driver application

    D. Windows 10 Driver Compatibility tool

11. You are the network administrator for your organization. Your organization has been using Windows 10 Enterprise. You need to run the Print Management tools from the command prompt. What command do you run?

    A. Printmgmt.exe

    B. PrintMig.exe

    C. Prtmgmt.exe

    D. Printbrm.exe

12. You are configuring power settings on your laptop. You configure the laptop to enter sleep mode after a specified period of inactivity. Which of the following will occur when the computer enters sleep mode?

    A. The computer will be shut down gracefully.

    B. Data will be saved to the hard disk.

    C. The monitor and hard disk will be turned off, but the computer will remain in a fully active state.

    D. The user session will not be available when you resume activity on the computer.

13. You are the administrator for a large organization that is moving to Windows 10. You need to set up a way that you can run multiple storage commands from a scripting tool. How can you set this up?

    A. Use SCCM for scripting.

    B. Use PowerShell for scripting.

    C. Use AD FS for scripting.

    D. Use Disk Administrator for scripting.

14. What is the CIDR equivalent for 255.255.255.224?

    A. /24

    B. /25

    C. /26

    D. /27

15. You have compressed a 4 MB file into 2 MB. You are copying the file to another computer that has a FAT32 partition. How can you ensure that the file will remain compressed?

    A. When you copy the file, use the XCOPY command with the /Comp switch.

    B. When you copy the file, use the Windows Explorer utility and specify the option Keep Existing Attributes.

    C. On the destination folder, make sure that you set the option Compress Contents To Save Disk Space in the folder's properties.

    D. You can't maintain disk compression on a non-NTFS partition.

16. You are the network administrator for Stellacon. Your network consists of 200 Windows 10 computers, and you want to assign static IP addresses rather than use a DHCP server. You want to configure the computers to reside on the 192.168.10.0 network. What subnet mask should you use with this network address?

    A. 255.0.0.0

    B. 255.255.0.0

    C. 255.255.255.0

    D. 255.255.255.255

17. You are using a laptop running Windows 10 Home. You want to synchronize files between your laptop and a network folder. Which of the following actions must you perform first in order to enable synchronization to occur between your laptop and the network folder?

    A. Upgrade your laptop to Windows 10 Enterprise.

    B. Enable one-way synchronization between the laptop and the network folder.

    C. Enable two-way synchronization between the laptop and the network folder.

    D. Configure the files on your laptop as read-only.

18. You have a DNS server that contains corrupt information. You fix the problem with the DNS server, but one of your users is complaining that they are still unable to access Internet resources. You verify that everything works on another computer on the same subnet. Which command can you use to fix the problem?

    A. ipconfig /flush

    B. ipconfig /flushdns

    C. ping /flush

    D. DNS /flushdns

19. You are the network administrator for a medium-sized company. Rick was the head of HR and recently resigned. John has been hired to replace Rick and has been given Rick's laptop. You want John to have access to all of the resources to which Rick had access. What is the easiest way to manage the transition?

    A. Rename Rick's account to John.

    B. Copy Rick's account and call the copied account John.

    C. Go into the Registry and do a search and replace to replace all of Rick's entries with John's name.

    D. Take ownership of all of Rick's resources and assign John Full Control to the resources.

20. Which of the following statements are true regarding the creation of a group in Windows 10? (Choose two.)

    A. Only members of the Administrators group can create users on a Windows 10 computer.

    B. Group names can be up to 64 characters.

    C. Group names can contain spaces.

    D. Group names can be the same as usernames but not the same as other group names on the computer.

21. You need to expand the disk space on your Windows 10 computer. You are considering using spanned volumes. Which of the following statements are true concerning spanned volumes? (Choose all that apply.)

    A. Spanned volumes can contain space from 2 to 32 physical drives.

    B. Spanned volumes can contain space from 2 to 24 physical drives.

    C. Spanned volumes can be formatted as FAT32 or NTFS partitions.

    D. Spanned volumes can be formatted only as NTFS partitions.

22. You have a network folder that resides on an NTFS partition on a Windows 10 computer. NTFS permissions and share permissions have been applied. Which of the following statements best describes how share permissions and NTFS permissions work together if they have been applied to the same folder?

    A. The NTFS permissions will always take precedence.

    B. The share permissions will always take precedence.

    C. The system will look at the cumulative share permissions and the cumulative NTFS permissions. Whichever set is less restrictive will be applied.

    D. The system will look at the cumulative share permissions and the cumulative NTFS permissions. Whichever set is more restrictive will be applied.

23. Your home computer network is protected by a firewall. You have configured your Windows 10 home computer to use Windows Mail. After you configure your email accounts, you discover that you are unable to send email messages from Windows Mail. Your email provider uses POP3 and SMTP. What port should you open on the firewall?

    A. 25

    B. 110

    C. 443

    D. 995

24. You need Windows 10 to be the primary operating system on a dual-boot machine. Which file do you configure for this?

    A. boot.ini

    B. bcdedit

    C. bcboot.ini

    D. bcdboot

25. Which of the following versions of Windows 10 can be upgraded to Windows 10 Enterprise edition? (Choose all that apply.)

   A. Windows 8.1 Home

   B. Windows 8.1 Professional

   C. Windows 8.1 Home Premium

   D. Windows 8.1 Enterprise

26. You are configuring a Windows 10 computer that is going to be used by your children. You are configuring access restrictions using the Parental Controls feature of Windows 10. Which of the following can be configured by setting Parental Controls? (Choose all that apply.)

   A. When your children can access the computer

   B. Which websites your children can view

   C. Which programs your children can access

   D. Which other computers on your home network your children can access

27. How do you access the Advanced Boot Options menu in Windows 10 during the boot process?

   A. Press the spacebar.

   B. Press F6.

   C. Press F8.

   D. Press F10.

28. You have a computer that runs Windows 10. Your computer has two volumes, C: and D:. Both volumes are formatted by using the NTFS file system. You need to disable previous versions on the D: volume. What should you do?

   A. From System Properties, modify the System Protection settings.

   B. From the properties of the D: volume, modify the Quota settings.

   C. From the properties of the D: volume, modify the Sharing settings.

   D. From the Disk Management snap-in, convert the hard disk drive that contains the D: volume to Dynamic.

29. Which utility is used to upgrade a FAT32 partition to NTFS?

   A. UPFS

   B. UPGRADE

   C. Disk Manager

   D. Convert

30. Your organization has created an application for its employees. You need to deploy the internally developed application to all employees while minimizing the costs. What's the best way to do that?

   A. Install the application one system at a time.

   B. Enable application sideloading.

   C. Purchase System Center and deploy the application.

   D. Run the Add-Application PowerShell cmdlet.

Part II: Exam 70-697, Configuring Windows Devices

31. What filename extension is applied by default to custom consoles that are created for the MMC?

   A. .mmc

   B. .msc

   C. .con

   D. .mcn

32. You want to create roaming profiles for users in the Sales department. They frequently log on at computers in a central area. The profiles should be configured as mandatory and roaming profiles. Which users are able to manage mandatory profiles on Windows 10 computers?

   A. The user who uses the profile

   B. Server operators

   C. Power users

   D. Administrators

33. Your employees use both desktops and tablets to access the company network. Your tablet users use a 4G mobile broadband Wi-Fi connection. You need to monitor how much data your users are using for this connection. How do you accomplish this?

   A. Configure the broadband connection as a metered network.

   B. Turn on network resource monitoring.

   C. Enable Performance Monitor.

   D. Enable tablet metering in the tablets' settings.

34. If you wanted to require that a user enter an Administrator password to perform administrative tasks, what type of user account should you create for the user?

   A. Administrator user account

   B. Standard user account

   C. Power user account

   D. Authenticated user account

35. You have installed a clean installation of Windows 10 on your computer. You want to create an image of the new installation to use as a basis for remote installs. What Windows 10 utility should you use to accomplish this?

A. WDS

B. Windows SIM

C. ImageX

D. Sysprep

36. Which of the following statements is true regarding the built-in Administrator account in Windows 10? (Choose all that apply.)

A. The built-in Administrator account does not exist in Windows 10.

B. The built-in Administrator account is disabled by default in Windows 10.

C. The built-in Administrator account has no permissions in Windows 10.

D. The built-in Administrator account is not a member of the Administrators group in Windows 10.

37. You have a user with limited vision. Which accessibility utility is used to read aloud screen text, such as the text in dialog boxes, menus, and buttons?

A. Read-Aloud

B. Orator

C. Dialog Manager

D. Narrator

38. You have just purchased a new computer that has Windows 10 preinstalled. You want to migrate existing users from a previous computer that was running Windows XP Professional. Which two files would you use to manage this process through the User State Migration Tool?

A. usmt.exe

B. ScanState.exe

C. LoadState.exe

D. Windows7Migrate.exe

39. You are the IT director for large company that has decided to move to the cloud. The company wants to use Azure Active Directory and Microsoft Intune. The company has been looking into this because users have been using multiple devices to get their job done. When your users get added to Intune and get licensed, how many devices can each user add by default?

A. Three

B. Four

C. Five

D. None. Device administrators are the only people who can add devices to Intune.

40. You are the network administrator for your company. Recently, one of your users in the Accounting department has reported that they were unsure whether a banking website was legitimate or not. You want to configure a utility that will verify whether a website is known to be fraudulent. Which utility should you configure?

  A. Pop-up Blocker

  B. RSS Reader

  C. Phishing Filter

  D. Add-on Manager

41. You have a user, Jan, who suspects that her Windows 10 computer has been infected with spyware. You remove the spyware from her computer and want to prevent spyware from infecting it in the future. Which of the following Windows 10 utilities should you configure?

  A. Windows Defender

  B. Phishing Filter

  C. Pop-up Blocker

  D. Windows OneCare

42. You are configuring power settings on your laptop. You configure the laptop to enter sleep mode after a specified period of inactivity. Which of the following will occur when the computer enters sleep mode?

  A. The computer will be shut down gracefully.

  B. Data will be saved to the hard disk.

  C. The monitor and hard disk will be turned off, but the computer will remain in a fully active state.

  D. The user session will not be available when you resume activity on the computer.

43. You are using Internet Explorer to access several RSS feeds that you subscribe to. One of the feeds stores only the 10 most recent updates. You want to ensure that the last 100 updates are stored. What should you do?

  A. Configure the RSS feed to automatically download attached files.

  B. Modify the schedule so that the RSS feed is updated more than once a day.

  C. Turn on feed reading view in IE.

  D. Modify the archive setting so that the last 100 items are stored.

44. What is the CIDR equivalent for 255.255.255.224?

  A. /24

  B. /25

  C. /26

  D. /27

45. You are configuring a new Windows 10 computer for a new employee. You configure the new user with a standard user account. Which of the following functions will the new employee be allowed to perform? (Choose all that apply.)

    A. Install a printer.

    B. Install network drivers.

    C. Configure WPA keys.

    D. Modify the Desktop settings.

46. You are the network administrator for Stellacon. Your network consists of 200 Windows 10 computers, and you want to assign static IP addresses rather than use a DHCP server. You want to configure the computers to reside on the 192.168.10.0 network. What subnet mask should you use with this network address?

    A. 255.0.0.0

    B. 255.255.0.0

    C. 255.255.255.0

    D. 255.255.255.255

47. You are using a laptop running Windows 10 Home. You want to synchronize files between your laptop and a network folder. Which of the following actions must you perform first in order to enable synchronization to occur between your laptop and the network folder?

    A. Upgrade your laptop to Windows 10 Enterprise.

    B. Enable one-way synchronization between the laptop and the network folder.

    C. Enable two-way synchronization between the laptop and the network folder.

    D. Configure the files on your laptop as read-only.

48. You have a DNS server that contains corrupt information. You fix the problem with the DNS server, but one of your users is complaining that they are still unable to access Internet resources. You verify that everything works on another computer on the same subnet. Which command can you use to fix the problem?

    A. `ipconfig /flush`

    B. `ipconfig /flushdns`

    C. `ping /flush`

    D. `DNS /flushdns`

49. Which of the following information can be configured on a VPN client so that it can access a VPN server? (Choose two.)

    A. IP address

    B. MAC address

    C. Domain name

    D. Connection address

50. Which of the following statements are true regarding the creation of a group in Windows 10? (Choose two.)

  A. Only members of the Administrators group can create users on a Windows 10 computer.

  B. Group names can be up to 64 characters.

  C. Group names can contain spaces.

  D. Group names can be the same as usernames but not the same as other group names on the computer.

51. You need to expand the disk space on your Windows 10 computer. You are considering using spanned volumes. Which of the following statements are true concerning spanned volumes? (Choose all that apply.)

  A. Spanned volumes can contain space from 2 to 32 physical drives.

  B. Spanned volumes can contain space from 2 to 24 physical drives.

  C. Spanned volumes can be formatted as FAT32 or NTFS partitions.

  D. Spanned volumes can be formatted only as NTFS partitions.

52. You have just installed Hyper-V on a server called ServerA and you have set up five new VM servers. You want to run PowerShell commands for the five VM servers from ServerA. How do you do this?

  A. Use the Invoke-Command cmdlet and specify the VMName parameter.

  B. Use the WinRM command -PowerShell.

  C. Use the PSCommands - enabled command.

  D. Just run the PowerShell commands with the -Name parameter.

53. Your home computer network is protected by a firewall. You have configured your Windows 10 home computer to use Windows Mail. After you configure your email accounts, you discover that you are unable to send email messages from Windows Mail. Your email provider uses POP3 and SMTP. What port should you open on the firewall?

  A. 25

  B. 110

  C. 443

  D. 995

54. You need Windows 10 to be the primary operating system on a dual-boot machine. Which file do you configure for this?

  A. boot.ini

  B. bcdedit

  C. bcboot.ini

  D. bcdboot

55. Which of the following versions of Windows 10 can be upgraded to Windows 10 Enterprise edition? (Choose all that apply.)

A. Windows 8 Home

B. Windows 8 Professional

C. Windows 8 Home Premium

D. Windows 8 Enterprise

56. You are configuring a Windows 10 computer that is going to be used by your children. You are configuring access restrictions using the Parental Controls feature of Windows 10. Which of the following can be configured by setting Parental Controls? (Choose all that apply.)

A. When your children can access the computer

B. Which websites your children can view

C. Which programs your children can access

D. Which other computers on your home network your children can access

57. How do you access the Advanced Boot Options menu in Windows 10 during the boot process?

A. Press the spacebar.

B. Press F6.

C. Press F8.

D. Press F10.

58. You have two remote sites with Windows 10 machines. You need to share data across the slow sites. What feature can help with this?

A. Link Detection

B. BranchCache

C. DirectAccess

D. DirectCache

59. Which utility is used to upgrade a FAT32 partition to NTFS?

A. UPFS

B. UPGRADE

C. Disk Manager

D. Convert

60. Your organization has created an application for its employees. You need to deploy the internally developed application to all employees while minimizing the costs. What's the best way to do that?

A. Install the application one system at a time.

B. Enable application sideloading.

C. Purchase System Center and deploy the application.

D. Run the Add-Application PowerShell cmdlet.

Answers to Assessment Test

Part I: Exam 70-698, Installing and Configuring Windows 10

1. D. Only members of the Administrators group can manage mandatory profiles. See Chapter 9 for more information.

2. B. When you create a custom console for the MMC, the .msc filename extension is automatically applied. See Chapter 4 for more information.

3. D. The feature the question is referring to is View Available Networks (VAN). Before Windows 10, when you used a wireless network adapter you would choose the wireless network that you wanted to connect to by using the wireless network adapter properties. In Windows 10, this is built into the operating system. See Chapter 1 for more information.

4. B. You would create a standard user account for the user. Standard users must provide the credentials of an administrator account when prompted by User Account Control (UAC) in order to perform administrative tasks. See Chapter 9 for more information.

5. C. You can use the DISM utility to create an image of a Windows 10 installation. After the image has been created, you can prepare the image with a utility such as the System Preparation Tool (Sysprep). The image can then be used for remote installations of Windows 10. See Chapter 2 for more information.

6. A. The Boot Configuration Data (BCD) store contains boot information parameters that were previously found in Boot.ini in older versions of Windows. To edit the boot options in the BCD store, use the bcdedit utility, which can be launched only from a command prompt. See Chapter 1 for more information.

7. D. The Narrator utility uses a sound output device to read onscreen text. See Chapter 5 for more information.

8. B, C. Windows 10 ships with a utility called the User State Migration Tool (USMT) that is used by administrators to migrate users from one computer to another via a command-line utility. The USMT consists of two executable files: ScanState.exe and LoadState.exe. See Chapter 2 for more information.

9. B. To get the latest drivers for any piece of hardware, you need to use the Upgrade Drivers button in Device Manager. After the upgrade button is chosen, you can use downloaded drivers or drivers from a new DVD. See Chapter 3 for more information.

10. A. Driver rollback allows you to replace a newly installed driver with the previous driver. You can do the driver rollback using the Device Manager utility. See Chapter 3 for more information.

11. D. The Printbrm.exe command should be run from a command prompt with administrative permission. This command is the command-line version of the Print Management tool. See Chapter 3 for more information.

12. B. Sleep mode is a combination of standby mode and hibernation mode. When sleep mode is configured, the user's session is quickly accessible on wakeup, but the data is saved to the hard disk. Sleep mode is the preferred power-saving mode in Windows 10. See Chapter 5 for more information.

13. B. PowerShell commands allow you to run multiple configurations by using scripts or even by using individual commands. See Chapter 4 for more information.

14. D. A subnet mask of 255.255.255.224 equals a CIDR of /27. CIDR is the number of on bits. See Chapter 7 for more information.

15. D. Windows 10 data compression is supported only on NTFS partitions. If you move the file to a FAT32 partition, then it will be stored as uncompressed. See Chapter 4 for more information.

16. C. You should use the subnet mask 255.255.255.0 on your network in this scenario. The IP network address 192.168.10.0 is a Class C address. Class C addresses, by default, use the subnet mask 255.255.255.0. The network portion of the address is 192.168.10, and the host portion of the address can be 1 to 254. See Chapter 7 for more information.

17. A. To enable synchronization of files between your laptop and a network folder, you must first upgrade your laptop to a version of Windows 10 that supports synchronization with network folders, such as Windows 10 Enterprise. Windows Sync Center also supports synchronization of files between computers and mobile devices. See Chapter 1 for more information.

18. B. The `ipconfig /flushdns` command is used to purge the DNS Resolver cache. The `ipconfig` command displays a computer's IP configuration. See Chapter 7 for more information.

19. A. The easiest way is to simply rename Rick's account to John. When you rename Rick's account to John, John will automatically have all of the rights and permissions to any resource that Rick had access to. See Chapter 6 for more information.

20. A, C. Only administrators can create new groups on a Windows 10 computer. Group names can contain up to 256 characters and can contain spaces. Group names must be unique to the computer, different from all the other usernames and group names that have been specified on that computer. See Chapter 9 for more information.

21. A, C. You can create a spanned volume from free space that exists on a minimum of 2 to a maximum of 32 physical drives. When the spanned volume is initially created in Windows 10, it can be formatted with FAT32 or NTFS. If you extend a volume that already contains data, however, the partition must be NTFS. See Chapter 4 for more information.

22. D. When both NTFS and share permissions have been applied, the system looks at the effective rights for NTFS and share permissions and then applies the most restrictive of the cumulative permissions. If a resource has been shared and you access it from the local computer where the resource resides, then you will be governed only by the NTFS permission. See Chapter 6 for more information.

23. A. Port 25 should be opened on the firewall. SMTP is used for outbound mail and uses port 25. POP3, which is used for receiving inbound mail, uses port 110. See Chapter 7 for more information.

24. B. You should configure the bcdedit utility to configure your boot order. See Chapter 1 for more information.

25. B, D. You can upgrade Windows 8 Professional and Windows 8 Enterprise to Windows 10 Enterprise edition. See Chapter 1 for more information.

26. A, B, C. Using Parental Controls, you can configure which websites your children can access, when they can use the computer, which games they can play, and which programs they can run, and you can view reports regarding their activity. See Chapter 5 for more information.

27. C. During the boot process, you are prompted to press F8 to access the Advanced Boot Options menu. See Chapter 10 for more information.

28. A. If you need to disable previous versions on the D: volume, this needs to be done from the System Protection settings from the computer system properties. See Chapter 10 for more information.

29. D. The Convert utility is used to convert a FAT32 partition to NTFS. See Chapter 4 for more information.

30. B. Applications that are developed by a company and are not signed by the Windows Store can be installed by the process of Sideloading. Sideloading allows companies to load applications into the Windows Store for deployment throughout a company. See Chapter 8 for more information.

Part II: Exam 70-697, Configuring Windows Devices

31. B. When you create a custom console for the MMC, the .msc filename extension is automatically applied. See Chapter 13 for more information.

32. D. Only members of the Administrators group can manage mandatory profiles. See Chapter 18 for more information.

33. A. Administrators have the ability to limit and monitor network usage by configuring the network as a metered network. Network metering allows network downloading to be watched or metered and then administrators can charge users or departments for the network usage. See Chapter 16 for more information.

34. B. You would create a standard user account for the user. Standard users must provide the credentials of an administrator account when prompted by User Account Control (UAC) in order to perform administrative tasks. See Chapter 18 for more information.

35. C. You can use the ImageX utility to create an image of a Windows 10 installation. After the image has been created, you can prepare the image with a utility such as the System Preparation Tool (Sysprep). The image can then be used for remote installations of Windows 10. See Chapter 12 for more information.

36. B. The built-in Administrator account is disabled by default in Windows 10. However, it can be enabled through Local Users and Groups or by modifying the Accounts: Administrator Account Status GPO setting. See Chapter 18 for more information.

37. D. The Narrator utility uses a sound output device to read onscreen text. See Chapter 15 for more information.

38. B, C. Windows 10 ships with a utility called the User State Migration Tool (USMT) that is used by administrators to migrate users from one computer to another via a command-line utility. The USMT consists of two executable files: ScanState.exe and LoadState.exe. See Chapter 12 for more information.

39. C. By default, licensed users can add up to five devices to their accounts. Device administrators have the ability to add devices to Intune, but users do have the ability to enroll up to five devices on their own. See Chapter 16 for more information.

40. C. Internet Explorer 11 ships with Phishing Filter, which can help verify whether a website is known to be fraudulent or not. Phishing Filter helps to prevent malicious websites from masquerading as a legitimate site in order to obtain your personal or financial information. See Chapter 17 for more information.

41. A. Windows Defender is an antispyware program included with Windows 10. It offers real-time protection from spyware and other unwanted software. You can also configure Windows Defender to scan for spyware on a regular basis. See Chapter 17 for more information.

42. B. Sleep mode is a combination of standby mode and hibernation mode. When sleep mode is configured, the user's session is quickly accessible on wakeup, but the data is saved to the hard disk. Sleep mode is the preferred power-saving mode in Windows 10. See Chapter 15 for more information.

43. D. Internet Explorer 11 provides the ability to read and subscribe to RSS feeds. You can configure several options for RSS feeds, such as how often the feed is checked for updates, whether attachments are automatically downloaded, and how many updates are stored for the feed. See Chapter 17 for more information.

44. D. A subnet mask of 255.255.255.224 equals a CIDR of /27. CIDR is the number of on bits. See Chapter 19 for more information.

45. A, C, D. Standard users are allowed to perform a variety of tasks, such as install printers, configure wireless keys, and modify their Desktop settings. See Chapter 18 for more information.

46. C. You should use the subnet mask 255.255.255.0 on your network in this scenario. The IP network address 192.168.10.0 is a Class C address. Class C addresses, by default, use the subnet mask 255.255.255.0. The network portion of the address is 192.168.10, and the host portion of the address can be 1 to 254. See Chapter 19 for more information.

47. A. To enable synchronization of files between your laptop and a network folder, you must first upgrade your laptop to a version of Windows 10 that supports synchronization with network folders, such as Windows 10 Enterprise. Windows Sync Center also supports synchronization of files between computers and mobile devices. See Chapter 11 for more information.

48. B. The `ipconfig /flushdns` command is used to purge the DNS Resolver cache. The `ipconfig` command displays a computer's IP configuration. See Chapter 19 for more information.

49. A, C. When you configure a VPN connection, you must specify the IP address or host domain name of the computer to which you'll connect. See Chapter 15 for more information.

50. A, C. Only administrators can create new groups on a Windows 10 computer. Group names can contain up to 256 characters and can contain spaces. Group names must be unique to the computer, different from all the other usernames and group names that have been specified on that computer. See Chapter 18 for more information.

51. A, C. You can create a spanned volume from free space that exists on a minimum of 2 to a maximum of 32 physical drives. When the spanned volume is initially created in Windows 10, it can be formatted with FAT32 or NTFS. If you extend a volume that already contains data, however, the partition must be NTFS. See Chapter 13 for more information.

52. A. Administrators can use PowerShell Direct to run PowerShell commands on a VM from the Hyper-V host. To do this, you need to run the following command, `Invoke-Command`, and you need to specify which VM you're connecting to (`-VMName` parameter). See Chapter 17 for more information.

53. A. Port 25 should be opened on the firewall. SMTP is used for outbound mail and uses port 25. POP3, which is used for receiving inbound mail, uses port 110. See Chapter 19 for more information.

54. B. You should configure the `bcdedit` utility to configure your boot order. See Chapter 11 for more information.

55. B, D. You can upgrade Windows 8 Professional and Windows 8 Enterprise to Windows 10 Enterprise edition. See Chapter 11 for more information.

56. A, B, C. Using Parental Controls, you can configure which websites your children can access, when they can use the computer, which games they can play, and which programs they can run, and you can view reports regarding their activity. See Chapter 15 for more information.

57. C. During the boot process, you are prompted to press F8 to access the Advanced Boot Options menu. See Chapter 10 for more information.

58. B. BranchCache allows multiple sites with slower links to share data quickly and efficiently. See Chapter 15 for more information.

59. D. The Convert utility is used to convert a FAT32 partition to NTFS. See Chapter 13 for more information.

60. B. Applications that are developed by a company and are not signed by the Windows Store can be installed by the process of sideloading. Sideloading allows companies to load applications into the Windows Store for deployment throughout a company. See Chapter 17 for more information.

Exam 70-698, Installing and Configuring Windows 10

PART

I

Chapter

1

Windows 10 Installation

MICROSOFT EXAM OBJECTIVES COVERED IN THIS CHAPTER:

✓ **Prepare for installation requirements.**

- This objective may include but is not limited to the following subobjectives: Determine hardware requirements and compatibility; choose between an upgrade and a clean installation; determine appropriate editions according to device type; determine requirements for particular features, such as Hyper-V, Cortana, Miracast, Virtual Smart Cards, and Secure Boot; determine and create appropriate installation media.

✓ **Install Windows.**

- This objective may include but is not limited to the following subobjectives: Perform clean installations, upgrade using Windows Update, upgrade using installation media, migrate from previous versions of Windows, install on bootable USB, configure Windows for additional regional and language support.

✓ **Configure updates.**

- This objective may include but is not limited to the following subobjectives: Configure Windows Update options; implement Insider Preview, Current Branch (CB), Current Branch for Business (CBB), and Long Term Servicing Branch (LTSB) scenarios; manage update history; roll back updates; update Windows Store apps.

This book is for exam 70-698, and even though it's a higher exam number, this is the first of two MCSA Windows 10 exams (70-698 and 70-697). If you are using both of the Sybex books for the Windows 10 MCSA, you will notice that many of the topics in these books are the same in both books. The reason for this is that no matter what test you take, installing Windows 10 is the same. It has the same control panel, the same applications, and the same way to configure the operating system.

So let me be the first to welcome you to Windows 10 and the beginning of a new journey. But as with the start of any journey, we must take our first steps. The first steps for this exam involves learning about the Windows 10 installation process. It is important that you understand the different versions of Windows 10 and which one is right for you and your organization.

In this chapter, I will show you the many different features of Windows 10 and then I will describe each edition. I will then show you how to install Windows 10 and also how to do an upgrade from a previous version.

Before you can install Windows 10, you must first make sure your hardware meets the minimum requirements and that your hardware is supported by the operating system. After we install the Windows 10 operating system, I will show you how to get upgrades for the Windows 10 system.

Understanding the Basics

Microsoft Windows 10 is the latest version of Microsoft's client operating system software. Windows 10 combines the best of Windows 7 and Windows 8, and it also makes it much easier to work within the cloud.

Microsoft has currently released six different versions of the Windows 10 operating system along with the announcement of a seventh:

- Windows 10 Home
- Windows 10 Professional
- Windows 10 Enterprise
- Windows 10 Education
- Windows 10 Mobility
- Windows 10 Mobility Enterprise
- Windows 10 Anniversary Edition

At the time this book was written, Windows 10 Anniversary Edition had not been released yet. Microsoft has stated that this version will be released by the end of 2016.

Microsoft also offers a slimmed-down version of some of these operating systems called "Windows 10 IoT Core." This version is one of the above Windows 10 versions that doesn't require a monitor or system. For example, you are building a toy robot and you want to load Windows 10 into his core computer. You can use the IoT versions to run the robot's functionality.

Windows 10 has been improved in many of the weak areas that plagued Windows 8. Windows 10 has a much faster boot time and shutdown compared to Windows 8. It also brings back the - Start button that we are all so familiar with from previous editions.

The Windows 10 operating system functions are also faster than their previous counterparts. The processes for opening, moving, extracting, compressing, and installing files and folders are more efficient than they were in previous versions of Microsoft's client operating systems.

Let's take a look at some of the features of each Windows 10 edition (this is just an overview of some of the benefits to using Windows 10). Table 1.1 shows some of the "core experiences" for each edition.

Two of the versions listed previously, Windows 10 Mobility and Windows 10 Mobility Enterprise, will not be covered in great detail in this book. If you go to Microsoft's website, you will see both listed and you can see what each offers. But neither of them can be put onto a network, so I don't cover them in this book unless applies to an exam objective.

TABLE 1.1   Windows 10 core experiences

Feature	Home	Pro	Enterprise	Education
Battery saver	•	•	•	•
Built-in ink support	•	•	•	•
Cortana integration	•	•	•	•
Customizable Start Menu	•	•	•	•
Enterprise-level biometric security	•	•	•	•
Fast startup with Hiberboot and InstantGo	•	•	•	•
"Hey Cortana" hands-free activation	•	•	•	•
Native facial and iris recognition	•	•	•	•
Native fingerprint recognition	•	•	•	•

TABLE 1.1   Windows 10 core experiences *(continued)*

Feature	Home	Pro	Enterprise	Education
Personal and proactive suggestions	•	•	•	•
Reading view	•	•	•	•
Reminders	•	•	•	•
Search web, device, and cloud	•	•	•	•
Snap apps (across screens on different monitors)	•	•	•	•
Snap assist (up to four apps on one screen)	•	•	•	•
Switch from PC to tablet mode	•	•	•	•
Talk or type naturally	•	•	•	•
TPM support	•	•	•	•
Virtual desktops	•	•	•	•
Windows Defender and Windows Firewall	•	•	•	•
Windows Update	•	•	•	•

The information in Table 1.1 and Table 1.2 was taken directly from Microsoft's website.

Now that we've looked at some of the Windows 10 core experiences, let's take a look at the business side. Table 1.2 shows each edition and what some of the "Business Experiences" are for those editions.

TABLE 1.2   Windows 10 business experiences

Feature	Home	Pro	Enterprise	Education
Ability to join Azure Active Directory		•	•	•
AppLocker			•	•
Assigned Access 8.1		•	•	•

Feature	Home	Pro	Enterprise	Education
BitLocker		•	•	•
BranchCache			•	•
Client Hyper-V		•	•	•
Credential Guard			•	•
Current Branch for Business		•	•	•
Device Encryption	•	•	•	•
Device Guard			•	•
Direct Access			•	•
Domain Join		•	•	•
Easy Upgrade from Home to Education Edition	•	•		•
Easy Upgrade from Pro to Enterprise Edition		•	•	
Enterprise Data Protection		•	•	•
Enterprise Mode Internet Explorer (EMIE)		•	•	•
Granular UX Control			•	•
Group Policy Management		•	•	•
Long Term Servicing Branch			•	
Microsoft Passport	•	•	•	•
Mobile device management	•	•	•	•
Remote Desktop		•	•	•
Side-loading of line-of-business apps	•	•	•	•
Start Screen Control with Group Policy			•	•
Trusted Boot		•	•	•
Windows Store for Business		•	•	•

TABLE 1.2   Windows 10 business experiences *(continued)*

Feature	Home	Pro	Enterprise	Education
Windows To Go Creator			•	•
Windows Update	•	•	•	•
Windows Update for Business		•	•	•

Windows 10 Features

Now that we have seen which editions contain which features, let's take a look at some of the Windows 10 features in greater detail. This section describes only a few of these features, but all features will be explained throughout this book.

Cortana Integration   Windows 10 comes with Cortana integration. Cortana is your very own personnel assistant. You can type in or ask Cortana a question, and Cortana will seek out the best possible answer based on your question.

Secure Boot   Windows 10 gives you the ability to use hardware-based virtualization that allows Windows 10 to prevent malware from running on your system. Windows 10 Secure Boot also prevents key processes from being tampered with because Windows 10 isolates these processes from the system.

Virtual Smart Cards   Windows 10 has started offering a new way to do two-factor authentication with virtual smart cards. Virtual smart cards help an IT department that doesn't want to invest in extra hardware and smart cards. Virtual smart cards use Trusted Platform Module (TPM) devices that allow for the same capabilities as physical smart cards with the physical hardware.

Miracast   Windows 10 allows you to project your Windows 10 laptop or mobile device to a projector or television. Miracast allows you to connect to an external device through the use of your mobile wireless display (WiDi) adapter.

Hyper-V   Windows 10 (except Home version) come with Hyper-V built into the operating system. Hyper-V is Microsoft's version of a virtual server.

Enterprise Data Protection   Windows 10 Enterprise Data Protection (EDP) helps protect corporate data in a world that is increasingly becoming a Bring Your Own Device (BYOD) environment. Since many organizations are allowing employees to connect their own devices to their network, the possibility of corporate data being compromised because of non-corporate programs running on these personnel devices is increasing. For example, many third-party apps may put corporate data at risk by accidently disclosing corporate information through the application.

Enterprise Data Protection helps protect information by separating corporate applications and corporate data from being disclosed by personal devices and personal applications.

Device Guard   Because employees can use multiple types of Windows 10 devices (Surface Pros, Windows Phones, and Windows 10 computer systems), Device Guard is a feature that helps guarantee that only trusted applications will run on any of these devices.

Device Guard uses both hardware and software security features to lock down a device so it can run only trusted and approved applications. This also helps protect against hackers running malicious software on these devices.

Microsoft Passport   Windows 10 allows administrators to replace passwords with other types of authentication on the operating system. Microsoft Passport allows for multifactor authentication by using a combination of an enrolled device and biometric authentication or a personal identification number (PIN).

Microsoft has encompassed the use of your Microsoft account with the use of your corporate account. So with Windows 10, Microsoft Passport can log you into your domain as well as into the cloud and Microsoft websites. The user will be required to verify their Microsoft Passport account, and that account will then be tied into a gesture or PIN, and from that point on, the user will not need to use a password to log in to the device and their protected resources. Because no password will be needed, this helps prevent hackers from using software to hack a password on an account.

Start Menu   Windows 10 has brought back the Start menu that users are familiar with. The Windows 10 Start menu combines the best of both Windows 7 and Windows 8. So the Start menu gives you a menu that we were familiar with in Windows 7 as well as the Live Tiles that users liked in Windows 8.

Microsoft Edge and Internet Explorer 11   Windows 10 has introduced a new way to surf the Internet with Microsoft Edge. But Windows 10 also still comes with Internet Explorer 11 in the event that you need to run ActiveX controls or run backward-compatible web services or sites.

Microsoft Edge allows users to start using many new Microsoft features, including Web Note (allows you to annotate, highlight, and call things out directly on web pages), Reading View (allows you to print and save as a PDF for easy reading), and Cortana (personal assistant).

Domain Join and Group Policy   Depending on the version of Windows 10 that you are using, administrators have the ability to join Windows 10 clients to either a corporate version of Active Directory or a cloud-based version of Azure Active Directory.

Windows Store for Business   Microsoft Store has included many applications that allow users to get better functionality and productivity out of their Windows 10 devices. One advantage for corporations is that they can create their own applications and load them into the Microsoft Store for users to download (called *sideloading*).

Mobile Device Management   Mobile Device Management (MDM) allows administrators to set up Windows 10 policies that can integrate many corporate scenarios, including the ability to control users' access to the Windows Store and the ability to use the corporate VPN. MDM also allows administrators to manage multiple users who have accounts set up on Microsoft Azure Active Directory (Azure AD). Windows 10 MDM support is based on the Open Mobile Alliance (OMA) Device Management (DM) protocol 1.2.1 specification.

Windows Feature Deprecation

With the release of its newest operating system, Microsoft has decided that some of the features you may be used to are no longer needed. Here are some of the features that have been deprecated:

- Windows 7 desktop gadgets will be removed as part of Windows 10.

- The Solitaire, Minesweeper, and Hearts games that come preinstalled on Windows 7 will be removed. Microsoft has released versions of Solitaire and Minesweeper called the "Microsoft Solitaire Collection" and "Microsoft Minesweeper."

- Mobile Device Management functionality will not be available in Windows 10 Home edition.

- Users with floppy drives will need to download the latest driver from Windows Update or from the manufacturer's website.

- Users who have Windows Live Essentials installed on their systems will lose the One-Drive application, which will be replaced with the inbox version of OneDrive.

- OneDrive will no longer support placeholder files in Windows 10. Windows 10 users can choose which folders they want to sync from OneDrive settings.

- When upgrading Windows 10 from previous versions of Windows operating systems that support Media Center, Windows Media Center will be removed. For a limited time on systems that were upgraded to Windows 10 from one of these versions of Windows, a DVD playback app, Windows DVD Player, will be installed. If the Windows DVD Player does not install immediately, it will be installed after the first successful Windows update.

Windows 10 Architecture

Windows 10 has limited the number of files that load at system startup to help with the core performance of the operating system. Microsoft has also removed many of the fluff items that Windows Vista used, allowing for better performance.

Microsoft offers both a 32-bit version and a 64-bit version of Windows 10. The terms *32-bit* and *64-bit* refer to the CPU, or processor. The number represents how the data is processed. It is processed either as 2^{32} or 2^{64}. The larger the number, the larger the amount of data that can be processed at any one time.

To get an idea of how 32-bit and 64-bit processors operate, think of a large highway with 32 lanes. Vehicles can travel on those 32 lanes only, so when traffic gets backed up, the result is delays. Now think of how many more vehicles can travel on a 64-lane highway. The problem here is that a 32-lane highway can't handle the number of vehicles a 64-lane highway can. You need to have the infrastructure to allow for that volume of vehicles. The same is true for computers. Your computer has to be configured to allow you to run a 64-bit processor.

So what does all of this mean to the common user or administrator? It's all about random access memory, or RAM. A 32-bit operating system can handle up to 4 GB of RAM, and a 64-bit processor can handle up to 16 exabytes of RAM. None of this is new. Although 64-bit processors are just starting to get accepted with Windows systems, other operating systems, such as Apple, have been using 64-bit processors for many years.

 Computer processors are typically rated by speed. The speed of the processor, or central processing unit (CPU), is rated by the number of clock cycles that can be performed in 1 second. This measurement is typically expressed in gigahertz (GHz). One GHz is one billion cycles per second. Keep in mind that processor architecture must also be taken into account when considering processor speed. A processor with a more efficient pipeline will be faster than a processor with a less-efficient pipeline at the same CPU speed.

Now that you have seen the new features of Windows 10, let's look at how to prepare the machine to install Windows 10.

Preparing to Install Windows 10

Installing Windows 10 can be relatively simple because of the installation wizard. The installation wizard will walk you through the entire installation of the operating system.

The most difficult part of installing Windows 10 is preparing and planning for the installation. One thing I often say to IT professionals is, "An hour of planning will save you days of work." Planning a Windows 10 rollout is one of the hardest and most important tasks that you will perform when installing Windows 10.

There are many decisions that should be made before you install Windows 10. The first decision is which version of Windows 10 you want to install. As mentioned previously, Microsoft has six different versions of the Windows 10 operating system. This allows an administrator to custom-fit a user's hardware and job function to the appropriate version of Windows 10. Many times, Microsoft releases multiple editions of the operating system contained within the same Windows 10 media disk. You can choose to unlock the one you want based on the product key you have. Let's take a closer look at the different versions of Windows 10.

 In this book, we will not talk much about Windows 10 Education. Windows 10 Education is the counterpart to Windows 10 Enterprise, but it is a volume-licensed version of Windows 10 that is specifically priced for educational institutions. Educational institutions receive the same Enterprise functionality, but they pay much less than a corporation.

Windows 10 Home

Windows 10 Home is the main operating system for home users. Windows 10 Home offers many features, including these:

- Broad application and device compatibility with unlimited concurrent applications
- A safe, reliable, and supported operating system
- Microsoft Passport
- HomeGroup, which allows a user to easily share media, documents, and printers across multiple PCs in homes or offices without the need of a domain
- Improved Taskbar and Jump Lists (Jump Lists is a feature in Windows 10 that allows you to quickly access files that you have been working on.)
- Live thumbnail previews and an enhanced visual experience
- Advanced networking support (ad hoc wireless networks and Internet connection sharing)
- View Available Networks (VAN) (Windows 10 by default has the ability, when you use a wireless network adapter, to choose the wireless network that you want to connect to by using the wireless network adapter properties.)
- Device Encryption
- Easy networking and sharing across all your PCs and devices
- Windows Update
- Multitouch
- Improved handwriting recognition

Windows 10 Professional

Windows 10 Professional is designed for small-business owners. Microsoft designed Windows 10 Professional for users to get more done and safeguard their data. Professional offers the following features:

- Broad application and device compatibility with unlimited concurrent applications
- A safe, reliable, and supported operating system
- Microsoft Passport
- Domain Join
- Improved Taskbar and Jump Lists
- Enterprise Mode Internet Explorer (EMIE)
- Advanced networking support (ad hoc wireless networks and Internet connection sharing)
- View Available Networks (VAN) (Windows 10 by default has the ability, when you use a wireless network adapter, to choose the wireless network that you want to connect to by using the wireless network adapter properties.)

- Mobility Center
- Action Center, which makes it easier to resolve many IT issues yourself
- Easy networking and sharing across all your PCs and devices
- Group Policy Management
- Windows Update and Windows Update for Business
- Multitouch
- Improved handwriting recognition
- Domain Join, which enables simple and secure server networking
- BitLocker, which protects data on removable devices
- Device Encryption
- Encrypting File System, which protects data
- Client Hyper-V
- Location Aware Printing, which helps find the right printer when moving between the office and home
- Start menu that includes Live Tiles

Windows 10 Enterprise

Windows 10 Enterprise is the version designed for midsize and large organizations. This operating system has the most features and security options of all Windows 10 versions. Here are some of the features:

- Broad application and device compatibility with unlimited concurrent applications
- A safe, reliable, and supported operating system
- Microsoft Passport
- Enterprise Mode Internet Explorer (EMIE)
- Group Policy Management
- Windows Update and Windows Update for Business
- Advanced networking support (ad hoc wireless networks and Internet connection sharing)
- View Available Networks (VAN) (Windows 10 by default has the ability, when you use a wireless network adapter, to choose the wireless network that you want to connect to by using the wireless network adapter properties.)
- Mobility Center
- Easy networking and sharing across all your PCs and devices
- Multitouch
- Start menu that includes Live Tiles

- Improved handwriting recognition
- Domain Join, which enables simple and secure server networking
- Device Encryption
- Encrypting File System, which protects data
- Location Aware Printing, which helps find the right printer when you are moving between the office and home
- Client Hyper-V
- Credential Guard
- Device Guard
- BitLocker, which protects data on removable devices
- DirectAccess, which links users to corporate resources from the road without a virtual private network (VPN)
- BranchCache, which makes it faster to open files and web pages from a branch office
- AppLocker, which restricts unauthorized software and also enables greater security hardware requirements

Before you can install the operating system, you must make sure the machine's hardware can handle the Windows 10 operating system.

To install Windows 10 successfully, your system must meet or exceed certain hardware requirements. Table 1.3 lists the minimum requirements for a Windows 10–capable PC.

TABLE 1.3   Hardware requirements

Component	Requirements
CPU (processor)	1 GHz or faster processor or system-on-a-chip (SoC)
Memory (RAM)	1 GB for 32-bit or 2 GB for 64-bit
Hard disk	16 GB for 32-bit OS or 20 GB for 64-bit OS
Video adapter	DirectX 9 or later with WDDM 1.0 driver
Optional drive	DVD-R/W drive
Network device	Compatible network interface card

The hardware requirements listed in Table 1.3 are those specified at the time this book was written. Always check the Microsoft website for the most current information.

The Windows 10–capable PC must meet or exceed the basic requirements to deliver the core functionality of the Windows 10 operating system. These requirements are based on the assumption that you are installing only the operating system, without any premium functionality. For example, you may be able to get by with the minimum requirements if you are installing the operating system just to learn the basics of the software. Remember, the better the hardware, the better the performance.

 Real World Scenario

Deciding on Minimum Hardware Requirements

The company you work for has decided that everyone will have their own laptop running Windows 10. You need to decide on the new computers' specifications for processor, memory, and disk space.

The first step is to determine which applications will be used. Typically, most users will work with an email program, a word processor, a spreadsheet application, presentation software, and maybe a drawing or graphics program. Additionally, an antivirus application will probably be used. Under these demands, a 1 GHz Celeron processor and 1 GB of RAM will make for a very slow-running machine. So for this usage, you can assume that the minimum baseline configuration would be higher than a 1 GHz processor with at least 2 GB of RAM.

Based on your choice of baseline configuration, you should then fit a test computer with the applications that will be used on it and test the configuration in a lab environment simulating normal use. This will give you an idea of whether the RAM and processor calculations you have made for your environment are going to provide a suitable response.

Today's disk drives have become capable of much larger capacity while dropping drastically in price. So for disk space, the rule of thumb is to buy whatever is the current standard. At the time this book was written, 500 GB drives were commonplace, which is sufficient for most users. If users plan to store substantial graphics or video files, you may need to consider buying larger-than-standard drives.

Also consider what the business requirements will be over the next 12 to 18 months. If you will be implementing applications that are memory or processor intensive, you may want to spec out the computers with hardware sufficient to support upcoming needs to avoid costly upgrades in the near future.

The requirements for the graphics card depend on the resolution at which you want to run. The required amount of memory is as follows:

- 64 MB is required for a single monitor at a resolution of 1,310,720 pixels or less, which is equivalent to a 1280×1024 resolution.

- 128 MB is required for a single monitor at a resolution of 2,304,000 pixels or less, which is equivalent to a 1920×1200 resolution.

- 256 MB is required for a single monitor at a resolution larger than 2,304,000 pixels.

Measurement Used for Disk Space and Memory

Hard disks are commonly rated by capacity. The following measurements are used for disk space and memory capacity:

- 1 MB (megabyte) = 1,024 KB (kilobytes)

- 1 GB (gigabyte) = 1,024 MB

- 1 TB (terabyte) = 1,024 GB

- 1 PB (petabyte) = 1,024 TB

- 1 EB (exabyte) = 1,024 PB

If you are not sure if your machine meets the minimum requirements, Microsoft includes some tools that can help you determine if a machine is Windows 10 compatible, which we will look at in the following sections.

The Hardware Compatibility List

Along with meeting the minimum requirements, whenever possible your hardware should appear on the *Hardware Compatibility List (HCL)*. The HCL is an extensive list of computers and peripheral hardware that have been tested with the Windows 10 operating system. To determine if your computer and peripherals are on the HCL, check the most up-to-date list at https://msdn.microsoft.com/en-us/library/windows/hardware/dn922588(v=vs.85).aspx.

The Windows 10 operating system requires control of the hardware for stability, efficiency, and security. The hardware and supported drivers on the HCL have been put through rigorous tests to ensure their compatibility with Windows 10. Microsoft guarantees that the items on the list meet the requirements for Windows 10 and do not have any incompatibilities that could affect the stability of the operating system.

If you call Microsoft for support, the first thing a Microsoft support engineer will ask about is your configuration. If you have any hardware that is not on the HCL, you may not be able to get support from Microsoft.

BIOS Compatibility

Before you install Windows 10, you should verify that your computer has the most current BIOS. This is especially important if your current BIOS does not include support for Advanced Configuration and Power Interface (ACPI) functionality. ACPI functionality is required for Windows 10 to function properly. Check the computer vendor's website for the latest BIOS version information.

Driver Requirements

To successfully install Windows 10, you must have the critical device drivers for your computer, such as the hard drive device driver. The Windows 10 media come with an extensive list of drivers. If your computer's device drivers are not on the Windows 10 installation media, you should check the device manufacturer's website.

New Install or Upgrade?

Once you've determined that your hardware meets the minimum requirements, you need to decide whether you want to do an upgrade or a clean install. An upgrade allows you to retain your existing operating system's applications, settings, and files. If you currently have a computer with Windows Vista, you are eligible to use an upgrade copy of Windows 10.

The bad news is that if you are moving from Windows Vista, Windows XP, or earlier versions of Windows to Windows 10, you must perform a clean install. (You can, however, use a third-party tool like the Laplink utility to migrate files and settings from Windows XP to Windows 10 on the same computer.)

You can perform an upgrade to Windows 10 if the following conditions are true:

- You are running Windows 7 or Windows 8.
- You want to keep your existing applications and preferences.
- You want to preserve any local users and groups you've created.

You must perform a clean install of Windows 10 if any of the following conditions are true:

- There is no operating system currently installed.
- You have an operating system installed that does not support an in-place upgrade to Windows 10 (such as DOS, Windows 9x, Windows NT, Windows Me, Windows 2000 Professional, Windows Vista, or Windows XP).
- You want to start from scratch, without keeping any existing preferences.
- You want to be able to dual-boot between Windows 10 and your previous operating system.

Table 1.4 shows each operating system that can be upgraded and the minimum edition of Windows 10 to which it should be upgraded.

TABLE 1.4 Windows 7 and Windows 8 upgrade options

From Current Edition	Windows 10 Edition
Windows 7 Starter	Windows 10 Home
Windows 7 Home Basic	Windows 10 Home

TABLE 1.4 Windows 7 and Windows 8 upgrade options *(continued)*

From Current Edition	Windows 10 Edition
Windows 7 Home Premium	Windows 10 Home
Windows 7 Professional	Windows 10 Pro
Windows 7 Ultimate	Windows 10 Pro
Windows 7 Enterprise	Windows 10 Enterprise
Windows Phone 8.1	Windows 10 Mobile
Windows 8.1 Home	Windows 10 Home
Windows 8.1 Pro	Windows 10 Pro
Windows 8.1 Enterprise	Windows 10 Enterprise
Windows 8.1 Pro for Students	Windows 10 Pro

Upgrade Considerations

Almost all Windows 7 and Windows 8 applications should run with the Windows 10 operating system. However, possible exceptions to this statement include the following:

- Applications that use file-system filters, such as antivirus software, may not be compatible.
- Custom power-management tools may not be supported.

Before upgrading to Windows 10, be sure to stop any antivirus scanners, network services, or other client software. These software packages may see the Windows 10 install as a virus and cause installation issues.

If you are performing a clean install to the same partition as an existing version of Windows, the contents of the existing Users (or Documents and Settings), Program Files, and Windows directories will be placed in a directory named Windows.old, and the old operating system will no longer be available.

Hardware Compatibility Issues

You need to ensure that you have Windows 10 device drivers for your hardware. If you have a video driver without a Windows 10–compatible driver, the Windows 10 upgrade will install the Standard VGA driver, which will display the video with an 800×600 resolution. Once you get the Windows 10 driver for your video, you can install it and adjust video properties accordingly.

Application Compatibility Issues

Not all applications that were written for earlier versions of Windows will work with Windows 10. After the upgrade, if you have application problems, you can address the problems in any of the following ways:

- If the application is compatible with Windows 10, reinstall the application after the upgrade is complete.

- If the application uses dynamic-link libraries (DLLs) and there are migration DLLs for the application, apply the migration DLLs.

- Use the Microsoft Application Compatibility Toolkit (ACT) to determine the compatibility of your current applications with Windows 10. ACT will determine which applications are installed, identify any applications that may be affected by Windows updates, and identify any potential compatibility problems with User Account Control and Internet Explorer. Reports can be exported for detailed analysis.

- If applications were written for earlier versions of Windows but are incompatible with Windows 10, use the Windows 10 Program Compatibility Wizard. From the Control Panel, click the Programs icon, and then click the Run Programs From Previous Versions link to start the Program Compatibility Wizard. If the application is not compatible with Windows 10, upgrade your application to a Windows 10–compliant version.

An Upgrade Checklist

Once you have made the decision to upgrade, you should develop a plan of attack. The following upgrade checklist (valid for upgrading from Windows 7 or Windows 8) will help you plan and implement a successful upgrade strategy:

- Verify that your computer meets the minimum hardware requirements for Windows 10.

- Be sure your hardware is on the HCL.

- Make sure you have the Windows 10 drivers for the hardware. You can verify this with the hardware manufacturer.

- To audit the current configuration and status of your computer, run the Get Windows 10 App tool from the Microsoft website, which also includes documentation on using the utility. It will generate a report of any known hardware or software compatibility issues based on your configuration. You should resolve any reported issues before you upgrade to Windows 10.

- Make sure your BIOS is current. Windows 10 requires that your computer has the most current BIOS. If it does not, it may not be able to use advanced power-management features or device-configuration features. In addition, your computer may cease to function during or after the upgrade. Use caution when performing BIOS updates because installing the incorrect BIOS can cause your computer to fail to boot.

- Take an inventory of your current configuration. This inventory should include documentation of your current network configuration, the applications that are installed, the hardware items and their configuration, the services that are running, and any profile and policy settings.

- Back up your data and configuration files. Before you make any major changes to your computer's configuration, you should back up your data and configuration files and then verify that you can successfully restore your backup. Chances are, if you have a valid backup, you won't have any problems. Likewise, if you don't have a valid backup, you will likely have problems.

- Delete any unnecessary files or applications, and clean up any program groups or program items you don't use. Theoretically, you want to delete all the junk on your computer before you upgrade. Think of this as the spring-cleaning step.

- Verify that there are no existing problems with your hard drive prior to the upgrade. Perform a disk scan, a current virus scan, and defragmentation. These too are spring-cleaning chores. This step just prepares your hard drive for the upgrade.

- Perform the upgrade. In this step, you upgrade from the Windows 7 or Windows 8 operating system to Windows 10.

- Verify your configuration. After Windows 10 has been installed, use the inventory to compare and test each element that was inventoried prior to the upgrade to verify that the upgrade was successful.

Handling an Upgrade Failure

Before you upgrade, you should have a contingency plan in place. Your plan should assume the worst-case scenario. For example, what happens if you upgrade and the computer doesn't work anymore? It is possible that, after checking your upgrade list and verifying that everything should work, your attempt at the actual upgrade may not work. If this happens, you may want to return your computer to the original, working configuration.

Indeed, I have made these plans, created my backups (two, just in case), verified them, and then had a failed upgrade anyway—only to discover that I had no clue where to find the original operating system CD. A day later, with the missing CD located, I was able to get up and running again. My problem was an older BIOS, and the manufacturer of my computer did not have an updated BIOS.

Disk Partitioning

Disk partitioning is the act of taking the physical hard drive and creating logical partitions. A logical drive is how space is allocated to the drive's primary and logical partitions. For example, if you have a 500 GB hard drive, you might partition it into three logical drives:

- C: drive, which might be 200 GB
- D: drive, which might be 150 GB
- E: drive, which might be 150 GB

The following sections detail some of the major considerations for disk partitioning:

Partition Size   One important consideration in your disk-partitioning scheme is determining the partition size. You need to consider the amount of space taken up by your operating system, the applications that will be installed, and the amount of stored data. It is also important to consider the amount of space required in the future.

Microsoft recommends that you allocate at least 16 GB of disk space for Windows 10. This allows room for the operating system files and for future growth in terms of upgrades and installation files that are placed with the operating system files.

The System and Boot Partitions   When you install Windows 10, files will be stored in two locations: the system partition and the boot partition. The system partition and the boot partition can be the same partition.

The system partition contains the files needed to boot the Windows 10 operating system. The system partition contains the Master Boot Record (MBR) and boot sector of the active drive partition. It is often the first physical hard drive in the computer and normally contains the necessary files to boot the computer. The files stored on the system partition do not take any significant disk space. The active partition is the system partition that is used to start your computer. The C: drive is usually the active partition.

The boot partition contains the Windows 10 operating system files. By default, the Windows operating system files are located in a folder named Windows.

Disk Partition Configuration Utilities   If you are partitioning your disk prior to installation, you can use several utilities, such as the DOS or Windows FDISK program, or a third-party utility, such as Norton's Partition Magic. You can also configure the disks during the installation of the Windows 10 operating system.

You might want to create only the first partition where Windows 10 will be installed. You can then use the Disk Management utility in Windows 10 to create any other partitions you need. The Windows 10 Disk Management utility is covered in Chapter 3, "Configuring Devices and Drivers."

Language and Locale

Language and locale settings determine the language the computer will use. Windows 10 supports many languages for the operating system interface and utilities.

Locale settings are for configuring the format for items such as numbers, currencies, times, and dates. For example, English for the United States specifies a short date as mm/dd/yyyy (month/day/year), while English for South Africa specifies a short date as yyyy/mm/dd (year/month/day).

It is very important to only choose the locales that this machine will need to use. The reason for this is that for every locale you choose, your system will get updates for all chosen locales that you set up.

Installing Windows 10

The first step to installing Windows 10 is to know what type of media you need to install the Windows 10 operating system. Windows 10 gives you multiple ways to do an install.

You can install Windows 10 either from the bootable DVD or through a network installation using files that have been copied to a network share point or USB device. You can also install Windows 10 by using a virtual hard drive (vhd). This option will be discussed in Chapter 2, "Installing in an Enterprise Environment." You can also launch the setup.exe file from within the Windows 10 operating system to upgrade your operating system.

To start the installation, you simply restart your computer and boot to the DVD. The installation process will begin automatically. You will walk through the steps of performing a clean install of Windows 10 from the DVD in Exercise 1.1.

If you are installing Windows 10 from the network, you need a distribution server and a computer with a network connection. A distribution server is a server that has the Windows 10 distribution files copied to a shared folder. The following steps are used to install Windows 10 over the network:

1. Boot the target computer.

2. Attach to the distribution server and access the share that has the files copied to it.

3. Launch setup.exe.

4. Complete the Windows 10 installation using either the clean install method or the upgrade method. These methods are discussed in detail in the following sections.

Performing a Clean Install of Windows 10

On any installation of Windows 10, there are three stages.

Collecting Information   During the collection phase of the installation, Windows 10 gathers the information necessary to complete the installation. This is where Windows 10 gathers your local time, location, keyboard, license agreement, installation type, and installation disk partition information.

Installing Windows   This section of the installation is where your Windows 10 files are copied to the hard disk and the installation is completed. This phase takes the longest because the files are installed.

Setting Up Windows   In this phase, you set up a username, computer name, and password; enter the product key; configure the security settings; and review the date and time. Once this is finished, your installation will be complete.

As explained earlier, you can run the installation from the optical media, from a USB, or over a network. The only difference in the installation procedure is your starting point: from your optical drive or USB or a network share. The steps in Exercise 1.1 and Exercise 1.2 assume you are using the Windows 10 DVD to install Windows 10.

Setting Up Your Computer for Hands-On Exercises

Before beginning Exercise 1.1, verify that your computer meets the requirements for installing Windows 10, as listed earlier in Table 1.3. For Exercise 1.1, it is assumed you are not currently running a previous version of Windows that will be upgraded.

The exercises in this book are based on your computer being configured in a specific manner. Your computer should have at least a 50 GB hard drive (this exceeds the basic minimums) that is configured with the minimum space requirements and partitions.

When you boot to the Windows 10 installation media, the Setup program will automatically start the Windows 10 installation. In Exercise 1.1, you will perform a clean install of Windows 10. This exercise assumes that you have access to Windows 10 Enterprise; other editions may vary slightly. You can also download an evaluation version of Windows 10 from the Microsoft website.

Also, I may list steps that you may not see or I may not list steps that you see—this is because my version of Windows may be different. For example, I am installing an MSDN Windows 10 Enterprise edition. At this time, I am not required to enter a license number during install. A normal version bought from a vendor may ask for the license during the actual install.

 I am loading Windows 10 Enterprise into a VMware Workstation virtual machine. Again, this may make your installation a little different than the steps listed in Exercise 1.1.

EXERCISE 1.1

Performing a Clean Install of Windows 10

1. Insert the Windows 10 DVD into a machine or virtual machine with no operating system and start the computer.

2. If you are directed to "Hit any key" to start the DVD, press Enter.

3. The first screen will ask you to enter your language, time and currency format, and keyboard or input method (see Figure 1.1). After filling in these fields, click Next.

FIGURE 1.1   Windows setup screen

4. On the next screen, click the Install Now button (see Figure 1.2).

FIGURE 1.2   Windows install screen

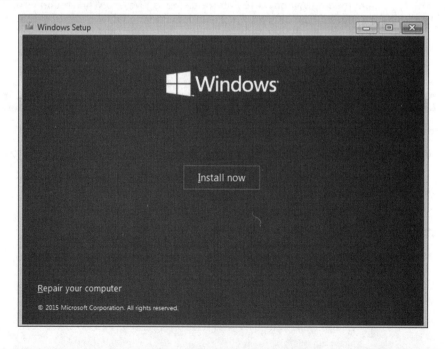

5. A message appears to tell you that the setup is starting. The licensing screen will be first. Read the license agreement and then check the I Accept The License Terms check box (see Figure 1.3). Click Next.

FIGURE 1.3 Windows license screen

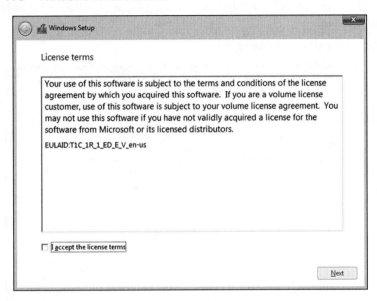

6. When asked which type of installation you want, click Custom (Advanced) as shown in Figure 1.4.

FIGURE 1.4 Type of install screen

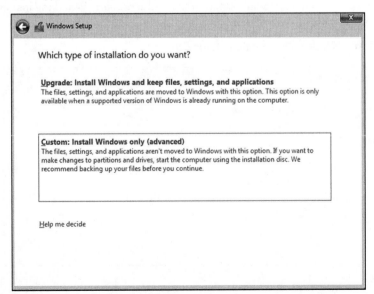

7. The next screen asks you to identify the disk to which you would like to install Windows 10. Choose an unformatted free space or a partition (partition will be erased) with at least 50 GB available. You can also click the Drive Options (Advanced) link to create and format your own partition as shown in Figure 1.5. After you choose your partition, click Next.

FIGURE 1.5 Windows disk setup screen

8. When your partition is set, the installation will start (as shown in Figure 1.6). You will see the progress of the installation during the entire process. When the installation is complete, the machine will reboot.

FIGURE 1.6 Windows installation status screen

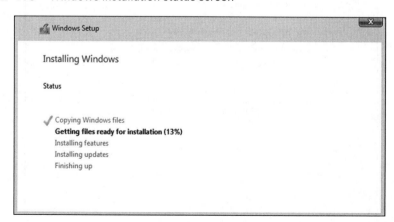

9. After the system restarts, a screen appears that asks if you want to use custom or express settings, as shown in Figure 1.7. Click the Use Express Settings button. The system will then restart.

FIGURE 1.7   Windows express settings screen

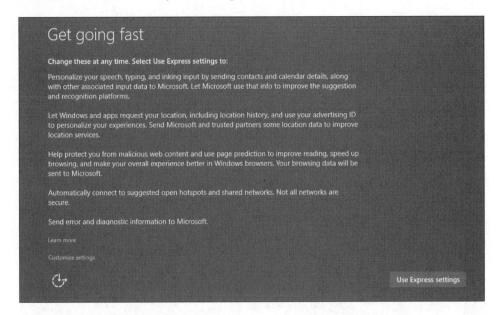

10. After the restart, a screen appears that asks you to choose how you will connect. Select Join A Domain (see Figure 1.8), and then click the Next button.

FIGURE 1.8   Choosing a domain

11. The next screen asks you to enter a username and password. Type in your username, password, and a password hint, as shown in Figure 1.9. Then click Next.

FIGURE 1.9   PC account screen

The Hi screen will appear, and the system will continue its setup. Then the system applications will be installed.

12. You will be asked if you want your system to be recognized by other systems on the network. This is a choice you can make. If you want other machines to see this Windows 10 system, choose Yes.

Once Windows 10 finishes its installation, you should see the Windows 10 desktop, as shown in Figure 1.10.

FIGURE 1.10 Windows 10 screen

Before we talk about the Windows 10 upgrade procedure, I want to quickly explain something that you saw during the Windows 10 install. In step 10, I had you choose Join A Domain instead of Azure AD. We will explore both of the choices in greater detail, but I wanted to quickly explain why we chose one over the other.

Microsoft offers two main networks: workgroup-based or domain-based. *Workgroups* (also referred to as peer-to-peer networks) is when you just connect your computers together directly to each other. A perfect example for most of us is what you do in your home network. Most home users connect their machines together without the use of a main server.

Corporations normally do things a bit differently than that. *Domains* are networks that are controlled by servers called domain controllers. Domain controllers are Windows servers that have a copy of a database called Active Directory (AD). Recently Microsoft took domain-based networks a step further by allowing companies to set up a cloud-based version of an Active Directory domain (Azure AD). This means that companies no longer need to maintain and manage their own domain controllers. Since most people don't have a cloud-based version of Azure AD, I had you choose the option Join A Domain so that we could finish the Windows 10 install.

We will go over all of these options in greater detail throughout this book, but I wanted to introduce you to these two Windows 10 options.

Performing an Upgrade to Windows 10

This section describes how to perform an upgrade to Windows 10 from Windows 8.1. Similar to a clean install, you can run the installation from the installation DVD, from a USB, or over a network. The only difference in the installation procedure is your starting point: from your optical or USB drive or from a network share. For the steps in the following sections, it is assumed that you are using the Windows 10 DVD to install the Windows 10 operating system.

Upgrading a Windows 7 or Windows 8.1 system to Windows 10 will save you a lot of time and trouble. Because we are upgrading the system, all of the user's data and applications will remain installed and most likely still work the exact same way. Sometimes when we upgrade a system, we run into problems with applications. But many times that is caused by a driver or a needed software update that will most likely solve the issue.

The three main steps in the Windows 10 upgrade process are very similar to the ones for a clean install. The three steps of upgrading to Windows 10 are as follows:

1. Collecting information

2. Installing Windows

3. Setting up Windows

In Exercise 1.2, you will go through the process of installing Windows 10 by upgrading Windows 8.1. As you can see in Figure 1.11, I have a Windows 8.1 Enterprise system that I will update to Windows 10 Enterprise.

FIGURE 1.11   Windows 8.1

EXERCISE 1.2

Upgrading Windows 8.1 to Windows 10

1. Insert the Windows 10 DVD. (We are upgrading Windows 8.1 Enterprise to Windows 10 Enterprise.)

2. If Autorun does not start, navigate to the DVD drive and click setup.exe. Once the setup starts (via either setup.exe or Autorun), click Run Setup.exe as shown in Figure 1.12.

FIGURE 1.12   DVD setup screen

3. If a pop-up box appears for User Account Control, click the Yes button (see Figure 1.13).

FIGURE 1.13   User Account Control screen

You should then see a message appear stating that Windows is preparing the system, as shown in Figure 1.14.

FIGURE 1.14   Preparing screen

4. You may be prompted to Get Important Updates. You can choose to either download the updates or not do them at this time. Make a choice and click the Next button. (During my installation, I decided to download the updates.)

5. The Microsoft Windows 10 license terms appear. Read the terms and then click Accept. (The installation will not allow you to continue until you click Accept.)

6. At the Ready To Install screen (shown in Figure 1.15), you can change what files and/ or apps you want to keep by clicking the Change What To Keep link. Once you're ready, click the Install button.

FIGURE 1.15   Ready To Install screen

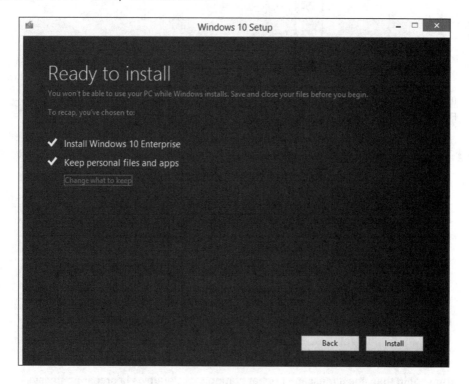

7. Windows 10 will begin to install (as shown in Figure 1.16). Your computer may restart multiple times. This is normal. As the upgrade status screen states, "Sit back and relax."

FIGURE 1.16 Installing Status screen

8. After the upgrade has completed, a welcome screen will be displayed, similar to the one shown in Figure 1.17. Click Next.

FIGURE 1.17 Welcome screen

9. At the Get Going Fast screen, click the Use Express Settings button.

10. At the New Apps screen, just click Next.

And that's it—Windows 10 is installed (see Figure 1.18). Congrats.

FIGURE 1.18 Windows 10 screen

Now that we have installed the Windows 10 operating system, let's take a look at how to change your system's locales. Earlier I explained that the locale settings help you with the systems language format, settings, and region-specific details.

In Exercise 1.3, I will show you how to change your current locale. This helps when you take your Windows 10 laptop, tablet, or phone to another part of the world.

EXERCISE 1.3

Configuring Locales

1. Click the Start button and choose Settings.

2. Once in the Settings screen, choose Time And Language.

3. This should place you on the Date & Time screen. Make sure that your time zone is set correctly. If it's not, pull down the Time Zone options and choose your time zone.

4. Scroll down and make sure the date and time formats are set the way you want. If they are not, click the Change Date And Time Formats link. Change the formats to the way you want them set.

5. Click the Region And Language link on the left-hand side.

6. Make sure the country or region is set properly. If you want to add a second language to this Windows 10 system, click the Add A Language link. Choose the language you want.

7. Once completed, close the Settings screen.

Troubleshooting Installation Problems

The Windows 10 installation process is designed to be as simple as possible. The chances for installation errors are greatly minimized through the use of wizards and the step-by-step process. However, it is possible that errors will occur.

Identifying Common Installation Problems

As most of you are aware, installations sometimes do get errors. You might encounter some of the following installation errors:

Media Errors   Media errors are caused by defective or damaged DVDs. To check the disc, put it into another computer and see if you can read it. Also check your disc for scratches or dirt—it may just need to be cleaned.

Insufficient Disk Space   Windows 10 needs at least 16 GB for the 32-bit OS and 20 GB for the 64-bit OS to execute properly. If the Setup program cannot verify that this space exists, the program will not let you continue.

Not Enough Memory   Make sure your computer has the minimum amount of memory required by Windows 10 (1 GB for 32-bit or 2 GB for 64-bit). Having insufficient memory may cause the installation to fail or blue-screen errors to occur after installation.

Not Enough Processing Power   Make sure your computer has the minimum processing power required by Windows 10 (1 GHz or faster processor or SoC). Having insufficient processing power may cause the installation to fail or blue-screen errors to occur after installation.

Hardware That Is Not on the HCL   If your hardware is not listed on the HCL, Windows 10 may not recognize the hardware or the device may not work properly.

Hardware with No Driver Support   Windows 10 will not recognize hardware without driver support.

Hardware That Is Not Configured Properly   If your hardware is Plug and Play (PnP) compatible, Windows 10 should configure it automatically. If your hardware is not Plug and

Play compatible, you will need to manually configure the hardware per the manufacturer's instructions.

Incorrect Product Key   Without a valid product key, the installation will not go past the Product Key screen. Make sure you have not typed in an incorrect key (check your Windows 10 installation folder or your computer case for this key).

Failure to Access TCP/IP Network Resources   If you install Windows 10 with typical settings, the computer is configured as a DHCP client. If there is no DHCP server to provide IP configuration information, the client will still generate an autoconfigured IP address but be unable to access network resources through TCP/IP if the other network clients are using DHCP addresses.

Installing Nonsupported Hard Drives   If your computer is using a hard disk that does not have a driver included on the Windows 10 media, you will receive an error message stating that the hard drive cannot be found. You should verify that the hard drive is properly connected and functional. You will need to obtain a disk driver for Windows 10 from the manufacturer and then specify the driver location by selecting the Load Driver option during partition selection.

Troubleshooting with Installation Log Files

When you install Windows 10, the Setup program creates several log files. You can view these logs to check for any problems during the installation process. Two log files are particularly useful for troubleshooting:

- The action log includes all of the actions that were performed during the setup process and a description of each action. These actions are listed in chronological order. The action log is stored as \Windows\setupact.log.

- The error log includes any errors that occurred during the installation. For each error, there is a description and an indication of the severity of the error. This error log is stored as \Windows\setuperr.log.

In Exercise 1.4, you will view the Windows 10 Setup logs to determine whether there were any problems with your Windows 10 installation.

EXERCISE 1.4

Troubleshooting Failed Installations with Setup Logs

1. Select Start ➢ Computer.

2. Double-click Local Disk (C:).

3. Double-click Windows.

4. In the Windows folder, double-click the Setupact.log file to view your action log in Notepad. When you are finished viewing this file, close Notepad.

5. Double-click the Setuperr.log file to view your error file in Notepad. If no errors occurred during installation, this file will be empty. When you are finished viewing this file, close Notepad.

6. Close the directory window.

Supporting Multiple-Boot Options

You may want to install Windows 10 but still be able to run other operating systems. *Dual-booting* or multibooting allows your computer to boot multiple operating systems. Your computer will be automatically configured for dual-booting if there was a dual-boot–supported operating system on your computer prior to the Windows 10 installation, you didn't upgrade from that operating system, and you installed Windows 10 into a different partition.

One reason for dual-booting is to test various systems. If you have a limited number of computers in your test lab and you want to be able to test multiple configurations, you should dual-boot. For example, you might configure one computer to dual-boot with Windows 7, Windows 8.1, and Windows 10.

Here are some keys to successful dual-boot configurations:

- Make sure you have plenty of disk space.

- Windows 10 must be installed on a separate partition in order to dual-boot with other operating systems.

- Install older operating systems before installing newer operating systems. If you want to support dual-booting with Windows 7 and Windows 10, Windows 7 must be installed first. If you install Windows 10 first, you cannot install Windows 7 without ruining your Windows 10 configuration.

- Do not install Windows 10 on a compressed volume unless the volume was compressed using NTFS compression.

Once you have installed each operating system, you can choose the operating system that you will boot to during the boot process. You will see a boot-selection screen that asks you to choose which operating system you want to boot.

The Boot Configuration Data (BCD) store contains boot information parameters that were previously found in boot.ini in older versions of Windows. To edit the boot options in the BCD store, use the bcdedit utility, which can be launched only from a command prompt. To open a command prompt window, you can do one of the following:

- Launch \Windows\system32\cmd.exe.

- Open the Run command by pressing the [Windows] key + R and then entering **cmd**.

- Type **cmd.exe** in the Search Programs And Files box and press Enter.

Once the command-prompt window is open, type **bcdedit** to launch the bcdedit utility. You can also type **bcdedit/?** to see all the different bcdedit commands. A few bcdedit commands may be needed when dual-booting a machine. Table 1.5 shows some of the bcdedit commands that may be needed when dual-booting.

TABLE 1.5   Bcdedit commands for dual-booting

Command	Explanation
/createstore	Creates a new empty boot configuration data store
/default	Allows you to specify which operating system will start when the time-out expires
/deletevalue	Allows you to delete a specified element from a boot entry
/displayorder	Shows the display order that the boot manager uses when showing the display order to the user
/export	Allows you to export the contents of the system store into a file
/import	Restores the system store by using the data file previously generated by using the /export option
/set	Allows you to set an entry option value
/store	Specifies the store to be used
/timeout	Specifies the amount of time used before the system boots into the default operating system

Using Windows Activation

Windows Activation is Microsoft's way of reducing software piracy. Unless you have a corporate license for Windows 10, you will need to perform post-installation activation. This can be done online or through a telephone call. Windows 10 will attempt automatic activation three days after you log on to it for the first time. There is a grace period when you will be able to use the operating system without activation. After the grace period expires, you will not be able to create new files or save changes to existing files until Windows 10 is activated. When the grace period runs out, the Windows Activation Wizard will automatically start (see Figure 1.19); it will walk you through the activation process. You may need to click the Change Product Key button and put in the license number that came with your Windows 10 copy.

FIGURE 1.19   The Windows Activation Wizard screen

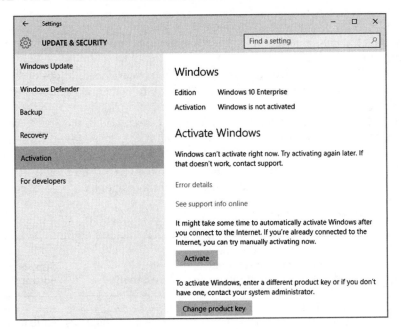

Windows Update

Windows Update is a utility that connects to the Microsoft website or to a local update server called a Windows Server Update Services (WSUS) server to ensure that the Windows 10 operating system (along with other Microsoft products) has the most up-to-date versions of Microsoft operating system files or software.

Some of the common update categories associated with Windows Update are as follows:

- Security updates
- Critical updates
- Service packs
- Drivers
- Product/Software updates
- Windows Store

So let's begin by looking at how Windows 10 updates get created by Microsoft.

The Update Process

To truly understand updates, you need to understand how the update process works with Microsoft. Microsoft normally releases updates to its products on Tuesdays (this is why we use the term *Patch Tuesdays*). But before that update gets released to the public, it has already been tested at Microsoft.

It all starts with the Windows engineering team adding new features and functionality to Windows using product cycles. These product cycles are comprised from three phases: development, testing, and release.

After the new Windows 10 features and functionality are developed, Microsoft employees test these updates out themselves on their own Windows 10 machines. This is referred to as "selfhost testing."

After the updates get tested at Microsoft, they then get released to the public. With Windows 10, Microsoft has introduced new ways to service updates. Microsoft's new servicing options are referred to as Current Branch (CB), Current Branch for Business (CBB), and Long-Term Servicing Branch (LTSB). Table 1.6 (taken directly from Microsoft's website) shows the different servicing options and the benefits of those options.

TABLE 1.6 Update Servicing Options

Servicing Option	Availability of Updates	Minimum length of servicing lifetime	Key benefits	Supported editions
Current Branch (CB)	Immediately after first published by Microsoft	Approximately 4 months	Makes new features available to users as soon as possible	Home, Pro, Education, Enterprise, IoT Core, Windows 10 IoT Core Pro (IoT Core Pro)
Current Branch for Business (CBB)	Approximately 4 months after first published by Microsoft	Approximately 8 months	Provides additional time to test new feature upgrades before deployment	Pro, Education, Enterprise, IoT Core Pro
Long-Term Servicing Branch (LTSB)	Immediately after published by Microsoft	10 Years	Enables long-term deployment of selected Windows 10 releases in low-change configurations	Enterprise LTSB

For more information on Microsoft servicing options, go to Microsoft's website:

```
https://technet.microsoft.com/en-us/itpro/windows/manage/
introduction-to-windows-10-servicing
```

Using Windows Update

There are two ways a user can receive updates: directly from Microsoft or using Microsoft Windows Server Update Services (WSUS). WSUS runs on a Windows server, and that server goes out to the Microsoft website and downloads the updates for your Windows clients. This allows client machines to receive their updates from a local server.

One advantage to using WSUS is that administrators can approve the updates before they get deployed to the client machines. Another advantage is that your clients only need to download updates locally, without using your Internet bandwidth.

     WSUS is discussed in detail in *MCSA: Windows Server 2012 R2 Complete Study Guide* by William Panek (Sybex, 2015).

If you want the Windows 10 clients to access and get their own updates, they would follow these steps to configure Windows Update:

1. Select Start ➢ Control Panel.

    - From Windows Icons View, select Windows Update.

    - From Windows Category View, select System And Security ➢ Windows Update.

2. Configure the options you want to use for Windows Update by clicking the Advanced Options link. The options you can access from Windows Update include the following:

    - Choose how updates are installed

        - This setting allows you to set how the machine updates are done. You can set this setting to Automatic or Notify to schedule a restart.

    - Give me updates for other Microsoft products

        - This setting allows you to get updates for other Microsoft products like Microsoft Office.

    - Defer Upgrades

        - When you choose to defer upgrades, new Windows features will not be downloaded or installed. Deferring upgrades doesn't apply security updates.

    - View Update History

        - This option allows you to see which updates have been loaded or not loaded.

    - Choose how updates are delivered

        - This option allows you to choose how you get your updates, either from Microsoft's website (internet) or from a WSUS server.

    - Get Insider Builds

        - This option allows you to join the Windows Insider Program and you'll be able to receive preview builds and give Microsoft feedback.

Check For Updates

When you click Check For Updates, Windows Update will retrieve a list of available updates from the Internet. You can then click View Available Updates to see what updates are available. Updates are marked as Important, Recommended, or Optional. Figure 1.20 shows the Check For Updates button.

FIGURE 1.20 Check For Updates button

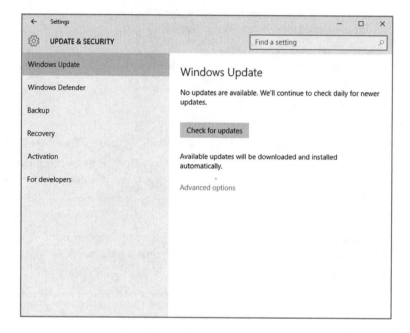

Installing Windows Service Packs

Service packs are updates to the Windows 10 operating system that include bug fixes and product enhancements. Some of the options that might be included in service packs are security fixes or updated versions of software, such as Internet Explorer.

Prior to installing a service pack, you should perform the following steps:

1. Back up your computer.

2. Check your computer to ensure that it is not running any malware or other unwanted software.

3. Check with your computer manufacturer to see whether there are any special instructions for your computer prior to installing the service pack.

You can download service packs from `https://support.microsoft.com/en-us/help/14162/windows-service-pack-and-update-center`.

You can also receive service packs via Windows Update, or you can pay for a copy of a service pack to be mailed to you on disk. Before you install a service pack, you should read the release notes that are provided on the Microsoft website.

Installing Windows Store Updates

Besides getting updates for the Windows 10 operating system and the different Microsoft products, you may also need to get updates for any of the applications, games, music, videos, and software that you downloaded from the Windows Store. To receive Windows Store updates, you need to go out to the Windows Store and then click on your user's account (see Figure 1.21).

FIGURE 1.21   Windows Store button

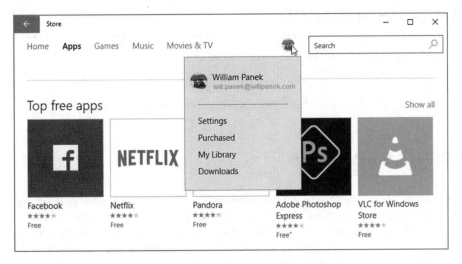

After you click on the Windows Store user's account, you click on the Downloads link. That will take you to the Downloads And Installs page (see Figure 1.22). Once on this page, click the Check For Updates button. This will allow you to download and install any Windows Store updates.

FIGURE 1.22   Check For Updates button

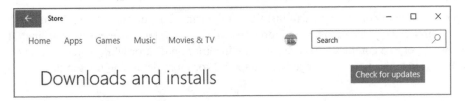

Summary

This chapter started with a discussion of the features included with Windows 10. We also took a look at the difference between 64-bit and 32-bit operating systems and showed some of the advantages that 64-bit entails, such as greater RAM and processor speed.

Then you learned about installing Windows 10. Installation is an easy process, but you must first make sure the machine is compatible with the Windows 10 operating system.

There are two main ways to install Windows 10: upgrade or clean install. You can upgrade a Windows 7 or Windows 8 machine to Windows 10. You can't upgrade Windows XP to Windows 10.

After the Windows 10 installation is complete, you'll want to make sure all updates and service packs are installed. You can use Windows Update to complete that task.

Video Resources

There are videos available for the following exercises:

1.1

1.2

You can access the videos at http://www.wiley.com/go/sybextestprep.

Exam Essentials

Understand the Windows 10 hardware requirements.   The minimum hardware requirements to run Windows 10 properly are 1 gigahertz (GHz) or faster processor or SoC, 1 gigabyte (GB) for 32-bit or 2 GB for 64-bit of RAM, 16 GB for 32-bit OS, 20 GB for 64-bit OS of hard drive space, DirectX 9 or later with WDDM 1.0 video driver, and a DVD-R/W drive or compatible network interface card.

Understand the Hardware Compatibility List.   The Hardware Compatibility List (HCL) is an extensive list of computers and peripheral hardware devices that have been tested with the Windows 10 operating system. The hardware and supported drivers on the HCL have been put through rigorous tests to ensure their compatibility with Windows 10. Microsoft guarantees that the items on the list meet the requirements for Windows 10 and do not have any incompatibilities that could affect the stability of the operating system.

Understand how to complete a clean install.   If your machine meets the minimum hardware requirements, you can install Windows 10. There are a few different ways to install Windows 10 onto a computer. You can use the installation disk or USB, install it over a network, or install it from an image (see Chapter 2 for more details on imaging).

Understand how to complete an upgrade.   You can't upgrade a Windows Vista machine to Windows 10. To complete an upgrade on a Windows 7 or Windows 8 machine, insert the Windows 10 DVD into the Windows machine or connect to the Windows 10 files over the network and complete an upgrade on the computer.

You can't upgrade a Windows XP machine directly to Windows 10. If the machine is running Windows XP, you have to use a migration tool to migrate all the user data from Windows XP to a Windows 10 machine.

Understand how to receive updates.   You need to understand how to set up and receive Microsoft updates for Windows 10, Microsoft products, and the Windows Store. Make sure you know the different settings for configuring update advanced options.

Review Questions

1. You are the administrator in charge of a computer that runs both Windows 7 and Windows 10. Windows 10 is installed on a different partition from Windows 7. You have to make sure that the computer always starts Windows 7 by default. What action should you perform?

   A. Run Bcdedit.exe and the /default parameter.

   B. Run Bcdedit.exe and the /bootcd parameter.

   C. Create a Boot.ini file in the root of the Windows 10 partition.

   D. Create a Boot.ini file in the root of the Windows 7 partition.

2. You are the administrator for a Windows 10 computer. You have decided to use Windows Update, but you want to be able to change the settings manually. What should you do?

   A. Log on to Windows 10 as a member of the Administrators group.

   B. From the local Group Policy, modify the Windows Update settings.

   C. Right-click Windows Update and select Run As Administrator.

   D. Right-click the command prompt, select Run As Administrator, and then run Wuapp.exe.

3. You are the administrator for a large organization. You have a Windows 10 Enterprise machine called Machine1. Machine1 is configured to receive updates from Microsoft's website. If a user is currently logged onto Machine1, you need to prevent Machine1 from restarting without the user's consent. How do you configure this?

   A. Configure the setting "Choose how updates are installed."

   B. Enable the "Defer Settings" button.

   C. Edit the "Schedule Automatic Updates" settings.

   D. Configure the setting "Choose how updates are delivered."

4. You are the IT manager for a medium-sized organization. Your organization is looking at upgrading its Windows XP machines to Windows 10. The managers have heard of a new feature that allows you to connect a device to the machine and then the Windows 10 operating system shows a graphic of the device for use. Which Windows 10 feature are they referring to?

   A. Device Manager

   B. Device Stage

   C. Staging Manager

   D. Add/Remove Hardware

5. You are the IT manager for your organization. The organization is looking at upgrading all of its machines from Windows XP to Windows 10. Many of the managers are concerned that their Windows XP applications won't be compatible with Windows 10. Which Windows 10 feature can you use to assure the managers that all of their Windows XP applications will continue to work?

   A. Windows XP Compatibility Checker

   B. Windows XP Application Center

   C. Windows Hyper-V client

   D. Windows XP Application Upgrade tool

6. You are the network administrator for a large company that wants all users to receive their updates from a local WSUS server. Currently all of your users receive their updates from the Internet. How do you configure the Windows 10 system to get the updates from a WSUS server?

    A. Configure the setting "Choose how updates are installed."

    B. Enable the "Defer Settings" button.

    C. Edit the "Schedule Automatic Updates" settings.

    D. Configure the setting "Choose how updates are delivered."

7. You are the IT administrator for a large computer-training company that uses laptops for all its employees. Currently the users have to connect to the wireless network through the wireless network adapter. Windows 10 now includes this built in as which feature?

    A. Available Network Finder (ANF)

    B. View Networks (VN)

    C. Network Availability Viewer (NAV)

    D. View Available Networks (VAN)

8. You are the network administrator for a midsized company. One of the managers has come into your office and asked you about setting up a network in his house. He wants to use Windows 10. What feature allows him to set up a home network using Windows 10?

    A. Home Networking

    B. HomeGroup

    C. Quick Connect

    D. Networking Groups

9. Which new Windows 10 feature allows you to quickly access files that you have been working on?

    A. Quick Connect

    B. Jump Lists

    C. File Finder

    D. Quick File Access

10. You are the IT manager for a pharmaceutical company. The company wants to create a medication dispenser that can be used on the floors of hospital units. The dispensers have to work through touch-screen technology. Which Windows 10 feature provides built-in touch-screen technology?

    A. Windows Touch Screen

    B. Windows Pure Touch

    C. Windows Touch

    D. Windows Pure Screen

Chapter

2

Installing in an Enterprise Environment

MICROSOFT EXAM OBJECTIVES COVERED IN THIS CHAPTER:

✓ **Installing Windows.**

- This objective may include but is not limited to the following subobjectives: Configure native boot scenarios, install to virtual hard disk (VHD), boot from VHD, install additional Windows features.

✓ **Implement Windows in an enterprise environment.**

- This objective may include but is not limited to the following subobjectives: Provision with the Windows Imaging and Configuration Designer (ICD) tool; implement Active Directory–based activation; implement volume activation using a Key Management Service (KMS); query and configure activation states using the command line.

✓ **Configure devices and device drivers.**

- This objective may include but is not limited to the following subobjectives: Use the Deployment Image and Service Management (DISM) tool to add packages.

✓ **Configure storage.**

- This objective may include but is not limited to the following subobjectives: Create and configure VHDs.

✓ **Perform post-installation configuration.**

- This objective may include but is not limited to the following subobjectives: Configure Hyper-V.

As you can see from the first chapter, installing Windows 10 is a quick and easy process. There may be times when you have to install Windows 10 in an enterprise environment and have to install hundreds of copies of Windows 10.

I will show you how to take a snapshot image of a Windows 10 system and how to move and manipulate these images. I will show you how to use images to install Windows 10 and the tools that can help you maintain those images.

I will also introduce you to Microsoft's virtualization servers called Hyper-V. I will show you how to create virtual hard drives (VHDs) and then use these VHDs to install Windows 10.

I will also start introducing you to networking and Active Directory and how we can use Active Directory–based activations.

Understanding Imaging

When I talk about installing Windows 10 into a corporate environment, I am talking about installing hundreds of Windows 10 machines on the network. Installing each machine one at a time is a slow and very time-consuming process.

Over the years, many IT people have used third-party tools to create images of a system that can be deployed later. An image is just a picture of an operating system that you can use later for multiple installations.

Disk imaging is the process of taking a checkpoint of a computer and then using that checkpoint to create new computers, thus allowing for automated deployments. The reference, or source, computer has Windows 10 installed and is configured with the settings and applications that should be installed on the target computers. The image (checkpoint) is then created and can be transferred to other computers, thus installing the operating system, settings, and applications that were defined on the reference computer.

So if an image is just a picture of an operating system, what tools can we use to take that picture? Well Microsoft provides us with some of these tools. Not only can we take a picture using the Microsoft tools, we can also deploy that image onto other machines. So let's start taking a look at some imaging tools.

An Overview of the System Preparation Tool and Disk Imaging

The *System Preparation Tool*, or *Sysprep* (Sysprep.exe), is used to prepare a computer for disk imaging, and the disk image can then be captured by using the Image Capture Wizard (an imaging-management tool included with Windows 10) or by using the Deployment Image Servicing and Management (DISM) utility.

 The Deployment Image Servicing and Management utility also gives you the ability to create an image. We will discuss DISM in greater detail throughout this chapter.

Sysprep is a free utility that comes on all Windows operating systems. By default, the Sysprep utility can be found on Windows Server 2012 R2 and Windows 10 operating systems in the \Windows\system32\sysprep directory.

Using Imaging Software

Using the System Preparation Tool and disk imaging is a good choice (and the one most commonly used in the real world) for automatic deployment when you have a large number of computers with similar configuration requirements or machines that need to be rebuilt frequently.

For example, StormWind Studios, a live online instructor-led computer training company, reinstalls the same software every few weeks for new classes. Imaging is a fast and easy way to simplify the deployment process.

Most organizations use images to create new machines quickly and easily, but they also use them to reimage end users' machines that crash.

In most companies, end users will have space on a server (home folders) to allow them to store data. We give our end users space on the server because this way we need to back up only the servers at night and not the end users' machines. If your end users place all of their important documents on the server, that information gets backed up.

Now, if we are also using images in our company and an end user's machine crashes, we just reload the image and they are backed up and running in minutes. Since their documents are being saved on the server, they do not lose any of their information.

Many organizations use third-party imaging software (such as Ghost) instead of using Sysprep.exe and Image Capture Wizard. This is another good way of imaging your Windows 10 machines. Just make sure your third-party software supports the Windows 10 operating system.

To perform an unattended installation, the System Preparation Tool prepares the reference computer by stripping away any computer-specific data, such as the security identifier (SID), which is used to uniquely identify each computer on the network; any event logs; and any other unique system information. The System Preparation Tool also detects any Plug and Play devices that are installed and can adjust dynamically for any computers that have different hardware installed.

When the client computer starts an installation using a disk image, you can customize what is displayed on the Windows Welcome screen and the options that are displayed through the setup process. You can also fully automate when and how the Windows Welcome screen is displayed during the installation process by using the /oobe (out-of-the-box experience) option with the System Preparation Tool and an answer file named Oobe.xml. The out-of-the-box experience makes the newly built system work as if you took the new system right out of the manufacturer's box.

Sysprep is a utility that is good only for setting up a new machine. You do not use Sysprep to image a computer for upgrading a current machine. There are a few switches that you can use in conjunction with Sysprep to configure the Sysprep utility for your specific needs. Table 2.1 shows you the important Sysprep switches and what they will do for you when used.

TABLE 2.1   Sysprep switches

Switch	Explanation
/pnp	Forces a mini-setup wizard to start at reboot so that all Plug and Play devices can be recognized.
/generalize	This allows Sysprep to remove all system-specific data from the Sysprep image. If you're running the GUI version of Sysprep, this is a check-box option.
/oobe	Initiates the Windows Welcome screen at the next reboot. This makes the machine work as if it's a first time bootup right out of the box.
/audit	Initiates Sysprep in audit mode.
/nosidgen	Sysprep does not generate a new SID on the computer restart. Forces a mini-setup on restart.
/reboot	Stops and restarts the computer system.
/quiet	Runs without any confirmation dialog messages being displayed.
/mini	Tells Sysprep to run the mini-setup on the next reboot.

 Real World Scenario

The SID Problem with Deployment Software

For many years, when you had to create many machines that each had a Microsoft operating system on it, you would have to use files to help deploy the multiple systems.

Then, multiple third-party companies came out with software that allowed you to take a picture of the Microsoft operating system, and you could deploy that picture to other machines. One advantage of this is that all the software that is installed on the system could also be part of that picture. This was a great way to copy all the software on a machine over to another machine.

There was one major problem for years—*security identifier (SID)* numbers. All computers get assigned a unique SID that represents them on a domain network. The problem for a long time was that when you copied a machine to another machine, the SID number was also copied.

Microsoft released Sysprep many years ago, and that helped solve this problem. Sysprep would allow you to remove the SID number so that a third-party software package could image it to another machine. Many third-party image software products now also remove the SID numbers, but Sysprep was one of the first utilities to help solve this problem.

When you decide to use Sysprep to set up your images, there are a few rules that you must follow for Sysprep to work properly:

- You can use images to restart the Windows activation clock. The Windows activation clock starts to decrease as soon as Windows starts for the first time. You can restart the Windows activation clock only three times using Sysprep.

- The computer on which you're running Sysprep has to be a member of a workgroup. The machine can't be part of a domain. If the computer is a member of the domain, when you run Sysprep, the computer will automatically be removed from the domain.

- When installing the image, the system will prompt you for a product key. During the install you can use an answer file, which in turn will have all the information needed for the install, and you will not be prompted for any information.

- A third-party utility or Image Capture Wizard is required to capture and deploy the image that is created from Sysprep.

- If you are using Sysprep to capture an NTFS partition, any files or folders that are encrypted will become corrupt and unreadable.

- One advantage to Sysprep and Windows 10 is that you can use Sysprep to prepare a new machine for duplication. You can use Sysprep to image a Windows 10 machine. The following steps are necessary to image a new machine:

    1. Install the Windows 10 operating system.

    2. Install all components on the OS.

    3. Run Sysprep /generalize to prepare the system for imaging.

    4. The system will reboot. After the computer reboots, use an image-capturing tool to capture your image.

Advantages of the System Preparation Tool

The following are advantages of using the System Preparation Tool as a method for automating Windows 10 installations:

- For large numbers of computers with similar hardware, it greatly reduces deployment time by copying the operating system, applications, and desktop settings from a reference computer to an image, which can then be deployed to multiple computers.

- Using disk imaging facilitates the standardization of desktops, administrative policies, and restrictions throughout an organization.

- Reference images can be copied across a network connection or through DVDs that are physically distributed to client computers.

Disadvantages of the System Preparation Tool

There are some disadvantages of using the System Preparation Tool as a method for automating Windows 10 installations:

- Image Capture Wizard, third-party imaging software, or hardware disk-duplication devices must be used for an image-based setup.

- The version of the System Preparation Tool that shipped with Windows 10 must be used. An older version of Sysprep cannot be used on a Windows 10 image.

- The System Preparation Tool will not detect any hardware that is not Plug and Play compliant.

In Exercise 2.1, you will use the System Preparation Tool to prepare the computer for disk imaging. The Sysprep utility must be run on a machine with a clean version of Windows 10. If you upgraded a Windows 7 or 8 machine to Windows 10, you will not be able to run the Sysprep utility.

EXERCISE 2.1

Prepare a System for Imaging by Using the System Preparation Tool

1. Log on to the source computer as Administrator, and if desired, install and configure any applications that should also be installed on the target computer.

2. Select Start ➢ Computer, and navigate to C:\%WINDIR%\System32\sysprep. Double-click the Sysprep application icon.

3. In the System Preparation Tool dialog box, select Enter System Out-Of-Box Experience (OOBE) in the system cleanup action.

4. Under the shutdown options, depending on the options selected, the System Preparation Tool will quit, the computer will shut down, or the computer will be rebooted into setup mode, where you will need to configure the setup options. Choose the Reboot option. Click OK.

5. After the system shuts down, you use an image capture tool to grab the image.

Overview of the Windows Assessment and Deployment Kit

Another way to install Windows 10 is to use the *Windows Assessment and Deployment Kit (ADK).* The Windows ADK is a set of utilities and documentation that allows an administrator to configure and deploy Windows operating systems. An administrator can use the Windows ADK to do the following:

- Windows Imaging and Configuration Designer (ICD)
- Windows Assessment Toolkit
- Windows Performance Toolkit

The Windows ADK can be installed and configured on the following operating systems:

- Windows 10
- Windows 7/8 with SP1
- Windows Server 2012 R2
- Windows Server 2012
- Windows Server 2008
- Windows Server 2008 R2
- Windows Server 2003 with SP2

The Windows ADK is a good solution for organizations that need to customize the Windows deployment environments. The Windows ADK allows an administrator to have the flexibility needed for mass deployments of Windows operating systems. Since every organization's needs are different, the Windows ADK allows you to use all or just some of the deployment tools available. It allows you to manage deployments by using some additional tools.

Windows Imaging and Configuration Designer (ICD)   The tools included with this part of the Windows ADK will allow an administrator to easily deploy and configure Windows operating systems and images.

Windows Application Compatibility Toolkit   When new Windows operating systems are installed, applications that ran on the previous version of Windows may not work properly. The Application Compatibility Toolkit allows an administrator to help solve these issues before they occur.

Windows Performance Toolkit   The Windows Performance Toolkit is a utility that will locate computers on a network and then perform a thorough inventory of them. This inventory can then be used to determine which machines can have Windows 10 installed.

Windows Imaging and Configuration Designer

The Windows Imaging and Configuration Designer (ICD) allows an administrator to work with images. The ICD allows an IT department to do the following:

- View and configure all of the settings and policies for a Windows 10 image or provisioning package

- Create Windows provisioning answer files
- Allow an answer file to add third-party drivers, apps, or other assets
- Create variants and specify the settings that apply to each variant
- Build and flash a Windows image
- Build a provisioning package

The Windows ICD gives an IT department many options on how to deploy and set up Windows 10 clients. Here are some of the functions that can be performed with the Windows ICD tools:

- Configure and edit images by using the Deployment Image Servicing and Management utility
- Create Windows Preinstallation Environment (Windows PE) images
- Migrate user data and profiles using the User State Migration Tool (USMT). This tool needs to be downloaded from Microsoft.
- Windows Imaging and Configuration Designer (Windows ICD)

Using Windows ICD to Create a Disk Image

After you've run the System Preparation Tool on the source computer, you can create an image from the installation, and you can then install the image on target computers. To create an image, you can use Image Capture Wizard, which is a utility that can be used to create and manage Windows image (.wim) files.

To run the Image Capture Wizard utility to create a disk image of a Windows 10 installation, follow these steps:

1. From the Windows ICD Start page, select New Windows Image Customization.
2. In the Enter Project Details window, specify a Name and Location for your project. Optionally, you can also enter a brief Description to describe your project.
3. Click Next.
4. If you selected New Windows Image Customization from the Start page, skip this step.
5. In the Select Project Workflow window, select Imaging from the list of available project workflows and then click Next.
6. In the Select Imaging Source Format window, select "The Windows image is based on a Windows image (WIM) file" and then click Next.
7. In the Select Image window, click Browse to launch File Explorer. Search and locate the path to the Install.wim file.

After you've selected the Install.wim file, all the Windows images in the .wim file are listed in the Available images panel. By default, the first Windows image in the list is selected, and the information about this image is displayed in the Image Information panel.

1. Select the Windows image that you want to use and then click Next.
2. Optional: If you have a provisioning package that contains customizations already configured in a different project and you want to reuse the customizations from this

package, click Browse in the Import A Provisioning Package screen to locate the provisioning package that was exported from another project.

3. Click Finish.

There is also a command-line version of the Windows ICD tool that you can use. The Microsoft exams have started using a lot of command-line utilities on their tests. So let's take a look at the Windows ICD command-line utility. The command that we use for this is icd.exe, as follows:

```
icd.exe <command> <parameters>
```

Table 2.2 describes some of the icd.exe command switches that you can use to configure the images.

TABLE 2.2   icd.exe switches

Switch	Description
/CustomizationXML	Identifies the location of the Windows provisioning XML file. This file holds the information for customization assets and settings.
/PackagePath	Identifies the location and the built provisioning package name where the package will be saved.
/StoreFile	Allows IT administrators to use their own settings store instead of the default store used by Windows ICD. If an IT administrator does not determine his or her own store, a default store that's common to all Windows editions will be loaded by Windows ICD.
/MSPackageRoot	Identifies the location of the root directory that holds the Microsoft packages that you downloaded from the Windows portal.
/OEMInputXML	Identifies the location to the OEMInput.xml file. This file defines a subset of settings that can be designed based on the image type.
/Variables	Identifies a macro pair that is separated by a semicolon, <name> and <value>.
Encrypted	Indicates whether or not the provisioning package should be created with encryption. Windows ICD will then automatically generate a decryption password that is included with the output.
Overwrite	Indicates whether or not to overwrite the existing provisioning package.
/?	Used to access the ICD help, which lists the switches and their descriptions for the ICD command-line tool.

After you create the disk image, the next step is to install it. In the next section, you'll learn how to install the disk image on a new machine.

Installing from a Disk Image

After you've run the System Preparation Tool and Image Capture Wizard on the source computer, you can copy the image and then install it on the target computer.

Once the image is copied, you should boot the destination computer into the Windows PE. If the computer has been used previously, it may be necessary to reformat the hard drive, which you can do using the diskpart command in Windows PE. If the image is stored over the network, you should then copy the image to the destination computer by using the net use [dir] [network share] and copy [file] [dir] commands. Then, you should use the /apply option of the Image Capture Wizard utility to apply the image to the local computer. If an answer file has not been deployed along with the image, you may have to apply such information as regional settings, the product key, the computer name, and the password to the new computer after the destination computer is rebooted.

In Exercise 2.2, you will use the stripped image that was created in Exercise 2.1 to simulate the process of continuing an installation from a disk image.

EXERCISE 2.2

Installing Windows 10 from a Disk Image

1. Boot the target computer into Windows PE.

2. Copy the image created in Exercise 2.1 to the local computer by using the following commands:

   ```
   net use z: \\Server\Images
   copy Z:\Images\image.wim E:
   ```

3. Apply the image to the target computer using the following Image Capture Wizard command:

   ```
   D:\ICD.exe /apply E:\Images\image.wim C:
   ```

When you install Windows 10, the installation wizard asks you questions such as your username and computer name. There is a way to answer these questions without actually being in front of the computer.

Using the Deployment Image Servicing and Management Tool

Deployment Image Servicing and Management (DISM.exe) is a command-line utility that allows you to manipulate a Windows image. DISM also allows you to prepare a Windows

PE image. DISM replaces multiple programs that were included with Windows 7/8. These programs include Package Manager (Pkgmgr.exe), PEimg, and Intlcfg. These tools have been consolidated into one tool (DISM.exe), and new functionality has been added to improve the experience for offline servicing.

DISM provides additional functionality when used with Windows 10 and Windows Server 2012 R2. You can use DISM to do the following:

- Add, remove, and enumerate packages
- Add, remove, and enumerate drivers
- Enable or disable Windows features
- Apply changes to an Unattend.xml answer file
- Configure international settings
- Upgrade a Windows image to a different edition
- Prepare a Windows PE 3.0 image

DISM works with all platforms (32-bit, 64-bit, and Itanium) and allows for the use of Package Manager scripts.

Table 2.3 describes the commands that can be used with DISM.exe.

TABLE 2.3 DISM.exe command-line commands

Command	Description
/Add-Driver	Adds third-party driver packages to an offline Windows image.
/Get-CurrentEdition	Displays the edition of the specified image.
/Get-Drivers	Displays basic information about driver packages in the online or offline image. By default, only third-party drivers will be listed.
/Get-DriverInfo	Displays detailed information about a specific driver package.
/Get-Help /?	Displays information about the option and the arguments.
/Get-TargetEditions	Displays a list of Windows editions that an image can be changed to.
/Remove-Driver	Removes third-party drivers from an offline image.
/Set-ProductKey:<productKey>	Can only be used to enter the product key for the current edition in an offline Windows image.

Understanding Hyper-V

In the following sections, I'll introduce you to Hyper-V. To begin, we'll take a look at virtualization and what types of virtualization exist. We will then discuss Hyper-V features and the Hyper-V architecture before finishing up with the Hyper-V requirements for software and hardware.

Hyper-V is very important to understand when working with Windows 10 because you can load a Windows 10 guest virtual machine onto a Hyper-V host system and you also have the ability to use Windows 10 as a Windows Hyper-V host.

Let's first make sure you understand what host and guest systems do. The Hyper-V machine that has another operating system running on top of it is a host. If you are running an operating system on top of another operating system, you are the guest system. So Windows 10 can be set up as a Hyper-V host or a Hyper-V guest.

So if you are running Windows Server 2012 R2 Hyper-V and the computer has issues, you can load the Server 2012 R2 Hyper-V virtual machines onto a Windows 10 Hyper-V host system. This gives you a temporary solution while the Windows Server 2012 R2 Hyper-V server gets repaired.

So why are we talking about Hyper-V in a Windows 10 deployment chapter? Because you can build a Windows 10 virtual machine and use that virtual machine to deploy Windows 10 operating systems throughout an organization.

What Is Virtualization?

Virtualization is a method for abstracting physical resources from the way they interact with other resources. For example, if you abstract the physical hardware from the operating system, you get the benefit of being able to move the operating system between different physical systems.

This is called *server virtualization*. But there are also other forms of virtualization available, such as presentation virtualization, desktop virtualization, and application virtualization. I will now briefly explain the differences between these forms of virtualization:

Server Virtualization   This basically enables multiple operating systems to run on the same physical server. Hyper-V is a server virtualization tool that allows you to move physical machines to virtual machines and manage them on a few physical servers. Thus, you will be able to consolidate physical servers.

Presentation Virtualization   When you use *presentation virtualization*, your applications run on a different computer and only the screen information is transferred to your computer. An example of presentation virtualization is Microsoft Remote Desktop Services in Windows Server 2012 R2.

Desktop Virtualization   *Desktop virtualization* provides you with a virtual machine on your desktop, comparable to server virtualization. You run your complete operating system and applications in a virtual machine so that your local physical machine just needs to run a very basic operating system. An example of this form of virtualization is Microsoft Windows 10 Hyper-V.

Application Virtualization   *Application virtualization* helps prevent conflicts between applications on the same PC. Thus, it helps you to isolate the application running environment from the operating system installation requirements by creating application-specific copies of all shared resources, and it helps reduce application-to-application incompatibility and testing needs. An example of an application virtualization tool is Microsoft Application Virtualization (App-V).

Installing the Hyper-V Role

Now it's time to see how to install the Hyper-V server role on both a Windows Server machine and a Windows 10 client. I'll show you how to install Hyper-V onto a Windows Server 2012 R2 system as well as how to load Hyper-V onto a Windows 10 Enterprise system.

So why am I showing both installations? Because you can load Windows 10 onto a Windows Server 2012 R2 Hyper-V server and you can use Windows 10 as a Hyper-V server.

Installing Hyper-V in Windows Server 2012 R2

You can install the Hyper-V server role on any Windows Server 2012 R2 installation. The server must meet both the hardware and software requirements. The installation process is simple, as Exercise 2.3 demonstrates.

EXERCISE 2.3

Installing Hyper-V in Windows Server 2012 R2

1. Open Server Manager.

2. In Server Manager, choose number 2, Add Roles And Features.

3. At the Select Installation Type page, choose the role-based or feature-based installation. Click Next.

4. On the Select Destination Server screen, choose Select A Server From The Server Pool and choose the server to which you want to add this role. Click Next.

5. On the Select Server Roles screen, click the check box next to Hyper-V. When the Add Features dialog box appears, click the Add Features button. Then click Next.

6. At the Select Features screen, just click Next.

7. At the Hyper-V introduction screen, just click Next.

8. At the Create Virtual Switches screen, choose your adapter and click Next.

9. At the Virtual Machine Migration screen, just click Next. You want to use migration only if you have multiple Hyper-V servers. Since we will have only one for this exercise, just skip this screen.

10. At the Default Stores screen, accept the defaults and click Next.

EXERCISE 2.3 *(continued)*

11. At the Confirmation screen, click the Install button.

12. After the installation is complete, click the Close button.

13. Restart your server.

Installing Hyper-V in Windows 10

You can install the Hyper-V server role on any Windows 10 Professional or Enterprise installation. The Windows 10 system must meet both the hardware and software requirements. The installation process is shown in Exercise 2.4.

EXERCISE 2.4

Installing Hyper-V on Windows 10

1. Right-click the Windows button and select Programs And Features.

2. Select the Turn Windows Features On Or Off option.

3. Select Hyper-V and click OK (as shown in Figure 2.1).

FIGURE 2.1   Installing Hyper-V

4. After the installation is complete, click the Close button.

5. Restart your system.

Now that you know how to install the Hyper-V roles onto a Windows 10 system using Programs And Features, let's install Hyper-V onto Windows 10 by using PowerShell. The following command is run in Windows PowerShell:

```
Enable-WindowsOptionalFeature -Online -FeatureName Microsoft-Hyper-V -All
```

The following PowerShell command is used to install Hyper-V into a Windows 10 image while it's an actual image:

```
DISM /Online /Enable-Feature /All /FeatureName:Microsoft-Hyper-V
```

Using Hyper-V Manager

Hyper-V Manager is the central management console to configure your server and create and manage your virtual machines, virtual networks, and virtual hard disks. Unlike Virtual Server 2005, where you managed all virtual machines through a web interface, Hyper-V Manager is managed through a Microsoft Management Console (MMC) snap-in.

You can access it by right-clicking the Start button ➤ Control Panel ➤ Administrative Tools ➤ Hyper-V Manager. Figure 2.2 shows how Hyper-V Manager looks once you start it.

FIGURE 2.2   Hyper-V Manager

Manage Virtual Switches

A virtual network provides the virtual links between nodes in either a virtual or physical network. Virtual networking in Hyper-V is provided in a secure and dynamic way because you can granularly define virtual network switches for their required usage. For example, you can define a private or internal virtual network if you don't want to allow your virtual machines to send packets to the physical network.

To allow your virtual machines to communicate with each other, you need virtual networks. Just like normal networks, virtual networks exist only on the host computer and allow you to configure how virtual machines communicate with each other, with the host, and with the network or the Internet. You manage virtual networks in Hyper-V using Virtual Switch Manager.

Using Virtual Switch Manager, you can create, manage, and delete virtual switches. You can define the network type as external, internal only, or private.

External   Any virtual machine connected to this virtual switch can access the physical network. You would use this option if you want to allow your virtual machines to access, for example, other servers on the network or the Internet. This option is used in production environments where your clients connect directly to the virtual machines.

Internal   This option allows virtual machines to communicate with each other as well as the host system but not with the physical network. When you create an internal network, it also creates a local area connection in Network Connections that allows the host machine to communicate with the virtual machines. You can use this if you want to separate your host's network from your virtual networks.

Private   When you use this option, virtual machines can communicate with each other but not with the host system or the physical network; thus, no network packets are hitting the wire. This option allows virtual machines on the same Hyper-V host to communicate without using any network traffic.

On the external and internal-only virtual networks, you also can enable virtual LAN (VLAN) identification. You can use VLANs to partition your network into multiple subnets using a VLAN ID. When you enable virtual LAN identification, the NIC that is connected to the switch will never see packets tagged with VLAN IDs. Instead, all packets traveling from the NIC to the switch will be tagged with the access mode VLAN ID as they leave the switch port. All packets traveling from the switch port to the NIC will have their VLAN tags removed. You can use this if you are already logically segmenting your physical machines and also use it for your virtual ones.

Managing Virtual Hard Disks

In addition to virtual networks, you need to manage virtual hard disks that you attach to your virtual machines. A virtual hard disk in Hyper-V, apart from a pass-through disk, is a VHD or VHDX file that basically simulates a hard drive on your virtual machine.

The following sections will first show you what types of virtual hard disks are available and then show you how to create them. You will also learn about what options are available to manage virtual hard disks.

Types of Hard Disks

Depending on how you want to use the disk, Hyper-V offers various types, as described in Table 2.4.

TABLE 2.4   Types of virtual hard disks

Type of Disk	Description	When to Use It
Dynamically expanding	This disk starts with a small VHD file and expands it on demand once an installation takes place. It can grow to the maximum size you defined during creation. You can use this type of disk to clone a local hard drive during creation.	This option is effective when you don't know the exact space needed on the disk and when you want to preserve hard disk space on the host machine. Unfortunately, it is the slowest disk type.
Fixed size	The size of the VHD file is fixed to the size specified when the disk is created. This option is faster than a dynamically expanding disk. However, a fixed-size disk uses up the maximum defined space immediately. This type is ideal for cloning a local hard drive.	A fixed-size disk provides faster access than dynamically expanding or differencing disks, but it is slower than a physical disk.
Differencing	This type of disk is associated in a parent-child relationship with another disk. The differencing disk is the child, and the associated virtual disk is the parent. Differencing disks include only the differences to the parent disk. By using this type, you can save a lot of disk space in similar virtual machines. This option is suitable if you have multiple virtual machines with the same operating systems.	Differencing disks are most commonly found in test environments and should not be used in production environments.
Physical (or pass-through disk)	The virtual machine receives direct pass-through access to the physical disk for exclusive use. This type provides the highest performance of all disk types and thus should be used for production servers where performance is the top priority. The drive is not available for other guest systems.	This type is used in high-end data centers to provide optimum performance for VMs. It's also used in failover cluster environments.

Creating Virtual Hard Disks

To help you gain practice in creating virtual hard disks, the following three exercises will teach you how to create a virtual machine, installing Hyper-V Integration Components, and creating a checkpoint of a virtual machine.

Changing Virtual Hard Disks

Hyper-V also provides two tools to manage virtual hard disks: Inspect Disk and Edit Disk. These tools are available on the Actions pane in Hyper-V Manager:

Inspect Disk   This provides you with information about the virtual hard disk. It shows you not only the type of the disk but also information like the maximum size for dynamically expanding disks and the parent VHD for differencing disks.

Edit Disk   This provides you with the Edit Virtual Hard Disk Wizard, which you can use to compact, convert, expand, merge, or reconnect hard disks.

Table 2.5 provides an overview of what you can do with the wizard.

TABLE 2.5   Edit Disk overview

Action	Description
Compact	Reduces the size of a dynamically expanding or differencing disk by removing blank space from deleted files.
Convert	Converts a dynamically expanding disk to a fixed disk or vice versa.
Expand	Increases the storage capacity of a dynamically expanding disk or a fixed virtual hard disk.
Merge	Merges the changes from a differencing disk into either the parent disk or another disk (applies to differencing disks only!).
Reconnect	If a differencing disk does not find its referring parent disk anymore, this option can reconnect the parent to the disk.

Configuring Virtual Machines

The following sections cover the topics of creating and managing virtual machines as well as how to back up and restore virtual machines using features like Import and Export and Checkpoints.

Creating and Managing Virtual Machines

It is important to learn how to create a virtual machine, how to change its configuration, and how to delete it. We will take a look at the Virtual Machine Connection tool and install the Hyper-V Integration Components onto a virtual machine.

Virtual machines define the child partitions in which you run operating system instances. Each virtual machine is separate and can communicate with the others only by using a virtual network. You can assign hard drive(s), virtual network(s), DVD drives, and other system components to it. A virtual machine is similar to an existing physical server, but it doesn't run on dedicated hardware anymore—it shares the hardware of the host system with the other virtual machines that run on the host.

Exercise 2.5 shows you how to create a new virtual machine.

EXERCISE 2.5

Creating a New Virtual Machine

1. Open Hyper-V Manager.

2. In Hyper-V Manager, on the Actions pane, choose New ➢ Virtual Machine.

3. In the New Virtual Machine Wizard, click Next on the Before You Begin page.

4. On the Specify Name And Location page, give your virtual machine a name and change the default location of the virtual machine configuration files. Click Next to continue.

5. On the Assign Memory page, define how much of your host computer's memory you want to assign to this virtual machine. Remember that once your virtual machine uses up all your physical memory, it will start swapping to disk, thus reducing the performance of all virtual machines. Click Next to continue.

6. On the Configure Networking page, select the virtual network that you previously configured using Virtual Network Manager. Click Next to continue.

7. On the next page, you configure your virtual hard disk. You can create a new virtual hard disk, select an existing disk, or choose to attach the hard disk later. Be aware that you can create only a dynamically expanding virtual disk on this page; you cannot create a differencing, physical, or fixed virtual hard disk here. However, if you created the virtual hard disk already, you can, of course, select it. Click Next to continue.

8. On the Installation Options page, you can select how you want to install your operating system. You have the option to install an operating system later, install the operating system from a boot CD/DVD-ROM where you can select a physical device or an image file (ISO file), install an operating system from a floppy disk image (VFD file, or a virtual boot floppy disk), or install an operating system from a network-based installation server. The last option will install a legacy network adapter to your virtual machine so you can boot from the network adapter. Select Install An Operating System Later and then click Next.

9. On the Completing The New Virtual Machine Wizard summary page, verify that all settings are correct. You also have the option to immediately start the virtual machine after creation. Click Next to create the virtual machine.

10. Repeat this process and create a few more virtual machines.

11. If you want to install an operating system on one of the VMs, start the VM, load a Windows 10 installation disk into the DVD, and then under the Media menu, choose DVD and Capture. Then just do a normal install.

After completing Exercise 2.5, you will have a virtual machine available in Hyper-V Manager. Initially, the state of the virtual machine will be Off. Virtual machines can have the following states: Off, Starting, Running, Paused, and Saved. You can change the state of a virtual machine in the Virtual Machines pane by right-clicking the virtual machine's name or by using the Virtual Machine Connection window.

Here is a list of some of the state options (when the VM is running) available for a virtual machine:

Start   Turn on the virtual machine. This is similar to pressing the power button when the machine is turned off. This option is available when your virtual machine is off or in saved state.

Turn Off   Turn off the virtual machine. This is similar to pressing the power off button on the computer. This option is available when your virtual machine is in running, saved, or paused state.

Shut Down   This option shuts down your operating system. You need to have the Hyper-V Integration Components installed on the operating system; otherwise, Hyper-V will not be able to shut down the system.

Save   The virtual machine is saved to disk in its current state. This option is available when your virtual machine is running or in paused state.

Pause   Pause the current virtual machine, but do not save the state to disk. You can use this option to quickly release processor utilization from this virtual machine to the host system.

Reset   Reset the virtual machine. This is like pressing the reset button on your computer. You will lose the current state and any unsaved data in the virtual machine. This option is available when your virtual machine is running or in paused state.

Resume   When your virtual machine is paused, you can resume it and bring it online again.

Installing Hyper-V Integration Components

Hyper-V Integration Components, also called Integration Services, are required to make your guest operating system "hypervisor aware." These components improve the performance of the guest operating system once the components are installed. On the architectural perspective, virtual devices are redirected directly via the VMBus; thus quicker access to resources and devices is provided.

If you do not install the Hyper-V Integration Components, the guest operating system uses emulation to communicate with the host's devices, which of course makes the guest operating system slower.

Exercise 2.6 shows you how to install Hyper-V Integration Components on one of your virtual machines running Windows 10.

EXERCISE 2.6

Installing Hyper-V Integration Components

1. Open Hyper-V Manager.

2. In Hyper-V Manager, in the Virtual Machines pane, right-click the virtual machine on which you want to install Hyper-V Integration Components and select Start.

3. Right-click the virtual machine again and select Connect. Meanwhile, your virtual machine should be already booting.

4. If you need to log in to the operating system of your virtual machine, you should do so.

5. Once the Windows desktop appears, you need to select Insert Integration Services Setup Disk from the Actions menu of your Virtual Machine Connection window.

6. Once the Hyper-V Integration Components are installed, you are asked to perform a reboot.

After the reboot, Hyper-V Integration Components are installed on your operating system, and you will be able to use them.

Managing Checkpoints

With virtual machine checkpoints (formerly known as virtual machine snapshots), you can save a copy of the virtual machine at any point in time, including while the virtual machine is running. You can take multiple checkpoints of a virtual machine and then revert it to any previous state by applying a checkpoint.

Using checkpoints makes it easier to diagnose the cause of errors by reducing the number of times you need to repeat a task or sequence within a virtual machine. The benefit is obvious; if you use checkpoints to revert to a previous virtual machine configuration, you do not need to copy virtual machines to keep a state. Thus, it is a quick and easy way to back up a certain state of your virtual machine.

You can create a checkpoint when a virtual machine is in a running, saved, or turned-off state. It's only from a paused state that you cannot perform a checkpoint.

In Exercise 2.7, you'll create and rename a checkpoint.

EXERCISE 2.7

Creating a Checkpoint of a Virtual Machine

1. Open Hyper-V Manager.

2. In Hyper-V Manager, in the Virtual Machines pane, right-click the virtual machine.

3. Select Checkpoints.

4. Once the checkpoint is taken, it should appear in the Checkpoints pane in Hyper-V Manager. Right-click the checkpoint and select Settings.

5. In the Settings window, on the Management pane, click Name and type in First CheckPoint as the name. You can also add some notes to make it easy to identify.

6. Click OK to apply the changes. You will now see that the checkpoint has a new name.

Technically speaking, when you make a checkpoint, the following files will be created in the virtual machine's checkpoints folder:

- A virtual machine configuration file
- Virtual machine saved state files
- Checkpoints differencing disks (AVHDs)

Once you create a checkpoint for a virtual machine, you will also have the Revert option available in the virtual machine name's pane in Hyper-V Manager. Reverting basically means that you restore the last checkpoint made. You'll also see the last checkpoint taken marked with a green arrow in the Checkpoints pane.

Settings   This opens the Settings window of the virtual machine. The only settings you can change are the Name and Notes fields. All others are read-only.

Apply   Applying a checkpoint to a virtual machine technically means that you copy the virtual machine state from the checkpoints to the active virtual machine. You can look at this as a "restore this checkpoint" option. Because you would lose all unsaved data and settings from the active virtual machine, you will be asked if you want to create another checkpoint before you apply this checkpoint. If you just click Apply, the active machine will be overwritten and reverted to the state it was in when the checkpoints was made. This checkpoint will not be removed.

Export   This allows you to export the checkpoint to another location.

Rename   You can change the name of the checkpoint without the need to open the settings.

Delete Checkpoints   Deleting a checkpoint is like deleting a backup file. You will no longer be able to restore to that point in time. Deleting a single checkpoint does not affect any other checkpoints that you made for this virtual machine. You will delete only the selected checkpoints. However, sometimes when you do delete a checkpoint, the system needs to merge the differencing disks. This occurs in the background when the virtual machine is not running. The user does not see when it happens.

Delete Checkpoints Subtree   This will delete the selected checkpoints and all checkpoints that are hierarchically underneath it. If you delete a checkpoint with only one sub-checkpoint, the configuration and saved state files for the checkpoints will be deleted and the checkpoint's differencing disks will be merged. If you have more sub-checkpoints, merging will not take place.

In Exercise 2.8, you will apply a checkpoint and thus revert to a previous virtual machine state.

EXERCISE 2.8

Applying a Checkpoint

1.   Open Hyper-V Manager.

2.   In Hyper-V Manager, in the Virtual Machines pane, click the virtual machine for which you created a checkpoint.

3.   In the Checkpoints pane, select First Checkpoints.

4.   In the First Checkpoints pane, under Actions, click Apply.

5.   In the Apply Checkpoints window, click Apply.

Moving Virtual Machines

There may be times when you need to move a virtual machine or its storage to another server or location. In this section, we will look at how to move virtual machines and storage.

When you are using Hyper-V, you cannot move the configuration files anymore. You need to use the Export feature to export the virtual machine and then use Import on the target machine to import the virtual machine to Hyper-V.

To export a virtual machine, it must be in either Off or Saved state. Open Hyper-V Manager, select the virtual machine you want to export, and either right-click the virtual machine and select Export or click Export on the virtual machine name's pane.

In this window, you can set the export path for the virtual machine and choose whether to export your virtual machine state data or not.

Once you check Don't Export Virtual Machine State Data, only the virtual machine's configuration files will be exported. The virtual hard disk and snapshots will not be exported.

In the export path, a folder with the name of the virtual machine is created along with the following subfolders:

Virtual Machines   This includes the virtual machine configuration files as well as the virtual machine state if the machine is saved.

Virtual Hard Disks   If you exported the state data, this folder will include your virtual hard disks VHD file(s).

Snapshots   If you exported the state data, this folder will include all snapshot files.

Once the virtual machine finishes exporting, you can move the export folder to the target machine if you did not store it directly on the server's disks. Open Hyper-V Manager and click Import Virtual Machine, which is located in the Actions pane.

The Import Virtual Machine dialog box asks you for the path to the exported virtual machine and allows you to decide if you want to reuse the old virtual machine ID.

You want to reuse old virtual machine IDs if you're moving all virtual machines from a host to a new target machine. The virtual machines are practically the same as on the source system. However, you do not want to reuse old virtual machine IDs if you used Export to clone a virtual machine.

When you import a virtual machine with state data, Hyper-V will use the import path for the virtual hard disks as well as snapshots in its virtual machine configuration XML. Thus, you're able to import an exported machine only once. For that reason, the import folder should already be on the host's target disk.

Booting from a VHD

What if you could build a Windows 10 virtual hard drive and then take that VHD to another machine running Windows 7 or Windows 8/8.1 and boot the machine up from the Windows 10 VHD? Well you can do just that. Windows 10 has the ability to boot up from a VHD.

So let's take a look at the process to do a Native Boot from a VHD. *Native Boot* means that you can boot up to a VHD without the need of having a virtual server or hypervisor on the system you're booting from.

1. First step is to create an MBR partitioned VHD on a GPT drive.

2. Then you need to apply the installation image to the VHD.

3. Finally, you need to set the Windows 10 VHD to boot.

So now that we know the process needed to boot from Windows 10, let's take a look at each step of the processes in greater detail.

Creating an MBR Partitioned VHD

So the first step to do a Native Boot from VHD is to create an MBR partitioned VHD. So the following steps are done on a Windows 7 Professional machine.

1. Open Computer Management ➢ Disk Management. If you're on Windows 8, right click the Start menu and choose Disk Management.

2. Under the Action menu, choose Create VHD (see Figure 2.3). This will start the Create VHD wizard.

FIGURE 2.3   Create VHD wizard

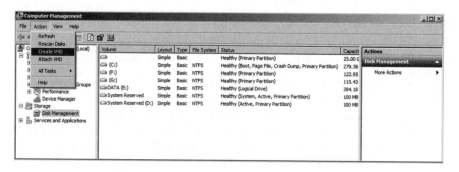

3. Next you will need to specify the location of the VHD folder on the GPT disk.

4. Then you will need to put in the desired size of the VHD.

5. Next you will need to choose between a VHD or VHDX. Windows 7 is only compatible with VHDs. Windows 8 can use the larger VHDX.

6. You will then choose between a fixed size VHD or dynamically expanding VHD.

7. After the creation of the VHD, the VHD will automatically be attached. The disk icon will be tinted blue.

8. Next you will need to right click on the VHD disk and select Initialize Disk. This will prepare the VHD disk for usage.

9. You will then choose the MBR partition style for initializing the disk.

10. The VHD disk will then be initialized. Next you will need to right click the unallocated space next to the disk and select New Simple Volume. This will launch the New Simple Volume Wizard.

11. Just go ahead and keep the defaults. This will use the entire disk.

12. Next we need to assign a drive letter to the volume. For example, assign the Z: to the drive.

13. We will format the partition next. Choose NTFS and label the partition (any label name is fine).

14. Finally, close the Disk Management MMC.

Applying the Windows 10 Image to the VHD

Now that we have created the VHD file, we need to apply an image to that VHD file. To do this, we will be using the DISM tool. Now if you are on Windows 7, you will need to download the Windows Assessment and Deployment Kit to use DISM. If you are on Windows 8 or higher, the DISM tool is included with the operating system.

1. First we will mount or install the VHD file. To do this, insert or mount the installation media for the VHD environment. The VHD image can also be extracted to a folder.

2. Next we will open an administrative Command Prompt or PowerShell session.

3. Finally we will apply the install.wim file from the Sources folder of the installation media to the VHD mounted at drive letter Z by entering the following command:

```
DISM /Apply-Image /ImageFile:D:\Sources\install.wim /Index:1 /ApplyDir:Z:\
```

 If the machine has been rebooted since the VHD was created, you may need to reattach the VHD (Z:). If this happened to you, open Disk Administrator, and under the Actions Menu, choose Attach VHD before running the above command.

4. You can now close the Command Prompt or PowerShell session.

Configuring the Boot Options

The final step in this process is configuring the boot options so that we can boot to the Windows 10 VHD. To do this, complete the following steps.

1. Open an administrative Command Prompt or PowerShell session.

2. Next we need to change the directory so we are in the System32 folder. You can use the following command to complete this step.

```
CD V:\Windows\System32
```

3. Enter the following command to add the VHD boot files to the system partition. This will allow the system to dual boot:

```
BCDBoot Z:\Windows
```

4. Finally, close the Command Prompt or PowerShell session and reboot the computer.

After the system reboots, you will be given a choice of which operating system you want to start. By choosing the Windows 10 operating system, you will boot up to Windows 10. The great thing about this is that you can keep Windows 7 or Windows 8 on that system and boot into the Windows 10 operating system anytime you want.

Installing Additional Windows Features to an Image

One advantage of images today is that there are tools that allow us to configure and maintain an image while it's still in the image format. If you think back a few years, we would create an image and use that image to deploy an operating system. If that operating system image needed to be changed, you would have to load the image onto a computer, make the changes you wanted to the operating system, and then recapture the image again for deployment.

Now, you no longer need to do that. We can configure or change an image while it's still an image. To do this, you will use the DISM tool. The following steps make up the process to add features to an image:

1. Mount an offline image for maintenance.

2. View available Windows features in the image.

3. Enable or disable Windows features.

4. Commit changes to the offline image.

Mounting an Offline Image for Maintenance

So the first step is to prepare the offline image for maintenance. To do this, we will mount the offline image. To mount an image for maintenance, you would complete the following steps:

1. First step is to open a command prompt with administrator privileges.

2. Now we need to run commands using DISM. We will run the /Get-ImageInfo DISM command to get the image number or name of the image we want to work on. In the following code, we will be looking at an image named Install.wim under a folder called Win10Image.

```
Dism /Get-ImageInfo /ImageFile:C:\Win10Image\install.wim
```

3. After we get the image name or index number, we will next mount the offline image so that we can work on it.

```
Dism /Mount-Image /ImageFile:C:\Win10Image\install.wim /Name:"Windows10
Image" /MountDir:C:\Win10Image\offline
```

Viewing the Available Windows Features

After the image has been mounted, we need to see what Windows features are available for installation. To complete this stage, we would do the following steps.

1. The first step is to open a command prompt with Administrator privileges.

2. Run the following command to see what features are available.

```
Dism /Image:C:\Win10Image\offline /Get-Features
```

3. Leave the command prompt open.

Enabling or Disabling a Windows Features

After we see what features are available, we can go ahead and enable the feature. The following command allows you to enable a feature in an offline image:

1. Run the following command to enable a feature. In this example, I am enabling FTP.

```
Dism /Image:C:\Win10Image\offline /Enable-Feature /FeatureName:FTP /All
```

You may also want to disable a feature that is already enabled on the image. To disable a feature, you would run the following command from the command prompt:

```
Dism /Image:C:\Win10Image\offline /Disable-Feature /FeatureName:FTP
```

Committing Changes to the Offline Image

After the changes have been made to the image, you need to commit the changes. To commit changes to the offline image, type in the following command from the administrative command prompt:

```
Dism /Unmount-Image /MountDir:C:\Win10Image\offline /Commit
```

Activating Machines in the Enterprise

In Chapter 1 "Windows 10 Installation," I talked about activating your Windows 10 system. In the following sections, I will show you how to do activations of Windows 10 in an enterprise environment.

This means that you can activate Windows 10 by using the Active Directory network. But before we talk about Active Directory–based activation, let's talk a little about networking.

Now we will cover networking in greater detail in Chapter 7, "Windows 10 Networking," but I wanted to give you some basic introductions so that you understand what Active Directory does.

Networking Basics

When we talk about Microsoft networking, we are talking about three ways to set up a network. You can set up a network as a HomeGroup, as a Workgroup, or as a Domain. Two of these (HomeGroups and Workgroups) are basically the same type of network setup. They are just two different ways to have the same outcome. So let's start by explaining what a HomeGroup or Workgroup network does.

HomeGroup or Workgroup networks are what we refer to as Peer-to-Peer networks. What that means is that the machines on that network work as a server and as a client machine. In a Peer-To-Peer network, there is no central database that controls the network.

 Microsoft doesn't use the term Peer-to-Peer. Its versions of Peer-to-Peer networks are called Workgroups and HomeGroups. Since there are two types of Peer-to-Peer networks for Windows 10, I will just refer to them as Peer-to-Peer for the remainder of the chapter.

There are many disadvantages to a Peer-to-Peer network. First, there is no centralized control of the network. Each machine has its own database that controls its operating system. This database is called a Security Account Management (SAM) database. The problem that you run into with a SAM is that every Windows 10 system has its own SAM. The SAMs are unique for each machine.

So what this means is that if I have 10 users that are using 10 machines, I need to create an account for each user on each machine (100 accounts). Each Windows 10 system needs to have its own users in its own SAM. Plus, even if the usernames and passwords are the same for each user on each machine, they are different users in the eyes of each Windows 10 system. Windows 10 only uses its local SAM database for authentication, and it will not share that SAM with any other Windows 10 system.

Next we can set up a domain-based network. Domain-based networks use Microsoft's Active Directory or Azure Active Directory, which is a single distributed database that contains all of the objects in your network. A domain is a logical grouping of objects into a distributed database. Some of these objects are user accounts, group accounts, and published objects (folders and printers).

The first of many advantages to Active Directory is centralized management. As just stated, the Active Directory database contains all the network information within a single, distributed, data repository. Because these network objects are all located in the same database, an administrator can easily manage the domain from one location.

So now that I have given you the basics, let's talk about how Active Directory can help you with your Windows activations.

Active Directory–Based Activation

In Chapter 1 I talked about activating your Windows 10 systems, but what if you had 100 or 1000 Windows systems that need to be activated? Would any of us want to walk from machine to machine to activate the systems one at a time? Well the answer is NO and Microsoft gives us some tools to help get the job done.

Active Directory–based activation allows you to use Active Directory to activate you systems. Now the real advantage to this is that you can not only activate your Windows 10 systems, you can activate Windows 8.1, Windows 8, Windows Server 2012 R2, or Windows Server 2012.

So how does the activation process work? Well, the Windows clients create an activation object in Active Directory by submitting a Key Management Service (KMS) host key. *KMS* is an activation service that companies can use to help activate Windows systems on their own networks. By using Active Directory–based activation and KMS, systems can be activated without the need of each Windows system contacting Microsoft for product activation.

To allow this process to work, you need to install a KMS host key on the Windows 10 system. This then allows the Windows 10 system to activate by locating the KMS server. Windows 10 clients will use DNS to find the KMS server on the network.

To set up Active Directory–based activation, administrators need to add the Volume Activation Services server role to a Windows Server. Administrators add the Volume Activation Services by using Server Manager.

Windows systems that are activated using Active Directory–based activation will continue to keep their activation status up-to-date every 7 days. What this means is that the Windows client will reactivate with the KMS server once a week. Now if the client system is away from the domain, the Windows system will keep its activation status for up to 180 days. If the system is off the domain for more than 180 days, the client will lose its activation status after the 180-day period runs out.

To configure KMS on a Windows 10 system, you would need to complete the following process using the command line:

1. Open an elevated command prompt.

2. Enter one of the following commands.

   - To install a KMS key, type **`slmgr.vbs /ipk <KmsKey>`**.

   - To activate online, type **`slmgr.vbs /ato`**.

   - To activate by using the telephone, type **`slui.exe 4`**.

3. After activating the KMS key, restart the Software Protection Service.

Summary

In this chapter, we discussed automated installation of Windows 10. Installing Windows 10 through an automated process is an effective way to install the Windows 10 operating system on multiple computers.

There are several methods for automated installation, including Windows Assessment and Deployment Kit (ADK), third-party applications, DISM, and using the System Preparation Tool.

The Windows 10 Assessment and Deployment Kit (ADK) is a set of utilities and documentation that allows an administrator to configure and deploy Windows operating systems.

You can also prepare an installation for imaging by using the System Preparation Tool (Sysprep.exe) and creating a disk image by using the Image Capture Wizard utility or a third-party utility.

I then talked to you about Hyper-V, virtual machines, and virtual hard drives. I explained how you can create VHDs and boot Windows 10 from a VHD.

Finally, I talked about activation and how you can do volume activation by using Active Directory-Activation along with the KMS server.

Video Resources

There are videos available for the following exercises:

2.1

2.3

You can access the videos at http://www.wiley.com/go/sybextestprep.

Exam Essentials

Understand the uses for Hyper-V.   Hyper-V is one way that Windows 10 can be deployed and tested as a guest on a Hyper-V server. You can also run Windows 10 as a host system and run other virtual machines from Windows 10.

Understand the features of Windows Assessment and Deployment Kit (ADK).   Know when it is appropriate to use Windows ADK and how DISM can be used to capture, deploy, and maintain images. I talked about how DISM can look at an image to see what Windows features are available for installation.

Be able to use disk images for installations.   Know how to perform installations of Windows 10 using the System Preparation Tool and DISM.

Understand the Microsoft activation options.   Know the different Microsoft activation options, including Active Directory-Activation services and KMS.

Review Questions

1. You are the network administrator for your organization. You have a reference computer that runs Windows 10. You need to create and deploy an image of the Windows 10 computer. You create an answer file named `answer.xml`. You have to make sure the installation applies the answer file after you deploy the image. Which command should you run before you capture the image?

    A. `ICD.exe /append answer.xml/check`

    B. `ICD.exe /mount answer.xml/verify`

    C. `Sysprep.exe/reboot/audit/unattend:answer.xml`

    D. `Sysprep.exe/generalize/oobe/unattend:answer.xml`

2. You have a Windows 10 Windows image (WIM) file that is mounted. You need to view the list of third-party drivers installed on the WIM. What should you do?

    A. Run DISM and specify the `/get-drivers` parameter.

    B. Run `Driverquery.exe` and use the `/si` parameter.

    C. From Device Manager, view all hidden drivers.

    D. From Windows Explorer, open the `mount` folder.

3. You are the network administrator for StormWind Studios. StormWind Studios does live online IT training all over the world. StormWind Studios uses images to install Windows 10 and Windows Server 2012 R2 on all of their studio computer systems. You need to add the FTP service to all of the Windows Server images. What tool would you use to manipulate the images while they are in the image format?

    A. Sysprep

    B. DISM

    C. WDS

    D. Active Directory-Activation utility

4. Your organization needs to add the FTP service to a Windows Server 2012 R2 image. The image is located in a folder called `Images\offline`. What DISM command would you use to install the FTP service?

    A. `Dism /Image:C:\Images\offline /Enable-Roles /RolesName:FTP`

    B. `Dism /Image:C:\Images\offline /Enable-Feature /FeatureName:TFTP /All`

    C. `Dism /Image:C:\Images\offline /Enable-Feature /FeatureName:FTP /All`

    D. `Dism /Image:C:\Images\offline /Enable-Roles /RoleName:FTP /All`

5. You are the administrator for a large company that is adding 500 Windows 10 systems. You want to do activations by using an activation service. What can you set up?

    A. KCC activation service

    B. DHCP server

    C. KMS service

    D. WDS server

6. You run a training department that needs the same software installed from scratch on the training computers each week. You decide to use Image Capture Wizard to deploy disk images. Which Windows 10 utility can you use in conjunction with Image Capture Wizard to create these disk images?

    A. UAF

    B. Answer Manager

    C. Setup Manager

    D. System Preparation Tool

7. You are the administrator for a midsize company and you are using Sysprep to prepare a Windows 10 system for imaging. You want to reset the Security ID (SID) and clear the event logs. What Sysprep options would you use?

    A. /oobe

    B. /generalize

    C. /audit

    D. /unattend

8. You are using Hyper-V for virtualization. You want to create a new virtual hard drive and you want all of the hard drive space to be created as soon as the VHD is created. What type of VHD do you want to use?

    A. Dynamically expanding

    B. Fixed

    C. Physical

    D. Differencing

9. You work for StormWind Studios as their IT manager. You want to have the machine boot up from a Windows 10 VHD. What is it called when a system boots up from a virtual hard disk without needing Hyper-V or a hypervisor?

    A. Native boot

    B. Virtual server

    C. VHD boot

    D. Virtual boot

10. You want to install a group of 25 computers using disk images created in conjunction with the System Preparation Tool. Your plan is to create an image from a reference computer and then copy the image to all the machines. You want the image to boot up as if it was a new machine out of the box. Which Sysprep.exe command-line option should you use to set this up?

    A. /specialize

    B. /generalize

    C. /oobe

    D. /quiet

Chapter

3

Configuring Devices and Drivers

MICROSOFT EXAM OBJECTIVES COVERED IN THIS CHAPTER:

✓ **Configure devices and device drivers.**

- This objective may include but is not limited to the following subobjectives: Install, update, disable, and roll back drivers; resolve driver issues; configure driver settings, including signed and unsigned drivers; manage driver packages; download and import driver packages.

✓ **Monitor Windows**

- This objective may include but is not limited to the following subobjectives: monitor and manage printers.

When discussing Windows 10, we must take a look at how hardware is set up and configured. Getting hardware up and running in today's operating systems is not usually a problem. With Plug and Play technology, the initial installation and configuration will typically go smoothly. However, the software controlling the hardware (drivers) will usually need to be updated over time and may need to be rolled back in case of an issue in a new package.

There will also be times when the drivers need to be installed manually for legacy hardware. You may also need to verify the hardware configuration and make adjustments. The utility provided to perform these functions is Device Manager.

Device Manager displays all installed hardware. It also keeps information on storage, both removable and fixed, and on communication devices like network interface cards and wireless and Bluetooth devices.

What you won't see for hardware in Device Manager are printers, unless of course they're USB. In that case, you will see the USB port and thus the printer will be identified, but you won't be able to configure the printer from Device Manager. You will use the Devices And Printers applet for configuring and troubleshooting printers. There is functionality in Windows 10 that integrates some Device Manager functionality into Devices And Printers. This functionality is known as Device Stage.

Configuring Hardware

Configuring hardware properly is one of the most important tasks when setting up Windows 10. Windows 10 has included some tools to help users and administrators configure their hardware properly.

In Windows 10, there is built-in functionality called *Device Stage*. Device Stage offers an enhanced graphic output, giving better details about and functionality to installed devices such as cameras. *Device Manager* works the same way in Windows 10 as it did in Windows 7 and Windows 8/8.1. *Device Manager* is designed to display information about the hardware installed on your computer and as an interface to add and configure new hardware.

Hardware today follows the Plug and Play standard, so most of the time simply connecting hardware will allow Device Manager to automatically configure it. Devices that are not Plug and Play compatible can be installed manually from Device Manager as well.

Understanding Device Stage

Throughout the evolution of technologies and PCs, one of the greatest features is how we can use such a wide array of devices on PCs. Device Manager has allowed us see all the hardware connected and make configuration changes, but utilizing the features of the devices themselves has been left up to programs outside the Windows interface. Windows 10 includes a specification for hardware vendors (knowing that most hardware comes with software for the user to interface with), allowing them to provide user access within Windows. This feature and specification is known as Device Stage. Windows 10 Devices And Printers (Figure 3.1) is the interface for displaying and accessing hardware that supports Device Stage.

FIGURE 3.1   Devices And Printers

Take, for example, a digital camera. Generally, when you connect a camera to a PC, the PC recognizes the device (this immediate recognition is called Plug and Play) and typically displays the camera as a mass storage device. Users wanting advanced features like downloading and editing the photos must use another program. When you plug in a device that supports Device Stage technology, on the other hand, Device Stage displays a single window that gives you easy access to common device tasks, such as, in the case of a camera, importing pictures, launching the vendor-supplied editing programs, and simply browsing pictures, all from one interface.

With Windows 10, you'll be able to access all of your connected and wireless devices from the single Devices And Printers screen, and some devices will be displayed in the Windows 10 enhanced Taskbar. From here, you can work with your devices, browse files they might contain, and manage device settings.

Wireless and Bluetooth devices are also supported by Device Stage, making management of these resources much easier for the end user. As portable devices are disconnected and reconnected, the Device Stage–driven Devices And Printers screen will update in real time. Exercise 3.1 will guide you through opening and viewing devices recognized on your Windows 10 machine. All of the following exercises in this chapter assume that you are in the icon view of Control Panel. To enable icon view, chose Control Panel, and in the right-hand corner, change the view to either large or small icons.

EXERCISE 3.1

Opening Devices And Printers to View Device Stage–Supported Devices

1. Right-click Start ➢ Control Panel ➢ Devices And Printers.

2. To see options specific to a device, right-click the device and choose Properties.

Even simpler, you can type **devices** into the integrated search box to launch Devices And Printers, the first applet in the search list.

Next, we'll take a look at using Device Manager to configure devices.

Using Device Manager

Device Manager is the component in Windows 10 you'll use to see which devices are connected to your machine. You can use Device Manager to ensure that all devices are working properly and to troubleshoot misbehaving devices. For each device installed, you can view specific properties down to the resources being used, such as the assigned I/O (input/output) port and IRQs (interrupt requests). Through Device Manager, you can take the following specific actions:

- View a list of all hardware installed on your computer
- Determine which device driver is installed for each device
- Manage and update device drivers
- Install new devices
- Disable, enable, and uninstall devices
- Use driver rollback to return to a previous version of a driver
- Troubleshoot device problems

More important, you can see which devices Windows 10 has recognized. That is, if you install or connect a new piece of hardware and Windows 10 doesn't recognize it at all, it won't be seen in Device Manager. This would be an unusual occurrence given the sophistication of today's hardware vendors and the Plug and Play standards that are implemented. However, using Device Manager is an important tool in seeing just which devices are known to Windows 10. Keep in mind that we've been using Device Manager for many versions of Windows, so what I'm discussing is applicable to legacy versions as well. In Exercise 3.2, you will view devices using Device Manager.

EXERCISE 3.2

Viewing Device Manager

1. Right-click Start ➤ Device Manager.

2. Click the triangle next to Network Adapters (or double-click Network Adapters) to expand Network Adapters.

The steps in Exercise 3.2 show one way to launch Device Manager, through Control Panel. This is a valid method that shows you where the application resides, but administrators can launch Device Manager in other ways.

You may want to try the following method to open Device Manager: right-click Start and then choose Device Manager. I also sometimes type **Device Manager** (or just **device**) into the Windows integrated search box and press Enter. All of these are means to the same end.

As shown in Figure 3.2, Device Manager has a fairly simple opening screen, but it has a lot of functionality behind it. From the opening screen, you get a good first feeling for the hardware that's installed and recognized and for any major issues, such as a device that's recognized but has no drivers installed or is not working correctly. You'll see a warning symbol displayed over the misbehaving device. For example, suppose you have just installed a new network adapter but the device does not seem to be working. You can open Device Manager and open the Network Adapter option to start the troubleshooting process. Figure 3.2 shows just such a network adapter.

FIGURE 3.2   Device Manager screen

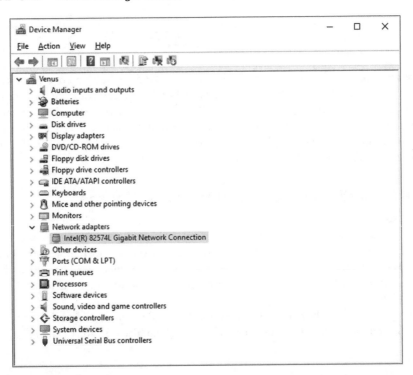

To continue troubleshooting the network adapter within Device Manager, you would right-click the misbehaving adapter and choose Properties to see its Properties dialog box (Figure 3.3). This is just a small part of the functionality within Device Manager.

FIGURE 3.3   Device Manager network adapter properties

There are many reasons to view the devices installed and configured on a machine. One reason is to verify the type and status of hardware. For example, if someone in your organization has given you documentation for a specific user machine that includes the machine's hardware specifications and you are concerned that the stated network adapter for the machine may not be the one actually installed, you can use Device Manager on the machine in question to see the network adapters Windows 10 recognizes in the machine.

Device Properties Available within Device Manager

Once you have opened Device Manager and have access to the installed devices on your machine, you can view their Properties dialog boxes. From there, you can view and change configuration parameters if necessary. You will find that the tabs available in the Properties dialog boxes will vary from device to device because the parameters that are available will vary with different hardware. Most devices will have at a minimum a General tab, a Driver tab, and a Details tab.

The Properties dialog box for most devices will include more specific tabs for the hardware configuration, such as for a network adapter, which also has an Advanced tab for more specific configuration parameters. Figure 3.4 shows a network adapter's Advanced tab and the Value drop-down box active to show possible choices.

FIGURE 3.4   Advanced network interface properties

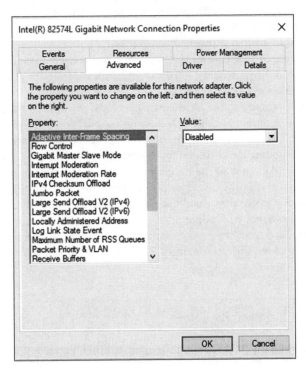

If you need to change the hardware configuration properties, Device Manager is the best way to access the parameters. Exercise 3.3 will show you how to view configurable properties for a network adapter through the Advanced tab.

EXERCISE 3.3

Configuring Network Adapter Advanced Properties

1.   Choose Start ➤ Device Manager.

2.   Click the triangle next to Network Adapters (or double-click Network Adapters) to expand it.

3.   Right-click your network adapter and select Properties.

4.   Choose the Advanced tab.

5.   Select various properties and view the parameters.

In addition to setting up devices, you will need to install and configure device drivers, which I will cover in the next section.

Installing and Updating Device Drivers

Device drivers are the controlling code actually interfacing the hardware components with the operating system. The commands are specific to each piece of hardware, and there may be different commands, memory locations, or actions, even within the same type of hardware. A network interface card (NIC) from one vendor may actually have a different set of instructions than a NIC from a different manufacturer.

An operating system or software works best when it can issue a standard command and have the same functionality across the hardware regardless of vendor. This is where *drivers* come in; the driver takes a standard instruction from the operating system and interprets and then issues the command to the hardware to perform the desired function.

Drivers need to be updated. For example, a command set for a driver may perform a function incorrectly. This can produce errors and would need to be fixed. The hardware vendor will typically update the driver to fix the problem. Oftentimes, new or improved functionality may be necessary, so the hardware vendor would need to change the driver code to add functionality or provide better performance, in turn leading to an update.

There are different ways to download and install drivers. Microsoft drivers can be downloaded using the Windows Update utility. Drivers from different manufacturers can normally be downloaded from the manufacturer's website. Just access their website, search the product, and download the latest drivers. Then you can install those drivers using the Device Manager.

 Real World Scenario

Driver Code Causing an Arbitrary Nonreproducible Error

While working on a consulting job for a company where I was installing a new program and hardware to provide bar code scanning, I was plagued by the bar code readers connected to PCs randomly failing.

The bar code readers seemed to install correctly, and they showed as functioning properly within Device Manager. However, periodically the hardware readers would fail to input data into the application I was using. I could reboot the affected machine and the bar code reader would work fine again (for a while). It's easy to blame the operating system because the reboot seemed to fix the problem, but the operating system wasn't to blame.

After several days of troubleshooting and working with the manufacturer, it was determined that the driver interfacing the operating system with the hardware was not releasing memory resources correctly, causing the driver to fail. We received an updated driver and applied the update to the machines, and the problem was resolved. Be careful not to blame the operating system prematurely, and be sure to investigate other areas for possible problems.

Typical first-time installation of drivers today happens automatically with the Plug and Play specification. After the hardware is installed, Windows 10 will recognize it and launch the driver installation program. Let's take, for example, the connection of a digital camera to the USB port of your computer.

Windows 10 will recognize that a device has been plugged in and will gather the information about the USB device. Windows 10 will then install the best driver it knows about (and if it doesn't know about the device, it will ask you how to proceed). Figure 3.5 shows the message indicating that the operating system found a driver and is installing it automatically.

FIGURE 3.5   Automatic driver installation

The installation completes and the device is now available in Device Manager. If you need to review the driver details for your newly installed device, the network adapter in this case, you can right-click the device in Device Manager and choose Properties. Figure 3.6 shows the right-click menu (also known as the context menu); note that the top choice in this menu is a quick launch to update the driver software.

FIGURE 3.6   Right-click menu for a device in Device Manager

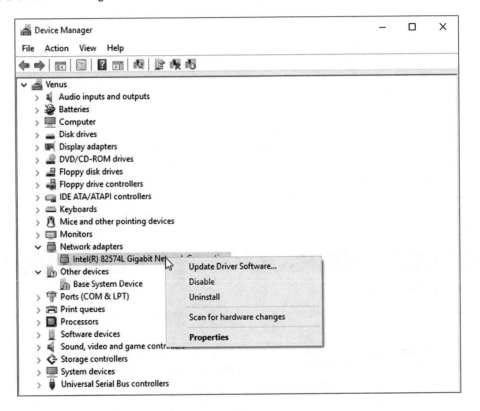

You may want to verify general information about the driver, like the provider or version. You can see that information in the Driver tab of the Properties dialog box. You can also choose to view the driver details, which are the supporting files and associated paths. Figure 3.7 shows the Driver tab for the network adapter.

FIGURE 3.7   Driver details within Device Manager

Sometimes when you're having issues with a hardware device, you will go online and read forums or use search engine queries to attempt to find resolution ideas from other administrators. Someone might mention that they had a problem with a specific driver for the hardware you're researching. They might even mention the exact version of the driver and suggest a fix. Having the ability to view information on drivers and update them is helpful in a situation such as this. Exercise 3.4 walks you through looking at driver details.

EXERCISE 3.4

Viewing Driver Details

1. Right-click Start ➢ Device Manager (or type **device manager** in the integrated search window).

2. Click the triangle next to the category in which you want to view driver details to expand the item list; you can also double-click the category name. For example, double-click the Network Adapters category to see the network connection to the machine.

3. Choose the Driver tab.

4. View the driver version.

5. Click the Driver Details button to see the files associated with the hardware.

Another task may be to update the drivers. In Exercise 3.5, we will look at updating a driver.

Updating a Driver

1. Right-click Start ➤ Device Manager (or type **device manager** in the integrated search window).

2. Click the triangle next to the category for which you want to update the driver to expand the item list; you can also double-click the category name.

3. Right-click the hardware item and select Properties.

4. Choose the Driver tab.

5. Click the Update Driver button; a window launches asking how you want to search for the driver.

6. Choose Search Automatically For Updated Driver Software to have Windows 10 search for you, or choose Browse My Computer For Driver Software if you have the new drivers already.

Windows 10 searches for and updates the drivers or reports back that you have the most current version.

Not only will you often need to update drivers because of a failure or hardware issue, but you will at times install new drivers for new or updated functionality. There will also be times when a hardware driver gets updated and the update breaks a piece of functioning hardware or doesn't solve a problem. In these cases, you will want to go back to the previous version, or "roll back" the driver. In Exercise 3.6, you will learn how to do a driver rollback.

Rolling Back a Driver

1. Right-click Start ➤ Device Manager (or type **device manager** in the integrated search window).

2. Click the triangle next to the category for which you want to roll back the driver to expand the item list; you can also double-click the category name.

3. Right-click the hardware item and select Properties.

4. Choose the Driver tab.

5. Click the Roll Back Driver button. Note that if the Roll Back Driver button is grayed out, there isn't a previous version of the driver available.

The previous driver will be installed and the hardware will return to its previous state of functionality.

The Driver tab for a piece of installed hardware in Device Manager also provides functionality for disabling and uninstalling a driver. Why would you want to disable a driver? There are several possibilities, but troubleshooting is one of the most common reasons.

Disabling the driver effectively disables the hardware; it will no longer function in the system. Uninstalling the device driver has a similar effect, but if the hardware is still installed, you can uninstall the driver and perform a scan to ensure that the hardware is still recognized and force a reinstallation.

I have often disabled a device from Device Manager to eliminate one part of an issue I am having with a system. If I'm confident that the problem is with the hardware, I will uninstall the driver and let the operating system reinstall it as part of the troubleshooting procedure. This works much of the time and is a good place to start. In Exercise 3.7, you will disable and enable a device driver.

EXERCISE 3.7

Disabling and Enabling a Device in Device Manager

1. Right-click Start ➢ Device Manager (or type **device manager** in the integrated search window).

2. Click the triangle next to the appropriate category to expand the item list; you can also double-click the category name.

3. Right-click the hardware item and select Properties. Note that you can select Disable directly from the context menu if desired.

4. Choose the Driver tab.

5. Click the Disable button. (This is a toggle button; it will be labeled Disable if the device is enabled and Enable if the device is disabled.)

6. The device driver and hence the device will be disabled and will no longer function. There will be a down arrow on the item in Device Manager, and the General tab will show that the device is disabled. Close the Properties dialog box for that device.

7. Right-click the hardware item and select Properties.

8. Choose the Driver tab.

9. Click the Enable button. This is a toggle button; it will say Enable if the device is disabled and Disable if the device is enabled.

10. The device driver will become enabled and the hardware will work as designed (barring any other issues).

11. Close Device Manager.

It may be beneficial at times to uninstall and reinstall a device driver. Many times when you do that, the default configuration parameters will be reset to their original specifications.

Any changes you have made will need to be reconfigured, but if the device driver worked previously and has stopped for some unknown reason (if you knew the reason, you'd simply fix it), uninstalling and reinstalling is worth a try. You may also consider using a different device driver than Windows 10 is set up to use via Plug and Play. Note that uninstalling a device driver does not delete the driver files from the machine; uninstalling the device driver removes the operating system configuration for the hardware.

You may want or need to find the driver files and delete them manually in some cases. Remember, you can find the files (and thus the filenames) from Driver Details within the Driver's tab of the Properties dialog box of the hardware within Device Manager.

If you have determined that the device driver for your misbehaving hardware is potentially causing the problem you are having, you can choose to uninstall and reinstall (automatically) the drivers. In Exercise 3.8, you will uninstall and then reinstall a device driver.

EXERCISE 3.8

Uninstalling and Reinstalling a Device Driver

1. Right-click Start ➤ Device Manager (or type **device manager** in the integrated search window).

2. Click the triangle next to the category for the device you want to uninstall to expand the item list; you can also double-click the category name.

3. Right-click the hardware item and select Properties. Note that you can select Uninstall directly from the context menu.

4. Choose the Driver tab.

5. Click the Uninstall button.

EXERCISE 3.8 *(continued)*

6. Click OK in the Confirm Device Uninstall dialog box. A progress box appears as the device driver is uninstalled. Once the driver is uninstalled, Device Manager will no longer show the device.

7. From Device Manager, choose the Action menu item and select Scan For Hardware Changes; alternatively, you can right-click the machine name in Device Manager and select Scan For Hardware Changes from the context menu.

Windows 10 will initiate the process of discovering the Plug and Play device and will reinstall the device driver configuration into the operating system. The hardware will be available again within Device Manager.

A lot of hardware manufacturers would like you to install the driver files and some software for their device before the operating system has a chance to discover it. This is often so that the software program controlling some of the hardware functionality will be installed first so its configuration file can accurately reference the installed drivers, or it can also be to add the driver files to the driver configuration directories of the operating system before the operating system discovers the device.

The process of adding the drivers is usually done by inserting and running a setup program from a provided CD or DVD. I will say the hardware vendors know what's best. As an admin, it's sometimes hard not to just install the hardware and go from there, but following the vendor's recommendations will most often produce a better result.

 Real World Scenario

Follow the Hardware Vendor's Recommendation

Like many other admins, I sometimes think I know the right way to proceed in installing a piece of hardware. Seriously, how hard can it be? I once installed a new wireless USB adapter into a machine I was using by just plugging it in despite the great big red sticker that said, "Run the setup on the CD FIRST!"

Sure enough, Windows found the adapter and proceeded to install the drivers. The hardware showed up in Device Manager but would not work. Now, being the good troubleshooter I am, I decided to run the Setup program on the CD. It turns out the driver files on the CD were a different version (actually older) than the installed files and Windows would not replace the installed drivers.

Even after I manually uninstalled them? Yes. I had to go back and find five different files in numerous locations and delete each one. Finding the files to delete was not a simple operation; a lot of online research went into solving this problem, and several hours of my time were wasted.

Simply following the hardware-vendor instructions would have been much easier. I did the same installation on another machine following the vendor recommendations, and everything worked perfectly. But then again, that's how we all learn these valuable lessons in life.

There are also situations we run into requiring a manual installation of hardware. There may be multiple reasons, including installation of legacy hardware, situations when drivers are not supplied in the operating system distribution files, or when drivers that may perform different functions from the default drivers are available. You can perform manual installations from Device Manager through the Add Hardware Wizard.

In the manual installation process, you can have Windows 10 go out to the Internet to find a current driver, or you can specify a location of your choosing locally. From Device Manager, you launch the Add Hardware Wizard (Figure 3.8) by choosing Add Legacy Hardware from either the Action menu or the context menu of the machine.

FIGURE 3.8   Add Hardware Wizard initial window

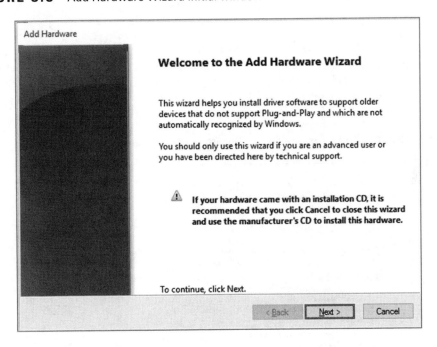

The next step is to tell Windows 10 where to look for the driver. This is the next page of the Add Hardware Wizard, as Figure 3.9 shows.

FIGURE 3.9   Driver file location choices

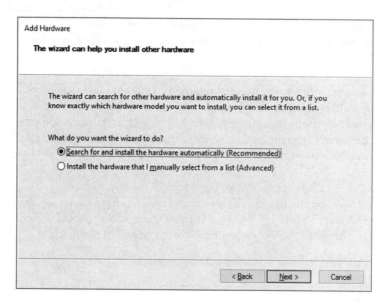

To choose a piece of hardware from a list of supplied drivers or, more importantly, to choose a specific path, select the option Install The Hardware That I Manually Select From A List (Advanced) and choose Next. This allows you to select a device type or choose Show All Devices (Figure 3.10); selecting Show All Devices and clicking Next will give you the ability to choose a location.

FIGURE 3.10   Add Hardware Device Wizard hardware-selection window

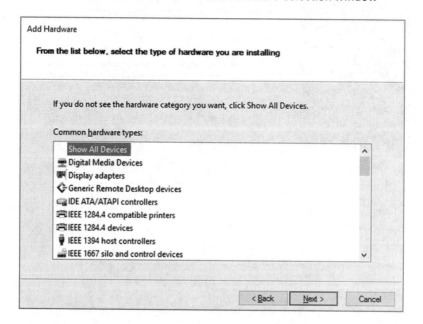

If you have a disk or have the appropriate drivers stored in an accessible location, click the Have Disk button (shown in Figure 3.11) and browse to the driver files you need to install. If all goes as planned, the hardware device drivers will be installed and Device Manager will display the newly installed hardware.

FIGURE 3.11   Add Hardware Device Wizard, Have Disk

Driver Signing

In this world of hackers and viruses, one issue that needs to be addressed is the possibility that drivers that are downloaded come from an unrepeatable source and have viruses or worms contained within the files. To help combat this problem, drivers that are created from reputable companies (like Dell or HP Compaq) assign a digital file certificate to the driver to show its validity.

One way to ensure that all the drivers on your machine are verified is to run `Sigverif.exe` from the Search Programs And Files box on the Start menu. Exercise 3.9 walks you through the steps of verifying the drivers on your machine.

Verifying Signed Drivers

1. Run the Sigverif.exe program by typing **Sigverif.exe** in the Search The Web And Windows box and then pressing Enter.

2. The File Signature Verification box appears. Click Start.

3. You will notice that the system scan begins. When the system has finished verifying the drivers, a message will appear stating that your files were all scanned. Click OK.

4. If there are any programs with unsigned drivers, they will be displayed at this time. Click Close to close the dialog box and then click Close to close the Sigverif.exe program.

Knowing how to properly install and configure drivers is an important part of an IT professional's job. Another task that we must perform is managing input/output devices.

Managing I/O Devices

The devices you use to get information into and out of your Windows 10 machine are your I/O (input/output) devices. I/O devices include removable storage, keyboard, mouse, scanner, and printer. Your devices may be connected to your computer by standard cabling or by USB, or they may use a wireless technology such as IrDA (infrared) or RF (radio frequency).

Configuring Removable Storage Devices

Removable storage devices have been part of our computing world since the beginning. CDs, DVDs, and floppy disks are examples of removable storage. Today, we're using other types of removable storage as well, including flash-based electronics like USB sticks, memory cards, USB or FireWire external hard drives, cameras, phones, and so on. Windows 10 installs drivers for these devices (or media) dynamically as the devices are connected.

We'll be concentrating in this section on dynamically connected devices utilizing the USB/FireWire connectivity and memory cards. These devices present challenges to the administrative team because end users utilizing the technology may not follow guidelines for protecting their data from loss or for keeping it secure.

Windows 10 includes improvements to the Safely Remove Hardware (eject) menu. For example, it's now possible to eject just one memory card (from a single hub) and keep the ports available for future use. Removable media are now listed under their label through

Devices And Printers (Figure 3.12) rather than just their drive letter as they were in previous versions of Windows. This is also part of the new Device Stage functionality of Windows 10; hardware vendors can include configuration information about portable devices and give users more resources from one location.

FIGURE 3.12   Devices And Printers with USB stick installed

There are considerations in terms of data access performance with the portable devices as well. To make data access and saves faster, it's possible to have the operating system cache the data and write it to the portable device later when there's free processor time. However, this allows the possibility of a user removing the portable device before the write is actually made, which would result in a loss of data.

Windows 10 defaults to writing the data immediately, minimizing the chance of data loss at the cost of performance. The configuration for optimizing the portable device for quick removal or better performance is found in the Policies tab of the Properties dialog box for the hardware device in Device Manager.

In Exercise 3.10, we will walk through the steps to configure input/output devices through the use of Device Manager.

EXERCISE 3.10

Configuring an Input/Output Device

1.   Right-click Start ➢ Device Manager (under Devices And Printers) or type **device manager** into the integrated search window of Windows 10.

2. Click the triangle next to Disk Drives (or double-click Disk Drives) to expand the item.

3. Right-click on one of the storage device items and select Properties.

4. Choose the Policies tab (see Figure 3.13).

FIGURE 3.13   Policies tab

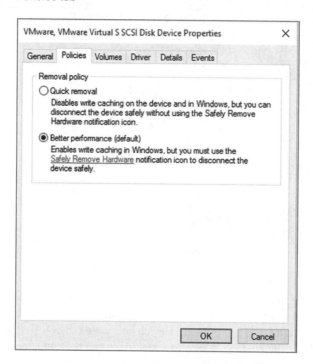

5. Select the Better Performance radio button and then click OK.

In Exercise 3.10, you changed the storage device to a write cache policy for better performance; this means writes to the portable device may be saved and written at a later time when the processor has clock cycles available. To ensure no loss of data, it is fairly important to properly eject the device through Windows 10 before physically removing it.

Choosing the icon in the Taskbar to eject the device initiates a stop for the hardware, forcing any cached writes in memory to be written to the device. You can also stop the portable hardware device from the Devices And Printers window by choosing Eject from the context menu of the device.

The device will close, meaning the writes have been made, and you will be presented with a window saying it's safe to remove the hardware.

Another important piece of hardware that needs to be configured is the printer. In the next section, we will discuss managing printers.

Managing Printers

Printers have been an issue for IT teams around the world and will continue to be as far as I can tell. Every new update/release/version of an operating system has new software intelligence to make the installation and maintenance easier, but printer technology continues to grow and hardware vendors continue to make changes.

The driver base for all the different printers out there is huge, and even for the same printer there are numerous variations. Printers themselves have lots of options that can be made available, and this all has to be controlled by the operating system, through the drivers.

The Printer vs. the Print Device

I have referred in the preceding portion of this chapter to printers and devices; I have been talking about the physical piece of hardware and its functions.

In the IT world, we need to distinguish between the functionality of the hardware and of the software (both the driver software and the controlling software).

To this end, a lot of us know the physical device that has paper in it as the print device, not "the printer." The printer is the software application on the local machine controlling the print device. The printer driver is the software shim between the operating system and the locally installed software (the printer).

You will find in most organizations that there is not a print device attached to every computer. They are usually shared among users. This is cost effective on many levels, but it tends to cause issues. Most of us, end users and the IT team, need to print something once in a while, and so we send our documents or web pages to the print device to be printed.

The print device may be connected to someone's machine and shared for others to use, or it may be a stand-alone device. You may have a server on your network that has one or more print devices attached, and everyone sends their documents to a central location. Each user machine will have a printer installed and the appropriate drivers to allow Windows 10 to send the document to the print device through the printer with the appropriate instructions.

Of course, the print device can't physically print a document at the speed at which the printer can send the data to it. This is where a software component called the spool (spooler, print spool, and so on) comes in. There need to be software components that can buffer the print job until the print device can complete it. In fact, there may be more than one user sending documents to be printed to the same print device at the same time, and the spool handles this as well.

What, No Spool?

I was working on a networking problem for a local veterinary clinic. The employees were complaining about issues they were having with their PCs being extremely slow sometimes but faster other times, and they were sure the network hardware was the cause. We discussed things that had changed recently—they had upgraded a piece of their software package to allow more functionality, which included having a couple of centralized printers for the docs and techs to use. It seemed as though every time someone printed, the network bogged down to the point of uselessness.

Casual discussions ensued. The network bog-down affected only the machine (or machines) actively sending a print job. Looking into the problem a little further showed that the vendor installation defaulted to printing directly to the print device, with no spooling. Each machine had to wait for the print job to complete before releasing any local resources (yes, that's right, not even background printing), and the other machines on the network ended up waiting as well. Allowing the machines to spool their print jobs solved the problem of slow networking (clearly not a networking issue in the end).

Installing Printers

Installing printers to a machine is done in two distinct ways: one where the print device is physically connected to the machine and one where it is not (it's connected over the network). There have to be software drivers in either case, and they can be on a CD/DVD, on a network share, downloaded on the Internet from the vendor, or even in the Windows distribution files. Printers in Windows 10 will be located in the Devices And Printers window and will allow the Device Stage configuration to accommodate a full range of functionality from this one location.

To add a printer to a machine locally, you will usually run the Setup program on the CD/DVD (following the manufacturer's instructions). The manufacturer's Setup program in a wizard format will ask the appropriate questions. You can set up the printer through Windows 10 as well as using the Add Printer functionality of Devices And Printers. To add a printer using the Windows 10 functionality, right-click Start ➤ Control Panel ➤ Devices And Printers ➤ Add A Printer, as shown in Figure 3.14. When USB printers are plugged in, they will be automatically detected and their drivers will be installed (or at least looked for automatically).

Choosing the Add A Printer menu item launches the Add Printer Wizard (starting at the screen shown in Figure 3.15) and brings up the screen where you can choose what printer you want to install. If the printer that you want to install is not in the list, you can choose the "The printer that I want isn't listed" link. If the printer wasn't listed, then the next screen allows you to make the choice of installing the printer by using the printer name, TCP/IP address, or Bluetooth discovery or by adding a local printer or network printer.

FIGURE 3.14   Adding a printer from Devices And Printers

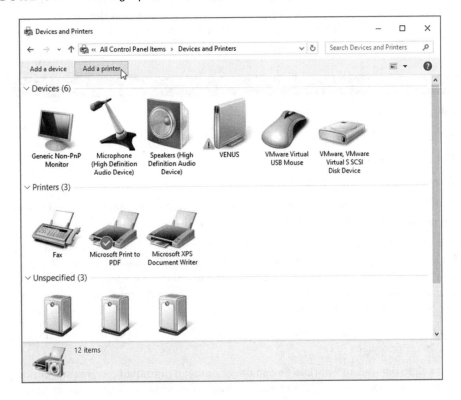

FIGURE 3.15   Add Printer Wizard local or remote choice

From the opening screen you can follow the steps in Exercise 3.11 to install the printer for a physically connected print device to a machine. We're going on the premise that the Setup program on the CD/DVD (if one existed) was not run, and we're installing the printer from the wizard associated with Windows.

EXERCISE 3.11

Installing a Printer

1. Right-click Start ➤ Control Panel ➤ Devices And Printers.

2. Choose Add A Printer.

3. Select the Add A Local Printer option.

4. In the Add Printer window, choose the Use An Existing Port radio button and use the drop-down window to select LPT1: (Printer Port). Then click Next.

5. Select the manufacturer of your print device and the printer model you want to install. If you don't find your model in the list, it wasn't included in the distribution files; you can click the Windows Update button to get more choices from Microsoft. If you still don't have your model available and you have the original disk, you can choose Have Disk and browse to the driver files.

6. If there was a driver previously installed, you will be given the option to use the existing driver or replace it.

7. After choosing the appropriate device driver or using the existing driver and clicking Next, enter a name for the printer. An intuitive name is always a good choice here. Enter the name and click Next.

8. You can make the print device available on the network by sharing it. The next page of the Add Printer Wizard gives you the opportunity to do so. After making your choice, click Next.

    Note that for most of the options within the wizard, you can change the values or function from the Properties dialog box if, for example, you change your mind later.

9. On the final page of the Add Printer Wizard, select the Set As The Default Printer check box (to make this the default printer for any application on the machine) and click Print A Test Page. Once the test page prints, click Finish. The printer for the locally connected print device is installed on the local machine.

Do not remove the printer you installed in this exercise. You will use it in a later exercise.

Once you have completed the Add Printer Wizard or let the hardware vendor's Setup program install your printer, you can open the Devices And Printers window and see it.

Using the context menu, you will have access to the Properties dialog box as well as some of the standard printing functions you've had in Windows in the past. As hardware vendors continue to implement functionality for Windows 10, you will have access to a full array of software components from the Devices And Printers window, at least for the vendors who are going to participate in the Device Stage specification.

What about installing a printer on a machine that needs to access a print device connected to another machine? In order to configure a printer to connect to a remote print device, you must launch the Add Printer Wizard and go through the process of installing the printer but point to a shared or stand-alone network printer by using the Add A Network, Wireless, Or Bluetooth Printer option.

Knowing that not all machines on any company's network are going to have print devices physically attached, there is functionality to allow sharing of networked devices and to install printers (software) on client machines. In Exercise 3.12, we will look at how to connect to a network printer.

EXERCISE 3.12

Installing a Shared Network Print Device

1.   Right-click Start ➤ Control Panel ➤ Devices And Printers.

2.   Choose the Add Printers menu item.

3.   Select Add A Network, Wireless Or Bluetooth Printer.

4.   The Add Printers Wizard will search the local network for print devices that are available.

5.   Select the networked print device from the Select A Printer section. If the device is not listed, you can choose The Printer That I Want Is Not Listed and enter the parameters for the networked print device.

The print device will be detected, the driver will be discovered and installed, and you will be able to use the printer. It will be available at this time in Devices And Printers.

Configuring Printers

Once the printer is installed for either a print device physically connected to the local machine or a network-connected print device, you can view the configuration parameters of the printer and modify them if necessary from the Properties dialog box. Access the property pages from Devices And Printers. Right-click the printer (Figure 3.16) and select Properties for the hardware properties or Printer Properties for the software components.

FIGURE 3.16   Printer context menu from Devices And Printers

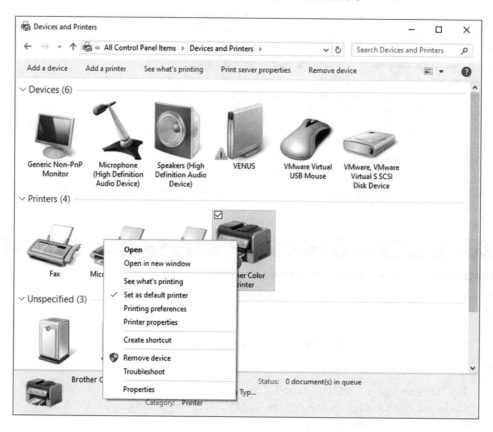

The Properties dialog boxes for printers follow a standard that Microsoft has in place, but the content is really up to the manufacturer. Some vendors will supply more information than others. Most printers will provide a basic set of pages (tabs):

General Tab   The printer name, location, and comments are displayed here. The model is typically shown as well as the features of the specific print device and available paper. The printer preferences page is available by clicking the Preferences button, and you can print a test page by clicking the Print Test Page button.

Sharing Tab   The Sharing tab allows you to share a printer if it wasn't shared during its installation or to stop sharing it if it was previously shared. You can also add drivers for other flavors of operating systems so the locally installed and shared printer can supply drivers for other machines attempting to connect and use it.

Ports Tab   Available ports and print devices connected to them can be viewed on the Ports tab. You can add a port, delete a port, and configure ports from the tab as well. Normally, operating systems just talk to the print device, but some print devices need to communicate with the operating system. This is known as bidirectional support (sending codes back from the print device to the printer for control).

Printer pooling is also available here. Printer pooling gives the IT staff the ability to configure multiple print devices (using identical drivers) to appear as one printer to connected users. The print jobs will be printed on one of the devices in the pool (first available print device prints the job). If a print device fails, the others will keep working, making life better for the users (always a goal). It is important to keep all print devices near each other in a printing pool because the print job will print to the next available device. If you scatter the devices all over the company, users will have to search for their print jobs.

Advanced Tab   The Advanced tab provides various configuration parameters to control the printer and print device functions. One of the available settings is what time the printer is available. You can set specific hours or allow the printer to always be available (see Figure 3.17). Configuring the installed print driver is also an option, as is adding a new driver (by launching the Add Printer Driver Wizard). Spool options include whether to spool or not and whether to start printing immediately upon job submission or start printing after the last page is spooled. The Advanced tab includes the following buttons:

> **Printing Defaults Button**   Launches the printer properties for the vendor as they apply to the documents.

FIGURE 3.17   The Advanced tab

Print Processor Button   Lets you choose whether to use the vendor-supplied print processor or the built-in Windows print processor. You can also choose the default data type to be sent to the print device.

Separator Page Button   Allows a specific page to be inserted between print jobs, making the separation of different documents easier.

Color Management Tab   If the print device has the capabilities of printing in color, there will be a Color Management tab. This tab gives you the ability to adjust the color management settings.

Security Tab   Group or user access permissions are controlled in the Security tab. Advanced permissions can be controlled here as well.

Device Settings Tab   Device settings–specific parameters for each print device are set up on the Device Settings tab (Figure 3.18). Items like Form To Tray Assignment, and other installable options for the print device are configurable here.

FIGURE 3.18   The Device Settings tab

Managing Documents

Once the configuration is complete and the printer and print device are working in harmony, life is good. You can see the status of the document currently being printed as well as documents waiting to be printed. This is what we call the queue. The queue used to be viewed by choosing the queue option in the context menu for the printer. Windows 10 calls it See What's Printing (Figure 3.20).

FIGURE 3.19   See What's Printing

Selecting See What's Printing opens the window that shows your printer's document/job control (Figure 3.20).

FIGURE 3.20   See What's Printing display window

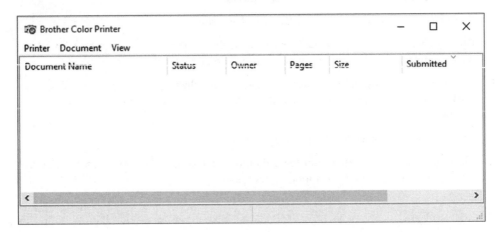

Device Stage allows you to select the context window from Devices And Printers. To get a graphical view of Device Stage, double-click the printer in Devices And Printers to get a consolidated view and the popular (as decided by the vendor) menu choices. Figure 3.21 shows a printer and its options as seen when you double-click it in Devices And Printers.

FIGURE 3.21   Printer window from Devices And Printers

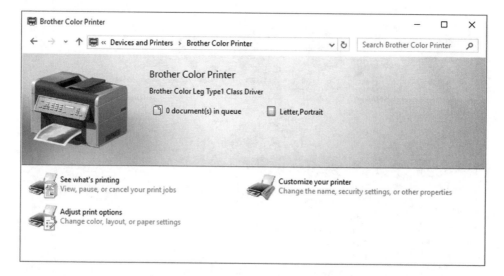

In Exercise 3.11 and Exercise 3.12, you installed printers for both a locally connected and a network-connected printer. In Exercise 3.13, let's take a look at sending a print job to the locally connected printer that you set up in Exercise 3.11 and view the document properties.

EXERCISE 3.13

Managing Documents in the Local Queue

1. Right-click Start ➤ Control Panel ➤ Devices And Printers.

2. Double-click the printer previously installed as the locally connected printer. If you haven't installed the printer yet, you can return to and complete Exercise 3.11.

3. To pause printing, open the printer window; double-click the See What's Printing area in the body of the window or single-click the Printer item in the top of the window.

4. Choose Printer ➤ Pause Printing from the menu.

5. View the status bar of the printer to verify that the printer is paused; there will also be a check mark next to Pause Printing in the menu.

Now let's send a test document to the paused locally connected printer:

1. From the Printer window, select Printer ➤ Properties.

2. On the General tab of the Properties window, click the Print Test Page button.

3. An information box will appear stating that a test page has been sent to the printer; click the Close button.

4. Click the OK button in the printer Properties window.

5. The Printer window will display the print job in the queue.

You can view document properties from a job in the print queue:

1. In the Printer window, single-click the document you want to view (the print job you want to view).

2. Choose Document ➤ Properties to view the document properties; you can also right-click the print job and select Properties from the context menu. The General tab will show you the document properties; the other tabs are vendor supplied to control additional printer functionality for the document.

3. Choose OK or Cancel to close the Properties window. OK will save any changes made and close the window; Cancel will close the window without saving any changes. If you have made any configuration changes, the Apply button will become available; selecting Apply saves any changes made but does not close the window.

Now, let's delete a document from the queue:

1. In the Printer window, single-click the job you want to cancel (the document you want to delete).

2. Choose Document ➤ Cancel From The Printer Window Menu Structure to delete the document. You can also right-click the document and select Cancel to delete the print job. Either method will prompt a confirmation message box asking Are You Sure You Want To Cancel The Document? Choose Yes.

3. The document will no longer be in the queue in the Printer window.

4. Choose Printer ➤ Close to close the Printer window.

Deleting Printers

There may also be times you will want to delete a printer, either one that's locally connected or a network printer, from your Windows 10 machine. This may be due to a replacement of an older print device or may be necessary when moving a user to a new print device. The removal will be performed from the Devices And Printers window. Removing a printer will remove the software configuration but not necessarily the driver files from the local machine. In Exercise 3.14, we will remove a printer.

EXERCISE 3.14

Removing a Printer from Devices And Printers

1. Right-click Start ➢ Control Panel ➢ Devices And Printers.

2. Right-click the printer you want to remove and select Remove Device from the context menu, or you can choose Remove Device from the menu of Devices And Printers to unpair the printer from the machine.

3. Click Yes in the dialog box with the question Are You Sure You Want To Remove This Device?

4. You are presented with a status box during the removal process, and then the device is no longer available in Devices And Printers.

Print Management Tool

The Print Management MMC snap-in is available in the Administrative Tools folder on computers running Windows 7/8/8.1/10, Windows Server 2008/2008 R2, and Windows Server 2012/2012 R2. Administrators can use the Print Management tools to install, manage, import/export print server settings, and view all of the printers and print servers throughout your company.

Administrators can use Print Management to install printers and to monitor print queues remotely. Print Management allows administrators to use filters to find printers that are in an error condition and to also receive email notifications or run scripts when a printer or print server needs attention. Depending on your printer, Print Management can also show administrators if a printer is low on ink or paper.

Print Management allows print administrators to have a single application where they can monitor and manage their printers. For example, Print Management allows an administrator to export print server information to a file and then take that file to another Windows system and import those print server settings into a new machine. This process is referred to as Print Server Migration.

Administrators can also use Print Management tools along with Group Policies. Group Policies are rules and policies that an administrator can set on a server and those policies will be deployed to your users and computers automatically through the network.

 Group Policy Objects (GPOs) will be discussed further throughout this book. I will also dive deeper into GPOs in Chapter 7, "Windows 10 Networking."

Print Management also gives administrators the ability to automatically search for and install network printers on their local network. Besides the Print Management MMC, there is a command-line utility that administrators can use, called `Printbrm.exe`, to manage their printers and print servers. When using the `Printbrm.exe` command, you must be in a command prompt with administrative privileges.

Print Management allows a printer administrator to complete some of the following tasks;

- Update and manage printer drivers
- Control printer driver installation
- Create new printer filters
- View extended features of the printers
- Pause or resume printing
- Cancel all print jobs
- List or remove printers from Active Directory
- Delete printers
- Import and export printer settings

In Exercise 3.15, we will use the Print Management Tools to export our print server settings to a file. You can then take that file and import the settings into another print server. This is a way to export printers from one server and load them onto another.

EXERCISE 3.15

Using the Print Management Tools

1. Right-click Start ➤ Control Panel ➤ Administrative Tools ➤ Print Management.

2. When the Print Management tool appears, right-click on Print Management and choose Migrate Printers (see Figure 3.22).

FIGURE 3.22   Migrate Printers option

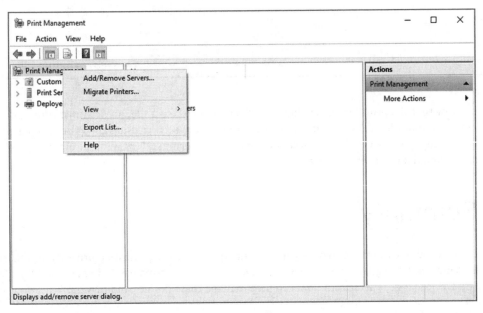

EXERCISE 3.15 *(continued)*

3. At the Getting Started With Print Migration screen, choose to export printer queues and print drivers to a file. Click Next.

4. Choose your print server and click Next.

5. A screen will appear showing you which objects will be exported. Click Next.

6. Type in a file name and location or click Browse to choose the file name and location. Click Next once completed.

7. The settings will be exported. Once the export is complete, click the Finish button as shown in Figure 3.23.

FIGURE 3.23   Export Complete screen

Now that the print server settings have been exported to a file, an administrator can now take that file to another machine and import those setting using the Print Management tools. This is an easy way for administrators to move print servers without manually rebuilding the print server settings.

Summary

Devices and hardware are two very important components that must be properly configured in Windows 10 to guarantee the best possible machine performance. Using Device Manager and Device Stage is an effective way to help manage these devices and drivers.

Another important task that we have to configure is setting up our print devices. The print devices are the physical machines that spit the print jobs out. The printer is the drivers that allow the print device to communicate with Windows 10.

Video Resources

There are videos available for the following exercises:

3.7

3.12

You can access the videos at `http://www.wiley.com/go/sybextestprep`.

Exam Essentials

Know how to verify whether drivers are signed.   Microsoft includes with Windows 10 a utility called `Sigverif.exe` for users to verify whether their drivers are digitally signed on their machines. `Sigverif.exe` will scan your machine and verify that all drivers are properly signed. If they are not signed, `Sigverif.exe` will show you which drivers are not signed.

Know how to configure devices and drivers.   Understand how to configure devices and drivers in Device Manager. Know how to roll back drivers and how to update drivers when newer versions are released. Know how to use Device Stage and how to add devices in Device Manager.

Know how to configure printers and print devices.   Understand how to configure printers and print devices in Devices And Printers. Know how to connect to a print device and how to manage the jobs that are sent to the printer.

Review Questions

1. You are the network administrator for your organization. You have been asked by the owner of the company to verify that all drivers installed on the Windows 10 machines are signed drivers. How do you accomplish this task?

   A. Run `Verify.exe` at the command prompt.

   B. Run a scan in Device Manager.

   C. Run `Sigverif.exe` at the command prompt.

   D. Run `Drivers.exe` at the command prompt.

2. You are the network administrator for your organization. You have a Windows 10 Enterprise system called PS1 that is configured with multiple shared print queues. You need to migrate the print queues to a new machine called PS2. How do you do that?

   A. Use the Migrate Printers utility in the Print Management tools.

   B. Use the Migrate Printers utility in the Control Panel.

   C. Use the Migrate Printers utility in the Devices And Printers utility.

   D. Use the Export Printers tool in the Print Management tools.

3. Your computer uses a SCSI adapter that supports a SCSI drive, which contains your Windows 10 system and boot partitions. After updating the SCSI driver, you restart your computer, and Windows 10 will load but with errors. You need to get this computer up and running as quickly as possible. Which of the following strategies should you try first to correct your problem?

   A. Restore your computer's configuration with your last backup.

   B. Boot your computer with the system image reload.

   C. Boot your computer and do a driver rollback.

   D. Boot your computer to the Recovery Console and manually copy the old driver back to the computer.

4. You are about to install a new driver for your CD-ROM drive, but you are not 100 percent sure that you are using the correct driver. Which of the following options will allow you to *most easily* return your computer to the previous state if the new driver is not correct?

   A. Safe Mode

   B. Roll Back Driver

   C. System Restore utility

   D. Startup Repair tool

5. You are the network administrator for your organization. Your organization has been using Windows 10 Enterprise. You need to run the Print Management tools from the command prompt. What command do you run?

   A. `Printmgmt.exe`

   B. `PrintMig.exe`

   C. `Prtmgmt.exe`

   D. `Printbrm.exe`

6. You are using Windows 10 Professional and you have a hardware component that is no longer needed. You do not want to delete the drivers but you do not want them active. What can you do to the drivers?

   A. Remove the drivers using Device Manager.

   B. Disable the drivers using Device Manager.

   C. Upgrade the drivers using Device Manager.

   D. Roll back the drivers using Device Manager.

7. You are the network administrator for a large organization. Your users are using Windows 10 Enterprise systems. One of your users just purchased a new laser printer. You need to install the printer onto the Windows 10 system. How do you achieve this?

   A. Use Device Manager.

   B. Use Printer Manager.

   C. Use Devices And Printers.

   D. Connect using the TCP/IP properties in Network Center.

8. You are the network administrator for a large organization. One of your users calls you and states that they think they are having issues with their network card. What tool can you use to see if the hardware is working properly?

   A. Device Hardware

   B. Manage Hardware

   C. Device Manager

   D. Device Configuration

9. You are the network administrator for a large organization. You have a Windows 10 machine that is working fine, but you downloaded and installed a newer version of the network adapter driver. After you load the driver, the network device stops working properly. Which tool should you use to help you fix the problem?

   A. Driver rollback

   B. Driver Repair utility

   C. Reverse Driver application

   D. Windows 10 Driver Compatibility tool

10. You are using Windows 10 Home and you want to update your video drivers. How do you accomplish this?

    A. Install new drivers using Driver Manager.

    B. Upgrade the drivers using Device Manager.

    C. Upgrade the drivers using Driver Manager.

    D. Install new drivers using Device Manager.

Chapter

4

Configuring Storage

MICROSOFT EXAM OBJECTIVES COVERED IN THIS CHAPTER:

✓ **Configure storage.**

- ■ This objective may include but is not limited to the following subobjectives: Configure disks, volumes, and file system options using Disk Management and Windows PowerShell; configure removable devices; create and configure storage spaces; troubleshoot storage and removable devices issues.

As you can see by the Configure Storage objectives, there are many things to discuss when it comes to storage. Not only are these topics important for the exam, but properly configuring your storage is a task that every IT professional should know how to accomplish because an improperly configured storage device can cause many issues for an IT team.

When you install Windows 10, you designate the initial configuration for your disks. Through Windows 10's utilities and features, you can change that configuration and perform disk-management tasks.

For file-system configuration, it is recommended that you use NTFS, although you could also format the disk drive as FAT32. You can also convert a FAT32 partition to NTFS. This chapter covers the features of each file system and how to use the Convert utility to convert to NTFS.

Another factor in disk management is choosing the configuration for your physical drives. Windows 10 supports basic, dynamic, and GUID Partition Table (GPT) disks. Dynamic disks are supported by Windows 10, Windows 8, Windows 7, Windows XP Professional, Windows Server 2003, Windows Server 2008, Windows Server 2008 R2, Windows Server 2012, and Windows Server 2012 R2. Dynamic disks allow you to create simple volumes, spanned volumes, and striped volumes. If your system is configured as a basic disk, in order to utilize volumes, you must first convert the machine's basic disks to dynamic disks.

Once you decide how your disks should be configured, you implement the disk configurations through the Disk Management utility. This utility helps you view and manage your physical disks and volumes. In this chapter, you will learn how to manage multiple types of storage and how to convert from basic storage to dynamic storage.

Understanding File Systems

A partition is a logical division of hard-drive space. Each partition you create under Windows 10 must have a file system associated with it. Partitions allow a single physical hard drive to be represented in the operating system as multiple drive letters and to be used as if there were multiple hard drives installed in the machine.

When selecting a file system, you can select FAT32 or NTFS. You typically select a file system based on the features you want to use and whether you will need to access the file system using other operating systems. If you have a FAT32 partition and want to update it to NTFS, you can use the Convert utility. The features of each file system and the procedure for converting file systems are covered in the following sections.

File System Selection

Your file system is used to track the storage of files on your hard drive in a way that is easily understood by end users while still allowing the operating system the ability to retrieve the files as requested. One of the fundamental choices associated with file management is the choice of your file system's configuration. It is recommended that you use the NTFS file system with Windows 10 because doing so will allow you to take advantage of features such as local security, file compression, and file encryption. You should choose the FAT32 file system only if you want to dual-boot your computer with a version of Windows that does not support NTFS because FAT32 is backward compatible with other operating systems.

Table 4.1 summarizes the capabilities of each file system, and they are described in more detail in the following sections. These volume size numbers were the current values at the time this book was written. Make sure you continue to check with Microsoft to see if the volume sizes have increased since this book's publication.

TABLE 4.1   File-system capabilities

Feature	Fat32	NTFS
Supporting operating systems	All Windows operating systems above Windows 95	Windows NT, Windows 2000, Windows XP, Windows Server 2003, Windows Vista, Windows 7, Windows 8, Windows 10, Windows Server 2008/2008 R2, and Windows Server 2012/2012 R2
Long filename support	Yes	Yes
Efficient use of disk space	Yes	Yes
Compression support	No	Yes
Encryption support	No	Yes
Support for local security	No	Yes
Support for network security	Yes	Yes
Maximum volume size	32 GB	16 TB with 4 KB clusters or 256 TB with 64 KB clusters

Windows 10 also supports Compact Disk File System (CDFS). However, CDFS cannot be managed. It is used only to mount and read CDs. Let's start looking at the supported disk file systems.

FAT32

FAT32 is an updated version of File Allocation Table (FAT). The FAT32 version was first shipped with Windows 95 OSR2 (Operating System Release 2) and can be used by every Windows operating system since.

One of the main advantages of FAT32 is its support for smaller cluster sizes, which results in more efficient space allocation than was possible with FAT16. Files stored on a FAT32 partition can use 20 to 30 percent less disk space than files stored on a FAT16 partition. FAT32 supports drive sizes from 512 MB up to 2 TB, although if you create and format a FAT32 partition through Windows 10, the FAT32 partition can only be up to 32 GB. Because of the smaller cluster sizes, FAT32 can also load programs up to 50 percent faster than FAT16 partitions can.

The main disadvantages of FAT32 compared to NTFS are that it does not provide as much support for larger hard drives and it does not provide very robust security options. It also doesn't offer native support for disk compression. Now that you understand FAT32, let's take a look at NTFS.

NTFS

NTFS, which was first used with the NT operating system, offers the highest level of service and features for Windows 10 computers. NTFS partitions can be up to 16 TB with 4 KB clusters or 256 TB with 64 KB clusters.

NTFS offers comprehensive folder-level and file-level security. This allows you to set an additional level of security for users who access the files and folders locally or through the network. For example, two users who share the same Windows 10 computer can be assigned different NTFS permissions so that one user has access to a folder but the other user is denied access to that folder. This is not possible on a FAT32 file system.

NTFS also offers disk-management features—such as compression and encryption capabilities—and data-recovery features. The disk-management features are covered later in this chapter. The data-recovery features are covered in Chapter 10, "Configuring Monitoring and Recovery."

You should also be aware that there are several different versions of NTFS. Every version of Windows 2000 uses NTFS 3.0. Windows 7/8/10, Windows Vista, Windows XP, Windows Server 2003, Windows Server 2008/2008 R2, and Windows Server 2012/2012 R2 use NTFS 3.1. NTFS versions 3.0 and 3.1 use similar disk formats, so Windows 2000 computers can access NTFS 3.1 volumes and Windows 10 computers can access NTFS 3.0 volumes. NTFS 3.1 includes the following features:

- When files are read or written to a disk, they can be automatically encrypted and decrypted.

- Reparse points are used with mount points to redirect data as it is written or read from a folder to another volume or physical disk.

- There is support for sparse files, which are used by programs that create large files but allocate disk space only as needed.

- Remote storage allows you to extend your disk space by making removable media (for example, external tapes) more accessible.
- It gives you the ability to resize volumes and partitions.
- You can use recovery logging on NTFS metadata, which is used for data recovery when a power failure or system problem occurs.

Now that you have seen the differences between FAT32 and NTFS, let's discuss how to convert a FAT32 drive to an NTFS drive.

File System Conversion

In Windows 10, you can convert FAT32 partitions to NTFS. File-system conversion is the process of converting one file system to another without the loss of data. If you format a drive, as opposed to converting it, all the data on that drive will be lost.

To convert a partition, you use the Convert command-line utility. The syntax for the Convert command is as follows:

```
Convert [drive:]/fs:ntfs
```

For example, if you wanted to convert your D: drive to NTFS, you would type the following from a command prompt:

```
Convert D:/fs:ntfs
```

When the conversion process begins, it will attempt to lock the partition. If the partition cannot be locked—perhaps because it contains the Windows 10 operating system files or the system's page file—the conversion will not take place until the computer is restarted.

In Exercise 4.1, you will convert your D: drive from FAT32 to NTFS. For this exercise, it is assumed that you have a D: drive that is formatted with the FAT32 file system. If you don't have a FAT32 drive, open Disk Management by right-clicking the Start button and choosing Disk Management. Click your C partition, right-click, and shrink the drive by only 5–10 GBs. Now create a simple volume and format it as FAT32.

Using the Convert Command

You can use the /v switch with the Convert command. This switch specifies that you want to use verbose mode, and all messages will be displayed during the conversion process. You can also use the /NoSecurity switch, which specifies that all converted files and folders will have no security applied by default, so they can be accessed by anyone.

EXERCISE 4.1

Converting a FAT32 Partition to NTFS

1. Copy some folders to the D: drive.

2. Select Start, and then type **cmd** into the Search box to open a command prompt.

3. In the Command Prompt dialog box, type Convert D: /fs:ntfs and press Enter.

4. After the conversion process is complete, close the Command Prompt dialog box.

5. Verify that the folders you copied in step 1 still exist on the partition.

Stopping a Conversion

If you choose to convert a partition from FAT32 to NTFS and the conversion has not yet taken place, you can cancel the conversion by editing the Registry with the REGEDIT or REGEDT32 command. The key that needs to be edited is

HKEY_LOCAL_MACHINE\System\CurrentControlSet\Control\SessionManager

The BootExecute value needs to be changed from autoconv\DosDevices\x:/FS:NTFS to autocheck autochk*.

Once you decide which file system you want to use, you need to decide what disk storage type you want to configure. Let's look at some of the disk storage options you have.

 Be careful when converting your file system. Once you change a FAT32 file system to NTFS, you cannot change it back without formatting the disk and losing your data.

Configuring NTFS

As mentioned earlier, NTFS has many advantages over FAT32. The main advantages are NTFS Security, compression, encryption (EFS), and quotas. Let's take a look at some of these advantages in greater detail.

NTFS Security One of the biggest advantages of NTFS is security. NTFS Security (as shown in Figure 4.1) is one of the most important aspects of an IT administrator's job.

An advantage of NTFS Security is that the security can be placed on individual files and folders. It does not matter whether you are local to the share (in front of the machine where the data is stored) or remote to the share (coming across the network to access the data), the security is always in place with NTFS. The default security permission is Users = Read on new folders or shares. Configuring NTFS Security and managing how it works with Shared Permissions are covered in Chapter 6, "Configuring Data Security."

FIGURE 4.1   NTFS Security tab

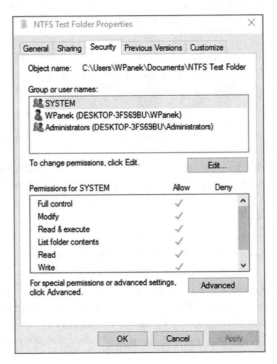

Compression   *Compression* helps compact files or folders to allow for more efficient use of hard drive space. For example, a file that usually takes up 20 MB of space might use only 13 MB after compression. To enable compression, just open the Advanced Attributes dialog box for a folder and check the Compress Contents To Save Disk Space box. Compression is covered in greater detail later in this chapter in the section "Managing Data Compression."

Encryption   *Encrypting File System (EFS)* allows a user or administrator to secure files or folders by using encryption. Encryption employs the user's security identification (SID) number to secure the file or folder. To implement encryption, open the Advanced Attributes dialog box for a folder, and check the Encrypt Contents To Secure Data box (see Figure 4.2).

FIGURE 4.2 Setting up encryption on a folder

If files are encrypted using EFS and an administrator has to unencrypt the files, there are two ways to do this. First, you can log in using the user's account (the account that encrypted the files) and unencrypt the files. Second, you can become a recovery agent and manually unencrypt the files.

Quotas   Disk *quotas* give administrators the ability to limit how much storage space a user can have on a hard drive. You have a few options available to you when you set up disk quotas. You can set up disk quotas based on volume or on users.

Setting Quotas by Volume   One way to set up disk quotas is by setting the quota by volume, on a per-volume basis. This means that if you have a hard drive with C:, D:, and E: volumes, you would have to set up three individual quotas (one for each volume). This is your umbrella. This is where you set up an entire disk quota based on the volume for all users.

Setting Quotas by User   You have the ability to set up quotas on volumes by user. Here is where you would individually let users have independent quotas that exceed your umbrella quota.

Specifying Quota Entries   You use quota entries to configure the volume and user quotas. You do this on the Quotas tab of the volume's Properties dialog box. (See Exercise 4.2.)

Creating Quota Templates   Quota templates are predefined ways to set up quotas. Templates allow you to set up disk quotas without needing to create a disk quota from scratch. One advantage of using a template is that when you want to set up disk quotas on multiple volumes (C:, D:, and E:) on the same hard drive, you do not need to re-create the quota on each volume.

Exercise 4.2 will show you how to set up an umbrella quota for all users. This is the disk quota that all users will then follow for whichever drive you set this up on.

EXERCISE 4.2

Configuring Disk Quotas

1. Open Windows Explorer.

2. Right-click the local disk (C:), and choose Properties.

3. Click the Quotas tab.

4. Check the Enable Quota Management check box. Also check the Deny Disk Space To Users Exceeding Quota Limit box.

5. Click the Limit Disk Space To option, and enter **1000MB** in the box.

6. Enter **750MB** in the Set Warning Level To boxes.

7. Click the Apply button. If a warning box appears, click OK. This warning is just informing you that the disk may need to be rescanned for the quota.

8. Now that you have set up an umbrella quota to cover everyone, close the disk quota tool.

Configuring Disk Storage

Windows 10 supports three types of disk storage: basic, dynamic, and GUID Partition Table (GPT). Basic storage is backward compatible with other operating systems and can be configured to support up to four partitions. Dynamic storage is supported by Windows 2000, Windows XP, Windows Vista, Windows 7, Windows 8, Windows 10, Windows Server 2003, Windows Server 2008, Windows Server 2008 R2, Windows Server 2012, and Windows Server 2012 R2 and allows storage to be configured as volumes. GPT support begins with the Windows 2003 SP1 release and allows you to configure volume sizes larger than 2 TB and up to 128 primary partitions. The following sections describe the basic storage, dynamic storage, and GPT storage configurations.

Basic Storage

Basic storage consists of primary and extended partitions and logical drives that exist within the extended partition. The first partition that is created on a hard drive is called a primary partition and is usually represented as the C: drive. Primary partitions use all of the space that is allocated to the partition, and a single drive letter is used to represent the partition. Only a single extended partition is allowed on any basic disk. Each physical drive can have up to four partitions. You can set up four primary partitions, or you can have three primary partitions and one extended partition. With an extended partition, you can allocate the space however you like, and each suballocation of space (called a logical drive) is represented by a different drive letter. For example, a 500 MB extended partition could have a 250 MB D: partition and a 250 MB E: partition.

At the highest level of disk organization, you have a physical hard drive. You cannot use space on the physical drive until you have logically partitioned the physical drive.

One of the advantages of using multiple partitions on a single physical hard drive is that each partition can have a different file system. For example, the C: drive might be FAT32 and the D: drive might be NTFS. Multiple partitions also make it easier to manage security requirements.

Basic storage is the default, and this is the type that many users continue to use. But what if you want some additional functionality from your storage type? Let's look at some of the more advanced disk storage options.

Dynamic Storage

Dynamic storage is a Windows 10 feature that consists of a dynamic disk divided into dynamic volumes. Dynamic volumes cannot contain partitions or logical drives.

Dynamic storage supports three dynamic volume types: simple volumes, spanned volumes, and striped volumes. Dynamic storage also supports a Redundant Array of Independent Disks (RAID), which will be discussed in the section "Understanding RAID" later in this chapter.

To set up dynamic storage, you convert or upgrade a basic disk to a dynamic disk. When converting a basic disk to dynamic, you do not lose any of your data. After the disk is converted, any partitions that existed on the basic disk are converted to dynamic simple volumes, and you can then create any additional dynamic volumes required within the dynamic disk.

You create dynamic storage with the Windows 10 Disk Management utility, which is discussed in the section "Using the Disk Management Utility" later in this chapter. Let's take a closer look at the different types of dynamic volumes.

Simple Volumes

A simple volume contains space from a single dynamic drive. The space from the single drive can be contiguous or noncontiguous. Simple volumes are used when you have enough disk space on a single drive to hold your entire volume. Figure 4.3 illustrates two simple volumes on a physical disk.

FIGURE 4.3   Two simple volumes

Simple Volume C:\
10 GB

Simple Volume D:\
10 GB

Physical Disk 0
20 GB

Spanned Volumes

A *spanned volume* consists of disk space on two or more dynamic drives; up to 32 dynamic drives can be used in a spanned volume configuration. Spanned volume sets are used to dynamically increase the size of a dynamic volume. When you create spanned volumes, the data is written sequentially, filling space on one physical drive before writing to space on the next physical drive in the spanned volume set. Typically, administrators use spanned volumes when they are running out of disk space on a volume and want to dynamically extend the volume with space from another hard drive or without using another drive letter.

You do not need to allocate the same amount of space to the volume set on each physical drive. This means you could combine 500 MB on one physical drive with two 750 MB volumes on other dynamic drives, as shown in Figure 4.4.

FIGURE 4.4   A spanned volume set

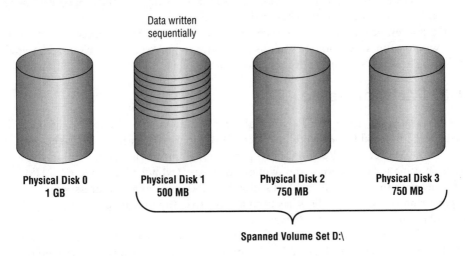

Because data is written sequentially, you do not see any performance enhancements with spanned volumes as you do with striped volumes (discussed next). The main disadvantage of spanned volumes is that if any drive in the spanned volume set fails, you lose access to all of the data in the spanned set.

Striped Volumes

A *striped volume* stores data in equal stripes between two or more (up to 32) dynamic drives, as illustrated in Figure 4.5. Since the data is written sequentially across the stripe, you can take advantage of multiple I/O performance and increase the speed at which data reads and writes take place. Typically, administrators use striped volumes when they want to combine the space of several physical drives into a single logical volume and increase disk performance.

FIGURE 4.5   A spanned volume set

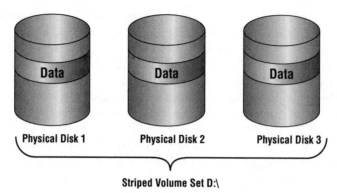

The main disadvantage of striped volumes is that if any drive in the striped volume set fails, you lose access to all of the data in the striped set.

In the last few years a new storage type has emerged in the Microsoft computer world, and as with most new technologies, it has some advantages over the previous technologies. Let's take a look at the newest advantageous storage type.

GUID Partition Table

The *GUID Partition Table (GPT)* is available for Windows 10 and was first introduced as part of the Extensible Firmware Interface (EFI) initiative from Intel. Basic and dynamic disks use the Master Boot Record (MBR) partitioning scheme that all operating systems have been using for years. Basic and dynamic disks use Cylinder-Head-Sector (CHS) addressing with the MBR scheme. CHS allows computers to assign addresses to data on the computer's hard-disk drives. This has been an effective way to store data on a hard drive, but there is a newer, more effective way.

The GPT disk-partitioning system uses the GPT to configure the disk area. GPT uses an addressing scheme called Logical Block Addressing (LBA), which is a newer method of accessing hard-disk drives. LBA uses a unique sector number only instead of using the cylinder, head, and sector number. Another advantage is that the GPT header and partition table are written to both the front and back ends of the disk, which provides for better redundancy.

The GPT disk-partitioning system gives you many benefits over using the MBR system:

- Allows a volume size larger than 2 TB
- Allows up to 128 primary partitions
- Used for both 32-bit and 64-bit Windows 10 editions
- Includes cyclic redundancy check (CRC) for greater reliability

However, there is one disadvantage to using the GPT drives. You can convert a GPT drive only if the disk is empty and unpartitioned. I will show you the steps to creating a GPT disk later in this chapter.

To convert any disk or format any volume or partition, you can use the Disk Management utility. I will show you how to manage your disks using the Disk Management utility later in this chapter.

Cloud-Based Storage

One of the fastest-growing parts of the IT world is cloud-based services. From cloud-based user storage to cloud-based corporate data storage, it seems like all we hear anymore is "cloud, cloud, cloud." Well, Microsoft has cloud-based subscription services called Microsoft Azure and OneDrive.

Microsoft Azure

Microsoft Azure (https://azure.microsoft.com/en-us/) can be used by almost any operating system on the market (Windows, Linux, etc.), by most applications (Java, .NET, PHP, etc.), and by most device types (Windows, Android, and iOS).

Microsoft Azure is different than many other cloud-based systems because Microsoft Azure doesn't make you choose either your network or the cloud. Many cloud-based service providers want you to use their cloud to run all of your applications and/or storage from their location. Microsoft Azure allows you to extend your current network infrastructure into the cloud to take full advantage of both worlds.

This way you can still have a full IT server room with full-time IT employees but get the benefits of storing data both locally and also in a cloud environment, which is then available from anywhere in the world.

Azure makes it easy to store documents in the cloud by using the Azure portal. The portal is the way that users and IT professionals can control and manage how data is stored in the cloud. The Azure portal allows you to do some of the following:

- Upload and download data to and from Azure
- Run reports showing the actual usage of each file share
- Adjust the quota sizes of your users
- Use the net use command-line utility to share files from a Windows client command prompt

One advantage to using Microsoft Azure is that you only pay for what you need. The more cloud-based storage you need, the more you pay for, and the less you need means less money. Table 4.2 shows you the maximum amount of data that can be stored on Microsoft Azure.

TABLE 4.2   Microsoft Azure data size availability

Operating System	Maximum Size of Data Source
Windows Server 2012 or above	54,400 GB
Windows 8 or above	54,400 GB
Windows Server 2008, Windows Server 2008 R2	1,700 GB
Windows 7	1,700 GB

If you decide that you want your company to use Microsoft Azure for some of its cloud-based storage or all of its cloud-based storage, please go to https://azure.microsoft.com/en-us/ to get the current subscription rates.

Microsoft OneDrive

Another Microsoft-based subscription is called OneDrive (used to be known as SkyDrive). Microsoft's OneDrive is built into Windows 10 by default (see Figure 4.6). OneDrive is a cloud-based storage subscription so home users can store their documents and then access those documents from anywhere in the world (provided that you have Internet access).

FIGURE 4.6 OneDrive welcome screen

OneDrive was designed for the average home user who is looking to store data in a safe, secure, cloud-based environment. OneDrive, when first released, was also a consideration for corporate environments, but with the release of Windows Azure, OneDrive is really intended for the home user or corporate user who wants to store some of their own personal documents in the cloud. Corporations would be more inclined to use Microsoft Azure and all of its corporate benefits.

If you or your company decides to purchase the Office 365 subscription, then OneDrive is included for cloud-based storage. If you didn't purchase Office 365, then you have to choose from one of the subscriptions shown in Table 4.3.

TABLE 4.3 OneDrive subscriptions

Amount of Storage	Subscription Monthly Fee
Office 365 + 1 TB included	$9.99
5 GB	Free
100 GB	$1.99
200 GB	$3.99

Please note that these were the current prices at the time this book was written and these prices may have changed. Be sure to check out Microsoft's OneDrive web page for current prices (https://onedrive.live .com/options/Upgrade).

Exercise 4.3 will show you how to set up a OneDrive account for your user account. To do this exercise, you must have a Microsoft account. You get 15 GB for free from Microsoft on the OneDrive cloud-based storage.

EXERCISE 4.3

Configuring OneDrive

1. Open OneDrive.

2. Log into OneDrive using your Microsoft account as shown in Figure 4.7.

3. You will get a screen that will show you where your files will be located on your system as shown in Figure 4.8. Click the Next button.

4. At the Sync files screen, choose what folders you want to sync with Microsoft and then click Next.

FIGURE 4.7 OneDrive login screen

FIGURE 4.8 OneDrive file location screen

A screen will appear telling you that your OneDrive is set up and ready to go (see Figure 4.9).

FIGURE 4.9   Open My OneDrive Folder screen

5. Click the Open My OneDrive Folder button to open your folders and Microsoft One-Drive.

6. Close OneDrive.

Cloud-based services will be discussed throughout this book.

Using the Disk Management Utility

The Disk Management utility is a Microsoft Management Console (MMC) snap-in that gives administrators a graphical tool for managing disks and volumes within Windows 10. In the following sections, you will learn how to access the Disk Management utility and use it to perform basic tasks, including managing basic storage and dynamic storage. You will also learn about troubleshooting disks through disk status codes.

But before we dive into the Disk Management utility, let's explore the MMC. It is important to understand the MMC since Disk Management (like many other tools) is actually an MMC snap-in.

Using the Microsoft Management Console

The *Microsoft Management Console (MMC)* is the console framework for application management. The MMC provides a common environment for snap-ins. Snap-ins are administrative tools developed by Microsoft or third-party vendors. Some of the MMC snap-ins that you may use are Computer Management, Active Directory Users and Computers, Active Directory Sites and Services, Active Directory Domains and Trusts, and DNS Management. When you look at the administrative tools, you know that each one of these tools are running inside of an MMC (shown in Figure 4.10).

FIGURE 4.10 The administrative tools running in MMCs

Knowing how to use and configure the MMC snap-ins will allow you to customize your work environment. For example, if you are in charge of Active Directory Users and Computers and DNS, you can add both of these snap-ins into the same window. This would then allow you to open just one application to configure all your tasks. The MMC offers many other benefits:

- The MMC is highly customizable—you add only the snap-ins you need.

- Snap-ins use a standard, intuitive interface, so they are easier to use than previous versions of administrative utilities.

- You can save customized MMCs and share them with other administrators.
- You can configure permissions so that the MMC runs in authoring mode, which an administrator can manage, or in user mode, which limits what users can access.
- You can use most snap-ins for remote computer management.

As shown in Figure 4.11, by default, the MMC contains three panes: a console tree on the left, a details pane in the middle, and an optional Actions pane on the right. The console tree lists the hierarchical structure of all snap-ins that have been loaded into the console. The details pane contains a list of properties or other items that are part of the snap-in that is highlighted in the console tree. The Actions pane provides a list of actions that the user can access depending on the item selected in the details pane.

FIGURE 4.11   The MMC tree, details pane, and Actions pane

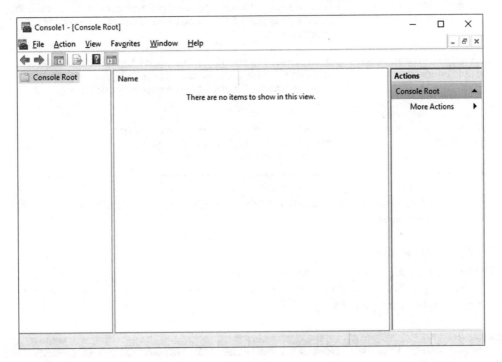

To open the MMC on a Windows 10 computer, click the Start button and type **MMC** in the Search dialog box. When you first open the MMC, it contains only the Console Root folder, as shown in Figure 4.11. The MMC does not have any default administrative functionality. It is simply a framework used to organize administrative tools through the addition of snap-in utilities.

The first thing that you should decide when using the MMC is which of the different administrative mode types you will employ. You need to decide which mode type is best suited to use for your organization.

Configuring MMC Modes

You can configure the MMC to run in author mode for full access to the MMC functions or in one of three user modes, which have more limited access to the MMC functions. To set a console mode, while in the MMC editor, select File ➤ Options to open the Options dialog box. In this dialog box, you can select from the console modes listed in Table 4.4.

TABLE 4.4   MMC modes

Console Mode	Description
Author mode	Allows use of all the MMC functions.
User mode—full access	Gives users full access to window-management commands, but they cannot add or remove snap-ins or change console properties.
User mode—limited access, multiple window	Allows users to create new windows but not close any existing windows. Users can access only the areas of the console tree that were visible when the console was last saved.
User mode—limited access, single window	Allows users to access only the areas of the console tree that were visible when the console was last saved, and they cannot create new windows.

After you decide which administrative role you are going to run, it's time to start configuring your MMC snap-ins.

Adding Snap-Ins

The biggest advantage of using the MMC is to configure snap-ins the way your organization needs them. Adding snap-ins is a simple and quick procedure. To add a snap-in to the MMC and save it, complete Exercise 4.4.

EXERCISE 4.4

Adding an MMC Snap-In

1. To start the MMC editor, click Start, type **MMC** into the search box, and press Enter.

2. From the main console window, select File ➤ Add/Remove Snap-In to open the Add Or Remove Snap-ins dialog box.

3. Highlight the snap-in you want to add (see Figure 4.12), and click the Add button.

4. If prompted, specify whether the snap-in will be used to manage the local computer or a remote computer. After you choose the MMCs you want in your custom snap-in (shown in Figure 4.13), click the Finish button.

FIGURE 4.12   The MMC Add Or Remove Snap-Ins screen

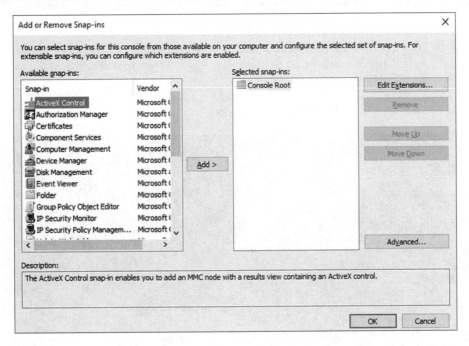

FIGURE 4.13   The MMC console screen

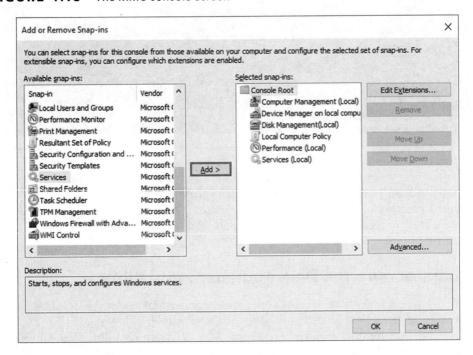

EXERCISE 4.4 *(continued)*

5.   When you have finished adding snap-ins, click OK.

6.   After you have added snap-ins to create a console, you can save it by selecting File ➢ Save As and entering a name for your console. Place the console on the Desktop as shown in Figure 4.14.

FIGURE 4.14   The MMC console on Desktop

You can save the console to a variety of locations, including a program group or the Desktop. By default, custom consoles have an `.msc` filename extension.

Many applications that are MMC snap-ins, including Disk Management, are already configured for you under the Administrative Tools section of Windows 10. Next, let's look at the Disk Management utility.

Understanding the Disk Management Utility

The Disk Management utility, located under the Computer Management snap-in by default, is a one-stop shop for configuring your disk options.

First of all, to have full permissions to use the Disk Management utility, you must be logged on with local Administrative privileges. You can access the Disk Management utility a few different ways. You can right-click Computer from the Start menu and select Manage, and then in Computer Management, select Disk Management. You could also use Control Panel ➢ Administrative Tools ➢ Computer Management.

Once you have launched Computer Management, you must expand the storage section of the console in order to access the Disk Management toolset. The Disk Management utility's opening window, shown in Figure 4.15, displays the following information:

- The volumes that are recognized by the computer

- The type of disk, either basic or dynamic

- The type of file system used by each partition

- The status of the partition and whether the partition contains the system or boot partition

- The capacity (amount of space) allocated to the partition

- The amount of free space remaining on the partition

- The amount of overhead associated with the partition

FIGURE 4.15   The Disk Management window

Windows 10 also includes a command-line utility called Diskpart, which can be used as a command-line alternative to the Disk Management utility. You can view all of the options associated with the Diskpart utility by typing **Diskpart** (as shown in Figure 4.16) at a command prompt and then typing **?** at the Diskpart prompt.

FIGURE 4.16 The Diskpart window

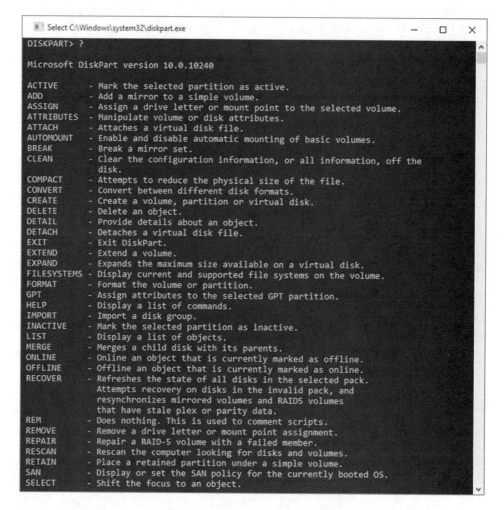

The Disk Management utility allows you to configure and manage your disks. Let's take a look at some of the tasks that you can perform in disk administration.

Managing Administrative Hard-Disk Tasks

The Disk Management utility allows you to perform a variety of hard-drive administrative tasks:

- View disk properties.
- View volume and local disk properties.
- Add a new disk.
- Create partitions and volumes.

- Upgrade a basic disk to a dynamic or GPT disk.

- Change a drive letter and path.

- Resize a volume or partition.

- Delete partitions and volumes.

These tasks are discussed in the sections that follow.

Viewing Disk Properties

To view the properties of a disk, right-click the disk number in the lower panel of the Disk Management main window and choose Properties from the context menu. This brings up the disk's Properties dialog box. Click the Volumes tab to see the volumes associated with the disk, as shown in Figure 4.17, which contains the following disk properties:

- The disk number

- The type of disk (basic, dynamic, CD-ROM, removable, DVD, or unknown)

- The status of the disk (online or offline)

- The partition style

- The capacity of the disk

- The amount of unallocated space on the disk

- The amount of space reserved on the disk

- The logical volumes that have been defined on the physical drive

FIGURE 4.17   The Volumes tab of a disk's Properties dialog box

> If you click the General tab of a disk's Properties dialog box, the hardware device type, the hardware vendor that produced the drive, the physical location of the drive, and the device status are displayed.

Viewing Volume and Local Disk Properties

On a dynamic disk, you manage volume properties. On a basic disk, you manage partition properties. Volumes and partitions perform the same function, and the options discussed in the following sections apply to both. (The examples here are based on a dynamic disk using a simple volume. If you are using basic storage, you will view the partition properties rather than the volume properties.)

To see the properties of a volume, right-click the volume in the upper panel of the Disk Management main window and choose Properties. This brings up the volume's Properties dialog box. Volume properties are organized on seven tabs: General, Tools, Hardware, Sharing, Security, Previous Versions, and Quota. The Security tab and Quota tab appear only for NTFS volumes. All these tabs are described in detail in the following list.

General   The information on the General tab of the volume's Properties dialog box, as shown in Figure 4.18, gives you a general idea of how the volume is configured. This dialog box shows the label, type, file system, used and free space, and capacity of the volume. The label is shown in an editable text box, and you can change it if desired. The space allocated to the volume is shown in a graphical representation as well as in text form.

FIGURE 4.18   General properties for a volume

The label on a volume or local disk is for informational purposes only. For example, depending on its use, you might give a volume a label such as APPS or ACCTDB.

The Disk Cleanup button starts the Disk Cleanup utility, which you can use to delete unnecessary files, thereby freeing disk space. This utility is discussed later in this chapter in the "Using the Disk Cleanup Utility" section.

This tab also allows you to configure compression for the volume and to indicate whether the volume should be indexed.

Tools   The Tools tab of the volume's Properties dialog box, shown in Figure 4.19, provides access to three tools.

FIGURE 4.19   The Tools tab of the volume's Properties dialog box

Click the Check button to run the Error-Checking utility to check the volume for errors. You may do this if you are experiencing problems accessing the volume or if the volume was open during a system restart that did not go through a proper shutdown sequence. This utility is covered in more detail in "Troubleshooting Disk Management," later in this chapter.

Click the Optimize button to run the Disk Defragmenter utility. This utility defragments files on the volume by storing the files contiguously on the hard drive.

Hardware   The Hardware tab of the volume's Properties dialog box, shown in Figure 4.20, lists the hardware associated with the disk drives that are recognized by the Windows 10 operating system. The bottom half of the dialog box shows the properties of the device that is highlighted in the top half of the dialog box.

FIGURE 4.20   The Hardware tab of the volume's Properties dialog box

For more details about a hardware item, highlight it and click the Properties button in the lower-right corner of the dialog box. This brings up a Properties dialog box for the item. Your Device Status field should report, "This device is working properly." If that's not the case, you can click the Troubleshoot button (it will appear if the device is not working properly) to get a troubleshooting wizard that will help you discover the problem.

Sharing   On the Sharing tab of the volume's Properties dialog box, shown in Figure 4.21, you can specify whether or not the volume is shared on the network. Volumes are not shared by default. Clicking the Advanced Sharing button will allow you to specify whether the volume is shared and, if so, what the name of the share should be. You will also be able to specify who will have access to the shared volume.

Security   The Security tab of the volume's Properties dialog box, shown in Figure 4.22, appears only for NTFS volumes. The Security tab is used to set the NTFS permissions for the volume.

FIGURE 4.21   The Sharing tab of the volume's Properties dialog box

FIGURE 4.22   The Security tab of the volume's Properties dialog box

Previous Versions   The Previous Versions tab displays shadow copies of the files that are created by System Restore, as shown in Figure 4.23. Shadow copies of files are backup copies created by Windows in the background to allow you to restore the system to a previous state. On the Previous Versions tab, you can select a copy of the volume and either view the contents of the shadow copy or copy the shadow copy to another location. If System Restore is not enabled, then shadow copies of a volume will not be created.

FIGURE 4.23   The Previous Versions tab of the volume's Properties dialog box

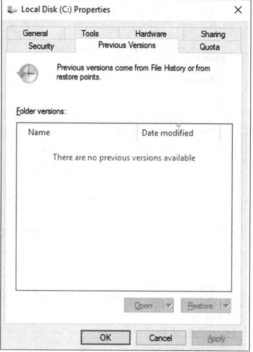

Quota   Quotas give you the ability to limit the amount of hard-disk space that a user can have on a volume or partition (see Figure 4.24). By default, quotas are disabled. To enable quotas, check the Enable Quota Management check box. There are a few options that can be configured when enabling quotas.

The Deny Disk Space To Users Exceeding Quota Limit check box is another option. When this box is enabled, any user who exceeds their quota limit will be denied disk storage. You can choose not to enable this option, which allows you to just monitor the quotas. You also have the ability to set the quota limit and warning size and to log all quota events as they happen.

FIGURE 4.24   The Quota tab of the volume's Properties dialog box

Adding a New Disk

New hard disks can be added to a system to increase the amount of disk storage you have. This is a fairly common task that you will need to perform as your application programs and files grow larger.

How you add a disk depends on whether your computer supports hot swapping of drives. Hot swapping is the process of adding a new hard drive while the computer is turned on. Most desktop computers do not support this capability. Remember, your user account must be a member of the Administrators group to install a new drive. The following list specifies configuration options:

Computer Doesn't Support Hot Swapping   If your computer does not support hot swapping, you must shut down the computer before you add a new disk. Then add the drive according to the manufacturer's directions. When you've finished, restart the computer. You should find the new drive listed in the Disk Management utility.

Computer Supports Hot Swapping   If your computer does support hot swapping, you don't need to turn off your computer first. Just add the drive according to the manufacturer's directions. Then open the Disk Management utility and select Action ➤ Rescan Disks. You should find the new drive listed in the Disk Management utility.

Creating Partitions and Volumes   Once you add a new disk, the next step is to create a partition (on a basic disk) or a volume (on a dynamic disk). Partitions and volumes fill similar roles in the storage of data on disks, and the processes for creating them are the same.

Creating a Volume or a Partition

Creating a volume or partition is a fairly easy process. To create the new volume or partition, right-click the unformatted free space and start the wizard.

Exercise 4.5 walks you through the New Volume Wizard for creating a new volume.

EXERCISE 4.5

Creating a New Volume

1. In the Disk Management utility, right-click an area of free storage space and choose the type of volume to create. If only one drive is installed, you will be able to create only a simple volume. You can click New Simple Volume to create a new simple volume.

2. The Welcome To The New Simple Volume Wizard appears. Click the Next button to continue.

3. The Select Volume Size screen appears. Select the size of volume to create, and then click Next to continue.

4. You should see the Assign Drive Letter Or Path screen. You can specify a drive letter, mount the volume as an empty folder, or choose not to assign a drive letter or drive path. If you choose to mount the volume into an empty folder, you can have a virtually unlimited number of volumes, negating the drive-letter limitation. If you choose not to assign a drive letter or path, users will not be able to access the volume. Make your selections, and click Next to continue (see Figure 4.25).

FIGURE 4.25   Assign Drive Letter Or Path screen

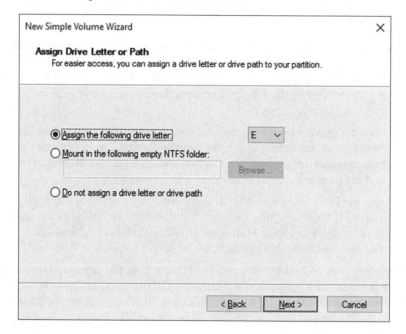

5. The Format Partition screen appears. This screen allows you to choose whether you will format the volume. If you choose to format the volume, you can format it as FAT32 or NTFS. You can also select the allocation unit size, enter a volume label (for information only), specify whether you would like to perform a quick format, and choose whether to enable file and folder compression (if available). After you've made your choices, click Next (see Figure 4.26).

FIGURE 4.26   Format Partition screen

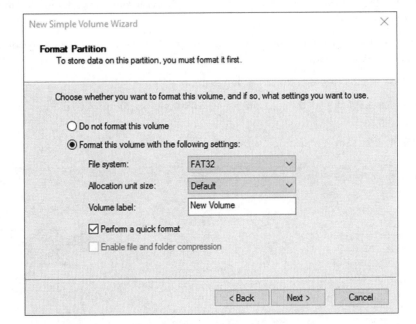

6. The Completing The New Volume Wizard screen appears. Verify your selections. If you need to change any of them, click the Back button to reach the appropriate screen. When everything is correctly set, click the Finish button.

Now that you know how to create a new volume or partition, let's see how to convert a basic disk to dynamic or GPT.

Upgrading a Basic Disk to a Dynamic or GPT Disk

When you perform a fresh installation of Windows 10, your drives are configured as basic disks. To take advantage of the features offered by Windows 10 dynamic or GPT disks, you must upgrade your basic disks to either of those disk configurations.

Upgrading basic disks to dynamic disks is a one-way process as far as preserving data is concerned and is a potentially dangerous operation. Before you perform this upgrade (or make any major change to your drives or volumes), create a new backup of the drive or volume and verify that you can successfully restore the backup before proceeding with the change.

Any basic disk can be converted to a dynamic disk, but only a disk with all unformatted free space can be converted to a GPT disk. Exercise 4.6 walks you through converting an MBR-based disk to a GPT disk.

Converting a Basic Disk to a GPT Disk

1. If the disk that you want to convert has partitions or volumes defined, first delete the partition or volume.

2. Open the Disk Management utility by clicking the Start button, right-clicking Computers, and choosing Manage.

3. Click Disk Management in the lower-left section.

4. Right-click the disk and choose Convert To GPT Disk (see Figure 4.27).

FIGURE 4.27   Format partition screen

5. After the disk converts, you can right-click the disk and see that the Convert To MBR Disk option is now available.

There are a few other methods for converting an MBR-based disk to a GPT disk. You can use the Diskpart utility and type in the Convert GPT command. You can also create a GPT disk when you first install a new hard drive. After you install the new hard drive, during the initialization phase, you can choose GPT Disk.

Another type of conversion that you may need to perform is that from a basic disk to a dynamic disk. Complete Exercise 4.7 to convert a basic disk to a dynamic disk.

EXERCISE 4.7

Converting a Basic Disk to a Dynamic Disk

1. In the Disk Management utility, right-click the disk you want to convert and select the Convert To Dynamic Disk option.

2. In the Convert To Dynamic Disk dialog box, check the disk that you want to convert and click OK.

3. In the Disks To Convert dialog box, click the Convert button.

4. A confirmation dialog box warns you that you will no longer be able to boot previous versions of Windows from this disk. Click the Yes button to continue to convert the disk.

As you are configuring the volumes or partitions on the hard drive, other things that you may need to configure are the drive letters and paths.

Changing the Drive Letters and Paths

There may be times when you need to change drive letters and paths when you add new equipment. Let's suppose you have a hard drive with two partitions: drive C: assigned as your first partition, and drive D: assigned as your second partition. Your DVD drive is assigned the drive letter E:. You add a new hard drive and partition it as a new volume. By default, the new partition is assigned as drive F:. If you want your logical drives to be listed before the DVD drive, you can use the Disk Management utility's Change Drive Letter And Paths option to reassign your drive letters.

When you need to reassign drive letters, right-click the volume for which you want to change the drive letter and choose Change Drive Letter And Paths. This brings up the dialog box shown in Figure 4.28. Click the Change button to access the Change Drive Letter Or Path dialog box shown in Figure 4.28. Use the drop-down list next to the Assign The Following Drive Letter option to select the drive letter you want to assign to the volume.

FIGURE 4.28   The dialog boxes for changing a drive letter or path

In Exercise 4.8, you will edit the drive letter of the partition you created.

EXERCISE 4.8

Editing a Drive Letter

1. Right-click Start ➢ Computer Management; then expand Storage ➢ Disk Management.

2. Right-click a drive that you have created and select Change Drive Letter And Paths.

3. In the Change Drive Letter And Paths dialog box, click the Change button.

4. In the Change Drive Letter Or Path dialog box, select a new drive letter and click OK.

5. In the dialog box that appears, click the Yes button to confirm that you want to change the drive letter.

Another activity that you may need to perform is deleting a partition or volume that you have created. The next section looks at these activities.

Deleting Partitions and Volumes

When configuring your hard disks, there may be a time that you want to reconfigure your drive by deleting the partitions or volumes on the hard drive. You may also want to delete a volume so that you can extend another volume. These are tasks that can be configured in Disk Management.

When deleting a volume or partition, you will see a warning that all the data on the partition or volume will be lost. You have to click Yes to confirm that you want to delete the volume or partition. This confirmation is important because once you delete a partition or volume, it's gone for good along with any data content that was contained within it.

The system volume, the boot volume, or any volume that contains the active paging (swap) file can't be deleted through the Disk Management utility. If you are trying to remove these partitions because you want to delete Windows 10, you can use a third-party disk-management utility.

In Exercise 4.9, you will delete a partition that you have created. Make sure that if you delete a partition or volume, it is empty; otherwise, back up all the data that you would like to retain before the deletion.

Deleting a Partition

1. In the Disk Management utility, right-click the volume or partition that you want to remove and choose Delete Volume.

2. A warning box appears, stating that once this volume is deleted, all data will be lost. Click Yes.

3. The volume will be removed, and the area will be returned as unformatted free space.

You may be worried about your users removing devices from their Windows 10 machines. Microsoft has helped you in this situation. You can use removable-device policies to help restrict your users from removing their hardware. Removable-device policies can be created through the use of a Group Policy Object (GPO) on the server. GPOs are policies that are set on a computer or user and allow you to manipulate the Windows 10 environment.

Now that we have explored some of the basic administrative tasks of Disk Management, let's look at how to manage storage.

Managing Storage

The Disk Management utility offers support for managing storage. You can create, delete, and format partitions or volumes on your hard drives. You can also extend or shrink volumes on dynamic disks. Additionally, you can delete volume sets and striped sets.

Managing Dynamic Storage

As noted earlier in this chapter, a dynamic disk can contain simple, spanned, or striped volumes. Through the Disk Management utility, you can create volumes of each type. You can also create an extended volume, which is the process of adding disk space to a single simple volume. The following sections describe these disk-management tasks.

Creating Simple, Spanned, and Striped Volumes

As explained earlier, you use the New Volume Wizard to create a new volume. To start the New Volume Wizard, in the Disk Management utility, right-click an area of free space where you want to create the volume. Then you can choose the type of volume you want to create: simple, spanned, or striped.

When you choose to create a spanned volume, you are creating a new volume from scratch that includes space from two or more physical drives, up to a maximum of 32 drives.

When you choose to create a striped volume, you are creating a new volume that combines free space from 2 to 32 drives into a single logical partition. The free space on all drives must be equal in size in a striped volume. Data in the striped volume is written across all drives in 64 KB stripes. (Data in spanned and extended volumes is written sequentially.) Striped volumes offer you better performance and are normally used for temporary files or folders. The problem with a striped volume is if you lose one of the drives in the volume, the entire striped volume is lost.

Another option that you have with volumes is to extend the volumes to create a larger storage area. In the next section, we will look at that process.

Creating Extended Volumes

When you create an extended volume, you are taking a single, simple volume (maybe one that is almost out of disk space) and adding more disk space to it, using free space that exists on the same physical hard drive. When the volume is extended, it is seen as a single drive letter. To extend a volume, the simple volume must be formatted as NTFS. You cannot extend a system or boot partition.

An extended volume is created when you are using only one physical drive. A spanned volume is created when you are using two or more physical drives. Exercise 4.10 shows you how to create an extended volume.

EXERCISE 4.10

Creating an Extended Volume

1. In the Disk Management utility, right-click the volume you want to extend and choose Extend Volume.

2. The Extend Volume Wizard starts. Click Next.

3. The Select Disks screen appears. As shown in Figure 4.29, you can specify the maximum size of the extended volume. The maximum size you can specify is determined by the amount of free space that exists in all of the dynamic drives on your computer. Click Next to continue.

4. The Completing The Extend Volume Wizard screen appears. Click the Finish button. You will see the new volume.

FIGURE 4.29   The Select Disks screen

Once a volume is extended, no portion of it can be deleted without losing data on the entire set. However, if there is unneeded space on a volume, you can shrink that volume without losing data by using the Shrink Volume option in Disk Management.

Real World Scenario

You're Running Out of Disk Space

Crystal, a user on your network, is running out of disk space. The situation needs to be corrected so she can be brought back up and running as quickly as possible. Crystal has a 250 GB drive (C:) that runs a very large customer database. She needs additional space added to the C: drive so the database will recognize the data because it must be stored on a single drive letter. Crystal's computer has a single SATA drive with nothing attached to the second SATA channel.

You have two basic options for managing space in this circumstance. One is to upgrade the disk to a larger disk, but this will necessitate reinstalling the OS and the applications and restoring the user's data. The other choice is to add a temporary second drive and extend the volume. This will at least allow Crystal to be up and running—but it should not be considered a permanent solution. If you do choose to extend the volume and then either drive within the volume set fails, the user will lose access to both drives. When Crystal's workload allows time for maintenance, you can replace the volume set with a single drive.

One issue you may run into with hard drives is that they go bad from time to time. If you have ever heard a hard drive fail, you know the sound: it is a distinct clicking. Once you have experienced it, you will never forget it. When drives go bad, Disk Management can help determine which drive and what the issue may be. Next, we will look at hard-disk errors.

Troubleshooting Disk Management

The Disk Management utility can be used to troubleshoot disk errors through a set of status codes; however, if a disk will not initialize, no status code will be displayed. Disks will not initialize if there is no valid disk signature.

The problem with disk errors is that you don't know when a disk fails or which disk failed. Disk Management can help you with this. When disks have problems or errors, status codes get assigned. Knowing what these codes mean will help you determine what the problem is and, more important, what steps need to be taken to fix the problem.

Understanding Disk Management Status Codes

The main window of the Disk Management utility displays the status of disks and volumes. The following list contains the possible status codes and a description of each code; these are very useful in troubleshooting disk problems:

Online   Indicates that the disk is accessible and that it is functioning properly. This is the normal disk status.

Online (Errors)   Used only with dynamic disks, this code indicates that I/O errors have been detected on the dynamic disk. One possible fix for this error is to right-click the disk and select Reactivate Disk to attempt to return the disk to Online status. This fix will work only if the I/O errors were temporary. You should immediately back up your data if you see this error and suspect that the I/O errors are not temporary.

Healthy   Specifies that the volume is accessible and functioning properly.

Healthy (At Risk)   Used to indicate that a dynamic volume is currently accessible but I/O errors have been detected on the underlying dynamic disk. This option is usually associated with Online (Errors) for the underlying disk.

Offline or Missing   Used only with dynamic disks, this code indicates that the disk is not accessible. This can occur if the disk is corrupted or the hardware has failed. If the error is not caused by hardware failure or major corruption, you may be able to reaccess the disk by using the Reactivate Disk option to return the disk to Online status. If the disk was originally offline and then the status changed to Missing, it indicates that the disk has become corrupted, has been powered down, or was disconnected.

Unreadable   This can occur on basic or dynamic disks. It indicates that the disk is inaccessible and might have encountered hardware errors, corruption, or I/O errors or that the system disk configuration database is corrupted. This message may also appear when a disk is spinning up while the Disk Management utility is rescanning the disks on the computer.

Failed   This can be seen with basic or dynamic volumes. It specifies that the volume can't be started. This can occur because the disk is damaged or the file system is corrupted. If this message occurs with a basic volume, you should check the underlying disk hardware. If the error occurs on a dynamic volume, verify that the underlying disks are online.

Unknown   Used with basic and dynamic volumes. It occurs if the boot sector for the volume becomes corrupted—for example, from a virus. This error can also occur if no disk signature is created for the volume.

Incomplete   Occurs when you move some but not all of the disks from a multidisk volume. If you do not complete the multivolume set, the data will be inaccessible.

Foreign   This error can occur if you move a dynamic disk from a computer running Windows 2000 (any version), Windows Server 2003, Windows Server 2008, Windows Server 2008 R2, Windows Server 2012/2012 R2, Windows XP Professional, Windows 7, Windows Vista, or Windows 8.1 to a Windows 10 computer. This error occurs because configuration data is unique to computers where the dynamic disk was created. You can correct this error by right-clicking the disk and selecting the Import Foreign Disks option. Any existing volume information will then be visible and accessible.

In addition to errors, there are some other issues that can arise when installing or configuring disks. One issue that may occur is that a disk fails to initialize when installed.

Troubleshooting Disks That Fail to Initialize

When you add a new disk to your computer in Windows 10, the disk does not initially contain a disk signature, which is required for the disk to be recognized by Windows. Disk signatures are at the end of the sector marker on the Master Boot Record (MBR) of the drive.

When you install a new drive and run the Disk Management utility, a wizard starts and lists all new disks that have been detected. The disk signature is written through this process. If you cancel the wizard before the disk signature is written, you will see the disk status Not Initialized. To initialize a disk, you right-click the disk you want to initialize and select the Initialize Disk option.

As you have now seen, Disk Management can be a very useful tool in your computer management arsenal. If you decide to format your partition or volume using NTFS, you then receive added benefits like compression, encryption (and therefore security), and quotas. In the following sections, we will take a closer look at compression and encryption.

Managing Data Compression

One of the advantages of using NTFS over FAT32 is the ability to compress data. I teach IT administrators data compression, and I like to refer to a well-known infomercial as an example. Have you seen the commercial where people put all of the blankets into a large bag and then hook a vacuum to the bag and suck all the air out? This is a great example of how compression works. Data compression is the process of storing data in a form that takes less space than uncompressed data.

If you have ever "zipped" or "packed" a file, you have used a form of data compression. The compression algorithms support cluster sizes only up to 4 KB, so if you are using larger cluster sizes, NTFS compression support is not available. If you have the Modify permission on an NTFS volume, you can manage data compression through Windows Explorer or the Compact command-line utility.

The following are some important points about compression:

- Files as well as folders in NTFS can be compressed and uncompressed. Files and folders are managed independently, which means that a compressed folder can contain uncompressed files and an uncompressed folder can contain compressed files.

- Access to compressed files by applications is transparent. For example, if you access a compressed file through Microsoft Word, the file will be uncompressed automatically when it is opened and then automatically compressed again when it is closed.

- Compression happens very quickly, but if, for example, you compress a 500 GB hard drive, there is no guarantee that there won't be any lag time on your machine or server.

- Data compression is available only on NTFS partitions. Because of this, if you copy or move a compressed folder or file to a FAT32 partition, Windows 10 automatically uncompresses the folder or file.

- Certain system files (e.g., Pagefile.sys) can't be compressed.

- You have the ability to show compressed files and folders with an alternate color.

In Exercise 4.11, you will compress and uncompress folders and files.

EXERCISE 4.11

Compressing and Uncompressing Folders

1. Select Start ➢ Run, and then type **Explorer** and click OK.

2. In Windows Explorer, find and select Computer, Local Disk (C:), and then a folder on the C: drive. The folder you select should contain files.

3. Right-click the folder and select Properties. In the General tab of the folder's Properties dialog box, note the value listed for Size On Disk. Then click the Advanced button.

4. In the Advanced Attributes dialog box, check the Compress Contents To Save Disk Space option and then click OK.

5. In the Confirm Attribute Changes dialog box, select the option Apply Changes To This Folder, Subfolders and Files. (If this confirmation dialog box does not appear, you can display it by clicking the Apply button in the Properties dialog box.) Click OK to confirm your changes.

6. On the General tab of the folder's Properties dialog box, note the value that now appears for Size On Disk. This size should have decreased because you compressed the folder.

To uncompress folders and files, repeat the steps in Exercise 4.11 and uncheck the Compress Contents To Save Disk Space option in the Advanced Attributes dialog box.

As I stated earlier, you can specify that compressed files be displayed in a different color from uncompressed files. To do so, in Windows Explorer select View ➤ Options. In the Options box, click the View tab, and under Files And Folders, check the Show Encrypted Or Compressed NTFS Files In Color option.

In addition to compressing files and folders in Windows Explorer, you can compress the files and folders using the Compact command-line utility.

Using the Compact Command-Line Utility

The command-line options for managing file and folder compression are Compact and Expand. You can access these commands from a command prompt. The Compact command offers you more control over file and folder compression than Windows Explorer. For example, you can use the Compact command with a batch script or to compress only files that meet a specific criterion (for example, all the DOC files in a specific folder). Some of the options that can be used with the Compact command are shown in Table 4.5.

TABLE 4.5 Compact commands options

Command	Description
/C	Compresses the specified file or folder
/U	Uncompresses the specified file or folder
/S:dir	Used to specify which folder should be compressed or uncompressed
/A	Displays any files that have been hidden or system file attributes
/I	Indicates that errors should be ignored
/F	Forces a file to be compressed
/Q	Used with reporting, to report only critical information
/?	Displays help

Another way that you can save disk space is by zipping folders. In the following section, we will discuss how to save space using zipped folders.

Using Compressed (Zipped) Folders

Windows 10 also supports compressed (zipped) folders. This feature is different from NTFS compressed folders. The advantage of using compressed (zipped) folders is that they are supported on FAT32 and NTFS volumes. In addition, you can use compressed (zipped) folders to share data with other programs that use zipped files. The downside to using compressed (zipped) folders is that it is slower than using NTFS compression.

Within Windows Explorer, you create a zipped folder (or file) by right-clicking the folder and selecting Send To ➤ Compressed (Zipped) Folder. You create a zipped file by right-clicking a file and selecting New ➤ Compressed (Zipped) Folder. When you create a compressed folder, it will be displayed as a folder with a zipper.

Understanding RAID

One concern for any computer department is the loss of data due to hard-drive failures. *Redundant Array of Independent Disks (RAID)* allows an administrator to recover data from a single hard-disk failure.

The important factor to remember about Microsoft software-based RAID is that you can recover from only a single disk failure. If multiple hard disks fail, RAID will no longer protect your system from data loss.

There are two types of RAID (called *RAID models*): hardware based and software based. Hardware RAID, which is the best option, is built into the physical hardware and must be supported by the disk controllers and hard drives. Software RAID is configured through the Windows operating system.

The downside to hardware RAID is cost. A server or computer that has hardware RAID built in can cost thousands of dollars. Software RAID is free, but remember the old saying "You get what you pay for."

In the next section, we will look at the different models of RAID and how each model operates.

RAID Levels

There are many different levels of RAID, but Microsoft Windows 10 allows for configuration of three main levels: RAID-0, RAID-1, and RAID-5. Let's take a look at each:

RAID-0 (Striped)   RAID-0 has no data recoverability, but it is used for better performance. With RAID-0 you can have a minimum of two hard disks, and these two disks work together as a single volume. Because the two disks work together, the disks both use their own read/write heads, giving you better performance.

The downside to RAID-0 is that if you lose either disk, you lose the entire striped volume. RAID-0 is good for temp files or noncritical data since RAID-0 is not recoverable in the event of a single hard-disk failure.

RAID-1 (Mirroring)   RAID-1, also known as mirroring, allows you to set up two volumes or disks that mirror each other. The advantage to mirroring is that if you lose one disk or volume, you can boot to the second disk or volume (the mirror) and recover your data. The downside to mirroring is that it is more expensive than other RAID options.

RAID-5 Volume   A RAID-5 volume, which many years ago was known as a stripe set with parity, uses a minimum of 3 disks (maximum of 32 disks) that work together as one volume. The advantage to a RAID-5 volume is that the volume uses a parity bit, which allows you to recover your data in the event of a single hard-disk failure.

When it comes to hardware RAID and software RAID, recoverability is night and day. Hardware RAID is much faster and easier when a hard disk fails. Many hardware RAID systems are hot swappable, meaning that when a disk fails, you just slide it out, insert a new disk, and RAID will then rebuild the drive and the system gets back to work.

This is not the case with software RAID. Recovering from a single hard-disk failure can take time, which in turn costs an organization money. Software RAID is set up through the Disk Management utility (explained earlier in this chapter) and is not available unless you have multiple hard disks installed in the Windows 10 machine. Another important thing to remember with software RAID is that hot swappable drives are not permitted. So it's always best to go with hardware-based RAID.

Storage Spaces

Storage Spaces in Windows 10 is another way to give your Windows 10 users data redundancy. This is just another advantage of Windows 10. Windows 10 administrators have the ability to group hard drives together into a storage pool. Windows 10 users can then use these storage pool capacities to turn the pools into individual storage spaces.

Storage spaces then show up in File Explorer as regular drives, but they are actually virtual drives created using the storage spaces. Users can use these drives just like any other hard drive in their system.

But when you set up the Storage Spaces, you can set them up so if you have at least two drives in the storage pool, you can create storage spaces that won't be affected by a drive failure. This gives you fault tolerance on the user's data.

Now why is this an actual advantage for Windows 10? Well, one of the biggest issues we have as administrators is our users running out of hard drive space. If we decide to use Storage Spaces and the user starts to run out of space, administrators can add more drives and increase the storage space on the user's Windows 10 system while also getting fault tolerance on the data.

To create storage spaces, you need at least one or more hard drives besides the drive on which Windows 10 is installed. One huge advantage is that these hard drives can be either internal or external hard drives, including solid-state drives. When it comes to building storage spaces, there are three main unique kinds based on your storage needs. Each one works like a version of RAID:

Simple Spaces   Simple storage spaces work the same as RAID-0 (striped volumes). Simple spaces are designed to give users increased performance but no data protection. These spaces are used best for files that don't need to be protected (temp files, music, etc.). This works great when you want better performance, and simple spaces only require at least one drive.

Mirror Spaces   Mirror storage spaces work just like RAID-1 (mirror), and they are designed to give you better performance while also giving your data protection from a single hard drive failure for a two-way mirror and a double hard drive failure from a three-way mirror.

Administrators can take mirror storage spaces even further by formatting them with the Resilient File System (ReFS). If the mirror storage space is formatted using ReFS, Windows will then automatically maintain the mirror's data integrity, making your data even more resilient to hard drive failures.

Parity Spaces   Parity storage spaces work a lot like RAID-5 volumes (stripe set with parity). To use parity spaces, you are required to have at least three drives to protect you from a single hard drive failure or seven drives to protect you from a double hard drive failure.

If you want to set up storage spaces, right-click the Start button and choose Control Panel. In the upper-right corner, change the View By option from Category to Large Icons. Scroll down to Storage Spaces and double-click Storage Spaces (see Figure 4.30).

FIGURE 4.30   The Storage Spaces icon in Control Panel

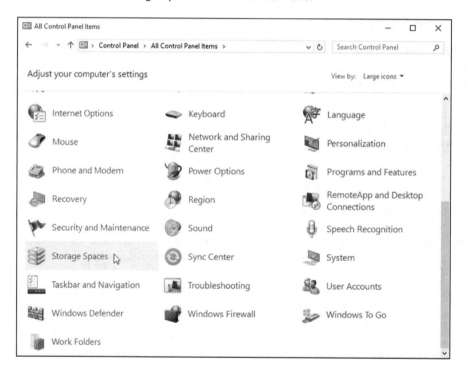

After you double-click and open Storage Spaces, you would complete the following steps to create a storage pool:

1. Click the "Create a new pool and storage space" link (shown in Figure 4.31).

2. Select the drives you want to add to the new storage space, and then click Create Pool.

3. Give the drive a name and letter, and then choose a layout (Simple, Two-Way Mirror, Three-Way Mirror, or Parity).

4. Enter the maximum size the storage space can reach, and then click Create Storage Space.

FIGURE 4.31   The link to create a new pool and storage space

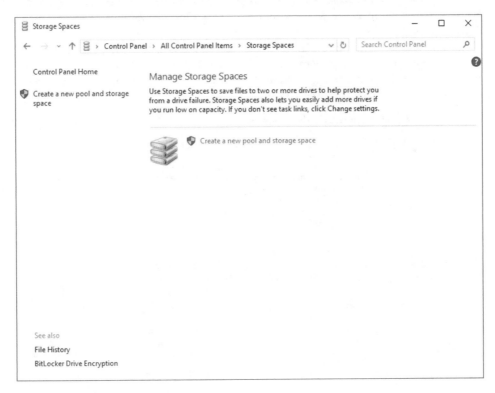

Now that you have seen how you can protect your data, we will look at how you can keep your disk volumes and partitions running at peak performance.

Using Disk-Maintenance Tools

Part of our job as IT professionals is to keep our systems running the best that they can. Most of us have seen machines running very quickly when they are new, but then they start to slow down over time, even when we do not install any new software.

Microsoft Windows 10 includes a few utilities that you can run to help keep your system running efficiently. In the next sections, we will discuss three of these utilities: Disk Optimization, Disk Cleanup, and Check Disk.

Using the Disk Optimization Utility

Data is normally stored sequentially on the disk as space is available. Optimization naturally occurs as users create, delete, and modify files. The access of noncontiguous data is transparent to the user; however, when data is stored in this manner, the operating system must search through the disk to access all the pieces of a file. This slows down data access. Disk optimization rearranges the existing files so they are stored contiguously, which optimizes access to them. In Windows 10, you use the Disk Optimization utility to optimize and defragment your disk.

To access the Disk Optimization utility, right-click Start ➤ Computer Management. Expand Storage and select Disk Management, right-click the drive, select the Tools tab, and then click the Optimize button. The Optimize Drives window appears (Figure 4.32); you can schedule when the disk optimizer should run or run the tool immediately.

FIGURE 4.32   The Optimize Drives window

In the next section we will look at another tool that is included with Windows 10—the Disk Cleanup utility.

Using the Disk Cleanup Utility

One concern that we as IT professionals face is how to conserve hard-disk space for our users. Hard drives continue to get larger and larger, but so do applications. This is where the Disk Cleanup utility can help.

The Disk Cleanup utility identifies areas of disk space that can be deleted to free up hard-disk space. Disk Cleanup works by identifying temporary files, Internet cache files, and unnecessary program files.

To access this utility, right-click Start ≻ Computer Management. Right-click the drive letter and choose Properties and then Disk Cleanup. The Disk Cleanup utility then runs and calculates the amount of disk space you can free up.

Complete Exercise 4.12 to run the Disk Cleanup utility on the Windows 10 operating system.

EXERCISE 4.12

Running the Disk Cleanup Utility

1. Right-click Start ≻ Computer Management.

2. Right-click the drive and choose Properties.

3. On the General tab, click the Disk Cleanup button.

   The Disk Cleanup utility will start to calculate the system data.

4. After the analysis is complete, you will see the Disk Cleanup dialog box (shown in Figure 4.33) listing files that are suggested for deletion and showing how much space will be gained by deleting those files. Click OK.

FIGURE 4.33   The Disk Cleanup dialog box

5. When you are asked to confirm that you want to delete the files, click the Yes button. The Disk Cleanup utility deletes the files and automatically closes the Disk Cleanup dialog box.

Another issue that you may run into is bad sectors on your hard disk. Windows 10 also includes a utility to help you troubleshoot disk devices and volumes.

Using the Check Disk Utility

If you are having trouble with your disk devices or volumes, you can use the Windows 10 Check Disk utility. This utility detects bad sectors, attempts to fix errors in the file system, and scans for and attempts to recover bad sectors. To use Check Disk, you must be logged in as a member of the Administrators group.

File system errors can be caused by a corrupted file system or by hardware errors. If you have software errors, the Check Disk utility may help you find them. There is no way to fix hardware errors through software, however. If you have excessive hardware errors, you should replace your disk drive.

Complete Exercise 4.13 to run the Check Disk utility.

EXERCISE 4.13

Using the Check Disk Utility

1. Select Start ➤ Computer Management, and then expand Storage and select Disk Management.

2. Right-click the C: drive and choose Properties.

3. Click the Tools tab, and then click the Check Now button.

4. In the Check Disk dialog box (shown in Figure 4.34), you can choose one or both of the options to automatically fix file system errors and to scan for and attempt recovery of bad sectors. For this exercise, check both of the check boxes. Then click the Start button.

FIGURE 4.34 The Check Disk dialog box

Another way to run the Check Disk utility is from the command line, using the command Chkdsk. Chkdsk is used to create and display a status report, which is based on the file system you are using.

PowerShell Disk Commands

As you can see from this chapter, there are many different ways to manage and configure disks and storage. But there is one way we haven't discussed yet, and that's with PowerShell commands.

PowerShell commands allow you to run multiple configurations by using scripts or even by using individual commands. So let's take a look at some of the different commands you can use. Table 4.6 looks at some of the different PowerShell commands.

TABLE 4.6   PowerShell commands

PowerShell Command	Description
Add-PhysicalDisk	This command will add a disk to a storage pool.
Clear-Disk	This command removes all partition information and erases all data on a disk.
Connect-VirtualDisk	Administrators use this command for connecting a disconnected virtual disk to a computer using Storage Spaces.
Disconnect-VirtualDisk	This command will disconnect a virtual disk from a computer.
Dismount-DiskImage	Administrators can use this command to dismount a VHD or ISO image from a machine.
Format-Volume	This command formats a volume on a drive.
Get-Disk	This command allows an operating system to see a disk.
Get-DiskImage	This command allows an operating system to see a disk image.
Get-FileIntegrity	Allows an administrator to check the integrity information for a file that is on an ReFS volume.
Get-Partition	This command allows an administrator to get a list of partitions on the system's disks.
Get-PhysicalDisk	This command gives you a list of all of your available physical disks.

TABLE 4.6   PowerShell commands *(continued)*

PowerShell Command	Description
Get-VirtualDisk	This command allows an operating system to see a virtual disk.
Get-Volume	This command shows you the volume object.
Initialize-Disk	This command allows you to initializes a disk for first-time use.
Invoke-Command	This command allows you to remotely execute PowerShell commands on another system.
Mount-DiskImage	Administrators can use this command to mount a VHD or ISO image. By doing this, the image will appear as a normal disk.
New-Partition	This allows administrators to create a new partition on an existing disk.
New-StoragePool	This command allows you to create a new storage pool of physical disks.
New-VirtualDisk	This command creates a new virtual disk in the specified storage pool.
New-Volume	This command allows you to create a new volume.
Remove-Partition	Administrators can use this command allows you to remove a partition.
Remove-PhysicalDisk	This command allows you to remove a disk.
Remove-VirtualDisk	Administrators can use this command allows you to remove a virtual disk.
Repair-VirtualDisk	This command allows you to repair a virtual disk.
Repair-Volume	Administrators can use this command allows you to repair a volume.
Resize-Partition	This command allows you to resize a partition.
Set-Partition	Administrators can use this command to set partition attributes, such as setting the partition to be active.
Set-PhysicalDisk	You can use this command to set disk attributes.

PowerShell Command	Description
Set-StoragePool	This command allows you to modify the properties of the specified storage pool.
Set-Volume	This command allows an administrator to set or change the file system label of a volume.
Update-Disk	Administrators can update cached information about a specified disk.
Update-StoragePool	This command will update the metadata of a Windows Server 2012 R2 storage pool.

Summary

There are two different ways that you can format your hard disk in a Windows 10 operating system: FAT32 and NTFS. NTFS has many advantages over FAT32, including security, encryption, disk quotas, and compression, just to name a few.

Besides the way you format your hard disk, you can configure your hard disk as a basic disk or a dynamic disk and must choose to either leave your disk partition system as the default MBR or choose to convert it to a GPT disk. You can use the Disk Management MMC snap-in to configure your hard disks and file system.

Another configurable option within the Disk Management utility is RAID. RAID-1 and RAID-5 allow you to recover your data in the event of a single hard-disk failure. RAID-0 allows you to achieve better performance but has no data recoverability in the event of a hard-disk failure. You also have Storage Spaces, which gives your data a way to have recoverability and larger disk pools.

After the hard disks are installed and configured, there will be some maintenance items that need to be tended to. The utilities that allow you to perform these maintenance activities include the Disk Defragmenter and Check Disk utilities.

Video Resources

There are videos available for the following exercises:

4.1
4.2
4.4

You can access the videos at http://www.wiley.com/go/sybextestprep.

Exam Essentials

Understand the different file format options.   There are two ways to format a hard disk in Windows 10: FAT32 and NTFS. Understand that NTFS offers many benefits over FAT32, including security, encryption, compression, and disk quotas.

Understand the different hard-disk storage types.   Windows 10 supports three types of disk storage: basic, dynamic, and GUID Partition Table (GPT). Basic storage is backward compatible with other operating systems and can be configured to support up to four partitions. Dynamic storage is supported by all Windows operating systems above Windows 2000 and allows storage to be configured as volumes. GPT storage allows you to configure volume sizes larger than 2 TB and up to 128 primary partitions.

Know Storage Spaces and Storage Pools.   Microsoft Windows 10 includes Storage Spaces and Storage Pools. Storage Spaces allows an administrator to combine drives to make a larger storage area. Storage Pools are for virtualization. To create Storage Pools, you group disks into Storage Spaces and then create virtual disks out of those Storage Spaces that are then called Storage Pools.

Know the disk-management utilities.   Microsoft Windows 10 includes a few utilities that you can run to help keep your system running efficiently. These utilities include Disk Defragmenter, Disk Cleanup, and Check Disk.

Review Questions

1. Will has installed Windows 10 on his Windows XP computer. The machine is now a dual-boot computer. He has FAT32 for Windows XP and NTFS for Windows 10. In addition, he boots his computer to Windows XP Professional for testing an application's compatibility with both operating systems. Which of the following file systems will be seen by both operating systems?

   A. Only the FAT32 partition will be seen by both operating systems.

   B. Only the NTFS partition will be seen by both operating systems.

   C. Neither the FAT32 partition nor the NTFS partition will be seen by both operating systems.

   D. Both the FAT32 partition and the NTFS partition will be seen by both operating systems.

2. You are the network administrator for a large organization. You have three external USB drives on a Windows 10 Enterprise system. You want to create a single volume using all three USB drives. You want the drive to be portable and resilient. How can you set the three USB drives into a single volume?

   A. Use Control Panel to create a drive space.

   B. Use the administrative tools to create a drive space.

   C. Use Control Panel to create a storage space.

   D. Use the administrative tools to create a storage space.

3. Alexandria is the payroll manager and stores critical files on her local drive for added security on her Windows 10 computer. She wants to ensure that she is using the disk configuration with the most fault tolerance and the highest level of consistent availability. Which of the following provisions should she use?

   A. Disk striping

   B. Spanned volumes

   C. Mirrored volumes

   D. Extended volumes

4. Paige is considering upgrading her basic disk to a dynamic disk on her Windows 10 computer. She asks you to help her understand the function of dynamic disks. Which of the following statements are true of dynamic disks in Windows 10?

   A. Dynamic disks can be recognized by older operating systems such as Windows NT 4 in addition to new operating systems such as Windows 10.

   B. Dynamic disks are supported only by Windows 2000 Server and Windows Server 2003.

   C. Dynamic disks support features such as simple partitions, extended partitions, spanned partitions, and striped partitions.

   D. Dynamic disks support features such as simple volumes, extended volumes, spanned volumes, mirrored volumes, and striped volumes.

5. Cindy is using Windows 10 on her laptop computer, and the C: partition is running out of space. You want to identify any areas of free space that can be reclaimed from temporary files. What utility should you use?

   A. Disk Cleanup

   B. Disk Manager

   C. Disk Administrator

   D. Disk Defragmenter

6. Rob is using Windows 10 to store video files. He doesn't access the files very often and wants to compress the files to utilize disk space more effectively. Which of the following options allows you to compress files in Windows 10?

   A. `JetPack.exe`

   B. `Cipher.exe`

   C. `Packer.exe`

   D. Windows Explorer

7. You are the administrator of a large organization. You have a Windows 10 Enterprise system with three hard disks. You need to change the hard disks from basic to dynamic disks. How can you do this?

   A. Use the `Cipher` command.

   B. Use the `Compact` command.

   C. Use the `Convert` command.

   D. Use the Administrative Disk tool.

8. You have compressed a 4 MB file into 2 MB. You are copying the file to another computer that has a FAT32 partition. How can you ensure that the file will remain compressed?

   A. When you copy the file, use the `XCOPY` command with the `/Comp` switch.

   B. When you copy the file, use the Windows Explorer utility and specify the option Keep Existing Attributes.

   C. On the destination folder, make sure that you set the option Compress Contents To Save Disk Space in the folder's properties.

   D. You can't maintain disk compression on a non-NTFS partition.

9. You are the administrator for a large organization that is moving to Windows 10. You need to set up a way that you can run multiple storage commands from a scripting tool. How can you set this up?

   A. Use SCCM for scripting.

   B. Use PowerShell for scripting.

   C. Use AD FS for scripting.

   D. Use Disk Administrator scripting.

10. What PowerShell command allows an operating system to see a new disk?

   A. `Dismount-DiskImage`

   B. `Format-Volume`

   C. `Get-Disk`

   D. `Get-DiskImage`

Chapter

5

Configuring the Windows 10 Environment

MICROSOFT EXAM OBJECTIVES COVERED IN THIS CHAPTER:

✓ **Perform post-installation configuration.**

- This objective may include but is not limited to the following subobjectives: Configure and customize start menu, desktop, taskbar, and notification settings, according to device type; configure accessibility options; configure Cortana; configure Microsoft Edge; configure Internet Explorer; configure power settings.

✓ **Configure advanced management tools.**

- This objective may include but is not limited to the following subobjectives: Configure services, configure Device Manager, configure and use the MMC, configure Task Scheduler, configure automation of management tasks using Windows PowerShell.

If you are studying for the 70-697 and the 70-698 exams, then some of this information may be a refresher for you if you started with 70-697. Control Panel is Control Panel no matter what test you're taking. But make sure you cover all the material in this chapter because there are subjects in this chapter, not needed for 70-697. So let's get started.

Now that Windows 10 is installed, it's time to start setting up some of the configuration options that we have. In this chapter, we will look at performing post-installation tasks like setting up and configuring the Start menu, the Device Manager, and Cortana.

Another section that we use in IT to configure the Windows 10 operating systems is the Control Panel. The Control Panel is one of the most important configuration tools for Windows 10. It includes many icons that can help you optimize, maintain, and personalize the operating system. One of the most important icons in Control Panel is the System icon. The System icon not only has operating-system information, it also allows you to configure devices, remote settings, and system protection.

Next we will talk about laptop users. If you use Windows 10 on a laptop computer, it is important to properly configure your power and mobility options. Configuring these options on a laptop will allow you to get the most out of your laptop and Windows 10. There are many different mobility options that you can choose from to help customize a laptop to each individual user.

We will also examine how services operate and how to configure your services to start manually or automatically. We will examine how to configure services in the event of a service error.

Managing Windows

Once the operating system is installed, the next thing we need to do in IT is manage the operating system. If Windows 10 is not properly configured, it may cause your IT department issues for a long time.

When you are the IT administrator for a company, you need to make sure that the Windows client systems are configured properly and, in most cases, the same.

There are many ways to do this, from individually configuring the Windows 10 systems to using Group Policy Objects (GPOs). Most companies are going to set Windows 10 configurations through the use of Windows Servers and GPOs, but you still need to understand each component and what it does so you can configure the proper settings.

The following sections describe many of the configuration options for customizing Windows 10 for each user's needs. We will start with configuring the Windows 10 desktop environment.

Manipulating the Desktop Environment

The Windows 10 desktop is the interface that appears when a user logs into the operating system. The desktop includes the wallpaper, Start menu, tiles, and icons (see Figure 5.1).

FIGURE 5.1 The default Windows 10 desktop

The Windows 10 Start menu, located at the bottom left of the desktop by default, includes the default All Apps section shown in Figure 5.2.

FIGURE 5.2 The All Apps section

The Windows 10 default desktop appears after a user has logged onto a Windows 10 computer for the first time. When you install a new instance of Windows 10, you will notice that the desktop is clean except for the Recycle Bin. You may also have a message on the desktop that states that the Windows 10 system has not been activated (as shown in Figure 5.3).

Users can then configure their desktops to suit their personal preferences and to work more efficiently. The following topics describe some of the common default options that appear on the Start menu, in the Most Used section, Control Panel, and All Apps section. This list includes some of the more commonly used applications and shortcuts; it's not a complete list of every application available to you.

FIGURE 5.3   The desktop with activation notice

 Depending on which version of Windows 10 you are using, these options may vary a bit.

Windows 10 Applications

The following are some of the applications for Windows 10. These are not all of the applications installed by default on Windows 10 but just a few to get you started.

Calculator   This shortcut starts the Calculator program. The Calculator works like any other store-bought calculator, and it can even be changed from a Standard calculator to a Scientific, Programmer, Converter, Volume, Length, Weight & Mass, or Temperature calculator.

Cortana   With this application, you can speak or type into the Windows 10 system, and your personnel assistant, Cortana, will try to find answers to any queries that you may have.

Getting Started   This is used to access preset tasks. Some of these tasks are Get To Know Windows 10 (see Figure 5.4), Microsoft Edge, Start Menu Tips, Setting Things Up, Get Connected, Cortana, Windows Hello, XBOX App, Entertainment, Office, Personalize And Settings, Saving And Syncing Content, Apps And Store, Continuum And Touch, and Ease Of Use.

FIGURE 5.4   Getting Started tasks

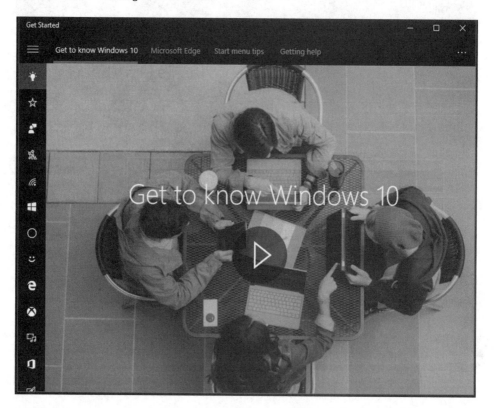

Get Skype   This app allows you to download and configure Skype. If your company uses Skype, Windows 10 gives you the ability to download and set up your Skype account with the Windows 10 operating system.

Maps   This app allows you to see the current location and area of the Windows 10 system. You can use Maps to search for locations and services (food, gas, directions, and so on), as shown in Figure 5.5.

FIGURE 5.5   Maps

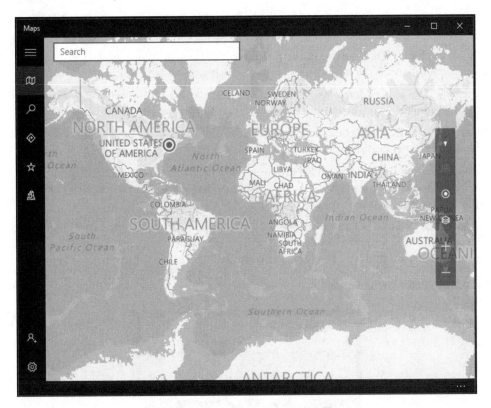

Microsoft Edge   This shortcut starts the built-in web browser. When used with an Internet connection, Microsoft Edge provides an interface for accessing the Internet or a local intranet.

OneDrive   This application allows you to connect with the Microsoft OneDrive cloud-based utility. You can use this application to share documents between the Windows 10 system and the OneDrive cloud-based subscription.

People   This application allows you to look up and work with your contacts. It enables you to use social media to connect people and contacts.

Windows Update   This shortcut allows you to receive updates and security patches for the Windows 10 operating system. You can receive updates from either Microsoft's web server or a Windows Server Update Services (WSUS) machine.

XPS Viewer   This application allows you to view Microsoft XML Paper Specification (.xps) files. The XPS viewer also allows you to print these files.

Windows 10 Accessories

Windows Accessories are some basic tools that are included with Windows 10 to help you do tasks from surfing the net to playing DVDs.

Internet Explorer   This shortcut starts the built-in web browser. When used with an Internet connection, Internet Explorer provides an interface for accessing the Internet or a local intranet.

Notepad   This application allows you to create text files. This is a great way to store notes on the Windows 10 system without using a full word processing application like Word.

Paint   This shortcut starts the Paint program. The Paint program is an application that allows you to change or manipulate graphics files.

Remote Desktop Connection   This program allows a user to connect remotely to another machine. To connect to another computer, Remote Desktop Connection must be enabled on the receiving computer.

Snipping Tool   This tool allows a user to capture an item on the desktop (see Figure 5.6). The user clicks the Snipping Tool and drags the cursor around an area that will then be captured. The captured area can then be drawn on, highlighted, or saved as a file.

FIGURE 5.6   Snipping tool

Sticky Notes   This application places a sticky note on the desktop, as shown in Figure 5.7. You can then type a message or reminder into the sticky note. It will remain on the desktop until you delete it.

FIGURE 5.7   Sticky Notes application

Settings   This application opens the Settings window. Inside the Settings window, you can configure your System, Devices, Network & Internet, Personalization, Accounts, Time & Language, Ease Of Access, Privacy, and Updates & Security settings (see Figure 5.8).

FIGURE 5.8   Settings window

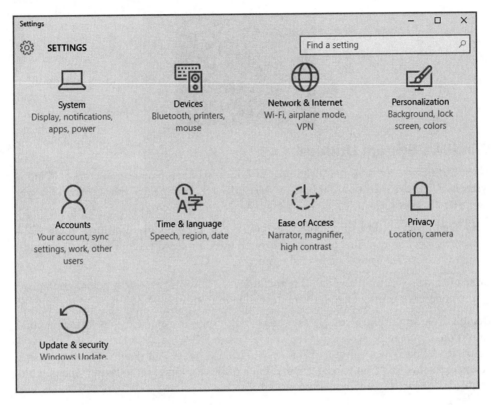

Store   This application allows you to download and purchase applications from the Microsoft Store. The Microsoft Store has thousands of business and personnel applications that you can use on Windows 10.

Windows Fax And Scan   This application allows you to create and manage scans and faxes. Windows Fax And Scan allows users to send or receive faxes from their workstation.

Windows Media Player   With this application, you can play all your media files, including videos, music, pictures, and recorded TV.

Windows Ease Of Access Tools

These tools are installed on a Windows 10 system to help individuals who have difficulty seeing the screen. The Ease Of Access tools can be accessed via Start ➤ All Apps ➤ Ease of Access and include a Magnifier, Narrator, On-Screen Keyboard, and Windows Speech Recognition, as shown in Figure 5.9.

FIGURE 5.9   Ease Of Access tools

Windows System Utilities

These utilities are the ones that help most IT administrators manage and control Windows systems. These are the tools that help us start, manage, and control the Windows 10 systems and applications.

Command Prompt   The Command Prompt is one of the most useful utilities to an IT administrator. You can run commands through the Command Prompt and program the Windows 10 system using system commands.

Control Panel   Control Panel holds many utilities and tools that allow you to configure your computer. It is discussed in greater detail later in this chapter.

Default Programs   When you choose the Default Programs shortcut, four different configuration items can be accessed (as shown in Figure 5.10): Set Your Default Programs, Associate A File Type Or Protocol With A Program, Change AutoPlay Settings, and Set Program Access And Computer Defaults. Each of these allows you to change the default programs that are used within Windows 10.

FIGURE 5.10   Default Programs

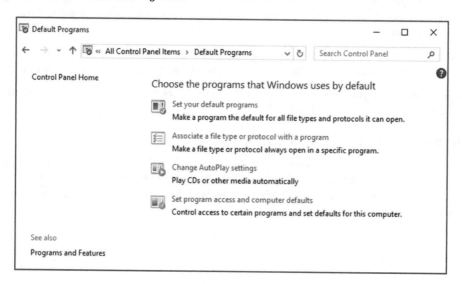

Devices   This shortcut opens the Devices section, where you can add or configure any of your hardware devices.

File Explorer   By default, this application shows all of the folders and files that are on the Windows 10 system. You can use this application to look at all of the files located on the Windows 10 system.

Run   You can either put in commands or run applications from the Run dialog box.

Task Manager   This is one of the few applications that I used as an IT director on a daily basis. The Task Manager allows you to see what applications are running on the Windows systems (including servers). The Task Manager also allows you to stop applications from running on a system.

This PC   This shortcut allows you to centrally manage your computer's files, hard drives, and devices with removable storage. It also allows you to manage system tasks and to view details about your computer.

Windows User's Tools

The Windows User's tools are the utilities we use to store and access user's data and documents. These are the applications and folders that we use to keep user data.

Desktop   This folder shows all of the applications that are located on the desktop.

Documents   By default, this folder stores the documents that are created. Each user has a unique Documents folder, so even if a computer is shared, each user will have his or her own personal folder.

Pictures   This application shows any pictures that are in the user's Pictures folder.

Music   This shortcut will show any music that is in the Music folder.

Videos   This shortcut shows you all of the videos that are stored on this Windows 10 system.

Shut Down or Restart   This button is used to shut down or restart the computer. There is an arrow next to the button that you can use to restart the machine or shut down the system.

The desktop also includes the Recycle Bin. The Recycle Bin is a special folder that holds the files and folders that have been deleted, assuming that your hard drive has enough free space to hold the deleted files. You can restore or permanently delete a file from the Recycle Bin by opening the Recycle Bin and right-clicking that file.

When configuring the desktop, you have the ability to decide between configuring a background of your choice as your desktop backdrop or you can choose one of the built-in desktop themes. Desktop themes are preset packages containing graphical appearance details used to customize the look and feel of an operating system.

Backgrounds are just the graphics that you decide to set as your wallpaper. To switch between different themes, right-click an area of open space on the desktop and select Personalize. In the Theme Settings dialog box, you can select the theme you want to use. You can additionally configure the desktop by customizing the Taskbar and Start menu, adding shortcuts, and setting display properties.

Configuring Personalization

To configure the Windows desktop and how it looks, right-click the Desktop and select Personalize. When you choose to Personalize the desktop, you have five different settings that you can configure (as shown in Figure 5.11).

FIGURE 5.11   Personalization screen

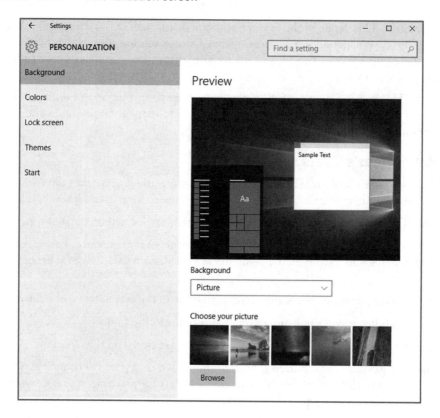

Background

This lets you pick your desktop background, which uses a picture or an HTML document as wallpaper. Setting up a desktop background can be as easy as picking a solid color and placing a picture of your favorite sports team or pet on top of it.

Windows 10 comes with some pictures already in the system, but you can basically turn any picture into your background desktop picture. As you can see in Figure 5.11, you can click the Browse button and choose the pictures that you want in your background.

Colors

This allows you to fine-tune the color and style of your windows background and accent. Windows 10 gives you the ability to automatically pick an accent color for your background, as shown in Figure 5.12.

FIGURE 5.12   Colors screen

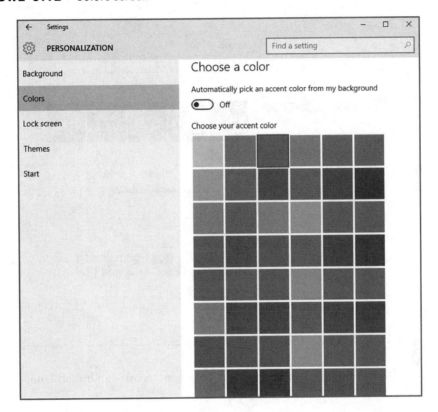

Windows 10 users also have the ability to automatically choose their own background colors. You can show colors on the Start screen, taskbar, and action center. You can also make the Start screen, taskbar, and Action Center transparent.

Lock Screen

This lets you select a screen saver that will start after the system has been idle for a specified amount of time. You can also specify a password that must be used to access the system after it has been idle. When the idle time has been reached and the screen saver is activated, the computer can also be set so that the Windows 10 system is locked (shown in Figure 5.13) and the password (or other authentication method) of the user who is currently logged on must be entered to unlock the computer again.

FIGURE 5.13 Lock Screen

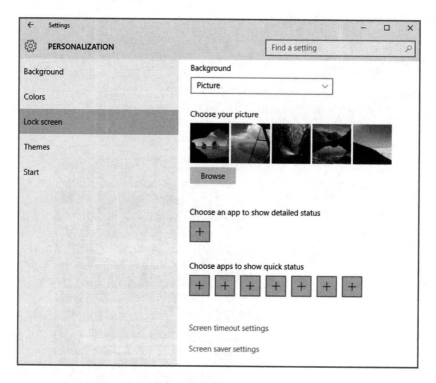

Windows 10 includes many different screen-saver options that can be used and configured:

- None
- 3D Text
- Blank
- Bubbles
- Mystify
- Photos
- Ribbons

Personalization Themes

This screen allows you to set the different themes that you can have for your desktop. Themes allow you to change the color pattern for all desktop and applications in one setting. The Themes screen (shown in Figure 5.14) also allows you to change the advanced sound settings, desktop icon settings, and mouse pointer settings.

FIGURE 5.14 Themes screen

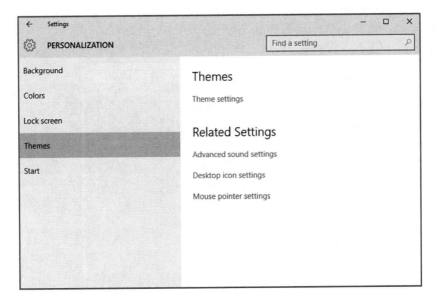

Advanced Sound Settings   This lets you choose the sounds that will be played based on the action taken. Each action can have its own sound. The Sound options also allow you to set up the external or internal speakers and microphones that you want to use. You can also calibrate different pieces of hardware.

Desktop Icon Settings   This allows you to customize the desktop icons. You also have the ability to change shortcut icons. Some of the icons that you can add to the desktop are the Computer icon, User's Files icon, Network icon, Recycle Bin icon, and Control Panel. You also have the ability to change icons at the screen.

Mouse Pointers Settings   This allows you to customize the appearance of the mouse pointers. It allows you to go from the traditional pointer to a Help Select, Busy, and Precision Select to just name a few. You can also change the Button options, Pointer options, Wheel options, and Hardware.

Personalization Start Screen

The Start section allows you to configure what you going to see on your Start menu and which folders appear on the Start. As you can see in Figure 5.15, you have the ability to set the following settings:

- Show most used apps
- Show recently added apps
- Use Start full screen
- Show recently opened items in Jump Lists on Start or the taskbar
- Choose which folders appear on Start

FIGURE 5.15   Start options

Now that we have looked at how to configure the Windows 10 desktop, let's go ahead and practice doing just that. Exercise 5.1 will walk you through the process of configuring your theme and choosing additional options.

EXERCISE 5.1

Configuring Windows 10 Desktop Options

1. Right-click an open area of the desktop and choose Personalize.

2. On the Background screen, either choose a new picture or use the pull-down under Background and choose Solid Color or Slideshow.

3. After you have set your new desktop, go to the Lock Screen page.

4. Scroll down and choose the link Screen Saver Settings.

5. Under the Screen Saver pull-down, choose 3D Text.

6. Click the Setting button. Make sure the radio button is set to Custom Text and put in the text you would like to see. Go ahead and change the font or size or rotation speed. Once completed, click the OK button. At the Screen Saver Settings screen, change the Wait Time setting to 15 minutes and then click the OK button.

7. Click the Themes screen. Click the Theme Settings link and choose a new theme that you like. You can also keep the current theme if you like that one. Hit the upper-right X to close the window once you're finished.

8. Click the Start screen. Make any changes that you want to change for your Start menu. Once you are finished, close the Personalization window.

 Real World Scenario

Configuring Personal Preferences

One thing that I noticed as an IT manager is that the most common configuration change made by users is to configure their desktop. This lets them use the computer more efficiently and often makes them more comfortable with the computer.

To help users work more efficiently with their computers, it's good to determine which applications or files are frequently and commonly used and verify that shortcuts or Start menu items are added for those elements. You can also remove shortcuts or Start menu items for elements that are seldom used or not used at all, helping to make the work area less cluttered and confusing.

Less-experienced users will feel more comfortable with their computer if they have a desktop that has been personalized to their preferences. This might include their choice of a desktop theme and screen saver.

Windows 10 includes several utilities for managing various aspects of the operating-system configuration. In the following sections, you will learn how to configure your operating system using Control Panel and the Registry Editor.

We will start with Control Panel and the different utilities included within it.

Using Control Panel

Control Panel is a set of GUI utilities that allow you to configure Registry settings without the need to use a registry editor. The Registry is a database used by the operating system to store configuration information.

You can configure the system by using the registry editor REGEDIT or REGEDT32. Windows 10 actually only uses the REGEDIT command. If you type REGEDT32, it just opens the REGEDIT command utility.

If you don't want to open the Registry directly but you still want to do some Registry changes, you can just use the Control Panel. So let's take a closer look at the utilities that are available through Control Panel. I have set Control Panel to Large Icons view, but you can set it to Small Icons view if you prefer (see Figure 5.16).

FIGURE 5.16   Control Panel

 If you keep the Control Panel view set to Category, you will not be able to follow along and see all the different items we are going to talk about. The Category view has all of these settings, but they are in different sections. I feel it's easier to understand each item using the Large Icons view.

Administrative Tools   This icon has multiple administrative tools that can help you configure and monitor the Windows 10 operating system. These tools include the following:

- Component Services
- Computer Management
- Defragment and Optimize Drives
- Disk Cleanup
- Event Viewer
- iSCSI Initiator
- Local Security Policy
- ODBC Data Sources (32-bit)
- ODBC Data Sources (64-bit)
- Performance Monitor
- Print Management
- Resource Monitor
- Services
- System Configuration
- System Information
- Task Scheduler
- Windows Firewall with Advanced Security
- Windows Memory Diagnostics

AutoPlay   This icon lets you configure media disks and will autoplay when inserted into the media player (see Figure 5.17). Each media type has different configuration settings, but the basic choices are as follows:

- Use AutoPlay for all media and devices
- Removable drive
- Camera Storage
- DVDs
- Blue-ray discs
- CDs
- Software
- Devices

FIGURE 5.17   AutoPlay options

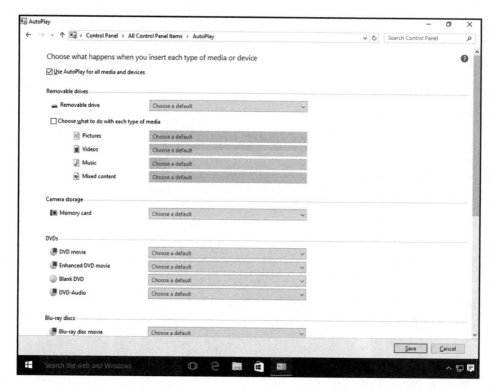

Backup And Restore (Windows 7)   The Backup And Restore icon allows you to configure your backup media. Users can make copies of all important data on their machine to avoid losing it in the event of a hardware failure or disaster. Backups will be discussed in greater detail in Chapter 10, "Configuring Monitoring and Recovery."

BitLocker Drive Encryption   BitLocker Drive Encryption helps prevent unauthorized users from accessing files stored on hard drives by encrypting the drive in its entirety. The user is able to use the computer as they normally would, but unauthorized users cannot read or use any of their files.

Color Management   The Color Management icon allows you to configure some of the video adapter's settings. You can configure the Windows color system defaults, the ICC Rendering Intent To WCS Gamut Mapping settings, and the display calibration. You can also change the system defaults to indicate how these items should be handled.

Credential Manager   Users can use the Credential Manager to store credentials such as usernames and passwords. These usernames and passwords get stored in vaults so that you can easily log onto computers or websites.

There are two sections in the Credential Manager: Web Credentials and Windows Credentials. You can add credentials by clicking the link next to each of the two credential sections.

Date And Time   The Date And Time icon allows you to configure your local date and time for the Windows 10 machine. You also have the ability to synchronize your clock with the Internet, as shown in Figure 5.18. Be aware that if your computer is a member of a domain, you will not see this screen and will not be able to synchronize your time with an Internet time server.

FIGURE 5.18   Time synchronization

Default Programs   The Default Programs icon allows you to choose the programs that Windows will use by default. For example, you can set Internet Explorer to be the default web browser.

Device Manager   The Device Manager icon allows you to configure the different devices on your Windows 10 machine. You can configure such devices as disk drives, display adapters, DVD/CD-ROM drives, monitors, and network adapters.

Devices And Printers   The Devices And Printers icon lets you add or configure the devices on your machine and your printers. This is where you add the printers that you have on your network.

Display   The Display icon allows you to configure your display. You can change the size of the text and other items on your screen. You also have the ability to change the resolution, calibrate colors, change display settings, adjust ClearType text, and change custom text size.

Ease Of Access Center   The Ease Of Access Center icon allows you to set up your accessibility options. These are settings that you can set for people with vision issues. The Ease of Access center allows you to configure voice narration (a computer voice tells you what your moussing over), an on screen keyboard, or start the magnifier (allows you to see everything magnified).

File Explorer Options   The File Explorer Options icon allows you to configure how you view folders on the Windows 10 machine by default. You have the ability to set up how you browse and navigate folders, which files and folders you can view (see Figure 5.19), and how folders are searched.

FIGURE 5.19 File Explorer Options

File History   File History allows users to save copies of their files so that you can get them back in the event of a file being lost or damaged. You have the ability to restore personal files, select drives, exclude folders, and even set advanced settings on the File History settings.

Flash Player (32-bit)   The Flash Player application allows you to set up how your Flash Player is going to operate and which applications the Flash Player will be associated with.

Fonts   This icon displays a screen where you can install, preview, delete, show, hide, and configure the fonts that the applications on your Windows 10 operating system can use. It enables you to get fonts online, adjust cleartext, find a character, and change font size.

HomeGroup   HomeGroups are small local networks that you can easily configure at home. When you install HomeGroups on your first computer, a password is assigned so that you can connect other computers to this HomeGroup. The password can be changed from the HomeGroup icon. HomeGroups are discussed in greater detail in Chapter 9, "Configuring Network Connectivity."

Be aware that if your computer is a member of a domain, you can belong to a HomeGroup that someone else creates but you cannot create your own HomeGroup.

Indexing Options   Windows uses indexing to perform very fast searches of common files on your computer. The Indexing Options feature gives you the ability to configure which files and applications get indexed.

Internet Options   The Internet Options icon allows you to configure how the Internet will operate (see Figure 5.20). From this icon you can configure your home page, browsing history, tabs, security, privacy, content, connections, and programs.

FIGURE 5.20   Internet Properties

Keyboard   The Keyboard properties allow you to configure how the keyboard will react when used. You can set the character repeat speed (how fast the keyboard will repeat what you are typing) and the cursor speed. You can also use these properties to configure the keyboard drivers.

Language   The Language application allows you to specify which languages you are going to be using on this Windows 10 system. The language at the top of your Language list is the primary language that the system will use.

Mail   You may or may not have this Mail application in Control Panel. If you have a mail client, such as Outlook, then the Mail application icon will be in Control Panel. If you don't have a mail client, then this icon will be missing from Control Panel.

When you configure the Mail properties, you set up your client-side mail settings. In the Mail properties, you can set up different user profiles (mailboxes) and the local mail servers or Internet mail servers to which they connect.

Mouse   Mouse properties give you the ability to configure how the mouse will operate. You can configure the buttons, click speed, ClickLock, pointer type, pointer options, center wheel, and hardware properties.

Network And Sharing Center   The Network And Sharing Center properties configure your Windows 10 machine to connect to a local network or the Internet. You can configure TCP/IP, set up a new network, connect to a network, choose a HomeGroup, and configure the network adapter. Network And Sharing Center is discussed in greater detail in Chapter 7, "Windows 10 Networking."

Personalization   Personalization allows you to set up your desktop environment to your liking. Personalization allows you to set up a desktop theme or background, system sounds, screen saver, desktop icons, mouse pointer, and account picture.

Phone And Modem   The Phone And Modem properties are used to set up local dialing properties and modem options. You can set up your dialing location, modem properties, and telephony providers.

Power Options   Power options allow a user to maximize their Windows 10 machine's performance and/or conserve energy. You can enter your own power restrictions to customize your machine. Power options are important settings when you are dealing with laptops. Since many laptops use batteries, power options allow you to get the most time from their batteries. Power management will be discussed later in this chapter in the section "Configuring Power Policies."

Programs And Features   The Programs And Features icon was the Add/Remove Programs icon in Windows XP. Programs And Features allows you to organize, uninstall, change, or repair programs and features.

The Programs And Features icon also allows you to choose which Windows 10 features you want installed on the machine, such as Indexing Services, Telnet Client, Telnet Server, and so on.

In Exercise 5.2, you'll install the Telnet client on the Windows 10 operating system.

EXERCISE 5.2

Installing New Features

1.   Open the Programs And Features tool by clicking Start ➢ Control Panel ➢ Programs And Features.

2.   Click the Turn Windows Features On Or Off link in the upper-left corner.

3. Scroll down the features list and check the Telnet Client check box (shown in Figure 5.21).

FIGURE 5.21   Telnet Client check box

4. Click OK.

 Real World Scenario

Using Telnet

As an IT manager, my job does not just consist of working on Windows machines. I also need to understand and work on routers.

You can use the Telnet client to connect to most routers. Using the Telnet client, you can configure the router to operate the way your organization needs it to operate.

I describe Windows Firewall later in this section; however, I do not recommend that you use Windows Firewall as your main line of defense against hackers. You need to purchase a good router/firewall to complete this task. Knowing how to configure the router using the Telnet client will help you accomplish your networking needs.

Recovery   The Recovery icon allows a user or administrator to recover the Windows 10 system to a previously captured restore point. System Restore is one of the first recovery options that should be considered when your Windows 10 system is experiencing problems. Recovery will be discussed in detail in Chapter 10.

Region   The Region tool allows you to configure your local regional settings as well as configure date and time formats.

RemoteApp And Desktop Connections   RemoteApp And Desktop Connections allows you to access programs and desktops on your network. To connect to these resources (remote applications and desktops), you must have the proper permission.

With RemoteApp And Desktop Connections, you can connect to either a remote computer or a virtual computer. To create a new connection, use the Set Up A New Connection Wizard included with the RemoteApp And Desktop Connections menu option.

Security And Maintenance   The Security And Maintenance utility has two configurable sections: Security and Maintenance. The Security section allows you to configure multiple options including:

- Network firewall, which helps protect your system from unauthorized connections and applications from running on you Windows 10 system.
- Spyware and unwanted software protection allows you to update Windows Defender.
    - Virus protection allows you to install and configure virus protection.
    - Windows Update allows you to update Windows 10.
    - Windows SmartScreen helps keep your PC safer by warning you before running unrecognized apps and files downloaded from the Internet.

The Maintenance section allows you to set up a Windows 10 maintenance schedule. You can also set up a HomeGroup, file history, drive status, and device software in this section.

Sound   The Sound icon allows you to configure your machine's audio. You can configure output (speakers and audio drivers) and your input devices (microphones).

Speech Recognition   The Speech Recognition icon allows you to configure your speech properties. Speech Recognition allows you to speak into the computer and have that speech be displayed on the system. Many programs, including Microsoft Office, can display the words onscreen as you speak them into the system. You can complete the following actions via the Speech Recognition icon:

- Start Speech Recognition
- Set up a microphone
- Take speech tutorials
- Train your computer to better understand you
- Open the Speech Reference Card, which allows you to view and print a list of common commands

Storage Spaces   Storage Spaces in Windows 10 is another way to give your Windows 10 users data redundancy. Storage Spaces allows an administrator to combine drives to make a larger storage area. Storage Spaces can be turned into Storage Pools (Storage Pools are for virtualization). To create Storage Pools, you group disks into Storage Spaces and then create virtual disks out of those Storage Spaces that are then called Storage Pools.

Sync Center   The Sync Center allows you to configure synchronization between the Windows 10 machine and a network server. The Sync Center also allows you to see when synchronization occurred, if the synchronization was successful, and if there were any errors.

System   The System icon is one of the most important icons in Control Panel. The System icon allows you to view which operating system your machine is using, view installed system resources (processor, RAM), change the computer name/domain/work-group, and activate Windows 10. From the System icon, you can also configure the following settings:

- Device Manager
- Remote Settings
- System Protection
- Advanced System Settings

Taskbar And Navigation   The Taskbar And Navigation icon allows you to configure how the Taskbar, Start menu, and toolbars will operate.

Troubleshooting   The Troubleshooting icon in Control Panel allows you to troubleshoot common Windows 10 problems within the following categories:

- Programs
- Hardware And Sound
- Network And Internet
- System And Security

User Accounts   The User Accounts icon allows you to create and modify local user accounts. With the User Account icon, you can perform the following tasks:

- Change user passwords
- Remove passwords
- Change the account picture
- Change the account name
- Change the account type
- Manage user accounts
- Change user-account control settings

Windows Defender   Windows Defender is a built-in Windows 10 application that protects your system from spyware. It is included free with the operating system, and once you turn it on, it starts automatically protecting your system. Windows Defender can operate in different modes:

Real-Time Protection   In Real-Time Protection mode, Windows Defender runs in the background and protects your system as you are working live on the Internet or a network.

Scanning Option   When you're in Scanning Option mode, you can run a system scan at any time to check for spyware. This option does not require Windows Defender to always be running.

Command-Line Utility   Windows Defender includes a command-line utility called MpCmdRun.exe, which allows you to automate the use of Windows Defender. The MpCmdRun.exe utility is located in the %ProgramFiles%\Windows Defender\ folder.

Windows Firewall   Windows Firewall helps prevent unauthorized users or hackers from accessing your Windows 10 machine from the Internet or the local network.

Windows To Go   Windows To Go gives an administrator or user the ability to provision Windows 10 onto an external USB drive. You can then use the USB drive (known as a Windows To Go workspace) to load a complete and managed Windows 10 system image into a managed or unmanaged Windows 10 host computer to boot and run the Windows 10 operating system.

Work Folders   Work Folders allows a user to make data files available on all of the devices that he or she uses. You can access that data even when the devices are offline.

Using the Microsoft Management Console

The Microsoft Management Console was covered in great detail in Chapter 4, "Configuring Storage," but because all of the previous application windows use the MMC, I am briefly covering it again.

Knowing that all of these applications use the MMC, you can create your own MMC windows. So let's take a look at creating a window with Disk Administrator and Services in the same console window. To do this, you would just complete the following steps:

1. Type **MMC** in Cortana and hit Enter.

2. Click Yes at the UAC dialog box.

3. In the MMC console, click File and then Add/Remove snap-in.

4. Click Disk Management and click the Add button. Make sure This Computer is chosen and click Finish.

5. Scroll down and choose Services and click the Add button. Choose Local Computer and click Finished.

6. Click the OK button.

7. Click File Save As and choose Desktop in the left pane. Name your console "Test" and click Save.

8. The new console should be on your desktop. Now when you want to open either the Disk Administrator or Services console, just open Test. Close the MMC.

Using the System Icon

The System icon (shown in Figure 5.22) in Control Panel is the gateway to a very useful set of utilities and tasks that can enable you to specify remote settings, device settings, system protection, and the computer name, among other things.

FIGURE 5.22   The System icon

Let's look at the different utilities and tasks that can be configured in System icon:

Windows Edition   The Windows Edition section shows you which edition of Windows the machine currently has installed. The Windows Edition section also shows whether service packs are installed.

System   The System section shows the following information about the system hardware:

- Processor
- Installed memory (RAM)
- System type
- Pen and touch-screen availability

Computer Name, Domain, And Workgroup Settings   In the Computer Name, Domain, And Workgroup Settings section, you can change the name of the computer system and also change the workgroup or domain. Windows 10 works well with Windows Server 2012 R2, which is explained in greater detail in Chapter 7.

Windows Activation The Windows Activation section allows you to activate your Windows 10 operating system and change your product key before activating.

If you look to the left side of the System window, you will see that there are four additional links: Device Manager, Remote Settings, System Protection, and Advanced System Settings. Let's take a look at some of these settings.

Device Manager The Device Manager link allows you to configure the different devices on your Windows 10 machine. You can configure such devices as disk drives, display adapters, DVD/CD-ROM drives, monitors, and network adapters.

Remote Settings In the Remote Settings section, you can set the Remote Assistance and Remote Desktop settings for the Windows 10 system. Windows Remote Assistance allows an administrator to connect to a machine and control the mouse and keyboard while the user is logged on with the administrator. This option can be enabled or disabled.

System Protection The System Protection section is for configuring restore points and recoverability for the Windows 10 operating system. You can also manage disk space and all of your restore points from the System Protection section.

Advanced System Settings The Advanced System Settings section allows you to set up such items as visual effects, processor scheduling, memory usage, virtual memory, desktop settings, system startup, and recoverability.

There are three main sections within the Advanced System Settings section:

Performance The Performance section allows you to configure the visual effects, the virtual memory, processor scheduling, and Data Execution Prevention for the Windows 10 operating system.

The virtual memory is a section of the hard drive that is used by the system and RAM. Think of RAM as a pitcher of water. As the water fills up the pitcher, the pitcher becomes full. Once it's full, more water would cause it to overflow. The virtual memory is the overflow for RAM. When RAM fills up, the oldest data in RAM gets put into the virtual memory. This way, the system does not need to look at an entire hard drive for that data. It finds it in the virtual memory.

The Data Execution Prevention section (found under the Settings button) helps protect against damage from viruses and other security threats.

User Profiles The User Profiles section allows you to copy, delete, or move a user's desktop profile to another location or user account.

Startup And Recovery The Startup And Recovery section allows you to configure which operating system will be booted by default (important for dual-booting machines) and what should happen when the system gets a startup error.

Let's now look at how to configure some of the options using the System icon. Complete Exercise 5.3 to change the computer name.

EXERCISE 5.3

Changing the Computer Name

1. Open the System tool by right-clicking Start ➤ System.

2. Under the Computer Name, Domain, And Workgroup settings section, click the Change Settings link.

3. Click the Change button in the To Rename This Computer section.

4. In the Computer Name field, rename your computer. Click OK.

5. A dialog box asking you to reboot the machine will appear. Click the OK button.

6. Click the Close button, and then click the Restart Now button.

Now that you have renamed the computer, let's look at how to configure performance options. Complete Exercise 5.4 to manipulate your system's virtual memory.

EXERCISE 5.4

Changing the System's Virtual Memory

1. Open the System tool by right-clicking Start ➤ System.

2. In the left side, click the Advanced System Settings link.

3. Under the Performance section, click the Settings button.

4. When the Performance option screen appears, click the Advanced tab.

5. In the Virtual Memory section, click the Change button.

6. Uncheck the Automatically Manage Paging File Size For All Drives check box.

7. Click the Custom Size radio button.

8. Set the Minimum and Maximum settings to two times the size of your RAM. For example, if your RAM is 4,096 MB, set the settings to 8,192 MB.

9. Click the Set button.

10. Click OK. Then click OK again at the Performance Options screen.

11. Close the System Properties screen.

Microsoft Windows 10 handles the virtual memory requirements by default, but I recommend increasing the virtual memory on your machine if hard drive space is available. I use the rule of thumb of one and a half to two times the size of RAM.

We have now talked about the Control Panel and the System icon, but we have not yet talked about the new Windows 10 Settings shortcut app. So in the next section, we are going to look at the Settings window.

Understanding the Settings Window

As stated earlier in the book, Windows 10 took the best of Windows 7 and Windows 8 to create Windows 10. When you click the Start menu, you will see an option called Settings (see Figure 5.23).

FIGURE 5.23   The Settings option

The Settings screen is a new way to configure different parts of the Windows 10 system. When you click the Settings option from the Start menu, you will see the Settings screen appear, as shown in Figure 5.24.

FIGURE 5.24   The Settings screen

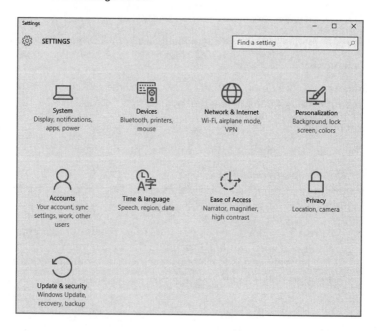

As you can see from Figure 5.24, the Settings Window has multiple sections of Windows 10 that you can configure. The following areas are settings that can be configured using the Settings screen:

- System
- Devices
- Network & Internet
- Personalization
- Accounts
- Time & Language
- Ease Of Access
- Privacy
- Updates & Security

Most of these sections have already been covered previously in this chapter, and many of the other sections (such as Accounts) will be covered in other chapters of the book. I just wanted to make sure that you understand that it's another way to configure many of the same options that we have already looked at.

The one area that I would recommend that you look at right away is the choice for Privacy. Microsoft has turned many features on where Microsoft and other third-party vendors can access data on your system and also get information on how you use your Windows 10 system. Take a few minutes to look through the Privacy section and make sure that nothing is on by default that you don't want turned on.

Using PowerShell

Another way to configure the Control Panel and its apps is to use PowerShell commands. So let's take a look at how to use PowerShell for configuration.

The first PowerShell command you need to understand is the Get-ControlPanelItem command. The Get-ControlPanelItem allows an administrator to find Control Panel items on a local computer by name, category, or description. Let's take a look at the Get-ControlPanelItem command to configure the Windows Firewall:

```
PS C:\> Get-ControlPanelItem -Name "Windows Firewall" | Show-ControlPanelItem
```

Table 5.1 shows some of the PowerShell configuration commands that you would use to help manage and configure the Windows 10 system.

TABLE 5.1 PowerShell configuration commands

Command	Description
Clear-EventLog	This commands allows an administrator to delete all entries from the event logs on a local or remote computer.
Debug-Process	Administrators use this command to debug processes running on a local computer.

TABLE 5.1   PowerShell configuration commands *(continued)*

Command	Description
Get-ComputerInfo	This commands returns the computer's system information.
Get-EventLog	Finds an event in a specific event log.
Get-Service	Finds a service on a Windows 10 system.
Get-TimeZone	Gets the system's time zone.
New-EventLog	Creates a new event log.
New-Service	This command allows an administrator to create a new service.
Remove-EventLog	This command deletes an event log.
Rename-Computer	This command allows an administrator to rename a computer.
Restart-Computer	This command reboots your system.
Restart-Service	This command restarts a service.
Resume-Service	This command resumes a service.
Set-TimeZone	Administrators can set the system's time zone.
Start-Process	This command allows you to start a process.
Start-Service	Administrators can start a service using this command.
Stop-Computer	This command shuts down a system.
Stop-Service	This command stops a service.
Test-Connection	Sends a ping to test NIC adapter settings.
Write-EventLog	This command writes an event to an event log.

Now that we have looked at how to do configurations for Windows 10, let's go ahead and take a look at how Windows 10 mobility works.

Configuring Mobility Options

So during this chapter we talked about all of the different icons in the Control Panel. Now we need to dive into a few of them in greater detail. The ones that we are going to discuss all have to deal with Windows 10 mobility.

Windows 10 is designed to be mobile, and it has many features that revolve around that. Here are some of the mobility issues that we need to cover: how to configure offline file policies, configure power policies, configure Windows To Go, configure Wi-Fi direct, and configure sync options using the Sync Center.

Configuring Offline Files and Synchronization

One of the advantages of Windows 10 is how the operating system works and synchronizes with other systems and data.

The term *synchronization* could mean different things to different people. We could be talking about synchronization of offline files and data, or we can be talking about synchronization between two systems like a Windows 10 system and cloud-based Azure or OneNote.

In this section, we will talk about both. We will address synchronization between offline and online files, and we will discuss synchronization between Windows 10 and cloud-based services.

Offline Files allows network files to be available to clients even when a network connection to the server is unavailable or slow. When a user is accessing a server that is unavailable or when the network connection is slower than a configurable threshold, files are then retrieved from the Offline Files folders.

The Offline Files feature is enabled by default on the following client computer operating systems: Windows 10 Professional, Windows 10 Enterprise, and Windows Education. This feature is turned off by default on Windows Server operating systems.

Because in many organizations Windows 10 will be loaded onto a laptop computer, offline file access can be an important part of how Windows clients stay current even while off the network.

When you decide to turn synchronization on, Windows will automatically keep track of your synchronization choices for you on all of your Windows 10 devices (as long as you are logged on to all of the Windows devices using the same account or have set up synchronization with the other accounts and your Microsoft account).

Users have the ability to choose what items that they want to synchronize. For example, users can synchronize passwords, web browser settings, File Explorer settings, and even notifications.

To truly have synchronization work the way that Microsoft has intended, you need to link all of your devices together using your Microsoft account or have your other accounts linked to your Microsoft account. This includes your school or work accounts all tied into one Microsoft account.

As an IT director for many years, I feel a bit uneasy about this idea. I truly believe that linking your personal accounts together to synchronize all of your personal data is a good way to go, but for obvious security reasons, I don't agree with corporate users linking into their personal accounts.

So how do we go about synchronizing everything in Windows 10 easily? The best method is to use the Sync Center in Control Panel (just right-click Start ➤ Control Panel ➤ Sync Center).

The Sync Center is built into Windows 10, and it's a one-stop shop for all of your synchronization needs, including working with offline files (see Figure 5.25).

FIGURE 5.25   The Sync Center

As you can see in Figure 5.25, you can set up synchronization between other devices and partnerships. The figure shows that you can also manage offline files. To manage offline files, you have to enable that on the Windows 10 system (done through Sync Center) and then also configure offline folder access with the Windows servers that you have at your company.

When you click the Manage Offline Folders link and enable offline folder access, you then have three tabs that can help you set up offline folder access properly:

Disk Usage   The Disk Usage tab will show you how much disk space is currently being reserved on the Windows 10 system for keeping offline files. You can change the amount of space that is set for the Windows 10 system by clicking the Change Limits button.

Encryption   To make sure that the offline files are encrypted while on the system, click the Encryption button. The files will get encrypted based on your user's Security Identification (SID) number. When you log into the Windows 10 account using the account with the matching SID number, the files will become automatically decrypted when they are opened. If someone with a different user ID (SID) number tries to access these files, he or she will be denied access.

Network   The Network tab allows you to set a time interval (such as 5 minutes), and when that interval is hit, the Windows 10 system will automatically check the network connection to make sure that the connection is not on a slow connection. For example, when you are at home and you don't have direct access to your network, the Windows system will automatically revert to using the offline files due to the connection being slow or not available.

Configuring Power Policies

Earlier in the chapter, we started talking about the Windows 10 Power options. Power options allow a user or administrator to maximize their Windows 10 machine's performance and/or conserve energy.

Administrators or users have the ability to enter your own power restrictions to customize their machine. Power options are important settings when you are dealing with laptops. Since many laptops use batteries, power options allow you to get the most time from their batteries.

Now here is the kicker! Depending on what type of system you are on, you will see different options when you look at your power plan options. For example, Figure 5.26 shows the power plan options for a desktop system. You can tell that the only real options you have is what happens when you choose when to turn off the display or change your power consumption options.

FIGURE 5.26   Desktop power plan options

However, if you look at Figure 5.27, you can see that you have additional options based on whether your laptop or tablet is plugged in. You will not have those options on a desktop, because most desktops can't work when unplugged (unless you have a magical desktop).

So setting up your power options really depends on what type of machine or tablet you're using. But some of the settings are the same no matter which one you use. The following are just some of the options that are the same no matter what type of Windows 10 system you're on:

- Require A Password On Wakeup
- Choose What The Power Button Does
- Create A Power Plan

Laptops will have additional choices, such as what happens when you close the lid of the laptop. No matter what type of system you are on, you can choose to go into advanced options and set very specific options on what system components would do while the system was running or while the system was idle.

FIGURE 5.27   Laptop power plan options

For example, you can tell the system when the network card or hard drive can go into a sleep mode based on idle time (amount of time while no one is working on the system). So if you want to configure each individual component and how it should work while active or idle, you can go into the advanced options and configure each component separately.

Managing Power States

In Windows 10, the Advanced Configuration Power Interface (ACPI) specifies different levels of power states:

- Fully active PC
- Sleep
- Hibernation
- Complete shutdown of PC

The sleep power state is a new power state introduced with Windows 10 that combines the features of hibernate and standby. When a computer enters the sleep power state, data, including window locations and running applications, is saved to memory, and that session is available within seconds when the computer wakes. The computer can thus be put into a power-saving state when not in use but allows quick access to the in-process user session, so the user can begin working more quickly than if the computer were shut down or put into hibernation.

Hibernation falls short of a complete shutdown of the computer. With hibernation, the computer saves your desktop state as well as any open files to the hard drive. To use the computer again, you need to press the power button. The computer should start more quickly than from a complete shutdown because it does not have to go through the complete startup process. You will have to again log onto the computer. Similar to when the computer is put into sleep mode, all the documents that were open when the computer went into hibernation are still available. With hibernation, you can easily resume work where you left off. You can configure your computer to hibernate through Power Options or by choosing Start and then clicking the arrow and selecting Hibernate from the dropdown menu. This option will appear only if hibernation has been enabled through Power Options.

The hibernation mode may not be available on your Windows 10 laptop machine by default. You must make sure your firmware can support hibernation before attempting to enable it. Now let's take a look at the different types of power options that you can configure.

Managing Power Options

You configure power options through the Power Options Properties dialog box. To access this dialog box, right-click Start ➤ Control Panel ➤ Power Options. The Power Options dialog box provides the ability to manage power plans and to control power options, such as when the display is turned off, when the computer sleeps, and what the power button does.

Configuring Power Plans

Windows 10 includes three configurable power plans: Balanced, Power Saver, and High Performance. Power plans control the trade-off between quick access to an existing computer session and energy savings. In Windows 10, each power plan contains default options that can be customized to meet the needs of various scenarios.

The Balanced power plan, as its name suggests, provides a balance between power savings and performance. By default, this plan is configured to turn off the display after 20 minutes and to put the computer to sleep after 1 hour of idle time. You can modify these times as needed. Other power options that you can modify include Wireless Adapter settings and Multimedia settings. Wireless adapters can be configured for maximum power savings or maximum performance. By default, the Balanced power plan configures wireless adapters for maximum performance. Additionally, you can configure the Multimedia settings so that the computer will not be put into sleep mode when sharing media. For example, if the computer is acting as a Media Center device, then you can configure the computer to remain on by setting the Prevent Idling To Sleep option so that other computers can connect to it and stream media from it even when the computer is not being used for other purposes.

The Power Saver power plan is optimized for power savings. By default, the display is configured to be turned off after 20 minutes of inactivity, and the computer will be put into sleep mode after 1 hour of inactivity. Additionally, this power plan configures hard disks to be turned off after 20 minutes of inactivity.

The High Performance power plan is configured to provide the maximum performance for portable computers. By default, the computer will never enter sleep mode, but the display will be turned off after 20 minutes. When this setting is configured, by default the Multimedia settings are configured with the new Allow The Computer To Enter Away Mode option. Away mode configures the computer to look like it's off to users but remain accessible for media sharing. For example, the computer can record television shows when in away mode. You can modify the existing power plans to suit your needs by clicking Change Plan Settings, or you can use the preconfigured power plans listed in Table 5.2.

TABLE 5.2   Windows 10 power plans

Power Plan	Turn Off Display	Put Computer to Sleep	Turn Hard Disks Off
Balanced	After 20 minutes	1 hour	
Power Saver	After 20 minutes	1 hour	After 20 minutes
High Performance	After 20 minutes	Never	

In Exercise 5.5, I will show you how to configure a power plan for your computer.

EXERCISE 5.5

Configuring a Power Plan

1. Right-click Start ➢ Power Options.

2. Select a power plan to modify from the Preferred Plans list, and click Change Plan Settings.

3. Configure the power-plan options for your computer based on your personal preferences. Click Change Advanced Power Settings to modify the advanced power settings. When all changes have been made, click Save Changes.

4. Close Control Panel.

Other desktop options you can use are the power button and switching users. Let's take a look at these features.

Configuring the Power Button

Unless you decide to run your computer 24 hours a day, you will eventually want to shut it down. By default, the Start menu has a power button. When you click this button, your machine will power off. But the power button does not have to be set to the Shut Down option. You can configure this button to Switch User, Logoff, Lock, Restart, or Shut Down.

You may have a machine that is shared by multiple users, and it may be better for you to have the Switch User button instead of the Shut Down button on the Start menu. Configuring the Switch User option would make it easier on your users.

In Exercise 5.6, you will configure the power button to allow the system to go into the Hibernate mode.

EXERCISE 5.6

Configuring the Power Button to Allow the System to Go into the Hibernate Mode

1. Right-click Start ➢ Power Options.

2. On the left side, click Choose What The Power Button Does.

3. From the Power Button Settings drop-down menu, choose Hibernate.

4. Click OK.

5. Click the power button and see if the system goes into the Hibernate mode. Once the system is brought out of the Hibernate mode, redo this exercise and choose Shut Down in step 3 to return the system to normal (if it was set to turn off).

After you decide how the power button is going to be used, you may want to configure some of the advanced power options. In the next section, we will look at the different power options.

Configuring Advanced Power Settings

Each power plan contains advanced settings that can be configured, such as when the hard disks will be turned off and whether a password is required on wakeup. To configure these advanced settings, right-click Start ➢ Control Panel ➢ Power Options and select the power plan to use. Then click Change Advanced Power Settings to open the Advanced Settings tab of the Power Options dialog box and modify the settings as desired (or restore the plan defaults).

For example, one option that you might want to change if you are using a mobile computer is the Power Buttons And Lid option, which configures what happens when you press the power button or close the lid of the mobile computer. When either of these actions occurs, the computer can be configured to do nothing, shut down, go into sleep mode, or go into hibernation mode.

Configuring Hibernation

Although sleep is the preferred power-saving mode in Windows 10, hibernation is still available for use. Hibernation for a computer means that anything stored in memory is written to your hard disk. This ensures that when your computer is shut down, you do not lose any of the information that is stored in memory. When you take your computer out of hibernation, it returns to its previous state by loading the hibernation reserved area of hard disk back into memory. To configure your computer to hibernate, complete the same steps as you did previously in Exercise 5.6.

Command-Line Configuration

Microsoft gives you the ability to configure and manage your power settings through the use of the command line. The Powercfg.exe tool allows you to control power settings and configure computers to default to hibernate or standby mode. The Powercfg.exe tool is installed with Windows 10 by default. Powercfg.exe has a few switches that provide you better functionality. Table 5.3 describes some of these switches.

TABLE 5.3   Powercfg.exe switches

Switch	Description
-change	Changes a setting in the current power scheme.
-changename	Changes the name of a power scheme. Also gives you the ability to change the description.
-delete	Deletes the power scheme of the GUID specified.
-deletesetting	Deletes a power setting.
-energy	Looks for common energy-efficiency and battery-life issues and displays these issues in an HTML format. This switch is used to identify problems with the power scheme.
-list	Shows all the power schemes in the current user's environment.
-query	Shows the content of a power scheme.
-qh	Displays the content (including hidden content) of the power scheme.
-waketimers	Enumerates the wake timers. If this is enabled, when the wake timer expires, the system will wake from hibernation or sleep state.

For a complete list of Powercfg.exe switches, visit the Microsoft website here:

https://technet.microsoft.com/en-us/library/cc748940%28v=ws.10%29.aspx?f=255&MSPPError=-2147217396

There is a useful tool when you're using a laptop on the battery that allows you to see how much time you have left until the battery dies. Let's take a look at the battery meter.

Managing Power Consumption Using the Battery Meter

Windows 10 includes a battery meter that you can use to monitor the battery-power consumption on your mobile computer (laptop or tablet). The battery meter also provides notification as to what power plan is being used.

The battery meter appears in the notification area of the Windows Taskbar and indicates the status of the battery, including the percentage of battery charge. As the battery charge gets lower, the battery meter provides a visual indication of the amount of charge left. For example, when the battery charge reaches the low-battery level, a red circle with a white *X* is displayed.

The battery meter also provides a quick method for changing the power plan in use on the computer. By clicking the battery-meter icon, you can select among the preferred power plans available with Windows 10.

Configuring Windows To Go

As stated earlier, Windows To Go gives an administrator or user the ability to provision Windows 10 onto an external USB drive. You can then use the USB drive (known as a Windows To Go workspace) to load a complete and managed Windows 10 system image into a managed or unmanaged Windows 10 host computer to boot and run the Windows 10 operating system.

Many of us carry a USB drive with us, or maybe you even carry one on your key ring. Well, think about having a copy of Windows 10 with you wherever and whenever you want to use it. So what are the requirements to set up a Windows To Go drive? Well, you need a USB drive certified for Windows To Go use and an image of Windows 10 Enterprise. If you try to load a USB that isn't certified, you will receive the error shown toward the bottom of Figure 5.28.

At the time that this book was written, the following list of USB drives are certified for Windows To Go:

- IronKey Workspace W700
- IronKey Workspace W500
- IronKey Workspace W300
- Kingston DataTraveler Workspace for Windows To Go
- Spyrus Portable Workplace
- Spyrus Secure Portable Workplace
- Spyrus Worksafe
- Super Talent Express RC4 for Windows To Go
- Super Talent Express RC8 for Windows To Go
- Western Digital My Passport Enterprise

FIGURE 5.28   USB non-compatible error

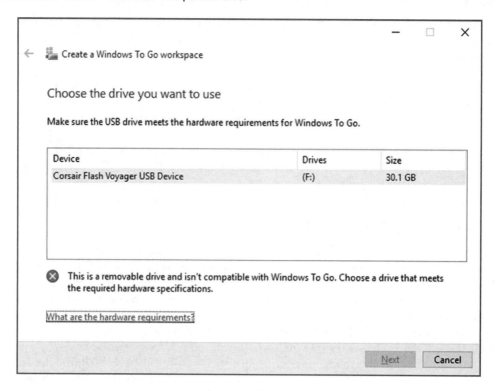

The information in Table 5.4 was taken directly from the Microsoft website regarding what is needed on the host's computer to be able to accept Windows To Go.

TABLE 5.4   Windows To Go host requirements

Item	Requirement
Boot process	Capable of USB boot
Firmware	USB boot enabled (PCs certified for use with Windows 7 or later can be configured to boot directly from USB; check with the hardware manufacturer if you are unsure of the ability of your PC to boot from USB.)
Processor architecture	Must support the image on the Windows To Go drive
External USB hubs	Not supported; connect the Windows To Go drive directly to the host machine
Processor	1 GHz or faster

Item	Requirement
RAM	2 GB or greater
Graphics	DirectX 9 graphics device with WDDM 1.2 or greater driver
USB port	USB 2.0 port or greater

To configure a Windows To Go USB drive, you need to complete the following steps:

1. Place a copy of a Windows 10 Enterprise image (.iso file) on the host computer you will use for image storage.

2. Open your Downloads folder on the host computer where you placed the .iso image, right-click the Windows image .iso file, and select MOUNT ISO. The .iso file will then appear as a disk drive on the host computer.

3. Right-click Start ➤ Control Panel.

4. In Control Panel, select Windows To Go.

5. Insert a compatible USB drive into a USB port on the host computer.

6. On the Choose The Drive You Want To Use page, all attached USB drives appear. Choose the compatible USB drive you want to use, and then click Next.

7. The mounted .iso file should now appear on the Choose A Windows 10 Image page. If for some reason you don't see the .iso file, select Add Search Location to choose the mounted .iso file. Select the file, and then click Next.

8. On the Set A BitLocker Password (Optional) page, select the Use BitLocker With My Windows To Go Workspace check box to protect the drive with BitLocker Drive Encryption.

9. Enter a BitLocker password, confirm it, and then click Next.

10. On the Ready To Create Your Windows To Go Workspace page, select Create to create the Windows To Go workspace.

11. Choose a boot (startup) option, and then select Yes to modify the Windows Boot Manager configuration to boot automatically from your Windows To Go workspace when the drive is connected to this host computer.

12. When provisioning is complete, select Save And Restart to restart the host computer.

Managing Windows 10 Services

A *service* is a program, routine, or process that performs a specific function within the Windows 10 operating system. You can manage services through the Services window, which can be accessed in a variety of ways. If you go through the Computer Management utility, you can just right-click Start ➤ Computer Management ➤ Services And Applications. You can also go through Administrative Tools in Control Panel.

The Services window lists the name of each service, a short description, the status, the startup type, and the logon account that is used to start it. To configure the properties of a service, double-click it to open its Properties dialog box, shown in Figure 5.29. This dialog box contains four tabs of options for services: General, Log On, Recovery, and Dependencies.

FIGURE 5.29   The Properties dialog box for a service

General   This tab allows you to view and configure the following options:

- The service display name
- The display name
- A description of the service
- The path to the service executable
- The startup type, which can be automatic, manual, or disabled
- The current service status
- Start parameters that can be applied when the service is started

In addition, the buttons across the lower part of the dialog box allow you change the service state to start, stop, and pause, and if the service is paused, you can also resume it.

Log On   The Log On tab allows you to configure the logon account that will be used to start the service. Choose the local system account or specify another logon account.

Recovery   The Recovery tab allows you to designate what action will be taken if the service fails to load. For the first, second, and subsequent failures, you can select a discrete action from the following list:

- Take No Action
- Restart The Service
- Run A Program
- Restart The Computer

If you choose Run A Program, specify it along with any command-line parameters. If you choose Restart The Computer, you can configure a message that will be sent to users who are connected to the computer before it is restarted. You can also specify how long until a machine is restarted if an error occurs.

Dependencies   The Dependencies tab lists any services that must be running in order for the specified service to start. If a service fails to start, you can use this information to examine the dependencies and then make sure each one is running. In the bottom panel, you can verify whether any other services depend on this service before you decide to stop it.

In Exercise 5.7, you will complete the steps needed to configure services in the Windows 10 operating system.

EXERCISE 5.7

Configuring Services

1. Start Computer Management by right-clicking Start ➤ Computer Management ➤ Services And Applications.

2. Click the Services link.

3. Scroll down the list and double-click Remote Desktop Configuration.

4. Under Startup Type, choose Automatic.

5. Under the Logon tab, click the This Account radio button.

6. Click the Browse button and choose the local administrator account. Click OK.

7. In the Password boxes, type and verify the administrator password.

8. In the Recovery tab, make sure the following settings are configured:

     Action: Response

     First Failure: Restart The Service

     Second Failure: Restart The Service

     Subsequent Failures: Take No Action

     Reset Fail Count After: 1 Day

     Restart Service After: 10 Minutes

EXERCISE 5.7 *(continued)*

9. Click the OK button.

10. Close the Computer Management MMC.

Services are just another troubleshooting and configuring tool that is part of your arsenal of troubleshooting techniques. Just remember that when your services are working properly, your Windows 10 operating system will be working properly.

Configuring Internet Browsers

Windows 10 comes with two ways to browse the Internet: Edge and IE11. Windows Internet Explorer 11, or IE11, is the latest web browser developed and released by Microsoft Corporation in the popular Internet Explorer series. IE11 is available for Windows 10 and Windows Server 2012 R2 versions.

With the explosion of Internet use—even for the inexperienced end user browsing the Internet for personal reasons as well as for those who use it for work-related tasks—enhancing the user interface (UI) while providing better levels of security (which include privacy) has been the focus in the development of both Edge and IE11.

Both browsers are loaded with user features to provide end users with a better and simpler way to get the information they desire from their browsing experience.

The features added to Edge and IE11 are designed to give end users an easy way to browse the Internet for the information they're looking for while providing a secure environment for networks by recognizing potentially bad sites (those attempting to sneak viruses or Trojan horses into the network), phishing sites (those that attempt to steal private information about the user), and invasive sites that users may go to either on purpose or inadvertently.

When comparing the two browsers, Edge and IE11, Edge has taken browsing a step further with the implementation of Cortana. Cortana can assist you while working with Edge.

Cortana

One of the configuration options that I see asked about on the Internet all the time is how to turn off Cortana. Well before we turn it off, let's talk about what Cortana can do for you.

Cortana is a powerful search and help utility. If your system has a microphone, then you can ask Cortana questions and Cortana will help find you an answer. If you don't have a microphone, then you can type in your questions and Cortana will try to help find you an answer.

To configure Cortana, click you mouse in the Cortana (Search the web and Windows) box. This will open Cortana up. Once Cortana is open, click on the little settings wheel to configure Cortana (see Figure 5.30).

FIGURE 5.30   Cortana Settings

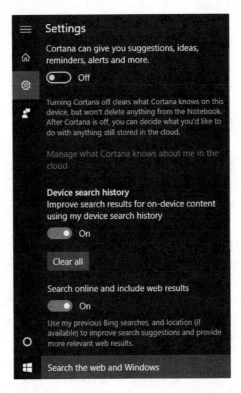

These settings allow you to configure Cortana or even turn off Cortana. If you decide to leave Cortana active, then you can clear your search history from the Cortana settings and you can also have Cortana search the local system for an answer or search the Web. After you set the configuration options that you want, close the Cortana settings box.

Browser Controls

When you open either Edge or IE11, one of the first things that will catch your attention is the simplified design. The most common controls, like tools and favorite buttons, are just a click away. You also have the ability to customize how the browser will look and which tools that you can use with the browser.

Pinning Sites to the Taskbar

Pinning sites to your Taskbar allows you to access the websites by clicking the pinned site at the bottom of the Taskbar. Pinning a site is a very easy process. Just drag the tab of the website to the Taskbar. An icon for the website will stay pinned until you remove it. When you click the pinned icon, the website will open within the Internet browser.

Searchable Address Bar

You have the ability to search the Internet directly from the Address bar. You still have the ability to enter a website's address and go directly to the website. But now you can enter a search term or incomplete address, thus launching a search using your currently selected search engine. You can choose which search engine you want to use by clicking the Address bar and choosing the search engine from the listed icons or adding a new search engine.

Security and Privacy Enhancements

IE11 and Edge have both included many security and privacy enhancements, including some of the following:

- ActiveX Filtering allows you to block ActiveX controls for any sites. You do have the ability to turn them back on for the sites that you trust.

- Domain highlighting allows you to see the real web address of a website you are visiting. This allows you to avoid websites that use misleading web addresses.

- SmartScreen Filter helps protect you from online phishing attacks, fraud, and spoofed or malicious websites.

- 128-bit Secure Sockets Layer (SSL) connection to use with secure websites.

- InPrivate Browsing allows you to use the Web without saving any data from the websites that are visited while the browser is in this mode.

Working with Web Slices

Web Slices allows your internet browser to check for updates to web page content you may frequently access. How many times in the course of the day do you check your local weather or stock quotes or even watch an auction item on eBay? Most of the time you either keep a tab open and refresh it periodically or revisit the website with the content you would like to review.

With Web Slices, you can add the piece of the web page with the content you're looking for to the Favorites bar, and the browser will check it for you when the content changes. With web slices, the browser can control how often the browser checks for changes.

Figure 5.31 shows the result of a Bing query for a weather forecast for Portsmouth, New Hampshire, and the Web Slice availability to the favorite's toolbar. Clicking the down arrow associated with the icon will display all of the Web Slices available on the current web page.

In previous versions of the Internet browsers, Web Slices appeared within the web page. Now they are shown with the feeds button, as shown in Figure 5.31.

When the user chooses a Web Slice icon, they'll see a confirmation box for adding the Web Slice to the Favorites bar. Once accepted, the Web Slice is available to be viewed at any time, even after you browse away from the originating page.

FIGURE 5.31   Web Slices

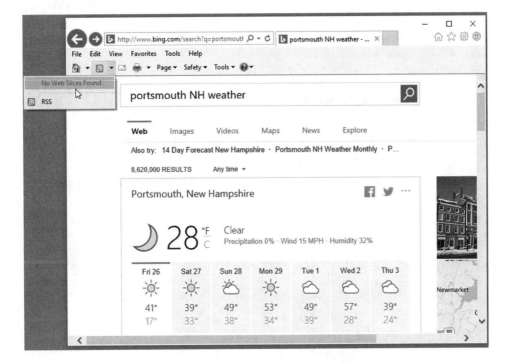

Using the Browser's Compatibility View

Windows Internet Explorer 11 and Edge are the new releases of Microsoft's web browser, and some websites may not be updated to use the new features or display their content correctly. Problems may exist with the display of misaligned images or text. By using Compatibility View, the browsers will display a web page the way it would have been displayed in previous versions, which should correct any display issues. To display a page in Compatibility View, click the Compatibility View Settings option in the tools (shown in Figure 5.32).

Once you have chosen Compatibility View for a website, you will not need to make the choice again. The browsers will display the site in Compatibility View the next time you browse to it. If the website gets updated in the future or you decide you would prefer to see it in the native standard mode, you can simply click the Compatibility View button again to return to the standard view. The Compatibility View option can also be selected from the Tools menu's Compatibility View menu option.

There is also a Compatibility View Settings option you can use to manage the sites currently set to be viewed in Compatibility View mode by adding or deleting sites by name. Many companies have extensive websites, and it may take time to update them to features. The Compatibility View Settings page has the default setting for all intranet sites to be displayed in Compatibility View. You also have to the choice to display all websites in Compatibility View.

FIGURE 5.32 Compatibility View Settings options

Using Protected Mode for IE11

Protected Mode is a feature of Windows 10 for Windows Internet Explorer 11 that forces IE to run in a protected, isolated memory space, preventing malicious code from directly writing data outside the `Temporary Internet Files` folder unless the program trying to write the information is specifically granted access by the user. Protected Mode is enabled by default and displayed in the lower-right section of Windows Internet Explorer 11.

You can install software through IE11, but you will need to explicitly allow the modification of the file structure of Windows 10 if the software is going to be installed outside the protected directory.

You can change out of Protected Mode from the Security tab of IE11's Internet options (via Tools ➤ Internet Options). You can also open Internet Options by typing **Internet options** into the integrated search box in Windows 10. You also have the option of double-clicking the Protected Mode: On text within Windows Internet Explorer 11 to open just the Security tab of Internet Options.

To toggle Protected Mode, click to select or deselect the Enable Protected Mode check box (this requires restarting Internet Explorer). It is recommended that Protected Mode remain active because it provides a greater level of security and safety for the user and does not prohibit an action (installing a program from IE11); it just requires interaction from the user to allow the modification, prompting at least a little thought about what's happening within Windows 10.

Using InPrivate Browsing and InPrivate Filtering

InPrivate Browsing provides some level of privacy to users using Windows Internet Explorer 11. The privacy maintained with InPrivate Browsing relates to a current browser where an InPrivate session has been enabled. The InPrivate session prevents the browsing history from being recorded and prevents temporary Internet files from being retained. Cookies, usernames, passwords, and form data will not remain in IE11 following the closing of the InPrivate session, nor will there be any footprints or data pertaining to the InPrivate Browsing session.

InPrivate Browsing keeps information from being saved to the local machine while the session is active, but don't get lulled into a false sense of security; malware, phishing, and other methods that send data out of the local machine are still valid and can provide personal information to a cybercriminal. In addition, employees visiting forbidden sites from work, for instance, could still be detected via forensics.

InPrivate Browsing is a good method of protecting user data if you are not surfing from your own machine or are surfing from a public location (always a bad place to leave personal information). InPrivate Browsing can also be used if you don't want anyone to be able to see data from your Internet browsing session.

There are several ways to launch an IE11 InPrivate Browsing session. One way is to open a new tab and select the Open An InPrivate Browsing Window option from the Browse With InPrivate section. This will open a new tab, and the tab will be an InPrivate session. You can also choose to open Windows Internet Explorer 11 and start an InPrivate session directly by choosing the Safety menu and selecting the InPrivate Browsing menu choice. Alternatively, you can open a new IE11 browser and press Ctrl+Shift+P.

InPrivate Filtering takes a slightly different approach in providing security and safety to the user who is surfing using Windows Internet Explorer 11. Many of today's websites gather content from different sources as they present a web page to you. Some of these sources are websites outside the main location, and they provide third-party companies with tracking information about where you surf and what you look at.

This information can then be used to provide statistics as well as send advertisements back to you. InPrivate Filtering provides an added layer of control for the user to decide what information third-party websites will have access to while the user is browsing, limiting the ability of third-party websites to track their browsing usage.

InPrivate Filtering is not enabled by default and must be enabled per browsing session. It is enabled from the Safety menu in IE11. You can alternatively use Ctrl+Shift+F to enable InPrivate Filtering.

The InPrivate Filtering dialog box is an alternate location for enabling InPrivate Filtering or disabling it. You open InPrivate Filtering from the Safety menu of Windows Internet Explorer 11.

Once you choose InPrivate Filtering, you will be given the option to have IE11 automatically block some third-party content or let the user select which third-party providers will receive the user's browsing information. You can always go back and change the options later or turn off InPrivate Filtering if you desire.

After InPrivate Filtering is enabled, you can see which pages have been blocked as third-party queries from the InPrivate Filtering Settings dialog box.

Another advantage of IE11 is that you can configure the web content filter. IE11 also allows you to set up and configure the Allow and Block lists. The Allow and Block lists are lists that you can subscribe to that will automatically filter out certain websites.

Configuring Windows Internet Explorer 11 Options

In addition to security and usability options that you can configure in IE11, you can configure other options for managing the browser. Many of the configurations we have discussed in this chapter (i.e., the Safety and Tools menu options) and have used to quickly change individual parameters are also available for modification within the Internet Options tabbed dialog box. The general parameters, security parameters, privacy configurations, content controls, connection settings, program options, and advanced settings available within Internet Options are discussed in the following sections.

General Parameters

You can open the Internet Properties tabbed dialog box by selecting the Tools menu and choosing the Internet Properties menu item or simply typing **Internet options** into the integrated search box of Windows 10. The General tab (Figure 5.33) allows you to change the default home page that displays when Windows Internet Explorer 11 is launched. An interesting feature here is that you can have more than one default home page. By entering more than one page in the Home Page text box, each time IE11 is launched all pages will open in their own tab.

FIGURE 5.33 General tab of IE11's Internet Properties

The General tab also allows you to control your browsing history, search, tabs, and appearance (including accessibility options) settings for the IE11 interface.

Security Parameters

The Security tab of IE11's (Figure 5.34) Internet Properties dialog box not only gives you access to control Protected Mode as discussed earlier but also gives you the ability to set security settings on the specific zones you may browse to as understood by Windows Internet Explorer 11. The zones are the Internet, Local Intranet, Trusted Sites, and Restricted Sites. You can set the behavior of IE11 individually for each zone and even individual sites within each zone. For example, if you add a website to the Local Intranet settings, you will not be asked to authenticate your credentials when connecting to the website.

FIGURE 5.34   Security tab of IE11's Internet Properties

Privacy Configurations

The Privacy tab of IE11's (Figure 5.35) Internet Properties allows the management of privacy settings for the Internet zone; this is the cookie management for specific sites. You can also control the settings for Pop-up Blocker and your InPrivate Filtering and InPrivate Browsing here.

FIGURE 5.35   Privacy tab of IE11's Internet Properties

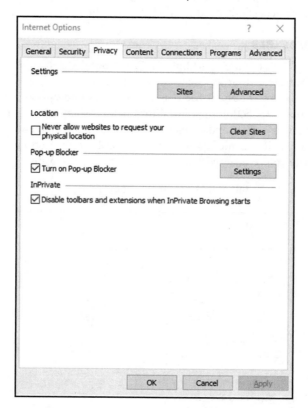

The pop-up blocker allows you to prevent unwanted Internet pop-ups from appearing while you are online. We have all been on websites where pop-up windows start appearing. With the IE11 pop-up blocker, you can prevent this from happening. To access the Pop-up Blocker Settings dialog box, you can click Start ➢ Internet Explorer ➢ Tools ➢ Pop-up Blocker ➢ Pop-up Blocker Settings.

To block cookies from any websites that do not have a compact privacy policy, you should set the privacy setting to High. The High setting prevents IE11 from saving cookies for websites that do not contain a compact privacy policy and cookies that have the potential of saving information that can be used to contact you without your explicit consent. Compact policies are used to indicate the privacy practices of a web service that uses cookies.

If you want to block any website from accessing cookies stored on the local computer, you should set the privacy setting to Block All Cookies. The Block All Cookies setting prevents cookies from being saved on the computer and prevents any existing cookies from being read by websites.

Content Control

Figure 5.36 shows the Content tab of Windows Internet Explorer 11's Internet Properties. There are controls to manage Certificates, Publishers, AutoComplete settings, and Feed and Web Slice settings.

FIGURE 5.36 Content tab of the Internet Properties dialog box

Certificate management for secure browsing is managed through the Content tab as well. You have the ability to manage AutoComplete functionality as well as RSS feeds and Web Slice data from within the Content tab.

The AutoComplete functionality allows IE11 to automatically fill in fields as you complete forms in IE11. It uses previously entered data to complete the fields on the form.

The Feeds And Web Slices section allows you to fill in what subscription feeds you belong to on the Internet and how often those feeds and slices will be updated along with other configuration options (i.e., playing a sound when the feed or slice is updated).

Connection Settings

The Connections tab of Windows Internet Explorer 11's Internet Properties dialog box allows you to manage the way IE11 gains access to the network. You can initiate the Connect To The Internet Wizard from this tab as well as set up a virtual private network (VPN). If you are using dial-up networking, this connection is also configured from the Connections tab. Local area network (LAN) general settings, which include specifying a proxy server if you need to use one (this is typical across many corporate sites, to provide a better level of anonymity for Internet surfing), are configured here as well.

Program Options

The Programs tab of the IE11 Internet Properties dialog box allows you to establish a default web browser. You can manage add-ons specific to IE11 in the Programs tab as well. Additionally, you can set up an application to allow for HTML editing and set up default programs to be used for Internet services such as email.

Advanced Options

The Advanced tab allows you to configure accessibility settings, browsing settings, international browsing settings, encoding settings, multimedia parameters, printing parameters, and general security settings. You can control whether links are underlined, whether pictures should be displayed, which versions of the secure communication protocols or SSL are used, background colors, and many other parameters.

In addition to being able to change the advanced settings, you have the option to restore advanced settings to their original configurations or to even reset Internet Explorer settings, which resets all IE11 settings (not just the advanced settings) to the default configuration.

Summary

Besides actually installing Windows 10, configuring the operating system properly is one of the most important tasks that an IT team can perform.

Configuring the desktop environment allows an administrator to configure an environment that is comfortable for the end user, which in turn makes the user more productive.

Understanding the Start menu and Control Panel icons allows you to configure and operate the Windows 10 applications more efficiently. Knowing how to configure the System icon properly in Control Panel allows you to fine-tune the Windows 10 operating system and get the best performance possible out of it.

In addition to using Control Panel to configure the Windows 10 operating system, you can edit the Registry directly using the REGEDIT or REGEDT32 utility. In Windows 10, REGEDT32 just opens REGEDIT.

Another important consideration when configuring Windows 10 is how the operating system will function when installed on a laptop or tablet (Windows Mobility). By configuring the mobility options on a laptop, you can allow that laptop to connect to data in multiple ways.

We also looked at services that run on Windows 10 and how to configure and troubleshoot them when they don't run properly.

Video Resources

There are videos available for the following exercises:
   5.1
   5.2
   5.3
   You can access the videos at http://www.wiley.com/go/sybextestprep.

Exam Essentials

Be able to configure Desktop settings.   Understand how to customize and configure the Windows 10 Desktop settings. This includes setting a desktop and also setting up desktop personalization. It is also important to know how to configure the Taskbar and Start menu.

Be able to support mobile computers through power-management features.   Understand the new power features that are available in Windows 10 and be able to configure a laptop computer to use them.

Understand remote connections.   Know how to configure and connect to machines through remote connections. You can use Remote Assistance, Remote Desktop, and a VPN.

Know how to configure services.   Understand how to stop, start, monitor, pause, and configure services on the Windows 10 operating system. Know how to configure the different properties available through services.

Review Questions

1. You are a consultant for a large organization. Some employees contact you at 11:00 p.m. and state that one of the servers is not working properly. No one is in the office to fix the problem. How can you connect to the server to fix the problem?

   A. Remote Desktop

   B. Hyper-V

   C. Remote Assistance

   D. Virtual PC

2. You have a user, Rob, who uses a laptop computer running Windows 10. You have configured the laptop to enter sleep mode after 30 minutes of inactivity. What will occur when the computer enters sleep mode?

   A. The data will be saved to the hard disk, and the computer will shut down.

   B. The data will be erased from RAM, and the computer will shut down.

   C. The monitor will be turned off, but the hard disks will remain active.

   D. The data will be saved to memory, and the computer will be put into a power-saving state.

3. You are an administrator for your company's network. You want to configure the clock to be displayed on the Desktop of your users' computers. How can you accomplish this task?

   A. Through Control Panel ➢ Personalization

   B. Through Control Panel ➢ Date And Time

   C. Through Control Panel ➢ Windows Sidebar Properties

   D. Through Control Panel ➢ Ease Of Access Center

4. A new employee named Crystal has been supplied with a Windows 10 laptop computer. You have configured Crystal's computer with the Power Saver power plan, and you used the default options. Which of the following will occur after 20 minutes of inactivity on Crystal's computer?

   A. The display will be turned off, but the hard disk will remain active.

   B. The hard disk will be turned off, but the display will remain active.

   C. Both the hard disk and the display will be turned off.

   D. No components will be turned off.

5. You are the network administrator for a medium-size company. You support all user Desktop issues. Gary is using the default Windows 10 Desktop on his laptop computer. Gary wants to change his Desktop settings. Which of the following options should Gary use to configure the Desktop in Windows 10?

   A. Right-click an empty space on the Desktop and choose Personalize from the context menu.

   B. Select Control Panel ➢ System.

   C. Right-click My Computer and choose Manage from the context menu.

   D. Right-click My Computer and choose Properties from the context menu.

6. You work on the help desk for a large company. One of your users calls you and reports that they just accidentally deleted their C:\Documents\Timesheet.xls file. What is the easiest way to recover this file?

  A. In Folder Options, click the Show Deleted Files option.

  B. In Folder Options, click the Undo Deleted Files option.

  C. Click the Recycle Bin icon on the Desktop and restore the deleted file.

  D. Restore the file from your most recent tape backup.

7. You are the system administrator for your company. You are configuring the services on a Windows 10 computer. You want to ensure that if a service fails to load, it will attempt to restart. Which tab of the service's Properties dialog box should you use?

  A. General

  B. Log On

  C. Recovery

  D. Dependencies

8. The system administrator of your network wants to edit the Registry, including setting security on the Registry keys. What primary utilities that support full editing of the Windows 10 Registry should the system administrator use? (Choose all that apply.)

  A. REGEDIT

  B. REDIT

  C. REGEDT32

  D. REGEDITOR

9. Kayla is dissatisfied with the configuration of her keyboard and mouse. She wants to reset the keyboard speed and the mouse pointer rate. Which utility should she use to configure the keyboard and mouse properties?

  A. Control Panel

  B. Computer Management

  C. Microsoft Management Console

  D. Registry Editor

10. Denise is using a laptop computer that uses ACPI. She wants to see what percentage of the battery power is still available. She also wants to know if hibernation has been configured. Which of the following utilities should she use?

  A. Device Manager

  B. Computer Manager

  C. Battery meter

  D. MMC

Chapter

6

Configuring Data Security

MICROSOFT EXAM OBJECTIVES COVERED IN THIS CHAPTER:

✓ **Configure data access and usage.**

- This objective may include but is not limited to the following subobjectives: Configure file and printer sharing and HomeGroup connections; configure folder shares, public folders, and OneDrive; configure file system permissions; configure OneDrive usage; troubleshoot data access and usage.

When it comes to working on a network, it doesn't matter if it's a small HomeGroup network or a large corporate data center; data security is one of the most important tasks that we have as IT personnel.

If you don't know how to protect your data, then you are just inviting hackers to have full reign of your network. We see companies getting hacked on the news on almost a weekly basis. But that is really not the worst of it. Most corporate hacks are done by your own users. That's right; the majority of hacks in the world are being done by the very same people who work for your company. This is why knowing how to properly configure your network's security is essential.

When you're configuring your company's data, you should make sure users only have the bare minimum security requirements to do their jobs. Never give users more access than what they need. This is the fine line we must all walk. Not enough access and your users can't do their jobs. Too much access and the users can do things that they are not supposed to.

In this chapter, I will show you the difference between shared permissions and NTFS security and how to configure them properly. I will also show you how to work with OneDrive. So let's begin with talking about configuring network resources.

Configuring Network Resources

To understand data security, we must first talk about why we set up networks. We have networks because we want to share corporate resources. Years ago, before most small companies had networks, we all used the network called sneakernet. This means that we had a pair of sneakers and we would copy files and folders from one system using floppy disks and then walk to another system to install the files. Larger companies had networks but most small companies just had multiple computers that were not connected together.

This was not very efficient. The reason we have networks is because we want to share network resources without the need to have individual copies of data on each machine. With a network, you can keep data on a server and allow hundreds of users to connect to that server to access the same data. But with this power comes great responsibility for protecting your data.

Microsoft has made networking so easy for the average user (using HomeGroups) that many of us even have networks in our own homes. Twenty years ago, this would have been a laughable statement.

When talking about Microsoft networking, there are three types of networks we need to talk about. Two of them are basically the same network but they are configured differently. The three Microsoft networks are domain-based, workgroup-based, and HomeGroup-based networks.

Domain-based networks have servers called Active Directory servers (called domain controllers) that maintain the users' account information in a central database. On a domain-based network, users get authenticated onto the network using Active Directory.

Workgroup networks and HomeGroup networks are both forms of peer-to-peer networks, which means that all computers work as both a client machine and a server machine. There are no central user databases and security is much more difficult to maintain and manage.

 We will discuss networking in greater detail in Chapter 7 "Windows 10 Networking."

So once you have decided to set up a network, the next step is setting up data protection. Setting up proper file and folder security is one of the most important tasks that an IT professional can perform. If permissions and security are not properly configured, users will be able to access resources that they shouldn't.

File and folder security defines what access a user has to local resources. You can limit access by applying security for files and folders. You should know what NTFS security permissions are and how they are applied.

In Windows 10, it is very easy to share folders. You can also apply security to shared folders in a manner that is similar to applying NTFS permissions. Once you share a folder, users with appropriate access rights can access the folders through a variety of methods.

When a user is created on a local Windows 10 system, or if the user is created on an Active Directory domain, the user gets a security identification (SID) number. It is important to remember that when you assign rights to a user, those rights and permissions get associated to the user's SID number and not the username. It's because of this that we can rename user accounts without any issues.

So before we talk about securing network data, let's take a look at how to configure the easiest Microsoft network, called HomeGroups.

Configuring HomeGroups in Windows 10

HomeGroup is a functionality of Windows 10 that simplifies the sharing of music, pictures, and documents within your small office or home network of Windows 10 PCs. HomeGroup allows you to share USB-connected printers too. If you have a printer installed on a Windows 10 computer and it's shared by HomeGroup, it is automatically installed onto the other HomeGroup-enabled Windows 10 PCs. Domain-joined computers cannot host a HomeGroup, but they can be a participant of a HomeGroup. All editions of Windows 10 can use HomeGroups, but only Home, Enterprise, or Professional edition can create a HomeGroup.

The first step in the process of using HomeGroup for sharing is to create a new HomeGroup or join an existing one. If the Windows 10 network-discovery feature does not find a HomeGroup, you will be asked to create a HomeGroup. In the Network and Sharing Center, select Choose HomeGroup and then click the Create A HomeGroup button (Figure 6.1).

FIGURE 6.1   Create a HomeGroup.

With Windows 10 network discovery turned on (the default), a HomeGroup is created automatically. You still need to join the HomeGroup to use the other shared resources and to share yours. From the Network and Sharing Center, you can join an existing HomeGroup by clicking the Join Now button, as shown in Figure 6.2.

FIGURE 6.2   Join an existing HomeGroup.

Part of joining a HomeGroup setup is defining the libraries that you want to make available to the other members of the HomeGroup. The HomeGroup libraries are the folders (Pictures, Music, Videos, Documents, and Printers) that you want to share. So you can choose which HomeGroup libraries that you want to share or not share. The next screen in the setup (Figure 6.3) lets you choose which resources you want to share.

FIGURE 6.3   HomeGroup sharing selections

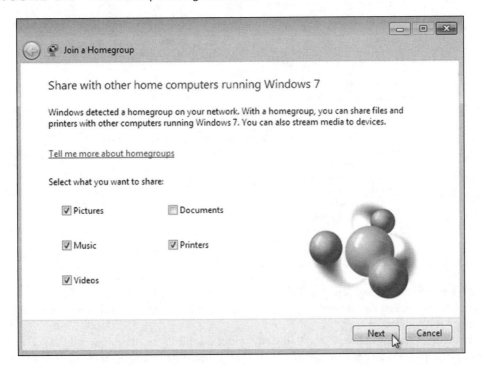

The next step is to enter the HomeGroup password. Windows 10, by default, will recognize a HomeGroup on the network. However, the other Windows 10 machines will not have access to the resources. Allowing any Windows 10 machine connecting to the network to automatically have shared resource access would be a huge security hole. To protect the Windows 10 user resources, a password must be entered to join a HomeGroup.

The password for the HomeGroup can be viewed or changed on the machine that established the HomeGroup. After other machines have joined, each machine has the ability to view or change the password. The initial machine in the HomeGroup will create a random secure password. To view and/or print the HomeGroup password, use the Choose HomeGroup And Sharing Options selection from the Network and Sharing Center, and then choose View Or Print The HomeGroup Password item, shown in Figure 6.4. Again, this can be done from any Windows 10 machine that is already a member of the HomeGroup but not from one that wants to join.

FIGURE 6.4   Change HomeGroup Settings screen

Figure 6.5 shows the View And Print Your HomeGroup Password screen. For simplicity here, I have changed the password to *password*, which is an example only and not recommended for your network.

Remember that Windows 10 will initially create a random secure password for the HomeGroup, and you need to visit the View And Print Your HomeGroup Password screen to find out what it is. You will probably want to change it. To change the password, choose the Change The Password option from the Change HomeGroup Settings page and then select Change The Password from the Change Your HomeGroup Password screen, as shown in Figure 6.6. When you change the HomeGroup password, you need to go to each of the other Windows 10 machines that are members of the HomeGroup and change the password there if you still want the others to share resources.

After the HomeGroup is set up, you can see the other members' resources from the HomeGroup option of Windows Explorer or even the Start menu if you customize the Start menu and have added HomeGroup to the displayed options. I have added the HomeGroup option to my Start menu, as shown in Figure 6.7 (depending on the Windows 10 version, this may be a bit different). To add the HomeGroup to the Start menu, right-click the Start menu and choose Control Panel. Once in Control Panel, make sure the view is set to Large Icons (in the upper-right corner of the window). Right-click the HomeGroup icon and choose Pin To My Start.

FIGURE 6.5   View And Print Your HomeGroup Password screen

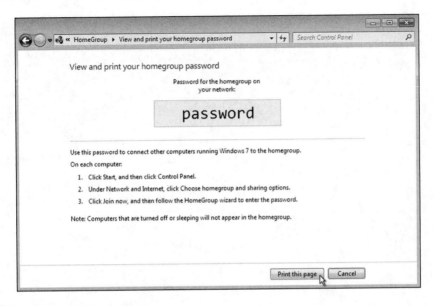

FIGURE 6.6   Change the HomeGroup password.

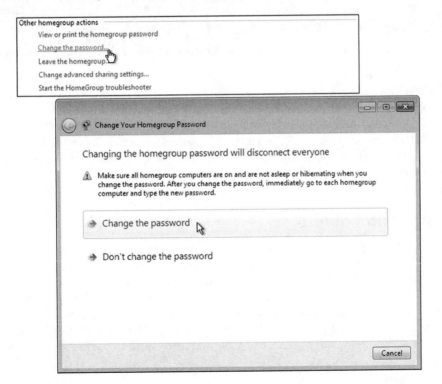

FIGURE 6.7 HomeGroup in the Start menu

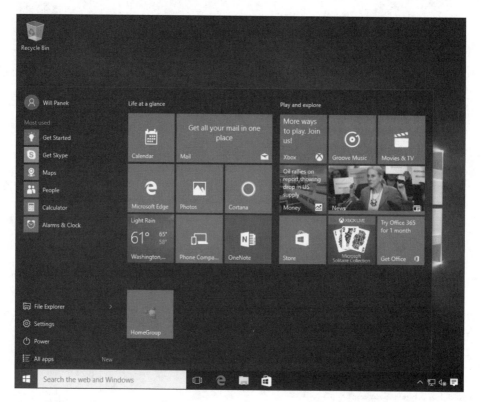

HomeGroups are a great option for users who want to share resources in the Windows 10 environment. But what if you still have non–Windows 10 machines? The legacy function of simply sharing resources and setting permissions still works for Windows 10 and will allow older operating systems to have access to resources shared on Windows 10 machines as well as allow users running Windows 10 to have access to the shared resources on older Windows operating systems.

Configuring Folders

Folders are just containers within a Windows 10 system. Think of folders as drawers in a large cabinet. Each drawer can contain its own unique items and each drawer can have its own security keys. Folders can be configured through the use of folder options.

The Windows 10 Folder Options dialog box allows you to configure many properties associated with files and folders, such as what you see when you access folders and how Windows searches through files and folders. To open the Folder Options dialog box, right-click Start ➤ File Explorer and then select View and then Option. You can also access

Folder Options by choosing Control Panel ➤ Large Icons View ➤ File Explorer Options. The Folder Options dialog box has three tabs: General, View, and Search. The options on each of these tabs are described in the following sections.

Folder General Options

The General tab, shown in Figure 6.8, includes the following options:

- Whether folders are opened all in the same window when a user is browsing folders or each folder is opened in a separate window
- Whether a user opens items with a single mouse click or a double-click
- Whether to show recently used files and folders in Quick access

FIGURE 6.8 The General tab of the Folder Options dialog box

Folder View Options

The View tab of the Folder Options dialog box, shown in Figure 6.9, is used to configure what users see when they open files and folders. For example, you can change the default setting so that hidden files and folders are displayed. Table 6.1 describes the View tab options.

FIGURE 6.9   The View tab of the Folder Options dialog box

TABLE 6.1   Folder view options

Option	Description	Default
Always Show Icons, Never Thumbnails	Shows icons instead of thumbnail previews for files.	Not selected
Always Show Menus	Shows the File, Edit, View, Tools, and Help menus when you're browsing for files.	Not selected
Display File Icon On Thumbnails	Displays the file icon on thumbnails.	Selected
Display File Size Information In Folder Tips	Specifies whether the file size is automatically displayed when you hover your mouse over a folder.	Selected
Display The Full Path In The Title Bar (Classic Theme Only)	Specifies whether the title bar shows an abbreviated path of your location. Selecting this option displays the full path, such as `C:\Word Documents\Sybex\Windows 10 Book\Chapter 9`, as opposed to showing an abbreviated path, such as `Chapter 9`.	Not selected

Option	Description	Default
Hidden Files And Folders	Specifies whether files and folders with the Hidden attribute are listed. Choosing Show Hidden Files, Folders, Or Drives displays these items.	Don't Show Hidden Files, Folders, And Drives
Hide Empty Drives	Prevents drives that are empty in the `Computer` folder from being displayed.	Selected
Hide Extensions For Known File Types	By default, filename extensions, which identify known file types (such as `.doc` for Word files and `.xls` for Excel files), are not shown. Disabling this option displays all filename extensions.	Selected
Hide Protected Operating System Files (Recommended)	By default, operating system files are not shown, which protects operating system files from being modified or deleted by a user. Deselecting this option displays the operating system files.	Selected
Launch Folder Windows In A Separate Process	By default, when you open a folder, it shares memory with the previous folders that were opened. Selecting this option opens folders in separate parts of memory, which increases the stability of Windows 10 but can slightly decrease the performance of the computer.	Not selected
Show Drive Letters	Specifies whether drive letters are shown in the `Computer` folder. When this option is disabled, only the name of the disk or device will be shown.	Selected
Show Encrypted Or Compressed NTFS Files In Color	Displays encrypted or compressed files in an alternate color when they are displayed in a folder window.	Selected
Show Pop-Up Description For Folder And Desktop Items	Displays whether a pop-up tooltip is displayed when you hover your mouse over files and folders.	Selected
Show Preview Handlers In Preview Pane	Shows the contents of files in the preview pane.	Selected
Use Check Boxes To Select Items	Adds a check box next to each file and folder so that one or more of them may be selected. Actions can then be performed on selected items.	Not selected

TABLE 6.1   Folder view options *(continued)*

Option	Description	Default
Use Sharing Wizard (Recommended)	Allows you to share a folder using a simplified sharing method.	Selected
When Typing Into List View	Selects whether text is automatically typed into the search box or whether the typed item is selected in the view.	Select The Typed Item In The View

Search Options

The Search tab of the Folder Options dialog box, shown in Figure 6.10, is used to configure how Windows 10 searches for files. You can choose for Windows 10 to search by filename only, by filenames and contents, or by a combination of the two, depending on whether indexing is enabled. You can also select from the following options:

- Don't use the index when searching in file folders for system files
- Include system directories in non-indexed locations
- Include compressed files in non-indexed locations
- Always search file names and contents (this might take several minutes)

FIGURE 6.10   The Search tab of the Folder Options dialog box

To search for files and folders, click Start ➢ Search and type your query in the search box. When searching for files or folders, you can use wildcards (*) to help find matches. So if I was looking for a .docx file, I could search *.docx to see all of the files that end in .docx.

Understanding Dynamic Access Control

One of the advantages of Windows Server 2012 R2 and Windows 10 is the ability to apply data governance to your file server. This will help control who has access to information and auditing. You get these advantages through the use of Dynamic Access Control (DAC). DAC allows you to identify data by using data classifications (both automatic and manual) and then control access to these files based on these classifications.

DAC also gives administrators the ability to control file access by using a central access policy. This central access policy will also allow an administrator to set up audit access to files for reporting and forensic investigation.

DAC allows an administrator to set up Active Directory Rights Management Service (AD RMS) encryption for Microsoft Office documents. For example, you can set up encryption for any documents that contain financial information.

DAC gives an administrator the flexibility to configure file access and auditing to domain-based file servers. To do this, DAC controls claims in the authentication token, resource properties, and conditional expressions within permission and auditing entries.

Administrators have the ability to give users access to files and folders based on Active Directory attributes. For example, a user named Dana is given access to the file server share because in the user's Active Directory (department attribute) properties, the value contains the attribute Sales.

Securing Access to Files and Folders

On NTFS partitions, you can specify the access each user has to specific folders or files on the partition based on the user's logon name and group associations. Access control consists of rights (which pertain to operations on the system) and permissions (which pertain to operations on specific objects). The owner of an object or any user who has the necessary rights to modify permissions can apply permissions to NTFS objects. If permissions are not explicitly granted within NTFS, then they are implicitly denied. Permissions can also be explicitly denied; explicit denials override explicitly granted permissions.

The following sections describe design goals for access control as well as how to apply NTFS permissions and some techniques for optimizing local access.

Considering Design Goals for Access Control

Before you start applying NTFS permissions to resources, you should develop design goals for access control as a part of your overall security strategy. Basic security strategy suggests that you provide each user and group with the minimum level of permissions needed for job functionality. The following list includes some of the considerations for planning access control:

- Defining the resources that are included within your network—in this case, the files and folders residing on the file system

- Defining which resources will put your organization at risk, including defining the resources and defining the risk of damage if a resource is compromised

- Developing security strategies that address possible threats and minimize security risks

- Defining groups that security can be applied to based on users within the group membership who have common access requirements, and applying permissions to groups as opposed to users

- Applying additional security settings through Group Policy if your Windows 10 clients are part of an Active Directory network

- Using additional security features, such as Encrypted File System (EFS), to provide additional levels of security or file auditing to track access to critical files and folders

After you have decided what your design goals are, you can start applying your NTFS permissions.

Applying NTFS Permissions

NTFS permissions control access to NTFS files and folders. Ultimately, the person who owns an object has complete control over the object. The owner or administrator can configure access by allowing or denying NTFS permissions to users and groups.

Normally, NTFS permissions are cumulative, based on group memberships. The user gets the highest level of security from all the different groups they belong to. However, if the user had been denied access through user or group membership, those deny permissions override the allowed permissions. Windows 10 offers seven levels of NTFS permissions, with one of them being special permissions:

Full Control   This permission allows the following rights:

- Traverse folders and execute files (programs) in the folders. The ability to traverse folders allows you to access files and folders in lower subdirectories, even if you do not have permissions to access specific portions of the directory path.

- List the contents of a folder and read the data in a folder's files.

- See a folder's or file's attributes.

- Change a folder's or file's attributes.

- Create new files and write data to the files.

- Create new folders and append data to the files.

- Delete subfolders and files.

- Delete files.

- Compress files.

- Change permissions for files and folders.

- Take ownership of files and folders.

If you select the Full Control permission, all permissions will be checked by default and can't be unchecked.

Any user with Full Control access can manage the security of a folder. However, to access folders, a user must have physical access to the computer as well as a valid logon name and password. By default, regular users can't access folders over the network unless the folders have been shared. Sharing folders is covered in the section "Creating and Managing Shared Folders" later in this chapter.

Modify   This permission allows the following rights:

- Traverse folders and execute files in the folders.
- List the contents of a folder and read the data in a folder's files.
- See a file's or folder's attributes.
- Change a file's or folder's attributes.
- Create new files and write data to the files.
- Create new folders and append data to the files.
- Delete files.

If you select the Modify permission, the Read & Execute, List Folder Contents, Read, and Write permissions will be checked by default and can't be unchecked.

Read & Execute   This permission allows the following rights:

- Traverse folders and execute files in the folders.
- List the contents of a folder and read the data in a folder's files.
- See a file's or folder's attributes.

If you select the Read & Execute permission, the List Folder Contents and Read permissions will be checked by default and can't be unchecked.

List Folder Contents   This permission allows the following rights:

- Traverse folders.
- List the contents of a folder.
- See a file's or folder's attributes.

Read   This permission allows the following rights:

- List the contents of a folder and read the data in a folder's files.
- See a file's or folder's attributes.
- View ownership.

Write   This permission allows the following rights:

- Overwrite a file.
- View file ownership and permissions.
- Change a file's or folder's attributes.
- Create new files and write data to the files.
- Create new folders and append data to the files.

Special Permissions This allows you to configure any permissions beyond the normal permissions, such as auditing, and to take ownership. To apply NTFS permissions, right-click the file or folder to which you want to control access, select Properties from the context menu, and then select the Security tab. The Security tab lists the users and groups who have been assigned permissions to the file or folder. When you click a user or group in the top half of the dialog box, you see the permissions that have been allowed or denied for that user or group in the bottom half (see Figure 6.11).

FIGURE 6.11 The object's Security tab

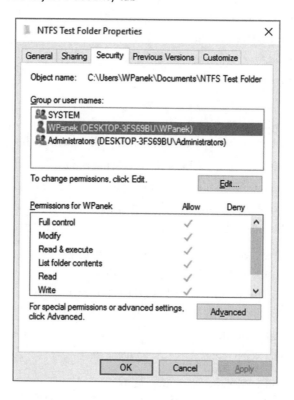

Exercise 6.1 walks you through assigning NTFS permissions.

EXERCISE 6.1

Managing NTFS Permissions

1. Right-click the file or folder to which you want to control access, select Properties from the context menu, and click the Security tab.

2. Click the Edit button to modify permissions.

3. Click the Add button to open the Select Users Or Groups dialog box. You can select users from the computer's local database or from the domain you are in (or trusted domains) by typing in the user or group name in the Enter The Object Names To Select portion of the dialog box and clicking OK.

   Through the Advanced button of the Security tab, you can configure more granular NTFS permissions, such as Traverse Folder and Read Attributes permissions.

4. You return to the Security tab of the folder Properties dialog box. Highlight a user or group in the top list box, and in the Permissions list, specify the NTFS permissions to be allowed or denied. When you have finished, click OK. To remove the NTFS permissions for a user, computer, or group, highlight that entity in the Security tab and click the Remove button. Be careful when you remove NTFS permissions. You won't be asked to confirm their removal as you are when deleting most other types of items in Windows 10.

Controlling Permission Inheritance

Normally, the directory structure is organized in a hierarchical manner. This means you are likely to have subfolders in the folders to which you apply permissions. In Windows 10, by default, the parent folder's permissions are applied to any files or subfolders in that folder as well as any subsequently created objects. These are called *inherited permissions*.

You can specify how permissions are inherited by subfolders and files by clicking the Advanced button on the Security tab of a folder's Properties dialog box. This calls up the Permissions tab of the Advanced Security Settings dialog box. To edit these options, click the Change Permissions button. You can edit the following options:

- Include Inheritable Permissions From This Object's Parent
- Replace All Existing Inheritable Permissions On All Descendants With Inheritable Permissions From This Object

If an Allow or Deny item in the Permissions list on the Security tab has a shaded check mark, this indicates that the permission was inherited from an upper-level folder. If a check mark is not shaded, it means the permission was applied at the selected folder. This is known as an explicitly assigned permission. Knowing which permissions are inherited and which are explicitly assigned is useful when you need to troubleshoot permissions.

Understanding Ownership and Security Descriptors

When an object is initially created on an NTFS partition, an associated security descriptor is created. A security descriptor contains the following information:

- The user or group who owns the object
- The users and groups who are allowed or denied access to the object
- The users and groups whose access to the object will be audited

After an object is created, the owner of the object has full permissions to change the information in the security descriptor, even for members of the Administrators group. You can view the owner of an object from the Security tab of the specified folder's Properties by clicking the Advanced button. Then click the Owner tab to see who the owner of the object is. From this dialog box, you can change the owner of the object.

Although the owner of an object can set its permissions so that the administrator can't access it, the administrator or any member of the Administrators group can take ownership of an object and thus manage the object's permissions. When you take ownership of an object, you can specify whether you want to replace the owner on subdirectories and subobjects of the object. If you would like to see who owns a directory, from the command prompt, type **dir /q**.

Determining and Viewing Effective Permissions for NTFS

To determine a user's effective permissions (the aggregate permissions the user has to a file or folder), add all of the permissions that have been allowed through the user's assignments based on that user's username and group associations. After you determine what the user is allowed, you subtract any permissions that have been denied the user through the username or group associations.

As an example, suppose user Marilyn is a member of both the Accounting and Execs groups. The following assignments have been made to the Accounting group permissions:

Permission	Allow	Deny
Full Control		
Modify	X	
Read & Execute	X	
List Folder Contents		
Read		
Write		

The following assignments have been made to the Execs group permissions:

Permission	Allow	Deny
Full Control		
Modify		
Read & Execute		
List Folder Contents		
Read	X	
Write		

To determine Marilyn's effective rights, you combine the permissions that have been assigned. The result is that Marilyn's effective rights are Modify, Read & Execute, and Read, so she effectively has Modify (the highest right).

As another example, suppose that user Dan is a member of both the Sales and Temps groups. The following assignments have been made to the Sales group permissions:

Permission	Allow	Deny
Full Control		
Modify	X	
Read & Execute	X	
List Folder Contents	X	
Read	X	
Write	X	

The following assignments have been made to the Temps group permissions:

Permission	Allow	Deny
Full Control		
Modify		X
Read & Execute		
List Folder Contents		
Read		
Write		X

To determine Dan's effective rights, you start by seeing what Dan has been allowed: Modify, Read & Execute, List Folder Contents, Read, and Write permissions. You then remove anything that he is denied: Modify and Write permissions. In this case, Dan's effective rights are Read & Execute, List Folder Contents, and Read.

If permissions have been applied at the user and group levels and inheritance is involved, it can sometimes be confusing to determine what the effective permissions are. To help identify which effective permissions will actually be applied, you can view them from the Effective Permissions tab of Advanced Security Settings, or you can use the ICACLS command-line utility.

To see what the effective permissions are for a user or group, you click the Select button and then type in the user or group name. Then click OK. If a box is checked and not shaded, then explicit permissions have been applied at that level. If the box is shaded, then the permissions to that object were inherited.

The ICACLS command-line utility can also be used to display or modify user access permissions. This command-line utility can help you troubleshoot any issues you may be having with user access. The options associated with the ICACLS command are as follows:

- /grant grants permissions.
- /remove revokes permissions.
- /deny denies permissions.
- /setintegritylevel sets an integrity level of Low, Medium, or High.

One issue that IT people run into is what happens to the security when you move or copy a file or folder. Let's take a look at NTFS permissions when they are moved or copied.

Determining NTFS Permissions for Copied or Moved Files

When you copy or move NTFS files, the permissions that have been set for those files might change. Use the following guidelines to predict what will happen:

- If you move a file from one folder to another folder on the same volume, the file will retain the original NTFS permissions.
- If you move a file from one folder to another folder between different NTFS volumes, the file is treated as a copy and will have the same permissions as the destination folder.
- If you copy a file from one folder to another folder on the same volume or on a different volume, the file will have the same permissions as the destination folder.
- If you copy or move a file or folder to a FAT partition, it will not retain any NTFS permissions.

A user's permissions and rights are automatically assigned to the user's security ID (SID) number and not the username. Because of this, you can rename user accounts. By renaming an account, you can give someone all the rights and permissions that someone else had who left the company. This is also why you can change someone's name if needed without changing their rights.

Managing Network Access

In every network, there are resources to which the users need to gain access. As IT professionals, we share these resources so that our users can do their jobs.

Sharing is the process of allowing network users access to a resource located on a computer. A network share provides a single location to manage shared data used by many users. Sharing also allows an administrator to install an application once, as opposed to installing it locally at each computer, and to manage the application from a single location.

The following sections describe how to create and manage shared folders and configure share permissions.

Creating and Managing Shared Folders

You can share a folder in two ways. To use the Sharing Wizard, right-click a folder and select Share. If the Sharing Wizard feature is enabled, you will see the File Sharing screen, where you can add local users. Alternatively, you can access the wizard by right-clicking a folder and then selecting Properties ➤ Sharing tab ➤ Share button.

However, you cannot use the Sharing Wizard to share resources with domain users. To share a folder with domain users, right-click the folder and select Properties, and then select the Sharing tab, shown in Figure 6.12.

FIGURE 6.12   The Sharing tab of a folder's Properties dialog box

The Share button will take you to the Sharing Wizard. To configure Advanced Sharing, click the Advanced Sharing button, which will open the Advanced Sharing dialog box.

When you share a folder, you can configure the options listed in Table 6.2.

TABLE 6.2 Shared folder options

Option	Description
Share This Folder	Makes the folder available through local access and network access.
Share Name	A descriptive name by which users will access the folder.
Comments	Additional descriptive information about the share (optional).
Limit The Number Of Simultaneous Users To	The maximum number of connections to the share at any one time. (No more than 20 users can simultaneously access a share on a Windows 10 computer.)
Permissions	How users will access the folder over the network.
Caching	How folders are cached when the folder is offline.

If you share a folder and then decide that you do not want to share it, just deselect the Share This Folder check box. You can easily tell that a folder has been shared by the group icon located at the bottom left of the folder icon.

Keep in mind the following guidelines regarding sharing:

- Only folders, not files, can be shared.
- Share permissions can be applied only to folders and not to files.
- If a folder is shared over the network and a user is accessing it locally, then share permissions will not apply to the local user; only NTFS permissions will apply if the file system is NTFS.
- If a shared folder is copied, the original folder will still be shared but not the copy.
- If a shared folder is moved, the folder will no longer be shared.
- If the shared folder will be accessed by a mixed environment of clients, including some that do not support long filenames, you should use the 8.3 naming format for files.
- Folders can be shared through the Net Share command-line utility.

Now let's take a look at configuring share permissions for your users.

Configuring Share Permissions

You can control users' access to shared folders from the network by assigning share permissions. Share permissions are less complex than NTFS permissions and can be applied only to folders (unlike NTFS permissions, which can be applied to files and folders).

To assign share permissions, click the Permissions button in the Advanced Sharing dialog box. This brings up the Share Permissions dialog box, shown in Figure 6.13.

FIGURE 6.13   The Share Permissions dialog box

You can assign three types of share permissions:

Full Control   Allows full access to the shared folder.

Change   Allows users to change data within a file or to delete files.

Read   Allows a user to view and execute files in the shared folder. Read is the default permission on shared folders for the Everyone group.

Shared folders do not use the same concept of inheritance as NTFS folders. If you share a folder, there is no way to block access to lower-level resources through share permissions. One thing that is the same between shared and NTFS is that all shared permissions are additive if you belong to multiple groups. This means that you add up all the permissions of the groups and get the highest permission.

NTFS vs. Share Permissions

When applying conflicting share and NTFS permissions, the most restrictive permissions win. Remember that share and NTFS permissions are both applied only when a user is accessing a shared resource over a network. Only NTFS permissions apply to a user accessing a resource locally. So, for example, if a user's NTFS security setting on a resource is Read and the share permission on the same resource is Full Control, the user would have only Read permission when they connect to the shared resource. The most restrictive set of permissions wins.

So to give you an example, let's look at the settings shown in Table 6.3 for the Apps folder and see how the effective permissions would apply.

TABLE 6.3   The Apps folder permissions

Group	NTFS Security	Shared Permission
Sales	Modify	Full Control
Marketing	Modify	Read

Looking at Table 6.3, you can see that the Sales group would have Modify access because the most restrictive permission between Modify and Full Control is Modify. The Marketing group would have Read only access because Read is more restrictive than Modify.

Configuring OneDrive

Windows 10 includes Microsoft OneDrive with the operating system. Microsoft OneDrive is a cloud-based storage system where corporate users or home users can store their data in the cloud. Microsoft OneDrive allows users to use up to 5 GB of cloud storage for free. Users have the ability to get more cloud-based storage by purchasing a higher subscription.

To set up a corporate user or home user with Microsoft OneDrive, you must first have a Microsoft account. You can create a Microsoft account at the time you are accessing OneDrive, as shown in Figure 6.14.

Once you have a Microsoft account, you then sign into the Microsoft OneDrive system where you can begin uploading data. Figure 6.15 shows Microsoft OneDrive from the Internet browser. Using the Internet browser, you can control the files that are located in the cloud.

FIGURE 6.14   Microsoft OneDrive sign-in screen

FIGURE 6.15   Microsoft OneDrive

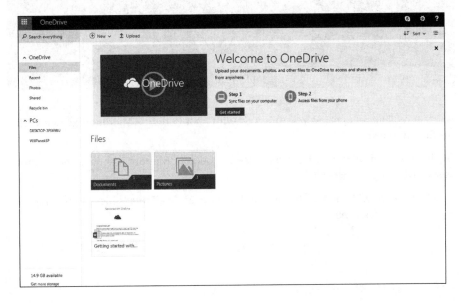

In Exercise 6.2, I will show you how to sign into your Microsoft OneDrive application.

EXERCISE 6.2

Logging into OneDrive

1. Click the Start button ➤ All Apps ➤ OneDrive, as shown in Figure 6.16 (Windows 10 Anniversary Edition may appear differently).

FIGURE 6.16 OneDrive menu option

2. A screen will appear asking you to log on with your Personal Microsoft account. Click the Sign In button.

3. On the Add Your Microsoft Account screen, type your Microsoft account name and password to log in, as shown in Figure 6.17.

4. Another screen will appear stating that this is your OneDrive folder (shown in Figure 6.18). Click Next.

FIGURE 6.17 OneDrive Login

FIGURE 6.18 This is your OneDrive folder screen.

5. The next screen will allow you to sync files with OneDrive. Choose which folders you want to sync and click Next, as shown in Figure 6.19.

FIGURE 6.19   Sync files screen

6. The next screen will tell you that you can start using OneDrive. Click the Open My OneDrive Folder button.

At this point you can start using OneDrive to create and upload files to the OneDrive cloud. In the left corner, next to the Home tab, you will see three lines. If you click those three lines, some options will appear. The bottom option allows you to change the OneDrive settings.

Inside those settings, you have the ability to change how often the system will sync with the cloud, which accounts will be associated to this OneDrive, and many other settings. The OneDrive cloud-based storage is a good way to back up some documents for protection from data loss.

Summary

In this chapter, we started looking at how to set up and configure folders on a Windows 10 and Windows Server 2012 R2 system. We talked about sharing those folders and how to grant access to those folders by using NTFS and shared permissions.

We also talked a Dynamic Access Control (DAC) and how Dynamic Access Control allows an administrator to identify data by using data classifications and then controlling access to these files based on these classifications.

DAC also gives administrators the ability to control file access by using a central access policy. This central access policy will also allow an administrator to set up audit access to files for reporting and forensic investigation.

Video Resources

There are videos available for the following exercise:

6.1

You can access the videos at http://www.wiley.com/go/sybextestprep.

Exam Essentials

Understand folder options.   Understand the purpose and features of using folders and files. Properly configuring folders and folder access is one of the most important tasks that we do on a daily basis.

Understand NTFS and share permissions.   Be able to configure security permissions and know the difference between NTFS and share permissions.

Understand OneDrive.   Be able to configure OneDrive for your Windows 10 system. Understand how OneDrive can back up your Windows 10 data.

Review Questions

1. You are asked by a family member to set up a network in their home. They have three machines in their home that are all connected by an ISP wireless router. The systems can't share documents because there is currently no network sharing in place. They want to be able to share audio and video files among their family. How can you easily set up a network? (Choose two.)

   A. Install a Windows Server 2008 R2 domain controller.

   B. Create a HomeGroup.

   C. All audio and video files should be moved to the HomeGroup libraries.

   D. Move all audio and video files to a shared folder on the Windows Server 2008 R2 machine.

2. William, the IT manager for your company, has been asked to give Jeff the rights to read and change documents in the StormWind Documents folder. The following table shows the current permissions on the shared folder:

Group/User	NTFS	Shared
Sales	Read	Change
Marketing	Modify	Change
R&D	Deny	Full Control
Finance	Read	Read
Jeff	Read	Change

   Jeff is a member of the Sales and Finance groups. When Jeff accesses the StormWind Documents folder, he can read all of the files, but the system won't let him change or delete files. What does William need to do to give Jeff the minimum amount of rights to do his job?

   A. Give Sales Full Control to shared permissions.

   B. Give Jeff Full Control to NTFS security.

   C. Give Finance Change to shared permissions.

   D. Give Finance Modify to NTFS security.

   E. Give Jeff Modify to NTFS security.

3. You are hired by a small family-owned company to set up a network for a business that is run out of the family's home. The company sells property and they have only five real estate agents. They can't afford a server and client access licenses. What type of network can you set up for them?

   A. Set up all Windows 10 clients on a domain.

   B. Create a HomeGroup.

   C. Set them up on Azure Active Directory.

   D. Load Windows Server 2012 R2 onto a Windows 10 system.

4. You have a network folder that resides on an NTFS partition on a Windows 10 computer. NTFS permissions and share permissions have been applied. Which of the following statements best describes how share permissions and NTFS permissions work together if they have been applied to the same folder?

   A. The NTFS permissions will always take precedence.

   B. The share permissions will always take precedence.

   C. The system will look at the cumulative share permissions and the cumulative NTFS permissions. Whichever set is less restrictive will be applied.

   D. The system will look at the cumulative share permissions and the cumulative NTFS permissions. Whichever set is more restrictive will be applied.

5. You are the network administrator for a medium-sized company. Rick was the head of HR and recently resigned. John has been hired to replace Rick and has been given Rick's laptop. You want John to have access to all of the resources to which Rick had access. What is the easiest way to manage the transition?

   A. Rename Rick's account to John.

   B. Copy Rick's account and call the copied account John.

   C. Go into the Registry and do a search and replace to replace all of Rick's entries with John's name.

   D. Take ownership of all of Rick's resources and assign John Full Control to the resources.

6. Jeff, the IT manager for StormWind Studios, has been asked to give Tom the rights to read and change documents in the StormWind Documents folder. The following table shows the current permissions on the shared folder:

Group/User	NTFS	Shared
Sales	Modify	Read
Marketing	Modify	Change
R&D	Deny	Full Control
Finance	Modify	Read
Tom	Modify	Read

   Tom is a member of the Sales and Finance groups. When Tom accesses the StormWind Documents folder, he can read all the files, but the system won't let him change or delete files. What do you need to do to give Tom the minimum amount of rights to do his job?

   A. Give Sales Full Control to shared permissions.

   B. Give Tom Full Control to NTFS security.

   C. Give Finance Change to shared permissions.

   D. Give Tom Change to shared permission.

7. You are the IT manager for your company. You have been asked to give the Admin group the rights to read, change, and assign permissions to documents in the Stormwind Documents folder. The following table shows the current permissions on the Stormwind Documents shared folder:

Group/User	NTFS	Shared
Sales	Read	Change
Marketing	Modify	Change
R&D	Deny	Full Control
Finance	Read	Read
Admin	Change	Change

What do you need to do to give the Admin group the rights to do their job? (Choose all that apply.)

A. Give Sales Full Control to shared permissions.

B. Give Full Control to NTFS security.

C. Give Admin Full Control to shared permissions.

D. Give Finance Modify to NTFS security.

E. Give Admin Full Control to NTFS security.

8. You are the IT manager for your company. You have been asked to give the Sales group the rights to read, change, and assign permissions to documents in the Stormwind Documents folder. The following table shows the current permissions on the Stormwind Documents shared folder:

Group/User	NTFS	Shared
Sales	Read	Change
Marketing	Modify	Change

What do you need to do to give the Sales group the rights to do their job? (Choose all that apply.)

A. Give Sales Full Control to shared permissions.

B. Give Sales Modify to NTFS security.

C. Give Marketing Change to shared permissions.

D. Give Sales Full Control to NTFS security.

9. You are the IT manager for your company. You have been asked to give the Marketing group the rights to read, change, and assign permissions to documents in the StormWind Documents folder. The following table shows the current permissions on the StormWind Documents shared folder:

Group/User	NTFS	Shared
Sales	Read	Change
Marketing	Modify	Read

What do you need to do to give the Marketing group the rights to do their job? (Choose all that apply.)

A. Give Marketing Full Control to shared permissions.

B. Give Sales Modify to NTFS security.

C. Give Marketing Change to shared permissions.

D. Give Sales Full Control to NTFS security.

10. You are the IT manager for your company. You have been asked to give the Sales group the rights to read, change, and assign permissions to documents in the Stormwind Documents folder. The following table shows the current permissions on the Stormwind Documents shared folder:

Group/User	NTFS	Shared
Sales	Read	Read
Marketing	Modify	Change

What do you need to do to give the Sales group the rights to do their job? (Choose all that apply.)

A. Give Sales Change to shared permissions.

B. Give Sales Modify to NTFS security.

C. Give Marketing Change to shared permissions.

D. Give Sales Full Control to NTFS security.

Chapter

7

Windows 10 Networking

MICROSOFT EXAM OBJECTIVES COVERED IN THIS CHAPTER:

✓ **Configure networking.**

▪ This objective may include but is not limited to the following subobjectives: Configure and support IPv4 and IPv6 network settings; configure name resolution; connect to a network; configure network locations; configure Windows Firewall; configure Windows Firewall with Advanced Security; configure network discovery; configure Wi-Fi settings; configure Wi-Fi Direct; troubleshoot network issues.

Before we talk about installing applications or user authentication on a Windows 10 system, I think it's important to understand how to set up a network. In most IT departments, you install applications through the network. Also, when your users authenticate, they normally authenticate onto a network.

For most of us, our Windows 10 devices will be configured on some type of a network. It doesn't matter if it's a home network or a corporate network, Windows 10 will normally belong to some type of network.

Because of this, it is very important to know how to properly configure and design a Windows network. In this chapter, we discuss Active Directory and how to configure Windows 10 to work within the Windows Server 2012 R2 domain environment. We will also look at connecting Windows 10 to a network by using either a wireless or wired connection and working with the Windows 10 HomeGroup.

Finally, we will look at how to protect your network by using the Windows 10 Firewall. The Windows 10 Firewall can help protect your client systems from being illegally breached, but when you're building a network, your Windows Firewall should *NOT* be your only firewall. Your network connection to the Internet should also be protected by some type of firewall, but that is an entirely different course (depending on your firewall type).

So let's begin this chapter with the basics and what networking is all about.

Understanding the Basics

Microsoft uses three networking models: domain-based networks, workgroup networks, and HomeGroup networks. HomeGroup networks and workgroup networks are basically the same type of network, called peer-to-peer. The difference between a workgroup and HomeGroup network is just how you set up the network.

The way you design your network is going to determine how you set up the rest of the computers and servers on that network. The choice you make here will be determined by many factors, including the number of users on your network and the amount of money you can spend.

Peer-to-Peer Networks

When setting up a Microsoft Windows *peer-to-peer network* (also referred to as a *workgroup* or *HomeGroup*), it is important to understand that all computers on the network are equal. All of the peer-to-peer computers, also referred to as *nodes*, simultaneously act as both clients and servers.

Peer-to-peer networks are typically any combination of Microsoft Windows XP, Windows Vista, Windows 7, Windows 8, and Windows 10 machines connected by a centralized device such as a router, switch, or hub (see Figure 7.1).

FIGURE 7.1   Peer-to-peer model

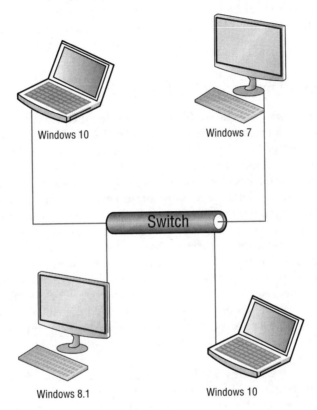

One of the biggest debates among IT professionals is when to use a peer-to-peer network. These types of networks have their place in the networking world. Most home networks use this type of configuration—where all of the computers are connected by a small Internet router. It's often the same for companies. You would use this network configuration in a small environment with 10 users or fewer. This enables small organizations to still share resources without needing expensive equipment, server software, or an internal IT department.

But there is a downside to peer-to-peer networks; the biggest issues are manageability and security. Many new IT people like working on a small peer-to-peer network because of its size, but no matter what, a network with 10 users and 10 computers can be very difficult to manage, and security is extremely difficult to set up. Because there is no server to centralize user accounts on a peer-to-peer network, each Microsoft Windows XP, Windows Vista, Windows 7, Windows 8, and Windows 10 computer must have a user account and password. So if you have 10 users and 10 computers and all 10 users must be able to access all 10 computers, you end up creating 100 accounts: 10 accounts on each machine times 10 machines.

Another disadvantage of peer-to-peer networks is backups. Most IT departments do not back up individual user machines, and because there is no centralized server for data storage when using a peer-to-peer network, data recoverability can be an issue.

Now that you have seen the advantages and disadvantages of a peer-to-peer network, let's discuss the advantages and disadvantages of a domain-based network.

Onsite Active Directory Networks

A *domain-based* network uses Microsoft's *Active Directory*, which is a single distributed database that contains all the objects in your network. A domain is a logical grouping of objects into a distributed database. Some of these objects are user accounts, group accounts, and published objects (folders and printers).

The first of many advantages to Active Directory is centralized management. As just stated, the Active Directory database contains all the network information within a single, distributed data repository. Because these network objects are all located in the same database, an administrator can easily manage the domain from one location.

Another major advantage to using Active Directory is domain security. An administrator has the advantage of creating a unique username and password for each user within the domain. These usernames and passwords can be used to access all resources that an individual has the proper rights to access. An administrator can determine, based on job function or position, which files or folders on the network a user should be granted access to and assign access to the user's single account. In our earlier peer-to-peer example, you needed to create 100 user accounts. With a domain, you would need to create only the 10 accounts, one per person.

An Active Directory structure is made up of one or more domains. As explained, a *domain* is a logical grouping of objects within your organization. For example, if we had the WillPanek.com domain, all users in that domain should be members of the WillPanek .com organization. The objects that are contained within a domain do not need to be in the same physical location. Domains can span the entire globe even though they are part of the same organization.

One of the advantages to using domains is the ability to have a *child domain*, which is a subdomain of another domain. You can build child domains based on physical locations, departments, and so forth. Figure 7.2 shows the hierarchy structure of WillPanek.com with its child domains (based on geographic location).

Microsoft Active Directory domains are represented as triangles. It is important to remember that when taking any Microsoft exam.

FIGURE 7.2   Domain structure

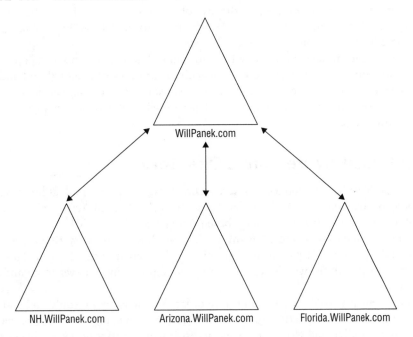

Child domains give you greater scalability. Active Directory has the ability to store millions of objects within a single domain, but child domains give an administrator the flexibility to design a structure that meets an organization's needs. For example, you may have a site located in a different state. Creating a child domain for that office allows that office to be an independent domain, and thus they can have their own security and domain settings. One or more domains that follow the same contiguous namespace are called a tree. For example, if my domain name is WillPanek.com and the child domains are NH.WillPanek.com, Arizona .WillPanek.com, and Florida.WillPanek.com, this would be a tree. All of these domains follow the WillPanek.com namespace.

When you set up child domains, the parent and child domains automatically establish a trust relationship. *Trusts* allow users to be granted access to resources in a domain even when their accounts reside in a different domain. To make administration of trust relationships easier, Microsoft has made transitive two-way trusts the default relationship between domains within a forest. A forest is all the trees that are part of your Active Directory structure, and they share a schema and global catalog. This means that by default, all domains within the same forest automatically trust one another. As shown in Figure 7.2, WillPanek.com automatically trusts NH.WillPanek.com, Arizona.WillPanek.com, and Florida.WillPanek.com. This means that all of the child domains implicitly trust one another.

The last Active Directory advantage that we will discuss is an extensible schema. The Active Directory schema contains all the objects and attributes of the database. For example, when you create a new user by using the Active Directory Users and Computers snap-in, the system asks you to fill in the user's first name, last name, username, password, and so forth. These fields are the attributes of the user object, and the way that the system knows to prompt for these fields is that the user object has these specific attributes assigned to it within the Active Directory schema. An administrator has the ability to change or expand these fields based on organizational needs.

The major disadvantage to an Active Directory model is cost. When setting up an Active Directory domain, an organization needs a machine that's powerful enough to handle the Windows Server 2012 R2 operating system. Also, most companies that decide to use a domain-based organization will require the IT personnel to manage and maintain the network infrastructure.

Cloud-Based Azure Active Directory

Now that you have been introduced to Active Directory, let's take a look at how you can have Microsoft manage your Active Directory with its cloud-based Active Directory called *Azure*. Azure is Microsoft's subscription-based Active Directory service.

If you are a small to midsized company and you don't want to worry about employing a full-time multi-person IT department, then this may be a great option for you. This allows Microsoft to deal with the worries of managing and maintaining a server room and all of the hardware.

All your company would need to do is hire or train someone who would add and maintain the actual Azure Active Directory accounts. This person could also work as the help desk or support individual. Now you have Microsoft worrying about the hardware and your IT people can focus on helping and maintaining users and accounts.

So how does Azure Active Directory compare when it comes to adding Windows 10 to the domain? It really doesn't matter. As long as you have Internet access to the cloud-based system, your Windows 10 accounts will work the same way as if the Active Directory was on premise.

Windows 10 includes a new feature for configuring and deploying corporation-owned Windows devices called Azure AD Join. Azure AD Join registers the Windows 10 devices in the Azure Active Directory, which then allows them to be accessible and managed by your organization.

The one nice advantage is that with Azure Active Directory, Windows 10 devices authenticate directly to Azure AD without the need of an onsite domain controller. But, if you want, you can still have a domain controller on site that works with the cloud-based Azure Active Directory.

When you are adding Windows 10 to Azure Active Directory, end users or domain admins can join their Windows 10 device (computer, tablet, or phone) to Azure AD during the out-of-box experience (OOBE). Because of this, organizations can assign devices to their users with no IT interaction or staging time.

Because of the Azure AD Join built into Windows 10, during the OOBE, the IT department would just add the device to the Azure Active Directory network.

Now that you understand the difference between a workgroup and a domain, let's go ahead and make sure that you understand some of the other networking terms that you will need to know.

Other Microsoft Networking Terms and Roles

Now that you have seen the different Microsoft networking models, let's talk about some of the server terminology that is used in the remainder of this chapter. You may be familiar with some of these terms, but it's always good to get a refresher.

Server A *server* is a machine that users connect to so they can access resources located on that machine. These resources can be files, printers, applications, and so forth. Usually, the type of server is dependent on the resource that the user needs. For example, a print server is a server that controls printers. A file server contains files. Application servers can run applications for the users. Sometimes you will hear a server referred to by the specific application that it may be running. For example, someone may say, "That's our SQL server" or "We have an Exchange server."

Domain Controller This is a server that contains a replica of the Active Directory database. As mentioned earlier in this chapter, Active Directory is the database that contains all the security objects in your network along with any resources that you publish to Active Directory. A *domain controller* is a server that contains this database. All domain controllers are equal in a Windows Server 2012 R2 network, and each can read from and write to the directory database unless it's a Read Only Domain Controller (RODC). Some domain controllers may contain extra roles, but they are all part of the same Active Directory network.

Member Server A *member server* is a server that is a member of a domain-based network but does not contain a copy of Active Directory. For example, it is recommended by Microsoft that a Microsoft Exchange server be loaded on a member server instead of a domain controller. Both domain controllers and member servers can act as file, print, or application servers. Your choice of server type depends on whether you need that server to have a replica of Active Directory.

Network Discovery *Network discovery* is a setting that determines whether your Windows 10 system can locate other computers and devices on the network and if other computers on the network can see your computer. To enable or disable Network Discovery, you need to complete the following steps:

1. In the Windows 10 search box, type **network**. Then click Change Advanced Sharing Settings on the left side.

2. Click Turn On/Turn Off Network Discovery, and then click the Save Changes button.

Standalone Server A *standalone server* is not a member of a domain. Many organizations may use this type of server for virtualization. For example, say you load Windows Server 2012 R2 with Hyper-V (Microsoft's virtualization server) on a standalone server. You can then create virtual machines that act as domain controllers to run the network.

Client Machine A *client machine* is a computer that normally is used by a company's end users. The most common operating systems for a client machine are Windows XP, Windows Vista, Windows 7, Windows 8, and Windows 10.

DNS Server A *Domain Name Service (DNS)* server has the DNS service running on it. DNS is a name-resolution service that resolves a hostname to a TCP/IP address (called forward lookup). DNS also has the ability to resolve a TCP/IP address to a name (called reverse lookup). When you install an operating system onto a computer, you assign that computer a hostname. The problem is that computers talk to each other by using TCP/IP addresses, such as, for example, 192.168.1.100. It would be very difficult for most users to remember all the different TCP/IP addresses on a network. So normally you connect to a machine by using its hostname. DNS does the conversion of hostname to TCP/IP address for you.

The easiest way to understand how this works is to think of your phone number. If someone wants to call you but doesn't have your telephone number, they can call Information. They give Information your name, and they get your phone number. This is basically how a network works as well. DNS is Information on your network. You give DNS a hostname, and it returns a network telephone number (TCP/IP address). DNS is a requirement if you want to install Active Directory. You can install DNS before or during the Active Directory installation, but DNS is required for an Active Directory installation to occur. DNS can help resolve either IPv4 or IPv6 TCP/IP addresses, both of which are explained later in this chapter, in the section "Understanding TCP/IP."

The reason that DNS can resolve both IPv4 and IPv6 is because of the Link Local Multicast Name Resolution, or LLMNR, protocol, which is based on DNS packet formats that allow both IPv4 and IPv6 hosts to perform name resolution for hosts on the same local network.

DHCP Server   A *Dynamic Host Configuration Protocol (DHCP)* server runs the DHCP service, which assigns TCP/IP information to your computers dynamically. Every computer needs three settings to operate properly (with the Internet and an intranet): a TCP/IP address, a subnet mask, and a default gateway (router address). Your computers can get this minimum information two ways: manually, where someone manually types in the TCP/IP information on the machine, or dynamically, where the DHCP service automatically assigns the machine an address. DHCP can assign more than just these three settings. DHCP can assign any TCP/IP configuration information, including the address of a DNS server, WINS server, time servers, and so forth.

Continuing with our scenario from the DNS server description, DHCP would be the phone company. DHCP is the component that assigns the telephone number (TCP/IP number).

If you are using DHCP and your Windows 10 machine receives a 169.254.*x.x* TCP/IPv4 address, your client is not able to connect to the DHCP server. Windows 10 machines will automatically assign themselves a 169.254.*x.x* TCP/IPv4 number when DHCP is unavailable. This is called Automatic Private IP Addressing (APIPA). DHCP can issue both IPv4 or IPv6 TCP/IP addresses.

Global Catalog   The *Global Catalog* is a database of all Active Directory objects in a forest with only a subset of the object attributes. Think of the Global Catalog as an index. If you needed to look something up in this Windows 10 book, you would go to the index and find what page you need to turn to. You would not just randomly look through the book for the information. This is the same purpose the Global Catalog serves in your Active Directory forest. When you need to find a resource in the domain (user, published printer, and so forth), you can search the Global Catalog to find its location.

Domain controllers need to use a Global Catalog to help with user authentication. Global Catalogs are a requirement on an Active Directory domain. All domain controllers can be Global Catalogs, but this is not always a good practice. Your network should have at least two Global Catalogs for redundancy, but too many can cause too much Global Catalog replication traffic unless you have a single-domain model.

Port Numbers   Port numbers are used by applications and services so that they can communicate with a network or a computer system. Think of port numbers as doorways that are used for the application or service. So for example, if a user wants to connect to the Internet, they use port number 80.

Configuring NIC Devices

Before you can connect a Windows 10 machine to the domain, you must set up the *network interface card (NIC)*—a hardware component used to connect computers or other devices to the network to allow the machines to communicate with each other. NICs are responsible for providing the physical connection that recognizes the physical address of the device where they are installed.

 The Open Systems Interconnection (OSI) model defines the encapsulation technique that builds the basic data structure for data transport across an internetwork. The OSI model provides interoperability among hardware vendors, network protocols, and applications. The physical address is the OSI model Layer 2 address or, for Ethernet technologies, the MAC (Media Access Control) address. This is not an IP address, which is the OSI Layer 3, or Network layer, also generically defined as the logical address.

We generically call the interface between our network devices and the software components of the machines *network adapters* (also referred to as a NIC). Most commonly, you see network adapters installed on computers, but you also see network adapters installed in network printers and specialized devices such as intrusion detection systems (IDSs) and firewalls. Network adapters do not need to be separate cards; they can be built in, as in the case of most PCs today or other network-ready devices such as network cameras and network media players. These adapters (and all other hardware devices) need a driver to communicate with the Windows 10 operating system.

Before you physically install a network adapter, it's important to read the vendor's instructions that come with the hardware. Most network adapters you get today should be self-configuring, using Plug and Play capabilities. After you install a network adapter that supports Plug and Play, it should work following the installation procedure (which should be automated if the vendor says it is). You might have to restart, but our operating systems are getting much better with this, and you might just get lucky and be ready to use the device immediately.

If you happen to have a network adapter that is not Plug and Play, the operating system should detect the new piece of hardware and start a wizard that leads you through the process of loading the adapter's driver and setting initial configuration parameters. You can see your network connection and manage the network connection properties through the Network and Sharing Center.

Configuring a Network Adapter

After you have installed the network adapter, you configure it through its Properties dialog box. You can get to the network adapter properties pages via the Network and Sharing Center (detailed in the section "Configuring Wireless Network Settings" later in this chapter), through Computer Management, or through Device Manager.

To use the Device Manager applet for the network adapter configuration, right-click Start and choose Device Manager. This launches the Device Manager MMC (Microsoft Management Console), shown in Figure 7.3.

FIGURE 7.3   Device Manager MMC

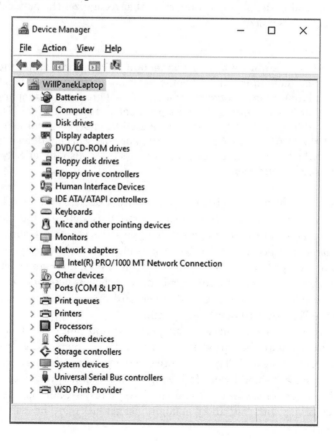

Figure 7.3 shows the Network Adapters device category expanded, and the adapter is installed in the machine. Accessing the network adapter properties allows us to view and change configuration parameters of the adapter. You do this by right-clicking the adapter in Device Manager and selecting Properties from the context menu. Each tab is detailed in the following list.

General Tab   The General tab of the Network Adapter Properties dialog box (Figure 7.4) shows the name of the adapter, the device type, the manufacturer, and the location. The Device Status box reports whether the device is working properly. If not, the Device Status box gives you an error code and a brief description of what Windows 10 identifies as the issue. You can perform an Internet search for the error code(s) if the text is not sufficient.

FIGURE 7.4   General tab of the Network Adapters Properties page

Advanced Tab   The contents of the Advanced tab of a Network Adapter's Properties dialog box vary depending on the network adapter and driver that you are using. Figure 7.5 shows an example of the Advanced tab for my Fast Ethernet adapter. To configure options in this dialog box, choose the property you want to modify in the Property list box and specify the desired value for the property in the Value box on the right.

FIGURE 7.5   Advanced tab of the Network Adapters Properties page

Driver Tab   The Driver tab of the Network Adapters Properties dialog box provides the following information about your driver:

- The driver provider
- The date the driver was released
- The driver version (useful in determining whether you have the latest driver installed)
- The digital signer (the company that provides the digital signature for driver signing)

The Driver tab for my adapter is shown in Figure 7.6. The information here varies from driver to driver and even from vendor to vendor. The Driver Details button on the Driver tab brings up the Driver File Details dialog box that provides the following details about the driver:

- The location of the driver file (useful for troubleshooting)
- The original provider of the driver
- The file version (useful for troubleshooting)
- Copyright information about the driver
- The digital signer for the driver

The Update Driver button starts a wizard to step you through upgrading the driver for an existing device. The Roll Back Driver button allows you to roll back to the previously installed driver if you update your network driver and encounter problems. In Figure 7.6, the Roll Back Driver button is grayed out (not available) because I have not updated the driver or a previous driver is not available. The Disable button is used to disable the device. After you disable the device, the Disable button changes into an Enable button, which you can use to enable the device. The Uninstall button removes the driver from your computer's configuration. You would uninstall the driver if you were going to remove the device from your system or if you want to completely remove the driver configuration from your system so you can reinstall it from scratch either automatically or manually.

FIGURE 7.6 Driver tab of the Network Adapters Properties page

Details Tab The Details tab of the network adapter's Properties dialog box lists the resource settings for your network adapter. Information found on the Details tab varies by hardware device. I have included the Details tab information from my adapter in Figure 7.7, with the Property drop-down list box set to Device description.

Events Tab The Events tab (Figure 7.8) of the network adapter's Properties dialog box shows you some of the device events that have happened to this piece of hardware. There is also a View All Events button that opens the Event Viewer MMC, which shows you all events for this device. This is a good way to look to see if there have been any events or issues (like errors or warnings) for the device.

FIGURE 7.7   Details tab of the Network Adapter Properties page

FIGURE 7.8   Events tab of the Network Adapter Properties page

Resources Tab   The Resources tab of the Network Adapter's Properties dialog box (Figure 7.9) lists the resource settings for your network adapter. Resources include interrupt request (IRQ), memory, and input/output (I/O) resources. This information can be important for troubleshooting if other devices are trying to use the same resource settings. This is not normally the case because Windows 10 and the Plug and Play specification should set up nonconflicting parameters. If there are issues, the Conflicting Device List box at the bottom of the Resources tab will show the conflicts.

FIGURE 7.9   Resources tab of the Network Adapter Properties page

Power Management Tab   The Power Management tab (Figure 7.10) of the network adapter's Properties dialog box allows you to set up how this device can save power on the system. For example, you can allow the system to turn off this device and also allow this device to wake the system from sleep mode.

FIGURE 7.10   Power Management tab of the Network Adapter Properties page

Troubleshooting a Network Adapter

When installing the NIC, you may encounter some problems or errors. Let's take a look at some NIC troubleshooting.

If your network adapter is not working, the problem might be with the hardware, the driver software, or the network protocols. We discuss the Layer 3 (Network layer) issues later in this chapter in the section "Understanding TCP/IP." The following are some common Layer 1 (Physical layer) and Layer 2 (Data Link layer) causes for network adapter problems:

Network Adapter Not on the HCL   If the device is not on the Hardware Compatibility List (HCL), use your Internet resources to see if others have discovered a solution, or contact the hardware vendor for advice.

Outdated Driver   Make sure that you have the most current driver for your adapter. You can have Windows 10 check for an updated driver from the Driver tab of the Properties page for the adapter by clicking the Update Driver button and having Windows search for a better driver, or you can check for the latest driver on the hardware vendor's website.

Network Adapter Not Recognized by Windows 10   Check Device Manager to see whether Windows 10 recognizes the adapter. If you don't see your adapter, you can try to manually install it.

Improperly Configured Network Card   Verify that the settings for the network card are correct for the parameters known within your network and for the hardware device the machine is connected to.

Cabling Problem   Make sure that all network cables are functioning and are the correct type. This includes making sure that the connector is properly seated, the cable is straight or crossed (depending on where it's plugged in), and the cable is not broken. This is usually done by looking at the little green light (LGL) on the network adapter card. This does not guarantee a good connection even if the LGLs are illuminated. A single conductor failure in a cable can still have a link light on, but data is not passing.

Bad Network Connection Device   Verify that all network connectivity hardware is properly working. For example, on a Fast Ethernet network, make sure the switch and port being used are functioning properly.

There are seven layers to the OSI model. Starting at Layer 7 and working down, they are Application, Presentation, Session, Transport, Network, Data Link, and Physical. You can remember this by using the phrase "All People Seem To Need Data Processing."

Configuring Wireless NIC Devices

Wireless technology has matured to the point of becoming cost effective and secure. The use of wireless network adapters is increasingly popular, scaling well out of the home and into the workplace. Windows 10 supports wireless auto configuration, which makes wireless network connections easy to use. Windows 10 will automatically discover the wireless networks available and connect your machine to the preferred wireless network.

One of the advantages to setting up Windows 10 and wireless connections is that once you have connected to a wireless access point (WAP), your Windows 10 will remember that and reconnect you to that preferred wireless network when your Windows 10 system is in range.

Configuring Wireless Network Settings

If you have a wireless network adapter compatible with Windows 10, it will be automatically recognized by the operating system. This can be a built-in adapter such as those most modern laptops come with, a wireless card you install in the machine, or even a wireless USB adapter. After it is installed, it is shown in Device Manager as well as in the Network and Sharing Center within the View Your Active Networks section.

We used Device Manager in the previous section for the network adapter configuration, so let's use the Network and Sharing Center for the wireless network configuration. Figure 7.11 shows the Network and Sharing Center with one active network, the wireless network connection called Trend.

FIGURE 7.11   Network and Sharing Center

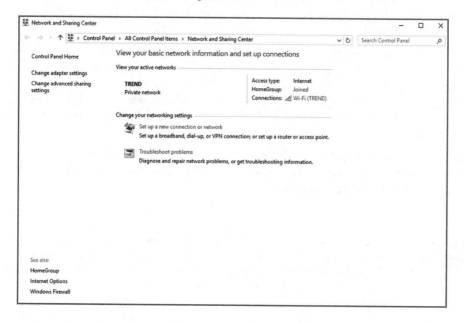

You can perform any of the following steps to access the Network and Sharing Center:

- Type **Network and Sharing Center** in the integrated search box of Windows 10.

- Right-click Start ➢ Control Panel ➢ Network And Internet ➢ Network And Sharing Center (if Control Panel view is Category).

- Right-click Start ➢ Control Panel ➢ Network And Sharing Center (if Control Panel view is Large Icons or Small Icons).

- Right-click the network icon in the lower-right taskbar and choose Open Network And Sharing Center.

- Click Start ➢ Settings ➢ Network and Internet and then choose either the Wi-Fi or Ethernet Connection link.

Viewing the Wireless Network Connection Status

From the Network and Sharing Center, you have easy access to the Wireless Network Connection Status window, which gives you an initial look at the status by providing the Layer 3 connectivity status (IPv4 and IPv6), media state, service set identifier (SSID) being used, how long the connection has been active (Duration), the negotiated speed of the connection, and the signal quality, as shown in Figure 7.12.

The Details button provides information such as the actual physical address (Layer 2), logical address (Layer 3), dynamic addressing parameters (DHCP), name-resolution items, and more. After you verify Physical layer parameters, this area is a great place to verify or troubleshoot logical (driver/software) issues.

FIGURE 7.12   Wireless Network Connection Status window

Viewing Wireless Network Connection Details

If you have a wireless adapter in your machine, perform Exercise 7.1 to view the network connection details for your wireless network connection.

EXERCISE 7.1

Viewing the Network Connection Details

1. Type **Network and Sharing Center** in the Windows 10 integrated search window; press Enter.

2. Select the Wireless Network Connection menu item from the View Your Active Networks section.

Click the Details button.

Review the network connection details for this connection.

The Wireless Network Connection Status window has an Activity section showing real-time traffic (in bytes) being sent from and received by the wireless network. From the

Wireless Network Connection Status window, you also have access to the Wireless Network Connection Properties, which includes access to the wireless adapter configuration pages.

You access the properties page by clicking the Properties button in the Activity section (refer back to Figure 7.12). The Wi-Fi Properties page has a Networking tab (see Figure 7.13) that shows which network adapter is being used for this connection (which you can change if you have more than one available).

FIGURE 7.13 Wi-Fi Properties window's Networking tab

The section that begins with "This connection uses the following items" displays the various clients, services, and protocols that are currently available for this connection.

You can install or uninstall network clients, network services, and network protocols by clicking the appropriate button. You can also view the client, service, or protocol properties if they are available by first highlighting the item from the list and then clicking the Properties button for the selected item. If the Properties button is gray, a properties page is not available for the item. From the Wireless Network Connection Properties window, you even have access to the network adapter's hardware configuration property pages. These are the same pages you have access to from Device Manager.

Perform Exercise 7.2 to access the network adapter properties from the Wireless Network Connection Properties page.

EXERCISE 7.2

Viewing Wireless Network Connection Properties

1. Type **Network and Sharing Center** in the Windows 10 integrated search window, and then press Enter.

2. Select the Wireless Network Connection menu item in the View Your Active Networks section.

3. Click the Properties button in the Activity section.

4. Click the Configure button.

5. View the various tabs regarding the network adapter properties.

6. Choose Cancel to return to the Wireless Network Connection Status window.

Configuring Wireless Network Security

Wireless network security is a very large piece of setting up our wireless networks. The focal point for this is the wireless access point or wireless router to which we connect. Whether you are using a small wireless network or a large wireless infrastructure, you should have a plan for secure communication and should configure wireless network security. There are several basic parameters you can configure on your network access devices to increase the security of a wireless network:

- Disable broadcast of the SSID, which is the name of the wireless network. When SSID broadcast is disabled, the wireless network cannot be detected automatically until you manually configure your wireless network card to connect to that SSID.

- Create a MAC address filter list so only specifically allowed wireless devices can connect to the wireless network, or you can require users attempting to connect to supply connection credentials.

- Enable encryption such as Wi-Fi Protected Access (WPA) or WPA2.

 Real World Scenario

Wireless Connection Infrastructure or Ad Hoc?

You might not always be connecting to an access point or router; these connections are considered infrastructure mode connections. An infrastructure mode connection is similar to a wired connection of a PC to an outlet. Instead, you might connect in an ad hoc fashion, which could be a computer-to-computer connection to share information with other wireless network devices without another wireless device acting as an intermediary.

Ad hoc connections exist in a wired environment as well, when we connect two PCs' NICs together by using an Ethernet crossover cable. Securing data transfer in an ad hoc wireless setup is just as important as it is in infrastructure mode because the data is still traversing between devices using radio frequency (RF) and network sniffers today running the wireless adapter promiscuously (in monitor mode) have no problem viewing the data stream. If the data stream is not encrypted, sniffers will have access to it.

For large implementations, there are several vendors supplying wireless access points under the control of a wireless director, which consists of software-based controllers that are responsible for allowing access points on the network, providing user access control, and enforcing encryption policies. For smaller implementations, this control functionality is done manually as the wireless routers or access points are set up.

The security policies put in place are configured on the wireless access device and the wireless client. Windows 10 client components must be set up to match the security settings of the wireless network access devices. During the setup of most wireless access devices provided by the hardware vendor, the administrator will configure the security parameters. Configuring can be done during the setup process and/or through a web browser that can access the wireless access device configuration pages.

Most of our current devices have a built-in web server to allow the HTTP connection from a web browser. Windows 10 also has the ability to configure the wireless access device if the hardware vendor makes it available. If there is no specific component written, you can launch the web browser–based configuration from a convenient location—the Network and Sharing Center.

Whether you have Windows 10 configure the wireless network connection or you perform the setup through the manufacturer's process, you still need to configure your Windows 10 client access.

If you have performed the simplest configuration and there are no security parameters configured (bad idea, by the way), Windows 10 will connect automatically with a quick window showing the wireless network it's connecting to and providing access without much user intervention. Even canceling the screens will produce a successful (nonsecure) connection. This simple configuration process makes connecting a home or small network easy and straightforward for nontechnical users. However, this is not a good solution.

If you have configured wireless network security (a good idea!), then you need to configure the Windows 10 client with the correct settings. Once again, the configuration screens are available from the convenient location known as the Network and Sharing Center.

In Exercise 7.3, you will access the Windows 10 client wireless network properties.

EXERCISE 7.3

Accessing the Windows 10 Wireless Properties

1. Type **Network and Sharing Center** in the Windows 10 integrated search window; press Enter.

2. Choose the Wireless Network Connection item within the View Your Active Networks section of the Network and Sharing Center.

3. Click the Wireless Properties button (shown in Figure 7.14) within the Connection area of the Wi-Fi Status window.

4. The Wireless Network Properties tabbed dialog box opens, displaying the current setup for the wireless network. Click Finish to close the window.

FIGURE 7.14   Wireless Properties button

From the Wireless Network Properties tabbed dialog box, you have the ability to set or change the Windows 10 client configuration. The first tab of the dialog box is the Connection tab (Figure 7.15), which displays the following information.

Name   The name assigned to the wireless network.

SSID   The SSID of the wireless connection. This defines a friendly name for the wireless network. This is normally an ASCII string and is usually broadcast by default, allowing a machine or users to select a wireless network with which to connect. Some wireless access devices will allow more than one SSID to be available (broadcast) at the same time, creating more than one wireless network within the same device.

Network Type   Displays the mode the wireless network is operating in. If the wireless network is in infrastructure mode, this parameter will be Access Point. If the wireless network is ad hoc, this will display Computer-To-Computer.

Network Availability   Displays to whom the wireless network is available—All Users or Me Only, for example.

Connect Automatically When This Network Is In Range   This option, when selected, allows automatic connection for this wireless network. Deselecting (clearing the check mark) requires the user to choose this wireless network for connection.

Look For Other Wireless Networks While Connecting To This Network   Windows 10 will attempt to look for other wireless network connections even though you are connected to a network at the time. This allows a user to see if there is a better network connection available even after you have connected to your wireless access point.

FIGURE 7.15   Wireless Network Properties dialog box's Connection tab

Connect Even If The Network Is Not Broadcasting Its Name (SSID)   If the wireless network you are attempting to connect to is not broadcasting its SSID, you must select this option to allow Windows 10 to automatically connect.

The second tab on the Wireless Network Properties dialog box is Security (Figure 7.16), which allows the configuration of the security parameters as defined in your security policy and configured on your wireless network access devices.

Figure 7.16 shows the Security tab's Security Type drop-down box with the WPA-Personal Security choice selected and Encryption Type with TKIP (Temporal Key Integrity Protocol) selected. You can also see the network security key as hidden text because the Show Characters check box is unchecked.

FIGURE 7.16 Wireless Network Properties Security tab

Configuring Wi-Fi Direct

Think about being able to connect to devices without the use of a WAP. What if we could connect devices directly to each other through the high-speed wireless adapters in those devices? That is exactly what Wi-Fi Direct enables us to do.

Wi-Fi Direct is a technology that allows us to directly access other devices without requiring a separate Wi-Fi access point. Windows 10 uses near-field communication (better known as NFC) technology to allow the Windows 10 system to locate other NFC Wi-Fi enabled devices so that they can be paired together.

When devices are trying to pair together, the Near Field Proximity (NFP) receives pairing information from the device that is trying to connect. NFP then passes the pairing information to Windows 10. Windows 10 Wi-Fi Direct will then automatically follow the Wi-Fi Alliance Out-Of-Box pairing procedures for the connection.

If the pairing process connects, Windows will prompt the user for permission for the connection. If permission is given, Windows 10 will then attempt to finalize the connection. From that point on, there is no other user interaction needed.

Windows 10 gives you the ability to set whether you want to pair with other devices or not. Figure 7.17 shows the Windows 10 Privacy settings and how Windows 10 will sync with other devices.

As you can see in Figure 7.17, you also have the ability to choose which applications can sync with devices. This gives an administrator or user better flexibility on whether to allow all applications to connect to all devices or only specific applications to connect.

FIGURE 7.17   Sync with devices

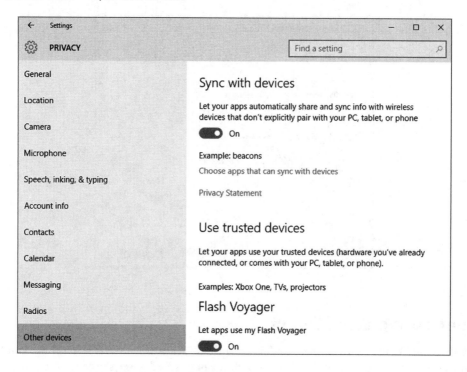

Troubleshooting Wireless Connectivity

There are a few common issues with wireless networking you can look at if you're having problems connecting to your wireless network. Following are a few problems and solutions:

Ensure that your wireless network card is enabled.   Here's one I see regularly: Many newer laptops and tablets have either a switch or a hot-key setting that enables and disables the wireless device. Often, a laptop switch will somehow be turned off, or a user will somehow press the key sequence to shut off the PC's wireless radio. The Physical layer is always a good place to start looking.

Ensure that your wireless card and the access devices are compatible.   Cards that are compatible with the 802.11b standard can connect to only 802.11b or 802.11b/g access devices configured to accept b. Cards using 802.11a can connect to only 802.11a or 802.11a/b/g access devices configured to accept a. An 802.11n card needs to connect to an 802.11n access device for efficiency, although most will autonegotiate to the best specification available. The specification you're using on the card has to be available and turned on in the wireless access device.

Ensure that the access point signal is available.   I find radio frequency (RF) to be a funny thing. You can't see it, and you assume that it is everywhere. Not a good assumption. The output power of the signal might be fine, but the RF power is absorbed or attenuated as it goes through walls, insulation, or water. You need to make sure there is nothing that might be causing interference of the wireless signal.

Ensure that the security parameters are configured alike.   The SSID, encryption type, encryption algorithm, and passphrase/security key have to be set the same on both the wireless access device and the wireless client. Here's another one I see quite often: In the desire to make the initial setup and the secure setup easier for end users, some hardware vendors have a nice little button that allows the network access device to negotiate a secure set of parameters with the client. In one instance, after the wireless network had been working correctly for a while, a failure showed the parameters to be incompatible, thanks in large part to someone pressing the easy button just before the failure.

Ensure automatic connections if the SSID is not being broadcast.   If you are having trouble connecting to a network that does not broadcast its SSID, select the Connect Even If The Network Is Not Broadcasting check box in the Wireless Network Properties dialog box. I have solved several wireless network connection issues with this fix.

Consider how a wireless router interfaces with hard-wired devices.   Many times when I go into a small or midsized network, I find that the company (or home user) is connected to a multifunction type of device. The wireless routers that are often deployed are really quite technologically sophisticated. They have switch ports for connecting hard-wired devices on the private network as well as an Internet port to connect to the outside world. The wireless portion of the device is like another switch port on the private side, allowing the wireless devices to interact with the hard-wired devices.

When I troubleshoot and eliminate issues, I start with the hard-wired devices and see whether they can communicate to each other and the outside (the other side of your wireless router). Try to communicate between the hard-wired and wireless as well, to eliminate the router components. It's also not the best idea to use the wireless network to configure the wireless devices. Configuring through the wireless interface will ultimately cause you to lose connectivity in the middle of a configuration and may force you to connect with the cable, often leaving the access point unusable until you complete the task you started wirelessly.

Understanding TCP/IP

Another item that we need to configure before we can connect a Windows 10 machine to the domain is the protocol that will allow the Windows 10 machine to communicate with other machines. *Transmission Control Protocol/Internet Protocol (TCP/IP)* is the most commonly used network protocol. It is actually a suite of protocols that have evolved into the industry standard for network, internetwork, and Internet connectivity.

As I explained earlier in this chapter, when I teach my Microsoft Windows classes (both server and client classes) I like to use the following example for TCP/IP. Don't think of TCP/IP as IP addresses, think of them as telephone numbers. That's right, think of them as telephone numbers. When you need to contact a server or a website, you call its telephone number (TCP/IP).

Just like telephone numbers, you may need to call Information to get someone's telephone number. Well, we have a form of information on our networks also. We call it Domain Name Service (DNS) servers. That's all DNS does. Its turns a name into a telephone number (name resolution). So when you type in www.willpanek.com, DNS turns willpanek.com into a TCP/IP number so that you can make your call to my website.

Now just as with telephone numbers, there must be some device that acts like the telephone company that issues us our telephone numbers. Well there is, and it's called a Dynamic Host Configuration Protocol (DHCP) server. DHCP gives your users a telephone (TCP/IP) number.

If you think of TCP/IP numbers as telephone numbers, I think it makes it much easier for anyone to understand why we use them and how they work.

> The main protocols providing basic TCP/IP services include Internet Protocol (IP), Transmission Control Protocol (TCP), User Datagram Protocol (UDP), Address Resolution Protocol (ARP), Internet Control Message Protocol (ICMP), and Internet Group Management Protocol (IGMP).

Benefits and Features of TCP/IP

TCP/IP as a protocol suite was accepted as an industry standard in the 1980s and continues to be the primary internetworking protocol today. For a default installation of Windows 10, IPv4 and IPv6 are both installed by default. TCP/IP has the following benefits:

- TCP/IP is the most common protocol and is supported by almost all network operating systems. It is the required protocol for Internet access.

- TCP/IP is dependable and scalable for use in small and large networks.

- Support is provided for connectivity across interconnected networks, independent of the operating systems being used at the upper end of the OSI model or the physical components at the lower end of the OSI model.

- TCP/IP provides standard routing services for moving packets over interconnected network segments. Dividing networks into multiple subnetworks (or subnets) optimizes network traffic and facilitates network management.

- TCP/IP is designed to provide data reliability by providing a connection at the Transport layer and verifying that each data segment is received and passed to the application requiring the data by retransmitting lost information.

- TCP/IP allows for the classification of data in regard to its importance with Quality of Service. This allows important time-sensitive streams of data, such as Voice over IP, to get preferential treatment.

- TCP/IP is designed to be fault tolerant. It is able to dynamically reroute packets if network links become unavailable, assuming alternate paths exist.

- Applications can provide services such as Dynamic Host Configuration Protocol (DHCP) for TCP/IP configuration and Domain Name Service (DNS) for hostname-to-IP-address resolution.

- Windows 10 continues to support Automatic Private IP Addressing (APIPA) used by small, local-connection-only networks without a DHCP server to allow Windows 10 to automatically assign an IP address to itself.

- Support for NetBIOS over TCP/IP (NetBT) is included in Windows 10. NetBIOS is a software specification used for identifying computer resources by name as opposed to IP address. We still use TCP/IP as the network protocol, so we map the NetBIOS name to an IP address.

- The inclusion of Alternate IP Configuration allows users to have a static and a DHCP-assigned IP address mapped to a single network adapter. This feature supports mobile users who roam between different network segments.

- IPv6 incorporates a much larger address space compared to IPv4 and, more important, incorporates many of the additional features of TCP/IP into a standardized protocol. This is important because a vendor that claims to support TCP/IP only has to support the 1980s version and may not support additional features such as Internet Protocol Security (IPSec). IPv6 as a standard includes these features, allowing a more robust network protocol.

Several of the features of TCP/IP included with Windows 10 are as follows:

- Allows a common structure for network communications across a wide variety of hardware and operating systems and a lot of applications that are specifically written to configure and control it.

- TCP/IP connectivity tools allowing access to a variety of hosts across a TCP/IP network. TCP/IP tools in Windows 10 include clients for HTTP, FTP, TFTP, Telnet, Finger, and so forth. Server components for the tools are available to install as well.

- Inclusion of a Simple Network Management Protocol (SNMP) agent that can be used to monitor performance and resource use of a TCP/IP host, server, or network hardware devices.

- TCP/IP management and diagnostic tools for maintenance and diagnostic support. TCP/IP management and diagnostic commands include `ipconfig`, `arp`, `ping`, `nbtstat`, `netsh`, `route`, `nslookup`, `tracert`, and `pathping`.

- Support for TCP/IP network printing, enabling you to print to networked print devices.

- Logical and physical multihoming, enabling multiple IP addresses on a single computer for single or multiple network adapters. Multiple network adapters installed on a single computer are normally associated with routing for internetwork connectivity.

- Support for internal IP routing, which enables a Windows 10 computer to route packets among multiple network adapters installed in one machine.

- Support for virtual private networks, which enable you to transmit data securely across a public network via encapsulated and encrypted packets.

Basics of IP Addressing and Configuration

Before you can configure TCP/IP, you should have a basic understanding of TCP/IP configuration and addressing. Let's review TCP/IP addressing. To configure a TCP/IP client, you must specify an IP address, subnet mask, and default gateway (if you're going to communicate outside your local network). Depending on your network, you might want to configure a DNS server, a domain name, or maybe even a WINS server.

You can see the Windows 10 IPv4 Properties window in Figure 7.18. I have included it here because I am going to discuss the different configuration items in the following sections. Although normally set up for automatic configuration, these parameters have been manually assigned in this figure for clarity.

FIGURE 7.18   Windows 10 TCP/IP version 4 properties

Understanding IPv4 Address Types

The IPv4 address scheme is one of two used by the Internet today, and TCP/IP is the only network protocol used by the Internet. There are three types of IPv4 addresses: broadcast, multicast, and unicast.

A *broadcast address* is read by all hosts that hear it (the broadcast will not go across a router, so only local devices hear the broadcast). The IPv4 broadcast address is 255.255.255.255; every single bit is a 1.

A *multicast address* is a special address that one or more devices will listen for by joining a multicast group. Only the local devices configured to listen for the address will respond and process the data in the multicast packet. A multicast address will have a value between 224 and 239 in the first octet (the leftmost number in the dotted decimal representation). A multicast example is 224.0.0.5.

A *unicast address* uniquely identifies a computer or device on the network. An IPv4 unicast address is a 32-bit address represented as dotted decimal (an example is 131.107.1.200). Each number in the dotted decimal notation is a decimal representation of 8 bits, and the value of each is between 0 and 255 (255 is the numerically largest value that 8 bits can represent). A portion of the IPv4 unicast address is used to identify the network the device is on (or the network of a destination device), and a portion is used to identify the individual host on the local network or the unique host on a remote network.

IPv4 Address Classes

There are three classes of unicast IP addresses defined. Depending on the class you use, different parts of the address show the default network portion of the address and the host address. Table 7.1 shows the three classes of network addresses and the number of networks and hosts available for each network class.

TABLE 7.1   IPv4 class assignments

Network Class	Address Range of First Octet	Number of Unique Networks Available	Number of Unique Hosts per Network
A	1–126	126	16,777,214
B	128–191	16,384	65,534
C	192–223	2,097,152	254

As you probably noticed, 127 is missing from the address ranges. 127.0.0.1 is the diagnostic loopback address, and because of that, no commercial TCP/IP range can start with 127.

The number of octets you can use for either the network ID or the host ID depends on which class you use for your network. For example, if I own a Class B address of

131.107.0.0, the first two octets (131.107) would be the network ID and the last two octets would be the host ID. Table 7.2 shows you the different classes and which octets are the network ID (represented by X) and which octets are the host ID (represented by Y). You are allowed to manipulate only the host IDs (Y) for your organization unless you are using a private IP address scheme.

TABLE 7.2 IPv4 network and host octets

Class	Example	Network ID	Host ID
A	17.1.10.10 (X.Y.Y.Y)	17 (X)	1.10.10 (Y.Y.Y)
B	131.107.14.240 (X.X.Y.Y)	131.107 (X.X)	14.240 (Y.Y)
C	192.168.1.10 (X.X.X.Y)	192.168.1 (X.X.X)	10 (Y)

IPv4 Subnet Mask

The *subnet mask* is used to specify which portion of the unicast IPv4 address defines the network value and which portion defines the unique host value. The subnet mask can be shown either as a dotted decimal, as with 255.255.255.0, or as a slash notation (called Classless Inter-Domain Routing, or CIDR), as in /24. The CIDR representation is the number of bits turned on in the subnet mask. For example, 255.255.224.0 is actually 11111111.11111111.11100000.00000000 (1s are on bits and 0s are off), which equals 19 bits turned on, or /19.

The standard for classful network addressing defines subnet masks for each class, as shown in Table 7.3.

TABLE 7.3 IPv4 default class subnet masks

Class	Default Mask	Slash Notation (CIDR)
A	255.0.0.0	/8
B	255.255.0.0	/16
C	255.255.255.0	/24

Another task of the subnet mask is to break down the ranges of your network. For example, 255.255.255.224 allows for six subnets. There should be six TCP/IP ranges that go with the six subnets. Table 7.4 shows the ranges for the different subnet masks.

TABLE 7.4   Subnet mask ranges

Subnet Mask Number	Ranges
255	1
254	2
252	4
248	8
240	16
224	32
192	64
128	128

What does this chart mean to you? Well, let's say that you have a subnet mask of 255.255.255.224. Because 224 allows for six subnets, the six ranges are in increments of 32. Table 7.5 shows a Class C subnet range for 224. Remember, in any range, you can't use the first number of the range (network ID) or the last number of any range (broadcast).

TABLE 7.5   Class C 224 subnet mask ranges

Subnets	Range	Usable
Range 1	32–63	33–62
Range 2	64–95	65–94
Range 3	96–127	97–126
Range 4	128–159	129–158
Range 5	160–191	161–190
Range 6	192–223	193–222

If this were a Class B subnet mask, the ranges would include a second octet that you would work with. Table 7.6 shows a Class B 224 subnet mask.

TABLE 7.6   Class B 224 subnet mask range

Subnets	Range	Usable
Range 1	32.0–63.255	32.1–63.254
Range 2	64.0–95.255	64.1–95.254
Range 3	96.0–127.255	96.1–127.254
Range 4	128.0–159.255	128.1–159.254
Range 5	160.0–191.255	160.1–191.254
Range 6	192.0–223.255	192.1–223.254

If this were a Class A subnet mask, the ranges would include three octets that you would work with. Table 7.7 shows a Class A 224 subnet mask.

TABLE 7.7   Class A 224 subnet mask range

Subnets	Range	Usable
Range 1	32.0.0–63.255.255	32.0.1–63.255.254
Range 2	64.0.0–95.255.255	64.0.1–95.255.254
Range 3	96.0.0–127.255.255	96.0.1–127.255.254
Range 4	128.0.0–159.255.255	128.0.1–159.255.254
Range 5	160.0.0–191.255.255	160.0.1–191.255.254
Range 6	192.0.0–223.255.255	192.0.1–223.255.254

Using IPv6 Addresses

Through most of this discussion, we have been referencing TCP/IP as the network protocol. However, you should remember that it is really a suite of protocols running in Layer 3 and Layer 4 of the OSI model. Internet Protocol (IP) is the Layer 3 protocol responsible for assigning devices globally unique addresses (that is, unique in a whole company for private addresses and unique across the whole Internet for public addresses).

When the TCP/IP standard was adopted in the 1980s, it was unimaginable that we would ever need more than 4 billion addresses that are possible with IPv4, but with the dramatic growth of the use of computers in the home and workplace today we do. In the 1990s, programmers realized that a new Layer 3 was going to be needed. This was not an easy task, and integration into the existing infrastructure was going to take a long time. An interim solution known as Network Address Translation (NAT) and Port Address Translation (PAT) emerged. NAT/PAT allowed more than one device to use the same IP address on a private network as long as there was one Internet address available. Cool enough, but this is not the real solution. IPv6 is the solution to the IPv4 address depletion.

As time has progressed from the IPv4 standard acceptance in the 1980s, we have needed new and better functionality. However, the way the standards process works around the world is that you can add functionality, but it may or may not be supported in any vendor's TCP/IPv4 network stack. What happened in IPv6 is that not only did the address space increase in size, but the additional functionality that may or may not have been included before has become part of the IPv6 standard.

For example, IPv4 is defined as having a variable-length header, which is cumbersome because we need to read an additional piece of data to see how big the header is. Most of the time, the header stays the same, so why not just fix its length and add an extension to the header if we need to carry more information? IPv6 uses a fixed-length IP header with the capability of carrying more information in an extension to the header, known as an *extension header*.

Microsoft has been including IPv6 in its operating systems since NT 4.0; it just has not been enabled by default. Windows 10 (as did Vista and Windows 7/8) natively supports both IPv4 and IPv6. The main differences you will notice between IPv4 and IPv6 are the format and size of the IP address. IPv6 addresses are 128 bits, typically written as eight groups of four hexadecimal characters. IPv4 addresses, as you saw earlier, are 32 bits—four decimal representations of eight bits. Each of the eight groups of characters in an IPv6 address is separated by a colon; for example, 2001:4860:0000:0000:0012:10FF:FECD:00EF.

Leading zeros can be omitted, so we can write our example address as 2001:4860:0:0: 12:10FF:FECD:EF. Additionally, a double colon can be used to compress a set of consecutive zeros, so we could write our example address as 2001:4860::12:10FF:FECD:EF. The IPv6 address is 128 bits; when you see a double colon, it's a variable that says to fill enough zeros within the colons to make the address 128 bits. You can have only one set of double colons; two variables in one address won't work.

Will IPv6 take over the global address space soon? Even with IPv4's lack of address space, we are going to continue to use it for many years. The integration of IPv6 into the infrastructure is going to happen as a joint venture with IPv4 and IPv6 running at the same time in the devices and on some networks.

There are many mechanisms for enabling IPv6 communications over an IPv4 network, including the following:

- Dual stack—A computer or device running both the IPv4 and IPv6 protocol stacks at the same time
- ISATAP—Intra-Site Automatic Tunnel Addressing Protocol

- 6to4—An encapsulation technique for putting IPv6 addresses inside IPv4 addresses
- Teredo tunneling—Another encapsulation technique for putting IPv6 traffic inside an IPv4 packet

Some IPv6-to-IPv4 dynamic translation techniques require that a computer's IPv4 address be used as the last 32 bits of the IPv6 address. When these translation techniques are used, it is common to write the last 32 bits as you would typically write an IPv4 address, such as 2001:4850::F8:192.168.122.26.

There are two ways to receive a TCP/IP address (for either IPv4 or IPv6): You can manually assign a TCP/IP address to the Windows 10 machine, or the Windows 10 machine can use DHCP.

There are several elements of the IPv4 protocol that could use some enhancements. Other elements have been added to IPv4 as extras to provide more functionality. IPv6 is designed to incorporate these enhancement/changes directly into the protocol specification.

The new concepts and new implementation of old concepts in IPv6 include the following:

- Larger address space (128-bit vs. 32-bit).
- Autoconfiguration of Internet-accessible addresses with or without DHCP (without DHCP it's called stateless autoconfiguration).
- More efficient IP header (fewer fields and no checksum).
- Fixed-length IP header (IPv4 header is variable length) with extension headers beyond the standard fixed length to provide enhancements.
- Built-in IP mobility and security (although available in IPv4, the IPv6 implementation is much better implementation).
- Built-in transition schemes to allow integration of the IPv4 and IPv6 spaces.
- ARP broadcast messages are replaced with multicast request.

128-bit Address Space   The new 128-bit address space will provide unique addresses for the foreseeable future. I would like to say we will never use up all the addresses, but history may prove me wrong. The number of unique addresses in the IPv6 space is 2^{128} or 3.4×10^{38} addresses. How big is that number? Enough for toasters and refrigerators (and maybe even cars) to all have their own addresses? Why yes, I believe it is.

For a point of reference, the nearest black hole to Earth is 1,600 light years away. If you were to stack 4 mm BB pellets from here to the nearest black hole and back, you would need 7.6×1021 BBs. This means you could uniquely address each BB from Earth to the black hole and back and still have quite a few addresses left over.

Or how about this: The IPv6 address space is big enough to provide well over 1 million addresses per square inch of the surface area of the earth (oceans included). No more running out of addresses for the Internet!

Stateful vs. Stateless Autoconfiguration   Autoconfiguration is another added/improved feature of IPv6. When you are choosing to use DHCP in IPv6, you can choose to set your systems up for Stateful or Stateless configuration. Stateful is what we currently do today with IPv4. Stateful means that DHCP is going to give our IPv6 clients all of their TCP/IP data (IP address, default gateway, and all DHCP options).

What if a Windows 10 client could ask the network itself what network it's on and, based on that information, create its own IP address and default gateway. Well, that is what Stateless configuration does. Stateless configuration means that the client's address is based on the router's advertisement messages. What this means is that the client creates their own IP address and default gateway based on the router's advertisement message and their MAC address. They can still get all of the other DHCP options, but they will not get an IP address and default gateway from DHCP.

Improved IPv6 Header   The IPv6 header is more efficient than the IPv4 header because it is fixed length (with extensions possible) and has only a few fields. The IPv6 header consists of a total of 40 bytes, which is broken down as follows: 32 bytes for source and destination IPv6 addresses and 8 bytes for version field, traffic class field, flow label field, payload length field, next header field, and hop limit field.

We don't waste time with a checksum validation anymore, and we don't have to include the length of the IP header since it's fixed in IPv6; the IP header is variable length in IPv4, so the length must be included as a field.

IPv6 Mobility   IPv6 is only a replacement of the OSI Layer 3 component; we are going to continue to use the TCP (and UDP) components as they currently exist; however, a TCP issue is addressed by IPv6. TCP is connection oriented, meaning we establish an end-to-end communication path with sequencing and acknowledgments before we ever send any data, and then we have to acknowledge all pieces of data sent. This is done through a combination of an IP address, port number, and port type (socket).

If the source IP address changes, the TCP connection may be disrupted. But then, how often does this happen? More and more often, because more people are walking around with a wireless laptop or a wireless Voice over IP (VoIP) telephone. IPv6 mobility adds the capability by establishing a TCP connection with a home address, and when changing networks, it continues to communicate with the original endpoint from a care-of address as it changes LANs, which sends all traffic back through the home address. The handing off of network addresses does not disrupt the TCP connection state (the original TCP port number and address stay intact).

Improved Security   IPv6 has security built in. Internet Protocol security (IPsec) is a component we use today to authenticate and encrypt secure tunnels from a source to a destination. This can be from the client to the server or between gateways. IPv4 lets us do this by enhancing IP header functionality (basically adding a second IP header while encrypting everything behind it). In IPv6, we add this as standard functionality by using extension headers. Extension headers are inserted into the packet only if they are needed. Each header has a "next header" field, which identifies the next piece of information. The extension headers currently identified for IPv6 are Hop-By-Hop Options, Routing, Fragment, Destination Options, Authentication, and Encapsulating Security Payload. The authentication header and Encapsulating Security Payload header are the IPsec-specific control headers.

IPv4-to-IPv6 Transmission   There are several mechanisms in place in IPv6 to make the IPv4 to IPv6 transition easy:

- A simple dual-stack implementation where both IPv4 and IPv6 are installed and used is certainly an option. In most situations (so far), this doesn't work so well because most of us aren't connected to an IPv6 network and our Internet connection is not IPv6 even if we're using IPv6 internally. So Microsoft includes other mechanisms that can be used in several different circumstances.

- *Intra-Site Automatic Tunnel Addressing Protocol (ISATAP)* is an automatic tunneling mechanism used to connect an IPv6 network to an IPv4 address space that does not use NAT. ISATAP treats the IPv4 space as one big logical link connection space.

- *6to4* is a mechanism used to transition to IPv4. This method, like ISATAP, treats the IPv4 address space as a Logical Link Layer with each IPv6 space in transition using a 6to4 router to create endpoints using the IPv4 space as a point-to-point connection (kind of like a WAN, eh?). 6to4 implementations still do not work well through a NAT, although a 6to4 implementation using an Application Layer Gateway (ALG) is certainly doable.

- *Teredo* is a mechanism that allows users behind a NAT to access the IPv6 space by tunneling IPv6 packets in UDP.

Pseduointerfaces are used in these mechanisms to create a usable interface for the operating system. Another interesting feature of IPv6 is that addresses are assigned to interfaces (or pseudointerfaces), not simply to the end node. Your Windows Server 2012 R2 will have several unique IPv6 addresses assigned.

New Broadcast Methods   IPv6 has moved away from using broadcasting. The three types of packets used in IPv6 are unicast, multicast, and anycast. IPv6 clients then must use one of these types to get the MAC address of the next Ethernet hop (default gateway). IPv6 makes use of multicasting for this along with new functionality of neighbor discovery. Not only does ARP utilize new functionality, but ICMP (also a Layer 3 protocol) is redone and known as ICMP6. ICMP6 is used for messaging (packet too large, time exceeded, and so on) as it was in IPv4, but it also is used for the messaging of IPv6 mobility. ICMP6 echo request and ICMP6 echo reply are still used for ping.

Additionally, there are several concepts to consider in IPv6 addressing. The format of the address has changed since IPv4 and we must get used to seeing/using it. There are three types of addresses we will use as well as predefined values used within the address space. You need to get used to seeing these addresses and being able to identify their uses.

IPv6 Address Format

For the design of IPv4 addresses, remember that we present addresses as octets or the decimal (base 10) representation of 8 bits. Four octets add up to the 32 bits required. IPv6 expands the address space to 128 bits, and the representation is for the most part shown in *hexadecimal* (a notation used to represent 8 bits using the values 0–9 and A–F). The following is an example of a full IPv6 address: 2001:0DB8:0000:0000:1234:0000:A9FE:133E.

You can tell the implementation of DNS will make life a lot easier for even those of us who like to ping the address in lieu of the name. Fortunately, DNS already has the ability to handle IPv6 addresses with the use of an AAAA record. (*A* is short for *alias*.) An A record in IPv4's addressing space is 32 bits, so an AAAA record—4 *As*—is 128 bits. The Windows Server 2012 R2 DNS server handles the AAAA and the reverse pointer (PTR) records for IPv6.

9.3.3.2 IPv6 Address Shortcuts

Here are some shortcuts you can use for writing an IPv6 address:

- :0: stands for:0000:

- You can leave out preceding 0s in any 16-bit word.

   For example, :DB8: and:0DB8: are equivalent.

- :: is a variable standing for enough zeros to round out the address to 128 bits.

   :: can be used only once in an address.

You can use these shortcuts to represent the example address 2001:0DB8:0000:0000:12 34:0000:A9FE:133E as shown here:

- Compress :0000: into :0:

   2001:0DB8:0000:0000:1234:0:A9FE:133E

- Eliminate preceding zeros:

   2001:DB8:0000:0000:1234:0:A9FE:133E

- Use the special variable shortcut for multiple zeros:

   2001:DB8::1234:0:A9FE:133E

You can also use *prefix notation* or slash notation when discussing IPv6 networks. The network of the example address can be represented as 2001:DB8:0000:0000:0000:0000:0 000:0000. This can also be expressed as 2001:DB8:: /32. The /32 indicates 32 bits of network, and 2001:DB8: is 32 bits of network.

IPv6 Address Assignment

So do we subnet IPv6? The answer depends on your definition of subnetting. If you are given 32 bits of network from your ISP, you have 96 bits to work with. If you use some of the 96 bits to route within your network infrastructure, then you are subnetting. In this context you do subnet IPv6. However, given the huge number of bits you have available, I can say with confidence that variable length subnet masking (VLSM) will no longer need to be implemented. For example, Microsoft has a network space of 2001:4898:: /32. That gives the administrators a space of 96 bits (2^{96} = 79,228,162,514,264,337,593,543,950,336 unique addresses using all 96 bits) to work with.

We can let Windows Server 2012 R2 dynamically or automatically assign its IPv6 address, or we can still assign it manually. With dynamic/automatic assignment, the IPv6 address is assigned either by a DHCPv6 server or by the Windows Server 2012 R2 machine itself. If no DHCPv6 server is configured, Windows Server 2012 R2 can query the local

LAN segment to find a router with a configured IPv6 interface. If so, the server will assign itself an address on the same IPv6 network as the router interface and set its default gateway to the router interface's IPv6 address.

To see your configured IP addresses (IPv4 and IPv6), you can still use the ipconfig command. We have configured a static IPv4 and IPv6 address on our server. The IPv6 address is the same as used in the previous example IPv6 address.

IPv6 Address Types

There are three types of addresses in IPv6: anycast, unicast, and multicast.

 You will notice that there is an absence of the broadcast type that is included in IPv4. IPv6 does not use broadcasts; they're replaced with multicasts.

Anycast Addresses   Anycast addresses are not really new. The concept of anycast existed in IPv4 but was not widely used. An anycast address is an IPv6 address assigned to multiple devices (usually different devices). When an anycast packet is sent, it is delivered to one of the devices, usually the closest one.

Unicast Addresses   A unicast packet uniquely identifies an interface of an IPv6 device. The interface can be a virtual or *pseudointerface* or a real (physical) interface.

 Real World Scenario

Unicast vs. Anycast

Unicast and anycast addresses look the same and may be indistinguishable from each other; it only depends on how many devices have the same address. If only one device has a globally unique IPv6 address, it's a unicast address; if more than one device has the same address, it's an anycast address. Both unicast and anycast are considered one-to-one communication, although you could say anycast is one-to-"one of many."

There are several types of unicast addresses, as described here:

Global Unicast Address   As of this writing, the *global unicast address* space is defined as 2000:: /3. 2001::/32 are the IPv6 addresses being issued to business entities. I mentioned before that Microsoft has been allocated 2001:4898:: /32. You'll find most example addresses listed as 2001:DB8:: /32; this space has been reserved for documentation. A DHCPv6 server would be set up with scopes (ranges of addresses to be assigned) within this address space. There are some special addresses and address formats you will see in use as well. Do you remember the loopback address in IPv4—127.0.0.1? In IPv6, the loopback address is::1 (or

0:0:0:0:0:0:0:0001). You may also see an address with dotted decimal used. A dual-stack Windows Server 2012 R2 may also show you FE80::5EFE:192.168.1.200. This address form is used in an integration/migration model of IPv6 (or if you just can't leave the dotted decimal era).

Link-Local Address *Link-local addresses* are defined as FE80:: /10. If you look at the `ipconfig` command, you will see the link-local IPv6 address as FE80::a425:ab9d:7da4:ccba. The last 8 bytes (64 bits) are random to ensure a high probability of randomness for the link-local address.

The link-local address is to be used on a single link (network segment) and should never be routed.

There is another form of the link-local IPv6 address called the Extended User Interface 64-bit (EUI-64) format. This is derived by using the MAC address of the physical interface and inserting an FFFE between the third and fourth bytes of the MAC. The first byte is also made 02, which sets the universal/local or U/L bit to 1 as defined in IEEE 802 frame specification. Again, looking at `ipconfig`, the EUI-64 address would take the physical (MAC) address 00–03–FF–11–02–CD and make the link-local IPv6 address FE80::0203:FFFF:FE11:02CD. I've left the preceding zeros in the link-local IPv6 address to make it easier for you to pick out the MAC address with the FFFE inserted.

AnonymousAddress Microsoft Server 2012 R2 uses the random address by default instead of EUI-64. The random value is called the AnonymousAddress in Microsoft Server 2012 R2. It can be modified to allow the use of EUI-64.

Unique Local Address The unique local address can be FC00 or FD00 and is used like the private address space of IPv4. Unique local addresses are described in RFC 4193. They are not expected to be routable on the global Internet. They are routable inside a more limited area, such as a site. They may also be routed between a limited set of sites.

Multicast Address Multicast addresses are one-to-many communication packets. Multicast packets are identifiable by their first byte (most significant byte, leftmost byte, leftmost 2 nibbles, leftmost 8 bits, etc.). A multicast address is defined as FF00::/8.

In the second byte shown (the 00 of FF00), the second 0 is what's called the scope. Interface local is 01; link-local is 02. FF01:: is an interface local multicast.

There are several well-known (already defined) multicast addresses. For example, if you want to send a packet to all nodes in the local link scope, you send the packet to FF02::1 (also shown as FF02:0:0:0:0:0:0:1). The all-routers multicast address is FF02::2.

We also use multicasting to get the logical link layer address (MAC address) of a device we are trying to communicate with. Instead of using the ARP mechanism of IPv4, IPv6 uses the ICMPv6 neighbor solicitation (NS) and neighbor advertisement (NA) messages. The NS and NA ICMPv6 messages are all part of the new Neighbor Discovery Protocol (NDP). This new ICMPv6 functionality also includes router solicitation and router advertisements as well as redirect messages (similar to the IPv4 redirect functionality).

Table 7.8 outlines the IPv6 address space known prefixes and some well-known addresses.

TABLE 7.8 IPv6 address space known prefixes and addresses

Address Prefix	Scope of Use
2000:: /3	Global unicast space prefix
FE80:: /10	Local link address prefix
FC00:: /7	Unique local unicast prefix
FF00:: /8	Multicast prefix
2001:DB8:: /32	Global unicast prefix used for documentation
::1	Reserved local loopback address
2001:0000: /32	Teredo prefix*
2002:: /16	6to4 prefix*

IPv6 Integration/Migration

It's time to get into the mindset of integrating IPv6 into your existing infrastructure with the longer goal of migrating over to IPv6. This is not going to be an "OK, Friday the Internet is changing over" rollout. We are going to bring about the change as a controlled implementation. It could easily be three to five years before a solid migration occurs and probably longer. The migration is just below getting the world migrated to the metric system on the overall timeline. The process of integration/migration is made up of several mechanisms:

- Dual stack—Simply running both IPv4 and IPv6 on the same network, utilizing the IPv4 address space for devices only using IPv4 addresses and utilizing the IPv6 address space for devices using IPv6 addresses

- Tunneling—Using an encapsulation scheme for transporting one address space inside another

- Address translation—Using a higher-level application to transparently change one address type (IPv4 or IPv6) to the other so end devices are unaware one address space is talking to another

IPv6 Dual Stack

The default implementation in Windows 10 is an enabled IPv6 configured along with IPv4; this is dual stack. The implementation can be dual IP Layer or dual TCP/IP stack. Windows 10 uses the dual IP Layer implementation. When an application queries a DNS server to resolve a hostname to an IP address, the DNS server may respond with an IPv4 address or an IPv6 address.

If the DNS server responds with both, Windows 10 will prefer the IPv6 addresses. Windows 10 can use both IPv4 and IPv6 addresses as necessary for network communication. When looking at the output of the ipconfig command, you will see both address spaces displayed.

IPv6 Tunneling

Windows 10 includes several tunneling mechanisms for tunneling IPv6 through the IPv4 address space. They include the following:

- ISATAP—Intra-Site Automatic Tunnel Addressing Protocol used for unicast IPv6 communication across an IPv4 infrastructure. ISATAP is enabled by default in Windows Server 2008.

- 6to4—Used for unicast IPv6 communication across an IPv4 infrastructure.

- Teredo—Used for unicast IPv6 communication with an IPv4 NAT implementation across an IPv4 infrastructure.

With multiple tunneling protocols available and enabled by default, you might ask what the difference is and why one is used over the others. They all allow us to tunnel IPv6 packets through the IPv4 address space (a really cool thing if you're trying to integrate/migrate).

ISATAP   ISATAP is the automatic tunnel addressing protocol providing IPv6 addresses based on the IPv4 address of the end interface (node). The IPv6 address is automatically configured on the local device, and the dual-stack machine can use either its IPv4 or IPv6 address to communicate on the local network (within the local network infrastructure). ISATAP can use the neighbor discovery mechanism to determine the router ID and network prefix where the device is located, thus making intrasite communication possible even in a routed infrastructure.

The format of an ISATAP address is [64 bits of prefix] [32 bits indicating ISATAP] [32 bits IPv4 address].

The center 32 bits indicating ISATAP are actually 0000:5EFE (when using private IPv4 addresses). The ISATAP address of my Windows 10 machine using the link-local IPv6 address is FE80::5EFE:192.168.1.200. Each node participating in the ISATAP infrastructure must support ISATAP. If you're routing through an IPv4 cloud, a border router (a router transitioning from an IPv6 to IPv4 space) must support ISATAP. Windows 10 can be configured as a border router and will forward ISATAP packets. ISATAP is experimental and is defined in RFC 4214.

6to4   6to4 specifies a procedure for IPv6 networks to communicate with each other through an IPv4 space without having the IPv6 nodes having to know what's going on.

The IPv6 nodes do not need to be dual stacked to make this happen. The border router is the device responsible for knowing about the IPv6-to-IPv4 transition. The IPv6 packets are encapsulated at the border router and decapsulated at the other end or on the way back. There is an assigned prefix for the 6to4 implementation; 2002:: /16. 6to4 is defined in RFC 3056.

Teredo   Teredo (named after a genus of shipworm that drills holes in the wood of ships) is a protocol designed to allow IPv6 addresses to be available to hosts through one or more layers of NAT. Teredo uses a process of tunneling packets through the IPv4 space using UDP. The Teredo service encapsulates the IPv6 data within a UDP segment (packet) and uses an IPv4 address to get through the IPv4 cloud. Having a Layer 4 (Transport Layer) available to use as a translation functionality is what gives us the ability to be behind a NAT. Teredo provides host-to-host communication and dynamic addressing for IPv6 nodes (dual stack), allowing the nodes to have access to resources in an IPv6 network and the IPv6 devices to have access to the IPv6 devices that have connectivity only to the IPv4 space (just as home users who have an IPv6-enabled operating system connecting to IPv6 resources and their home ISP have only IPv4 capabilities). Teredo is defined in RFC 4380.

In Windows 10, an IPv4 Teredo server is identified and configured (using the netsh command interface). The Teredo server provides connectivity resources (address) to the Teredo client (the node that has access to the IPv4 Internet and needs access to an IPv6 network/ Internet). A Teredo relay is a component used by the IPv6 router to receive traffic destined for Teredo clients and forward the traffic appropriately. The defined prefix for Teredo addresses is 2001:: /32 (does it look better like this? – 2001:0000:: /32). Teredo does add overhead like all the implementations discussed. It is generally accepted that we should use the simplest model available. However, in the process of integration/migration for most of us behind a NAT, Teredo will be the process to choose.

From Windows 10, use the ipconfig /all command to view the default configurations including IPv4 and IPv6. You may notice a notation we didn't discuss: the percent sign at the end of the IPv6 address. The number after the percent sign is the virtual interface identifier used by Windows 10.

Information Commands Useful with IPv6

There are numerous commands you can use to view, verify, and configure the network parameters of Windows 10. You can use the netsh command set and the route command set, as well as the standard ping and tracert functions.

Use the netsh command interface to examine and configure IPv6 functionality (as well as the provided dialog boxes if you like). The netsh command issued from the command interpreter changes into a network shell (netsh) where you can configure and view both IPv4 and IPv6 components.

Don't forget to use the ever-popular route print command to see the Windows 10 routing tables (IPv4 and IPv6). The other diagnostic commands are still available for IPv4 as well as IPv6. In previous versions of Microsoft operating systems, ping was the IPv4 command and ping6 was the IPv6 command.

This has changed for Windows 10; ping works for both IPv4 and IPv6 to test Layer 3 connectivity to remote devices. The IPv4 tracert command was tracert6 for IPv6. The command is now tracert for both IPv4 and IPv6 and will show you every Layer 3 (IP) hop from source to destination (assuming all the administrators from here to there want you to see the hops and are not blocking ICMP and also assuming there are not IP tunnels your packets are traversing; you won't see the router hops in the tunnel either).

Overall, the consortium of people making up development of the Internet and Internet protocols have tried to make all changes to communication infrastructures easy to implement (this is a daunting task with so many vendors and various infrastructures currently in place).

The goal is not to daze and confuse administrators; it's to provide the most flexibility with the greatest functionality. IPv6 is going to provide the needed Layer 3 (Network

Layer, Global Addressing Layer, Logical Addressing Layer. . . call it what you like) functionality for the foreseeable future.

Configuring TCP/IP on Windows 10

Windows 10 can use either IPv4 or IPv6 to communicate with other machines on a network, but the Windows 10 machine must receive the TCP/IP address. There are two ways that a Windows 10 machine can get a TCP/IP address: statically or dynamically.

Assigning Static TCP/IP Numbers

As an administrator, it may be necessary to configure a Windows 10 machine manually (static configuration). To do so, you must know the following:

- Which TCP/IP address the machine will receive
- What the subnet mask is for the segment
- What the default gateway (router's TCP/IP address) is
- What the DNS server TCP/IP addresses are

Complete Exercise 7.4 to configure a Windows 10 machine to use a static TCP/IP address. This example uses TCP/IP addresses for a local network, but you can use your own TCP/IP addresses if you know what they should be.

EXERCISE 7.4

Configuring a Static TCP/IP Address

1. Type **Network and Sharing Center** in the Windows 10 integrated search box.

2. In the Network And Sharing Center window, click the Local Area Connection item in the View Your Active Networks section.

3. Click the Properties button from the Activity section of the Local Area Connection Status box.

4. In the Local Area Connection Properties dialog box, click to highlight (do not deselect the check box) Internet Protocol Version 4 (TCP/IPv4) and click the Properties button. Manual configuration will work with both IPv4 and IPv6.

5. Under the General tab, click the Use The Following IP Address radio button. Type in the following (unless you want or know your own settings):

    IP Address: **192.168.1.50**

    Subnet Mask: **255.255.255.0**

    Default Gateway: **192.168.1.1**

6. Click the Use The Following DNS Server Addresses radio button and type **4.2.2.2** (unless you want to use your own settings) in the TCP/IP Address field.

7. Click OK.

Configuring a Windows 10 Machine to Use DHCP

Dynamic IP configuration assumes that you have a DHCP server on your network that is reachable by the DHCP clients. DHCP servers are configured to automatically provide DHCP clients with all their IP configuration information, including IP address, subnet mask, and DNS server.

For large networks, DHCP is the easiest and most reliable way of managing IP configurations. By default, a Windows 10 machine is configured as a DHCP client for dynamic IP configuration.

Complete Exercise 7.5 to configure a Windows 10 machine to use a dynamic IP configuration.

EXERCISE 7.5

Using DHCP

1. Type **Network and Sharing Center** in the Windows 10 integrated search box.

2. In the Network And Sharing Center window, click the Local Area Connection item in the View Your Active Networks section.

3. Click the Properties button from the Activity section of the Local Area Connection Status box.

4. In the Local Area Connection Properties dialog box, click to select (do not deselect the check box) Internet Protocol Version 4 (TCP/IPv4) and click the Properties button. DHCP will work with both IPv4 and IPv6.

5. Choose the Obtain An IP Address Automatically radio button from the General tab of the Internet Protocol Version 4 (TCP/IPv4) Properties dialog box.

6. Choose the Obtain DNS Server Address Automatically radio button from the General tab of the Internet Protocol Version 4 (TCP/IPv4) Properties dialog box.

7. To use this configuration, click OK to accept the selection and close the dialog box. To exit without saving (if you had a valid static configuration), choose Cancel.

If you are using DHCP and you are not connecting to other machines properly, you can type **ipconfig /all** at a command prompt to see what your TCP/IP address is. If your TCP/IP address starts with 169.254.*x.x*, you are not connecting to the DHCP server. Instead, your Windows 10 machine is using APIPA.

Understanding APIPA

Automatic Private IP Addressing (APIPA) is used to automatically assign private IP addresses for home or small business networks that contain a single subnet, have no DHCP server, and are not using static IP addressing. If APIPA is being used, clients will be able to communicate only with other clients on the same subnet that are also using APIPA. The benefit of using APIPA in small networks is that it is less tedious and has less chance of configuration errors than statically assigning IP addresses and configuration.

APIPA is used with Windows 10 under the following conditions:

- When the client is configured as a DHCP client but no DHCP server is available to service the DHCP request

- When the client originally obtained a DHCP lease from a DHCP server but when the client tried to renew the DHCP lease, the DHCP server was unavailable and the lease period expired

APIPA uses a Class B network address space that has been reserved for its use. The address space is the 169.254.0.0 network, where the range of 169.254.0.1–169.254.255.254 is available for the host to assign to itself. APIPA uses the following process:

1. The Windows 10 client attempts to use a DHCP server for its configuration, but no DHCP servers respond.

2. The Windows 10 client selects a random address from the 169.254.0.1–169.254.255.254 range of addresses and will use a subnet mask of 255.255.0.0.

3. The client uses a duplicate address-detection method to verify that the address it selected is not already in use on the network.

4. If the address is already in use, the client repeats steps 1 and 2. If the address is not already in use, the client configures its network interface with the address it randomly selected. Given the number of the address the APIPA client can select from (65,534 addresses), the odds of selecting a duplicate are very slim.

5. The Windows 10 network client continues to search for a DHCP server every five minutes. If a DHCP server replies to the request, the APIPA configuration is dropped, and the client receives new IP configuration settings from the DHCP server.

You can determine whether your network interface has been configured using APIPA by looking at your IP address from the command prompt by using the `ipconfig /all` command.

Testing Your IP Configuration

After you have installed and configured the TCP/IP settings, you can test the IP configuration by using the `ipconfig`, `ping`, and `nbtstat` commands. These commands are also useful in troubleshooting IP configuration errors. You can also graphically view connection details through the Local Area Connection Status section of the Network and Sharing Center.

Using the *ipconfig* Command

The `ipconfig` command displays your IP configuration. Table 7.9 lists the command switches that you can use with the `ipconfig` command.

TABLE 7.9   ipconfig switches

Switch	Description
/?	Shows all of the help options for ipconfig
/all	Shows verbose information about your IP configuration, including your computer's physical address, the DNS server you are using, and whether you are using DHCP
/allcompartments	Shows IP information for all compartments
/release	Releases an IPv4 address that has been assigned through DHCP
/release6	Releases an IPv6 address that has been assigned through DHCP
/renew	Renews an IPv4 address through DHCP
/renew6	Renews an IPv6 address through DHCP
/flushdns	Purges the DNS resolver cache
/registerdns	Refreshes DHCP leases and re-registers DNS names
/displaydns	Displays the contents of the DNS resolver cache
/showclassid	Lists the DHCP class IDs allowed by the computer
/setclassID	Allows you to modify the DHCP class ID

Using Other TCP/IP Commands

You can use numerous commands to view, verify, and configure the network parameters of Windows 10. Specifically, you can use the netsh command set and the route command set as well as the standard ping and tracert functions.

Use the netsh command interface to examine and configure IPv6 functionality (as well as the provided dialog boxes if you want). The netsh command issued from the command interpreter changes into a network shell (netsh) where you can configure and view both IPv4 and IPv6 components. Don't forget to use the ever-popular route print command to see the Windows 10 routing tables (IPv4 and IPv6). In previous versions of Microsoft operating systems, ping was the IPv4 command, and ping6 was the IPv6 command. This has changed for Windows 10; ping works for both IPv4 and IPv6 to test Layer 3 connectivity to remote devices. The IPv4 tracert command was tracert6 for IPv6. As already mentioned, the command is now tracert for both IPv4 and IPv6 and will show you every

Layer 3 (IP) hop from source to destination (assuming all the administrators from here to there want you to see the hops and are not blocking ICMP and also assuming there are no IP tunnels your packets are traversing, or you won't see the router hops in the tunnel either).

TCP/IP Troubleshooting

If you are having trouble connecting to network resources, consider the following:

- If you can access resources on your local subnet but not on a remote subnet, check the default gateway settings on your computer. Pinging a remote host and receiving a Destination Unreachable message is also related to default gateway misconfiguration.

- If you can access some but not all resources on your local subnet or remote subnet, you should check your subnet mask settings, the wiring to those resources, or the devices between your computer and those resources.

- Use the **ipconfig** utility to ensure that you are not configured with an APIPA address. If you are, determine why you are not receiving IP settings from your DHCP server.

- If you can access a resource (for example, by pinging a computer) by IP address but not by name, check the DNS settings on your computer.

After we have TCP/IP set up on our Windows 10 machine, we can connect the Windows 10 machine to the network. In the next section, we will look at how to do that.

Configuring Windows 10 on a Network

In a corporate environment, the client machines (Windows XP, Windows Vista, Windows 7/8/8.1, and Windows 10) will be connected to the domain environment either from the Windows 10 operating system domain or from Active Directory. Having the Windows 10 machine on the network offers many benefits to administration:

- You can deploy GPOs from one location instead of LGPOs on each machine.

- Users can store their data on a server. This way, the nightly backups capture user information. Most Windows 10 machines will *not* be backed up separately.

- You can manage users and groups from one central location (Active Directory) instead of on each Windows 10 machine.

- You can manage resource security on servers instead of on each Windows 10 machine.

Another type of network on which you may have to set up Windows 10 is a HomeGroup environment. HomeGroups allow you to easily connect two or more PCs running Windows 10 on your home network. Windows 10 searches for your home network, and if one is found, it connects after you enter the HomeGroup password. If a home network is not found, a networking wizard automatically creates a password for the HomeGroup. This password allows you to connect all of your other computers to the same network, and it can be changed any time after the installation of Windows 10.

Adding Windows 10 to the Domain

It does not matter which way you choose to connect the machine to the domain. I usually connect the Windows 10 machine through the Windows operating system. Many IT administrators add the Windows 10 system by using the Active Directory Users and Computers MMC, but either way does the same task.

Complete Exercise 7.6 to connect a Windows 10 machine to a Windows Server 2012 R2 domain via the Windows 10 OS. To complete this exercise, you will need to have a Windows Server 2012 R2 domain that the Window 10 machine can connect to.

EXERCISE 7.6

Connecting a Windows 10 Machine to the Domain

1. On the Windows 10 machine, right-click Start and choose System.

2. Under the Computer Name, Domain, And Workgroup section, click the Change Settings link.

3. Click the Change button next to the To Rename This Computer Or Change Its Domain Or Workgroup section.

4. In the Member Of section, click the Domain radio button (shown in Figure 7.19) and type in the name of your Windows Server 2012 R2 domain.

FIGURE 7.19   Computer Name/Domain Changes screen

5. A Credentials box appears, asking for a username and password. Enter an account with administrative credentials to join the machine to the domain. Click OK.

6. A dialog box stating that you are part of the domain appears. Click OK and reboot the machine.

7. From the Windows 10 machine, log on to the domain with your username and password.

You also have the ability to create the computer account in the Active Directory Users and Computers MMC snap-in. Complete Exercise 7.7 to add the Windows 10 machine to the domain from the Active Directory snap-in. To complete this exercise, you will need a Windows Server 2012 R2 domain that you can add the Windows 10 machine to.

EXERCISE 7.7

Adding Windows 10 to the Domain via Active Directory

1. From the Windows Server 2012 R2 domain controller machine, click Start ➢ Administrative Tools ➢ Active Directory Users And Computers.

2. Expand the domain and right-click the Computers OU. Choose New ➢ Computer.

3. In the Computer Name field, type the name of the Windows 10 computer. Click OK.

4. Double-click the new Windows 10 computer in the right-hand window to open the properties.

5. Take a look at the different tabs, and then click the Cancel button.

Joining and Sharing HomeGroups in Windows 10

HomeGroup is a function of Windows 10 that simplifies the sharing of music, pictures, and documents within your small office or home network of Windows 10 PCs. HomeGroup allows you to share USB-connected printers too. If you have a printer installed on a Windows 10 computer and it's shared by HomeGroup, it is automatically installed onto the other HomeGroup-enabled Windows 10 PCs. Domain-joined computers cannot host a HomeGroup, but they can be a participant of a HomeGroup. All editions of Windows 10 can use HomeGroups.

The first step in the process of using HomeGroup for sharing is to create a new HomeGroup or join an existing one. If the Windows 10 network-discovery feature does not find a HomeGroup, you will be asked to create a HomeGroup. In the Control Panel, select the HomeGroup link and then click the Create A HomeGroup button (Figure 7.20).

FIGURE 7.20 Create a HomeGroup.

You will then walk through the Create a HomeGroup wizard. During the wizard, you will be asked what folders you want to share with other members of the HomeGroup (shown in Figure 7.21).

FIGURE 7.21 HomeGroup folders

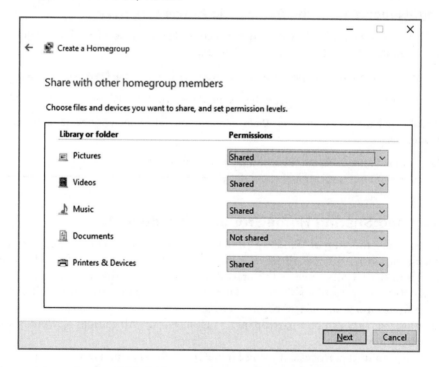

After you have chosen which folders you want to share, you will be given a password that will allow other Windows clients to join the HomeGroup. You can change this password after it has been set by going back into the HomeGroup link (in Control Panel) and choose the Change The Password link.

Now once the HomeGroup is created, other Windows 10 clients can be added. When other Windows 10 clients join the HomeGroup, they will be able to choose the resources that they want to make available to the other members of the HomeGroup. The next step is to enter the HomeGroup password.

Windows 10, by default, will recognize a HomeGroup on the network you're connected to. However, the other Windows 10 machines will not have access to the resources unless they join the HomeGroup. This is very important because allowing just any Windows 10 machine connecting to the network to automatically have shared resource access would be a huge security hole. So to protect Windows 10 user data, a password must be entered to join a HomeGroup before you can access other HomeGroup resources.

After other machines have joined, each machine has the ability to view or change the password. Remember that Windows 10 will initially create a random secure password for the HomeGroup, and you need to visit the View And Print Your HomeGroup Password link to find out what it is. You will probably want to change it. Again, to change the password, choose the Change The Password link from the Change HomeGroup Settings page, as shown in Figure 7.22. When you change the HomeGroup password, you need to go to each of the other Windows 10 machines that are members of the HomeGroup and change the password there if you still want the others to share resources.

FIGURE 7.22   Change HomeGroup Settings screen

After the HomeGroup is set up, you can see the other members' resources from the HomeGroup option of Windows Explorer or even the Start menu if you customize the Start menu and have added HomeGroup to the displayed options.

HomeGroups are a great option for users who want to share resources in the Windows 10 environment. But what if you still have non–Windows 10 machines? The legacy function of simply sharing resources and setting permissions still works for Windows 10 and will allow older operating systems to have access to resources shared on Windows 10 machines as well as allow users running Windows 10 to have access to the shared resources on Vista and XP.

Configuring Windows Firewall

Windows Firewall, which is included with Windows 10, helps prevent unauthorized users or malicious software from accessing your computer. Windows Firewall does not allow unsolicited traffic, which is traffic that was not sent in response to a request, to pass through the firewall.

Understanding the Windows Firewall Basics

You configure Windows Firewall by right-clicking Start ➢ Control Panel ➢ Large Icons View ➢ Windows Firewall. You can then decide what firewall options you want to set (as shown in Figure 7.23), like changing firewall notifications, turning the Windows Firewall on or off, restoring defaults, configuring advanced settings, and troubleshooting.

FIGURE 7.23   Windows Firewall settings dialog box

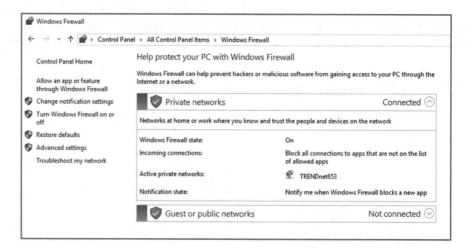

The Windows Firewall settings dialog box allows you to turn Windows Firewall on or off for both private and public networks. The On setting will block incoming sources, and the Turn off Windows Firewall setting will allow incoming sources to connect.

There is also a check box for Block All Incoming Connections. This feature allows you to connect to networks that are not secure. When Block All Incoming Connections is enabled, all incoming connections (even ones allowed in the allowed apps list) will be blocked by Windows Firewall.

Windows Firewall with Advanced Security

You can configure more-advanced settings by configuring Windows Firewall with Advanced Security (WFAS). To do so, right-click Start ➢ Control Panel ➢ Large Icons

View ➤ Windows Firewall ➤ Advanced Settings. The Windows Firewall With Advanced Security dialog box appears, as shown in Figure 7.24.

FIGURE 7.24   Windows Firewall With Advanced Security

The scope pane to the left shows that you can set up specific inbound and outbound rules, connection security rules, and monitoring rules. The central area shows an overview of the firewall's status when no rule is selected in the left pane. When a rule is selected, the central area shows the rule's settings. The right pane shows the same actions as the Action menu on the top. These are just shortcuts to the different actions that can be performed in Windows Firewall. Let's take a more detailed look at some of the elements in Windows Firewall.

Inbound and Outbound Rules

Inbound and outbound rules consist of many preconfigured rules that can be enabled or disabled. Obviously, inbound rules (see Figure 7.25) monitor inbound traffic, and outbound rules monitor outbound traffic. By default, many are disabled. Double-clicking a rule will bring up its Properties dialog box (Figure 7.26).

FIGURE 7.25 Inbound rules

FIGURE 7.26 An inbound rule's Properties dialog box

You can filter the rules to make them easier to view. Filtering can be based on the profile the rule affects, on whether the rule is enabled or disabled, or on the rule group. You can filter a rule by clicking which filter type you want to use in the right pane or by clicking the Actions menu on the top of the screen.

If you can't find a rule that is appropriate for your needs, you can create a new rule by right-clicking Inbound Rules or Outbound Rules in the scope pane and then selecting New Rule. The New Inbound (or Outbound) Rule Wizard will launch, and you will be asked whether you want to create a rule based on a particular program, protocol or port, pre-defined category, or custom settings.

As you are setting up the firewall rules, you have the ability to configure authenticated exceptions. No matter how well your system security is set up, there are almost always times when computers on your network can't use IPsec. This is when you set up authenticated exceptions. It's important to understand that when you set up these authenticated exceptions, you are reducing the security of the network because it allows computers to send unprotected IPsec network traffic. So make sure that the computers that are added to the authenticated exceptions list are managed and trusted computers only. Table 7.10 shows you some of the most common port numbers and what those port numbers are used for.

TABLE 7.10   Common port numbers

Port Number	Associated Application or Service
20	FTP Data
21	FTP Control
22	Secure Shell (SSH)
23	Telnet
25	SMTP
53	DNS
67/68	DHCP/BOOTP
80	HTTP
102	Microsoft Exchange Server
110	POP3
443	HHTPS (HTTP with SSL)

Complete Exercise 7.8 to create a new inbound rule that will allow only encrypted TCP traffic.

EXERCISE 7.8

Creating a New Inbound Rule

1. Right-click Start ➢ Control Panel ➢ Large Icon View ➢ Windows Firewall.

2. Click Advanced Settings on the left side.

3. Right-click Inbound Rules and select New Rule.

4. Choose a rule type. For this exercise, choose Custom so you can see all the options available to you. Then click Next.

5. At the Program screen, choose All Programs. Then click Next.

6. Choose the protocol type as well as the local and remote port numbers that are affected by this rule. For this exercise, choose TCP, and ensure that All Ports is selected for both Local Port and Remote Port. Click Next to continue.

7. At the Scope screen, choose Any IP Address for both local and remote. Then click Next.

8. At the Action screen, choose Allow The Connection Only If It Is Secure. Click Next.

9. At the Users screen, you can experiment with these options if you want by entering users to both sections. Once you click one of the check boxes, the Add and Remove buttons become available. Click Next to continue.

10. At the Computers screen, you can choose what computers you will authorize or allow through this rule (exceptions). Again, you can experiment with these options if you want. Click Next to continue.

11. At the Profiles screen, choose which profiles will be affected by this rule. Select one or more profiles and click Next.

12. Give your profile a name and description, and then click Finish. Your custom rule will appear in the list of inbound rules, and the rule will be enabled.

13. Double-click your newly created rule. Notice that you can change the options that you previously configured.

14. Delete the rule by right-clicking the new rule and choosing Delete. A dialog box will appear asking you if you are sure. Click Yes.

15. Close the Windows Firewall.

Connection Security Rules

Connection security rules are used to configure how and when authentication occurs. These rules do not specifically allow connections; that's the job of inbound and outbound rules. You can configure the following connection security rules:

- Isolation: To restrict a connection based on authentication criteria

- Authentication Exemption: To specify computers that are exempt from authentication requirements

- Server-to-Server: To authenticate connections between computers
- Tunnel: To authenticate connections between gateway computers
- Custom

Monitoring

The Monitoring section shows detailed information about the firewall configurations for the Domain Profile, Private Profile, and Public Profile settings. These network location profiles determine what settings are enforced for private networks, public networks, and networks connected to a domain.

 Real World Scenario

Use More Than Just Windows Firewall

When doing consulting, it always makes me laugh when I see small to midsized companies using Microsoft Windows Firewall and no other protection. Microsoft Windows Firewall should be your *last* line of defense. You need to make sure that you have good hardware firewalls that separate your network from the world.

Also watch Windows Firewall when it comes to printing. I have run into many situations where a printer that needs to communicate with the operating system has issues when Windows Firewall is enabled. If this happens, make sure that the printer is allowed in the Allowed Programs section of the Windows Firewall.

Summary

In this chapter, we discussed the different types of Windows networks: domain based and peer-to-peer (workgroup) based. We also discussed a newer, easier way to set up a workgroup-based network by using HomeGroups.

Computers need to use a communication device called a NIC device in order to communicate with each other across the network. You can set up Windows 10 to use both wired and wireless NIC devices. Windows 10 also has new features included to help with setting up your wireless networks.

To allow computers to communicate on a network, you must use a *protocol*—a set of communication standards that all computers will use. The main protocol that Windows 10 uses is TCP/IP. There are two versions of TCP/IP that Windows 10 can use, IPv4 and IPv6. IPv4 is the most commonly used protocol, but IPv6 is the newest version of TCP/IP and gives organizations flexibility and growth potential.

Finally, we also discussed using Windows Firewall with Advanced Security. Windows Firewall helps prevent unauthorized users from connecting to the Windows 10 operating system. Windows Firewall is an extra line of defense, but it *should not* replace a perimeter firewall for your network.

Video Resources

There are videos available for the following exercises:

7.1

7.2

7.4

You can access the videos at http://www.wiley.com/go/sybextestprep.

Exam Essentials

Understand Microsoft networking.   Know the difference between the Microsoft networks that you can set up. Know the difference between workgroups and domains. Know about working with Azure Active Directory vs. onsite Active Directory.

Understand how to configure network settings.   Know how to install and configure both wired and wireless networks. Understand how Windows 10 has built-in wireless network support. Know how to set up your preferred wireless network.

Understand IPv4 and IPv6.   Know and understand IPv4 and IPv6. Understand how to configure and maintain both IPv4 and IPv6 networks. Know how to subnet an IPv4 network. Understand that APIPA will automatically assign an IP address to a Windows 10 machine if DHCP is not available.

Know how to configure Windows Firewall.   Know how to set up and maintain Windows Firewall with Advanced Security. Know that you can set up inbound and outbound rules by using Windows Firewall. Know how to allow or deny applications by using Windows Firewall.

Review Questions

1. You have two DHCP servers on your network. Your computer accidentally received the wrong IP and DNS server configuration from a DHCP server that was misconfigured. The DHCP server with the incorrect configuration has been disabled. What commands could you use to release and renew your computer's DHCP configuration? (Choose two.)

    A. `ipconfig /release`

    B. `ipconfig /registerdhcp`

    C. `ipconfig /renew`

    D. `ipconfig /flushdhcp`

2. You are the network administrator for your company. Your service provider has assigned you the network address 192.168.154.0. You have been granted the entire range to use. What class of address have you been assigned?

    A. Class A

    B. Class B

    C. Class C

    D. Class D

3. You are the network administrator for your company. After configuring a new computer and connecting it to the network, you discover that you cannot access any of the computers on the remote subnet by IP address. You can access some of the computers on the local subnet by IP address. What is the most likely problem?

    A. Incorrectly defined IP address

    B. Incorrectly defined subnet mask

    C. Incorrectly defined default gateway

    D. Incorrectly defined DNS server

4. A user cannot access a server in the domain. After troubleshooting, you determine that the user cannot access the server by name but can access the server by IP address. What is the most likely problem?

    A. Incorrectly defined IP address

    B. Incorrectly defined subnet mask

    C. Incorrectly defined DHCP server

    D. Incorrectly defined DNS server

5. You have a Windows 10 machine that needs to have a static TCP/IP address. You assign the IP address to the machine and you now want to register the computer with DNS. How can you do this from the Windows 10 machine?

    A. `ipconfig /renewdns`

    B. `ipconfig /flushdns`

    C. `ipconfig /dns`

    D. `ipconfig /registerdns`

6. You have been hired as a TCP/IP contractor for an organization who wants to redo their network. The company currently uses a 192.168.x.x class but they are projecting a hiring of over 500 new employees this year. They currently have 175 employees. They do not want to buy a new TCP/IP class. What can you do to help them? (Choose all that apply.)

   A. Change the network to 10.0.0.0/8.

   B. Change the network to 172.16.0.0/16.

   C. Change the network to 224.10.0.0/24.

   D. Change the network to 192.10.0.0/24.

7. You are hired by a small company to set up a network. The company sells pocket watches and they have only five employees. They can't afford a server and client access licenses. What type of network can you set up for them?

   A. Set up all Windows 10 clients on a workgroup.

   B. Create a HomeGroup.

   C. Set them up on Azure Active Directory.

   D. Load Windows Server 2012 R2 onto a Windows 10 system.

8. Which of the following IP addresses are Class A addresses? (Choose all that apply.)

   A. 131.107.10.15

   B. 128.10.14.1

   C. 10.14.100.240

   D. 65.102.17.9

9. You are the network administrator for a small organization. Your organization has implemented Windows 10 on all client machines. You want to implement another line of security on the Windows 10 machine so unauthorized users can't access the machines. What can you implement on the Windows 10 machines?

   A. Windows Data Protection

   B. Windows Encryption Protection

   C. Windows Firewall

   D. Windows Secure Data Protocol

10. You are the network administrator for a large organization with many laptop users who go on the road. Your organization would like to start moving away from users connecting in by VPN to get data. They have decided that they want to start moving the entire IT department to the cloud. What version of Active Directory can they start using?

   A. Azure Active Directory

   B. OneDrive

   C. Windows Server 2012 R2 Active Directory

   D. DirectAccess

Chapter

8

Installing Applications

MICROSOFT EXAM OBJECTIVES COVERED IN THIS CHAPTER:

✓ **Implement apps.**

- This objective may include but is not limited to the following subobjectives: Configure desktop apps, configure startup options, configure Windows features, configure Windows Store, implement Windows Store apps, implement Windows Store for Business, provision packages, create packages, use deployment tools, use the Windows Assessment and Deployment Kit (ADK).

Now that the Windows 10 system is properly set up, it's time to start working with applications. When discussing applications on Windows 10, we could be looking at another complete book. There are so many applications that you can install on Windows 10 that there would be no way to cover them all. So we are going to focus on the applications that are included with the Windows 10 system or applications that you can download from Microsoft.

I will also talk about some of the different ways to install applications on a Windows 10 device. For example, years ago we in IT would take disks from PC to PC to install software. Then Microsoft introduced tools that allowed us to deploy software remotely. Now with Microsoft cloud-based services, you can install applications to machines anywhere in the world.

Also, with the popularity of the Windows Store, users can buy their own applications for Windows 10. IT departments also have the ability to set up a Windows Store for their company. Users can then install corporate applications from the company's Window Store. So let's look at implementing applications on Windows 10.

Understanding Deployment Options

So the first thing that every IT department needs to decide is how they are going to install the corporate applications onto the Windows 10 machines.

There are many different options when trying to decide how to deploy your Windows 10 applications. IT departments can use System Center Configuration Manager to deploy software. Companies can also use other deployment options like Group Policy Objects, the Windows 10 Application Deployment toolkit, the Windows Store, and Windows Assessment and Deployment Kit (ADK). So let's start looking at some of the different methods that an IT department can use.

Understanding System Center

When talking about Microsoft System Center, we have to be a bit more specific because there are many different versions of Microsoft System Center. So we are going to focus on Microsoft System Center 2012 R2 Configuration Manager.

Microsoft System Center 2012 R2 Configuration Manager supports application deployment for Windows 10. System Center is a third-party Microsoft application deployment tool that you can download from Microsoft.

 Unless your company is a Microsoft partner or has a subscription for MSDN, you can download and use System Center for a limited time before Microsoft will require a license.

One of the nice advantages to using System Center Configuration Manager is that you can also use it to deploy Windows 10 to machines. So you get the best of both worlds: Windows 10 and application deployment.

Another advantage of using System Center is that you can integrate it with using Microsoft cloud-based services like Intune. By using these applications in conjunction with each other, IT departments have the ability to manage desktops, laptops, Macs, and Unix/ Linux servers. IT departments would also be able to manage cloud-based mobile devices running Windows, iOS, and Android. The advantage to all of this is that you can manage all of these devices from a single management console.

To deploy applications using System Center Configuration Manager, you need to create an application package that can be deployed to your Windows 10 systems. To create applications for deployment, you must make sure that the applications have the ability to be deployed using the Windows Installer package (.msi) format. To create the System Center deployment package, you would need to complete the following steps:

 These steps will assume that you already have an .msi package to deploy. In these steps, my .msi file will be called WP.msi. I will use ServerA as the server where the .msi package resides and the directory will be called \Deployment\software\Test App. The .msi file resides in the Test App folder.

1. In the System Center Configuration Manager Console, under the Software Library workspace, expand Application Management.

2. Right-click on the OSD (Operating System Deployment) folder and select Create Application. This will start the Create Application Wizard.

3. On the General page, choose the Automatically Detect Information About This Application From Installation Files radio button. There are two settings that need to be completed under this radio button called Type and Location.

4. In the Type setting choose Windows Installer (*.msi file).

5. In the Location setting type in the location of the .msi files (\ServerA\Deployment\ Software\Test App\WP.msi).

6. Click Next. System Center Configuration Manager will prepare the MSI file for deployment.

7. When the Import Information page appears, review the information and make sure everything is correct. If it is correct, click Next.

8. On the General Information page, name the application **WP Install**. Then you will need to click the Next button two more times and then finally click Close.

Using the Windows 10 Application Deployment Tool

Microsoft has developed a tool called the Windows 10 Application Deployment toolkit. This tool allows an IT department to deploy Windows applications from a Windows 10 system to a Windows mobile device like a Surface Pro. The Windows 10 Application Deployment toolkit is a command-line utility called WinAppDeployCmd.exe.

The Windows 10 Application Deployment toolkit is included with Windows 10 SDK (Software Development Kit). You can download a standalone version of the Windows 10 SDK from Microsoft's website. Go to

https://developer.microsoft.com/en-US/windows/downloads/windows-10-sdk

The WinAppDeployCmd.exe tool allows you to deploy .appx deployment packages. To create your own .appx packages, you can use an application called MakeAppx.exe. The MakeAppx.exe tool allows an administrator to create an application package from files and turn that application into an .appx package that you can deploy using the WinAppDeployCmd.exe utility.

To learn more about the MakeAppx.exe tool, visit Microsoft's website at https://msdn.microsoft.com/en-us/library/windows/desktop/hh446767(v=vs.85).aspx

After an administrator creates the .appx package, the administrator would then move the package to a Windows 10 machine. You would then connect your mobile device to that Windows 10 machine and use the WinAppDeployCmd.exe tool to deploy the .appx package to that mobile device. Even though the .appx filename extension is normally used by Visual Studio, there is no need to load or use Visio Studio to create or deploy these .appx files.

After downloading and installing the Windows 10 SDK package, you can then use the WinAppDeployCmd.exe command-line utility. The WinAppDeployCmd.exe files will be located in the C:\Program Files (x86)\Windows Kits\10\bin\x86 directory.

The WinAppDeployCmd.exe command-line utility does not install any certificates that may be required for the applications to run. To run the application, the Windows 10 mobile device must either be in developer mode or already have the needed certificate installed for the application to be installed and run properly.

The `WinAppDeployCmd.exe` command-line utility can be run independently or in a batch file. Table 8.1 shows you some of the available commands and switches that you can use with the `WinAppDeployCmd.exe` utility.

TABLE 8.1   `WinAppDeployCmd.exe` commands and switches

Command/Switch	Description
devices	This command will show you the list of available network devices.
install	This command is used to install a Windows 10 application package to a target device.
list	This command shows an administrator the list of apps installed on the specified target device.
uninstall	This command uninstalls an application from the target device.
update	This command allows an administrator to update an application that is already installed on a device.
-f (-file)	This switch is used to show the file path for the application package to install, update, or uninstall.
-h (-help)	This switch shows an administrator all of the commands, options, and arguments for the WinAppDeployCmd tool.
-ip	This switch allows you to specify a TCP/IP address of a target device.

Deploying Software with the Windows Assessment and Deployment Kit (ADK)

Another way to install an application onto a Windows 10 system is to use the Windows Assessment and Deployment Kit (ADK). As explained in Chapter 2, "Installing in an Enterprise Environment," the Windows ADK is a set of utilities and documentation that allows an administrator to configure and deploy Windows operating systems and applications. In Chapter 2, I explained how to use this utility to install Windows 10. Now I will talk about how to use this tool to deploy applications.

The Windows ADK is a good solution for organizations that need to customize the Windows deployment environments. The Windows ADK allows an administrator to have the flexibility needed for mass deployments of applications. Since every organization's needs are different, the Windows ADK allows you to use all or just some of the application deployment tools available. It allows you to manage application deployments by using some additional tools. Let's take a look at just some of the tools that you can use with the Windows ADK.

Windows Imaging and Configuration Designer (ICD)

The tools included with this part of the Windows ADK will allow an administrator to easily deploy and configure Windows operating systems and images. These images can have applications pre-installed on the image.

Administrators who decide to use the Imaging and Configuration Designer will also get another utility referred to as provisioning packages. There are going to be times when you want an easy way to configure your Windows 10 machines and mobile devices without using an image. This is exactly what provisioning does.

Administrators can quickly and easily enroll Windows 10 computers and mobile devices into a single management console where all configuration and deployment options can be configured. Microsoft recommends provisioning for small to midsized companies that run between 10 to 200 users. The reason for this recommendation is it allows a company with a smaller IT department an easy way to configure and manage both Windows 10 PC and mobile devices.

Provisioning doesn't require a lot of training to use, and it can be configured simply enough by just writing a few simple commands. Provisioning gives an IT department a lot of flexibility, and it allows you to quickly configure a new device without using an image. It also allows you to configure multiple devices by creating just one provisioning package.

One nice advantage of provisioning is the ability to configure these devices even without network connectivity. Provisioning packages can be installed using a removable device such as a USB drive or an SD card or even by email.

To use package provisioning, you must install the Windows ADK software package and then choose the Windows Imaging and Configuration Designer (ICD) to create a provisioning package (.ppkg). To create a provisioning package, an administrator would need to complete the following steps:

1. Open the Windows ICD start page and select New Provisioning Package.

2. In the Enter Project Details window, specify the Name of your project and the Location of your project. Administrators should also enter a brief Description and click the Next button.

3. At the Select Windows Edition window, choose the Windows operating system for which you want to create this provisioning package. Administrators can choose the default setting of Common To All Windows Editions. After you choose which Windows edition you want this package to use, click the Next button.

4. If you have another provisioning package that you want to reuse, click the Browse button on the Import A Provisioning Package screen. Click the Finish button either after you added another package or just when you get to this screen (if you don't have another package to install).

5. In the Customizations page, select what you want to customize from the Available Customizations panel. This can include the following items:

- Applications
- Driver set
- Drivers
- Features on demand
- Language packages
- Reference device data
- Settings
- Windows updates

6. After you complete choosing which customization configurations you want, choose Export from the main menu drop-down and then select Provisioning Package.

7. At the Provisioning Package Configuration screen, describe the provisioning package by filling in all of the fields, and then click the Next button.

8. At the security window, choose the type of encryption that you want on the package. Administrators can also enable package signing for extra security. Security is not needed to create a provisioning package, but it is heavily recommended. Click the Next button.

9. Specify the output location of where you want this built provisioning package. By default, Windows ICD uses the project folder as the output location. Click the Next button.

10. Finally, click Build to start building the package. If your provisioning package gets an error message, it will show the error and a link to the project folder. Administrators can look at the logs to try to figure out what caused the error. If you are able to fix the issue, try rebuilding the package again. If the provisioning package is successful, you will see the name of the provisioning package, the output directory, and project directory.

If you would like additional information on creating and deploying provisioning packages, check out Microsoft's website at https://msdn.microsoft.com/library/windows/hardware/dn916107(v=vs.85).aspx

Application Compatibility Toolkit

The Application Compatibility Toolkit for Windows 10 is shipping with the Windows 10 ADK. When new Windows operating systems are installed, applications that ran on the previous version of Windows may not work properly. The Application Compatibility Toolkit allows an administrator to help solve these issues before they occur.

Mobile Software Tracing

Event Tracing for Windows (ETW) lets you log kernel or application-defined events to a log file. Administrators can use this log file to debug an application and/or determine if there are performance issues occurring within the application.

Windows Performance Toolkit

Windows Performance Toolkit contains monitoring tools that produce performance profiles of Windows operating systems and applications. The Windows Performance Toolkit includes two independent utilities: Windows Performance Recorder (WPR) and Windows Performance Analyzer (WPA).

Windows Performance Recorder (WPR)   WPR is a powerful recording utility that creates event logs for Windows. Administrators can run WPR from the user interface or from the command line. WPR provides built-in profile settings that administrators can use to select the events that are going to be recorded.

Windows Performance Analyzer (WPA)   WPA is an analysis utility that combines a user interface with advanced graphing capabilities and data tables that can be pivoted and that have full text search capabilities.

Volume Activation Management Tool (VAMT)

One of the new tools included with the Windows Assessment and Deployment Kit is the Volume Activation Management Tool (VAMT). The VAMT allows administrators to automate and manage activation keys and the activation process. The VAMT allows administrators to work with activation and volume activation licensing for Windows operating systems and other Microsoft products.

VAMT can work with Multiple Activation Keys (MAK) and the Windows Key Management Services as long as your Windows system works with version 3.0 of the Microsoft Management Console. VAMT can be installed on Windows 7 or higher and Windows Server 2008 and higher.

The VAMT will work with different versions of license keys, including Multiple Activation Key (MAK), Key Management Service (KMS) host keys (CSVLK), and KMS client setup keys (GVLK).

So when an administrator decides that they want to start using the VAMT utility, there are a few requirements. First off, to use the VAMT utility requires local administrator privileges on any computers that you want to manage. You need to have administrative rights in order to deposit confirmation IDs (CIDs), get the client application license status, and install product keys. For networks using Active Directory, I would recommend that you use Active Directory-based activation. No matter which type of VAMT you want to use, there are a few steps in order to make it work:

1. Log in as an administrator or use elevated privileges.
2. Install the Windows ADK.

3. Ensure that Volume Activation Management Tool and Microsoft SQL Server 2012 Express are selected to be installed.

4. Click Install.

Understanding GPO Deployments

Windows Server 2012 R2 gives you the ability to deploy software without installing any other software. Administrators can deploy applications through the use of a Group Policy Object (GPO). Group Policy Objects are just policies or rules that can be placed on network users or computers.

Windows Server 2012 R2 group policies are designed to provide system administrators with the ability to customize end-user settings and to place restrictions on the types of actions those users can perform. Group policies can be easily created by system administrators and then later applied to one or more users or computers within the environment. Although they ultimately do affect Registry settings, it is much easier to configure and apply settings through the use of Group Policy than it is to make changes to each computer's Registry manually. To make management easy, Microsoft has set up Windows Server 2008, Windows Server 2008 R2, Windows Server 2012, and Windows Server 2012 R2 so that Group Policy settings are all managed from within the Microsoft Management Console (MMC) in the Group Policy Management Console (GPMC).

GPOs act as containers for the settings made within Group Policy files, which simplifies the management of settings. For example, as a system administrator, you might have different policies for users and computers in different departments. Based on these requirements, you could create a GPO for members of the Sales department and another for members of the Engineering department. Then you could apply the GPOs to the OU for each department. Another important concept you need to understand is that Group Policy settings are hierarchical; that is, system administrators can apply Group Policy settings at four different levels. These levels determine the GPO processing priority:

Local Every Windows operating system computer has one Group Policy Object that is stored locally. This GPO functions for both the computer and user Group Policy processing. Local GPOs can't install applications to a Windows 10 system.

Sites At the highest level, system administrators can configure GPOs to apply to entire sites within an Active Directory environment. These settings apply to all of the domains and servers that are part of a site. Group Policy settings managed at the site level may apply to more than one domain within the same forest. Therefore, they are useful when you want to make settings that apply to all of the domains within an Active Directory tree or forest.

Domains Domains are the third level to which system administrators can assign GPOs. GPO settings placed at the domain level will apply to all of the User and Computer objects within the domain. Usually, system administrators make master settings at the domain level.

Organizational Units (OU) The most granular level of settings for GPOs is the OU level. By configuring Group Policy options for OUs, system administrators can take advantage of the hierarchical structure of Active Directory. If the OU structure is planned well, you will find it easy to make logical GPO assignments for various business units at the OU level.

Based on the business need and the organization of the Active Directory environment, system administrators might decide to set up Group Policy settings at any of these four levels. Because the settings are cumulative by default, a User object might receive policy settings from the site level, from the domain level, and from the OUs in which it is contained.

There are two main methods of making programs available to end users using Active Directory: assigning and publishing. Both assigning and publishing applications greatly ease the process of deploying and managing applications in a network environment.

In the following sections, you'll look at how the processes of assigning and publishing applications can make life easier for IT staff and users alike. The various settings for assigned and published applications are managed through the use of GPOs.

Assigning Applications

Software applications can be assigned to users and computers. *Assigning* a software package makes the program available for automatic installation. The applications advertise their availability to the affected users or computers by placing icons on the Start menu.

When applications are assigned to a user, programs will be advertised to the user regardless of which computer they are using. That is, icons for the advertised program will appear within the Start menu regardless of whether the program is installed on that computer. If the user clicks an icon for a program that has not yet been installed on the local computer, the application will automatically be accessed from a server and it will be installed.

When an application is assigned to a computer, the program is made available to any users of the computer. For example, all users who log on to a computer that has been assigned Microsoft Office 2013 will have access to the components of the application. If the user did not previously install Microsoft Office 2013, they will be prompted for any required setup information when the program first runs.

Generally, applications that are required by the vast majority of users should be assigned to computers. This reduces the amount of network bandwidth required to install applications on demand and improves the end-user experience by preventing the delay involved when installing an application the first time it is accessed. Any applications that may be used by only a few users (or those with specific job tasks) should be assigned to users.

Publishing Applications

When applications are *published*, they are advertised, but no icons are automatically created. Instead, the applications are made available for installation using the Add Or Remove Programs icon in Control Panel.

Installing Applications

As IT professionals, many of us think of managing applications simply as installing applications on the computer. But there are other details that may need to be configured to allow applications to run faster and more efficiently.

As operating systems evolve, one issue that you can run into is that your applications may not work properly on the newer version of the operating system. Microsoft has developed a few different ways to help you combat this issue.

Using the Upgrade Analytics Tool

When new Windows operating systems are installed, applications that ran on the previous version of Windows may not work properly. The Upgrade Analytics tool allows an administrator to help solve these issues before they occur.

The Upgrade Analytics tool allows IT professionals to decide if an application is compatible with the Windows 10 operating system before rolling out the new Windows 10 OS to the entire network. Upgrade Analytics also allows IT departments to decide how updating to Windows 10 will impact the applications on the domain.

IT professionals can use the Upgrade Analytics features to do the following:

- Verify that all of the corporate applications and computer hardware are compatible with Windows 10.

- Test the corporate applications for issues related to User Account Control (UAC).

- Test the corporate web applications and websites for compatibility with new versions and security updates to Windows Internet Explorer.

After installing ACT, there are three phases of how Upgrade Analytics works within the network.

Phase 1: Collecting Your Compatibility Data   Phase 1 consists of your IT department collecting all compatibility data from the software packages as well as creating and configuring your data-collection packages (DCPs). Phase 1 also includes information about how to distribute your DCPs and how to perform common collection tasks, such as importing or exporting DCP settings.

Phase 2: Analyzing Your Compatibility Data   Phase 2 analyzes the information that you collected in Phase 1. Phase 2 allows an administrator to gather information and procedures and to filter and organize the data collected in Phase 1. Phase 2 also provides information about your application compatibility reports, issues, and solutions.

Phase 3: Testing and Mitigating Your Compatibility Issues   Phase 3 consist of testing guidance and procedures for using the development tools. These tools include the Standard User Analyzer (SUA), the Internet Explorer Compatibility Test Tool (IECTT), and the Compatibility Administrator, which allow administrators to fix their compatibility issues. Phase 3 also consists of information about the application fix (also known as Shims) library and the known Internet Explorer security feature issues.

Understanding Application Fix (Shims)

When new operating systems get released, older applications may not run, and you may not be able to get a newer version of the application. For example, a vendor that sold you an application may have gone out of business, but the application is still needed in your organization.

If you install the application on Windows 10, there may be issues. This is where Shims will apply. The *Shims* is a coding fix that allows the application to function properly.

The Shim Infrastructure consists of application programming interface (API) hooking. This means the Shim Infrastructure uses linking to redirect API calls from the Windows operating system to the alternative code called the shim.

To have Shims created, you must first contact Microsoft. Microsoft must create the Shim; Microsoft does not offer any custom tools to allow for private creation. Microsoft does include shims with Windows 10, and new shims will be available through Windows Update as they are created.

File Extension Association

When dealing with applications and software packages, you may need to associate a file extension (shown in Figure 8.1) with a software package. For example, you may want all files with the filename extension .asx to be played through Windows Media Player. You have the ability to set these file-extension associations in Default Programs in Control Panel. Within Default Programs, there is link called "Associate a file type or protocol with a specific program."

FIGURE 8.1   Filename-extension association

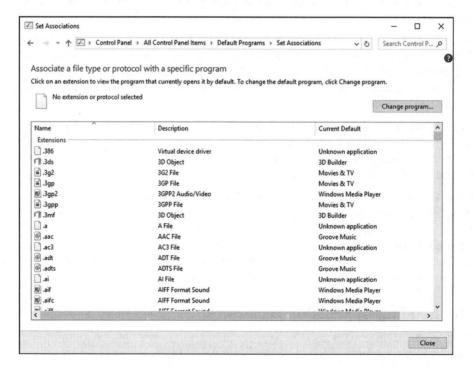

Windows Features

Many users do not even know that there are many Windows applications and features available for them to use. To access the different features in Windows 10, users can access the Apps and Features section of the system settings or they can access Programs and Features from the Control Panel.

These two areas allow users to add features as they are required or wanted. Many IT departments remove this feature from users by using a GPO, but if your organization has decided to allow your users to add what features they need, make sure you teach your users that there are features available on demand in these two sections.

Configuring Startup Options

One of the best advantages of Windows 10 is that it is very customizable. Companies have many ways to set up their user's Windows 10 system for standardization. For example, companies may want to deploy customized startup options. Companies that decide to use a standard Windows 10 startup can help improve performance because no matter what Windows 10 system you use at work, they all look and operate the same way.

To configure the startup options for your users, you will want to use GPOs. GPOs will allow you to customize settings for users based on sites, domains, or OUs. Many companies create OUs based on departments. So for example, the Sales department will have its own OU and Marketing will have its own OU. Once you have decided how you want to configure Active Directory OUs, you can decide how you want to customize the startup options.

Some of the different options that you can set up using a GPO are things like Remove Logoff on the Start menu, Remove frequent programs from the Start menu, Remove All Programs list from the Start menu, Prevent users from customizing their Start Screen, Prevent changes to Taskbar and Start Menu Settings, and many others.

To learn more about GPO settings that apply to Windows 10 Startup Options and Taskbar, go to Microsoft's website for more details: https://technet.microsoft.com/en-us/itpro/windows/manage/ windows-10-start-layout-options-and-policies

Using Hyper-V for Desktop Applications

Virtualization—the ability to run one operating system on top of another—is sweeping the computer industry. Microsoft has a virtualization environment called *Hyper-V* that can operate on its client software. Hyper-V allows you to create and manage virtual machines without the need for a server operating system on different hardware. The advantage of virtualization is that you can run multiple operating systems like Windows XP, Windows Vista, Windows 7, Windows 8/8.1, and Windows 10 all on the same hardware.

Hyper-V gives you the ability to set up virtualization on a client operating system. This is very beneficial for anyone in the industry who has to do testing or configuration. Hyper-V on Windows 10 is not really meant to run a network as Hyper-V on Windows Server 2012 R2 does, but it does give an administrator the ability to test software and patches before installing them live on a network or running applications in an operating system other than the installed one. Also, it is beneficial to research problems in a controlled environment and not on a live system where you can end up doing more harm than good.

Finally, Hyper-V gives you a training advantage. Think about having the ability to train users on a real product like Windows Server 2012 R2 or Windows 10 without needing to purchase additional equipment. Hyper-V allows you to train users on products and software while using only one machine. I will now briefly explain the differences between these forms of virtualization:

Server Virtualization   This basically enables multiple servers to run on the same physical server. Hyper-V is a server virtualization tool that allows you to move physical machines to virtual machines and manage them on a few physical servers. Thus, you will be able to consolidate physical servers.

Presentation Virtualization   When you use *presentation virtualization*, your applications run on a different computer and only the screen information is transferred to your computer. An example of presentation virtualization is Microsoft Remote Desktop Services in Windows Server 2012 R2.

Desktop Virtualization   *Desktop virtualization* provides you with a virtual machine on your desktop, comparable to server virtualization. You run your complete operating system and applications in a virtual machine so that your local physical machine just needs to run a very basic operating system. An example of this form of virtualization is Microsoft Virtual PC.

Application Virtualization   *Application virtualization* helps prevent conflicts between applications on the same PC. Thus, it helps you to isolate the application running environment from the operating system installation requirements by creating application-specific copies of all shared resources, and it helps reduce application-to-application incompatibility and testing needs. An example of an application virtualization tool is Microsoft Application Virtualization (App-V).

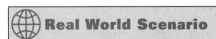

Real World Scenario

Hyper-V Advantages

As an instructor and consultant, I can't say enough about how valuable Hyper-V can be as a tool. I have used it on many occasions to either test a piece of software before installation or find an answer to a problem in a controlled environment.

At the time this book is being written, I use Microsoft Windows 7 Professional on my laptop. On that same laptop I have a version of virtualization with both Windows Server 2012 R2 and Windows 10 Professional operating system virtual machines.

While I am on a client site or while I am in the classroom, having a way to test and research problems using multiple operating systems on one client computer system is invaluable.

Hyper-V Features

As a lead-in to the virtualization topic and Hyper-V, I will start with a list of key features. This should provide you with a quick, high-level view of this feature before we dig deeper into the technology.

Key Features of Hyper-V

The following list briefly describes the key features of Hyper-V:

Hyper-V Architecture   The hypervisor-based architecture, which has a 64-bit micro-kernel, provides an array of device support as well as performance and security improvements.

Operating System Support   Both 32-bit and 64-bit operating systems can run simultaneously in Hyper-V. Also, different platforms like Windows, Linux, and others are supported.

Support for Symmetric Multiprocessors   Support for up to four processors in a virtual machine environment provides you with the ability to run applications as well as multiple virtual machines faster.

Network Load Balancing   Hyper-V provides support for *Windows Network Load Balancing (NLB)* to balance the network load across virtual machines on different servers.

New Hardware Architecture   Hyper-V's architecture provides improved utilization of resources like networking and disks. This allows an IT department the ability to run multiple operating systems on the same host without each system interfering with the other systems.

Quick Migration   Hyper-V's *Quick Migration* feature provides you with the functionality to run virtual machines in a clustered environment with switchover capabilities when there is a failure. Thus, you can reduce downtime and achieve higher availability of your virtual machines.

Virtual Machine Snapshot   You can take snapshots of running virtual machines, which provides you with the capability to recover to any previous virtual machine snapshot state quickly and easily.

Resource Metering   Hyper-V *resource metering* allows an organization to track usage within the businesses departments. It allows an organization to create a usage-based billing solution that adjusts to the provider's business model and strategy.

Scripting   Using the Windows Management Instrumentation (WMI) interfaces and APIs, you can easily build custom scripts to automate processes in your virtual machines. Administrators also have the ability to use PowerShell cmdlets to do scripting.

RemoteFX   Windows 10 Hyper-V RemoteFX allows for an enhanced user experience for RemoteFX desktops by providing a 3D virtual adapter, intelligent codecs, and the ability to redirect USB devices in virtual machines.

Fibre Channel   The virtual Fibre Channel feature allows you to connect to the Fibre Channel storage unit from within the virtual machine. *Virtual Fibre Channel* allows an administrator to use their existing Fibre Channel to support virtualized workloads. Hyper-V users have the ability to use Fibre Channel storage area networks (SANs) to virtualize the workloads that require direct access to SAN logical unit numbers (LUNs).

Enhanced Session Mode   Enhanced Session Mode enhances the interactive session of the Virtual Machine Connection for Hyper-V administrators who want to connect to their virtual machines. It gives administrators the same functionality as a remote desktop connection when the administrator is interacting with a virtual machine.

In previous versions of Hyper-V, the virtual machine connection gave you limited functionality while you connected to the virtual machine screen, keyboard, and mouse. An administrator could use an RDP connection to get full redirection abilities, but that would require a network connection to the virtual machine host.

Enhanced Session Mode gives administrators the following benefits for local resource redirection:

- Display configuration
- Audio
- Printers
- Clipboard
- Smart cards
- Drives
- USB devices
- Supported Plug and Play devices

Shared Virtual Hard Disk   Windows 10 Hyper-V has a feature called Shared Virtual Hard Disk; Shared Virtual Hard Disk allows an administrator to cluster virtual machines together by using the shared virtual hard disk (VHDX) files.

Shared virtual hard disk allows an administrator to build a high availability infrastructure which is very important if you are setting up either a private cloud deployment or a cloud-hosted environment for managing large workloads. Shared virtual hard disks allow two or more virtual machines to access the same virtual hard disk (VHDX) file.

Automatic Virtual Machine Activation (AVMA)   Automatic Virtual Machine Activation (AVMA) is a new feature that allows administrators to install virtual machines on a properly activated Windows 10 system without the need to manage individual product keys for each virtual machine. When using AVMA, virtual machines get bound to the licensed Hyper-V server as soon as the virtual machine starts.

Dynamic Memory   *Dynamic Memory* is a feature of Hyper-V that allows it to balance memory automatically among running virtual machines. Dynamic Memory allows Hyper-V to adjust the amount of memory available to the virtual machines in response to the needs of the virtual machine. It is currently available for Hyper-V in Windows 10.

Installing Hyper-V

To run Hyper-V, you need a minimum processor of an x64-compatible processor with Intel VT or AMD-V technology enabled. Hardware Data Execution Prevention (DEP), specifically Intel XD bit (execute disable bit) or AMD NX bit (no execute bit), must be available and enabled. Minimum: 1.4 GHz. Recommended: 2 GHz or faster.

Your system memory (RAM) should be at minimum at least 1 GB of RAM, but recommended is at least 2 GB RAM or greater (additional RAM is required for each running guest operating system) with a maximum of 1 TB.

Your system's hard drive should be a minimum of 8 GB, recommended 20 GB or greater. (Additional disk space is needed for each guest operating system.)

You can load Hyper-V on some versions of the following operating systems: Windows 10, Windows 8/8.1, and Windows Server 2008/2008 R2 and 2012/2012 R2. As for Windows 10 Hyper-V, you need to use one of the following versions: Enterprise, Professional, or Education. Exercise 8.1 walks you through the process of installing the Hyper-V role on Windows 10 Enterprise.

EXERCISE 8.1

Installing Hyper-V

1. Open the Programs And Features tool by clicking Start ➤ Control Panel ➤ Programs And Features.

2. Click the Turn Windows Features On Or Off link in the upper-left corner.

3. Scroll down the features list and check the Hyper-V check box (shown in Figure 8.2). Click Next.

FIGURE 8.2   Hyper-V check box

4.   The installation wizard will take a few minutes to install Hyper-V. Once Windows has finished installing Hyper-V, click the Close button.

5.   Restart your server.

 After you have installed Hyper-V and you create your virtual machines, there may be a time when you need to remotely execute Power-Shell commands on a virtual machine. To do this, you need to run the Invoke-Command command and specify which VM you're connecting to (the -VMName parameter).

Configuring User Experience Virtualization (UE-V)

To help you fully understand the benefits of Microsoft User Experience Virtualization (UE-V), I need to explain the benefits of roaming profiles. Roaming profiles were used to allow a user to go from one system to another but still have the exact same desktop and settings. Well, UE-V is roaming profiles on steroids.

Microsoft UE-V is a virtualization platform that allows users to move from one Windows system to another, but they get to keep the same Windows operating system and all of their settings. This allows users to feel comfortable moving from one device to another because their current operating system and settings follow them wherever they go.

So how does UE-V actually allow users to move around? UE-V uses XML templates that allow users to save their operating system and settings. Actually, with the use of the XML template files, you can choose which settings get saved and moved between Windows operating systems. The XML templates know exactly how all of the application settings are saved throughout the file system.

Microsoft UE-V provides the following benefits:

- Administrators have the ability to specify exactly which application and desktop settings synchronize between the operating systems.

- Administrator have the ability to create their own custom templates for third-party applications.

- Users have the ability to recover their settings and applications after any type of hardware changes.

- Users can access their settings from any location and on any Windows device.

UE-V Components

Now that you understand UE-V, let's take a look at some of the components needed to make it all work properly. Table 8.2 lists all of the different components and describes what each component does.

TABLE 8.2 UE-V components

Component	Description
UE-V agent	The UE-V agent gets installed on every Windows operating system that you want to synchronize settings with. The UE-V agent also observes all of the applications and settings for the Windows operating system.
Settings packages	UE-V agents take all of the settings and applications on a system and turn those into an application package. These application packages are created locally, and then they are copied to a shared network location.
Settings storage share	Administrators must create a network share that will house all of the setting packages. The UE-V agent will verify that the network share is configured properly, and then the UE-V agent will create a hidden system folder for the user's settings.
Settings location templates	XML templates are used to synchronize the application and settings files. UE-V includes a few templates by default, but you have the ability to create your own.
Windows apps list	The Windows apps list is used to determine which Windows applications will get synchronized. UE-V uses the Windows apps list to know which apps and files get copied to the settings package.

Installing and Configuring UE-V

Installing UE-V is not a very complicated process. First thing that you must do is download the Microsoft Desktop Optimization Pack (MDOP). Microsoft UE-V is part of the MDOP software package. Then you need to create a network share where you can store your UE-V templates. After the share is created, you must make sure that you set up the permissions properly on that shared drive. After you have created the network share, you then have to install the UE-V agent. The UE-V agent allows the Windows operating system to share its settings to the network. Then you just need to test your configurations, and you are all set. To set up the UE-V agent, you need to run the following executable along with the path of the network share:

```
AgentSetup.exe SettingsStoragePath=\\server\settingsshare\%username%
```

When you install UE-V, certain Windows files and apps get stored automatically. The following list shows some of the apps and files that get copied automatically.

UE-V synchronizes settings for some Microsoft applications by default. Here is a partial list of just some of the applications that get synchronized by default:

- Microsoft Office 2013 applications (UE-V 2.1 SP1 and 2.1)

- Microsoft Office 2010 applications (UE-V 2.1 SP1, 2.1, and 2.0)

- Microsoft Office 2007 applications (UE-V 2.0 only)

- Internet Explorer 8, 9, and 10

- Internet Explorer 11 in UE-V 2.1 SP1 and 2.1

- Windows applications, such as Xbox

- Windows desktop applications, such as Microsoft Calculator, Notepad, and WordPad

- Windows Settings, such as desktop background or wallpaper

> Since the Microsoft Desktop Optimization Pack is needed to do this installation, I did not include a lab. If you have the ability to download the MDOP, go to `https://technet.microsoft.com/en-us/library/dn479305(v=vs.85).aspx` to get step-by-step procedures for installing and using UE-V.

Understanding AppLocker

Since we're talking about how we should support applications, then we also need to look at how we lock down applications. AppLocker is a feature included with Windows (Windows 7 and higher) that allows administrators to lock out certain applications from running. AppLocker can also be run from a GPO on a Windows Server (2008 and above) to lock an application out of the entire domain.

AppLocker allows administrators to control how network users can access and use certain files like executables (.exe and .com), scripts (.ps1, .bat, .cmd, .vbs, and .js), DLLs (.dll and .ocx), and Windows Installer files (.msi and .msp). AppLocker allows you to do the following;

- Test the AppLocker policy before implementing it by using the audit-only mode.

- Set file attribute rules using the application's digital signature, product name, filename, or even file version.

- Place rules on individuals or security groups.

- Set exceptions for any rule.

- Administrators have the ability to import or export rules.

- AppLocker can be managed by using PowerShell cmdlets.

When you're setting an AppLocker rule, all files for that rule will be denied from working unless you create a rule exemption. If there are no AppLocker rules for a specific file format, then all of those files will be allowed to work on the system. When setting AppLocker rules, the rules can be allowed or denied:

Allow   Administrators have the ability to determine which files are permitted to run in the corporate environment. Administrators also have the ability to configure exceptions to the rules.

Deny   Administrators have the ability to determine which files are *not* permitted to run in the corporate environment. Administrators also have the ability to configure exceptions to the rules.

Understanding Azure

Before I start talking about Azure, you first must understand that Azure is more than one thing—it's like a suite of tools and applications. Azure is a subscription-based service from Microsoft that offers many resources to help any size organization get the most out of Microsoft products. Figure 8.3 shows just some of the services offered by Azure. You have the ability to use Azure Active Directory, Azure backups, Windows applications, Azure virtual machines, and Windows Servers, among many other things.

FIGURE 8.3   Azure options

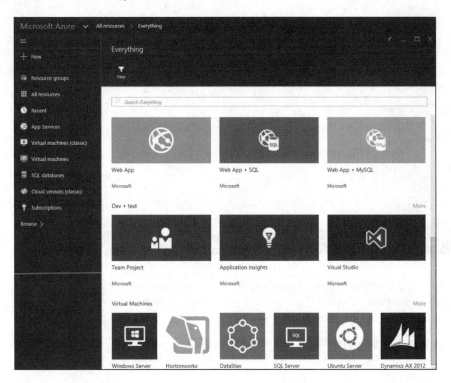

Azure Active Directory is the Microsoft version of Directory Services. In short, Active Directory is a set of services that help you secure and manage your network. There are multiple components of Active Directory:

- Active Directory Domain Services (AD DS)
- Active Directory Certificate Services (AD CS)
- Active Directory Federation Services (AD FS)
- Active Directory Rights Management Services (AD RMS)
- Active Directory Lightweight Directory Services (AD LDS)

Let's look at some of the Azure applications (some of which are shown in Figure 8.4) that you can configure and manage, starting with All Items in the upper-left corner.

FIGURE 8.4   Azure applications

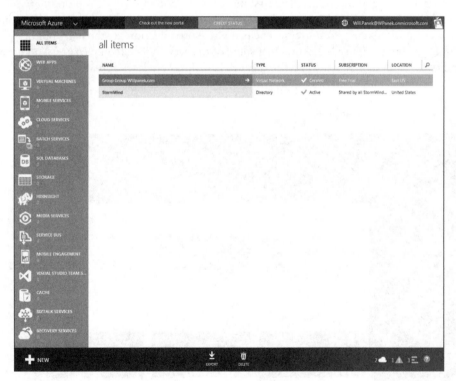

All Items   The All Items feature shows you all of the applications and services that you currently subscribe to. The All Items feature allows you to manage and manipulate all of your services from one location.

Web Apps   The Web Apps feature allows developers to quickly develop, deploy, and manage websites and web apps. Developers can build web apps using .NET, Node.js, PHP,

Python, and Java. Developers can use a single backend to create web apps and mobile apps for employees or customers.

Virtual Machines   The Virtual Machine feature allows IT administrators to quickly create and manage cloud-based virtual machines. The Virtual Machines feature allows an administrator to quickly deploy a wide range of computing solutions and pay by the minute for the use of the virtual machines. The Virtual Machine feature allows an administrator to work with multiple operating systems, including Windows, Linux, Microsoft SQL Server, Oracle, IBM, SAP, and Azure BizTalk Services.

Cloud Services   Azure Cloud Services allows an organization to create, package, and deploy applications and services to the cloud with the click of a button. Once an organization creates an application, Microsoft does the rest. Azure handles all aspects, from provisioning and load-balancing to health monitoring. Your organization's application is supported by an industry-leading 99.95-percent guaranteed uptime.

Batch Services   Azure Batch services allow you to execute large-scale batch jobs. Administrators have the ability to run these batch jobs either on demand or on a schedule.

SQL Databases   Azure SQL Database is a database service modeled after the Microsoft SQL Server software. The one major advantage of using the cloud-based version of SQL services is that you get all of the benefits of SQL, like performance, scalability, no down-time, business continuity, and data protection—all with near-zero administration. This gives your organization the ability to focus on application development instead of focusing on managing virtual machines and infrastructure. The SQL Database feature is available in Basic, Standard, and Premium service tiers.

Storage   Azure Storage provides organizations with the ability to store and retrieve large amounts of data in the cloud. Administrators have the ability to store data, such as documents and media files, while giving your organization scalability, reliability, and redundancy. Through the use of Microsoft's Azure cloud-based system, you get a cost-efficient way to store all of your company's data in one location.

HDInsight   Azure HDInsight is an Apache Hadoop server located in the cloud. Using HDInsight allows an organization to handle any amount of data on demand, from gigabytes to petabytes.

Media Services   Azure Media Services gives a company the ability to enable enterprise streaming solutions worldwide. Azure Media Services allows a company to have a powerful and scalable cloud-based encoding, encryption, and streaming system.

Service Bus   Azure Service Bus is a cloud-based messaging system for connecting applications, services, and devices. The real advantage of using Azure Service Bus is that you can connect any of these items wherever the items are located. You can even use Service Bus to connect other devices, like tablets or phones, to an application or each other.

Mobile Engagement   The Mobile Engagement feature gives an organization the ability to have real-time analytics. Using these analytics allows an IT department to solve problems with their network or applications. For example, you can see if your network is having bottlenecks and take measures to help solve the bottleneck.

Visual Studio Team Services   Visual Studio is one of the most popular ways for developers to create packages. Visual Studio Team Services allows developers to plan, build, and send software across a multitude of operating systems. Since this is a cloud-based app, the advantage of using Visual Studio Team Services is that you get the benefits of Visual Studio without having the need to install or configure a single Windows server.

Cache   Microsoft Azure Cache allows quick access to your corporate applications without the need to have a lot of memory local on your system. The Cache is a cloud-based memory system that is a scalable solution that allows corporations to create applications by providing fast access to data.

BizTalk Services   BizTalk Services allows cloud-based applications to communicate with each other or with on-premise applications. Because cloud-based apps run in their own cloud space, there is an issue with messaging and transport protocol mismatches. This is where BizTalk can help. BizTalk bridges the gap between the apps and your onsite services.

Recovery Services   Azure Recovery Services allows an organization to back up and recover their data in the cloud. Recovery Services is a subscription-based backup service that is controlled by Microsoft.

Scheduler   Azure Scheduler allows an administrator to schedule jobs in the cloud that consistently initiate service requests inside or outside of Azure. Administrators have the ability to run tasks right away, on a recurring schedule, or in the future.

API Management   Microsoft Azure API (application program interface) Management allows an administrator to manage APIs among internal departments, partners, and developers. API Management allows administrators to use the tools needed for provisioning user roles, developing usage plans and quotas, applying policies, and monitoring alerts.

Networks   Azure Virtual Network allows you to create an isolated and secure environment that you can run virtual machines and applications in. Administrators can use private IP addresses, subnets, access control policies, and almost anything that you can do with a physical network.

RemoteApp   Azure RemoteApp allows an administrator to provide secure, remote access to applications from multiple user devices. Azure RemoteApp allows users to host temporary Terminal Server sessions in the cloud. These Terminal Server sessions can be used and shared by other users in your network. RemoteApp is discussed in greater detail in the "Using Azure RemoteApp" section that follows this list of apps.

Active Directory   Azure Active Directory allows an organization to use and manage an Active Directory network without the need of setting up Windows Servers. Users can still use a single sign-on for any cloud-based or web application.

Marketplace   Azure Marketplace is your one-stop store for thousands of software applications, developer services, and data. These applications are automatically configured for use with Microsoft Azure.

Using Azure RemoteApp

As stated earlier in the chapter, Azure RemoteApp allows an administrator to provide secure, remote access to applications from multiple user devices. Azure RemoteApp allows users to host temporary Terminal Server sessions in the cloud. These Terminal Server sessions can be used and shared by other users in your network.

Azure RemoteApp allows users to share resources and applications on any device type. It can do this because your organization's applications are hosted in the cloud. Since all of your applications are cloud-based, any device with Internet access can then gain access to the applications. The one main advantage of using Azure RemoteApp is that you do not need to build and use servers in your organization to run your apps. After you upload your applications to the cloud, you then manage all of your applications through the Azure portal.

Then after the applications are loaded to the cloud, your users can access those applications from any device in the world. It does not matter on the application. Any application that is loaded to the cloud can then be accessed from the cloud. Users will need to download the Azure RemoteApp client to have web access for Azure RemoteApp.

If you want your users to have web access to Azure RemoteApp, you need to download a RemoteApp client on your device. To do this, go to www .remoteapp.windowsazure.com/en/clients.aspx.

Since the applications are loaded onto virtual machines, the applications can be accessed by any type of device, including Apple devices and Android devices. Azure RemoteApp even supports application streaming for both 32-bit and 64-bit applications as long as they are loaded onto a Windows Server 2012 R2 virtual machine.

Creating Collections in Azure RemoteApp

The first thing you need to do to Azure RemoteApp is set up your application collections. Collections are just storage containers for applications and users. Every software image gets its own collection in the cloud.

Let's take a look at how to create an Office 2013 collection. Exercise 8.2 walks you through the creation of a collection for Office 2013.

EXERCISE 8.2

Creating a Collection

1. Open the Azure portal.

2. In the tree on the left, scroll down until you see RemoteApp. Click the RemoteApp feature (shown in Figure 8.5).

FIGURE 8.5 RemoteApp feature

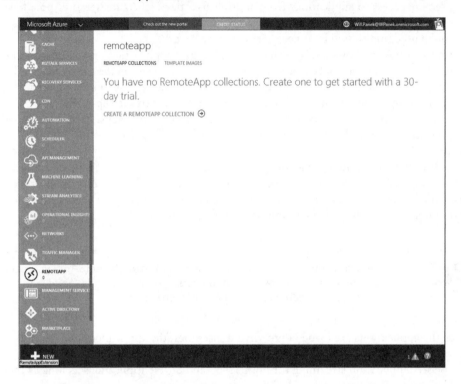

3. Click the Create a RemoteApp Collection link.

4. Click the Quick Create option and then enter a name for your collection (see Figure 8.6).

FIGURE 8.6 Quick Create option

5. Select your region. If your region is not listed, choose the closest region to your own.

6. Select the billing plan you want to use. For this exercise, select the Basic package.

7. Finally, select the Office 2013 Professional image. This image contains Office 2013 apps. This image is good only for trial collections. You can't use this image in a production environment.

8. Click the Create RemoteApp Collection link.

Sharing an Application

Now that you have created a collection, you have to share the application so that users can gain access. To share the application, follow the steps in Exercise 8.3.

EXERCISE 8.3

Sharing the Collection

1. Open the Azure portal.

2. In the tree on the left, scroll down until you see RemoteApp. Click the RemoteApp feature.

3. Click the arrow to the right of the collection name that you created in Exercise 8.2.

4. Click the Publishing tab on the top. Click Publish at the bottom of the screen, and then click Publish Start Menu Programs.

5. Next, you need to select the apps that you want to publish. For this exercise, I chose Word. Click Complete. You will then need to wait for the application to complete its publishing.

6. Once the application has completed publishing, click the User Access tab to add the users who will require access to the application. Enter each user's email address and then click Save.

Setting Up RemoteApp Connection Feeds

One of the issues that previous versions of RemoteApp encountered was that the applications ran in a web page and needed to be started from a web location. With Windows Server 2008 R2 and 2012/2012 R2 and Windows 7/8/8.1/10, you can now add the program to the users' Start menu. This gives your users the same program startup as if they had the program installed on their machine.

RemoteApp along with Desktop Connections allow for a feature called RemoteApp and Desktop Connection Feed. When using RemoteApp and Desktop Connection Feed, your users will subscribe to a RemoteApp programs feed (a URL). Once your clients subscribe to the feed, the application will be displayed on the users' Start menu.

To set up the RemoteApp and Desktop Connection feed, you need to create a new feed in Control Panel. To complete these steps, you will need to get the URL of the feed. To do this, go into the Azure Portal ➤ RemoteApp and then click the collection you created. There will be a URL link that you can use for the feed. You have to create a published feed on a virtual machine to get a proper URL and then use that link for setting up the feed. The following steps walk you through how you would set up a feed on a Windows 10 machine:

1. Open RemoteApp And Desktop Connections in Control Panel (shown in Figure 8.7).

FIGURE 8.7   RemoteApp And Desktop Connections

2. Click the Access RemoteApp And Desktops link on the left side of the screen.

3. Enter the URL of the collection feed and click Next.

4. On the Ready To Setup The Connection screen, click Next.

5. On the sign-in screen, enter your credentials. Click OK.

6. On the Summary screen, click the Finish button.

7. Start the application by accessing your system's Start menu.

Using Device Redirection

RemoteApp device redirection allows an administrator to configure a Windows system so that your users' devices can interact with the remote applications. For example, if you want to set up Skype through RemoteApp, a user would still need his or her camera and microphone to work with the RemoteApp version of Skype.

Administrators have the ability to set up RemoteApp device redirection through the use of a GPO, or they can set up the collection to automatically use redirection. To set up the collection for redirection, you would need to run some PowerShell commands. Table 8.3 lists some of the PowerShell commands and describes what they do.

TABLE 8.3 RemoteApp PowerShell commands

PowerShell Command	Description
`Set-AzureRemoteAppCollection -CollectionName <collection name> -CustomRdpProperty "drivestoredirect: s:*'nusbdevicestoredirect:s:*"`	This command sets the custom RDP properties.
`Get-AzureRemoteAppCollection -CollectionName <collection name>`	This command shows you a list of what custom RDP properties are configured.
`Set-AzureRemoteAppCollection -Collection-Name <collection name> -CustomRdpProperty "drivestoredirect:s:*"`	This command shows you how to set up hard-drive redirection.
`Set-AzureRemoteAppCollection -CollectionName <collection name> -CustomRdpProperty "drivestoredirect: s:*'nusbdevicestoredirect:s:*"`	This command shows you how to set up USB and hard-drive redirection.
`Install-Module AzureRM Install-AzureRM`	These commands allow you to install the Azure Resource Manager modules.
`Install-Module Azure`	This command installs the Azure Service Management module.
`Import-AzureRM`	This command imports AzureRM modules.
`Import-Module Azure`	This command imports the Azure Service Management module.
`Set-Mailbox`	This command allows you to manipulate an Office 365 mailbox.

To configure RemoteApp redirection by using a Group Policy Object, you would complete the following steps:

 For this example, I am showing you how to configure USB redirection on a system. I am showing you how to set up a local Group Policy in the event that you do not have a Windows Server set up. If you do want to do this for a domain, create a new GPO in the Group Policy Management MMC and then follow these steps.

1. Open the Local Group Policy Editor by typing **gpedit.msc** into the Windows 10 Search window.

2. Expand Computer Configuration\Policies\Administrative Templates\Windows Components\Remote Desktop Services\Remote Desktop Connection Client\RemoteFX USB Device Redirection.

3. Double-click the "Allow RDP redirection of other supported RemoteFX USB devices from this computer" option.

4. Select Enabled, and then choose Administrators And Users in the RemoteFX USB Redirection Access Rights.

5. Close the Group Policy Editor.

6. Restart the computer.

Understanding Shared Computer Activation

There may be a time when you need to set up Office 365 ProPlus to multiple users on the same computer within your organization. To do this, you must set up shared computer activation (SharedComputerLicensing value).

Shared computer activation allows an administrator to set up Office 365 ProPlus on a single computer for multiple users. This can be useful for schools, hospitals, and hotels. Let's say that you have multiple hotel front-desk staff members who need to access data on the same remote server—this is where shared computer activation can help.

Shared computer activation is used only when you have multiple people using the same computer. If you have users in your network that each has his or her own system, you would not use shared computer activation; you would use product key activation for Office 365 ProPlus.

 To set up shared computer activation, you must use the Office Deployment Tool. For information about setting up shared computer activation, visit the Microsoft website: https://technet.microsoft.com/en-us/library/dn782860.aspx?f=255&MSPPError=-2147217396

Understanding App-V

Microsoft Application Virtualization (App-V) is included with the Microsoft Desktop Optimization Pack (MDOP). App-V gives an organization the ability to make applications available to corporate users without installing the application on the end user's system. App-V allows applications to be managed centrally without the worry of applications conflicting with one another.

App-V allows administrators to deploy applications as services, and App-V allows those applications to be deployed anywhere. App-V allows applications to get transferred from locally installed applications to the cloud.

One real nice advantage of App-V is that when new operating systems and applications get released, there is no need to constantly upgrade your users' systems to run those new applications. Since the applications are virtualized, they can run on older operating systems. When talking about App-V, we need to take a look at some of the components needed. Table 8.4 shows the different components required for App-V.

TABLE 8.4 App-V components

Component	Description
App-V Management Server	Administrators can manage the App-V infrastructure from the Management Server. App-V Management Server allows you to set up virtual applications to the App-V Desktop Client and the Remote Desktop Services Client.
App-V Publishing Server	This server hosts streaming virtual applications and also allows App-V–specific employees to gain access to virtual applications.
App-V Desktop Client	This accesses the virtual applications along with client application publication. Desktop client also manages virtual environments and stores employee-specific application settings.
App-V Remote Desktop Services (RDS) Client	This allows Remote Desktop Session Host servers to work in conjunction with the App-V Desktop Client for shared desktop sessions. This is very useful for tablets connecting to corporate applications. If the tablet can't run the application, the tablet user can connect to the Remote Desktop services to access the application.
App-V Sequencer	This tool allows administrators to convert normal applications into virtual applications through the use of a wizard.
Disconnected Operation Mode	The disconnected operation mode allows App-V Desktop Clients to run applications even when the client cannot connect to the App-V Management Server. This allows laptops to continue to access App-V applications even when not connected to the network or the Internet.

Supporting the Windows Store

The Microsoft Windows Store is a one-stop shop for all Microsoft devices. The Windows Store allows users to find and download applications for business and personal use. The Windows Store allows you to download everything from business applications that you can use to create spreadsheets to Xbox games that will allow you to game it out.

There are two ways to use the Windows Store. You can allow your users to find applications and download their own Windows Store applications to their corporate machine. This is not the way that I would go. The second option is to create your own corporate Windows Store for Business. This way you can test and choose which applications that users can use.

The Windows Store for Business allows an IT team to find, purchase, manage, test and distribute Windows Store applications that are approved by your organization.

You can browse the Windows Store from your PC, tablet, or phone, and you can quickly and easily get free and paid content including games, music, movies, TV shows, and applications. So if your company is looking for free applications to improve business, the Windows Store can help.

One of the advantages to using the Windows Store is that all applications on the store are watched by Microsoft and require a digital certificate to make sure that they are legitimate. If an application is not signed, it will be removed from the Microsoft Store. This also means that you can't build your own apps and place them into the Windows Store without the same security measures. There are methods of loading corporate apps so that only corporate users can gain access to those apps, and that is referred to as sideloading.

Sideloading is the process of loading apps onto your corporate users with the need of a digital signature or the security rules that follow the Microsoft Store or Windows 10.

So what must you do if you want to build your own apps and place them onto the Windows Store? Well, you have to use one of Microsoft's tools that allow you to certify your applications, and those tools include the `MakeCert.exe` and `Pvk2Pfx.exe` tools that are included with the Windows Driver Kit (WDK).

Installing and Managing Software by Using Microsoft Office 365 and Windows Store Apps

One of the best advantages to using the Windows Store is that you can pretty much find and download any application that you need to help your business be more efficient. This can also be one of the biggest issues that an IT department can face. Normally an IT department needs to verify and test all applications before deploying them to the corporate network.

Now your users can find the specific applications that they think will help them do their jobs better and download just those applications. However, IT departments have the ability to turn off the Windows Store through the use of a GPO or local policy, which allows them to maintain more control.

If your IT department does not care about users downloading applications, then the Windows Store is for you. It's very easy to install applications from the Windows Store. You just go to the Windows Store, search for the application that you are looking for, and then click the download button next to that application. Normally the applications will have a small fee associated with them, but many of them are free.

Maintaining and updating applications is also a very easy process. To make sure that your applications get updated whenever there is an update available, just follow these steps:

1. On the Start screen, click the Store icon on the taskbar to open the Windows Store.

2. On the top Windows Store menu, click the picture next to the Search box and then choose Settings.

3. Under App Updates, set the Update Apps Automatically slide bar to On, as shown in Figure 8.8.

When you have finished, close the Windows Store Settings window.

FIGURE 8.8 Windows Store Settings

Let's take a look at some of the other things that you can set while on the Settings page for the Windows Store. Users or administrators also have the ability to show products on tiles, require a sign-in for purchases, and manage the devices that are loaded onto the Windows Store.

Now that you know how to get applications from the Windows Store, let's take a look at how to load corporate applications through the process of sideloading.

Sideloading Apps into Online and Offline Images

There will be a time when you or someone in your company may have to build or support a custom-made Line of Business (LOB) application. Companies build and use LOB apps because they have a very special need and can't find a software package to help solve that need.

Sideloading is the process of loading a Windows Store application without needing to publish the software application and download it from the store. Users can install the software package directly. Windows 10 sideloading has changed since Windows 8 in the following ways:

- Administrators have the ability to unlock a device for sideloading using an enterprise GPO policy.

- Software license keys are not required to install the application.

- Devices do not have to be part of the domain to get an application sideloaded.

Sideloading is not a very difficult process to complete. It is just a few settings along with the use of some PowerShell commands. To enable the systems to accept sideloading, complete the following steps:

1. Open Settings.
2. Click Update & Security ➢ For Developers.
3. Under the Use Developer Features section, choose Sideload Apps, as shown in Figure 8.9.

FIGURE 8.9 Windows sideloading

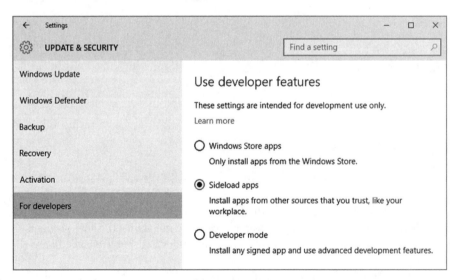

Once the system is enabled to allow applications to be sideloaded, you then need to run some PowerShell commands to make that happen. Navigate to the Windows PowerShell prompt and run the following commands (where "*TestApp*" is the path and name of the package file you created):

```
import-module appx
add-appxpackage "TestApp"
```

Integrating Microsoft Accounts Including Personalization Settings

Normally in the corporate world, we all get issued a corporate username and password so that we can log into the network and access corporate resources. But what if we wanted to access both corporate and personal data from the Internet? That's where integrating your Microsoft online account and your domain account can be beneficial.

Windows 10 gives you the ability to use both a corporate username and personal user account within the same Windows 10 account. Users can link their online accounts with their corporate accounts. So if you have your own personal cloud-based account as well as a corporate account, you can set it up so that you only log in once but have access to both accounts.

Users who decide to link their Microsoft accounts with their corporate accounts have the ability to gain access to applications and games from the Microsoft Windows Store using one account. One of the benefits of tying both accounts together is that once you've completed this setup, the Accounts Wizard will have you establish a PIN at the end. After it's all set, you will log in using the PIN from that point on.

So how do we link the two accounts together? Exercise 8.4 walks you through how to tie both accounts together. After the exercise is complete, your local account will switch to your Microsoft account after you restart your system.

EXERCISE 8.4

Setting the Microsoft Account

1. Click the Start button and then choose Settings. In the Settings window, choose Accounts (shown in Figure 8.10).

2. In the Accounts window, click the "Sign in with a Microsoft account instead" link (shown in Figure 8.11).

FIGURE 8.10 Settings window

FIGURE 8.11 Accounts window

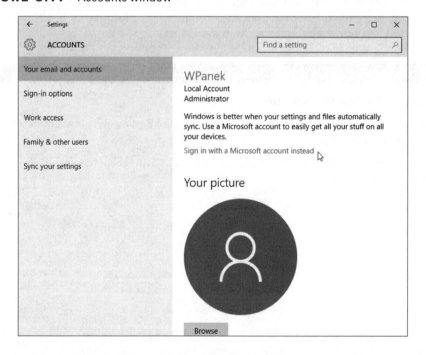

3.   A new window will appear that states, "Make it your." Type in your Microsoft online username and password. Then click the Sign In button.

4.   If a box pops up asking for your Windows network password, enter it and click Next. If you don't have a password, just click Next.

5.   The screen will ask you to enter a PIN. Click the Set A PIN button (shown in Figure 8.12) and set your PIN.

FIGURE 8.12   PIN button

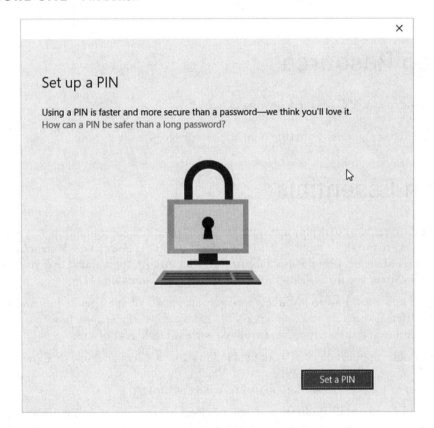

6.   After the PIN is completed, you are all set. Close the Accounts window.

Summary

Managing Windows software is a very important component that must be properly configured in Windows 10 to guarantee the best possible performance. In the event that the Windows software packages can't be run on the Windows 10 operating system, there are other options for you to run software with Windows 10.

The first thing you need to figure out is how you are going to deploy applications to the Windows 10 systems. Administrators can use System Center Configuration Manager, Group Policy Objects, the Windows 10 Application Deployment tool, the Windows Store, and Windows Assessment and Deployment Kit (ADK).

You can use Hyper-V to create other operating systems on the Windows 10 system. Administrators can also use application virtualization (App-V) to run applications in the cloud. Administrators can also use the cloud to deploy applications by using RemoteApp.

We also talked about how to use the Windows Store and the Windows Store for Business to help your organization manage, deploy, and test Windows Store applications that you want to use.

Video Resources

There is a video available for the following exercise:
8.4
You can access the video at http://www.wiley.com/go/sybextestprep.

Exam Essentials

Know the different ways to deploy applications.   Know the different methods that an administrator can use to install an application to a Windows 10 device. You can use System Center Configuration Manager, Group Policy Objects, the Windows 10 Application Deployment tool, the Windows Store, and the Windows Assessment and Deployment Kit (ADK).

Understand and know how to install Hyper-V.   Understand what Hyper-V does and know all of the different components of a Hyper-V virtual machine. Understand how to configure virtual machines and the components that make virtual machines operate.

Know how older applications can work in Windows 10.   Understand how to allow older applications to work with Windows 10. You can run applications in Hyper-V or Compatibility Mode or use shims that are created by Microsoft.

Understand how to install applications from the cloud.   You can use Azure RemoteApp to help control and manage how applications get deployed. RemoteApp allows you to download applications to many different Windows device types.

Understand Application Virtualization.   Know how to use application virtualization (App-V) and know how to run applications from the cloud without the need to deploy the applications to users' hardware.

Know the Windows Store.   Know how to use the Windows Store to your organization's benefits. This means decide what applications you will allow your users to access from the Windows Store and test and manage those applications from one location.

Review Questions

1. You are the administrator for a midsized company. You need to deploy an application onto a Windows 10 mobile device. You want to create a provisioning package (.ppkg) to deploy the application. What application do you need to install to create a provisioning package? (Choose two. Each answer is part of the solution.)

   A. Windows Imaging and Configuration Designer (ICD)

   B. Windows Assessment and Deployment Kit (ADK)

   C. Windows Provisioning Package Kit (PPK)

   D. Windows GPO

2. You are the network administrator for a large organization that needs to deploy an application to all employees. The application was built in-house and is not Windows Store signed. How can you still load the application onto user's machines?

   A. Sideloading

   B. BranchCache

   C. Application compatibility mode

   D. App-V

3. Will is your network manager. Will wants to start using App-V but Will doesn't want applications to be run while users are disconnected from the network. What option can you tell Will about to stop users from running App-V applications while offline?

   A. Tell Will to disable the Disconnected Operation Mode.

   B. Tell Will to enable Terminal Services.

   C. Tell Will to enable Remote Desktop Services.

   D. Tell Will that there is no way to stop App-V applications from running while offline.

4. You are the network administrator for your organization. You are asked by your manager to modify the associations of a few file extensions that are associated with Internet Explorer. How can you accomplish this task?

   A. In Control Panel, open Default Programs and then click Set Associations. Set the proper file extensions.

   B. In Internet Explorer, set extensions on the Extension tab.

   C. In Control Panel, open System and then click Set Associations. Set the proper file extensions.

   D. In Internet Explorer, set extensions on the Advanced tab.

5. You are the network administrator for your organization. Your organization has deployed Azure RemoteApp collections by configuring a custom template image. This image is going to contain Microsoft Office 365 ProPlus. Your organization needs to guarantee that multiple employees can run Office 365 ProPlus from the image all at the same time. What do you need to include in your configuration file?

   A. `<Property Name="SHUTDOWNAPP" Value = "True"/>`

   B. `<Property Name="SharedComputerLicensing" Value = "1"/>`

   C. `<Property Name="ACTIVATEAPP" Value = "1"/>`

   D. `<Property Name="OFFICE365ProPlus" Value = "1"/>`

6. Your company has decided to start using AppLocker GPOs to control application access. Jeff, StormWind Studio's IT Manager, would like to test the AppLocker policy before implementing it. How can Jeff test the AppLocker policy?

   A. In the Group Policy Manager, run the Group Policy Results Wizard.

   B. In the Group Policy Manager, run the Group Policy Modeling Wizard.

   C. In the Group Policy Manager, enforce the new AppLocker policy in Audit-Only mode.

   D. In the Group Policy Manager, run the Group Policy Test Wizard.

7. You are the network manager for a large organization. You have decided to implement Hyper-V and set up all servers as virtual machines. You want to see how much usage each department is using for the Hyper-V virtual machines. How do you monitor virtual machine usage?

   A. Hyper-V Resource Monitor

   B. Hyper-V Performance Monitor

   C. Hyper-V Resource Metering

   D. Windows Server 2012 R2 Server Monitor

8. You are the network administrator for a large organization. You have installed Hyper-V on a server called ServerA, and you have set up four new VM servers. You want to run Power-Shell commands for the VM servers from ServerA. How do you do this?

   A. Use the `Invoke-Command` cmdlet and specify the `VMName` parameter.

   B. Use the `WinRM` command `-PowerShell`.

   C. Use the `PSCommands–enabled` command.

   D. Just run the PowerShell commands with the `-Name` parameter.

9. You are the network administrator for a large organization. You have deployed a software package to all of the Windows computers in your domain. You want to set up a GPO so that some employees have no access to the application. How do you accomplish this?

   A. Set up a restriction server and place all of your restricted employees onto that server.

   B. Configure BitLocker.

   C. Configure AppLocker.

   D. Configure each Windows 10 system to use user policies.

10. You are the administrator of a large organization. Your company has developed an application for your employees. You need to deploy the internally developed application to all employees while minimizing the costs. What's the best way to do that?

   A. Install the application one system at a time.

   B. Enable application sideloading.

   C. Purchase System Center and deploy the application.

   D. Run the `Add-Application` PowerShell cmdlet.

Chapter

9

Managing Authorization and Authentication

MICROSOFT EXAM OBJECTIVES COVERED IN THIS CHAPTER:

✓ **Configure authorization and authentication.**

- This objective may include but is not limited to: Identifying and resolving issues related to the following: Configure Microsoft Passport, configure picture passwords and biometrics, configure workgroups, configure domain settings, configure Home-Group settings, configure Credential Manager, configure local accounts, configure Microsoft accounts, configure Device Registration, configure Windows Hello, configure Device Guard, configure Credential Guard, configure Device Health Attestation, configure UAC behavior.

✓ **Configure authorization and authentication.**

- This objective may include but is not limited to: Identifying and resolving issues related to the following: Choose the appropriate remote management tools; configure remote management settings; modify settings remotely by using the Microsoft Management Console (MMC) or Windows Power-Shell; configure Remote Assistance, including Easy Connect; configure Remote Desktop; configure remote PowerShell.

Now that we have discussed networking and basic Windows 10 configuration, we need to look at one of the most important topics to discuss, authorization and authentication.

Understanding how users authenticate onto your network and knowing some of the tricks on how to secure your network and users is one of the most important tasks that administrators must perform.

One administrative job that we need to perform is creating user and group accounts. Without a user account, a user cannot log on to a computer, server, or network. When users log on, they supply a username and password. Then their user accounts are validated by a security mechanism. In Windows 10, users can log on to a computer locally, or if the machine is a member of an Active Directory domain, the user can authenticate against a local copy of Active Directory or a cloud-based copy of Active Directory.

Groups are used to ease network administration by grouping users who have similar permission requirements. Groups are an important part of network management. Many administrators are able to accomplish the majority of their management tasks through the use of groups; they rarely assign permissions to individual users. Windows 10 includes built-in local groups, such as Administrators and Backup Operators.

You create and manage local groups through the Local Users and Groups utility. With this utility, you can add groups, change group membership, rename groups, and delete groups.

Windows 10 also offers a wide variety of security options. If the Windows 10 computer is a part of a domain, you can apply security through Group Policy Objects using the Group Policy Management Console. If the Windows 10 computer is not a part of a domain, then you can use Local Group Policy Objects to manage local security.

Understanding User Accounts

When you install Windows 10, several user accounts are created automatically. Additionally, you can create new user accounts. As you already know, user accounts allow a user to log on to machines and access resources.

You can create local user accounts, which reside locally on the Windows 10 machine. Such accounts cannot be utilized to gain access to any resources hosted on the network. If you have installed Active Directory either in the cloud (Azure Active Directory) or on a network that has a Windows Server 2012/2012 R2, Windows Server 2008/2008 R2, Windows Server 2003, or Windows Server 2000 domain controller, your network can have domain user accounts as well.

In the following sections, you will learn about the different account types: the default user accounts that are created by Windows 10 and the difference between local and domain user accounts.

Account Types

Windows 10 supports two basic types of user accounts: administrator and standard user (see Figure 9.1). Each of these accounts is used for specific reasons.

FIGURE 9.1   Choosing an account type

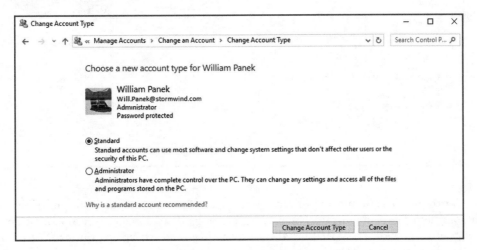

Administrator   The Administrator account type provides unrestricted access for performing administrative tasks. As a result, administrator accounts should be used only for performing administrative tasks and should not be used for normal computing tasks.

Only administrator accounts can change the Registry. This is important to know because when most software is installed onto a Windows 10 machine, the Registry gets changed. This is why you need administrator rights to install most software.

Standard User   The standard user account type should be assigned to every user of the computer. Standard user accounts can perform most day-to-day tasks, such as running Microsoft Word, accessing email, using Internet Explorer, and so on. Running as a standard user increases security by limiting the possibility of a virus or other malicious code from infecting the computer. Standard user accounts are unable to make system-wide changes, which also helps to increase security.

When you install Windows 10, by default, there are premade accounts called built-in accounts. Let's take a look at them.

Built-In Accounts

When installed into a workgroup environment, Windows 10 has five built-in accounts, which are created automatically at the time you install the operating system (see Figure 9.2). Figure 9.2 also shows the accounts that I created while writing this book.

FIGURE 9.2   The five built-in accounts

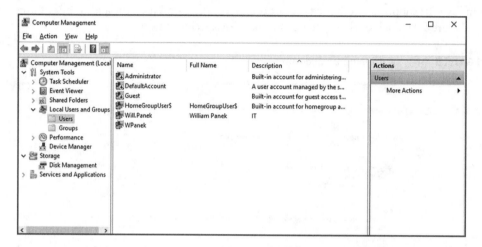

Administrator   The Administrator account is a special account that has full control over the computer. The Administrator account can perform all tasks, such as creating users and groups, managing the filesystem, installing applications, and setting up printing. Note that the Administrator account is disabled by default.

DefaultAccount   This is a user account created by the system and used by the system. This account is a member of the HomeUsers group and the System Managed Accounts group.

Guest   The Guest account allows users to access the computer even if a person does not have a unique username and password. Because of the inherent security risks associated with this type of user, the Guest account is disabled by default. When this account is enabled, it is usually given very limited privileges.

**HomeGroupUser$**   The HomeGroupUser$ account is created by default to allow this machine to connect to other machines within the same HomeGroup network. This account is created by default as soon as you set up a HomeGroup.

Initial User   The Initial User account uses the name of the registered user. By default, the initial user is a member of the Administrators group.

By default, the name Administrator is given to a user account that is a member of the Administrators group. However, in Windows 10, this user account is disabled by default. You can increase the computer's security by leaving this account disabled and assigning other users to the Administrators group. This way, a malicious user will be unable to log on to the computer using the Administrator user account.

All five of these users are considered local users, and their permissions are contained to the Windows 10 machine. If the user's account needs to access resources on machines other than their own, you can have a user log in to the Windows 10 computer as a remote user (a user who is not in front of the machine they're logging on to), and this would be considered a domain user's account. Let's take a look at the difference between these account types.

Local and Domain User Accounts

Windows 10 supports two kinds of users: local users and domain users. Local users get set up on each Windows 10 client system. The Windows 10 system can be part of a workgroup or it can be a stand-alone system. A computer that is running Windows 10 has the ability to store its own user accounts database. The user accounts stored at the local computer are known as *local user accounts*.

Workgroups are networks that have user databases on each individual Windows 10 machine. However, you can share resources on the workgroup network.

Domains

Domains are networks where there is a centralized security database (Active Directory), and you can control all of your users and groups from one central location.

Active Directory is a directory service that stores information in a central database, which allows users to have a single user account for the network. The user accounts stored in Active Directory's central database are called *domain user accounts*. Active Directory is available in two different models. There is a cloud-based Active Directory called Azure Active Directory and a server-based version that runs on Windows Server 2012/2012 R2, Windows Server 2008/2008 R2, Windows Server 2003, and Windows 2000 Server platforms.

Workgroups

You can log on locally to a Windows 10 computer using a locally stored user account, or you can log on to a domain using an Active Directory account. When you install Windows 10 on a computer, you specify that the computer will be a part of a workgroup, which implies a local logon, or that it will be a part of a domain, which implies a domain logon.

On all Windows versions except domain controllers, you can create local users through the Local Users and Groups utility, as described in the section "Working with

User Accounts" later in this chapter. On Windows Server domain controllers (Windows Server 2000 and above), you manage users with the Microsoft Active Directory Users and Computers MMC.

> Active Directory is covered in detail in *MCSA Windows Server 2012 R2 Complete Study Guide: Exams 70–410, 70–411, 70–412, and 70–417* by William Panek (Sybex, 2016).

Workplace Join

There may be times when you need someone to gain access to a domain resource but that person doesn't have a domain account. That's where Workplace Join can help. Workplace Join is a Windows tool that you can download and use on your domain.

Workplace Join allows an end user to use a corporate email address and password to connect a Windows system (Windows phone, tablet, or operating system) to a domain. The email address and password are then sent to an Active Directory server to be verified. The server can be set to then send a message to the device to confirm that the device should be given access to the domain. After the verification is done, Workplace Join creates a new device object in Active Directory and installs a certificate onto the Windows device.

Logging Off

No matter what type of account you have, you will eventually need to log off the Windows 10 system. When users are ready to stop working, they should either log off or shut down the system. A user can do either of these by right-clicking the Windows Start button and choosing Shut Down or Sign Out.

Working with User Accounts

To set up and manage your local user accounts, you use the Local Users and Groups utility or the User Accounts option in Control Panel. With either option, you can create, disable, delete, and rename user accounts as well as change user passwords.

Windows 10 includes User Account Control (UAC), which provides an additional level of security by limiting the level of access that users have when performing normal, everyday tasks. When needed, users can gain elevated access for specific administrative tasks.

Using the Local Users and Groups Utility

There are two common methods for accessing the Local Users and Groups utility:

- Load Local Users and Groups as a Microsoft Management Console (MMC) snap-in.

- Access the Local Users and Groups utility through the Computer Management utility.

If your computer doesn't have a custom MMC configured, the quickest way to access the Local Users and Groups utility is through the Computer Management utility.

In Exercise 9.1, you will add the Local Users and Groups snap-in MMC to the desktop. This exercise needs to be completed in order to complete other exercises in this chapter.

EXERCISE 9.1

Adding the Local Users and Groups Snap-in

1. In the Search box, type MMC and press Enter.

2. If a warning box appears, click Yes.

3. Select File ➢ Add/Remove Snap-in.

4. Scroll down the list and highlight Local Users And Groups, and then click the Add button (shown in Figure 9.3).

FIGURE 9.3   MMC snap-ins

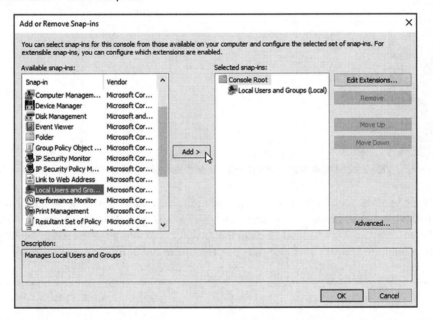

5. In the Choose Target Machine dialog box, click the Finish button to accept the default selection of Local Computer.

6. Click OK in the Add Or Remove Snap-ins dialog box.

7. In the MMC window, right-click the Local Users And Groups folder and choose New Window From Here. You will see that Local Users and Groups is now the main window.

EXERCISE 9.1 *(continued)*

8. Click File ➢ Save As. Name the console **Local Users and Groups** and choose Desktop under the Save In pull-down box. Click the Save button. This is creating the shortcut shown in Figure 9.4 for you to use in exercises throughout this chapter.

FIGURE 9.4   Local Users and Groups MMC

9. Close the MMC snap-in. You should now see the Local Users and Groups snap-in on the Desktop. You can also open the Local Users and Groups MMC from the Computer Management utility, which you'll do in Exercise 9.2. Complete the following exercise for opening the Local Users and Groups utility from the Computer Management utility.

EXERCISE 9.2

Accessing Local Users and Groups via the Computer Management Utility

1. Right-click the Start button and then choose Computer Management.

2. In the Computer Management window, expand the System Tools folder and then the Local Users and Groups folder.

Using the User Accounts Option in Control Panel

Now let's look at an alternative way to configure local users and groups through the *User Accounts Control (UAC)* Control Panel option, which provides the ability to manage user accounts in addition to configuring parental controls. To access the User Accounts Control Panel option, right-click Start ➤ Control Panel ➤ User Accounts. Table 9.1 briefly describes the configurable options in the User Accounts option in Control Panel.

TABLE 9.1   Configurable user-account options in Control Panel

Option	Explanation
Change Your Password	Allows you to change a user's password.
Change Your Account Name	Allows you to rename the account.
Change Your Account Type	Allows you to change your account type between the standard user and administrator account type.
Manage Another Account	Allows you to configure other accounts on the Windows 10 machine.
Change User Account Control Settings	Allows you to set the level of notification displayed through pop-up messages when changes are made to your computer. These notifications can prevent potentially hazardous programs from being loaded onto the operating system.
Manage Your Credentials	Allows you to set up credentials so you can easily connect to websites that require usernames and passwords or computers that require certificates.
Manage Your File Encryption Certificates	Allows you to manage your file-encryption certificates.
Configure Advanced User Profile Properties	Takes you directly to the User's Profile dialog box in Control Panel ➤ System ➤ Advanced ➤ System Settings.
Change My Environment Variables	Allows you to access the Environment Variables dialog box directly.

Creating New Users

To create users on a Windows 10 computer, you must be logged on as a user with permission to create a new user, which means your account must be a member of the Administrators group.

When you create a new user, there are many options that you have to configure. Table 9.2 describes all the options available in the New User dialog box. (You access this dialog box through the MMC, which is detailed in Exercise 9.3 later in this chapter.)

TABLE 9.2 User account options available in the New User dialog box

Option	Description
User Name	Defines the username for the new account. Choose a name that is consistent with your naming convention (e.g., WPanek). This is the only required field. Usernames are not case sensitive.
Full Name	Allows you to provide more-detailed name information. This typically consists of the user's first and last names (e.g., Will Panek). By default, this field contains the same name as the User Name field.
Description	Typically used to specify a title and/or location (e.g., Sales-Nashville) for the account, but it can be used to provide any additional information about the user.
Password	Assigns the initial password for the user. For security purposes, avoid using readily available information about the user. Passwords are case sensitive.
Confirm Password	Confirms that you typed the password the same way two times to verify that you entered the password correctly.
User Must Change Password At Next Logon	If enabled, forces the user to change the password the first time they log on. This is done to increase security. By default, this option is selected.
User Cannot Change Password	If enabled, prevents a user from changing their password. This is useful for accounts such as Guest and accounts that are shared by more than one user. By default, this option is not selected.
Password Never Expires	If enabled, specifies that the password will never expire, even if a password policy has been specified. For example, you might enable this option if this is a service account and you do not want the administrative overhead of managing password changes. By default, this option is not selected.
Account Is Disabled	If enabled, specifies that this account cannot be used for logon purposes. For example, you might select this option for template accounts or if an account is not currently being used. It helps keep inactive accounts from posing security threats. By default, this option is not selected.

In the following sections, you will learn about username rules and conventions and security identifiers.

Username Rules and Conventions

The only real requirement for creating a new user is that you provide a valid username. To be valid, the name must follow the Windows 10 rules for usernames. However, it's also a good idea to have your own rules for usernames, which form your naming convention.

The following are the Windows 10 rules for usernames:

- A username must be from 1 to 20 characters.

- The username must be unique among all the other user and group names stored on the computer.

- The username cannot contain any of the following characters:

  / \ [ ]:; | =, + ? < > " @

- A username cannot consist exclusively of periods or spaces.

Keeping the Windows 10 rules in mind, you should choose a naming convention (a consistent naming format) for your company. For example, your naming convention might be to use the last name and first initial, so for a user named William Panek, the username would be WillP or WilliamP. Another naming convention might use the first initial and last name, for the username WPanek. This is the naming convention followed by many midsize and larger organizations. You could base usernames on the naming convention your company has defined for email names so that the logon name and the name in the email address match.

You should also provide a mechanism that will accommodate duplicate names. For example, if you have a user named Jane Smith and a user named John Smith, you might use a middle initial for usernames, such as JDSmith and JRSmith. It is also a good practice to come up with a naming convention for groups, printers, and computers.

 Real World Scenario

Naming-Convention Considerations

As an IT manager, I don't recommend using first name, first initial of last name (WilliamP) as a naming convention. In a midsize-to-large company, there is the possibility of having two WilliamPs, but the odds that you will have two WPaneks are rare.

If you choose to use the first name, first initial of last name option, it can be a lot of work to go back and change this format later if the company grows. Choose a naming convention that can grow with the company.

When creating users, it's important to make sure that your usernames and passwords are as strong as possible. The reason that you want strong security is because when a user logs into a system, the user's credentials are placed into the computer's Local Security Authority Subsystem Service (LSASS) process memory. This is done so that the credentials can be used by the account during a session connection.

Credentials will also get stored on the Windows 10 authoritative databases, such as the SAM database and in the database that is used by Active Directory Domain Services (AD DS). Therefore, it's important to make your usernames and passwords strong so that hackers have the hardest time to hack into a system and steal these cached credentials.

Now let's take a look at how user accounts get security ID numbers associated with them and how those numbers affect your accounts.

Security Identifiers

When you create a new user account, a *security identifier (SID)* is automatically created for the user account. The username is a property of the SID. For example, a user SID might look like this:

```
S-1-5-21-823518204-746137067-120266-629-500
```

It's apparent that using SIDs for user identification would make administration a nightmare. Fortunately, for your administrative tasks, you see and use the username instead of the SID.

SIDs have several advantages. Because Windows 10 uses the SID as the user object, you can easily rename a user while retaining all the user's properties. All security settings get associated with the SID, not the user account. Every time you create a new user, a unique SID gets associated. This ensures that if you delete and re-create a user account with the same username, the new user account will not have any of the properties of the old account because it is based on a new, unique SID. Even if the username is the same as a previously deleted account, the system still sees the account as a new user.

Because every user account gets a unique SID number, it is a good practice to disable rather than delete accounts for users who leave the company or have an extended absence. If you ever need to access the disabled account again, you have the ability to do so.

Secure Channel

Another part of authentication and encrypted communications between a client and a server is a mechanism called *Secure Channel*. Secure Channel, also known as Schannel, is a set of security protocols that help offer secure encrypted communications and authentication between a client and a server.

Schannel is a security package that uses the following four protocols on the Windows platforms:

- Transport Layer Security (TLS 1.1)
- Transport Layer Security (TLS 1.2)
- Secure Sockets Layer (SSL 3.0)
- Secure Sockets Layer (SSL 2.0)

To create an Schannel connection, the clients and servers are both required to obtain Schannel credentials and create a security session. Once the client and server connection is obtained, the security credentials become available. If a connection is lost for any reason, the client and server can automatically renegotiate the connection and finish all communications.

Creating a New Local User Account

Complete Exercise 9.3 to create a new local user account. Before you complete the following steps, make sure you are logged on as a user with permissions to create new user accounts and have already added the Local Users and Groups snap-in to the MMC (Exercise 9.1). I created bogus usernames; you can change these to whatever names you want to use, but I refer to the ones I created in other exercises.

EXERCISE 9.3

Creating New Users via the MMC

1. Open the Local Users and Groups MMC Desktop shortcut that you created in Exercise 9.1, and expand the Local Users and Groups snap-in. If a dialog box appears, click Yes.

2. Highlight the Users folder and select Action ➤ New User. The New User dialog box appears, as shown in Figure 9.5.

FIGURE 9.5   New User dialog box

3. In the User Name text box, type **APanek**.

EXERCISE 9.3 *(continued)*

4. In the Full Name text box, type **Alexandria Panek**.

5. In the Description text box, type **Operations Manager**.

6. Leave the Password and Confirm Password text boxes empty. Make sure you uncheck the User Must Change Password At Next Logon option, and accept the defaults for the remaining check boxes. Click the Create button to add the user.

7. Use the New User dialog box to create four more users, filling out the fields as follows:

   User Name: **PPanek**; Full Name: **Paige Panek**

   User Name: **GWashington**; Full Name: **George Washington**

   User Name: **JAdams**; Full Name: **John Adams**

   User Name: **ALincoln**; Full Name: **Abe Lincoln**

8. After you've finished creating all of the users, click the Close button to exit the New User dialog box.

 You can also create users through the command-line utility NET USER. For more information about this command, type **NET USER /?** at the command prompt.

Disabling User Accounts

When a user account is no longer needed, the account should be disabled or deleted. After you've disabled an account, you can later reenable it to restore it with all of its associated user properties. An account that is deleted, however, can never be recovered unless you complete a restore from a backup.

You might disable an account because a user will not be using it for a period of time, perhaps because that employee is going on vacation or taking a leave of absence. Another reason to disable an account is that you're planning to put another user in that same function and would like to reuse the account.

For example, suppose that Gary, the engineering manager, quits. If you disable his account, when your company hires a new engineering manager, you can simply rename Gary's user account (to the username for the new manager), enable it, and reset the password. This ensures that the user who takes over Gary's position will have all the same user properties and own all the same resources.

Disabling accounts also provides a security mechanism for special situations. For example, if your company is laying off a group of people, as a security measure you could disable their accounts at the same time the layoff notices are given out. This prevents those users from inflicting any damage to the company's files after they receive their layoff notice. (Note, however, that this won't affect users who are already logged in.)

In Exercise 9.4, you will disable a user account. Before you complete this exercise, you should have created new users in Exercise 9.3.

EXERCISE 9.4

Disabling User Accounts

1. Open the Local Users and Groups MMC Desktop shortcut that you created in Exercise 9.1 and expand the Local Users and Groups snap-in.

2. Open the Users folder. Double-click user PPanek to open her Properties dialog box.

3. In the General tab, check the Account Is Disabled box. Click OK.

4. Close the Local Users and Groups MMC.

5. Log off and attempt to log on as PPanek. This should fail because the account is now disabled.

6. Log back on using your user account.

 You can also access a user's properties by highlighting the user, right-clicking, and selecting Properties.

When a user has left the company for a long period of time and you know you no longer need the user account, you can delete it. Let's take a look at how to delete user accounts.

Deleting User Accounts

As noted in the preceding section, you should disable a user account if you are not sure whether the account will ever be needed again. But if the account has been disabled and you know that the user account will never need to be accessed again, you should delete the account.

To delete a user, open the Local Users and Groups utility, highlight the user account you wish to delete, click Action to bring up the menu shown in Figure 9.6, and then select Delete. You can also delete an account by clicking the account and pressing the Delete key on the keyboard.

Because deleting an account is a permanent action, you will see the dialog box shown in Figure 9.7 asking you to confirm that you really wish to delete the account. After you click the Yes button here, you will not be able to re-create or reaccess the account (unless you restore your local user accounts database from a backup).

FIGURE 9.6 Deleting a user account

FIGURE 9.7 Confirming account deletion

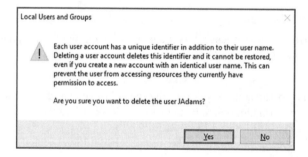

Complete Exercise 9.5 to delete a user account. These steps assume you have completed Exercises 9.2, 9.3, and 9.4.

EXERCISE 9.5

Deleting a User Account

1. Open the Local Users and Groups MMC Desktop shortcut and expand the Local Users and Groups snap-in.

2. Expand the Users folder and single-click user JAdams to select his user account.

3. Select Action ➢ Delete. The dialog box for confirming user deletion appears.

4. Click the Yes button to confirm that you wish to delete this user.

5. Close the Local Users and Groups MMC.

Now that you have disabled and deleted accounts, let's take a look at how to rename a user's account.

Renaming User Accounts

Once an account has been created, you can rename it at any time. Renaming a user account allows the account to retain all the associated user properties such as group memberships and assigned permissions even though the username is being changed.

You might want to rename a user account because the user's name has changed (for example, the user gets married) or because the name was spelled incorrectly. Also, as explained in the section "Disabling User Accounts," you can rename an existing user's account for a new user, such as someone hired to take an ex-employee's position, when you want the new user to have the same properties.

Complete Exercise 9.6 to rename a user account. These steps assume you have completed Exercises 9.2 through 9.5.

EXERCISE 9.6

Renaming a User Account

1. Open the Local Users and Groups MMC Desktop shortcut and expand the Local Users and Groups snap-in.

2. Open the Users folder and highlight user ALincoln.

3. Select Action ➤ Rename.

4. Type the username **RReagan** and press Enter. Notice that the Full Name field retains the original Full Name property of Abe Lincoln in the Local Users and Groups utility.

5. Double-click RReagan to open the properties and change the user's full name to Ronald Reagan.

6. Click the User Must Change Password At Next Logon check box.

7. Click OK.

8. Close the Local Users and Groups MMC.

Renaming a user does not change any hard-coded names, such as the name of the user's home folder. If you want to change these names as well, you need to modify them manually—for example, through Windows Explorer. (Note that there is a small possibility that you'll have to change the Registry to point to the new name.)

Another very common task that we must deal with is changing the user's password. Let's take a look at how to do that.

Changing a User's Password

What should you do if a user forgets his or her password and can't log on? As the administrator, you can change the user's password, which they can then use.

It is very important as IT managers and IT administrators that we teach our users proper security measures that go along with password protection. As you have all probably seen before, the users who tape their password to their monitors or under the keyboards are not following correct security precautions. It's our job as IT professionals to teach our users proper security, and it always amazes me when I do consulting how many IT departments don't teach their users properly.

Complete Exercise 9.7 to change a user's password. This exercise assumes you have completed Exercises 9.2 onward.

EXERCISE 9.7

Changing a User's Password

1. Open the Local Users and Groups MMC Desktop shortcut and expand the Local Users and Groups snap-in.

2. Open the Users folder and highlight user APanek.

3. Select Action ➢ Set Password. The Set Password dialog box appears.

4. A warning appears, indicating the risks involved in changing the password. Select Proceed.

5. Type the new password and then confirm the password. Click OK.

6. Close the Local Users and Groups MMC.

Using a Microsoft Passport, Pictures, and Biometrics

Now that we have looked at how to set up and manage local and domain accounts, let's look at how you can use other options to help you log into your system or network.

Those of us who have been certified for a long time are quite familiar with using a Microsoft account to log into the Microsoft websites. Now we can use this same account to log into our computer and networks.

Microsoft Passports are Microsoft accounts that you can use to authenticate to a domain, to a cloud-based domain, or to a computer. To do this, you need to link your Microsoft account to your Windows 10 system.

Linking your Windows 10 system is an easy two-step verification process with Microsoft Passport enrollment. When you set up a Microsoft Passport on the device, you can set up the system to use Windows Hello or a PIN.

Windows Hello allows you to sign in to your Windows 10 devices with just a look or a touch. Windows Hello can be set up so that you can use biometrics, face recognition, or even an iris scan. To configure Windows Hello options, click the Start menu and choose Settings. Once you're in the settings, choose Accounts.

You also have the ability to set up Microsoft Passport to use a PIN. This is a secure number that you input instead of a username and password. You may be thinking to yourself that a PIN doesn't seem as secure as a username and password, but actually that is not true.

PINs can be very complex and include special characters and letters, both uppercase and lowercase. So that means that you can have a PIN of 1234 or a PIN of 1234Wi!!Panek1001. Also, PINs are tied directly to a machine and not to an account, so when you set up a PIN, it's good for that machine only. Because of this, PINs are actually better than a password that can be used anywhere on the network. If someone steals your password, they can access your account from anywhere. This is not the case with a PIN, because anyone trying to use it would also need access to your machine.

Windows 10 also gives you the ability to set up your logon for use with a picture. When you decide to use a picture for authentication, you first choose your picture and then you add three gestures onto the picture. You can draw straight lines, circles, squares, or anything you want. Then when you log on to the system, you just re-create the gestures on the picture and the system logs you in.

Using Device Guard

So far we have been discussing how to secure your computer or network based on username, passwords, biometrics, and Microsoft Passport, but there are other ways to help lock your Windows 10 systems down. One of those ways is Device Guard.

Device Guard is an enterprise set of hardware and software security features that when used together can lock a system down so that only trusted applications can run on the operating system. Administrators have the ability to define policies, and it is these policies that help Windows 10 lock down applications that do not meet the policies that your organization has defined.

If an administrator has created a policy and an application does not meet the criteria of the defined policies, the application will not run. This is very useful when it comes to unauthorized people trying to access your network. Even if a hacker gets into the Windows 10 operating system and takes control of the kernel, because of the policies that you have created, it is almost impossible that any unauthorized software will be able to run.

As long as you are using Windows 10 Enterprise or Education, Device Guard can be used with virtualization-based security policies. This is possible because Device Guard works in conjunction with the Hyper-V hypervisor. Because of this, Device Guard can help protect applications and operating systems that run within the Hyper-V application.

The advantage to Device Guard is that it works on two levels, the kernel mode code integrity (KMCI) and user mode code integrity (UMCI). Because Device Guard works at both levels, it helps protect against hardware- and software-based threats.

Understanding Device Guard Protection

In Table 9.3, I will show you some of the different features available that can help protect against multiple types of threats.

TABLE 9.3 Device Guard features

Security Threat	Device Guard Feature
Boot attacks	To help protect against attacks at system startup, Device Guard includes a feature called Universal Extensible Firmware Interface (UEFI) Secure Boot. This feature protects the system from hacks during the boot process and also from malicious firmware installations. Because of the Device Guard security features, the UEFI is locked down (Boot order, Boot entries, Secure Boot, Virtualization extensions, IOMMU, Microsoft UEFI CA) and changes can't be made to compromise the system.
Control of kernel	To help protect against kernel invasions, Device Guard uses virtualization-based security (VBS). VBS helps guard the Hyper-V hypervisor, which in turn protects the kernel and the operating system. After an administrator enables VBS, VBS tightens the default kernel-mode code integrity policy (which help protect system files or bad drivers from being deployed) or the configurable code integrity policy.
Direct Memory Access (DMA) based attacks	With this policy, virtualization-based security (VBS) uses input/output memory management units (IOMMUs) to evaluate memory usage. This policy helps determine if the memory access is accepted or denied.
New malware	This policy helps protect against kernel invasions by protecting against code integrity policies. Administrators have the ability to control a whitelist of software that is allowed to run. This way, if a hacker tries to run a malicious piece of code that has not been whitelisted, it will not run.
Unassigned code	When hackers build malicious code, the one advantage we have in IT is that the code is not signed by an authorized vendor. Because of this, administrators can set up code integrity policies with catalog files. This policy will immediately help protect against many known and unknown threats. The one drawback to this policy is that many organizations use unsigned line-of-business (LOB) applications.

Managing Device Guard

When talking about Device Guard, there are many different ways that an administrator can configure it. Let's take a look at some of the different options available for managing and configuring Device Guard.

Group Policy

One of the ways that you can configure Device Guard is through the use of a Group Policy Object (GPO). You can configure the GPOs using the Windows Server 2012 R2 Group Policy Management console or directly through a local GPO within Windows 10.

GPOs provide a template that allows an administrator to manage and configure the hardware-based security features in Device Guard that you would like to enable and deploy. You can manage Device Guard settings and your other network settings within the same GPO.

Microsoft System Center Configuration Manager

Administrators also have the ability to use System Center Configuration Manager to easily deploy and manage catalog files, code integrity policies, and hardware-based security features.

Windows PowerShell

You can use Windows PowerShell to create and service code integrity policies. Table 9.4 shows Windows PowerShell commands for managing Device Guard.

TABLE 9.4   Device Guard PowerShell Commands

PowerShell Command	Description
Add-SignerRule	Allows an administrator to create a signer rule and add that rule to a policy.
ConvertFrom-CIPolicy	This command allows an administrator to convert an .xml file into binary format. These files contain code integrity policies.
Get-CIPolicy	Allows an administrator to view the rules in a code integrity policy.
Get-CIPolicyIdInfo	Allows an administrator to view code integrity policy information.
Get-SystemDriver	Administrators can view the drivers on a system.
Merge-CIPolicy	This command allows an administrator to merge the rules of several code Integrity policy files.

TABLE 9.4   Device Guard PowerShell Commands *(continued)*

PowerShell Command	Description
New-CIPolicy	Allows an administrator to create a code integrity policy as an .xml file.
New-CIPolicyRule	Administrators can create code integrity policy rules for drivers.
Set-CIPolicyIdInfo	This command allows an administrator to modify the name and ID of a code integrity policy.
Set-CIPolicyVersion	This command allows an administrator to modify the version number of a policy.
Set-HVCIOptions	Administrators can change hypervisor code integrity options for a specific policy.
Set-RuleOption	This command allows an administrator to modify the rule options in a code integrity policy.

Understanding Credential Guard

Another new security feature introduced with Windows 10 Enterprise and Windows Server 2016 is Credential Guard. Credential Guard relies on Hyper-V based security measures to help operating systems run only software with the appropriate security privileges. Credential Guard helps stop unauthorized access to credentials thus stopping many types of security threats.

When a user sends a username and password to a domain controller, after the domain controller authenticates the user and the Windows 10 system, a domain token (sometimes referred to as a Kerberos ticket) is issued to the user. Credential Guard helps protect against attacks that specifically target this authentication process.

Credential Guard Protection

One of the advantages of Credential Guard is that hardware can be secured. Credential Guard can help secure your hardware by using virtualization-based security and a feature called secure boot. By securing the Windows 10 hardware, you can also secure the Windows 10 operating system.

One of the nicest advantages of using Credential Guard is its ease to manage and deploy. Credential Guard can be configured by using a Group Policy Object, from a Windows 10 command prompt, or by using Windows PowerShell. But before we look at managing Credential Guard, let's take a look at each security measure.

Virtualization-Based Security

One of the greatest advantages of virtualization is that each guest operating system runs independent of every other guest operating system. So basically that means that each operating system works as if it's on its own physical piece of hardware. Credential Guard uses a security feature that works along the same way. The Windows services that manage domain authentication credentials are separated into their own special environment that is separated from the Windows 10 operating system.

It is because of this separation that you get added protection to your Windows environment. Virtualization-based security protects against credential theft attack techniques that are used in most credential attacks. Many types of attacks that run in the Windows operating system run using administrative privileges. Because virtualization-based security separates authentication credentials into their own special environment, it protects system credentials from being extracted by the hackers or malware programs that are running on the operating system.

Secure Boot

Secure boot is another way that Windows 10 can help protect your hardware because secure boot verifies that only manufacture trusted firmware gets used by the system. This can protect your system from hackers and hacks that attack the system's firmware. But, as with any good thing, there could also be issues. Secure boot may possibly cause issues with things like hardware (high-end graphics cards) or operating systems such as Linux or previous version of Windows.

So one thing that you may need to know is actually how to disable secure boot in the event that is does conflict with some hardware. There are normally two ways that you can disable secure boot, through the BIOS or through the Windows 10 bootup process. If you need to disable secure boot, you would complete the following steps:

1. Open the PC BIOS menu, or from the Windows 10 operating system, hold the Shift key while selecting Restart. Then choose Troubleshoot ➢ Advanced Options: UEFI Firmware Settings.

2. Under the Secure Boot setting (normally under the Security or Boot tab) and set it to Disabled.

3. Save the changes and reboot the system.

To re-enable secure boot, you would do the same procedure except you would choose enable under the Secure Boot option.

Configuring Device Health Attestation

In today's Bring Your Own Device (BYOD) world, many companies allow users to bring their own personal devices into work. The issue with this is that you have no idea what security measures they have on their machines. Something new with Windows 10 is the ability to check the health of your computers and make sure that they meet certain system requirements. This is where device health attestation comes into play.

Administrators can use the Configuration Manager console in device health attestation to view the status of Windows 10 machines on your network and make sure that they meet the minimum requirements that your organization sets.

Administrators can now view the computer systems that are onsite or even managed through the cloud using Microsoft Intune. Administrators have the ability to determine whether reporting is done through the onsite infrastructure or through the cloud. The advantage of being able to work with both cloud-based and internal computers is if your company doesn't have current Internet access, you can still use the device health attestation utility.

Device health attestation allows an administrator to verify that client systems have TPM enabled, proper BIOS configurations, and boot security measures enabled.

Device Health Attestation Requirements

If you want to use device health attestation on your network or in the cloud, your systems must meet some minimum requirements:

- Windows 10

- Windows Server 2016 with device health attestation enabled

- TPM 2 enabled

- Internet communication needs to be established between your Configuration Manager client agent and has.spserv.microsoft.com (port 443) Health Attestation service.

After you have met the minimum requirements for your systems, then we have to configure our systems to run device health attestation:

1. In the Configuration Manager console, choose Administration ➤ Overview ➤ Client Settings. Choose the Computer Agent tab.

2. In the Default Settings dialog box, choose Computer Agent and then scroll down to Enable Communication With Health Attestation Service and choose Yes. Click OK.

Another piece that we may need to configure is enabling on-premises health attestation service:

1. In the Configuration Manager console, navigate to Administration ➤ Overview ➤ Client Settings. You will then need to set Use On-Premises Health Attestation Service to Yes.

2. Specify the On-Premise Health Attestation Service URL and then click OK.

Managing User Properties

For more control over user accounts, you can configure user properties. Through the user's Properties dialog box, you can change the original password options, add the user to existing groups, and specify user profile information.

To open a user's Properties dialog box, access the Local Users and Groups utility, open the Users folder, and double-click the user account. The user's Properties dialog box has tabs for the three main categories of properties: General, Member Of, and Profile.

The General tab contains the information you supplied when you set up the new user account, including the full name and a description, the password options you selected, and whether the account is disabled. If you want to modify any of these properties after you've created the user, simply open the user's Properties dialog box and make the changes on the General tab (Figure 9.8).

FIGURE 9.8   General tab of the user's Properties dialog box

You can use the Member Of tab to manage the user's membership in groups, and the Profile tab lets you set properties to customize the user's environment. The following sections discuss the Member Of and Profile tabs in detail.

Managing User Group Membership

The Member Of tab of the user's Properties dialog box displays all the groups that the user belongs to, as shown in Figure 9.9. From this tab, you can add the user to an existing group or remove the user from a group. To add a user to a group, click the Add button and select the group that the user should belong to. If you want to remove the user from a group, highlight the group and click the Remove button.

FIGURE 9.9   The Member Of tab of the user's Properties dialog box

Complete Exercise 9.8 to add a user to an existing group. These steps assume you have completed Exercises 9.2 onward.

EXERCISE 9.8

Adding a User to an Existing Group

1. Open the Local Users and Groups MMC Desktop snap-in that you created previously.

2. Open the Users folder and double-click user APanek. The APanek Properties dialog box appears.

3. Select the Member Of tab and click the Add button. The Select Groups dialog box appears.

4. Under Enter The Object Names To Select, type **Backup Operators**, and click the Check Names button. After the name is confirmed, click OK.

5. Click OK to close the APanek Properties dialog box.

Now let's take a look at the Profile tab and what options can be configured within that tab.

Setting Up User Profiles, Logon Scripts, and Home Folders

The Profile tab of the user's Properties dialog box, shown in Figure 9.10, allows you to customize the user's environment. Here, you can specify the following items for the user:

- User profile path
- Logon script
- Home folder

FIGURE 9.10   The Profile tab of the user's Properties dialog box

The following sections describe how these properties work and when you might want to use them.

Setting a User's Profile Path

User profiles contain information about the Windows 10 environment for a specific user. For example, profile settings include the Desktop arrangement, program groups, and screen colors that users see when they log on.

Each time you log on to a Windows 10 computer, the system checks to see if you have a local user profile in the Users folder, which was created on the boot partition when you installed Windows 10. The first time users log on, they receive a default user profile. A folder that matches the user's logon name is created for the user in the Users folder. The user profile folder that is created holds a file called NTUSER.DAT as well as subfolders that contain directory links to the user's Desktop items.

In Exercise 9.9, you'll create two new users and set up local user profiles.

EXERCISE 9.9

Setting Up User Profiles

1. Using the Local Users and Groups utility, create two new users: WPanek and CPanek. Deselect the User Must Change Password At Next Logon option for each user.

2. Select Start ➢ All Programs ➢ Accessories ➢ Windows Explorer. Expand Computer ➢ Local Disk (C:) ➢ Users. Notice that the Users folder does not contain user profile folders for the new users.

3. Log off and log on as WPanek.

4. Right-click an open area on the Desktop and select Personalize. In the Personalization dialog box, select a color scheme and click Apply, and then click OK.

5. Right-click an open area on the Desktop and select New ➢ Shortcut. In the Create Shortcut dialog box, type **CALC** to open the Calculator program. Accept CALC as the name for the shortcut and click Finish.

6. Log off as WPanek and log on as CPanek. Notice that user PPanek sees the Desktop configuration stored in the default user profile.

7. Log off as CPanek and log on as WPanek. Notice that WPanek sees the Desktop configuration you set up in steps 3, 4, and 5.

8. Log off as WPanek and log on as your user account. Open Windows Explorer. Expand Computer ➢ Local Disk (C:) ➢ Users. Notice that this folder now contains user profile folders for WPanek and CPanek.

The drawback of local user profiles is that they are available only on the computer where they were created. For example, suppose all of your Windows 10 computers are a part of a domain and you use only local user profiles. User Rick logs on at Computer A and creates a customized user profile. When he logs on to Computer B for the first time, he will receive the default user profile rather than the customized user profile he created on Computer A. To enable users to access their user profile from any computer they log on to, you need to use roaming profiles; however, these require the use of a network server because they can't be stored on a local Windows 10 computer.

In the next sections, you will learn about how roaming profiles and mandatory profiles can be used. To have a roaming profile or a mandatory profile, your computer must be a part of a network with server access.

Using Roaming Profiles

A *roaming profile* is stored on a network server and allows a user to access their user profile regardless of the client computer to which they're logged on. Roaming profiles provide a consistent desktop for users who move around, no matter which computer they access. Even if the server that stores the roaming profile is unavailable, the user can still log on using a local profile.

If you are using roaming profiles, the contents of the user's systemdrive:\Users\ UserName folder will be copied to the local computer each time the roaming profile is accessed. If you have stored large files in any subfolders of your user profile folder, you may notice a significant delay when accessing your profile remotely as opposed to locally. If this problem occurs, you can reduce the amount of time the roaming profile takes to load by moving the subfolder to another location, such as the user's home directory, or you can use Group Policy Objects within Active Directory to specify that specific folders should be excluded when the roaming profile is loaded.

Using Mandatory Profiles

A *mandatory profile* is a profile that can't be modified by the user. Only members of the Administrators group can manage mandatory profiles. You can create mandatory profiles for a single user or a group of users. You might consider creating mandatory profiles for users who should maintain consistent desktops.

For example, suppose you have a group of 20 salespeople who know enough about system configuration to make changes but not enough to fix any problems they create. For ease of support, you could use mandatory profiles. This way, all of the salespeople will always have the same profile, which they will not be able to change.

The mandatory profile is stored in a file named NTUSER.MAN. To create a mandatory profile, you just change the user's roaming profile extension to .man, and the profile will become mandatory. A user with a mandatory profile can set different desktop preferences while logged on, but those settings will not be saved when the user logs off.

There are two folders where the profiles are stored. They are Username and Username.v2 (*Username* will be replaced with the user's name). The difference is that if you are using Windows XP, the profile gets placed in the *Username* folder. If the users are using Windows Vista, Windows 7/8/8.1, Windows 10, or Windows Server 2008, the user profile gets placed in the *Username.v2* folder.

Now let's look at a second type of mandatory profile, called super-mandatory profile.

Using Super-Mandatory Profiles

A *super-mandatory profile* is a mandatory user profile with an additional layer of security. With mandatory profiles, a temporary profile is created if the mandatory profile is not available when a user logs on. However, when super-mandatory profiles are configured, temporary profiles are not created if the mandatory profile is not available over the network, and the user is unable to log on to the computer.

The process for creating super-mandatory profiles is similar to that for creating mandatory profiles, except that instead of renaming the user folder *Username.v2* as you would for a mandatory profile, you name the folder *Username.man*. User profiles become *super-mandatory* when the folder name of the profile path ends in .man, as in, for example, *server**share**APanek.man*\. Only system administrators can make changes to mandatory user profiles.

 Real World Scenario

Copying User Profiles

Within your company, you have a user, Paige, who logs in with two different user accounts. One account is a regular user account, and the other is an Administrator account used for administration tasks only.

When Paige established all her Desktop preferences and installed the computer's applications, they were installed with the Administrator account. Now, when she logs in with the regular user account, she can't access the Desktop and profile settings that were created for her as an administrative user.

To solve this problem, you can copy a local user profile from one user to another (for example, from Paige's administrative account to her regular user account) by choosing Control Panel ➤ System ➤ Advanced System Settings ➤ User Profiles Settings. When you copy a user profile, the following items are copied: favorites, cookies, documents, Start menu items, and other unique user Registry settings.

Using Logon Scripts

Another configurable element within the Profile tab of the user's properties is logon scripts—files that run every time a user logs on to the network. They are usually batch files, but they can be any type of executable file. Logon scripts are either created by the admin or just grabbed off the Internet. Creating these scripts is beyond the scope of this book.

You might use logon scripts to set up drive mappings or to run a specific executable file each time a user logs on to the computer. For example, you could run an inventory-management file that collects information about the computer's configuration and sends that data to a central management database. Logon scripts are also useful for compatibility with non–Windows 10 operating systems for users who want to log on but still maintain consistent settings with their native operating system.

To run a logon script for a user, enter the script name in the Logon Script text box in the Profile tab of the user's Properties dialog box.

Setting Up Home Folders

Users usually store their personal files and information in a private folder called a home folder. In the Profile tab of the user's Properties dialog box, you can specify the location of a home folder as a local folder or a network folder. The main reason you give your users a home folder on the server is because the servers are usually the only machines that get backed up. Most companies do not back up individual users' machines. If your users place all their important documents in the home folder location on the network, those documents will get backed up as part of the nightly backup.

To specify a local folder, choose the Local Path option and type the path in the text box next to that option. To specify a network path for a folder, choose the Connect option and specify a network path using a Universal Naming Convention (UNC) path. A UNC path consists of the computer name and the share that has been created on the computer. When connecting to a UNC name, the network folder you are connecting to should already be created and shared. For example, if you wanted to connect to a folder called \Users\Will on a server called SALES, you'd choose the Connect option, select a drive letter that would be mapped to the home directory, and then type **\\SALES\Users\ Will** in the To box.

If the home folder you are specifying does not exist, Windows 10 will attempt to create the folder for you. You can also use the variable %username% in place of a specific user's name. The %username% will automatically change to the name of the user you are currently working on.

WARNING

Be careful when you're specifying your home folder. If you make a mistake when typing in the path for the directory, Windows will create a folder for you that is improperly named.

Complete Exercise 9.10 to assign a home folder to a user. These steps assume you have completed Exercises 9.2 onward.

EXERCISE 9.10

Assigning Home Folders

1. Open the Local Users and Groups MMC Desktop shortcut and expand the Local Users and Groups snap-in.

2. Open the Users folder and double-click user GWashington. The GWashington Properties dialog box appears.

3. Select the Profile tab and click the Local Path radio button to select it.

4. Specify the home folder path by typing **C:\HomeFolders\GWashington** in the text box for the Local Path option. Then click OK.

5. Use Windows Explorer to verify that this folder was created.

6. Close the Local Users and Groups MMC.

🌐 **Real World Scenario**

Using Home Folders to Keep Files Backed Up

As an administrator for a large network, one of my primary responsibilities is to make sure that all data is backed up daily. This has become difficult because daily backup of each user's local hard drive is impractical. You can also have problems with employees deleting important corporate information as they are leaving the company.

After examining the contents of a typical user's local drive, you will realize that most of the local disk space is taken up by the operating system and the user's stored applications. This information does not change and does not need to be backed up. What you are primarily concerned with is backing up the user's data.

To more effectively manage this data and accommodate the necessary backup, you should create home folders for each user and store them on a network share. This allows the data to be backed up daily, to be readily accessible should a local computer fail, and to be easily retrieved if the user leaves the company.

Here are the steps to create a home folder that resides on the network:

1. Decide which server will store the users' home folders.

2. Create a directory structure that will store the home folders efficiently (for example, C:\HOME).

3. Create a single share to the user's home folder. (You can do this by right-clicking the home folder and choosing Properties.)

4. Use NTFS and share permissions to ensure that only the specified user has permissions to their home folder.

5. Specify the location of the home folder through the Profile tab of the user's Properties dialog box.

Troubleshooting User Account Authentication

When a user attempts to log on through Windows 10 and is unable to be authenticated, you will need to track down the reason for the problem.

If a local user is having trouble logging on, the problem may be with the username, the password, or the user account itself. The following are some common causes of local logon errors:

Because many of these same issues happen when logging on to a domain from a Windows 10 machine, these approaches can be used for both local logons and domain logons.

Incorrect Username   You can verify that the username is correct by checking the Local Users and Groups utility. Verify that the name was spelled correctly.

Incorrect Password   Remember that passwords are case sensitive. Is the Caps Lock key on? If you see any messages relating to an expired password or locked-out account, the reason for the problem is obvious. If necessary, you can assign a new password through the Local Users and Groups utility.

Prohibitive User Rights   Does the user have permission to log on locally at the computer? By default, the Log On Locally user right is granted to the Users group, so all users can log on to Windows 10 computers.

However, if this user right was modified, you will see an error message stating that the local policy of this computer does not allow interactive logon. The terms *interactive logon* and *local logon* are synonymous and mean that the user is logging on at the computer where the user account is stored on the computer's local database.

A Disabled or Deleted Account   You can verify whether an account has been disabled by checking the account properties through the Local Users and Groups utility. If the account is no longer in the database, then it has most likely been deleted.

A Domain Account Logon at the Local Computer   If a computer is a part of a domain, the logon dialog box has options for logging on to the domain or to the local computer. Make sure the user has chosen the correct option.

Managing and Creating Groups

Groups are an important part of network management. Many administrators are able to accomplish the majority of their management tasks through the use of groups; they rarely assign permissions to individual users.

Windows 10 includes built-in local groups (such as Administrators and Backup Operators) that already have all the permissions needed to accomplish specific tasks. Windows 10 also uses built-in special groups in which users are placed automatically when they meet certain criteria.

You can create and manage local groups (but not special groups) through the Local Users and Groups utility. With this utility, you can add groups, change group membership, rename groups, and delete groups.

One misconception about groups is that they have to work with Group Policy Objects (GPOs). This is not correct. Group Policy Objects are sets of rules that allow you to set computer-configuration and user-configuration options that apply to users or computers for a Site, Domain, or OU.

Using Built-In Groups

On a Windows 10 computer, built-in local groups have already been created and assigned all necessary permissions to accomplish basic tasks. In addition, there are built-in special groups that the Windows 10 system handles automatically. These groups are described in the following sections.

Built-in Local Groups

A local group is a group that is stored on the local computer's accounts database. You can add users to these groups and can manage the groups directly on a Windows 10 computer. By default, some the following local groups are created on Windows 10 computers:

- Administrators
- Backup Operators
- Cryptographic Operators
- Distributed COM Users
- Event Log Readers
- Guests
- IIS_IUSRS
- Network Configuration Operators
- Performance Log Users
- Performance Monitor Users
- Power Users
- Remote Desktop Users
- Replicator
- Users

I will briefly describe each group, its default permissions, and the users assigned to the group by default.

If possible, you should add users to the built-in local groups rather than creating new groups from scratch. This simplifies administration because the built-in groups already have the appropriate permissions. All you need to do is add the users you want to be members of the group.

Administrators   The Administrators group has full permissions and privileges. Its members can grant themselves any permissions they do not have by default to manage all the objects on the computer. (Objects include the filesystem, printers, and account management.) By default, the Administrator account, which is disabled by default, and the Initial User account are members of the Administrators local group.

 Assign users to the Administrators group with caution since they will have full permissions to manage the computer.

Members of the Administrators group can perform the following tasks:

- Install the operating system.
- Install and configure hardware device drivers.
- Install system services.
- Install service packs, hot fixes, and Windows updates.
- Upgrade the operating system.
- Repair the operating system.
- Install applications that modify the Windows system files.
- Configure password policies.
- Configure audit policies.
- Manage security logs.
- Create administrative shares.
- Create administrative accounts.
- Modify groups and accounts that have been created by other users.
- Remotely access the Registry.
- Stop or start any service.
- Configure services.
- Increase and manage disk quotas.
- Increase and manage execution priorities.
- Remotely shut down the system.
- Assign and manage user rights.
- Reenable locked-out and disabled accounts.
- Manage disk properties, including formatting hard drives.
- Modify systemwide environment variables.
- Access any data on the computer.
- Back up and restore all data.

Backup Operators   Members of the Backup Operators group have permissions to back up and restore the filesystem, even if the filesystem is NTFS and they have not been assigned permissions to access the filesystem. However, the members of Backup Operators can access the filesystem only through the Backup utility. To access the file system directly, Backup Operators must have explicit permissions assigned. There are no default members of the Backup Operators local group.

Cryptographic Operators   The Cryptographic Operators group has access to perform cryptographic operations on the computer. There are no default members of the Cryptographic Operators local group.

Distributed COM Users   The Distributed COM Users group has the ability to launch and run Distributed COM objects on the computer. There are no default members of the Distributed COM Users local group.

Event Log Readers   The Event Log Readers group has access to read the event log on the local computer. There are no default members of the Event Log Readers local group.

Guests   The Guests group has limited access to the computer. This group is provided so that you can allow people who are not regular users to access specific network resources. As a general rule, most administrators do not allow Guest access because it poses a potential security risk. By default, the Guest user account is a member of the Guests local group.

IIS_IUSRS   The IIS_IUSRS group is used by Internet Information Services (IIS). The NT AUTHORITY\IUSR user account (premade for IIS) is a member of the IIS_IUSRS group by default.

Network Configuration Operators   Members of the Network Configuration Operators group have some administrative rights to manage the computer's network configuration, such as, for example, editing the computer's TCP/IP settings.

Performance Log Users   The Performance Log Users group has the ability to access and schedule logging of performance counters and can create and manage trace counters on the computer. There are no default members of this group.

Performance Monitor Users   The Performance Monitor Users group has the ability to access and view performance counter information on the computer. Users who are members of this group can access performance counters both locally and remotely. There are no default members of this group.

Power Users   The Power Users group is included in Windows 10 for backward compatibility to ensure that computers upgraded from Windows XP function as before with regard to folders that allow access to members of the group. Otherwise, the Power Users group has limited administrative rights. There are no default members of this group.

Remote Desktop Users   The Remote Desktop Users group allows members of the group to log on remotely for the purpose of using the Remote Desktop service. There are no default members of this group.

Replicator   The Replicator group is intended to support directory replication, which is a feature used by domain servers. Only domain users who will start the replication service should be assigned to this group. The Replicator local group has no default members.

Users   The Users group is intended for end users who should have very limited system access. If you have installed a fresh copy of Windows 10, the default settings for the Users group prohibit its members from compromising the operating system or program files. By default, all users who have been created on the computer, except Guest, are members of the Users local group.

Special Groups

Special groups are premade groups that can be used by the system or by administrators. Membership in special groups is automatic if certain criteria are met. You cannot manage special groups through the Local Users and Groups utility, but an administrator can add special groups to resources. The following text describes the special groups that are built into Windows 10.

Anonymous Logon   This group includes users who access the computer through anonymous logons. When users gain access through special accounts created for anonymous access to Windows 10 services, they become members of the Anonymous Logon group.

Authenticated Users   This group includes users who access the Windows 10 operating system through a valid username and password. Users who can log on belong to the Authenticated Users group.

Batch   This group includes users who log on as a user account that is used only to run a batch job.

Creator Owner   This is the account that created or took ownership of an object. This is typically a user account. Each object (files, folders, printers, and print jobs) has an owner. Members of the Creator Owner group have special permissions to resources. For example, if you are a regular user who has submitted 12 print jobs to a printer, you can manipulate your print jobs as Creator Owner, but you can't manage any print jobs submitted by other users.

Dialup   This group includes users who log on to the network from a dial-up connection.

Everyone   This group includes anyone who could possibly access the computer—all users who have been defined on the computer (including Guest), plus (if your computer is a part of a domain) all users within the domain. If the domain has trust relationships with other domains, all users in the trusted domains are part of the Everyone group as well. The exception to automatic group membership with the Everyone group is that members of the Anonymous Logon group are not included as a part of the Everyone group.

Interactive   This group includes all users who use the computer's resources locally.

Network   This group includes users who access the computer's resources over a network connection.

Service   This group includes users who log on as a user account that is used only to run a service. You can configure the use of user accounts for logon through the Services program.

System   There are times when the Windows 10 operating system will access functions within the system. When the operating system accesses these functions, it does it as a system user. When the system accesses specific functions as a user, that process becomes a member of the System group.

Terminal Server User   This group includes users who log on through Terminal Services.

Creating Groups

To create a group, you must be logged on as a member of the Administrators group. The Administrators group has full permissions to manage users and groups.

Keep your naming conventions in mind when assigning names to groups, just as you do when choosing usernames. Consider the following guidelines:

- The group name should be descriptive; for example, Accounting Data Users.
- The group name must be unique to the computer and different from all other group names and usernames that exist on that computer.
- Group names can be up to 256 characters. It is best to use alphanumeric characters for ease of administration. The backslash (\) character is not allowed.

Creating groups is similar to creating users, and it is a fairly easy process. After you've added the Local Users and Groups MMC or used Local Users and Groups through the Computer Management utility, expand it to see the Users and Groups folders. Right-click the Groups folder and select New Group from the context menu. This brings up the New Group dialog box, shown in Figure 9.11.

FIGURE 9.11   The New Group dialog box

The only required entry in the New Group dialog box is the group name. If appropriate, you can enter a description for the group, and you can add (or remove) group members. When you're ready to create the new group, click the Create button.

Complete Exercise 9.11 to create two new local groups. (Creating domain groups is beyond the scope of this book.)

Creating Local Groups

1. Open the Admin Console MMC Desktop shortcut you created and expand the Local Users and Groups snap-in.

2. Right-click the Groups folder and select New Group.

3. In the New Group dialog box, type **Data Users** in the Group Name text box. Click the Create button.

4. Repeat step 3, but type **Application Users** in the Group Name text box.

After the groups are created, you will have to manage the groups and their membership. In the next section, we will look at managing groups.

Managing Group Membership

After you've created a group, you can add members to it. As mentioned earlier, you can put the same user in multiple groups. You can easily add and remove users through a group's Properties dialog box, shown in Figure 9.12. To access a group's Properties dialog box from the Groups folder in the Local Users and Groups utility, double-click the name of the group you want to manage.

FIGURE 9.12 Group's Properties dialog box

From the group's Properties dialog box, you can change the group's description and add or remove group members. When you click the Add button to add members, the Select Users dialog box appears (Figure 9.13).

FIGURE 9.13   The Select Users dialog box

In the Select Users dialog box, you enter the object names of the users you want to add. You can use the Check Names button to validate the users against the database. Select the user accounts you wish to add and click Add. Click the OK button to add the selected users to the group.

To remove a member from the group, select the member in the Members list of the Properties dialog box and click the Remove button.

In Exercise 9.12, you'll create new user accounts and then add these users to one of the groups you created in the previous steps.

EXERCISE 9.12

Adding Accounts to Groups

1. Open the Local Users and Groups MMC shortcut you created and expand the Local Users and Groups snap-in.

2. Create two new users: JDoe and DDoe. Deselect the User Must Change Password At Next Logon option for each user.

3. Expand the Groups folder.

4. Double-click the Data Users group.

5. In the Data Users Properties dialog box, click the Add button.

6. In the Select Users dialog box, type the username **JDoe**; then click OK.

7. Click Add and type the username **DDoe**; then click OK.

8. In the Data Users Properties dialog box, you will see that the users have both been added to the group. Click OK to close the group's Properties dialog box.

There may come a point when a specific group is no longer needed. In the next section, we will look at how to delete a group from the Local Users and Groups utility.

Deleting Groups

If you are sure that you will never again want to use a particular group, you can delete it. Once a group is deleted, you lose all permissions assignments that have been specified for the group.

To delete a group, right-click the group name and choose Delete from the context menu. You will see a warning that once a group is deleted, it is gone for good. Click the Yes button if you're sure you want to delete the group.

If you delete a group and give another group the same name, the new group won't be created with the same properties as the deleted group because, like users, groups get unique SIDs assigned at the time of creation.

Creating users and groups is one of the most important tasks that we as IT members can do. On a Windows 10 machine, creating users and groups is an easy and straightforward process.

Now that you understand how to create users and groups, you need to know how to manage Windows 10 security using GPOs and LGPOs. We'll look at that next.

Managing Security Using GPOs and LGPOs

Windows 10 offers a wide variety of security options. If the Windows 10 computer is a part of a domain, then you can apply security through a Group Policy Object using the Group Policy Management Console. If the Windows 10 computer is not a part of a domain, then you use Local Group Policy Objects to manage local security.

Additionally, you can use policies to help manage user accounts. Account policies control the logon environment for the computer, such as password and logon restrictions. Local policies specify what users can do once they log on and include auditing, user rights, and security options. You can also manage critical security features through the Windows Security Center.

Understanding the GPO and LGPO Basics

The tools you use to manage Windows 10 computer security configurations depend on whether the Windows 10 computer is a part of a Windows 2000, Windows 2003, Windows 2008, Windows 2008/2008 R2, or Windows Server 2012/2012 R2 domain environment.

If the Windows 10 client is not a part of a domain, then you apply security settings through *Local Group Policy Objects (LGPOs)*. LGPOs are sets of security configuration settings that are applied to users and computers. LGPOs are created and stored locally on the Windows 10 computer.

If your Windows 10 computer is a part of a domain, which uses the services of Active Directory, then you typically manage and configure security through Group Policy Objects (GPOs). Active Directory is the database that contains all your domain user and group accounts along with all other domain objects.

Group Policy Objects are policies that can be applied to either users or computers in the domain. The Group Policy Management Console (GPMC) is a Microsoft Management Console (MMC) snap-in that is used to configure and manage GPOs for users and computers via Active Directory.

Windows 10 computers that are part of a domain still have LGPOs, and you can use LGPOs in conjunction with the Active Directory group policies (GPOs).

 Usage of Group Policy Objects for domains is covered in greater detail in my book *MCSA Windows Server 2012 R2 Complete Study Guide: Exams 70–410, 70–411, 70–412, and 70–417* (Sybex, 2016).

The settings you can apply through the Group Policy utility within Active Directory are more comprehensive than the settings you can apply through LGPOs. Table 9.5 lists some of the options that can be set for GPOs within Active Directory and which of those options can be applied through LGPOs.

TABLE 9.5 Group Policy and LGPO setting options

Group Policy Setting	Available for LGPO?
Software installation	No
Remote Installation Services	Yes
Scripts	Yes
Printers	Yes
Security settings	Yes
Policy-based QOS	Yes
Administrative templates	Yes
Folder redirection	No
Internet Explorer configuration	Yes

Now that we have looked at LGPOs, let's look at some of the tools available for creating and managing them.

Using the Group Policy Result Tool

When a user logs on to a computer or domain, a resulting set of policies to be applied is generated based on the LGPOs, site GPOs, domain GPOs, and OU GPOs. The overlapping nature of group policies can make it difficult to determine what group policies will actually be applied to a computer or user.

To help determine what policies will actually be applied, Windows 10 includes the Group Policy Result Tool, also known as the *Resultant Set of Policy (RSoP)*. You can access this tool through the GPResult command-line utility. The gpresult command displays the set of policies that were enforced on the computer and the specified user during the logon process.

The gpresult command will display the RSoP for the computer and user who is currently logged in. Several switches can be used with the gpresult command; Table 9.6 shows the different switches that can be used for the gpresult command.

TABLE 9.6   gpresult switches

Switch	Explanation
/F	Forces gpresult to override the filename specified in the /X or /H command
/H	Saves the report in an HTML format
/P	Specifies the password for a given user context
/R	Displays RSoP summary data
/S	Specifies the remote system to connect to
/U	Specifies the user context under which the command should be executed
/V	Specifies that verbose information should be displayed
/X	Saves the report in XML format
/Z	Specifies that the super-verbose information should be displayed
/?	Shows all the gpresult command switches
/scope	Specifies whether the user or the computer settings need to be displayed
/User	Specifies the username for which the RSoP data is to be displayed

In the next section, we will look at how to create and apply Local Group Policy Objects to the Windows 10 machine.

Managing and Applying LGPOs

Policies that have been linked through Active Directory will, by default, take precedence over any established local group policies. Local group policies are typically applied to computers that are not part of a network or are in a network that does not have a domain controller and thus does not use Active Directory.

Pre-Vista versions of Windows contained only one Local Group Policy Object that applied to all of the computer's users unless NTFS permissions were applied to the LGPO. However, Windows 10 and Windows Vista changed that with the addition of *Multiple Local Group Policy Objects (MLGPOs)*. MLGPOs are applied in the following hierarchical order:

1. Local Computer Policy

2. Administrators and Non-Administrators Local Group Policy

3. User-Specific Group Policy

The Local Computer Policy is the only LGPO that includes computer and user settings; the other LGPOs contain only user settings. Settings applied here will apply to all users of the computer.

The Administrators LGPO is applied to users who are members of the built-in local Administrators group. As you might guess, the Non-Administrators LGPO is applied to users who are not members of the local Administrators group. Because each user of a computer can be classified as an administrator or a non-administrator, either one policy or the other will apply.

User-Specific LGPOs are also included with Windows 10. These LGPOs make it possible for specific policy settings to apply to a single user.

As with Active Directory GPOs, any GPO settings applied lower in the hierarchy will override GPO settings applied higher in the hierarchy by default. For example, any User-Specific GPO settings will override any conflicting Administrator/Non-Administrator GPO settings or Local Computer Policy settings. And, of course, any AD GPO settings will still override any conflicting LGPO settings.

> Domain administrators can disable LGPOs on Windows 10 computers by enabling the Turn Off Local Group Policy Objects Processing Domain GPO setting under Computer Configuration\Administrative Templates\ System\Group Policy.

You apply an LGPO to a Windows 10 computer through the Group Policy Object Editor snap-in within the MMC. Figure 9.14 shows the Local Computer Policy for a Windows 10 computer.

FIGURE 9.14 Local Computer Policy

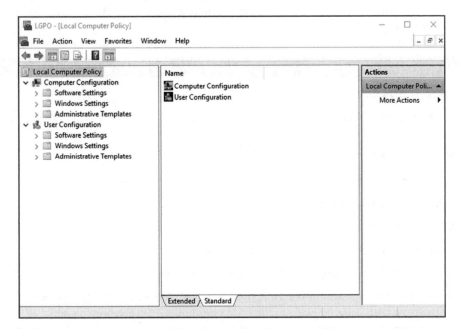

Complete Exercise 9.13 to add the Local Computer Policy snap-in to the MMC.

EXERCISE 9.13

Adding the Local Computer Policy Snap-in

1. Open the Local Users and Groups MMC shortcut by typing **MMC** in the Search Programs And Files box.

2. A User Account Control dialog box appears. Click Yes.

3. Select File ➢ Add/Remove Snap-in.

4. Highlight the Group Policy Object Editor snap-in and click the Add button.

5. The Group Policy Object specifies Local Computer by default. Click the Finish button.

6. In the Add Or Remove Snap-Ins dialog box, click OK.

7. In the left pane, right-click the Local Computer Policy and choose New Windows From Here.

8. Choose File ➢ Save As and name the console **LGPO**. Make sure you save it to the Desktop. Click Save.

9. Close the Local Users and Groups MMC.

Now we will look at how to open an LGPO for a specific user account on a Windows 10 machine. Complete Exercise 9.14 to access the Administrators, Non-Administrators, and User-Specific LGPOs.

Accessing an LGPO

1. Open the Local Users and Groups MMC shortcut by typing **MMC** in the Windows 10 Search box.

2. Select File ➢ Add/Remove Snap-In.

3. Highlight the Group Policy Object Editor snap-in and click the Add button.

4. Click Browse so that you can browse for a different GPO.

5. Click the Users tab.

6. Select the user you want to access and click OK.

7. In the Select Group Policy Object dialog box, click Finish.

8. In the Add Or Remove Snap-Ins dialog box, click OK. You may close the console when you have finished looking at the LGPO settings for the user you chose.

Notice that the Administrators, Non-Administrators, and User-Specific LGPOs contain only User Configuration settings, not Computer Configuration settings.

Now let's take a look at the different security settings that can be configured in the LGPO.

Configuring Local Security Policies

Through the use of the Local Computer Policy, you can set a wide range of security options under Computer Configuration\Windows Settings\Security Settings.

This portion of the Local Computer Policy is also known as the Local Security Policy. The following sections describe in detail how to apply security settings through LGPOs. The main areas of security configuration of the LGPO are as follows:

Account Policies   Account policies are used to configure password and account lockout features. Some of these settings include password history, maximum password age, minimum password age, minimum password length, password complexity, account lockout duration, account lockout threshold, and whether to reset the account lockout counter afterward.

Local Policies   Local policies are used to configure auditing, user rights, and security options.

Windows Firewall with Advanced Security   Windows Firewall with Advanced Security provides network security for Windows computers. Through this LGPO, you can set domain, private, and public profiles. You can also set this LGPO to authenticate communications between computers and inbound/outbound rules.

Network List Manager Policies   This section allows you to set the network name, icon, and location group policies. Administrators can set Unidentified Networks, Identifying Networks, and All Networks.

Public Key Policies   Use the Public Key Policies settings to specify how to manage certificates and certificate life cycles.

Software Restriction Policies   The settings under Software Restriction Policies allow you to identify malicious software and control that software's ability to run on the Windows 10 machine. These policies allow an administrator to protect the Microsoft Windows 10 operating system against security threats such as viruses and Trojan horse programs.

Application Control Policies   This section allows you to set up AppLocker. You can use AppLocker to configure a Denied list and an Accepted list for applications. Applications that are configured on the Denied list will not run on the system, and applications on the Accepted list will operate properly.

IP Security Policies on Local Computer   This section allows you to configure the IPSec policies. IPSec is a way to secure data packets at the IP level of the message.

Advanced Audit Policy Configuration   Advanced Audit Policy Configuration settings can be used to provide detailed control over audit policies. This section also allows you to configure auditing to help show administrators either successful or unsuccessful attacks on their network.

You can also access the Local Security Policy by running secpol.msc or by opening Control Panel and selecting Administrative Tools ➢ Local Security Policy.

Now that you have seen all the options in the security section of the LGPO, let's take a look at account policies and local policies in more detail.

Using Account Policies

Account policies are used to specify the user account properties that relate to the logon process. They allow you to configure computer security settings for passwords and account-lockout specifications.

If security is not an issue—perhaps because you are using your Windows 10 computer at home—then you don't need to bother with account policies. If, on the other hand, security is important—for example, because your computer provides access to payroll information—then you should set very restrictive account policies.

 Account policies at the LGPO level apply only to local user accounts, not domain accounts. To ensure that user account security is configured for domain user accounts, you need to configure these policies at the domain GPO level.

To access the Account Policies folder from the MMC, follow this path: Local Computer Policy ➢ Computer Configuration ➢ Windows Settings ➢ Security Settings ➢ Account Policies. In the following sections, you will learn about the password policies and account-lockout policies that define how security is applied to account policies.

Setting Password Policies

Password policies ensure that security requirements are enforced on the computer. It is important to understand that password policies are set on a per-computer basis; they cannot be configured for specific users. Figure 9.15 shows the password policies, which are described in Table 9.7.

FIGURE 9.15 The password policies

TABLE 9.7   Password policy options

Policy	Description	Default	Minimum	Maximum
Enforce Password History	Keeps track of user's password history	Remember 0 passwords	Same as default	Remember 24 passwords
Maximum Password Age	Determines maximum number of days user can keep valid password	Keep password for 42 days	Keep password for 1 day	Keep password for up to 999 days
Minimum Password Age	Specifies how long password must be kept before it can be changed	0 days (password can be changed immediately)	Same as default	998 days
Minimum Password Length	Specifies minimum number of characters password must contain	0 characters (no password required)	Same as default	14 characters
Password Must Meet Complexity Requirements	Requires that passwords meet minimum levels of complexity	Disabled	No minimum	No maximum
Store Passwords Using Reversible Encryption	Specifies higher level of encryption for stored user passwords	Disabled	No minimum	No maximum

You can use the password policies in Table 9.7 as follows:

Enforce Password History   Prevents users from repeatedly using the same passwords. Users must create a new password when their password expires or is changed.

Maximum Password Age   Forces users to change their passwords after the maximum password age is exceeded. Setting this value to 0 will specify that the password will never expire.

Minimum Password Age   Prevents users from changing their passwords several times in rapid succession in order to defeat the purpose of the Enforce Password History policy.

Minimum Password Length   Ensures that a user creates a password and specifies the length requirement for that password. If this option isn't set, users are not required to create a password at all.

Password Must Meet Complexity Requirements Passwords must be six characters or longer and cannot contain the user's account name or any part of the user's full name. In addition, passwords must contain three of the following four character types:

- English uppercase characters (A through Z)
- English lowercase characters (a through z)
- Decimal digits (0 through 9)
- Symbols (such as !, @, #, $, and %)

Store Passwords Using Reversible Encryption Provides a weaker level of security for user passwords. This is required for Challenge Handshake Authentication Protocol (CHAP) authentication through remote access or Internet Authentication Services (IAS) and for Digest Authentication with Internet Information Services (IIS).

Complete Exercise 9.15 to configure password policies for your computer. These steps assume that you have added the Local Computer Policy snap-in to the MMC in Exercise 9.1.

EXERCISE 9.15

Configuring Password Policy

1. Open the LGPO MMC shortcut that you created earlier.

2. Expand the Local Computer Policy snap-in.

3. Expand the folders as follows: Computer Configuration ➤ Windows Settings ➤ Security Settings ➤ Account Policies ➤ Password Policy.

4. Open the Enforce Password History policy. On the Local Security Setting tab, specify that five passwords will be remembered. Click OK.

5. Open the Maximum Password Age policy. On the Local Security Setting tab, specify that the password expires in 60 days. Click OK.

Let's now look at how to set and manage the policies in the Account Lockout Policies section.

Setting Account-Lockout Policies

The account-lockout policies specify how many invalid logon attempts should be tolerated. You configure the account-lockout policies so that after x number of unsuccessful logon attempts within y number of minutes, the account will be locked for a specified amount of time or until the administrator unlocks it.

Account-lockout policies are similar to a bank's arrangements for ATM access-code security. You have a certain number of chances to enter the correct PIN. That way, anyone who steals your card can't just keep guessing your access code until they get it right. Typically, after three unsuccessful attempts, the ATM takes the card. Then you need to request a new card from the bank. Figure 9.16 shows the account-lockout policies, which are described in Table 9.8.

FIGURE 9.16   Account-lockout policies

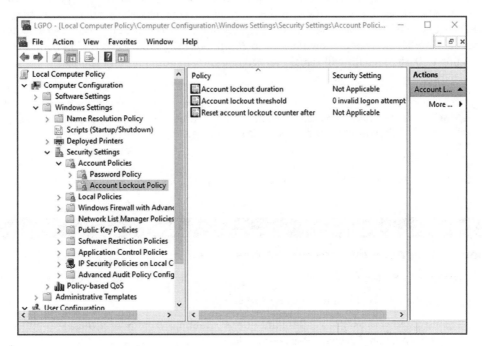

TABLE 9.8   Account-lockout policy options

Policy	Description	Default	Minimum	Maximum
Account Lockout Duration	Specifies how long account will remain locked if the account lockout threshold is reached	Disabled (If Account Lockout Threshold is enabled, 30 minutes.)	Same as default.	99,999 minutes
Account Lockout Threshold	Specifies number of invalid attempts allowed before account is locked out	0 (Disabled; account will not be locked out.)	Same as default.	999 attempts
Reset Account Lockout Counter After	Specifies how long counter will remember unsuccessful logon attempts	Disabled (If Account Lockout Threshold is enabled, 30 minutes.)	Same as default; if enabled, must be equal to or less than the Account Lockout Duration value.	99,999 minutes

The Account Lockout Duration and Reset Account Lockout Counter After policies will be disabled until a value is specified for the Account Lockout Threshold policy. After the Account Lockout Threshold policy is set, the Account Lockout Duration and Reset Account Lockout Counter After policies will be set to 30 minutes. If you set Account Lockout Duration to 0, the account will remain locked out until an administrator unlocks it.

 The Reset Account Lockout Counter After value must be equal to or less than the Account Lockout Duration value.

Complete Exercise 9.16 to configure account-lockout policies and test their effects.

EXERCISE 9.16

Configuring Account-Lockout Policies

1. Open the LGPO MMC shortcut.

2. Expand the Local Computer Policy snap-in.

3. Expand the folders as follows: Computer Configuration ➢ Windows Settings ➢ Security Settings ➢ Account Policies ➢ Password Policy.

4. Open the Account Lockout Threshold policy. On the Local Security Setting tab, specify that the account will lock after three invalid logon attempts. Click OK.

5. Accept the suggested value changes for the Account Lockout Duration and Reset Account Lockout Counter After policies by clicking OK.

6. Open the Account Lockout Duration policy. On the Local Security Setting tab, specify that the account will remain locked for 5 minutes. Click OK.

7. Accept the suggested value changes for the Reset Account Lockout Counter After policy by clicking OK.

8. Log off your Administrator account. Try to log on as one of the accounts that have been created on this Windows 10 machine and enter an incorrect password four times.

9. After you see the error message stating that the referenced account has been locked out, log on as an administrator.

10. To unlock the account, open the Local Users and Groups snap-in in the MMC, expand the Users folder, and double-click the user.

11. On the General tab of the user's Properties dialog box, click to remove the check mark from the Account Is Locked Out check box. Then click OK.

Using Local Policies

As you learned in the preceding section, account policies are used to control logon procedures. When you want to control what a user can do after logging on, you use local policies. With local policies, you can implement auditing, specify user rights, and set security options.

To use local policies, first add the Local Computer Policy snap-in to the MMC. Then, from the MMC, follow this path to access the Local Policies folders: Local Computer Policy ➢ Computer Configuration ➢ Windows Settings ➢ Security Settings ➢ Local Policies. Figure 9.17 shows the three Local Policies folders: Audit Policy, User Rights Assignment, and Security Options. We will look at Audit Policy and User Rights Assignment in the following sections.

FIGURE 9.17   Accessing the Local Policies folders

Setting Audit Policies

Audit policies can be implemented to track the success or failure of specified user actions. You audit events that pertain to user management through the audit policies. By tracking certain events, you can create a history of specific tasks, such as user creation and successful or unsuccessful logon attempts. You can also identify security violations that arise when users attempt to access system management tasks for which they do not have permission.

🌐 Real World Scenario

Auditing Failed Attempts

As an IT manager, you have to make sure that you monitor failed attempts to access resources. A failed attempt to access a resource usually means that someone tried to access the resource and was denied because of insufficient privileges.

Users who try to go to areas for which they do not have permission usually fall into two categories: hackers and people who are just curious to see what they can get away with. Both are very dangerous.

If a user is trying to access an area in which they do not belong, make sure to warn the user. This is very common on a network and needs to be nipped in the bud.

When you define an audit policy, you can choose to audit success or failure of specific events. The success of an event means that the task was successfully accomplished. The failure of an event means that the task was not successfully accomplished.

By default, auditing is not enabled, and it must be manually configured. Once auditing has been configured, you can see the results of the audit in the security log using the Event Viewer utility.

> Only members of the Administrators group can view the security log in Event Viewer.

Figure 9.18 shows the audit policies, which are described in Table 9.9.

TABLE 9.9   Audit-policy options

Policy	Description
Audit Account Logon Events	Tracks when a user logs on or logs off either their local machine or the domain (if domain auditing is enabled).
Audit Account Management	Tracks user and group account creation, deletion, and management actions, such as password changes.
Audit Directory Service Access	Tracks directory service accesses.
Audit Logon Events	Audits events related to logon, such as running a logon script, accessing a roaming profile, and accessing a server.

Policy	Description
Audit Object Access	Enables auditing of access to files, folders, and printers.
Audit Policy Change	Tracks any changes to the audit policies, trust policies, or user rights assignment policies.
Audit Privilege Use	Tracks users exercising a user right.
Audit Process Tracking	Tracks events such as activating a program, accessing an object, and exiting a process.
Audit System Events	Tracks system events such as shutting down or restarting the computer as well as events that relate to the security log in Event Viewer.

FIGURE 9.18   Audit policies

After you set the Audit Object Access policy to enable auditing of object access in the object's properties, you must enable file auditing through NTFS security or print auditing through printer security.

Complete Exercise 9.17 to configure audit policies and view their results.

EXERCISE 9.17

Configuring Audit Policies

1. Open the LGPO MMC shortcut.

2. Expand the Local Computer Policy snap-in.

3. Expand the folders as follows: Computer Configuration ➤ Windows Settings ➤ Security Settings ➤ Local Policies ➤ Audit Policy.

4. Open the Audit Account Logon Events policy. Check the Success and Failure boxes. Click OK.

5. Open the Audit Account Management policy. Check the Success and Failure boxes. Click OK.

6. Log off of your Administrator account. Attempt to log back on to your Administrator account using an incorrect password. The logon should fail (because the password is incorrect).

7. Log on as an administrator.

8. Select Start, right-click Computer, and choose Manage to open Event Viewer.

9. From Event Viewer, open the Security log by selecting Windows Logs ➤ Security. You should see the audited events listed with a Task Category of Credential Validation.

Assigning User Rights

The user-rights policies determine what rights a user or group has on the computer. User rights, also called privileges, apply to the system. They are not the same as permissions, which apply to a specific object. An example of a user right is Back Up Files And Directories. This right allows a user to back up files and folders even if the user does not have permissions that have been defined through NTFS filesystem permissions. The other user rights are similar because they deal with system access as opposed to resource access.

Figure 9.19 shows the first several user-rights policies; all of the policies are described in Table 9.10.

TABLE 9.10 User Rights Assignment policy options

Right	Description
Access Credential Manager As A Trusted Caller	Used to back up and restore Credential Manager.
Access This Computer From The Network	Allows a user to access the computer from the network.

Right	Description
Act As Part Of The Operating System	Allows low-level authentication services to authenticate as any user.
Add Workstations To Domain	Allows a user to create a computer account on the domain.
Adjust Memory Quotas For A Process	Allows you to configure how much memory can be used by a specific process.
Allow Log On Locally	Allows a user to log on at the physical computer.
Allow Log On Through Remote Desktop Services	Gives a user permission to log on through Remote Desktop Services.
Back Up Files And Directories	Allows a user to back up all files and directories regardless of how the file and directory permissions have been set.
Bypass Traverse Checking	Allows a user to pass through and traverse the directory structure, even if that user does not have permissions to list the contents of the directory.
Change The System Time	Allows a user to change the internal time and date on the computer.
Change The Time Zone	Allows a user to change the time zone.
Create A Pagefile	Allows a user to create or change the size of a page file.
Create A Token Object	Allows a process to create a token if the process uses an internal API to create the token.
Create Global Objects	Allows a user to create global objects when connected using Terminal Server.
Create Permanent Shared Objects	Allows a process to create directory objects through Object Manager.
Create Symbolic Links	Allows a user to create a symbolic link.
Debug Programs	Allows a user to attach a debugging program to any process.
Deny Access To This Computer From The Network	Allows you to deny specific users or groups access to this computer from the network. Overrides the Access This Computer From The Network policy for accounts present in both policies.

TABLE 9.10   User Rights Assignment policy options *(continued)*

Right	Description
Deny Log On As A Batch Job	Allows you to prevent specific users or groups from logging on as a batch file. Overrides the Log On As A Batch Job policy for accounts present in both policies.
Deny Log On As A Service	Allows you to prevent specific users or groups from logging on as a service. Overrides the Log On As A Service policy for accounts present in both policies.
Deny Log On Locally	Allows you to deny specific users or groups access to the computer locally. Overrides the Log On Locally policy for accounts present in both policies.
Deny Log On Through Terminal Services	Specifies that a user is not able to log on through Terminal Services.
Enable Computer And User Accounts To Be Trusted For Delegation	Allows a user or group to set the Trusted For Delegation setting for a user or computer object. A user or computer that is trusted for delegation can access resources on another computer using delegated credentials of a client.
Force Shutdown From A Remote System	Allows the system to be shut down by a user at a remote location on the network.
Generate Security Audits	Allows a user, group, or process to make entries in the security log.
Impersonate A Client After Authentication	Enables programs running on behalf of a user to impersonate a client.
Increase A Process Working Set	The working set of a process is the current set of pages in the virtual address space of the process that resides in physical memory. This setting allows you to increase the size of the process working set.
Increase Scheduling Priority	Specifies that a process can increase or decrease the priority that is assigned to another process.
Load And Unload Device Drivers	Allows a user to dynamically unload and load device drivers. This right does not apply to Plug and Play drivers.
Lock Pages In Memory	Allows an account to create a process that runs only in physical RAM, preventing it from being paged.

Right	Description
Log On As A Batch Job	Allows a process to log on to the system and run a file that contains one or more operating system commands.
Log On As A Service	Allows a service to log on in order to run.
Manage Auditing And Security Log	Allows a user to enable object access auditing for files and other Active Directory objects. This right does not allow a user to enable general object access auditing in the Local Security Policy.
Modify An Object Label	Allows a user to change the integrity level of files, folders, or other objects.
Modify Firmware Environment Variables	Allows a user to install or upgrade Windows. It also allows a user or process to modify the firmware environment variables stored in NVRAM of non-x86-based computers. This right does not affect the modification of system environment variables or user environment variables.
Perform Volume Maintenance Tasks	Allows a user to perform volume maintenance tasks such as defragmentation and error checking.
Profile Single Process	Allows a user to monitor nonsystem processes through performance-monitoring tools.
Profile System Performance	Allows a user to monitor system processes through performance-monitoring tools.
Remove Computer From Docking Station	Allows a user to undock a laptop through the Windows 10 user interface.
Replace A Process Level Token	Allows a process, such as Task Scheduler, to call an API to start another service.
Restore Files And Directories	Allows a user to restore files and directories regardless of file and directory permissions.
Shut Down The System	Allows a user to shut down the Windows 10 computer locally.
Synchronize Directory Service Data	Allows a user to synchronize Active Directory data.
Take Ownership Of Files Or Other Objects	Allows a user to take ownership of system objects, such as files, folders, printers, and processes.

FIGURE 9.19   User-rights policies

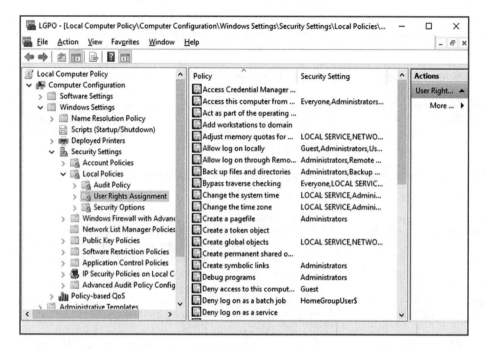

In Exercise 9.18, you'll apply a user-rights policy.

EXERCISE 9.18

Applying a User-Rights Policy

1. Open the LGPO MMC shortcut.

2. Expand the Local Computer Policy snap-in.

3. Expand the folders as follows: Computer Configuration ➢ Windows Settings ➢ Security Settings ➢ Local Policies ➢ User Rights Assignment.

4. Open the Log On As A Service user right.

5. Click the Add User Or Group button. The Select Users Or Groups dialog box appears.

6. Click the Advanced button, and then select Find Now.

7. Select a user. Click OK.

8. Click OK in the Select Users Or Groups dialog box.

9. In the Log On As A Service Properties dialog box, click OK.

Configuring User Account Control

Most administrators have had to wrestle with the balance between security and enabling applications to run correctly. In the past, some applications simply would not run correctly under Windows unless the user running the application was a local administrator.

Unfortunately, granting local administrator permissions to a user also allows the user to install software and hardware, change configuration settings, modify local user accounts, and delete critical files. Even more troubling is the fact that malware that infects a computer while an administrator is logged in is able to perform administrative functions.

The problem is that many applications require that users have permissions to write to protected folders and to the Registry. Windows 10's solution is *User Account Control (UAC)*. UAC enables non-administrator users to perform standard tasks, such as install a printer, configure a VPN or wireless connection, and install updates, while preventing them from performing administrative tasks such as installing applications.

Privilege Elevation

UAC protects computers by requiring privilege elevation for all users, even users who are members of the local Administrators group. As you have no doubt seen by now, UAC will prompt you for permission when performing a task that requires privilege elevation. This prevents malware from silently launching processes without your knowledge.

Privilege elevation is required for any feature that contains the security shield. For example, the small shield shown on the Change Date And Time button in the Date And Time dialog box indicates an action that requires privilege elevation.

Now let's take a look at how to elevate privileges for users and executables.

Elevated Privileges for Users

By default, local administrators are logged on as standard users. When administrators attempt to perform a task that requires privilege elevation, they are prompted for confirmation by default. This can require administrators to authenticate when performing a task that requires privilege elevation by changing the User Account Control: Behavior Of The Elevation Prompt For Administrators In Admin Approval Mode policy setting to Prompt For Credentials. On the other hand, if you don't want UAC to prompt administrators for confirmation when elevating privileges, you can change the policy setting to Elevate Without Prompting.

Non-administrator accounts are called standard users. When standard users attempt to perform a task that requires privilege elevation, they are prompted for a password of a user account that has administrative privileges. You cannot configure UAC to automatically allow standard users to perform administrative tasks, nor can you configure UAC to prompt a standard user for confirmation before performing administrative tasks. The UAC does this automatically. If you do not want standard users to be prompted at all for credentials when attempting to perform administrative tasks, you change the User

Account Control: Behavior Of The Elevation Prompt For Standard Users policy setting to Automatically Deny Elevation Requests.

The built-in Administrator account, though disabled by default, is not affected by UAC. UAC will not prompt the built-in Administrator account for elevation of privileges. Thus, it is important to use a normal user account whenever possible and use the built-in Administrator account only when absolutely necessary.

 With the Default UAC setting enabled, a user's desktop will be dimmed when they are notified of a change to the computer. The administrator or user must either approve or deny the request in the UAC dialog box before the user can do anything else on that computer. This is known as the *secure desktop.* You have the ability to turn off the secure desktop by modifying either the Local Security Policy or the Registry.

Complete Exercise 9.19 to see how UAC affects administrator and non-administrator accounts differently.

EXERCISE 9.19

Seeing How UAC Affects Accounts

1. Log on to Windows 10 as a non-administrator account.

2. Right-click Start ➢ Control Panel ➢ Large Icons View ➢ Windows Firewall.

3. Click the Turn Windows Firewall On Or Off link on the left side. The UAC box should prompt you for permission to continue. Click Yes. You should be denied access to the Windows Firewall Settings dialog box.

4. In the Users and Groups MMC, enable the Administrator account and also reset the Administrator's password.

5. Log off and log on as the Administrator account.

6. Right-click Start ➢ Control Panel ➢ *Large Icons View* ➢ Windows Firewall.

7. Click the Turn Windows Firewall On Or Off link.

8. You should automatically be taken to the Windows Firewall screen. Close the Windows Firewall screen.

Let's now take a look at elevating privileges for executable applications.

Elevated Privileges for Executables

You can also enable an executable file to run with elevated privileges. To do so, you can right-click a shortcut or executable and select Run As Administrator. The elevation applies to this session only.

But what if you need to configure an application to always run with elevated privileges for a user? To do so, log in as an administrator, right-click a shortcut or executable, and select Properties. On the Compatibility tab, check the Run This Program As An Administrator check box. If the Run This Program As An Administrator check box is unavailable, the program is blocked from permanently running as an administrator because the program doesn't need administrative privileges or you are not logged on as an administrator.

Registry and File Virtualization

Many applications that are installed on a Windows 10 machine need to have access to the Registry. By default, Windows 10 protects the Registry from non-administrator accounts, but a feature called Registry and File Virtualization enables non-administrator users to run applications that previously required administrative privileges to run correctly. As discussed earlier, some applications write to the Registry and to protected folders, such as C:\Windows and C:\Program Files. For non-administrator users, Windows 10 redirects any attempts to write to protected locations to a per-user location. By doing so, Windows 10 enables users to use the application successfully while it protects critical areas of the system.

Understanding Smart Cards

Another way to help secure Windows 10 is by using smart cards. *Smart cards* are plastic cards (the size of a credit card) that can be used in combination with other methods of authentication. This process of using a smart card along with another authentication method is called two-factor authentication or *multi-factor authentication*. Authentication is the process of using user credentials to log on to either the local Windows 10 machine or the domain.

Multi-factor authentication support allows you to increase the security of many critical functions of your company, including client authentication, interactive logon, and document signing.

Multi-factor authentication (using smart cards) is now easier than ever to use and deploy because of the new features included with all versions of Windows 10.

Enhanced Support for Smart Card–Related Plug and Play and the Personal Identity Verification (PIV) Standard   This allows users of Windows 10 to use smart cards from vendors who publish their drivers through Windows Update, allowing Windows 10 to use the smart card without special middleware. These drivers are downloaded in the same way as drivers for other Windows devices. When a smart card that is PIV-compliant is placed into a smart-card reader, Windows 10 will try to download a current driver from Windows Update. If a driver is not available, the PIV-compliant minidriver that is included with Windows 10 is used for the smart card.

Encrypting Drives with BitLocker   If your users are using Windows 10 Enterprise or Professional, the users can choose to encrypt their removable media by turning on BitLocker and then choosing the smart-card option to unlock the drive. Windows will then retrieve the correct minidriver for the smart card and allow the operation to complete.

Smart-Card Domain Logon   When using Windows 10, the correct minidriver for a smart card is automatically retrieved. This allows a new smart card to authenticate with the domain controller without requiring the user to install or configure additional middleware.

Document and Email Signing   Windows 10 users can use smart cards to sign an email or document. XML Paper Specification (XPS) documents can also be signed without additional software.

Use with Line-of-Business Applications   Using Windows 10 smart cards allows applications that use Cryptography Next Generation (CNG) or CryptoAPI to retrieve the correct minidriver at runtime. This eliminates the need for middleware.

When you decide to use multi-factor authentication, you are deciding to use a process that will require certificate authorities (CAs). CAs are servers that are running the certificate services on them. When you move forward with the decision to use smart cards, you will then need to install and configure CAs to make all of the components work together.

CAs are built on Windows Server operating systems, and if your Windows 10 users are having issues logging into the Windows 10 operating systems using smart cards, then you must check the server CAs to make sure that they are configured and running properly.

> Certificate Servers are covered in greater detail in *MCSA Windows Server 2012 R2 Complete Study Guide: Exams 70–410, 70–411, 70–412, and 70–417* by William Panek (Sybex, 2016).

There are two types of smart cards: physical and virtual. Physical smart cards are cards that look like ATM cards. Most of them have either a magnetic strip or chip built into the physical card. To use a physical smart card, you need a smart card reader. This is a device that either connects to a computer or is built into a computer and you place the physical smart card into the reader. You then enter a PIN into the system and the machine is unlocked or logged into the network.

There is a downside to using physical smart cards, which is that they can get lost or misplaced. When I implemented a smart card system into a previous company, we ended up replacing one-fourth of all cards in the first month due to loss or damage.

This is where virtual smart cards can be an advantage. Virtual smart cards use a cryptographic key technology that is stored on the actual Windows 10 computer, as long as that computer has a Trusted Platform Module (TPM) installed on the motherboard.

Virtual smart cards offer the security benefits of two-factor authentication without the price of physical cards and readers. This is possible because of the TPM technology. TPM devices allow us to use cryptographic capabilities, the same as physical smart cards do, but without the cards. Virtual smart cards give us the same benefits as physical cards, including non-exportability, anti-hammering, and isolated cryptography.

Non-exportability TPM technology is built to be tamper proof. When a system uses TPM encryption, the TPM encryption is specific to the machine that installed it. Because of this, you can't take a virtual smart card from one system and use it on another.

Anti-hammering (Lockout) Smart cards use PINs to unlock the system. If a PIN is entered incorrectly, the TPM uses an Anti-hammering technology that locks the system from further attempts for a specific amount of time.

Isolated Cryptography TPMs are the only mechanism on a Windows 10 system that loads a copy of the private keys. These keys are not loaded into the system's memory, and because only TPM has the keys, the keys stay isolated and inaccessible to anything or anyone.

Virtual smart cards function the same way as physical smart cards that are continuously inserted into a system. The machine gets the same benefits and results. To set up virtual smart cards, you need to build a certificate authority (CA) server in your organization, and all of your Windows clients need to be Windows 7 or higher.

After the CA is built, you then need to build a certificate template for the virtual smart cards to use. Then, to create the TPM virtual smart card for a Windows 10 system, open a command prompt with Administrative credentials on a Windows 10 domain computer and type in the following command:

```
tpmvscmgr.exe create /name tpmvsc /pin default /adminkey random /generate
```

After you run this command, you will create a virtual smart card with the name `tpmvsc`. The system will then prompt you for a PIN. You will need to enter and confirm a PIN of at least eight characters. After a few seconds, the process will complete. The TPM application (`tpmvscmgr.exe`) will then provide you with the device instance ID for the virtual smart card. You may want to store this ID in case you will need it to manage or remove the virtual smart card later.

Finally, you will need to enroll the certificate into the CA by requesting a new certificate and then choosing the TPM Virtual Smart Card Logon check box. When you are prompted for a device, select the Microsoft virtual smart card that you created earlier.

Configuring Remote Management

End-user support is a major concern and a time-consuming endeavor for most IT departments. Anything you can do to provide a more efficient solution to user issues is a major benefit. Basic telephone or chat support works in many cases, but what if you could see what the end user sees or even interface with their machine? By using Remote Assistance and Remote Desktop, you can.

Remote Assistance in Windows provides many enhancements over previous versions, including improvements in security, performance, and usability. Windows 10 goes even further by adding Easy Connect, which makes it even easier for novice users to request help from expert users. Group Policy support has been increased. There is command-line functionality (meaning you can add scripting), bandwidth optimization, logging, and even more.

Remote Desktop is a tool that allows you to take control of a remote computer's keyboard, video, and mouse. This tool does not require someone collaborating with you on the remote computer. Remote Desktop is used to access remote machines' applications and troubleshoot issues as well as meet end-user needs where you want complete control of the remote machine. Let's start the discussion with Remote Assistance.

In the following sections, we will also look at how to use virtual private networks (VPNs). We will look at how to configure VPNs and the protocols that work with VPNs.

Remote Assistance

Remote Assistance provides a method for inviting help by instant message, email, a file, or now an Easy Connect option. To use Remote Assistance, the computer requesting help and the computer providing help must have Remote Assistance capabilities and the feature enabled, and both computers must have network connectivity (they have to be able to talk to each other).

Remote Assistance is designed to have an expert user (the assistor) provide assistance to a novice user (assistee). When assisting a novice user, the expert can use text-based chat built into Remote Assistance. The expert can also take control of a novice user's desktop (with permission, of course). Here are two common examples of when you would use Remote Assistance:

- Diagnosing problems that are difficult to explain or reproduce. Remote Assistance can allow an expert to remotely view the computer, and the novice user can show the expert an error or problem.

- Guiding a novice user to perform a complex set of actions. The expert can also take control of the computer and complete the tasks if necessary.

Easy Connect

The Easy Connect method for getting remote assistance is new for Windows 10. Easy Connect uses Peer Name Resolution Protocol (PNRP) to set up direct peer-to-peer transfer using a central machine on the Internet to establish the connection. PNRP uses IPv6 and Teredo tunneling to register a machine as globally unique. You're not using IPv6? You are with PNRP; Windows 10 (as well as Windows 7/8, Windows Server 2008/2008 R2, and Windows Server 2012/2012 R2) has IPv6 turned on natively as well as the currently used standard of IPv4. We discussed IPv6 in detail in Chapter 7, "Windows 10 Networking," but to give you an idea, you can see the structure of the PNRP Teredo IPv6 packet in Figure 9.20.

FIGURE 9.20   Teredo and IPv6 PNRP structure

To establish a Remote Assistance session with a user using Easy Connect, the novice should open the Windows Remote Assistance screen by right clicking Start ➤ System ➤ Remote Settings ➤ Windows Remote Assistance. You can also launch the Windows Remote Assistance screen by typing **msra** in the integrated search box next to the Start menu.

Remote Assistance can also be incorporated in Group Policy in an enterprise environment by having the expert user configured as a Helper for users in the enterprise (by domain or OU). Once configured as a Helper, the expert can initiate a Remote Assistance session by issuing the command msra /offerra. This will bring up the Who Do You Want To Help Remote Assistance screen.

The expert can also include the novice user's IP address or computer name as an option to the offerRA switch to initiate the Remote Assistance session in one stop (e.g., msra /offerra *ipaddress | computername*).

There are several msra.exe switches available to further control the establishment of the Remote Assistance session for both the novice and the expert user. Table 9.11 highlights many of the switches.

TABLE 9.11   MSRA command-line switches

Switch	OS Availability	Functionality
/?	Vista and above	Displays the help options.
/novice	Vista and above	Starts Remote Assistance at the Invite screen.
/expert	Vista and above	Starts Remote Assistance at the Help Someone screen.
/offerRA *ip | computer*	Vista and above	Starts Remote Assistance at the Expert Initiated screen or with the options, by automatically initiating with the novice user (used with Group Policy configured in an enterprise environment).

TABLE 9.11   MSRA command-line switches *(continued)*

Switch	OS Availability	Functionality
/email *password*	Vista and above	Creates an email invitation to be sent to an expert user to request assistance using the novice's default email program; a random password will be generated and needs to be conveyed to the expert, or alternatively a password can be specified with the password option and conveyed to the expert.
/saveasfile *path password*	Vista and above	Creates a file invitation to be given to an expert user to request assistance; a random password will be generated, or optionally a password can be specified with the *password* option and conveyed to the expert.
/openfile *path*	Vista and above	Used to open the invitation file sent to the expert; can be local or on a shared network drive; the expert will enter the password given to the user when the session was initiated.
/geteasyhelp	Windows 7 and above	Starts a novice user's Remote Assistance session using Easy Connect; presents the novice with the password to convey to the expert user.
/offereasyhelp	Windows 7 and above	Starts an expert user's Remote Assistance session using Easy Connect; presents the expert user with the screen to enter the password from the novice user.
/getcontacthelp *address*	Windows 7 and above	Reestablishes a Remote Assistance session from a novice user's machine to the address from the previous session. The address is in the RAContactHistory.xml file as a 20-byte hexadecimal string with a .RAContact extension.
/offercontacthelp *address*	Windows 7 and above	Reestablishes a Remote Assistance session from an expert user's machine to the address from the previous session. The address is in the RAContactHistory.xml file as a 20-byte hexadecimal string with a .RAContact extension.

Whichever way the novice or the expert launches the feature, the Windows Remote Assistance screen will become available (see Figure 9.21). To start using Easy Connect, the novice user will select Invite Someone You Trust To Help You.

FIGURE 9.21   Remote Assistance initial screen

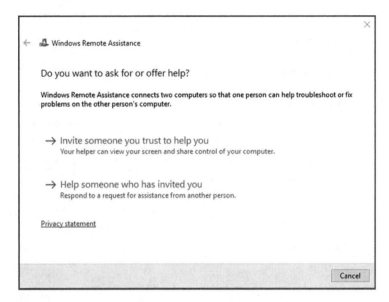

One nice feature of Easy Connect is that if the novice user has established an Easy Connect session previously with an expert user, the screen after selecting Use Easy Connect will offer the novice the ability to connect to the same expert. The novice user can also choose to invite someone new and/or delete the old contact. The expert user will have the same option after choosing Use Easy Connect from the machine used for a previous Easy Connect session.

After the Use Easy Connect option is selected, Windows 10 will verify network connectivity briefly. This is the point at which the PNRP actions take place and the novice user's information is added to a cloud on the Internet. The cloud is the group of machines holding little pieces of information—the identifiers of users needing connectivity, set up in a peer-to-peer sharing environment. PNRP uses this distributed infrastructure for its peer-to-peer name resolution. The novice user's contact information is entered into the PNRP cloud, and an associated password is created and displayed to the novice user.

The novice user will now relay the password to the expert by text message, telephone, or any convenient conversation method. The novice will simply have to wait for the expert to initiate their part. The novice user will still have to accept the connection once the expert starts the remote assistance session.

The expert user needs to start a Remote Assistance session the same way the novice did in Figure 9.21, but the expert will choose Help Someone Who Has Invited You from the Windows Remote Assistance screen.

The expert user will be presented a dialog box to use an invitation file, and then after they choose the file, they will be prompted to enter the password (Figure 9.22) to connect to the Remote Assistance session.

FIGURE 9.22 Remote Assistance screen for entering a password

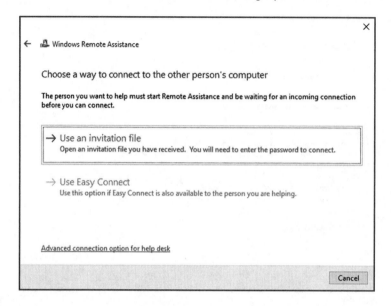

After a few moments of querying the PNRP cloud and finding the connection information that provides the path back to the novice user, Remote Assistance presents the novice user with a confirmation box verifying that the user wants to allow help from the expert.

The novice user will then have a control bar on their screen indicating that the Remote Assistance session is active. From this control bar, the novice can initiate a chat session with the expert and modify some general session settings (bandwidth, logging, contact information exchange, and sharing control).

The expert user will be shown the novice user's Desktop within a separate Remote Assistance window. The expert user will also have some general configuration-setting capabilities as well as an option to request control of the novice user's desktop. The novice user will, of course, be allowed to accept or reject the expert's request.

The expert and novice user can now have an interactive session in which the necessary assistance can be provided. This method of help really takes out the "can you tell me what you see on your screen" issues between two users. The Easy Connect feature takes one more problem out of the equation, getting a novice user to send an invitation to another user. The one caveat here is that both users must be using Windows 10 for Easy Connect to be an option.

Now what if the user is not available to send you the invitation? You can still connect to a user's computer using Remote Desktop, which I will discuss in the next section.

Remote Desktop

Remote Desktop is a tool in Windows 10 that allows you to take control of a remote computer's keyboard, video, and mouse. This tool does not require someone to be available to collaborate with you on the remote computer. While the remote computer is being accessed, locally it remains locked and any actions that are performed remotely will not be visible to the monitor that is attached to the remote computer.

Windows 10 Remote Desktop is, again, an enhanced version of the remote desktop functionality that has been with us for many of the previous versions of Windows, both client and server operating systems. Remote Desktop uses Remote Desktop Protocol (RDP) to provide the data between a host and a client machine. Windows 10 Remote Desktop features are as follows:

- RDP Core Performance Enhancements.

- True Multi-Monitor Support.

- Direct 2D and Direct 3D 10.1 Application Support.

- Bi-directional Audio Support.

- Multimedia and Media Foundation Support.

- Remote FX has a few end-user enhancements for RDP. These enhancements allow for an enhanced desktop environment within your corporate network.

There are many uses for Remote Desktop, but the most common use is that of the administrator attempting to perform a task on an end user's machine (or on a server).

Another use is the end user connecting to a machine from their home or on the road. If you have noticed the enhancements of Remote Desktop (which are enhancements to RDP), you can see that one of the main goals of enhancing Remote Desktop is to make the user experience as comfortable and seamless as possible.

 Real World Scenario

Using Remote Desktop Functionality

I have mentioned many times using Remote Desktop for troubleshooting client computers. As an administrator, I like to just take control of an end-user machine and fix it. Although this can be done in Remote Assistance, the end user is required to allow us to have access and then can watch what we do. In Remote Desktop, we just take control and close the interactive session at the remote machine (yes, the remote end user can block us or take over the session, but not if they want their problem solved).

But there are other uses as well. We provide servers with resources to our clients, and the servers may need to be changed or updated on a regular basis (sometimes a couple of changes in a day). Remote Desktop allows us to maintain our servers from wherever we are without impacting the clients or other administrators.

Remote Desktop Connection Options

When connecting to a Remote Desktop host machine, several options are available to enhance the client user session. The options allow configuration for general settings, display options, local resource access, programs to be executed on startup, the user experience, and advanced options for security and Remote Desktop gateway access. The options become available by clicking the Options button in the lower-left area of the initial Remote Desktop Connection screen. Figure 9.23 shows the options window displayed.

FIGURE 9.23   Remote Desktop options

From the General tab, you can select the target remote computer and username. You can save the user credentials from this tab as well. You can save the connection settings to a file or open an existing RDP file from the General tab.

From the Display tab you can choose the size of the display screen. This is also where you select the option to use multiple monitors. The color depth (color quality) is also selected in the Display tab. The option to display the connection bar when using full-screen display is available here as well.

From the Local Resources tab you can configure remote audio settings, keyboard settings, and local device and resource access.

The Programs tab for Remote Desktop options allows the selection of a program to run at connection startup. The program name and path are specified, as is a startup folder if necessary.

The end-user experience is important to the overall success of using Remote Desktop in the user environment. Remote Desktop can be used to provide a user with the ability to connect to their machine and "remote in." The most seamless environment from the user to the remote location is desirable, but that will be dependent on the bandwidth available. The more bandwidth, the more high-end features can be made available to the end user.

This is also nice for the administrator who is working on an end-user machine. The Experience tab allows the configuration of the end-user experience.

Controlling the behavior of the Remote Desktop connection with regard to security is configured on the Advanced tab of the Remote Desktop options dialog box. The Advanced tab also supports the configuration of a Remote Desktop gateway to allow Remote Desktop connections to be established from any Internet location through SSL. The user must still be authorized and the Remote Desktop client must still be available.

In Exercise 9.20, you will enable the Windows 10 machine to allow Remote Desktop connections. It is up to the company to decide whether all user machines are to be configured this way when you install Windows 10 or whether you should do this only when it becomes necessary for a given computer.

EXERCISE 9.20

Enabling Remote Desktop

1. Open the System tool by right clicking Start ➤ Control Panel ➤ System.

2. In the left-hand side, click the Remote Settings link.

3. In the Remote Desktop section, click the radio button that allows connections from computers running any version of Remote Desktop (Less Secure).

4. Make sure the Allow Remote Assistance Connections To This Computer check box is checked.

5. Click OK.

6. Close the System Properties screen.

One way a Windows 10 user can connect to a server is through the use of a virtual private network connection. In the next section, we will look at how to configure a VPN connection on Windows 10.

Configuring a VPN Connection

A virtual private network is a way to establish a connection between a client machine (VPN client) and server machine (VPN server). A VPN gives you the ability to connect (called *tunneling*) to a server through the use of the Internet or a dial-up connection (hopefully not dial-up), typically with the intention of accessing resources that are available on the network where the VPN server is connected. The VPN server acts as a bridge for the external user connecting from the Internet or other external connections point to the internal network. In a nutshell, a VPN allows you to connect to a private network from a public network.

VPN connections can be secured using various protocols. The following list shows you some of the tunneling protocols that can be used when connecting a Windows 10 machine to a remote server:

Internet Key Exchange version 2 (IKEv2)   Windows 10 can connect to a Windows Server VPN using the *Internet Key Exchange version 2 (IKEv2)* VPN tunneling protocol. The IKEv2 VPN protocol is the newest VPN protocol out of all of the following protocols and can be used with Windows Server 2012/2012 R2 and Windows Server 2016. The main advantage of using the IKEv2 VPN protocol is that it allows for the interruptions of the network connection. IKEv2 will then automatically restore the VPN connection after the network connection is restored. This feature is referred to as VPN Reconnect and it is automatically built into the IKEv2 protocol.

Secure Socket Tunneling Protocol   *Secure Socket Tunneling Protocol (SSTP)* was released with Windows Server 2008 and is one of the tunneling protocols available with a Windows Server 2008/2008 R2 server and Windows 7 machines and later. SSTP works by allowing encapsulated Point-to-Point Protocol (PPP) packets to be transmitted over an HTTPS connection. Because of this, firewalls or Network Address Translation (NAT) devices allow SSTP VPN connections to be more easily established. SSTP is the best choice for securing a VPN connection.

Point-to-Point Tunneling Protocol   *Point-to-Point Tunneling Protocol (PPTP)* is one of the predecessors to SSTP, and it also allows point-to-point packets to have encryption for secure connections. PPTP uses TCP/IP for the encryption. PPTP encapsulates PPP frames in IP and uses the TCP for the management side of PPTP.

Layer 2 Tunneling Protocol   *Layer 2 Tunneling Protocol (L2TP)* is a tunneling protocol that has no encryption included in the protocol. L2TP uses the IP Security protocol (IPSec) to make L2TP secure. L2TP with IPSec is a much more secure tunneling option than PPTP.

To set up an outbound client VPN connection in Windows 10, you use the Network and Sharing Center. In Exercise 9.21, you will set up a new VPN connection.

EXERCISE 9.21

Setting Up a VPN Connection

1. Start the Network and Sharing Center by right clicking Start ➤ Control Panel ➤ Network And Sharing Center.

2. Choose the Set Up A New Connection Or Network link.

3. Choose Connect To A Workplace. Click Next.

4. Choose the Use My Internet Connection (VPN) option.

5. The Connect To A Workplace screen appears. You need to type in the TCP/IP address of a VPN server and name this VPN connection. In this window, you also have the ability to use a smart card, to allow other people to use this connection, and to set up the VPN but not connect at this time (the option I chose). After you type in a TCP/IP address and name the VPN connection, click Next.

6. The next screen asks you for your logon credentials. Type in your username, password, and domain name. Click Create.

   Now that the connection is created, I'll show you the steps needed to use it.

7. In the lower-right corner, click on your network connection.

8. A box appears showing your connections. To connect to the VPN connection, choose the corresponding link.

9. When the Connect dialog box appears, make sure your username, password, and domain name are present and click the Connect button.

10. After the connection is established, close it and close the Network and Sharing Center.

Transparent Caching

Windows 10 has a feature called *transparent caching* to help reduce the time needed for retrieving shared files and folders. Transparent caching reduces the time required to access files for the second and subsequent times across a slow network.

In previous versions of Windows, to access a file across a slower network, client computers had to retrieve the file from the server computer. But now with Windows 10 transparent caching, computers can cache these remote files, thus reducing the number of times a computer might retrieve the same data.

When a user opens a file for the first time, Windows 10 accesses the file from the server and then stores the file in the cache of the local disk. From that point on, the user reads the same cached file instead of reading it from the server computer.

To make sure the file is accurate, the Windows 10 client always contacts the server to ensure that the cached copy is up to date. The file would not be accessible if the server is unavailable. Transparent caching is not enabled by default on fast networks. Transparent caching can be enabled through the use of a group policy.

Broadband Tethering

One nice advantage to Windows 10 and mobility is Broadband Tethering. Let's all pretend that we are at a large Microsoft conference and only one of us in our group can get onto the Internet. Windows 10 Broadband Tethering allows at least 10 devices to connect to your Internet connection and use your Internet for their access. As long as their devices have Broadband enabled capabilities, they will be able to connect to your system and use the Internet.

When you set up the Broadband Tethering, you can setup a connection name and password for all of the other users in your group to connect to your system.

All you need to do is go to your Windows 10 mobile device (in Figure 9.24), I'm using a Windows 10 Surface Pro, and you just need to open your Internet connection by sharing the connection.

FIGURE 9.24   Manage Wi-Fi settings

As you can see in Figure 9.25, once you open the connection, you need to set up a password (at least eight characters), and then you can share that password with the other members of your group with whom you want to allow your Internet connection to be shared.

FIGURE 9.25   Manage Wi-Fi Settings password

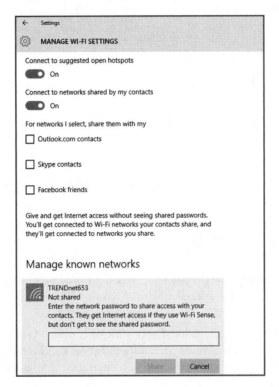

Summary

In this chapter, you learned how to create and manage user and group accounts. We looked at the different tools that can be used to create users in Windows 10.

We also looked at Windows 10 security. We reviewed the difference between LGPOs, which are applied at the local computer level, and GPOs, which are applied through a Windows 2003, 2008, 2008 R2, 2012/2012 R2, and 2016 domain and how they are applied.

We looked at account policies, which control the logon process. The two types of account policies are password and account lockout policies. We also looked at local policies, which control what a user can do at the computer. The three types of local policies are audit, user rights, and security options policies.

Finally, we looked at how administrators can do remote administration and many of the different utilities that we can use to make sure that our hardware and boot up process is secure.

Video Resources

There are videos available for the following exercises:

9.1

9.3

9.4

You can access the videos at http://www.wiley.com/go/sybextestprep.

Exam Essentials

Be able to create and manage user accounts.   When creating user accounts, be aware of the requirements for doing so. Understand User Account Control. Know how to rename and delete user accounts. Be able to manage all user properties.

Know how to configure and manage local user authentication.   Understand the options that can be configured to manage local user authentication and when these options would be used to create a more secure environment. Be able to specify where local user authentication options are configured.

Know how to manage local groups.   Understand the local groups that are created on Windows 10 computers by default, and be familiar with the rights each group has. Know how to create and manage new groups.

Know how to set local group policies.   Understand the purpose of account policies and local policies. Know the purpose and implementation of account policies for managing password policies and account lockout policies. Understand the purpose and implementation of local policies and how they can be applied to users and groups for audit policies, user rights assignments, and security options.

Understand User Account Control.   Understand the purpose and features of User Account Control. Be familiar with Registry and file virtualization. Understand privilege elevation. Know the basics of the new UAC Group Policy settings.

Review Questions

1. You are the network administrator for a Fortune 500 company. The Accounting department has recently purchased a custom application for running financial models. To run properly, the application requires that you make some changes to the computer policy. You decide to deploy the changes through a Local Group Policy setting. You suspect that the policy is not being applied properly because of a conflict somewhere with another Local Group Policy setting. What command should you run to see a list of how the group policies have been applied to the computer and the user?

   A. gpresult

   B. gporesult

   C. gpaudit

   D. gpinfo

2. You have a Windows 10 computer that is located in an unsecured area. You want to track usage of the computer by recording user logon and logoff events. To do this, which of the following auditing policies must be enabled?

   A. Audit Account Logon Events

   B. Audit Account Management

   C. Audit Process Tracking

   D. Audit System Events

3. You are the administrator for a printing company. After you configure the Password Must Meet Complexity Requirements policy, several users have problems when changing their passwords. Which of the following passwords meet the minimum complexity requirements? (Choose all that apply.)

   A. abc12345678

   B. Abcde!

   C. 1247445Np

   D. !@#$%^&*(-[]

4. You are the system administrator for Stellacon Corp. You have a computer that is shared by many users. You want to ensure that when users press Ctrl+Alt+Del to log on, they do not see the name of the last user. What do you configure?

   A. Set the security option Clear User Settings When Users Log Off.

   B. Set the security option Interactive Logon: Do Not Display Last User Name In Logon Screen.

   C. Set the security option Prevent Users From Seeing Last User Name.

   D. Configure nothing; this is the default setting.

5. You are the administrator of a large company. You believe that your network's security has been compromised. You do not want hackers to be able to repeatedly attempt user logon with different passwords. What Local Security Policy box should you define?

    A. Password Policy

    B. Audit Policy

    C. Security Options

    D. Account Lockout Policy

6. You have recently hired Will as an assistant for network administration. You have not decided how much responsibility you want Will to have. In the meantime, you want Will to be able to restore files on Windows 10 computers in your network, but you do not want Will to be able to run the backups. What is the minimum assignment that will allow Will to complete this task?

    A. Add Will to the Administrators group.

    B. Grant Will the Read right to the root of each volume he will back up.

    C. Add Will to the Backup Operators group.

    D. Grant Will the user right Restore Files and Directories.

7. You are the network administrator of a medium-size company. Your company requires a fair degree of security, and you have been tasked with defining and implementing a security policy. You have configured password policies so that users must change their passwords every 30 days. Which password policy would you implement if you want to prevent users from reusing passwords they have used recently?

    A. Passwords Must Be Advanced

    B. Enforce Password History

    C. Passwords Must Be Unique

    D. Passwords Must Meet Complexity Requirements

8. You have a network folder that resides on an NTFS partition on a Windows 10 computer. NTFS permissions and share permissions have been applied. Which of the following statements best describes how share permissions and NTFS permissions work together if they have been applied to the same folder?

    A. The NTFS permissions will always take precedence.

    B. The share permissions will always take precedence.

    C. The system will look at the cumulative share permissions and the cumulative NTFS permissions. Whichever set is less restrictive will be applied.

    D. The system will look at the cumulative share permissions and the cumulative NTFS permissions. Whichever set is more restrictive will be applied.

9. You are the network administrator for a bookstore. You install Windows 10 on a new computer. Before you connect the computer to the Internet, you want to ensure that the appropriate features are enabled. You open Windows Security Center and notice that there are features that need to be addressed. Which of the following features are not included with Windows 10?

    A. Firewall protection

    B. Spyware protection

    C. Virus protection

    D. Automatic update protection

10. You are the Active Directory administrator for your company. A Windows 10 computer has been purchased for the Finance department, and you want to monitor it for unauthorized access. You configure the Audit Object Access policy to audit both success and failure events. However, when you look at the security event log a few days later, you do not see any entries related to file access. What is the most likely reason for this behavior?

    A. Auditing has not been enabled for the appropriate files and folders.

    B. A conflicting Group Policy setting is overriding your configuration.

    C. Another administrator has disabled your Group Policy setting.

    D. Object access events are found in the system event log.

Chapter

10

Configuring Monitoring and Recovery

MICROSOFT EXAM OBJECTIVES COVERED IN THIS CHAPTER:

✓ **Configure system and data recovery.**

- This objective may include but is not limited to the following subobjectives: Configure a recovery drive, configure a system restore, perform a refresh or recycle, perform a driver rollback, configure restore points, resolve hardware and device issues, interpret data from Device Manager, restore previous versions of files and folders, configure File History, recover files from OneDrive, use Windows Backup and Restore, perform a backup and restore with WBAdmin, perform recovery operations using Windows Recovery.

✓ **Monitor Windows.**

- This objective may include but is not limited to the following subobjectives: Configure and analyze Event Viewer logs, configure event subscriptions, monitor performance using Task Manager, monitor performance using Resource Monitor, monitor performance using Performance Monitor and Data Collector Sets, monitor system resources, configure indexing options, manage client security by using Windows Defender, evaluate system stability using Reliability Monitor, troubleshoot performance issues.

One of the tasks that administrators will need to do on a daily basis is fixing Windows 10 systems that are having issues.

There are many ways to determine what issues a Windows 10 system may be having, and there are many tools to help you solve the issues.

The best way to protect any Windows 10 system is to make sure the users' files are stored on a network server and backed up daily. But there may be times when you need to back up the Windows 10 system.

Windows 10 includes a full backup and restore application (Backup and Restore [Windows 7]) that allows a user or an administrator to maintain a backup copy of any of the Windows 10 component files and data files that are considered critical to the operation of your day-to-day business.

There may also be times when Windows 10 doesn't start properly and an administrator will need to identify and resolve the Windows error to get the system booting up properly again. There are many different utilities that allow you to troubleshoot and fix startup issues, including Safe Mode, Last Known Good Configuration, Startup Repair tool, Backup and Restore Center, Driver Rollback, and doing a System Restore.

Finally, there will be times when an administrator needs to monitor the Windows 10 system. Sometimes, performance optimization can feel like a luxury, but it can be very important, especially if you can't get your Windows 10 system to run applications the way they are intended to run. The Windows 10 operating system has been specifically designed to keep your mission-critical applications and data accessible even in times of failures.

The most common cause of such problems is a hardware configuration issue. Poorly written device drivers and unsupported hardware can cause problems with system stability. Failed hardware components (such as system memory) may do so as well. Memory chips can be faulty, electrostatic discharge can ruin them, and other hardware issues can occur. No matter what, a problem with your memory chip spells disaster for your Windows 10 system.

Usually, third-party hardware vendors provide utility programs with their computers that can be used for performing hardware diagnostics on machines to help you find problems. These utilities are a good first step to resolving intermittent problems, but Windows 10 comes with many utilities that can help you diagnose and fix your issues.

In this chapter, I'll cover the tools and methods used for measuring performance and troubleshooting failures in Windows 10. Before you dive into the technical details, however, you should thoroughly understand what you're trying to accomplish and how you'll meet this goal.

One of the Microsoft objectives under Monitoring Windows is using Windows Defender. Windows Defender is not covered in this chapter because it is covered in detail in Chapter 5, "Configuring the Windows 10 Environment."

Understanding Recovery

One of the worst events you may experience is a computer that won't boot. An even worse experience is discovering that there is no recent backup for that computer. The first step in preparing for disaster recovery is to expect that a disaster will happen at some point and ensure to take proactive measures to plan your recovery before the failure occurs. Here are some of the preparations you can take:

- Keep your computer up to date with Windows Update (covered in Chapter 1, "Windows 10 Installation").

- Perform regular system backups.

- Use current software to scan for malware (such as viruses, spyware, and adware), and make sure you have the most recent updates.

- Perform regular administrative functions, such as monitoring the logs in the Event Viewer utility.

No matter how many safeguards you enact, eventually you'll likely need to recover a system. Table 10.1 summarizes all of the Windows 10 utilities and options you can use to assist in performing system recovery. All these Windows 10 recovery techniques are covered in detail in this chapter.

TABLE 10.1 Windows 10 recovery techniques

Recovery Technique	When to Use
Event Viewer	If the Windows 10 operating system can be loaded through normal mode or Safe Mode, one of the first places to look for hints about the problem is Event Viewer. Event Viewer displays System, Security, and Application logs.
Safe Mode	This is generally your starting point for system recovery. Safe Mode loads the absolute minimum of services and drivers that are needed to boot Windows 10. If you can boot your computer to Safe Mode and you suspect that you have a system conflict, you can temporarily disable an application or processes, troubleshoot services, or uninstall software.
Startup Repair tool	If your computer will not boot to Safe Mode, you can use the Startup Repair tool to replace corrupted system files. This option will not help if you have hardware errors, however.
Backup and Restore	You should use this utility to safeguard your computer. If necessary, you can use the Backup and Restore (Windows 7) utility to restore personal files from backup media and to restore a complete image of your computer.

TABLE 10.1 Windows 10 recovery techniques *(continued)*

Recovery Technique	When to Use
Driver Rollback	If you install a driver that causes issues on your system, you can use the Driver Rollback utility to return the driver to its previous version. Use Device Manager to access the Driver Rollback utility. Right-click the hardware component and choose Properties. Then click the Driver tab, and the Roll Back Driver button (Driver Rollback) will be there.
System Restore	System Restore is used to create known checkpoints of your system's configuration. In the event that your system becomes misconfigured, you can restore the system configuration to an earlier version of the checkpoint.

Knowing the Advanced Boot Options

The Windows 10 advanced boot options can be used to troubleshoot errors that keep Windows 10 from successfully booting. Figure 10.1 shows the Advanced Boot Options screen. These advanced boot options are covered in this section.

FIGURE 10.1 Advanced Boot Options screen

To access the Windows 10 advanced boot options, start or reboot the computer and press the F8 key after the firmware POST process but before Windows 10 is loaded. This will bring up the Advanced Boot Options menu, which offers numerous options for booting Windows 10.

Starting in Safe Mode

When your computer will not start, one of the fundamental troubleshooting techniques is to simplify the configuration as much as possible. This is especially important when you do not know the cause of your problem and you have a complex configuration. After you have simplified the configuration, you can determine whether the problem is in the basic configuration or is a result of your complex configuration.

If the problem is in the basic configuration, you have a starting point for troubleshooting. If the problem is not in the basic configuration, you should proceed to restore each configuration option you removed, one at a time. This helps you to identify what is causing the error.

If Windows 10 will not load, you can attempt to load the operating system in *Safe Mode*. When you run Windows 10 in Safe Mode, you are simplifying your Windows configuration as much as possible. Safe Mode loads only the drivers needed to get the computer up and running.

The drivers that are loaded with Safe Mode include basic ones for the mouse, monitor, keyboard, hard drive, standard video driver, and default system services.

Safe Mode is considered a diagnostic mode, so you do not have access to all of the features and devices in Windows 10 that you have access to when you boot normally, including networking capabilities.

Windows 10 offers a few Startup settings when you're trying to repair your Windows 10 system. Figure 10.2 shows the Startup Settings that are offered when you boot into Startup Settings.

FIGURE 10.2 Startup Settings screen

Startup Settings

Press a number to choose from the options below:

Use number keys or functions keys F1-F9.

1) Enable debugging
2) Enable boot logging
3) Enable low-resolution video
4) Enable Safe Mode
5) Enable Safe Mode with Networking
6) Enable Safe Mode with Command Prompt
7) Disable driver signature enforcement
8) Disable early launch anti-malware protection
9) Disable automatic restart after failure

Press F10 for more options
Press Enter to return to your operating system

When the Startup Settings screen appears, you then have the ability to choose to enter a Safe Mode (three versions). Once a computer is booted into Safe Mode, you will see the text *Safe Mode* in the four corners of your desktop, as shown in Figure 10.3.

FIGURE 10.3   A computer running in Safe Mode

If you boot to Safe Mode, check all of your computer's hardware and software settings in Device Manager and try to determine why Windows 10 will not boot properly. After you take steps to fix the problem, try to boot to Windows 10 as you normally would.

In Exercise 10.1, you will boot your computer to Safe Mode.

EXERCISE 10.1

Booting Your Computer to Safe Mode

1. Turn on the Windows 10 system.

2. During the boot process, press the F8 key to access the Boot Options menu.

3. At the Recovery screen, choose See Advanced Repair Options, as shown in Figure 10.4.

FIGURE 10.4   Recovery screen

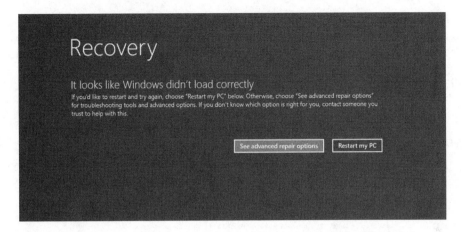

4.   At the Choose An Option screen, choose the Troubleshoot option.

5.   At the Troubleshoot screen, choose Advanced Options (shown in Figure 10.5).

FIGURE 10.5   Troubleshoot screen

6.   At the Advanced Options screen, choose Startup Settings.

7.   At the Startup Settings screen, click the Restart button. The system will reboot into the Startup Settings screen.

8.   At the Startup Settings screen, choose 5) Enable Safe Mode With Networking.

9.   When Windows 10 starts, log in.

Don't restart your computer yet; you will do this as a part of the next exercise.

Enabling Boot Logging

Boot logging creates a log file that tracks the loading of drivers and services. When you choose the Enable Boot Logging option from the Advanced Boot Options menu, Windows 10 loads normally, not in Safe Mode. This allows you to log all of the processes that take place during a normal boot sequence.

This log file can be used to troubleshoot the boot process. When logging is enabled, the log file is written to \WINDOWS\Ntbtlog.txt. A sample of the Ntbtlog.txt file is shown in Figure 10.6.

FIGURE 10.6   A Windows 10 boot log file

In Exercise 10.2, you will examine the boot log file that was created by default during Exercise 10.1.

EXERCISE 10.2

Using Boot Logging

1. Click Windows Explorer (the folder icon on the taskbar) and browse to C:\WINDOWS\Ntbtlog.txt. Double-click this file.

2. Examine the contents of your boot log file.

3. Shut down your computer and restart it without using Advanced Boot Options.

The boot log file is cumulative. Each time you boot to Safe Mode, you are writing to this file. This enables you to make changes, reboot, and see whether you have fixed any problems. If you want to start from scratch, you should manually delete this file and reboot to an Advanced Boot Options menu selection that supports logging (Enable Boot Logging).

Using Other Startup Setting Options

In this section, you will learn about additional Startup Settings menu modes. These include the following options:

1) Enable Debugging   This runs the Kernel Debugger, if it is installed. The Kernel Debugger is an advanced troubleshooting utility.

2) Enable Boot Logging   When you enable boot logging, a file is created called `Ntbtlog.txt`. This file lists all the drivers that are installed during startup and that might be useful for advanced troubleshooting.

3) Enable Low-Resolution Video   This loads a standard VGA driver without starting the computer in Safe Mode. You might use this mode if you changed your video driver, did not test it, and tried to boot to Windows 10 with a bad driver that would not allow you to access video. The Enable VGA mode bails you out by loading a default driver, providing access to video so that you can properly install (and test!) the correct driver for your computer.

Safe Mode starts Windows 10 at a resolution of 800×600.

4) Enable Safe Mode   As explained previously, entering into Safe Mode allows the system to boot up with only the minimum drivers needed to make the system operate.

5) Enable Safe Mode With Networking   This is the same as the Safe Mode option but adds networking features. You might use this mode if you need networking capabilities to download drivers or service packs from a network location.

6) Enable Safe Mode With Command Prompt   This starts the computer in Safe Mode, but after you log in to Windows 10, only a command prompt is displayed. This mode does not provide access to the desktop. Experienced troubleshooters use this mode.

7) Disable Driver Signature Enforcement   This allows drivers to be installed even if they do not contain valid signatures.

8) Disable Early Launch Anti-malware Protection   Windows 10 has a feature called Secure Boot. Secure Boot helps protect the Windows boot configuration and its components. Secure Boot also loads an Early Launch Anti-malware (ELAM) driver. Choosing this option disables the Early Launch Anti-malware driver.

9) Disable Automatic Restart After Failure   This prevents Windows from restarting when a critical error causes Windows to fail. This option should be used only when Windows fails every time you restart, preventing you from accessing the desktop or any configuration options.

10) Press Enter to Return to Your Operating System   This boots the Windows 10 system in the default manner. This option is on the Advanced Boot Options menu in case you accidentally hit F8 during the boot process but really wanted to boot Windows 10 normally.

11) Launch Recovery Environment   The Windows 10 Recovery Environment (WinRE) is used to repair common causes of bootable operating systems problems. By default, WinRE is preloaded into the Windows 10 for Desktop editions (Home, Pro, Enterprise, and Education).

Understanding System Restore

System restores are actually a two-part process to make work. First in the Windows 10 operating system, you create system restore points. These are snapshots of the Windows 10 system so in the event that you need to revert to one of these snapshots, you can.

So after you create some system restore points, the System Restore option in the Advanced Options allows you to revert your PC to an earlier point in time. Restore points are generated when an administrator or user installs a new application, driver, or Windows update or when you manually create a restore point.

When you restore to a previous point, the user's personal files won't be affected, but restores do remove applications, drivers, and updates installed after the restore point was made.

To enable System Protection (needed to create restore points), in Control Panel, choose the System icon. When the System Properties window appears, choose the System Protection tab. Click the Configure button (see Figure 10.7) to turn System Protection on.

FIGURE 10.7   Configure button for System Protection

Once you have enabled System Protection in Control Panel, you then need to open the System Restore application. To do that, you follow these steps:

1. Right-click the Start button and then select Control Panel.

2. Choose Control Panel ➢ Recovery.

3. In the Recovery window, choose Configure System Restore (as shown in Figure 10.8).

FIGURE 10.8   Open System Restore

4. At the next screen, click the Create button. This will allow you to create a system restore point.

The steps to create restore points as well as restore and clean up old restore points will be explained in the section "Maintaining Windows 10 with Backup and Restore," later in this chapter.

Before you can use the system restore to fix a crashed computer, you need to create a recovery drive. Recovery drives allow you to create a backup drive in the event that a PC can't start. After the recovery drive is created, you can then use that drive to recover from a system crash.

To use the recovery drive to fix a crashed computer, boot the system into the Advanced options and then choose System Restore. Then it will ask you for a username and then a password and the system will continue using one of the restore points that was selected.

Using the System Image Recovery

Another way to protect your Windows 10 computer system is to create and use system images. System images are exact copies of the Windows 10 drive. System images, by default, include the drives that are needed for Windows to function properly. System images include Windows and all of the system settings, programs, and files.

System images work well in the event of a major hard disk or computer crash. System images allow you to restore all of the contents of the crashed system and get the system back up and running. When you restore a crashed system from an image, the entire system is restored. It's a complete restore of the computer system. This means that you can't pick and choose what programs you want to install. It's an all-or-nothing restore.

This is the reason why you should also make sure that you do regular backups. By making sure all of your backups are up to date and by making sure you have a system image, you are completely covered in the event of a major crash.

To create a system image, right-click the Start menu and choose Control Panel. In the Control Panel, open File History. Once you're in the File History application, click the System Image Backup link in the lower-left corner (see Figure 10.9).

FIGURE 10.9   System Image Backup

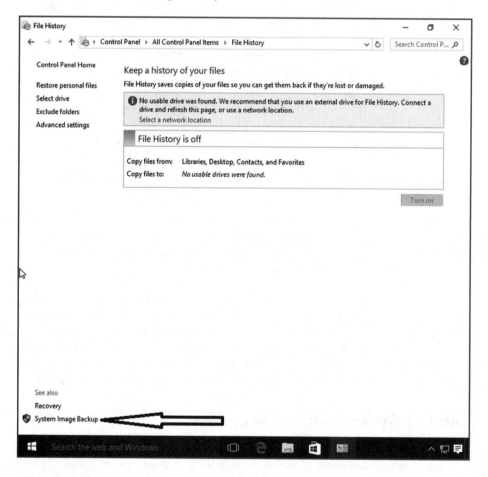

The steps to create a System Image Backup will be explained in later in this chapter in the section "Maintaining Windows 10 with Backup and Restore."

Using the Startup Repair Tool

Another option that is available in the Advanced Options menu is the Startup Repair tool. If your Windows 10 computer will not boot because of missing or corrupted system files, you can use the *Startup Repair tool* to correct these problems. Startup Repair cannot repair hardware failures. Additionally, Startup Repair cannot recover personal files that have been corrupted, damaged by viruses, or deleted. To ensure that you can recover your personal files, you should use the Backup and Restore utility discussed in the next section.

If Startup Repair is unable to correct the problem, you might have to reinstall Windows 10, but this should be done as a last resort. This is one reason you should always back up your Windows 10 machine.

Maintaining Windows 10 with Backup and Restore

The Windows 10 *Backup and Restore utility* enables you to create and restore backups. Backups protect your data in the event of system failure by storing the data on another medium, such as a hard disk, CD, DVD, or network location. If your original data is lost because of corruption, deletion, or media failure, you can restore the data by using your backup.

To access Backup and Restore, type **backup and restore** in the Windows 10 search box. Alternatively, you can choose Start ➤ Control Panel, choose either the small or large icon view, and then click Backup And Restore (Windows 7). Backup and Restore is shown in Figure 10.10.

FIGURE 10.10   Windows 10 Backup and Restore

Creating a Backup

You can see in Figure 10.10 that no backups of this Windows 10 machine have been taken. To set up a backup, choose the Set Up Backup link in the right side of the **Backup And Restore** window. Choosing Set Up Backup launches a wizard that takes you through the process of creating a backup. The Backup Wizard first asks you for a location to save your backup. This location can be a hard disk (removable or fixed), a CD, a DVD, or even a network location (if you have Windows 10 Premium or Ultimate).

Next, you are asked to either let Windows 10 choose the files and folders to back up or let you manually select the resources you want to back up. In your manual selection, you can choose just the data libraries of Windows 10 for you as a user or other users. You can also choose to create a backup of the Windows 10 system files. If you want to choose other files and folders, you have the option of selecting any resources individually on your hard disk(s).

The final page of the wizard enables you to view the items you have selected as well as set up a schedule for your backups to occur. If you're happy with the setup, click the Save Settings And Run Backup button. The backup commences, and you are able to restore the resources if necessary in the future. Figure 10.11 shows my Windows 10 machine right after I chose to save the settings and run a backup. You can see the backup in progress and the date and time of my last backup.

FIGURE 10.11   Windows 10 backup status

Windows 10 *cannot* back up encrypted files. To back up encrypted files, you need to manually copy all encrypted files to an external hard drive or decrypt the files before the backup.

In Exercise 10.3, you will make a backup of your files. This exercise assumes that you haven't yet configured an automatic backup.

EXERCISE 10.3

Backing Up Files

1. Right-click Start ➤ Control Panel ➤ Backup And Restore (Windows 7).

2. Click the Back Up Now button.

3. Select the location where you want to save your backup, and then click Next. In our example, we will use our D: drive.

4. The What Do You Want To Back Up? screen appears. Click the Let Me Choose radio button and then click Next.

5. Select the files that you would like to back up. Click Next.

6. At the Review Your Backup Settings screen, you can select how often you want a backup to be automatically performed. To start the backup, click the Save Settings And Run Backup button.

    Windows begins backing up files, and a progress indicator indicates how the backup is progressing.

7. When the backup is complete, click Close.

After you have created your backup, you can restore system files and user data files with the Backup and Restore utility.

Restoring Files from a Backup

If you have lost or destroyed files that you still want on your Windows 10 system, you can restore them from your backup. To restore files to your computer, launch the Backup and Restore program by typing **backup and restore** in the Windows 10 search box. Assuming the media where your backup was saved is available, you can click the Restore My Files button.

Clicking the Restore My Files button launches a restore wizard that prompts you to search for the files you want to restore. You can select multiple files and folders. When you have selected all the files and folders you want to restore, click Next, and you will have one final option: to restore to the original location or pick an alternative location for restoration. After you make the restore-location decision, choose Restore. The restore operation commences, and your original files and folders are available for you from the backup media.

You also have options in the Backup And Restore window to restore all users' files or to select another backup to restore files from. You would use this second option if you saved your backup to multiple locations and the last one (the one listed in the backup section) is not the set of backup files you want to use in your current session. Other than just restoring files and folders, you have the choice to use other advanced backup options.

In Exercise 10.4, you will restore some files. This exercise assumes that you created a backup in Exercise 10.3.

EXERCISE 10.4

Restoring Files

1. Right-click Start ➢ Control Panel ➢ Backup And Restore (Windows 7).

2. Click the Restore My Files button.

3. At the Restore Files screen, click the Browse For Folders button.

4. Click the Microsoft Windows Backup link in the left window. Then double-click the backup that you created in the previous exercise. Choose the folder that you want to restore (I chose the Program Files folder, but you need to choose a folder with enough free space) and click Add. Click Next to continue.

5. Select whether you want files saved in the original location or a different location. To begin the restore, click Restore.

6. When the restore is complete, click Finish.

Recovering Files from OneDrive

As explained in Chapter 4, "Configuring Storage," Microsoft has a subscription-based storage system called OneDrive. Microsoft's OneDrive is built into Windows 10 by default. OneDrive is a cloud-based storage subscription service so home users can store their documents and then access those documents from anywhere in the world (provided that you have Internet access).

OneDrive was designed for the average home user who is looking to store data in a safe, secure, cloud-based environment. OneDrive, when first released, was also a consideration for corporate environments, but with the release of Windows Azure, OneDrive is really intended for the home user or corporate user who wants to store some of their own personal documents in the cloud. Corporations would be more inclined to use Microsoft Azure with all of its corporate benefits.

Exercise 10.5 will show you how to set up a OneDrive account for your user account. To do this, you must have a Microsoft account. You get 5 GB for free from Microsoft on the OneDrive cloud-based storage.

NOTE   If you did Exercise 4.3 in Chapter 4, "Configuring Storage," please skip the following exercise.

EXERCISE 10.5

Configuring OneDrive

1. Open OneDrive.

2. Log into OneDrive using your Microsoft account.

3. You will get a screen that shows where your files will be located on your system. Click the Next button.

4. At the Sync Files screen, choose what folders you want to sync with Microsoft and then click Next.

    A screen will appear telling you that your OneDrive is set up and ready to go.

5. Click the Open My OneDrive Folder button to open your folders and Microsoft OneDrive.

6. Close OneDrive.

Now that the OneDrive subscription has been set up, you can recover files and folders by clicking Windows Explorer and then choosing OneDrive from the left side. You can recover any of the files and folders that were stored on OneDrive.

Using the Wbadmin Command Utility

Administrators have the ability to configure and manage backups and restores through the command prompt using a utility called Wbadmin. The Wbadmin.exe command replaces the Ntbackup.exe command that was released with previous versions of Windows. Wbadmin allows you to back up and restore your operating system, volumes, files, folders, and applications all from a command prompt.

You must be a member of the Administrators group to configure a regularly scheduled backup. To perform any other tasks using Wbadmin, you must be a member of either the Backup Operators group or the Administrators group, or you must have been delegated the appropriate permissions.

To run the Wbadmin.exe command, you must start it from an elevated command prompt. To do this, click Start, right-click the command prompt, and then click Run As Administrator.

Table 10.2 shows the Windows 10 Wbadmin command switches and their descriptions.

TABLE 10.2   Wbadmin switches

Command	Description
Wbadmin Start Backup	Runs a one-time backup
Wbadmin Stop job	Stops the currently running backup or recovery job

TABLE 10.2   Wbadmin switches *(continued)*

Command	Description
Wbadmin get versions	Shows the details of a backup
Wbadmin get items	Lists items contained in a backup
Wbadmin get status	Shows the status of the currently running operation

Using Advanced Backup Options

In the main Backup And Restore window, you have options in the left pane to turn off the schedule, create a system image, and create a system repair disk.

Choosing the Turn Off Schedule option lets you take your backup out of the current backup scheduling as seen in Task Scheduler. Creating a system image lets you back up critical operating system files for restoration later if your operating system becomes corrupt. Creating a system repair disc allows you to create a bootable disc with which you will have a limited set of repair utilities and the ability to restore your backup files if necessary.

Creating a System Image

A *system image* enables you to take a snapshot of the entire hard disk and capture that image to a specific location so you can restore that image at a later date.

To create a system image of your entire computer, select the Create A System Image link on the left side of the Backup And Restore utility. When creating a system image, you can save that image to a hard disk, a DVD, or a network location.

In Exercise 10.6, you will create a system image and save it to a local hard disk.

EXERCISE 10.6

Creating a System Image

1. Right-click Start ➤ Control Panel ➤ Backup And Restore (Windows 7).

2. Click the Create A System Image link on the left side.

3. Choose the location where you want to save the image. I am choosing the local D: drive. Click Next.

4. At the Confirm screen, click Start Backup.

5. A dialog box may appear, asking whether you want to create a system repair disc. Click the No button. If you want to create a system repair disc, you will need a DVD burner and a DVD.

6. When the image is complete, click the Close button.

After you create a system image, you may need to restore it. Let's take a look at the steps needed to complete a restore.

Restoring an Image

When you need to restore an image, you will use the System Image Recovery tool. To restore an image using this tool, you must perform the following steps:

1. Boot your computer by using the Windows 10 media, or use the recovery partition instructions provided by your computer manufacturer.

2. When the Install Windows dialog box appears, select the language, the time and currency format, and the keyboard or input method. Click Next to continue.

3. The Install Now button appears in the center of the screen. Click Repair Your Computer in the lower-left corner.

4. Select the operating system to recover and click Next. If you do not see your operating system, you might need to load your hard-disk drivers by clicking the Load Drivers button.

5. The System Recovery Options dialog box appears. You can choose one of the following options:

    -   Startup Repair

    -   System Restore

    -   Windows Complete PC Restore

    -   Windows Memory Diagnostic Tool

    -   Command Prompt

    Choose Windows Complete PC Restore to continue.

6. Select the recommended image, or select Restore A Different Backup. Click Next to continue.

7. If you selected Restore A Different Backup, follow the prompts to select the location of the image and the image you want to restore.

8. You will be asked to review your selections. Click Finish to continue.

9. You will be asked to confirm your decision. Click the check box and click OK to restore the image.

 If you were not provided the Windows 10 media when you purchased your computer, the computer manufacturer might have placed the files on a recovery partition. Check with the manufacturer for more information.

Using System Protection

System Protection is a feature of Windows 10 that creates a backup and saves the configuration information of your computer's system files and settings on a regular basis. System Protection saves multiple previous versions of saved configurations rather than just overwriting them. This makes it possible to return to multiple configurations in your Windows 10 history, known as *restore points*. These restore points are created before most significant events, such as installing a new driver. Restore points are also created automatically every seven days. System Protection is turned on by default in Windows 10 for any drive formatted with NTFS.

You manage System Protection and the restore points from the System Protection tab of the System Properties dialog box. You can also access this tab directly by typing **restore point** into the Windows 10 search box or by clicking the Recovery icon in Control Panel.

Clicking the System Restore button launches the System Restore Wizard, which walks you through the process of returning Windows 10 to a previous point in time.

Also within the System Protection tab of the System Properties dialog box is the Protection Settings section, where you can configure any of your available drives. Select the drive for which you would like to modify the configuration and click the Configure button. The System Protection configuration dialog box for the drive appears.

The System Protection dialog box allows you to enable or disable system protection for the drive. When you enable protection, you can opt for previous versions of files or previous versions of files and system settings. You also have the ability to set the maximum disk space that your restore points will use for storage. Another function of the System Protection dialog box for the selected disk is to delete all restore points (including system settings and previous versions of files) by clicking the Delete button.

One tool included with restore points is shadow copies. Shadow copies are copies of files and folders that Windows automatically saves as part of a restore point. Normally, restore points are made only once a day if you have enabled System Protection. If System Protection is enabled, Windows will then automatically create shadow copies of files that have been modified since the last restore point was made.

One advantage of using restore points and shadow copies is the ability to restore files and folders using the Previous Versions tab. When you click any folder and choose Properties, the last tab on the right is Previous Versions. You can easily restore any folder by choosing one of these previous versions.

Creating Restore Points

Restore points contain Registry and system information as it was at a certain point in time. These restore points are created at the following times:

- Weekly
  - Before installing applications or drivers
  - Before significant system events

- Before System Restore is used to restore files (so you can undo the changes if necessary)
- Manually upon request

In Exercise 10.7, you will manually create a restore point.

EXERCISE 10.7

Creating a Restore Point

1. Right-click Start ➢ Control Panel ➢ System ➢ Advanced System Settings.

2. When the System Properties dialog box appears, click the System Protection tab.

3. Click the Create button on the bottom of the screen.

4. At the System Protection dialog box, enter a description for the restore point. Click Create.

5. A dialog box states that the restore point was created. Click Close.

Restoring Restore Points

You can restore previously created restore points with System Restore. The restore operation will restore system files and settings but will not affect your personal files.

WARNING   System Restore will also remove any programs that have been installed since the restore point was created.

In Exercise 10.8, you will revert your system configuration to a previously captured restore point.

EXERCISE 10.8

Restoring a Restore Point

1. Right-click Start ➢ Control Panel ➢ System ➢ Advanced System Settings.

2. When the System Properties dialog box appears, click the System Protection tab.

3. Click the System Restore button. Click Next at the Welcome screen to continue.

4. Choose the restore point created in the previous exercise and click Next to continue.

5. Review your restore point selection, and click Finish to continue.

6. Click Yes to confirm that you want System Restore to continue.

7. System Restore will restore your system and reboot your computer to apply the changes. You should see a message stating that System Restore has restored your computer. Click OK to close the dialog box.

Cleaning Up Old Restore Points

One problem with creating multiple restore points is that they start to take up a large amount of your hard disk. You will need to clean up old restore points from time to time, and you can accomplish this task by using the Disk Cleanup utility.

The Disk Cleanup utility removes temporary files, empties the Recycle Bin, and removes a variety of system files and other items that you no longer need. When using the Disk Cleanup utility, you can also click the More Options tab and choose Programs And Features and System Restore And Shadow Copies to clean them up as well.

The More Options tab is available when you choose to clean up files from all users on the computer.

To use the Disk Cleanup utility, right-click Start ➢ Control Panel ➢ Administrative Tools ➢ Disk Cleanup.

Using the Recycle Bin

Now we are going to talk about an icon that we have seen on our desktop for many years called the Recycle Bin. The Recycle Bin is a temporary storage container that holds deleted files. The advantage of having a temporary storage container is that you can restore or recycle the files to their original location. So basically, it allows you to undelete a deleted file.

When a file or folder is deleted on a computer, it isn't actually deleted. When files or folders get deleted, they get placed into the Recycle Bin. This works well because if you change your mind or realize that you actually need the file or folder, you can undelete it and it gets restored. The Recycle Bin allows you to perform a refresh or recycle of files that were deleted but shouldn't have been.

The Recycle Bin allows you to restore files or folders multiple ways. You can right-click the item and choose Restore or you can use the Manage tab (as shown in Figure 10.12).

FIGURE 10.12 Manage tab in Recycle Bin

In Exercise 10.9, you will create a document and then delete the document. Then you will use the Recycle Bin to restore the document to its original location.

EXERCISE 10.9

Using the Recycle Bin

1. On the Windows 10 desktop, right-click and choose New Text Document.

2. Create a new test document called **Test.txt**.

3. After the document is created, right-click the document and choose Delete.

4. Double-click to open the Recycle Bin.

5. You can either right-click the Test.txt document and choose Restore or click the document, and then on the Manage tab, choose Restore The Selected Item.

6. Close the Recycle Bin, and the document should be back on the desktop.

Monitoring Windows

Because performance monitoring and optimization are vital functions in network environments of any size, Windows 10 includes several monitoring and performance tools.

Introducing Performance Monitor

The first and most useful tool is the Windows 10 *Performance Monitor,* which was designed to allow users and system administrators to monitor performance statistics for various operating system parameters. Specifically, you can collect, store, and analyze information about CPU, memory, disk, and network resources using this tool, and these are only a handful of the things you can monitor. By collecting and analyzing performance values, system administrators can identify many potential problems.

You can use the Performance Monitor in the following ways:

Performance Monitor ActiveX Control   The Windows 10 Performance Monitor is an ActiveX control that you can place within other applications. Examples of applications that can host the Performance Monitor control include web browsers and client programs such as Microsoft Word and Microsoft Excel. This functionality can make it easy for application developers and system administrators to incorporate the Performance Monitor into their own tools and applications.

Performance Monitor MMC   For more common performance monitoring functions, you'll want to use the built-in Microsoft Management Console (MMC) version of the Performance Monitor.

Data Collector Sets   Windows 10 Performance Monitor includes the Data Collector Set. This tool works with performance logs, telling Performance Monitor where the logs are stored and when the log needs to run. The Data Collector Sets also define the credentials used to run the set.

To access the Performance Monitor MMC, you open Administrative Tools and then choose Performance Monitor. This launches the Performance MMC and loads and initializes Performance Monitor with a handful of default counters.

You can choose from many different methods of monitoring performance when you are using Performance Monitor. A couple of examples are listed here:

- You can look at a snapshot of current activity for a few of the most important counters. This allows you to find areas of potential bottlenecks and monitor the load on your servers at a certain point in time.

- You can save information to a log file for historical reporting and later analysis. This type of information is useful, for example, if you want to compare the load on your servers from three months ago to the current load.

You'll get to take a closer look at this method and many others as you examine Performance Monitor in more detail.

In the following sections, you'll learn about the basics of working with the Windows 10 Performance Monitor and other performance tools. Then you'll apply these tools and techniques when you monitor the performance of your network.

 Your Performance Monitor grows as your system grows, and whenever you add services to Windows 10, you also add to what you can monitor. You should make sure that, as you install services, you take a look at what it is you can monitor.

Deciding What to Monitor

The first step in monitoring performance is to decide *what* you want to monitor. In Windows 10, the operating system and related services include hundreds of performance statistics that you can track easily. For example, you may want to monitor the processor. This is just one of many items that can be monitored. All performance statistics fall into three main categories that you can choose to measure:

Performance Objects A *performance object* within Performance Monitor is a collection of various performance statistics that you can monitor. Performance objects are based on various areas of system resources. For example, there are performance objects for the processor and memory as well as for specific services.

Counters *Counters* are the actual parameters measured by Performance Monitor. They are specific items that are grouped within performance objects. For example, within the Processor performance object, there is a counter for % Processor Time. This counter displays one type of detailed information about the Processor performance object (specifically, the amount of total CPU time all of the processes on the system are using). Another set of counters you can use will allow you to monitor print servers.

Instances Some counters will have *instances*. An instance further identifies which performance parameter the counter is measuring. A simple example is a server with two CPUs. If you decide you want to monitor processor usage (using the Processor performance object)—specifically, utilization (the % Total Utilization counter)—you must still specify *which* CPU(s) you want to measure. In this example, you would have the choice of monitoring either of the two CPUs or a total value for both (using the Total instance).

To specify which performance objects, counters, and instances you want to monitor, you add them to Performance Monitor using the Add Counters dialog box. Figure 10.13 shows the various options that are available when you add new counters to monitor using Performance Monitor.

The items that you will be able to monitor will be based on your hardware and software configuration. For example, if you have not installed and configured Hyper-V, the options available within the Hyper-V Server performance object will not be available. Or, if you have multiple network adapters or CPUs on the Windows 10 system, you will have the option of viewing each instance separately or as part of the total value.

FIGURE 10.13   Adding a new Performance Monitor counter

Viewing Performance Information

The Windows 10 Performance Monitor was designed to show information in a clear and easy-to-understand format. Performance objects, counters, and instances may be displayed in each of three views. This flexibility allows system administrators to quickly and easily define the information they want to see once and then choose how it will be displayed based on specific needs. Most likely, you will use only one view, but it's helpful to know what other views are available depending on what it is you are trying to assess.

You can use the following main views to review statistics and information on performance:

Graph View　The *Graph view* is the default display that is presented when you first access the Windows 10 Performance Monitor. The chart displays values using the vertical axis and time using the horizontal axis. This view is useful if you want to display values over a period of time or see the changes in these values over that time period. Each point that is plotted on the graph is based on an average value calculated during the sample interval for the measurement being made. For example, you may notice overall CPU utilization starting at a low value at the beginning of the chart and then becoming much higher during later measurements. This indicates that the server has become busier (specifically, with CPU-intensive processes). Figure 10.14 provides an example of the Graph view.

FIGURE 10.14　Viewing information in Performance Monitor Graph view

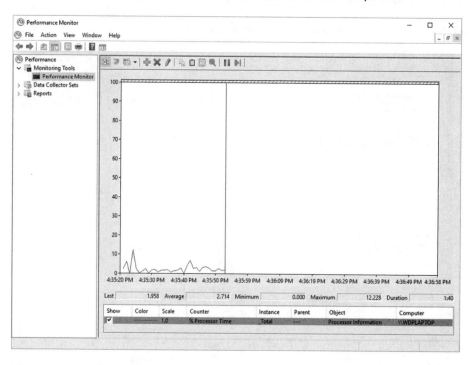

Histogram View　The *Histogram view* shows performance statistics and information using a set of relative bar charts. This view is useful if you want to see a snapshot of the latest value for a given counter. For example, if you were interested in viewing a snapshot of current system performance statistics during each refresh interval, the length of each of the bars in the display would give you a visual representation of each value. It would also allow you to compare measurements visually relative to each other. You can set the histogram to display an average measurement as well as minimum and maximum thresholds. Figure 10.15 shows a typical Histogram view.

Report View　Like the Histogram view, the *Report view* shows performance statistics based on the latest measurement. You can see an average measurement as well as minimum and maximum thresholds. This view is most useful for determining exact values because it provides information in numeric terms, whereas the Chart and Histogram views provide information graphically. Figure 10.16 provides an example of the type of information you'll see in the Report view.

FIGURE 10.15 Viewing information in Performance Monitor Histogram view

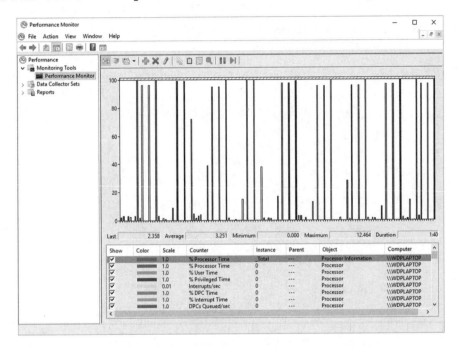

FIGURE 10.16 Viewing information in Performance Monitor Report view

Managing Performance Monitor Properties

You can specify additional settings for viewing performance information within the properties of Performance Monitor. You can access these options by clicking the Properties button in the Taskbar or by right-clicking the Performance Monitor display and selecting Properties. You can change these additional settings by using the following tabs:

General Tab On the General tab (shown in Figure 10.17), you can specify several options that relate to Performance Monitor views:

FIGURE 10.17 General tab of the Performance Monitor Properties dialog box

- You can enable or disable legends (which display information about the various counters), the value bar, and the toolbar.

- For the Report and Histogram views, you can choose which type of information is displayed. The options are Default, Current, Minimum, Maximum, and Average. What you see with each of these options depends on the type of data being collected. These options are not available for the Graph view because the Graph view displays an average value over a period of time (the sample interval).

- You can also choose the graph elements. By default, the display will be set to update every second. If you want to update less often, you should increase the number of seconds between updates.

Source Tab On the Source tab (shown in Figure 10.18), you can specify the source for the performance information you want to view. Options include current activity (the default setting) or data from a log file. If you choose to analyze information from a log file, you can also specify the time range for which you want to view statistics. I'll cover these selections in the next section.

FIGURE 10.18 Source tab of the Performance Monitor Properties dialog box

Data Tab The Data tab (shown in Figure 10.19) lists the counters that have been added to the Performance Monitor display. These counters apply to the Chart, Histogram, and Report views. Using this interface, you can also add or remove any of the counters and change the properties, such as the width, style, and color of the line and the scale used for display.

FIGURE 10.19 The Data tab of the Performance Monitor Properties dialog box

Graph Tab On the Graph tab (shown in Figure 10.20), you can specify certain options that will allow you to customize the display of Performance Monitor views. First you can specify what type of view you want to see (Line, Histogram, or Report). Then you can add a title for the graph, specify a label for the vertical axis, choose to display grids, and specify the vertical scale range.

FIGURE 10.20 The Graph tab of the Performance Monitor Properties dialog box

Appearance Tab Using the Appearance tab (see Figure 10.21), you can specify the colors for the areas of the display, such as the background and foreground. You can also specify the fonts that are used to display counter values in Performance Monitor views. You can change settings to find a suitable balance between readability and the amount of information shown on one screen. Finally, you can set up the properties for a border.

Now that you have an idea of the types of information Performance Monitor tracks and how this data is displayed, we'll take a look at another feature—saving and analyzing performance data.

FIGURE 10.21   The Appearance tab of the Performance Monitor Properties dialog box

Saving and Analyzing Data with Performance Logs and Alerts

One of the most important aspects of monitoring performance is that it should be done over a given period of time (referred to as a *baseline*). So far, I have shown you how you can use Performance Monitor to view statistics in real time. I have, however, also alluded to using Performance Monitor to save data for later analysis. Now let's take a look at how you can do this.

When viewing information in Performance Monitor, you have two main options with respect to the data on display:

View Current Activity   When you first open the Performance icon from the Administrative Tools folder, the default option is to view data obtained from current system information. This method of viewing measures and displays various real-time statistics on the system's performance.

View Log File Data   This option allows you to view information that was previously saved to a log file. Although the performance objects, counters, and instances may appear to be the same as those viewed using the View Current Activity option, the information itself was actually captured at a previous point in time and stored into a log file.

Log files for the View Log File Data option are created in the Performance Logs And Alerts section of the Windows 10 Performance tool.

Three items allow you to customize how the data is collected in the log files:

Counter Logs   *Counter logs* record performance statistics based on the various performance objects, counters, and instances available in Performance Monitor. The values are updated based on a time interval setting and are saved to a file for later analysis.

Circular Logging   In *circular logging*, the data that is stored within a file is overwritten as new data is entered into the log. This is a useful method of logging if you want to record information only for a certain time frame (for example, the past four hours). Circular logging also conserves disk space by ensuring that the performance log file will not continue to grow over certain limits.

Linear Logging   In *linear logging*, data is never deleted from the log files, and new information is added to the end of the log file. The result is a log file that continually grows. The benefit is that all historical information is retained.

Now that you have an idea of the types of functions that are supported by the Windows 10 Performance tools, you can learn how you can apply this information to the task at hand—monitoring and troubleshooting your Windows network.

 Real World Scenario

Real-World Performance Monitoring

In our daily jobs as system engineers and administrators, we come across systems that are in need of our help. . .and may even ask for it. You, of course, check your Event Viewer and Performance Monitor and perform other tasks that help you troubleshoot. But what is really the most common problem that occurs? From my experience, I'd say that you suffer performance problems many times if your Windows 10 operating system is installed on a subpar system. Either the system's hardware minimum requirements weren't addressed or the operating system is not configured properly.

Using Other Performance-Monitoring Tools

Performance Monitor allows you to monitor different parameters of the Windows 10 operating system and associated services and applications. However, you can also use three other tools to monitor performance in Windows 10. They are Reliability Monitor, Task Manager, and Event Viewer. All three of these tools are useful for monitoring different areas of overall system performance and for examining details related to specific system events. In the following sections, you'll take a quick look at these tools and how you can best use them.

Reliability Monitor

Windows 10 Reliability Monitor is part of the Windows Reliability and Performance Monitor snap-in for Microsoft Management Console (MMC). The easiest way to access the Reliability Monitor is to type **perfmon /rel** in the Start Search box and press Enter.

The Reliability Monitor provides a system stability overview and allows an administrator to get details about events that may be impacting the Windows 10 reliability. Reliability Monitor calculates a stability index based on a certain period of time and it then shows that stability index in the System Stability Chart.

The Reliability Monitor shows information, all on their own separate lines, about application failures, Windows failures, miscellaneous failures, warnings, and information.

The Reliability Monitor shows an administrator a period of time on the Windows 10 system and the administrator can click on any of the events during that specific period of time and see what Information, Warnings, or Errors that may have happened during that time period.

Administrators can then use the information gathered by the Reliability Monitor to help diagnose the issues that the Windows 10 system may be having.

Task Manager

Performance Monitor is designed to allow you to keep track of specific aspects of system performance over time. But what do you do if you want to get a quick snapshot of what the local system is doing? Creating a System Monitor chart, adding counters, and choosing a view is overkill. Fortunately, the Windows 10 Task Manager has been designed to provide a quick overview of important system performance statistics without requiring any configuration. Better yet, it's always readily available.

You can easily access Task Manager in several ways:

- Right-click the Windows Taskbar, and then click Task Manager.

- Press Ctrl+Alt+Del, and then select Task Manager.

- Press Ctrl+Shift+Esc.

- Type **Taskman** in the Windows Search box.

Each of these methods allows you to access a snapshot of the current system performance quickly.

Once you access Task Manager, you will see the following seven tabs:

 These tabs can be different on Windows client machines. For example, Windows 10 Home can vary from Windows 10 Enterprise.

Processes Tab   The Processes tab shows you all the processes that are currently running on the local computer. By default, you'll be able to view how much CPU time and memory a particular process is using. By clicking any of the columns, you can quickly sort by the data values in that particular column. This is useful, for example, if you want to find out which processes are using the most memory on your server.

By accessing the performance objects in the View menu, you can add columns to the Processes tab. Figure 10.22 shows a list of the current processes running on a Windows 10 computer.

FIGURE 10.22 Viewing process statistics and information using Task Manager

Performance Tab   One of the problems with using Performance Monitor to get a quick snapshot of system performance is that you have to add counters to a chart. Most system administrators are too busy to take the time to do this when all they need is basic CPU and memory information. That's where the Performance tab of Task Manager comes in. Using the Performance tab, you can view details about how memory is allocated on the computer and how much of the CPU is utilized (see Figure 10.23).

App History   This tab shows you all of the recent applications that have been running on the Windows 10 system. Users have the ability to Delete Usage History from this tab.

FIGURE 10.23 Viewing CPU and memory performance information using Task Manager

Startup The Startup tab shows an administrator or user which applications get started when the machine first starts up. Some applications require that services start at system startup for the applications to run properly.

Users Tab The Users tab (see Figure 10.24) lists the currently active user accounts. This is particularly helpful if you want to see who is online and quickly log off or disconnect users.

Details Tab The Details tab (see Figure 10.25) shows you what applications are currently running on the system. From this location, you can stop an application from running by right-clicking the application and choosing Stop. You also have the ability to set your affinity level here. By setting the affinity, you can choose which applications will use which processors on your system.

FIGURE 10.24 Viewing user information using Task Manager

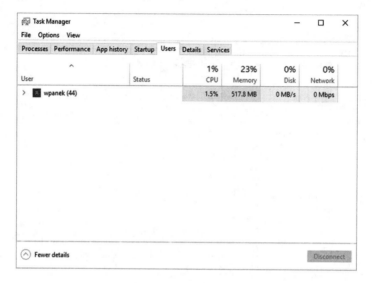

FIGURE 10.25 Viewing currently running applications using Task Manager

Services Tab　The Services tab (see Figure 10.26) shows you what services are currently running on the system. From this location, you can stop a service from running by right-clicking the service and choosing Stop. The Open Services link launches the Services MMC.

FIGURE 10.26　Viewing services information using Task Manager

Name	PID	Description	Status	Group
ZuneWlanCfgSvc		Zune Wireless Configuration Ser...	Stopped	
ZuneNetworkSvc		Zune Network Sharing Service	Stopped	
WSearch	2660	Windows Search	Running	
WMZuneComm		Zune Windows Mobile Connecti...	Stopped	
WMPNetworkSvc		Windows Media Player Network ...	Stopped	
wmiApSrv		WMI Performance Adapter	Stopped	
WinDefend	2584	Windows Defender Service	Running	
WdNisSvc	5540	Windows Defender Network Insp...	Running	
wbengine		Block Level Backup Engine Service	Stopped	
VSS		Volume Shadow Copy	Stopped	
vpnagent	1884	Cisco AnyConnect Secure Mobili...	Running	
VMwareHostd	6068	VMware Workstation Server	Running	
VMware NAT Service	2848	VMware NAT Service	Running	
VMUSBArbService	3136	VMware USB Arbitration Service	Running	
VMnetDHCP	2888	VMware DHCP Service	Running	
VMAuthdService	2832	VMware Authorization Service	Running	
vds		Virtual Disk	Stopped	
VaultSvc	804	Credential Manager	Running	
UI0Detect		Interactive Services Detection	Stopped	
TrustedInstaller		Windows Modules Installer	Stopped	
TieringEngineService		Storage Tiers Management	Stopped	
Te.Service		Te.Service	Stopped	
Stereo Service	1204	NVIDIA Stereoscopic 3D Driver S...	Running	

Task Manager — File　Options　View — Processes　Performance　App history　Startup　Users　Details　**Services** — Fewer details | Open Services

As you can see, Task Manager is useful for providing important information about the system quickly. Once you get used to using Task Manager, you won't be able to get by without it!

> Make sure that you use Task Manager and familiarize yourself with all that it can do; you can end processes that have become intermittent, kill applications that may hang the system, view NIC performance, and so on. In addition, you can access this tool quickly to get an idea of what could be causing you problems. Event Viewer and Performance Monitor are both great tools for getting granular information on potential problems.

Event Viewer

Event Viewer is also useful for monitoring network information. Specifically, you can use the logs to view any information, warnings, or alerts related to the proper functioning of the network (see Figure 10.27). You can access Event Viewer by selecting Administrative Tools ➤ Event Viewer or by right-clicking the Start button and choosing Event Viewer. Clicking any of the items in the left pane displays the various events that have been logged for each item.

FIGURE 10.27 Event Viewer

Each event that is preceded by a blue "i" icon designates that these events are informational and do not indicate problems with the network. Rather, they record benign events such as Microsoft Office startup or a service starting.

Problematic or potentially problematic events are indicated by a yellow warning icon or a red error icon (see Figure 10.28). Warnings usually indicate a problem that wouldn't prevent a service from running but might cause undesired effects with the service in question.

Error events almost always indicate a failed service, application, or function. For instance, if the dynamic registration of a DNS client fails, Event Viewer will generate an error. As you can see, errors are more severe than warnings because, in the case of DNS, the DNS client cannot participate in DNS at all.

FIGURE 10.28   Information, errors, and warnings in Event Viewer

Double-clicking any event opens its Event Properties dialog box, as shown in Figure 10.29, which displays a detailed description of the event.

Event Viewer can display thousands of different events, so it would be impossible to list them all here. The important points of which you should be aware are the following:

- Information events are always benign.

- Warnings indicate noncritical problems.

- Errors indicate show-stopping events.

Let's discuss some of the logs and the ways that you can view data:

Applications and Services   The *applications and services logs* are part of Event Viewer where applications (for example, Hardware events) and services log their events. Internet Explorer events would be logged in this part of Event Viewer. An important log in this section is the Key Management Service log (see Figure 10.30). This is where all of your Key Management Service events get stored.

FIGURE 10.29 An Event Properties dialog box

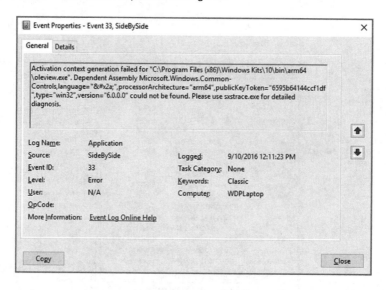

FIGURE 10.30 The applications and services logs

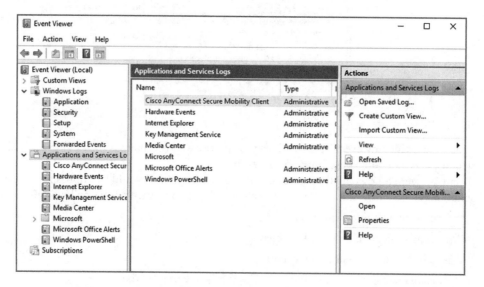

Custom Views *Custom views* allow you to filter events (see Figure 10.31) to create your own customized look. You can filter events by event level (critical, error, warning, and so on), by logs, and by source. You also have the ability to view events occurring within a specific timeframe. This allows you to look only at the events that are important to you.

FIGURE 10.31   Create Custom View dialog box

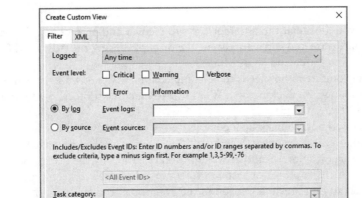

Subscriptions   *Subscriptions* allow a user to receive alerts about events that you predefine. In the Subscription Properties dialog box (see Figure 10.32), you can define what type of events you want notifications about and the notification method. The Subscriptions section is an advanced alerting service to help you watch for events.

FIGURE 10.32   Subscription Properties dialog box

Summary

In this chapter, you looked at the different ways to recover and protect your Windows 10 machine from hardware and software issues. We discussed using the Advanced Boot Options such as Safe Mode and VGA Mode.

Another important item that needs to be completed on a Windows 10 machine is Backup and Restore (Windows 7). Backing up a Windows 10 machine protects data in the event of a hardware or software failure.

We also discussed how to back up a complete copy of Windows 10 by using images. An image allows you to copy the entire Windows 10 machine and then reimage the machine in the event of a major failure. Another way to protect data is by the use of shadow copies. Shadow copies, which are a part of System Protection, allow you to keep previous versions of data and revert to that previous version in the event of a problem.

The chapter also covered monitoring the Windows 10 system. Monitoring performance on Windows 10 is imperative to rooting out any issues that may affect your network. If your systems are not running at their best, your end users may experience issues such as latency, or worse, you may experience corruption in your network data. Either way, it's important to know how to monitor the performance of your systems.

We also examined how to use the various performance-related tools that are included with Windows 10. Tools such as Performance Monitor, Task Manager, and Event Viewer can help you diagnose and troubleshoot system performance issues. These tools will help you find typical problems related to memory, disk space, and any other hardware-related issues you may experience. Knowing how to use tools to troubleshoot and test your systems is imperative, not only to passing the exam, but also to performing your duties at work. To have a smoothly running network environment, it is vital that you understand the issues related to the reliability and performance of your Windows 10 systems.

Video Resources

There are no videos for this chapter.

Exam Essentials

Understand the different options for managing system recovery.   Know how to use the Startup Repair tool, System Restore, and the Backup and Restore Center and when it is appropriate to use each option.

Be able to perform file recovery with the Backup and Restore Center and shadow copies.   Understand the options that are supported through the Backup and Restore (Windows 7) Center and the files that are backed up using this tool. Know how to manually create a shadow copy and how to keep only the last shadow copy version.

Know how to troubleshoot using Advanced Boot Options.   Be able to list the options that can be accessed through Advanced Boot Options, and know when it is appropriate to use each option. Know the difference between Last Known Good Configuration, Safe Mode, and VGA Mode.

Know the importance of common performance counters.   Several important performance-related counters deal with general system performance. Know the importance of monitoring memory, print server, CPU, and network usage on a busy server.

Understand the role of other troubleshooting tools.   Windows Task Manager and Event Viewer can both be used to diagnose and troubleshoot configuration- and performance-related issues.

Understand how to troubleshoot common sources of server reliability problems.   Windows 10 has been designed to be a stable, robust, and reliable operating system. Should you experience intermittent failures, you should know how to troubleshoot device drivers and buggy system-level software.

Review Questions

1. You need to stop an application from running in Task Manager. Which tab would you use to stop an application from running?

    A. Performance

    B. Users

    C. Options

    D. Details

2. You have a computer that runs Windows 10. You upgrade the network adapter driver on the computer. After the upgrade, you can no longer access network resources. You open Device Manager and see a warning symbol next to the network adapter. You need to restore access to network resources. What should you do?

    A. Roll back the network adapter driver.

    B. Assign a static IP address to the network adapter.

    C. Disable the network adapter and scan for hardware changes.

    D. Uninstall the network adapter and scan for hardware changes.

3. You need to back up the existing data on a computer before you install a new application. You also need to ensure that you are able to recover individual user files that are replaced or deleted during the installation. What should you do?

    A. Create a system restore point.

    B. Perform an Automated System Recovery (ASR) backup and restore.

    C. In the Backup And Restore Center window, click the Back Up Now button.

    D. In the Backup And Restore Center window, click the Back Up Computer button.

4. Your data-recovery strategy must meet the following requirements:

    ▪ Back up all data files and folders in C:\Data.

    ▪ Restore individual files and folders in C:\Data.

    ▪ Ensure that data is backed up to and restored from external media.

    What should you do?

    A. Use the Previous Versions tab to restore the files and folders.

    B. Use the System Restore feature to perform backup and restore operations.

    C. Use the NTBackup utility to back up and restore individual files and folders.

    D. Use the Backup and Restore Center to back up and restore files.

5. You need to ensure that you can recover system configuration and data if your computer hard disk fails. What should you do?

   A. Create a system restore point.

   B. Create a backup of all file categories.

   C. Create a Backup and Restore image.

   D. Perform an Automated System Recovery (ASR) backup.

6. You have a computer that runs Windows 10. Your computer has two volumes, C: and D:. Both volumes are formatted by using the NTFS file system. You need to disable previous versions on the D: volume. What should you do?

   A. From System Properties, modify the System Protection settings.

   B. From the properties of the D: volume, modify the Quota settings.

   C. From the properties of the D: volume, modify the Sharing settings.

   D. From the Disk Management snap-in, convert the hard disk drive that contains the D: volume to Dynamic.

7. You have a computer that runs Windows 10. You configure a backup job to back up all files and folders on an external NTFS file system hard disk drive. The backup job fails to back up all files that have the encryption attribute set. You need to back up all encrypted files. The backed-up files must remain encrypted. What should you do?

   A. Manually copy the encrypted files to the external hard disk drive.

   B. Schedule a backup job to occur when you are not logged on to the computer.

   C. Enable Volume Shadow Copy on the external drive and schedule a backup job.

   D. Add the certificate of the local administrator account to the list of users who can transparently access the files, and schedule a backup job.

8. You have a computer that runs Windows 10. You use Windows Backup and Restore to create a backup image. You need to perform a complete restore of the computer. What are two possible ways to begin the restore? (Each correct answer presents a complete solution. Choose two.)

   A. Open the Windows Backup and Restore Center and click Advanced Restore.

   B. Open the Windows Backup and Restore Center and click Restore Computer.

   C. Start your computer. From the Advanced Boot Options menu, select Repair Your Computer.

   D. Start the computer by using the Windows 10 installation media. Select Repair Your Computer.

9. You are the network administrator for your organization. You are asked by a junior administrator when he should create restore points. Which of the following are times when restore points should be created? (Choose all that apply.)

A. Every day

B. Before installing applications or drivers

C. Before significant system events

D. Before System Restore is used to restore files (so you can undo the changes if necessary)

10. You install Windows 10 on a new computer. You update the video card driver and restart the computer. When you start the computer, the screen flickers and then goes blank. You restart the computer and receive the same result. You need to configure the video card driver. What should you do first?

A. Restart the computer in Safe Mode.

B. Restart the computer in Debugging Mode.

C. Restart the computer in low-resolution video mode.

D. Insert the Windows 10 installation media into the computer, restart, and use System Recovery to perform a startup repair.

Exam 70-697, Configuring Windows Devices

Chapter

11

Installing Windows 10

MICROSOFT EXAM OBJECTIVES COVERED IN THIS CHAPTER:

✓ **Migrate and configure user data.**

- This objective may include but is not limited to the following subobjectives: migrate user profiles; configure folder location; configure profiles including profile version, local, roaming, and mandatory.

✓ **Configure and manage updates.**

- This objective may include but is not limited to the following subobjectives: Configure update settings, configure Windows Update policies, manage update history, roll back updates, update Windows Store apps.

Welcome to Windows 10 and the future of Microsoft Windows computing. In previous editions of Microsoft Windows, Microsoft introduced the networking world to using the cloud for storage. Windows 10 starts to take this even further.

But let's start at the beginning. Before you can master any Microsoft product, you must know about the different versions of Windows 10 and also how to properly install Windows 10. In this chapter, I will show you the many different features of Windows 10 and describe each edition. I will then show you how to install Windows 10 and set up the user profiles. This is a straightforward process that can be highly automated and user friendly.

Preparing for the installation of Windows 10 involves making sure your hardware meets the minimum requirements and is supported by the operating system. Another consideration when installing Windows 10 is whether you are going to upgrade from a previous version of Windows or install a clean copy on your computer. An upgrade attempts to preserve existing settings; a clean install puts a fresh copy of the operating system on your computer. Installation preparation also involves making choices about your system's configuration, such as selecting a disk-partitioning scheme.

To complete the Windows 10 installation, you will need to activate the product through Windows Activation. This process is used to reduce software piracy. After Windows 10 is installed, you can keep the operating system up-to-date with postinstallation updates.

Introducing Windows 10

Microsoft Windows 10 is the newest version of Microsoft's client operating system software. Windows 10 combines the best of Windows 7 and Windows 8.

At the time this book was written, Microsoft has currently released six different versions of the Windows 10 operating system:

- Windows 10 Home
- Windows 10 Professional
- Windows 10 Enterprise
- Windows 10 Education
- Windows 10 Mobility
- Windows 10 Mobility Enterprise

Two of the versions listed previously will not be covered in this book, Windows 10 Mobility and Windows 10 Mobility Enterprise. If you go to Microsoft's website, you will see both listed and you can see what each offers. But neither of them can be put onto a network, so we don't cover them in this book.

Windows 10 has been improved in many of the weak areas that plagued Windows 8. Windows 10 has a much faster boot time and shutdown compared to Windows 8. It also brings back the previous Start button that we are all so familiar with from previous editions.

The Windows 10 operating system functions are also faster than their previous counterparts. The processes for opening, moving, extracting, compressing, and installing files and folders are more efficient than they were in previous versions of Microsoft's client operating systems.

Let's take a look at some of the features of each Windows 10 edition (this is just an overview of some of the benefits to using Windows 10). Table 11.1 shows each edition and what some of the "core experiences" are for those editions.

 The information in Table 11.1 and Table 11.2 was taken directly from Microsoft's website.

TABLE 11.1 Windows 10 core experiences

Feature	Home	Pro	Enterprise	Education
Battery saver	●	●	●	●
Built-in ink support	●	●	●	●
Cortana integration	●	●	●	●
Customizable Start Menu	●	●	●	●
Enterprise-level biometric security	●	●	●	●
Fast startup with Hiberboot and InstantGo	●	●	●	●
"Hey Cortana" hands-free activation	●	●	●	●
Native facial and iris recognition	●	●	●	●
Native fingerprint recognition	●	●	●	●

TABLE 11.1 Windows 10 core experiences *(continued)*

Feature	Home	Pro	Enterprise	Education
Personal and proactive suggestions	●	●	●	●
Reading view	●	●	●	●
Reminders	●	●	●	●
Search web, device, and cloud	●	●	●	●
Snap apps (across screens on different monitors)	●	●	●	●
Snap assist (up to four apps on one screen)	●	●	●	●
Switch from PC to tablet mode	●	●	●	●
Talk or type naturally	●	●	●	●
TPM support	●	●	●	●
Virtual desktops	●	●	●	●
Windows Defender and Windows Firewall	●	●	●	●
Windows Update	●	●	●	●

Now that we've looked at some of the Windows 10 core experiences, let's take a look at the business side. Table 11.2 shows each edition and what some of the "Business Experiences" are for those editions.

TABLE 11.2 Windows 10 business experiences

Feature	Home	Pro	Enterprise	Education
Ability to join Azure Active Directory		●	●	●
AppLocker			●	●
Assigned Access 8.1		●	●	●
BitLocker		●	●	●
BranchCache			●	●

Feature	Home	Pro	Enterprise	Education
Client Hyper-V		•	•	•
Credential Guard			•	•
Current Branch for Business		•	•	•
Device Encryption	•	•	•	•
Device Guard			•	•
Direct Access			•	•
Domain Join		•	•	•
Easy Upgrade from Home to Education Edition	•	•		•
Easy Upgrade from Pro to Enterprise Edition		•	•	
Enterprise Data Protection		•	•	•
Enterprise Mode Internet Explorer (EMIE)		•	•	•
Granular UX Control			•	•
Group Policy Management		•	•	•
Long Term Servicing Branch			•	
Microsoft Passport	•	•	•	•
Mobile device management	•	•	•	•
Remote Desktop		•	•	•
Side-loading of line-of-business apps	•	•	•	•
Start Screen Control with Group Policy			•	•
Trusted Boot		•	•	•
Windows Store for Business		•	•	•
Windows To Go Creator			•	•
Windows Update	•	•	•	•
Windows Update for Business		•	•	•

Windows 10 Features

Now that we have seen which editions contain which features, let's take a look at some of the Windows 10 features in greater detail. This section describes only a few of these features, but all features will be explained throughout this book.

Cortana Integration   Windows 10 comes with Cortana integration. Cortana is your very own personnel assistant. You can type in or ask Cortana a question, and Cortana will seek out the best possible answer based on your question.

Secure Boot   Windows 10 gives you the ability to use hardware-based virtualization that allows Windows 10 to prevent malware from running on your system. Windows 10 Secure Boot also prevents key processes from being tampered with because Windows 10 isolates these processes from the system.

Enterprise Data Protection   Windows 10 Enterprise Data Protection (EDP) helps protect corporate data in a world that is increasingly becoming a Bring Your Own Device (BYOD) environment. Since many organizations are allowing employees to connect their own devices to their network, the possibility of corporate data being compromised because of non-corporate programs running on these personnel devices is increasing. For example, many third-party apps may put corporate data at risk by accidently disclosing corporate information through the application.

Enterprise Data Protection helps protect information by separating corporate applications and corporate data from being disclosed by personal devices and personal applications.

Device Guard   Because employees can use multiple types of Windows 10 devices (Surface Pros, Windows Phones, and Windows 10 computer systems), Device Guard is a feature that helps guarantee that only trusted applications will run on any of these devices.

Device Guard uses both hardware and software security features to lock down a device so it can run only trusted and approved applications. This also helps protect against hackers from running malicious software on these devices.

Microsoft Passport   Windows 10 allows administrators to replace passwords with other types of authentication on the operating system. Microsoft Passport allows for multifactor authentication by using a combination of an enrolled device and biometric authentication or a personal identification number (PIN).

Microsoft has encompassed the use of your Microsoft account with the use of your corporate account. So with Windows 10, Microsoft Passport can log you into your domain as well as into the cloud and Microsoft websites. The user will be required to verify their Microsoft Passport account, and that account will then be tied into a gesture or PIN, and from that point on, the user will not need to use a password to log in to the device and their protected resources. Because no password will be needed, this helps prevent hackers from using software to hack a password on an account.

Start Menu   Windows 10 has brought back the Start Menu that users are familiar with. The Windows 10 Start Menu combines the best of both Windows 7 and Windows 8. So the Start Menu gives you a menu that we were familiar with in Windows 7 as well as the Live Tiles that users liked in Windows 8.

Microsoft Edge and Internet Explorer 11   Windows 10 has introduced a new way to surf the Internet with Microsoft Edge. But Windows 10 also still comes with Internet Explorer 11 in the event that you need to run ActiveX controls or run backward-compatible web services or sites.

Microsoft Edge allows users to start using many new Microsoft features, including Web Note (allows you to annotate, highlight, and call things out directly on web pages), Reading View (allows you to print and save as a PDF for easy reading), and Cortana (personal assistant).

Domain Join and Group Policy   Depending on the version of Windows 10 that you are using, administrators have the ability to join Windows 10 clients to either a corporate version of Active Directory or a cloud-based version of Azure Active Directory.

Windows Store for Business   Microsoft Store has included many applications that allow users to get better functionality and productivity out of their Windows 10 devices. One advantage for corporations is that they can create their own applications and load them into the Microsoft Store for users to download (called *sideloading*).

Mobile Device Management   Mobile Device Management (MDM) allows administrators to set up Windows 10 policies that can integrate many corporate scenarios, including the ability to control users' access to the Windows Store and the ability to use the corporate VPN. MDM also allows administrators to manage multiple users who have accounts set up on Microsoft Azure Active Directory (Azure AD). Windows 10 MDM support is based on the Open Mobile Alliance (OMA) Device Management (DM) protocol 1.2.1 specification.

 Real World Scenario

Choosing an Appropriate Operating System

As an IT consultant, I have clients who want to stay on the leading edge of technology but don't have the money to replace all of their equipment. This is where I have to convince the client that it is better to slowly migrate their equipment.

Try presenting a timeline to your customers or organization that shows the migration to Windows 10. Your clients will be happy, and you will have the time needed to migrate your organization.

I understand that if you are reading this book, there is the strong likelihood that you are getting ready to install or upgrade to Windows 10 in your organization.

Microsoft has taken the best of Windows 7 and Windows 8 and created Windows 10. In a corporate environment, if you have machines running Windows 8, most will have a free upgrade to Windows 10, which will improve performance. But if you have clients who are comfortable and happy with Windows 7, a decision will need to be made about whether to stay with Windows 7 or upgrade to Windows 10.

Windows Feature Deprecation

With the release of its newest operating system, Microsoft has decided that some of the features you may be used to are no longer needed. Here are some of the features that have been deprecated:

- Windows 7 desktop gadgets will be removed as part of Windows 10.

- The Solitaire, Minesweeper, and Hearts games that come preinstalled on Windows 7 will be removed. Microsoft has released versions of Solitaire and Minesweeper called the "Microsoft Solitaire Collection" and "Microsoft Minesweeper."

- Mobile Device Management functionality will not be available in Windows 10 Home edition.

- Users with floppy drives will need to download the latest driver from Windows Update or from the manufacturer's website.

- Users who have Windows Live Essentials installed on their systems will lose the One-Drive application, which will be replaced with the inbox version of OneDrive.

- OneDrive will no longer support placeholder files in Windows 10. Windows 10 users can choose which folders they want to sync from OneDrive settings.

- When upgrading Windows 10 with versions of previous operating systems that support Media Center, Windows Media Center will be removed. For a limited time on systems that were upgraded to Windows 10 from one of these versions of Windows, a DVD playback app, Windows DVD Player, will be installed. If the Windows DVD Player does not install immediately, it will be installed after the first successful Windows update.

Windows 10 Architecture

Windows 10 has limited the number of files that load at system startup to help with the core performance of the operating system. Microsoft has also removed many of the fluff items that Windows Vista used, allowing for better performance.

Microsoft offers both a 32-bit version and a 64-bit version of Windows 10. The terms *32-bit* and *64-bit* refer to the CPU, or processor. The number represents how the data is processed. It is processed either as 2^{32} or 2^{64}. The larger the number, the larger the amount of data that can be processed at any one time.

To get an idea of how 32-bit and 64-bit processors operate, think of a large highway with 32 lanes. Vehicles can travel on those 32 lanes only, so when traffic gets backed up, the result is delays. Now think of how many more vehicles can travel on a 64-lane highway. The problem here is that a 32-lane highway can't handle the number of vehicles a 64-lane highway can. You need to have the infrastructure to allow for that volume of vehicles. The same is true for computers. Your computer has to be configured to allow you to run a 64-bit processor.

So what does all of this mean to the common user or administrator? It's all about random access memory, or RAM. A 32-bit operating system can handle up to 4 GB of RAM, and a 64-bit processor can handle up to 16 exabytes of RAM. None of this is new. Although 64-bit processors are just starting to get accepted with Windows systems, other operating systems, such as Apple, have been using 64-bit processors for many years.

Computer processors are typically rated by speed. The speed of the processor, or central processing unit (CPU), is rated by the number of clock cycles that can be performed in 1 second. This measurement is typically expressed in gigahertz (GHz). One GHz is one billion cycles per second. Keep in mind that processor architecture must also be taken into account when considering processor speed. A processor with a more efficient pipeline will be faster than a processor with a less-efficient pipeline at the same CPU speed.

Now that you have seen the new features of Windows 10, let's look at how to prepare the machine to install Windows 10.

Preparing to Install Windows 10

Installing Windows 10 can be relatively simple because of the installation wizard. The installation wizard will walk you through the entire installation of the operating system.

The most difficult part of installing Windows 10 is preparing and planning for the installation. One thing I often say to IT professionals is, "An hour of planning will save you days of work." Planning a Windows 10 rollout is one of the hardest and most important tasks that you will perform when installing Windows 10.

There are many decisions that should be made before you install Windows 10. The first decision is which version of Windows 10 you want to install. As mentioned previously, Microsoft has six different versions of the Windows 10 operating system. This allows an administrator to custom-fit a user's hardware and job function to the appropriate version of Windows 10. Many times, Microsoft releases multiple editions of the operating system contained within the same Windows 10 media disk. You can choose to unlock the one you want based on the product key you have. Let's take a closer look at the different versions of Windows 10.

> In this book, we will not talk much about Windows 10 Education. Windows 10 Education is the counterpart to Windows 10 Enterprise, but it is a volume-licensed version of Windows 10 that is specifically priced for educational institutions. Educational institutions receive the same Enterprise functionality, but they pay much less than a corporation.

Windows 10 Home

Windows 10 Home is the main operating system for home users. Windows 10 Home offers many features, including these:

- Broad application and device compatibility with unlimited concurrent applications
- A safe, reliable, and supported operating system
- Microsoft Passport
- HomeGroup, which allows a user to easily share media, documents, and printers across multiple PCs in homes or offices without the need of a domain
- Improved Taskbar and Jump Lists (Jump Lists is a feature in Windows 10 that allows you to quickly access files that you have been working on.)
- Live thumbnail previews and an enhanced visual experience
- Advanced networking support (ad hoc wireless networks and Internet connection sharing)
- View Available Networks (VAN) (Windows 10 by default has the ability, when you use a wireless network adapter, to choose the wireless network that you want to connect to by using the wireless network adapter properties.)
- Device Encryption
- Easy networking and sharing across all your PCs and devices
- Windows Update
- Multitouch
- Improved handwriting recognition

Windows 10 Professional

Windows 10 Professional is designed for small-business owners. Microsoft designed Windows 10 Professional for users to get more done and safeguard their data. Professional offers the following features:

- Broad application and device compatibility with unlimited concurrent applications
- A safe, reliable, and supported operating system
- Microsoft Passport
- Domain Join
- Improved Taskbar and Jump Lists
- Enterprise Mode Internet Explorer (EMIE)
- Advanced networking support (ad hoc wireless networks and Internet connection sharing)
- View Available Networks (VAN) (Windows 10 by default has the ability, when you use a wireless network adapter, to choose the wireless network that you want to connect to by using the wireless network adapter properties.)
- Mobility Center
- Action Center, which makes it easier to resolve many IT issues yourself
- Easy networking and sharing across all your PCs and devices
- Group Policy Management
- Windows Update and Windows Update for Business
- Multitouch
- Improved handwriting recognition
- Domain Join, which enables simple and secure server networking
- BitLocker, which protects data on removable devices
- Device Encryption
- Encrypting File System, which protects data
- Client Hyper-V
- Location Aware Printing, which helps find the right printer when moving between the office and home
- Start Menu that includes Live Tiles

Windows 10 Enterprise

Windows 10 Enterprise is the version designed for midsize and large organizations. This operating system has the most features and security options of all Windows 10 versions. Here are some of the features:

- Broad application and device compatibility with unlimited concurrent applications.
- A safe, reliable, and supported operating system.
- Microsoft Passport.
- Enterprise Mode Internet Explorer (EMIE).

- Group Policy Management.

- Windows Update and Windows Update for Business.

- Advanced networking support (ad hoc wireless networks and Internet connection sharing).

- View Available Networks (VAN). Windows 10 by default has the ability, when you use a wireless network adapter, to choose the wireless network that you want to connect to by using the wireless network adapter properties.

- Mobility Center.

- Easy networking and sharing across all your PCs and devices.

- Multitouch.

- Start menu that includes Live Tiles.

- Improved handwriting recognition.

- Domain Join, which enables simple and secure server networking.

- Device Encryption.

- Encrypting File System, which protects data.

- Location Aware Printing, which helps find the right printer when you are moving between the office and home.

- Client Hyper-V.

- Credential Guard.

- Device Guard.

- BitLocker, which protects data on removable devices.

- DirectAccess, which links users to corporate resources from the road without a virtual private network (VPN).

- BranchCache, which makes it faster to open files and web pages from a branch office.

- AppLocker, which restricts unauthorized software and also enables greater security hardware requirements

Before you can install the operating system, you must make sure the machine's hardware can handle the Windows 10 operating system.

To install Windows 10 successfully, your system must meet or exceed certain hardware requirements. Table 11.3 lists the minimum requirements for a Windows 10–capable PC.

TABLE 11.3   Hardware requirements

Component	Requirements
CPU (processor)	1 GHz or faster processor or system-on-a-chip (SoC)
Memory (RAM)	1 GB for 32-bit or 2 GB for 64-bit

Component	Requirements
Hard disk	16 GB for 32-bit OS 20 GB for 64-bit OS
Video adapter	DirectX 9 or later with WDDM 1.0 driver
Optional drive	DVD-R/W drive
Network device	Compatible network interface card

The hardware requirements listed in Table 11.3 are those specified at the time this book was written. Always check the Microsoft website for the most current information.

The Windows 10–capable PC must meet or exceed the basic requirements to deliver the core functionality of the Windows 10 operating system. These requirements are based on the assumption that you are installing only the operating system, without any premium functionality. For example, you may be able to get by with the minimum requirements if you are installing the operating system just to learn the basics of the software. Remember, the better the hardware, the better the performance.

 Real World Scenario

Deciding on Minimum Hardware Requirements

The company you work for has decided that everyone will have their own laptop running Windows 10. You need to decide on the new computers' specifications for processor, memory, and disk space.

The first step is to determine which applications will be used. Typically, most users will work with an email program, a word processor, a spreadsheet, presentation software, and maybe a drawing or graphics program. Additionally, an antivirus application will probably be used. Under these demands, a 1 GHz Celeron processor and 1 GB of RAM will make for a very slow-running machine. So for this usage, you can assume that the minimum baseline configuration would be higher than a 1 GHz processor with at least 2 GB of RAM.

Based on your choice of baseline configuration, you should then fit a test computer with the applications that will be used on it and test the configuration in a lab environment simulating normal use. This will give you an idea of whether the RAM and processor calculations you have made for your environment are going to provide a suitable response.

Today's disk drives have become capable of much larger capacity while dropping drastically in price. So for disk space, the rule of thumb is to buy whatever is the current standard. At the time this book was written, 500 GB drives were commonplace, which is sufficient for most users. If users plan to store substantial graphics or video files, you may need to consider buying larger-than-standard drives.

Also consider what the business requirements will be over the next 12 to 18 months. If you will be implementing applications that are memory or processor intensive, you may want to spec out the computers with hardware sufficient to support upcoming needs to avoid costly upgrades in the near future.

The requirements for the graphics card depend on the resolution at which you want to run. The required amount of memory is as follows:

- 64 MB is required for a single monitor at a resolution of 1,310,720 pixels or less, which is equivalent to a 1280×1024 resolution.

- 128 MB is required for a single monitor at a resolution of 2,304,000 pixels or less, which is equivalent to a 1920×1200 resolution.

- 256 MB is required for a single monitor at a resolution larger than 2,304,000 pixels.

Measurement Used for Disk Space and Memory

Hard disks are commonly rated by capacity. The following measurements are used for disk space and memory capacity:

- 1 MB (megabyte) = 1,024 KB (kilobytes)

- 1 GB (gigabyte) = 1,024 MB

- 1 TB (terabyte) = 1,024 GB

- 1 PB (petabyte) = 1,024 TB

- 1 EB (exabyte) = 1,024 PB

If you are not sure if your machine meets the minimum requirements, Microsoft includes some tools that can help you determine if a machine is Windows 10 compatible, which we will look at in the following sections.

The Hardware Compatibility List

Along with meeting the minimum requirements, whenever possible your hardware should appear on the *Hardware Compatibility List (HCL)*. The HCL is an extensive list of computers and peripheral hardware that have been tested with the Windows 10 operating system. To determine if your computer and peripherals are on the HCL, check the most up-to-date list at

https://msdn.microsoft.com/en-us/library/windows/hardware/
dn922588(v=vs.85).aspx

The Windows 10 operating system requires control of the hardware for stability, efficiency, and security. The hardware and supported drivers on the HCL have been put through rigorous tests to ensure their compatibility with Windows 10. Microsoft guarantees that the items on the list meet the requirements for Windows 10 and do not have any incompatibilities that could affect the stability of the operating system.

If you call Microsoft for support, the first thing a Microsoft support engineer will ask about is your configuration. If you have any hardware that is not on the HCL, you may not be able to get support from Microsoft.

BIOS Compatibility

Before you install Windows 10, you should verify that your computer has the most current BIOS. This is especially important if your current BIOS does not include support for Advanced Configuration and Power Interface (ACPI) functionality. ACPI functionality is required for Windows 10 to function properly. Check the computer vendor's website for the latest BIOS version information.

Driver Requirements

To successfully install Windows 10, you must have the critical device drivers for your computer, such as the hard drive device driver. The Windows 10 media come with an extensive list of drivers. If your computer's device drivers are not on the Windows 10 installation media, you should check the device manufacturer's website.

New Install or Upgrade?

Once you've determined that your hardware meets the minimum requirements, you need to decide whether you want to do an upgrade or a clean install. An upgrade allows you to retain your existing operating system's applications, settings, and files. If you currently have a computer with Windows Vista, you are eligible to use an upgrade copy of Windows 10.

The bad news is that if you are moving from Windows Vista, Windows XP, or earlier versions of Windows to Windows 10, you must perform a clean install. (You can, however, use the Windows Easy Transfer utility to migrate files and settings from Windows XP to Windows 10 on the same computer.)

You can perform an upgrade to Windows 10 if the following conditions are true:

- You are running Windows 7 or Windows 8.

- You want to keep your existing applications and preferences.

- You want to preserve any local users and groups you've created.

You must perform a clean install of Windows 10 if any of the following conditions are true:

- There is no operating system currently installed.
- You have an operating system installed that does not support an in-place upgrade to Windows 10 (such as DOS, Windows 9x, Windows NT, Windows Me, Windows 2000 Professional, Windows Vista, or Windows XP).
- You want to start from scratch, without keeping any existing preferences.
- You want to be able to dual-boot between Windows 10 and your previous operating system.

Table 11.4 shows each operating system that can be upgraded and the edition of Windows 10 to which it should be upgraded.

TABLE 11.4   Windows 7 and Windows 8 upgrade options

From Current Edition	Windows 10 Edition
Windows 7 Starter	Windows 10 Home
Windows 7 Home Basic	Windows 10 Home
Windows 7 Home Premium	Windows 10 Home
Windows 7 Professional	Windows 10 Pro
Windows 7 Ultimate	Windows 10 Pro
Windows 7 Enterprise	Windows 10 Enterprise
Windows Phone 8.1	Windows 10 Mobile
Windows 8.1 Home	Windows 10 Home
Windows 8.1 Pro	Windows 10 Pro
Windows 8.1 Enterprise	Windows 10 Enterprise
Windows 8.1 Pro for Students	Windows 10 Pro

Upgrade Considerations

Almost all Windows 7 and Windows 8 applications should run with the Windows 10 operating system. However, possible exceptions to this statement include the following:

- Applications that use file-system filters, such as antivirus software, may not be compatible.
- Custom power-management tools may not be supported.

Before upgrading to Windows 10, be sure to stop any antivirus scanners, network services, or other client software. These software packages may see the Windows 10 install as a virus and cause installation issues.

If you are performing a clean install to the same partition as an existing version of Windows, the contents of the existing Users (or Documents and Settings), Program Files, and Windows directories will be placed in a directory named Windows.old, and the old operating system will no longer be available.

Hardware Compatibility Issues

You need to ensure that you have Windows 10 device drivers for your hardware. If you have a video driver without a Windows 10–compatible driver, the Windows 10 upgrade will install the Standard VGA driver, which will display the video with an 800×600 resolution. Once you get the Windows 10 driver for your video, you can install it and adjust video properties accordingly.

Application Compatibility Issues

Not all applications that were written for earlier versions of Windows will work with Windows 10. After the upgrade, if you have application problems, you can address the problems in any of the following ways:

- If the application is compatible with Windows 10, reinstall the application after the upgrade is complete.
- If the application uses dynamic-link libraries (DLLs) and there are migration DLLs for the application, apply the migration DLLs.
- Use the Microsoft Application Compatibility Toolkit (ACT) to determine the compatibility of your current applications with Windows 10. ACT will determine which applications are installed, identify any applications that may be affected by Windows updates, and identify any potential compatibility problems with User Account Control and Internet Explorer. Reports can be exported for detailed analysis.
- If applications were written for earlier versions of Windows but are incompatible with Windows 10, use the Windows 10 Program Compatibility Wizard. From the Control Panel, click the Programs icon, and then click the Run Programs From Previous Versions link to start the Program Compatibility Wizard. If the application is not compatible with Windows 10, upgrade your application to a Windows 10–compliant version.

An Upgrade Checklist

Once you have made the decision to upgrade, you should develop a plan of attack. The following upgrade checklist (valid for upgrading from Windows 7 or Windows 8) will help you plan and implement a successful upgrade strategy:

- Verify that your computer meets the minimum hardware requirements for Windows 10.

- Be sure your hardware is on the HCL.

- Make sure you have the Windows 10 drivers for the hardware. You can verify this with the hardware manufacturer.

- To audit the current configuration and status of your computer, run the Get Windows 10 App tool from the Microsoft website, which also includes documentation on using the utility. It will generate a report of any known hardware or software compatibility issues based on your configuration. You should resolve any reported issues before you upgrade to Windows 10.

- Make sure your BIOS is current. Windows 10 requires that your computer has the most current BIOS. If it does not, it may not be able to use advanced power-management features or device-configuration features. In addition, your computer may cease to function during or after the upgrade. Use caution when performing BIOS updates because installing the incorrect BIOS can cause your computer to fail to boot.

- Take an inventory of your current configuration. This inventory should include documentation of your current network configuration, the applications that are installed, the hardware items and their configuration, the services that are running, and any profile and policy settings.

- Back up your data and configuration files. Before you make any major changes to your computer's configuration, you should back up your data and configuration files and then verify that you can successfully restore your backup. Chances are, if you have a valid backup, you won't have any problems. Likewise, if you don't have a valid backup, you will likely have problems.

- Delete any unnecessary files or applications, and clean up any program groups or program items you don't use. Theoretically, you want to delete all the junk on your computer before you upgrade. Think of this as the spring-cleaning step.

- Verify that there are no existing problems with your hard drive prior to the upgrade. Perform a disk scan, a current virus scan, and defragmentation. These too are spring-cleaning chores. This step just prepares your hard drive for the upgrade.

- Perform the upgrade. In this step, you upgrade from the Windows 7 or Windows 8 operating system to Windows 10.

- Verify your configuration. After Windows 10 has been installed, use the inventory to compare and test each element that was inventoried prior to the upgrade to verify that the upgrade was successful.

Handling an Upgrade Failure

Before you upgrade, you should have a contingency plan in place. Your plan should assume the worst-case scenario. For example, what happens if you upgrade and the computer doesn't work anymore? It is possible that, after checking your upgrade list and verifying that everything should work, your attempt at the actual upgrade may not work. If this happens, you may want to return your computer to the original, working configuration.

Indeed, I have made these plans, created my backups (two, just in case), verified them, and then had a failed upgrade anyway—only to discover that I had no clue where to find the original operating system CD. A day later, with the missing CD located, I was able to get up and running again. My problem was an older BIOS, and the manufacturer of my computer did not have an updated BIOS.

Disk Partitioning

Disk partitioning is the act of taking the physical hard drive and creating logical partitions. A logical drive is how space is allocated to the drive's primary and logical partitions. For example, if you have a 500 GB hard drive, you might partition it into three logical drives:

- C: drive, which might be 200 GB
- D: drive, which might be 150 GB
- E: drive, which might be 150 GB

The following sections detail some of the major considerations for disk partitioning:

Partition Size   One important consideration in your disk-partitioning scheme is determining the partition size. You need to consider the amount of space taken up by your operating system, the applications that will be installed, and the amount of stored data. It is also important to consider the amount of space required in the future.

Microsoft recommends that you allocate at least 16 GB of disk space for Windows 10. This allows room for the operating system files and for future growth in terms of upgrades and installation files that are placed with the operating system files.

The System and Boot Partitions   When you install Windows 10, files will be stored in two locations: the system partition and the boot partition. The system partition and the boot partition can be the same partition.

The system partition contains the files needed to boot the Windows 10 operating system. The system partition contains the Master Boot Record (MBR) and boot sector of the active drive partition. It is often the first physical hard drive in the computer and normally contains the necessary files to boot the computer. The files stored on the system partition do not take any significant disk space. The active partition is the system partition that is used to start your computer. The C: drive is usually the active partition.

The boot partition contains the Windows 10 operating system files. By default, the Windows operating system files are located in a folder named Windows.

Disk Partition Configuration Utilities If you are partitioning your disk prior to installation, you can use several utilities, such as the DOS or Windows FDISK program, or a third-party utility, such as Norton's Partition Magic. You can also configure the disks during the installation of the Windows 10 operating system.

You might want to create only the first partition where Windows 10 will be installed. You can then use the Disk Management utility in Windows 10 to create any other partitions you need. The Windows 10 Disk Management utility is covered in Chapter 13, "Configuring Storage and Security."

Language and Locale

Language and locale settings determine the language the computer will use. Windows 10 supports many languages for the operating system interface and utilities.

Locale settings are for configuring the format for items such as numbers, currencies, times, and dates. For example, English for the United States specifies a short date as mm/dd/yyyy (month/day/year), while English for South Africa specifies a short date as yyyy/mm/dd (year/month/day).

Installing Windows 10

You can install Windows 10 either from the bootable DVD or through a network installation using files that have been copied to a network share point or USB device. You can also launch the setup.exe file from within the Windows 10 operating system to upgrade your operating system.

To start the installation, you simply restart your computer and boot to the DVD. The installation process will begin automatically. You will walk through the steps of performing a clean install of Windows 10 from the DVD in Exercise 11.1.

If you are installing Windows 10 from the network, you need a distribution server and a computer with a network connection. A distribution server is a server that has the Windows 10 distribution files copied to a shared folder. The following steps are used to install Windows 10 over the network:

1. Boot the target computer.

2. Attach to the distribution server and access the share that has the files copied to it.

3. Launch setup.exe.

4. Complete the Windows 10 installation using either the clean install method or the upgrade method. These methods are discussed in detail in the following sections.

Performing a Clean Install of Windows 10

On any installation of Windows 10, there are three stages.

Collecting Information   During the collection phase of the installation, Windows 10 gathers the information necessary to complete the installation. This is where Windows 10 gathers your local time, location, keyboard, license agreement, installation type, and installation disk partition information.

Installing Windows   This section of the installation is where your Windows 10 files are copied to the hard disk and the installation is completed. This phase takes the longest because the files are installed.

Setting Up Windows   In this phase, you set up a username, computer name, and password; enter the product key; configure the security settings; and review the date and time. Once this is finished, your installation will be complete.

As explained earlier, you can run the installation from the optical media, from a USB, or over a network. The only difference in the installation procedure is your starting point: from your optical drive or USB or a network share. The steps in Exercise 11.1 and Exercise 11.2 assume you are using the Windows 10 DVD to install Windows 10.

Setting Up Your Computer for Hands-On Exercises

Before beginning Exercise 11.1, verify that your computer meets the requirements for installing Windows 10, as listed earlier in Table 11.3. For Exercise 11.1, it is assumed you are not currently running a previous version of Windows that will be upgraded.

The exercises in this book are based on your computer being configured in a specific manner. Your computer should have at least a 50 GB hard drive (this exceeds the basic minimums) that is configured with the minimum space requirements and partitions.

When you boot to the Windows 10 installation media, the Setup program will automatically start the Windows 10 installation. In Exercise 11.1, you will perform a clean install of Windows 10. This exercise assumes that you have access to Windows 10 Enterprise; other editions may vary slightly. You can also download an evaluation version of Windows 10 from the Microsoft website.

Also, I may list steps that you may not see or I may not list steps that you see—this is because my version of Windows may be different. For example, I am installing an MSDN Windows 10 Enterprise edition. At this time, I am not required to enter a license number during install. A normal version bought from a vendor may ask for the license during the actual install.

I am loading Windows 10 Enterprise into a VMware Workstation virtual machine. Again, this may make your installation a little different than the steps listed in Exercise 11.1.

EXERCISE 11.1

Performing a Clean Install of Windows 10

1. Insert the Windows 10 DVD into a machine or virtual machine with no operating system and start the computer.

2. If you are directed to "Hit any key" to start the DVD, press Enter.

3. The first screen will ask you to enter your language, time and currency format, and keyboard or input method (see Figure 11.1). After filling in these fields, click Next.

FIGURE 11.1   Windows Setup screen

4. On the next screen, click the Install Now button (see Figure 11.2).

FIGURE 11.2 Windows install screen

5. A message appears to tell you that the setup is starting. The licensing screen will be first. Read the license agreement and then check the I Accept The License Terms check box (see Figure 11.3). Click Next.

FIGURE 11.3 Windows license screen

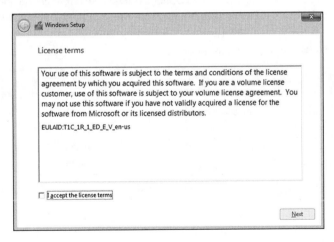

6. When asked which type of installation you want, click Custom (Advanced) as shown in Figure 11.4.

FIGURE 11.4 Type of install screen

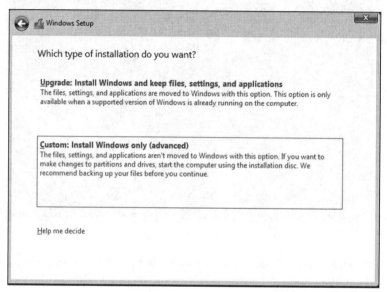

7. The next screen asks you to identify the disk to which you would like to install Windows 10. Choose an unformatted free space or a partition (partition will be erased) with at least 50 GB available. You can also click the Drive Options (Advanced) link to create and format your own partition as shown in Figure 11.5. After you choose your partition, click Next.

FIGURE 11.5 Windows disk setup screen

8. When your partition is set, the installation will start (as shown in Figure 11.6). You will see the progress of the installation during the entire process. When the installation is complete, the machine will reboot.

FIGURE 11.6 Windows installation status screen

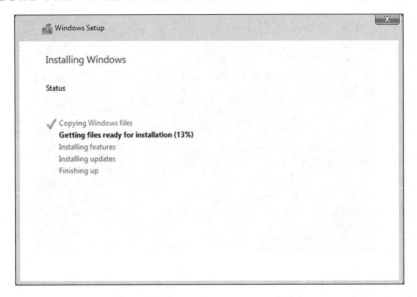

9. After the system restarts, a screen appears that asks if you want to use custom or express settings, as shown in Figure 11.7. Click the Use Express Settings button. The system will then restart.

FIGURE 11.7 Windows express settings screen

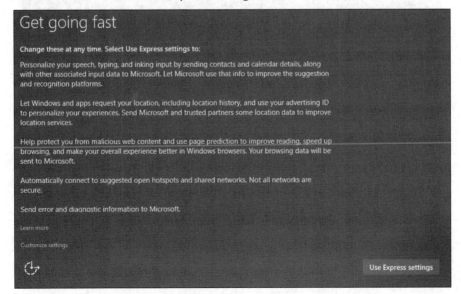

10. After the restart, a screen appears that asks you to choose how you will connect. Select Join A Domain (see Figure 11.8), and then click the Next button.

FIGURE 11.8   Choosing a domain

11. The next screen asks you to enter a username and password. Type in your username, password, and a password hint, as shown in Figure 11.9. Then click Next.

FIGURE 11.9   PC account screen

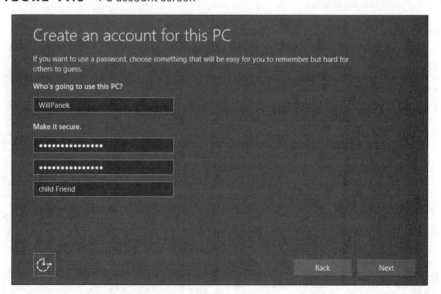

The Hi screen will appear, and the system will continue its setup. Then the system applications will be installed.

12. You will be asked if you want your system to be recognized by other systems on the network. This is a choice you can make. If you want other machines to see this Windows 10 system, choose Yes.

Once Windows 10 finishes its installation, you should see the Windows 10 desktop, as shown in Figure 11.10.

FIGURE 11.10   Windows 10 screen

Before we talk about the Windows 10 upgrade procedure, I want to quickly explain something that you saw during the Windows 10 install. In step 10, I had you choose Join A Domain instead of Azure AD. We will explore both of the choices in greater detail, but I wanted to quickly explain why we chose one over the other.

Microsoft offers two main networks: workgroup-based or domain-based. *Workgroups* (also referred to also as peer-to-peer networks) is when you just connect your computers together directly to each other. A perfect example for most of us is what you do in your home network. Most home users connect their machines together without the use of a main server.

Corporations normally do things a bit differently than that. *Domains* are networks that are controlled by servers called domain controllers. Domain controllers are Windows servers that have a copy of a database called Active Directory (AD). Recently Microsoft took domain-based networks a step further by allowing companies to set up a cloud-based version of an Active Directory domain (Azure AD). This means that companies no longer need to maintain and manage their own domain controllers. Since most people don't have a cloud-based version of Azure AD, I had you choose the option Join A Domain so that we could finish the Windows 10 install.

We will go over all of these options in greater detail throughout this book, but I wanted to introduce you to these two Windows 10 options.

Performing an Upgrade to Windows 10

This section describes how to perform an upgrade to Windows 10 from Windows 8.1. Similar to a clean install, you can run the installation from the installation DVD, from a USB, or over a network. The only difference in the installation procedure is your starting point: from your optical or USB drive or from a network share. For the steps in the following sections, it is assumed that you are using the Windows 10 DVD to install the Windows 10 operating system.

Upgrading a Windows 7 or Windows 8.1 system to Windows 10 will save you a lot of time and trouble. Because we are upgrading the system, all of the user's data and applications will remain installed and most likely still work the exact same way. Sometimes when we upgrade a system, we run into problems with applications. But many times that is caused by a driver or a needed software update that will most likely solve the issue.

The three main steps in the Windows 10 upgrade process are very similar to the ones for a clean install. The three steps of upgrading to Windows 10 are as follows:

1. Collecting information

2. Installing Windows

3. Setting up Windows

In Exercise 11.2, you will go through the process of installing Windows 10 by upgrading Windows 8.1. As you can see in Figure 11.11, I have a Windows 8.1 Enterprise system that I will update to Windows 10 Enterprise.

FIGURE 11.11   Windows 8.1

EXERCISE 11.2

Upgrading Windows 8.1 to Windows 10

1. Insert the Windows 10 DVD. (We are upgrading Windows 8.1 Enterprise to Windows 10 Enterprise.)

2. If Autorun does not start, navigate to the DVD drive and click setup.exe. Once the setup starts (via either setup.exe or Autorun), click Run Setup.exe as shown in Figure 11.12.

FIGURE 11.12   DVD setup screen

3. If a pop-up box appears for User Account Control, click the Yes button (see Figure 11.13).

FIGURE 11.13 User Account Control screen

You should then see a message appear stating that Windows is preparing the system, as shown in Figure 11.14.

FIGURE 11.14 Preparing screen

4. You may be prompted to Get Important Updates. You can choose to either download the updates or not do them at this time. Make a choice and click the Next button. (During my installation, I decided to download the updates.)

5. The Microsoft Windows 10 license terms appear. Read the terms and then click Accept. (The installation will not allow you to continue until you click Accept.)

6. At the Ready To Install screen (shown in Figure 11.15), you can change what files and/ or apps you want to keep by clicking the Change What To Keep link. Once you're ready, click the Install button.

FIGURE 11.15   Ready To Install screen

7. Windows 10 will begin to install (as shown in Figure 11.16). Your computer may restart multiple times. This is normal. As the upgrade status screen states, "Sit back and relax."

FIGURE 11.16   Installing Status screen

8. After the upgrade has completed, a welcome screen will be displayed, similar to the one shown in Figure 11.17. Click Next.

FIGURE 11.17 Welcome screen

9. At the Get Going Fast screen, click the Use Express Settings button.

10. At the New Apps screen, just click Next.

And that's it—Windows 10 is installed (see Figure 11.18). Congrats.

FIGURE 11.18 Windows 10 screen

Troubleshooting Installation Problems

The Windows 10 installation process is designed to be as simple as possible. The chances for installation errors are greatly minimized through the use of wizards and the step-by-step process. However, it is possible that errors will occur.

Identifying Common Installation Problems

As most of you are aware, installations sometimes do get errors. You might encounter some of the following installation errors:

Media Errors   Media errors are caused by defective or damaged DVDs. To check the disc, put it into another computer and see if you can read it. Also check your disc for scratches or dirt—it may just need to be cleaned.

Insufficient Disk Space   Windows 10 needs at least 16 GB for the 32-bit OS and 20 GB for the 64-bit OS to execute properly. If the Setup program cannot verify that this space exists, the program will not let you continue.

Not Enough Memory   Make sure your computer has the minimum amount of memory required by Windows 10 (1 GB for 32-bit or 2 GB for 64-bit). Having insufficient memory may cause the installation to fail or blue-screen errors to occur after installation.

Not Enough Processing Power   Make sure your computer has the minimum processing power required by Windows 10 (1 GHz or faster processor or SoC). Having insufficient processing power may cause the installation to fail or blue-screen errors to occur after installation.

Hardware That Is Not on the HCL   If your hardware is not listed on the HCL, Windows 10 may not recognize the hardware or the device may not work properly.

Hardware with No Driver Support   Windows 10 will not recognize hardware without driver support.

Hardware That Is Not Configured Properly   If your hardware is Plug and Play (PnP) compatible, Windows 10 should configure it automatically. If your hardware is not Plug and Play compatible, you will need to manually configure the hardware per the manufacturer's instructions.

Incorrect Product Key   Without a valid product key, the installation will not go past the Product Key screen. Make sure you have not typed in an incorrect key (check your Windows 10 installation folder or your computer case for this key).

Failure to Access TCP/IP Network Resources   If you install Windows 10 with typical settings, the computer is configured as a DHCP client. If there is no DHCP server to provide IP configuration information, the client will still generate an autoconfigured IP address but be unable to access network resources through TCP/IP if the other network clients are using DHCP addresses.

Installing Nonsupported Hard Drives   If your computer is using a hard disk that does not have a driver included on the Windows 10 media, you will receive an error message stating that the hard drive cannot be found. You should verify that the hard drive is properly connected and functional. You will need to obtain a disk driver for Windows 10 from the manufacturer and then specify the driver location by selecting the Load Driver option during partition selection.

Troubleshooting with Installation Log Files

When you install Windows 10, the Setup program creates several log files. You can view these logs to check for any problems during the installation process. Two log files are particularly useful for troubleshooting:

- The action log includes all of the actions that were performed during the setup process and a description of each action. These actions are listed in chronological order. The action log is stored as \Windows\setupact.log.

- The error log includes any errors that occurred during the installation. For each error, there is a description and an indication of the severity of the error. This error log is stored as \Windows\setuperr.log.

In Exercise 11.3, you will view the Windows 10 Setup logs to determine whether there were any problems with your Windows 10 installation.

EXERCISE 11.3

Troubleshooting Failed Installations with Setup Logs

1. Select Start ➢ Computer.

2. Double-click Local Disk (C:).

3. Double-click Windows.

4. In the Windows folder, double-click the Setupact.log file to view your action log in Notepad. When you are finished viewing this file, close Notepad.

5. Double-click the Setuperr.log file to view your error file in Notepad. If no errors occurred during installation, this file will be empty. When you are finished viewing this file, close Notepad.

6. Close the directory window.

Migrating Files and Settings

Rather than perform an in-place upgrade, you can choose to migrate your files and settings from an existing installation. In this case, you can use the *User State Migration Tool (USMT)*. USMT can help you migrate user profiles, configure folder locations for uploads and downloads of user data, and configure profile versions: local, roaming, and mandatory.

User State Migration Tool

You can download a utility called USMT that is used by administrators to migrate large numbers of users over automated deployments. USMT for Windows 10 is now part of the Windows Assessment and Deployment Kit (ADK). USMT is similar to Windows Easy Transfer, with the following differences:

- USMT is more configurable and can use XML files to specify which files and settings are transferred.

- USMT is scriptable and uses command-line utilities to save and restore user files and settings.

USMT consists of two executable files: `Scanstate.exe` and `Loadstate.exe`. In addition, there are three premade migration-rule information files: `Migapp.xml`, `Migsys.xml`, and `Miguser.xml`. Finally, you can create a `Config.xml` file that specifies what should and should not be migrated. The purpose of these files is as follows:

- `Scanstate.exe` collects user data and settings information based on the configuration of the `Migapp.xml`, `Migsys.xml`, and `Miguser.xml` files and stores it as an image file. ScanState is used on the machine you are migrating from.

- `Loadstate.exe` then deposits the information that is collected to a computer running a fresh copy of Windows 10. The `Config.xml` file can be used to help exclude files and settings during the LoadState process. The LoadState command is used to bring the user data that was collected from the ScanState utility over to the new Windows 10 system.

The following information is migrated:

- From each user:
  - Documents
  - Video
  - Music
  - Pictures
  - Desktop files
  - Start menu
  - Quick Launch toolbar
  - Internet Explorer Favorites
- From the All Users profile:
  - Shared documents
  - Shared video
  - Shared music
  - Shared desktop files
  - Shared pictures
  - Shared Start menu
  - Shared Internet Explorer Favorites

- Files with certain filename extensions, including .doc, .dot, .rtf, .txt, .wps, .wri, .xls, .csv, .wks, .ppt, .pps, .pot, .pst, and more
- Access control lists (ACLs)

USMT will not migrate hardware settings, drivers, passwords, application binaries, synchronization files, DLL files, or other executables.

A decision point that exists while using USMT is to determine if you want to perform a side-by-side installation or a wipe-and-load installation.

Side-by-Side Installation   A side-by-side installation means that you have the new computer and the old computer. You use ScanState to collect the user's data. You then store that data on an intermediate store. After the installation of Windows 10 on a new machine, you use LoadState to move the data from the intermediate store to the new computer.

Wipe-and-Load Installation   A wipe-and-load installation means that you have the old computer only. You will install Windows 10 on the same machine as the previous operating system. You use ScanState to collect the user's data. You then store that data on an intermediate store. After the installation of Windows 10 on the machine, you use LoadState to move the data from the intermediate store to the old computer.

USMT is downloadable software from Microsoft's website. In its simplest form, you use USMT in the following manner:

1. Run Scanstate.exe on the source computer. Scanstate.exe will copy the user state data to an intermediate store. The intermediate store (for example, a CD-RW) must be large enough to accommodate the data that will be transferred. Scanstate.exe would commonly be executed as a shortcut sent to users that they would deploy in the evening or through a scheduled script.

2. Install a fresh copy of Windows 10 on the target computer.

3. Run Loadstate.exe on the target computer. Loadstate.exe will access the intermediate store to restore the user settings.

When you use USMT, you can create a script that can be run manually or can be used as an automated process at a scheduled time. Table 11.5 defines the options for the Scanstate .exe and Loadstate.exe commands.

TABLE 11.5   Options for Scanstate.exe and Loadstate.exe

Option	Description
/config	Specifies the Config.xml file that should be used
/encrypt	Encrypts the store (Scanstate.exe only)
/decrypt	Decrypts the store (Loadstate.exe only)
/nocompress	Disables data compression

Option	Description
/genconfig	Generates a Config.xml file but does not create a store
/targetxp	Optimizes ScanState for use with Windows XP
/all	Migrates all users
/ue	User exclude: excludes the specified user
/ui	User include: includes the specified user
/uel	Excludes user based on last login time
/v verboselevel	Used to identify what verbosity level will be associated with the log file on a scale of 0–13, with 0 being the least verbose

Migrating Profiles

Even an operating system that you install has a user profile. User profiles are created when a user logs into a system for the first time. The user profile is a group of settings that make the computer look and work the way you want it to. It contains your settings for desktop backgrounds, screen savers, pointer preferences, sound settings, and other features. Each user account has at least one user profile associated with it. To view the user profiles on a system, you view the Advanced tab of the System Properties (see Figure 11.19).

FIGURE 11.19   User Profiles Settings button

User profiles ensure that your personal preferences are used whenever you log on to Windows. User profiles are not user accounts; rather, they specify how the user account's desktop and settings are configured.

There are different types of user accounts: local, roaming, and mandatory. *Local profiles* are used when you log into a local system or a network system that doesn't use network profiles.

A local profile can be saved to a network location, and then the user's network account can point to that network profile location. This is referred to as a *roaming profile*. Roaming profiles are just local profiles saved to a network location. No matter which system you log into on your network, your desktop and user profile will be the same. The profile follows the user.

To copy a local profile to the network, click the user's profile and then click the Copy To button (see Figure 11.20). Place the user's profile on a network share, and then in the Active Directory account properties for that user, point to the network profile (for example, *Server**ShareName**UserName*). You have now created a roaming profile.

FIGURE 11.20   Local user profiles

To change a roaming profile to a *mandatory profile* (a profile that is mandatory), just change the name of the user profile with the extension of .man. So, for example, if Will Panek's roaming profile is called NTuser.dat, you would change it to NTuser.man. By adding the .man extension, you have made the profile mandatory. Now the user would have to use this profile when he or she logs into the network.

Supporting Multiple-Boot Options

You may want to install Windows 10 but still be able to run other operating systems. *Dual-booting* or multibooting allows your computer to boot multiple operating systems. Your computer will be automatically configured for dual-booting if there was a dual-boot–supported operating system on your computer prior to the Windows 10 installation, you didn't upgrade from that operating system, and you installed Windows 10 into a different partition.

One reason for dual-booting is to test various systems. If you have a limited number of computers in your test lab and you want to be able to test multiple configurations, you should dual-boot. For example, you might configure one computer to dual-boot with Windows 7, Windows 8.1, and Windows 10.

Here are some keys to successful dual-boot configurations:

- Make sure you have plenty of disk space.

- Windows 10 must be installed on a separate partition in order to dual-boot with other operating systems.

- Install older operating systems before installing newer operating systems. If you want to support dual-booting with Windows 7 and Windows 10, Windows 7 must be installed first. If you install Windows 10 first, you cannot install Windows 7 without ruining your Windows 10 configuration.

- Do not install Windows 10 on a compressed volume unless the volume was compressed using NTFS compression.

Once you have installed each operating system, you can choose the operating system that you will boot to during the boot process. You will see a boot-selection screen that asks you to choose which operating system you want to boot.

The Boot Configuration Data (BCD) store contains boot information parameters that were previously found in boot.ini in older versions of Windows. To edit the boot options in the BCD store, use the bcdedit utility, which can be launched only from a command prompt. To open a command prompt window, you can do the following:

1. Launch \Windows\system32\cmd.exe.

2. Open the Run command by pressing the [Windows] key + R and then entering **cmd**.

3. Type **cmd.exe** in the Search Programs And Files box and press Enter.

Once the command-prompt window is open, type bcdedit to launch the **bcdedit** utility. You can also type **bcdedit/?** to see all the different bcdedit commands. A few bcdedit commands may be needed when dual-booting a machine. Table 11.6 shows some of the bcdedit commands that may be needed when dual-booting.

TABLE 11.6   Bcdedit commands for dual-booting

Command	Explanation
/createstore	Creates a new empty boot configuration data store
/default	Allows you to specify which operating system will start when the time-out expires
/deletevalue	Allows you to delete a specified element from a boot entry

TABLE 11.6 Bcdedit commands for dual-booting *(continued)*

Command	Explanation
/displayorder	Shows the display order that the boot manager uses when showing the display order to the user
/export	Allows you to export the contents of the system store into a file
/import	Restores the system store by using the data file previously generated by using the /export option
/set	Allows you to set an entry option value
/store	Specifies the store to be used
/timeout	Specifies the amount of time used before the system boots into the default operating system

Using Windows Activation

Windows Activation is Microsoft's way of reducing software piracy. Unless you have a corporate license for Windows 10, you will need to perform postinstallation activation. This can be done online or through a telephone call. Windows 10 will attempt automatic activation three days after you log on to it for the first time. There is a grace period when you will be able to use the operating system without activation. After the grace period expires, you will not be able to create new files or save changes to existing files until Windows 10 is activated. When the grace period runs out, the Windows Activation Wizard will automatically start (see Figure 11.21); it will walk you through the activation process. You may need to click the Change Product Key button and put in the license number that came with your Windows 10 copy.

Using Windows Update

Windows Update is a utility that connects to the Microsoft website and checks to ensure that you have the most up-to-date versions of Microsoft products.

Some of the common update categories associated with Windows Update are as follows:

- Critical updates
- Service packs
- Drivers

FIGURE 11.21   The Windows Activation Wizard screen

Follow these steps to configure Windows Update:

1. Select Start ➢ Control Panel.

   - From Windows Icons View, select Windows Update.
   - From Windows Category View, select System And Security ➢ Windows Update.

2. Configure the options you want to use for Windows Update by clicking the Advanced Options link. The options you can access from Windows Update include the following:

   - Choose how updates are installed
   - Give me updates for other Microsoft products
   - Defer Upgrades
   - View Update History
   - Choose how updates are delivered
   - Get Insider Builds

Check For Updates

When you click Check For Updates, Windows Update will retrieve a list of available updates from the Internet. You can then click View Available Updates to see what updates are available. Updates are marked as Important, Recommended, or Optional. Figure 11.22 shows the Check for Updates button.

FIGURE 11.22   Check for updates button

There are two ways a user can receive updates: directly from Microsoft or using Microsoft Windows Server Update Service (WSUS). WSUS runs on a Windows server, and that server goes out to the Microsoft website and downloads the updates for your Windows clients. This allows client machines to receive their updates from a local server.

One advantage to using WSUS is that administrators can approve the updates before they get deployed to the client machines. Another advantage is that your clients only need to download updates locally, without using your Internet bandwidth.

   WSUS is discussed in detail in *MCSA: Windows Server 2012 R2 Complete Study Guide* by William Panek (Sybex, 2015).

Using Command-Line Options

Command-line options are becoming more and more popular among administrators and users. Windows Update has a few command-line options that can be used to help configure and maintain it. First, to start Windows Update from a command prompt, you can type **wuapp.exe**. Another command-line option that works with Windows Update is called Windows Update Automatic Update Client (wuauclt.exe), which offers the following options:

Detectnow   When working with WSUS, waiting for detection to start can become very time-consuming. So Microsoft has added an option to allow you to initiate the process of detecting available updates right away. To run the detectnow option, type the following command at the command prompt: **wuauclt.exe /detectnow**.

Reportnow This command allows you to send all queued reporting events to the server asynchronously. To execute this command, type **wuauclt.exe /reportnow** at the command prompt.

Resetauthorization WSUS uses a cookie on Windows 10 client computers to store different types of information. By default, an hour after the cookie is created, it expires. If you need the cookie to expire now, you can use the resetauthorization option along with the detectnow option. Using these options will expire the cookie, initiate detection, and have WSUS update computer group membership. To execute this command, type **wuauclt.exe /resetauthorization /detectnow** at the command prompt.

Installing Windows Service Packs

Service packs are updates to the Windows 10 operating system that include bug fixes and product enhancements. Some of the options that might be included in service packs are security fixes or updated versions of software, such as Internet Explorer.

Prior to installing a service pack, you should perform the following steps:

1. Back up your computer.
2. Check your computer to ensure that it is not running any malware or other unwanted software.
3. Check with your computer manufacturer to see whether there are any special instructions for your computer prior to installing the service pack.

You can download service packs from

http://windows.microsoft.com/en-US/windows/downloads/service-packs

You can also receive service packs via Windows Update, or you can pay for a copy of a service pack to be mailed to you on disk. Before you install a service pack, you should read the release notes that are provided on the Microsoft website.

Summary

This chapter started with a discussion of the features included with Windows 10. We also took a look at the difference between 64-bit and 32-bit operating systems and showed some of the advantages that 64-bit entails, such as greater RAM and processor speed.

Then you learned about installing Windows 10. Installation is an easy process, but you must first make sure the machine is compatible with the Windows 10 operating system.

There are two main ways to install Windows 10: upgrade or clean install. You can upgrade a Windows 7 or Windows 8 machine to Windows 10. You can migrate the user's data and information from a Windows XP machine, but there is no direct upgrade option.

After the Windows 10 installation is complete, you'll want to make sure all updates and service packs are installed. You can use Windows Update to complete that task.

Video Resources

There are videos available for the following exercises:

    11.1

    11.2

You can access the videos at www.wiley.com/go/sybextestprep on the Other Study Tools tab.

Exam Essentials

Understand the Windows 10 hardware requirements. The minimum hardware requirements to run Windows 10 properly are 1 gigahertz (GHz) or faster processor or SoC, 1 gigabyte (GB) for 32-bit or 2 GB for 64-bit of RAM, 16 GB for 32-bit OS 20 GB for 64-bit OS of hard drive space, DirectX 9 or later with WDDM 1.0 video driver, and a DVD-R/W drive or compatible network interface card.

Understand the Hardware Compatibility List. The Hardware Compatibility List (HCL) is an extensive list of computers and peripheral hardware devices that have been tested with the Windows 10 operating system. The hardware and supported drivers on the HCL have been put through rigorous tests to ensure their compatibility with Windows 10. Microsoft guarantees that the items on the list meet the requirements for Windows 10 and do not have any incompatibilities that could affect the stability of the operating system.

Understand how to complete a clean install. If your machine meets the minimum hardware requirements, you can install Windows 10. There are a few different ways to install Windows 10 onto a computer. You can use the installation disk or USB, install it over a network, or install it from an image (see Chapter 12, "Automated Windows 10 Deployments," for more details on imaging).

Understand how to complete an upgrade. You can't upgrade a Windows Vista machine to Windows 10. To complete an upgrade on a Windows 7 or Windows 8 machine, insert the Windows 10 DVD into the Windows machine or connect to the Windows 10 files over the network and complete an upgrade on the computer.

You can't upgrade a Windows XP machine directly to Windows 10. If the machine is running Windows XP, you have to use a migration tool to migrate all the user data from Windows XP to a Windows 10 machine.

Understand how to migrate a user to Windows 10. If you can't perform an upgrade on the computer, you can choose to migrate the user's files and settings from an existing installation. In this case, you can use the User State Migration Tool (USMT).

Review Questions

1. You are the administrator in charge of a computer that runs both Windows 7 and Windows 10. Windows 10 is installed on a different partition from Windows 7. You have to make sure that the computer always starts Windows 7 by default. What action should you perform?

   A. Run Bcdedit.exe and the /default parameter.

   B. Run Bcdedit.exe and the /bootcd parameter.

   C. Create a Boot.ini file in the root of the Windows 10 partition.

   D. Create a Boot.ini file in the root of the Windows 7 partition.

2. You are the administrator for a Windows 10 computer. You have decided to use Windows Update, but you want to be able to change the settings manually. What should you do?

   A. Log on to Windows 10 as a member of the Administrators group.

   B. From the local Group Policy, modify the Windows Update settings.

   C. Right-click Windows Update and select Run As Administrator.

   D. Right-click the command prompt, select Run As Administrator, and then run Wuapp.exe.

3. You have two computers: System1 and System2. System1 runs the Windows 7 operating system, and System2 runs Windows 10. You need to migrate the profiles and user files from System1 to System2. You need to identify how much space is required to complete the migration. What action should you perform?

   A. On System1, run Loadstate c:\store /nocompress.

   B. On System2, run Loadstate \\system1\store /nocompress.

   C. On System1, run Scanstate c:\store /nocompress /p.

   D. On System2, run Scanstate \\system1\store /nocompress /p.

4. You are the IT manager for a medium-size organization. Your organization is looking at upgrading its Windows XP machines to Windows 10. The managers have heard of a new feature that allows you to connect a device to the machine and then the Windows 10 operating system shows a graphic of the device for use. Which Windows 10 feature are they referring to?

   A. Device Manager

   B. Device Stage

   C. Staging Manager

   D. Add/Remove Hardware

5. You are the IT manager for your organization. The organization is looking at upgrading all of its machines from Windows XP to Windows 10. Many of the managers are concerned that their Windows XP applications won't be compatible with Windows 10. Which

Windows 10 feature can you use to assure the managers that all of their Windows XP applications will continue to work?

A. Windows XP Compatibility Checker

B. Windows XP Application Center

C. Windows Hyper-V client

D. Windows XP Application Upgrade tool

6. You are the network administrator for a midsize company that needs to convert all of its Windows XP machines to Windows 10. How can the IT department put Windows 10 on all the Windows XP machines without losing any of the users' information?

A. Upgrade all the Windows XP machines to Windows 10.

B. Format all the XP machines and do a clean install of Windows 10.

C. Use a migration tool to migrate all the users' data and then load a clean copy of Windows 10.

D. Do nothing. The Windows XP machines can't be upgraded without losing all the users' data.

7. You are the IT administrator for a large computer-training company that uses laptops for all its employees. Currently the users have to connect to the wireless network through the wireless network adapter. Windows 10 now includes this built in as which feature?

A. Available Network Finder (ANF)

B. View Networks (VN)

C. Network Availability Viewer (NAV)

D. View Available Networks (VAN)

8. You are the network administrator for a midsize company. One of the managers has come into your office and asked you about setting up a network in his house. He wants to use Windows 10. What feature allows him to set up a home network using Windows 10?

A. Home Networking

B. HomeGroup

C. Quick Connect

D. Networking Groups

9. Which new Windows 10 feature allows you to quickly access files that you have been working on?

A. Quick Connect

B. Jump Lists

C. File Finder

D. Quick File Access

10. You are the IT manager for a pharmaceutical company. The company wants to create a medication dispenser that can be used on the floors of hospital units. The dispensers have to work through touch-screen technology. Which Windows 10 feature provides built-in touch-screen technology?

   A. Windows Touch Screen

   B. Windows Pure Touch

   C. Windows Touch

   D. Windows Pure Screen

Chapter

12

Automated Windows 10 Deployments

MICROSOFT EXAM OBJECTIVES COVERED IN THIS CHAPTER:

✓ **Configure Hyper-V.**

  ▪ This objective may include but is not limited to the following subobjectives: Create and configure virtual machines including integration services, create and manage checkpoints, create and configure virtual switches, create and configure virtual disks, move a virtual machine's storage.

Installing Windows 10 is quick and easy, but as an IT manager or IT professional, you may have to install hundreds of copies of Windows 10. It is not a good practice to install them one at a time. It's important to understand how to automate a Windows 10 deployment for the Windows 10 (70-697) exam, but you'll also use automated deployments in a corporate environment. Many companies use third-party tools to create and deploy Windows 10 machines, but there are other ways.

You can automate the installation of Windows 10 in several ways. You can install Windows 10 by using an unattended installation, by using Windows Deployment Services (WDS) to remotely deploy unattended installations (which requires a Windows Server 2012 R2 machine), by using Hyper-V, or by using the System Preparation Tool for disk imaging. To help customize these options for automating remote installations, you can also use answer files to provide answers to the questions that are normally asked during the installation process. After you've installed Windows 10, you can also automate the installation of applications by using Windows Installer packages.

This chapter also includes the following topics:

- An overview of the automated deployment options

- How to access the deployment tools available for Windows 10 and the use of unattended installation

- WDS

- How the System Preparation Tool (along with Image Capture Wizard) is used to create disk images for automated installation

- How to use Windows System Image Manager (SIM) to create unattended answer files

I will also talk about how to set up and configure Hyper-V. Windows 10 can be loaded onto a Windows Server 2012 R2 Hyper-V server, or Windows 10 can also act as a Hyper-V server.

Understanding Automated Deployment Options

If you need to install Windows 10 on multiple computers, you could manually install the operating system on each computer, as described in Chapter 11, "Installing Windows 10." However, automating the deployment process will make your job easier, more efficient, and more cost-effective if you have a large number of client computers on which to install Windows 10.

Windows 10 comes with several utilities that can be used for deploying and automating the Windows 10 installation. With access to multiple utilities with different functionality, administrators have increased flexibility in determining how to best deploy Windows 10 within a large corporate environment.

The following sections contain overviews of the automated deployment options, which will help you choose which solution is best for your requirements and environment. Each utility will then be covered in more detail throughout this chapter. The options for automated deployment of Windows 10 are as follows:

- Microsoft Deployment Toolkit (MDT) 2013 Update 1

- Unattended installation, or unattended setup, which uses Setup.exe

- WDS, which requires Windows Server 2012 R2 for deployment

- Windows 10 Assessment and Deployment Kit (ADK), which also includes the System Preparation Tool (Sysprep.exe), used to create images or clones

- Windows Imaging and Configuration Designer (Windows ICD)

Table 12.3, later in the chapter, summarizes the features and requirements of each installation deployment option.

> Another option that you have to deploy Windows 10 is through System Center Configuration Manager (SCCM). Since SCCM is its own application, it is beyond the scope of this book. You can learn more about SCCM on the Microsoft website at http://www.microsoft.com.

An Overview of the Microsoft Deployment Toolkit 2013

Microsoft released a deployment assistance toolset called the *Microsoft Deployment Toolkit (MDT) 2013*. It is used to automate desktop and server deployment. MDT provides an administrator with the following benefits:

- Administrative tools that allow for the deployment of desktops and servers through the use of a common console (see Figure 12.1)

- Quicker deployments and the capabilities of having standardized desktop and server images and security

- Zero-touch deployments of Windows 10, Windows Server 2012 and 2012 R2, Windows Server 2008, Windows Server 2008 R2, and Windows 7 and 8

FIGURE 12.1 MDT console

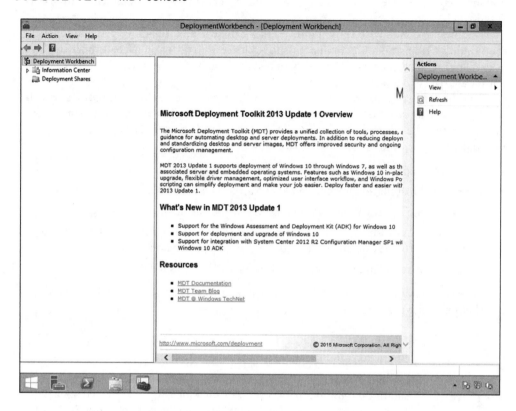

To install the MDT 2013 package onto your computer (regardless of the operating system being deployed), you must first meet the minimum requirements of MDT. These components need to be installed only on the computer where MDT 2013 is being installed:

- You can install MDT 2013 on any of the following operating systems: Windows 10, Windows 7, Windows 8, Windows 8.1, Windows Server 2008 R2, Windows Server 2012, or Windows Server 2012 R2.

- The Windows Assessment and Deployment Kit (ADK) for Windows 10 is required for all deployment scenarios.

- System Center 2012 R2 Configuration Manager Service Pack 1 with the Windows ADK for Windows 10 is required for zero-touch installation (ZTI) and user-driven installation (UDI) scenarios.

- If you are using ZTI and/or UDI, you are allowed to add the MDT SQL database to any version of System Center Configuration Manager with SQL technology; if you are using LTI, you must use a separately licensed SQL Server product to host your MDT SQL database.

You can install MDT 2013 without installing Windows (ADK) first, but you will not be able to use the package fully until Windows (ADK) is installed.

In Exercise 12.1, you will download and install MDT 2013. You can install MDT 2013 on the Windows 10 operating system machine that you installed in Chapter 11. If you decide to install the MDT 2013 onto a server or production machine, I recommend that you perform a full backup before completing Exercise 12.1. Installing MDT 2013 will replace any previous version of MDT that the machine may currently be using.

EXERCISE 12.1

Downloading and Installing MDT 2013

To download and install MDT 2013, follow these steps:

1. Download the MDT 2013 Update 1 utility from the Microsoft website (https://www .microsoft.com/en-us/download/details.aspx?id=48595).

2. Click the Download button.

3. You get a screen asking you to "Choose the download you want." Choose the x64 or x86 version. Click Next.

4. A message box may appear asking if you want to run or save the MDT. I clicked the down arrow next to Save and saved the files into the downloads directory.

5. Double-click MicrosoftDeploymentToolkit_xxx.exe to start the installation.

6. At the Welcome screen, click Next as shown in Figure 12.2.

    FIGURE 12.2 MDT Setup Wizard Welcome screen

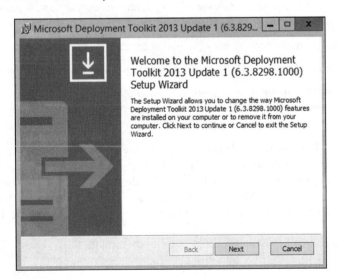

7. At the License screen, click the I Accept The Terms In The License Agreement button and click Next.

8. At the Custom Setup screen, click the down arrow next to Microsoft Deployment Toolkit and choose Entire Feature Will Be Installed On Local Hard Drive. Click Next as shown in Figure 12.3.

FIGURE 12.3   MDT Custom Setup screen

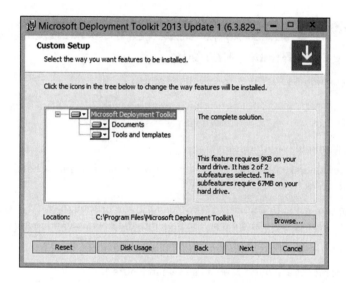

9. At the Customer Experience Improvement Program screen, choose if you want to participate or not and choose Next.

10. At the Ready To Install screen, click the Install button.

11. If a User Account Control dialog box appears, click the Yes button.

12. When the installation completes, click the Finish button.

Now that you have installed MDT 2013, you are going to configure the package. In Exercise 12.2, you will configure MDT 2013 and set up a distribution share and database. I am creating the MDT 2013 on a Windows Server 2012 R2 so that we can distribute Windows 10. Make sure the Windows Assessment and Deployment Kit (ADK) for Windows 10 is installed, because it is required for all deployment scenarios.

EXERCISE 12.2

Configuring MDT 2013

To configure MDT 2013, follow these steps:

1. Create a shared folder on your network called `Distribution`, and give the Everyone group full control to the folder for this exercise.

2. Open the MDT workbench by choosing Start ➢ down arrow ➢ Microsoft Development Toolkit ➢ Deployment Workbench.

3. If the User Account Control box appears, click Yes.

4. In the left pane, click Deployment Shares, and then right-click the deployment shares and choose New Deployment Share.

5. The New Deployment Share Wizard begins (as shown in Figure 12.4). On the first screen, you will choose the directory where the deployments will be stored. Click the Browse button and choose the Distribution share that you created in step 1. Then click Next.

FIGURE 12.4   New Deployment Share Wizard screen

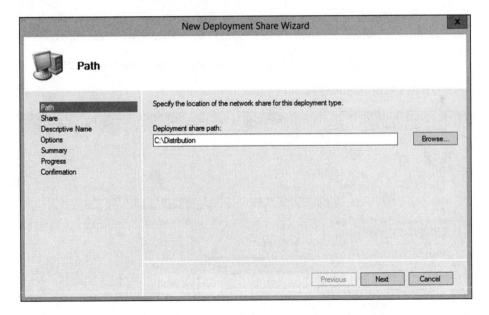

6. On the Share Name screen, accept the default, Distribution. Click Next.

7. On the Descriptive Name screen, accept the default description name (as shown in Figure 12.5) and click Next.

FIGURE 12.5 Descriptive Name screen

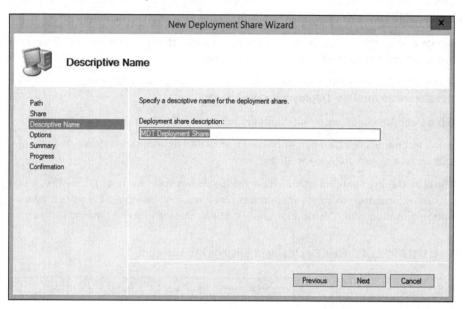

8. On the Options screen, make sure all check boxes are checked, as shown in Figure 12.6.

FIGURE 12.6 Options screen

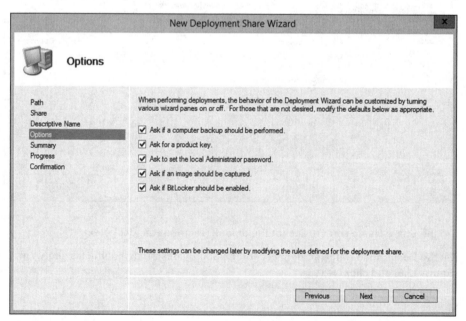

9. On the Summary screen, look over the options and click the Next button.

10. The installation Progress screen will show you how the installation is performing. When the installation is complete, click the Finish button.

    The new deployment share is set up and ready to start deploying. Now an operating system needs to be set up in the MDT 2013 for deployment.

11. Close the MDT workbench.

Now that you have seen how to install the MDT 2013 utility, let's take a look at some other ways to automatically install Windows 10.

An Overview of Unattended Installation

Unattended installation is a practical method of automating deployments when you have a large number of clients to install and the computers require different hardware and software configurations. Unattended installations allow you to create customized installations that are specific to your environment. Custom installations can support custom hardware and software installations.

Unattended installations utilize an answer file called Autounattend.xml to provide configuration information during the installation process. Think about the Windows 10 installation from the previous chapter. You are asked for your locale, type of installation, and so on. The answer file allows these questions to be answered without user interaction. In addition to providing standard Windows 10 configuration information, the answer file can provide installation instructions for applications, additional language support, service packs, and device drivers.

With an unattended installation, you can use a distribution share to install Windows 10 on the target computers. You can also use a Windows 10 DVD with an answer file located on the root of the DVD, on a floppy disk, or on a universal flash device (UFD), such as an external USB flash drive.

Unattended installations allow you to create customized installations that are specific to your environment. Custom installations can support custom hardware and software installations. Since the answer file for Windows 10 is in XML format, all custom configuration information can be contained within the Autounattend.xml file. This is different from past versions of Windows, where creating automated installation routines for custom installations required multiple files to be used. In addition to providing standard Windows 10 configuration information, you can use the answer file to provide installation instructions for applications, additional language support, service packs, and device drivers.

If you use a distribution share, it should contain the Windows 10 operating system image and the answer file to respond to installation configuration queries. The target computer must be able to connect to the distribution share over the network. After the distribution share and target computers are connected, you can initiate the installation process. Figure 12.7 illustrates the unattended installation process.

FIGURE 12.7 Unattended installation with distribution share and a target computer

Distribution Share

Target

Stores:
Windows 10 Image File
Answer File (Unattend.xml)

Requires:
Network Connection

Advantages of Unattended Installation

In a midsize or large organization, it just makes sense to use automated setups. As stated earlier, it is nearly impossible to install Windows 10 one at a time on hundreds of machines. But there are many advantages to using unattended installations as a method for automating Windows 10:

- Unattended installation saves time and money because users do not have to interactively respond to each installation query.

- It can be configured to provide automated query response while still selectively allowing users to provide specified input during installation.

- It can be used to install clean copies of Windows 10 or upgrade an existing operating system (providing it is on the list of permitted operating systems) to Windows 10.

- It can be expanded to include installation instructions for applications, additional language support, service packs, and device drivers.

- The physical media for Windows 10 does not need to be distributed to all computers on which it will be installed.

Disadvantages of Unattended Installation

As stated earlier, a manual installation is not practical for mass installations. But one of the biggest disadvantages to performing an unattended installation is that an administrator does not physically walk through the installation of Windows 10. A client operating system is one of the most important items that you will install onto a machine. As an IT manager and consultant, I have always felt better physically installing a client operating system. This way, if there are any glitches, I can see and deal with them immediately. If something happens during an unattended install, you may never know it, but the end user may experience small issues throughout the lifetime of the machine.

Two other disadvantages of using unattended installations as a method for automating Windows 10 installations are listed here:

- They require more initial setup than a standard installation of Windows 10.

- Someone must have access to each client computer and must initiate the unattended installation process on the client side.

An Overview of Windows Deployment Services

Windows Deployment Services (WDS) is an updated version of Remote Installation Services (RIS). WDS is a suite of components that allows you to remotely install Windows 10 on client computers.

A WDS server installs Windows 10 on the client computers, as illustrated in Figure 12.8. The WDS server must be configured with the Preboot Execution Environment (PXE) boot files, the images to be deployed to the client computers, and the answer file. WDS client computers must be PXE-capable. PXE is a technology that is used to boot to the network when no operating system or network configuration has been installed and configured on a client computer.

FIGURE 12.8 Windows Deployment Services (WDS) uses a WDS server and WDS clients.

WDS Server

Stores:
PXE Boot Files and Boot Images
Windows 10 Boot Images
Answer File(s)

WDS Client

Requires:
PXE-Compatible Boot

The WDS clients access the network with the help of a Dynamic Host Configuration Protocol (DHCP) server. This allows the WDS client to remotely install the operating system from the WDS server. The network environment must be configured with a DHCP server, a Domain Name System (DNS) server, NTFS Volumes, and Active Directory to connect to the WDS server. No other client operating system is required to connect to the WDS server. Remote installation is a good choice for automatic deployment when you need to deploy to large numbers of computers and the client computers are PXE-compliant.

Advantages of WDS

The advantages of using WDS as a method for automating Windows 10 installations are as follows:

- WDS allows an IT department to remotely install Windows operating systems throughout the network. This advantage helps reduce the difficulty and IT manpower cost compared to a manual installation.
- WDS allows an IT department to deploy multiple images for mixed environments including Windows 7, Windows 8, Windows 10, and Windows Server.

- WDS allows IT departments to use Windows setups including Windows Preinstallation Environment (Windows PE), .wim files, and image-based setups.

- WDS uses multicasting to allow for the transmitting data and imaging data to communicate to each other.

- An IT department can create reference images using the Windows Imaging and Configuration Designer (Windows ICD) to customize Windows 10 images.

- WDS allows an IT administrator to install a driver package to the server and configure the drivers to be deployed to client computers at the same time the image is installed.

- WDS allows IT departments to standardize Windows 10 installations throughout a group or organization.

- The physical media for Windows 10 does not need to be distributed to all computers that will be installed.

- End-user installation deployment can be controlled through the Group Policy utility. For example, you can configure what choices a user can access or are automatically specified through the end-user Setup Wizard.

Disadvantages of WDS

The disadvantages of using WDS as a method for automating Windows 10 installations include the following:

- WDS can be used only if your network is running Windows Server 2008, Windows Server 2008 R2, Windows Server 2012, or Windows Server 2012 R2 with Active Directory installed.

- The clients that use WDS must be PXE compatible or have a discovery image.

You can configure WDS on a Windows Server 2012 or Windows Server 2012 R2 computer by using the Windows Deployment Services Configuration Wizard or by using the WDSUTIL command-line utility. Table 12.1 describes the WDSUTIL command-line options.

TABLE 12.1   WDSUTIL command-line options

WDSUTIL Option	Description
/initialize-server	Initializes the configuration of the WDS server
/uninitialized-server	Undoes any changes made during the initialization of the WDS server
/add	Adds images and devices to the WDS server
/convert-ripimage	Converts Remote Installation Preparation (RIPrep) images to WIM images

WDSUTIL Option	Description
/remove	Removes images from the server
/set	Sets information in images, image groups, WDS servers, and WDS devices
/get	Gets information from images, image groups, WDS servers, and WDS devices
/new	Creates new capture images or discover images
/copy-image	Copies images from the image store
/export-image	Exports to WIM files images contained within the image store
/start	Starts WDS services
/stop	Stops WDS services
/disable	Disables WDS services
/enable	Enables WDS services
/approve-autoadddevices	Approves Auto-Add devices
/reject-autoadddevices	Rejects Auto-Add devices
/delete-autoadddevices	Deletes records from the Auto-Add database
/update	Uses a known-good resource to update a server resource

An Overview of the System Preparation Tool and Disk Imaging

The *System Preparation Tool,* or *Sysprep* (Sysprep.exe), is used to prepare a computer for disk imaging, and the disk image can then be captured using Image Capture Wizard (an imaging-management tool included with Windows 10) or third-party imaging software. Sysprep is a free utility that comes on all Windows operating systems. By default, the Sysprep utility can be found on Windows Server 2012 R2 and Windows 10 operating systems in the \Windows\system32\sysprep directory.

Disk imaging is the process of taking a checkpoint of a computer and then using that checkpoint to create new computers, thus allowing for automated deployments. The reference, or source, computer has Windows 10 installed and is configured with the settings and applications that should be installed on the target computers. The image (checkpoint) is then created and can be transferred to other computers, thus installing the operating system, settings, and applications that were defined on the reference computer.

Using Imaging Software

Using the System Preparation Tool and disk imaging is a good choice (and the one most commonly used in the real world) for automatic deployment when you have a large number of computers with similar configuration requirements or machines that need to be rebuilt frequently.

For example, StormWind Studios, an online computer education company, reinstalls the same software every few week for new classes. Imaging is a fast and easy way to simplify the deployment process.

Most organizations use images to create new machines quickly and easily, but they also use them to reimage end users' machines that crash.

In most companies, end users will have space on a server (home folders) to allow them to store data. We give our end users space on the server because this way we need to back up only the servers at night and not the end users' machines. If your end users place all of their important documents on the server, that information gets backed up.

Now, if we are also using images in our company and an end user's machine crashes, we just reload the image and they are backed up and running in minutes. Since their documents are being saved on the server, they do not lose any of their information.

Many organizations use third-party imaging software (such as Ghost) instead of using Sysprep.exe and Image Capture Wizard. This is another good way of imaging your Windows 10 machines. Just make sure your third-party software supports the Windows 10 operating system.

To perform an unattended installation, the System Preparation Tool prepares the reference computer by stripping away any computer-specific data, such as the security identifier (SID), which is used to uniquely identify each computer on the network; any event logs; and any other unique system information. The System Preparation Tool also detects any Plug and Play devices that are installed can adjust dynamically for any computers that have different hardware installed.

When the client computer starts an installation using a disk image, you can customize what is displayed on the Windows Welcome screen and the options that are displayed through the setup process. You can also fully automate when and how the Windows Welcome screen is displayed during the installation process by using the /oobe (out-of-the-box experience) option with the System Preparation Tool and an answer file named Oobe.xml.

The out-of-the-box experience makes the newly built system work as if you took the new system right out of the manufacturer's box.

Sysprep is a utility that is good only for setting up a new machine. You do not use Sysprep to image a computer for upgrading a current machine. There are a few switches that you can use in conjunction with Sysprep to configure the Sysprep utility for your specific needs. Table 12.2 shows you the important Sysprep switches and what they will do for you when used.

TABLE 12.2   Sysprep switches

Switch	Explanation
/pnp	Forces a mini-setup wizard to start at reboot so that all Plug and Play devices can be recognized.
/generalize	This allows Sysprep to remove all system-specific data from the Sysprep image. If you're running the GUI version of Sysprep, this is a check-box option.
/oobe	Initiates the Windows Welcome screen at the next reboot.
/audit	Initiates Sysprep in audit mode.
/nosidgen	Sysprep does not generate a new SID on the computer restart. Forces a mini-setup on restart.
/reboot	Stops and restarts the computer system.
/quiet	Runs without any confirmation dialog messages being displayed.
/mini	Tells Sysprep to run the mini-setup on the next reboot.

 Real World Scenario

The SID Problem with Deployment Software

For many years, when you had to create many machines that each had a Microsoft operating system on it, you would have to use files to help deploy the multiple systems.

Then, multiple third-party companies came out with software that allowed you to take a picture of the Microsoft operating system, and you could deploy that picture to other machines. One advantage of this is that all the software that is installed on the system could also be part of that picture. This was a great way to copy all the software on a machine over to another machine.

There was one major problem for years—*security identifier (SID)* numbers. All computers get assigned a unique SID that represents them on a domain network. The problem for a long time was that when you copied a machine to another machine, the SID number was also copied.

Microsoft released Sysprep many years ago, and that helped solve this problem. Sysprep would allow you to remove the SID number so that a third-party software package could image it to another machine. Many third-party image software products now also remove the SID numbers, but Sysprep was one of the first utilities to help solve this problem.

When you decide to use Sysprep to set up your images, there are a few rules that you must follow for Sysprep to work properly:

- You can use images to restart the Windows activation clock. The Windows activation clock starts to decrease as soon as Windows starts for the first time. You can restart the Windows activation clock only three times using Sysprep.

- The computer on which you're running Sysprep has to be a member of a work-group. The machine can't be part of a domain. If the computer is a member of the domain, when you run Sysprep, the computer will automatically be removed from the domain.

- When installing the image, the system will prompt you for a product key. During the install you can use an answer file, which in turn will have all the information needed for the install, and you will not be prompted for any information.

- A third-party utility or Image Capture Wizard is required to deploy the image that is created from Sysprep.

- If you are using Sysprep to capture an NTFS partition, any files or folders that are encrypted will become corrupt and unreadable.

One advantage to Sysprep and Windows 10 is that you can use Sysprep to prepare a new machine for duplication. You can use Sysprep to image a Windows 10 machine. The following steps are necessary to image a new machine:

1. Install the Windows 10 operating system.

2. Install all components on the OS.

3. Run Sysprep /generalize to create the image.

When you image a computer using the Windows Sysprep utility, a Windows image (.wim) file is created. Most third-party imaging software products can work with the Windows image file.

Advantages of the System Preparation Tool

The following are advantages of using the System Preparation Tool as a method for automating Windows 10 installations:

- For large numbers of computers with similar hardware, it greatly reduces deployment time by copying the operating system, applications, and desktop settings from a reference computer to an image, which can then be deployed to multiple computers.

- Using disk imaging facilitates the standardization of desktops, administrative policies, and restrictions throughout an organization.

- Reference images can be copied across a network connection or through DVDs that are physically distributed to client computers.

Disadvantages of the System Preparation Tool

There are some disadvantages of using the System Preparation Tool as a method for automating Windows 10 installations:

- Image Capture Wizard, third-party imaging software, or hardware disk-duplication devices must be used for an image-based setup.

- The version of the System Preparation Tool that shipped with Windows 10 must be used. An older version of Sysprep cannot be used on a Windows 10 image.

- The System Preparation Tool will not detect any hardware that is not Plug and Play compliant.

Overview of the Windows Assessment and Deployment Kit

Another way to install Windows 10 is to use the *Windows Assessment and Deployment Kit (ADK)*. The Windows ADK is a set of utilities and documentation that allows an administrator to configure and deploy Windows operating systems. An administrator can use the Windows ADK to do the following:

- Windows Imaging and Configuration Designer (ICD)
- Windows Assessment Toolkit
- Windows Performance Toolkit

The Windows ADK can be installed and configured on the following operating systems:

- Windows 10
- Windows 7/8 with SP1
- Windows Server 2012 R2
- Windows Server 2012
- Windows Server 2008

- Windows Server 2008 R2
- Windows Server 2003 with SP2

The Windows ADK is a good solution for organizations that need to customize the Windows deployment environments. The Windows ADK allows an administrator to have the flexibility needed for mass deployments of Windows operating systems. Since every organization's needs are different, the Windows ADK allows you to use all or just some of the deployment tools available. It allows you to manage deployments by using some additional tools.

Windows Imaging and Configuration Designer (ICD)   The tools included with this part of the Windows ADK will allow an administrator to easily deploy and configure Windows operating systems and images.

Windows Assessment Toolkit   When new Windows operating systems are installed, applications that ran on the previous version of Windows may not work properly. The Application Compatibility Toolkit allows an administrator to help solve these issues before they occur.

Windows Performance Toolkit   The Windows Performance Toolkit is a utility that will locate computers on a network and then perform a thorough inventory of them. This inventory can then be used to determine which machines can have Windows 10 installed.

Windows Imaging and Configuration Designer

The Windows Imaging and Configuration Designer (ICD) allows an administrator to work with images. The ICD allows an IT department to do the following;

- View and configure all of the settings and policies for a Windows 10 image or provisioning package
- Create Windows provisioning answer files
- Allow an answer file to add third-party drivers, apps, or other assets
- Create variants and specify the settings that apply to each variant
- Build and flash a Windows image
- Build a provisioning package

The Windows ICD gives an IT department many options on how to deploy and set up Windows 10 clients. Here are some of the functions that can be performed with the Windows ICD tools:

- Configure and edit images by using the Deployment Image Servicing and Management (DISM) utility
- Create Windows Preinstallation Environment (Windows PE) images
- Migrate user data and profiles using the User State Migration Tool (USMT)
- Windows Imaging and Configuration Designer (Windows ICD)

Summary of Windows 10 Deployment Options

Table 12.3 summarizes the installation tools and files that are used with unattended, automated installations of Windows 10, the associated installation method, and a description of each tool.

TABLE 12.3   Summary of Windows 10 unattended deployment utilities

Tool or File	Automated Installation Option	Description
Setup.exe	Unattended installation	Program used to initiate the installation process
Autounattend.xml	Unattended installation	Answer file used to customize installation queries
Windows System Image Manager	Unattended installation	Program used to create answer files to be used for unattended installations
Image Capture Wizard.exe	Sysprep	Command-line utility that works in conjunction with Sysprep to create and manage Windows 10 image files for deployment
Sysprep.exe	Sysprep	System Preparation Tool, which prepares a source reference computer that will be used in conjunction with a distribution share or with disk duplication through Image Capture Wizard, third-party software, or hardware disk-duplication devices

The Windows 10 installation utilities and resources relating to automated deployment are found in a variety of locations. Table 12.4 provides a quick reference for each utility or resource and its location.

TABLE 12.4   Location of Windows 10 deployment utilities and resources

Utility	Location
Sysprep.exe	Included with Windows 10; installed to %WINDIR%\system32\sysprep
Image Capture Wizard.exe	Installed with the WAIK; installed to C:\ProgramFiles\ Windows AIK\Tools\x86\Image Capture Wizard.exe
Windows System Image Manager	Installed with WAIK; installed to C:\ProgramFiles\Windows AIK\Tools\Image Manager\ ImgMgr.exe

Deploying Unattended Installations

You can deploy Windows 10 installations or upgrades through a Windows 10 distribution DVD or through a distribution server that contains Windows 10 images and associated files, such as Autounattend.xml for unattended installations. Using a DVD can be advantageous if the computer on which you want to install Windows 10 is not connected to the network or is connected via a low-bandwidth network. It is also typically faster to install a Windows 10 image from DVD than to use a network connection.

Unattended installations rely on options configured in an answer file that is deployed with the Windows 10 image. Answer files are XML files that contain the settings that are typically supplied by the installer during attended installations of Windows 10. Answer files can also contain instructions for how programs and applications should be run.

The Windows Setup program is run to install or upgrade to Windows 10 from computers that are running compatible versions of Windows, as discussed in Chapter 11. In fact, Windows Setup is the basis for the other types of installation procedures I'll be discussing in this chapter, including unattended installations, WDS, and image-based installations.

The Windows Setup program (Setup.exe) replaces Winnt32.exe and Winnt.exe, which are the setup programs used in versions of Windows prior to Windows 7/8. Although it's a graphical tool, Windows Setup can be run from the command line. For example, you can use the following command to initiate an unattended installation of Windows 10:

setup.exe /unattend:answerfile

The Windows Setup program has several command-line options that can be applied. Table 12.5 describes the Setup.exe command-line options.

TABLE 12.5 Setup.exe **command-line options and descriptions**

Setup.exe Option	Description
/1394debug: channel [baudrate:baudrate]	Enables kernel debugging over a FireWire (IEEE 1394) port for troubleshooting purposes. The [baudrate] optional parameter specifies the baud rate for data transfer during the debugging process.
/debug:port [baudrate:baudrate]	Enables kernel debugging over the specified port for troubleshooting purposes. The [baudrate] optional parameter specifies the baud rate for data transfer during the debugging process.
/dudisable	Used to prevent a dynamic update from running during the installation process

Setup.exe Option	Description
/emsport:{com1|com2|usebiossettings|off}[/emsbaudrate:baudrate]	Configures EMS to be enabled or disabled. The [baudrate] optional parameter specifies the baud rate for data transfer during the debugging process.
/m:folder_name	Used with Setup to specify that replacement files should be copied from the specified location. If the files are not present, Setup will use the default location.
/noreboot	Normally, when the down-level phase of Setup.exe is complete, the computer restarts. This option specifies that the computer should not restart so that you can execute another command prior to the restart.
/tempdrive:drive letter	Specifies the location that will be used to store the temporary files for Windows 10 and the installation partition for Windows 10.
/unattend:[answerfile]	Specifies that you will be using an unattended installation for Windows 10. The answerfile variable points to the custom answer file you will use for installation.

Next we'll look at the System Preparation Tool (Sysprep); using it is one of many ways to install Windows 10 automatically.

Using the System Preparation Tool to Prepare an Installation for Imaging

You can use disk images to install Windows 10 on computers that have similar hardware configurations. Also, if a computer is having technical difficulties, you can use a disk image to quickly restore it to a baseline configuration.

To create a disk image, you install Windows 10 on the source computer with the configuration that you want to copy and use the System Preparation Tool to prepare the installation for imaging. The source computer's configuration should also include any applications that should be installed on target computers.

Once you have prepared the installation for imaging, you can use imaging software such as Image Capture Wizard to create an image of the installation.

The System Preparation Tool (Sysprep.exe) is included with Windows 10, in the %WINDIR%\system32\sysprep directory. When you run this utility on the source computer, it strips out information that is unique for each computer, such as the SID. Table 12.6 defines the command options that you can use to customize the Sysprep.exe operation.

TABLE 12.6   System Preparation Tool command-line options

Switch	Description
/audit	Configures the computer to restart into audit mode, which allows you to add drivers and applications to Windows or test the installation prior to deployment
/generalize	Removes any unique system information from the image, including the SID and log information
/oobe	Specifies that the Windows Welcome screen should be displayed when the computer reboots
/quiet	Runs the installation with no user interaction
/quit	Specifies that the System Preparation Tool should quit after the specified operations have been completed
/reboot	Restarts the target computer after the System Preparation Tool completes
/shutdown	Specifies that the computer should shut down after the specified operations have been completed
/unattend	Indicates the name and location of the answer file to use

In the following sections, you will learn how to create a disk image and how to copy and install from it.

Preparing a Windows 10 Installation

To run the System Preparation Tool and prepare an installation for imaging, take the following steps:

1. Install Windows 10 on a source computer. The computer should have a similar hardware configuration to that of the destination computer(s). The source computer should not be a member of a domain. (See Chapter 11 for instructions on installing Windows 10.)

2. Log on to the source computer as Administrator and, if desired, install and configure any applications, files (such as newer versions of Plug and Play drivers), or custom settings (for example, a custom desktop) that will be applied to the target computer(s).

3. Verify that your image meets the specified configuration criteria and that all applications are properly installed and working.

4. Select Start ➢ Computer, and navigate to C:\%WINDIR%\System32\sysprep. Double-click the Sysprep application icon.

5. The Windows System Preparation Tool dialog box appears. Select the appropriate options for your configuration.

6. If configured to do so, Windows 10 will be rebooted into setup mode, and you will be prompted to enter the appropriate setup information.

7. You will now be able to use imaging software to create an image of the computer to deploy to other computers.

In Exercise 12.3, you will use the System Preparation Tool to prepare the computer for disk imaging. The Sysprep utility must be run on a machine with a clean version of Windows 10. If you upgraded a Windows 7 or Windows 8 machine to Windows 10, you will not be able to run the Sysprep utility.

EXERCISE 12.3

Preparing a System for Imaging by Using the System Preparation Tool

1. Log on to the source computer as Administrator and, if desired, install and configure any applications that should also be installed on the target computer.

2. Select Start ➢ Computer, and navigate to C:\%WINDIR%\System32\sysprep. Double-click the Sysprep application icon.

3. In the System Preparation Tool dialog box, select Enter System Out-Of-Box Experience (OOBE) in the system cleanup action.

4. Under the shutdown options, depending on the options selected, the System Preparation Tool will quit, the computer will shut down, or the computer will be rebooted into setup mode, where you will need to configure the setup options. Choose the Reboot option. Click OK.

5. Configure the Sysprep utility and name the image **image.wim**.

After creating the Sysprep image, you need to use some type of third-party software to capture it. Windows includes a utility called Image Capture Wizard for just that purpose.

Using Windows Imaging and Configuration Designer (Windows ICD) to Create a Disk Image

After you've run the System Preparation Tool on the source computer, you can create an image from the installation, and you can then install the image on target computers. To create an image, you can use Image Capture Wizard, which is a utility that can be used to create and manage Windows image (.wim) files.

To run the Image Capture Wizard utility to create a disk image of a Windows 10 installation, follow these steps:

1. From the Windows ICD Start page, select New Windows Image Customization.

2. In the Enter Project Details window, specify a Name and Location for your project. Optionally, you can also enter a brief Description to describe your project.

3. Click Next.

4. If you selected New Windows Image Customization from the Start page, skip this step.

   In the Select Project Workflow window, select Imaging from the list of available project workflows and then click Next.

5. In the Select Imaging Source Format window, select "The Windows image is based on a Windows image (WIM) file" and then click Next.

6. In the Select Image window, click Browse to launch File Explorer. Search and locate the path to the Install.wim file.

   After you've selected the Install.wim file, all the Windows images in the .wim file are listed in the Available images panel. By default, the first Windows image in the list is selected, and the information about this image is displayed in the Image Information panel.

7. Select the Windows image that you want to use and then click Next.

8. Optional: If you have a provisioning package that contains customizations already configured in a different project and you want to reuse the customizations from this package, click Browse in the Import A Provisioning Package screen to locate the provisioning package that was exported from another project.

9. Click Finish.

There is also a command-line version of the Windows (ICD) tool that you can use. The Microsoft exams have started using a lot of command-line utilities on their tests. So let's take a look at the Windows (ICD) command-line utility. The command that we use for this is icd.exe, as follows:

icd.exe <command> <parameters>

Table 12.7 describes some of the icd.exe command switches that you can use to configure the images.

TABLE 12.7 icd.exe switches

Switch	Description
/CustomizationXML	Identifies the location of the Windows provisioning XML file. This file holds the information for customization assets and settings.
/PackagePath	Identifies the location and the built provisioning package name where the package will be saved.
/StoreFile	Allows IT administrators to use their own settings store instead of the default store used by Windows ICD. If an IT administrator does not determine his or her own store, a default store that's common to all Windows editions will be loaded by Windows ICD.

Switch	Description
/MSPackageRoot	Identifies the location of the root directory that holds the Microsoft packages that you downloaded from the Windows portal.
/OEMInputXML	Identifies the location to the OEMInput.xml file. This file defines a subset of settings that can be designed based on the image type.
/Variables	Identifies a macro pair that is separated by a semicolon, *<name>* and *<value>*.
Encrypted	Indicates whether or not the provisioning package should be created with encryption. Windows ICD will then automatically generate a decryption password that is included with the output.
Overwrite	Indicates whether or not to overwrite the existing provisioning package.
/?	Used to access the ICD help, which lists the switches and their descriptions for the ICD command-line tool.

After you create the disk image, the next step is to install it. In the next section, you'll learn how to install the disk image on a new machine.

Installing from a Disk Image

After you've run the System Preparation Tool and Image Capture Wizard on the source computer, you can copy the image and then install it on the target computer.

Once the image is copied, you should boot the destination computer into the Windows PE. If the computer has been used previously, it may be necessary to reformat the hard drive, which you can do using the diskpart command in Windows PE. If the image is stored over the network, you should then copy the image to the destination computer by using the net use [*dir*] [*network share*] and copy [*file*] [*dir*] commands. Then, you should use the /apply option of the Image Capture Wizard utility to apply the image to the local computer. If an answer file has not been deployed along with the image, you may have to apply such information as regional settings, the product key, the computer name, and the password to the new computer after the destination computer is rebooted.

In Exercise 12.4, you will use the stripped image that was created in Exercise 12.3 to simulate the process of continuing an installation from a disk image.

EXERCISE 12.4

Installing Windows 10 from a Disk Image

1. Boot the target computer into Windows PE.

2. Copy the image created in Exercise 12.3 to the local computer by using the following commands:

   ```
   net use z: \\Server\Images
   copy  Z:\Images\image.wim E:
   ```

3. Apply the image to the target computer using the following Image Capture Wizard command:

   ```
   D:\ICD.exe /apply E:\Images\image.wim C:
   ```

When you install Windows 10, the installation wizard asks you questions such as your username and computer name. There is a way to answer these questions without actually being in front of the computer.

Using the Deployment Image Servicing and Management Tool

Deployment Image Servicing and Management (DISM.exe) is a command-line utility that allows you to manipulate a Windows image. DISM also allows you to prepare a Windows PE image. DISM replaces multiple programs that were included with Windows 7/8. These programs include Package Manager (Pkgmgr.exe), PEimg, and Intlcfg. These tools have been consolidated into one tool (DISM.exe), and new functionality has been added to improve the experience for offline servicing.

DISM provides additional functionality when used with Windows 10 and Windows Server 2012 R2. You can use DISM to do the following:

- Add, remove, and enumerate packages
- Add, remove, and enumerate drivers
- Enable or disable Windows features
- Apply changes to an Unattend.xml answer file
- Configure international settings
- Upgrade a Windows image to a different edition
- Prepare a Windows PE 3.0 image

DISM works with all platforms (32-bit, 64-bit, and Itanium) and allows for the use of Package Manager scripts.

Table 12.8 describes the commands that can be used with DISM.exe.

TABLE 12.8 DISM.exe command-line commands

Command	Description
/Add-Driver	Adds third-party driver packages to an offline Windows image.
/Get-CurrentEdition	Displays the edition of the specified image.
/Get-Drivers	Displays basic information about driver packages in the online or offline image. By default, only third-party drivers will be listed.
/Get-DriverInfo	Displays detailed information about a specific driver package.
/Get-Help /?	Displays information about the option and the arguments.
/Get-TargetEditions	Displays a list of Windows editions that an image can be changed to.
/Remove-Driver	Removes third-party drivers from an offline image.
/Set-ProductKey:<productKey>	Can only be used to enter the product key for the current edition in an offline Windows image.

Using Windows System Image Manager to Create Answer Files

Answer files are automated installation scripts used to answer the questions that appear during a normal Windows 10 installation. You can use answer files with Windows 10 unattended installations, disk image installations, or WDS installations. Setting up answer files allows you to easily deploy Windows 10 to computers that may not be configured in the same manner, with little or no user intervention. Because answer files are associated with image files, you can validate the settings within an answer file against the image file.

You can create answer files by using the Windows System Image Manager (Windows SIM) utility. There are several advantages to using Windows SIM to create answer files:

- You can easily create and edit answer files through a graphical interface, which reduces syntax errors.

- It simplifies the addition of user-specific or computer-specific configuration information.

- You can validate existing answer files against newly created images.

- You can include additional application and device drivers in the answer file.

In the following sections, you will learn about options that can be configured through Windows SIM, how to create answer files with Windows SIM, how to format an answer file, and how to manually edit answer files.

Configuring Components through Windows System Image Manager

You can use Windows SIM to configure a wide variety of installation options. The following list defines which components can be configured through Windows SIM and gives a short description of each component:

auditSystem   Adds additional device drivers, specifies firewall settings, and applies a name to the system when the image is booted into audit mode. Audit mode is initiated by using the sysprep/audit command.

auditUser   Executes RunSynchronous or RunAsynchronous commands when the image is booted into audit mode. Audit mode is initiated by using the sysprep/audit command.

generalize   Removes system-specific information from an image so that the image can be used as a reference image. The settings specified in the generalize component will be applied only if the sysprep/generalize command is used.

offlineServicing   Specifies the language packs and packages to apply to an image prior to the image being extracted to the hard disk.

oobeSystem   Specifies the settings to apply to the computer the first time the computer is booted into the Windows Welcome screen, which is also known as the Out-Of-Box Experience (OOBE). To boot to the Welcome screen, the sysprep/oobe command should be used.

specialize   Configures the specific settings for the target computer, such as network settings and domain information. This configuration pass is used in conjunction with the generalize configuration pass.

Windows PE   Sets the Windows PE–specific configuration settings as well as several Windows Setup settings, such as partitioning and formatting the hard disk, selecting an image, and applying a product key.

Understanding Hyper-V

In the following sections, I'll introduce you to Hyper-V. To begin, we'll take a look at virtualization and what types of virtualization exist. We will then discuss Hyper-V features and the Hyper-V architecture before finishing up with the Hyper-V requirements for software and hardware.

Hyper-V is very important to understand when working with Windows 10 because you can load a Windows 10 guest virtual machine onto a Hyper-V host system and you also have the ability to use Windows 10 as a Windows Hyper-V host.

Let's first make sure you understand what host and guest systems do. The Hyper-V machine that has another operating system running on top of it is a host. If you are running an operating system on top of another operating system, you are the guest system. So Windows 10 can be set up as a Hyper-V host or a Hyper-V guest.

So if you are running Windows Server 2012 R2 Hyper-V and the computer has issues, you can load the Server 2012 R2 Hyper-V virtual machines onto a Windows 10 Hyper-V host system. This gives you a temporary solution while the Windows Server 2012 R2 Hyper-V server gets repaired.

So why are we talking about Hyper-V in a Windows 10 deployment chapter? Because you can build a Windows 10 virtual machine and use that virtual machine to deploy Windows 10 operating systems throughout an organization.

What Is Virtualization?

Virtualization is a method for abstracting physical resources from the way they interact with other resources. For example, if you abstract the physical hardware from the operating system, you get the benefit of being able to move the operating system between different physical systems.

This is called *server virtualization*. But there are also other forms of virtualization available, such as presentation virtualization, desktop virtualization, and application virtualization. I will now briefly explain the differences between these forms of virtualization:

Server Virtualization   This basically enables multiple operating systems to run on the same physical server. Hyper-V is a server virtualization tool that allows you to move physical machines to virtual machines and manage them on a few physical servers. Thus, you will be able to consolidate physical servers.

Presentation Virtualization   When you use *presentation virtualization*, your applications run on a different computer and only the screen information is transferred to your computer. An example of presentation virtualization is Microsoft Remote Desktop Services in Windows Server 2012 R2.

Desktop Virtualization   *Desktop virtualization* provides you with a virtual machine on your desktop, comparable to server virtualization. You run your complete operating system and applications in a virtual machine so that your local physical machine just needs to run a very basic operating system. An example of this form of virtualization is Microsoft Windows 10 Hyper-V.

Application Virtualization   *Application virtualization* helps prevent conflicts between applications on the same PC. Thus, it helps you to isolate the application running environment from the operating system installation requirements by creating application-specific copies of all shared resources, and it helps reduce application-to-application incompatibility and testing needs. An example of an application virtualization tool is Microsoft Application Virtualization (App-V).

Installing the Hyper-V Role

Now it's time to see how to install the Hyper-V server role on both a Windows Server machine and a Windows 10 client. I'll show you how to install Hyper-V onto a Windows Server 2012 R2 system as well as how to load Hyper-V onto a Windows 10 Enterprise System.

So why am I showing both installations? Because you can load Windows 10 onto a Windows Server 2012 R2 Hyper-V server and you can use Windows 10 as a Hyper-V server.

Installing Hyper-V in Windows Server 2012 R2

You can install the Hyper-V server role on any Windows Server 2012 R2 installation. The server must meet both the hardware and software requirements. The installation process is simple, as Exercise 12.5 demonstrates.

EXERCISE 12.5

Installing Hyper-V in Windows Server 2012 R2

1. Open Server Manager.

2. In Server Manager, choose number 2, Add Roles And Features.

3. At the Select Installation Type page, choose the role-based or feature-based installation. Click Next.

4. On the Select Destination Server screen, choose Select A Server From The Server Pool and choose the server to which you want to add this role. Click Next.

5. On the Select Server Roles screen, click the check box next to Hyper-V. When the Add Features dialog box appears, click the Add Features button. Then click Next.

6. At the Select Features screen, just click Next.

7. At the Hyper-V introduction screen, just click Next.

8. At the Create Virtual Switches screen, choose your adapter and click Next.

9. At the Virtual Machine Migration screen, just click Next. You want to use migration only if you have multiple Hyper-V servers. Since we will have only one for this exercise, just skip this screen.

10. At the Default Stores screen, accept the defaults and click Next.

11. At the Confirmation screen, click the Install button.

12. After the installation is complete, click the Close button.

13. Restart your server.

Installing Hyper-V in Windows 10

You can install the Hyper-V server role on any Windows 10 Professional or Enterprise installation. The Windows 10 system must meet both the hardware and software requirements. The installation process is shown in Exercise 12.6.

EXERCISE 12.6

Installing Hyper-V on Windows 10

1. Right-click the Windows button and select Programs And Features.

2. Select the Turn Windows Features On Or Off option.

3. Select Hyper-V and click OK (as shown in Figure 12.9).

  FIGURE 12.9 Installing Hyper-V

4. After the installation is complete, click the Close button.

5. Restart your system.

Now that you know how to install the Hyper-V roles onto a Windows 10 system using Programs And Features, let's install Hyper-V onto Windows 10 by using PowerShell. The following command is run in Windows PowerShell:

```
Enable-WindowsOptionalFeature -Online -FeatureName Microsoft-Hyper-V –All
```

The following PowerShell command is used to install Hyper-V into a Windows 10 image while it's an actual image:

```
DISM /Online /Enable-Feature /All /FeatureName:Microsoft-Hyper-V
```

Using Hyper-V Manager

Hyper-V Manager is the central management console to configure your server and create and manage your virtual machines, virtual networks, and virtual hard disks. Unlike Virtual Server 2005, where you managed all virtual machines through a web interface, Hyper-V Manager is managed through a Microsoft Management Console (MMC) snap-in.

You can access it by right-clicking the Start button ➤ Control Panel ➤ Administrative Tools ➤ Hyper-V Manager. Figure 12.10 shows how Hyper-V Manager looks once you start it.

FIGURE 12.10   Hyper-V Manager

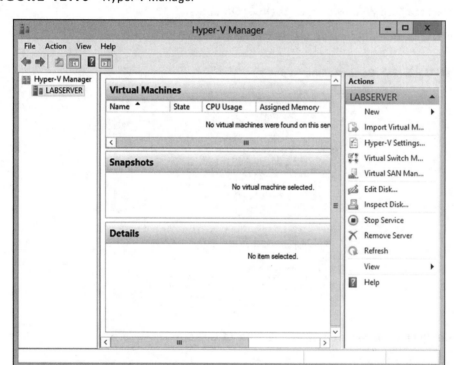

Manage Virtual Switches

A virtual network provides the virtual links between nodes in either a virtual or physical network. Virtual networking in Hyper-V is provided in a secure and dynamic way because you can granularly define virtual network switches for their required usage. For example, you can define a private or internal virtual network if you don't want to allow your virtual machines to send packets to the physical network.

To allow your virtual machines to communicate with each other, you need virtual networks. Just like normal networks, virtual networks exist only on the host computer and allow you to configure how virtual machines communicate with each other, with the host, and with the network or the Internet. You manage virtual networks in Hyper-V using Virtual Switch Manager.

Using Virtual Switch Manager, you can create, manage, and delete virtual switches. You can define the network type as external, internal only, or private.

External   Any virtual machine connected to this virtual switch can access the physical network. You would use this option if you want to allow your virtual machines to access, for example, other servers on the network or the Internet. This option is used in production environments where your clients connect directly to the virtual machines.

Internal   This option allows virtual machines to communicate with each other as well as the host system but not with the physical network. When you create an internal network, it also creates a local area connection in Network Connections that allows the host machine to communicate with the virtual machines. You can use this if you want to separate your host's network from your virtual networks.

Private   When you use this option, virtual machines can communicate with each other but not with the host system or the physical network; thus, no network packets are hitting the wire. This option allows virtual machines on the same Hyper-V host to communicate without using any network traffic.

On the external and internal-only virtual networks, you also can enable virtual LAN (VLAN) identification. You can use VLANs to partition your network into multiple subnets using a VLAN ID. When you enable virtual LAN identification, the NIC that is connected to the switch will never see packets tagged with VLAN IDs. Instead, all packets traveling from the NIC to the switch will be tagged with the access mode VLAN ID as they leave the switch port. All packets traveling from the switch port to the NIC will have their VLAN tags removed. You can use this if you are already logically segmenting your physical machines and also use it for your virtual ones.

Managing Virtual Hard Disks

In addition to virtual networks, you need to manage virtual hard disks that you attach to your virtual machines. A virtual hard disk in Hyper-V, apart from a pass-through disk, is a VHD or VHDX file that basically simulates a hard drive on your virtual machine.

The following sections will first show you what types of virtual hard disks are available and then show you how to create them. You will also learn about what options are available to manage virtual hard disks.

Types of Hard Disks

Depending on how you want to use the disk, Hyper-V offers various types, as described in Table 12.9.

TABLE 12.9   Types of virtual hard disks

Type of Disk	Description	When to Use It
Dynamically expanding	This disk starts with a small VHD file and expands it on demand once an installation takes place. It can grow to the maximum size you defined during creation. You can use this type of disk to clone a local hard drive during creation.	This option is effective when you don't know the exact space needed on the disk and when you want to preserve hard disk space on the host machine. Unfortunately, it is the slowest disk type.
Fixed size	The size of the VHD file is fixed to the size specified when the disk is created. This option is faster than a dynamically expanding disk. However, a fixed-size disk uses up the maximum defined space immediately. This type is ideal for cloning a local hard drive.	A fixed-size disk provides faster access than dynamically expanding or differencing disks, but it is slower than a physical disk.
Differencing	This type of disk is associated in a parent-child relationship with another disk. The differencing disk is the child, and the associated virtual disk is the parent. Differencing disks include only the differences to the parent disk. By using this type, you can save a lot of disk space in similar virtual machines. This option is suitable if you have multiple virtual machines with the same operating systems.	Differencing disks are most commonly found in test environments and should not be used in production environments.
Physical (or pass-through disk)	The virtual machine receives direct pass-through access to the physical disk for exclusive use. This type provides the highest performance of all disk types and thus should be used for production servers where performance is the top priority. The drive is not available for other guest systems.	This type is used in high-end data centers to provide optimum performance for VMs. It's also used in failover cluster environments.

Creating Virtual Hard Disks

To help you gain practice in creating virtual hard disks, the following three exercises will teach you how to create a differencing hard disk, how to clone an existing disk by creating a new disk, and how to configure a physical or pass-through disk to your virtual machine. First, in Exercise 12.7, you will learn how to create a differencing virtual hard disk.

EXERCISE 12.7

Creating a Differencing Hard Disk

1. Open Hyper-V Manager.

2. In Hyper-V Manager, on the Actions pane, choose New ➢ Hard Disk.

3. In the New Virtual Hard Disk Wizard, click Next on the Before You Begin page.

4. On the Choose Disk Format screen, choose VHDX and click Next. The size of your VHDs determines which format you should choose. If you're going to have a VHD larger than 2 TB, use VHDX. If your VHD is less than 2 TB, then you should use VHD.

5. On the Choose Disk Type page, select Fixed Size and click Next.

6. On the Specify Name And Location page, enter the new name of the child disk (for example, **newvirtualharddisk.vhd**). You can also modify the default location of the new VHD file if you want. Click Next to continue.

7. Next, on the Configure Disk page, you need to specify the size of the VHD file. Choose a size based on your hard disk and then click Next to continue. I used 60 GB as the test size.

8. On the Completing The New Virtual Hard Disk Wizard page, verify that all settings are correct, and click Finish to create the hard disk.

Changing Virtual Hard Disks

Hyper-V also provides two tools to manage virtual hard disks: Inspect Disk and Edit Disk. These tools are available on the Actions pane in Hyper-V Manager:

Inspect Disk This provides you with information about the virtual hard disk. It shows you not only the type of the disk but also information like the maximum size for dynamically expanding disks and the parent VHD for differencing disks.

Edit Disk This provides you with the Edit Virtual Hard Disk Wizard, which you can use to compact, convert, expand, merge, or reconnect hard disks.

Table 12.10 provides an overview of what you can do with the wizard.

TABLE 12.10 Edit Disk overview

Action	Description
Compact	Reduces the size of a dynamically expanding or differencing disk by removing blank space from deleted files.
Convert	Converts a dynamically expanding disk to a fixed disk or vice versa.

TABLE 12.10   Edit Disk overview *(continued)*

Action	Description
Expand	Increases the storage capacity of a dynamically expanding disk or a fixed virtual hard disk.
Merge	Merges the changes from a differencing disk into either the parent disk or another disk (applies to differencing disks only!).
Reconnect	If a differencing disk does not find its referring parent disk anymore, this option can reconnect the parent to the disk.

Configuring Virtual Machines

The following sections cover the topics of creating and managing virtual machines as well as how to back up and restore virtual machines using features like Import and Export and Checkpoints.

Creating and Managing Virtual Machines

It is important to learn how to create a virtual machine, how to change its configuration, and how to delete it. We will take a look at the Virtual Machine Connection tool and install the Hyper-V Integration Components onto a virtual machine.

Virtual machines define the child partitions in which you run operating system instances. Each virtual machine is separate and can communicate with the others only by using a virtual network. You can assign hard drive(s), virtual network(s), DVD drives, and other system components to it. A virtual machine is similar to an existing physical server, but it doesn't run on dedicated hardware anymore—it shares the hardware of the host system with the other virtual machines that run on the host.

Exercise 12.8 shows you how to create a new virtual machine.

EXERCISE 12.8

Creating a New Virtual Machine

1. Open Hyper-V Manager.

2. In Hyper-V Manager, on the Actions pane, choose New ➢ Virtual Machine.

3. In the New Virtual Machine Wizard, click Next on the Before You Begin page.

4. On the Specify Name And Location page, give your virtual machine a name and change the default location of the virtual machine configuration files. Click Next to continue.

5. On the Assign Memory page, define how much of your host computer's memory you want to assign to this virtual machine. Remember that once your virtual machine uses up all your physical memory, it will start swapping to disk, thus reducing the performance of all virtual machines. Click Next to continue.

6. On the Configure Networking page, select the virtual network that you previously configured using Virtual Network Manager. Click Next to continue.

7. On the next page, you configure your virtual hard disk. You can create a new virtual hard disk, select an existing disk, or choose to attach the hard disk later. Be aware that you can create only a dynamically expanding virtual disk on this page; you cannot create a differencing, physical, or fixed virtual hard disk here. However, if you created the virtual hard disk already, you can, of course, select it. Click Next to continue.

8. On the Installation Options page, you can select how you want to install your operating system. You have the option to install an operating system later, install the operating system from a boot CD/DVD-ROM where you can select a physical device or an image file (ISO file), install an operating system from a floppy disk image (VFD file, or a virtual boot floppy disk), or install an operating system from a network-based installation server. The last option will install a legacy network adapter to your virtual machine so you can boot from the network adapter. Select Install An Operating System Later and then click Next.

9. On the Completing The New Virtual Machine Wizard summary page, verify that all settings are correct. You also have the option to immediately start the virtual machine after creation. Click Next to create the virtual machine.

10. Repeat this process and create a few more virtual machines.

11. If you want to install an operating system on one of the VMs, start the VM, load a Windows 10 installation disk into the DVD, and then under the Media menu, choose DVD and Capture. Then just do a normal install.

After completing Exercise 12.8, you will have a virtual machine available in Hyper-V Manager. Initially, the state of the virtual machine will be Off. Virtual machines can have the following states: Off, Starting, Running, Paused, and Saved. You can change the state of a virtual machine in the Virtual Machines pane by right-clicking the virtual machine's name or by using the Virtual Machine Connection window.

Here is a list of some of the state options (when the VM is running) available for a virtual machine:

Start   Turn on the virtual machine. This is similar to pressing the power button when the machine is turned off. This option is available when your virtual machine is off or in saved state.

Turn Off   Turn off the virtual machine. This is similar to pressing the power off button on the computer. This option is available when your virtual machine is in running, saved, or paused state.

Shut Down   This option shuts down your operating system. You need to have the Hyper-V Integration Components installed on the operating system; otherwise, Hyper-V will not be able to shut down the system.

Save   The virtual machine is saved to disk in its current state. This option is available when your virtual machine is running or in paused state.

Pause   Pause the current virtual machine, but do not save the state to disk. You can use this option to quickly release processor utilization from this virtual machine to the host system.

Reset   Reset the virtual machine. This is like pressing the reset button on your computer. You will lose the current state and any unsaved data in the virtual machine. This option is available when your virtual machine is running or in paused state.

Resume   When your virtual machine is paused, you can resume it and bring it online again.

Installing Hyper-V Integration Components

Hyper-V Integration Components, also called Integration Services, are required to make your guest operating system "hypervisor aware." These components improve the performance of the guest operating system once the components are installed. On the architectural perspective, virtual devices are redirected directly via the VMBus; thus quicker access to resources and devices is provided.

If you do not install the Hyper-V Integration Components, the guest operating system uses emulation to communicate with the host's devices, which of course makes the guest operating system slower.

Exercise 12.9 shows you how to install Hyper-V Integration Components on one of your virtual machines running Windows 10.

EXERCISE 12.9

Installing Hyper-V Integration Components

1. Open Hyper-V Manager.

2. In Hyper-V Manager, in the Virtual Machines pane, right-click the virtual machine on which you want to install Hyper-V Integration Components and select Start.

3. Right-click the virtual machine again and select Connect. Meanwhile, your virtual machine should be already booting.

4. If you need to log in to the operating system of your virtual machine, you should do so.

5. Once the Windows desktop appears, you need to select Insert Integration Services Setup Disk from the Actions menu of your Virtual Machine Connection window.

6. Once the Hyper-V Integration Components are installed, you are asked to perform a reboot.

After the reboot, Hyper-V Integration Components are installed on your operating system, and you will be able to use them.

Managing Checkpoints

With virtual machine checkpoints (formerly known as virtual machine snapshots), you can save a copy of the virtual machine at any point in time, including while the virtual machine is running. You can take multiple checkpoints of a virtual machine and then revert it to any previous state by applying a checkpoint.

Using checkpoints makes it easier to diagnose the cause of errors by reducing the number of times you need to repeat a task or sequence within a virtual machine. The benefit is obvious; if you use checkpoints to revert to a previous virtual machine configuration, you do not need to copy virtual machines to keep a state. Thus, it is a quick and easy way to back up a certain state of your virtual machine.

You can create a checkpoint when a virtual machine is in a running, saved, or turned-off state. It's only from a paused state that you cannot perform a checkpoint.

In Exercise 12.10, you'll create and rename a checkpoint.

EXERCISE 12.10

Creating a Checkpoint of a Virtual Machine

1. Open Hyper-V Manager.

2. In Hyper-V Manager, in the Virtual Machines pane, right-click the virtual machine.

3. Select Checkpoints.

4. Once the checkpoint is taken, it should appear in the Checkpoints pane in Hyper-V Manager. Right-click the checkpoint and select Settings.

5. In the Settings window, on the Management pane, click Name and type in **First CheckPoint** as the name. You can also add some notes to make it easy to identify.

6. Click OK to apply the changes. You will now see that the checkpoint has a new name.

Technically speaking, when you make a checkpoint, the following files will be created in the virtual machine's checkpoints folder:

- A virtual machine configuration file
- Virtual machine saved state files
- Checkpoints differencing disks (AVHDs)

Once you create a checkpoint for a virtual machine, you will also have the Revert option available in the virtual machine name's pane in Hyper-V Manager. Reverting basically means that you restore the last checkpoint made. You'll also see the last checkpoint taken marked with a green arrow in the Checkpoints pane.

Settings   This opens the Settings window of the virtual machine. The only settings you can change are the Name and Notes fields. All others are read-only.

Apply   Applying a checkpoint to a virtual machine technically means that you copy the virtual machine state from the checkpoints to the active virtual machine. You can look at this as a "restore this checkpoint" option. Because you would lose all unsaved data and settings from the active virtual machine, you will be asked if you want to create another checkpoint before you apply this checkpoint. If you just click Apply, the active machine will be overwritten and reverted to the state it was in when the checkpoints was made. This checkpoint will not be removed.

Export   This allows you to export the checkpoint to another location.

Rename   You can change the name of the checkpoint without the need to open the settings.

Delete Checkpoints   Deleting a checkpoint is like deleting a backup file. You will no longer be able to restore to that point in time. Deleting a single checkpoint does not affect any other checkpoints that you made for this virtual machine. You will delete only the selected checkpoints. However, sometimes when you do delete a checkpoint, the system needs to merge the differencing disks. This occurs in the background when the virtual machine is not running. The user does not see when it happens.

Delete Checkpoints Subtree   This will delete the selected checkpoints and all checkpoints that are hierarchically underneath it. If you delete a checkpoint with only one sub-checkpoint, the configuration and saved state files for the checkpoints will be deleted and the checkpoint's differencing disks will be merged. If you have more sub-checkpoints, merging will not take place.

In Exercise 12.11, you will apply a checkpoint and thus revert to a previous virtual machine state.

EXERCISE 12.11

Applying a Checkpoint

1.   Open Hyper-V Manager.

2.   In Hyper-V Manager, in the Virtual Machines pane, click the virtual machine for which you created a checkpoint.

3.   In the Checkpoints pane, select First Checkpoints.

4.   In the First Checkpoints pane, under Actions, click Apply.

5.   In the Apply Checkpoints window, click Apply.

Moving Virtual Machines

There may be time when you need to move a virtual machine or its storage to another server or location. In this section, we will look at how move virtual machines and storage.

Using Hyper-V, you cannot move the configuration files anymore. You need to use the Export feature to export the virtual machine and then use Import on the target machine to import the virtual machine to Hyper-V.

To export a virtual machine, it must be in either Off or Saved state. Open Hyper-V Manager, select the virtual machine you want to export, and either right-click the virtual machine and select Export or click Export on the virtual machine name's pane.

In this window, you can set the export path for the virtual machine and choose whether to export your virtual machine state data or not.

Once you check Don't Export Virtual Machine State Data, only the virtual machine's configuration files will be exported. The virtual hard disk and snapshots will not be exported.

In the export path, a folder with the name of the virtual machine is created along with the following subfolders:

Virtual Machines   This includes the virtual machine configuration files as well as the virtual machine state if the machine is saved.

Virtual Hard Disks   If you exported the state data, this folder will include your virtual hard disks VHD file(s).

Snapshots   If you exported the state data, this folder will include all snapshot files.

Once the virtual machine finishes exporting, you can move the export folder to the target machine if you did not store it directly on the server's disks. Open Hyper-V Manager and click Import Virtual Machine, which is located in the Actions pane.

The Import Virtual Machine dialog box asks you for the path to the exported virtual machine and allows you to decide if you want to reuse the old virtual machine ID.

You want to reuse old virtual machine IDs if you're moving all virtual machines from a host to a new target machine. The virtual machines are practically the same as on the source system. However, you do not want to reuse old virtual machine IDs if you used Export to clone a virtual machine.

When you import a virtual machine with state data, Hyper-V will use the import path for the virtual hard disks as well as snapshots in its virtual machine configuration XML. Thus, you're able to import an exported machine only once. For that reason, the import folder should already be on the host's target disk.

Summary

In this chapter, we discussed automated installation of Windows 10. Installing Windows 10 through an automated process is an effective way to install the Windows 10 operating system on multiple computers.

There are several methods for automated installation: unattended installations, Windows Deployment Services (WDS), Windows Assessment and Deployment Kit (ADK), third-party applications, unattended installations, and using the System Preparation Tool along with Image Capture Wizard.

Windows Deployment Services (WDS) is an updated version of Remote Installation Services (RIS). WDS is a suite of components that allows you to remotely install Windows 10 on client computers.

The Windows 10 Assessment and Deployment Kit (ADK) is a set of utilities and documentation that allows an administrator to configure and deploy Windows operating systems.

You can use unattended answer files to automatically respond to the queries that are generated during the normal installation process.

You can also prepare an installation for imaging by using the System Preparation Tool (Sysprep.exe) and creating a disk image by using the Image Capture Wizard utility or a third-party utility.

Microsoft Deployment Toolkit (MDT) 2013 Update 1 is a way of automating desktop and server deployment. With the MDT, an administrator can deploy desktops and servers through the use of a common console, which allows for quicker deployments, having standardized desktop and server images and security and zero-touch deployments of Windows 10, Windows 8, Windows 7, Windows Server 2008, Windows Server 2008 R2, Windows Server 2012, and Windows Server 2012 R2.

Video Resources

There are videos available for the following exercises:

12.1

12.3

You can access the videos at www.wiley.com/go/sybextestprep on the Other Study Tools tab.

Exam Essentials

Know the difference between the various unattended installation methods.   Understand the various options available for unattended installations of Windows 10 and when it is appropriate to use each installation method.

Understand the uses for Hyper-V.   Hyper-V is one way that Windows 10 can be deployed and tested as a guest on a Hyper-V server. You can also run Windows 10 as a host system and run other virtual machines from Windows 10.

Understand the features and uses of WDS.   Know when it is appropriate to use WDS to manage unattended installations. Be able to list the requirements for setting up WDS servers and WDS clients. Be able to complete an unattended installation using WDS.

Be able to use disk images for unattended installations.   Know how to perform unattended installations of Windows 10 using the System Preparation Tool and disk images.

Know how to use Windows System Image Manager to create and edit answer files.   Understand how to access and use Windows System Image Manager to create answer files. Be able to edit the answer files and know the basic options that can be configured for them.

Understand the Microsoft Deployment Toolkit (MDT) 2013 Update 1.   Know that the MDT is a way of automating desktop and server deployment. Understand that the MDT allows an administrator to deploy desktops and servers through the use of a common console.

Review Questions

1. You are the network administrator for your organization. You have a reference computer that runs Windows 10. You need to create and deploy an image of the Windows 10 computer. You create an answer file named `answer.xml`. You have to make sure the installation applies the answer file after you deploy the image. Which command should you run before you capture the image?

    A. `ICD.exe /append answer.xml/check`

    B. `ICD.exe /mount answer.xml/verify`

    C. `Sysprep.exe/reboot/audit/unattend:answer.xml`

    D. `Sysprep.exe/generalize/oobe/unattend:answer.xml`

2. You have a Windows 10 Windows Image (WIM) that is mounted. You need to view the list of third-party drivers installed on the WIM. What should you do?

    A. Run DISM and specify the `/get-drivers` parameter.

    B. Run `Driverquery.exe` and use the `/si` parameter.

    C. From Device Manager, view all hidden drivers.

    D. From Windows Explorer, open the `mount` folder.

3. You are the network administrator for a large organization. You are in charge of developing a plan to install 200 Windows 10 computers in your company's data center. You decide to use WDS. You are using a Windows Server 2012 R2 domain and have verified that your network meets the requirements for using WDS. What command-line utility should you use to configure the WDS server?

    A. Image Capture Wizard

    B. WDSUTIL

    C. `Setup.exe`

    D. The WDS icon in Control Panel

4. Will is the network manager for a large company. He has been tasked with creating a deployment plan to automate installations for 100 computers that need to have Windows 10 installed. Will wants to use WDS for the installations. To fully automate the installations, he needs to create an answer file. Will does not want to create the answer files with a text editor. What other program can he use to create unattended answer files via a GUI interface?

    A. Image Capture Wizard

    B. Answer Manager

    C. Windows System Image Manager

    D. System Preparation Tool

5. Bob is using WDS to install 100 clients that are identically configured. The first 65 computers are installed with no problems. When he tries to install the other 35, the

machines all receive a 169.254.*x*.*x* number along with an error. Which of the following would cause this failure?

A. The WDS server has been authorized to serve only 65 clients.

B. The WINS server is no longer available.

C. The DHCP server does not have enough IP addresses to allocate to the WDS clients.

D. The network bandwidth has become saturated.

6. You run a training department that needs the same software installed from scratch on the training computers each week. You decide to use Image Capture Wizard to deploy disk images. Which Windows 10 utility can you use in conjunction with Image Capture Wizard to create these disk images?

A. UAF

B. Answer Manager

C. Setup Manager

D. System Preparation Tool

7. You are trying to decide whether you want to use WDS as a method of installing Windows 10 within your company. Which of the following options is *not* an advantage to using a WDS automated installation?

A. The Windows 10 security is retained when you restart the computer.

B. Windows 10 installation media does not need to be deployed to each computer.

C. Unique information is stripped out of the installation image so that it can be copied to other computers.

D. You can quickly recover the operating system in the event of a system failure.

8. You are the network manager of XYZ Corporation. You are in charge of developing an automated deployment strategy for rolling out new Windows 10 computers. You want to install a WDS server and are evaluating whether an existing server can be used as a WDS server for Windows 10 deployment. Which of the following is *not* a requirement for configuring the WDS server?

A. The remote installation folder must be NTFS version 3.0 or later.

B. The remote installation folder must reside on the system partition.

C. RIS must be installed on the server.

D. The existing server must run Windows Server 2003 with Service Pack 1 installed.

9. You are using WDS to install 20 Windows 10 computers. When the clients attempt to use WDS, they are not able to complete the unattended installation. You suspect that the WDS server has not been configured to respond to client requests. Which one of the following utilities would you use to configure the WDS server to respond to client requests?

A. Active Directory Users and Computers

B. Active Directory Users and Groups

C. WDS MMC snap-in

D. WDSMAN

10. You want to install a group of 25 computers using disk images created in conjunction with the System Preparation Tool. Your plan is to create an image from a reference computer and then copy the image to all the machines. You do not want to create an SID on the destination computer when you use the image. Which `Sysprep.exe` command-line option should you use to set this up?

   A. `/specialize`

   B. `/generalize`

   C. `/oobe`

   D. `/quiet`

Chapter

13

Configuring Storage and Security

MICROSOFT EXAM OBJECTIVES COVERED IN THIS CHAPTER:

✓ **Support data storage.**

- ▪ This objective may include but is not limited to the following subobjectives: identifying and resolving issues related to the following: DFS client including caching settings, storage spaces including capacity and fault tolerance, OneDrive.

✓ **Configure file and folder access.**

- ▪ This objective may include but is not limited to the following subobjectives: encrypt files and folders by using EFS, configure NTFS permissions, configure disk quotas, configure file access auditing, configure authentication and authorization.

✓ **Support data security.**

- ▪ This objective may include but is not limited to the following subobjectives: encrypting File System (EFS) including Data Recovery Agent.

As you've probably noticed, there are a few different Microsoft objectives covered for the Microsoft Windows 10 (70-697) exam in this chapter. Not only are these topics important for the exam, but properly configuring your storage is a task that every IT professional should know how to accomplish because an improperly configured storage device can cause many issues for an IT team.

When you install Windows 10, you designate the initial configuration for your disks. Through Windows 10's utilities and features, you can change that configuration and perform disk-management tasks.

For file-system configuration, it is recommended that you use NTFS, although you could also format the disk drive as FAT32. You can also convert a FAT32 partition to NTFS. This chapter covers the features of each file system and how to use the Convert utility to convert to NTFS.

Another factor in disk management is choosing the configuration for your physical drives. Windows 10 supports basic, dynamic, and GUID Partition Table (GPT) disks. Dynamic disks are supported by Windows 10, Windows 8, Windows 7, Windows XP Professional, Windows Server 2003, Windows Server 2008, Windows Server 2008 R2, Windows Server 2012, and Windows Server 2012 R2. Dynamic disks allow you to create simple volumes, spanned volumes, and striped volumes. If your system is configured as a Basic Disk, in order to utilize volumes, you must first convert the machine's basic disks to dynamic disks.

Once you decide how your disks should be configured, you implement the disk configurations through the Disk Management utility. This utility helps you view and manage your physical disks and volumes. In this chapter, you will learn how to manage multiple types of storage and how to convert from basic storage to dynamic storage.

The other disk-management features covered in this chapter are data compression, data encryption (EFS), disk defragmentation, disk cleanup, and disk error checking.

Understanding File Systems

A partition is a logical division of hard-drive space. Each partition you create under Windows 10 must have a file system associated with it. Partitions allow a single physical hard drive to be represented in the operating system as multiple drive letters and to be used as if there were multiple hard drives installed in the machine.

When selecting a file system, you can select FAT32 or NTFS. You typically select a file system based on the features you want to use and whether you will need to access the file system using other operating systems. If you have a FAT32 partition and want to update it to NTFS, you can use the Convert utility. The features of each file system and the procedure for converting file systems are covered in the following sections.

File System Selection

Your file system is used to track the storage of files on your hard drive in a way that is easily understood by end users while still allowing the operating system the ability to retrieve the files as requested. One of the fundamental choices associated with file management is the choice of your file system's configuration. It is recommended that you use the NTFS file system with Windows 10 because doing so will allow you to take advantage of features such as local security, file compression, and file encryption. You should choose the FAT32 file system only if you want to dual-boot your computer with a version of Windows that does not support NTFS because FAT32 is backward compatible with other operating systems.

Table 13.1 summarizes the capabilities of each file system, and they are described in more detail in the following sections. These volume size numbers are the current values at the time this book was written. Make sure you continue to check with Microsoft to see if the volume sizes have increased since this book's publication.

TABLE 13.1 File-system capabilities

Feature	FAT32	NTFS
Supporting operating systems	All Windows operating systems above Windows 95	Windows NT, Windows 2000, Windows XP, Windows Server 2003, Windows Vista, Windows 7, Windows 8, Windows 10, Windows Server 2008/2008 R2, and Windows Server 2012/2012 R2
Long filename support	Yes	Yes
Efficient use of disk space	Yes	Yes
Compression support	No	Yes
Encryption support	No	Yes
Support for local security	No	Yes
Support for network security	Yes	Yes
Maximum volume size	32 GB	16 TB with 4 KB clusters or 256 TB with 64 KB clusters

Windows 10 also supports Compact Disk File System (CDFS). However, CDFS cannot be managed. It is used only to mount and read CDs. Let's start looking at the supported disk file systems.

FAT32

FAT32 is an updated version of File Allocation Table (FAT). The FAT32 version was first shipped with Windows 95 OSR2 (Operating System Release 2) and can be used by every Windows operating system since.

One of the main advantages of FAT32 is its support for smaller cluster sizes, which results in more efficient space allocation than was possible with FAT16. Files stored on a FAT32 partition can use 20 to 30 percent less disk space than files stored on a FAT16 partition. FAT32 supports drive sizes from 512 MB up to 2 TB, although if you create and format a FAT32 partition through Windows 10, the FAT32 partition can only be up to 32 GB. Because of the smaller cluster sizes, FAT32 can also load programs up to 50 percent faster than FAT16 partitions can.

The main disadvantages of FAT32 compared to NTFS are that it does not provide as much support for larger hard drives and it does not provide very robust security options. It also doesn't offer native support for disk compression. Now that you understand FAT32, let's take a look at NTFS.

NTFS

NTFS, which was first used with the NT operating system, offers the highest level of service and features for Windows 10 computers. NTFS partitions can be up to 16 TB with 4 KB clusters or 256 TB with 64 KB clusters.

NTFS offers comprehensive folder-level and file-level security. This allows you to set an additional level of security for users who access the files and folders locally or through the network. For example, two users who share the same Windows 10 computer can be assigned different NTFS permissions so that one user has access to a folder but the other user is denied access to that folder. This is not possible on a FAT32 file system.

NTFS also offers disk-management features—such as compression and encryption capabilities—and data-recovery features. The disk-management features are covered later in this chapter. The data-recovery features are covered in Chapter 20, "Configuring Recovery."

You should also be aware that there are several different versions of NTFS. Every version of Windows 2000 uses NTFS 3.0. Windows 7/8/10, Windows Vista, Windows XP, Windows Server 2003, Windows Server 2008/2008 R2, and Windows Server 2012/2012 R2 use NTFS 3.1. NTFS versions 3.0 and 3.1 use similar disk formats, so Windows 2000 computers can access NTFS 3.1 volumes and Windows 10 computers can access NTFS 3.0 volumes. NTFS 3.1 includes the following features:

- When files are read or written to a disk, they can be automatically encrypted and decrypted.

- Reparse points are used with mount points to redirect data as it is written or read from a folder to another volume or physical disk.

- There is support for sparse files, which are used by programs that create large files but allocate disk space only as needed.
- Remote storage allows you to extend your disk space by making removable media (for example, external tapes) more accessible.
- It gives you the ability to resize volumes and partitions.
- You can use recovery logging on NTFS metadata, which is used for data recovery when a power failure or system problem occurs.

Now that you have seen the differences between FAT32 and NTFS, let's discuss how to convert a FAT32 drive to an NTFS drive.

File System Conversion

In Windows 10, you can convert FAT32 partitions to NTFS. File-system conversion is the process of converting one file system to another without the loss of data. If you format a drive, as opposed to converting it, all the data on that drive will be lost.

To convert a partition, you use the Convert command-line utility. The syntax for the Convert command is as follows:

```
Convert [drive:]/fs:ntfs
```

For example, if you wanted to convert your D: drive to NTFS, you would type the following from a command prompt:

```
Convert D:/fs:ntfs
```

When the conversion process begins, it will attempt to lock the partition. If the partition cannot be locked—perhaps because it contains the Windows 10 operating system files or the system's page file—the conversion will not take place until the computer is restarted.

In Exercise 13.1, you will convert your D: drive from FAT32 to NTFS. For this exercise, it is assumed that you have a D: drive that is formatted with the FAT32 file system. If you don't have a FAT32 drive, open Disk Management by right-clicking the Start button and choose Disk Management. Click your C partition, right-click and shrink the drive by only 5–10 GBs. Now create a simple volume and format it as FAT32.

Using the Convert **Command**

You can use the /v switch with the Convert command. This switch specifies that you want to use verbose mode, and all messages will be displayed during the conversion process. You can also use the /NoSecurity switch, which specifies that all converted files and folders will have no security applied by default, so they can be accessed by anyone.

EXERCISE 13.1

Converting a FAT32 Partition to NTFS

1. Copy some folders to the D: drive.

2. Select Start, and then type **cmd** into the Search box to open a command prompt.

3. In the Command Prompt dialog box, type **Convert D: /fs:ntfs** and press Enter.

4. After the conversion process is complete, close the Command Prompt dialog box.

5. Verify that the folders you copied in step 1 still exist on the partition.

Stopping a Conversion

If you choose to convert a partition from FAT32 to NTFS and the conversion has not yet taken place, you can cancel the conversion by editing the Registry with the REGEDIT or REGEDT32 command. The key that needs to be edited is

HKEY_LOCAL_MACHINE\System\CurrentControlSet\Control\SessionManager

The BootExecute value needs to be changed from autoconv\DosDevices\x:/FS:NTFS to autocheck autochk*.

Once you decide which file system you want to use, you need to decide what disk storage type you want to configure. Let's look at some of the disk storage options you have.

 Be careful when converting your file system. Once you change a FAT32 file system to NTFS, you cannot change it back without formatting the disk and losing your data.

Configuring NTFS

As mentioned earlier, NTFS has many advantages over FAT32. The main advantages are NTFS Security, compression, encryption (EFS), and quotas. Let's take a look at some of these advantages in greater detail.

NTFS Security   One of the biggest advantages of NTFS is security. NTFS Security (as shown in Figure 13.1) is one of the most important aspects of an IT administrator's job. An advantage of NTFS Security is that the security can be placed on individual files and folders. It does not matter whether you are local to the share (in front of the machine where the data is stored) or remote to the share (coming across the network to access the data); the security is always in place with NTFS. The default security permission is Users = Read on new folders or shares. Configuring NTFS Security and managing how it works with Shared Permissions are covered in Chapter 14, "Managing Data Access."

FIGURE 13.1   NTFS Security tab

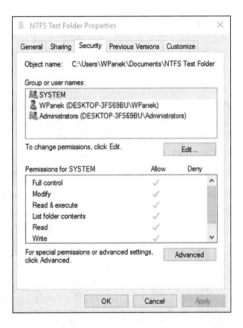

Compression   *Compression* helps compact files or folders to allow for more efficient use of hard drive space. For example, a file that usually takes up 20 MB of space might use only 13 MB after compression. To enable compression, just open the Advanced Attributes dialog box for a folder and check the Compress Contents To Save Disk Space box. Compression is covered in greater detail later in this chapter in the "Managing Data Compression" section.

Encryption   *Encrypting File System (EFS)* allows a user or administrator to secure files or folders by using encryption. Encryption employs the user's security identification (SID) number to secure the file or folder. To implement encryption, open the Advanced Attributes dialog box for a folder, and check the Encrypt Contents To Secure Data box (see Figure 13.2).

FIGURE 13.2   Setting up encryption on a folder

If files are encrypted using EFS and an administrator has to unencrypt the files, there are two ways to do this. First, you can log in using the user's account (the account that encrypted the files) and unencrypt the files. Second, you can become a recovery agent and manually unencrypt the files. EFS is covered in greater detail in the section "Managing Data Encryption with EFS" later in this chapter.

Quotas   Disk *quotas* give administrators the ability to limit how much storage space a user can have on a hard drive. You have a few options available to you when you set up disk quotas. You can set up disk quotas based on volume or on users.

> **Setting Quotas by Volume**   One way to set up disk quotas is by setting the quota by volume, on a per-volume basis. This means that if you have a hard drive with C:, D:, and E: volumes, you would have to set up three individual quotas (one for each volume). This is your umbrella. This is where you set up an entire disk quota based on the volume for all users.
>
> **Setting Quotas by User**   You have the ability to set up quotas on volumes by user. Here is where you would individually let users have independent quotas that exceed your umbrella quota.
>
> **Specifying Quota Entries**   You use quota entries to configure the volume and user quotas. You do this on the Quotas tab of the volume's Properties dialog box. (See Exercise 13.2.)
>
> **Creating Quota Templates**   Quota templates are predefined ways to set up quotas. Templates allow you to set up disk quotas without needing to create a disk quota from scratch. One advantage of using a template is that when you want to set up disk quotas on multiple volumes (C:, D:, and E:) on the same hard drive, you do not need to re-create the quota on each volume.

Exercise 13.2 will show you how to set up an umbrella quota for all users. This is the disk quota that all users will then follow for whichever drive you set this up on.

EXERCISE 13.2

Configuring Disk Quotas

1. Open Windows Explorer.

2. Right-click the local disk (C:), and choose Properties.

3. Click the Quotas tab.

4. Check the Enable Quota Management check box. Also check the Deny Disk Space To Users Exceeding Quota Limit box.

5. Click the Limit Disk Space To option, and enter **1000MB** in the box.

6. Enter **750MB** in the Set Warning Level To boxes.

7. Click the Apply button. If a warning box appears, click OK. This warning is just informing you that the disk may need to be rescanned for the quota.

8. Now that you have set up an umbrella quota to cover everyone, close the disk quota tool.

Configuring Disk Storage

Windows 10 supports three types of disk storage: basic, dynamic, and GUID Partition Table (GPT). Basic storage is backward compatible with other operating systems and can be configured to support up to four partitions. Dynamic storage is supported by Windows 2000, Windows XP, Windows Vista, Windows 7, Windows 8, Windows 10, Windows Server 2003, Windows Server 2008, Windows Server 2008 R2, Windows Server 2012, and Windows Server 2012 R2 and allows storage to be configured as volumes. GPT support begins with the Windows 2003 SP1 release and allows you to configure volume sizes larger than 2 TB and up to 128 primary partitions. The following sections describe the basic storage, dynamic storage, and GPT storage configurations.

Basic Storage

Basic storage consists of primary and extended partitions and logical drives that exist within the extended partition. The first partition that is created on a hard drive is called a primary partition and is usually represented as the C: drive. Primary partitions use all of the space that is allocated to the partition, and a single drive letter is used to represent the partition. Only a single extended partition is allowed on any basic disk. Each physical drive can have up to four partitions. You can set up four primary partitions, or you can have three primary partitions and one extended partition. With an extended partition, you can allocate the space however you like, and each suballocation of space (called a logical drive) is represented by a different drive letter. For example, a 500 MB extended partition could have a 250 MB D: partition and a 250 MB E: partition.

At the highest level of disk organization, you have a physical hard drive. You cannot use space on the physical drive until you have logically partitioned the physical drive.

One of the advantages of using multiple partitions on a single physical hard drive is that each partition can have a different file system. For example, the C: drive might be FAT32 and the D: drive might be NTFS. Multiple partitions also make it easier to manage security requirements.

Basic storage is the default, and this is the type that many users continue to use. But what if you want some additional functionality from your storage type? Let's look at some of the more advanced disk storage options.

Dynamic Storage

Dynamic storage is a Windows 10 feature that consists of a dynamic disk divided into dynamic volumes. Dynamic volumes cannot contain partitions or logical drives.

Dynamic storage supports three dynamic volume types: simple volumes, spanned volumes, and striped volumes. Dynamic storage also supports a Redundant Array of Independent Disks (RAID), which will be discussed in the "Understanding RAID" section of this chapter.

To set up dynamic storage, you convert or upgrade a basic disk to a dynamic disk. When converting a basic disk to dynamic, you do not lose any of your data. After the disk is converted, any partitions that existed on the basic disk are converted to dynamic simple volumes, and you can then create any additional dynamic volumes required within the dynamic disk.

You create dynamic storage with the Windows 10 Disk Management utility, which is discussed in the "Using the Disk Management Utility" section of this chapter. Let's take a closer look at the different types of dynamic volumes.

Simple Volumes

A *simple volume* contains space from a single dynamic drive. The space from the single drive can be contiguous or noncontiguous. Simple volumes are used when you have enough disk space on a single drive to hold your entire volume. Figure 13.3 illustrates two simple volumes on a physical disk.

FIGURE 13.3 Two simple volumes

Simple Volume C:\
10 GB

Simple Volume D:\
10 GB

Physical Disk 0
20 GB

Spanned Volumes

A *spanned volume* consists of disk space on two or more dynamic drives; up to 32 dynamic drives can be used in a spanned volume configuration. Spanned volume sets are used to dynamically increase the size of a dynamic volume. When you create spanned volumes, the data is written sequentially, filling space on one physical drive before writing to space on the next physical drive in the spanned volume set. Typically, administrators use spanned volumes when they are running out of disk space on a volume and want to dynamically extend the volume with space from another hard drive or without using another drive letter.

You do not need to allocate the same amount of space to the volume set on each physical drive. This means you could combine 500 MB on one physical drive with two 750 MB volumes on other dynamic drives, as shown in Figure 13.4.

FIGURE 13.4   A spanned volume set

Because data is written sequentially, you do not see any performance enhancements with spanned volumes as you do with striped volumes (discussed next). The main disadvantage of spanned volumes is that if any drive in the spanned volume set fails, you lose access to all of the data in the spanned set.

Striped Volumes

A *striped volume* stores data in equal stripes between two or more (up to 32) dynamic drives, as illustrated in Figure 13.5. Since the data is written sequentially across the stripe, you can take advantage of multiple I/O performance and increase the speed at which data reads and writes take place. Typically, administrators use striped volumes when they want to combine the space of several physical drives into a single logical volume and increase disk performance.

FIGURE 13.5   A spanned volume set

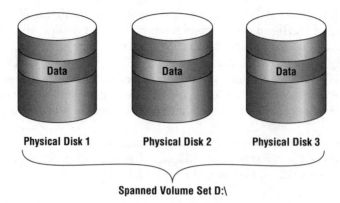

Spanned Volume Set D:\

The main disadvantage of striped volumes is that if any drive in the striped volume set fails, you lose access to all of the data in the striped set.

In the last few years a new storage type has emerged in the Microsoft computer world, and as with most new technologies, it has some advantages over the previous technologies. Let's take a look at the newest advantageous storage type.

GUID Partition Table

The *GUID Partition Table (GPT)* is available for Windows 10 and was first introduced as part of the Extensible Firmware Interface (EFI) initiative from Intel. Basic and dynamic disks use the Master Boot Record (MBR) partitioning scheme that all operating systems have been using for years. Basic and dynamic disks use Cylinder-Head-Sector (CHS) addressing with the MBR scheme. CHS allows computers to assign addresses to data on the computer's hard-disk drives. This has been an effective way to store data on a hard drive, but there is a newer, more effective way.

The GPT disk-partitioning system uses the GPT to configure the disk area. GPT uses an addressing scheme called Logical Block Addressing (LBA), which is a newer method of accessing hard-disk drives. LBA uses a unique sector number only instead of using the cylinder, head, and sector number. Another advantage is that the GPT header and partition table are written to both the front and back ends of the disk, which provides for better redundancy.

The GPT disk-partitioning system gives you many benefits over using the MBR system:

- Allows a volume size larger than 2 TB
- Allows up to 128 primary partitions
- Used for both 32-bit and 64-bit Windows 10 editions
- Includes cyclic redundancy check (CRC) for greater reliability

However, there is one disadvantage to using the GPT drives. You can convert a GPT drive only if the disk is empty and unpartitioned. I will show you the steps to creating a GPT disk later in this chapter.

To convert any disk or format any volume or partition, you can use the Disk Management utility. I will show you how to manage your disks using the Disk Management utility in the "Using the Disk Management Utility" section, later in this chapter.

Cloud-Based Storage

One of the fastest-growing parts of the IT world is cloud-based services. From cloud-based user storage to cloud-based corporate data storage, it seems like all we hear anymore is "cloud, cloud, cloud."

Well, Microsoft has cloud-based subscription services called Microsoft Azure and OneDrive.

Microsoft Azure

Microsoft Azure (https://azure.microsoft.com/en-us/) can be used by almost any operating system on the market (Windows, Linux, etc.), by most applications (Java, .NET, PHP, etc.), and by most device types (Windows, Android, and iOS).

Microsoft Azure is different than many other cloud-based systems because Microsoft Azure doesn't make you choose either your network or the cloud. Many cloud-based service providers want you to use their cloud to run all of your applications and/or storage from their location. Microsoft Azure allows you to extend your current network infrastructure into the cloud to take full advantage of both worlds.

This way you can still have a full IT server room with full-time IT employees but get the benefits of storing data both locally and also in a cloud environment, which is then available from anywhere in the world.

Azure makes it easy to store documents in the cloud by using the Azure portal. The portal is the way that users and IT professionals can control and manage how data is stored in the cloud. The Azure portal allows you to do some of the following:

- Upload and download data to and from Azure
- Run reports showing the actual usage of each file share
- Adjust the quota sizes of your users
- Use the net use command-line utility to share files from a Windows client command prompt

One advantage to using Microsoft Azure is that you only pay for what you need. The more cloud-based storage you need, the more you pay for and the less you need means less money. Table 13.2 shows you the maximum amount of data that can be stored on Microsoft Azure.

TABLE 13.2   Microsoft Azure data size availability

Operating System	Maximum Size of Data Source
Windows Server 2012 or above	54,400 GB
Windows 8 or above	54,400 GB

TABLE 13.2   Microsoft Azure data size availability *(continued)*

Operating System	Maximum Size of Data Source
Windows Server 2008, Windows Server 2008 R2	1,700 GB
Windows 7	1,700 GB

If you decide that you want your company to use Microsoft Azure for some of its cloud-based storage or all of its cloud-based storage, please go to https://azure.microsoft.com/en-us/ to get the current subscription rates.

Microsoft OneDrive

Another Microsoft-based subscription is called OneDrive (used to be known as SkyDrive). Microsoft's OneDrive is built into Windows 10 by default (see Figure 13.6). OneDrive is a cloud-based storage subscription so home users can store their documents and then access those documents from anywhere in the world (provided that you have Internet access).

FIGURE 13.6   OneDrive welcome screen

OneDrive was designed for the average home user who is looking to store data in a safe, secure, cloud-based environment. OneDrive, when first released, was also a consideration for corporate environments, but with the release of Windows Azure, OneDrive is really intended for the home user or corporate user who wants to store some of their own personal documents in the cloud. Corporations would be more inclined to use Microsoft Azure and all of its corporate benefits.

If you or your company decides to purchase the Office 365 subscription, then OneDrive is included for cloud-based storage. If you didn't purchase Office 365, then you have to choose from one of the subscriptions shown in Table 13.3.

TABLE 13.3 OneDrive Subscriptions

Amount of Storage	Subscription Monthly Fee
Office 365 + 1 TB included	$9.99
5 GB	Free
100 GB	$1.99
200 GB	$3.99

Please note that these are the current prices at the time this book was written and these prices may have changed. Be sure to check out Microsoft's OneDrive web page for current prices (https://onedrive.live.com/options/Upgrade).

Exercise 13.3 will show you how to set up a OneDrive account for your user account. To do this access, you must have a Microsoft account. You get 15 GB for free from Microsoft on the OneDrive cloud-based storage.

EXERCISE 13.3

Configuring OneDrive

1. Open OneDrive.

2. Log into OneDrive using your Microsoft account as shown in Figure 13.7.

FIGURE 13.7 OneDrive login screen

3. You will get a screen that will show you where your files will be located on your system as shown in Figure 13.8. Click the Next button.

FIGURE 13.8 OneDrive file location screen

4. At the Sync files screen, choose what folders that you want to sync with Microsoft and then click Next.

A screen will appear telling you that your OneDrive is set up and ready to go (see Figure 13.9).

FIGURE 13.9   Open My OneDrive Folder screen

5. Click the Open My OneDrive Folder button to open your folders and Microsoft OneDrive.

6. Close OneDrive.

Cloud-based services will be discussed throughout this book.

Using the Disk Management Utility

The Disk Management utility is a Microsoft Management Console (MMC) snap-in that gives administrators a graphical tool for managing disks and volumes within Windows 10. In this section, you will learn how to access the Disk Management utility and use it to perform basic tasks, including managing basic storage, and dynamic storage. You will also learn about troubleshooting disks through disk status codes.

But before we dive into the Disk Management utility, let's explore the MMC. It is important to understand the MMC since Disk Management (like many other tools) is actually an MMC snap-in.

Using the Microsoft Management Console

The *Microsoft Management Console (MMC)* is the console framework for application management. The MMC provides a common environment for snap-ins. Snap-ins are administrative tools developed by Microsoft or third-party vendors. Some of the MMC snap-ins that you may use are Computer Management, Active Directory Users and Computers, Active Directory Sites and Services, Active Directory Domains and Trusts, and DNS Management. When you look at the administrative tools, you know that each one of these tools are running inside of an MMC (shown in Figure 13.10).

FIGURE 13.10   The administrative tools running in MMCs

Knowing how to use and configure the MMC snap-ins will allow you to customize your work environment. For example, if you are in charge of Active Directory Users and Computers and DNS, you can add both of these snap-ins into the same window. This would then allow you to open just one application to configure all your tasks. The MMC offers many other benefits:

- The MMC is highly customizable—you add only the snap-ins you need.
- Snap-ins use a standard, intuitive interface, so they are easier to use than previous versions of administrative utilities.
- You can save customized MMCs and share them with other administrators.
- You can configure permissions so that the MMC runs in authoring mode, which an administrator can manage, or in user mode, which limits what users can access.
- You can use most snap-ins for remote computer management.

As shown in Figure 13.11, by default, the MMC contains three panes: a console tree on the left, a details pane in the middle, and an optional Actions pane on the right. The console tree lists the hierarchical structure of all snap-ins that have been loaded into the console. The details pane contains a list of properties or other items that are part of the snap-in that is highlighted in the console tree. The Actions pane provides a list of actions that the user can access depending on the item selected in the details pane.

FIGURE 13.11   The MMC tree, details pane, and Actions pane

To open the MMC on a Windows 10 computer, click the Start button and type **MMC** in the Search dialog box. When you first open the MMC, it contains only the Console Root folder, as shown in Figure 13.11. The MMC does not have any default administrative functionality. It is simply a framework used to organize administrative tools through the addition of snap-in utilities.

The first thing that you should decide when using the MMC is which of the different administrative mode types you will employ. You need to decide which mode type is best suited to use for your organization.

Configuring MMC Modes

You can configure the MMC to run in author mode for full access to the MMC functions or in one of three user modes, which have more limited access to the MMC functions. To set a console mode, while in the MMC editor, select File ➤ Options to open the Options dialog box. In this dialog box, you can select from the console modes listed in Table 13.4.

TABLE 13.4   MMC modes

Console Mode	Description
Author mode	Allows use of all the MMC functions.
User mode—full access	Gives users full access to window-management commands, but they cannot add or remove snap-ins or change console properties.
User mode—limited access, multiple window	Allows users to create new windows but not close any existing windows. Users can access only the areas of the console tree that were visible when the console was last saved.
User mode—limited access, single window	Allows users to access only the areas of the console tree that were visible when the console was last saved, and they cannot create new windows.

After you decide which administrative role you are going to run, it's time to start configuring your MMC snap-ins.

Adding Snap-Ins

The biggest advantage of using the MMC is to configure snap-ins the way your organization needs them. Adding snap-ins is a simple and quick procedure. To add a snap-in to the MMC and save it, complete Exercise 13.4.

EXERCISE 13.4

Adding an MMC Snap-In

1. To start the MMC editor, click Start, type **MMC** into the search box, and press Enter.

2. From the main console window, select File ➤ Add/Remove Snap-In to open the Add Or Remove Snap-ins dialog box.

3. Highlight the snap-in you want to add (see Figure 13.12), and click the Add button.

FIGURE 13.12   The MMC Add Or Remove Snap-Ins screen

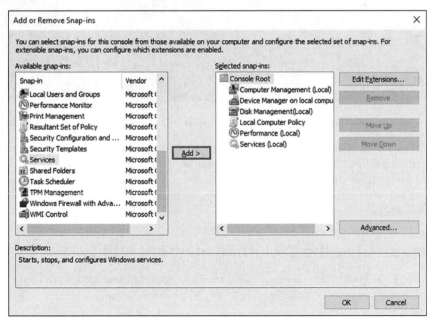

4. If prompted, specify whether the snap-in will be used to manage the local computer or a remote computer. After you choose the MMCs you want in your custom snap-in (shown in Figure 13.13), click the Finish button.

FIGURE 13.13   The MMC console screen

5. When you have finished adding snap-ins, click OK.

6. After you have added snap-ins to create a console, you can save it by selecting File ➢ Save As and entering a name for your console. Place the console on the desktop as shown in Figure 13.14.

FIGURE 13.14   The MMC console on desktop

You can save the console to a variety of locations, including a program group or the desktop. By default, custom consoles have an `.msc` filename extension.

Many applications that are MMC snap-ins, including Disk Management, are already configured for you under the Administrative Tools section of Windows 10. Next, let's look at the Disk Management utility.

Understanding the Disk Management Utility

The Disk Management utility, located under the Computer Management snap-in by default, is a one-stop shop for configuring your disk options.

First of all, to have full permissions to use the Disk Management utility, you must be logged on with local Administrative privileges. You can access the Disk Management utility a few different ways. You can right-click Computer from the Start menu and select Manage, and then in Computer Management, select Disk Management. You could also use Control Panel ➤ Administrative Tools ➤ Computer Management.

Once you have launched Computer Management, you must expand the storage section of the console in order to access the Disk Management toolset. The Disk Management utility's opening window, shown in Figure 13.15, displays the following information:

- The volumes that are recognized by the computer

- The type of disk, either basic or dynamic

- The type of file system used by each partition

- The status of the partition and whether the partition contains the system or boot partition

- The capacity (amount of space) allocated to the partition

- The amount of free space remaining on the partition

- The amount of overhead associated with the partition

FIGURE 13.15   The Disk Management window

Windows 10 also includes a command-line utility called Diskpart, which can be used as a command-line alternative to the Disk Management utility. You can view all of the options associated with the Diskpart utility by typing **Diskpart** (as shown in Figure 13.16) at a command prompt and then typing **?** at the Diskpart prompt.

FIGURE 13.16 The Diskpart window

The Disk Management utility allows you to configure and manage your disks. Let's take a look at some of the tasks that you can perform in disk administration.

Managing Administrative Hard-Disk Tasks

The Disk Management utility allows you to perform a variety of hard-drive administrative tasks:

- View disk properties.
- View volume and local disk properties.
- Add a new disk.
- Create partitions and volumes.
- Upgrade a basic disk to a dynamic or GPT disk.
- Change a drive letter and path.
- Resize a volume or partition.
- Delete partitions and volumes.

These tasks are discussed in the sections that follow.

Viewing Disk Properties

To view the properties of a disk, right-click the disk number in the lower panel of the Disk Management main window and choose Properties from the context menu. This brings up the disk's Properties dialog box. Click the Volumes tab to see the volumes associated with the disk, as shown in Figure 13.17, which contains the following disk properties:

- The disk number
- The type of disk (basic, dynamic, CD-ROM, removable, DVD, or unknown)
- The status of the disk (online or offline)
- The partition style
- The capacity of the disk
- The amount of unallocated space on the disk
- The amount of space reserved on the disk
- The logical volumes that have been defined on the physical drive

FIGURE 13.17 The Volumes tab of a disk's Properties dialog box

 If you click the General tab of a disk's Properties dialog box, the hardware device type, the hardware vendor that produced the drive, the physical location of the drive, and the device status are displayed.

Viewing Volume and Local Disk Properties

On a dynamic disk, you manage volume properties. On a basic disk, you manage partition properties. Volumes and partitions perform the same function, and the options discussed in the following sections apply to both. (The examples here are based on a dynamic disk using a simple volume. If you are using basic storage, you will view the partition properties rather than the volume properties.)

To see the properties of a volume, right-click the volume in the upper panel of the Disk Management main window and choose Properties. This brings up the volume's Properties dialog box. Volume properties are organized on seven tabs: General, Tools, Hardware, Sharing, Security, Previous Versions, and Quota. The Security tab and Quota tab appear only for NTFS volumes. All these tabs are described in detail in the following text.

General   The information on the General tab of the volume's Properties dialog box, as shown in Figure 13.18, gives you a general idea of how the volume is configured. This dialog box shows the label, type, file system, used and free space, and capacity of the volume. The label is shown in an editable text box, and you can change it if desired. The space allocated to the volume is shown in a graphical representation as well as in text form.

FIGURE 13.18   General properties for a volume

The label on a volume or local disk is for informational purposes only. For example, depending on its use, you might give a volume a label such as APPS or ACCTDB.

The Disk Cleanup button starts the Disk Cleanup utility, which you can use to delete unnecessary files, thereby freeing disk space. This utility is discussed later in this chapter in the "Using the Disk Cleanup Utility" section.

This tab also allows you to configure compression for the volume and to indicate whether the volume should be indexed.

Tools   The Tools tab of the volume's Properties dialog box, shown in Figure 13.19, provides access to three tools.

FIGURE 13.19   The Tools tab of the volume's Properties dialog box

Click the Check Now button to run the Error-Checking utility to check the volume for errors. You may do this if you are experiencing problems accessing the volume or if the volume was open during a system restart that did not go through a proper shutdown sequence. This utility is covered in more detail in "Troubleshooting Disk Management," later in this chapter.

Click the Optimize Now button to run the Disk Defragmenter utility. This utility defragments files on the volume by storing the files contiguously on the hard drive.

Hardware   The Hardware tab of the volume's Properties dialog box, shown in Figure 13.20, lists the hardware associated with the disk drives that are recognized by the Windows 10 operating system. The bottom half of the dialog box shows the properties of the device that is highlighted in the top half of the dialog box.

FIGURE 13.20 The Hardware tab of the volume's Properties dialog box

For more details about a hardware item, highlight it and click the Properties button in the lower-right corner of the dialog box. This brings up a Properties dialog box for the item. Your Device Status field should report, "This device is working properly." If that's not the case, you can click the Troubleshoot button (it will appear if the device is not working properly) to get a troubleshooting wizard that will help you discover the problem.

Sharing   On the Sharing tab of the volume's Properties dialog box, shown in Figure 13.21, you can specify whether or not the volume is shared on the network. Volumes are not shared by default. Clicking the Advanced Sharing button will allow you to specify whether the volume is shared and, if so, what the name of the share should be. You will also be able to specify who will have access to the shared volume.

Security   The Security tab of the volume's Properties dialog box, shown in Figure 13.22, appears only for NTFS volumes. The Security tab is used to set the NTFS permissions for the volume.

Previous Versions   The Previous Versions tab displays shadow copies of the files that are created by System Restore, as shown in Figure 13.23. Shadow copies of files are backup copies created by Windows in the background to allow you to restore the system to a previous state. On the Previous Versions tab, you can select a copy of the volume and either view the contents of the shadow copy or copy the shadow copy to another location. If System Restore is not enabled, then shadow copies of a volume will not be created.

FIGURE 13.21   The Sharing tab of the volume's Properties dialog box

FIGURE 13.22   The Security tab of the volume's Properties dialog box

FIGURE 13.23 The Previous Versions tab of the volume's Properties dialog box

Quota Quotas give you the ability to limit the amount of hard-disk space that a user can have on a volume or partition (see Figure 13.24). By default, quotas are disabled. To enable quotas, check the Enable Quota Management check box. There are a few options that can be configured when enabling quotas.

FIGURE 13.24 The Quota tab of the volume's Properties dialog box

The Deny Disk Space To Users Exceeding Quota Limit check box is another option. When this box is enabled, any user who exceeds their quota limit will be denied disk storage. You can choose not to enable this option, which allows you to just monitor the quotas. You also have the ability to set the quota limit and warning size and to log all quota events as they happen.

Adding a New Disk

New hard disks can be added to a system to increase the amount of disk storage you have. This is a fairly common task that you will need to perform as your application programs and files grow larger.

How you add a disk depends on whether your computer supports hot swapping of drives. Hot swapping is the process of adding a new hard drive while the computer is turned on. Most desktop computers do not support this capability. Remember, your user account must be a member of the Administrators group to install a new drive. The following list specifies configuration options:

Computer Doesn't Support Hot Swapping   If your computer does not support hot swapping, you must shut down the computer before you add a new disk. Then add the drive according to the manufacturer's directions. When you've finished, restart the computer. You should find the new drive listed in the Disk Management utility.

Computer Supports Hot Swapping   If your computer does support hot swapping, you don't need to turn off your computer first. Just add the drive according to the manufacturer's directions. Then open the Disk Management utility and select Action ➤ Rescan Disks. You should find the new drive listed in the Disk Management utility.

Creating Partitions and Volumes   Once you add a new disk, the next step is to create a partition (on a basic disk) or a volume (on a dynamic disk). Partitions and volumes fill similar roles in the storage of data on disks, and the processes for creating them are the same.

Creating a Volume or a Partition

Creating a volume or partition is a fairly easy process. To create the new volume or partition, right-click the unformatted free space and start the wizard.

Exercise 13.5 walks you through the New Volume Wizard for creating a new volume.

EXERCISE 13.5

Creating a New Volume

1. In the Disk Management utility, right-click an area of free storage space and choose the type of volume to create. If only one drive is installed, you will be able to create only a simple volume. You can click New Simple Volume to create a new simple volume.

2. The Welcome To The New Simple Volume Wizard appears. Click the Next button to continue.

3. The Select Volume Size screen appears. Select the size of volume to create, and then click Next to continue.

4. You should see the Assign Drive Letter Or Path screen. You can specify a drive letter, mount the volume as an empty folder, or choose not to assign a drive letter or drive path. If you choose to mount the volume into an empty folder, you can have a virtually unlimited number of volumes, negating the drive-letter limitation. If you choose not to assign a drive letter or path, users will not be able to access the volume. Make your selections, and click Next to continue (see Figure 13.25).

FIGURE 13.25 Assign Drive Letter Or Path screen

5. The Format Partition screen appears. This screen allows you to choose whether you will format the volume. If you choose to format the volume, you can format it as FAT32 or NTFS. You can also select the allocation unit size, enter a volume label (for information only), specify whether you would like to perform a quick format, and choose whether to enable file and folder compression. After you've made your choices, click Next (see Figure 13.26).

FIGURE 13.26   Format Partition screen

6.   The Completing The New Volume Wizard screen appears. Verify your selections. If you need to change any of them, click the Back button to reach the appropriate screen. When everything is correctly set, click the Finish button.

Now that you know how to create a new volume or partition, let's see how to convert a basic disk to dynamic or GPT.

Upgrading a Basic Disk to a Dynamic or GPT Disk

When you perform a fresh installation of Windows 10, your drives are configured as basic disks. To take advantage of the features offered by Windows 10 dynamic or GPT disks, you must upgrade your basic disks to either of those disk configurations.

WARNING   Upgrading basic disks to dynamic disks is a one-way process as far as preserving data is concerned and is a potentially dangerous operation. Before you perform this upgrade (or make any major change to your drives or volumes), create a new backup of the drive or volume and verify that you can successfully restore the backup before proceeding with the change.

Any basic disk can be converted to a dynamic disk, but only a disk with all unformatted free space can be converted to a GPT disk. Exercise 13.6 walks you through converting an MBR-based disk to a GPT disk.

EXERCISE 13.6

Converting a Basic Disk to a GPT Disk

1. If the disk that you want to convert has partitions or volumes defined, first delete the partition or volume.

2. Open the Disk Management utility by clicking the Start button, right-clicking Computers, and choosing Manage.

3. Click Disk Management in the lower-left section.

4. Right-click the disk and choose Convert To GPT Disk (see Figure 13.27).

FIGURE 13.27   Format Partition Screen

5. After the disk converts, you can right-click the disk and see that the Convert To MBR Disk option is now available.

There are a few other methods for converting an MBR-based disk to a GPT disk. You can use the Diskpart utility and type in the Convert GPT command. You can also create a GPT disk when you first install a new hard drive. After you install the new hard drive, during the initialization phase, you can choose GPT Disk.

Another type of conversion that you may need to perform is that from a basic disk to a dynamic disk. Complete Exercise 13.7 to convert a basic disk to a dynamic disk.

EXERCISE 13.7

Converting a Basic Disk to a Dynamic Disk

1. In the Disk Management utility, right-click the disk you want to convert and select the Convert To Dynamic Disk option.

2. In the Convert To Dynamic Disk dialog box, check the disk that you want to convert and click OK.

3. In the Disks To Convert dialog box, click the Convert button.

4. A confirmation dialog box warns you that you will no longer be able to boot previous versions of Windows from this disk. Click the Yes button to continue to convert the disk.

As you are configuring the volumes or partitions on the hard drive, other things that you may need to configure are the drive letters and paths.

Changing the Drive Letters and Paths

There may be times when you need to change drive letters and paths when you add new equipment. Let's suppose you have a hard drive with two partitions: drive C: assigned as your first partition and drive D: assigned as your second partition. Your DVD drive is assigned the drive letter E:. You add a new hard drive and partition it as a new volume. By default, the new partition is assigned as drive F:. If you want your logical drives to be listed before the DVD drive, you can use the Disk Management utility's Change Drive Letter And Paths option to reassign your drive letters.

When you need to reassign drive letters, right-click the volume for which you want to change the drive letter and choose Change Drive Letter And Paths. This brings up the dialog box shown in Figure 13.28. Click the Change button to access the Change Drive Letter Or Path dialog box shown in Figure 13.28. Use the drop-down list next to the Assign The Following Drive Letter option to select the drive letter you want to assign to the volume.

FIGURE 13.28 The dialog boxes for changing a drive letter or path

In Exercise 13.8, you will edit the drive letter of the partition you created.

EXERCISE 13.8

Editing a Drive Letter

1. Right-click Start ➤ Computer Management; then expand Storage ➤ Disk Management.

2. Right-click a drive that you have created and select Change Drive Letter And Paths.

3. In the Change Drive Letter And Paths dialog box, click the Change button.

4. In the Change Drive Letter Or Path dialog box, select a new drive letter and click OK.

5. In the dialog box that appears, click the Yes button to confirm that you want to change the drive letter.

Another activity that you may need to perform is deleting a partition or volume that you have created. The next section looks at these activities.

Deleting Partitions and Volumes

When configuring your hard disks, there may be a time that you want to reconfigure your drive by deleting the partitions or volumes on the hard drive. You may also want to delete a volume so that you can extend another volume. These are tasks that can be configured in Disk Management.

When deleting a volume or partition, you will see a warning that all the data on the partition or volume will be lost. You have to click Yes to confirm that you want to delete the volume or partition. This confirmation is important because once you delete a partition or volume, it's gone for good along with any data content that was contained within it.

 The system volume, the boot volume, or any volume that contains the active paging (swap) file can't be deleted through the Disk Management utility. If you are trying to remove these partitions because you want to delete Windows 10, you can use a third-party disk-management utility.

In Exercise 13.9, you will delete a partition that you have created. Make sure that if you delete a partition or volume, it is empty; otherwise, back up all the data that you would like to retain before the deletion.

EXERCISE 13.9

Deleting a Partition

1. In the Disk Management utility, right-click the volume or partition that you want to remove and choose Delete Volume.

2. A warning box appears, stating that once this volume is deleted, all data will be lost. Click Yes.

3. The volume will be removed, and the area will be returned as unformatted free space.

You may be worried about your users removing devices from their Windows 10 machines. Microsoft has helped you in this situation. You can use removable-device policies to help restrict your users from removing their hardware. Removable-device policies can be created through the use of a Group Policy Object (GPO) on the server. GPOs are policies that are set on a computer or user and allow you to manipulate the Windows 10 environment.

Now that we have explored some of the basic administrative tasks of Disk Management, let's look at how to manage storage.

Managing Storage

The Disk Management utility offers support for managing storage. You can create, delete, and format partitions or volumes on your hard drives. You can also extend or shrink volumes on dynamic disks. Additionally, you can delete volume sets and striped sets.

Managing Dynamic Storage

As noted earlier in this chapter, a dynamic disk can contain simple, spanned, or striped volumes. Through the Disk Management utility, you can create volumes of each type. You can also create an extended volume, which is the process of adding disk space to a single simple volume. The following sections describe these disk-management tasks.

Creating Simple, Spanned, and Striped Volumes

As explained earlier, you use the New Volume Wizard to create a new volume. To start the New Volume Wizard, in the Disk Management utility right-click an area of free space where you want to create the volume. Then you can choose the type of volume you want to create: simple, spanned, or striped.

When you choose to create a spanned volume, you are creating a new volume from scratch that includes space from two or more physical drives, up to a maximum of 32 drives.

When you choose to create a striped volume, you are creating a new volume that combines free space from 2 to 32 drives into a single logical partition. The free space on all drives must be equal in size in a striped volume. Data in the striped volume is written across all drives in 64 KB stripes. (Data in spanned and extended volumes is written sequentially.) Striped volumes offer you better performance and are normally used for temporary files or folders. The problem with a striped volume is if you lose one of the drives in the volume, the entire striped volume is lost.

Another option that you have with volumes is to extend the volumes to create a larger storage area. In the next section, we will look at that process.

Creating Extended Volumes

When you create an extended volume, you are taking a single, simple volume (maybe one that is almost out of disk space) and adding more disk space to it, using free space that exists on the same physical hard drive. When the volume is extended, it is seen as a single drive letter. To extend a volume, the simple volume must be formatted as NTFS. You cannot extend a system or boot partition.

An extended volume is created when you are using only one physical drive. A spanned volume is created when you are using two or more physical drives. Exercise 13.10 shows you how to create an extended volume.

EXERCISE 13.10

Creating an Extended Volume

1. In the Disk Management utility, right-click the volume you want to extend and choose Extend Volume.

2. The Extend Volume Wizard starts. Click Next.

3. The Select Disks screen appears. As shown in Figure 13.29, you can specify the maximum size of the extended volume. The maximum size you can specify is determined by the amount of free space that exists in all of the dynamic drives on your computer. Click Next to continue.

FIGURE 13.29 The Select Disks screen

> **4.** The Completing The Extend Volume Wizard screen appears. Click the Finish button. You will see the new volume.

Once a volume is extended, no portion of it can be deleted without losing data on the entire set. However, if there is unneeded space on a volume, you can shrink that volume without losing data by using the Shrink Volume option in Disk Management.

 Real World Scenario

You're Running Out of Disk Space

Crystal, a user on your network, is running out of disk space. The situation needs to be corrected so she can be brought back up and running as quickly as possible. Crystal has a 250 GB drive (C:) that runs a very large customer database. She needs additional space added to the C: drive so the database will recognize the data because it must be stored on a single drive letter. Crystal's computer has a single SATA drive with nothing attached to the second SATA channel.

You have two basic options for managing space in this circumstance. One is to upgrade the disk to a larger disk, but this will necessitate reinstalling the OS and the applications and restoring the user's data. The other choice is to add a temporary second drive and extend the volume. This will at least allow Crystal to be up and running—but it should not be considered a permanent solution. If you do choose to extend the volume and then either drive within the volume set fails, the user will lose access to both drives. When Crystal's workload allows time for maintenance, you can replace the volume set with a single drive.

One issue you may run into with hard drives is that they go bad from time to time. If you have ever heard a hard drive fail, you know the sound: it is a distinct clicking. Once you have experienced it, you will never forget it. When drives go bad, Disk Management can help determine which drive and what the issue may be. Next, we will look at hard-disk errors.

Troubleshooting Disk Management

The Disk Management utility can be used to troubleshoot disk errors through a set of status codes; however, if a disk will not initialize, no status code will be displayed. Disks will not initialize if there is no valid disk signature.

The problem with disk errors is that you don't know when a disk fails or which disk failed. Disk Management can help you with this. When disks have problems or errors, status codes get assigned. Knowing what these codes mean will help you determine what the problem is and, more important, what steps need to be taken to fix the problem.

Understanding Disk Management Status Codes

The main window of the Disk Management utility displays the status of disks and volumes. The following list contains the possible status codes and a description of each code; these are very useful in troubleshooting disk problems:

Online Indicates that the disk is accessible and that it is functioning properly. This is the normal disk status.

Online (Errors) Used only with dynamic disks, this code indicates that I/O errors have been detected on the dynamic disk. One possible fix for this error is to right-click the disk and select Reactivate Disk to attempt to return the disk to Online status. This fix will work only if the I/O errors were temporary. You should immediately back up your data if you see this error and suspect that the I/O errors are not temporary.

Healthy Specifies that the volume is accessible and functioning properly.

Healthy (At Risk) Used to indicate that a dynamic volume is currently accessible but I/O errors have been detected on the underlying dynamic disk. This option is usually associated with Online (Errors) for the underlying disk.

Offline or Missing Used only with dynamic disks, this code indicates that the disk is not accessible. This can occur if the disk is corrupted or the hardware has failed. If the error is not caused by hardware failure or major corruption, you may be able to reaccess the disk by using the Reactivate Disk option to return the disk to Online status. If the disk was originally offline and then the status changed to Missing, it indicates that the disk has become corrupted, has been powered down, or was disconnected.

Unreadable This can occur on basic or dynamic disks. It indicates that the disk is inaccessible and might have encountered hardware errors, corruption, or I/O errors or that the system disk configuration database is corrupted. This message may also appear when a disk is spinning up while the Disk Management utility is rescanning the disks on the computer.

Failed This can be seen with basic or dynamic volumes. It specifies that the volume can't be started. This can occur because the disk is damaged or the file system is corrupted. If this message occurs with a basic volume, you should check the underlying disk hardware. If the error occurs on a dynamic volume, verify that the underlying disks are online.

Unknown Used with basic and dynamic volumes. It occurs if the boot sector for the volume becomes corrupted—for example, from a virus. This error can also occur if no disk signature is created for the volume.

Incomplete Occurs when you move some but not all of the disks from a multidisk volume. If you do not complete the multivolume set, the data will be inaccessible.

Foreign This error can occur if you move a dynamic disk from a computer running Windows 2000 (any version), Windows Server 2003, Windows 2008, Windows Server

2008 R2, Windows Server 2012/2012 R2, Windows XP Professional, Windows 7, Windows Vista, or Windows 8.1 to a Windows 10 computer. This error occurs because configuration data is unique to computers where the dynamic disk was created. You can correct this error by right-clicking the disk and selecting the Import Foreign Disks option. Any existing volume information will then be visible and accessible.

In addition to errors, there are some other issues that can arise when installing or configuring disks. One issue that may occur is that a disk fails to initialize when installed.

Troubleshooting Disks That Fail to Initialize

When you add a new disk to your computer in Windows 10, the disk does not initially contain a disk signature, which is required for the disk to be recognized by Windows. Disk signatures are at the end of the sector marker on the Master Boot Record (MBR) of the drive.

When you install a new drive and run the Disk Management utility, a wizard starts and lists all new disks that have been detected. The disk signature is written through this process. If you cancel the wizard before the disk signature is written, you will see the disk status Not Initialized. To initialize a disk, you right-click the disk you want to initialize and select the Initialize Disk option.

As you have now seen, Disk Management can be a very useful tool in your computer management arsenal. If you decide to format your partition or volume using NTFS, you then receive added benefits like compression, encryption (and therefore security), and quotas. In the following sections, we will take a closer look at compression and encryption.

Managing Data Compression

One of the advantages of using NTFS over FAT32 is the ability to compress data. I teach IT Administrators data compression, and I like to refer to a well-known infomercial as an example. Have you seen the commercial where people put all of the blankets into a large bag and then hook a vacuum to the bag and suck all the air out? This is a great example of how compression works. Data compression is the process of storing data in a form that takes less space than uncompressed data.

If you have ever "zipped" or "packed" a file, you have used a form of data compression. The compression algorithms support cluster sizes only up to 4 KB, so if you are using larger cluster sizes, NTFS compression support is not available. If you have the Modify permission on an NTFS volume, you can manage data compression through Windows Explorer or the Compact command-line utility.

The following are some important points about compression:

- Files as well as folders in NTFS can be compressed and uncompressed. Files and folders are managed independently, which means that a compressed folder can contain uncompressed files, and an uncompressed folder can contain compressed files.

- Access to compressed files by applications is transparent. For example, if you access a compressed file through Microsoft Word, the file will be uncompressed automatically when it is opened and then automatically compressed again when it is closed.

- Compression happens very quickly, but if, for example, you compress a 500 GB hard drive, there is no guarantee that there won't be any lag time on your machine or server.

- Data compression is available only on NTFS partitions. Because of this, if you copy or move a compressed folder or file to a FAT32 partition, Windows 10 automatically uncompresses the folder or file.

- Certain system files (e.g., Pagefile.sys) can't be compressed.

- You have the ability to show compressed files and folders with an alternate color.

In Exercise 13.11, you will compress and uncompress folders and files.

EXERCISE 13.11

Compressing and Uncompressing Folders

1. Select Start ➤ Run, and then type **Explorer** and click OK.

2. In Windows Explorer, find and select Computer, Local Disk (C:), and then a folder on the C: drive. The folder you select should contain files.

3. Right-click the folder and select Properties. In the General tab of the folder's Properties dialog box, note the value listed for Size On Disk. Then click the Advanced button.

4. In the Advanced Attributes dialog box, check the Compress Contents To Save Disk Space option (see Figure 13.30). Then click OK.

FIGURE 13.30   The Advanced Attributes dialog box

5. In the Confirm Attribute Changes dialog box, select the option Apply Changes To This Folder, Subfolders and Files. (If this confirmation dialog box does not appear, you can

display it by clicking the Apply button in the Properties dialog box.) Click OK to confirm your changes.

6. On the General tab of the folder's Properties dialog box, note the value that now appears for Size On Disk. This size should have decreased because you compressed the folder.

To uncompress folders and files, repeat the steps in Exercise 13.11 and uncheck the Compress Contents To Save Disk Space option in the Advanced Attributes dialog box.

As I stated earlier, you can specify that compressed files be displayed in a different color from uncompressed files. To do so, in Windows Explorer select View ➤ Options. In the Options box, click the View tab and under Files And Folders, check the Show Encrypted Or Compressed NTFS Files In Color option.

In addition to compressing files and folders in Windows Explorer, you can compress the files and folders using the Compact command-line utility.

Using the Compact Command-Line Utility

The command-line options for managing file and folder compression are Compact and Expand. You can access these commands from a command prompt. The Compact command offers you more control over file and folder compression than Windows Explorer. For example, you can use the Compact command with a batch script or to compress only files that meet a specific criterion (for example, all the DOC files in a specific folder). Some of the options that can be used with the Compact command are shown in Table 13.5.

TABLE 13.5   Compact commands

Command	Description
/C	Compresses the specified file or folder
/U	Uncompresses the specified file or folder
/S:dir	Used to specify which folder should be compressed or uncompressed
/A	Displays any files that have been hidden or system file attributes
/I	Indicates that errors should be ignored
/F	Forces a file to be compressed
/Q	Used with reporting, to report only critical information
/?	Displays help

Another way that you can save disk space is by zipping folders. In the following section, we will discuss how to save space using zipped folders.

Using Compressed (Zipped) Folders

Windows 10 also supports compressed (zipped) folders. This feature is different from NTFS compressed folders. The advantage of using compressed (zipped) folders is that they are supported on FAT32 and NTFS volumes. In addition, you can use compressed (zipped) folders to share data with other programs that use zipped files. The downside to using compressed (zipped) folders is that it is slower than using NTFS compression.

Within Windows Explorer, you create a zipped folder (or file) by right-clicking the folder and selecting Send To ➤ Compressed (Zipped) Folder. You create a zipped file by right-clicking a file and selecting New ➤ Compressed (Zipped) Folder. When you create a compressed folder, it will be displayed as a folder with a zipper.

Understanding Distributed File System

One problem that network administrators have is deciding how to share folders and communicating to the end users how to find the shares. For example, if you share a folder called Stormwind Documents on server A, how do you make sure that your users will find the folder and the files within it? The users have to know the server name and the share name. This can be a huge problem if you have hundreds of shares on multiple servers. If you want to have multiple copies of the folder called Stormwind Documents for fault tolerance and load balancing, the problem becomes even more complicated.

Distributed File System (DFS) in Windows Server 2012 R2 offers a simplified way for users to access geographically dispersed files. DFS allows you to set up a tree structure of virtual directories that allow users to connect to shared folders throughout the entire network.

Administrators have the ability to take shared folders that are located on different servers and transparently connect them to one or more DFS namespaces—virtual trees of shared folders throughout an organization. The advantage of using DFS is that if one of the folders becomes unavailable, DFS has failover capability that will allow your users to connect to the data on a different server.

Administrators can use the DFS tools to choose which shared folders will appear in the namespace and also to decide how the names of these shared folders will show up in the virtual tree listing. Administrators can then deploy the DFS shared folders to the Windows 10 DFS clients.

Advantages of DFS

One of the advantages of DFS is that when a user views this virtual tree, the shared folders appear to be located on a single machine. The following list includes some other advantages of DFS:

Simplified Data Migration   DFS gives you the ability to move data from one location to another without the user needing to know the physical location of the data. Because the users do not need to know the physical location of the shared data, administrators can simply move data from one location to another.

Security Integration   Administrators do not need to configure additional security for the DFS shared folders. The shared folders use the NTFS and shared folder permissions that an administrator has already assigned when the share was set up.

Access-Based Enumeration (ABE)   This DFS feature (disabled by default) displays only the files and folders that a user has permissions to access. If a user does not have access to a folder, Windows hides the folder from the user's DFS view. This feature is not active if the user is viewing the files and folders locally.

Types of DFS

The following are types of DFS:

DFS Replication   Administrators have the ability to manage replication scheduling and bandwidth throttling using the DFS management console. Replication is the process of sharing data between multiple machines. As explained earlier in the section, replicated shared folders allow you to balance the load and have fault tolerance. DFS also has read-only replication folders.

DFS Namespaces   The DFS Namespace service is the virtual tree listing in the DFS server. An administrator can set up multiple namespaces on the DFS, allowing for multiple virtual trees within DFS. DFS Namespaces was once known as Distributed File System in Windows 2000 Server and Windows Server 2003 (in case you still use Server 2003).

Now that you understand DFS and how it works, let's talk about DFS and Windows 10. Windows 10 allows you to use DFS by using the DFS client. After DFS is installed properly on the Windows Server 2012 R2 system, Windows 10 can then access the DFS namespace.

 Most Windows clients need to install the proper system updates to get the DFS drivers for client-side configurations. When deploying DFS, make sure your clients have all of their current updates.

DFS is a nice advantage for allowing users to find data, but now we are going to take a look at how your users can protect their data with data encryption. In the following section, we will discuss the benefits of using data encryption.

Managing Data Encryption with EFS

Data encryption is a way to increase data security. Encryption is the process of translating data into code that is not easily accessible to users other than the person who encrypted the data. Once data has been encrypted, you must have the correct key to decrypt the data. Unencrypted data is known as plain text, and encrypted data is known as *ciphertext*.

The *Encrypting File System* (EFS) is the Windows 10 technology that is used to store encrypted files on NTFS partitions. Encrypted files add an extra layer of security to your file system. A user with the proper key can transparently access encrypted files. A user without the proper key is denied access. If the user who encrypted the files is unavailable, you can use the data recovery agent (DRA) to provide the proper key to decrypt folders or files. The following EFS features are among those included with Windows 10:

- Automatic color-coding of encrypted files in green text so you can easily identify files that have been encrypted
- Support so that offline folders can also be encrypted
- A shell user interface (UI) that is used to support encrypted files for multiple users
- Control over who can read the encrypted files

In the following sections, you will learn how to encrypt and decrypt data, create and manage DRAs, recover encrypted files, share encrypted files, and use the Cipher utility.

Encrypting and Decrypting Folders and Files

To use EFS, a user specifies that a folder or file on an NTFS partition should be encrypted. The encryption is transparent to users. However, when other users try to access the file, they will not be able to unencrypt it—even if those users have Full Control NTFS permissions. Instead, they will receive an error message.

 Windows 10 does not allow you to have a folder or file compressed and encrypted at the same time.

In Exercise 13.12, you will use EFS to encrypt a folder. Before encrypting any data, you will create a new user.

EXERCISE 13.12

Encrypting a Folder

1. To create a new user, right-click Start ➤ Computer Management. Under System Tools, expand Local Users And Groups and right-click the Users folder. Choose New User.

2. Create a new user named **Paige** and make her password **P@ssw0rd**. Deselect the User Must Change Password At Next Logon option for this user. Click Create.

3. Close Computer Management.

4. Select the File Explorer icon on the Taskbar.

5. In Windows Explorer, find and select a folder on the C: drive. The folder you select should contain files. Right-click the folder and select Properties.

6. On the General tab of the folder's Properties dialog box, click the Advanced button.

7. In the Advanced Attributes dialog box, check the Encrypt Contents To Secure Data option. Then click OK.

8. In the Confirm Attribute Changes dialog box (if this dialog box does not appear, click the Apply button in the Properties dialog box to display it), select Apply Changes To This Folder, Subfolders And Files. Then click OK.

9. Log off as Administrator and log on as Paige.

10. Open Windows Explorer and attempt to access one of the files in the folder you encrypted. You should receive an error message stating that the file is not accessible.

11. Log off as Paige and log on as Administrator.

To decrypt folders and files, repeat the steps in Exercise 13.10, but uncheck the Encrypt Contents To Secure Data option in the Advanced Attributes dialog box.

The problem here is that the user who encrypts the data is the only one who can open the files. But the owner of the data can share the encrypted files with other users. In the next section, we will look at how to share your encrypted data with other users.

Managing EFS File Sharing

In Windows 10, it is possible to share encrypted files with other people or between multiple computers. To share encrypted files, you must have a valid EFS certificate for the user who should have access to the file. By implementing EFS file sharing, you provide an additional level of recovery in the event that the person who encrypted the files is unavailable.

Complete Exercise 13.13 to implement EFS file sharing.

EXERCISE 13.13

Implementing EFS File Sharing

1. Encrypt the file if it is not already encrypted (see Exercise 13.12 for the steps involved).

2. Through Windows Explorer, access the encrypted file's properties. At the bottom of the dialog box, click the Advanced button.

3. The Advanced Attributes dialog box appears. In the Compress Or Encrypt Attributes section of the Advanced Attributes dialog box, click the Details button, which brings up the Encryption Details dialog box.

4. In the Encryption Details dialog box, click the Add button to add any additional users who should have access to the encrypted file (provided they have a valid certificate for EFS in Active Directory or that you have imported a valid certificate onto the local computer).

5. Close the Properties box for the folder.

Recovering Encrypted Files

Someone may have encrypted files or folders and then left the company. There are a few different ways to unencrypt the data so you can continue to use the files or folders, as you'll see in the next sections.

Using the DRA

If a user who encrypted folders or files is unavailable or no longer with the company and you need to decrypt the folders or files, you can use the DRA to access the encrypted files. DRAs are implemented differently depending on the version of your operating system and the configuration of your computer:

- For Windows 10 computers that are a part of a Windows 2012 R2 Active Directory domain, the domain Administrator user account is automatically assigned the role of DRA.

- For Windows 10 computers that are installed as stand-alone computers or if the computer is a part of a workgroup, no default DRA is assigned.

You should use extreme caution when using EFS on a stand-alone Windows 10 computer. If the key used to encrypt the files is lost, there is no default recovery process, and all access to the files will be lost.

Creating a DRA on a Stand-Alone Windows 10 Computer

If Windows 10 is installed on a stand-alone computer or on a computer that is part of a workgroup, then no DRA is created by default. To manually create a DRA, you may use the Cipher command-line utility as follows:

```
Cipher/R:filename
```

The /R switch is used to generate two files, one with a .pfx filename extension and one with a .cer extension. The PFX file is used for data recovery, and the CER file includes a self-signed EFS recovery agent certificate.

The CER file (self-signed public key certificate) can then be imported into the local security policy, and the PFX file (private key) can be stored in a secure location. Cipher is explained further in the next section.

Once you have created the public and private keys to be used with EFS, you can specify the DRA through Local Security Policy, using the steps in Exercise 13.14.

EXERCISE 13.14

Using the Local Security Policy

1. Through Local Security Policy, which can be accessed through Administrative Tools or the Local Computer Policy MMC snap-in, expand Public Key Policies ➢ Encrypting File System (as shown in Figure 13.31).

FIGURE 13.31   Local Security Policy

2. Right-click Encrypting File System and select Add Data Recovery Agent.

3. The Add Recovery Agent Wizard starts. Click the Next button to continue.

4. The Select Recovery Agents screen appears (shown in Figure 13.32). Click the Browse Folders button to access the CER file you created with the `Cipher/R:`*filename* command. Select the certificate and click Next.

FIGURE 13.32   Select Recovery Agents

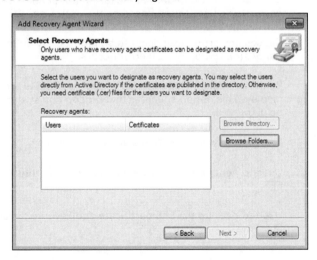

5. The Completing The Add Recovery Agent Wizard screen appears. Confirm that the settings are correct and click the Finish button.

You will see the DRA listed in the Local Security Settings dialog box, under Encrypting File System. If the DRA has the private key to the DRA certificate (that was created through Cipher/R:*filename*), the DRA can decrypt files in the same manner as the user who originally encrypted the file. Once the encrypted files are opened by a DRA, they are available as unencrypted files and can be stored as either encrypted or unencrypted files.

Using the Cipher Utility

Cipher is a command-line utility that can be used to encrypt files on NTFS volumes. The syntax for the Cipher command is as follows:

```
Cipher /[command parameter] [filename]
```

Table 13.6 lists common command parameters associated with the Cipher command.

TABLE 13.6 Cipher command parameters

Parameter	Description
/E	Specifies that files or folders should be encrypted. Any files that are subsequently added to the folder will be encrypted.
/D	Specifies that files or folders should be decrypted. Any files that are subsequently added to the folder will not be encrypted.
/S:dir	Specifies that subfolders of the target folder should also be encrypted or decrypted based on the option specified.
/I	Causes any errors that occur to be ignored. By default, the Cipher utility stops whenever an error occurs.
/H	By default, files with hidden or system attributes are omitted from display. This option specifies that hidden and system files should be displayed.
/K	Creates a new certificate file and certificate key.
/R	Used to generate a recovery agent key and certificate for use with EFS.
/X	Used to back up the EFS certificate and key into the specified filename.

Exercise 13.15 will show you how to use the Cipher utility to encrypt files. Make sure that you have encrypted a folder on the C: drive before completing these steps.

EXERCISE 13.15

Using the Cipher Utility

1. Right-click Start ➤ Command Prompt (Admin).

2. In the Command Prompt dialog box, type **C:** and press Enter to access the C: drive.

3. From the C:\> prompt, type *cipher*. You will see a list of folders and files and the state of encryption. The folder you encrypted should be indicated by an E.

4. Type **MD TEST** and press Enter to create a new folder named Test.

5. Type **cipher /e test** and press Enter. You will see a message verifying that the folder was encrypted.

In the next section, we will look at how to protect your data using Redundant Array of Independent Disks.

Understanding RAID

One concern for any computer department is the loss of data due to hard-drive failures. *Redundant Array of Independent Disks (RAID)* allows an administrator to recover data from a single hard-disk failure.

The important factor to remember about Microsoft software-based RAID is that you can recover from only a single disk failure. If multiple hard disks fail, RAID will no longer protect your system from data loss.

There are two types of RAID (called *RAID models*): hardware based and software based. Hardware RAID, which is the best option, is built into the physical hardware and must be supported by the disk controllers and hard drives. Software RAID is configured through the Windows operating system.

The downside to hardware RAID is cost. A server or computer that has hardware RAID built in can cost thousands of dollars. Software RAID is free, but remember the old saying "You get what you pay for."

In the next section, we will look at the different models of RAID and how each model operates.

RAID Levels

There are many different levels of RAID, but Microsoft Windows 10 allows for configuration of three main levels: RAID-0, RAID-1, and RAID-5. Let's take a look at each:

RAID-0 (Striped)   RAID-0 has no data recoverability, but it is used for better performance. With RAID-0 you can have a minimum of two hard disks, and these two disks work together as a single volume. Because the two disks work together, the disks both use their own read/write heads, giving you better performance.

The downside to RAID-0 is that if you lose either disk, you lose the entire striped volume. RAID-0 is good for temp files or noncritical data since RAID-0 is not recoverable in the event of a single hard-disk failure.

RAID-1 (Mirroring)   RAID-1, also known as mirroring, allows you to set up two volumes or disks that mirror each other. The advantage to mirroring is that if you lose one disk or volume, you can boot to the second disk or volume (the mirror) and recover your data. The downside to mirroring is that it is more expensive than other RAID options.

RAID-5 Volume   A RAID-5 volume, which many years ago was known as a stripe set with parity, uses a minimum of 3 disks (maximum of 32 disks) that work together as one volume. The advantage to a RAID-5 volume is that the volume uses a parity bit, which allows you to recover your data in the event of a single hard-disk failure.

When it comes to hardware RAID and software RAID, recoverability is night and day. Hardware RAID is much faster and easier when a hard disk fails. Many hardware RAID systems are hot swappable, meaning that when a disk fails, you just slide it out, insert a new disk, and RAID gets back to work.

This is not the case with software RAID. Recovering from a single hard-disk failure can take time, which in turn costs an organization money. Software RAID is set up through the Disk Management utility (explained earlier in this chapter) and is not available unless you have multiple hard disks installed in the Windows 10 machine.

Storage Spaces

Storage Spaces in Windows 10 is another way to give your Windows 10 users data redundancy. This is just another advantage of Windows 10 and that advantage is called Storage Spaces. Windows 10 administrators have the ability to group hard drives together into a storage pool. Windows 10 users can then use these storage pool capacities to turn the pools into individual storage spaces.

Storage spaces then show up in File Explorer as regular drives, but they are actually virtual drives created using the storage spaces. Users can use these drives just like any other hard drive in their system.

But when you set up the Storage Spaces, you can set them up so if you have at least two drives in the storage pool, you can create storage spaces that won't be affected by a drive failure. This gives you fault tolerance on the user's data.

Now why is this an actual advantage for Windows 10? Well, one of the biggest issues we have as administrators is our users running out of hard drive space. If we decide to use Storage Spaces and the user starts to run out of space, administrators can add more drives and increase the storage space on the user's Windows 10 system while also getting fault tolerance on the data.

To create storage spaces, you need at least one or more hard drives besides the drive on which Windows 10 is installed. One huge advantage is that these hard drives can be either internal or external hard drives, including solid-state drives. When it comes to building storage spaces, there are three main unique kinds based on your storage needs. Each one works like a version of RAID:

Simple Spaces   Simple storage spaces work the same as RAID-0 (striped volumes). Simple spaces are designed to give users increased performance but no data protection. These spaces are used best for files that don't need to be protected (temp files, music, etc.). The works great when you want better performance, and simple spaces only require at least one drive.

Mirror Spaces   Mirror storage spaces work just like RAID-1 (mirror), and they are designed to give you better performance while also giving your data protection from a single hard drive failure for a two-way mirror and a double hard drive failure from a three-way mirror.

Administrators can take mirror storage spaces even further by formatting them with the Resilient File System (ReFS). If the mirror storage space is formatted using ReFS, Windows will then automatically maintain the mirror's data integrity, making your data even further resilient to hard drive failures.

Parity Spaces   Parity storage spaces work a lot like RAID 5 volumes (stripe set with parity). To use parity spaces you are required to have at least three drives to protect you from a single hard drive failure or seven drives to protect you from a double hard drive failure.

If you want to set up storage spaces, right-click the Start button and choose Control Panel. In the upper-right corner, change the View By option from Category to Large Icons. Scroll down to Storage Spaces and double-click Storage Spaces (see Figure 13.33).

FIGURE 13.33   The Storage Spaces icon in Control Panel

After you double-click and open Storage Spaces, you would complete the following steps to create a storage pool:

1. Click the "Create a new pool and storage space" link (shown in Figure 13.34).

   FIGURE 13.34 The link to create a new pool and storage space

   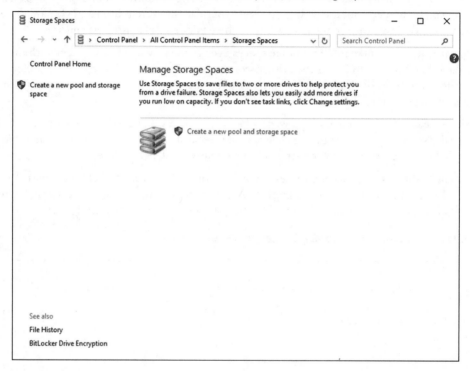

2. Select the drives you want to add to the new storage space, and then click or click Create Pool.

3. Give the drive a name and letter, and then choose a layout (Simple, Two-Way Mirror, Three-Way Mirror, or Parity).

4. Enter the maximum size the storage space can reach, and then click Create Storage Space.

Now that you have seen how you can protect your data, in the next section, we will look at how you can keep your disk volumes and partitions running at peak performance.

Using Disk-Maintenance Tools

Part of our job as IT professionals is to keep our systems running the best that they can. Most of us have seen machines running very quickly when they are new, but then they start to slow down over time, even when we do not install any new software.

Microsoft Windows 10 includes a few utilities that you can run to help keep your system running efficiently. In the next sections we will discuss three of these utilities: Disk Optimization utility, Disk Cleanup, and Check Disk.

Using the Disk Optimization Utility

Data is normally stored sequentially on the disk as space is available. Optimization naturally occurs as users create, delete, and modify files. The access of noncontiguous data is transparent to the user; however, when data is stored in this manner, the operating system must search through the disk to access all the pieces of a file. This slows down data access. Disk optimization rearranges the existing files so they are stored contiguously, which optimizes access to them. In Windows 10, you use the Disk Optimization utility to optimize and defragment your disk.

To access the Disk Optimization utility, right-click Start ➤ Computer Management. Expand Storage and select Disk Management, right-click the drive, select the Tools tab, and then click the Optimize button. The Optimize window appears (Figure 13.35); you can schedule when the disk optimizer should run or run the tool immediately.

FIGURE 13.35 The Optimize Drives window

In the next section we will look at another tool that is included with Windows 10—the Disk Cleanup utility.

Using the Disk Cleanup Utility

One concern that we as IT professionals face is how to conserve hard-disk space for our users. Hard drives continue to get larger and larger, but so do applications. This is where the Disk Cleanup utility can help.

The Disk Cleanup utility identifies areas of disk space that can be deleted to free up hard-disk space. Disk Cleanup works by identifying temporary files, Internet cache files, and unnecessary program files.

To access this utility, right-click Start ➢ Computer Management. Right-click the drive letter and choose Properties and then Disk Cleanup. The Disk Cleanup utility then runs and calculates the amount of disk space you can free up.

Complete Exercise 13.16 to run the Disk Cleanup utility on the Windows 10 operating system.

EXERCISE 13.16

Running the Disk Cleanup Utility

1. Right-click Start ➢ Computer Management.

2. Right-click the drive and choose Properties.

3. On the General tab, click the Disk Cleanup button.

    The Disk Cleanup utility will start to calculate the system data.

4. After the analysis is complete, you will see the Disk Cleanup dialog box (shown in Figure 13.36) listing files that are suggested for deletion and showing how much space will be gained by deleting those files. Click OK.

FIGURE 13.36 The Disk Cleanup dialog box

5.   When you are asked to confirm that you want to delete the files, click the Yes button. The Disk Cleanup utility deletes the files and automatically closes the Disk Cleanup dialog box.

Another issue that you may run into is bad sectors on your hard disk. Windows 10 also includes a utility to help you troubleshoot disk devices and volumes.

Using the Check Disk Utility

If you are having trouble with your disk devices or volumes, you can use the Windows 10 Check Disk utility. This utility detects bad sectors, attempts to fix errors in the file system, and scans for and attempts to recover bad sectors. To use Check Disk, you must be logged in as a member of the Administrators group.

File system errors can be caused by a corrupted file system or by hardware errors. If you have software errors, the Check Disk utility may help you find them. There is no way to fix hardware errors through software, however. If you have excessive hardware errors, you should replace your disk drive.

Complete Exercise 13.17 to run the Check Disk utility.

EXERCISE 13.17

Using the Check Disk Utility

1.   Select Start ➢ Computer Management, and then expand Storage and select Disk Management.

2.   Right-click the C: drive and choose Properties.

3.   Click the Tools tab, and then click the Check Now button.

4.   In the Check Disk dialog box (shown in Figure 13.37), you can choose one or both of the options to automatically fix file system errors and to scan for and attempt recovery of bad sectors. For this exercise, check both of the check boxes. Then click the Start button.

FIGURE 13.37   The Check Disk dialog box

Another way to run the Check Disk utility is from the command line, using the command Chkdsk. Chkdsk is used to create and display a status report, which is based on the file system you are using.

Summary

There are two different ways that you can format your hard disk in a Windows 10 operating system: FAT32 and NTFS. NTFS has many advantages over FAT32, including security, encryption, disk quotas, and compression, just to name a few.

Besides the way you format your hard disk, you can configure your hard disk as a basic disk or a dynamic disk and must choose to either leave your disk partition system as the default MBR or choose to convert it to a GPT disk. You can use the Disk Management MMC snap-in to configure your hard disks and file system.

Another configurable option within the Disk Management utility is RAID. RAID-1 and RAID-5 allow you to recover your data in the event of a single hard-disk failure. RAID-0 allows you to achieve better performance but has no data recoverability in the event of a hard-disk failure. You also have Storage Spaces, which gives your data a way to have recoverability and larger disk pools.

After the hard disks are installed and configured, there will be some maintenance items that need to be tended to. The utilities that allow you to perform these maintenance activities include the Disk Defragmenter and Check Disk utilities.

In the next chapter, we will examine how to manage data access on the Windows 10 operating system.

Video Resources

There are videos available for the following exercises:

13.1

13.2

13.4

You can access the videos at www.wiley.com/go/sybextestprep on the Other Study Tools tab.

Exam Essentials

Understand the different file format options.   There are two ways to format a hard disk in Windows 10: FAT32 and NTFS. Understand that NTFS offers many benefits over FAT32, including security, encryption, compression, and disk quotas.

Understand the different hard-disk storage types.   Windows 10 supports three types of disk storage: basic, dynamic, and GUID Partition Table (GPT). Basic storage is backward compatible with other operating systems and can be configured to support up to four partitions. Dynamic storage is supported by all Windows operating systems above Windows 2000 and allows storage to be configured as volumes. GPT storage allows you to configure volume sizes larger than 2 TB and up to 128 primary partitions.

Know Storage Spaces.   Microsoft Windows 10 includes Storage Spaces, which can help you create disks into storage pools, which can then be turned into storage spaces. Storage spaces allow you to take multiple disks and create drives with fault tolerance.

Understand Encrypted File Systems   Know that data encryption is a way to increase data security. Encryption is the process of translating data into code that is not easily accessible to users other than the person who encrypted the data.

Understand Distributed File Systems   Distributed File System (DFS) in Windows Server 2012 R2 offers a simplified way for users to access geographically dispersed files. DFS allows you to set up a tree structure of virtual directories that allow users to connect to shared folders throughout the entire network.

Know the disk-management utilities.   Microsoft Windows 10 includes a few utilities that you can run to help keep your system running efficiently. These utilities include Disk Defragmenter, Disk Cleanup, and Check Disk.

Review Questions

1. Will has installed Windows 10 on his Windows XP computer. The machine is now a dual-boot computer. He has FAT32 for Windows XP and NTFS for Windows 10. In addition, he boots his computer to Windows XP Professional for testing an application's compatibility with both operating systems. Which of the following file systems will be seen by both operating systems?

   A. Only the FAT32 partition will be seen by both operating systems.

   B. Only the NTFS partition will be seen by both operating systems.

   C. Neither the FAT32 partition nor the NTFS partition will be seen by both operating systems.

   D. Both the FAT32 partition and the NTFS partition will be seen by both operating systems.

2. You are the network administrator for a large company that has decided to use EFS. You have two Windows 10 machines, named machine1 and machine2. Both of these Windows 10 machines are part of a Windows Server 2012 R2 domain. From machine1, you can recover all EFS encrypted files for all users in the entire domain. You need to be able to do the same from machine2. How do you accomplish this task?

   A. From machine1, export the DRA certificate and import that certificate onto machine2.

   B. On a domain controller, add machine1 as the master EFS machine.

   C. From machine1, export the DRA certificate and import that certificate onto the EFS server.

   D. On a domain controller, add machine2 as the EFS recovery agent machine.

3. Alexandria is the payroll manager and stores critical files on her local drive for added security on her Windows 10 computer. She wants to ensure that she is using the disk configuration with the most fault tolerance and the highest level of consistent availability. Which of the following provisions should she use?

   A. Disk striping

   B. Spanned volumes

   C. Mirrored volumes

   D. Extended volumes

4. Paige is considering upgrading her basic disk to a dynamic disk on her Windows 10 computer. She asks you to help her understand the function of dynamic disks. Which of the following statements are true of dynamic disks in Windows 10?

   A. Dynamic disks can be recognized by older operating systems such as Windows NT 4 in addition to new operating systems such as Windows 10.

   B. Dynamic disks are supported only by Windows 2000 Server and Windows Server 2003.

   C. Dynamic disks support features such as simple partitions, extended partitions, spanned partitions, and striped partitions.

    D. Dynamic disks support features such as simple volumes, extended volumes, spanned volumes, mirrored volumes, and striped volumes.

5. Cindy is using Windows 10 on her laptop computer, and the C: partition is running out of space. You want to identify any areas of free space that can be reclaimed from temporary files. What utility should you use?

    A. Disk Cleanup

    B. Disk Manager

    C. Disk Administrator

    D. Disk Defragmenter

6. Rob is using Windows 10 to store video files. He doesn't access the files very often and wants to compress the files to utilize disk space more effectively. Which of the following options allows you to compress files in Windows 10?

    A. `JetPack.exe`

    B. `Cipher.exe`

    C. `Packer.exe`

    D. Windows Explorer

7. Crystal wants the highest level of security possible for her data. She stores the data on an NTFS partition and has applied NTFS permissions. Now she wants to encrypt the files through EFS (Encrypting File System). Which command-line utility can she use to manage data encryption?

    A. Encrypt

    B. Cipher

    C. Crypto

    D. EDS

8. You have compressed a 4 MB file into 2 MB. You are copying the file to another computer that has a FAT32 partition. How can you ensure that the file will remain compressed?

    A. When you copy the file, use the XCOPY command with the /Comp switch.

    B. When you copy the file, use the Windows Explorer utility and specify the option Keep Existing Attributes.

    C. On the destination folder, make sure that you set the option Compress Contents To Save Disk Space in the folder's properties.

    D. You can't maintain disk compression on a non-NTFS partition.

9. Julie wants to allow her assistant, Tylor, access to several files that she has encrypted with EFS. How can she allow Tylor to access the files on her computer?

    A. Julie should export and email her encryption key to Tylor.

    B. Julie should configure NTFS permissions to provide Tylor with full access to the files.

    C. Julie should import Tylor's encryption key and add Tylor's certificate to each file to which Tylor should have access.

    D. Julie should configure share permissions to provide Tylor with full access to the files over the network.

10. Will is the manager of Human Resources in your company. He is concerned that members of the Administrators group, who have implied access to all NTFS resources, will be able to easily view the contents of the sensitive personnel files. How can you apply the highest level of security to the payroll files?

   A. Apply NTFS permissions to the files.

   B. Encrypt the files with EFS.

   C. Secure the files with the Secure.exe command.

   D. Encrypt the files with HSP.

Chapter 14

Managing Data Access

MICROSOFT EXAM OBJECTIVES COVERED IN THIS CHAPTER:

✓ **Support data security.**

- This objective may include but is not limited to the following subobjectives: Identifying and resolving issues related to the following: Permissions including share, NTFS, and Dynamic Access Control (DAC); access to removable media; BitLocker and BitLocker To Go including Data Recovery Agent and Microsoft BitLocker Administration and Monitoring (MBAM).

✓ **Configure shared resources.**

- This objective may include but is not limited to the following subobjectives: Configure shared folder permissions, configure HomeGroup settings, configure libraries, configure shared printers, configure OneDrive.

✓ **Configure security for mobile devices.**

- This objective may include but is not limited to the following subobjectives: Configure BitLocker, configure startup key storage.

One of the most fundamental tasks in network management is setting up user's rights and permissions. This is by far one of the most important tasks that we as IT members face every day. Too much access and your users can cause issue. Not enough access and your users can't do their job.

One way to help make sure that your users don't have more permissions or security than they need is to use groups. Groups are used to ease network administration by grouping users together who have similar permission requirements. Groups are an important part of network management.

We will dive into user accounts and groups in Chapter 18, "Managing Identity and Authorization," but you still need to understand how NTFS and shared resources work together and how to secure the network hardware. So that's where this chapter comes into play.

In this chapter, we will also talk about users accessing resources on a network. If you think about it, that's one of the main reasons we set up networks, to share resources. If we didn't have resources that users needed access to, why even bother setting up a network? So we will talk about sharing resources and assigning permissions to those shares.

You will then learn about NTFS security and share permissions and how they work independently and together. Finally, this chapter will introduce you to some of the Windows 10 security options, including BitLocker. So let's start exploring ways to make your data more secure.

Managing File and Folder Security

Setting up proper file and folder security is one of the most important tasks that an IT professional can perform. If permissions and security are not properly configured, users will be able to access resources that they shouldn't. File and folder security defines what access a user has to local resources. You can limit access by applying security for files and folders. You should know what NTFS security permissions are and how they are applied.

A powerful feature of networking is the ability to allow network access to local folders. In Windows 10, it is very easy to share folders. You can also apply security to shared folders in a manner that is similar to applying NTFS permissions. Once you share a folder, users with appropriate access rights can access the folders through a variety of methods.

When a user is created on a local Windows 10 system or if the user is created on an Active Directory domain, the user gets a Security Identification (SID) number. It is important to remember that when you assign rights to a user, those rights and permissions get associated to the user's SID number and not the username. It's because of this that we can rename user accounts without any issues.

Before diving into the security nitty-gritty, you need to know about the folder options. So let's start with that discussion.

Folder Options

The Windows 10 Folder Options dialog box allows you to configure many properties associated with files and folders, such as what you see when you access folders and how Windows searches through files and folders. To open the Folder Options dialog box, right-click Start ➢ File Explorer and then select View and then Option. You can also access Folder Options by choosing Control Panel ➢ *Large Icons View* ➢ File Explorer Options. The Folder Options dialog box has three tabs: General, View, and Search. The options on each of these tabs are described in the following sections.

Folder General Options

The General tab, shown in Figure 14.1, includes the following options:

- Whether folders are opened all in the same window when a user is browsing folders or each folder is opened in a separate window

- Whether a user opens items with a single mouse click or a double-click

- Whether to have the navigation pane show all folders and automatically expand to the current folder

FIGURE 14.1   The General tab of the Folder Options dialog box

Folder View Options

The View tab of the Folder Options dialog box, shown in Figure 14.2, is used to configure what users see when they open files and folders. For example, you can change the default setting so that hidden files and folders are displayed. Table 14.1 describes the View tab options.

FIGURE 14.2   The View tab of the Folder Options dialog box

TABLE 14.1   Folder view options

Option	Description	Default
Always Show Icons, Never Thumbnails	Shows icons for files instead of thumbnail previews.	Not selected
Always Show Menus	Shows the File, Edit, View, Tools, and Help menus when you're browsing for files.	Not selected
Display File Icon On Thumbnails	Displays the file icon on thumbnails.	Selected

Option	Description	Default
Display File Size Information In Folder Tips	Specifies whether the file size is automatically displayed when you hover your mouse over a folder.	Selected
Display The Full Path In The Title Bar (Classic Theme Only)	Specifies whether the title bar shows an abbreviated path of your location. Selecting this option displays the full path, such as C:\Word Documents\ Sybex\Windows 10 Book\Chapter 19, as opposed to showing an abbreviated path, such as Chapter 19.	Not selected
Hidden Files And Folders	Specifies whether files and folders with the Hidden attribute are listed. Choosing Show Hidden Files, Folders, Or Drives displays these items.	Don't Show Hidden Files, Folders, And Drives
Hide Empty Drives	Prevents drives that are empty in the Computer folder from being displayed.	Selected
Hide Extensions For Known File Types	By default, filename extensions, which identify known file types (such as .doc for Word files and .xls for Excel files), are not shown. Disabling this option displays all filename extensions.	Selected
Hide Protected Operating System Files (Recommended)	By default, operating system files are not shown, which protects operating system files from being modified or deleted by a user. Deselecting this option displays the operating system files.	Selected
Launch Folder Windows In A Separate Process	By default, when you open a folder, it shares memory with the previous folders that were opened. Selecting this option opens folders in separate parts of memory, which increases the stability of Windows 10 but can slightly decrease the performance of the computer.	Not selected
Show Drive Letters	Specifies whether drive letters are shown in the Computer folder. When this option is disabled, only the name of the disk or device will be shown.	Selected

TABLE 14.1   Folder view options *(continued)*

Option	Description	Default
Show Encrypted Or Compressed NTFS Files In Color	Displays encrypted or compressed files in an alternate color when they are displayed in a folder window.	Selected
Show Pop-Up Description For Folder And Desktop Items	Displays whether a pop-up tooltip is displayed when you hover your mouse over files and folders.	Selected
Show Preview Handlers In Preview Pane	Shows the contents of files in the preview pane.	Selected
Use Check Boxes To Select Items	Adds a check box next to each file and folder so that one or more of them may be selected. Actions can then be performed on selected items.	Not selected
Use Sharing Wizard (Recommended)	Allows you to share a folder using a simplified sharing method.	Selected
When Typing Into List View	Selects whether text is automatically typed into the search box or whether the typed item is selected in the view.	Select The Typed Item In The View

Search Options

The Search tab of the Folder Options dialog box, shown in Figure 14.3, is used to configure how Windows 10 searches for files. You can choose for Windows 10 to search by filename only, by filenames and contents, or by a combination of the two, depending on whether indexing is enabled. You can also select from the following options:

- Include subfolders
- Find partial matches
- Use natural language searches
- Don't use the index when searching in file folders for system files
- Include system directories in non-indexed locations
- Include compressed files in non-indexed locations

FIGURE 14.3   The Search tab of the Folder Options dialog box

To search for files and folders, click Start ➢ Search and type your query in the search box.

Understanding Dynamic Access Control

One of the advantages of Windows Server 2012 R2 and Windows 10 is the ability to apply data governance to your file server. This will help control who has access to information and auditing. You get these advantages through the use of Dynamic Access Control (DAC). DAC allows you to identify data by using data classifications (both automatic and manual) and then control access to these files based on these classifications.

DAC also gives administrators the ability to control file access by using a central access policy. This central access policy will also allow an administrator to set up audit access to files for reporting and forensic investigation.

DAC allows an administrator to set up Active Directory Rights Management Service (AD RMS) encryption for Microsoft Office documents. For example, you can set up encryption for any documents that contain financial information.

DAC gives an administrator the flexibility to configure file access and auditing to domain-based file servers. To do this, DAC controls claims in the authentication token, resource properties, and conditional expressions within permission and auditing entries.

Administrators have the ability to give users access to files and folders based on Active Directory attributes. For example, a user named Dana is given access to the file server share because in the user's Active Directory (department attribute) properties, the value contains the value Sales.

Securing Access to Files and Folders

On NTFS partitions, you can specify the access each user has to specific folders or files on the partition based on the user's logon name and group associations. Access control consists of rights (which pertain to operations on the system) and permissions (which pertain to operations on specific objects). The owner of an object or any user who has the necessary rights to modify permissions can apply permissions to NTFS objects. If permissions are not explicitly granted within NTFS, then they are implicitly denied. Permissions can also be explicitly denied; explicit denials override explicitly granted permissions.

The following sections describe design goals for access control as well as how to apply NTFS permissions and some techniques for optimizing local access.

Considering Design Goals for Access Control

Before you start applying NTFS permissions to resources, you should develop design goals for access control as a part of your overall security strategy. Basic security strategy suggests that you provide each user and group with the minimum level of permissions needed for job functionality. The following list includes some of the considerations for planning access control:

- Defining the resources that are included within your network—in this case, the files and folders residing on the file system

- Defining which resources will put your organization at risk, including defining the resources and defining the risk of damage if the resource is compromised

- Developing security strategies that address possible threats and minimize security risks

- Defining groups that security can be applied to based on users within the group membership who have common access requirements, and applying permissions to groups as opposed to users

- Applying additional security settings through Group Policy if your Windows 10 clients are part of an Active Directory network

- Using additional security features, such as Encrypted File System (EFS), to provide additional levels of security or file auditing to track access to critical files and folders

After you have decided what your design goals are, you can start applying your NTFS permissions.

Applying NTFS Permissions

NTFS permissions control access to NTFS files and folders. Ultimately, the person who owns an object has complete control over the object. The owner or administrator can configure access by allowing or denying NTFS permissions to users and groups.

Normally, NTFS permissions are cumulative, based on group memberships. The user gets the highest level of security from all the different groups they belong to. However, if the user had been denied access through user or group membership, those deny permissions override the allowed permissions. Windows 10 offers seven levels of NTFS permissions, plus special permissions:

Full Control   This permission allows the following rights:

- Traverse folders and execute files (programs) in the folders. The ability to traverse folders allows you to access files and folders in lower subdirectories, even if you do not have permissions to access specific portions of the directory path.
- List the contents of a folder and read the data in a folder's files.
- See a folder's or file's attributes.
- Change a folder's or file's attributes.
- Create new files and write data to the files.
- Create new folders and append data to the files.
- Delete subfolders and files.
- Delete files.
- Compress files.
- Change permissions for files and folders.
- Take ownership of files and folders.

If you select the Full Control permission, all permissions will be checked by default and can't be unchecked.

Any user with Full Control access can manage the security of a folder. However, to access folders, a user must have physical access to the computer as well as a valid logon name and password. By default, regular users can't access folders over the network unless the folders have been shared. Sharing folders is covered in the section "Creating and Managing Shared Folders," later in this chapter.

Modify   This permission allows the following rights:

- Traverse folders and execute files in the folders.
- List the contents of a folder and read the data in a folder's files.
- See a file's or folder's attributes.
- Change a file's or folder's attributes.
- Create new files and write data to the files.
- Create new folders and append data to the files.
- Delete files.

If you select the Modify permission, the Read & Execute, List Folder Contents, Read, and Write permissions will be checked by default and can't be unchecked.

Read & Execute   This permission allows the following rights:

- Traverse folders and execute files in the folders.
- List the contents of a folder and read the data in a folder's files.
- See a file's or folder's attributes.

If you select the Read & Execute permission, the List Folder Contents and Read permissions will be checked by default and can't be unchecked.

List Folder Contents   This permission allows the following rights:

- Traverse folders.
- List the contents of a folder.
- See a file's or folder's attributes.

Read   This permission allows the following rights:

- List the contents of a folder and read the data in a folder's files.
- See a file's or folder's attributes.
- View ownership.

Write   This permission allows the following rights:

- Overwrite a file.
- View file ownership and permissions.
- Change a file's or folder's attributes.
- Create new files and write data to the files.
- Create new folders and append data to the files.

Special Permissions   This allows you to configure any permissions beyond the normal permissions, such as auditing, and to take ownership. To apply NTFS permissions, right-click the file or folder to which you want to control access, select Properties from the context menu, and then select the Security tab. The Security tab lists the users and groups who have been assigned permissions to the file or folder. When you click a user or group in the top half of the dialog box, you see the permissions that have been allowed or denied for that user or group in the bottom half (see Figure 14.4).

FIGURE 14.4   The object's Security tab

Exercise 14.1 walks you through assigning NTFS permissions.

Managing NTFS Permissions

1. Right-click the file or folder to which you want to control access, select Properties from the context menu, and click the Security tab.

2. Click the Edit button to modify permissions.

3. Click the Add button to open the Select Users Or Groups dialog box. You can select users from the computer's local database or from the domain you are in (or trusted domains) by typing in the user or group name in the Enter The Object Names To Select portion of the dialog box and clicking OK.

    Through the Advanced button of the Security tab, you can configure more granular NTFS permissions, such as Traverse Folder and Read Attributes permissions.

4. You return to the Security tab of the folder Properties dialog box. Highlight a user or group in the top list box, and in the Permissions list, specify the NTFS permissions to be allowed or denied. When you have finished, click OK. To remove the NTFS permissions for a user, computer, or group, highlight that entity in the Security tab and click the Remove button. Be careful when you remove NTFS permissions. You won't be asked to confirm their removal as you are when deleting most other types of items in Windows 10.

Controlling Permission Inheritance

Normally, the directory structure is organized in a hierarchical manner. This means you are likely to have subfolders in the folders to which you apply permissions. In Windows 10, by default, the parent folder's permissions are applied to any files or subfolders in that folder as well as any subsequently created objects. These are called *inherited permissions*.

You can specify how permissions are inherited by subfolders and files by clicking the Advanced button on the Security tab of a folder's Properties dialog box. This calls up the Permissions tab of the Advanced Security Settings dialog box. To edit these options, click the Change Permissions button. You can edit the following options:

- Include Inheritable Permissions From This Object's Parent

- Replace All Existing Inheritable Permissions On All Descendants With Inheritable Permissions From This Object

If an Allow or Deny item in the Permissions list on the Security tab has a shaded check mark, this indicates that the permission was inherited from an upper-level folder. If a check mark is not shaded, it means the permission was applied at the selected folder. This is known as an explicitly assigned permission. Knowing which permissions are inherited and which are explicitly assigned is useful when you need to troubleshoot permissions.

Understanding Ownership and Security Descriptors

When an object is initially created on an NTFS partition, an associated security descriptor is created. A security descriptor contains the following information:

- The user or group who owns the object
- The users and groups who are allowed or denied access to the object
- The users and groups whose access to the object will be audited

After an object is created, the owner of the object has full permissions to change the information in the security descriptor, even for members of the Administrators group. You can view the owner of an object from the Security tab of the specified folder's Properties by clicking the Advanced button. Then click the Owner tab to see who the owner of the object is. From this dialog box, you can change the owner of the object.

Although the owner of an object can set its permissions so that the administrator can't access it, the administrator or any member of the Administrators group can take ownership of an object and thus manage the object's permissions. When you take ownership of an object, you can specify whether you want to replace the owner on subdirectories and subobjects of the object. If you would like to see who owns a directory, from the command prompt, type **dir /q**.

Determining and Viewing Effective Permissions for NTFS

To determine a user's effective permissions (the aggregate permissions the user has to a file or folder), add all of the permissions that have been allowed through the user's assignments based on that user's username and group associations. After you determine what the user is allowed, you subtract any permissions that have been denied the user through the username or group associations.

As an example, suppose user Marilyn is a member of both the Accounting and Execs groups. The following assignments have been made to the Accounting group permissions:

Permission	Allow	Deny
Full Control		
Modify	X	
Read & Execute	X	
List Folder Contents		
Read		
Write		

The following assignments have been made to the Execs group permissions:

Permission	Allow	Deny
Full Control		
Modify		
Read & Execute		
List Folder Contents		
Read	X	
Write		

To determine Marilyn's effective rights, you combine the permissions that have been assigned. The result is that Marilyn's effective rights are Modify, Read & Execute, and Read, so she effectively has Modify (the highest right).

As another example, suppose that user Dan is a member of both the Sales and Temps groups. The following assignments have been made to the Sales group permissions:

Permission	Allow	Deny
Full Control		
Modify	X	
Read & Execute	X	
List Folder Contents	X	
Read	X	
Write	X	

The following assignments have been made to the Temps group permissions:

Permission	Allow	Deny
Full Control		
Modify		X
Read & Execute		
List Folder Contents		
Read		
Write		X

To determine Dan's effective rights, you start by seeing what Dan has been allowed: Modify, Read & Execute, List Folder Contents, Read, and Write permissions. You then remove anything that he is denied: Modify and Write permissions. In this case, Dan's effective rights are Read & Execute, List Folder Contents, and Read.

If permissions have been applied at the user and group levels and inheritance is involved, it can sometimes be confusing to determine what the effective permissions are. To help identify which effective permissions will actually be applied, you can view them from the Effective Permissions tab of Advanced Security Settings, or you can use the ICACLS command-line utility.

To see what the effective permissions are for a user or group, you click the Select button and then type in the user or group name. Then click OK. If a box is checked and not shaded, then explicit permissions have been applied at that level. If the box is shaded, then the permissions to that object were inherited.

The ICACLS command-line utility can also be used to display or modify user access permissions. The options associated with the ICACLS command are as follows:

- /grant grants permissions.

- /remove revokes permissions.

- /deny denies permissions.

- /setintegritylevel sets an integrity level of Low, Medium, or High.

One issue that IT people run into is what happens to the security when you move or copy a file or folder. Let's take a look at NTFS permissions when they are moved or copied.

Determining NTFS Permissions for Copied or Moved Files

When you copy or move NTFS files, the permissions that have been set for those files might change. Use the following guidelines to predict what will happen:

- If you move a file from one folder to another folder on the same volume, the file will retain the original NTFS permissions.

- If you move a file from one folder to another folder between different NTFS volumes, the file is treated as a copy and will have the same permissions as the destination folder.

- If you copy a file from one folder to another folder on the same volume or on a different volume, the file will have the same permissions as the destination folder.

- If you copy or move a file or folder to a FAT partition, it will not retain any NTFS permissions.

User's permissions and rights are automatically assigned to the user's Security ID (SID) number and not the username. Because of this, you can rename user accounts. By renaming an account, you can give someone all the rights and permissions that someone else had who left the company. This is also why you can change someone's name if needed without changing their rights.

Managing Network Access

In every network, there are resources to which the users need to gain access. As IT professionals, we share these resources so that our users can do their jobs.

Sharing is the process of allowing network users access to a resource located on a computer. A network share provides a single location to manage shared data used by many users. Sharing also allows an administrator to install an application once, as opposed to installing it locally at each computer, and to manage the application from a single location.

The following sections describe how to create and manage shared folders and configure share permissions.

Creating and Managing Shared Folders

You can share a folder in two ways. To use the Sharing Wizard, right-click a folder and select Share. If the Sharing Wizard feature is enabled, you will see the File Sharing screen, where you can add local users. Alternatively, you can access the wizard by right-clicking a folder and then selecting Properties ➤ Sharing tab ➤ Share button.

However, you cannot use the Sharing Wizard to share resources with domain users. To share a folder with domain users, right-click the folder and select Properties, and then select the Sharing tab, shown in Figure 14.5.

FIGURE 14.5   The Sharing tab of a folder's Properties dialog box

The Share button will take you to the Sharing Wizard. To configure Advanced Sharing, click the Advanced Sharing button, which will open the Advanced Sharing dialog box.

When you share a folder, you can configure the options listed in Table 14.2.

TABLE 14.2 Shared folder options

Option	Description
Share This Folder	Makes the folder available through local access and network access
Share Name	A descriptive name by which users will access the folder
Comments	Additional descriptive information about the share (optional)
Limit The Number Of Simultaneous Users To	The maximum number of connections to the share at any one time (no more than 10 users can simultaneously access a share on a Windows 10 computer)
Permissions	How users will access the folder over the network
Caching	How folders are cached when the folder is offline

If you share a folder and then decide that you do not want to share it, just deselect the Share This Folder check box. You can easily tell that a folder has been shared by the group icon located at the bottom left of the folder icon.

Keep in mind the following guidelines regarding sharing:

- Only folders, not files, can be shared.
- Share permissions can be applied only to folders and not to files.
- If a folder is shared over the network and a user is accessing it locally, then share permissions will not apply to the local user; only NTFS permissions will apply.
- If a shared folder is copied, the original folder will still be shared but not the copy.
- If a shared folder is moved, the folder will no longer be shared.
- If the shared folder will be accessed by a mixed environment of clients, including some that do not support long filenames, you should use the 8.3 naming format for files.
- Folders can be shared through the Net Share command-line utility.

Now let's take a look at configuring share permissions for your users.

Configuring Share Permissions

You can control users' access to shared folders from the network by assigning share permissions. Share permissions are less complex than NTFS permissions and can be applied only to folders (unlike NTFS permissions, which can be applied to files and folders).

To assign share permissions, click the Permissions button in the Advanced Sharing dialog box. This brings up the Share Permissions dialog box, shown in Figure 14.6.

FIGURE 14.6 The Share Permissions dialog box

You can assign three types of share permissions:

Full Control Allows full access to the shared folder.

Change Allows users to change data within a file or to delete files.

Read Allows a user to view and execute files in the shared folder. Read is the default permission on shared folders for the Everyone group.

Shared folders do not use the same concept of inheritance as NTFS folders. If you share a folder, there is no way to block access to lower-level resources through share permissions. One thing that is the same between shared and NTFS is that all shared permissions are additive if you belong to multiple groups. This means that you add up all the permissions of the groups and get the highest permission.

When applying conflicting share and NTFS permissions, the most restrictive permissions win. Remember that share and NTFS permissions are both applied only when a user is accessing a shared resource over a network. Only NTFS permissions apply to a user accessing a resource locally. So, for example, if a user's NTFS security setting on a resource is

Read and the share permission on the same resource is Full Control, the user would have only Read permission when they connect to the shared resource. The most restrictive set of permissions wins.

Configuring OneDrive

Windows 10 includes Microsoft OneDrive with the operating system. Microsoft OneDrive is a cloud-based storage system where corporate users or home users can store their data in the cloud. Microsoft OneDrive allows users to use up to 15 GB of cloud storage for free without a subscription. Users have the ability to get more cloud-based storage by purchasing a higher subscription.

To set up a corporate user or home user with Microsoft OneDrive, you must first have a Microsoft account. You can create a Microsoft account at the time you are accessing OneDrive, as shown in Figure 14.7.

FIGURE 14.7   Microsoft OneDrive sign-in screen

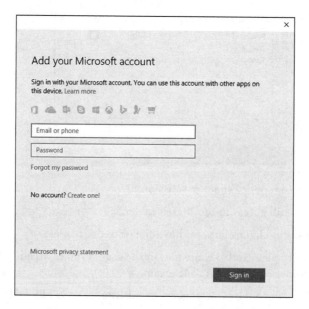

Once you have a Microsoft account, you then sign into the Microsoft OneDrive system where you can begin uploading data. Figure 14.8 shows Microsoft OneDrive from the Internet browser. Using the Internet browser, you can control the files that are located in the cloud.

FIGURE 14.8   Microsoft OneDrive

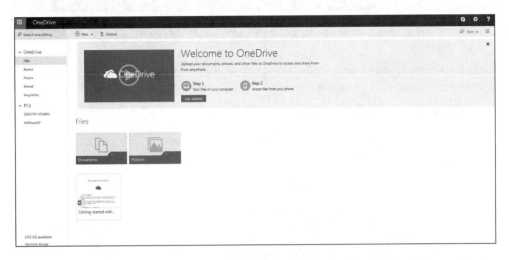

In Exercise 14.2, I will show you how to sign into your Microsoft OneDrive application.

EXERCISE 14.2

Logging into OneDrive

1. Click the Start button ➤ All Apps ➤ OneDrive, as shown in Figure 14.9.

    FIGURE 14.9   OneDrive menu option

    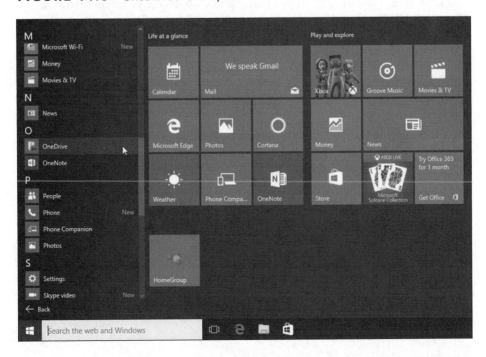

2. A screen will appear asking you to log on with Personal Microsoft account. Click the Sign In button.

3. On the Add Your Microsoft Account screen, type in your Microsoft account name and password to log in, as shown in Figure 14.10.

FIGURE 14.10 OneDrive login

4. Another screen will appear stating that this is your OneDrive folder (shown in Figure 14.11). Click Next.

FIGURE 14.11 This is your OneDrive folder screen.

5. The next screen will allow you to sync files with OneDrive. Choose which folders you want to sync and click Next, as shown in Figure 14.12.

FIGURE 14.12   Sync files screen

6. The next screen will tell you that you can start using OneDrive. Click the Open My OneDrive Folder button.

At this point you can start using OneDrive to create and upload files to the OneDrive cloud. In the left corner, next to the Home tab, you will see three lines. If you click those three lines, some options will appear. The bottom option allows you to change the OneDrive settings.

Inside those settings, you have the ability to change how often the system will sync with the cloud, which accounts will be associated to this OneDrive, and many other settings. The OneDrive cloud-based storage is a good way to back up some documents for protection of data loss.

When Windows 7 was released, Microsoft created an easy way for users to set up networks at home even if they don't know much about networking. In the next section, we will look at using Windows 10 HomeGroups.

Joining and Sharing HomeGroups in Windows 10

HomeGroup is a functionality of Windows 10 that simplifies the sharing of music, pictures, and documents within your small office or home network of Windows 10 PCs. HomeGroup allows you to share USB-connected printers too. If you have a printer installed on a Windows 10 computer and it's shared by HomeGroup, it is automatically installed onto the other HomeGroup-enabled Windows 10 PCs. Domain-joined computers cannot host a HomeGroup, but they can be a participant of a HomeGroup. All editions of Windows 10 can use HomeGroups, but only Home, Enterprise, or Professional edition can create a HomeGroup.

The first step in the process of using HomeGroup for sharing is to create a new HomeGroup or join an existing one. If the Windows 10 network-discovery feature does not find a HomeGroup, you will be asked to create a HomeGroup. In the Network and Sharing Center, select Choose HomeGroup and then click the Create A HomeGroup button (Figure 14.13).

FIGURE 14.13   Create a HomeGroup.

With Windows 10 network discovery turned on (the default), a HomeGroup is created automatically. You still need to join the HomeGroup to use the other shared resources and to share yours. From the Network and Sharing Center, you can join an existing HomeGroup by clicking the Join Now button, as shown in Figure 14.14.

Part of joining a HomeGroup setup is defining the libraries that you want to make available to the other members of the HomeGroup. The HomeGroup libraries are the folders (Pictures, Music, Videos, Documents, and Printers) that you want to share. So you can choose which HomeGroup libraries that you want to share or not share. The next screen in the setup (Figure 14.15) lets you choose which resources you want to share.

FIGURE 14.14   Join an existing HomeGroup.

FIGURE 14.15   HomeGroup sharing selections

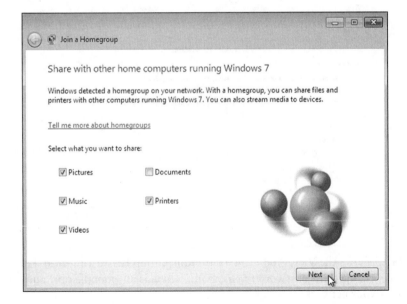

The next step is to enter the HomeGroup password. Windows 10, by default, will recognize a HomeGroup on the network. However, the other Windows 10 machines will not have access to the resources. Allowing any Windows 10 machine connecting to the network to automatically have shared resource access would be a huge security hole. To protect the Windows 10 user resources, a password must be entered to join a HomeGroup.

The password for the HomeGroup can be viewed or changed on the machine that established the HomeGroup. After other machines have joined, each machine has the ability to view or change the password. The initial machine in the HomeGroup will create a random secure password. To view and/or print the HomeGroup password, use the Choose HomeGroup And Sharing Options selection from the Network and Sharing Center, and then choose View Or Print The HomeGroup Password item, shown in Figure 14.16. Again, this can be done from any Windows 10 machine that is already a member of the HomeGroup but not from one that wants to join.

FIGURE 14.16 Change HomeGroup Settings screen

Figure 14.17 shows the View And Print Your HomeGroup Password screen. For simplicity here, I have changed the password to *password*, which is an example only and not recommended for your network.

FIGURE 14.17   View And Print Your HomeGroup Password screen

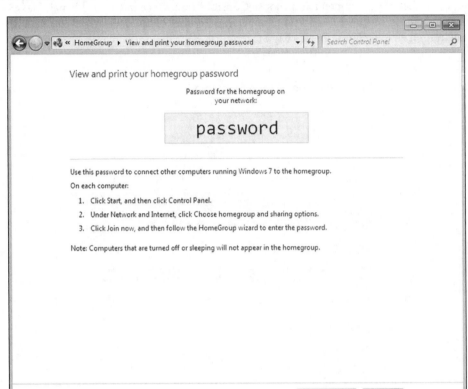

Remember that Windows 10 will initially create a random secure password for the HomeGroup, and you need to visit the View And Print Your HomeGroup Password screen to find out what it is. You will probably want to change it. To change the password, choose the Change The Password option from the Change HomeGroup Settings page and then select Change The Password from the Change Your HomeGroup Password screen, as shown in Figure 14.18. When you change the HomeGroup password, you need to go to each of the other Windows 10 machines that are members of the HomeGroup and change the password there if you still want the others to share resources.

After the HomeGroup is set up, you can see the other members' resources from the HomeGroup option of Windows Explorer or even the Start menu if you customize the Start menu and have added HomeGroup to the displayed options. I have added the HomeGroup option to my Start menu, as shown in Figure 14.19. To add the HomeGroup to the Start menu, right-click the Start menu and choose Control Panel. Once in Control Panel, make sure the view is set to Large Icons (in the upper-right corner of the window). Right-click the HomeGroup icon and choose Pin To My Start.

FIGURE 14.18   Change the HomeGroup password.

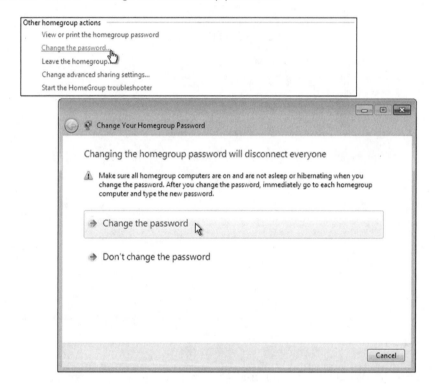

HomeGroups are a great option for users who want to share resources in the Windows 10 environment. But what if you still have non–Windows 10 machines? The legacy function of simply sharing resources and setting permissions still works for Windows 10 and will allow older operating systems to have access to resources shared on Windows 10 machines as well as allow users running Windows 10 to have access to the shared resources on older Windows operating systems.

In the following sections, I will show you how to start protecting your hardware from data loss or theft by securing your hardware.

FIGURE 14.19   HomeGroup in the Start menu

Understanding Hardware Security

One issue that IT members have to face is the protection of not only our data but also the hardware that the data resides on. (You may remember a case a few years back when an individual stole some hard drives from a VA office.) Let's take a look at a security measure that will help you protect your data drives from physically being taken.

We must make sure that if anyone steals hardware from our corporation or from our server rooms that the data that they are stealing is secured and can't be used. This is where BitLocker can help.

Using BitLocker Drive Encryption

To prevent individuals from stealing your computer and viewing personal and sensitive data found on your hard disk, some editions of Windows come with a new feature called *BitLocker Drive Encryption*. BitLocker encrypts the entire system drive.

BitLocker allows you to configure security for mobile devices by locking the physical drives. If someone steals a hard drive or external drive that has BitLocker on the drive, that drive will not function properly on another computer system.

When you use BitLocker, new files added to the BitLocker drive are encrypted automatically, and files moved from this drive to another drive or computers are decrypted automatically.

Only Windows 10 Enterprise, Professional, and Education, Windows 8 Pro and Enterprise, Windows 7 Pro and Enterprise, Windows Server 2008 and 2008 R2, and Windows Server 2012 and 2012 R2 include BitLocker Drive Encryption, and only the operating system drive (usually C:) or internal hard drives can be encrypted with BitLocker. Files on other types of drives must be encrypted using BitLocker To Go. BitLocker To Go allows you to put BitLocker on removable media such as external hard disks or USB drives.

BitLocker uses a Trusted Platform Module (TPM) version 1.2 or higher to store the security startup key. A TPM is a chip that is found in newer computers. If you do not have a computer with a TPM, you can store the startup key on a removable USB drive. If you don't have a system with TPM, you will need to turn off the TPM setting in the local computer settings as shown in Figure 14.20. The USB drive will be required each time you start the computer so that the system drive can be decrypted.

FIGURE 14.20   Changing the TPM settings

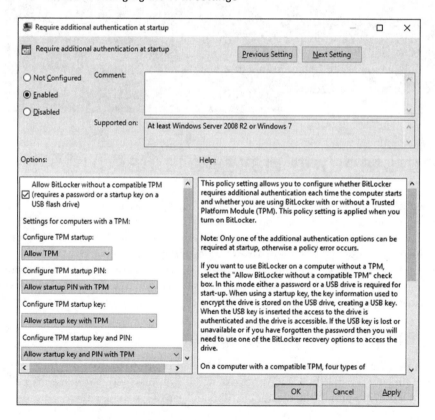

If the TPM discovers a potential security risk, such as a disk error or changes made to BIOS, hardware, system files, or startup components, the system drive will not be unlocked until you enter the 48-digit BitLocker recovery password or use a USB drive with a recovery key as a recovery agent.

BitLocker must be set up either within the Local Group Policy editor or through the BitLocker icon in Control Panel. One advantage of using BitLocker is that you can prevent any unencrypted data from being copied onto a removable disk, thus protecting the computer.

BitLocker Recovery Password

The BitLocker recovery password is very important. Do not lose it or you may not be able to unlock the drive. Even if you do not have a TPM, be sure to keep your recovery password in case your USB drive becomes lost or corrupted.

BitLocker requires that you have a hard disk with at least two partitions, both formatted with NTFS. One partition will be the system partition that will be encrypted. The other partition will be the active partition that is used to start the computer. This partition will remain unencrypted.

Features of BitLocker

As with any version of Windows, Microsoft continues to improve on technologies for Windows Server 2012 R2 and Windows 10. The following sections cover some of the features of BitLocker.

BitLocker Provisioning

In previous versions of BitLocker (Windows 7), the BitLocker provisioning (system and data volumes) was completed during the post-installation of the BitLocker utility. The BitLocker provisioning was done either through the command-line interface (CLI) or Control Panel. In the Windows 8, Windows 10, and Windows Server 2012 R2 version of BitLocker, an administrator can choose to provision BitLocker before the operating system is even installed.

Administrators have the ability to enable BitLocker, prior to the operating system deployment, from the Windows Preinstallation Environment (WinPE). BitLocker is applied to the formatted volume, and BitLocker encrypts the volume prior to running the Windows setup process.

If an administrator wants to check the status of BitLocker on a particular volume, the administrator can view the status of the drive in either the BitLocker Control Panel applet or Windows Explorer.

Encrypting Used Disk Space Only

Windows 10 BitLocker has a requirement that all data and free space on the drive has to be encrypted. Because of this, the encryption process can take a very long time on larger volumes. In Windows 10 BitLocker, administrators have the ability to encrypt either the entire volume or just the space being used. When you choose to encrypt the Used Disk Space Only option, only the section of the drive that has data will be encrypted. Because of this, encryption is completed much faster.

Standard User PIN and Password Change

One issue that BitLocker has had is that you need to be a local administrator to configure BitLocker on operating system drives. This can be an issue in a large organization due to the fact deploying the Trusted Platform Module (TPM) + PIN to a large number of computers can be very challenging.

Even with the new operating system changes, administrative privileges are still needed to configure BitLocker, but now your users have the ability to change the BitLocker PIN for the operating system or change the password on the data volumes.

When a user gets to choose their own PIN and password, they normally choose something that has meaning and something easy for them to remember. That is a good thing and a bad thing. It's good because when your users choose their own PIN and password, normally they don't need to write it down—they just know it. It's bad because if anyone knows the user well, they can have an easier time figuring out the person's PIN and password. Even when you allow your users to choose their own PIN and password, make sure you set a GPO to require password complexity.

Network Unlock

One of the new features of BitLocker is called Network Unlock. *Network Unlock* allows administrators to easily manage desktop and servers that are configured to use BitLocker. Network Unlock allows an administrator to configure BitLocker to unlock automatically an encrypted hard drive during a system reboot when that hard drive is connected to their trusted corporate environment. For this to function properly on a system, there has to be a DHCP driver implementation in that system's firmware.

If your operating system volume is also protected by the TPM + PIN protection, the administrator has to be sure to enter the PIN at the time of the reboot. This protection can actually make using Network Unlock more difficult to use, but they can be used in combination.

Support for Encrypted Hard Drives for Windows

One of the new advantages of using BitLocker is *Full Volume Encryption (FVE)*. BitLocker provides built-in encryption for Windows data files and Windows operating system files. The advantage of this type of encryption is that encrypted hard drives that use *Full Disk Encryption (FDE)* get each block of the physical disk space encrypted. Because each physical block gets encrypted, it offers much better encryption. The only downside to this is because each physical block is encrypted, it adds some degradation to the hard drive speed. So, as an administrator, you have to decide if you want better speeds or better security on your hard disk.

Windows 7 and 2008 R2 vs. Windows 10 and 2012 R2

When reading a book on a new operating system, the first question most of us have is what's the difference between Windows 7 and Windows 2008 R2 versus Windows 10 and Windows Server 2012 R2. Table 14.3 shows you many of the common features and how they worked then and now.

TABLE 14.3   BitLocker then and now

Feature	Windows 7/Server 2008 R2	Windows 10/Server 2012 R2
Reset the BitLocker PIN or password	The user's privileges must be set to an administrator if you want to reset the BitLocker PIN on an operating system drive and the password on a fixed or removable data drive.	Standard users now have the ability to reset the BitLocker PIN and password on operating system drives, fixed data drives, and removable data drives.
Disk encryption	When BitLocker is enabled, the entire disk is encrypted.	When BitLocker is enabled, users have the ability to choose whether to encrypt the entire disk or only the used space on the disk.
Hardware Encrypted Drive support	Not supported.	If the Windows logo hard drive comes pre-encrypted from the manufacturer, BitLocker is supported.
Unlocking using a network-based key to provide dual-factor authentication	Not available.	If a computer is rebooted on a trusted corporate wired network, the key protector then allows a key to unlock and skip the PIN entry.
Protection for clusters	Not available.	Windows Server 2012 R2 BitLocker includes the ability to support cluster shared volumes and failover clusters as long as they are running in a domain that was established by a Windows Server 2012 R2 domain controller with the Kerberos Key Distribution Center Service enabled.

TABLE 14.3 BitLocker then and now *(continued)*

Feature	Windows 7/Server 2008 R2	Windows 10/Server 2012 R2
Linking a BitLocker key protector to an Active Directory account	Not available.	BitLocker allows a user, group, or computer account in Active Directory to be tied to a key protector. This key protector allows a protected data volumes to be unlocked.

In Exercise 14.3, you will enable BitLocker on the Windows 10 system.

EXERCISE 14.3

Using BitLocker in Windows 10

1. Right-click the Start button and choose Control Panel.

2. Change the View By: Category to Large Icons by using the pull-down menu.

3. Choose the BitLocker Drive Encryption icon, as shown in Figure 14.21.

FIGURE 14.21 Choosing the BitLocker icon

4. Click the link that says "Turn on BitLocker."

5. On the Choose How To Unlock The Drive screen, click the "Enter a password" link.

6. Enter a password, reenter the password, and click the Next button.

7. Pick one of the options on the How Do You Want To Save The Recovery Key screen, and then click Next.

8. On the Choose How Much You Want To Encrypt screen, choose to encrypt used disk space or the entire drive. I am choosing the entire drive.

9. On the Are You Ready To Encrypt The Drive? screen, click Continue.

    The drive will be encrypted. You can unencrypt the drive at any time by choosing Unencrypt Drive from the BitLocker icon in Control Panel.

Using the BitLocker Administration and Monitoring Utility

Microsoft BitLocker Administration and Monitoring (MBAM) is part of the Microsoft Desktop Optimization Pack (MDOP) and will allow the IT department to use enterprise-based utilities for managing and maintaining BitLocker and BitLocker To Go. As I talked about BitLocker, one of the hardest components of BitLocker is managing and maintaining BitLocker deployment and key recovery. This is where MBAM comes in to play.

MBAM helps IT departments simplify BitLocker deployment and key recovery while also providing centralized compliance monitoring and reporting. MBAM also helps minimize the money related to provisioning and supporting encrypted BitLocker drives.

As explained, BitLocker helps protect against the theft of hardware, and MBAM helps an IT department administer BitLocker in an easy-to-use administrative Microsoft Management Console (MMC) interface.

Overview of MBAM

Microsoft has created MBAM 2.5 to help administrators handle and administer BitLocker and BitLocker To Go. MBAM offers many of the following features:

- Allows IT administrators to automatically set up client computers to use encrypted volumes across the entire enterprise.

- Allows corporate security personnel to rapidly determine if the corporate compliances have been met, and it also allows them to check the state of individual computers throughout the network.

- IT members can use Microsoft System Center Configuration Manager to have a centralized reporting and hardware management utility that works with MBAM.

- Helps IT departments to rapidly assist end users with BitLocker PIN and recovery key requests.

- Allows corporate users to recover their own encrypted devices by using the MBAM Self-Service Portal.

- Give corporations piece of mind that their users can work anywhere in the world with the knowledge that corporate data is being protected.

MBAM is part of the Microsoft Desktop Optimization Pack (MDOP) down-loadable utility, but your network must meet certain requirements. Many of these requirements require server installations and are beyond the scope of this book. To learn more about MBAM, go to the following Microsoft website to see all of the requirements:

https://technet.microsoft.com/en-us/library/mt427465.aspx

Understanding Smart Cards

Another way to help secure Windows 10 is by using smart cards. *Smart cards* are plastic cards (the size of a credit card) that can be used in combination with other methods of authentication. This process of using a smart card along with another authentication method is called two-factor authentication or *multifactor authentication*. Authentication is the process of using user credentials to log on to either a local Windows 10 machine or a domain.

Smart card support allows you to increase the security of many critical functions of your company, including client authentication, interactive logon, and document signing.

Smart cards are now easier than ever to use and deploy because of the new features included with all versions of Windows 10.

Enhanced Support for Smart Card–Related Plug and Play and the Personal Identity Verification (PIV) Standard   This allows users of Windows 10 to use smart cards from vendors who publish their drivers through Windows Update, allowing Windows 10 to use the smart card without special middleware. These drivers are downloaded in the same way as drivers for other Windows devices are downloaded. When a smart card that is PIV compliant is placed into a smart-card reader, Windows 10 will try to download a current driver from Windows Update. If a driver is not available, the PIV-compliant minidriver that is included with Windows 10 is used for the smart card.

Encrypting Drives with BitLocker   If your users are using Windows 10 Enterprise or Professional, the users can choose to encrypt their removable media by turning on BitLocker and then choosing the smart-card option to unlock the drive. Windows will then retrieve the correct minidriver for the smart card and allow the operation to complete.

Smart-Card Domain Logon   When using Windows 10, the correct minidriver for a smart card is automatically retrieved. This allows a new smart card to authenticate with the domain controller without requiring the user to install or configure additional middleware.

Document and Email Signing   Windows 10 users can use smart cards to sign an email or document. XML Paper Specification (XPS) documents can also be signed without additional software.

Use with Line-of-Business Applications   Using Windows 10 smart cards allows applications that use Cryptography Next Generation (CNG) or CryptoAPI to retrieve the correct minidriver at runtime. This eliminates the need for middleware.

Summary

In this chapter, we started looking at how to set up and configure folders on a Windows 10 and Windows Server 2012 R2 system. We talked about sharing those folders and how to grant access to those folders by using NTFS and shared permissions.

We also talked a Dynamic Access Control (DAC) and how Dynamic Access Control allows an administrator to identify data by using data classifications and then controlling access to these files based on these classifications.

DAC also gives administrators the ability to control file access by using a central access policy. This central access policy will also allow an administrator to set up audit access to files for reporting and forensic investigation.

We also talked about BitLocker and BitLocker To Go including Data Recovery Agent and Microsoft BitLocker Administration and Monitoring (MBAM).

We then finished the chapter by talking about two-factor authentication using smart cards. Smart cards and user accounts will be discussed in greater detail in Chapter 18 "Managing Identity and Authorization."

Video Resources

There are videos available for the following exercises:

14.1

14.3

You can access the videos at www.wiley.com/go/sybextestprep on the Other Study Tools tab.

Exam Essentials

Understand folder options.   Understand the purpose and features of using folders and files. Properly configuring folders and folder access is one of the most important tasks that we do on a daily basis.

Understand NTFS and share permissions.   Be able to configure security permissions and know the difference between NTFS and share permissions.

Know how to use BitLocker Drive Encryption. Understand the purpose and requirements of BitLocker Drive Encryption. Know which editions of Windows 10 (Enterprise, Education, and Professional) include BitLocker.

Understand Microsoft BitLocker Administration and Monitoring (MBAM). Understand the purpose and requirements of MBAM. MBAM allows an IT department to manage all of your BitLocker setting through the use of one application.

Understand Smartcards. You need to understand smart cards and two-factor authentication. The reason it is called two-factor authentication is because you need the smart card and the PIN (two factors).

Review Questions

1. You are hired by a friend to set up a network in their home. They have four machines in their home that are all connected by an ISP wireless router. The systems can't share documents because there is currently no network sharing in place. They want to be able to share audio and video files among their family. How can you easily set up a network? Choose two.

    A. Install a Windows Server 2008 R2 domain controller.

    B. Create a HomeGroup.

    C. All audio and video files should be moved to the HomeGroup libraries.

    D. Move all audio and video files to a shared folder on the Windows Server 2008 R2 machine.

2. You are the network administrator for a large organization. You have a Windows 10 machine that needs to prevent any user for copying unencrypted files from the Windows 10 machine to any removable disk. How do you accomplish this task?

    A. Within the System icon in Control Panel, set the BitLocker Drive encryption.

    B. Within the Hardware icon in Control Panel, set the BitLocker Drive encryption.

    C. Within the Device Manager icon in Control Panel, set the BitLocker Drive encryption.

    D. Within a Local Group Policy, set the BitLocker Drive encryption.

3. Which editions of Windows 10 can you enable BitLocker? Choose all that apply.

    A. Windows 10 Education Edition

    B. Windows 10 Basic Edition

    C. Windows 10 Professional Edition

    D. Windows 10 Enterprise Edition

4. You have a network folder that resides on an NTFS partition on a Windows 10 computer. NTFS permissions and share permissions have been applied. Which of the following statements best describes how share permissions and NTFS permissions work together if they have been applied to the same folder?

    A. The NTFS permissions will always take precedence.

    B. The share permissions will always take precedence.

    C. The system will look at the cumulative share permissions and the cumulative NTFS permissions. Whichever set is less restrictive will be applied.

    D. The system will look at the cumulative share permissions and the cumulative NTFS permissions. Whichever set is more restrictive will be applied.

5. You are the network administrator for a medium-sized company. Rick was the head of HR and recently resigned. John has been hired to replace Rick and has been given Rick's laptop. You want John to have access to all of the resources to which Rick had access. What is the easiest way to manage the transition?

    A. Rename Rick's account to John.

    B. Copy Rick's account and call the copied account John.

C. Go into the Registry and do a search and replace to replace all of Rick's entries with John's name.

D. Take ownership of all of Rick's resources and assign John Full Control to the resources.

6. Jeff, the IT manager for Stormwind, has been asked to give Tom the rights to read and change documents in the Stormwind Documents folder. The following table shows the current permissions on the shared folder:

Group/User	NTFS	Shared
Sales	Read	Change
Marketing	Modify	Change
R&D	Deny	Full Control
Finance	Read	Read
Tom	Read	Change

Tom is a member of the Sales and Finance groups. When Tom accesses the Stormwind Documents folder, he can read all the files, but the system won't let him change or delete files. What do you need to do to give Tom the minimum amount of rights to do his job?

A. Give Sales Full Control to shared permissions.

B. Give Tom Full Control to NTFS security.

C. Give Finance Change to shared permissions.

D. Give Finance Modify to NTFS security.

E. Give Tom Modify to NTFS security.

7. You are the IT manager for your company. You have been asked to give the Admin group the rights to read, change, and assign permissions to documents in the Stormwind Documents folder. The following table shows the current permissions on the Stormwind Documents shared folder:

Group/User	NTFS	Shared
Sales	Read	Change
Marketing	Modify	Change
R&D	Deny	Full Control
Finance	Read	Read
Admin	Change	Change

What do you need to do to give the Admin group the rights to do their job? (Choose all that apply.)

A. Give Sales Full Control to shared permissions.

B. Give Full Control to NTFS security.

C. Give Admin Full Control to shared permissions.

D. Give Finance Modify to NTFS security.

E. Give Admin Full Control to NTFS security.

8. Vincent is an instructor for Stormwind, and he is talking to Jeff, the company's IT manager. Vince asks Jeff to implement some type of two-factor authentication. What can Jeff install to complete this request?

A. Passwords and usernames

B. Retina scanners

C. Fingerprint scanners

D. Smart cards

9. You are using Windows 10 and you have created a file with called "my text" in Notepad and has a .txt extension type. You need to change the extension type from .txt to .vbx. What setting do you need to change on the folder so that you can see the extension types?

A. Uncheck Hide Extensions For Known File Types

B. Check Unhide Extensions For Files

C. Check show Extensions For Files

D. Uncheck Hide All File Types

10. The owner of your company has come to you and stated that they want all of the hardware on all systems to use BitLocker and BitLocker To Go. What utility should you install to help manage and maintain BitLocker and BitLocker To Go?

A. MAAM

B. MBAM

C. MNBM

D. MABM

Chapter

15

Managing the Windows 10 Environment

MICROSOFT EXAM OBJECTIVES COVERED IN THIS CHAPTER:

✓ **Configure mobility options.**

 ▪ This objective may include but is not limited to the following subobjectives: Configure offline file policies, configure power policies, configure Windows To Go, configure sync options, configure Wi-Fi direct, files, powercfg, Sync Center.

✓ **Configure remote connections.**

 ▪ This objective may include but is not limited to the following subobjectives: Configure remote authentication, configure Remote Desktop settings, configure VPN connections and authentication, enable VPN reconnect, configure broadband tethering.

After you've installed Windows 10, you will need to configure the system. In this chapter, we will examine the process of configuring the Windows 10 environment, beginning with an overview of the main configuration utilities.

Control Panel is one of the most important configuration tools for Windows 10. It includes many icons that can help you optimize, maintain, and personalize the operating system. One of the most important icons in Control Panel is the System icon. The System icon not only has operating-system information, but it also allows you to configure devices, remote settings, and system protection.

If you use Windows 10 on a laptop computer, it is important to properly configure your power and mobility options. Configuring these options on a laptop will allow you to get the most out of your laptop and Windows 10. There are many different mobility options that you can choose from to help customize the laptop to each individual user.

We will also examine how services operate and how to configure your services to start manually or automatically. We will examine how to configure services in the event of a service error.

Configuring the Windows 10 Operating System

After Windows 10 is installed, the next important step is configuration. If a Windows 10 machine is not configured properly, it may not run properly. When you are the IT administrator for a company, you need to make sure that the Windows client systems are configured properly and, in most cases, the same.

There are many ways to do this, from individually configuring the Windows 10 systems to using Group Policy Objects (GPOs). Most companies are going to set Windows 10 configurations through the use of Windows Servers and GPOs, but you still need to understand each component and what it does so you can configure the proper settings.

The following sections describe many of the configuration options for customizing Windows 10 for each user's needs. We will start with configuring the Windows 10 desktop environment.

Configuring the Desktop Environment

The Windows 10 desktop is the interface that appears when a user logs into the operating system. The desktop includes the wallpaper, Start menu, tiles, and icons (see Figure 15.1).

FIGURE 15.1   The default Windows 10 desktop

The Windows 10 Start menu, located at the bottom left of the desktop by default, includes the default All Apps section shown in Figure 15.2.

FIGURE 15.2 The All Apps section

The Windows 10 default desktop appears after a user has logged onto a Windows 10 computer for the first time. When you install a new instance of Windows 10, you will notice that the desktop is clean except for the Recycle Bin. You may also have a message on the desktop that states that the Windows 10 system has not been activated (as shown in Figure 15.3).

Users can then configure their desktops to suit their personal preferences and to work more efficiently. The following list describes some of the common default options that appear on the Start menu, in the Most Used section, Control Panel, and All Apps section. This list includes some of the more commonly used applications and shortcuts; it's not a complete list of every application available to you.

Depending on which version of Windows 10 you are using, these options may vary a bit.

FIGURE 15.3   The desktop with activation notice

Windows Applications

The following are some of the applications for Windows 10. These are not all of the applications installed by default on Windows 10 but just a few to get you started.

Calculator   This shortcut starts the Calculator program. The Calculator works like any other store-bought calculator, and it can even be changed from a Standard calculator to a Scientific, Programmer, Converter, Volume, Length, Weight & Mass, or Temperature calculator.

Cortana   With this application, you can speak or type into the Windows 10 system, and your personnel assistant, Cortana, will try to find answers to any queries that you may have.

Getting Started   This is used to access preset tasks. Some of these tasks are Get To Know Windows 10 (see Figure 15.4), Microsoft Edge, Start Menu Tips, Setting Things Up, Get Connected, Cortana, Windows Hello, XBOX App, Entertainment, Office, Personalize And Settings, Saving And Syncing Content, Apps And Store, Continuum And Touch, and Ease Of Use.

FIGURE 15.4   Getting Started tasks

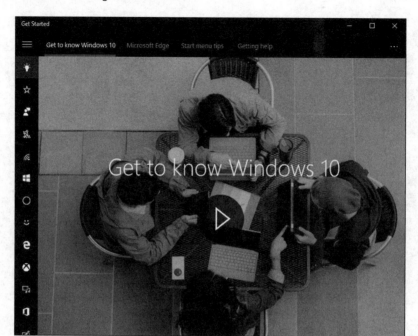

Get Skype   This app allows you to download and configure Skype. If your company uses Skype, Windows 10 gives you the ability to download and set up your Skype account with the Windows 10 operating system.

Maps   This app allows you to see the current location and area of the Windows 10 system. You can use Maps to search for locations and services (food, gas, directions, etc.), as shown in Figure 15.5.

Microsoft Edge   This shortcut starts the built-in web browser. When used with an Internet connection, Microsoft Edge provides an interface for accessing the Internet or a local intranet.

OneDrive   This application allows you to connect with the Microsoft OneDrive cloud-based utility. You can use this application to share documents between the Windows 10 system and the OneDrive cloud-based subscription.

People   This application allows you to look up and work with your contacts. It enables you to use social media to connect people and contacts.

Windows Update   This shortcut allows you to receive updates and security patches for the Windows 10 operating system. You can receive updates from either Microsoft's web server or a Windows Server Update Services (WSUS) machine.

FIGURE 15.5 Maps

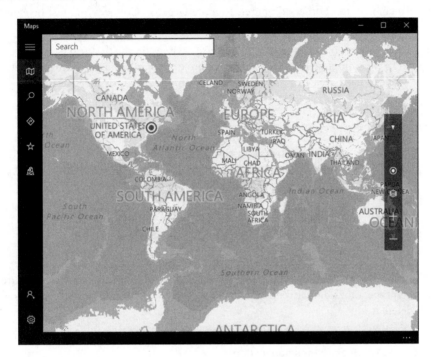

XPS Viewer   This application allows you to view Microsoft XML Paper Specification (.xps) files. The XPS viewer also allows you to print these files.

Windows Accessories

Windows Accessories are some basic tools that are included with Windows 10 to help you do tasks from surfing the net to playing DVDs.

Internet Explorer   This shortcut starts the built-in web browser. When used with an Internet connection, Internet Explorer provides an interface for accessing the Internet or a local intranet.

Microsoft Edge   There is another Internet browser on Windows 10 called Edge. Microsoft Edge gives you new ways to find pages, read and write on the Web, plus help from Cortana when you need it.

Notepad   This application allows you to create text files. This is a great way to store notes on the Windows 10 system without using a full word processing application like Word.

Paint   This shortcut starts the Paint program. The Paint program is an application that allows you to change or manipulate graphics files.

Remote Desktop Connection   This program allows a user to connect remotely to another machine. To connect to another computer, Remote Desktop Connection must be enabled on the receiving computer.

Snipping Tool   This tool allows a user to capture an item on the desktop (see Figure 15.6). The user clicks the Snipping Tool and drags the cursor around an area that will then be captured. The captured area can then be drawn on, highlighted, or saved as a file.

FIGURE 15.6   Snipping Tool

Sticky Notes   This application places a sticky note on the desktop, as shown in Figure 15.7. You can then type a message or reminder into the sticky note. It will remain on the desktop until you delete it.

FIGURE 15.7   Sticky Notes application

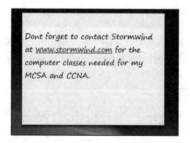

Settings   This application opens the Settings window. Inside the Settings window, you can configure your System, Devices, Network & Internet, Personalization, Accounts, Time & Language, Ease Of Access, Privacy, and Updates & Security (see Figure 15.8).

Store   This application allows you to download and purchase applications from the Microsoft Store. The Microsoft Store has thousands of business and personnel applications that you can use on Windows 10.

Windows Fax And Scan   This application allows you to create and manage scans and faxes. Windows Fax And Scan allows users to send or receive faxes from their workstation.

FIGURE 15.8   Settings window

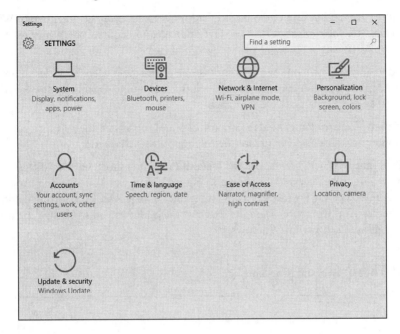

Windows Media Player   With this application, you can play all your media files, including videos, music, pictures, and recorded TV.

Windows Ease Of Access Tools

These tools are installed on a Windows 10 system to help individuals who have difficulty seeing the screen. The Ease Of Access tools can be accessed via Start ➤ All Apps ➤ Ease of Access and include a Magnifier, Narrator, On-Screen Keyboard, and Windows Speech Recognition, as shown in Figure 15.9.

FIGURE 15.9   Ease Of Access tools

Windows System Utilities

These utilities are the ones that help most IT administrators manage and control Windows systems. These are the tools that help us start, manage, and control the Windows 10 systems and applications.

Command Prompt   The Command Prompt is one of the most useful utilities to an IT administrator. You can run commands through the Command Prompt and program the Windows 10 system using system commands.

Control Panel   Control Panel holds many utilities and tools that allow you to configure your computer. It is discussed in greater detail later in this chapter.

Default Programs   When you choose the Default Programs shortcut, four different configuration items can be accessed (as shown in Figure 15.10): Set Your Default Programs, Associate A File Type Or Protocol With A Program, Change AutoPlay Settings, and Set Program Access And Computer Defaults. Each of these allows you to change the default programs that are used within Windows 10.

FIGURE 15.10   Default Programs

Devices   This shortcut opens the Devices section, where you can add or configure any of your hardware devices.

File Explorer   By default, this application shows all of the folders and files that are on the Windows 10 system. You can use this application to look at all of the files located on the Windows 10 system.

Run   You can either put in commands or run applications from the Run dialog box.

Task Manager   This is one of the few applications that I used as an IT director on a daily basis. The Task Manager allows you to see what applications are running on the Windows systems (including servers). The Task Manager also allows you to stop applications from running on a system. This utility will be explained in greater detail throughout this book.

This PC   This shortcut allows you to centrally manage your computer's files, hard drives, and devices with removable storage. It also allows you to manage system tasks and other places and to view details about your computer.

Windows User's Tools

The Windows User's tools are the utilities we use to store and access user's data and documents. These are the applications and folders that we use to keep user data.

Desktop   This folder shows all of the applications that are located on the desktop.

Documents   By default, this folder stores the documents that are created. Each user has a unique Documents folder, so even if a computer is shared, each user will have his or her own personal folder.

Pictures   This application shows any pictures that are in the user's Pictures folder.

Music   This shortcut will show any music that is in the Music folder.

Videos   This shortcut shows you all of the videos that are stored on this Windows 10 system.

Shut Down or Restart   This button is used to shut down or restart the computer. There is an arrow next to the button that you can use to restart the machine or shut down the system.

The desktop also includes the Recycle Bin. The Recycle Bin is a special folder that holds the files and folders that have been deleted, assuming that your hard drive has enough free space to hold the deleted files. You can restore or permanently delete a file from the Recycle Bin by opening the Recycle Bin and right-clicking that file.

When configuring the desktop, you have the ability to decide between configuring a background of your choice as your desktop backdrop or you can choose one of the built-in desktop themes. Desktop themes are a preset package containing graphical appearance details, used to customize the look and feel of an operating system.

Backgrounds are just the graphics that you decide to set as your wallpaper. To switch between different themes, right-click an area of open space on the desktop and select Personalize. In the Theme Settings dialog box, you can select the theme you want to use. You can additionally configure the desktop by customizing the taskbar and Start menu, adding shortcuts, and setting display properties.

Configuring Personalization

To configure the Windows desktop and how it looks, right-click the Desktop and selecting Personalize. When you choose to Personalize the desktop, you have five different settings that you can configure (as shown in Figure 15.11).

FIGURE 15.11   Personalization screen

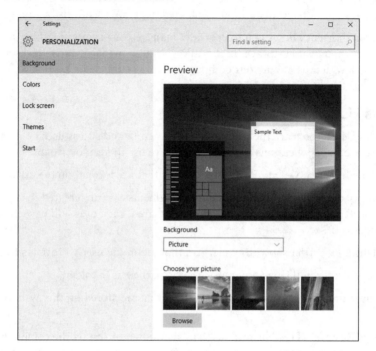

Background

This lets you pick your desktop background, which uses a picture or an HTML document as wallpaper. Setting up a desktop background can be as easy as picking a solid color and placing a picture of your favorite sports team or pet on top of it.

Windows 10 comes with some pictures already in the system, but you can basically turn any picture into your background desktop picture. As you can see in Figure 15.11, you can click the Browse button and choose the pictures that you want in your background.

Colors

This allows you to fine-tune the color and style of your windows background and accent. Windows 10 gives you the ability to automatically pick an accent color for your background, as shown in Figure 15.12.

Windows 10 users also have the ability to automatically choose their own background colors. You can show colors on the Start screen, taskbar, and action center. You can also make the Start screen, taskbar, and action center transparent.

FIGURE 15.12   Colors screen

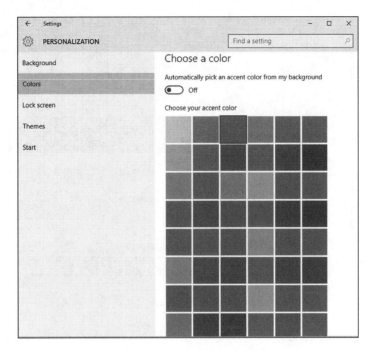

Lock Screen

This lets you select a screen saver that will start after the system has been idle for a specified amount of time. You can also specify a password that must be used to access the system after it has been idle. When the idle time has been reached and the screen saver is activated, the computer can also be set so that the Windows 10 system is locked (shown in Figure 15.13) and the password (or other authentication method) of the user who is currently logged on must be entered to unlock the computer again.

Windows 10 includes many different screen-saver options that can be used and configured:

- None
- 3D Text
- Blank
- Bubbles
- Mystify
- Photos
- Ribbons

FIGURE 15.13   Lock Screen

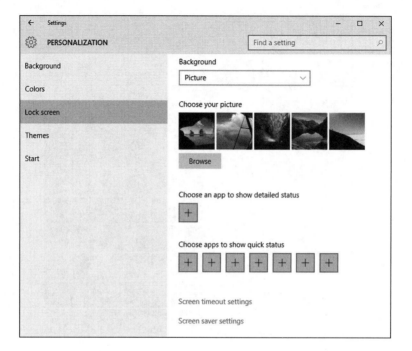

Personalization Themes

This screen allows you to set the different themes that you can have for your desktop. Themes allow you to change the color pattern for all desktop and applications in one setting. The Themes screen (shown in Figure 15.14) also allows you to change the advanced sound settings, desktop icon settings, and mouse pointer settings.

Advanced Sound Settings   This lets you choose the sounds that will be played based on the action taken. Each action can have its own sound. The Sound options also allow you to set up the external or internal speakers and microphones that you want to use. You can also calibrate different pieces of hardware.

Desktop Icon Settings   This allows you to customize the desktop icons. You also have the ability to change shortcut icons. Some of the icons that you can add to the desktop are the Computer icon, User's Files icon, Network icon, Recycle Bin icon, and Control Panel. You also have the ability to change icons at the screen.

Mouse Pointers Settings   This allows you to customize the appearance of the mouse pointers. It allows you to go from the traditional pointer to a Help Select, Busy, and Precision Select to just name a few. You can also change the Button options, Pointer Options, Wheel options, and Hardware.

FIGURE 15.14   Themes screen

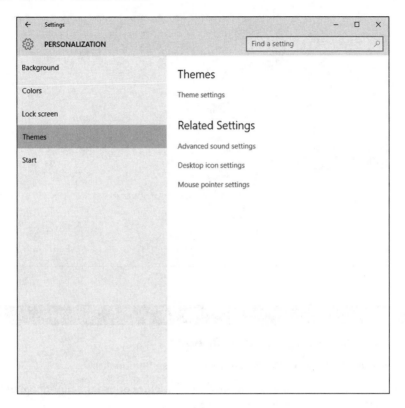

Personalization Start Screen

The Start section allows you to configure what you going to see on your Start menu and which folders appear on the Start. As you can see in Figure 15.15, you have the ability to set the following settings;

- Show most used apps
- Show recently added apps
- Use Start full screen
- Show recently opened items in Jump Lists on Start or the taskbar
- Choose which folders appear on Start

Now that we have looked at how to configure the Windows 10 desktop, let's go ahead and practice doing just that. Exercise 15.1 will walk you through the process of configuring your theme and choosing additional options.

FIGURE 15.15 Start options

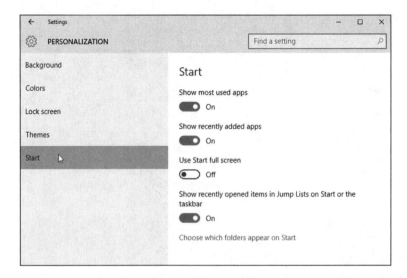

EXERCISE 15.1

Configuring Windows 10 Desktop Options

1. Right-click an open area of the desktop and choose Personalize.

2. On the Background screen, either choose a new picture or use the pull-down under Background and choose Solid Color or Slideshow.

3. After you have set your new desktop, go to the Lock Screen page.

4. Scroll down and choose the link "Screen saver settings."

5. Under the Screen Saver pull-down, choose 3D Text.

6. Click the Setting button. Make sure the radio button is set for Custom Text and put in the text you would like to see. Go ahead and change the font or size or rotation speed. Once completed, click the OK button. At the Screen Saver Settings screen, change the Wait Time to 15 minutes and then click the OK button.

7. Click the Themes screen. Click the Theme Settings link and choose a new theme that you like. You can also keep the current theme if you like that one. Hit the upper-right X to close the window once you're finished.

8. Click the Start screen. Make any changes that you want to change for your Start menu. Once you are finished, close the Personalization window.

Windows 10 includes several utilities for managing various aspects of the operating-system configuration. In the following sections, you will learn how to configure your operating system using Control Panel and the Registry Editor.

We will start with Control Panel and the different utilities included within it.

Using Control Panel

Control Panel is a set of GUI utilities that allow you to configure Registry settings without the need to use a Registry Editor. The Registry is a database used by the operating system to store configuration information.

Let's take a closer look at the utilities that are available through Control Panel. I have set Control Panel to Large Icons view, but you can set it to Small Icons view if you prefer (see Figure 15.16).

If you keep the Control Panel view set to Category, you will not be able to follow along and see all the different items we are going to talk about. The Category view has all of these settings, but they are in different sections. I feel it's easier to understand each item using the Large Icons view.

FIGURE 15.16   Control Panel

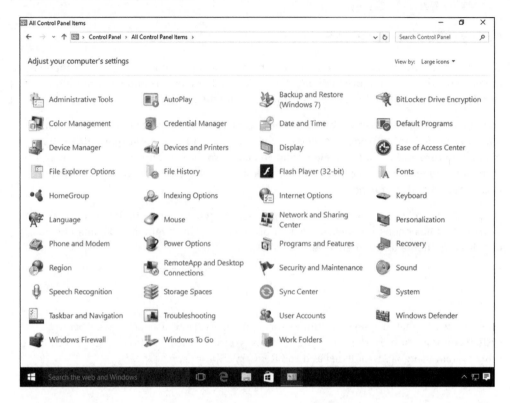

Administrative Tools   This icon has multiple administrative tools that can help you configure and monitor the Windows 10 operating system. These tools include the following:

- Component Services
- Computer Management
- Defragment and Optimize Drives
- Disk Cleanup
- Event Viewer
- iSCSI Initiator
- Local Security Policy
- ODBC Data Sources (32-bit)
- ODBC Data Sources (64-bit)
- Performance Monitor
- Print Management
- Resource Monitor
- Services

- System Configuration
- System Information
- Task Scheduler
- Windows Firewall with Advanced Security
- Windows Memory Diagnostics

AutoPlay　This icon lets you configure media disks and will autoplay when inserted into the media player (see Figure 15.17). Each media type has different configuration settings, but the basic choices are as follows:

- Use AutoPlay for all media and devices
- Removable drive
- Camera Storage
- DVDs
- Blue-ray discs
- CDs
- Software
- Devices

FIGURE 15.17　AutoPlay options

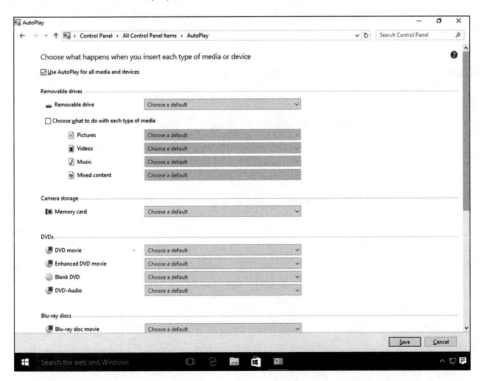

Backup And Restore (Windows 7)   The Backup And Restore icon allows you to configure your backup media. Users can make copies of all important data on their machine to avoid losing it in the event of a hardware failure or disaster. Backups will be discussed in greater detail in Chapter 20, "Configuring Recovery."

BitLocker Drive Encryption   BitLocker Drive Encryption helps prevent unauthorized users from accessing files stored on hard drives by encrypting the drive in its entirety. The user is able to use the computer as they normally would, but unauthorized users cannot read or use any of their files. BitLocker Drive Encryption will be discussed in greater detail in Chapter 16, "Planning and Managing Microsoft Intune."

Color Management   The Color Management icon allows you to configure some of the video adapter's settings. You can configure the Windows color system defaults, the ICC Rendering Intent to WCS Gamut Mapping settings, and the display calibration. You can also change the system defaults to indicate how these items should be handled.

Credential Manager   Users can use the Credential Manager to store credentials such as usernames and passwords. These usernames and passwords get stored in vaults so that you can easily log onto computers or websites.

There are two sections in the Credential Manager: Web Credentials and Windows Credentials. You can add credentials by clicking the link next to each of the two credential sections.

Date And Time   The Date And Time icon allows you to configure your local date and time for the Windows 10 machine. You also have the ability to synchronize your clock with the Internet, as shown in Figure 15.18. Be aware that if your computer is a member of a domain, you will not see this screen and will not be able to synchronize your time with an Internet time server.

FIGURE 15.18   Time synchronization

Default Programs   The Default Programs icon allows you to choose the programs that Windows will use by default. For example, you can set Internet Explorer to be the default web browser.

Device Manager   The Device Manager icon allows you to configure the different devices on your Windows 10 machine. You can configure such devices as disk drives, display adapters, DVD/CD-ROM drives, monitors, and network adapters.

Devices And Printers   The Devices And Printers icon lets you add or configure the devices on your machine and your printers. This is where you add the printers that you have on your network.

Display   The Display icon allows you to configure your display. You can change the size of the text and other items on your screen. You also have the ability to change the resolution, calibrate colors, change display settings, adjust ClearType text, and change custom text size.

Ease Of Access Center   The Ease Of Access Center icon allows you to set up your accessibility options.

File Explorer Options   The Folder Options icon allows you to configure how you view folders on the Windows 10 machine by default. You have the ability to set up how you browse and navigate folders, which files and folders you can view (see Figure 15.19), and how folders are searched.

File History   File History allows users to save copies of their files so that you can get them back in the event of a file being lost or damaged. You have the ability to restore personal files, select drives, exclude folders, and even set advanced settings on the File History settings.

FIGURE 15.19   Folder Options

Flash Player (32-bit)   The Flash Player application allows you to set up how your Flash Player is going to operate and which applications the Flash Player will be associated with.

Fonts   This icon displays a screen where you can install, preview, delete, show, hide, and configure the fonts that the applications on your Windows 10 operating system can use. It enables you to get fonts online, adjust cleartext, find a character, and change font size.

HomeGroup   HomeGroups are small local networks that you can easily configure at home. When you install HomeGroups on your first computer, a password is assigned so that you can connect other computers to this HomeGroup. The password can be changed from the HomeGroup icon. HomeGroups are discussed in greater detail in Chapter 19, "Configuring Network Connectivity."

Be aware that if your computer is a member of a domain, you can belong to a HomeGroup that someone else creates but you cannot create your own HomeGroup.

Indexing Options   Windows uses indexing to perform very fast searches of common files on your computer. The Indexing Options feature gives you the ability to configure which files and applications get indexed.

Internet Options   The Internet Options icon allows you to configure how the Internet will operate (see Figure 15.20). From this icon you can configure your home page, browsing history, tabs, security, privacy, content, connections, and programs. Internet Explorer will be discussed in greater detail in Chapter 17, "Configuring Applications."

FIGURE 15.20   Internet Properties

Keyboard   The Keyboard properties allow you to configure how the keyboard will react when used. You can set the character repeat speed (how fast the keyboard will repeat what you are typing) and the cursor speed. You can also use these properties to configure the keyboard drivers.

Language   The Language application allows you to specify which languages you are going to be using on this Windows 10 system. The language at the top of your Language list is the primary language that the system will use.

Mail   You may or may not have this Mail application in Control Panel. If you have a mail client, such as Outlook, then the Mail application icon will be in Control Panel. If you don't have a mail client, then this icon will be missing from Control Panel.

When you configure the Mail properties, you set up your client-side mail settings. In the Mail properties, you can set up different user profiles (mailboxes) and the local mail servers or Internet mail servers to which they connect.

Mouse   Mouse properties give you the ability to configure how the mouse will operate. You can configure the buttons, click speed, ClickLock, pointer type, pointer options, center wheel, and hardware properties.

Network And Sharing Center   The Network And Sharing Center properties configure your Windows 10 machine to connect to a local network or the Internet. You can configure TCP/IP, set up a new network, connect to a network, choose a homegroup, and configure the network adapter. Network And Sharing Center is discussed in greater detail in Chapter 19.

Personalization   Personalization allows you to set up your desktop environment to your liking. Personalization allows you to set up a desktop theme or background, system sounds, screen saver, desktop icons, mouse pointer, and account picture.

Phone And Modem   The Phone And Modem properties are used to set up local dialing properties and modem options. You can set up your dialing location, modem properties, and telephony providers.

Power Options   Power options allow a user to maximize their Windows 10 machine's performance and/or conserve energy. You can enter your own power restrictions to customize your machine. Power options are important settings when you are dealing with laptops. Since many laptops use batteries, power options allow you to get the most time from their batteries. Power management will be discussed later in this chapter.

Programs And Features   The Programs And Features icon was the Add/Remove Programs icon in Windows XP. Programs And Features allows you to organize, uninstall, change, or repair programs and features.

The Programs And Features icon also allows you to choose which Windows 10 features you want installed on the machine, such as Indexing Services, Telnet Client, Telnet Server, and so on.

In Exercise 15.2, you'll install the Telnet client on the Windows 10 operating system.

EXERCISE 15.2

Installing Features

1. Open the Programs And Features tool by clicking Start ➢ Control Panel ➢ Programs And Features.

2. Click the Turn Windows Features On Or Off link in the upper-left corner.

3. Scroll down the features list and check the Telnet Client check box (shown in Figure 15.21).

FIGURE 15.21 Telnet Client check box

4. Click OK.

 Real World Scenario

Using Telnet

As an IT manager, my job does not just consist of working on Windows machines. I also need to understand and work on routers.

You can use the Telnet client to connect to most routers. Using the Telnet client, you can configure the router to operate the way your organization needs it to operate.

I describe Windows Firewall later in this section; however, I do not recommend that you use Windows Firewall as your main line of defense against hackers. You need to purchase a good router/firewall to complete this task. Knowing how to configure the router using the Telnet client will help you accomplish your networking needs.

Recovery   The Recovery icon allows a user or administrator to recover the Windows 10 system to a previously captured restore point. System Restore is one of the first recovery options that should be considered when your Windows 10 system is experiencing problems. Recovery will be discussed in detail in Chapter 19.

Region   The Region tool allows you to configure your local regional settings as well as configure date and time formats.

RemoteApp And Desktop Connections   RemoteApp And Desktop Connections allows you to access programs and desktops on your network. To connect to these resources (remote applications and desktops), you must have the proper permission.

With RemoteApp And Desktop Connections, you can connect to either a remote computer or a virtual computer. To create a new connection, use the Set Up A New Connection Wizard included with the RemoteApp And Desktop Connections menu option.

Security And Maintenance   The Security And Maintenance utility has two configurable sections: Security and Maintenance. The Security section allows you to configure three different options:

- Spyware and unwanted software protection allows you to update Windows Defender.
- Virus protection allows you to install and configure virus protection.
- Windows Update allows you to update Windows 10.

The Maintenance section allows you to set up a Windows 10 Maintenance schedule. You can also set up a HomeGroup, file history, drive status, and device software in this section.

Sound   The Sound icon allows you to configure your machine's audio. You can configure output (speakers and audio drivers) and your input devices (microphones).

Speech Recognition   The Speech Recognition icon allows you to configure your speech properties. Speech Recognition allows you to speak into the computer and have that speech be displayed on the system. Many programs, including Microsoft Office, can display the words onscreen as you speak them into the system. You can complete the following actions via the Speech Recognition icon:

- Start Speech Recognition
- Set up a microphone
- Take speech tutorials
- Train your computer to better understand you
- Open the Speech Reference Card, which allows you to view and print a list of common commands

Storage Spaces   Storage Spaces in Windows 10 is another way to give your Windows 10 users data redundancy. Windows 10 administrators have the ability to group hard drives together into a storage pools. Windows 10 users can then use these storage pool capacities to turn the pools into individual Storage Spaces. You can configure your Storage Pools in this application.

Sync Center   The Sync Center allows you to configure synchronization between the Windows 10 machine and a network server. The Sync Center also allows you to see when synchronization occurred, if the synchronization was successful, and if there were any errors.

System   The System icon is one of the most important icons in Control Panel. The System icon allows you to view which operating system your machine is using, view installed system resources (processor, RAM), change the computer name/domain/workgroup, and activate Windows 10. From the System icon, you can also configure the following settings:

- Device Manager
- Remote Settings
- System Protection
- Advanced System Settings

Taskbar And Navigation   The Taskbar And Navigation icon allows you to configure how the taskbar, Start menu, and toolbars will operate.

Troubleshooting   The Troubleshooting icon in Control Panel allows you to troubleshoot common Windows 10 problems within the following categories:

- Programs
- Hardware And Sound
- Network And Internet
- System And Security

User Accounts   The User Accounts icon allows you to create and modify local user accounts. With the User Account icon, you can perform the following tasks:

- Change user passwords
- Remove passwords
- Change the account picture
- Change the account name
- Change the account type
- Manage user accounts
- Change user-account control settings

Windows Defender   Windows Defender is a built-in Windows 10 application that protects your system from spyware. It is included free with the operating system, and once you turn it on, it starts automatically protecting your system. Windows Defender can operate in different modes:

Real-Time Protection   In Real-Time Protection mode, Windows Defender runs in the background and protects your system as you are working live on the Internet or a network.

Scanning Option   When you're in Scanning Option mode, you can run a system scan at any time to check for spyware. This option does not require Windows Defender to always be running.

Command-Line Utility   Windows Defender includes a command-line utility called MpCmdRun.exe, which allows you to automate the use of Windows Defender. The MpCmdRun.exe utility is located in the %ProgramFiles%\Windows Defender\ folder.

Windows Firewall   Windows Firewall helps prevent unauthorized users or hackers from accessing your Windows 10 machine from the Internet or the local network. Windows Firewall is explained in detail in Chapter 19.

Windows To Go   Windows To Go gives an administrator or user the ability to provision Windows 10 onto an external USB drive. You can then use the USB drive (known as a Windows To Go workspace) to load a complete and managed Windows 10 system image into a managed or unmanaged Windows 10 host computer to boot and run the Windows 10 operating system.

Work Folders   Work Folders allow a user to make data files available on all of the devices that he or she uses. You can access that data even when the devices are offline.

Now that we have taken a brief look at most of the icons in Control Panel, let's look at the System icon in greater detail.

Understanding the System Icon

The System icon (shown in Figure 15.22) in Control Panel is the gateway to a very useful set of utilities and tasks that can enable you to specify remote settings, device settings, system protection, and the computer name, among other things.

FIGURE 15.22   The System page

Let's look at the different utilities and tasks that can be configured in Control Panel:

Windows Edition The Windows Edition section shows you which edition of Windows the machine currently has installed. The Windows Edition section also shows whether service packs are installed.

System The System section shows the following information about the system hardware:

- Processor
- Installed memory (RAM)
- System type
- Pen and touch-screen availability

Computer Name, Domain, And Workgroup Settings In the Computer Name, Domain, And Workgroup settings section, you can change the name of the computer system and also change the workgroup or domain. Windows 10 works well with Windows Server 2012 R2, which is explained in greater detail in Chapter 19.

Windows Activation The Windows Activation section allows you to activate your Windows 10 operating system and change your product key before activating.

If you look to the left side of the System windows, you will see that there are four additional links: Device Manager, Remote Settings, System Protection, and Advanced System Settings. Let's take a look at some of these settings.

Device Manager The Device Manager icon allows you to configure the different devices on your Windows 10 machine. You can configure such devices as disk drives, display adapters, DVD/CD-ROM drives, monitors, and network adapters.

Remote Settings In the Remote section, you can set the Remote Assistance and Remote Desktop settings for the Windows 10 system. Windows Remote Assistance allows an administrator to connect to a machine and control the mouse and keyboard while the user is logged on with the administrator. This option can be enabled or disabled.

System Protection The System Protection section is for configuring restore points and recoverability for the Windows 10 operating system. You can also manage disk space and all of your restore points from the System Protection section.

Advanced System Settings The Advanced System Settings section allows you to set up such items as visual effects, processor scheduling, memory usage, virtual memory, desktop settings, system startup, and recoverability.

There are three main sections within the Advanced System Settings section:

Performance The Performance section allows you to configure the visual effects, the virtual memory, processor scheduling, and Data Execution Prevention for the Windows 10 operating system.

The virtual memory is a section of the hard drive that is used by the system and RAM. Think of RAM as a pitcher of water. As the water fills up the pitcher, the pitcher becomes full. Once it's full, more water would cause it to overflow. The virtual memory is the overflow for RAM. When RAM fills up, the oldest data in RAM gets put into the virtual memory. This way, the system does not need to look at an entire hard drive for that data. It finds it in the virtual memory.

The Data Execution Prevention section (found under the Settings button) helps protect against damage from viruses and other security threats.

User Profiles   The User Profiles section allows you to copy, delete, or move a user's desktop profile to another location or user account.

Startup And Recovery   The Startup And Recovery section allows you to configure which operating system will be booted by default (important for dual-booting machines) and what should happen when the system gets a startup error.

Let's now look at how to configure some of the options using the System icon. Complete Exercise 15.3 to change the computer name.

EXERCISE 15.3

Changing the Computer Name

1. Open the System tool by right-clicking Start ➤ Control Panel ➤ System.

2. Under the Computer Name, Domain, And Workgroup settings section, click the Change Settings link.

3. Click the Change button in the To Rename This Computer section.

4. In the Computer Name field, rename your computer. Click OK.

5. A dialog box asking you to reboot the machine will appear. Click the OK button.

6. Click the Close button, and then click the Restart Now button.

Now that you have renamed the computer, let's look at how to configure performance options. Complete Exercise 15.4 to manipulate your system's virtual memory.

EXERCISE 15.4

Changing the System's Virtual Memory

1. Open the System tool by right-clicking Start ➤ Control Panel ➤ System.

2. In the left side, click the Advanced System Settings link.

3. Under the Performance section, click the Settings button.

4. When the Performance option screen appears, click the Advanced tab.

5. In the Virtual Memory section, click the Change button.

6. Uncheck the Automatically Manage Paging File Size For All Drives check box.

7. Click the Custom Size radio button.

EXERCISE 15.4 *(continued)*

8. Set the Minimum and Maximum settings to two times the size of your RAM. For example, if your RAM is 4,096 MB, set the settings to 8,192 MB.

9. Click the Set button.

10. Click OK. Then click OK again at the Performance Options screen.

11. Close the System Properties screen.

Microsoft Windows 10 handles the virtual memory requirements by default, but I recommend increasing the virtual memory on your machine if hard drive space is available. I use the rule of thumb of one and a half to two times the size of RAM.

We have now talked about the Control Panel and the System icon, but we have not yet talked about the new Windows 10 Settings shortcut app. So in the next section, we are going to look at the Settings window.

Understanding the Settings Window

As stated earlier in the book, Windows 10 took the best of both Windows 7 and Windows 8 and created Windows 10. When you click the Start menu, you will see an option called Settings (see Figure 15.23).

FIGURE 15.23   The Settings option

The Settings screen is a new way to configure different parts of the Windows 10 system. When you click the Settings option from the Start menu, you will see the Settings screen appear, as shown in Figure 15.24.

FIGURE 15.24   The Settings screen

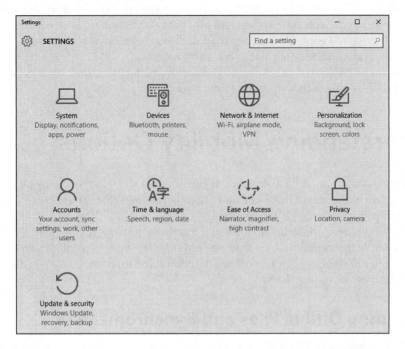

As you can see from Figure 15.24, the Settings Window has multiple sections of Windows 10 that you can configure. The following areas are settings that can be configured using the Settings screen:

- System
- Devices
- Network & Internet
- Personalization
- Accounts
- Time & Language
- Ease of Access
- Privacy
- Updates & Security

Most of these sections have already been covered previously in this chapter, and many of the other sections (such as Accounts) will be covered in other chapters of the book. I just wanted to make sure that you understand that it's another way to configure many of the same options that we have already looked at.

The one area that I would recommend that you look at right away is the choice for Privacy. Microsoft has turned many features on where Microsoft and other third-party vendors can access data on your system and also get information on how you use your Windows 10 system. Take a few minutes to look through the Privacy section and make sure that nothing is on by default that you don't want turned on.

Now that we have looked at how to do configurations for Windows 10, let's go ahead and take a look at how Windows 10 mobility works.

Understanding Mobility Options

So during this chapter we talked about all of the different icons in the Control Panel. Now we need to dive into a few of them in greater detail. The ones that we are going to discuss all have to deal with Windows 10 mobility.

Windows 10 is designed to be mobile and it has many features that revolve around that. Here are some of the mobility issues that we need to cover: how to configure offline file policies, configure power policies, configure Windows To Go, configure Wi-Fi direct, and configure sync options using the Sync Center.

Configuring Offline Files and Synchronization

One of the advantages of Windows 10 is how the operating system works and synchronizes with other systems and data.

The term *synchronization* could mean different things to different people. We could be talking about synchronization of offline files and data, or we can be talking about synchronization between two systems like a Windows 10 system and cloud-based Azure or OneNote.

In this section, we will talk about both. We will address synchronization between offline and online files, and we will discuss synchronization between Windows 10 and cloud-based services.

Offline Files allows network files to be available to clients even when a network connection to the server is unavailable or slow. When a user is accessing a server that is unavailable or when the network connection is slower than a configurable threshold, files are then retrieved from the Offline Files folders.

The Offline Files feature is enabled by default on the following client computer operating systems: Windows 10 Professional, Windows 10 Enterprise, and Windows Education. This feature is turned off by default on Windows Server operating systems.

Because in many organizations Windows 10 will be loaded onto a laptop computer, offline file access can be an important part of how Windows clients stay current even while off the network.

When you decide to turn synchronization on, Windows will automatically keep track of your synchronization choices for you on all of your Windows 10 devices (as long as you are logged on to all of the Windows devices using the same account or have set up synchronization with the other accounts and your Microsoft account).

Users have the ability to choose what items that they want to synchronize. For example, users can synchronize passwords, web browser settings, File Explorer settings, and even notifications.

To truly have synchronization work the way that Microsoft has intended, you need to link all of your devices together using your Microsoft account or have your other accounts linked to your Microsoft account. This includes your school or work accounts all tied into one Microsoft account.

As an IT director for many years, I feel a bit uneasy about this idea. I truly believe that linking your personal accounts together to synchronize all of your personal data is a good way to go, but for obvious security reasons, I don't agree with corporate users linking into their personal accounts.

So how do we go about synchronizing everything in Windows 10 easily? The best method is to use the Sync Center in Control Panel (just right-click the Start ➤ Control Panel ➤ Sync Center).

The Sync Center is built into Windows 10, and it's a one-stop shop for all of your synchronization needs, including working with offline files (see Figure 15.25).

FIGURE 15.25   The Sync Center

As you can see in Figure 15.25, you can set up synchronization between other devices and partnerships. The figure shows you can also manage offline files. To manage offline files, you have to enable that on the Windows 10 system (done through Sync Center) and then also configure offline folder access with the Windows servers that you have at your company.

When you click the link to Manage Offline Folders and enable offline folder access, you then have three tabs that can help you set up offline folder access properly:

Disk Usage   The Disk Usage tab will show you how much disk space is currently being reserved on the Windows 10 system for keeping offline files. You can change the amount of space that is set for the Windows 10 system by clicking the Change Limits button.

Encryption   To make sure that the offline files are encrypted while on the system, click the Encryption button. The files will get encrypted based on your user's Security Identification (SID) number. When you log into the Windows 10 account using the account with the matching SID number, the files will become automatically decrypted when they are opened. If someone with a different user ID (SID) number tries to access these files, he or she will be denied access.

Network   The Network tab allows you to set a time interval (such as 5 minutes), and when that interval is hit, the Windows 10 system will automatically check the network connection to make sure that the connection is not on a slow connection. For example, when you are at home and you don't have direct access to your network, the Windows system will automatically revert to using the offline files due to the connection being slow or not available.

Configuring Power Policies

Earlier in the chapter, we started talking about the Windows 10 Power options. Power options allow a user or administrator to maximize their Windows 10 machine's performance and/or conserve energy.

Administrators or users have the ability to enter your own power restrictions to customize their machine. Power options are important settings when you are dealing with laptops. Since many laptops use batteries, power options allow you to get the most time from their batteries.

Now here is the kicker! Depending on what type of system you are on, you will see different options when you look at your power plan options. For example, Figure 15.26 shows the power plan options for a desktop system. You can tell that the only real options you have is what happens when you choose when to turn off the display or change your power consumption options.

FIGURE 15.26   Desktop power plan options

However, if you look at Figure 15.27, you can see that you have additional options based on whether your laptop or tablet is plugged in. You will not have those options on a desktop, because most desktops can't work when unplugged (unless you have a magical desktop).

FIGURE 15.27 Laptop power plan options

So setting up your power options really depends on what type of machine or tablet you're using. But some of the settings are the same no matter which one you use. The following are just some of the options that are the same no matter what type of Windows 10 system you're on:

- Require a password on wakeup
- Choose what the power button does
- Create a power plan

Laptops will have additional choices such as what happens when you close the lid of the laptop. No matter what type of system you are on, you can choose to go into advanced options and set very specific options on what system components would do while the system was running or while the system was idle.

For example, you can tell the system when the network card or hard drive can go into a sleep mode based on idle time (amount of time while no one is working on the system). So if you want to configure each individual component and how it should work while active or idle, you can go into the advanced options and configure each component separately.

Managing Power States

In Windows 10, the Advanced Configuration Power Interface (ACPI) specifies different levels of power states:

- Fully active PC
- Sleep
- Hibernation
- Complete shutdown of PC

The sleep power state is a new power state introduced with Windows 10 that combines the features of hibernate and standby. When a computer enters the sleep power state, data, including window locations and running applications, is saved memory, and that session is available within seconds when the computer wakes. The computer can thus be put into a power-saving state when not in use but allows quick access to the in-process user session, so the user can begin working more quickly than if the computer were shut down or put into hibernation.

Hibernation falls short of a complete shutdown of the computer. With hibernation, the computer saves your desktop state as well as any open files to the hard drive. To use the computer again, you need to press the power button. The computer should start more quickly than from a complete shutdown because it does not have to go through the complete startup process. You will have to again log onto the computer. Similar to when the computer is put into sleep mode, all the documents that were open when the computer went into hibernation are still available. With hibernation, you can easily resume work where you left off. You can configure your computer to hibernate through Power Options or by choosing Start and then clicking the arrow and selecting Hibernate from the drop-down menu. This option will appear only if hibernation has been enabled through Power Options.

The hibernation mode may not be available on your Windows 10 laptop machine by default. You must make sure your firmware can support hibernation before attempting to enable it. Now let's take a look at the different types of power options that you can configure.

Managing Power Options

You configure power options through the Power Options Properties dialog box. To access this dialog box, right-click Start ➤ Control Panel ➤ Power Options. The Power Options dialog box provides the ability to manage power plans and to control power options, such as when the display is turned off, when the computer sleeps, and what the power button does.

Configuring Power Plans

Windows 10 includes three configurable power plans: Balanced, Power Saver, and High Performance. Power plans control the trade-off between quick access to an existing computer session and energy savings. In Windows 10, each power plan contains default options that can be customized to meet the needs of various scenarios.

The Balanced power plan, as its name suggests, provides a balance between power savings and performance. By default, this plan is configured to turn off the display after 20 minutes and to put the computer to sleep after 1 hour of idle time. You can modify these times as needed. Other power options that you can modify include Wireless Adapter settings and Multimedia settings. Wireless adapters can be configured for maximum power savings or maximum performance. By default, the Balanced power plan configures wireless adapters for maximum performance. Additionally, you can configure the Multimedia settings so that the computer will not be put into sleep mode when sharing media. For example, if the computer is acting as a Media Center device, then you can configure the computer to remain on by setting the Prevent Idling To Sleep option so that other computers can connect to it and stream media from it even when the computer is not being used for other purposes.

The Power Saver power plan is optimized for power savings. By default, the display is configured to be turned off after 20 minutes of inactivity, and the computer will be put into sleep mode after 1 hour of inactivity. Additionally, this power plan configures hard disks to be turned off after 20 minutes of inactivity.

The High Performance power plan is configured to provide the maximum performance for portable computers. By default, the computer will never enter sleep mode, but the display will be turned off after 20 minutes. When this setting is configured, by default the Multimedia settings are configured with the new Allow The Computer To Enter Away Mode option. Away mode configures the computer to look like it's off to users but remain accessible for media sharing. For example, the computer can record television shows when in away mode. You can modify the existing power plans to suit your needs by clicking Change Plan Settings, or you can use the preconfigured power plans listed in Table 15.1.

TABLE 15.1   Windows 10 power plans

Power Plan	Turn Off Display	Put Computer to Sleep	Turn Hard Disks Off
Balanced	After 20 minutes	1 hour	
Power Saver	After 20 minutes	1 hour	After 20 minutes
High Performance	After 20 minutes	Never	

In Exercise 15.5, I will show you how to configure a power plan for your computer.

EXERCISE 15.5

Configuring a Power Plan

1.   Right-click Start ➢ Control Panel ➢ Power Options.

2.   Select a power plan to modify from the Preferred Plans list, and click Change Plan Settings.

3.   Configure the power-plan options for your computer based on your personal preferences. Click Change Advanced Power Settings to modify the advanced power settings. When all changes have been made, click Save Changes.

4.   Close Control Panel.

Other desktop options you can use are the power button and switching users. Let's take a look at these features.

Configuring the Power Button

Unless you decide to run your computer 24 hours a day, you will eventually want to shut it down. By default, the Start menu has a power button. When you click this button, your machine will power off. But the power button does not have to be set to the Shut Down option. You can configure this button to Switch User, Logoff, Lock, Restart, or Shut Down.

You may have a machine that is shared by multiple users, and it may be better for you to have the Switch User button instead of the Shut Down button on the Start menu. Configuring the Switch User option would make it easier on your users.

In Exercise 15.6, you will configure the power button to the Switch User option.

EXERCISE 15.6

Configuring the Power Button to the Switch User Option

1. Right-click Start ➢ Control Panel ➢ Power Options.

2. On the left side, click Choose what the power button does.

3. From the Power Button Settings drop-down menu, choose Hibernate.

4. Click OK.

5. Click the power button and see if the system goes into the Hibernate mode. Once the system is brought out of the Hibernate mode, redo this exercise and choose Shut Down in step 3 to return the system to normal (if it was set to turn off).

After you decide how the power button is going to be used, you may want to configure some of the advanced power options. In the next section, we will look at the different power options.

Configuring Advanced Power Settings

Each power plan contains advanced settings that can be configured, such as when the hard disks will be turned off and whether a password is required on wakeup. To configure these advanced settings, right-click Start ➢ Control Panel ➢ Power Options and select the power plan to use. Then click Change Advanced Power Settings to open the Advanced Settings tab of the Power Options dialog box and modify the settings as desired (or restore the plan defaults).

For example, one option that you might want to change if you are using a mobile computer is the Power Buttons And Lid option, which configures what happens when you press the power button or close the lid of the mobile computer. When either of these actions occurs, the computer can be configured to do nothing, shut down, go into sleep mode, or go into hibernation mode.

Configuring Hibernation

Although sleep is the preferred power-saving mode in Windows 10, hibernation is still available for use. Hibernation for a computer means that anything stored in memory is written to your hard disk. This ensures that when your computer is shut down, you do not lose any of the information that is stored in memory. When you take your computer out of hibernation, it returns to its previous state by loading the hibernation reserved area of hard disk back into memory. To configure your computer to hibernate, complete the same steps as you did previously in Exercise 15.6.

Command-Line Configuration

Microsoft gives you the ability to configure and manage your power settings through the use of the command line. The Powercfg.exe tool allows you to control power settings and configure computers to default to hibernate or standby mode. The Powercfg.exe tool is installed with Windows 10 by default. Powercfg.exe has a few switches that provide you better functionality. Table 15.2 describes some of these switches.

TABLE 15.2 Powercfg.exe switches

Switch	Description
-change	Changes a setting in the current power scheme.
-changename	Changes the name of a power scheme. Also gives you the ability to change the description.
-delete	Deletes the power scheme of the GUID specified.
-deletesetting	Deletes a power setting.
-energy	Looks for common energy-efficiency and battery-life issues and displays these issues in an HTML format. This switch is used to identify problems with the power scheme.
-list	Shows all the power schemes in the current user's environment.
-query	Shows the content of a power scheme.
-qh	Displays the content (including hidden content) of the power scheme.
-waketimers	Enumerates the wake timers. If this is enabled, when the wake timer expires, the system will wake from hibernation or sleep state.

For a complete list of Powercfg.exe switches, visit the Microsoft website here:

https://technet.microsoft.com/en-us/library/
cc748940%28v=ws.10%29.aspx?f=255&MSPPError=-2147217396

There is a useful tool when you're using a laptop on the battery that allows you to see how much time you have left until the battery dies. Let's take a look at the battery meter.

Managing Power Consumption Using the Battery Meter

Windows 10 includes a battery meter that you can use to monitor the battery-power consumption on your mobile computer (laptop or tablet). The battery meter also provides notification as to what power plan is being used.

The battery meter appears in the notification area of the Windows taskbar and indicates the status of the battery, including the percentage of battery charge. As the battery charge gets lower, the battery meter provides a visual indication of the amount of charge left. For example, when the battery charge reaches the low-battery level, a red circle with a white X is displayed.

The battery meter also provides a quick method for changing the power plan in use on the computer. By clicking the battery-meter icon, you can select among the preferred power plans available with Windows 10.

Configuring Windows To Go

As stated earlier, Windows To Go gives an administrator or user the ability to provision Windows 10 onto an external USB drive. You can then use the USB drive (known as a Windows To Go workspace) to load a complete and managed Windows 10 system image into a managed or unmanaged Windows 10 host computer to boot and run the Windows 10 operating system.

Many of us carry a USB drive with us or maybe even on your key ring. Well, think about having a copy of Windows 10 with you wherever and whenever you want to use it. So what are the requirements to set up a Windows To Go drive? Well, you need a USB drive certified for Windows To Go use and an image of Windows 10 Enterprise. If you try to load a USB that isn't certified, you will receive the error, as shown in Figure 15.28.

FIGURE 15.28   USB non-compatible error

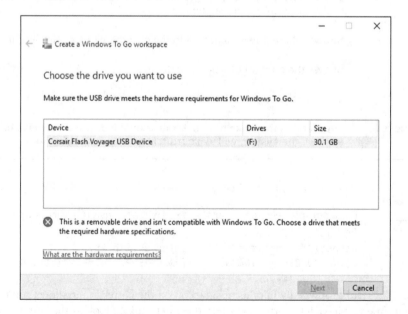

At the time that this book was written, the following list of USB drives are certified for Windows To Go:

- IronKey Workspace W700
- IronKey Workspace W500
- IronKey Workspace W300
- Kingston DataTraveler Workspace for Windows To Go
- Spyrus Portable Workplace
- Spyrus Secure Portable Workplace
- Spyrus Worksafe
- Super Talent Express RC4 for Windows To Go
- Super Talent Express RC8 for Windows To Go
- Western Digital My Passport Enterprise

The information in Table 15.3 was taken directly from the Microsoft website regarding what is needed on the host's computer to be able to accept Windows To Go.

TABLE 15.3   Windows To Go Host requirements

Item	Requirement
Boot Process	Capable of USB boot
Firmware	USB boot enabled (PCs certified for use with Windows 7 or later can be configured to boot directly from USB; check with the hardware manufacturer if you are unsure of the ability of your PC to boot from USB)
Processor architecture	Must support the image on the Windows To Go drive
External USB Hubs	Not supported; connect the Windows To Go drive directly to the host machine
Processor	1 Ghz or faster
RAM	2 GB or greater
Graphics	DirectX 9 graphics device with WDDM 1.2 or greater driver
USB port	USB 2.0 port or greater

To configure a Windows To Go USB drive, you need to complete the following steps:

1. Place a copy of a Windows 10 Enterprise image (.iso file) on the host computer you will use for image storage.

2. Open your Downloads folder on the host computer where you placed the .iso image, right-click the Windows image .iso file, and select MOUNT ISO. The .iso file will then appear as a disk drive on the host computer.

3. Right-click Start ➢ Control Panel.

4. In Control Panel, select Windows To Go.

5. Insert a compatible USB drive into a USB port on the host computer.

6. On the Choose the Drive You Want to Use page, all attached USB drives appear. Choose the compatible USB drive you want to use, and then click Next.

7. The mounted .iso file should now appear on the Choose a Windows 10 Image page. If for some reason you don't see the .iso file, select Add Search Location to choose the mounted .iso file. Select the file, and then click Next.

8. On the Set a BitLocker Password (Optional) page, select the Use BitLocker With My Windows To Go Workspace check box to protect the drive with BitLocker Drive Encryption.

9. Enter a BitLocker password, confirm it, and then click Next.

10. On the Ready to Create Your Windows to Go Workspace page, select Create to create the Windows To Go workspace.

11. Choose a boot (startup) option, and then select Yes to modify the Windows Boot Manager configuration to boot automatically from your Windows To Go workspace when the drive is connected to this host computer.

12. When provisioning is complete, select Save And Restart to restart the host computer.

Configuring Wi-Fi Direct

To understand Wi-Fi Direct, you must first understand a bit about Wi-Fi and how it's used to connect to a network. So let's think about most of our home networks. You go to a big-box store to buy (or maybe order online) a wireless access point (WAP) such as Netgear or Linksys. Most of us have these at home connected to our Internet provider.

So we buy a wireless access point (WAP) like Netgear or Linksys and connect it to our Internet provider. We then connect our home systems to the wireless access points and BOOM, we all have Internet access.

Now think about being able to connect to devices without the use of a WAP. What if we could connect devices directly to each other through the high-speed wireless adapters in those devices? That is exactly what Wi-Fi Direct enables us to do.

Wi-Fi Direct is a technology that allows us to directly access other devices without requiring a separate Wi-Fi access point. Windows 10 uses near-field communication (better known as NFC) technology to allow the Windows 10 system to locate other NFC Wi-Fi enabled devices so that they can be paired together.

When devices are trying to pair together, the Near Field Proximity (NFP) receives pairing information from the device that is trying to connect. NFP then passes the pairing information to Windows 10. Windows 10 Wi-Fi Direct will then automatically follow the Wi-Fi Alliance Out-Of-Box pairing procedures for the connection.

If the pairing process connects, Windows will prompt the user for permission for the connection. If permission is given, Windows 10 will then attempt to finalize the connection. From that point on, there is no other user interaction needed.

Windows 10 gives you the ability to set whether you want to pair with other devices or not. Figure 15.29 shows the Windows 10 Privacy settings and how Windows 10 will sync with other devices.

FIGURE 15.29   Sync with devices

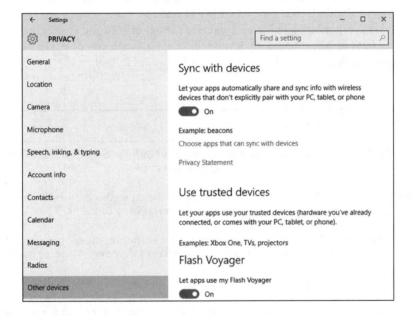

As you can see in Figure 15.29, you also have the ability to choose which applications can sync with devices. This gives an administrator or user better flexibility on whether to allow all applications to connect to all devices or only specific applications to connect.

Now that we have looked at how to use applications to configure the Windows 10 system, let's look at how we can configure the Windows 10 system by using the Registry.

Using the Registry Editor

You use the Registry Editor program to edit the Registry. This utility is designed for advanced configuration of the system. Usually, when you make changes to your configuration, you use other utilities, such as Control Panel, which was discussed in the previous section.

WARNING   Only experienced administrators should use the Registry Editor. It is intended for making configuration changes that can be made only directly through the Registry. For example, you might edit the Registry to specify an alternate location for a print-spool folder. Improper changes to the Registry can cause the computer to fail to boot. Use the Registry Editor with extreme caution.

Windows 10 uses the REGEDIT or REGEDT32 program as the primary utility for Registry editing in Windows 10. It does not matter which program you use; both support full editing of the Registry. To use REGEDIT, select Start and type **REGEDIT** in the Search dialog box. To use REGEDT32, type **REGEDT32** into the Search dialog box.

The Registry is organized in a hierarchical tree format of keys and subkeys that represent logical areas of computer configuration. By default, when you open the Registry Editor, you see five Registry key listings, as described in Table 15.4.

TABLE 15.4   Registry keys

Registry Key	Description
HKEY_CLASSES_ROOT	Configuration information used by Windows Explorer to properly associate file types with applications.
HKEY_CURRENT_USER	Configuration information for the user who is currently logged onto the computer. This key is a subkey of the HKEY_USERS key.
HKEY_LOCAL_MACHINE	Computer hardware configuration information. This computer configuration is used regardless of the user who is logged in.
HKEY_USERS	Configuration information for all users of the computer.
HKEY_CURRENT_CONFIG	Configuration of the hardware profile that is used during system startup.

Earlier in this chapter, I showed you that Remote Desktop Connection is one of the configurable Windows 10 options. In the next section, we will look at configuring different ways to remotely connect using the Windows 10 operating system and how to allow others to remotely connect to you for assistance.

Configuring Remote Connections

End-user support is a major concern and a time-consuming endeavor for most IT departments. Anything you can do to provide a more efficient solution to user issues is a major benefit. Basic telephone or chat support works in many cases, but what if you could see what the end user sees or even interface with their machine? By using Remote Assistance and Remote Desktop, you can.

Remote Assistance in Windows provides many enhancements over previous versions, including improvements in security, performance, and usability. Windows 10 goes even further by adding Easy Connect, which makes it easier for novice users to request help from expert users. Group Policy support has been increased. There is command-line functionality (meaning you can add scripting), bandwidth optimization, logging, and more.

Remote Desktop is a tool that allows you to take control of a remote computer's keyboard, video, and mouse. This tool does not require someone collaborating with you on the remote computer. Remote Desktop is used to access remote machines' applications and troubleshoot issues as well as meet end-user needs where you want complete control of the remote machine.

We'll start the discussion with Remote Assistance. Later in this section, we will also look at how to use virtual private networks (VPNs). We will look at how to configure VPNs and the protocols that work with VPNs.

Remote Assistance

Remote Assistance provides a method for inviting help by instant message, email, a file, or now an Easy Connect option. To use Remote Assistance, the computer requesting help and the computer providing help must have Remote Assistance capabilities and the feature enabled, and both computers must have network connectivity (they have to be able to talk to each other).

Remote Assistance is designed to have an expert user (the assistor) provide assistance to a novice user (assistee). When assisting a novice user, the expert can use text-based chat built into Remote Assistance. The expert can also take control of a novice user's desktop (with permission, of course). Here are two common examples of when you would use Remote Assistance:

- Diagnosing problems that are difficult to explain or reproduce. Remote Assistance can allow an expert to remotely view the computer, and the novice user can show the expert an error or problem.

- Guiding a novice user to perform a complex set of actions. The expert can also take control of the computer and complete the tasks if necessary.

Easy Connect

The Easy Connect method for getting remote assistance is new for Windows 10. Easy Connect uses Peer Name Resolution Protocol (PNRP) to set up direct peer-to-peer transfer using a central machine on the Internet to establish the connection. PNRP uses IPv6 and Teredo tunneling to register a machine as globally unique. You're not using IPv6? You are with PNRP; Windows 10 (as well as Windows 7/8, Windows Server 2008/2008 R2, and Windows Server 2012/2012 R2) has IPv6 turned on natively as well as the currently used standard of IPv4. We'll discuss IPv6 in more detail in a later chapter, but to give you an idea, you can see the structure of the PNRP Teredo IPv6 packet in Figure 15.30.

To establish a Remote Assistance session with a user using Easy Connect, the novice should open the Windows Remote Assistance screen by right-clicking Start ➤ System ➤ Remote Settings ➤ Remote tab. You can also launch the Windows Remote Assistance screen by typing **msra** in the integrated search box next to the Start menu.

FIGURE 15.30 Teredo and IPv6 PNRP structure

Remote Assistance can also be incorporated in Group Policy in an enterprise environment by having the expert user configured as a Helper for users in the enterprise (by domain or OU). Once configured as a Helper, the expert can initiate a Remote Assistance session by issuing the command msra /offerra. This will bring up the Who Do You Want To Help Remote Assistance screen.

The expert can also include the novice user's IP address or computer name as an option to the offerRA switch to initiate the Remote Assistance session in one stop (e.g., msra / offerra *ipaddress | computername*).

There are several msra.exe switches available to further control the establishment of the Remote Assistance session for both the novice and the expert user. Table 15.5 highlights many of the switches.

TABLE 15.5 MSRA command-line switches

Switch	OS Availability	Functionality
/?	Vista and above	Displays the help options.
/novice	Vista and above	Starts Remote Assistance at the Invite screen.
/expert	Vista and above	Starts Remote Assistance at the Help Someone screen.
/offerRA *ip | computer*	Vista and above	Starts Remote Assistance at the Expert Initiated screen or with the options, by automatically initiating with the novice user (used with Group Policy configured in an enterprise environment).
/email *password*	Vista and above	Creates an email invitation to be sent to an expert user to request assistance using the novice's default email program; a random password will be generated and needs to be conveyed to the expert, or alternatively a password can be specified with the password option and conveyed to the expert.

Switch	OS Availability	Functionality
/saveasfile *path password*	Vista and above	Creates a file invitation to be given to an expert user to request assistance; a random password will be generated, or optionally a password can be specified with the *password* option and conveyed to the expert.
/openfile *path*	Vista and above	Used to open the invitation file sent to the expert; can be local or on a shared network drive; the expert will enter the password given to the user when the session was initiated.
/geteasyhelp	Windows 7 and above	Starts a novice user's Remote Assistance session using Easy Connect; presents the novice with the password to convey to the expert user.
/offereasyhelp	Windows 7 and above	Starts an expert user's Remote Assistance session using Easy Connect; presents the expert user with the screen to enter the password from the novice user.
/getcontacthelp *address*	Windows 7 and above	Reestablishes a Remote Assistance session from a novice user's machine to the address from the previous session. The address is in the RAContactHistory.xml file as a 20-byte hexadecimal string with an .RAContact extension.
/offercontacthelp *address*	Windows 7 and above	Reestablishes a Remote Assistance session from an expert user's machine to the address from the previous session. The address is in the RAContactHistory.xml file as a 20-byte hexadecimal string with an .RAContact extension.

Whichever way the novice or the expert launches the feature, the Windows Remote Assistance screen will become available (see Figure 15.31). To start using Easy Connect, the novice user will select Invite Someone You Trust To Help You.

One nice feature of Easy Connect is that if the novice user has established an Easy Connect session previously with an expert user, the screen after selecting Use Easy Connect will offer the novice the ability to connect to the same expert. The novice user can also choose to invite someone new and/or delete the old contact. The expert user will have the same option after choosing Use Easy Connect from the machine used for a previous Easy Connect session.

After the Use Easy Connect option is selected, Windows 10 will verify network connectivity briefly. This is the point at which the PNRP actions take place and the novice user's information is added to a cloud on the Internet. The cloud is the group of machines holding little pieces of information—the identifiers of users needing connectivity, set up in a peer-to-peer sharing environment. PNRP uses this distributed infrastructure for its peer-to-peer name resolution. The novice user's contact information is entered into the PNRP cloud, and an associated password is created and displayed to the novice user.

FIGURE 15.31   Remote Assistance initial screen

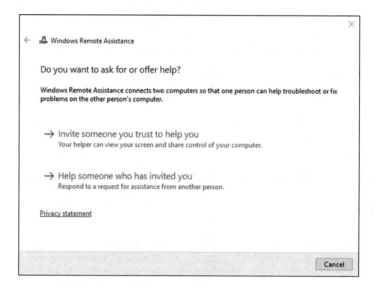

The novice user will now relay the password to the expert by text message, telephone, or any convenient conversation method. The novice will simply have to wait for the expert to initiate their part. The novice user will still have to accept the connection once the expert starts the remote assistance session.

The expert user needs to start a Remote Assistance session the same way the novice did in Figure 15.31, but the expert will choose "Help Someone Who Has Invited You" from the Windows Remote Assistance screen.

The expert user will be presented a dialog box to "use an invitation file" (Figure 15.32) and then, after choosing the file, will be prompted to enter the password to connect to the Remote Assistance session.

After a few moments of querying the PNRP cloud and finding the connection information that provides the path back to the novice user, Remote Assistance presents the novice user a confirmation box verifying that the user wants to allow help from the expert.

The novice user will then have a control bar on their screen indicating that the Remote Assistance session is active. From this control bar, the novice can initiate a chat session with the expert and modify some general session settings (bandwidth, logging, contact information exchange, and sharing control).

The expert user will be shown the novice user's desktop within a separate Remote Assistance window. The expert user will also have some general configuration-setting capabilities as well as an option to request control of the novice user's desktop. The novice user will, of course, be allowed to accept or reject the expert's request.

FIGURE 15.32   Remote Assistance screen for entering a password

The expert and novice user can now have an interactive session in which the necessary assistance can be provided. This method of help really takes out the "can you tell me what you see on your screen" issues between two users. The Easy Connect feature takes one more problem out of the equation, getting a novice user to send an invitation to another user. The one caveat here is that both users must be using Windows 10 for Easy Connect to be an option.

Now what if the user is not available to send you the invitation? You can still connect to a user's computer using Remote Desktop, which I will discuss in the next section.

Remote Desktop

Remote Desktop is a tool in Windows 10 that allows you to take control of a remote computer's keyboard, video, and mouse. This tool does not require someone to be available to collaborate with you on the remote computer. While the remote computer is being accessed, locally it remains locked and any actions that are performed remotely will not be visible to the monitor that is attached to the remote computer.

Windows 10 Remote Desktop is, again, an enhanced version of the remote desktop functionality that has been with us for many of the previous versions of Windows, both client and server operating systems. Remote Desktop uses Remote Desktop Protocol (RDP) to provide the data between a host and a client machine. Windows 10 Remote Desktop features are as follows:

- RDP Core Performance Enhancements
- True Multi-Monitor Support

- Direct 2D and Direct 3D 10.1 Application Support

- Bi-directional Audio Support

- Multimedia and Media Foundation Support

- Remote FX has a few end-user enhancements for RDP. These enhancements allow for an enhanced desktop environment within your corporate network.

There are many uses for Remote Desktop, but the most common use is that of the administrator attempting to perform a task on an end user's machine (or on a server).

Another use is the end user connecting to a machine from their home or on the road. If you have noticed the enhancements of Remote Desktop (which are enhancements to RDP), you can see that one of the main goals of enhancing Remote Desktop is to make the user experience as comfortable and seamless as possible.

 Real World Scenario

Using Remote Desktop Functionality

As an administrator, I like to just take control of an end-user machine and fix it. Although this can be done in Remote Assistance, the end user is required to allow us to have access and then can watch what I do. In Remote Desktop, I just take control and close the interactive session at the remote machine (yes, the remote end user can block us or take over the session, but not if they want their problem solved).

But there are other uses as well. I provide servers with resources to our clients, and that server may need to be changed or updated on a regular basis (sometimes a couple of changes in a day). Remote Desktop allows me to maintain our servers from wherever we are without impacting the clients or other administrators.

Remote Desktop Connection Options

When connecting to a Remote Desktop host machine, several options are available to enhance the client user session. The options allow configuration for general settings, display options, local resource access, programs to be executed on startup, the user experience, and advanced options for security and Remote Desktop gateway access. The options become available by clicking the Options button in the lower-left area of the initial Remote Desktop Connection screen. Figure 15.33 shows the options window displayed.

From the General tab, you can select the target remote computer and username. You can save the user credentials from this tab as well. You can save the connection settings to a file or open an existing RDP file from the General tab.

From the Display tab you can choose the size of the display screen. This is also where you select the option to use multiple monitors. The color depth (color quality) is also selected in the Display tab. The option to display the connection bar when using full-screen display is available here as well.

FIGURE 15.33   Remote Desktop options

From the Local Resources tab you can configure remote audio settings, keyboard settings, and local device and resource access.

The Programs tab for Remote Desktop options allows the selection of a program to run at connection startup. The program name and path are specified, as is a startup folder if necessary.

The end-user experience is important to the overall success of using Remote Desktop in the user environment. Remote Desktop can be used to provide a user with the ability to connect to their machine and "remote in." The most seamless environment from the user to the remote location is desirable, but that will be dependent on the bandwidth available. The more bandwidth, the more high-end features can be made available to the end user.

This is also nice for the administrator who is working on an end-user machine. The Experience tab allows the configuration of the end-user experience.

Controlling the behavior of the Remote Desktop connection with regard to security is configured on the Advanced tab of the Remote Desktop options dialog box. The Advanced tab also supports the configuration of a Remote Desktop gateway to allow Remote Desktop connections to be established from any Internet location through SSL. The user must still be authorized, and the Remote Desktop client must still be available.

One very cool feature of using RDP is that if you connect from a touch-compatible device, your RDP session will have touch, regardless if the target machine has a touch screen. For example, if you are on a surface Pro and you RDP into a Windows 10 desktop without a touch-capable monitor, you will be able to control the Windows 10 desktop with touch options of the Surface Pro.

In Exercise 15.7, you will enable the Windows 10 machine to allow Remote Desktop connections. It is up to the company to decide whether all user machines are to be configured this way when you install Windows 10 or whether you should do this only when it becomes necessary for a given computer.

EXERCISE 15.7

Enabling Remote Desktop

1. Open the System tool by right-clicking Start ≻ Control Panel ≻ System.

2. On the left-hand side, click the Remote Settings link.

3. In the Remote Desktop section, click the radio button that allows connections from computers running any version of Remote Desktop (Less Secure).

4. Make sure the Allow Remote Assistance Connections To This Computer check box is checked.

5. Click OK.

6. Close the System Properties screen.

One way a Windows 10 user can connect to a server is through the use of a virtual private network connection. In the next section, we will look at how to configure a VPN connection on Windows 10.

Configuring a VPN Connection

A virtual private network is a way to establish a connection between a client machine (VPN client) and server machine (VPN server). A VPN gives you the ability to connect (called *tunneling*) to a server through the use of the Internet or a dial-up connection (hopefully not dial-up), typically with the intention of accessing resources that are available on the network where the VPN server is connected. The VPN server acts as a bridge for the external user connecting from the Internet or other external connections point, to the internal network. In a nutshell, a VPN allows you to connect to a private network from a public network.

VPN connections can be secured using various protocols. The following list shows you some of the tunneling protocols that can be used when connecting a Windows 10 machine to a remote server:

Internet Key Exchange version 2 (IKEv2)   Windows 10 can connect to a Windows Server VPN using the *Internet Key Exchange version 2 (IKEv2)* VPN tunneling protocol. The IKEv2 VPN protocol is the newest VPN protocol out of all of the following protocols and can be used with Windows Server 2012/2012 R2. The main advantage of using the IKEv2 VPN protocol is that it allows for the interruptions of the network connection. IKEv2 will then automatically restore the VPN connection after the network connection is restored. This feature is referred to as VPN Reconnect, and it is automatically built into the IKEv2 protocol.

Secure Socket Tunneling Protocol   *Secure Socket Tunneling Protocol (SSTP)* was released with Windows Server 2008 and is one of the tunneling protocols available with a Windows Server 2008/2008 R2 server and Windows 7 machines and later. SSTP works by allowing encapsulated Point-to-Point Protocol (PPP) packets to be transmitted over an HTTPS connection. Because of this, firewalls or Network Address Translation (NAT) devices allow SSTP VPN connections to be more easily established. SSTP is the best choice for securing a VPN connection.

Point-to-Point Tunneling Protocol   *Point-to-Point Tunneling Protocol (PPTP)* is one of the predecessors to SSTP, and it also allows point-to-point packets to have encryption for secure connections. PPTP uses TCP/IP for the encryption. PPTP encapsulates PPP frames in IP and uses the TCP for the management side of PPTP.

Layer 2 Tunneling Protocol   *Layer 2 Tunneling Protocol (L2TP)* is a tunneling protocol that has no encryption included in the protocol. L2TP uses the IP Security protocol (IPSec) to make L2TP secure. L2TP with IPSec is a much more secure tunneling option than PPTP.

To set up an outbound client VPN connection in Windows 10, you use the Network And Sharing Center. In Exercise 15.8, you will set up a new VPN connection.

EXERCISE 15.8

Setting Up a VPN Connection

1. Start the Network And Sharing Center by right-clicking Start ➢ Control Panel ➢ Network And Sharing Center.

2. Choose the Set Up A New Connection Or Network link.

3. Choose Connect To A Workplace. Click Next.

4. Choose the Use My Internet Connection (VPN) option.

5. The Connect To A Workplace screen appears. You need to type in the TCP/IP address of a VPN Server and name this VPN connection. In this window, you also have the ability to use a smart card, to allow other people to use this connection, and to set up the VPN but not connect at this time (the option I chose). After you type in a TCP/IP address and name the VPN connection, click Next.

6. The next screen asks you for your logon credentials. Type in your username, password, and domain name. Click Create.

   Now that the connection is created, I'll show you the steps needed to use it.

7. In the lower-right corner, click your network connection.

8. A box appears showing your connections. To connect to the VPN connection, choose the corresponding link.

9. When the Connect dialog box appears, make sure your username, password, and domain name are present and click the Connect button.

10. After the connection is established, close it and close the Network and Sharing Center.

Transparent Caching

Windows 10 has a feature called *transparent caching* to help reduce the time needed for retrieving shared files and folders. Transparent caching reduces the time required to access files for the second and subsequent times across a slow network.

In previous versions of Windows, to access a file across a slower network, client computers had to retrieve the file from the server computer. But now with Windows 10 transparent caching, computers can cache these remote files, thus reducing the number of times a computer might retrieve the same data.

When a user opens a file for the first time, Windows 10 accesses the file from the server and then stores the file in the cache of the local disk. From that point on, the user reads the same cached file instead of reading it from the server computer.

To make sure the file is accurate; the Windows 10 client always contacts the server to ensure the cached copy is up to date. The file would not be accessible if the server is unavailable. Transparent caching is not enabled by default on fast networks. Transparent caching can be enabled through the use of a group policy.

Broadband Tethering

One nice advantage to Windows 10 and mobility is Broadband Tethering. Let's all pretend that we are at a large Microsoft conference and only one of us in our group can get onto the Internet. Windows 10 Broadband Tethering allows at least 10 devices to connect to your Internet connection and use your Internet for their access. As long as their devices have Broadband-enabled capabilities, they will be able to connect to your system and use the Internet.

When you set up the Broadband Tethering, you can set up a connection name and password for all of the other users in your group to connect to your system.

All you need to do is go to your Windows 10 mobile device (in Figure 15.34), I'm using a Windows 10 Surface Pro, and you just need to open your Internet connection by sharing the connection.

As you can see in Figure 15.35, once you open the connection up, you need to set up a password (at least eight characters), and then you can share that password with the other members of your group who you want to allow your Internet to be shared with.

In the next section, we will look at how to configure Windows 10 Services.

FIGURE 15.34   Manage Wi-Fi Settings

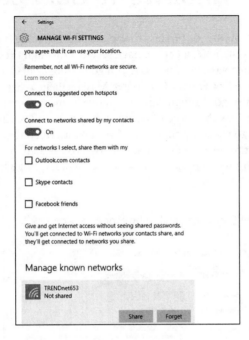

FIGURE 15.35   Manage Wi-Fi Settings password

Managing Windows 10 Services

A *service* is a program, routine, or process that performs a specific function within the Windows 10 operating system. You can manage services through the Services window, which can be accessed in a variety of ways. If you go through the Computer Management utility, you can just right-click Start ➢ Computer Management ➢ Services And Applications. You can also go through Administrative Tools in Control Panel.

The Services window lists the name of each service, a short description, the status, the startup type, and the logon account that is used to start it. To configure the properties of a service, double-click it to open its Properties dialog box, shown in Figure 15.36. This dialog box contains four tabs of options for services: General, Log On, Recovery, and Dependencies.

FIGURE 15.36   The Properties dialog box for a service

General   This tab allows you to view and configure the following options:

- The service display name
- The display name
- A description of the service
- The path to the service executable
- The startup type, which can be automatic, manual, or disabled

- The current service status
- Start parameters that can be applied when the service is started

In addition, the buttons across the lower part of the dialog box allow you change the service state to start, stop, pause, or if paused you can also resume the service.

Log On   The Log On tab allows you to configure the logon account that will be used to start the service. Choose the local system account or specify another logon account.

Recovery   The Recovery tab allows you to designate what action will be taken if the service fails to load. For the first, second, and subsequent failures, you can select a discrete action from the following list:

- Take No Action
- Restart The Service
- Run A Program
- Restart The Computer

If you choose Run A Program, specify it along with any command-line parameters. If you choose Restart The Computer, you can configure a message that will be sent to users who are connected to the computer before it is restarted. You can also specify how long until a machine is restarted if an error occurs.

Dependencies   The Dependencies tab lists any services that must be running in order for the specified service to start. If a service fails to start, you can use this information to examine the dependencies and then make sure each one is running. In the bottom panel, you can verify whether any other services depend on this service before you decide to stop it.

In Exercise 15.9, you will complete the steps needed to configure services in the Windows 10 operating system.

EXERCISE 15.9

Configuring Services

1. Start Computer Management by right-clicking Start ➢ Computer Management ➢ Services And Applications.

2. Click the Services link.

3. Scroll down the list and double-click Remote Desktop Configuration.

4. Under Startup Type, choose Automatic.

5. Under the Logon tab, click the This Account radio button.

6. Click the Browse button and choose the local administrator account. Click OK.

7. In the Password boxes, type and verify the administrator password.

8. In the Recovery tab, make sure the following settings are configured:

   Action: Response

   First Failure: Restart The Service

   Second Failure: Restart The Service

   Subsequent Failures: Take No Action

   Reset Fail Count After: 1 Day

   Restart Service After: 10 Minutes

9. Click the OK button.

10. Close the Computer Management MMC.

Services are just another troubleshooting and configuring tool that is part of your arsenal of troubleshooting techniques. Just remember that when your services are working properly, your Windows 10 operating system will be working properly.

Summary

Besides actually installing Windows 10, configuring the operating system properly is one of the most important tasks that an IT team can perform.

Configuring the desktop environment allows an administrator to configure an environment that is comfortable for the end user, which in turn makes the user more productive.

Understanding the Start menu and Control Panel icons allows you to configure and operate the Windows 10 applications more efficiently. Knowing how to configure the System icon properly in Control Panel allows you to fine-tune the Windows 10 operating system and get the best performance possible out of it.

In addition to using Control Panel to configure the Windows 10 operating system, you can edit the Registry directly using the REGEDIT or REGEDT32 utility.

Another important consideration when configuring Windows 10 is how the operating system will function when installed on a laptop or tablet (Windows Mobility). By configuring the mobility options on a laptop, you can allow that laptop to connect to their data in multiple ways.

We also looked at services that run on Windows 10 and how to configure and troubleshoot them when they don't run properly.

Video Resources

There are videos available for the following exercises:

15.1

15.2

15.3

You can access the videos at www.wiley.com/go/sybextestprep on the Other Study Tools tab.

Exam Essentials

Be able to configure Desktop settings.   Understand how to customize and configure the Windows 10 Desktop settings. This includes setting a desktop and also setting up desktop personalization. It is also important to know how to configure the Taskbar and Start menu.

Be able to support mobile computers through power-management features.   Understand the new power features that are available in Windows 10 and be able to configure a laptop computer to use them.

Understand remote connections.   Know how to configure and connect to machines through remote connections. You can use Remote Assistance, Remote Desktop, and a VPN.

Know how to configure services.   Understand how to stop, start, monitor, pause, and configure services on the Windows 10 operating system. Know how to configure the different properties available through services.

Review Questions

1. You are the system administrator for your company. You are configuring the services on a Windows 10 computer. You want to ensure that if a service fails to load, it will attempt to restart. Which tab of the service's Properties dialog box should you use?

   A. General

   B. Log On

   C. Recovery

   D. Dependencies

2. The system administrator of your network wants to edit the Registry, including setting security on the Registry keys. What primary utilities that support full editing of the Windows 10 Registry should the system administrator use? (Choose all that apply.)

   A. REGEDIT

   B. REDIT

   C. REGEDT32

   D. REGEDITOR

3. Kayla is dissatisfied with the configuration of her keyboard and mouse. She wants to reset the keyboard speed and the mouse pointer rate. Which utility should she use to configure the keyboard and mouse properties?

   A. Control Panel

   B. Computer Management

   C. Microsoft Management Console

   D. Registry Editor

4. Denise is using a laptop computer that uses ACPI. She wants to see what percentage of the battery power is still available. She also wants to know if hibernation has been configured. Which of the following utilities should she use?

   A. Device Manager

   B. Computer Manager

   C. Battery meter

   D. MMC

5. You are administering a computer that is used by several customer-support representatives for your company. The support representatives use a custom application to report support incidents. After the application is updated, it stops functioning properly, and one of the programmers who wrote the application indicates that a Registry change needs to be made to the computer. You need to ensure that the change is applied for each user of the computer. Which Registry key should you modify?

   A. HKEY_CLASSES_ROOT

   B. HKEY_CURRENT_USER

   C. HKEY_LOCAL_MACHINE

   D. HKEY_USERS

6. You have a user, Rob, who uses a laptop computer running Windows 10. You have configured the laptop to enter sleep mode after 30 minutes of inactivity. What will occur when the computer enters sleep mode?

   A. The data will be saved to the hard disk, and the computer will shut down.

   B. The data will be erased from RAM, and the computer will shut down.

   C. The monitor will be turned off, but the hard disks will remain active.

   D. The data will be saved to memory, and the computer will be put into a power-saving state.

7. You want to speed up the resume time on your computer after it is put into hibernation mode. You have installed a hybrid hard-disk drive into your Windows 10 computer. Which technology should you use to accomplish your goal?

   A. ReadyDrive

   B. ReadyBoost

   C. Superfetch

   D. SuperDrive

8. A new employee named Crystal has been supplied with a Windows 10 laptop computer. You have configured Crystal's computer with the Power Saver power plan, and you used the default options. Which of the following will occur after 20 minutes of inactivity on Crystal's computer?

   A. The display will be turned off, but the hard disk will remain active.

   B. The hard disk will be turned off, but the display will remain active.

   C. Both the hard disk and the display will be turned off.

   D. No components will be turned off.

9. You are the network administrator for a medium-size company. You support all user Desktop issues. Gary is using the default Windows 10 Desktop on his laptop computer. Gary wants to change his Desktop settings. Which of the following options should Gary use to configure the Desktop in Windows 10?

   A. Right-click an empty space on the Desktop and choose Personalize from the context menu.

   B. Select Control Panel ➢ System.

   C. Right-click My Computer and choose Manage from the context menu.

   D. Right-click My Computer and choose Properties from the context menu.

10. You work on the help desk for a large company. One of your users calls you and reports that they just accidentally deleted their C:\Documents\Timesheet.xls file. What is the easiest way to recover this file?

    A. In Folder Options, click the Show Deleted Files option.

    B. In Folder Options, click the Undo Deleted Files option.

    C. Click the Recycle Bin icon on the Desktop and restore the deleted file.

    D. Restore the file from your most recent tape backup.

Chapter

16

Planning and Managing Microsoft Intune

MICROSOFT EXAM OBJECTIVES COVERED IN THIS CHAPTER:

✓ **Manage devices with Microsoft Intune.**

- This objective may include but is not limited to the following subobjectives: Provision user accounts, enroll devices, view and manage all managed devices, configure the Microsoft Intune subscriptions, configure the Microsoft Intune connector site system role, manage user and computer groups, configure monitoring and alerts, manage policies, manage remote computers.

✓ **Deploy software updates by using Microsoft Intune.**

- This objective may include but is not limited to the following subobjectives: Use reports and In-Console Monitoring to identify required updates, approve or decline updates, configure automatic approval settings, configure deadlines for update installations, deploy third-party updates.

✓ **Support mobile devices.**

- This objective may include but is not limited to the following subobjectives: Support mobile device policies including security policies, remote access, and remote wipe; support mobile access and data synchronization including Work Folders and Sync Center; support broadband connectivity including broadband tethering and metered networks; support Mobile Device Management by using Microsoft Intune, including Windows Phone, iOS, and Android.

✓ **Support Windows Store and cloud apps.**

- This objective may include but is not limited to the following subobjectives: Deeplink apps by using Microsoft Intune; sideload apps by using Microsoft Intune.

✓ **Support desktop apps.**

- This objective may include but is not limited to the following subobjective: Deploy desktop apps by using Microsoft Intune.

In this chapter, we will start diving into the world of the cloud. I am going to talk about Microsoft Intune and how you can manage devices and software by using Microsoft Intune. I will show you how to set up and configure an Intune subscription and how you can use that subscription to help your network users get the most out of the network resources and software.

I will start the chapter by talking about managing devices using Intune. I will show you how to provision user accounts and enroll devices. I will also discuss how to manage and configure devices using the Microsoft Intune subscription.

I will then continue the discussion by showing you how to deploy and configure updates using Intune. I will show you how to use the In-Console monitoring tools and how to approve and decline updates.

I will then talk about working with mobile devices including Windows tablets, broadband metering, and tethering, as well as how to wipe mobile devices for employees who leave the company.

I will then show you how to use Intune to help deploy and maintain your company's software packages. I will also talk to you about sideloading applications into your users' devices and the different types of reports that you can run to check on the various hardware and software in your environment.

Let's get started by discussing how you can use Microsoft Intune to help manage and maintain your corporate devices.

Managing Devices with Microsoft Intune

The first thing we need to discuss in this chapter is exactly what Microsoft Intune is. Microsoft Intune is a device management system (see Figure 16.1). *Microsoft Intune* allows administrators to manage mobile devices, mobile applications, and PC management capabilities all from the cloud.

Administrators using Intune can provide their users with access to corporate applications, data, and resources from almost anywhere and on almost any device while also keeping corporate information secure.

FIGURE 16.1   Microsoft Intune dashboard

Microsoft Intune also helps you save money because it allows you to license users instead of devices. So if you have a user who works from multiple devices (laptop, tablet, and Windows Phone), you pay only once for the user license instead of multiple times for all of the user's devices.

Administrators can use Microsoft Intune to support and manage Windows 10. Administrators can use Intune on a Windows 10 device for the following:

- Enrollment
- Organization resource access
- Application management
- Policies
- Inventory
- Reporting
- Remote wipe

Microsoft Intune is built on Microsoft Azure Active Directory and System Center. Active Directory is a Directory Services database created by Microsoft. Directory Services was originally designed by Novell, and starting in Windows Server 2000, Microsoft's version—Active Directory—was introduced to the world. To put this in an easy way to think about, Active Directory is just a database that allows administrators to control access to the network.

Microsoft has now taken Active Directory to a new level with cloud-based Active Directory, or Azure Active Directory. Now instead of requiring your organization to buy Windows Server and the required hardware, you can just use a cloud-based version of Active Directory.

Azure Active Directory will be covered again in Chapters 17, "Configuring Applications," and in even greater detail in Chapter 19, "Configuring Network Connectivity."

Microsoft System Center Configuration Manager allows administrators to have a wide-ranging solution for change and configuration management. Configuration Manager allows an administrator to perform the following tasks:

- Deploy corporate operating systems, applications, and updates
- Monitor and fix computers for compliance requirements
- Monitor hardware and software inventory
- Remotely administer devices

Understanding Microsoft Intune Benefits

Microsoft Intune has many different benefits to help an IT department be more productive and keep its systems running all on the same software. Intune provides an IT department the ability to keep corporate data secure while allowing users to access the same company software from any device that they want to work from. Here are some other Intune benefits:

- Multiple device enrollments for users. Licenses are per user and not per device, so users can work from multiple devices.
- Corporate data security for users and applications like Microsoft Exchange, Outlook, and Office.
- The ability to use Office 365 from any approved device.
- Since Microsoft Intune is a cloud-based system, the IT department is not required to build an infrastructure. This saves the additional cost of buying and maintaining hardware and software.
- Microsoft Intune extends your System Center Configuration Manager through both the cloud and on-premise versions by connecting the two systems together through the use of an application connector.
- Microsoft 24/7 support is available through worldwide phone support or online support. Also, administrators have access to Microsoft.com for Intune FAQs and its knowledge base.
- Corporations have multiple licensing options available to them to choose from. Intune is also part of the Enterprise Mobility Suite by default.

Configuring Intune Subscriptions

When you are deciding about using Microsoft Intune, you must think about the subscription type that you want. You can start with a free 30-day trial or move directly into a full paid subscription. Either choice allows you to start managing mobile devices and corporate computers immediately.

One of the nice advantages to the Intune subscriptions is that if you decide to add at least 150 user licenses, you get to use Microsoft's FastTrack Benefits Center. This benefit also allows a Microsoft specialist to work with your organization. This Microsoft specialist then helps you get the most out of using Intune and all of its benefits.

To start using Microsoft Intune is a very easy and free process. You go out to Microsoft's website and sign up for a free 30-day trial of Intune. Then you start adding your users, groups, and devices. Then if you decide that Microsoft Intune is right for your organization, you can sign up for one of their monthly rates.

Once you have decided to take that next step, you need to start redesigning your company's infrastructure to include the cloud-based subscription. This can be as easy as setting up your DNS servers to include the cloud-based services or as complex as adding all of your devices to the cloud and phasing out many of the infrastructure servers that you currently have running in house.

Whatever you decide, one of the most important phases of moving to a cloud-based system is planning. Once you have made the decision to move to the cloud, that's when the real work happens. Here are some questions to think about:

- Will you be moving all users to Azure Active Directory?

- Will you be using the cloud just for device and software deployment?

- Will you be phasing out in-house equipment?

- Will you allow users to use their own devices (Bring Your Own Device—BYOD)?

- If users use their personal devices, will you supply them with corporate software applications?

- Will you be using Office 2013 or Office 365?

When you sign up for a Microsoft Intune account, you will choose a domain for your Intune subscription. After you sign up for your Intune subscription, Microsoft will send you an email that will have your Intune information contained within the email. Figure 16.2 shows an example of the information contained within the Microsoft Intune email.

In Exercise 16.1, I will show you how to set up a free Microsoft Intune 30-day trial account. You will need to complete this exercise to do some of the other exercises in this chapter.

FIGURE 16.2   Microsoft Intune email

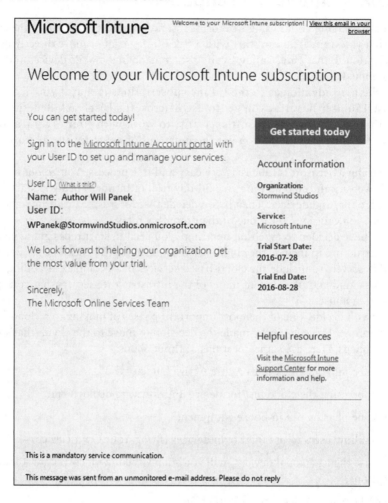

Setting Up a Microsoft Intune Account

1. Go to the Microsoft Intune website (http://www.microsoft.com/en-us/server-cloud/products/microsoft-intune/overview.aspx).

2. Click the Try Now button.

3. On the Welcome to Microsoft Intune page, fill out the required information (Country, First Name, Last Name, etc., as shown in Figure 16.3), and then click Next.

FIGURE 16.3   Microsoft Intune signup

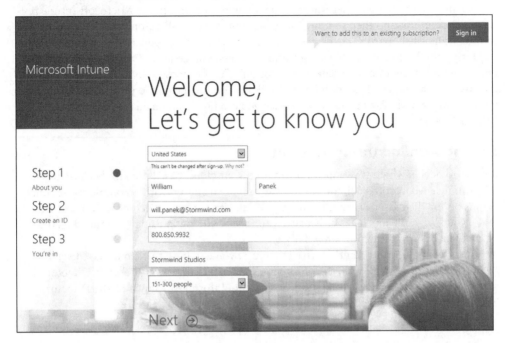

4. On the Create Username screen, create a username and password. Click Next.

5. You will need to prove you're not an Internet robot by verifying your account. Type in a cell phone number so that a verification code can be texted to you. Then enter the code and click Verify. Then click the Create my Account link.

6. You will get a screen with a link to your portal and your username. Print this page for later use.

7. Type the portal link into your web browser and then enter your username and password.

8. In the lower-left corner of the Menu window, click the Intune link to bring up the Intune dashboard.

Provisioning User Accounts

Once you have decided to sign up for the Microsoft Intune subscription, you next need to start assigning your corporate users and groups to Intune. By assigning users and groups, you are choosing which individuals get to access the cloud-based services of Intune, and the IT department gets to start using all of the Intune benefits.

As stated previously, once you sign up for the Microsoft Intune subscription, you will receive an email with your user information along with a link to the Microsoft Intune portal. Click that link and then sign in. Once you sign in, you will automatically be redirected to the Intune Dashboard. This is where you can start creating your users and groups.

During the Microsoft Intune subscription process, you create a domain name, and that domain is added to a Microsoft extension by default. So, if I choose a domain named Stormwind, then the default Microsoft subscription will look like Stormwind.onmicrosoft.com. If your company already owns its own domain name, then you can use that domain instead of the default Microsoft option.

Setting Administrator Accounts

Be sure to decide which way you want to set up your cloud-based domain because if you decide to use Microsoft's default, all of your users will end up with an onmicrosoft.com extension for their User Principal Names (UPNs). Using a pre-owned domain name can make your life in IT much easier because your users will log in using the same domain name that they are using now on a daily basis.

When setting up your Azure Active Directory, you can have this cloud-based version of Active Directory work with the on-premise server-based version of Active Directory by using the Azure Active Directory (AD) Connect tool (formerly known as the Directory Synchronization tool, the Directory Sync tool, or the DirSync.exe tool).

You can download the Azure Active Directory Connect tool from the Microsoft website https://www.microsoft.com/en-us/download/details.aspx?id=47594.

The Azure Active Directory (AD) Connect tool is a server-based application that can be installed onto a server that is currently joined to your local domain. The connect tool allows your corporate onsite users to synchronize to your cloud-based services.

When you decide to connect your Azure Active Directory to your onsite server-based Active Directory, user administration becomes much easier for your IT department. It allows your users to use a single sign-on to access both the local resources and the cloud-based resources. When users have to log in using different accounts, it puts more stress on an IT department and/or help desk.

The first users that you should add to Microsoft Intune are your administrators. By adding the administrators first, then they can start to help also build other user accounts. When you are choosing administrative privileges, you can choose from three administrator types: Tenant Administrator, Service Administrator, or Device Enrollment Manager. Let's take a look at each of these administrator's permissions.

Tenant Administrator

Organizations have the ability to set an administrator up as tenant administrators. Tenant Administrators are used for very specific tasks. Normally, Tenant Administrators are assigned only one dministrator role. This one administrative role determines the administrative scope for the user and the tasks they can manage. Tenant Administrators can be any of the following roles:

Billing Administrator   The Billing Administrator makes purchases, handles company subscriptions, manages support items, and handles service health issues.

Global Administrator   The Global Administrator has the ability to access all administrative features. By default, the administrator who signs up for the Intune subscription is the Global Administrator for your organization.

- Global Administrators are the only administrators who can assign other administrator their rights.
- Organizations have the ability to have more than one Global Administrator within your organization.

Password Administrator   Password Administrators have the ability to deal with user password issues like resetting passwords, managing requests, and monitoring service health. Password Administrators are allowed to reset passwords for users and other password administrators.

Service Support Administrator   Service Support Administrators can manage service requests, and they can handle service health requests.

User Management Administrator   User Management Administrators can deal with user issues like resetting passwords, handling service health requests, and managing user accounts and groups.

Service Administrator

This is a tough role to truly understand because Intune doesn't assign a Service Administrator role. Actually, the Service Administrator role is just a Tenant Administrator role with the Global Administrator permission assigned to the individual who signed up for the Microsoft Intune subscription. Service Administrators use the administrative console to handle the daily tasks for Intune.

Device Enrollment Manager

One of the great benefits of using Microsoft Intune is the ability of users to enroll multiple devices. By default, each user can enroll five devices if they want. If you want a user to help other users enroll devices, then you can also make a user a Device Enrollment Manager. This role allows an administrator or user the ability to enroll devices for other users. This is also useful for companies that have kiosk-type machines. Your Device Enrollment Manager can enroll these types of systems.

Creating a User in Intune

Once you have decided to use Microsoft Intune, you must start setting up user accounts within Intune so that your users can start accessing the benefits of using Intune.

For users to access Intune, they must have a valid license. When a user has a valid user license, they can then enroll up to five of their devices. This way they can use different devices to do different tasks from both work and home.

When adding users into the Intune portal, you can do it either one user at a time or by bulk import from a CSV file. When adding users, you must assign licenses to each of these users. No matter how you add a user, adding a license to that user is not necessary at the time the user is created. But a license must be associated to that user before that user can access Intune.

If you decide to import your users from your on-site Active Directory to the cloud, the users will *not* have a license. You will be required to assign licenses to your users after the Active Directory merger to Intune.

Let's take a look at how easy it is to create a new user. In Exercise 16.2, I will walk you through the process of creating a new user in the Intune Management Console.

EXERCISE 16.2

Adding Users into Microsoft Intune

1. Open the Microsoft Intune portal by clicking the link in the email that you received from creating your subscription in Exercise 16.1.

2. Once you're in the Intune Dashboard, click the Users link under Management.

3. In the center of the console under Users, you will see a New button with a down arrow. Click New and choose User (shown in Figure 16.4).

FIGURE 16.4 Intune new user

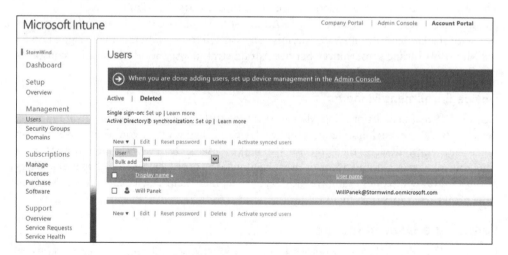

4. If you are asked to re-log back in, enter your Intune username and password.

5. On the New User Details screen, enter the user's First Name, Last Name, Display Name, and Username (see Figure 16.5). Click Next.

FIGURE 16.5   Intune New User Details

6. On the Assign Role screen, you must decide if this new user should have administrative rights and which type. You can choose Yes or No on this step. (I chose Yes, gave the user global administrator privileges, and set up an email address for administrative emails.) Click Next.

7. At the Group screen, just click Next. You will add users to a group in another exercise.

8. At the Send Results In An Email screen, make sure there is an email address for this user and click Create.

9. At the Results screen, print out the user's temporary password (see Figure 16.6). Click Finish.

FIGURE 16.6   Intune New User Results page

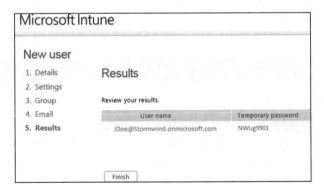

10. Close the Intune portal.

Now that we have looked at creating a user in the Intune Management Console, let's take a look at how to create device groups.

Creating Device Groups

Creating groups in Intune helps administrators have more flexibility when it comes to Intune management. Administrators can set up groups based on devices, users, geographic locations, departments, or even hardware types.

There are two main types of groups in Microsoft Intune: device groups and user groups. The groups are created in about the same way, but deciding which groups to create is when the planning and decision making takes place.

When creating new device groups, you can choose which types of devices you want to manage. For example, you can choose mobile devices or all devices. Also, when creating groups, you must add your groups to a parent group. For devices, the parent group is called All Devices. As you create more groups, those groups can become parent groups to other groups.

It is very important to understand that when you create a child group off a parent group, that child group can't be moved to another parent group without deleting the group. So for example, let's say that I have a group called Corporate and a group called NH. If I create a child group called Portsmouth under Corporate and then want it to be a child group off the NH group, I have to delete the Portsmouth group and re-create it under NH. It's important to understand that when you delete groups, the users do *not* get deleted when the groups get deleted.

Administrators create device groups to help deploy applications and updates to specific devices. In Exercise 16.3, I will show you how to create a device group using the Microsoft Intune Management Console.

EXERCISE 16.3

Creating a Device Group

1. Open the Microsoft Intune portal and sign in.

2. In the Intune Management Console, click the Groups link on the left side.

3. In the window on the right, under Tasks, click the Create Group link (shown in Figure 16.7).

FIGURE 16.7 Choosing the Create Group task

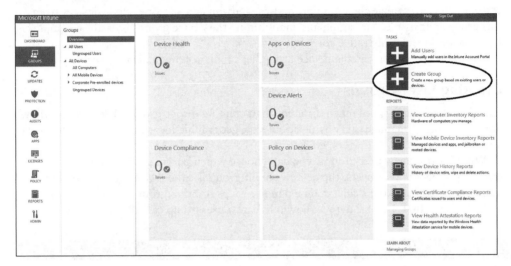

4. At the Create Group screen, under Group Name type **My Devices**. You can add a description to the Description section. Under the section called Select, choose a parent group, click the All Devices choice, and then click Next.

5. At the Define Membership Criteria screen, choose what type of devices you want to include. For this exercise, we are changing the device type from Mobile to All Devices. Click Next.

6. At the Define Direct Membership screen, you can include or exclude devices from this group. Since this group was created using all devices, we are not going to exclude anything. Just click Next.

7. At the Summary screen, verify that everything is correct and click the Finish button (shown in Figure 16.8).

FIGURE 16.8 Create Group Summary screen

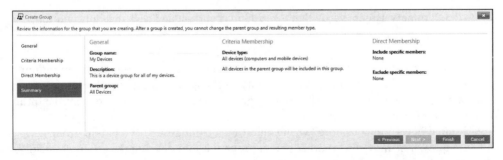

After you create the group, you can view and manage it from the Intune administrative console. You can change the group properties, and you can add or exclude devices from this group at any time. Managing and maintaining the device groups is easily accomplished from the Intune administrative console.

Now that you have created a device group, let's look at how to create a security group.

Creating User Groups

Creating user groups is not much different than creating device groups. User groups allow administrators to manage users by position type, geographic location, or even by hierarchy (executives, directors, managers, etc.).

When creating new user groups, you can choose which parent group you want your group to be part of. For users, the default parent group is called All Users. As you create more groups, those groups can become parent groups to other groups.

In Exercise 16.4, I will show you how to create a user group called Intune Users.

EXERCISE 16.4

Creating a Security User Group

1. Open the Microsoft Intune portal and sign in.

2. In the Intune Management Console, click the Groups link on the left side.

3. In the window on the right, under Tasks, click the Create Group link.

4. At the Create Group screen, under Group Name type **Intune Users**. You can add a description to the Description section. Under Select A Parent Group, click the All Users choice and then click Next.

5. At the Define Membership Criteria screen, choose what type of users you want to include. For this exercise, we are using All Users in the Parent group. Click Next.

6. At the Define Direct Membership screen, you can include or exclude users from this group. Since this group was created using all users, we are not going to exclude anyone. Just click Next.

7. At the Summary screen, verify that everything is correct and click the Finish button.

After you create the security group, you can manage that group from the Intune administrative console. Administrators have the ability to change the group membership at any time. Managing and maintaining the security groups is easily accomplished from the Intune administrative console.

As I stated in the previous note, when you create a child group off a parent group, that child group can't be moved to another parent group without deleting the group. Remember, when you delete groups, the users do *not* get deleted when the groups are deleted.

Now that you have seen how to create users and groups in Intune, let's look at how to set up Intune policies.

Creating Intune Policies

Administrators have the ability to place rules on security settings, firewall settings, and endpoint protection settings on their Intune mobile devices and applications. Think of Intune policies as network Group Policies. These are rules that you can put on devices or users.

Once you decide to move to Microsoft Intune for your devices, it's important to use Intune policies to help manage the devices on your network and set up endpoint protection. Microsoft Intune helps your IT staff deploy devices and applications, and Intune policies allow the IT team to manage the settings on these deployments. When you build a policy, you can deploy that policy to the user groups that you set up in the previous section. Then when the user logs in to Intune, the policy becomes their baseline policy.

You can create policies for the different types of devices available for Microsoft Intune. You can create policies for Android, iOS, Mac OS X, Windows, software, Computer Manager, and common mobile device settings.

In Exercise 16.5, I will walk you through the steps required to set up a Microsoft Intune policy. Administrators have the option to change the policy at any time.

EXERCISE 16.5

Creating an Intune Policy

1. Open the Intune administration portal.

2. In the left pane, click the Policy icon (see Figure 16.9).

FIGURE 16.9   Policy screen

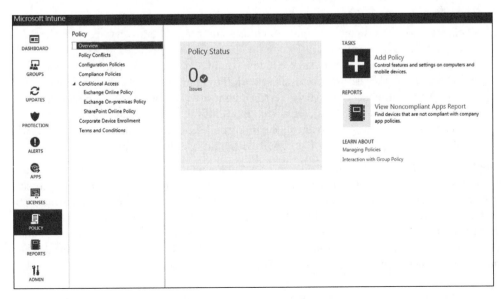

3. In the Tasks section on the Policy Status page, click the Add Policy link.

4. In the policy list, expand the platform you want to create a policy for; select Windows ➢ General Configuration ➢ Windows 10 Desktop And Mobile And Later. Under the General Configuration section, click the Create And Deploy A Custom Policy radio button. Then click the Create Policy button.

5. In the Create Policy window, type in a policy name and description. Then choose which policies you want to enforce under the Password, Encryption, System, Cloud, Applications, Apps, Device Capabilities, Hardware, Features, and Update sections. Click the Save Policy button.

6. If prompted to deploy this policy now, click the No button. If you want to deploy the policy, go ahead and click Yes, but for these exercises we do not want to configure live settings in a test environment.

7. To apply the policy to a user or device group, click the policy and then right-click the policy and choose Manage Deployment.

8. When prompted to select the groups to which you want to deploy this policy, select Intune Users from the previous exercise, and click Add. Then click OK.

Now that we have looked at how to set up Intune users, groups, and policies, it's time to look at how an administrator enrolls devices in Intune.

Enrolling Devices Using Intune

To take advantage of using Intune, you must enroll devices into the Intune system. To enroll clients into this system, you must download the Intune client software onto the devices that need to be enrolled.

For some of the devices on the market today, you may need to take additional steps in order for them to work with your Intune network. For example, to use the Apple iOS, an Apple Push Notification service (APNs) certificate must be imported from Apple so that you can manage iOS devices. This certificate allows Intune administrators to manage iOS.

When an administrator goes to enroll the many different devices on the Intune network, as stated, some of the different devices require different installation options.

Apple iOS   Administrators need to import an Apple Push Notification service certificate from Apple so that you can manage iOS devices. Administrators need to open the Microsoft Intune administration portal and go to Administration ➢ Mobile Device Management ➢ iOS and Mac OS X ➢ Download the APNs Certificate Requests (see Figure 16.10). Administrators then must save the certificate signing request (.csr) file locally. The .csr file is used to request a trust relationship certificate from the Apple Push Certificates Portal. The administrator then needs to click the Upload The APNs Certificate.

FIGURE 16.10   Upload An APNs Certificate screen

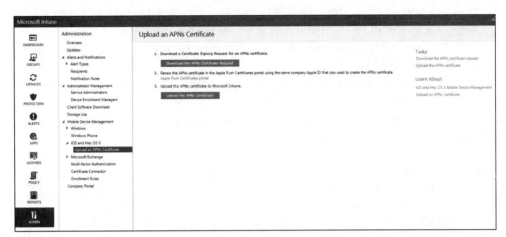

Android Devices   No additional configurations in the Intune console are needed to enable Android mobile device enrollment.

Windows Phone   Administrators must set up some management requirements before Windows Phones will work with your Intune network. DNS administrators need to create CNAME records in order for users to connect to the Intune network resources. Windows Phones also require a certificate to establish encrypted communications between the client device and the Intune cloud-based system.

Windows Devices   Windows devices are connected basically the same way as Windows Phones. The DNS administrator has to create a CNAME record, and then applications can be sideloaded into the Windows computer. Users can also connect to Intune by using the Intune Management Portal.

Sideloading applications using Intune will be explained in greater detail later in this chapter. Sideloading basically means loading pre-bought or company applications using the Windows Store, Intune, or images.

Administrators can use the Mobile Device Management (MDM) tools to help your company users enroll different devices and manage their Intune accounts. MDM provides the following benefits:

- MDM gives users the capabilities of enrolling their own devices through the use of the self-service Company Portal app. After users enroll their devices, they can install corporate applications.

- Once a device is enrolled, MDM helps deploy certificates, Wi-Fi, VPN, and email profiles automatically. This allows users to have access to corporate resources with the necessary security configuration options.

- MDM allows administrators to use broad management tools for managing mobile devices, passcode resets, device lockouts, and data encryption and to fully wipe a stolen device to help protect against corporate data loss.

- MDM helps simplify the enrollment of corporate devices using bulk enrollment tools like the Apple Configurator.

- MDM allows administrators to easy enroll Apple iOS devices with the Device Enrollment Program (DEP).

- MDM allows administrators to enforce a much stricter lockdown policy for iOS, Android, and Windows Phone devices.

To enroll clients into the Intune network, you can install the software in a variety of ways. The company administrator can provide an installation package to allow users to enroll their systems. Administrators can set up a Group Policy that can be used to enroll the computer into Intune, or users can self-enroll using the Intune portal.

If you decide to use MDM, you must first set up the mobile device management authority. This enables management of device platforms and allows your devices to be enrolled via the Company Portal app.

In Exercise 16.6, I will walk you through how to install and enroll your Windows 10 laptop or desktop in Microsoft Intune.

EXERCISE 16.6

Enrolling a Device in Intune

1. Enter the address of the Microsoft Intune portal into your web browser.

2. Click the Enroll button (see Figure 16.11).

FIGURE 16.11 Enroll screen

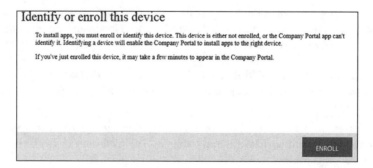

3. On the Enroll Your Computer screen, click the Download Software button (see Figure 16.12).

FIGURE 16.12   Download Software button

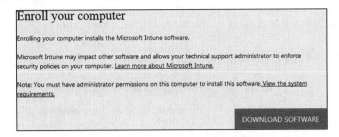

4. If the Save As box appears, click the Save File button (see Figure 16.13). If the download automatically starts, go to step 5.

FIGURE 16.13   Save File dialog box

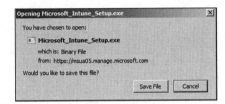

5. Once the file is downloaded, click the Run button.

6. The Microsoft Intune login screen will appear, as shown in Figure 16.14. Log into Microsoft Intune.

FIGURE 16.14   Microsoft Intune login screen

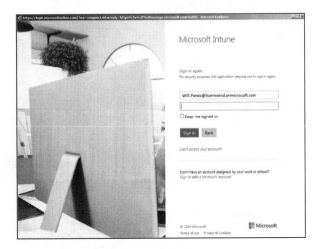

7. On the Welcome To Microsoft Intune Setup Wizard screen, click Next (see Figure 16.15).

   FIGURE 16.15   Welcome to Microsoft Intune

8. Microsoft Intune will be installed. If a User Account Control box appears, click Yes.

9. On the Complete screen, click the Finish button.

10. Log back into the Microsoft Intune portal.

11. If the message states that the computer is still not recognized, click the message. A box will appear, asking if you now want your computer to be enrolled. Click the radio button next to your system name and click the Select button, as shown in Figure 16.16.

    FIGURE 16.16   Select your device

    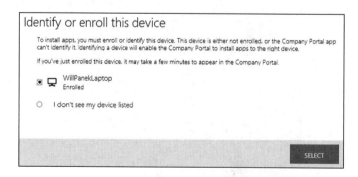

12. If you refresh your Intune portal, you will see your newly connected device. Click the device and it will show you the device settings, as shown in figure 16.17.

FIGURE 16.17   Device Settings in Intune

13. Close the Intune portal.

Configuring the Intune Connector Site

To understand how connectors work, you must first understand what a connector does and why we use them in the computer industry. Connectors allow different types of devices to communicate with each other. So, for example, let's say you had a Microsoft Exchange server and a UNIX-based mail server. You would add a connector into the Exchange server so that it could communicate and understand the UNIX mail server. That's how Intune connectors work also.

Intune connectors allow Microsoft Intune to communicate and understand other types of devices and software. So if you decide to use Azure Active Directory and Azure Exchange, you can install a connector so that Azure Exchange can work with the corporate Exchange mail server.

Exchange devices have the ability to be managed through both the on-premise Exchange servers and the hosted Exchange servers in the cloud. The Exchange connector connects your users with your Exchange deployments, and the connector lets you manage your mobile devices through the Intune console.

Administrators who have been using System Center Configuration Manager to manage their computers, Macs, and UNIX-based devices can add the Intune connector so that they can manage all of these devices from one console.

To configure connectors, in the Intune Management Console click the Admin link. Then expand the Mobile Device Management section. You would then click the device or software package and set up the connector.

Configuring Intune Alerts

One of the advantages of using Intune is the ability to monitor and see alerts within Intune. There are different levels of severity within the alerts. Table 16.1 shows you the different alert types and what each type means.

TABLE 16.1 Intune alert types

Alert	Description
● Critical	This alert shows you that you have a serious issue that needs to be investigated and fixed.
⚠ Warning	This alert shows you that there may be an issue but that issue is not very serious at this time. These alerts need to be investigated to make sure that they do not become a problem in the future.
ℹ Informational	This alert shows you that there is some information about a product but it's not a problem. For example, an informational alert may tell you that there is an upgrade to a connector that you have installed.

When dealing with Intune monitoring and alerts, there are a few settings that you can set up to help configure how alerts work. For example, under the Alerts And Notifications section, you can set up recipients who will receive emails when alerts happen.

So if you get a critical error, an email can be sent to an administrator so that the IT department can work on resolving the issue as fast as possible. If you don't set up email alerts, someone will need to monitor the Intune system daily to watch for issues. Intune administrators have the ability to set different email recipients for different alert types. So critical alerts can go to one IT person, and warnings can go to another.

Administrators also have the ability to enable or disable certain alert types. So if you are getting a warning that you know is not going to affect your Intune system, you can disable the warning to remove it completely. This way it's not a message your Intune administrators need to see on a daily basis.

To configure your alerts and notifications, in the Intune Management Console click the Admin link. Then expand Alerts and Notifications. You can then create new alert rules and notifications.

Supporting Applications

Microsoft Intune gives an organization the ability to deploy and maintain software from the cloud. The advantage to this is that the software issued through Intune is licensed to the user and not the hardware. So what this means is that you can deploy a copy of Office to a user using multiple devices, and when that user works on corporate data, that data is secure. That's the real advantage to Intune. This allows your users to work securely from their iPhone, Windows laptops, or tablet.

Microsoft Intune also allows an organization to use their current business apps by using the Intune App Wrapping tool. The Intune App Wrapping tool is a command line application that builds a package around the in-house application. Then the business application can be managed by the Intune mobile application management policies.

The Intune App Wrapping tool also gives you secure data viewing through the Intune Managed Browser, AV Player, Image viewer, and the PDF viewer. Administrators also have the ability to deny specific applications or web addresses from being accessed from specific types of mobile devices. Finally, when dealing with corporate data and security, administrators have the ability to wipe out a device in the event that the device is stolen, the device is lost, or the employee leaves the company.

Deploying Applications Using Intune

The way that we do business in the corporate world continues to change on a daily basis. Today, many of our users bring in their own devices. Because of BYOD, it is getting harder for IT departments to deploy software.

As stated earlier in this chapter, Microsoft Intune (Figure 16.18) is a cloud-based desktop and mobile device management tool. Intune helps IT departments provide their users with access to company applications, data, and resources. The users have the ability to access these resources from any type of device (i.e., Apple, Android, or Windows devices).

FIGURE 16.18   Microsoft Intune

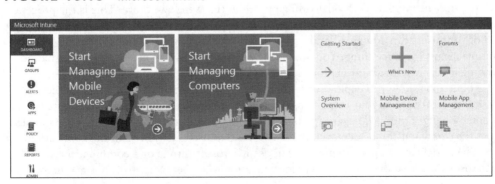

One of the issues that we face as IT administrators is that we have multiple copies of software throughout a company and multiple version types (Apple versions of Office compared to Windows versions). Let's take a look at Office as an example. Many times we have older versions of Office (Office 2010) and newer versions of Office (Office 2016/ Office 365).

This is where Microsoft Intune can help out an IT department. You can upload software packages to Intune and your users can get current copies of the software from the web. Also, Intune helps your organization protect its software by giving you extra security and features. Intune also allows you to set up application management policies that allow an IT department to manage applications on different devices.

As long as a device is compatible with Microsoft Intune, you can deploy the applications to that device. Depending on the device and the application, deployment options may vary. Administrators have the ability to upload their applications to Microsoft Intune or link a Windows Store application to Microsoft Intune storage.

To deploy applications using Intune, you must use the proper software installation type based on the different devices that your users may be using. Microsoft gives you a trial subscription of 2 GB of cloud storage. You can purchase more storage depending on how much money you want to spend.

Intune Software Publisher

To make an application available for your users to deploy, you must upload the installation package and then publish the package. As soon as you add or modify an application to Microsoft Intune, the Microsoft Intune Software Publisher starts. Then from the publisher you can choose and configure the software installation type.

To use the Microsoft Intune Software Publisher, you must have Microsoft .NET 4.0 installed on the Windows system. After you install .NET, restart the system and you should be able to use the Microsoft Intune Software Publisher.

Sideload Apps by Using Microsoft Intune

Sideloading an application means that you are loading an application that you already own or one that your company created into a delivery system (i.e., Intune, Microsoft Store, or images).

You may be familiar with sideloading apps into the Windows Store. This is the process of building or buying your own application and then adding it to the Windows Store so that all of your users can download and use that app. Sideloading an application into Microsoft Intune means the same thing. You are taking an application that you built or bought and adding it into Microsoft Intune for user downloads.

Think about how you deploy software today. You buy a package and either manually install the software to your users or use some type of deployment package like System Center Configuration Manager. The only difference now is that the application gets loaded into the cloud and can be deployed to any device that is compatible with the application.

When sideloading applications you can use Microsoft Intune or a combination of Microsoft Intune and System Center Configuration Manager. Microsoft has a Windows

Intune connector that allows Intune to work directly with System Center Configuration Manager. Here are the steps required to sideload applications into Microsoft Intune:

1. Upload your application into Microsoft Intune. To do this, click the Add Apps link (shown in Figure 16.19).

FIGURE 16.19 The Add Apps link

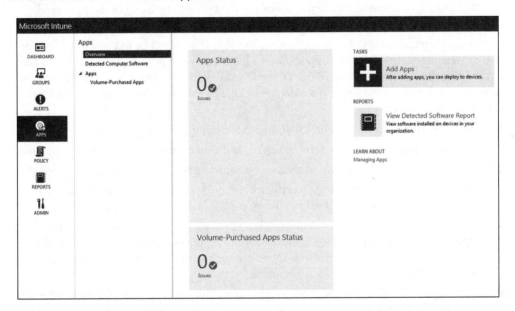

2. A dialog box will appear asking you if you want to download a setup.exe file. Click Yes. This is the Microsoft Intune Software Publisher. After it is downloaded, click the exe. The Software Publisher dialog box will appear, asking if you want to install. Click Run (shown in Figure 16.20).

FIGURE 16.20 Install the Intune Software Publisher

3. The Microsoft Intune Software Publisher sign-in screen will appear. Enter the credentials for a Microsoft account tied to Intune and click the Sign In link.

4. At the Software Setup page, choose the Windows application package software installer type and the Universal Naming Convention (UNC) path to the application.

5. When the Software Description page appears, choose the publisher, user-friendly name, and description of the app. Click Next.

   When the Add Software Wizard is complete, the app will be listed in the Managed Software node in the Software workspace.

Once an application is uploaded to Intune, the next step would be to deploy the application to your users. To deploy the application to the users, you assign the application to the created Windows Intune groups. While in the Windows Intune portal, you would click the Apps link and then choose the app for deployment. The following steps describe how to deploy the application:

1. Open the Microsoft Intune administrator console and click the Apps link.

2. Select the application that you want to deploy, and then click the Manage Deployment link.

3. Choose the user or device groups that you want to deploy the application to.

4. On the Deployment Action page, configure for approval (Required, Available, Not Applicable, or Uninstall) or deadline (when the application must be installed).

5. If the application that you are deploying has the ability to be configured by a mobile application management policy, then the Mobile App Management page will be displayed. On this page an administrator can choose the mobile application management policy that they want with this application.

6. If the application that you are deploying has the ability to be configured by a VPN profile, then the VPN Profile page will be displayed. Here is where you can choose the iOS apps with the VPN profile.

After the application is set up and ready for deployment, an administrator can always go back into the application properties and make changes. To view the properties of an application, click the app and choose the View Properties link. There are three tabs for the software properties.

General The General tab allows an administrator to see the applications general information and its installation status.

Devices The Device tab allows an administrator to see the devices that have successfully installed the application.

Users The Users tab allows an administrator to see the users that have successfully installed the application.

Deep-Link Applications by Using Microsoft Intune

One of the nice advantages of using Windows 10 is that you can purchase Windows store applications. After you purchase the applications, you can deploy the Windows Store application (deep-link) to all of your users.

Supporting Broadband Connectivity

Administrators have a few weapons in their broadband arsenal. Two different options that we can set up as administrators are the ability to see how much network or software bandwidth is being used (metering) and how we can set up our Windows 10 devices to use our cellular Internet connections (tethering).

Understanding Metering

Administrators have the ability to limit and monitor network usage by configuring the network as a metered network. Network metering allows network downloading to be watched or metered, and then administrators can charge users or departments for the network usage.

This is becoming something that many IT departments have started doing due to budgeting. Many IT departments are non-revenue-generating departments, and because of this, it can be difficult for an IT administrator to get a budget passed. But with network metering, you can charge other departments for the amount of bandwidth and network that is being used.

When setting up your company's Internet connection, your ISP has the ability to charge by the amount of data used. That's called a metered Internet connection. If you have a metered Internet connection, setting your network connection to metered in Windows can help you reduce the amount of data you send and receive. To set this up in Windows, you would take the following steps:

1. Click Start ➤ Settings, and then tap Network & Internet.

2. Tap or click the Wi-Fi link and then, under Metered Connection, turn the Set As a Metered Connection option on or off.

Administrators also have the ability to limit how much bandwidth a user or department gets to use when downloading applications. This is referred to as *software metering*.

To set up software metering, an administrator must use a combination of Microsoft Windows Intune and System Center Configuration Monitor.

Understanding Broadband Tethering

Tethering allows a user to use their Windows 10 mobile device through their cellular phone. If you have a Windows 10 mobile device and want it to access the Internet, you can go through your cell coverage to get online.

Tethering can also be connecting one mobile device to another mobile device for Internet access. For example, let's say I have an iPad with cellular Internet connection. I can connect another Windows 10 tablet to that iPad to gain Internet access. So tethering is the ability to connect one device to another for Internet access. Before you set up tethering, here are a few things that you should know:

- There may be extra charges when connecting your data connection with another device.

- Applications and updates may not be downloaded over a metered connection, and by default, tethered and mobile broadband connections are metered.

- Many cellular carriers require that you pay an extra fee for allowing your phone to be a hotspot for tethering. To enable tethering on most devices, you set up your mobile device as an Internet hotspot.

Understanding Data Synchronization

Data synchronization allows you to synchronize your devices with your servers. These servers can be network-based or cloud-based. Administrators have the ability to synchronize work folders, and they can also use the Sync Center to use one application for all of their synchronization needs.

To enable synchronization on the Windows 10 device, click the Start button and choose Settings. When you are in the Settings window, click the Accounts link to set up your user accounts and synchronization (see Figure 16.21).

FIGURE 16.21   Data synchronization

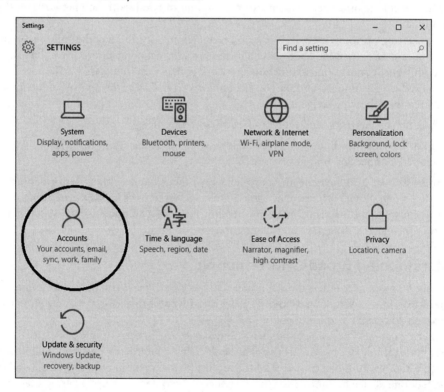

Once you enter into the Accounts link, you can choose the bottom option (Sync Your Settings) to set up all of your synchronization settings (see Figure 16.22).

One of the final things that you want to look at in the Accounts link is the Work Access link. The Work Access link allows you to connect your device to your work or school, sign in to Azure, and enroll in device management (see Figure 16.23).

FIGURE 16.22   Sync Your Settings

FIGURE 16.23   Work Access link

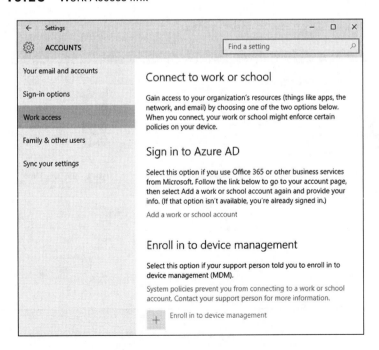

Understanding Updates

Deploying updates can be a very difficult process for many organizations. Depending on the number of users that you have and the number of applications that each user uses, updates can be a very time-consuming process.

Many organizations install a Microsoft server called Windows Server Update Services (WSUS). WSUS servers allow administrators to deploy Microsoft product updates to computers that are running the Windows operating system. Administrators can manage all of their organization's Microsoft updates from one application.

The downside to WSUS is that it is used for Microsoft updates. So you can deploy updates to all of your applications, Microsoft and Non-Microsoft, by using the Intune management portal.

Deploying Software Updates Using Intune

When you decide to use Intune to deploy your updates, you get a lot of options that you get to consider and set up. For example, do you want to approve all of your updates or do you want the updates to automatically deploy? Many administrators like to approve all of their updates so that they have a chance to test them first before deploying.

As updates become available from Microsoft or from any third-party software vendor that your company is using, a notification will be displayed on the Overview page of the Updates workspace (see Figure 16.24).

FIGURE 16.24 Overview of update types

Once an administrator sees these notifications, they can click the notification link and view the information about the update. After viewing the update information, the administrator can then decide if they want to approve or deny the update.

If you have been in the IT industry long enough, you have run into the situation when you did a software update and then the software stopped performing properly. Now, with the ability to test and approve updates in Intune, you can solve this issue. You can guarantee that the update will work as needed or deny the update from being deployed.

This is just one of the options that you have when using Intune updates. Let's take a look at some of the other settings that you need to plan out before setting up your Intune updates.

Identifying Required Updates

When you decide to use Intune for updates, you need to decide which type of updates that you want to install. Administrators have the ability to choose what type of updates they want to install.

All Updates   The All Updates section means just that, all updates. Every possible update that can be deployed will be shown under the All Updates section.

Critical Updates   Critical updates are updates that are released to fix a specific issue that is for a critical bug that is not security related.

Security Updates   Security updates are updates that need to be applied to fix a security issue. These security issues are used by hackers to either hack into a device or software.

Definition Updates   Definition updates are normally software updates that contain additions to a product's definition database. Definition databases get used to identify objects that have very specific attributes. These attributes look for malicious code, phishing websites, or junk mail.

Service Packs   Service packs are a collective set of all current hotfixes, security updates, critical updates, and updates. Normally service packs also contain additional fixes for known issues that are found since the release of the product. Service packs may also contain customer requested design changes or features.

Update Rollups   Update rollup updates are current hotfixes, security updates, critical updates, and updates that are bundled together for easy deployment. Update rollups are normally used to target a specific component or software package.

Mandatory Updates   Mandatory updates are updates that are released to either fix or replace a software or hardware issue. Mandatory updates are required to run or the device or Windows system may stop functioning properly.

Non-Microsoft Updates   Non-Microsoft updates are updates for third-party software and hardware devices. These are updates that other vendors release for solving problems or improving their product.

Approving or Declining Updates

One of the best advantages to using any update service is the ability to either approve or deny updates. Plus, having the ability to approve updates gives you the ability to test the updates first.

In today's virtualization world testing updates can be easier than before. It's easy to set up a virtual server just for update testing without spending thousands of dollars on new hardware. Let's take a look at the steps necessary to approve or deny updates:

1. Open the Microsoft Intune administration console. Then click the Updates link ➤ Overview ➤ New to approve.

2. Select any of the updates and then look at the update description at the bottom of the page. Once you know you want to approve the update, click the Approve link on the top of the page. If you want to approve multiple updates at the same time, hold down the Ctrl key as you select each update and then click Approve.

3. On the Select Groups page, select which group you want to deploy the updates to and then click the Add button. Once you done choosing your groups, click Next.

4. On the Deployment Action page, you have two options to choose from. You can either approve or deny the update.

   - Under the Approval list, Administrators can choose to do the following:
     - Required Install—Installs the update on the computers that were chosen in the specified group.
     - Do Not Install—Allows you to use update reporting but the update is not installed.
     - Available Install—The user has the ability to choose if they want the update to install from the Company Portal.
     - Uninstall—Removes the update from the computers in the listed group.

   - Under the Deadline list, administrators can choose to do the following:
     - None—This choice sets no deadline for the installation of the update, and users can choose to install or ignore the update as long as the update remains in the list.
     - As Soon As Possible—This choice forces the update to be installed on the computers at the next possible opportunity.
     - Custom—This choice allows administrators to specify the date and time that approved updates will be installed.
     - One Week, Two Weeks, One Month—This choice forces the update to install within the specified time period.

5. Click Finish to save the settings.

6. You can check the details pane at the bottom of the All Updates page for information about the updates.

Configuring Automatic Approval

Another option that administrators can set is the ability to automatically configure updates for automatic approvals. To set this up, administrators would complete the following steps:

1. Open the Microsoft Intune administration console. Then click the Configure Updates link.

2. In the Automatic Approval Rules section (see Figure 16.25) under the Server Settings: Updates page, click the New button.

FIGURE 16.25   Automatic Approval Rules

3. On the General page, type in the approval rule name and optional description. Click Next.

4. On the Product Categories page, select the products for which you want to have automatic updates. Click Next.

5. On the Update Classifications page, choose the update classifications that have automatic approval. Click Next.

6. On the Deployment page, choose the devices that these automatic approvals will apply to and click Add. Click Next.

7. On the Summary page, review your settings and then click the Finish button.

Deploying Third-Party Updates

Microsoft Intune has one advantage over using other types of update servers (like WSUS) because Intune can also update third-party non-Microsoft updates. This is very useful when deploying applications like virus protection. The virus list constantly needs to be updated, and Intune can help administrators achieve this.

To deploy software updates to non-Microsoft vendors, you would use the Upload Update Wizard. The Upload Update Wizard helps an administrator get their updates into the cloud storage space. After they are uploaded, administrators can then approve or deny the updates to specific groups. To launch the Upload Update wizard, you would click the Add Updates link (see Figure 16.26).

FIGURE 16.26 Add Updates link

Using the Intune Reports

One of the best tools that Microsoft Intune offers is the ability to obtain all of the different types of reports. The Intune reports help an administrator monitor the status of their enrolled devices and see if there are any issues that need to be addressed. The reports also allow an administrator to examine both the hardware and software inventory.

To access the many different reports available in Intune, you open the Intune Management Console and click the Reports link on the left side (shown in Figure 16.27).

FIGURE 16.27   Reports link

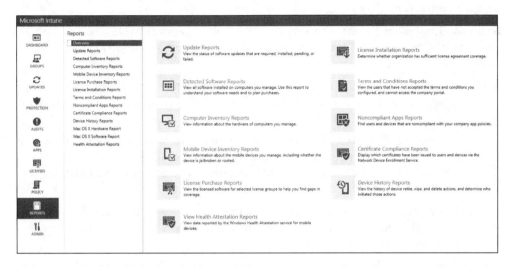

The following descriptions are of just some of the reports that you can run as an administrator to get information about your updates and about your hardware.

Update Report   Running this report allows administrators to see the software updates that were successfully installed on computers in your organization along with information about updates that failed, are pending, or are needed.

Detected Software Report   This report allows administrators to see what software was installed on the computers throughout your organization. This report also includes the software version that was installed. Administrators have the ability to filter the information and display only specific software publishers and specific software categories. Administrators can also get more details by clicking the directional arrow next to the list item.

Computer Inventory Report   Running this report will help administrators get detailed information about the managed computers in the organization. Administrators can use this report for planning hardware purchases and also to get a better understanding about the hardware needs of the users in your organization.

Mobile Device Inventory Report   Administrators can use this report to gather information about the mobile devices in their organization. Administrators have the ability to filter the information that is displayed. Some of this information includes the groups the device belongs to and the operating system that is running on the device.

License Purchase Report   This report allows an administrator to see the software titles for all licensed software in selected license groups. License reports are not an exact list of software that is being used or proof of the software compliance. The report is used by administrators as a tool to help you make licensing decisions for your organization.

License Installation Report   Administrators can use this report to compare installed software with your current license agreement coverage.

Terms and Conditions Report   This report allows administrators to see whether users have accepted the terms and conditions that you deployed and which version they accepted.

Noncompliant Apps Report   Administrators can use this report to see information about users who have applications installed that are on your lists of compliant and noncompliant apps.

Certificate Compliance Report   This report allows you to see which certificates have been installed to users and devices through the Network Device Enrollment Service (NDES). NDES allows hardware, like routers, to be able to receive a certificate even though the router can't request a certificate.

Device History Report   Administrators can use this report to see a historical log of retired, wiped, and delete actions that have been performed. Administrators use this report to see who initiated actions on devices in the past.

Mac OS X Report   This report is run to show you the Mac OS X groups and what software and hardware that they run. This report allows administrators to watch the Apple devices enrolled into the Intune cloud system.

Summary

In this chapter, we talked about the cloud and Microsoft Intune. I showed you how Microsoft Intune can help you manage devices and software. I showed you how to set up and configure an Intune subscription and how you can use that subscription to help your network users get the most out of their network resources and software.

I also talked about managing devices using Intune. I showed you how to provision user accounts and enroll devices. I also discussed how to manage and configure devices using the Microsoft Intune subscription.

I then continued the chapter by discussing how to deploy and configure software and updates using Intune. I showed you how to use the In-Console monitoring tool and how to approve and decline updates.

I then talked about how to work with mobile devices including Windows tablets, broadband metering, and tethering, and I also showed you how to wipe mobile devices for employees who leave the company. I then showed you how to use Intune to help deploy and maintain your company's software packages and updates.

Finally, we looked at the different types of reports that an administrator can run using Intune. These reports can help you see what devices still need updates and also what hardware may need to be installed or replaced.

Video Resources

There are no videos for this chapter.

Exam Essentials

Understand Microsoft Intune.   Understand what Microsoft Intune can do to help your network. Make sure you understand how users and devices get connected to Intune.

Know how to configure a Microsoft Intune Subscription.   Understand how to set up and manage a Microsoft Intune Subscription. Understand how to configure a device to use Microsoft Intune.

Understand the Microsoft Intune benefits.   Understand what Microsoft Intune benefits can be used in a corporate environment. Understand how these benefits, like remote wipe, can help you protect corporate data.

Understand the Azure Active Directory (AD) Connect tool.   Understand that Administrators can connect their cloud-based version of Active Directory (Azure Active Directory) with their on-premise server-based version of Active Directory by using the Azure Active Directory (AD) Connect tool.

Understand Intune Connectors.   Understand Microsoft Intune Connectors allow Microsoft Intune to work with software within a network. The connector allows the cloud-based software to communicate properly with the infrastructure based software.

Understand Intune Alerts.   Understand each type of Intune alerts and which alerts are important to fix immediately or which alerts just are giving you information. Understand how to set up notifications for each alert type.

Know how to work with Intune Reports.   Understand that the different reports help an administrator monitor the status of Intune managed devices. These reports give you information on the status of software updates, software installed, and certificate compliance. Understand how reports also let you examine the inventory of your network's hardware and software.

Review Questions

1. You are the network administrator for your organization. Your users use both desktops and tablets to access the network. Your tablet users use a 4G mobile broadband Wi-Fi connection. You need to watch how much data your users are using on this connection. How do you do that?

    A. Configure the broadband connection as a metered network.

    B. Turn on network resource monitoring.

    C. Enable performance monitor.

    D. Enable tablet metering in the tablets settings.

2. You are the network administrator for a company that has a Microsoft Intune subscription. You have decided to set up three Intune Security groups called CorpGroup, NHGroup, and Portsmouth. CorpGroup is a parent group to Portsmouth. Portsmouth has 75 users in the group. You realized that you need to make NHGroup the parent to Portsmouth. What is the first thing that you need to do?

    A. Edit the security properties of CorpGroup.

    B. Edit the security properties of NHGroup.

    C. Remove all 75 users from Portsmouth

    D. Delete Portsmouth and then re-create the Portsmouth group under NHGroup.

3. You are the IT manager of a large manufacturing company. Sales personnel are allowed to bring their own personal Windows 10 devices to the office. The company allows the sales people to install company software and use their devices to retrieve company mail by using the management infrastructure agent. One of your salespeople reports that their Windows 10 laptop was stolen while at the airport. You need to make sure that no one can steal any of the corporate data or access any corporate emails. Which two actions should you perform? Each correct answer presents part of the solution.

    A. Prevent the computer from connecting to the corporate wireless network.

    B. Remove the computer from the management infrastructure.

    C. Reset the user's password.

    D. Do a remote wipe on the users laptop.

4. You are the IT director for a large school system. The school has decided that students can bring in their own devices to do school work with. Your organization uses Microsoft Azure Active Directory and Intune for all of the student's applications and network authentication. You need to be sure that students that are using IPADs as well as Windows 10 devices have full access. What do you need to do to be sure that all iOS devices can get access?

    A. Add a Student Portal app from the Apple App Store.

    B. Create a device enrollment manager account.

    C. Configure an Intune Service Connector for Exchange.

    D. Import an Apple Push Notification service (APNs) certificate.

5. You are the administrator for Stormwind Studios. Stormwind has subscribed to Microsoft Intune. All of your client computers are running Windows 10 Enterprise. Users are complaining that they get prompted to restart their systems after mandatory updates. You need to stop the prompts from appearing on the clients Windows 10 systems following their updates. Which Intune policy template should you use?

    A. Microsoft Intune Agent Settings.

    B. Windows Intune Policy Configuration.

    C. Microsoft Intune Security Settings.

    D. You need to create a Custom Windows 10 Policy.

6. You are the IT Manager for WillPanek.com. The company has an Active Directory domain and a cloud-based Azure Active Directory. The two are synchronized by using the Azure Active Directory Synchronization Tool. The company also uses System Center Configuration Manager. You need to use Configuration Manager to manage devices registered with Intune. What do you need to do to accomplish this? (Choose two.)

    A. Create a new device enrollment manager account in Microsoft Intune.

    B. In Microsoft Intune, configure an Active Directory Connector.

    C. Configure the Microsoft Intune Connector role in Configuration Manager.

    D. Create the Microsoft Intune subscription in Configuration Manager.

7. You are the administrator of your organization's Active Directory domain. The owners of the company want to move to the cloud by using Azure Active Directory. You need to be able to have the on-site version of Active Directory work with the cloud-based Azure Active Directory. What do you need to install to make this happen?

    A. The Active Directory (AD) user connector

    B. Azure Active Directory (AD) Connect tool

    C. Microsoft Intune Connection tool

    D. Microsoft Intune single sign-on tool

8. You are the IT director for large company that has decided to move to the cloud. The company wants to use Azure Active Directory and Microsoft Intune. The company has been looking into this because users have been using multiple devices to get their job done. When your users get added to Intune and get licensed, how many devices can each user add by default?

    A. 3

    B. 4

    C. 5

    D. None. Device Administrators are the only person who can add devices to Intune.

9. You are the administrator of a company that builds its own applications. You have decided that you want to install a company application to all employees by using the Windows Store. Which term is used to refer to installing corporate apps through the Windows Store?

    A. WS Installations

    B. BranchCache

    C. Image installation

    D. Sideloading

10. You are the IT Director for Stormwind training studios. Your company has decided to start using Microsoft Intune for all of their software deployments. You want to set up a notification system so that you see all alerts and that you IT Manager only gets notified for Critical alerts. How do you accomplish this? (Choose all that apply.)

    A. Set up all event notifications for the IT Manager in Intune.

    B. Set up all event notifications for the IT Director in Intune.

    C. Set up Critical event notifications for the IT Manager in Intune.

    D. Set up Critical event notifications for the IT Manager in Intune.

Chapter

17

Configuring Applications

MICROSOFT EXAM OBJECTIVES COVERED IN THIS CHAPTER:

✓ **Deploy and manage Azure RemoteApp.**

    ■ This objective may include but is not limited to the follow-ing subobjectives: Configure RemoteApp and Desktop Con-nections settings, configure Group Policy Objects (GPOs) for signed packages, subscribe to the Azure RemoteApp and Desktop Connections feeds, export and import Azure RemoteApp configurations, support iOS and Android, con-figure remote desktop web access for Azure RemoteApp distribution.

✓ **Support desktop apps.**

    ■ This objective may include but is not limited to the follow-ing subobjectives: The following support considerations including: Desktop app compatibility using Application Com-patibility Toolkit (ACT) including shims and compatibility database; desktop application co-existence using Hyper-V, Azure RemoteApp, and App-V; installation and configuration of User Experience Virtualization (UE-V).

✓ **Support Windows Store and cloud apps.**

    ■ This objective may include but is not limited to the follow-ing subobjectives: Install and manage software by using Microsoft Office 365 and Windows Store apps, sideload apps into online and offline images, integrate Microsoft account including personalization settings.

In this chapter, we will look at how to configure applications on Windows 10. One of the issues with applications is that they may not work properly on a newer operating system. We will look at the ways to allow older applications to work on Windows 10.

We will also look at two different ways to browse the Internet: Edge and Internet Explorer. As the Internet and the World Wide Web have increased exponentially in both content and features, Microsoft has continually enhanced and added new functionality to its browser. The current version is Windows Internet Explorer 11, or IE11.

With the increase in the functionality of browsers and in their ease of use, there has been an increase in the way websites are used to provide content for end users in the public space (Internet browsing) as well as for private corporate browsing. With the introduction of IE11, Microsoft has taken the usability that end users want to new levels as well as provided a good deal of security enhancement. This gives the user the best and easiest browsing environment and provides a balance of security information about the sites and pages being viewed.

Supporting Desktop Applications

As IT professionals, many of us think of managing applications simply as installing applications on the computer. But there are other details that may need to be configured to allow applications to run faster and more efficiently.

As operating systems evolve, one issue that you can run into is that your applications may not work properly on the newer version of the operating system. Microsoft has developed a few different ways to help you combat this issue.

Using the Application Compatibility Toolkit (ACT)

When new Windows operating systems are installed, applications that ran on the previous version of Windows may not work properly. The Application Compatibility Toolkit (ACT) allows an administrator to help solve these issues before they occur.

The Application Compatibility Toolkit allows IT professionals to decide if an application is compatible with the Windows 10 operating system before rolling out the new Windows 10 OS to the entire network. ACT also allows IT departments to decide how updating to Windows 10 will impact the applications on the domain.

IT professionals can use the ACT features to do the following:

- Verify that all of the corporate applications and computer hardware are compatible with Windows 10.
- Test the corporate applications for User Account Control (UAC)–related issues.
- Test the corporate web applications and websites for compatibility with new versions and security updates to Windows Internet Explorer.

After installing ACT, there are three phases of how ACT works within the network.

Phase 1: Collecting Your Compatibility Data   Phase 1 consists of your IT department collecting all compatibility data from the software packages as well as creating and configuring your data-collection packages (DCPs). Phase 1 also includes information about how to distribute your DCPs and how to perform common collection tasks, such as importing or exporting DCP settings.

Phase 2: Analyzing Your Compatibility Data   Phase 2 analyzes the information that you collected in Phase 1. Phase 2 allows an administrator to gather information and procedures and to filter and organize the data collected in Phase 1. Phase 2 also provides information about your application compatibility reports, issues, and solutions.

Phase 3: Testing and Mitigating Your Compatibility Issues   Phase 3 consist of testing guidance and procedures for using the development tools. These tools include the Standard User Analyzer (SUA), the Internet Explorer Compatibility Test Tool (IECTT), and the Compatibility Administrator, which allow administrators to fix their compatibility issues. Phase 3 also consists of information about the application fix (also known as "Shims") library, and the known Internet Explorer security feature issues.

Understanding Application Fix (Shims)

When new operating systems get released, older applications may not run, and you may not be able to get a newer version of the application. For example, a vendor that sold you an application may have gone out of business, but the application is still needed in your organization.

If you install the application on Windows 10, there may be issues. This is where Shims will apply. The *Shims* is a coding fix that allows the application to function properly.

The Shim Infrastructure consists of application programming interface (API) hooking. This means the Shim Infrastructure uses linking to redirect API calls from the Windows operating system to the alternative code called the shim.

To have Shims created, you must first contact Microsoft. Microsoft must create the Shim; Microsoft does not offer any custom tools to allow for private creation. Microsoft does include shims with Windows 10, and new shims will be available through Windows Update as they are created.

File Extension Association

When dealing with applications and software packages, you may need to associate a file extension (shown in Figure 17.1) with a software package. For example, you may want all files with the filename extension `.asx` to be played through Windows Media Player. You have the ability to set these file-extension associations in Default Programs in Control Panel. Within Default Programs, there is link called "Associate a file type or protocol with a specific program."

FIGURE 17.1   Filename-extension association

Using Hyper-V for Desktop Applications

Virtualization—the ability to run one operating system on top of another—is sweeping the computer industry. Microsoft has a virtualization environment called *Hyper-V* that can operate on its client software. Hyper-V allows you to create and manage virtual machines without the need for a server operating system on different hardware. The advantage of virtualization is that you can run multiple operating systems like Windows XP, Windows Vista, Windows 7, Windows 8/8.1, or Windows 10 all on the same hardware.

Hyper-V gives you the ability to set up virtualization on a client operating system. This is very beneficial for anyone in the industry who has to do testing or configuration. Hyper-V on Windows 10 is not really meant to run a network as Hyper-V on Windows Server 2012 R2 does, but it does give an administrator the ability to test software and patches before installing them live on a network or running applications in an operating system other than the installed one. Also, it is beneficial to research problems in a controlled environment and not on a live system where you can end up doing more harm than good.

Finally, Hyper-V gives you a training advantage. Think about having the ability to train users on a real product like Windows Server 2012 R2 or Windows 10 without needing to purchase additional equipment. Hyper-V allows you to train users on products and software while using only one machine. I will now briefly explain the differences between these forms of virtualization:

Server Virtualization   This basically enables multiple servers to run on the same physical server. Hyper-V is a server virtualization tool that allows you to move physical machines to virtual machines and manage them on a few physical servers. Thus, you will be able to consolidate physical servers.

Presentation Virtualization   When you use *presentation virtualization*, your applications run on a different computer and only the screen information is transferred to your computer. An example of presentation virtualization is Microsoft Remote Desktop Services in Windows Server 2012 R2.

Desktop Virtualization   *Desktop virtualization* provides you with a virtual machine on your desktop, comparable to server virtualization. You run your complete operating system and applications in a virtual machine so that your local physical machine just needs to run a very basic operating system. An example of this form of virtualization is Microsoft Virtual PC.

Application Virtualization   *Application virtualization* helps prevent conflicts between applications on the same PC. Thus, it helps you to isolate the application running environment from the operating system installation requirements by creating application-specific copies of all shared resources, and it helps reduce application-to-application incompatibility and testing needs. An example of an application virtualization tool is Microsoft Application Virtualization (App-V).

 Real World Scenario

Hyper-V Advantages

As an instructor and consultant, I can't say enough about how valuable Hyper-V can be as a tool. I have used it on many occasions to either test a piece of software before installation or find an answer to a problem in a controlled environment.

At the time this book is being written, I use Microsoft Windows 7 Professional on my laptop. On that same laptop I have a version of virtualization with both Windows Server 2012 R2 and Windows 10 Professional operating system virtual machines.

While I am on a client site or while I am in the classroom, having a way to test and research problems using multiple operating systems on one client computer system is invaluable.

Hyper-V Features

As a lead-in to the virtualization topic and Hyper-V, I will start with a list of key features, followed by a list of supported guest operating systems. This should provide you with a quick, high-level view of this feature before we dig deeper into the technology.

Key Features of Hyper-V

The following list briefly describes the key features of Hyper-V:

New Architecture   The hypervisor-based architecture, which has a 64-bit micro-kernel, provides an array of device support as well as performance and security improvements.

Operating System Support   Both 32-bit and 64-bit operating systems can run simultaneously in Hyper-V. Also, different platforms like Windows, Linux, and others are supported.

Support for Symmetric Multiprocessors   Support for up to four processors in a virtual machine environment provides you with the ability to run applications as well as multiple virtual machines faster.

Network Load Balancing   Hyper-V provides support for *Windows Network Load Balancing (NLB)* to balance the network load across virtual machines on different servers.

New Hardware Architecture   Hyper-V's architecture provides improved utilization of resources like networking and disks. This allows an IT department the ability to run multiple operating systems on the same host without each system interfering with the other systems.

Quick Migration   Hyper-V's *Quick Migration* feature provides you with the functionality to run virtual machines in a clustered environment with switchover capabilities when there is a failure. Thus, you can reduce downtime and achieve higher availability of your virtual machines.

Virtual Machine Snapshot   You can take snapshots of running virtual machines, which provides you with the capability to recover to any previous virtual machine snapshot state quickly and easily.

Resource Metering   Hyper-V *resource metering* allows an organization to track usage within the businesses departments. It allows an organization to create a usage-based billing solution that adjusts to the provider's business model and strategy.

Scripting   Using the Windows Management Instrumentation (WMI) interfaces and APIs, you can easily build custom scripts to automate processes in your virtual machines. Administrators also have the ability to use PowerShell cmdlets to do scripting.

RemoteFX   Windows 10 Hyper-V RemoteFX allows for an enhanced user experience for RemoteFX desktops by providing a 3D virtual adapter, intelligent codecs, and the ability to redirect USB devices in virtual machines.

Fibre Channel   The virtual Fibre Channel feature allows you to connect to the Fibre Channel storage unit from within the virtual machine. *Virtual Fibre Channel* allows an administrator to use their existing Fibre Channel to support virtualized workloads. Hyper-V users have the ability to use Fibre Channel storage area networks (SANs) to virtualize the workloads that require direct access to SAN logical unit numbers (LUNs).

Enhanced Session Mode   Enhanced Session Mode enhances the interactive session of the Virtual Machine Connection for Hyper-V administrators who want to connect to their virtual machines. It gives administrators the same functionality as a remote desktop connection when the administrator is interacting with a virtual machine.

In previous versions of Hyper-V, the virtual machine connection gave you limited functionality while you connected to the virtual machine screen, keyboard, and mouse. An administrator could use an RDP connection to get full redirection abilities, but that would require a network connection to the virtual machine host.

Enhanced Session Mode gives administrators the following benefits for local resource redirection:

- Display configuration
- Audio
- Printers
- Clipboard
- Smart cards
- Drives
- USB devices
- Supported Plug and Play devices

Shared Virtual Hard Disk   Windows 10 Hyper-V has a feature called Shared Virtual Hard Disk; Shared Virtual Hard Disk allows an administrator to cluster virtual machines together by using the shared virtual hard disk (VHDX) files.

Shared virtual hard disk allows an administrator to build a high availability infrastructure which is very important if you are setting up either a private cloud deployment or a cloud-hosted environment for managing large workloads. Shared virtual hard disks allow two or more virtual machines to access the same virtual hard disk (VHDX) file.

Automatic Virtual Machine Activation (AVMA)   Automatic Virtual Machine Activation (AVMA) is a new feature that allows administrators to install virtual machines on a properly activated Windows 10 system without the need to manage individual product keys for each virtual machine. When using AVMA, virtual machines get bound to the licensed Hyper-V server as soon as the virtual machine starts.

Dynamic Memory   *Dynamic Memory* is a new feature of Hyper-V that allows it to balance memory automatically among running virtual machines. Dynamic Memory allows Hyper-V to adjust the amount of memory available to the virtual machines in response to the needs of the virtual machine. It is currently available for Hyper-V in Windows 10.

Installing Hyper-V

To run Hyper-V, you need a minimum processor of an x64-compatible processor with Intel VT or AMD-V technology enabled. Hardware Data Execution Prevention (DEP), specifically Intel XD bit (execute disable bit) or AMD NX bit (no execute bit), must be available and enabled. Minimum: 1.4 GHz. Recommended: 2 GHz or faster.

Your system memory (RAM) should be at minimum at least 1 GB of RAM, but recommended is at least 2 GB RAM or greater (additional RAM is required for each running guest operating system) with a maximum of 1 TB.

Your system's hard drive should be a minimum of 8 GB, recommended 20 GB or greater. (Additional disk space needed for each guest operating system.).

You can load Hyper-V on some versions of the following operating systems: Windows 10, Windows 8/8.1, and Windows Server 2008/2008 R2 and 2012/2012 R2. As for as Windows 10 Hyper-V, you need to use one of the following versions: Enterprise, Professional, or Education. Exercise 17.1 walks you through the process of installing the Hyper-V role on Windows 10 Enterprise.

EXERCISE 17.1

Installing Hyper-V

1. Open the Programs And Features tool by clicking Start ➤ Control Panel ➤ Programs And Features.

2. Click the Turn Windows Features On Or Off link in the upper-left corner.

3. Scroll down the features list and check the Hyper-V check box (shown in Figure 17.2). Click Next.

   FIGURE 17.2   Hyper-V check box

4. The installation wizard will take a few minutes to install Hyper-V. Once Windows has finished installing Hyper-V, click the Close button.

5. Restart your server.

There may be a time when you need to remotely execute PowerShell commands on a virtual machine. To do this, you need to run the Invoke-Command command and specify which VM you're connecting to (the -VMName parameter).

Configuring User Experience Virtualization (UE-V)

To help you fully understand the benefits of Microsoft User Experience Virtualization (UE-V), I need to explain the benefits of roaming profiles. Roaming profiles were used to allow a user to go from one system to another but still have the exact same desktop and settings. Well UE-V is roaming profiles on steroids.

Microsoft UE-V is a virtualization platform that allows users to move from one Windows system to another but they get to keep the same Windows operating system and all of their settings. This allows users to feel comfortable moving from one device to another because their current operating system and settings follow them wherever they go.

So how does UE-V actually allow users to move around? UE-V uses XML templates that allow users to save their operating system and settings. Actually, with the use of the XML template files, you can choose which settings get saved and moved between Windows operating systems. The XML templates know exactly how all of the application settings are saved throughout the file system.

Microsoft UE-V provides the following benefits:

- Administrators have the ability to specify exactly which application and desktop settings synchronize between the operating systems.

- Administrator have the ability to create their own custom templates for third-party applications.

- Users have the ability to recover their settings and applications after any type of hardware changes.

- Users can access their settings from any location and on any Windows device.

UE-V Components

Now that you understand UE-V, let's take a look at some of the components needed to make it all work properly. Table 17.1 lists all of the different components and describes what each component does.

TABLE 17.1   UE-V components

Component	Description
UE-V agent	The UE-V agent gets installed on every Windows operating system that you want to synchronize settings with. The UE-V agent also observes all of the applications and settings for the Windows operating system.
Settings packages	UE-V agents take all of the settings and applications on a system and turn those into an application package. These application packages are created locally, and then they are copied to a shared network location.
Settings storage share	Administrators must create a network share that will house all of the setting packages. The UE-V agent will verify that the network share is configured properly, and then the UE-V agent will create a hidden system folder for the user's settings.
Settings location templates	XML templates are used to synchronize the application and settings files. UE-V includes a few templates by default, but you have the ability to create your own.
Windows apps list	The Windows apps list is used to determine which Windows applications will get synchronized. UE-V uses the Windows apps list to know which apps and files get copied to the settings package.

Installing and Configuring UE-V

Installing UE-V is not a very complicated process. First thing that you must do is download the Microsoft Desktop Optimization Pack (MDOP). Microsoft UE-V is part of the MDOP software package. Then you need to create a network share that we can store your UE-V templates at. After the share is created, you must make sure that you set up the permissions properly on that shared drive. After you have created the network share, you then have to install the UE-V agent. The UE-V agent allows the Windows operating system to share its settings to the network. Then you just need to test your configurations, and you are all set. To set up the UE-V agent, you need to run the following executable along with the path of the network share:

```
AgentSetup.exe SettingsStoragePath=\\server\settingsshare\%username%
```

When you install UE-V, certain Windows files and apps get stored automatically. The following list shows some of the apps and files that get copied automatically.

UE-V synchronizes settings for some Microsoft applications by default. Here is a partial list of just some of the applications that get synchronized by default:

- Microsoft Office 2013 applications (UE-V 2.1 SP1 and 2.1)
- Microsoft Office 2010 applications (UE-V 2.1 SP1, 2.1, and 2.0)

- Microsoft Office 2007 applications (UE-V 2.0 only)
- Internet Explorer 8, 9, and 10
- Internet Explorer 11 in UE-V 2.1 SP1 and 2.1
- Windows applications, such as Xbox
- Windows desktop applications, such as Microsoft Calculator, Notepad, and WordPad
- Windows settings, such as desktop background or wallpaper

 Since the Microsoft Desktop Optimization Pack is needed to do this installation, I did not include a lab. If you have the ability to download the MDOP, go to `https://technet.microsoft.com/en-us/library/dn479305(v=vs.85)` `.aspx` to get step-by-step procedures for installing and using UE-V.

Understanding AppLocker

Since we're talking about how we should support applications, then we also need to look at how we lock down applications. AppLocker is a feature included with Windows (Windows 7 and higher) that allows administrators to lock out certain applications from running. AppLocker can also be run from a GPO on a Windows Server (2008 and above) to lock an application out of the entire domain.

AppLocker allows administrators to control how network users can access and use certain files like executables (`.exe` and `.com`), scripts (`.ps1`, `.bat`, `.cmd`, `.vbs`, and `.js`), DLLs (`.dll` and `.ocx`), and Windows Installer files (`.msi` and `.msp`). AppLocker allows you to do the following;

- Test the AppLocker policy before implementing it by using the audit-only mode.
- Set file attribute rules using the application's digital signature, product name, filename, or even file version.
- Place rules on individuals or security groups.
- Set exceptions for any rule.
- Administrators have the ability to import or export rules.
- AppLocker can be managed by using PowerShell cmdlets.

When setting an AppLocker rule, all files for that rule will be denied from working unless you create a rule exemption. If there are no AppLocker rules for a specific file format, then all of those files will be allowed to work on the system. When setting AppLocker rules, the rules can be allowed or denied.

Allow: Administrators have the ability to determine which files are permitted to run in the corporate environment. Administrators also have the ability to configure exceptions to the rules.

Deny: Administrators have the ability to determine which files are *not* permitted to run in the corporate environment. Administrators also have the ability to configure exceptions to the rules.

Understanding Azure

Before I start talking about Azure, you first must understand that Azure is more than one thing—it's like a suite of tools and applications. Azure is a subscription-based service from Microsoft that offers many resources to help any size organization get the most out of Microsoft products. Figure 17.3 shows just some of the services offered by Azure. You have the ability to use Azure Active Directory, Azure backups, Windows applications, Azure virtual machines, and Windows Servers, among many other things.

FIGURE 17.3   Azure options

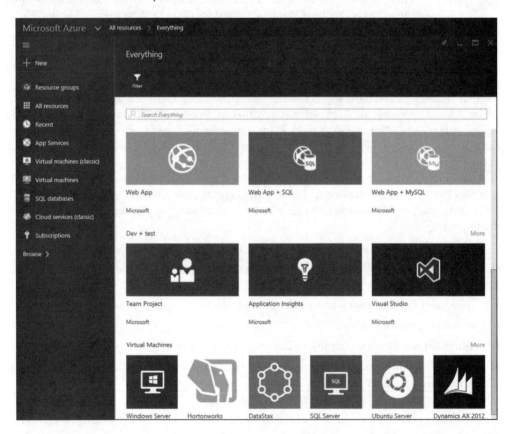

Azure Active Directory is the Microsoft version of Directory Services. In short, Active Directory is a set of services that help you secure and manage your network. There are multiple components of Active Directory:

- Active Directory Domain Services (AD DS)
- Active Directory Certificate Services (AD CS)

- Active Directory Federation Services (AD FS)
- Active Directory Rights Management Services (AD RMS)
- Active Directory Lightweight Directory Services (AD LDS)

 I will talk about Active Directory in greater detail in Chapter 19, "Configuring Network Connectivity."

Let's look at some of the Azure applications (some of which are shown in Figure 17.4) that you can configure and manage, starting with All Items in the upper-left corner.

FIGURE 17.4 Azure applications

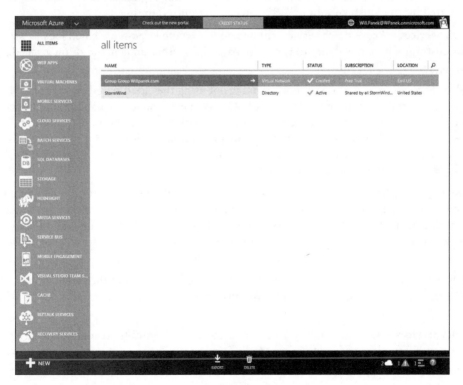

All Items The All Items feature shows you all of the applications and services that you currently subscribe to. The All Items feature allows you to manage and manipulate all of your services from one location.

Web Apps   The Web Apps feature allows developers to quickly develop, deploy, and manage websites and web apps. Developers can build web apps using .NET, Node.js, PHP, Python, and Java. Developers can use a single backend to create web apps and mobile apps for employees or customers.

Virtual Machines   The Virtual Machine feature allows IT Administrators to quickly create and manage cloud-based virtual machines. The Virtual Machines feature allows an administrator to quickly deploy a wide range of computing solutions and pay by the minute for the use of the virtual machines. The Virtual Machine Feature allows an administrator to work with multiple operating systems including Windows, Linux, Microsoft SQL Server, Oracle, IBM, SAP, and Azure BizTalk Services.

Cloud Services   Azure Cloud Services allows an organization to create, package, and deploy applications and services to the cloud with the click of a button. Once an organization creates an application, Microsoft does the rest. Azure handles all aspects from provisioning, load-balancing, and health monitoring. Your organization's application is supported by an industry-leading 99.95-percent guaranteed uptime.

Batch Services   Azure Batch services allow you to execute large-scale batch jobs. Administrators have the ability to run these batch jobs either on demand or on a schedule.

SQL Databases   Azure SQL Database is a database service modeled after the Microsoft SQL Server software. The one major advantage of using the cloud-based version of SQL services is that you get all of the benefits of SQL like performance, scalability, no downtime, business continuity, and data protection—all with near-zero administration. This gives your organization the ability to focus on application development instead of focusing on managing virtual machines and infrastructure. The SQL Database feature is available in Basic, Standard, and Premium service tiers.

Storage   Azure Storage provides organizations with the ability to store and retrieve large amounts of data in the cloud. Administrators have the ability to store data, such as documents and media files, while giving your organization scalability, reliability, and redundancy. Through the use of Microsoft's Azure cloud-based system, you get a cost-efficient way to store all of your company's data in one location.

HDInsight   Azure HDInsight is an Apache Hadoop server located in the cloud. Using HDInsight allows an organization to handle any amount of data on demand, from gigabytes to petabytes.

Media Services   Azure Media Services gives a company the ability to enable enterprise streaming solutions worldwide. Azure Media Services allows a company to have a powerful and scalable cloud-based encoding, encryption, and streaming system.

Service Bus   Azure Service Bus is a cloud-based messaging system for connecting applications, services, and devices. The real advantage of using Azure Service Bus is that you can connect any of these items wherever the items are located. You can even use Service Bus to connect other devices like tablets or phones to an application or each other.

Mobile Engagement   The Mobile Engagement feature gives an organization the ability to have real-time analytics. Using these analytics allows an IT department to solve problems with their network or applications. For example, you can see if your network is having bottlenecks and take measure to help solve the bottleneck.

Visual Studio Team Services   Visual Studio is one of the most popular ways for developers to create packages. Visual Studio Team Services allows developers to plan, build, and send software across a multitude of operating systems. Since this is a cloud-based app, the advantage of using Visual Studio Team Services is that you get the benefits of Visual Studio without having the need to install or configure a single Windows server.

Cache   Microsoft Azure Cache allows quick access to your corporate applications without the need to have a lot of memory local on your system. The Cache is a cloud-based memory system that is a scalable solution that allows corporations to create applications by providing fast access to data.

BizTalk Services   BizTalk Services allows cloud-based applications to communicate with each other or with on-premise applications. Because cloud-based apps run in their own cloud space, there is an issue with messaging and transport protocol mismatches. This is where BizTalk can help. BizTalk bridges the gap between the apps and your onsite services.

Recovery Services   Azure Recovery Services allows an organization to back up and recover their data in the cloud. Recovery Services is a subscription-based backup service that is controlled by Microsoft.

Scheduler   Azure Scheduler allows an administrator to schedule jobs in the cloud that consistently initiate service requests inside or outside of Azure. Administrators have the ability to run tasks right away, on a recurring schedule, or in the future.

API Management   Microsoft Azure API (application program interface) Management allows an administrator to manage APIs among internal departments, partners, and developers. API Management allows administrators to use the tools needed for provisioning user roles, developing usage plans and quotas, applying policies, and monitoring alerts.

Networks   Azure Virtual Network allows you to create an isolated and secure environment that you can run virtual machines and applications in. Administrators can use private IP addresses, subnets, access control policies, and almost anything that you can do with a physical network.

RemoteApp   Azure RemoteApp allows an administrator to provide secure, remote access to applications from multiple user devices. Azure RemoteApp allows users to host temporary Terminal Server sessions in the cloud. These Terminal Server sessions can be used and shared by other users in your network. RemoteApp is discussed in greater detail in the "Using Azure RemoteApp and App-V" section that follows this list of apps.

Active Directory   Azure Active Directory allows an organization to use and manage an Active Directory network without the need of setting up Windows Servers. Users can still use a single sign-on for any cloud-based or web application.

Marketplace   Azure Marketplace is your one-stop store for thousands of software applications, developer services, and data. These applications are automatically configured for use with Microsoft Azure.

Using Azure RemoteApp

As stated earlier in the chapter, Azure RemoteApp allows an administrator to provide secure, remote access to applications from multiple user devices. Azure RemoteApp allows users to host temporary Terminal Server sessions in the cloud. These Terminal Server sessions can be used and shared by other users in your network.

Azure RemoteApp allows users to share resources and applications on any device type. It can do this because your organization's applications are hosted in the cloud. Since all of your applications are cloud-based, any device with Internet access can then gain access to the applications. The one main advantage of using Azure RemoteApp is that you do not need to build and use servers in your organization to run your apps. After you upload your applications to the cloud, you then manage all of your applications through the Azure portal.

Then after the applications are loaded to the cloud, your users can access those applications from any device in the world. It does not matter on the application. Any application that is loaded to the cloud can then be accessed from the cloud. Users will need to download the Azure RemoteApp client to have web access for Azure RemoteApp.

> If you want your users to have web access to Azure RemoteApp, you need to download a RemoteApp client on your device. To do this, go to https://www.remoteapp.windowsazure.com/en/clients.aspx.

Since the applications are loaded onto virtual machines, the applications can be accessed by any type of device, including Apple devices and Android devices. Azure RemoteApp even supports application streaming for both 32-bit and 64-bit applications as long as they are loaded onto a Windows Server 2012 R2 virtual machine.

Creating Collections in Azure RemoteApp

The first thing you need to do to Azure RemoteApp is set up your application collections. Collections are just storage containers for applications and users. Every software image gets its own collection in the cloud.

Let's take a look at how to create an Office 2013 collection. Exercise 17.2 walks you through the creation of a collection for Office 2013.

Creating a Collection

1. Open the Azure portal.

2. In the tree on the left, scroll down until you see RemoteApp. Click the RemoteApp feature (shown in Figure 17.5).

FIGURE 17.5   RemoteApp feature

3. Click the Create a RemoteApp Collection link.

4. Click the Quick Create option and then enter a name for your collection (see Figure 17.6).

5. Select your region. If your region is not listed, choose the closest region to your own.

6. Select the billing plan you want to use. For this exercise, select the Basic package.

7. Finally, select the Office 2013 Professional image. This image contains Office 2013 apps. This image is good only for trial collections. You can't use this image in a production environment.

8. Click the Create RemoteApp Collection link.

FIGURE 17.6 Quick Create option

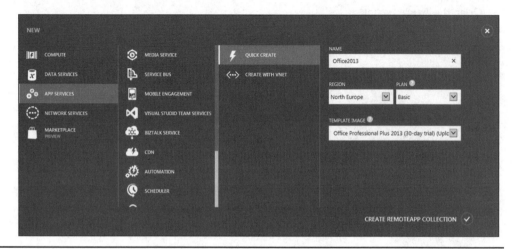

Sharing an Application

Now that you have created a collection, you have to share the application so that users can gain access. To share the application, follow the steps in Exercise 17.3.

EXERCISE 17.3

Sharing the Collection

1. Open the Azure portal.

2. In the tree on the left, scroll down until you see RemoteApp. Click the RemoteApp feature.

3. Click the arrow to the right of the collection name that you created in Exercise 17.2.

4. Click the Publishing tab on the top. Click Publish at the bottom of the screen, and then click Publish Start Menu Programs.

5. Next, you need to select the apps that you want to publish. For this exercise, I chose Word. Click Complete. You will then need to wait for the application to complete its publishing.

6. Once the application has completed publishing, click the User Access tab to add the users who will require access to the application. Enter each user's email address and then click Save.

Setting Up RemoteApp Connection Feeds

One of the issues that previous versions of RemoteApp encountered was that the applications ran in a web page and needed to be started from a web location. With Windows Server 2008 R2 and 2012/2012 R2 and Windows 7/8/8.1/10, you can now add the program to the users' Start menu. This gives your users the same program startup as if they had the program installed on their machine.

RemoteApp along with Desktop Connections allow for a feature called RemoteApp and Desktop Connection Feed. When using RemoteApp and Desktop Connection Feed, your users will subscribe to a RemoteApp programs feed (a URL). Once your clients subscribe to the feed, the application will be displayed on the users' Start menu.

To set up the RemoteApp and Desktop Connection feed, you need to create a new feed in Control Panel. To complete these steps, you will need to get the URL of the feed. To do this, go into the Azure Portal ➤ RemoteApp and then click the collection you created. There will be a URL link that you can use for the feed. You have to create a published feed on a virtual machine to get a proper URL and then use that link for setting up the feed. The following steps walk you through how you would set up a feed on a Windows 10 machine:

1. Open RemoteApp And Desktop Connections in Control Panel (shown in Figure 17.7).

FIGURE 17.7   RemoteApp And Desktop Connections

2. Click the Access RemoteApp And Desktops link on the left side of the screen.

3. Enter the URL of the collection feed and click Next.

4. On the Ready To Setup The Connection screen, click Next.

5. On the sign-in screen, enter your credentials. Click OK.

6. On the Summary screen, click the Finish button.

7. Start the application by accessing your system's Start menu.

Using Device Redirection

RemoteApp device redirection allows an administrator to configure a Windows system so that your users' devices can interact with the remote applications. For example, if you want to set up Skype through RemoteApp, a user would still need his or her camera and microphone to work with the RemoteApp version of Skype.

Administrators have the ability to set up RemoteApp device redirection through the use of a GPO, or they can set up the collection to automatically use redirection. To set up the collection for redirection, you would need to run some PowerShell commands. Table 17.2 lists some of the PowerShell commands and describes what they do.

TABLE 17.2   RemoteApp PowerShell commands

PowerShell Command	Description
Set-AzureRemoteAppCollection -CollectionName <collection name> -CustomRdpProperty "drivestoredirect: s:*'nusbdevicestoredirect:s:*"	This command sets the custom RDP properties.
Get-AzureRemoteAppCollection -CollectionName <collection name>	This command shows you a list of what custom RDP properties are configured.
Set-AzureRemoteAppCollection -CollectionName <collection name> -CustomRdpProperty "drivestoredirect:s:*"	This command shows you how to set up hard-drive redirection.
Set-AzureRemoteAppCollection -CollectionName <collection name> -CustomRdpProperty "drivestoredirect: s:*'nusbdevicestoredirect:s:*"	This command shows you how to set up USB and hard-drive redirection.
Install-Module AzureRM Install-AzureRM	These commands allow you to install the Azure Resource Manager modules.
Install-Module Azure	This command installs the Azure Service Management module.
Import-AzureRM	This command imports AzureRM modules.
Import-Module Azure	This command imports the Azure Service Management module.
Set-Mailbox	This command allows you to manipulate an Office 365 mailbox.

To configure RemoteApp redirection by using a Group Policy Object, you would complete the following steps:

For this example, I am showing you how to configure USB redirection on a system. I am showing you how to set up a local Group Policy in the event that you do not have a Windows Server setup. If you do want to do this for a domain, create a new GPO in the Group Policy Management MMC and then follow these steps.

1. Open the Local Group Policy Editor by typing **gpedit.msc** into the Windows 10 Search window.
2. Expand Computer Configuration\Policies\Administrative Templates\Windows Components\Remote Desktop Services\Remote Desktop Connection Client\RemoteFX USB Device Redirection.
3. Double-click the "Allow RDP redirection of other supported RemoteFX USB devices from this computer" option.
4. Select Enabled, and then choose Administrators And Users in the RemoteFX USB Redirection Access Rights.
5. Close the Group Policy Editor.
6. Restart the computer.

Understanding Shared Computer Activation

There may be a time when you need to set up Office 365 ProPlus to multiple users on the same computer within your organization. To do this, you must set up shared computer activation (SharedComputerLicensing value).

Shared computer activation allows an administrator to set up Office 365 ProPlus on a single computer for multiple users. This can be useful for schools, hospitals, and hotels. Let's say that you have multiple hotel front-desk staff members who need to access data on the same remote server—this is where shared computer activation can help.

Shared computer activation is used only when you have multiple people using the same computer. If you have users in your network that each has his or her own system, you would not use shared computer activation; you would use product key activation for Office 365 ProPlus.

To set up shared computer activation, you must use the Office Deployment Tool. For information about setting up shared computer activation, visit the Microsoft website https://technet.microsoft.com/en-us/library/dn782860.aspx?f=255&MSPPError=-2147217396.

Understanding App-V

Microsoft Application Virtualization (App-V) is included with the Microsoft Desktop Optimization Pack (MDOP). App-V gives an organization the ability to make applications available to corporate users without installing the application on the end user's system. App-V allows applications to be managed centrally without the worry of applications conflicting with one another.

App-V allows administrators to deploy applications as services, and App-V allows those applications to be deployed anywhere. App-V allows applications to get transferred from locally installed applications to the cloud.

One real nice advantage of App-V is that when new operating systems and applications get released, there is no need to constantly upgrade your users' systems to run those new applications. Since the applications are virtualized, they can run on older operating systems. When talking about App-V, we need to take a look at some of the components needed. Table 17.3 shows the different components required for App-V.

TABLE 17.3 App-V components

Component	Description
App-V Management Server	Administrators can manage the App-V infrastructure from the Management Server. App-V Management Server allows you to set up virtual applications to the App-V Desktop Client and the Remote Desktop Services Client.
App-V Publishing Server	This server hosts streaming virtual applications and also allows App-V–specific employees to gain access to virtual applications.
App-V Desktop Client	This accesses the virtual applications along with client application publication. Desktop client also manages virtual environments and stores employee-specific application settings.
App-V Remote Desktop Services (RDS) Client	This allows Remote Desktop Session Host servers to work in conjunction with the App-V Desktop Client for shared desktop sessions. This is very useful for tablets connecting to corporate applications. If the tablet can't run the application, the tablet user can connect to the Remote Desktop services to access the application.
App-V Sequencer	This tool allows administrators to convert normal applications into virtual applications through the use of a wizard.
Disconnected Operation Mode	The disconnected operation mode allows App-V Desktop Clients to run applications even when the client cannot connect to the App-V Management Server. This allows laptops to continue to access App-V applications even when not connected to the network or the Internet.

Supporting the Windows Store

The Microsoft Windows Store is a one-stop shop for all Microsoft devices. The Windows Store allows users to find and download applications for business and personal use. The Windows Store allows you to download everything from business applications that you can use to create spreadsheets to Xbox games that will allow you to game it out.

You can browse the Windows Store from your PC, tablet, or phone, and you can quickly and easily get free and paid content including games, music, movies, TV shows, and applications. So if your company is looking for free applications to improve business, the Windows Store can help.

One of the advantages to using the Windows Store is that all applications on the store are watched by Microsoft and require a digital certificate to make sure that they are legitimate. If an application is not signed, it will be removed from the Microsoft Store. This also means that you can't build your own apps and place them into the Windows Store without the same security measures. There are methods of loading corporate apps so that only corporate users can gain access to those apps, and that is referred to as sideloading.

Sideloading is the process of loading apps onto your corporate users with the need of a digital signature or the security rules that follow the Microsoft Store.

So what must you do if you want to build your own apps and place them onto the Windows Store? Well, you have to use one of Microsoft's tools that allow you to certify your applications, and those tools include the `MakeCert.exe` and `Pvk2Pfx.exe` tools that are included with the Windows Driver Kit (WDK).

Installing and Managing Software by Using Microsoft Office 365 and Windows Store Apps

One of the best advantages to using the Windows Store is that you can pretty much find and download any application that you need to help your business be more efficient. This can also be one of the biggest issues that an IT department can face. Normally an IT department needs to verify and test all applications before deploying them to the corporate network.

Now your users can find the specific applications that they think will help them do their jobs better and download just those applications. However, IT departments have the ability to turn off the Windows Store through the use of a GPO or local policy, which allows them to maintain more control.

If your IT department does not care about users downloading applications, then the Windows Store is for you. It's very easy to install applications from the Windows Store. You just go to the Windows Store, search for the application that you are looking for, and then click the download button next to that application. Normally the applications will have a small fee associated with them, but many of them are free.

Maintaining and updating applications is also a very easy process. To make sure that your applications get updated whenever there is an update available, just follow these steps:

1. On the Start screen, click the Store icon on the taskbar to open the Windows Store.

2. On the top Windows Store menu, click the picture next to the Search box and then choose Settings.

3. Under App Updates, set the Update Apps Automatically slide bar to On, as shown in Figure 17.8.

FIGURE 17.8   Windows Store Settings

4. When you have finished, close the Windows Store Settings window.

Let's take a look at some of the other things that you can set while on the Settings page for the Windows Store. Users or administrators also have the ability to show products on tiles, require a sign-in for purchases, and manage the devices that are loaded onto the Windows Store.

Now that you know how to get applications from the Windows Store, let's take a look at how to load corporate applications through the process of sideloading.

Sideloading Apps into Online and Offline Images

There will be a time when you or someone in your company may have to build or support a custom-made Line of Business (LOB) application. Companies build and use LOB apps because they have a very special need and can't find a software package to help solve that need.

Sideloading is the process of loading a Windows Store application without needing to publish the software application and download it from the store. Users can install the software package directly. Windows 10 sideloading has changed since Windows 8 in the following ways:

- Administrators have the ability to unlock a device for sideloading using an enterprise GPO policy.
- Software license keys are not required to install the application.
- Devices do not have to be part of the domain to get an application sideloaded.

Sideloading is not a very difficult process to complete. It is just a few settings along with the use of some PowerShell commands. To enable the systems to accept sideloading, complete the following steps:

1. Open Settings.
2. Click Update & Security ➢ For Developers.
3. Under the Use Developer Features section, choose Sideload Apps, as shown in Figure 17.9.

FIGURE 17.9   Windows sideloading

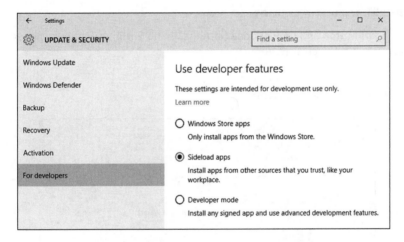

Once the system is enabled to allow applications to be sideloaded, you then need to run some PowerShell commands to make that happen. Navigate to the Windows PowerShell prompt and run the following commands (where "*TestApp*" is the path and name of the package file you created):

```
import-module appx
add-appxpackage "TestApp"
```

Integrating Microsoft Accounts Including Personalization Settings

Normally in the corporate world, we all get issued a corporate username and password so that we can log into the network and access corporate resources. But what if we wanted to access both corporate and personal data from the Internet? That's where integrating your Microsoft online account and your domain account can be beneficial.

Windows 10 gives you the ability to use both a corporate username and personal user account within the same Windows 10 account. Users can link their online accounts with their corporate accounts. So if you have your own personal cloud-based account as well as a corporate account, you can set it up so that you only log in once but have access to both accounts.

Users who decide to link their Microsoft accounts with their corporate accounts have the ability to gain access to applications and games from the Microsoft Windows Store using one account. One of the benefits of tying both accounts together is that once you've completed this setup, the Accounts Wizard will have you establish a PIN at the end. After it's all set, you will log in using the PIN from that point on.

So how do we link the two accounts together? Exercise 17.4 walks you through how to tie both accounts together. After the exercise is complete, your local account will switch to your Microsoft account after you restart your system.

EXERCISE 17.4

Setting the Microsoft Account

1. Click the Start button and then choose Settings. In the Settings window, choose Accounts (shown in Figure 17.10).

FIGURE 17.10   Settings window

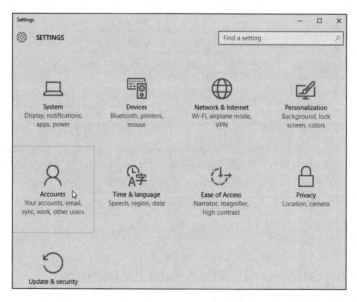

2. In the Accounts window, click the "Sign in with a Microsoft account instead" link (shown in Figure 17.11).

FIGURE 17.11   Accounts window

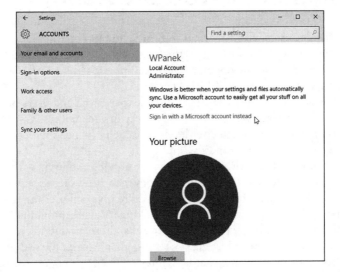

3. A new window will appear that states "Make it your." Type in your Microsoft online username and password. Then click the Sign In button.

4. If a box pops up asking for your Windows network password, enter it and click Next. If you don't have a password, just click Next.

5. The screen will ask you to enter a PIN. Click the Set A PIN button (shown in Figure 17.12) and set your PIN.

FIGURE 17.12   PIN button

6. After the PIN is completed, you are all set. Close the Accounts window.

Understanding Web Browsers

Windows 10 provides users with two ways to browse the Internet: Edge and IE11. Windows Internet Explorer 11, or IE11, is the latest web browser developed and released by Microsoft Corporation in the popular Internet Explorer series. IE11 is available for Windows 10 and Windows Server 2012 R2 versions.

With the explosion of Internet use—from the inexperienced end users browsing the Internet for personal reasons to those who use it for work-related tasks—enhancing the user interface (UI) while providing better levels of security (which include privacy) has been the focus in the development of both Edge and IE11.

Both browsers are loaded with user features that provide end users with a better and simpler way to get the information they desire from their browsing experience.

The features added to Edge and IE11 are designed to give end users an easy way to browse the Internet for the information they're looking for while providing a secure environment for networks by recognizing potentially bad sites (those attempting to sneak viruses or Trojan horses into the network), phishing sites (those that attempt to steal private information about the user), or invasive sites that users may go to either on purpose or inadvertently.

When comparing the two browsers, Edge and IE11, Edge has taken browsing a step further with the implementation of Cortana. Cortana can assist you while working with Edge.

Browser Controls

When you open either Edge or IE11, one of the first things that will catch your attention is the simplified design. The most common controls, like tools and favorite buttons, are just a click away. You also have the ability to customize how the browser will look and which tools you can use with the browser.

Pinning Sites to the Taskbar

Pinning sites to your taskbar allows you to access the websites by clicking the pinned site at the bottom of the taskbar. Pinning a site is an easy process. Just drag the tab of the website to the taskbar. An icon for the website will stay pinned until you remove it. When you click the pinned icon, the website will open within the Internet browser.

Searchable Address Bar

You have the ability to search the Internet directly from the Address bar. You still have the ability to enter a website's address and go directly to the website. But now you can enter a search term or incomplete address, thus launching a search using your currently selected search engine. You can choose which search engine you want to use by clicking the Address bar and choosing the search engine from the listed icons or adding a new search engine.

Security and Privacy Enhancements

IE11 and Edge have both included many security and privacy enhancements, including some of the following:

- ActiveX Filtering allows you to block ActiveX controls for any sites. You do have the ability to turn them back on for the sites that you trust.

- Domain highlighting allows you to see the real web address of a website you are visiting. This allows you to avoid websites that use misleading web addresses. Domain highlighting is discussed in detail later in this section.

- SmartScreen Filter helps protect users from online phishing attacks, fraud, and spoofed or malicious websites. SmartScreen Filter is discussed in detail later in this section.

- 128-bit Secure Sockets Layer (SSL) connection to use with secure websites.

- InPrivate Browsing allows you to use the Web without saving any data from the websites that are visited while the browser is in this mode.

Working with Web Slices

Web Slices allow your Internet browser (IE, not Edge) to check for updates to web page content you may frequently access. How many times in the course of the day do you check your local weather or stock quotes or even watch an auction item on eBay? Most of the time, you either keep a tab open and refresh it periodically or revisit the website with the content you would like to review.

With Web Slices, you can add the piece of the web page with the content you're looking for to the Favorites bar, and the browser will check it for you when the content changes. With Web Slices, the browser can control how often the browser checks for changes.

Figure 17.13 shows the result of a Bing query for the weather forecast for Portsmouth, New Hampshire, and the Web Slice availability to the Favorites toolbar. Clicking the down arrow associated with the icon will display all of the Web Slices available on the current web page.

FIGURE 17.13 Web Slice

In previous versions of the Internet browsers, Web Slices use to appear within the web page. Now the Web Slices are displayed with the feeds button, as shown in Figure 17.13.

When the user chooses a Web Slice icon, he or she will see a confirmation box for adding the Web Slice to the Favorites bar. Once accepted, the Web Slice is available to be viewed at any time, even after the user browses away from the originating page.

Using the Browser Compatibility View

Windows Internet Explorer 11 is the new release of Microsoft's IE web browser, and some websites may not be updated to use the new features or display their content correctly. Problems may exist displaying misaligned images or text. By using Compatibility View in IE11 (not available in Edge), the browser will display a web page the way it would have been displayed in previous versions, which should correct any display issues. To display a page in Compatibility View, click the Compatibility View option in the tools (shown in Figure 17.14).

FIGURE 17.14 Compatibility View option

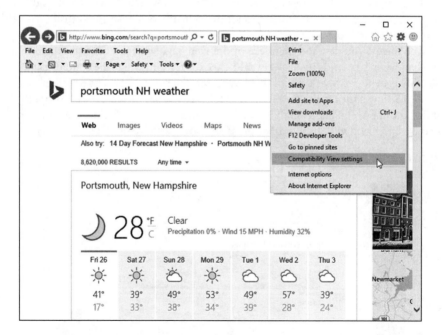

Once you have chosen Compatibility View for a website, you will not need to make the choice again. The browsers will display the site in Compatibility View the next time you browse to it. If the website gets updated in the future or you decide you would prefer to see it in the native standard mode, you can simply click the Compatibility View option again to return to the standard view. The Compatibility View option can also be selected from the Tools menu's Compatibility View menu option.

There is also a Compatibility View Settings option you can use to manage the sites currently set to be viewed in Compatibility View mode by adding or deleting sites by name. Many companies have extensive websites, and it may take time to update them to features. The Compatibility View Settings page has the default setting for all intranet sites to be displayed in Compatibility View. You also have to the choice to display all websites in Compatibility View.

Using Protected Mode for IE11

Protected Mode is a feature of Windows 10 for Windows Internet Explorer 11 that forces IE to run in a protected, isolated memory space, preventing malicious code from directly writing data outside the `Temporary Internet Files` folder unless the program trying to write the information is specifically granted access by the user. Protected Mode is enabled by default and displayed in the lower-right section of Windows Internet Explorer 11.

You can install software through IE11, but you will need to explicitly allow the modification of the file structure of Windows 10 if the software is going to be installed outside the protected directory.

You can change out of Protected Mode from the Security tab of IE11's Internet options (via Tools ➤ Internet Options). You can also open Internet Options by typing **Internet options** into the integrated search box in Windows 10. You also have the option of double-clicking the Protected Mode: On text within Windows Internet Explorer 11 to open just the Security tab of Internet Options.

To toggle Protected Mode, click to select or deselect the Enable Protected Mode check box (this requires restarting Internet Explorer). It is recommended that Protected Mode remain active because it provides a greater level of security and safety for the user and does not prohibit an action (such as installing a program from IE11); it just requires interaction from the user to allow the modification, prompting at least a little thought about what's happening within Windows 10.

Using InPrivate Browsing and InPrivate Filtering

InPrivate Browsing provides some level of privacy to users using Windows Internet Explorer 11 and Edge. The privacy maintained with InPrivate Browsing relates to a current browser where an InPrivate session has been enabled. The InPrivate session prevents the browsing history from being recorded and prevents temporary Internet files from being retained. Cookies, usernames, passwords, and form data will not remain in IE11 following the closing of the InPrivate session, nor will there be any footprints or data pertaining to the InPrivate Browsing session.

InPrivate Browsing keeps information from being saved to the local machine while the session is active, but don't get lulled into a false sense of security; malware, phishing, and other methods that send data out of the local machine are still valid and can provide personal information to a cybercriminal. In addition, employees visiting forbidden sites from work, for instance, could still be detected via forensics.

InPrivate Browsing is a good method of protecting user data if you are not surfing from your own machine or are surfing from a public location (always a bad place to leave personal information). InPrivate Browsing can also be used if you don't want anyone to be able to see data from your Internet browsing session.

There are several ways to launch an IE11 InPrivate Browsing session. One way is to open a new tab and select the Open An InPrivate Browsing Window option from the Browse With InPrivate section. This will open a new tab, and the tab will be an InPrivate session. You can also choose to open Windows Internet Explorer 11 and start an InPrivate session directly by choosing the Safety menu and selecting the InPrivate Browsing menu choice. Alternatively, you can open a new IE11 browser and press Ctrl+Shift+P.

InPrivate Filtering (IE 11 only) takes a slightly different approach in providing security and safety to the user who is surfing using Windows Internet Explorer 11. Many of today's websites gather content from different sources as they present a web page to you. Some of these sources are websites outside the main location, and they provide third-party companies with tracking information about where you surf and what you look at.

This information can then be used to provide statistics as well as send advertisements back to you. InPrivate Filtering provides an added layer of control for the user to decide what information third-party websites will have access to while the user is browsing, limiting the ability of third-party websites to track their browsing usage.

InPrivate Filtering is not enabled by default and must be enabled per browsing session. It is enabled from the Safety menu in IE11. You can alternatively use Ctrl+Shift+F to enable InPrivate Filtering.

The InPrivate Filtering dialog box is an alternate location for enabling InPrivate Filtering or disabling it. You open InPrivate Filtering from the Safety menu of Windows Internet Explorer 11.

Once you choose InPrivate Filtering, you will be given the option to have IE11 automatically block some third-party content or let the user select which third-party providers will receive the user's browsing information. You can always go back and change the options later or turn off InPrivate Filtering if you desire.

After InPrivate Filtering is enabled, you can see which pages have been blocked as third-party queries from the InPrivate Filtering Settings dialog box.

Another advantage of IE11 is that you can configure the web content filter. IE11 also allows you to set up and configure the Allow and Block lists. The Allow and Block lists are lists that you can subscribe to that will automatically filter out certain websites.

Configuring Windows Internet Explorer 11 Options

In addition to security and usability options that you can configure in IE11, you can configure other options for managing the browser. Many of the configurations we have discussed in this chapter (i.e., the Safety or Tools menu options) and have used to quickly change individual parameters are also available for modification within the Internet Options tabbed dialog box. The general parameters, security parameters, privacy configurations, content controls, connection settings, program options, and advanced settings available within Internet Options are discussed in the following sections.

General Parameters

You can open the Internet Properties tabbed dialog box by selecting the Tools menu and choosing the Internet Properties menu item or by simply typing **Internet options** into the integrated search box of Windows 10. The General tab (shown in Figure 17.15) allows you to change the default home page that displays when Windows Internet Explorer 11 is launched. One interesting feature here is that you can have more than one default home page. By entering more than one page in the Home Page text box, each time IE11 is launched, all pages will open in their own tab.

FIGURE 17.15   General tab of IE11's Internet Properties

The General tab also allows you to control your Browsing History, Search, Tabs, and Appearance (including accessibility options) settings for the IE11 interface.

Security Parameters

The Security tab of IE11's Internet Properties dialog box (shown in Figure 17.16) not only gives you access to control Protected Mode as discussed earlier in this section but also gives you the ability to set security settings on the specific zones you may browse to as understood by Windows Internet Explorer 11. The zones are the Internet, Local Intranet, Trusted Sites, and Restricted Sites. You can set the behavior of IE11 individually for each zone and even individual sites within each zone. For example, if you add a website to the Local

Intranet settings, you will not be asked to authenticate your credentials when connecting to the website.

FIGURE 17.16   Security tab of IE11's Internet Properties

Privacy Configurations

The Privacy tab of IE11's Internet Properties (shown in Figure 17.17) allows the management of privacy settings for the Internet Zone; this is the cookie management for specific sites. You can also control the settings for Pop-up Blocker and your InPrivate Filtering and InPrivate Browsing here.

The Pop-up Blocker allows you to prevent unwanted Internet pop-ups from appearing while you are online. We have all been on websites where pop-up windows start appearing. With the IE11 Pop-up Blocker, you can prevent this from happening. To access the Pop-up Blocker Settings dialog box, click Start ➤ Internet Explorer ➤ Tools ➤ Pop-up Blocker ➤ Pop-up Blocker Settings.

To block cookies from any websites that do not have a compact privacy policy, you should set the privacy setting to High. The High setting prevents IE11 from saving cookies for websites that do not contain a compact privacy policy and cookies that have the potential of saving information that can be used to contact you without your explicit consent. Compact policies are used to indicate the privacy practices of a web service that uses cookies.

FIGURE 17.17   Privacy tab of IE11's Internet Properties

If you want to block any website from accessing cookies stored on the local computer, you should set the privacy setting to Block All Cookies. The Block All Cookies setting prevents cookies from being saved on the computer and prevents any existing cookies from being read by websites.

Content Control

Figure 17.18 shows the Content tab of Windows Internet Explorer 11's Internet Properties. There are Parental Controls to manage which sites are available through web filtering and to monitor website access through an Activity Monitor. There has to be a privileged account with a password set to enforce Parental Controls. InPrivate Browsing is not allowed when Parental Controls are in place.

Content Advisor settings allow a display of rated sites as users browse to different locations. (Sites can be rated based on factors such as fear, tobacco, alcohol, nudity, drugs, gambling, and so on.)

Certificate management for secure browsing is managed through the Content tab as well. You have the ability to manage AutoComplete functionality as well as RSS feeds and Web Slice data from within the Content tab.

FIGURE 17.18   Content tab of the Internet Properties dialog box

The AutoComplete functionality allows IE11 to automatically fill in fields as you complete forms in IE11. It uses previously entered data to complete the fields on the form.

The Feeds And Web Slices section allows you to fill in what subscription feeds you belong to on the Internet and how often those feeds and slices will be updated along with other configuration options (i.e., playing a sound when the feed or slice is updated).

Connection Settings

The Connections tab of Windows Internet Explorer 11's Internet Properties dialog box allows you to manage the way IE11 gains access to the network. You can initiate the Connect to The Internet Wizard from this tab as well as set up a virtual private network (VPN). If you are using dial-up networking, this connection is also configured from the Connections tab. Local area network (LAN) general settings, which includes specifying a proxy server if you need to use one (this is typical across many corporate sites, to provide a better level of anonymity for Internet surfing), are configured here as well.

Program Options

The Programs tab of the IE11 Internet Properties dialog box allows you to establish a default web browser. You can manage add-ons specific to IE11 in the Programs tab as well.

Additionally, you can set up an application to allow for HTML editing and set up default programs to be used for Internet services such as email.

Advanced Options

The Advanced tab allows you to configure accessibility settings, browsing settings, international browsing settings, encoding settings, multimedia parameters, printing parameters, and general security settings. You can control whether links are underlined, whether pictures should be displayed, which versions of the secure communication protocols or SSL are used, background colors, and many other parameters.

In addition to being able to change the advanced settings, you have the option to restore advanced settings to their original configurations or to even reset Internet Explorer settings, which resets all IE11 settings (not just the advanced settings) to the default configuration.

Summary

Managing Windows software is a very important component that must be properly configured in Windows 10 to guarantee the best possible performance. In the event that the Windows Software packages can't be run on the Windows 10 operating system, there are other options for you to run software with Windows 10.

You can use Hyper-V to create other operating systems on the Windows 10 system. Administrators can also use application virtualization (App-V) to run applications in the cloud. Administrators can also use the cloud to deploy applications by using RemoteApp.

We also talked about how to make sure that applications are going to continue to work properly by testing them through the Application Compatibility Toolkit (ACT).

Another application that is very important to most of us is Internet Explorer. Edge and Internet Explorer 11 are both included with Windows 10, and they have many new features and security enhancements so that the user can get the most out of their browsing experience.

Video Resources

There is a video available for the following exercise:

   17.4

You can access the video at www.wiley.com/go/sybextestprep on the Other Study Tools tab.

Exam Essentials

Understand and know how to install Hyper-V.   Understand what Hyper-V does and know all of the different components of a Hyper-V virtual machine. Understand how to configure virtual machines and the components that make virtual machines operate.

Know how older applications can work in Windows 10.   Understand how to allow older applications to work with Windows 10. You can run applications in Hyper-V or Compatibility Mode or use shims that are created by Microsoft.

Understand how to install applications from the cloud.   You can use Azure RemoteApp to help control and manage how applications get deployed. RemoteApp allows you to download applications to many different Windows device types.

Understand Application Virtualization   Know how to use application virtualization (App-V) and know how to run applications from the cloud without the need to deploy the applications to users' hardware.

Be able to configure privacy settings in IE11 and Edge.   Know how to enable and disable cookies. Know when it is useful to use cookies and when cookies should be blocked. Cookies are files that are placed on your system. Not having files placed on your system increases security. Know how to set an InPrivate session to verify that nothing is saved during an Internet session.

Review Questions

1. You are the network administrator for your organization. Your organization has started using App-V. You notice that laptop users are still able to access App-V applications even when they are not connected to the network. You want to stop this from happening. What do you do?

    A. Disable the Disconnected Operation Mode.

    B. Enable Terminal Services.

    C. Enable Remote Desktop Services.

    D. Discontinue laptops from using App-V.

2. You are the network administrator for your organization. You are asked by your manager to modify the associations of a few file extensions that are associated with Internet Explorer. How can you accomplish this task?

    A. In Control Panel, open Default Programs and then click Set Associations. Set the proper file extensions.

    B. In Internet Explorer, set extensions on the Extension tab.

    C. In Control Panel, open System and then click Set Associations. Set the proper file extensions.

    D. In Internet Explorer, set extensions on the Advanced tab.

3. You are the network administrator for a large organization. You are in charge of implementing company policies. One company policy states that you have to prevent Internet Explorer from saving any data during a user's browsing session. How do you accomplish this?

    A. Set the Internet Security settings to Disabled.

    B. Run the browsers in InPrivate sessions.

    C. Disable InPrivate sessions.

    D. Private sessions should be enabled.

4. You are the network administrator for a large organization. A user calls you and says that when they try to connect to the internal website, they are prompted for authentication. The user has the rights to access the internal site due to the fact that all users and computers are part of a domain and the internal website uses Integrated Windows Authentication. How do you make sure that the user is automatically authenticated when they connect?

    A. Change the user's local permissions to Administrator.

    B. The Local sites URL should be added to the Local Intranet zone.

    C. The Local sites security credentials should be added to the trusted sites zone.

    D. The Internet security level should be lowered to lowest.

5. You are the network administrator for your organization. Your organization has deployed Azure RemoteApp collections by configuring a custom template image. This image is going to contain Microsoft Office 365 ProPlus. Your organization needs to guarantee that multiple employees can run Office 365 ProPlus from the image all at the same time. What do you need to include in your configuration file?

   A. `<Property Name="SHUTDOWNAPP" Value = "True"/>`

   B. `<Property Name="SharedComputerLicensing" Value = "1"/>`

   C. `<Property Name="ACTIVATEAPP" Value = "1"/>`

   D. `<Property Name="OFFICE365ProPlus" Value = "1"/>`

6. Your company has decided to start using AppLocker GPOs to control application access. Jeff, Stormwind's IT Manager, would like to test the AppLocker policy before implementing it. How can Jeff test the AppLocker policy?

   A. In the Group Policy Manager, run the Group Policy Results Wizard.

   B. In the Group Policy Manager, run the Group Policy Modeling Wizard.

   C. In the Group Policy Manager, enforce the new AppLocker policy in Audit-Only mode.

   D. In the Group Policy Manager, run the Group Policy Test Wizard.

7. You are the administrator of an organization who has decided to use Microsoft Azure Active Directory cloud-based services. You have set up a corporate subscription for Microsoft Office 365. Each employee gets a mailbox stored in Office 365 and also an email for the corporate network. After buying out another company, you need to add a third email address to each user. How can you do this?

   A. In Active Directory Sites And Services, edit the email attribute for each employee.

   B. In Active Directory Domains And Trusts, edit the email attribute for each employee.

   C. Use the Set-Mailbox cmdlet from the Azure Active Directory Module for PowerShell.

   D. Use the Set-Mailbox cmdlet from the Active Directory Module for PowerShell.

8. You are the network administrator for a large organization. You have installed Hyper-V on a server called ServerA, and you have set up four new VM servers. You want to run PowerShell commands for the VM servers from ServerA. How do you do this?

   A. Use the Invoke-Command cmdlet and specify the VMName parameter.

   B. Use the WinRM command -PowerShell.

   C. Use the PSCommands–enabled command.

   D. Just run the PowerShell commands with the -Name parameter.

9. You are the network administrator for a large organization. You have deployed a software package to all of the Windows computers in your domain. You want to set up a GPO so that some employees have no access to the application. How do you accomplish this?

   A. Set up a restriction server and place all of your restricted employees onto that server.

   B. Configure BitLocker.

   C. Configure AppLocker.

   D. Configure each Windows 10 system to use user policies.

10. You are the administrator of a large organization. Your company has developed an application for your employees. You need to deploy the internally developed application to all employees while minimizing the costs. What's the best way to do that?

   A. Install the application one system at a time.

   B. Enable application sideloading.

   C. Purchase System Center and deploy the application.

   D. Run the Add-Application PowerShell cmdlet.

Chapter

18

Managing Identity and Authorization

MICROSOFT EXAM OBJECTIVES COVERED IN THIS CHAPTER:

✓ **Support authentication and authorization.**

- This objective may include but is not limited to: Identifying and resolving issues related to the following: Multi-factor authentication including certificates, Microsoft Passport, virtual smart cards, picture passwords, and biometrics; workgroup vs. domain, Homegroup, computer and user authentication including secure channel, account policies, credential caching, and Credential Manager; local account vs. Microsoft account; Workplace Join; Configuring Windows Hello.

This may be one of the most important chapters in this study guide. Setting up users, groups, and security involves some of the most critical tasks that any IT manager needs to perform.

One of the most fundamental tasks in network management is creating user and group accounts. Without a user account, a user cannot log on to a computer, server, or network. When users log on, they supply a username and password. Then their user accounts are validated by a security mechanism. In Windows 10, users can log on to a computer locally, or if the machine is a member of an Active Directory domain, the user can authenticate against a local copy of Active Directory or a cloud-based copy of Active Directory.

Groups are used to ease network administration by grouping users who have similar permission requirements. Groups are an important part of network management. Many administrators are able to accomplish the majority of their management tasks through the use of groups; they rarely assign permissions to individual users. Windows 10 includes built-in local groups, such as Administrators and Backup Operators.

You create and manage local groups through the Local Users and Groups utility. With this utility, you can add groups, change group membership, rename groups, and delete groups.

Windows 10 also offers a wide variety of security options. If the Windows 10 computer is a part of a domain, you can apply security through Group Policy Objects using the Group Policy Management Console. If the Windows 10 computer is not a part of a domain, then you can use Local Group Policy Objects to manage local security.

Overview of Windows 10 User Accounts

When you install Windows 10, several user accounts are created automatically. Additionally, you can create new user accounts. As you already know, user accounts allow a user to log on to machines and access resources.

You can create local user accounts, which reside locally on the Windows 10 machine. Such accounts cannot be utilized to gain access to any resources hosted on the network. If you have installed Active Directory either in the cloud (Azure Active Directory) or on a network that has a Windows Server 2012/2012 R2, Windows Server 2008/2008 R2, Windows Server 2003, or Windows Server 2000 domain controller, your network can have domain user accounts as well.

In the following sections, you will learn about the different account types: the default user accounts that are created by Windows 10 and the difference between local and domain user accounts.

Account Types

Windows 10 supports two basic types of user accounts: administrator and standard user (see Figure 18.1). Each of these accounts is used for specific reasons.

FIGURE 18.1   Choosing an account type

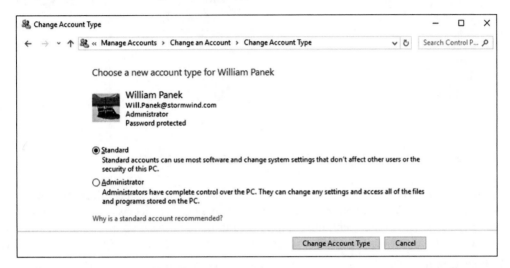

Administrator   The administrator account type provides unrestricted access for performing administrative tasks. As a result, administrator accounts should be used only for performing administrative tasks and should not be used for normal computing tasks.

Only administrator accounts can change the Registry. This is important to know because when most software is installed onto a Windows 10 machine, the Registry gets changed. This is why you need administrator rights to install most software.

Standard User   The standard user account type should be assigned to every user of the computer. Standard user accounts can perform most day-to-day tasks, such as running Microsoft Word, accessing email, using Internet Explorer, and so on. Running as a standard user increases security by limiting the possibility of a virus or other malicious code from infecting the computer. Standard user accounts are unable to make system-wide changes, which also helps to increase security.

When you install Windows 10, by default, there are premade accounts called built-in accounts. Let's take a look at them.

Built-In Accounts

When installed into a workgroup environment, Windows 10 has five built-in accounts, which are created automatically at the time you install the operating system (see Figure 18.2). Figure 18.2 also shows the accounts that I created while writing this book.

FIGURE 18.2   The five built-in accounts

Administrator   The Administrator account is a special account that has full control over the computer. The Administrator account can perform all tasks, such as creating users and groups, managing the filesystem, installing applications, and setting up printing. Note that the Administrator account is disabled by default.

DefaultAccount   This is a user account created by the system and used by the system. This account is a member of the HomeUsers group and the System Managed Accounts group.

Guest   The Guest account allows users to access the computer even if a person does not have a unique username and password. Because of the inherent security risks associated with this type of user, the Guest account is disabled by default. When this account is enabled, it is usually given very limited privileges.

**HomeGroupUser$**   The HomeGroupUser$ account is created by default to allow this machine to connect to other machines within the same HomeGroup network. This account is created by default as soon as you set up a HomeGroup.

Initial User   The Initial User account uses the name of the registered user. By default, the initial user is a member of the Administrators group.

By default, the name Administrator is given to a user account that is a member of the Administrators group. However, in Windows 10, this user account is disabled by default. You can increase the computer's security by leaving this account disabled and assigning other users to the Administrators group. This way, a malicious user will be unable to log on to the computer using the Administrator user account.

All five of these users are considered local users, and their permissions are contained to the Windows 10 machine. If the user's account needs to access resources on machines other than their own, you can have a user log in to the Windows 10 computer as a remote user (a user who is not in front of the machine they're logging on to), and this would be considered a domain user's account. Let's take a look at the difference between these account types.

Local and Domain User Accounts

Windows 10 supports two kinds of users: local users and domain users. Local users get set up on each Windows 10 client system. The Windows 10 system can be part of a workgroup or it can be a stand-alone system. A computer that is running Windows 10 has the ability to store its own user accounts database. The user accounts stored at the local computer are known as *local user accounts*.

Workgroups are networks that have user databases on each individual Windows 10 machine. However, you can share resources on the workgroup network.

Domains

Domains are networks where there is a centralized security database (Active Directory), and you can control all of your users and groups from one central location.

Active Directory is a directory service that stores information in a central database, which allows users to have a single user account for the network. The user accounts stored in Active Directory's central database are called *domain user accounts*. Active Directory is available in two different models. There is a cloud-based Active Directory called Azure Active Directory and a server-based version that runs on Windows Server 2012/2012 R2, Windows Server 2008/2008 R2, Windows Server 2003, and Windows 2000 Server platforms.

Workgroups

You can log on locally to a Windows 10 computer using a locally stored user account, or you can log on to a domain using an Active Directory account. When you install Windows 10 on a computer, you specify that the computer will be a part of a workgroup, which implies a local logon, or that it will be a part of a domain, which implies a domain logon.

On all Windows versions except domain controllers, you can create local users through the Local Users and Groups utility, as described in the section "Working with User Accounts" later in this chapter. On Windows Server domain controllers (Windows Server 2000 and above), you manage users with the Microsoft Active Directory Users and Computers MMC.

 NOTE   Active Directory is covered in detail in *MCSA Windows Server 2012 R2 Complete Study Guide: Exams 70-410, 70-411, 70-412, and 70-417,* by William Panek (Sybex, 2016).

Workplace Join

There may be times when you need someone to gain access to a domain resource but that person doesn't have a domain account. That's where Workplace Join can help. Workplace Join is a Windows tool that you can download and use on your domain.

Workplace Join allows an end user to use a corporate email address and password to connect a Windows system (Windows phone, tablet, or operating system) to a domain. The email address and password are then sent to an Active Directory server to be verified. The server can be set to then send a message to the device to confirm that the device should be given access to the domain. After the verification is done, Workplace Join creates a new device object in Active Directory and installs a certificate onto the Windows device.

Logging Off

No matter what type of network you have, you will eventually need to log off the Windows 10 system. When users are ready to stop working, they should either log off or shut down the system. A user can do either of these by right-clicking the Windows Start button and choosing Shut Down or Sign Out.

Working with User Accounts

To set up and manage your local user accounts, you use the Local Users and Groups utility or the User Accounts option in Control Panel. With either option, you can create, disable, delete, and rename user accounts as well as change user passwords.

Windows 10 includes User Account Control (UAC), which provides an additional level of security by limiting the level of access that users have when performing normal, everyday tasks. When needed, users can gain elevated access for specific administrative tasks.

Using the Local Users and Groups Utility

There are two common methods for accessing the Local Users and Groups utility:

- Load Local Users and Groups as a Microsoft Management Console (MMC) snap-in.
- Access the Local Users and Groups utility through the Computer Management utility.

If your computer doesn't have a custom MMC configured, the quickest way to access the Local Users and Groups utility is through the Computer Management utility.

In Exercise 18.1, you will add the Local Users and Groups snap-in MMC to the desktop. This exercise needs to be completed in order to complete other exercises in this chapter.

EXERCISE 18.1

Adding the Local Users and Groups Snap-in

1. In the Search box, type **MMC** and press Enter.

2. If a warning box appears, click Yes.

3. Select File ➤ Add/Remove Snap-in.

4. Scroll down the list and highlight Local Users And Groups, and then click the Add button (shown in Figure 18.3).

FIGURE 18.3   MMC snap-ins

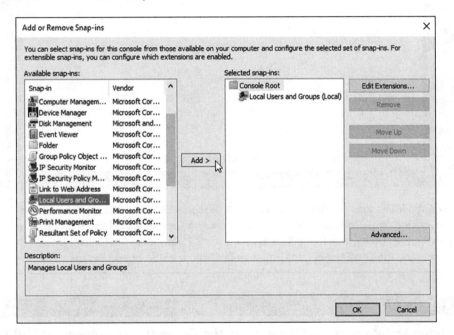

5. In the Choose Target Machine dialog box, click the Finish button to accept the default selection of Local Computer.

6. Click OK in the Add Or Remove Snap-ins dialog box.

7. In the MMC window, right-click the Local Users And Groups folder and choose New Window From Here. You will see that Local Users and Groups is now the main window.

8. Click File ➤ Save As. Name the console **Local Users and Groups** and choose Desktop under the Save In pull-down box. Click the Save button. This is creating the shortcut shown in Figure 18.4 for you to use in exercises throughout this chapter.

FIGURE 18.4   Local Users and Groups MMC

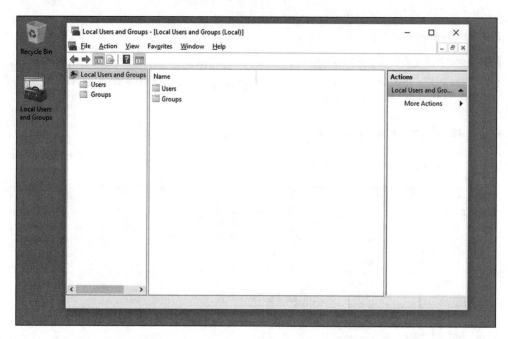

9. Close the MMC snap-in. You should now see the Local Users and Groups snap-in on the Desktop. You can also open the Local Users and Groups MMC from the Computer Management utility, which you'll do in Exercise 18.2. Complete the following exercise for opening the Local Users and Groups utility from the Computer Management utility.

EXERCISE 18.2

Accessing Local Users and Groups via the Computer Management Utility

1. Right-click the Start button and then choose Computer Management.

2. In the Computer Management window, expand the System Tools folder and then the Local Users and Groups folder.

Using the User Accounts Option in Control Panel

Now let's look at an alternative way to configure local users and groups through the *User Accounts Control (UAC)* Control Panel option, which provides the ability to manage user accounts in addition to configuring parental controls. To access the User Accounts

Control Panel option, right-click Start ➤ Control Panel ➤ User Accounts. Table 18.1 briefly describes the configurable options in the User Accounts option in Control Panel.

TABLE 18.1   Configurable user-account options in Control Panel

Option	Explanation
Change Your Password	Allows you to change a user's password.
Change Your Account Name	Allows you to rename the account.
Change Your Account Type	Allows you to change your account type between the standard user and administrator account type.
Manage Another Account	Allows you to configure other accounts on the Windows 10 machine.
Change User Account Control Settings	Allows you to set the level of notification displayed through pop-up messages when changes are made to your computer. These notifications can prevent potentially hazardous programs from being loaded onto the operating system.
Manage Your Credentials	Allows you to set up credentials so you can easily connect to websites that require usernames and passwords or computers that require certificates.
Manage Your File Encryption Certificates	Allows you to manage your file-encryption certificates.
Configure Advanced User Profile Properties	Takes you directly to the User's Profile dialog box in Control Panel ➤ System ➤ Advanced ➤ System Settings.
Change My Environment Variables	Allows you to access the Environment Variables dialog box directly.

Creating New Users

To create users on a Windows 10 computer, you must be logged on as a user with permission to create a new user, which means your account must be a member of the Administrators group.

When you create a new user, there are many options that you have to configure. Table 18.2 describes all the options available in the New User dialog box. (You access this dialog box through the MMC, which is detailed in Exercise 18.3 later in this chapter.)

TABLE 18.2 User account options available in the New User dialog box

Option	Description
User Name	Defines the username for the new account. Choose a name that is consistent with your naming convention (e.g., WPanek). This is the only required field. Usernames are not case-sensitive.
Full Name	Allows you to provide more-detailed name information. This typically consists of the user's first and last names (e.g., Will Panek). By default, this field contains the same name as the User Name field.
Description	Typically used to specify a title and/or location (e.g., Sales-Nashville) for the account, but it can be used to provide any additional information about the user.
Password	Assigns the initial password for the user. For security purposes, avoid using readily available information about the user. Passwords are case-sensitive.
Confirm Password	Confirms that you typed the password the same way two times to verify that you entered the password correctly.
User Must Change Password At Next Logon	If enabled, forces the user to change the password the first time he or she logs on. This is done to increase security. By default, this option is selected.
User Cannot Change Password	If enabled, prevents a user from changing their password. This is useful for accounts such as Guest and accounts that are shared by more than one user. By default, this option is not selected.
Password Never Expires	If enabled, specifies that the password will never expire, even if a password policy has been specified. For example, you might enable this option if this is a service account and you do not want the administrative overhead of managing password changes. By default, this option is not selected.
Account Is Disabled	If enabled, specifies that this account cannot be used for logon purposes. For example, you might select this option for template accounts or if an account is not currently being used. It helps keep inactive accounts from posing security threats. By default, this option is not selected.

In the following sections, you will learn about username rules and conventions and security identifiers.

Username Rules and Conventions

The only real requirement for creating a new user is that you provide a valid username. To be valid, the name must follow the Windows 10 rules for usernames. However, it's also a good idea to have your own rules for usernames, which form your naming convention.

The following are the Windows 10 rules for usernames:

- A username must be from 1 to 20 characters.
- The username must be unique among all the other user and group names stored on the computer.
- The username cannot contain any of the following characters:

    / \ [ ] : ; | = , + ? < > " @

- A username cannot consist exclusively of periods or spaces.

Keeping the Windows 10 rules in mind, you should choose a naming convention (a consistent naming format) for your company. For example, your naming convention might be to use the last name and first initial, so for a user named William Panek, the username would be WillP or WilliamP. Another naming convention might use the first initial and last name, for the username WPanek. This is the naming convention followed by many midsize and larger organizations. You could base usernames on the naming convention your company has defined for email names so that the logon name and the name in the email address match.

You should also provide a mechanism that will accommodate duplicate names. For example, if you have a user named Jane Smith and a user named John Smith, you might use a middle initial for usernames, such as JDSmith and JRSmith. It is also a good practice to come up with a naming convention for groups, printers, and computers.

 Real World Scenario

Naming-Convention Considerations

As an IT manager, I don't recommend using first name, first initial of last name (WilliamP) as a naming convention. In a midsize-to-large company, there is the possibility of having two WilliamPs, but the odds that you will have two WPaneks are rare.

If you choose to use the first name, first initial of last name option, it can be a lot of work to go back and change this format later if the company grows. Choose a naming convention that can grow with the company.

When creating users, it's important to make sure that your usernames and passwords are as strong as possible. The reason that you want strong security is because when a user logs into a system, the user's credentials are placed into the computer's Local Security Authority

Subsystem Service (LSASS) process memory. This is done so that the credentials can be used by the account during a session connection.

Credentials will also get stored on the Windows 10 authoritative databases, such as the SAM database and in the database that is used by Active Directory Domain Services (AD DS). Therefore, it's important to make your usernames and passwords strong so that hackers have the hardest time to hack into a system and steal these cached credentials.

Now let's take a look at how user accounts get security ID numbers associated with them and how those numbers affect your accounts.

Security Identifiers

When you create a new user account, a *security identifier (SID)* is automatically created for the user account. The username is a property of the SID. For example, a user SID might look like this:

```
S-1-5-21-823518204-746137067-120266-629-500
```

It's apparent that using SIDs for user identification would make administration a nightmare. Fortunately, for your administrative tasks, you see and use the username instead of the SID.

SIDs have several advantages. Because Windows 10 uses the SID as the user object, you can easily rename a user while retaining all the user's properties. All security settings get associated with the SID, not the user account. Every time you create a new user, a unique SID gets associated. This ensures that if you delete and re-create a user account with the same username, the new user account will not have any of the properties of the old account because it is based on a new, unique SID. Even if the username is the same as a previously deleted account, the system still sees the account as a new user.

Because every user account gets a unique SID number, it is a good practice to disable rather than delete accounts for users who leave the company or have an extended absence. If you ever need to access the disabled account again, you have the ability to do so.

Secure Channel

Another part of authentication and encrypted communications between a client and a server is a mechanism called *Secure Channel*. Secure Channel, also known as Schannel, is a set of security protocols that help offer secure encrypted communications and authentication between a client and a server.

Schannel is a security package that uses the following four protocols on the Windows platforms:

- Transport Layer Security (TLS 1.1)
- Transport Layer Security (TLS 1.2)
- Secure Sockets Layer (SSL 3.0)
- Secure Sockets Layer (SSL 2.0)

To create a Schannel connection, the clients and servers are both required to obtain Schannel credentials and create a security session. Once the client and server connection is obtained, the security credentials become available. If a connection is lost for any reason, the client and server can automatically renegotiate the connection and finish all communications.

Creating a New Local User Account

Complete Exercise 18.3 to create a new local user account. Before you complete the following steps, make sure you are logged on as a user with permissions to create new user accounts and have already added the Local Users and Groups snap-in to the MMC (Exercise 18.1). I created bogus usernames; you can change these to whatever names you want to use, but I refer to the ones I created in other exercises.

EXERCISE 18.3

Creating New Users via the MMC

1. Open the Local Users and Groups MMC Desktop shortcut that you created in Exercise 18.1, and expand the Local Users and Groups snap-in. If a dialog box appears, click Yes.

2. Highlight the Users folder and select Action ➢ New User. The New User dialog box appears, as shown in Figure 18.5.

FIGURE 18.5 New User dialog box

3. In the User Name text box, type **APanek**.

4. In the Full Name text box, type **Alexandria Panek**.

5. In the Description text box, type **Operations Manager**.

EXERCISE 18.3 *(continued)*

6. Leave the Password and Confirm Password text boxes empty. Make sure you uncheck the User Must Change Password At Next Logon option, and accept the defaults for the remaining check boxes. Click the Create button to add the user.

7. Use the New User dialog box to create four more users, filling out the fields as follows:

   User Name: **PPanek**; Full Name: **Paige Panek**

   User Name: **GWashington**; Full Name: **George Washington**

   User Name: **JAdams**; Full Name: **John Adams**

   User Name: **ALincoln**; Full Name: **Abe Lincoln**

8. After you've finished creating all of the users, click the Close button to exit the New User dialog box.

 You can also create users through the command-line utility NET USER. For more information about this command, type **NET USER /?** at the command prompt.

Disabling User Accounts

When a user account is no longer needed, the account should be disabled or deleted. After you've disabled an account, you can later reenable it to restore it with all of its associated user properties. An account that is deleted, however, can never be recovered unless you complete a restore from a backup.

You might disable an account because a user will not be using it for a period of time, perhaps because that employee is going on vacation or taking a leave of absence. Another reason to disable an account is that you're planning to put another user in that same function and would like to reuse the account.

For example, suppose that Gary, the engineering manager, quits. If you disable his account, when your company hires a new engineering manager, you can simply rename Gary's user account (to the username for the new manager), enable it, and reset the password. This ensures that the user who takes over Gary's position will have all the same user properties and own all the same resources.

Disabling accounts also provides a security mechanism for special situations. For example, if your company is laying off a group of people, as a security measure you could disable their accounts at the same time the layoff notices are given out. This prevents those users from inflicting any damage to the company's files after they receive their layoff notice. (Note, however, that this won't affect users who are already logged in.)

In Exercise 18.4, you will disable a user account. Before you complete this exercise, you should have created new users in Exercise 18.3.

EXERCISE 18.4

Disabling User Accounts

1. Open the Local Users and Groups MMC Desktop shortcut that you created in Exercise 18.1 and expand the Local Users and Groups snap-in.

2. Open the Users folder. Double-click user PPanek to open her Properties dialog box.

3. In the General tab, check the Account Is Disabled box. Click OK.

4. Close the Local Users and Groups MMC.

5. Log off and attempt to log on as PPanek. This should fail because the account is now disabled.

6. Log back on using your user account.

 You can also access a user's properties by highlighting the user, right-clicking, and selecting Properties.

When a user has left the company for a long period of time and you know you no longer need the user account, you can delete it. Let's take a look at how to delete user accounts.

Deleting User Accounts

As noted in the preceding section, you should disable a user account if you are not sure whether the account will ever be needed again. But if the account has been disabled and you know that the user account will never need to be accessed again, you should delete the account.

To delete a user, open the Local Users and Groups utility, highlight the user account you wish to delete, click Action to bring up the menu shown in Figure 18.6, and then select Delete. You can also delete an account by clicking the account and pressing the Delete key on the keyboard.

FIGURE 18.6   Deleting a user account

Because deleting an account is a permanent action, you will see the dialog box shown in Figure 18.7, asking you to confirm that you really wish to delete the account. After you click the Yes button here, you will not be able to re-create or reaccess the account (unless you restore your local user accounts database from a backup).

FIGURE 18.7   Confirming account deletion

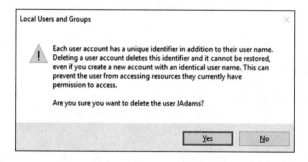

Complete Exercise 18.5 to delete a user account. These steps assume you have completed Exercises 18.2, 18.3, and 18.4.

Deleting a User Account

1. Open the Local Users and Groups MMC Desktop shortcut and expand the Local Users and Groups snap-in.

2. Expand the Users folder and single-click user JAdams to select his user account.

3. Select Action ➤ Delete. The dialog box for confirming user deletion appears.

4. Click the Yes button to confirm that you wish to delete this user.

5. Close the Local Users and Groups MMC.

Now that you have disabled and deleted accounts, let's take a look at how to rename a user's account.

Renaming User Accounts

Once an account has been created, you can rename it at any time. Renaming a user account allows the account to retain all the associated user properties such as group memberships and assigned permissions even though the username is being changed.

You might want to rename a user account because the user's name has changed, for example, the user gets married, or because the name was spelled incorrectly. Also, as explained in the section "Disabling User Accounts," you can rename an existing user's account for a new user, such as someone hired to take an ex-employee's position, when you want the new user to have the same properties.

Complete Exercise 18.6 to rename a user account. These steps assume you have completed Exercises 18.2 through 18.5.

Renaming a User Account

1. Open the Local Users and Groups MMC Desktop shortcut and expand the Local Users and Groups snap-in.

2. Open the Users folder and highlight user ALincoln.

3. Select Action ➤ Rename.

4. Type the username **RReagan** and press Enter. Notice that the Full Name field retains the original Full Name property of Abe Lincoln in the Local Users and Groups utility.

5. Double-click RReagan to open the properties and change the user's full name to Ronald Reagan.

6. Click the User Must Change Password At Next Logon check box.

7. Click OK.

8. Close the Local Users and Groups MMC.

Renaming a user does not change any hard-coded names, such as the name of the user's home folder. If you want to change these names as well, you need to modify them manually—for example, through Windows Explorer. (Note that there is a small possibility that you'll have to change the Registry to point to the new name.)

Another very common task that we must deal with is changing the user's password. Let's take a look at how to do that.

Changing a User's Password

What should you do if a user forgets his or her password and can't log on? As the administrator, you can change the user's password, which he or she can then use.

It is very important as IT managers and IT administrators that we teach our users proper security measures that go along with password protection. As you have all probably seen before, the users who tape their password to their monitors or under the keyboards are not following correct security precautions. It's our job as IT professionals to teach our users proper security, and it always amazes me when I do consulting how many IT departments don't teach their users properly.

Complete Exercise 18.7 to change a user's password. This exercise assumes you have completed Exercises 18.2 onward.

Changing a User's Password

1. Open the Local Users and Groups MMC Desktop shortcut and expand the Local Users and Groups snap-in.

2. Open the Users folder and highlight user APanek.

3. Select Action ➤ Set Password. The Set Password dialog box appears.

4. A warning appears, indicating the risks involved in changing the password. Select Proceed.

5. Type the new password and then confirm the password. Click OK.

6. Close the Local Users and Groups MMC.

Using a Microsoft Passport, Pictures, and Biometrics

Now that we have looked at how to set up and manage local and domain accounts, let's look at how you can use other options to help you log into your system or network.

Those of us who have been certified for a long time are quite familiar with using a Microsoft account to log into the Microsoft websites. Now we can use this same account to log into our computer and networks.

Microsoft Passports are Microsoft accounts that you can use to authenticate to a domain, to a cloud-based domain, or to a computer. To do this, you need to link your Microsoft account to your Windows 10 system.

Linking your Windows 10 system is an easy two-step verification process with Microsoft Passport enrollment. When you set up a Microsoft Passport on the device, you can set up the system to use Windows Hello or a PIN.

Windows Hello allows you to sign in to your Windows 10 devices with just a look or a touch. Windows Hello can be set up so that you can use biometrics, face recognition, or even an iris scan. To configure Windows Hello options, click the Start menu and choose Settings. Once you're in the settings, choose Accounts.

You also have the ability to set up Microsoft Passport to use a PIN number. This is a secure number that you input instead of a username and password. You may be thinking to yourself that a PIN doesn't seem as secure as a username and password, but actually that is not true.

PINs can be very complex and include special characters and letters, both uppercase and lowercase. So that means that you can have a PIN of 1234 or a PIN of 1234Wi!!Panek1001. Also, PINs are tied directly to a machine and not to an account, so when you set up a PIN, it's good for that machine only. Because of this, PINs are actually better than a password that can be used anywhere on the network. If someone steals your password, they can access your account from anywhere. This is not the case with a PIN, because anyone trying to use it would also need access to your machine.

Windows 10 also gives you the ability to set up your logon for use with a picture. When you decide to use a picture for authentication, you first choose your picture and then you add three gestures onto the picture. You can draw straight lines, circles, squares, or anything you want. Then when you log on to the system, you just re-create the gestures on the picture and the system logs you in.

Managing User Properties

For more control over user accounts, you can configure user properties. Through the user's Properties dialog box, you can change the original password options, add the user to existing groups, and specify user profile information.

To open a user's Properties dialog box, access the Local Users and Groups utility, open the Users folder, and double-click the user account. The user's Properties dialog box has tabs for the three main categories of properties: General, Member Of, and Profile.

The General tab contains the information you supplied when you set up the new user account, including the full name and a description, the password options you selected, and whether the account is disabled. If you want to modify any of these properties after you've created the user, simply open the user's Properties dialog box and make the changes on the General tab (Figure 18.8).

FIGURE 18.8   General tab of the user's Properties dialog box

You can use the Member Of tab to manage the user's membership in groups, and the Profile tab lets you set properties to customize the user's environment. The following sections discuss the Member Of and Profile tabs in detail.

Managing User Group Membership

The Member Of tab of the user's Properties dialog box displays all the groups that the user belongs to, as shown in Figure 18.9. From this tab, you can add the user to an existing group or remove the user from a group. To add a user to a group, click the Add button and select the group that the user should belong to. If you want to remove the user from a group, highlight the group and click the Remove button.

FIGURE 18.9 The Member Of tab of the user's Properties dialog box

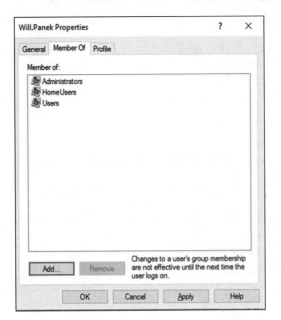

Complete Exercise 18.8 to add a user to an existing group. These steps assume you have completed Exercises 18.2 onward.

Adding a User to an Existing Group

1. Open the Local Users and Groups MMC Desktop snap-in that you created previously.

2. Open the Users folder and double-click user APanek. The APanek Properties dialog box appears.

3. Select the Member Of tab and click the Add button. The Select Groups dialog box appears.

4. Under Enter The Object Names To Select, type **Backup Operators**, and click the Check Names button. After the name is confirmed, click OK.

5. Click OK to close the APanek Properties dialog box.

Now let's take a look at the Profile tab and what options can be configured within that tab.

Setting Up User Profiles, Logon Scripts, and Home Folders

The Profile tab of the user's Properties dialog box, shown in Figure 18.10, allows you to customize the user's environment. Here, you can specify the following items for the user:

- User profile path
- Logon script
- Home folder

FIGURE 18.10   The Profile tab of the user's Properties dialog box

The following sections describe how these properties work and when you might want to use them.

Setting a User's Profile Path

User profiles contain information about the Windows 10 environment for a specific user. For example, profile settings include the Desktop arrangement, program groups, and screen colors that users see when they log on.

Each time you log on to a Windows 10 computer, the system checks to see if you have a local user profile in the Users folder, which was created on the boot partition when you installed Windows 10. The first time users log on, they receive a default user profile. A folder that matches the user's logon name is created for the user in the Users folder. The user profile folder that is created holds a file called NTUSER.DAT as well as subfolders that contain directory links to the user's Desktop items (as shown previously in Figure 18.10).

In Exercise 18.9, you'll create two new users and set up local user profiles.

EXERCISE 18.9

Setting Up User Profiles

1. Using the Local Users and Groups utility, create two new users: WPanek and CPanek. Deselect the User Must Change Password At Next Logon option for each user.

2. Select Start ➢ All Programs ➢ Accessories ➢ Windows Explorer. Expand Computer ➢ Local Disk (C:) ➢ Users. Notice that the Users folder does not contain user profile folders for the new users.

3. Log off and log on as WPanek.

4. Right-click an open area on the Desktop and select Personalize. In the Personalization dialog box, select a color scheme and click Apply, and then click OK.

5. Right-click an open area on the Desktop and select New ➢ Shortcut. In the Create Shortcut dialog box, type **CALC** to open the Calculator program. Accept CALC as the name for the shortcut and click Finish.

6. Log off as WPanek and log on as CPanek. Notice that user PPanek sees the Desktop configuration stored in the default user profile.

7. Log off as CPanek and log on as WPanek. Notice that WPanek sees the Desktop configuration you set up in steps 3, 4, and 5.

8. Log off as WPanek and log on as your user account. Open Windows Explorer. Expand Computer ➢ Local Disk (C:) ➢ Users. Notice that this folder now contains user profile folders for WPanek and CPanek.

The drawback of local user profiles is that they are available only on the computer where they were created. For example, suppose all of your Windows 10 computers are a part of a domain and you use only local user profiles. User Rick logs on at Computer A and creates a customized user profile. When he logs on to Computer B for the first time, he will receive the default user profile rather than the customized user profile he created on Computer A. To enable users to access their user profile from any computer they log on to, you need to use roaming profiles; however, these require the use of a network server because they can't be stored on a local Windows 10 computer.

In the next sections, you will learn about how roaming profiles and mandatory profiles can be used. To have a roaming profile or a mandatory profile, your computer must be a part of a network with server access.

Using Roaming Profiles

A *roaming profile* is stored on a network server and allows a user to access their user profile regardless of the client computer to which they're logged on. Roaming profiles provide a consistent desktop for users who move around, no matter which computer they access. Even if the server that stores the roaming profile is unavailable, the user can still log on using a local profile.

If you are using roaming profiles, the contents of the user's systemdrive:\Users\ UserName folder will be copied to the local computer each time the roaming profile is accessed. If you have stored large files in any subfolders of your user profile folder, you may notice a significant delay when accessing your profile remotely as opposed to locally. If this problem occurs, you can reduce the amount of time the roaming profile takes to load by moving the subfolder to another location, such as the user's home directory, or you can use Group Policy Objects within Active Directory to specify that specific folders should be excluded when the roaming profile is loaded.

Using Mandatory Profiles

A *mandatory profile* is a profile that can't be modified by the user. Only members of the Administrators group can manage mandatory profiles. You can create mandatory profiles for a single user or a group of users. You might consider creating mandatory profiles for users who should maintain consistent desktops.

For example, suppose you have a group of 20 salespeople who know enough about system configuration to make changes but not enough to fix any problems they create. For ease of support, you could use mandatory profiles. This way, all of the salespeople will always have the same profile, which they will not be able to change.

The mandatory profile is stored in a file named NTUSER.MAN. To create a mandatory profile, you just change the user's profile extension to .man, and the profile will become mandatory. A user with a mandatory profile can set different desktop preferences while logged on, but those settings will not be saved when the user logs off.

There are two folders where the profiles are stored. They are *Username* and *Username*.v2 (*Username* will be replaced with the user's name). The difference is that if you are using Windows XP, the profile gets placed in the *Username* folder. If the users are using Windows Vista, Windows 7/8/8.1, Windows 10, or Windows Server 2008, the user profile gets placed in the *Username*.v2 folder.

You can use only roaming profiles as mandatory profiles. Mandatory profiles do not work for local user profiles.

Now let's look at a second type of mandatory profile called super-mandatory profile.

Using Super-Mandatory Profiles

A *super-mandatory profile* is a mandatory user profile with an additional layer of security. With mandatory profiles, a temporary profile is created if the mandatory profile is not available when a user logs on. However, when super-mandatory profiles are configured, temporary profiles are not created if the mandatory profile is not available over the network, and the user is unable to log on to the computer.

The process for creating super-mandatory profiles is similar to that for creating mandatory profiles, except that instead of renaming the user folder *Username.v2* as you would for a mandatory profile, you name the folder *Username.man*. User profiles become *super-mandatory* when the folder name of the profile path ends in .man, for example, \\server\share\APanek.man\. Only system administrators can make changes to mandatory user profiles.

 Real World Scenario

Copying User Profiles

Within your company, you have a user, Paige, who logs in with two different user accounts. One account is a regular user account, and the other is an Administrator account used for administration tasks only.

When Paige established all her Desktop preferences and installed the computer's applications, they were installed with the Administrator account. Now, when she logs in with the regular user account, she can't access the Desktop and profile settings that were created for her as an administrative user.

To solve this problem, you can copy a local user profile from one user to another (for example, from Paige's administrative account to her regular user account) by choosing Control Panel ➢ System ➢ Advanced System Settings ➢ User Profiles Settings. When you copy a user profile, the following items are copied: favorites, cookies, documents, Start menu items, and other unique user Registry settings.

Using Logon Scripts

Another configurable element within the Profile tab of the user's properties is logon scripts—files that run every time a user logs on to the network. They are usually batch files, but they can be any type of executable file. Logon scripts are either created by the admin or just grabbed off the Internet. Creating these scripts is beyond the scope of this book.

You might use logon scripts to set up drive mappings or to run a specific executable file each time a user logs on to the computer. For example, you could run an inventory-management file that collects information about the computer's configuration and sends that data to a central management database. Logon scripts are also useful for compatibility with non–Windows 10 operating systems for users who want to log on but still maintain consistent settings with their native operating system.

To run a logon script for a user, enter the script name in the Logon Script text box in the Profile tab of the user's Properties dialog box.

Setting Up Home Folders

Users usually store their personal files and information in a private folder called a home folder. In the Profile tab of the user's Properties dialog box, you can specify the location of a home folder as a local folder or a network folder. The main reason you give your users a home folder on the server is because the servers are usually the only machines that get backed up. Most companies do not back up individual users' machines. If your users place all their important documents in the home folder location on the network, those documents will get backed up as part of the nightly backup.

To specify a local folder, choose the Local Path option and type the path in the text box next to that option. To specify a network path for a folder, choose the Connect option and specify a network path using a Universal Naming Convention (UNC) path. A UNC consists of the computer name and the share that has been created on the computer. When connecting to a UNC name, the network folder you are connecting to should already be created and shared. For example, if you wanted to connect to a folder called \Users\Will on a server called SALES, you'd choose the Connect option, select a drive letter that would be mapped to the home directory, and then type **\\SALES\Users\Will** in the To box.

If the home folder you are specifying does not exist, Windows 10 will attempt to create the folder for you. You can also use the variable %username% in place of a specific user's name. The %username% will automatically change to the name of the user you are currently working on.

WARNING
Be careful when you're specifying your home folder. If you make a mistake when typing in the path for the directory, Windows will create a bogus-named folder for you.

Complete Exercise 18.10 to assign a home folder to a user. These steps assume you have completed Exercises 18.2 onward.

EXERCISE 18.10

Assigning Home Folders

1. Open the Local Users and Groups MMC Desktop shortcut and expand the Local Users and Groups snap-in.

2. Open the Users folder and double-click user GWashington. The GWashington Properties dialog box appears.

3. Select the Profile tab and click the Local Path radio button to select it.

4. Specify the home folder path by typing **C:\HomeFolders\GWashington** in the text box for the Local Path option. Then click OK.

5. Use Windows Explorer to verify that this folder was created.

6. Close the Local Users and Groups MMC.

🌐 Real World Scenario

Using Home Folders to Keep Files Backed Up

As an administrator for a large network, one of my primary responsibilities is to make sure that all data is backed up daily. This has become difficult because daily backup of each user's local hard drive is impractical. You can also have problems with employees deleting important corporate information as they are leaving the company.

After examining the contents of a typical user's local drive, you will realize that most of the local disk space is taken by the operating system and the user's stored applications. This information does not change and does not need to be backed up. What you are primarily concerned with is backing up the user's data.

To more effectively manage this data and accommodate the necessary backup, you should create home folders for each user and store them on a network share. This allows the data to be backed up daily, to be readily accessible should a local computer fail, and to be easily retrieved if the user leaves the company.

Here are the steps to create a home folder that resides on the network:

1. Decide which server will store the users' home folders.

2. Create a directory structure that will store the home folders efficiently (for example, C:\HOME).

3. Create a single share to the user's home folder. (You can do this by right-clicking the home folder and choosing Properties.)

4. Use NTFS and share permissions to ensure that only the specified user has permissions to their home folder.

5. Specify the location of the home folder through the Profile tab of the user's Properties dialog box.

Troubleshooting User Account Authentication

When a user attempts to log on through Windows 10 and is unable to be authenticated, you will need to track down the reason for the problem.

If a local user is having trouble logging on, the problem may be with the username, the password, or the user account itself. The following are some common causes of local logon errors.

> Because many of these same issues happen when logging on to a domain from a Windows 10 machine, these approaches can be used for both local logons and domain logons.

Incorrect Username   You can verify that the username is correct by checking the Local Users and Groups utility. Verify that the name was spelled correctly.

Incorrect Password   Remember that passwords are case-sensitive. Is the Caps Lock key on? If you see any messages relating to an expired password or locked-out account, the reason for the problem is obvious. If necessary, you can assign a new password through the Local Users and Groups utility.

Prohibitive User Rights   Does the user have permission to log on locally at the computer? By default, the Log On Locally user right is granted to the Users group, so all users can log on to Windows 10 computers.

However, if this user right was modified, you will see an error message stating that the local policy of this computer does not allow interactive logon. The terms *interactive logon* and *local logon* are synonymous and mean that the user is logging on at the computer where the user account is stored on the computer's local database.

A Disabled or Deleted Account   You can verify whether an account has been disabled by checking the account properties through the Local Users and Groups utility. If the account is no longer in the database, then it has most likely been deleted.

A Domain Account Logon at the Local Computer   If a computer is a part of a domain, the logon dialog box has options for logging on to the domain or to the local computer. Make sure the user has chosen the correct option.

Managing and Creating Groups

Groups are an important part of network management. Many administrators are able to accomplish the majority of their management tasks through the use of groups; they rarely assign permissions to individual users.

Windows 10 includes built-in local groups (such as Administrators and Backup Operators) that already have all the permissions needed to accomplish specific tasks. Windows 10 also uses built-in special groups in which users are placed automatically when they meet certain criteria.

You can create and manage local groups (but not special groups) through the Local Users and Groups utility. With this utility, you can add groups, change group membership, rename groups, and delete groups.

> One misconception about groups is that they have to work with Group Policy Objects (GPOs). This is not correct. Group Policy Objects are sets of rules that allow you to set computer-configuration and user-configuration options that apply to users or computers. Group Policies, on the other hand, are typically used with Active Directory and are applied as Group Policy Objects.

Using Built-In Groups

On a Windows 10 computer, built-in local groups have already been created and assigned all necessary permissions to accomplish basic tasks. In addition, there are built-in special groups that the Windows 10 system handles automatically. These groups are described in the following sections.

Built-in Local Groups

A local group is a group that is stored on the local computer's accounts database. You can add users to these groups and can manage the groups directly on a Windows 10 computer. By default, some the following local groups are created on Windows 10 computers:

- Administrators
- Backup Operators
- Cryptographic Operators
- Distributed COM Users
- Event Log Readers
- Guests
- IIS_IUSRS
- Network Configuration Operators
- Performance Log Users
- Performance Monitor Users
- Power Users
- Remote Desktop Users
- Replicator
- Users

I will briefly describe each group, its default permissions, and the users assigned to the group by default.

If possible, you should add users to the built-in local groups rather than creating new groups from scratch. This simplifies administration because the built-in groups already have the appropriate permissions. All you need to do is add the users you want to be members of the group.

Administrators   The Administrators group has full permissions and privileges. Its members can grant themselves any permissions they do not have by default to manage all the objects on the computer. (Objects include the filesystem, printers, and account management.) By default, the Administrator account, which is disabled by default, and the Initial User account are members of the Administrators local group.

Assign users to the Administrators group with caution since they will have full permissions to manage the computer.

Members of the Administrators group can perform the following tasks:

- Install the operating system.
- Install and configure hardware device drivers.
- Install system services.
- Install service packs, hot fixes, and Windows updates.
- Upgrade the operating system.
- Repair the operating system.
- Install applications that modify the Windows system files.
- Configure password policies.
- Configure audit policies.
- Manage security logs.
- Create administrative shares.
- Create administrative accounts.
- Modify groups and accounts that have been created by other users.
- Remotely access the Registry.
- Stop or start any service.
- Configure services.
- Increase and manage disk quotas.
- Increase and manage execution priorities.
- Remotely shut down the system.
- Assign and manage user rights.
- Reenable locked-out and disabled accounts.
- Manage disk properties, including formatting hard drives.
- Modify systemwide environment variables.

- Access any data on the computer.
- Back up and restore all data.

Backup Operators   Members of the Backup Operators group have permissions to back up and restore the filesystem, even if the filesystem is NTFS and they have not been assigned permissions to access the filesystem. However, the members of Backup Operators can access the filesystem only through the Backup utility. To access the filesystem directly, Backup Operators must have explicit permissions assigned. There are no default members of the Backup Operators local group.

Cryptographic Operators   The Cryptographic Operators group has access to perform cryptographic operations on the computer. There are no default members of the Cryptographic Operators local group.

Distributed COM Users   The Distributed COM Users group has the ability to launch and run Distributed COM objects on the computer. There are no default members of the Distributed COM Users local group.

Event Log Readers   The Event Log Readers group has access to read the event log on the local computer. There are no default members of the Event Log Readers local group.

Guests   The Guests group has limited access to the computer. This group is provided so that you can allow people who are not regular users to access specific network resources. As a general rule, most administrators do not allow Guest access because it poses a potential security risk. By default, the Guest user account is a member of the Guests local group.

IIS_IUSRS   The IIS_IUSRS group is used by Internet Information Services (IIS). The NT AUTHORITY\IUSR user account (premade for IIS) is a member of the IIS_IUSRS group by default.

Network Configuration Operators   Members of the Network Configuration Operators group have some administrative rights to manage the computer's network configuration, for example, editing the computer's TCP/IP settings.

Performance Log Users   The Performance Log Users group has the ability to access and schedule logging of performance counters and can create and manage trace counters on the computer. There are no default members of this group.

Performance Monitor Users   The Performance Monitor Users group has the ability to access and view performance counter information on the computer. Users who are members of this group can access performance counters both locally and remotely. There are no default members of this group.

Power Users   The Power Users group is included in Windows 10 for backward compatibility to ensure that computers upgraded from Windows XP function as before with regard to folders that allow access to members of the group. Otherwise, the Power Users group has limited administrative rights. There are no default members of this group.

Remote Desktop Users   The Remote Desktop Users group allows members of the group to log on remotely for the purpose of using the Remote Desktop service. There are no default members of this group.

Replicator The Replicator group is intended to support directory replication, which is a feature used by domain servers. Only domain users who will start the replication service should be assigned to this group. The Replicator local group has no default members.

Users The Users group is intended for end users who should have very limited system access. If you have installed a fresh copy of Windows 10, the default settings for the Users group prohibit its members from compromising the operating system or program files. By default, all users who have been created on the computer, except Guest, are members of the Users local group.

Special Groups

Special groups are premade groups that can be used by the system or by administrators. Membership in special groups is automatic if certain criteria are met. You cannot manage special groups through the Local Users and Groups utility, but an administrator can add special groups to resources. The following text describes the special groups that are built into Windows 10.

Anonymous Logon This group includes users who access the computer through anonymous logons. When users gain access through special accounts created for anonymous access to Windows 10 services, they become members of the Anonymous Logon group.

Authenticated Users This group includes users who access the Windows 10 operating system through a valid username and password. Users who can log on belong to the Authenticated Users group.

Batch This group includes users who log on as a user account that is used only to run a batch job.

Creator Owner This is the account that created or took ownership of an object. This is typically a user account. Each object (files, folders, printers, and print jobs) has an owner. Members of the Creator Owner group have special permissions to resources. For example, if you are a regular user who has submitted 12 print jobs to a printer, you can manipulate your print jobs as Creator Owner, but you can't manage any print jobs submitted by other users.

Dialup This group includes users who log on to the network from a dial-up connection.

Everyone This group includes anyone who could possibly access the computer—all users who have been defined on the computer (including Guest), plus (if your computer is a part of a domain) all users within the domain. If the domain has trust relationships with other domains, all users in the trusted domains are part of the Everyone group as well. The exception to automatic group membership with the Everyone group is that members of the Anonymous Logon group are not included as a part of the Everyone group.

Interactive This group includes all users who use the computer's resources locally.

Network This group includes users who access the computer's resources over a network connection.

Service This group includes users who log on as a user account that is used only to run a service. You can configure the use of user accounts for logon through the Services program.

System   There are times when the Windows 10 operating system will access functions within the system. When the operating system accesses these functions, it does it as a system user. When the system accesses specific functions as a user, that process becomes a member of the System group.

Terminal Server User   This group includes users who log on through Terminal Services.

Creating Groups

To create a group, you must be logged on as a member of the Administrators group. The Administrators group has full permissions to manage users and groups.

Keep your naming conventions in mind when assigning names to groups, just as you do when choosing usernames. Consider the following guidelines:

- The group name should be descriptive; for example, Accounting Data Users.

- The group name must be unique to the computer and different from all other group names and usernames that exist on that computer.

- Group names can be up to 256 characters. It is best to use alphanumeric characters for ease of administration. The backslash (\) character is not allowed.

Creating groups is similar to creating users, and it is a fairly easy process. After you've added the Local Users and Groups MMC or used Local Users and Groups through the Computer Management utility, expand it to see the Users and Groups folders. Right-click the Groups folder and select New Group from the context menu. This brings up the New Group dialog box, shown in Figure 18.11.

FIGURE 18.11   The New Group dialog box

The only required entry in the New Group dialog box is the group name. If appropriate, you can enter a description for the group, and you can add (or remove) group members. When you're ready to create the new group, click the Create button.

Complete Exercise 18.11 to create two new local groups. (Creating domain groups is beyond the scope of this book.)

EXERCISE 18.11

Creating Local Groups

1. Open the Admin Console MMC Desktop shortcut you created and expand the Local Users and Groups snap-in.

2. Right-click the Groups folder and select New Group.

3. In the New Group dialog box, type **Data Users** in the Group Name text box. Click the Create button.

4. Repeat step 3, but type **Application Users** in the Group Name text box.

After the groups are created, you will have to manage the groups and their membership. In the next section, we will look at managing groups.

Managing Group Membership

After you've created a group, you can add members to it. As mentioned earlier, you can put the same user in multiple groups. You can easily add and remove users through a group's Properties dialog box, shown in Figure 18.12. To access a group's Properties dialog box from the Groups folder in the Local Users and Groups utility, double-click the name of the group you want to manage.

FIGURE 18.12   Group's Properties dialog box

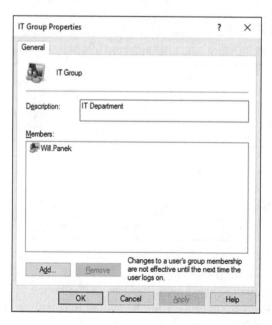

From the group's Properties dialog box, you can change the group's description and add or remove group members. When you click the Add button to add members, the Select Users dialog box appears (Figure 18.13).

FIGURE 18.13   The Select Users dialog box

In the Select Users dialog box, you enter the object names of the users you want to add. You can use the Check Names button to validate the users against the database. Select the user accounts you wish to add and click Add. Click the OK button to add the selected users to the group.

To remove a member from the group, select the member in the Members list of the Properties dialog box and click the Remove button.

In Exercise 18.12, you'll create new user accounts and then add these users to one of the groups you created in the previous steps.

EXERCISE 18.12

Adding Accounts to Groups

1. Open the Local Users and Groups MMC shortcut you created and expand the Local Users and Groups snap-in.

2. Create two new users: JDoe and DDoe. Deselect the User Must Change Password At Next Logon option for each user.

3. Expand the Groups folder.

4. Double-click the Data Users group.

5. In the Data Users Properties dialog box, click the Add button.

6. In the Select Users dialog box, type the username **JDoe**; then click OK.

7. Click Add and type the username **DDoe**; then click OK.

8. In the Data Users Properties dialog box, you will see that the users have both been added to the group. Click OK to close the group's Properties dialog box.

There may come a point when a specific group is no longer needed. In the next section, we will look at how to delete a group from the Local Users and Groups utility.

Deleting Groups

If you are sure that you will never again want to use a particular group, you can delete it. Once a group is deleted, you lose all permissions assignments that have been specified for the group.

To delete a group, right-click the group name and choose Delete from the context menu. You will see a warning that once a group is deleted, it is gone for good. Click the Yes button if you're sure you want to delete the group.

If you delete a group and give another group the same name, the new group won't be created with the same properties as the deleted group because, like users, groups get unique SIDs assigned at the time of creation.

Creating users and groups is one of the most important tasks that we as IT members can do. On a Windows 10 machine, creating users and groups is an easy and straightforward process.

Now that you understand how to create users and groups, you need to know how to manage Windows 10 security using GPOs and LGPOs. We'll look at that next.

Managing Security Using GPOs and LGPOs

Windows 10 offers a wide variety of security options. If the Windows 10 computer is a part of a domain, then you can apply security through a Group Policy Object using the Group Policy Management Console. If the Windows 10 computer is not a part of a domain, then you use Local Group Policy Objects to manage local security.

Additionally, you can use policies to help manage user accounts. Account policies control the logon environment for the computer, such as password and logon restrictions. Local policies specify what users can do once they log on and include auditing, user rights, and security options. You can also manage critical security features through the Windows Security Center.

Understanding the GPO and LGPO Basics

The tools you use to manage Windows 10 computer security configurations depend on whether the Windows 10 computer is a part of a Windows 2000, Windows 2003, Windows 2008, Windows 2008/2008 R2, or Windows Server 2012/2012 R2 domain environment.

If the Windows 10 client is not a part of a domain, then you apply security settings through *Local Group Policy Objects (LGPOs)*. LGPOs are sets of security configuration settings that are applied to users and computers. LGPOs are created and stored locally on the Windows 10 computer.

If your Windows 10 computer is a part of a domain, which uses the services of Active Directory, then you typically manage and configure security through Group Policy Objects (GPOs). Active Directory is the database that contains all your domain user and group accounts along with all other domain objects.

Group Policy Objects are policies that can be applied to either users or computers in the domain. The Group Policy Management Console (GPMC) is a Microsoft Management Console (MMC) snap-in that is used to configure and manage GPOs for users and computers via Active Directory.

Windows 10 computers that are part of a domain still have LGPOs, and you can use LGPOs in conjunction with the Active Directory group policies (GPOs).

 Usage of Group Policy Objects for domains is covered in greater detail in my book *MCSA Windows Server 2012 R2 Complete Study Guide: Exams 70-410, 70-411, 70-412, and 70-417* (Sybex, 2016).

The settings you can apply through the Group Policy utility within Active Directory are more comprehensive than the settings you can apply through LGPOs. Table 18.3 lists some of the options that can be set for GPOs within Active Directory and which of those options can be applied through LGPOs.

TABLE 18.3 Group Policy and LGPO setting options

Group Policy Setting	Available for LGPO?
Software installation	No
Remote Installation Services	Yes
Scripts	Yes
Printers	Yes
Security settings	Yes
Policy-based QOS	Yes
Administrative templates	Yes
Folder redirection	No
Internet Explorer configuration	Yes

Now that we have looked at LGPOs, let's look at some of the tools available for creating and managing them.

Using the Group Policy Result Tool

When a user logs on to a computer or domain, a resulting set of policies to be applied is generated based on the LGPOs, site GPOs, domain GPOs, and OU GPOs. The overlapping nature of group policies can make it difficult to determine what group policies will actually be applied to a computer or user.

To help determine what policies will actually be applied, Windows 10 includes the Group Policy Result Tool, also known as the *Resultant Set of Policy (RSoP)*. You can access this tool through the GPResult command-line utility. The gpresult command displays the set of policies that were enforced on the computer and the specified user during the logon process.

The gpresult command will display the RSoP for the computer and user who is currently logged in. Several switches can be used with the gpresult command; Table 18.4 shows the different switches that can be used for the gpresult command.

TABLE 18.4   gpresult switches

Switch	Explanation
/F	Forces gpresult to override the filename specified in the /X or /H command
/H	Saves the report in an HTML format
/P	Specifies the password for a given user context
/R	Displays RSoP summary data
/S	Specifies the remote system to connect to
/U	Specifies the user context under which the command should be executed
/V	Specifies that verbose information should be displayed
/X	Saves the report in XML format
/Z	Specifies that the super-verbose information should be displayed
/?	Shows all the gpresult command switches
/scope	Specifies whether the user or the computer settings need to be displayed
/User	Specifies the username for which the RSoP data is to be displayed

In the next section, we will look at how to create and apply Local Group Policy Objects to the Windows 10 machine.

Managing and Applying LGPOs

Policies that have been linked through Active Directory will, by default, take precedence over any established local group policies. Local group policies are typically applied to computers that are not part of a network or are in a network that does not have a domain controller and thus does not use Active Directory.

Pre-Vista versions of Windows contained only one Local Group Policy Object that applied to all of the computer's users unless NTFS permissions were applied to the LGPO. However, Windows 10 and Windows Vista changed that with the addition of *Multiple Local Group Policy Objects (MLGPOs)*. MLGPOs are applied in the following hierarchical order:

1. Local Computer Policy
2. Administrators and Non-Administrators Local Group Policy
3. User-Specific Group Policy

The Local Computer Policy is the only LGPO that includes computer and user settings; the other LGPOs contain only user settings. Settings applied here will apply to all users of the computer.

The Administrators LGPO is applied to users who are members of the built-in local Administrators group. As you might guess, the Non-Administrators LGPO is applied to users who are not members of the local Administrators group. Because each user of a computer can be classified as an administrator or a non-administrator, either one policy or the other will apply.

User-Specific LGPOs are also included with Windows 10. These LGPOs make it possible for specific policy settings to apply to a single user.

As with Active Directory GPOs, any GPO settings applied lower in the hierarchy will override GPO settings applied higher in the hierarchy by default. For example, any User-Specific GPO settings will override any conflicting Administrator/Non-Administrator GPO settings or Local Computer Policy settings. And, of course, any AD GPO settings will still override any conflicting LGPO settings.

 Domain administrators can disable LGPOs on Windows 10 computers by enabling the Turn Off Local Group Policy Objects Processing Domain GPO setting under Computer Configuration\Administrative Templates\ System\Group Policy.

You apply an LGPO to a Windows 10 computer through the Group Policy Object Editor snap-in within the MMC. Figure 18.14 shows the Local Computer Policy for a Windows 10 computer.

FIGURE 18.14   Local Computer Policy

Complete Exercise 18.13 to add the Local Computer Policy snap-in to the MMC.

EXERCISE 18.13

Adding the Local Computer Policy Snap-In

1. Open the Local Users and Groups MMC shortcut by typing **MMC** in the Search Programs And Files box.

2. A User Account Control dialog box appears. Click Yes.

3. Select File ➢ Add/Remove Snap-in.

4. Highlight the Group Policy Object Editor snap-in and click the Add button.

5. The Group Policy Object specifies Local Computer by default. Click the Finish button.

6. In the Add Or Remove Snap-Ins dialog box, click OK.

7. In the left pane, right-click the Local Computer Policy and choose New Windows From Here.

8. Choose File ➢ Save As and name the console **LGPO**. Make sure you save it to the Desktop. Click Save.

9. Close the Local Users and Groups MMC.

Now we will look at how to open an LGPO for a specific user account on a Windows 10 machine. Complete Exercise 18.14 to access the Administrators, Non-Administrators, and User-Specific LGPOs.

EXERCISE 18.14

Accessing an LGPO

1. Open the Local Users and Groups MMC shortcut by typing **MMC** in the Windows 10 Search box.

2. Select File ➢ Add/Remove Snap-In.

3. Highlight the Group Policy Object Editor snap-in and click the Add button.

4. Click Browse so that you can browse for a different GPO.

5. Click the Users tab.

6. Select the user you want to access and click OK.

7. In the Select Group Policy Object dialog box, click Finish.

8. In the Add Or Remove Snap-Ins dialog box, click OK. You may close the console when you have finished looking at the LGPO settings for the user you chose.

 Notice that the Administrators, Non-Administrators, and User-Specific LGPOs contain only User Configuration settings, not Computer Configuration settings.

Now let's take a look at the different security settings that can be configured in the LGPO.

Configuring Local Security Policies

Through the use of the Local Computer Policy, you can set a wide range of security options under `Computer Configuration\Windows Settings\Security Settings`.

This portion of the Local Computer Policy is also known as the Local Security Policy. The following sections describe in detail how to apply security settings through LGPOs. The main areas of security configuration of the LGPO are as follows:

Account Policies Account policies are used to configure password and account lockout features. Some of these settings include password history, maximum password age, minimum password age, minimum password length, password complexity, account lockout duration, account lockout threshold, and whether to reset the account lockout counter afterward.

Local Policies   Local policies are used to configure auditing, user rights, and security options.

Windows Firewall with Advanced Security   Windows Firewall with Advanced Security provides network security for Windows computers. Through this LGPO, you can set domain, private, and public profiles. You can also set this LGPO to authenticate communications between computers and inbound/outbound rules.

Network List Manager Policies   This section allows you to set the network name, icon, and location group policies. Administrators can set Unidentified Networks, Identifying Networks, and All Networks.

Public Key Policies   Use the Public Key Policies settings to specify how to manage certificates and certificate life cycles.

Software Restriction Policies   The settings under Software Restriction Policies allow you to identify malicious software and control that software's ability to run on the Windows 10 machine. These policies allow an administrator to protect the Microsoft Windows 10 operating system against security threats such as viruses and Trojan horse programs.

Application Control Policies   This section allows you to set up AppLocker. You can use AppLocker to configure a Denied list and an Accepted list for applications. Applications that are configured on the Denied list will not run on the system, and applications on the Accepted list will operate properly.

IP Security Policies on Local Computer   This section allows you to configure the IPsec policies. IPsec is a way to secure data packets at the IP level of the message.

Advanced Audit Policy Configuration   Advanced Audit Policy Configuration settings can be used to provide detailed control over audit policies. This section also allows you to configure auditing to help show administrators either successful or unsuccessful attacks on their network.

> You can also access the Local Security Policy by running secpol.msc or by opening Control Panel and selecting Administrative Tools ➢ Local Security Policy.

Now that you have seen all the options in the security section of the LGPO, let's take a look at account policies and local policies in more detail.

Using Account Policies

Account policies are used to specify the user account properties that relate to the logon process. They allow you to configure computer security settings for passwords and account-lockout specifications.

If security is not an issue—perhaps because you are using your Windows 10 computer at home—then you don't need to bother with account policies. If, on the other hand, security is important—for example, because your computer provides access to payroll information—then you should set very restrictive account policies.

> Account policies at the LGPO level apply only to local user accounts, not domain accounts. To ensure that user account security is configured for domain user accounts, you need to configure these policies at the domain GPO level.

To access the Account Policies folder from the MMC, follow this path: Local Computer Policy ➤ Computer Configuration ➤ Windows Settings ➤ Security Settings ➤ Account Policies. In the following sections, you will learn about the password policies and account-lockout policies that define how security is applied to account policies.

Setting Password Policies

Password policies ensure that security requirements are enforced on the computer. It is important to understand that password policies are set on a per-computer basis; they cannot be configured for specific users. Figure 18.15 shows the password policies, which are described in Table 18.5.

FIGURE 18.15   The password policies

TABLE 18.5   Password policy options

Policy	Description	Default	Minimum	Maximum
Enforce Password History	Keeps track of user's password history	Remember 0 passwords	Same as default	Remember 24 passwords
Maximum Password Age	Determines maximum number of days user can keep valid password	Keep password for 42 days	Keep password for 1 day	Keep password for up to 999 days
Minimum Password Age	Specifies how long password must be kept before it can be changed	0 days (password can be changed immediately)	Same as default	998 days
Minimum Password Length	Specifies minimum number of characters password must contain	0 characters (no password required)	Same as default	14 characters
Password Must Meet Complexity Requirements	Requires that passwords meet minimum levels of complexity	Disabled	No minimum	No maximum
Store Passwords Using Reversible Encryption	Specifies higher level of encryption for stored user passwords	Disabled	No minimum	No maximum

You can use the password policies in Table 18.5 as follows:

Enforce Password History   Prevents users from repeatedly using the same passwords. Users must create a new password when their password expires or is changed.

Maximum Password Age   Forces users to change their passwords after the maximum password age is exceeded. Setting this value to 0 will specify that the password will never expire.

Minimum Password Age   Prevents users from changing their passwords several times in rapid succession in order to defeat the purpose of the Enforce Password History policy.

Minimum Password Length   Ensures that a user creates a password and specifies the length requirement for that password. If this option isn't set, users are not required to create a password at all.

Password Must Meet Complexity Requirements   Passwords must be six characters or longer and cannot contain the user's account name or any part of the user's full name. In addition, passwords must contain three of the following four character types:

- English uppercase characters (A through Z)
- English lowercase characters (a through z)
- Decimal digits (0 through 9)
- Symbols (such as !, @, #, $, and %)

Store Passwords Using Reversible Encryption   Provides a higher level of security for user passwords. This is required for Challenge Handshake Authentication Protocol (CHAP) authentication through remote access or Internet Authentication Services (IAS) and for Digest Authentication with Internet Information Services (IIS).

Complete Exercise 18.15 to configure password policies for your computer. These steps assume that you have added the Local Computer Policy snap-in to the MMC in Exercise 18.1.

EXERCISE 18.15

Configuring Password Policy

1. Open the LGPO MMC shortcut that you created earlier.

2. Expand the Local Computer Policy snap-in.

3. Expand the folders as follows: Computer Configuration ➤ Windows Settings ➤ Security Settings ➤ Account Policies ➤ Password Policy.

4. Open the Enforce Password History policy. On the Local Security Setting tab, specify that five passwords will be remembered. Click OK.

5. Open the Maximum Password Age policy. On the Local Security Setting tab, specify that the password expires in 60 days. Click OK.

Let's now look at how to set and manage the policies in the Account Lockout Policies section.

Setting Account-Lockout Policies

The account-lockout policies specify how many invalid logon attempts should be tolerated. You configure the account-lockout policies so that after x number of unsuccessful logon attempts within y number of minutes, the account will be locked for a specified amount of time or until the administrator unlocks it.

Account-lockout policies are similar to a bank's arrangements for ATM access-code security. You have a certain number of chances to enter the correct PIN. That way, anyone who steals your card can't just keep guessing your access code until they get it right. Typically, after three unsuccessful attempts, the ATM takes the card. Then you need to request a new card from the bank. Figure 18.16 shows the account-lockout policies, which are described in Table 18.6.

FIGURE 18.16   Account-lockout policies

TABLE 18.6   Account-lockout policy options

Policy	Description	Default	Minimum	Maximum
Account Lockout Duration	Specifies how long account will remain locked if the account lockout threshold is reached	Disabled (If Account Lockout Threshold is enabled, 30 minutes.)	Same as default.	99,999 minutes
Account Lockout Threshold	Specifies number of invalid attempts allowed before account is locked out	0 (Disabled; account will not be locked out.)	Same as default.	999 attempts
Reset Account Lockout Counter After	Specifies how long counter will remember unsuccessful logon attempts	Disabled (If Account Lockout Threshold is enabled, 30 minutes.)	Same as default; if enabled, must be equal to or less than the Account Lockout Duration value.	99,999 minutes

The Account Lockout Duration and Reset Account Lockout Counter After policies will be disabled until a value is specified for the Account Lockout Threshold policy. After the Account Lockout Threshold policy is set, the Account Lockout Duration and Reset Account Lockout Counter After policies will be set to 30 minutes. If you set Account Lockout Duration to 0, the account will remain locked out until an administrator unlocks it.

> The Reset Account Lockout Counter After value must be equal to or less than the Account Lockout Duration value.

Complete Exercise 18.16 to configure account-lockout policies and test their effects.

EXERCISE 18.16

Configuring Account-Lockout Policies

1. Open the LGPO MMC shortcut.

2. Expand the Local Computer Policy snap-in.

3. Expand the folders as follows: Computer Configuration ➢ Windows Settings ➢ Security Settings ➢ Account Policies ➢ Password Policy.

4. Open the Account Lockout Threshold policy. On the Local Security Setting tab, specify that the account will lock after three invalid logon attempts. Click OK.

5. Accept the suggested value changes for the Account Lockout Duration and Reset Account Lockout Counter After policies by clicking OK.

6. Open the Account Lockout Duration policy. On the Local Security Setting tab, specify that the account will remain locked for 5 minutes. Click OK.

7. Accept the suggested value changes for the Reset Account Lockout Counter After policy by clicking OK.

8. Log off your Administrator account. Try to log on as one of the accounts that have been created on this Windows 10 machine and enter an incorrect password four times.

9. After you see the error message stating that the referenced account has been locked out, log on as an administrator.

10. To unlock the account, open the Local Users and Groups snap-in in the MMC, expand the Users folder, and double-click the user.

11. On the General tab of the user's Properties dialog box, click to remove the check mark from the Account Is Locked Out check box. Then click OK.

Using Local Policies

As you learned in the preceding section, account policies are used to control logon procedures. When you want to control what a user can do after logging on, you use local policies. With local policies, you can implement auditing, specify user rights, and set security options.

To use local policies, first add the Local Computer Policy snap-in to the MMC. Then, from the MMC, follow this path to access the Local Policies folders: Local Computer Policy ➤ Computer Configuration ➤ Windows Settings ➤ Security Settings ➤ Local Policies. Figure 18.17 shows the three Local Policies folders: Audit Policy, User Rights Assignment, and Security Options. We will look at Audit Policy and User Rights Assignment in the following sections.

FIGURE 18.17   Accessing the Local Policies folders

Setting Audit Policies

Audit policies can be implemented to track the success or failure of specified user actions. You audit events that pertain to user management through the audit policies. By tracking certain events, you can create a history of specific tasks, such as user creation and successful or unsuccessful logon attempts. You can also identify security violations that arise when users attempt to access system management tasks for which they do not have permission.

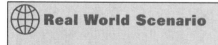
Real World Scenario

Auditing Failed Attempts

As an IT manager, you have to make sure that you monitor failed attempts to access resources. A failed attempt to access a resource usually means that someone tried to access the resource and was denied because of insufficient privileges.

Users who try to go to areas for which they do not have permission usually fall into two categories: hackers and people who are just curious to see what they can get away with. Both are very dangerous.

If a user is trying to access an area in which they do not belong, make sure to warn the user. This is very common on a network and needs to be nipped in the bud.

When you define an audit policy, you can choose to audit success or failure of specific events. The success of an event means that the task was successfully accomplished. The failure of an event means that the task was not successfully accomplished.

By default, auditing is not enabled, and it must be manually configured. Once auditing has been configured, you can see the results of the audit in the security log using the Event Viewer utility.

Only members of the Administrators group can view the security log in Event Viewer.

Figure 18.18 shows the audit policies, which are described in Table 18.7.

FIGURE 18.18 Audit policies

After you set the Audit Object Access policy to enable auditing of object access in the object's properties, you must enable file auditing through NTFS security or print auditing through printer security.

Complete Exercise 18.17 to configure audit policies and view their results.

EXERCISE 18.17

Configuring Audit Policies

1. Open the LGPO MMC shortcut.

2. Expand the Local Computer Policy snap-in.

3. Expand the folders as follows: Computer Configuration ➢ Windows Settings ➢ Security Settings ➢ Local Policies ➢ Audit Policy.

4. Open the Audit Account Logon Events policy. Check the Success and Failure boxes. Click OK.

5. Open the Audit Account Management policy. Check the Success and Failure boxes. Click OK.

6. Log off of your Administrator account. Attempt to log back on to your Administrator account using an incorrect password. The logon should fail (because the password is incorrect).

7. Log on as an administrator.

8. Select Start, right-click Computer, and choose Manage to open Event Viewer.

9. From Event Viewer, open the Security log by selecting Windows Logs ➢ Security. You should see the audited events listed with a Task Category of Credential Validation.

TABLE 18.7 Audit-policy options

Policy	Description
Audit Account Logon Events	Tracks when a user logs on or logs off either their local machine or the domain (if domain auditing is enabled).
Audit Account Management	Tracks user and group account creation, deletion, and management actions, such as password changes.
Audit Directory Service Access	Tracks directory service accesses.
Audit Logon Events	Audits events related to logon, such as running a logon script, accessing a roaming profile, and accessing a server.
Audit Object Access	Enables auditing of access to files, folders, and printers.
Audit Policy Change	Tracks any changes to the audit policies, trust policies, or user rights assignment policies.
Audit Privilege Use	Tracks users exercising a user right.
Audit Process Tracking	Tracks events such as activating a program, accessing an object, and exiting a process.
Audit System Events	Tracks system events such as shutting down or restarting the computer as well as events that relate to the security log in Event Viewer.

Assigning User Rights

The user-rights policies determine what rights a user or group has on the computer. User rights, also called privileges, apply to the system. They are not the same as permissions, which apply to a specific object. An example of a user right is Back Up Files And Directories. This right allows a user to back up files and folders even if the user does not have permissions that have been defined through NTFS filesystem permissions. The other user rights are similar because they deal with system access as opposed to resource access.

Figure 18.19 shows the first several user-rights policies; all of the policies are described in Table 18.8.

FIGURE 18.19   User-rights policies

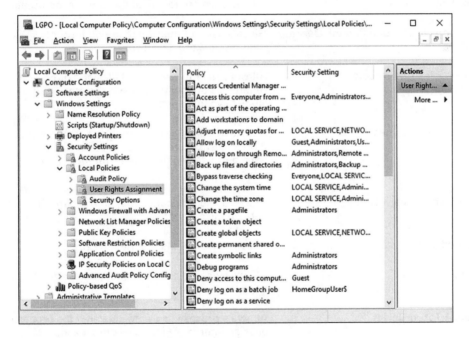

In Exercise 18.18, you'll apply a user-rights policy.

TABLE 18.8   User Rights Assignment policy options

Right	Description
Access Credential Manager As A Trusted Caller	Used to back up and restore Credential Manager.
Access This Computer From The Network	Allows a user to access the computer from the network.

TABLE 18.8 User Rights Assignment policy options *(continued)*

Right	Description
Act As Part Of The Operating System	Allows low-level authentication services to authenticate as any user.
Add Workstations To Domain	Allows a user to create a computer account on the domain.
Adjust Memory Quotas For A Process	Allows you to configure how much memory can be used by a specific process.
Allow Log On Locally	Allows a user to log on at the physical computer.
Allow Log On Through Remote Desktop Services	Gives a user permission to log on through Remote Desktop Services.
Back Up Files And Directories	Allows a user to back up all files and directories regardless of how the file and directory permissions have been set.
Bypass Traverse Checking	Allows a user to pass through and traverse the directory structure, even if that user does not have permissions to list the contents of the directory.
Change The System Time	Allows a user to change the internal time and date on the computer.
Change The Time Zone	Allows a user to change the time zone.
Create A Pagefile	Allows a user to create or change the size of a page file.
Create A Token Object	Allows a process to create a token if the process uses an internal API to create the token.
Create Global Objects	Allows a user to create global objects when connected using Terminal Server.
Create Permanent Shared Objects	Allows a process to create directory objects through Object Manager.
Create Symbolic Links	Allows a user to create a symbolic link.
Debug Programs	Allows a user to attach a debugging program to any process.

Right	Description
Deny Access To This Computer From The Network	Allows you to deny specific users or groups access to this computer from the network. Overrides the Access This Computer From The Network policy for accounts present in both policies.
Deny Log On As A Batch Job	Allows you to prevent specific users or groups from logging on as a batch file. Overrides the Log On As A Batch Job policy for accounts present in both policies.
Deny Log On As A Service	Allows you to prevent specific users or groups from logging on as a service. Overrides the Log On As A Service policy for accounts present in both policies.
Deny Log On Locally	Allows you to deny specific users or groups access to the computer locally. Overrides the Log On Locally policy for accounts present in both policies.
Deny Log On Through Terminal Services	Specifies that a user is not able to log on through Terminal Services.
Enable Computer And User Accounts To Be Trusted For Delegation	Allows a user or group to set the Trusted For Delegation setting for a user or computer object. A user or computer that is trusted for delegation can access resources on another computer using delegated credentials of a client.
Force Shutdown From A Remote System	Allows the system to be shut down by a user at a remote location on the network.
Generate Security Audits	Allows a user, group, or process to make entries in the security log.
Impersonate A Client After Authentication	Enables programs running on behalf of a user to impersonate a client.
Increase A Process Working Set	The working set of a process is the current set of pages in the virtual address space of the process that resides in physical memory. This setting allows you to increase the size of the process working set.
Increase Scheduling Priority	Specifies that a process can increase or decrease the priority that is assigned to another process.

TABLE 18.8 User Rights Assignment policy options *(continued)*

Right	Description
Load And Unload Device Drivers	Allows a user to dynamically unload and load device drivers. This right does not apply to Plug and Play drivers.
Lock Pages In Memory	Allows an account to create a process that runs only in physical RAM, preventing it from being paged.
Log On As A Batch Job	Allows a process to log on to the system and run a file that contains one or more operating system commands.
Log On As A Service	Allows a service to log on in order to run.
Manage Auditing And Security Log	Allows a user to enable object access auditing for files and other Active Directory objects. This right does not allow a user to enable general object access auditing in the Local Security Policy.
Modify An Object Label	Allows a user to change the integrity level of files, folders, or other objects.
Modify Firmware Environment Variables	Allows a user to install or upgrade Windows. It also allows a user or process to modify the firmware environment variables stored in NVRAM of non-x86-based computers. This right does *not* affect the modification of system environment variables or user environment variables.
Perform Volume Maintenance Tasks	Allows a user to perform volume maintenance tasks such as defragmentation and error checking.
Profile Single Process	Allows a user to monitor nonsystem processes through performance-monitoring tools.
Profile System Performance	Allows a user to monitor system processes through performance-monitoring tools.
Remove Computer From Docking Station	Allows a user to undock a laptop through the Windows 10 user interface.
Replace A Process Level Token	Allows a process, such as Task Scheduler, to call an API to start another service.

Right	Description
Restore Files And Directories	Allows a user to restore files and directories regardless of file and directory permissions.
Shut Down The System	Allows a user to shut down the Windows 10 computer locally.
Synchronize Directory Service Data	Allows a user to synchronize Active Directory data.
Take Ownership Of Files Or Other Objects	Allows a user to take ownership of system objects, such as files, folders, printers, and processes.

EXERCISE 18.18

Applying a User-Rights Policy

1. Open the LGPO MMC shortcut.

2. Expand the Local Computer Policy snap-in.

3. Expand the folders as follows: Computer Configuration ➢ Windows Settings ➢ Security Settings ➢ Local Policies ➢ User Rights Assignment.

4. Open the Log On As A Service user right.

5. Click the Add User Or Group button. The Select Users Or Groups dialog box appears.

6. Click the Advanced button, and then select Find Now.

7. Select a user. Click OK.

8. Click OK in the Select Users Or Groups dialog box.

9. In the Log On As A Service Properties dialog box, click OK.

Configuring User Account Control

Most administrators have had to wrestle with the balance between security and enabling applications to run correctly. In the past, some applications simply would not run correctly under Windows unless the user running the application was a local administrator.

Unfortunately, granting local administrator permissions to a user also allows the user to install software and hardware, change configuration settings, modify local user accounts, and delete critical files. Even more troubling is the fact that malware that infects a computer while an administrator is logged in is able to perform administrative functions.

The problem is that many applications require that users have permissions to write to protected folders and to the Registry. Windows 10's solution is *User Account Control (UAC)*. UAC enables non-administrator users to perform standard tasks, such as install a printer, configure a VPN or wireless connection, and install updates, while preventing them from performing administrative tasks such as installing applications.

Privilege Elevation

UAC protects computers by requiring privilege elevation for all users, even users who are members of the local Administrators group. As you have no doubt seen by now, UAC will prompt you for permission when performing a task that requires privilege elevation. This prevents malware from silently launching processes without your knowledge.

Privilege elevation is required for any feature that contains the security shield. For example, the small shield shown on the Change Date And Time button in the Date And Time dialog box indicates an action that requires privilege elevation.

Now let's take a look at how to elevate privileges for users and executables.

Elevated Privileges for Users

By default, local administrators are logged on as standard users. When administrators attempt to perform a task that requires privilege escalation, they are prompted for confirmation by default. This can require administrators to authenticate when performing a task that requires privilege escalation by changing the User Account Control: Behavior Of The Elevation Prompt For Administrators In Admin Approval Mode policy setting to Prompt For Credentials. On the other hand, if you don't want UAC to prompt administrators for confirmation when elevating privileges, you can change the policy setting to Elevate Without Prompting.

Non-administrator accounts are called standard users. When standard users attempt to perform a task that requires privilege elevation, they are prompted for a password of a user account that has administrative privileges. You cannot configure UAC to automatically allow standard users to perform administrative tasks, nor can you configure UAC to prompt a standard user for confirmation before performing administrative tasks. The UAC does this automatically. If you do not want standard users to be prompted at all for credentials when attempting to perform administrative tasks, you change the User Account Control: Behavior Of The Elevation Prompt For Standard Users policy setting to Automatically Deny Elevation Requests.

The built-in Administrator account, though disabled by default, is not affected by UAC. UAC will not prompt the built-in Administrator account for elevation of privileges. Thus, it is important to use a normal user account whenever possible and use the built-in Administrator account only when absolutely necessary.

> With the Default UAC setting enabled, a user's desktop will be dimmed when they are notified of a change to the computer. The administrator or user must either approve or deny the request in the UAC dialog box before the user can do anything else on that computer. This is known as the *secure desktop*. You have the ability to turn off the secure desktop by modifying either the Local Security Policy or the Registry.

Complete Exercise 18.19 to see how UAC affects administrator and non-administrator accounts differently.

EXERCISE 18.19

Seeing How UAC Affects Accounts

1. Log on to Windows 10 as a non-administrator account.

2. Right-click Start ➢ Control Panel ➢ Large Icons View ➢ Windows Firewall.

3. Click the Turn Windows Firewall On Or Off link on the left side. The UAC box should prompt you for permission to continue. Click Yes. You should be denied access to the Windows Firewall Settings dialog box.

4. In the Users and Groups MMC, enable the Administrator account and also reset the Administrator's password.

5. Log off and log on as the Administrator account.

6. Right-click Start ➢ Control Panel ➢ *Large Icons View* ➢ Windows Firewall.

7. Click the Turn Windows Firewall On Or Off link.

8. You should automatically be taken to the Windows Firewall screen. Close the Windows Firewall screen.

Let's now take a look at elevating privileges for executable applications.

Elevated Privileges for Executables

You can also enable an executable file to run with elevated privileges. To do so, you can right-click a shortcut or executable and select Run As Administrator. The elevation applies to this session only.

But what if you need to configure an application to always run with elevated privileges for a user? To do so, log in as an administrator, right-click a shortcut or executable, and select Properties. On the Compatibility tab, check the Run This Program As An Administrator check box. If the Run This Program As An Administrator check box is unavailable, the program is blocked from permanently running as an administrator because the program doesn't need administrative privileges or you are not logged on as an administrator.

Registry and File Virtualization

Many applications that are installed on a Windows 10 machine need to have access to the Registry. By default, Windows 10 protects the Registry from non-administrator accounts, but a feature called Registry and File Virtualization enables non-administrator users to run applications that previously required administrative privileges to run correctly. As discussed earlier, some applications write to the Registry and to protected folders, such as C:\Windows and C:\Program Files. For non-administrator users, Windows 10 redirects any attempts to write to protected locations to a per-user location. By doing so, Windows 10 enables users to use the application successfully while it protects critical areas of the system.

Understanding Smart Cards

Another way to help secure Windows 10 is by using smart cards. *Smart cards* are plastic cards (the size of a credit card) that can be used in combination with other methods of authentication. This process of using a smart card along with another authentication method is called two-factor authentication or *multi-factor authentication*. Authentication is the process of using user credentials to log on to either the local Windows 10 machine or the domain.

Multi-factor authentication support allows you to increase the security of many critical functions of your company, including client authentication, interactive logon, and document signing.

Multi-factor authentication (using smart cards) is now easier than ever to use and deploy because of the new features included with all versions of Windows 10.

Enhanced Support for Smart Card–Related Plug and Play and the Personal Identity Verification (PIV) Standard   This allows users of Windows 10 to use smart cards from vendors who publish their drivers through Windows Update, allowing Windows 10 to use the smart card without special middleware. These drivers are downloaded in the same way as drivers for other Windows devices. When a smart card that is PIV-compliant is placed into a smart-card reader, Windows 10 will try to download a current driver from Windows Update. If a driver is not available, the PIV-compliant minidriver that is included with Windows 10 is used for the smart card.

Encrypting Drives with BitLocker   If your users are using Windows 10 Enterprise or Professional, the users can choose to encrypt their removable media by turning on BitLocker and then choosing the smart-card option to unlock the drive. Windows will then retrieve the correct minidriver for the smart card and allow the operation to complete.

Smart-Card Domain Logon   When using Windows 10, the correct minidriver for a smart card is automatically retrieved. This allows a new smart card to authenticate with the domain controller without requiring the user to install or configure additional middleware.

Document and Email Signing   Windows 10 users can use smart cards to sign an email or document. XML Paper Specification (XPS) documents can also be signed without additional software.

Use with Line-of-Business Applications   Using Windows 10 smart cards allows applications that use Cryptography Next Generation (CNG) or CryptoAPI to retrieve the correct minidriver at runtime. This eliminates the need for middleware.

When you decide to use multi-factor authentication, you are deciding to use a process that will require certificate authorities (CAs). CAs are servers that are running the certificate services on them. When you move forward with the decision to use smart cards, you will then need to install and configure CAs to make all of the components work together.

CAs are built on Windows Server operating systems, and if your Windows 10 users are having issues logging into the Windows 10 operating systems using smart cards, then you must check the server CAs to make sure that they are configured and running properly.

 Certificate Servers are covered in greater detail in *MCSA Windows Server 2012 R2 Complete Study Guide: Exams 70-410, 70-411, 70-412, and 70-417* by William Panek (Sybex, 2016).

There are two types of smart cards: physical and virtual. Physical smart cards are cards that look like ATM cards. Most of them have either a magnetic strip or chip built into the physical card. To use a physical smart card, you need a smart card reader. This is a device that either connects to a computer or is built into a computer and you place the physical smart card into the reader. You then enter a PIN into the system and the machine is unlocked or logged into the network.

There is a downside to using physical smart cards, which is that they can get lost or misplaced. When I implemented a smart card system into a previous company, we ended up replacing one-fourth of all cards in the first month due to loss or damage.

This is where virtual smart cards can be an advantage. Virtual smart cards use a cryptographic key technology that is stored on the actual Windows 10 computer, as long as that computer has a Trusted Platform Module (TPM) installed on the motherboard.

Virtual smart cards offer the security benefits of two-factor authentication without the price of physical cards and readers. This is possible because of the TPM technology. TPM devices allow us to use cryptographic capabilities, the same as physical smart cards do, but without the cards. Virtual smart cards give us the same benefits as physical cards, including non-exportability, anti-hammering, and isolated cryptography.

Non-exportability   TPM technology is built to be tamper proof. When a system uses TPM encryption, the TPM encryption is specific to the machine that installed it. Because of this, you can't take a virtual smart card from one system and use it on another.

Anti-hammering (Lockout)   Smart cards use PINs to unlock the system. If a PIN is entered incorrectly, the TPM uses an Anti-hammering technology that locks the system from further attempts for a specific amount of time.

Isolated Cryptography   TPMs are the only mechanism on a Windows 10 system that loads a copy of the private keys. These keys are not loaded into the system's memory, and because only TPM has the keys, the keys stay isolated and inaccessible to anything or anyone.

Virtual smart cards function the same way as physical smart cards that are continuously inserted into a system. The machine gets the same benefits and results. To set up virtual smart cards, you need to build a certificate authority (CA) server in your organization, and all of your Windows clients need to be Windows 8 or higher.

After the CA is built, you then need to build a certificate template for the virtual smart cards to use. Then, to create the TPM virtual smart card for a Windows 10 system, open a command prompt with Administrative credentials on a Windows 10 domain computer and type in the following command:

```
tpmvscmgr.exe create /name tpmvsc /pin default /adminkey random /generate
```

After you run this command, you will create a virtual smart card with the name tpmvsc. The system will then prompt you for a PIN. You will need to enter and confirm a PIN of at least eight characters. After a few seconds, the process will complete. The TPM application (tpmvscmgr.exe) will then provide you with the device instance ID for the virtual smart card. You may want to store this ID in case you will need it to manage or remove the virtual smart card later.

Finally, you will need to enroll the certificate into the CA by requesting a new certificate and then choosing the TPM Virtual Smart Card Logon check box. When you are prompted for a device, select the Microsoft virtual smart card that you created earlier.

Summary

In this chapter, you learned how to create and manage user and group accounts. We looked at the different tools that can be used to create users in Windows 10.

We also looked at Windows 10 security. We reviewed the difference between LGPOs, which are applied at the local computer level, and GPOs, which are applied through a Windows 2003, 2008, 2008 R2, or 2012/2012 R2 domain, and how they are applied.

We looked at account policies, which control the logon process. The two types of account policies are password and account lockout policies. We also looked at local policies, which control what a user can do at the computer. The three types of local policies are audit, user rights, and security options policies.

Video Resources

There are videos available for the following exercises:

18.1

18.3

18.4

You can access the videos at www.wiley.com/go/sybextestprep on the Other Study Tools tab.

Exam Essentials

Be able to create and manage user accounts.   When creating user accounts, be aware of the requirements for doing so. Understand User Account Control. Know how to rename and delete user accounts. Be able to manage all user properties.

Know how to configure and manage local user authentication.   Understand the options that can be configured to manage local user authentication and when these options would be used to create a more secure environment. Be able to specify where local user authentication options are configured.

Know how to manage local groups.   Understand the local groups that are created on Windows 10 computers by default, and be familiar with the rights each group has. Know how to create and manage new groups.

Know how to set local group policies.   Understand the purpose of account policies and local policies. Know the purpose and implementation of account policies for managing password policies and account lockout policies. Understand the purpose and implementation of local policies and how they can be applied to users and groups for audit policies, user rights assignments, and security options.

Understand User Account Control.   Understand the purpose and features of User Account Control. Be familiar with Registry and file virtualization. Understand privilege escalation. Know the basics of the new UAC Group Policy settings.

Review Questions

1. You are the administrator for a large training company. You have decided that everyone needs to configure the Password Must Meet Complexity Requirements policy. Users are not sure what they can use. You decide to send an email out showing people examples of what types of passwords they can use. Which of the following passwords meet the minimum complexity requirements? (Choose all that apply.)

    A. aBcdEfG1!

    B. Abc-de!

    C. Kl982!@#$%^&*

    D. 123456789nA

2. You are setting up a machine for a home user who does not know much about computers. You do not want to make the user a local administrator, but you do want to give this user the right to change Windows Updates manually. How can you configure this?

    A. Modify the LGPO for Windows Update to allow the user to make changes manually.

    B. Explain to the user how to log on as the Administrator account.

    C. Set Windows Update modifications to anyone.

    D. This can't be done. Only administrators can change Windows Update.

3. You are the administrator for a large organization with multiple Windows Server 2012 R2 domain controllers and multiple domains. You have a Windows 10 machine that is set up for all users to access. You have an application called `StellApp.exe` that everyone on this Windows 10 computer can use except for the Sales group. How do you stop the Sales group from accessing this one application?

    A. Deny the Everyone group the rights to the application.

    B. Create an executable rule from the Application Control Policy.

    C. Create a security role from the Application Control Policy.

    D. Give the Everyone group full control to the application.

4. You have a Windows 10 machine that multiple users access. All users have the rights to use USB removable devices, but you need to deny one user access to USB removable devices. How do you accomplish this?

    A. Deny the one user from using the machine.

    B. Set a USB rule on Hardware Manager.

    C. Deny all users from using USB devices.

    D. Create a removable storage access policy through an LGPO.

5. You are the system administrator for a large organization. You have a Windows 10 machine that all users can access. There is a folder on the Windows 10 machine called Apps. You need to set up auditing on this folder. How do you accomplish this task?

    A. From the Local Group Policy, enable Directory Service Access.

    B. From the Local Group Policy, enable Audit Object Access.

    C. From the Local Group Policy, enable Account Access.

    D. From the Local Group Policy, enable File And Folder Access.

6. Your company, Stormwind, requires that you implement security and you have been asked to define and implement a security policy. You have configured password policies so that users must change their passwords every month. Users are not allowed to use any of their previous 24 passwords. Which password policy would you implement if you want to prevent users from reusing passwords?

    A. Passwords Must Be Advanced

    B. Enforce Password History

    C. Passwords Must Be Unique

    D. Passwords Must Meet Complexity Requirements

7. You are the network administrator for a large organization. You have a Windows 10 machine that needs to prevent any user from copying unencrypted files from the Windows 10 machine to any removable disk. How do you accomplish this task?

    A. Within the System icon in Control Panel, set the BitLocker Drive Encryption.

    B. Within the Hardware icon in Control Panel, set the BitLocker Drive Encryption.

    C. Within the Device Manager icon in Control Panel, set the BitLocker Drive Encryption.

    D. Within a Local Group Policy, set the BitLocker Drive Encryption.

8. In which editions of Windows 10 can you enable UAC? (Choose all that apply.)

    A. Windows 10 Home edition

    B. Windows 10 Education edition

    C. Windows 10 Professional edition

    D. Windows 10 Enterprise edition

9. A salesperson in your company purchases a new laptop with Windows 10 installed. She asks you to configure it for her. You create a standard local user account for her. Which of the following tasks can she perform by default?

    A. Change date and time settings

    B. Change time-zone settings

    C. Check Device Manager

    D. Enable parental controls

10. Your network's security has been breached. You are trying to redefine security so that a user cannot repeatedly attempt user logon with different passwords. To accomplish this, which of the following items in the Local Security Policy box should you define?

    A. Password Policy

    B. Account Lockout Policy

    C. Audit Policy

    D. Security Options

Chapter

19

Configuring Network Connectivity

MICROSOFT EXAM OBJECTIVES COVERED IN THIS CHAPTER:

✓ **Configure IP settings.**

- This objective may include but is not limited to the following subobjectives: Configure name resolution, connect to a network, configure network locations.

✓ **Configure networking settings.**

- This objective may include but is not limited to the following subobjectives: Connect to a wireless network, manage preferred wireless networks, configure network adapters, configure location-aware printing.

✓ **Configure and maintain network security.**

- This objective may include but is not limited to the following subobjectives: Configure Windows Firewall, configure Windows Firewall with Advanced Security, configure connection security rules (IPsec), configure authenticated exceptions, configure network discovery.

In most organizations, Windows 10 machines will be configured as a member of a domain. Therefore, it's very important to know how to properly configure Windows 10 in a domain environment.

In this chapter, we discuss Active Directory and how to configure Windows 10 to work within the Windows Server 2012 R2 domain environment. We will look at how to connect to a Windows Server 2012 R2 domain by using both IPv4 and IPv6. We will also look at connecting Windows 10 to a network by using either a wireless or wired connection and working with the Windows 10 HomeGroup.

We will look at how to protect your network by using the Windows 10 Firewall. We discuss the different ways that you can manage your network and Windows 10 machines remotely.

Another technology that we present in this chapter is virtualization. This is one of the fastest growing and hottest technologies to hit the market in the past few years. Server virtualization gives an organization the ability to run multiple operating systems, called *virtual machines*, on a single physical machine. We will look at how to install and configure Windows 10 to run as a virtual machine.

Understanding Networking

Microsoft uses two networking models: domain-based networks and peer-to-peer networks. The way you design your network is going to determine how you set up the rest of the computers and servers on that network. The choice you make here will be determined by many factors, including the number of users on your network and the amount of money you can spend.

Windows Peer-to-Peer Network

When setting up a Microsoft Windows *peer-to-peer network* (also referred to as a *workgroup*), it is important to understand that all computers on the network are equal. All of the peer-to-peer computers, also referred to as *nodes*, simultaneously act as both clients and servers.

Peer-to-peer networks are typically any combination of Microsoft Windows XP, Windows Vista, Windows 7, Windows 8, and Windows 10 machines connected by a centralized device such as a router or hub (see Figure 19.1).

FIGURE 19.1   Peer-to-peer model

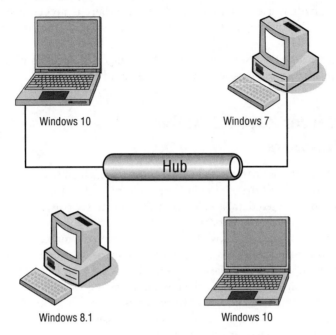

Windows 10

Windows 7

Hub

Windows 8.1

Windows 10

 To learn more about Microsoft networks, see *MCSA Windows Server 2012 R2 Complete Study Guide: Exams 70-410, 70-411, 70-412, and 70-417,* by William Panek (Sybex, 2015).

One of the biggest debates among IT professionals is when to use a peer-to-peer network. These types of networks have their place in the networking world. Most home networks use this type of configuration—where all of the computers are connected by a small Internet router. It's often the same for companies. You would use this network configuration in a small environment with 10 users or fewer. This enables small organizations to still share resources without needing expensive equipment, server software, or an internal IT department.

But there is a downside to peer-to-peer networks; the biggest issue is manageability and security. Many new IT people like working on a small peer-to-peer network because of its size, but no matter what, a network with 10 users and 10 computers can be very difficult to manage and security is extremely difficult to set up. Because there is no server to centralize user accounts on a peer-to-peer network, each Microsoft Windows XP, Windows Vista, Windows 7, Windows 8, and Windows 10 computer must have a user account and password. So if you have 10 users and 10 computers and all 10 users must be able to access all 10 computers, you end up creating 100 accounts: 10 accounts on each machine times 10 machines.

Another disadvantage of peer-to-peer networks is backups. Most IT departments do not back up individual user machines, and because there is no centralized server for data storage when using a peer-to-peer network, data recoverability can be an issue.

Now that you have seen the advantages and disadvantages of a peer-to-peer network, let's discuss the advantages and disadvantages of a domain-based network.

Windows Server 2012 R2 Active Directory Network

A *domain-based network* uses Microsoft's *Active Directory*, which is a single distributed database that contains all the objects in your network. A domain is a logical grouping of objects into a distributed database. Some of these objects are user accounts, group accounts, and published objects (folders and printers).

The first of many advantages to Active Directory is centralized management. As just stated, the Active Directory database contains all the network information within a single, distributed, data repository. Because these network objects are all located in the same database, an administrator can easily manage the domain from one location.

Another major advantage to using Active Directory is domain security. An administrator has the advantage of creating a single username and password for all users within the domain. This username and password can be used to access all resources that an individual has the proper rights to access. An administrator can determine, based on job function or position, which files or folders on the network a user should be granted access to, and assign access to the user's single account. In our earlier peer-to-peer example, you needed to create 100 user accounts. With a domain, you would need to create only the 10 accounts, one per person.

An Active Directory structure is made up of one or more domains. As explained, a *domain* is a logical grouping of objects within your organization. For example, if we had the Stormwind.com domain, all users in that domain should be members of the Stormwind.com organization. The objects that are contained within a domain do not need to be in the same physical location. Domains can span the entire globe even though they are part of the same organization.

One of the advantages to using domains is the ability to have a *child domain*, which is a subdomain of another domain. You can build child domains based on physical locations, departments, and so forth. Figure 19.2 shows the hierarchy structure of Stormwind.com with its child domains (based on geographic location).

Microsoft Active Directory domains are represented as triangles. It is important to remember that when taking any Microsoft exam.

FIGURE 19.2   Domain structure

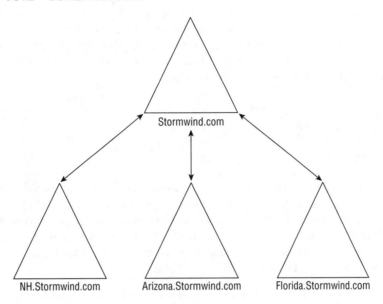

Child domains give you greater scalability. Active Directory has the ability to store millions of objects within a single domain, but child domains give an administrator the flexibility to design a structure that meets an organization's needs. For example, you may have a site located in a different state. Creating a child domain for that office allows that office to be an independent domain, and thus they can have their own security and domain settings. One or more domains that follow the same contiguous namespace are called a tree. For example, if my domain name is Stormwind.com and the child domains are NH.Stormwind.com, Arizona.Stormwind.com, and Florida.Stormwind.com, this would be a tree. All of these domains follow the Stormwind.com namespace.

When you set up child domains, the parent and child domains automatically establish a trust relationship. *Trusts* allow users to be granted access to resources in a domain even when their accounts reside in a different domain. To make administration of trust relationships easier, Microsoft has made transitive two-way trusts the default relationship between domains within a forest. A forest is all the trees that are part of your Active Directory structure, and they share a schema and Global Catalog. This means that by default, all domains within the same forest automatically trust one another. As shown in Figure 19.2, Stormwind.com automatically trusts NH.Stormwind.com, Arizona.Stormwind.com, and Florida.Stormwind.com. This means that all of the child domains implicitly trust one another.

The last Active Directory advantage that we will discuss is an extensible schema. The Active Directory schema contains all the objects and attributes of the database. For example, when you create a new user by using the Active Directory Users and Computers snap-in, the system asks you to fill in the user's first name, last name, username, password, and so forth. These fields are the attributes of the user object, and the way that the system knows to prompt for these fields is that the user object has these specific attributes assigned to it within the Active Directory schema. An administrator has the ability to change or expand these fields based on organizational needs.

 Real World Scenario

Extending the Schema

You may be asking yourself why an organization would need to extend the schema. Many years ago, when I got out of the military and before I got into the computer industry, I used to cast toilets for American Standard. I made 50 toilets a day. When working for American Standard, I had an employee number of 343. All my toilets were stamped 343 (so the company knew who made the product) on the base of the toilet. My time card did not even have my name, just my number.

This number is an example of a field that would need to be added to a schema. I would have an account in Active Directory with my name, but there would need to be a field that showed my employee number. You may have to adjust your Active Directory schema based on your organization's requirements.

The major disadvantage to an Active Directory model is cost. When setting up an Active Directory domain, an organization needs a machine that's powerful enough to handle the Windows Server 2012 R2 operating system. Also, most companies that decide to use a domain-based organization will require the IT personnel to manage and maintain the network infrastructure.

Cloud-Based Azure Active Directory

Now that you have been introduced to Active Directory, let's take a look at how you can have Microsoft manage your Active Directory with their cloud-based Active Directory called *Azure*. Azure is Microsoft's subscription-based Active Directory.

If you are a small- to mid-size company and you don't want to worry about employing a full-time multi-person IT department, then this may be a great option for you. This allows Microsoft to deal with the worries of managing and maintaining a server room and all of the hardware.

All your company would need to do is hire or train someone who would add and maintain the actual Azure Active Directory accounts. This person could also work as the help desk or support individual. Now you have Microsoft worrying about the hardware and your IT people can focus on helping and maintaining users and accounts.

So how does Azure Active Directory compare when it comes to adding Windows 10 to the domain? It really doesn't matter. As long as you have Internet access to the cloud-based system, your Windows 10 accounts will work the same way as if the Active Directory was on premise.

Windows 10 includes a new feature for configuring and deploying corporation-owned Windows devices called Azure AD Join. Azure AD Join registers the Windows 10 devices in the Azure Active Directory, which then allows them to be accessible and managed by your organization.

The one nice advantage is that with Azure Active Directory, Windows 10 devices authenticate directly to Azure AD without the need of an onsite domain controller. But, if you want, you can still have a domain controller on site that works with the cloud-based Azure Active Directory.

When you are adding Windows 10 to Azure Active Directory, end-users or domain admins can join their Windows 10 device (computer, tablet, or phone) to Azure AD during the out-of-box experience (OOBE). Because of this, organizations can assign devices to their users with no IT interaction or staging time.

Because of the Azure AD Join built into Windows 10, during the OOBE, the IT department would just add the device to the Azure Active Directory network.

Now that you understand the difference between a workgroup and a domain, let's go ahead and make sure that you understand some of the other networking terms that you will need to know.

Other Microsoft Networking Terms and Roles

Now that you have seen the different Microsoft networking models, let's talk about some of the server terminology that is used in the remainder of this chapter. You may be familiar with some of these terms, but it's always good to get a refresher.

Server   A *server* is a machine that users connect to so they can access resources located on that machine. These resources can be files, printers, applications, and so forth. Usually, the type of server is dependent on the resource that the user needs. For example, a print server is a server that controls printers. A file server contains files. Application servers can run applications for the users. Sometimes you will hear a server referred to by the specific application that it may be running. For example, someone may say, "That's our SQL server" or "We have an Exchange server."

Domain Controller   This is a server that contains a replica of the Active Directory database. As mentioned earlier in this chapter, Active Directory is the database that contains all the security objects in your network along with any resources that you publish to Active Directory. A *domain controller* is a server that contains this database. All domain controllers are equal in a Windows Server 2012 R2 network, and each can read from and write to the directory database. Some domain controllers may contain extra roles, but they all part of the same Active Directory.

Member Server   A *member server* is a server that is a member of a domain-based network but does not contain a copy of Active Directory. For example, it is recommended by Microsoft that a Microsoft Exchange server be loaded on a member server instead of a domain controller. Both domain controllers and member servers can act as file, print, or application servers. Your choice of server type depends on whether you need that server to have a replica of Active Directory.

Network Discovery   *Network discovery* is a setting that determines whether your Windows 10 system can locate other computers and devices on the network and if other computers on the network can see your computer. To enable or disable Network Discovery, you need to complete the following steps:

1. In the Windows 10 search box, type **network**. Then click Change Advanced Sharing Settings on the left side.

2. Click Turn On/Turn Off Network Discovery, and then click the Save Changes button.

Standalone Server   A *standalone server* is not a member of a domain. Many organizations may use this type of server for virtualization. For example, say you load Windows Server 2012 R2 with Hyper-V (Microsoft's virtualization server) on a standalone server. You can then create virtual machines that act as domain controllers to run the network.

Client Machine   A *client machine* is a computer that normally is used by a company's end users. The most common operating systems for a client machine are Windows XP, Windows Vista, Windows 7, Windows 8, and Windows 10.

DNS Server   A *Domain Name Service (DNS)* server has the DNS service running on it. DNS is a name-resolution service that resolves a hostname to a TCP/IP address (called forward lookup). DNS also has the ability to resolve a TCP/IP address to a name (called reverse lookup). When you install an operating system onto a computer, you assign that computer a hostname. The problem is that computers talk to each other by using TCP/IP addresses, for example, 192.168.1.100. It would be very difficult for most users to remember all the different TCP/IP addresses on a network. So normally you connect to a machine by using its hostname. DNS does the conversion of hostname to TCP/IP address for you.

The easiest way to understand how this works is to think of your phone number. If someone wants to call you but doesn't have your telephone number, they can call Information. They give Information your name, and they get your phone number. This is basically how a network works as well. DNS is Information on your network. You give DNS a hostname, and it returns a network telephone number (TCP/IP address). DNS is a requirement if you want to install Active Directory. You can install DNS before or during the Active Directory installation. DNS can help resolve either IPv4 or IPv6 TCP/IP addresses, both of which are explained later in this chapter, in the section "Understanding TCP/IP."

The reason that DNS can resolve both IPv4 and IPv6 is because of the Link Local Multicast Name Resolution, or LLMNR, protocol, which is based on DNS packet formats that allow both IPv4 and IPv6 hosts to perform name resolution for hosts on the same local network.

DHCP Server   A *Dynamic Host Configuration Protocol (DHCP)* server runs the DHCP service, which assigns TCP/IP information to your computers dynamically. Every computer needs three settings to operate properly (with the Internet and intranet): a TCP/IP address, a subnet mask, and a default gateway (router address). Your computers can get this minimum information two ways: manually, where someone manually types in the TCP/IP information on the machine, or dynamically, where the DHCP service automatically assigns the machine an address. DHCP can assign more than just these three settings. DHCP can assign any TCP/IP configuration information, including the address of a DNS server, WINS server, time servers, and so forth.

Continuing with our scenario from "DNS Server," DHCP would be the phone company. DHCP is the component that assigns the telephone number (TCP/IP number).

If you are using DHCP and your Windows 10 machine receives a 169.254.*x.x* TCP/IPv4 address, your client is not able to connect to the DHCP server. Windows 10 machines will automatically assign themselves a 169.254.*x.x* TCP/IPv4 number when DHCP is unavailable. This is called Automatic Private IP Addressing (APIPA). DHCP can issue either IPv4 or IPv6 TCP/IP addresses.

Global Catalog   The *Global Catalog* is a database of all Active Directory objects in a forest with only a subset of the object attributes. Think of the Global Catalog as an index. If you needed to look something up in this Windows 10 book, you would go to the index and find what page you need to turn to. You would not just randomly look through the book for the information. This is the same purpose the Global Catalog serves in your Active Directory forest. When you need to find a resource in the domain (user, published printer, and so forth), you can search the Global Catalog to find its location.

Domain controllers need to use a Global Catalog to help with user authentication. Global Catalogs are a requirement on an Active Directory domain. All domain controllers can be Global Catalogs, but this is not always a good practice. Your network should have at least two Global Catalogs for redundancy, but too many can cause too much Global Catalog replication traffic unless you have a single-domain model.

Location Aware Printing   Location Aware Printing allows you to choose different default printers for different networks. This was introduced in Windows 7, and it allowed your system to connect to the printer that was on your current network. So if you were on your home network, it would automatically print to your home printer, and if you were at work, it work automatically choose your work printer.

One of the objectives listed at the beginning of the chapter was location-aware printing. At the time this book was written, Microsoft announced that the location-aware printing feature that was introduced in Windows 7 was being removed. I listed it in the event that Microsoft adds it back into Windows 10.

Configuring Windows 10 NIC Devices

Before you can connect a Windows 10 machine to the domain, you must set up the *network interface card (NIC)*—a hardware component used to connect computers or other devices to the network to allow the machines to communicate with each other. NICs are responsible for providing the physical connection that recognizes the physical address of the device where they are installed.

> The Open System Interconnection (OSI) model defines the encapsulation technique that builds the basic data structure for data transport across an internetwork. The OSI model provides interoperability among hardware vendors, network protocols, and applications. The physical address is the OSI model Layer 2 address or, for Ethernet technologies, the MAC (Media Access Control) address. This is not an IP address, which is the OSI Layer 3 or Network Layer address, also generically defined as the logical address.

We generically call the interface between our network devices and the software components of the machines *network adapters* (also referred to as a NIC). Most commonly, you see network adapters installed on computers, but you also see network adapters installed in network printers and specialized devices such as Intrusion Detection Systems (IDSs) and firewalls. Network adapters do not need to be separate cards; they can be built in, as in the case of most PCs today or other network-ready devices such as network cameras or network media players. These adapters (and all other hardware devices) need a driver to communicate with the Windows 10 operating system.

Before you physically install a network adapter, it's important to read the vendor's instructions that come with the hardware. Most network adapters you get today should be self-configuring, using Plug and Play capabilities. After you install a network adapter that supports Plug and Play, it should work following the installation procedure (which should be automated if the vendor says it is). You might have to restart, but our operating systems are getting much better with this, and you might just get lucky and be ready to use the device immediately.

If you happen to have a network adapter that is not Plug and Play, the operating system should detect the new piece of hardware and start a wizard that leads you through the process of loading the adapter's driver and setting initial configuration parameters. You can see your network connection and manage the network connection properties through the Network and Sharing Center.

Configuring a Network Adapter

After you have installed the network adapter, you configure it through its Properties dialog box. You can get to the network adapter properties pages via the Network and Sharing

Center (detailed in the "Configuring Wireless Network Settings" section later in this chapter), through Computer Management, or through Device Manager.

To use the Device Manager applet for the network adapter configuration, right-click the Start and choose Device Manager. This launches Device Manager (see Figure 19.3) MMC (Microsoft Management Console).

FIGURE 19.3   Device Manager MMC

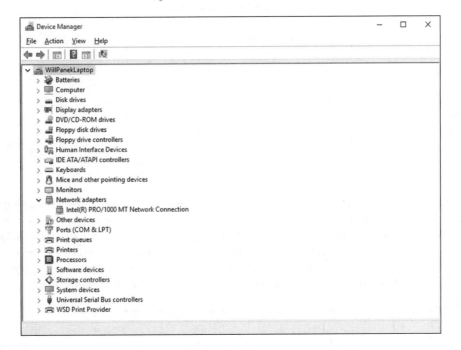

Figure 19.3 shows the Network Adapters device category expanded, and the adapter is installed in the machine. Accessing the network adapter properties allows us to view and change configuration parameters of the adapter. You do this by right-clicking the adapter in Device Manager and selecting Properties from the context menu. Each tab is detailed in the following paragraphs.

General Tab   The General tab of the Network Adapter Properties dialog box (Figure 19.4) shows the name of the adapter, the device type, the manufacturer, and the location. The Device Status box reports whether the device is working properly. If not, the Device Status box gives you an error code and a brief description of what Windows 10 identifies as the issue. You can perform an Internet search for the error code(s) if the text is not sufficient.

FIGURE 19.4   General tab of the Network Adapters Properties page

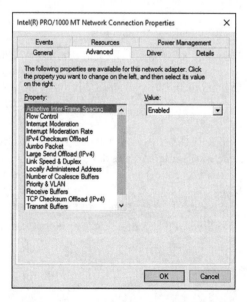

Advanced Tab   The contents of the Advanced tab of a Network Adapter's Properties dialog box vary depending on the network adapter and driver that you are using. Figure 19.5 shows an example of the Advanced tab for my Fast Ethernet adapter. To configure options in this dialog box, choose the property you want to modify in the Property list box and specify the desired value for the property in the Value box on the right. I have selected the Connection Type property and opened the drop-down list box to show you the options for my network adapter.

FIGURE 19.5   Advanced tab of the Network Adapters Properties page

Driver Tab   The Driver tab of the Network Adapters Properties dialog box provides the following information about your driver:

- The driver provider
- The date the driver was released
- The driver version (useful in determining whether you have the latest driver installed)
- The digital signer (the company that provides the digital signature for driver signing)

The Driver tab for my adapter is shown in Figure 19.6. The information here varies from driver to driver and even from vendor to vendor.

FIGURE 19.6   Driver tab of the Network Adapters Properties page

The **Driver Details button** on the Driver tab brings up the Driver File Details dialog box that provides the following details about the driver:

- The location of the driver file (useful for troubleshooting)
- The original provider of the driver
- The file version (useful for troubleshooting)
- Copyright information about the driver
- The digital signer for the driver

The **Update Driver button** starts a wizard to step you through upgrading the driver for an existing device.

The Roll Back Driver button allows you to roll back to the previously installed driver if you update your network driver and encounter problems. In Figure 19.6, the Roll Back Driver button is grayed out (not available) because I have not updated the driver or a previous driver is not available.

The Disable button is used to disable the device. After you disable the device, the Disable button changes into an Enable button, which you can use to enable the device.

The Uninstall button removes the driver from your computer's configuration. You would uninstall the driver if you were going to remove the device from your system or if you want to completely remove the driver configuration from your system so you can reinstall it from scratch either automatically or manually.

Details Tab The Details tab of the network adapter's Properties dialog box lists the resource settings for your network adapter. Information found on the Details tab varies by hardware device. I have included the Details tab information from my adapter in Figure 19.7, with the Property drop-down list box expanded to show the options for my hardware.

FIGURE 19.7 Details tab of the Network Adapter Properties page

Events Tab   The Events tab (Figure 19.8) of the network adapter's Properties dialog box shows you some of the device events that have happened to this piece of hardware. There is also a View All Events button that opens the Event Viewer MMC, which shows you all events for this device. This is a good way to look to see if there have been any events or issues (like errors or warnings) to the device.

FIGURE 19.8   Events tab of the Network Adapter Properties page

Resources Tab   The Resources tab of the Network Adapter's Properties dialog box (Figure 19.9) lists the resource settings for your network adapter. Resources include interrupt request (IRQ), memory, and input/output (I/O) resources. This information can be important for troubleshooting if other devices are trying to use the same resource settings. This is not normally the case because Windows 10 and the Plug and Play specification should set up nonconflicting parameters. If there are issues, the Conflicting Device List box at the bottom of the Resources tab will show the conflicts.

Power Management Tab   The Power Management tab (Figure 19.10) of the network adapter's Properties dialog box allows you to set up how this device can save power on the system. For example, you can allow the system to turn off this device and also allow this device to wake the system from sleep mode.

FIGURE 19.9   Resources tab of the Network Adapter Properties page

FIGURE 19.10   Power Management tab of the Network Adapter Properties page

Troubleshooting a Network Adapter

When installing the NIC, you may encounter some problems or errors. Let's take a look at some NIC troubleshooting.

If your network adapter is not working, the problem might be with the hardware, the driver software, or the network protocols. We discuss the Layer 3 (Network Layer) issues later in this chapter in the section "Understanding TCP/IP." The following are some common Layer 1 (Physical Layer) and Layer 2 (Data Link Layer) causes for network adapter problems:

Network Adapter Not on the HCL   If the device is not on the Hardware Compatibility List (HCL), use your Internet resources to see if others have discovered a solution, or contact the hardware vendor for advice.

Outdated Driver   Make sure that you have the most current driver for your adapter. You can have Windows 10 check for an updated driver from the Driver tab of the Properties page for the adapter by clicking the Update Driver button and having Windows search for a better driver, or you can check for the latest driver on the hardware vendor's website.

Network Adapter Not Recognized by Windows 10   Check Device Manager to see whether Windows 10 recognizes the adapter. If you don't see your adapter, you can try to manually install it.

Improperly Configured Network Card   Verify that the settings for the network card are correct for the parameters known within your network and for the hardware device the machine is connected to.

Cabling Problem   Make sure that all network cables are functioning and are the correct type. This includes making sure that the connector is properly seated, the cable is straight or crossed (depending on where it's plugged in), and the cable is not broken. This is usually done by looking at the little green light (LGL) on the network adapter card. This does not guarantee a good connection even if the LGLs are illuminated. A single conductor failure in a cable can still have a link light on, but data is not passing.

Bad Network Connection Device   Verify that all network connectivity hardware is properly working. For example, on a Fast Ethernet network, make sure the switch and port being used are functioning properly.

 There are seven layers to the OSI model. Starting at Layer 7 and working down, they are Application, Presentation, Session, Transport, Network, Data-Link, and Physical. You can remember this by using the phrase "All People Seem To Need Data Processing."

Configuring Wireless NIC Devices

Wireless technology has matured to the point of becoming cost effective and secure. The use of wireless network adapters is increasingly popular, scaling well out of the home and into the workplace. Windows 10 supports wireless auto configuration, which makes wireless network connections easy to use. Windows 10 will automatically discover the wireless networks available and connect your machine to the preferred wireless network.

One of the advantages to setting up Windows 10 and wireless connections is that once you have connected to a wireless access point, your Windows 10 will remember that and reconnect you to that preferred wireless network when your Windows 10 system is in range.

Configuring Wireless Network Settings

If you have a wireless network adapter compatible with Windows 10, it will be automatically recognized by the operating system. This can be a built-in adapter such as most modern laptops come with, a wireless card you install in the machine, or even a wireless USB adapter. After it is installed, it is shown in Device Manager as well as in the Network and Sharing Center within the View Your Active Networks section.

We used Device Manager in the previous section for the network adapter configuration, so let's use the Network and Sharing Center for the wireless network configuration. Figure 19.11 shows the Network and Sharing Center with one active network, the Wireless Network Connection called Trend.

FIGURE 19.11 Network and Sharing Center

You can perform any of the following steps to access the Network and Sharing Center:

- Type **Network and Sharing Center** in the integrated search box of Windows 10.
- Right-click Start ➤ Control Panel ➤ Network And Internet ➤ Network And Sharing Center (if Control Panel view is Category).

- Right-click Start ➤ Control Panel ➤ Network And Sharing Center (if Control Panel view is Large Icons or Small Icons).

- Right-click the network icon in the lower-right taskbar and choose Open Network And Sharing Center.

- Click Start ➤ Settings ➤ Network and Internet and then choose either the Wi-Fi or Ethernet Connection link.

Viewing the Wireless Network Connection Status

From the Network and Sharing Center, you have easy access to the Wireless Network Connection Status window, which gives you an initial look at the status by providing the Layer 3 connectivity status (IPv4 and IPv6), media state, service set identifier (SSID) being used, how long the connection has been active (Duration), the negotiated speed of the connection, and the signal quality, as shown in Figure 19.12.

FIGURE 19.12 Wireless Network Connection Status

The Details button provides information such as the actual physical address (Layer 2), logical address (Layer 3), dynamic addressing parameters (DHCP), name-resolution items, and more. After verifying Physical Layer parameters, this area is a great place to verify or troubleshoot logical (driver/software) issues.

Viewing Wireless Network Connection Details

If you have a wireless adapter in your machine, perform Exercise 19.1 to view the Network Connection Details for your Wireless Network Connection.

EXERCISE 19.1

Viewing the Network Connection Details

1. Type **Network and Sharing Center** in the Windows 10 integrated search window; press Enter.

2. Select the Wireless Network Connection menu item from the View Your Active Networks section.

3. Click the Details button.

4. Review the network connection details for this connection.

The Wireless Network Connection Status window has an Activity section showing real-time traffic (in bytes) being sent from and received by the wireless network. From the Wireless Network Connection Status window, you also have access to the Wireless Network Connection Properties, which includes access to the wireless adapter configuration pages.

You access the properties page by clicking the Properties button in the Activity section (refer back to Figure 19.12). The Wi-Fi Properties page has a Networking tab (see Figure 19.13) that shows which network adapter is being used for this connection (which you can change if you have more than one available).

FIGURE 19.13 Wi-Fi Properties window's Networking tab

The section that begins with "This connection uses the following items" displays the various clients, services, and protocols that are currently available for this connection.

You can install or uninstall network clients, network services, and network protocols by clicking the appropriate button. You can also view the client, service, or protocol properties if they are available by first highlighting the item from the list and then clicking the Properties button for the selected item. If the Properties button is gray, a properties page is not available for the item. From the Wireless Network Connection Properties window, you even have access to the network adapter's hardware configuration property pages. These are the same pages you have access to from Device Manager.

Perform Exercise 19.2 to access the network adapter properties from the Wireless Network Connection Properties page.

EXERCISE 19.2

Viewing Wireless Network Connection Properties

1. Type **Network and Sharing Center** in the Windows 10 integrated search window, and then press Enter.

2. Select the Wireless Network Connection menu item in the View Your Active Networks section.

3. Click the Properties button in the Activity section.

4. Click the Configure button.

5. View the various tabs regarding the network adapter properties.

6. Choose Cancel to return to the Wireless Network Connection Status window.

Configuring Wireless Network Security

Wireless network security is a very large piece of setting up our wireless networks. The focal point for this is the wireless access point or wireless router to which we connect. Whether you are using a small wireless network or a large wireless infrastructure, you should have a plan for secure communication and should configure wireless network security. There are several basic parameters you can configure on your network access devices to increase the security of a wireless network:

- Disable broadcast of the SSID, which is the name of the wireless network. When SSID broadcast is disabled, the wireless network cannot be detected automatically until you manually configure your wireless network card to connect to that SSID.

- Create a MAC address filter list so only specifically allowed wireless devices can connect to the wireless network, or you can require users attempting to connect to supply connection credentials.

- Enable encryption such as Wi-Fi Protected Access (WPA) or WPA2.

Real World Scenario

Wireless Connection Infrastructure or Ad Hoc?

You might not always be connecting to an access point or router; these connections are considered infrastructure mode connections. An infrastructure mode connection is similar to a wired connection of a PC to an outlet. Instead, you might connect in an ad hoc fashion, which could be a computer-to-computer connection to share information with other wireless network devices without another wireless device acting as an intermediary.

Ad hoc connections exist in a wired environment as well, when we connect two PCs' NICs together by using an Ethernet crossover cable. Securing data transfer in an ad hoc wireless setup is just as important as it is in infrastructure mode, because the data is still traversing between devices using radio frequency (RF), and network sniffers today running the wireless adapter promiscuously (in monitor mode) have no problem viewing the data stream. If the data stream is not encrypted, sniffers will have access to it.

For large implementations, there are several vendors supplying wireless access points under the control of a wireless director, which consists of software-based controllers that are responsible for allowing access points on the network, providing user access control, and enforcing encryption policies. For smaller implementations, this control functionality is done manually as the wireless routers or access points are set up.

The security policies put in place are configured on the wireless access device and the wireless client. Windows 10 client components must be set up to match the security settings of the wireless network access devices. During the setup of most wireless access devices provided by the hardware vendor, the administrator will configure the security parameters. Configuring can be done during the setup program and/or through a web browser that can access the wireless access device configuration pages.

Most of our current devices have a built-in web server to allow the HTTP connection from a web browser. Windows 10 also has the ability to configure the wireless access device if the hardware vendor makes it available. If there is no specific component written, you can launch the web browser–based configuration from a convenient location—the Network and Sharing Center.

Whether you have Windows 10 configure the wireless network connection or you perform the setup through the manufacturer's process, you still need to configure your Windows 10 client access.

If you have performed the simplest configuration and there are no security parameters configured (bad idea, by the way), Windows 10 will connect automatically with a quick window showing the wireless network it's connecting to and providing access without much user intervention. Even canceling the screens will produce a successful (nonsecure) connection. This simple configuration process makes connecting a home or small network easy and straightforward for nontechnical users. However, this is not a good solution.

If you have configured wireless network security (a good idea!), then you need to configure the Windows 10 client with the correct settings. Once again, the configuration screens are available from the convenient location known as the Network and Sharing Center.

In Exercise 19.3, you will access the Windows 10 client wireless network properties.

EXERCISE 19.3

Accessing the Windows 10 Wireless Properties

1. Type **Network and Sharing Center** in the Windows 10 integrated search window; press Enter.

2. Choose the Wireless Network Connection item within the View Your Active Networks section of the Network and Sharing Center.

3. Click the Wireless Properties button (shown in Figure 19.14) within the Connection area of the Wireless Network Connection Status window.

FIGURE 19.14 Wireless Properties button

4. The Wireless Network Properties tabbed dialog box opens, displaying the current setup for the wireless network. Click Finish to close the window.

From the Wireless Network Properties tabbed dialog box, you have the ability to set or change the Windows 10 client configuration. The first tab of the dialog box is the Connection tab (Figure 19.15), which displays the following information.

FIGURE 19.15 Wireless Network Properties dialog box's Connection tab

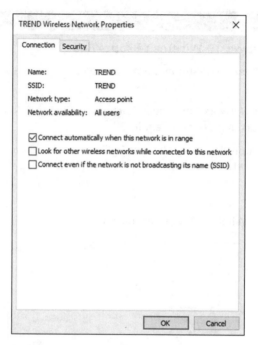

Name   The name assigned to the wireless network.

SSID   The SSID of the wireless connection. This defines a friendly name for the wireless network. This is normally an ASCII string and is usually broadcast by default, allowing a machine or users to select a wireless network with which to connect. Some wireless access devices will allow more than one SSID to be available (broadcast) at the same time, creating more than one wireless network within the same device.

Network Type   Displays the mode the wireless network is operating in. If the wireless network is in infrastructure mode, this parameter will be Access Point. If the wireless network is ad hoc, this will display Computer-To-Computer.

Network Availability   Displays to whom the wireless network is available—All Users or Me Only, for example.

Connect Automatically When This Network Is In Range   This option, when selected, allows automatic connection for this wireless network. Deselecting (clearing the check mark) requires the user to choose this wireless network for connection.

Look For Other Wireless Networks While Connecting To This Network Windows 10 will attempt to look for other wireless network connections even though you are connected to a network at the time. This allows a user to see if there is a better network connection available even after you have connected to your wireless access point.

Connect Even If The Network Is Not Broadcasting Its Name (SSID) If the wireless network you are attempting to connect to is not broadcasting its SSID, you must select this option to allow Windows 10 to automatically connect.

The second tab on the Wireless Network Properties dialog box is Security (Figure 19.16), which allows the configuration of the security parameters as defined in your security policy and configured on your wireless network access devices.

Figure 19.16 shows the Security tab's Security Type drop-down box with the WPA-Personal Security choice selected and Encryption Type with TKIP (Temporal Key Integrity Protocol) selected. You can also see the Network Security Key as hidden text because the Show Characters check box is unchecked.

FIGURE 19.16   Wireless Network Properties Security tab

Troubleshooting Wireless Connectivity

There are a few common issues with wireless networking you can look at if you're having problems connecting to your wireless network. Following are a few problems and solutions:

Ensure that your wireless network card is enabled. Here's one I see regularly: Many newer laptops and tablets have either a switch or a hot-key setting that enables and disables the wireless device. Often, a laptop switch will somehow be turned off, or a user will somehow press the key sequence to shut off the PC's wireless radio. The Physical Layer is always a good place to start looking.

Ensure that your wireless card and the access devices are compatible.   Cards that are compatible with the 802.11b standard can connect to only 802.11b or 802.11b/g access devices configured to accept b. Cards using 802.11a can connect to only 802.11a or 802.11a/b/g access devices configured to accept a. An 802.11n card needs to connect to an 802.11n access device for efficiency, although most will autonegotiate to the best specification available. The specification you're using on the card has to be available and turned on in the wireless access device.

Ensure that the access point signal is available.   I find radio frequency (RF) to be a funny thing. You can't see it, and you assume that it is everywhere. Not a good assumption. The output power of the signal might be fine, but the RF power is absorbed or attenuated as it goes through walls, insulation, or water. You need to make sure there is nothing that might be causing interference of the wireless signal.

Ensure that the security parameters are configured alike.   The SSID, encryption type, encryption algorithm, and passphrase/security key have to be set the same on both the wireless access device and the wireless client. Here's another one I see quite often: In the desire to make the initial setup and the secure setup easier for end users, some hardware vendors have a nice little button that allows the network access device to negotiate a secure set of parameters with the client. In one instance, after the wireless network had been working correctly for a while, a failure showed the parameters to be incompatible, thanks in large part to someone pressing the easy button just before the failure.

Ensure automatic connections if the SSID is not being broadcast.   If you are having trouble connecting to a network that does not broadcast its SSID, select the Connect Even If The Network Is Not Broadcasting check box in the Wireless Network Properties dialog box. I have solved several wireless network connection issues with this fix.

Consider how a wireless router interfaces with hard-wired devices.   Many times when I go into a small or midsize network, I find that the company (or home user) is connected to a multifunction type of device. The wireless routers that are often deployed are really quite technologically sophisticated. They have switch ports for connecting hard-wired devices on the private network as well as an Internet port to connect to the outside world. The wireless portion of the device is like another switch port on the private side, allowing the wireless devices to interact with the hard-wired devices.

When I troubleshoot and eliminate issues, I start with the hard-wired devices and see whether they can communicate to each other and the outside (the other side of your wireless router). Try to communicate between the hard-wired and wireless as well, to eliminate the router components. It's also not the best idea to use the wireless network to configure the wireless devices. Configuring through the wireless interface will ultimately cause you to lose connectivity in the middle of a configuration and may force you to connect with the cable, often leaving the access point unusable until you complete the task you started wirelessly.

Understanding TCP/IP

Another item that we need to configure before we can connect a Windows 10 machine to the domain is the protocol that will allow the Windows 10 machine to communicate with other machines. *Transmission Control Protocol/Internet Protocol (TCP/IP)* is the most commonly used network protocol. It is actually a suite of protocols that have evolved into the industry standard for network, internetwork, and Internet connectivity.

The main protocols providing basic TCP/IP services include Internet Protocol (IP), Transmission Control Protocol (TCP), User Datagram Protocol (UDP), Address Resolution Protocol (ARP), Internet Control Message Protocol (ICMP), and Internet Group Management Protocol (IGMP).

Benefits and Features of TCP/IP

TCP/IP as a protocol suite was accepted as an industry standard in the 1980s and continues to be the primary internetworking protocol today. For a default installation of Windows 10, IPv4 and IPv6 are both installed by default. TCP/IP has the following benefits:

- TCP/IP is the most common protocol and is supported by almost all network operating systems. It is the required protocol for Internet access.

- TCP/IP is dependable and scalable for use in small and large networks.

- Support is provided for connectivity across interconnected networks, independent of the operating systems being used at the upper end of the OSI model or the physical components at the lower end of the OSI model.

- TCP/IP provides standard routing services for moving packets over interconnected network segments. Dividing networks into multiple subnetworks (or subnets) optimizes network traffic and facilitates network management.

- TCP/IP is designed to provide data reliability by providing a connection at the Transport layer and verifying that each data segment is received and passed to the application requiring the data by retransmitting lost information.

- TCP/IP allows for the classification of data in regard to its importance with Quality of Service. This allows important time-sensitive streams of data, such as Voice over IP, to get preferential treatment.

- TCP/IP is designed to be fault tolerant. It is able to dynamically reroute packets if network links become unavailable, assuming alternate paths exist.

- Applications can provide services such as Dynamic Host Configuration Protocol (DHCP) for TCP/IP configuration and Domain Name Service (DNS) for hostname-to-IP address resolution.

- Windows 10 continues to support Automatic Private IP Addressing (APIPA) used by small, local-connection-only networks without a DHCP server, to allow Windows 10 to automatically assign an IP address to itself.

- Support for NetBIOS over TCP/IP (NetBT) is included in Windows 10. NetBIOS is a software specification used for identifying computer resources by name as opposed to IP address. We still use TCP/IP as the network protocol, so we map the NetBIOS name to an IP address.

- The inclusion of Alternate IP Configuration allows users to have a static and a DHCP-assigned IP address mapped to a single network adapter. This feature supports mobile users who roam between different network segments.

- IPv6 incorporates a much larger address space compared to IPv4 and, more importantly, incorporates many of the additional features of TCP/IP into a standardized protocol. This is important because a vendor that claims to support TCP/IP only has to support the 1980s version and may not support additional features such as Internet Protocol security (IPSec). IPv6 as a standard includes these features, allowing a more robust network protocol.

Several of the features of TCP/IP included with Windows 10 are as follows:

- Allows a common structure for network communications across a wide variety of hardware and operating systems and a lot of applications that are specifically written to configure and control it.

- TCP/IP connectivity tools allowing access to a variety of hosts across a TCP/IP network. TCP/IP tools in Windows 10 include clients for HTTP, FTP, TFTP, Telnet, Finger, and so forth. Server components for the tools are available to install as well.

- Inclusion of a Simple Network Management Protocol (SNMP) agent that can be used to monitor performance and resource use of a TCP/IP host, server, or network hardware devices.

- TCP/IP management and diagnostic tools for maintenance and diagnostic support. TCP/IP management and diagnostic commands include `ipconfig`, `arp`, `ping`, `nbtstat`, `netsh`, `route`, `nslookup`, `tracert`, and `pathping`.

- Support for TCP/IP network printing, enabling you to print to networked print devices.

- Logical and physical multihoming, enabling multiple IP addresses on a single computer for single or multiple network adapters. Multiple network adapters installed on a single computer are normally associated with routing for internetwork connectivity.

- Support for internal IP routing, which enables a Windows 10 computer to route packets among multiple network adapters installed in one machine.

- Support for virtual private networks, which enable you to transmit data securely across a public network via encapsulated and encrypted packets.

Basics of IP Addressing and Configuration

Before you can configure TCP/IP, you should have a basic understanding of TCP/IP configuration and addressing. Let's review TCP/IP addressing. To configure a TCP/IP client, you must specify an IP address, subnet mask, and default gateway (if you're going to communicate outside your local network). Depending on your network, you might want to configure a DNS server, a domain name, or maybe even a WINS server.

You can see the Windows 10 IPv4 Properties window in Figure 19.17. I have included it here because I am going to discuss the different configuration items in the following sections. Although normally set up for automatic configuration, these parameters have been manually assigned in this figure for clarity. Later in this section you will go through the configuration steps and learn how to access this window.

FIGURE 19.17   Windows 10 TCP/IP version 4 properties

Understanding IPv4 Address Types

The IPv4 address scheme is one of two used by the Internet today, and TCP/IP is the only network protocol used by the Internet. There are three types of IPv4 addresses: broadcast, multicast, and unicast.

A *broadcast address* is read by all hosts that hear it (the broadcast will not go across a router, so only local devices hear the broadcast). The IPv4 broadcast address is 255.255.255.255; every single bit is a 1.

A *multicast address* is a special address that one or more devices will listen for by joining a multicast group. Only the local devices configured to listen for the address will respond and process the data in the multicast packet. A multicast address will have a value between 224 and 239 in the first octet (the leftmost number in the dotted decimal representation). A multicast example is 224.0.0.5.

A *unicast address* uniquely identifies a computer or device on the network. An IPv4 unicast address is a 32-bit address represented as dotted decimal (an example is 131.107.1.200). Each number in the dotted decimal notation is a decimal representation of 8 bits, and the value of each is between 0 and 255 (255 is the numerically largest value that 8 bits can represent). A portion of the IPv4 unicast address is used to identify the network the device is on (or the network of a destination device), and a portion is used to identify the individual host on the local network or the unique host on a remote network.

IPv4 Address Classes

There are three classes of unicast IP addresses defined. Depending on the class you use, different parts of the address show the default network portion of the address and the host address. Table 19.1 shows the three classes of network addresses and the number of networks and hosts available for each network class.

TABLE 19.1   IPv4 class assignments

Network Class	Address Range of First Octet	Number of Unique Networks Available	Number of Unique Hosts per Network
A	1–126	126	16,777,214
B	128–191	16,384	65,534
C	192–223	2,097,152	254

 As you probably noticed, 127 is missing from the address ranges. 127.0.0.1 is the diagnostic loopback address, and because of that, no commercial TCP/IP range can start with 127.

The number of octets you can use for either the network ID or the host ID depends on which class you use for your network. For example, if I own a Class B address of 131.107.0.0, the first two octets (131.107) would be the network ID and the last two octets would be the host ID. Table 19.2 shows you the different classes and which octets are the network ID (represented by X) and which octets are the host ID (represented by Y). You are allowed to manipulate only the host IDs (Y) for your organization unless you are using a private IP address scheme.

TABLE 19.2   IPv4 network and host octets

Class	Example	Network ID	Host ID
A	17.1.10.10 (X.Y.Y.Y)	17 (X)	1.10.10 (Y.Y.Y)
B	131.107.14.240 (X.X.Y.Y)	131.107 (X.X)	14.240 (Y.Y)
C	192.168.1.10 (X.X.X.Y)	192.168.1 (X.X.X)	10 (Y)

IPv4 Subnet Mask

The *subnet mask* is used to specify which portion of the unicast IPv4 address defines the network value and which portion defines the unique host value. The subnet mask can be shown either as a dotted decimal, as with 255.255.255.0, or as a slash notation (called Classless Inter-Domain Routing, or CIDR), as in /24. The CIDR representation is the number of bits turned on in the subnet mask. For example, 255.255.224.0 is actually 11111111.11111111.11100000.00000000 (1s are on bits and 0s are off), which equals 19 bits turned on, or /19.

The standard for classful network addressing defines subnet masks for each class, as shown in Table 19.3.

TABLE 19.3   IPv4 default class subnet masks

Class	Default Mask	Slash Notation (CIDR)
A	255.0.0.0	/8
B	255.255.0.0	/16
C	255.255.255.0	/24

Another task of the subnet mask is to break down the ranges of your network. For example, 255.255.255.224 allows for six subnets. There should be six TCP/IP ranges that go with the six subnets. Table 19.4 shows the ranges for the different subnet masks.

TABLE 19.4   Subnet mask ranges

Subnet Mask Number	Ranges
255	1
254	2

TABLE 19.4 Subnet mask ranges *(continued)*

Subnet Mask Number	Ranges
252	4
248	8
240	16
224	32
192	64
128	128

What does this chart mean to you? Well, let's say that you have a subnet mask of 255.255.255.224. Because 224 allows for six subnets, the six ranges are in increments of 32. Table 19.5 shows a Class C subnet range for 224. Remember, in any range, you can't use the first number of the range (network ID) or the last number of any range (broadcast).

TABLE 19.5 Class C 224 subnet mask ranges

Subnets	Range	Usable
Range 1	32–63	33–62
Range 2	64–95	65–94
Range 3	96–127	97–126
Range 4	128–159	129–158
Range 5	160–191	161–190
Range 6	192–223	193–222

If this were a Class B subnet mask, the ranges would include a second octet that you would work with. Table 19.6 shows a Class B 224 subnet mask.

TABLE 19.6 Class B 224 subnet mask range

Subnets	Range	Usable
Range 1	32.0–63.255	32.1–63.254
Range 2	64.0–95.255	64.1–95.254

Subnets	Range	Usable
Range 3	96.0–127.255	96.1–127.254
Range 4	128.0–159.255	128.1–159.254
Range 5	160.0–191.255	160.1–191.254
Range 6	192.0–223.255	192.1–223.254

If this were a Class A subnet mask, the ranges would include three octets that you would work with. Table 19.7 shows a Class A 224 subnet mask.

TABLE 19.7   Class A 224 subnet mask range

Subnets	Range	Usable
Range 1	32.0.0–63.255.255	32.0.1–63.255.254
Range 2	64.0.0–95.255.255	64.0.1–95.255.254
Range 3	96.0.0–127.255.255	96.0.1–127.255.254
Range 4	128.0.0–159.255.255	128.0.1–159.255.254
Range 5	160.0.0–191.255.255	160.0.1–191.255.254
Range 6	192.0.0–223.255.255	192.0.1–223.255.254

Using IPv6 Addresses

Through most of this section, we have been referencing TCP/IP as the network protocol. However, you should remember that it is really a suite of protocols running in Layer 3 and Layer 4 of the OSI model. Internet Protocol (IP) is the Layer 3 protocol responsible for assigning devices globally unique addresses (that is, unique in a whole company for private addresses and unique across the whole Internet for public addresses).

When the TCP/IP standard was adopted in the 1980s, it was unimaginable that we would ever need more than 4 billion addresses that are possible with IPv4, but with the dramatic growth of computers in the home and workplace today we do. In the 1990s, programmers realized that a new Layer 3 was going to be needed. This was not an easy task, and integration into the existing infrastructure was going to take a long time. An interim solution known as NAT and PAT emerged. NAT/PAT allowed more than one device to use the same IP address on a private network as long as there was one Internet address available. Cool enough, but this is not the real solution. IPv6 is the solution to the IPv4 address depletion.

As time has progressed from the IPv4 standard acceptance in the 1980s, we have needed new and better functionality. However, the way the standards process works around the world is that you can add functionality, but it may or may not be supported in any vendor's TCP/IPv4 network stack. What happened in IPv6 is not only did the address space increase in size, but the additional functionality that may or may not have been included before has become part of the IPv6 standard.

For example, IPv4 is defined as having a variable-length header, which is cumbersome because we need to read an additional piece of data to see how big the header is. Most of the time, the header stays the same, so why not just fix its length and add an extension to the header if we need to carry more information? IPv6 uses a fixed-length IP header with the capability of carrying more information in an extension to the header, known as an *extension header*.

Microsoft has been including IPv6 in its operating systems since NT 4.0; it just has not been enabled by default. Windows 10 (as did Vista and Windows 7/8) natively supports both IPv4 and IPv6. The main differences you will notice between IPv4 and IPv6 are the format and size of the IP address. IPv6 addresses are 128 bits, typically written as eight groups of four hexadecimal characters. IPv4 addresses, as you saw earlier, are 32 bits—four decimal representations of eight bits. Each of the eight groups of characters in an IPv6 address is separated by a colon; for example, 2001:4860:0000:0000:0012:10FF:FE CD:00EF.

Leading zeros can be omitted, so we can write our example address as 2001:4860:0:0:12:10FF:FECD:EF. Additionally, a double colon can be used to compress a set of consecutive zeros, so we could write our example address as 2001:4860::12:10FF:FECD:EF. The IPv6 address is 128 bits; when you see a double colon, it's a variable that says to fill enough zeros within the colons to make the address 128 bits. You can have only one set of double colons; two variables in one address won't work.

Will IPv6 take over the global address space soon? Even with IPv4's lack of address space, we are going to continue to use it for many years. The integration of IPv6 into the infrastructure is going to happen as a joint venture with IPv4 and IPv6 running at the same time in the devices and on some networks.

There are many mechanisms for enabling IPv6 communications over an IPv4 network, including the following:

- Dual stack—A computer or device running both the IPv4 and IPv6 protocol stacks at the same time

- ISATAP—Intra-Site Automatic Tunnel Addressing Protocol

- 6to4—An encapsulation technique for putting IPv6 addresses inside IPv4 addresses

- Teredo tunneling—Another encapsulation technique for putting IPv6 traffic inside an IPv4 packet

Some IPv6-to-IPv4 dynamic translation techniques require that a computer's IPv4 address be used as the last 32 bits of the IPv6 address. When these translation techniques are used, it is common to write the last 32 bits as you would typically write an IPv4 address, such as 2001:4850::F8:192.168.122.26.

There are two ways to receive a TCP/IP address (for either IPv4 or IPv6): You can manually assign a TCP/IP address to the Windows 10 machine, or the Windows 10 machine can use DHCP.

There are several elements of the IPv4 protocol that could use some enhancements. Other elements have been added to IPv4 as extras to provide more functionality. IPv6 is designed to incorporate these enhancement/changes directly into the protocol specification.

The new concepts and new implementation of old concepts in IPv6 include the following:

- Larger address space (128-bit vs. 32-bit).

- Autoconfiguration of Internet-accessible addresses with or without DHCP (without DHCP it's called stateless autoconfiguration).

- More efficient IP header (fewer fields and no checksum).

- Fixed-length IP header (IPv4 header is variable length) with extension headers beyond the standard fixed length to provide enhancements.

- Built-in IP mobility and security (although available in IPv4, the IPv6 implementation is much better implementation).

- Built-in transition schemes to allow integration of the IPv4 and IPv6 spaces.

- ARP broadcast messages are replaced with multicast request.

128-bit Address Space   The new 128-bit address space will provide unique addresses for the foreseeable future. We would like to say we will never use up all the addresses, but history may prove us wrong. The number of unique addresses in the IPv6 space is 2^{128} or 3.4×10^{38} addresses. How big is that number? Enough for toasters and refrigerators (and maybe even cars) to all have their own addresses? Why yes, we believe it is.

For a point of reference, the nearest black hole to Earth is 1,600 light years away. If you were to stack 4mm BB pellets from here to the nearest black hole and back, you would need 7.6×1021 BBs. This means you could uniquely address each BB from Earth to the black hole and back and still have quite a few addresses left over.

Or how about this: the IPv6 address space is big enough to provide well over 1 million addresses per square inch of the surface area of the earth (oceans included). No more running out of addresses for the Internet!

Stateful vs. Stateless Autoconfiguration   Autoconfiguration is another added/improved feature of IPv6. When you are choosing to use DHCP in IPv6, you can choose to set your systems up for Stateful or Stateless configuration. Stateful is what we currently do today with IPv4. Stateful means that DHCP is going to give our IPv6 clients all of their TCP/IP data (IP address, default gateway, and all DHCP options).

What if a Windows 10 client could ask the network itself what network it's on and, based on that information, create its own IP address and default gateway. Well, that is what Stateless configuration does. Stateless configuration means that the client's address is based on the router's advertisement messages. What this means is that the client creates their own

IP address and default gateway based on the router's advertisement message and their MAC address. They can still get all of the other DHCP options, but they will not get an IP address and default gateway from DHCP.

Improved IPv6 Header   The IPv6 header is more efficient than the IPv4 header because it is fixed length (with extensions possible) and has only a few fields. The IPv6 header consists of a total of 40 bytes, which is broken down as follows:

> 32 bytes for source and destination IPv6 addresses
>
> 8 bytes for version field, traffic class field, flow label field, payload length field, next header field, and hop limit field

We don't waste time with a checksum validation anymore, and we don't have to include the length of the IP header since it's fixed in IPv6; the IP header is variable length in IPv4, so the length must be included as a field.

IPv6 Mobility   IPv6 is only a replacement of the OSI layer 3 component; we are going to continue to use the TCP (and UDP) components as they currently exist; however, a TCP issue is addressed by IPv6. TCP is connection oriented, meaning we establish an end-to-end communication path with sequencing and acknowledgments before we ever send any data, and then we have to acknowledge all pieces of data sent. This is done through a combination of an IP address, port number, and port type (socket).

If the source IP address changes, the TCP connection may be disrupted. But then, how often does this happen? More and more often, because more people are walking around with a wireless laptop or a wireless Voice Over IP (VoIP) telephone. IPv6 mobility adds the capability by establishing a TCP connection with a home address, and when changing networks, it continues to communicate with the original endpoint from a care-of address as it changes LANs, which sends all traffic back through the home address. The handing off of network addresses does not disrupt the TCP connection state (the original TCP port number and address stay intact).

Improved Security   IPv6 has security built in. Internet Protocol security (IPsec) is a component we use today to authenticate and encrypt secure tunnels from a source to a destination. This can be from the client to the server or between gateways. IPv4 lets us do this by enhancing IP header functionality (basically adding a second IP header while encrypting everything behind it). In IPv6, we add this as standard functionality by using extension headers. Extension headers are inserted into the packet only if they are needed. Each header has a "next header" field, which identifies the next piece of information. The extension headers currently identified for IPv6 are Hop-By-Hop Options, Routing, Fragment, Destination Options, Authentication, and Encrypted Security Payload. The authentication header and Encapsulating Security Payload header are the IPsec-specific control headers.

IPv4-to-IPv6 Transmission   There are several mechanisms in place in IPv6 to make the IPv4 to IPv6 transition easy:

> A simple dual-stack implementation where both IPv4 and IPv6 are installed and used is certainly an option. In most situations (so far) this doesn't work so well, because most of

us aren't connected to an IPv6 network and our Internet connection is not IPv6 even if we're using IPv6 internally. So Microsoft includes other mechanisms that can be used in several different circumstances.

Intra-Site Automatic Tunnel Addressing Protocol (ISATAP) is an automatic tunneling mechanism used to connect an IPv6 network to an IPv4 address space that does not use NAT. ISATAP treats the IPv4 space as one big logical link connection space.

6to4 is a mechanism used to transition to IPv4. This method, like ISATAP, treats the IPv4 address space as a Logical Link Layer with each IPv6 space in transition using a 6to4 router to create endpoints using the IPv4 space as a point-to-point connection (kind of like a WAN, eh?). 6to4 implementations still do not work well through a NAT, although a 6to4 implementation using an Application Layer Gateway (ALG) is certainly doable.

Teredo is a mechanism that allows users behind a NAT to access the IPv6 space by tunneling IPv6 packets in UDP.

Pseduointerfaces are used in these mechanisms to create a usable interface for the operating system. Another interesting feature of IPv6 is that addresses are assigned to interfaces (or pseudointerfaces), not simply to the end node. Your Windows Server 2008 will have several unique IPv6 addresses assigned.

New Broadcast Methods   IPv6 has moved away from using broadcasting. The three types of packets used in IPv6 are unicast, multicast, and anycast. IPv6 clients then must use one of these types to get the MAC address of the next Ethernet hop (default gateway). IPv6 makes use of multicasting for this along with new functionality of neighbor discovery. Not only does ARP utilize new functionality, but ICMP (also a Layer 3 protocol) is redone and known as ICMP6. ICMP6 is used for messaging (packet too large, time exceeded, and so on) as it was in IPv4, but it also is used for the messaging of IPv6 mobility. ICMP6 echo request and ICMP6 echo reply are still used for ping.

Additionally, there are several concepts to consider in IPv6 addressing. The format of the address has changed since IPv4 and we must get used to seeing/using it. There are three types of addresses we will use as well as predefined values used within the address space. You need to get used to seeing these addresses and being able to identify their uses.

IPv6 Address Format

For the design of IPv4 addresses, remember that we present addresses as octets or the decimal (base 10) representation of 8 bits. Four octets add up to the 32 bits required. IPv6 expands the address space to 128 bits, and the representation is for the most part shown in *hexadecimal* (a notation used to represent 8 bits using the values 0–9 and A–F). The following is an example of a full IPv6 address: 2001:0DB8:0000:0000:1234:0000:A9FE:133E.

You can tell the implementation of DNS will make life a lot easier for even those of us who like to ping the address in lieu of the name. Fortunately, DNS already has the ability to handle IPv6 address with the use of an AAAA record. (*A* is short for *alias*.) An A record in IPv4's addressing space is 32 bits, so an AAAA record—4 *A*s—is 128 bits. The Windows

Server 2012 R2 DNS server handles the AAAA and the reverse pointer (PTR) records for IPv6.

IPv6 Address Shortcuts

Here are some shortcuts you can use for writing an IPv6 address:

- :0: stands for :0000:
- You can leave out preceding 0s in any 16-bit word.

  For example, :DB8: and :0DB8: are equivalent.
- :: is a variable standing for enough zeros to round out the address to 128 bits.

  :: can be used only once in an address.

You can use these shortcuts to represent the example address 2001:0DB8:0000:0000:1234:0000:A9FE:133E as shown here:

- Compress :0000: into :0:

  2001:0DB8:0000:0000:1234:0:A9FE:133E
- Eliminate preceding zeros:

  2001:DB8:0000:0000:1234:0:A9FE:133E
- Use the special variable shortcut for multiple zeros:

  2001:DB8::1234:0:A9FE:133E

You can also use *prefix notation* or slash notation when discussing IPv6 networks. The network of the example address can be represented as 2001:DB8:0000:0000:0000:0000:0000:0000. This can also be expressed as 2001:DB8:: /32. The /32 indicates 32 bits of network, and 2001:DB8: is 32 bits of network.

IPv6 Address Assignment

So do we subnet IPv6? The answer depends on your definition of subnetting. If you are given 32 bits of network from your ISP, you have 96 bits to work with. If you use some of the 96 bits to route within your network infrastructure, then you are subnetting. In this context you do subnet IPv6. However, given the huge number of bits you have available, we can say with confidence that VLSM will no longer need to be implemented. For example, Microsoft has a network space of 2001:4898:: /32. That gives the administrators a space of 96 bits ($296 = 79,228,162,514,264,337,593,543,950,336$ unique addresses using all 96 bits) to work with.

We can let Windows Server 2012 R2 dynamically or automatically assign its IPv6 address, or we can still assign it manually. With dynamic/automatic assignment, the IPv6 address is assigned either by a DHCPv6 server or by the Windows Server 2012 R2 machine itself. If no DHCPv6 server is configured, the Windows Server 2012 R2 can query the local LAN segment to find a router with a configured IPv6 interface. If so, the server will assign itself an address on the same IPv6 network as the router interface and set its default gateway to the router interface's IPv6 address.

To see your configured IP addresses (IPv4 and IPv6), you can still use the `ipconfig` command. We have configured a static IPv4 and IPv6 address on our server. The IPv6 address is the same as used in the previous example IPv6 address.

IPv6 Address Types

There are three types of addresses in IPv6: anycast, unicast, and multicast.

> You will notice that there is an absence of the broadcast type that is included in IPv4. IPv6 does not use broadcasts; they're replaced with multicasts.

Anycast Addresses   Anycast addresses are not really new. The concept of anycast existed in IPv4 but was not widely used. An anycast address is an IPv6 address assigned to multiple devices (usually different devices). When an anycast packet is sent, it is delivered to one of the devices, usually the closest one.

Unicast Addresses   A unicast packet uniquely identifies an interface of an IPv6 device. The interface can be a virtual or *pseudointerface* or a real (physical) interface.

 Real World Scenario

Unicast vs. Anycast

Unicast and anycast addresses look the same and may be indistinguishable from each other; it only depends on how many devices have the same address. If only one device has a globally unique IPv6 address, it's a unicast address; if more than one device has the same address, it's an anycast address. Both unicast and anycast are considered one-to-one communication, although you could say anycast is one-to-"one of many."

There are several types of unicast addresses, as described here:

Global Unicast Address   As of this writing, the *global unicast address* space is defined as 2000:: /3. 2001::/32 are the IPv6 addresses being issued to business entities. I mentioned before Microsoft has been allocated 2001:4898:: /32. You'll find most example addresses listed as 2001:DB8:: /32; this space has been reserved for documentation. A DHCPv6 server would be set up with scopes (ranges of addresses to be assigned) within this address space. There are some special addresses and address formats you will see in use as well. Do you remember the loopback address in IPv4—127.0.0.1? In IPv6 the loopback address is ::1 (or 0:0:0:0:0:0:0:0001). You may also see an address with dotted decimal used. A dual-stack Windows Server 2012 R2 may also show you FE80::5EFE:192.168.1.200. This address form is used in an integration/migration model of IPv6 (or if you just can't leave the dotted-decimal era).

Link-Local Address   *Link-local addresses* are defined as FE80:: /10. If you look at the ipconfig command, you will see the link-local IPv6 address as FE80::a425:ab9d:7da4:ccba. The last 8 bytes (64 bits) are random to ensure a high probability of randomness for the link-local address.

The link-local address is to be used on a single link (network segment) and should never be routed.

There is another form of the link-local IPv6 address called the Extended User Interface 64-bit (EUI-64) format. This is derived by using the MAC address of the physical interface and inserting an FFFE between the third and fourth bytes of the MAC. The first byte is also made 02, which sets the universal/local or U/L bit to 1 as defined in IEEE 802 frame specification. Again, looking at ipconfig, the EUI-64 address would take the physical (MAC) address 00-03-FF-11-02-CD and make the link-local IPv6 address FE80::0203:FFFF:FE11:02CD. I've left the preceding zeros in the link-local IPv6 address to make it easier for you to pick out the MAC address with the FFFE inserted.

AnonymousAddress   Microsoft Server 2012 R2 uses the random address by default instead of EUI-64. The random value is called the AnonymousAddress in Microsoft Server 2012 R2. It can be modified to allow the use of EUI-64.

Unique Local Address   The unique local address can be FC00 or FD00 and is used like the private address space of IPv4. Unique local addresses as describe in RFC 4193. They are not expected to be routable on the global Internet. They are routable inside a more limited area, such as a site. They may also be routed between a limited set of sites.

Multicast Address   Multicast addresses are one-to-many communication packets. Multicast packets are identifiable by their first byte (most significant byte, leftmost byte, leftmost 2 nibbles, leftmost 8 bits, etc.). A multicast address is defined as FF00::/8.

In the second byte shown (the 00 of FF00), the second 0 is what's called the scope. Interface local is 01; link-local is 02. FF01:: is an interface local multicast.

There are several well-known (already defined) multicast addresses. For example, if you want to send a packet to all nodes in the local link scope, you send the packet to FF02::1 (also shown as FF02:0:0:0:0:0:0:1). The all-routers multicast address is FF02::2.

We also use multicasting to get the logical link Layer address (MAC address) of a device we are trying to communicate with. Instead of using the ARP mechanism of IPv4, IPv6 uses the ICMPv6 neighbor solicitation (NS) and neighbor advertisement (NA) messages. The NS and NA ICMPv6 messages are all part of the new Neighbor Discovery Protocol (NDP). This new ICMPv6 functionality also includes router solicitation and router advertisements as well as redirect messages (similar to the IPv4 redirect functionality).

Table 19.8 outlines the IPv6 address space known prefixes and some well-known addresses.

TABLE 19.8   IPv6 address space known prefixes and addresses

Address Prefix	Scope of Use
2000:: /3	Global unicast space prefix
FE80:: /10	Local link address prefix
FC00:: /7	Unique local unicast prefix
FF00:: /8	Multicast prefix
2001:DB8:: /32	Global unicast prefix used for documentation
::1	Reserved local loopback address
2001:0000: /32	Teredo prefix*
2002:: /16	6to4 prefix*

IPv6 Integration/Migration

It's time to get into the mindset of integrating IPv6 into your existing infrastructure with the longer goal of migrating over to IPv6. This is not going to be an "OK, Friday the Internet is changing over" rollout. We are going to bring about the change as a controlled implementation. It could easily be three to five years before a solid migration occurs and probably longer. The migration is just below getting the world migrated to the metric system on the overall timeline. The process of integration/migration is made up of several mechanisms:

- Dual stack—Simply running both IPv4 and IPv6 on the same network, utilizing the IPv4 address space for devices only using IPv4 addresses and utilizing the IPv6 address space for devices using IPv6 addresses.

- Tunneling—Using an encapsulation scheme for transporting one address space inside another.

- Address translation—Using a higher-level application to transparently change one address type (IPv4 or IPv6) to the other so end devices are unaware one address space is talking to another.

IPv6 Dual Stack

The default implementation in Windows 10 is an enabled IPv6 configured along with IPv4; this is dual stack. The implementation can be dual IP Layer or dual TCP/IP stack. Windows 10 uses the dual IP Layer implementation. When an application queries a DNS server to resolve a hostname to an IP address, the DNS server may respond with an IPv4 address or an IPv6 address. If the DNS server responds with both, Windows 10 will prefer the IPv6 addresses. Windows 10 can use both IPv4 and IPv6 addresses as necessary for network communication. When looking at the output of the `ipconfig` command, you will see both address spaces displayed.

IPv6 Tunneling

Windows Server 2012 R2 includes several tunneling mechanisms for tunneling IPv6 through the IPv4 address space. They include the following:

- ISATAP—Intra-Site Automatic Tunnel Addressing Protocol used for unicast IPv6 communication across an IPv4 infrastructure. ISATAP is enabled by default in Windows Server 2008.

- 6to4—Used for unicast IPv6 communication across an IPv4 infrastructure.

- Teredo—Used for unicast IPv6 communication with an IPv4 NAT implementation across an IPv4 infrastructure.

With multiple tunneling protocols available and enabled by default, you might ask what the difference is and why one is used over the others. They all allow us to tunnel IPv6 packets through the IPv4 address space (a really cool thing if you're trying to integrate/migrate).

ISATAP   ISATAP is the automatic tunnel addressing protocol providing IPv6 addresses based on the IPv4 address of the end interface (node). The IPv6 address is automatically configured on the local device, and the dual-stack machine can use either its IPv4 or IPv6 address to communicate on the local network (within the local network infrastructure). ISATAP can use the neighbor discovery mechanism to determine the router ID and network prefix where the device is located, thus making intrasite communication possible even in a routed infrastructure.

The format of an ISATAP address is [64 bits of prefix] [32 bits indicating ISATAP] [32 bits IPv4 Address].

The center 32 bits indicating ISATAP are actually 0000:5EFE (when using private IPv4 addresses). The ISATAP address of our example Windows Server 2012 R2 machine using the link-local IPv6 address is FE80::5EFE:192.168.1.200. Each node participating in the ISATAP infrastructure must support ISATAP. If you're routing through an IPv4 cloud, a border router (a router transitioning from an IPv6 to IPv4 space) must support ISATAP. Windows Server 2012 R2 can be configured as a border router and will forward ISATAP packets. ISATAP is experimental and is defined in RFC 4214.

6to4   6to4 specifies a procedure for IPv6 networks to communicate with each other through an IPv4 space without having the IPv6 nodes having to know what's going on.

The IPv6 nodes do not need to be dual stacked to make this happen. The border router is the device responsible for knowing about the IPv6-to-IPv4 transition. The IPv6 packets are encapsulated at the border router and decapsulated at the other end or on the way back. There is an assigned prefix for the 6to4 implementation, 2002:: /16. 6to4 is defined in RFC 3056.

Teredo   Teredo (named after a genus of shipworm that drills holes in the wood of ships) is a protocol designed to allow IPv6 addresses to be available to hosts through one or more layers of NAT. Teredo uses a process of tunneling packets through the IPv4 space using UDP. The Teredo service encapsulates the IPv6 data within a UDP segment (packet) and uses an IPv4 address to get through the IPv4 cloud. Having a Layer 4 (Transport Layer) available to use as a translation functionality is what gives us the ability to be behind a NAT. Teredo provides host-to-host communication and dynamic addressing for IPv6 nodes (dual stack), allowing the nodes to have access to resources in an IPv6 network and the IPv6 devices to have access to the IPv6 devices that have connectivity only to the IPv4 space (just as home users who have an IPv6-enabled operating system connecting to IPv6 resources and their home ISP have only IPv4 capabilities). Teredo is defined in RFC 4380.

In Windows 10, an IPv4 Teredo server is identified and configured (using the `netsh` command interface). The Teredo server provides connectivity resources (address) to the Teredo client (the node that has access to the IPv4 Internet and needs access to an IPv6 network/ Internet. A Teredo relay is a component used by the IPv6 router to receive traffic destined for Teredo clients and forward the traffic appropriately. The defined prefix for Teredo address is 2001:: /32 (does it look better like this? – 2001:0000:: /32). Teredo does add overhead like all the implementations discussed. It is generally accepted that we should use the simplest model available. However, in the process of integration/migration for most of us behind a NAT, Teredo will be the process to choose.

From Windows 10, use the `ipconfig /all` command to view the default configurations including IPv4 and IPv6. You may notice a notation we didn't discuss: the percent sign at the end of the IPv6 address. The number after the percent sign is the virtual interface identifier used by Windows 10.

Information Commands Useful with IPv6

There are numerous commands you can use to view, verify, and configure the network parameters of Windows Server 2012 R2. You can use the `netsh` command set and the `route` command set, as well as the standard `ping` and `tracert` functions.

Use the `netsh` command interface to examine and configure IPv6 functionality (as well as the provided dialog boxes if you like). The `netsh` command issued from the command interpreter changes into a network shell (netsh) where you can configure and view both IPv4 and IPv6 components.

Don't forget to use the ever-popular `route print` command to see the Windows 10 routing tables (IPv4 and IPv6). The other diagnostic commands are still available for IPv4 as well as IPv6. In previous versions of Microsoft operating systems, `ping` was the IPv4 command and `ping6` was the IPv6 command.

This has changed for Windows 10; `ping` works for both IPv4 and IPv6 to test Layer 3 connectivity to remote devices. The IPv4 `tracert` command was `tracert6` for IPv6. The command is now `tracert` for both IPv4 and IPv6 and will show you every Layer 3 (IP) hop from source to destination (assuming all the administrators from here to there want you to see the hops and are not blocking ICMP and also assuming there are not IP tunnels your packets are traversing, you won't see the router hops in the tunnel either).

If you are using DHCP and you are not connecting to other machines properly, you can type ipconfig /all at a command prompt to see what your TCP/IP address is. If your TCP/IP address starts with 169.254.*x.x*, you are not connecting to the DHCP server. Instead, your Windows 10 machine is using APIPA.

Understanding APIPA

Automatic Private IP Addressing (APIPA) is used to automatically assign private IP addresses for home or small business networks that contain a single subnet, have no DHCP server, and are not using static IP addressing. If APIPA is being used, clients will be able to communicate only with other clients on the same subnet that are also using APIPA. The benefit of using APIPA in small networks is that it is less tedious and has less chance of configuration errors than statically assigning IP addresses and configuration.

APIPA is used with Windows 10 under the following conditions:

- When the client is configured as a DHCP client, but no DHCP server is available to service the DHCP request.

- When the client originally obtained a DHCP lease from a DHCP server, but when the client tried to renew the DHCP lease, the DHCP server was unavailable and the lease period expired.

APIPA uses a Class B network address space that has been reserved for its use. The address space is the 169.254.0.0 network, where the range of 169.254.0.1–169.254.255.254 is available for the host to assign to itself. APIPA uses the following process:

1. The Windows 10 client attempts to use a DHCP server for its configuration, but no DHCP servers respond.

2. The Windows 10 client selects a random address from the 169.254.0.1–169.254.255.254 range of addresses and will use a subnet mask of 255.255.0.0.

3. The client uses a duplicate address-detection method to verify that the address it selected is not already in use on the network.

4. If the address is already in use, the client repeats steps 1 and 2. If the address is not already in use, the client configures its network interface with the address it randomly selected. Given the number of the address the APIPA client can select from (65,534 addresses), the odds of selecting a duplicate are very slim.

5. The Windows 10 network client continues to search for a DHCP server every five minutes. If a DHCP server replies to the request, the APIPA configuration is dropped, and the client receives new IP configuration settings from the DHCP server.

You can determine whether your network interface has been configured using APIPA by looking at your IP address from the command prompt by using the ipconfig /all command.

Testing Your IP Configuration

After you have installed and configured the TCP/IP settings, you can test the IP configuration by using the ipconfig, ping, and nbtstat commands. These commands are also useful in troubleshooting IP configuration errors. You can also graphically view connection details through the Local Area Connection Status section of the Network and Sharing Center.

Using the ipconfig Command

The `ipconfig` command displays your IP configuration. Table 19.9 lists the command switches that you can use with the `ipconfig` command.

TABLE 19.9   `ipconfig` switches

Switch	Description
/?	Shows all of the help options for `ipconfig`
/all	Shows verbose information about your IP configuration, including your computer's physical address, the DNS server you are using, and whether you are using DHCP
/allcompartments	Shows IP information for all compartments
/release	Releases an IPv4 address that has been assigned through DHCP
/release6	Releases an IPv6 address that has been assigned through DHCP
/renew	Renews an IPv4 address through DHCP
/renew6	Renews an IPv6 address through DHCP
/flushdns	Purges the DNS Resolver cache
/registerdns	Refreshes DHCP leases and re-registers DNS names
/displaydns	Displays the contents of the DNS Resolver Cache
/showclassid	Lists the DHCP class IDs allowed by the computer
/setclassID	Allows you to modify the DHCP class ID

Using Other TCP/IP Commands

You can use numerous commands to view, verify, and configure the network parameters of Windows 10. Specifically, you can use the `netsh` command set and the `route` command set, as well as the standard `ping` and `tracert` functions.

Use the `netsh` command interface to examine and configure IPv6 functionality (as well as the provided dialog boxes if you want). The `netsh` command issued from the command interpreter changes into a network shell (netsh) where you can configure and view both IPv4 and IPv6 components.

Don't forget to use the ever-popular route print command to see the Windows 10 routing tables (IPv4 and IPv6). In previous versions of Microsoft operating systems, ping was the IPv4 command, and ping6 was the IPv6 command. This has changed for Windows 10; ping works for both IPv4 and IPv6 to test Layer 3 connectivity to remote devices. The IPv4 tracert command was tracert6 for IPv6. As already mentioned, the command is now tracert for both IPv4 and IPv6 and will show you every Layer 3 (IP) hop from source to destination (assuming all the administrators from here to there want you to see the hops and are not blocking ICMP and also assuming there are no IP tunnels your packets are traversing, or you won't see the router hops in the tunnel either).

TCP/IP Troubleshooting

If you are having trouble connecting to network resources, consider the following:

- If you can access resources on your local subnet but not on a remote subnet, check the default gateway settings on your computer. Pinging a remote host and receiving a Destination Unreachable message is also related to default gateway misconfiguration.

- If you can access some but not all resources on your local subnet or remote subnet, you should check your subnet mask settings, the wiring to those resources, or the devices between your computer and those resources.

- Use the ipconfig utility to ensure that you are not configured with an APIPA address. If you are, determine why you are not receiving IP settings from your DHCP server.

- If you can access a resource (for example, by pinging a computer) by IP address but not by name, check the DNS settings on your computer.

After we have TCP/IP set up on our Windows 10 machine, we can connect the Windows 10 machine to the network. In the next section, we will look at how to do that.

Configuring Windows 10 on a Network

In a corporate environment, the client machines (Windows XP, Windows Vista, Windows 7/8/8.1, and Windows 10) will be connected to the domain environment either from the Windows 10 operating system domain or from Active Directory. Having the Windows 10 machine on the network offers many benefits to administration:

- You can deploy GPOs from one location instead of LGPOs on each machine.

- Users can store their data on a server. This way, the nightly backups capture user information. Most Windows 10 machines will *not* be backed up separately.

- You can manage users and groups from one central location (Active Directory) instead of on each Windows 10 machine.

- You can manage resource security on servers instead of on each Windows 10 machine.

Another type of network on which you may have to set up Windows 10 is a HomeGroup environment. HomeGroups allow you to easily connect two or more PCs running Windows 10 on your home network. Windows 10 searches for your home network, and if one is found, it connects after you enter the HomeGroup password. If a home network is not found, a networking wizard automatically creates a password for the HomeGroup. This password allows you to connect all of your other computers to the same network, and it can be changed any time after the installation of Windows 10.

Adding Windows 10 to the Domain

It does not matter which way you choose to connect the machine to the domain. I usually connect the Windows 10 machine through the Windows operating system, but either way does the same task.

Having the Windows 10 machine on the domain offers many benefits to administration:

- You can deploy GPOs from one location instead of LGPOs on each machine.

- Users can back up their data to a server. This way, the nightly backups cover user information. Most Windows 10 machines will *not* be backed up separately.

- You can manage users and groups from one central location (Active Directory) instead of on each Windows 10 machine.

- You can manage security to resources on servers instead of resources on each Windows 10 machine.

Complete Exercise 19.6 to connect a Windows 10 machine to a Windows Server 2012 R2 domain via the Windows 10 OS. To complete this exercise, you will need to have a Windows Server 2012 R2 domain that the Window 10 machine can connect to.

EXERCISE 19.6

Connecting a Windows 10 Machine to the Domain

1. On the Windows 10 machine, right-click Start and System.

2. Under the Computer Name, Domain, And Workgroup section, click the Change Settings link.

3. Click the Change button next to the To Rename This Computer Or Change Its Domain Or Workgroup section.

4. In the Member Of section, click the Domain radio button (shown in Figure 19.18) and type in the name of your Windows Server 2012 R2 domain.

5. A Credentials box appears, asking for a username and password. Enter an account with administrative credentials to join the machine to the domain. Click OK.

6. A dialog box stating that you are part of the domain appears. Click OK and reboot the machine.

7. From the Windows 10 machine, log on to the domain with your username and password.

EXERCISE 19.6 *(continued)*

FIGURE 19.18 Computer Name/Domain Changes screen

You also have the ability to create the computer account in the Active Directory Users and Computers MMC snap-in. Complete Exercise 19.7 to add the Windows 10 machine to the domain from the Active Directory snap-in. To complete this exercise, you will need a Windows Server 2012 R2 domain that you can add the Windows 10 machine to.

EXERCISE 19.7

Adding Windows 10 to the Domain via Active Directory

1. From the Windows Server 2012 R2 machine, click Start ➢ Administrative Tools ➢ Active Directory Users And Computers.

2. Expand the domain and right-click the Computers OU. Choose New ➢ Computer.

3. In the Computer Name field, type in the name of the Windows 10 computer. Click OK.

4. Double-click the new Windows 10 computer in the right-hand window to open the properties.

5. Take a look at the different tabs, and then click the Cancel button.

Joining and Sharing HomeGroups in Windows 10

HomeGroup is a function of Windows 10 that simplifies the sharing of music, pictures, and documents within your small office or home network of Windows 10 PCs. HomeGroup allows you to share USB-connected printers too. If you have a printer installed on a Windows 10 computer and it's shared by HomeGroup, it is automatically installed onto the other HomeGroup-enabled Windows 10 PCs. Domain-joined computers cannot host a

HomeGroup, but they can be a participant of a HomeGroup. All editions of Windows 10 can use HomeGroups.

The first step in the process of using HomeGroup for sharing is to create a new HomeGroup or join an existing one. If the Windows 10 network-discovery feature does not find a HomeGroup, you will be asked to create a HomeGroup. In the Control Panel, select the HomeGroup link and then click the Create A HomeGroup button (Figure 19.19).

FIGURE 19.19   Create a HomeGroup.

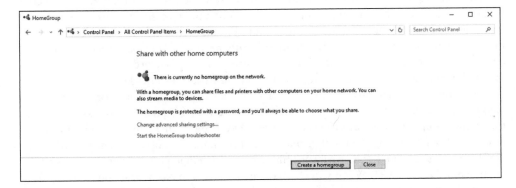

You will then walk through the Create a HomeGroup wizard. During the wizard, you will be asked what folders you want to share with other members of the HomeGroup (shown in Figure 19.20).

FIGURE 19.20   HomeGroup folders

After you have chosen which folders you want to share, you will be given a password that will allow other Windows clients to join the HomeGroup. You can change this password after it has been set by going back into the HomeGroup link (in Control Panel) and choose the Change The Password link.

Now once the HomeGroup is created, other Windows 10 clients can be added. When other Windows 10 clients join the HomeGroup, they will be able to choose the resources that they want to make available to the other members of the HomeGroup. The next step is to enter the HomeGroup password.

Windows 10, by default, will recognize a HomeGroup on the network you're connected to. However, the other Windows 10 machines will not have access to the resources unless they join the HomeGroup. This is very important because allowing just any Windows 10 machine connecting to the network to automatically have shared resource access would be a huge security hole. So to protect Windows 10 user data, a password must be entered to join a HomeGroup before you can access other HomeGroup resources.

After other machines have joined, each machine has the ability to view or change the password. Remember that Windows 10 will initially create a random secure password for the HomeGroup, and you need to visit the View And Print Your HomeGroup Password link to find out what it is. You will probably want to change it. Again, to change the password, choose the Change The Password link from the Change HomeGroup Settings page, as shown in Figure 19.21. When you change the HomeGroup password, you need to go to each of the other Windows 10 machines that are members of the HomeGroup and change the password there if you still want the others to share resources.

FIGURE 19.21   Change HomeGroup Settings screen

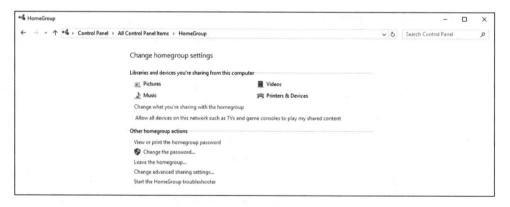

After the HomeGroup is set up, you can see the other members' resources from the HomeGroup option of Windows Explorer or even the Start menu if you customize the Start menu and have added HomeGroup to the displayed options.

HomeGroups are a great option for users who want to share resources in the Windows 10 environment. But what if you still have non–Windows 10 machines? The legacy function of simply sharing resources and setting permissions still works for Windows 10 and will allow older operating systems to have access to resources shared on Windows 10 machines, as well as allow users running Windows 10 to have access to the shared resources on Vista and XP.

Understanding Network Printing

One advantage to setting up any type of network is the ability to use network printers. Network printers are normal printers that are connected to the internal network that users can access.

Think back a few years and remember the days that when you wanted to have a printer, you had to have a print device physically connected to your machine. Now you can just place the print device in a centrally located area, plug it into the network, connect your users to the printer, and start printing.

When it comes to network printing, Windows 10 has made some improvements to help you find and use network printers. One of the improvements is called location-aware printing. Location-aware printing allows a network user to choose different default printers for different networks. For example, you can have a default printer set up at work and a different default printer set up at home. This is very useful for those individuals using laptop computers.

Location-aware printing is available for Windows 10 Professional, Enterprise, and Ultimate editions. Location-aware printing matches the default printer with a network name. This allows you to have different default printers for different networks. Windows 10 can retrieve the network name from multiple sources, such as the name of the domain the Windows 10 machine is connected to or the station identification of the wireless router at your home.

To configure location-aware printing, go into the Devices and Printers Control Panel application. Then select the installed printer and click the Manage Default Printers command in the menu bar on top. Once the Manage Default Printers dialog box opens, you can select a different default printer for each network you visit.

Location-aware printing was removed in the November 2015 update. But it is still listed as a Microsoft test objective, so we added it to be safe.

Configuring Windows Firewall

Windows Firewall, which is included with Windows 10, helps prevent unauthorized users or malicious software from accessing your computer. Windows Firewall does not allow unsolicited traffic, which is traffic that was not sent in response to a request, to pass through the firewall.

Understanding the Windows Firewall Basics

You configure Windows Firewall by right-clicking Start ➢ Control Panel ➢ Large Icons View ➢ Windows Firewall. You can then decide what firewall options you want to set (as shown in Figure 19.22) like changing firewall notifications, turning the Windows Firewall on or off, restoring defaults, setting advanced settings, and troubleshooting.

FIGURE 19.22   Windows Firewall settings dialog box

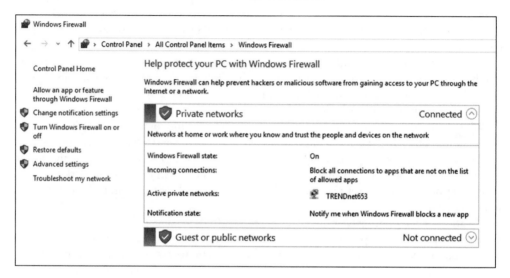

The Windows Firewall settings dialog box allows you to turn Windows Firewall on or off for both private and public networks. The On setting will block incoming sources, and the Turn off Windows Firewall setting will allow incoming sources to connect.

There is also a check box for Block All Incoming Connections. This feature allows you to connect to networks that are not secure. When Block All Incoming Connections is enabled, all incoming connections (even ones allowed in the allowed apps list) will be blocked by Windows Firewall.

Windows Firewall with Advanced Security

You can configure more-advanced settings by configuring Windows Firewall with Advanced Security (WFAS) by right-clicking Start ➤ Control Panel ➤ Large Icons View ➤ Windows Firewall ➤ Advanced Settings. The Windows Firewall With Advanced Security dialog box appears, as shown in Figure 19.23.

The scope pane to the left shows that you can set up specific inbound and outbound rules, connection security rules, and monitoring rules. The central area shows an overview of the firewall's status when no rule is selected in the left pane. When a rule is selected, the central area shows the rule's settings. The right pane shows the same actions as the Action menu on the top. These are just shortcuts to the different actions that can be performed in Windows Firewall. Let's take a more detailed look at some of the elements in Windows Firewall.

FIGURE 19.23   Windows Firewall With Advanced Security

Inbound and Outbound Rules

Inbound and outbound rules consist of many preconfigured rules that can be enabled or disabled. Obviously, inbound rules (see Figure 19.24) monitor inbound traffic, and outbound rules monitor outbound traffic. By default, many are disabled. Double-clicking a rule will bring up its Properties dialog box (Figure 19.25).

You can filter the rules to make them easier to view. Filtering can be based on the profile the rule affects, on whether the rule is enabled or disabled, or on the rule group. You can filter a rule by clicking which filter type you want to use in the right pane or by clicking the Actions menu on the top of the screen.

If you can't find a rule that is appropriate for your needs, you can create a new rule by right-clicking Inbound Rules or Outbound Rules in the scope pane and then selecting New Rule. The New Inbound (or Outbound) Rule Wizard will launch, and you will be asked whether you want to create a rule based on a particular program, protocol or port, predefined category, or custom settings.

As you are setting up the firewall rules, you have the ability to configure authenticated exceptions. No matter how well your system security is set up, there are almost always times when computers on your network can't use IPsec. This is when you set up authenticated exceptions. It's important to understand that when you set up these authenticated exceptions, you are reducing the security of the network because it allows computers to send unprotected IPsec network traffic. So make sure that the computers that are added to the authenticated exceptions list are managed and trusted computers only.

FIGURE 19.24   Inbound rules

FIGURE 19.25   An inbound rule's Properties dialog box

Complete Exercise 19.8 to create a new inbound rule that will allow only encrypted TCP traffic.

EXERCISE 19.8

Creating a New Inbound Rule

1. Right-click Start ➤ Control Panel ➤ Large Icon View ➤ Windows Firewall.

2. Click Advanced Settings on the left side.

3. Right-click Inbound Rules and select New Rule.

4. Choose a rule type. For this exercise, choose Custom so you can see all the options available to you. Then click Next.

5. At the Program Screen, choose All Programs. Then click Next.

6. Choose the protocol type, as well as the local and remote port numbers that are affected by this rule. For this exercise, choose TCP, and ensure that All Ports is selected for both Local Port and Remote Port. Click Next to continue.

7. At the Scope Screen, choose Any IP Address for both local and remote. Then click Next.

8. At the Action screen, choose Allow The Connection Only If It Is Secure. Click Next.

9. At the Users screen, you can experiment with these options if you want by entering users to both sections. Once you click one of the check boxes, the Add and Remove buttons become available. Click Next to continue.

10. At the Computers screen, you can choose what computers you will authorize or allow through this rule (exceptions). Again, you can experiment with these options if you want. Click Next to continue.

11. At the Profiles screen, choose which profiles will be affected by this rule. Select one or more profiles and click Next.

12. Give your profile a name and description, and then click Finish. Your custom rule will appear in the list of inbound rules, and the rule will be enabled.

13. Double-click your newly created rule. Notice that you can change the options that you previously configured.

14. Delete the rule by right-clicking the new rule and choosing Delete. A dialog box will appear asking you if you are sure. Click Yes.

15. Close the Windows Firewall.

Connection Security Rules

Connection security rules are used to configure how and when authentication occurs. These rules do not specifically allow connections; that's the job of inbound and outbound rules. You can configure the following connection security rules:

- Isolation: To restrict a connection based on authentication criteria

- Authentication Exemption: To specify computers that are exempt from authentication requirements

- Server-to-Server: To authenticate connections between computers
- Tunnel: To authenticate connections between gateway computers
- Custom

Monitoring

The Monitoring section shows detailed information about the firewall configurations for the Domain Profile, Private Profile, and Public Profile settings. These network location profiles determine what settings are enforced for private networks, public networks, and networks connected to a domain.

Real World Scenario

Use More Than Just Windows Firewall

When doing consulting, it always makes me laugh when I see small to midsize companies using Microsoft Windows Firewall and no other protection. Microsoft Windows Firewall should be your last line of defense. You need to make sure that you have good hardware firewalls that separate your network from the world.

Also watch Windows Firewall when it comes to printing. I have run into many situations where a printer that needs to communicate with the operating system has issues when Windows Firewall is enabled. If this happens, make sure that the printer is allowed in the Allowed Programs section.

Summary

In this chapter, we discussed the different types of Windows networks: domain based and peer-to-peer (workgroup) based. We also discussed a newer, easier way to set up a workgroup-based network by using HomeGroups.

Computers need to use a communication device called a NIC device in order to communicate with each other across the network. You can set up Windows 10 to use both wired and wireless NIC devices. Windows 10 also has new features included to help with setting up your wireless networks.

To allow computers to communicate on a network, you must use a *protocol*—a set of communication standards that all computers will use. The main protocol that Windows 10 uses is TCP/IP. There are two versions of TCP/IP that Windows 10 can use, IPv4 and IPv6. IPv4 is the most commonly used protocol, but IPv6 is the newest version of TCP/IP and gives organizations flexibility and growth potential.

Finally, we also discussed using Windows Firewall with Advanced Security. Windows Firewall helps prevent unauthorized users from connecting to the Windows 10 operating system. Windows Firewall is an extra line of defense, but it *should not* replace a perimeter firewall for your network.

Video Resources

There are videos available for the following exercises:

19.1

19.2

19.4

You can access the videos at www.wiley.com/go/sybextestprep on the Other Study Tools tab.

Exam Essentials

Understand Microsoft networking.   Know the difference between the Microsoft networks that you can set up. Know the difference between workgroups and domains. Know about working with Azure Active Directory vs. Onsite Active Directory.

Understand how to configure network settings.   Know how to install and configure both wired and wireless networks. Understand how Windows 10 has built-in wireless network support. Know how to set up your preferred wireless network.

Understand IPv4 and IPv6.   Know and understand IPv4 and IPv6. Understand how to configure and maintain both IPv4 and IPv6 networks. Know how to subnet an IPv4 network. Understand that APIPA will automatically assign an IP address to a Windows 10 machine if DHCP is not available.

Know how to configure Windows Firewall.   Know how to set up and maintain Windows Firewall with Advanced Security. Know that you can set up inbound and outbound rules by using Windows Firewall. Know how to allow or deny applications by using Windows Firewall.

Review Questions

1. You are the network administrator for a small organization that has decided to implement Microsoft Active Directory. Your organization is worried because the budget does not allow them to purchase new hardware for the Active Directory installation. The server room has a UNIX server it uses for file and DNS access. What option can you tell them about that will allow the organization to have Active Directory?

    A. Use Microsoft OneDrive to install Active Directory.

    B. Install Active Directory on the UNIX system.

    C. Subscribe to Azure Active Directory.

    D. Tell them that without the new hardware, there is no way to install Active Directory.

2. You are the network administrator for a midsize company that uses Windows Server 2012 R2 and Windows 10. All Windows 10 machines receive their IP address from DHCP. You have a Windows 10 machine and need to identify its IPv6 address. How can you accomplish this task? (Choose all that apply.)

    A. Click Details from the network connection status.

    B. Type **ipconfig /all** at the command prompt.

    C. Type **ipconfig /view** at the command prompt.

    D. Choose Properties of My Computer.

3. You are hired by friends to set up a network in their home. They have four Windows 10 devices in their home that are all connected by a router. There is currently no network in place. They want to be able to share audio and video files among their family members. How can you set up the network? (Choose two.)

    A. Install a Windows Server 2012 R2 domain controller.

    B. Create a HomeGroup.

    C. All audio and video files should be moved to the media library and accessible through HomeGroup.

    D. Move all audio and video files to a shared folder on the Windows Server 2012 R2 machine.

4. You are the network administrator for an organization with two sites, as shown in Figure 19.26. You need to install a new Windows 10 machine into site 1. Which TCP/IP address can you assign to the new Windows 10 machine?

    A. 192.168.2.32

    B. 192.168.2.31

    C. 192.168.2.41

    D. 192.168.2.63

FIGURE 19.26   Network layout

Windows Server 2012 R2
192.168.2.98
255.255.225.224
Gateway 192.168.2.97

Main Branch

Site 1

IP address
192.168.2.62/27

Windows 10 system
192.168.2.33
255.255.255.224
Gateway 192.168.2.62

New Windows 10 System

5. You are the network administrator for a large organization that has decided to use IPv6 and DHCP. You want to set up the network so that all Windows 10 systems using IPv6 get all of their information through DHCP including IP address and default gateway. How would you set up the network?

A.   Set up a stateful network.

B.   Set up a stateless network.

C.   Set up DNS to use DHCP.

D.   Set Active Directory static IP addresses.

6. You are the network administrator for a midsize company that uses both desktops and laptops. All laptops use Windows 10 and have been connected to a wireless access point. You disable the SSID, and now your laptops can no longer connect to the access point. What do you need to do to allow the laptops to connect?

A.   Reboot the laptops.

B.   Modify the wireless network connection settings on the laptops.

    C. Reboot the access point.

    D. Disconnect and reconnect the laptops to the domain.

7. You have a Windows 10 system that is having issues connecting to other machines on the network. You want to see the TCP/IP details to make sure that the user is using DHCP and that the assigned IP address is accurate. What command-line utility and switch can you use to do this?

    A. Route Add

    B. Ipconfig /FlushDNS

    C. Ipconfig /all

    D. Tracert

8. You are the network administrator for a midsize company that uses both desktops and laptops. All laptops use Windows 10 and have been connected to a wireless access point that is configured to use Advanced Encryption Standard (AES) security. There is no pre-shared password key being used. You need to connect a new Windows 10 laptop to the access point. How would you set up the security setting on the laptop?

    A. WPA2-Personal

    B. WPA2-Enterprise

    C. WPA-Personal

    D. WAP security

9. You are the network administrator for a large organization that uses Windows Server 2012 R2 and Windows 10. You have decided to set up a tunnel between two locations. You want to set the tunnel up so that it uses IPv6. What protocol can you use that allows for IPv4 and IPv6 on your network and to use IPv6 with the tunneling?

    A. IPv4to6

    B. 6v4

    C. ISATAP

    D. TUNISA

10. You are the network administrator for a small organization that has decided to switch the company's TCP/IP subnet mask. The organization has chosen to use 255.255.255.240. What is the increment for subnet ranges in a 240 subnet mask?

    A. 4

    B. 8

    C. 16

    D. 32

Chapter

20

Configuring Recovery

MICROSOFT EXAM OBJECTIVES COVERED IN THIS CHAPTER:

✓ **Configure system recovery.**

- This objective may include but is not limited to the following subobjectives: Configure a recovery drive, configure system restore, perform a refresh or recycle, perform a driver rollback, configure restore points.

✓ **Configure file recovery.**

- This objective may include but is not limited to the following subobjectives: Restore previous versions of files and folders, configure File History, recover files from OneDrive.

Every administrator should take measures to safeguard against disaster. Keeping backups is an important component of disaster preparedness and recovery. Windows 10 has a full backup and restore application (Backup and Restore [Windows 7]) to enable you to maintain a backup copy of any of the Windows 10 component files and data files that are considered critical to the operation of your day-to-day business. You can use the backup of the files to restore files if they become unusable for various reasons such as becoming corrupt, deleted, or even modified.

If you can't start Windows 10, there are several options and utilities that can be used to identify and resolve Windows errors. The following is a broad list of troubleshooting options (details on these options are provided throughout the chapter):

- Event Viewer
- Safe Mode
- Last Known Good Configuration
- Startup Repair tool
- Backup and Restore Center
- Driver Rollback
- System Restore

Safeguarding and Recovery Basics

One of the worst events you may experience is a computer that won't boot. An even worse experience is discovering that there is no recent backup for that computer. The first step in preparing for disaster recovery is to expect that a disaster will happen at some point and ensure to take proactive measures to plan your recovery before the failure occurs. Here are some of the preparations you can take:

- Keep your computer up to date with Windows Update (covered in Chapter 11, "Installing Windows 10").
- Perform regular system backups.
- Use current software to scan for malware (such as viruses, spyware, and adware), and make sure you have the most recent updates.
- Perform regular administrative functions, such as monitoring the logs in the Event Viewer utility.

No matter how many safeguards you enact, eventually you'll likely need to recover a system. Table 20.1 summarizes all of the Windows 10 utilities and options you can use to assist in performing system recovery. All these Windows 10 recovery techniques are covered in detail in this chapter.

TABLE 20.1   Windows 10 recovery techniques

Recovery Technique	When to Use
Event Viewer	If the Windows 10 operating system can be loaded through normal mode or Safe Mode, one of the first places to look for hints about the problem is Event Viewer. Event Viewer displays System, Security, and Application logs.
Safe Mode	This is generally your starting point for system recovery. Safe Mode loads the absolute minimum of services and drivers that are needed to boot Windows 10. If you can boot your computer to Safe Mode and you suspect that you have a system conflict, you can temporarily disable an application or processes, troubleshoot services, or uninstall software.
Startup Repair tool	If your computer will not boot to Safe Mode, you can use the Startup Repair tool to replace corrupted system files. This option will not help if you have hardware errors, however.
Backup and Restore	You should use this utility to safeguard your computer. If necessary, you can use the Backup and Restore (Windows 7) utility to restore personal files from backup media and to restore a complete image of your computer.
Driver Rollback	If you install a driver that causes issues on your system, you can use the Driver Rollback utility to return the driver to its previous version. Use Device Manager to access the Driver Rollback utility. Right-click the hardware component and choose Properties. Then click the Driver tab, and the Roll Back Driver button (Driver Rollback) will be there.
System Restore	System Restore is used to create known checkpoints of your system's configuration. In the event that your system becomes misconfigured, you can restore the system configuration to an earlier version of the checkpoint.

Using Advanced Boot Options

The Windows 10 advanced boot options can be used to troubleshoot errors that keep Windows 10 from successfully booting. Figure 20.1 shows the Advanced Boot Options screen. These advanced boot options are covered in this section.

FIGURE 20.1 Advanced Boot Options screen

 To access the Windows 10 advanced boot options, start or reboot the computer and press the F8 key after the firmware POST process but before Windows 10 is loaded. This will bring up the Advanced Boot Options menu, which offers numerous options for booting Windows 10.

Starting in Safe Mode

When your computer will not start, one of the fundamental troubleshooting techniques is to simplify the configuration as much as possible. This is especially important when you do not know the cause of your problem and you have a complex configuration. After you have simplified the configuration, you can determine whether the problem is in the basic configuration or is a result of your complex configuration.

If the problem is in the basic configuration, you have a starting point for troubleshooting. If the problem is not in the basic configuration, you should proceed to restore each configuration option you removed, one at a time. This helps you to identify what is causing the error.

If Windows 10 will not load, you can attempt to load the operating system in *Safe Mode*. When you run Windows 10 in Safe Mode, you are simplifying your Windows configuration as much as possible. Safe Mode loads only the drivers needed to get the computer up and running.

The drivers that are loaded with Safe Mode include basic ones for the mouse, monitor, keyboard, hard drive, standard video driver, and default system services.

Safe Mode is considered a diagnostic mode, so you do not have access to all of the features and devices in Windows 10 that you have access to when you boot normally, including networking capabilities.

Windows 10 offers a few Startup settings when you're trying to repair your Windows 10 system. Figure 20.2 shows the Startup Settings that are offered when you boot into Startup Settings.

FIGURE 20.2   Startup Settings screen

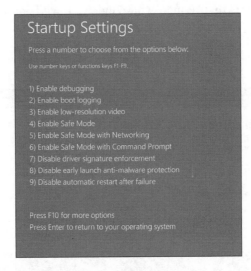

When the Startup Settings screen appears, you then have the ability to choose to enter a Safe Mode (three versions). Once a computer is booted into Safe Mode, you will see the text *Safe Mode* in the four corners of your desktop, as shown in Figure 20.3.

FIGURE 20.3   A computer running in Safe Mode

If you boot to Safe Mode, check all of your computer's hardware and software settings in Device Manager and try to determine why Windows 10 will not boot properly. After you take steps to fix the problem, try to boot to Windows 10 as you normally would.

In Exercise 20.1, you will boot your computer to Safe Mode.

EXERCISE 20.1

Booting Your Computer to Safe Mode

1. Turn on the Windows 10 system.

2. During the boot process, press the F8 key to access the Boot Options menu.

3. At the Recovery screen, choose See Advanced Repair Options, as shown in Figure 20.4.

   FIGURE 20.4 Recovery screen

   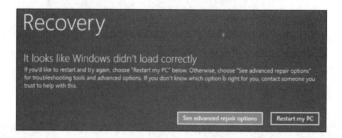

4. At the Choose An Option screen, choose the Troubleshoot option.

5. At the Troubleshoot screen, choose Advanced Options (shown in Figure 20.5).

   FIGURE 20.5 Troubleshoot screen

6. At the Advanced Options screen, choose Startup Settings.

7. At the Startup Settings screen, click the Restart button. The system will reboot into the Startup Settings screen.

8. At the Startup Settings screen, choose 5) Enable Safe Mode With Networking.

9. When Windows 10 starts, log in.

Don't restart your computer yet; you will do this as a part of the next exercise.

Enabling Boot Logging

Boot logging creates a log file that tracks the loading of drivers and services. When you choose the Enable Boot Logging option from the Advanced Boot Options menu, Windows 10 loads normally, not in Safe Mode. This allows you to log all of the processes that take place during a normal boot sequence.

This log file can be used to troubleshoot the boot process. When logging is enabled, the log file is written to \WINDOWS\Ntbtlog.txt. A sample of the Ntbtlog.txt file is shown in Figure 20.6.

FIGURE 20.6   A Windows 10 boot log file

```
ntbtlog - Notepad                                    —    □    ×
File  Edit  Format  View  Help
Microsoft (R) Windows (R) Version 10.0 (Build 10586)
 1 23 2016 13:59:10.279
BOOTLOG_LOADED \SystemRoot\system32\ntoskrnl.exe
BOOTLOG_LOADED \SystemRoot\system32\hal.dll
BOOTLOG_LOADED \SystemRoot\system32\kd.dll
BOOTLOG_LOADED \SystemRoot\system32\mcupdate_GenuineIntel.dll
BOOTLOG_LOADED \SystemRoot\System32\drivers\werkernel.sys
BOOTLOG_LOADED \SystemRoot\System32\drivers\CLFS.SYS
BOOTLOG_LOADED \SystemRoot\System32\drivers\tm.sys
BOOTLOG_LOADED \SystemRoot\system32\PSHED.dll
BOOTLOG_LOADED \SystemRoot\system32\BOOTVID.dll
BOOTLOG_LOADED \SystemRoot\System32\drivers\cmimcext.sys
BOOTLOG_LOADED \SystemRoot\System32\drivers\ntosext.sys
BOOTLOG_LOADED \SystemRoot\system32\CI.dll
BOOTLOG_LOADED \SystemRoot\System32\drivers\msrpc.sys
BOOTLOG_LOADED \SystemRoot\System32\drivers\FLTMGR.SYS
BOOTLOG_LOADED \SystemRoot\System32\drivers\ksecdd.sys
BOOTLOG_LOADED \SystemRoot\System32\drivers\clipsp.sys
BOOTLOG_LOADED \SystemRoot\system32\drivers\Wdf01000.sys
BOOTLOG_LOADED \SystemRoot\system32\drivers\WDFLDR.SYS
BOOTLOG_LOADED \SystemRoot\System32\Drivers\acpiex.sys
BOOTLOG_LOADED \SystemRoot\System32\Drivers\WppRecorder.sys
BOOTLOG_LOADED \SystemRoot\System32\Drivers\cng.sys
BOOTLOG_LOADED \SystemRoot\System32\drivers\ACPI.sys
```

In Exercise 20.2, you will examine the boot log file that was created by default during Exercise 20.1.

EXERCISE 20.2

Using Boot Logging

1. Click Windows Explorer (the folder icon on the taskbar) and browse to `C:\WINDOWS\ Ntbtlog.txt`. Double-click this file.

2. Examine the contents of your boot log file.

3. Shut down your computer and restart it without using Advanced Boot Options.

The boot log file is cumulative. Each time you boot to Safe Mode, you are writing to this file. This enables you to make changes, reboot, and see whether you have fixed any problems. If you want to start from scratch, you should manually delete this file and reboot to an Advanced Boot Options menu selection that supports logging (Enable Boot Logging).

Using Other Startup Setting Options

In this section, you will learn about additional Startup Settings menu modes. These include the following options:

1) **Enable Debugging**   This runs the Kernel Debugger, if it is installed. The Kernel Debugger is an advanced troubleshooting utility.

2) **Enable Boot Logging**   When you enable boot logging, a file is created called `Ntbtlog.txt`. This file lists all the drivers that are installed during startup and that might be useful for advanced troubleshooting.

3) **Enable Low-Resolution Video**   This loads a standard VGA driver without starting the computer in Safe Mode. You might use this mode if you changed your video driver, did not test it, and tried to boot to Windows 10 with a bad driver that would not allow you to access video. The Enable VGA mode bails you out by loading a default driver, providing access to video so that you can properly install (and test!) the correct driver for your computer.

Safe Mode starts Windows 10 at a resolution of 800×600.

4) **Enable Safe Mode**   As explained previously, entering into Safe Mode allows the system to boot up with only the minimum drivers needed to make the system operate.

5) Enable Safe Mode With Networking   This is the same as the Safe Mode option but adds networking features. You might use this mode if you need networking capabilities to download drivers or service packs from a network location.

6) Enable Safe Mode With Command Prompt   This starts the computer in Safe Mode, but after you log in to Windows 10, only a command prompt is displayed. This mode does not provide access to the desktop. Experienced troubleshooters use this mode.

7) Disable Driver Signature Enforcement   This allows drivers to be installed even if they do not contain valid signatures.

8) Disable Early Launch Anti-malware Protection   Windows 10 has a feature called Secure Boot. Secure Boot helps protect the Windows boot configuration and its components. Secure Boot also loads an Early Launch Anti-malware (ELAM) driver. Choosing this option disables the Early Launch Anti-malware driver.

9) Disable Automatic Restart After Failure   This prevents Windows from restarting when a critical error causes Windows to fail. This option should be used only when Windows fails every time you restart, preventing you from accessing the desktop or any configuration options.

Press Enter to Return to Your Operating System   This boots the Windows 10 system in the default manner. This option is on the Advanced Boot Options menu in case you accidentally hit F8 during the boot process but really wanted to boot Windows 10 normally.

Launch Recovery Environment   The Windows 10 Recovery Environment (WinRE) is used to repair common causes of bootable operating systems problems. By default, WinRE is preloaded into the Windows 10 for Desktop editions (Home, Pro, Enterprise, and Education).

Understanding System Restore

System restores are actually a two-part process to make work. First in the Windows 10 operating system, you create system restore points. These are snapshots of the Windows 10 system so in the event that you need to revert to one of these snapshots, you can.

So after you create some system restore points, the System Restore option in the Advanced Options allows you to revert your PC to an earlier point in time. Restore points are generated when an administrator or user installs a new application, driver, Windows update, or when you manually create a restore point.

When you restore to a previous point, the user's personal files won't be affected, but restores do remove applications, drivers, and updates installed after the restore point was made.

To enable System Protection (needed to create restore points), in Control Panel, choose the System icon. When the System Properties window appears, choose the System Protection tab. Click the Configure button (see Figure 20.7) to turn System Protection on.

FIGURE 20.7 Configure button for System Protection

Once you have enabled System Protection in Control Panel, you then need to open the System Restore application. To do that, you follow these steps:

1. Right-click the Start button and then select Control Panel.

2. Choose Control Panel ➢ Recovery.

3. In the Recovery window, choose Configure System Restore (as shown in Figure 20.8).

FIGURE 20.8 Open System Restore

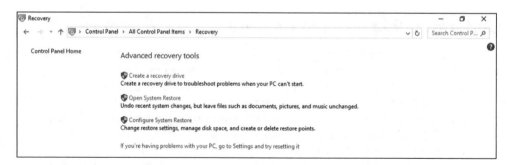

4. At the next screen, click the Create button. This will allow you to create a system restore point.

The steps to create restore points as well as restore and clean up old restore points will be explained in the section "Maintaining Windows 10 with Backup and Restore," later in this chapter.

Before you can use the system restore to fix a crashed computer, you need to create a recovery drive. Recovery drives allow you to create a backup drive in the event that a PC can't start. After the recovery drive is created, you can then use that drive to recover from a system crash.

To use the recovery drive to fix a crashed computer, boot the system into the Advanced options and then choose System Restore. Then it will ask you for a username and then a password and the system will continue using one of the restore points that was selected.

Using the System Image Recovery

Another way to protect your Windows 10 computer system is to create and use system images. System images are exact copies of the Windows 10 drive. System images, by default, include the drives that are needed for Windows to function properly. System images include Windows and all of the system settings, programs, and files.

System images work well in the event of a major hard disk or computer crash. System images allow you to restore all of the contents of the crashed system and get the system back up and running. When you restore a crashed system from an image, the entire system is restored. It's a complete restore of the computer system. This means that you can't pick and choose what programs you want to install. It's an all-or-nothing restore.

This is the reason why you should also make sure that you do regular backups. By making sure all of your backups are up to date and by making sure you have a system image, you are completely covered in the event of a major crash.

To create a system image, right-click the Start menu and choose Control Panel. In the Control Panel, open File History. Once you're in the File History application, click the System Image Backup link in the lower-left corner (see Figure 20.9).

FIGURE 20.9   System Image Backup

The steps to create a System Image Backup will be explained in "Maintaining Windows 10 with Backup and Restore."

Using the Startup Repair Tool

Another option that is available in the Advanced Options menu is the Startup Repair tool. If your Windows 10 computer will not boot because of missing or corrupted system files, you can use the *Startup Repair tool* to correct these problems. Startup Repair cannot repair hardware failures. Additionally, Startup Repair cannot recover personal files that have been corrupted, damaged by viruses, or deleted. To ensure that you can recover your personal files, you should use the Backup and Restore utility discussed in the next section.

If Startup Repair is unable to correct the problem, you might have to reinstall Windows 10, but this should be done as a last resort. This is one reason why you should always back up your Windows 10 machine.

Maintaining Windows 10 with Backup and Restore

The Windows 10 *Backup and Restore utility* enables you to create and restore backups. Backups protect your data in the event of system failure by storing the data on another medium, such as a hard disk, CD, DVD, or network location. If your original data is lost because of corruption, deletion, or media failure, you can restore the data by using your backup.

To access Backup and Restore, type **backup and restore** in the Windows 10 search box. Alternatively, you can choose Start ➤ Control Panel, choose either the small or large icon view, and then click Backup And Restore (Windows 7). Backup and Restore is shown in Figure 20.10.

Creating a Backup

You can see in Figure 20.10 that no backups of this Windows 10 machine have been taken. To set up a backup, choose the Set Up Backup link in the right side of the Backup And Restore window. Choosing Set Up Backup launches a wizard that takes you through the process of creating a backup. The Backup Wizard first asks you for a location to save your backup. This location can be a hard disk (removable or fixed), a CD, a DVD, or even a network location (if you have Windows 10 Premium or Ultimate).

FIGURE 20.10 Windows 10 Backup and Restore

Next, you are asked to either let Windows 10 choose the files and folders to back up or let you manually select the resources you want to back up. In your manual selection, you can choose just the data libraries of Windows 10 for you as a user or other users. You can also choose to create a backup of the Windows 10 system files. If you want to choose other files and folders, you have the option of selecting any resources individually on your hard disk(s).

The final page of the wizard enables you to view the items you have selected as well as set up a schedule for your backups to occur. If you're happy with the setup, click the Save Settings And Run Backup button. The backup commences, and you are able to restore the resources if necessary in the future. Figure 20.11 shows my Windows 10 machine right after I chose to save the settings and run a backup. You can see the backup in progress and the date and time of my last backup.

Windows 10 *cannot* back up encrypted files. To back up encrypted files, you need to manually copy all encrypted files to an external hard drive or decrypt the files before the backup.

In Exercise 20.3, you will make a backup of your files. This exercise assumes that you haven't yet configured an automatic backup.

FIGURE 20.11 Windows 10 backup status

EXERCISE 20.3

Backing Up Files

1. Right-click Start ➤ Control Panel ➤ Backup And Restore (Windows 7).

2. Click the Back Up Now button.

3. Select the location where you want to save your backup, and then click Next. In our example, we will use our D: drive.

4. The What Do You Want To Back Up? screen appears. Click the Let Me Choose radio button and then click Next.

5. Select the files that you would like to back up. Click Next.

6. At the Review Your Backup Settings screen, you can select how often you want a backup to be automatically performed. To start the backup, click the Save Settings And Run Backup button.

   Windows begins backing up files, and a progress indicator indicates how the backup is progressing.

7. When the backup is complete, click Close.

After you have created your backup, you can restore system files and user data files with the Backup and Restore utility.

Restoring Files from a Backup

If you have lost or destroyed files that you still want on your Windows 10 system, you can restore them from your backup. To restore files to your computer, launch the Backup and Restore program by typing **backup and restore** in the Windows 10 search box. Assuming the media where your backup was saved is available, you can click the Restore My Files button.

Click the Restore My Files button to launch a restore wizard that prompts you to search for the files you want to restore. You can select multiple files and folders. When you have selected all the files and folders you want to restore, click Next, and you will have one final option: to restore to the original location or pick an alternative location for restoration. After you make the restore-location decision, choose Restore. The restore operation commences, and your original files and folders are available for you from the backup media.

You also have options in the Backup And Restore window to restore all users' files or to select another backup to restore files from. You would use this second option if you saved your backup to multiple locations and the last one (the one listed in the backup section) is not the set of backup files you want to use in your current session. Other than just restoring files and folders, you have the choice to use other advanced backup options.

In Exercise 20.4, you will restore some files. This exercise assumes that you created a backup in Exercise 20.3.

EXERCISE 20.4

Restoring Files

1.   Right-click Start ➤ Control Panel ➤ Backup And Restore (Windows 7).

2.   Click the Restore My Files button.

3.   At the Restore Files screen, click the Browse For Folders button.

4.   Click the Microsoft Windows Backup link in the left window. Then double-click the backup that you created in the previous exercise. Choose the folder that you want to restore (we chose the Program Files folder, but you need to choose a folder with enough free space) and click Add. Click Next to continue.

5.   Select whether you want files saved in the original location or a different location. To begin the restore, click Restore.

6.   When the restore is complete, click Finish.

Recovering Files from OneDrive

As explained in Chapter 13, "Configuring Storage and Security," Microsoft has a subscription-based storage system called OneDrive. Microsoft's OneDrive is built into Windows 10 by default. OneDrive is a cloud-based storage subscription so home users can store their documents and then access those documents from anywhere in the world (provided that you have Internet access).

OneDrive was designed for the average home user who is looking to store data in a safe, secure, cloud-based environment. OneDrive, when first released, was also a consideration for corporate environments, but with the release of Windows Azure, OneDrive is really intended for the home user or corporate user who wants to store some of their own personal documents in the cloud. Corporations would be more inclined to use Microsoft Azure and all of its corporate benefits.

Exercise 20.5 will show you how to set up a OneDrive account for your user account. To do this, you must have a Microsoft account. You get 5 GB for free from Microsoft on the OneDrive cloud-based storage.

If you did Exercise 3.3 in Chapter 13, "Configuring Storage and Security," please skip the following exercise.

EXERCISE 20.5

Configuring OneDrive

1. Open OneDrive.

2. Log into OneDrive using your Microsoft account.

3. You will get a screen that shows where your files will be located on your system. Click the Next button.

4. At the Sync Files screen, choose what folders that you want to sync with Microsoft and then click Next.

    A screen will appear telling you that your OneDrive is set up and ready to go.

5. Click the Open My OneDrive Folder button to open your folders and Microsoft OneDrive.

6. Close OneDrive.

Now that the OneDrive subscription has been set up, you can recover files and folders from clicking Windows Explorer and then choosing OneDrive from the left side. You can recover any of the files and folders that were stored on OneDrive.

Using the Wbadmin Command Utility

Administrators have the ability to configure and manage backups and restores through the command prompt using a utility called Wbadmin. The Wbadmin.exe command replaces the Ntbackup.exe command that was released with previous versions of Windows. Wbadmin allows you to back up and restore your operating system, volumes, files, folders, and applications all from a command prompt.

You must be a member of the Administrators group to configure a regularly scheduled backup. To perform any other tasks using Wbadmin, you must be a member of either the Backup Operators group or the Administrators group, or you must have been delegated the appropriate permissions.

To run the Wbadmin.exe command, you must start it from an elevated command prompt. To do this, click Start, right-click the command prompt, and then click Run As Administrator.

Table 20.2 shows the Windows 10 Wbadmin command switches and their descriptions.

TABLE 20.2   Wbadmin switches

Command	Description
Wbadmin Start Backup	Runs a one-time backup
Wbadmin Stop job	Stops the currently running backup or recovery
Wbadmin get versions	Shows the details of a backup
Wbadmin get items	Lists items contained in a backup
Wbadmin get status	Shows the status of the currently running operation

Using Advanced Backup Options

In the main Backup And Restore window, you have options in the left pane to turn off the schedule, create a system image, and create a system repair disk.

Choosing the Turn Off Schedule option lets you take your backup out of the current backup scheduling as seen in Task Scheduler. Creating a system image lets you back up critical operating system files for restoration later if your operating system becomes corrupt. Creating a system repair disc allows you to create a bootable disc with which you will have a limited set of repair utilities and the ability to restore your backup files if necessary.

Creating a System Image

A *system image* enables you to take a snapshot of the entire hard disk and capture that image to a specific location so you can restore that image at a later date.

To create a system image of your entire computer, select the Create A System Image link on the left side of the Backup And Restore utility. When creating a system image, you can save that image to a hard disk, a DVD, or a network location.

In Exercise 20.6, you will create a system image and save it to a local hard disk.

EXERCISE 20.6

Creating a System Image

1. Right-click Start ➤ Control Panel ➤ Backup And Restore (Windows 7).

2. Click the Create A System Image link on the left side.

3. Choose the location where you want to save the image. We are choosing the local D: drive. Click Next.

4. At the Confirm screen, click Start Backup.

5. A dialog box may appear, asking whether you want to create a system repair disc. Click the No button. If you want to create a system repair disc, you will need a DVD burner and DVD.

6. When the image is complete, click the Close button.

After you create a system image, you may need to restore it. Let's take a look at the steps needed to complete a restore.

Restoring an Image

When you need to restore an image, you will use the System Image Recovery tool. To restore an image using this tool, you must perform the following steps:

1. Boot your computer by using the Windows 10 media, or use the recovery partition instructions provided by your computer manufacturer.

2. When the Install Windows dialog box appears, select the language, the time and currency format, and the keyboard or input method. Click Next to continue.

3. The Install Now button appears in the center of the screen. Click Repair Your Computer in the lower-left corner.

4. Select the operating system to recover and click Next. If you do not see your operating system, you might need to load your hard-disk drivers by clicking the Load Drivers button.

5. The System Recovery Options dialog box appears. You can choose one of the following options:

   - Startup Repair
   - System Restore
   - Windows Complete PC Restore
   - Windows Memory Diagnostic Tool
   - Command Prompt

   Choose Windows Complete PC Restore to continue.

6. Select the recommended image, or select Restore A Different Backup. Click Next to continue.

7. If you selected Restore A Different Backup, follow the prompts to select the location of the image and the image you want to restore.

8. You will be asked to review your selections. Click Finish to continue.

9. You will be asked to confirm your decision. Click the check box and click OK to restore the image.

 If you were not provided the Windows 10 media when you purchased your computer, the computer manufacturer might have placed the files on a recovery partition. Check with the manufacturer for more information.

Using System Protection

System Protection is a feature of Windows 10 that creates a backup and saves the configuration information of your computer's system files and settings on a regular basis. System Protection saves multiple previous versions of saved configurations rather than just overwriting them. This makes it possible to return to multiple configurations in your Windows 10 history, known as *restore points*. These restore points are created before most significant events, such as installing a new driver. Restore points are also created automatically every seven days. System Protection is turned on by default in Windows 10 for any drive formatted with NTFS.

You manage System Protection and the restore points from the System Protection tab of the System Properties dialog box. You can also access this tab directly by typing **restore point** into the Windows 10 search box or by clicking the Recovery icon in Control Panel.

Clicking the System Restore button launches the System Restore Wizard, which walks you through the process of returning Windows 10 to a previous point in time.

Also within the System Protection tab of the System Properties dialog box is the Protection Settings section, where you can configure any of your available drives. Select the drive for which you would like to modify the configuration and click the Configure button. The System Protection configuration dialog box for the drive appears.

The System Protection dialog box allows you to enable or disable system protection for the drive. When you enable protection, you can opt for previous versions of files or previous versions of files and system settings. You also have the ability to set the maximum disk space that your restore points will use for storage. Another function of the System Protection dialog box for the selected disk is to delete all restore points (including system settings and previous versions of files) by clicking the Delete button.

One tool included with restore points is shadow copies. Shadow copies are copies of files and folders that Windows automatically saves as part of a restore point. Normally, restore points are made only once a day if you have enabled System Protection. If System

Protection is enabled, Windows will then automatically create shadow copies of files that have been modified since the last restore point was made.

One advantage of using restore points and shadow copies is the ability to restore files and folders using the Previous Versions tab. When you click any folder and choose Properties, the last tab on the right is Previous Versions. You can easily restore any folder by choosing one of these previous versions.

Creating Restore Points

Restore points contain Registry and system information as it was at a certain point in time. These restore points are created at the following times:

- Weekly
- Before installing applications or drivers
- Before significant system events
- Before System Restore is used to restore files (so you can undo the changes if necessary)
- Manually upon request

In Exercise 20.7, you will manually create a restore point.

EXERCISE 20.7

Creating a Restore Point

1. Right-click Start ➤ Control Panel ➤ System ➤ Advanced System Settings.

2. When the System Properties dialog box appears, click the System Protection tab.

3. Click the Create button on the bottom of the screen.

4. At the System Protection dialog box, enter a description for the restore point. Click Create.

5. A dialog box states that the restore point was created. Click Close.

Restoring Restore Points

You can restore previously created restore points with System Restore. The restore operation will restore system files and settings but will not affect your personal files.

 WARNING   System Restore will also remove any programs that have been installed since the restore point was created.

In Exercise 20.8, you will revert your system configuration to a previously captured restore point.

EXERCISE 20.8

Restoring a Restore Point

1. Right-click Start ➢ Control Panel ➢ System ➢ Advanced System Settings.

2. When the System Properties dialog box appears, click the System Protection tab.

3. Click the System Restore button. Click Next at the Welcome screen to continue.

4. Choose the restore point created in the previous exercise and click Next to continue.

5. Review your restore point selection, and click Finish to continue.

6. Click Yes to confirm that you want System Restore to continue.

7. System Restore will restore your system and reboot your computer to apply the changes. You should see a message stating that System Restore has restored your computer. Click OK to close the dialog box.

Cleaning Up Old Restore Points

One problem with creating multiple restore points is that they start to take up a large amount of your hard disk. You will need to clean up old restore points from time to time, and you can accomplish this task by using the Disk Cleanup utility.

The Disk Cleanup utility removes temporary files, empties the Recycle Bin, and removes a variety of system files and other items that you no longer need. When using the Disk Cleanup utility, you can also click the More Options tab and choose Programs And Features and System Restore And Shadow Copies to clean them up as well.

 The More Options tab is available when you choose to clean up files from all users on the computer.

To use the Disk Cleanup utility, right-click Start ➢ Control Panel ➢ Administrative Tools ➢ Disk Cleanup.

Using the Recycle Bin

Now we are going to talk about an icon that we have seen on our desktop for many years called the Recycle Bin. The Recycle Bin is a temporary storage container that holds deleted files. The advantage of have a temporary storage container is that you can restore or recycle the files to their original location. So basically it allows you to undelete a deleted file.

When a file or folder is deleted on a computer, it isn't actually deleted. When files or folders get deleted, they get placed into the Recycle Bin. This works well because if you change your mind or realize that you actually need the file or folder, you can undelete it and it gets restored. The Recycle Bin allows you to perform a refresh or recycle of files that were deleted but shouldn't have been.

The Recycle Bin allows you to restore files or folders multiple ways. You can right-click the item and choose Restore or you can use the Manage tab (as shown in Figure 20.12).

FIGURE 20.12   Manage tab in Recycle Bin

In Exercise 20.9, you will create a document and then delete the document. Then you will use the Recycle Bin to restore the document to its original location.

EXERCISE 20.9

Using the Recycle Bin

1. On the Windows 10 desktop, right-click and choose New Text Document.

2. Create a new test document called **Test.txt**.

3. After the document is created, right-click the document and choose Delete.

4. Double-click to open the Recycle Bin.

5. You can either right-click the Test.txt document and choose Restore, or click the document and then on the Manage tab choose Restore The Selected Item.

6. Close the Recycle Bin, and the document should be back on the desktop.

Summary

In this chapter, you looked at the different ways to recover and protect your Windows 10 machine from hardware and software issues. We discussed using the Advanced Boot Options such as Safe Mode, Debugging Mode, and VGA Mode.

Another important item that needs to be completed on a Windows 10 machine is Backup and Restore (Windows 7). Backing up a Windows 10 machine protects data in the event of a hardware or software failure.

We also discussed how to back up a complete copy of Windows 10 by using images. An image allows you to copy the entire Windows 10 machine and then reimage the machine in the event of a major failure. Another way to protect data is by the use of shadow copies. Shadow copies, which are a part of System Protection, allow you to keep previous versions of data and revert to that previous version in the event of a problem.

Video Resources

There are no videos for this chapter.

Exam Essentials

Understand the different options for managing system recovery.   Know how to use the Startup Repair tool, System Restore, and the Backup and Restore Center and when it is appropriate to use each option.

Be able to perform file recovery with the Backup and Restore Center and shadow copies.   Understand the options that are supported through the Backup and Restore (Windows 7) Center and the files that are backed up using this tool. Know how to manually create a shadow copy and how to keep only the last shadow copy version.

Know how to troubleshoot using Advanced Boot Options.   Be able to list the options that can be accessed through Advanced Boot Options, and know when it is appropriate to use each option. Know the difference between Last Known Good Configuration, Safe Mode, Debugging Mode, and VGA Mode.

Review Questions

1. You are the network administrator for a large organization that uses both Windows Server 2012 R2 and Windows 10. One of the Windows 10 machines needs to be backed up daily. You perform an image backup on the Windows 10 machine. The Windows 10 machine then gets struck by a virus and will not start up properly. What can you do to get the Windows 10 machine up and running the fastest possible way?

    A. Because of the virus, the best thing is to rebuild the machine from scratch.

    B. Start the computer from the Windows 10 DVD and then use the System Image Recovery tool.

    C. Start the computer from the Windows 10 DVD and then use the Image Restore utility.

    D. Use a Windows 10 boot disk and run the Image Restore utility.

2. You need to back up Windows 10, but the backup must be backed up to a local disk drive. When you start the backup, you see the screen shown in Figure 20.13.

FIGURE 20.13   Backup and Restore (Windows 7) error

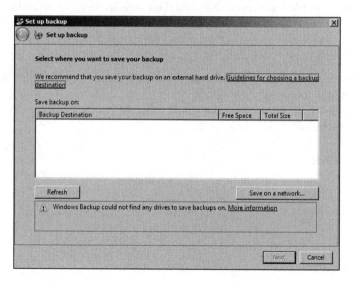

What action do you need to perform?

    A. Log on as the backup administrator.

    B. Log on as the system administrator.

    C. Add a local hard disk to the machine by using Computer Management and then run the backup again.

    D. Run the backup utility in protected mode.

3. You are the system administrator for a large organization that uses Windows Server 2012 R2 and Windows 10. You have a Windows 10 machine and have enabled System Protection. You want the machine to retain only the last System Protection snapshot that was taken. What should you do?

    A. Run Disk Cleanup for System Restore and then run Shadow Copies.

    B. Disable Shadow Copies and run System Protection.

    C. Set the Keep Only Last Shadow Copy option in System Protection.

    D. Enable Shadow Copies and then set the Keep Only Last Shadow Copy option.

4. You are the network administrator for a small company. You manage the computers for the Marketing department, all of which are running the Windows 10 operating system. You are making several configuration changes to the manager's computer to enhance performance. Before you make any changes, you want to create a restore point that can be used if any problems arise. How do you manually create a restore point?

    A. By using the System Restore utility

    B. By using the System Protection tab of the System Properties dialog box

    C. By using the System Configuration utility

    D. By using the Startup Repair tool

5. Your computer uses a SCSI adapter that supports a SCSI drive, which contains your Windows 10 system and boot partitions. After updating the SCSI driver, you restart your computer, but Windows 10 will not load. You need to get this computer up and running as quickly as possible. Which of the following repair strategies should you try first to correct your problem?

    A. Restore your computer's configuration with your last backup.

    B. Boot your computer with the System Image reload.

    C. Boot your computer with the Safe Mode option and do a driver rollback.

    D. Boot your computer to the Recovery Console and manually copy the old driver back to the computer.

6. You are about to install a new driver for your CD-ROM drive, but you are not 100 percent sure that you are using the correct driver. Which of the following options will allow you to *most easily* return your computer to the previous state if the new driver is not correct?

    A. Safe Mode

    B. Roll Back Driver

    C. System Restore utility

    D. Startup Repair tool

7. After you updated Will's computer, his system files became corrupted due to a virus and now need to be restored. Which of the following processes should you use to fix the problem?

    A. Restore a backup.

    B. Restore an image.

    C. Use the Startup Repair tool.

    D. Boot to Safe Mode.

8. You are unable to boot your Windows 10 computer, so you decide to boot the computer to Safe Mode. Which of the following statements regarding Safe Mode is false?

   A. When the computer is booted to Safe Mode, there is no network access.

   B. Safe Mode loads all the drivers for the hardware that is installed on the computer.

   C. When you run Safe Mode, boot logging is automatically enabled.

   D. When you run Safe Mode, the screen resolution is set to 800×600.

9. You have been having problems with your Windows 10 computer. You decide to start the computer by using the Enable Boot Logging option on the Advanced Boot Options menu. Where can you find the log file that is created?

   A. `\Windows\ntbtlog.txt`

   B. `\Windows\System32\ntbtlog.txt`

   C. `\Windows\ntboot.log`

   D. `\Windows\System32\ntboot.log`

10. You have purchased a new computer with Windows 10 installed. After modifying the system so that it is configured just how you want it, you want to back up the system so that if anything happens, you can restore the files and settings. Which of the following should you do?

    A. Back up your files by using the Back Up Files button in the Backup and Restore Center.

    B. Create an image of your computer by using the Create An Image link in the Backup and Restore Center.

    C. Use the System Repair tool to make an image of your computer.

    D. Use Shadow Copies to create a previous version of the files.

Appendix A

Answers to Review Questions

Chapter 1: Windows 10 Installation

1. A. The Boot Configuration Data (BCD) store contains boot information parameters that were previously found in Boot.ini in older versions of Windows. To edit the boot options in the BCD store, use the bcdedit utility, which can be launched only from a command prompt.

2. B. By modifying the changes on the local Group Policy, you can manually configure your Windows Update settings. You can automatically configure the Windows Update settings by creating a server-issued Group Policy Object (GPO).

3. A. In the "Choose how updates are installed" setting, you can use the drop-down setting to configure how the computer restarts after an update is done. You can choose either schedule a restart or restart automatically.

4. B. Device Stage is part of the Windows 10 operating system family. Device Stage allows you to connect a compatible device to your PC, and a picture of the device will appear. This allows you to easily share files between devices and computers.

5. C. With Windows Hyper-V client, an organization that chooses to upgrade to Windows 10 will still have the ability to run older Windows XP applications on a virtual Windows XP system.

6. D. In the "Choose how updates are delivered" setting, this option allows you to choose how you get your updates. You can receive your updates from either the Microsoft's website (Internet) or from a WSUS server.

7. D. The feature the question is referring to is View Available Networks (VAN). Before Windows 10, when you used a wireless network adapter, you would choose the wireless network that you wanted to connect to by using the wireless network adapter properties. In Windows 10, this is built into the operating system.

8. B. HomeGroup provides an easy way to set up a network using Windows 10. Windows 10 will search for your home network, and if it is found, it will connect after the HomeGroup password is entered. If a home network is not found, a networking wizard will automatically create a password for the HomeGroup so other computers can join.

9. B. Jump Lists is a new feature in Windows 10 that allows you to quickly access files that you have been working on. Another advantage to using Jump Lists is that certain applications, such as Windows Media Player, can be preset, and in the case of Internet Explorer, you could view all the recent websites that you have visited.

10. C. Windows Touch allows you to control the operating system and its applications by using a touch screen. Touch screens can be placed on laptops, tabletops, GPS devices, phones, and now the Windows 10 operating system.

Chapter 2: Installing in an Enterprise Environment

1. **D.** You would use the Sysprep utility. The `/generalize` options prevents system-specific information from being included in the image.

2. **A.** The DISM utility with the `/get-drivers` switch allows you to find out which drivers are installed on the WIM.

3. **B.** You would use the DISM utility to manage and manipulate an image while it's in the image format. With DISM you can create, deploy, and manage your images.

4. **C.** To add FTP to an image, you would use the DISM command with the `Enable-Feature` switch. With the `Enable-Feature` switch, you must include the FeatureName.

5. **C.** KMS is an activation service that companies can use to help activate Windows systems on their own network. By using Active Directory–based activation and KMS, systems can be activated without the need of each Windows system contacting Microsoft for product activation.

6. **D.** Once you have a reference computer installed, you can use the System Preparation Tool to prepare the computer to be used with disk imaging. Image Capture Wizard is a utility that can be used to create a disk image after it is prepared using the System Preparation Tool. The image can then be transferred to the destination computer(s).

7. **B.** Using the `/generalize` switch, the system is getting prepared for imaging. Also, all of the unique system information, including the SID number, is removed from the image.

8. **B.** The size of the VHD file is fixed to the size specified when the disk is created. This option is faster than a dynamically expanding disk. However, a fixed-size disk uses up the maximum defined space immediately.

9. **A.** Native Boot means that you can boot up to a VHD without the need of having a virtual server or hypervisor on the system you're booting from.

10. **C.** The `/oobe` option initiates the Windows Welcome screen at the next reboot. This makes the machine work as if it's a first time boot-up right out of the box.

Chapter 3: Configuring Devices and Drivers

1. **C.** Running the `Sigverif.exe` program will run a check against all the drivers installed on your machine and then notify you of any drivers that are unsigned.

2. A. The Print Management tool has a utility called Migrate Printers. This utility allows an administrator to migrate the print server queues from one machine and transfer those print settings to another machine.

3. C. If you need to get a stalled computer up and running as quickly as possible, you should start with the Driver Rollback option. This option is used when you've made changes to your computer's hardware drivers and now you have issues.

4. B. The Roll Back Driver option is the easiest way to roll back to a known good driver. You could also use the System Restore utility to roll back your computer to a known restore point if you make harmful changes to your computer, but Driver Rollback is easier and faster.

5. D. The `Printbrm.exe` command should be run from a command prompt with administrative permission. This command is the command-line version of the Print Management tool.

6. B. By disabling the drivers, the drivers are still installed on the Windows 10 system but they are not active. Administrators like to use the disable so the user can always re-enable the drivers later for use.

7. C. To install a printer on Windows 10, you would use the Devices And Printers MMC. Once in the MMC snap-in, choose the Add Printer link and walk through the printer installation wizard.

8. C. Device Manager is the utility included with Windows 10 that allows you to configure and manage your devices and hardware. You can also configure your drivers within Device Manager.

9. A. Driver rollback allows you to replace a newly installed driver with the previous driver. You can do the driver rollback using the Device Manager utility.

10. B. To get the latest drivers for any piece of hardware, you need to use the Upgrade Drivers button in Device Manager. After the upgrade button is chosen, you can use downloaded drivers or drivers from a new DVD.

Chapter 4: Configuring Storage

1. D. Both Windows 10 and Windows XP Professional support FAT32 and NTFS, so both file systems will be viewable on both operating systems.

2. C. Storage Spaces allows you to take multiple drives and turn them into a single volume. To create storage spaces, you need to connect at least two or more internal or external drives.

3. C. Windows 10 supports mirrored volumes, which allow you to have fault tolerance in the event of a single hard-disk failure.

4. D. Dynamic disks are supported by all Windows operating systems above Windows Server 2000. Windows 10 supports mirrored volumes.

5. A. The Disk Cleanup utility is used to identify areas of space that may be reclaimed through the deletion of temporary files or Recycle Bin files.

6. D. In Windows 10, one way you can compress files is through Windows Explorer. Windows 10 has no programs called Packer, and JetPack is for compressing JET databases. The Cipher program is used to encrypt or decrypt files. The command-line option for managing file and folder compression is `compact`.

7. C. The `convert` command allows you to convert a basic disk to a dynamic disk. Administrators have the ability to change a disk from basic to dynamic without losing any data.

8. D. Windows 10 data compression is supported only on NTFS partitions. If you move the file to a FAT32 partition, then it will be stored as uncompressed.

9. B. PowerShell commands allow you to run multiple configurations by using scripts or even by using individual commands.

10. C. The PowerShell command to allow an operating system to see a new disk is `Get-Disk`. The `Get-DiskImage` command allows an operating system to see a disk image.

Chapter 5: Configuring the Windows 10 Environment

1. A. Remote Desktop allows you to connect to a machine and take over the session. Remote Assistance requires that a user invite you to the connection.

2. D. When the computer enters sleep mode, the data will be saved to memory, and the computer will be put into a power-saving state. Sleep mode combines the features of standby and hibernation so that all data is saved, but the computer restores faster than if the computer was put into hibernation mode.

3. B. You can configure notification area options, such as displaying the clock and stock ticker, through Control Panel ➤ Date And Time. Windows 10 has removed the Windows Sidebar.

4. C. When a Windows 10 computer is configured with the Power Saver power plan, the computer's display and hard disk will be turned off after 20 minutes of inactivity in order to conserve energy. The computer will be put into sleep mode after one hour of inactivity when the Power Saver power plan is used.

5. A. The easiest way to configure the Desktop is by right-clicking an open area of the Desktop and choosing Personalize.

6. C. The easiest way to recover a deleted file is to restore it from the Recycle Bin. The Recycle Bin holds all of the files and folders that have been deleted as long as there is space on the disk. From this utility, you can retrieve or permanently delete files.

7. C. You can configure what actions will occur if the service fails to start on the Recovery tab of the service's Properties dialog box. For example, you can configure the service to attempt to restart, or you can configure the computer to reboot.

8. A, C. In Windows 10, you can edit the Registry with REGEDIT or REGEDT32. You should always use extreme caution when editing the Registry because improper configurations can cause the computer to fail to boot.

9. A. You configure keyboard and mouse properties in Control Panel.

10. C. On a laptop computer, Denise can use the battery meter to view the amount of battery power available and to change the power plan configured for the computer.

Chapter 6: Configuring Data Security

1. B, C. Create a new HomeGroup and set the password. Use that password and join all computers to the same HomeGroup. By default, all files in the HomeGroup libraries are available to all members of the HomeGroup.

2. E. By giving Jeff Modify on the NTFS security setting, William is giving him just enough to do his job. William could also give Sales or Finance the Modify permission, but then everyone in those groups would be able to delete, change, and do more than they all need to do. Also, Jeff does not need Full Control to change or delete files.

3. B. Create a HomeGroup and add all the real estate agents to the HomeGroup. Because the company is never going to get any larger, there is no reason to have them use any version of Active Directory or Windows Server.

4. D. When both NTFS and share permissions have been applied, the system looks at the effective rights for NTFS and share permissions and then applies the most restrictive of the cumulative permissions. If a resource has been shared and you access it from the local computer where the resource resides, then you will be governed only by the NTFS permissions.

5. A. The easiest way to manage this transition is to simply rename Rick's account to John. It is very important to remember that rights and permissions get associated to a user's SID number and not a username. When you rename Rick's account to John, John will automatically have all of the rights and permissions to any resource that Rick had access to.

6. D. By giving Tom Change on the shared permission setting, you're giving him just enough to do his job. You could also give Sales or Finance the Change shared security, but then everyone in those groups would be able to delete, change, and do more than they all need to do.

7. C, E. The Admin group needs Full Control on the NTFS security and shared permission settings in order to do their job. To be able to give other users permissions, you must have the Full Control permission.

8. B. The Sales group needs Modify on the NTFS security and Change shared permission settings in order to do their job.

9. C. Since they have Modify on NTFS and Read on Shared, right now they only have Read. The Marketing group needs Change on the Shared permission settings in order to do their job.

10. A, B. The Sales group needs Modify on the NTFS security and Change shared permission settings in order to do their job.

Chapter 7: Windows 10 Networking

1. A, C. The `ipconfig /release` and the `ipconfig /renew` commands will allow your machine to receive a new IP address from the DHCP server.

2. C. Because the first octet starts with 192, it's a Class C. If the first octet starts with 1–126, it's a Class A. 128–191 is a Class B, and 192–223 is a Class C.

3. C. The default gateway is the router's IP address. The default gateway allows you to get from your subnet to another subnet.

4. D. The DNS server turns a hostname into an IP address so you can connect to a machine by the machine name. If you can connect to a machine by using the TCP/IP address but not the name, DNS is the issue.

5. D. `Ipconfig /registerdns` will automatically register the Windows 10 machine with the DNS server. The registration will include the Windows 10 machine name and the IP address.

6. A, B. You have to use either a Class A or Class B. Class C addresses can only handle 254 users. 10.x.x.x and 172.16.x.x are both able to handle the 675 users and they are both internal private address schemes that anyone can use.

7. A. Create a new Workgroup and add all the employees to the Workgroup. You don't want to use a HomeGroup because even though its five users, you need to make sure that permissions are setup properly so that users can't look at data of other users. Because they are never going to get any larger, there is no reason to have them use any version of Active Directory or Windows Server.

8. C, D. Class A addresses go from 1–126 (127 is used for the loopback address). Class B addresses go from 128–191, and Class C addresses are from 192–223.

9. C. Windows Firewall, which is included with Windows 10, helps to prevent unauthorized users or malicious software from accessing your computer. Windows Firewall does not allow unsolicited traffic (traffic that was not sent in response to a request) to pass through the firewall.

10. A. Azure is Microsoft's cloud-based Active Directory subscription. Azure is great if you don't want to deal with the worries of managing and maintaining a server room and all of the hardware, and it's also great for accessing Active Directory from anywhere in the world.

Chapter 8: Installing Applications

1. A, B. Administrators would use the Windows Assessment and Deployment Kit (ADK) and the Windows Imaging and Configuration Designer (ICD) to create a provisioning package (.ppkg).

2. A. Applications that are developed by a company and are not signed by the Windows Store can be installed by the process of Sideloading. Sideloading allows companies to load applications into the Windows Store for deployment throughout a company.

3. A. The disconnected operation mode allows App-V Desktop Clients to run applications even when the client cannot connect to the App-V Management Server. This allows laptops to continue to access App-V applications even when not connected to the network or Internet. To stop that from happening, you must disable the disconnected operation mode.

4. A. The Default Programs icon in Control Panel allows you to set file extension associations to the various programs in Windows 10.

5. B. Shared computer activation (SharedComputerLicensing) allows an administrator to set up Office 365 ProPlus on a single computer for multiple users.

6. C. Administrators can test AppLocker policies before implementing them by using the audit-only mode.

7. C. Hyper-V resource metering allows an organization to track usage within the businesses departments. It allows an organization to create a usage-based billing solution that adjusts to the provider's business model and strategy.

8. A. Administrators can use PowerShell Direct to run PowerShell commands on a VM from the Hyper-V host. To do this, you need to run `Invoke-Command` and specify which VM you're connecting to (i.e., use the `VMName` parameter).

9. C. AppLocker is a feature included with Windows (Windows 7 and higher) that allows administrators to lock out certain applications from running.

10. B. Applications that are developed by a company and are not signed by the Windows Store can be installed by the process of sideloading. Sideloading allows a company to load applications into the Windows Store for deployment throughout the company.

Chapter 9: Managing Authorization and Authentication

1. A. The Group Policy Result Tool is accessed through the GPResult command-line utility. The `gpresult` command displays the resulting set of policies that were enforced on the computer and the specified user during the logon process.

2. A. Audit Account Logon Events is used to track when a user logs on, logs off, or makes a network connection. You can configure auditing for success or failure, and audited events can be tracked through Event Viewer.

3. B, C. The password Abcde! meets complexity requirements because it is at least six characters long and contains an uppercase letter, lowercase letters, and a symbol. The password 1247445Np meets complexity requirements because it is at least six characters long and contains an uppercase letter, a lowercase letter, and numbers. Complex passwords must be at least six characters long and contain three of the four types of characters—uppercase letters, lowercase letters, numbers, and symbols.

4. B. The security option Interactive Logon: Do Not Display Last User Name In Logon Screen is used to prevent the last username in the logon screen from being displayed in the logon dialog box. This option is commonly used in environments where computers are used publicly.

5. D. Account Lockout Policy, a subset of Account Policies, is used to specify options that prevent a user from attempting multiple failed logon attempts. If the Account Lockout Threshold value is exceeded, the account will be locked. The account can be reset based on a specified amount of time or through administrator intervention.

6. D. The Restore Files and Directories user right allows a user to restore files and directories regardless of file and directory permissions. Assigning this user right is an alternative to making a user a member of the Backup Operators group.

7. B. The Enforce Password History policy allows the system to keep track of a user's password history for up to 24 passwords. This prevents a user from using the same password over and over again.

8. D. When both NTFS and share permissions have been applied, the system looks at the effective rights for NTFS and share permissions and then applies the most restrictive of the cumulative permissions. If a resource has been shared and you access it from the local computer where the resource resides, then you will be governed only by the NTFS permissions.

9. C. Virus protection is not included with Windows 10 and should be purchased separately. Windows Firewall, Windows Defender (spyware protection), and Windows Update (automatic updates) are included with Windows 10.

10. A. The most likely reason there are no file access entries in the security event log is that you did not enable auditing for the appropriate files and folders. This behavior is true of print auditing as well.

Chapter 10: Configuring Monitoring and Recovery

1. D. All of the applications that are running on the Windows 10 machine will show up under the Details tab. Right-click the application and end the process.

2. **A.** The Roll Back Driver option is the fastest way to return the driver to the previous version. You could also use System Restore, but Driver Rollback is easier and faster.

3. **C.** The Back Up Now button allows you to start a backup and configure a Windows 10 backup.

4. **D.** If you need to back up and restore your Windows 10 machine, you need to use the Windows 10 Backup and Restore Center.

5. **C.** Using images allows you to back up and restore your entire Windows 10 machine instead of just certain parts of data.

6. **A.** If you need to disable previous versions on the D: volume, this needs to be done from the System Protection settings from the computer system properties.

7. **A.** You have to manually copy all the encrypted files because the backup software will not work with the encrypted files in Windows 10.

8. **C, D.** There are two ways to repair system files on Windows 10. You can do it by using the installation disc and choosing Repair during the installation, or you can boot to the advanced options and select Repair Your Computer.

9. **A, B, C, D.** Restore points allow you to bring your system back to a previous point in time, and they should be created at all of the times listed.

10. **A.** Starting the computer in Safe Mode loads the basic VGA drivers and allows you to fix any video issues, including using the Driver Rollback utility.

Chapter 11: Installing Windows 10

1. **A.** The Boot Configuration Data (BCD) store contains boot information parameters that were previously found in Boot.ini in older versions of Windows. To edit the boot options in the BCD store, use the bcdedit utility, which can be launched only from a command prompt.

2. **B.** By modifying the changes on the local Group Policy, you can manually configure your Windows Update settings. You can automatically configure the Windows Update settings by creating a server-issued Group Policy Object (GPO).

3. **C.** Scanstate.exe collects user data and settings information based on the configuration of the Migapp.xml, Migsys.xml, and Miguser.xml files and stores it as an image file. Loadstate.exe then deposits the information that is collected to a computer running a fresh copy of Windows 10.

4. **B.** Device Stage is part of the Windows 10 operating system family. Device Stage allows you to connect a compatible device to your PC, and a picture of the device will appear. This allows you to easily share files between devices and computers.

5. C. With the Windows Hyper-V client, an organization that chooses to upgrade to Windows 10 will still have the ability to run older Windows XP applications on a virtual Windows XP system.

6. C. You can't upgrade Windows XP to Windows 10, so you must use a migration tool to migrate all the users' data and then install a clean copy of Windows 10.

7. D. The feature the question is referring to is View Available Networks (VAN). Before Windows 10, when you used a wireless network adapter, you would choose the wireless network that you wanted to connect to by using the wireless network adapter properties. In Windows 10, this is built into the operating system.

8. B. HomeGroup provides an easy way to set up a network using Windows 10. Windows 10 will search for your home network, and if it is found, it will connect after the HomeGroup password is entered. If a home network is not found, a networking wizard will automatically create a password for the HomeGroup so other computers can join.

9. B. Jump Lists is a feature in Windows 10 that allows you to quickly access files that you have been working on. Another advantage to using Jump Lists is that certain applications, such as Windows Media Player, can be preset, and in the case of Internet Explorer, you could view all the recent websites that you have visited.

10. C. Windows Touch allows you to control the operating system and its applications by using a touch screen. Touch screens can be placed on laptops, tabletops, GPS devices, phones, and now on the Windows 10 operating system.

Chapter 12: Automated Windows 10 Deployments

1. D. You would use the Sysprep utility. The /generalize options prevents system-specific information from being included in the image.

2. A. The DISM utility with the /get-drivers switch allows you to find out which drivers are installed on the WIM.

3. B. WDSUTIL is a command-line utility that can be used to configure the WDS server. Several other configuration options need to be specified on the WDS server, and you can set them using WDSUTIL.

4. C. Windows System Image Manager (SIM) is used to create unattended answer files in Windows 10. It uses a GUI-based interface to set up and configure the most common options that are used within an answer file.

5. C. To access the WDS server, the WDS clients must be able to access the DHCP server. Each WDS client will use an IP address from the DHCP server's scope, so you should ensure that the DHCP server has enough addresses to accommodate all of the WDS clients.

6. D. Once you have a reference computer installed, you can use the System Preparation Tool to prepare the computer to be used with disk imaging. Image Capture Wizard is a utility that can be used to create a disk image after it is prepared using the System Preparation Tool. The image can then be transferred to the destination computer(s).

7. C. Unique information is stripped out of the installation image when you use the System Preparation Tool to create a disk image—for example, the unique SID that is applied to every computer. Unique information is then generated when the target computer is installed.

8. B. When you configure your WDS server, the remote installation folder should not reside on the system partition.

9. C. You enable WDS servers to respond to client requests through the Windows Deployment Services (WDS) Microsoft Management Console (MMC) snap-in. In the PXE Properties dialog box, enable the option Respond To Client Computers.

10. B. The /generalize option prevents system-specific information from being included in the image. The Sysprep.exe command can be used with a variety of options. You can see a complete list by typing **sysprep/?** at a command-line prompt.

Chapter 13: Configuring Storage and Security

1. D. Both Windows 10 and Windows XP Professional support FAT32 and NTFS, so both file systems will be viewable on both operating systems.

2. A. In Windows 10, it is possible to share encrypted files with another person or between computers. To share encrypted files, you must have a valid EFS certificate for the user who should have access to the files.

3. C. Windows 10 supports mirrored volumes, which allow you to have fault tolerance in the event of a single hard-disk failure.

4. D. Dynamic disks are supported by all Windows operating systems above Windows Server 2000. Windows 10 supports mirrored volumes.

5. A. The Disk Cleanup utility is used to identify areas of space that may be reclaimed through the deletion of temporary files or Recycle Bin files.

6. D. In Windows 10, one way you can compress files is through Windows Explorer. Windows 10 has no programs called Packer, and JetPack is for compressing JET databases. The Cipher program is used to encrypt or decrypt files. The command-line option for managing file and folder compression is compact.

7. B. The Cipher utility is used to encrypt or decrypt files. Windows 10 doesn't have a program called Encrypt, Crypto, or EDS. If you want to manage file encryption through a GUI utility, you can use Windows Explorer.

8. D. Windows 10 data compression is supported only on NTFS partitions. If you move the file to a FAT32 partition, then it will be stored as uncompressed.

9. C. To allow Tylor to access her encrypted files, Julie should import Tylor's encryption key and then add that key to each file to which Tylor should have access. Adding share permissions or NTFS permissions will not allow another user to access an encrypted file unless that user's encryption key has been added to the file. Exporting and emailing Julie's key to Tylor will not allow Tylor to access the file.

10. B. You can increase the level of security on folders and files on an NTFS partition by using EFS. Only a user who is configured as a DRA with the correct private key or who has explicitly been provided permission can access this data.

Chapter 14: Managing Data Access

1. B, C. Create a new HomeGroup and set the password. Use that password and join all computers to the same HomeGroup. By default, all files in the HomeGroup libraries are available to all members of the HomeGroup.

2. D. Windows 10 comes with a feature called BitLocker Drive Encryption. BitLocker encrypts the entire system drive. New files added to this drive are encrypted automatically. To configure BitLocker, you must either use a Local Group Policy or use the BitLocker icon in Control Panel.

3. A, C, D. BitLocker Drive Encryption is a data protection feature available in Windows Education, Enterprise, and Professional editions of Windows 10.

4. D. When both NTFS and share permissions have been applied, the system looks at the effective rights for NTFS and share permissions and then applies the most restrictive of the cumulative permissions. If a resource has been shared and you access it from the local computer where the resource resides, then you will be governed only by the NTFS permissions.

5. A. The easiest way to manage this transition is to simply rename Rick's account to John. It is very important to remember that rights and permissions get associated to a user's SID number and not a username. By renaming Rick's account to John, John will automatically have all of the rights and permissions to any resource that Rick had access to.

6. E. By giving Tom Modify on the NTFS security setting, you're giving him just enough to do his job. You could also give Sales or Finance the Modify permission, but then everyone in those groups would be able to delete, change, and do more than they all need. Also, Tom does not need Full Control to change or delete files.

7. C, E. The Admin group needs Full Control on the NTFS security and shared permission settings in order to do their job. To be able to give other users permissions, you must have the Full Control permission.

8. D. Smart cards are plastic cards (the size of a credit card) that can be used in combination with other methods of authentication. This process of using a smart card along

with another authentication method is called two-factor authentication or multifactor authentication.

9. A. File extensions for known files are hidden by default. If you want to be able to see the file extension for all files, you must uncheck the Hide Extensions For Known File Types box.

10. B. Microsoft BitLocker Administration and Monitoring (MBAM) will allow the IT department to use enterprise-based utilities for managing and maintaining BitLocker and BitLocker To Go.

Chapter 15: Managing the Windows 10 Environment

1. C. You can configure what actions will occur if the service fails to start on the Recovery tab of the service's Properties dialog box. For example, you can configure the service to attempt to restart, or you can configure the computer to reboot.

2. A, C. In Windows 10, you can edit the Registry with REGEDIT or REGEDT32. You should always use extreme caution when editing the Registry because improper configurations can cause the computer to fail to boot.

3. A. You configure keyboard and mouse properties in Control Panel.

4. C. On a laptop computer, Denise can use the battery meter to view the amount of battery power available and to change the power plan configured for the computer.

5. C. You will need to make the Registry modification in the HKEY_LOCAL_MACHINE Registry key. This key provides configuration information that is accessible regardless of who is logged onto the computer.

6. D. When the computer enters sleep mode, the data will be saved to memory, and the computer will be put into a power-saving state. Sleep mode combines the features of standby and hibernation so that all data is saved, but the computer restores faster than if the computer was put into hibernation mode.

7. A. You should use the Windows ReadyDrive technology to help speed the resume time of your computer after it has been put into hibernation mode. ReadyDrive is a new technology that is used in conjunction with hybrid hard-disk drives, which combine flash memory with standard hard-disk technology. This allows data to be stored in flash memory, which enables the hard disk to remain spun down longer and also improves the time required for the computer to resume after being put into hibernation mode.

8. C. When a Windows 10 computer is configured with the Power Saver power plan, the computer's display and hard disk will be turned off after 20 minutes of inactivity in order to conserve energy. The computer will be put into sleep mode after one hour of inactivity when using the Power Saver power plan.

9. A. The easiest way to configure the Desktop is by right-clicking an open area of the desktop and choosing Personalize.

10. C. The easiest way to recover a deleted file is to restore it from the Recycle Bin. The Recycle Bin holds all of the files and folders that have been deleted as long as there is space on the disk. From this utility, you can retrieve or permanently delete files.

Chapter 16: Planning and Managing Microsoft Intune

1. A. Administrators have the ability to limit and monitor network usage by configuring the network as a metered network. Network metering allows network downloading to be watched or metered, and then administrators can charge users or departments for the network usage.

2. D. Microsoft Intune does not allow you to change a security group parent. When you delete a group, the users are not deleted, and so the only way to change a group's parent group is to create the security group under the parent. So, Portsmouth needs to be re-created under NHGroup, and then the users need to be re-added to Portsmouth.

3. C, D. As long as the salesperson's personally owned Windows 10 laptop is being managed by the management infrastructure agent, administrators can use the remote wipe feature. When you do a remote wipe, all of the company's data gets wiped from the device.

4. D. An Apple Push Notification service (APNs) certificate must be imported from Apple so that the school can manage iOS devices. This certificate allows Intune administrators to manage iOS.

5. A. To configure the update restart prompt setting, you must configure the Microsoft Intune Agent Settings policy. Setting the "Prompt user to restart Windows during Intune client agent mandatory updates" to No, this would stop users from receiving restart prompts after mandatory updates.

6. C, D. If using Configuration Manger, administrators must configure Configuration Manager to manage mobile devices. To do this, it requires administrators to create a Windows Intune subscription and use a connector to synchronize user accounts.

7. B. Administrators can have the cloud-based version of Active Directory (Azure Active Directory) work with the on-premise server-based version of Active Directory by using the Azure Active Directory (AD) Connect tool (formerly known as the Directory Synchronization tool, the Directory Sync tool, or the DirSync.exe tool).

8. C. By default, licensed users can add up to five devices to their accounts. Device Administrators have the ability to add devices to Intune, but users do have the ability to enroll five devices on their own.

9. D. Sideloading an application means that you are loading an application that you already own or one that your company created into a delivery system (i.e., Intune, Microsoft Store, or images).

10. B, C. Intune administrators have the ability to set up different notifications to different emails based on alert type. So, you can send all alerts, critical alerts, warnings, and informational alerts to different IT members.

Chapter 17: Configuring Applications

1. A. The disconnected operation mode allows App-V Desktop Clients to run applications even when the client cannot connect to the App-V Management Server. This allows laptops to continue to access App-V applications even when not connected to the network or Internet. To stop that from happening, you must disable the disconnected operation mode.

2. A. The Default Programs icon in Control Panel allows you to set file extension associations to the various programs in Windows 10.

3. B. An InPrivate session prevents the browsing history from being recorded and does not allow temporary Internet files to be retained. Cookies, usernames, passwords, and form data will not remain in IE11 and Edge following the closing of the InPrivate session, nor will there be any footprints or data pertaining to the InPrivate browsing session.

4. B. Because all users and computers are part of the domain and the internal website uses Integrated Windows Authentication, once you add the URL to the Local Intranet zone properties, Windows Authentication will take over.

5. B. Shared computer activation (SharedComputerLicensing) allows an administrator to set up Office 365 ProPlus on a single computer for multiple users.

6. C. Administrators can test AppLocker policies before implementing them by using the audit-only mode.

7. C. The Azure Active Directory Module for PowerShell Set-Mailbox cmdlet allows you to manipulate an Office 365 mailbox.

8. A. Administrators can use PowerShell Direct to run PowerShell commands on a VM from the Hyper-V host. To do this, you need to run Invoke-Command and specify which VM you're connecting to (i.e., the VMName parameter).

9. C. AppLocker is a feature included with Windows (Windows 7 and higher) that allows administrators to lock out certain applications from running.

10. B. Applications that are developed by a company and are not signed by the Windows Store can be installed by the process of sideloading. Sideloading allows a company to load applications into the Windows Store for deployment throughout the company.

Chapter 18: Managing Identity and Authorization

1. **A, D.** The password aBcdEfG1! meets complexity requirements because it is at least six characters long and contains an uppercase letter, lowercase letters, and a symbol. The password 123456789nA meets complexity requirements because it is at least six characters long and contains an uppercase letter, a lowercase letter, and numbers. Complex passwords must be at least six characters long and contain three of the four types of characters—uppercase letters, lowercase letters, numbers, and symbols.

2. **A.** You do not want this user to have any administrator rights. To allow this user to change Windows Update manually, you must set this in an LGPO.

3. **B.** Application Control Policy (AppLocker) allows you to configure a Denied list and an Accepted list for applications or users. Applications that are configured on the Denied list will not run on the system or cannot be run by specific groups, and applications on the Accepted list will operate properly.

4. **D.** LGPOs are policies that you can set on a local Windows 10 machine to limit hardware and user usage. You also have the ability to control individual users within the Local Group Policy.

5. **B.** Audit Object Access enables auditing of access to files, folders, and printers.

6. **B.** The Enforce Password History policy allows the system to keep track of a user's password history for up to 24 passwords. This prevents a user from using the same password over and over again.

7. **D.** Windows 10 comes with a new feature called BitLocker Drive Encryption. BitLocker encrypts the entire system drive. New files added to this drive are encrypted automatically. To configure BitLocker, you must either use a Local Group Policy or use the BitLocker icon in Control Panel.

8. **A, B, C, D.** UAC is available in all Windows 10 editions.

9. **B.** As a standard user, the salesperson can change time-zone settings. Changing the date and time settings, checking Device Manager, and enabling parental controls require administrative privileges. Any action that requires administrative privileges will be marked with a shield icon.

10. **B.** Account Lockout Policy, a subset of Account Policies, is used to specify options that prevent a user from attempting multiple failed logon attempts. If the Account Lockout Threshold value is exceeded, the account will be locked. The account can be reset based on a specified amount of time or through administrator intervention.

Chapter 19: Configuring Network Connectivity

1. C. Subscribing to Azure Active Directory allows a small to midsize company to have Active Directory without the need of purchasing new hardware.

2. A, B. You can see what the IPv6 address is by clicking the Details button from the network connection status or by typing **ipconfig /all**. There is no such command as ipconfig / view, and the My Computer properties will not show IP address configuration information.

3. B, C. Create a new HomeGroup and set the password. Use that password and join all computers to the same HomeGroup. By putting all files in the media library, they will be available to all members of the HomeGroup.

4. C. The company's subnet mask is 255.255.224.0. This subnet mask uses subnet ranges of 32. So, the subnet's layout is 32–63, 64–95, 96–127, 128–159, 160–191, and 192–223. Now when you subnet, you can't use the first or last number of any range. The first number represents the network ID, and the last number represents the broadcast. Because the router and the one Windows 10 computer fall within the 32–63 range, your new Windows 10 machine must fall within this range. 32 is the network ID and can't be used, and 63 is the broadcast and can't be used. So, the only available addresses are from 33–62, and the only available unused IP address in that range is 192.168.2.41.

5. A. Stateful is what we currently do today with IPv4. Stateful means that DHCP is going to give our IPv6 clients all of their TCP/IP data (IP address, default gateway, and all DHCP options). Stateless configuration means that the client's address is based on the router's advertisement messages. Clients create their own IP address and default gateway based on the router's advertisement message and their MAC address. They can still get all of the other DHCP options, but they will not get an IP address and default gateway from DHCP.

6. B. You need to change the wireless network connection settings on the laptop to allow these laptop users to connect to the reconfigured access point.

7. C. Ipconfig / all shows verbose information about your IP configuration, including your computer's physical address, the DNS server you are using, and whether you are using DHCP.

8. B. When it comes to WPA, there are two versions: WPA2-Personal and WPA2-Enterprise. WPA2-Personal allows you to set up WPA2 by using a shared password key. WPA2-Enterprise allows you to set up WPA2 by using a server for verification. Because all users are using AES with no shared password key, WPA2-Enterprise is the setting that you would choose.

9. C. ISATAP is the automatic tunnel addressing protocol providing IPv6 addresses based on the IPv4 address of the end interface (node). The IPv6 address is automatically configured on the local device, and the dual-stack machine can use either its IPv4 or IPv6 address to communicate on the local network.

10. C. On a 240 subnet mask, the ranges go by 16. Because this is a Class C, the ranges would be 16–31, 32–47, 48–63, 64–79, 80–95, 96–111, 112–127, 128–143, 144–159, 160–175, 176–191, 192–207, 208–223, and 224–239. Remember that in a Class C address, these are not all usable. You have to subtract the first number (network ID) and the last number (broadcast).

Chapter 20: Configuring Recovery

1. B. After starting the machine with the Windows 10 DVD, you can use the System Image Recovery tool to reload the backup image that you created.

2. C. When you are using the backup utility and no local disks are present, you must either configure an installed disk or physically install a hard disk before running the backup utility.

3. A. You have to run the Disk Cleanup utility to delete the previous versions and then run Shadow Copies in System Protection. There is no Keep Only Last Shadow Copy option.

4. B. To manually create a restore point or to restore your computer to a previous restore point, you use the System Protection tab of the System Properties dialog box. Although System Restore uses restore points, you do not use the System Restore utility to create a restore point.

5. C. If you need to get a stalled computer up and running as quickly as possible, you should start with the Driver Rollback option. This option is used when you've made changes to your computer's hardware drivers and now you have issues.

6. B. The Roll Back Driver option is the easiest way to roll back to a known good driver. You could also use the System Restore utility to roll back your computer to a known restore point if you make harmful changes to your computer, but Driver Rollback is easier and faster.

7. C. To quickly repair the system files, you can use the Startup Repair tool. You can restore an image by using the Backup and Repair Center, but it is faster to use the Startup Repair tool. Additionally, you will not lose any personal files by using the Startup Repair tool. Alternatively, you could try to use System Restore to go back to a previous checkpoint.

8. B. When you run your computer in Safe Mode, you simplify your Windows 10 configuration. Only the drivers that are needed to get the computer up and running are loaded.

9. A. When you enable boot logging, the file created is \Windows\ntbtlog.txt. This log file is used to troubleshoot the boot process.

10. B. You should create an image of your computer by using the Create An Image link in the Backup and Restore Center. Images back up everything on your computer. File backups cannot be used to back up system files and settings.

Appendix B

Windows 10 PowerShell Commands

One of the things that Microsoft has changed recently on the exam is that there are more PowerShell commands that administrators need to know. This appendix contains a list of PowerShell commands that you should know before taking the Windows 10 exams. These PowerShell commands can be on both Microsoft exams 70-698 and exam 70-697.

PowerShell Command	Description
Add-PhysicalDisk	This command will add a disk to a storage pool.
Add-SignerRule	Allows an administrator to create a signer rule and add that rule to a policy.
Clear-Disk	This command removes all partition information and erases all data on a disk.
Clear-EventLog	This commands allows an administrator to delete all entries from the event logs on a local or remote computer.
Connect-VirtualDisk	Administrators use this command for connecting a disconnected virtual disk to a computer using Storage Spaces.
ConvertFrom-CIPolicy	This command allows an administrator to convert an .xml file into binary format. These files contain Code Integrity Policies.
Debug-Process	Administrators use this command to debug processes running on a local computer.
Disconnect-VirtualDisk	This command will disconnect a virtual disk from a computer.
DISM /Apply-Image /ImageFile:D:\Sources\install.wim /Index:1 /ApplyDir:Z:\	Applying an image to a VHD file using the DISM tool. It will apply the install.wim file from the Source folder of the installation media to the VHD mounted at drive letter Z.
DISM /Online /Enable-Feature /All /FeatureName:Microsoft-Hyper-V	Installs Hyper-V into a Windows 10 image while it's an actual image.

PowerShell Command	Description
Dismount-DiskImage	Administrators can use this command to dismount a VHD or ISO image from a machine.
Enable-WindowsOptionalFeature -Online -FeatureName Microsoft-Hyper-V -All	Installs Hyper-V onto Windows 10.
Format-Volume	This command formats a volume on a drive.
Get-AppLockerPolicy -Effective	Returns the effective AppLocker policy on the local computer.
Get-AzureRemoteAppCollection -CollectionName <collection name>	This command shows you a list of what custom RDP properties are configured.
Get-CIPolicy	Allows an administrator to view the rules in a Code Integrity policy.
Get-CIPolicyIdInfo	Allows an administrator to view Code Integrity policy information.
Get-ComputerInfo	This commands returns the computer's system information.
Get-Disk	This command allows an operating system to see a disk.
Get-DiskImage	This command allows an operating system to see a disk image.
Get-EventLog	Finds an event in a specific event log.
Get-FileIntegrity	Allows an administrator to check the integrity information for a file that is on an ReFS volume.
Get-Partition	This command allows an administrator to get a list of partitions on the system's disks.
Get-PhysicalDisk	This command gives you a list of all of your available physical disks.
Get-Service	Finds a service on a Windows 10 system.
Get-SystemDriver	Administrators can view the drivers on a system.
Get-TimeZone	Gets the system's time zone.

PowerShell Command	Description
Get-VirtualDisk	This command allows an operating system to see a virtual disk.
Get-Volume	This command shows you the volume object.
Import-AzureRM	This command imports AzureRM modules.
import-module appx add-appxpackage "TestApp"	Allows an application to be sideloaded. "TestApp" is the path and name of the package file you created.
Import-Module Azure	This command imports the Azure Service Management module.
Initialize-Disk	This command allows you to initializes a disk for first-time use.
Install-Module Azure	This command installs the Azure Service Management module.
Install-Module AzureRM Install-AzureRM	These commands allow you to install the Azure Resource Manager modules.
Invoke-Command	This command allows you to remotely execute PowerShell commands on another system.
Merge-CIPolicy	This command allows an administrator to merge the rules of several Code Integrity policy files.
Mount-DiskImage	Administrators can use this command to mount a VHD or ISO image. By doing this, the image will appear as a normal disk.
New-CIPolicy	Allows an administrator to create a Code Integrity policy as an .xml file.
New-CIPolicyRule	With this command, administrators can create Code Integrity policy rules for drivers.
New-EventLog	Creates a new event log.
New-Partition	This allows administrators to create a new partition on an existing disk.

PowerShell Command	Description
New-Service	This command allows an administrator to create a new service.
New-StoragePool	This command allows you to create a new storage pool of physical disks.
New-VirtualDisk	This command creates a new virtual disk in the specified storage pool.
New-Volume	This command allows you to create a new volume.
Remove-EventLog	This command deletes an event log.
Remove-Partition	Administrators can use this command allows you to remove a partition.
Remove-PhysicalDisk	This command allows you to remove a disk.
Remove-VirtualDisk	Administrators can use this command allows you to remove a virtual disk.
Rename-Computer	This command allows an administrator to rename a computer.
Repair-VirtualDisk	This command allows you to repair a virtual disk.
Repair-Volume	Administrators can use this command allows you to repair a volume.
Resize-Partition	This command allows you to resize a partition.
Restart-Computer	This command reboots your system.
Restart-Service	This command restarts a service.
Resume-Service	This command resumes a service.
Set-AzureRemoteAppCollection -CollectionName <collection name> -CustomRdpProperty "drivestoredirect: s:*'nusbdevicestoredirect:s:*"	This command sets the custom RDP properties.

PowerShell Command	Description
Set-AzureRemoteAppCollection -CollectionName <collection name> -CustomRdpProperty "drivestoredirect:s:*"	This command shows you how to set up hard-drive redirection.
Set-AzureRemoteAppCollection -CollectionName <collection name> -CustomRdpProperty "drivestoredirect: s:*'nusbdevicestoredirect:s:*"	This command shows you how to set up USB and hard-drive redirection.
Set-CIPolicyIdInfo	This command allows an administrator to modify the name and ID of a Code Integrity policy.
Set-CIPolicyVersion	This command allows an administrator to modify the version number of a policy.
Set-HVCIOptions	Administrators can change hypervisor Code Integrity options for a specific policy.
Set-Mailbox	This command allows you to manipulate an Office 365 mailbox.
Set-Partition	Administrators can use this command to set partition attributes, such as setting the partition to be active.
Set-PhysicalDisk	You can use this command to set disk attributes.
Set-RuleOption	This command allows an administrator to modify the rule options in a Code Integrity policy.
Set-StoragePool	This command allows you to modify the properties of the specified storage pool.
Set-TimeZone	Administrators can set the system's time zone.
Set-Volume	This command allows an administrator to set or change the file system label of a volume.
Start-Process	This command allows you to start a process.
Start-Service	Administrators can start a service using this command.
Stop-Computer	This command shuts down a system.

PowerShell Command	Description
Stop-Service	This command stops a service.
Test-Connection	Sends a ping to test NIC adapter settings.
Update-Disk	Administrators can update cached information about a specified disk.
Update-StoragePool	This command will update the metadata of a Windows Server 2012 R2 storage pool.
Write-EventLog	This command writes an event to an event log.

Index

Note to the Reader: Throughout this index, page numbers in **bold** indicate primary discussions of a topic. *Italicized* page numbers indicate illustrations. Commands and computer entries are indicated with a special font.

Numbers

6to4 mechanisms, 308, 312–313, 945, 950
32-bit processors, 10–11, 513
64-bit processors, 10–11, 513
128-bit address space, 306, 943

A

ABE (Access-Based Enumeration), in DFS, 643
access control. *See also* DAC (Dynamic Access Control); data security
applying NTFS permissions, 668–671
configuring OneDrive, *678–681*
configuring share permissions, 676–678
controlling permissions inheritance, 671
creating/managing shared folders, 675–676
design goals, 668
determining/viewing NTFS permissions, 672–674
dynamic, 667
exam objectives, 695–696
folder options, 663–666
joining/sharing HomeGroups, *682–687*
managing file and folder security, 662–663
managing network access, 675
overview of, 662
ownership and security descriptors, 672
review questions and answers, 697–699, 1009–1010
search options, 666–667
securing files and folders, 668
access points
ad hoc connections without, 291–292
near-field communications vs., 295
network type as, 293, *294*
troubleshooting, 296–297, 934

Access-Based Enumeration (ABE), in DFS, 643
accessibility features. *See* Ease of Access Center
accessories, Windows 10, **707–709**
account policies
configuring, 885
using, 886–887
account-lockout policies
overview of, 424–426
setting, 889–891
accounts
group. *See* groups
user. *See* user accounts
accounts, Intune, **769–784**
adding users, 771–774
configuring alerts, 784, *784*
configuring connector site, 783–784
creating device groups, 774–776
creating policies, 777–778
creating user groups, 776–777
enrolling devices, 778–783
setting up administrator accounts, 770–771
setting up generally, 768–769
setting up users and groups, 769–770
accounts, linking Microsoft accounts with corporate accounts, 367–369, 827–829
ACPI (Advanced Configuration Power Interface)
BIOS compatibility, 16
managing power states, 212–213, 736
Windows 10 requirements, 519
ACT (Application Compatibility Toolkit)
application compatibility issues, 19
troubleshooting installation issues, 55, 339
using, 804–805
action logs, 36, 538
activation notices, desktop, *705*
Active Directory. *See* AD (Active Directory)

Active Directory Certificate Services
 (AD CS), 814
Active Directory Domain Services
 (AD DS), 814
Active Directory Federation Services (AD
 FS), 815
Active Directory Lightweight Directory
 Services (AD LDS), 815
Active Directory Rights Management Service
 (AD RMS)
  Active Directory components, 815
  setting up with DAC, 249, 667
Active Directory Users and Computers, 958
ActiveX Filtering, for browser security and
 privacy, 831
AD (Active Directory). *See also* Azure Active
 Directory
  activating systems with, 76–78
  adding Windows 10 to domain via, 321
  components, 814–815
  domain controllers, 277
  domain structure, *913*
  domain user accounts, 379
  domain-based networks, 274–276
  domains, 274, *275*, 849
  Global Catalog database, 278–279
  member servers, 277
  networks, 912–914
  Rights Management Service for, 249
  SID (Security Identification) number,
   662–663
AD CS (Active Directory Certificate
 Services), 814
AD DS (Active Directory Domain Services),
 814
AD FS (Active Directory Federation
 Services), 815
ad hoc mode, wireless connection options,
 291–292, 930
AD LDS (Active Directory Lightweight
 Directory Services), 815
AD RMS (Active Directory Rights
 Management Service)
  Active Directory components, 815
  setting up with DAC, 249, 667
Add Hardware Wizard, *95–97*
Add or Remove Snap-ins dialog box, *381*
Add Printer Wizard, *103*
Address bar, searching Internet from, 830
Address Resolution Protocol (ARP), 298

address translation, 949
ADK (Assessment and Deployment Kit),
 337–341
  about, 337–338
  administrative features, 55
  creating ICD disk image, 55–58, 338–339
  event tracing, 340
  installing Windows 10 with, 55–58, 78
  VAMT in, 340–341
  Windows Performance Toolkit in, 340
Administrative Tools
  Control Panel, *718*
  list of, 193, 718–719
  running in MMCs, *616*
Administrator account
  account types, 377, 847
  built-in user accounts, 378, 848
  choosing account type, 377
  malicious users and, 379
administrators
  account types, 377–379, 847
  activation keys and process management
   tools for, 340–341
  auditing failed attempts, 428
  built-in user accounts, 378, 848
  configuring user account control,
   435–437
  controlling file access, 249
  debugging apps, 340
  deploying software, 337–341
  locking out applications, 352–353
  managing groups, 407–415
  managing mandatory profiles, 403
  managing Windows configurations, 176–177
  personalizing desktop, 191
  provisioning packages, 338–339
  Registry and File Virtualization
   feature, 437
  setting up Intune accounts, 770–771
  setting up shared computer activation, 362
  solving app compatibility issues, 19,
   55, 339
Administrators group
  creating groups, 877
  group accounts, 874
  managing/applying LGPOs, 883
  permissions and privileges of, 409
Advanced Attributes dialog box, folder
 properties, *640*
Advanced Audit Policy Configuration, 886

advanced backup options, 987
advanced boot options, **460–469, 973–982**
  accessing, 461
  boot logging, 464–465, 977–978
  illustrated, *460*
  overview of, 973–974
  Safe Mode, *461–463,* 974–977
  start up options, 978–979
  Startup Repair tool, 982
  Startup Settings, *461,* 465–466, *975*
  system images, 981–982
  System Restore, 979–981
Advanced Configuration Power Interface.
  See ACPI (Advanced Configuration
  Power Interface)
advanced power settings, 738
Advanced System Settings, 728
Advanced tab
  Internet Options dialog box, 232
  Network Adapters Properties dialog box,
   281, *282*
  Properties dialog box, 107–108
alerts, Intune, *784, 784*
alerts, subscriptions and, 497
All Apps section (Windows 10 Start menu),
  178, 704
All Items feature, Azure, 815
Android devices, enrolling in Intune, 779
Anniversary Edition, 5
anonymous addresses, IPv6, 948
Anonymous Logon group, 411, 876
answer files, creating with SIM utility,
  579–580
anycast addresses, IPv6, 308, 310,
  945, 947
API (application programming interface)
  API hooking in Shim Infrastructure, 805
  Azure applications, 817
APIPA (Automatic Private IP Addressing)
  overview of, 316–317, 954
  TCP/IP and, 936
  Windows 10 support, 299
APNs (Apple Push Notifications), enrolling
  Apple devices in Intune, 778–780
Appearance tab (Performance Monitor),
  486, *487*
Apple iOS devices, enrolling in Intune,
  778–780
Application Compatibility Toolkit. *See* ACT
  (Application Compatibility Toolkit)

Application Control Policies, local security
  policies, 886
application programming interface (API)
  API hooking in Shim Infrastructure, 805
  Azure applications, 817
application virtualization. *See also* App-V
  (Application Virtualization), 581, 807
applications. *See also* apps
  Application Compatibility Toolkit,
   804–805
  applying permissions to, 260
  App-V and, 824, *824*
  assigning, 342
  Azure, 354–356, 815–818
  collections, *357–359*
  compatibility, 19, 521
  deploying. *See* deploying applications
  deploying with Intune. *See* deploying
   applications, with Intune
  desktop applications. *See* desktop
   applications
  disk imaging, 566
  file extensions, 805–806
  fixing older applications using Shims, 805
  installing. *See* installing applications
  installing/managing with Office 365 and
   Windows Store, 825–826
  integrating Microsoft accounts and
   personalization settings, 827–829
  locking, 813
  locking out, 352–353
  publishing, 342
  redirecting calls with Shim Infrastructure,
   343–344, 370
  reducing piracy, 544
  Registry and File Virtualization feature
   for, 437
  remote. *See* RemoteApp And Desktop
   Connections
  running upgrade analytics, 343
  sharing, 820
  sideloading, 364, 366–367, 826–827
  upgrade to Windows 10 and,
   520–521
  virtualization, 61, 346
  Windows 10, *179–181*
AppLocker, 352–353, 813
apps. *See also* applications
  building and placing in Windows
   Store, *825*

deploying to all users (deep-link), 788
installing/managing apps with Office 365
and Windows Store, 826
integrating Microsoft accounts and
personalization settings, 827–829
sideloading, 786–788, 826–827
Apps folder, 260
App-V (Application Virtualization)
components, 824
exam objectives, 840
Hyper-V and, 807
overview of, 362–363, 824
running applications in cloud, 370
types of virtualization, 581
appx packages, 336–337
architecture, Windows 10, 10–11, 512–513
ARP (Address Resolution Protocol), 298
Assessment and Deployment Kit. See ADK
(Assessment and Deployment Kit)
audit policies
Advanced Audit Policy Configuration, 886
options, 429–430
setting, 427–430, 892–894
Authenticated Users group, 876
authentication. See also GPOs (Group Policy
Objects); groups; LGPOs (Local Group
Policy Objects); user accounts
Credential Guard, 396–397
device health attestation, 397–398
exam objectives, 451–452, 905
logon errors during, 406–407
Microsoft Passport, 392–393, 863
multifactor authentication using smart
cards, 902–904
password security, 889
Remote Assistance, 440–444
Remote Desktop, 440, 444–447
review questions and answers, 453–455,
1004–1005
Secure Channel, 386–387, 856
smart cards for multifactor
authentication, 437, 694–695,
902–904
troubleshooting, 871–872
user profiles for, 401–404
user rights and, 896–897
video resources, 452
authorization. See authentication
autoconfiguration, in IPv6, 943
automatic driver installation, 89

Automatic Private IP Addressing. See APIPA
(Automatic Private IP Addressing)
automatic restarts after failure, 466
Automatic Virtual Machine Activation
(AVMA), 809
AutoPlay
configuring media disks, 193, 719
options, 194, 719
Autounattend.xml, for unattended
deployment, 571
AVMA (Automatic Virtual Machine
Activation), 809
Azure, 353–363, 814–823
about, 353–356
applications, 815–818
cloud-based storage, 611–612
creating collections in RemoteApp,
818–820
device redirection, 360–362,
822–823
exam objectives, 840
features, 131–132, 276
Intune built on, 765
OneDrive vs., 132–133
options and applications, 353–356
overview of, 814–815
review questions and answers, 841–843,
1012
setting up RemoteApp feeds, 359–360,
821, 821
shared computer activation, 823
sharing applications, 820
using RemoteApp, 357–362, 818
Azure Active Directory
Azure features, 818
components, 354, 814–815
Connect tool, 770
domain user accounts and, 379
Microsoft Intune and, 765
networks, 914–915
overview of, 276
using, 354, 379
Azure RemoteApp
creating collections, 818–820
device redirection, 822–823
overview of, 817
PowerShell commands, 822
setting up connection feeds, 821, 821
sharing applications, 820
using, 818

B

background (desktop), personalization options, 186, 712
Backup and Restore, **469–472, 982–989**
  advanced backup options, 987
  choosing from Control Panel, 469, *469*
  creating backups, 470–471, 982–984
  creating system image, 474–475, 987–988
  exam objectives, 457
  features, 194, 459
  overview of, 972
  restoring files from backup, 471–472, 985
  restoring files from OneDrive, 985–986
  restoring system image, 988–989
  Wbadmin.exe command, 986–987
  in Windows 7, 720
Backup Operators group, 410, 875
backups. *See also* Backup and Restore
  advanced options, 987
  creating, 470–471, 982–984
  files to home folders, 871
  peer-to-peer network, 274
  restoring files, 471–472, 985
  of system image, 467–468
  tips for making home folder, 406
  using WBadmin, 473–474
Balanced power plan, 213–214, 736–737
basic storage
  basic disks, 151–153
  disk storage options, 127–128, 607–608
  upgrading basic disk to dynamic or GPT disk, 631–633
Batch group, 876
batch services, Azure, 816
battery meter, managing power consumption, 217, 740
BCD (Boot Configuration Data), 543
bcedit utility, managing multiple-boot option, 37–38, *543–544*
billing administrators account, Intune, 771
biometrics
  for logging in, 863
  in Windows Hello, 393

BIOS compatibility, Windows OSs, 16, 519
BitLocker Drive Encryption
  choosing from Control Panel, 194, 720
  comparing in Windows versions, 691–692
  encrypting hard disks, 902
  encrypting removable media, 902
  features, 689–691
  for hardware security, 687–689
  Microsoft BitLocker Administration and Monitoring, 693–694
  recovery password, 689
  Trusted Platform Module and, *688*
  using in Windows 10, 692, *692*
  using with smart cards, 694
Bluetooth. *See also* configuring devices and drivers
  Device Manager displaying, 82
  Device Stage supporting, 84
  printers discovering, 102, 105
Boot Configuration Data (BCD), 543
boot logging, enabling, 464–465, 977–978
boot options, advanced. *See* advanced boot options
boot partitions, 21, 523
booting
  accessing Advanced Boot Options, 461
  configuring dual-booting, 37–38
  installing Windows 10 from bootable DVD, 22
  protecting against boot attacks, 394
  to Safe Mode, *462–463*
  Secure Boot, 397
  from VHD, 71–74
Broadband Tethering
  Intune and, 789–790
  managing Wi-Fi settings, *450–451, 755*
  overview of, 449–451, 754–755
broadcasts
  addresses for, 300
  IPv4, 937
  IPv6, 308
  SSID, 291, 294, *294*
browsers. *See* web browsers
bug fixes, in service packs, 547
built-in groups, 873–876
built-in user accounts, 847–849
business experiences, Windows 10, *508–509*
button, power, 214–215, 737

C

cabling, network, 287, 925
cache
    Azure applications, 817
    transparent caching, 449, 754
calculator, Windows applications, 705
CAs (certificate authorities), 438–439, 903
Category view, Control Panel, 192
CB (Current Branch) service option, 40
CBB (Current Branch for Business) service
    option, 40
CDFS (Compact Disk File System), 121
CDs. *See also* DVDs
    CDFS, 121
    installing hardware drivers, 94–95, 97
    setting up printers, 102
central processing units. *See* CPUs (central
    processing units)
certificate authorities (CAs), 438–439, 903
change permission (share), *259, 259,* 677
Check Disk
    dialog box, *168, 655*
    troubleshooting with, 168–169, 655–656
Check For Updates button, *42–43*
checkpoints, virtual machines, 69–70,
    591–592
child domains, 274–275, 912–913
Chkdsk command. *See* Check Disk
CHS (Cylinder-Head-Sector), in disk storage,
    610
Cipher command
    overview of, 648–649
    parameters, *648*
ciphertext. *See also* encryption, 643
circular logging, 488
classes, IPv4 addresses, 938, *938*
clean install
    exam objectives, 44
    performing, **22–29, 524–532**
    upgrade vs., 17, 512, **519–523**
    Windows versions requiring, 17, 18
cleanup utility. *See* Disk Cleanup
clients
    AD on network, 319–323
    configuring Telnet, 199
    defined, 277
    managing security using GPOs and
        LGPOs, 415–417
    network terminology and roles, 916
    peer-to-peer network computers as, 272

remote connections to, 445–447
clock speed, CPU, 513
cloud-based storage, **131–135, 611–615**
    Azure Active Directory, 276
    Azure data size availability, *131, 611–612*
    Azure features, 816
    configuring OneDrive, *613–615,*
        678–681
    domain user accounts and, 379
    OneDrive login screen and file location
        screen, *134*
    OneDrive welcome screen, *132*
    overview of Azure, 131–132, 611–612
    overview of OneDrive, 132–135,
        612–613
CNG (Cryptography Next Generation), *695,*
    903
collections, application, 357–359
Color Management, Control Panel, 194, 720
color options, desktop personalization, 187,
    187, 712–713
command-line. *See also* commands
    command prompt, 184, 710
    creating users, 388
    DISM.exe options, *579*
    WDSUTIL options, 564–565
    Windows Defender mode for, 202
    Windows Update options, 546–547
commands
    dual-boot, 37–38
    IPv6, 314–315, 951–952
    PowerShell, 169–171, 207–208, 350,
        395–396, 1018–1023
    REGEDIT/REGEDIT32, 192
    TCP/IP, 317–319
Compact Disk File System (CDFS), 121
Compact utility
    managing file and folder compression,
        161, 641–642
    options, *161, 641*
compatibility
    application. *See* ACT (Application
        Compatibility Toolkit)
    hardware. *See* HCL (Hardware
        Compatibility List)
    Windows To Go USB drives, 217–218
    wireless connectivity, 934
Compatibility View, web browsers, 225,
    226, 832–833
compression, **639–642**
    adding/removing, 160–161

Compact and Expand utilities, 161, 641–642
configuring NTFS, 125
of folders, 640–641
NTFS, 605
overview of, 639–640
supported in NTFS, 159–160
using compressed (zipped) folders, 161–162, 642
Computer Management
  Check Disk, 655–656
  configuring services, 757–758
  Disk Cleanup, 654, *654*
  Local Users and Groups, 382, 850
  Optimize Drives window, 653, *653*
Computer Name, Domain, And Workgroup Settings, *320*, 728–729
computers. *See also* upgrade, to Windows 10
  BIOS compatibility with Windows, 16
  capturing target image, *54*
  checking for system files on recovery partition, 475
  client, 277, 445–447
  device drivers, 17
  dual-boot configurations, 37–38
  GPO and LGPO security, 415–417
  hardware compatibility, 16
  hardware requirements, 14–16
  HomeGroup for non-Windows 10, 323
  hot swapping, 149
  joining domains, 27
  language and locale settings, 21, 34–35
  modifying HomeGroup passwords for, 241–243
  naming/renaming, 205, 729
  partitioning disks, 20–21
  port numbers, 279, 327
  power plans, 211–214
  recovery techniques, 459–460
  setting up, 23
  shared activation of, 362
  sharing resources with non-Windows 10, 244
  starting in Safe Mode, *461–463*
  startup options, 345
configuring devices and drivers, **81–117**
  automatic driver installation, *89*
  device health attestation setup, 397–398
  Device Manager for, 82–83, 84–85

Device Stage for, 82–84
exam objectives, 81, 115
installing/updating drivers, 88–97
opening devices and printers, 84
overview, 114–115
Print Management MMC snap-in, 112–114
printers, **101–114**
removable storage devices, 98–101
review questions and answers, 116–117, 999–1000
updating drivers, 88, 91
video resources, 115
configuring Windows 10 environment. *See also* mobility options, **175–235**
accessories, **707–709**
advanced power settings, 738
applications, **705–707**
background options, 712
battery meter for managing power consumption, 740
Broadband Tethering, 754–755
changing computer name, 729
changing virtual memory, 729–730
color options, 712–713
Control Panel options, 191–202, **717–727**
desktop, 177–191, **703–705**, 716
Ease of Access tools, 709, *709*
editing Registry, 743–744
exam objectives, 175, 233, 759
hibernation, 738–739
Internet browsers, 222–232
MMC and, 202
mobility options, 209–219, 732
offline files and synchronization, 732–734
overview of, 232, 702–703
personalization features, 711–712
power button, 737
power plans, 736–737
power policies, 734–735
power settings from command-line, 739
power states, 736
PowerShell commands, 207–208
preferences, 717
Remote Assistance, 745–749
remote connections, 744–745
Remote Desktop, 749–752
review questions and answers, 234–235, 760–761, 1001–1002, 1010–1011

screen savers, 713–714
services, 219–222, 756–758
Settings window, 206–207, *730–732*
start options, 715–716
syncing with devices, *743*
System icon, 203–206, 727–729
system utilities, 710–711
themes, 714–715
transparent caching, 449, 754
turning features on/off, 724, *724*
user tools, 711
video resources, 232–233
VPN connections, 752–754
Wi-Fi Direct, 742–743
Windows To Go, 740–742
configuring Windows 10, on networks,
    956–961
    adding to domain, *320*, 957–958
    joining/sharing HomeGroups, *322–323*,
        958–961
    overview of, 319–323, 956–957
    understanding network printing, 961
Connect tool, Azure Active Directory, 770
connections
    network. *See* network connections
    remote. *See* remote connections
Connections tab (Internet Options dialog
    box), 231
connectors, Intune, 783–784
Content tab (Internet Options dialog box),
    230–231
Control Panel
    about, 176, 184
    defined, 191
    installing features, 198–199, 345
    overview of, 191–192
    troubleshooting with, 201
    utilities, **193–202**, **717–727**
    view options, 192
controls, Web browser, 830–831
Convert command, 123–124, 603–604
copying user profiles, 404
core experiences, Windows 10, *507–508*
Cortana
    integration in Windows 10, 510
    overview of, 179, 705
counters
    adding Performance Monitor, *481*
    defined, 480
    logs, 488

CPUs (central processing units)
    Hyper-V requirements, 809
    Hyper-V support for symmetric
        multiprocessors, 808
    insufficient processing power, 35
    Windows 10 architecture, 10–11, 513
    Windows 10 hardware requirements, 14,
        516–517
Creator Owner group, 876
Credential Guard, 396–397
Credential Manager, Control Panel, 194, 720
critical updates, 793
CryptoAPI, 695, 903
Cryptographic Operators group, 875
cryptography. *See also* encryption, 904
Cryptography Next Generation (CNG),
    695, 903
Current Branch (CB) service option, 40
Current Branch for Business (CBB) service
    option, 40
Custom (Advanced) Installs. *See* clean install
Cylinder-Head-Sector (CHS), in disk
    storage, 610

D

DAC (Dynamic Access Control), 249, 265,
    667
dashboard, Microsoft Intune, *765*
Data Collector Sets, 479
Data Execution Prevention (DEP), 809
data files. *See also* data security
    accessing, *192*, 202
    compressing, 159–162
    restoring from backup, 471–472
data security, **237–269**
    configuring NTFS folders and files,
        244–256
    exam objectives, 237, 265
    HomeGroup networks and, **239–244**
    NTFS file and folder permissions,
        249–256
    overview, 238, 265
    review questions and answers, 266–268,
        1002–1003
    setting up OneDrive for, 260–264
    share permissions for, 257–260
    video resources, 265
data synchronization, Intune, *790–791*

Data tab (Properties dialog box), 485, *485*
Date And Time, Control Panel, 195, *195*
Date and Time, Control Panel, 720
debugging, Startup Settings options,
    465, 978
deep-link, deploying apps to all users, 788
default account, 378
default desktop, 177–179, *703*
Default Programs
    choosing program to be used by default,
        195, 721
    configuration items associated with,
        710, *710*
    setting file extensions, 806
    system utilities, 184, *184*
DefaultAccount, built-in user accounts, 848
deleting, 465
    checkpoints and subtrees, 70
    groups, 415, 880
    partitions and volumes, 154–155
    printers, 111–112
    user accounts, 389–391, 407, 859–861
DEP (Data Execution Prevention), 809
DEP (Device Enrollment Program), 780
Dependencies tab (Properties dialog box),
    services, 221
deploying applications. *See also* ADK
    (Assessment and Deployment Kit);
    DISM (Deployment Image Servicing and
    Management), **334–342**
    ACT, 339
    ETW, 340
    GPO deployments, 341–342
    .msi file deployments, 334–336
    solving compatibility issues, 19, 55, 339
    tools for, 337–341
    VAMT, 340–341
    Windows Performance Toolkit, 340
deploying applications, with Intune, **785–789**
    Microsoft Intune Software Publisher, 786
    overview of, 785–786
    sideloading apps, 786–788
    Windows Store apps to all users
        (deep-link), 788
deploying installations. *See also* Hyper-V
    Assessment and Deployment Kit,
        569–570
    configuring deployment toolkit, *559–561*
    Deployment Image Servicing and
        Management, 578–579

from disk image, *565–569, 573–575,*
    577–578
downloading and installing deployment
    toolkit, *557–558*
exam essentials, *594*
Imaging and Configuration Designer,
    570, 575–577
Microsoft Deployment Toolkit, *555–558*
options, *554–555*
overview of, *554*
review questions and answers, *595–597,*
    1007–1008
System Image Manager (SIM) utility,
    579–580
unattended installations, *561–562, 572–573*
utilities for, *571, 571*
Windows Deployment Services, *563–565*
Deployment Image Servicing and
    Management. *See* DISM (Deployment
    Image Servicing and Management)
deprecated features, Windows 10, 512
design goals, access control, 668
desktop, 177–191
    accessories, 182–183
    with activation notices, *705*
    All Apps section, *704*
    colors for, *187*, 187
    configuring, 190–191, *703–705*
    default, 177–179, *703*
    Ease of Access tools, 183, *184*
    personalization, 186, *186*, 189, 716
    screen savers, 187–188
    Settings app, 182, *183*
    Start screen, *190*, 190
    user preferences, 191
    Windows User's tools, 185
desktop applications, **804–813**
    ACT (Application Compatibility Toolkit),
        804–805
    AppLocker, 813
    exam objectives, 840
    file extensions, 805–806
    Hyper-V and, **806–811**
    review questions and answers, 841–843,
        1012
    Shims fixing older applications, 805
    UE-V (User Experience Virtualization),
        811–813
    Windows 10 applications, *179–181*
desktop computers. *See* computers

Desktop folder, user tools, 711
desktop icons, themes, 714
desktop screen
    installing Windows 10, *531*
    upgrade to Windows 10, *536*
desktop virtualization
    defined, 581
    Hyper-V, 807
    Hyper-V and, 346
    what is virtualization, 60–61
Details tab (Network Adapters Properties
    dialog box), 283, *284*
Detectnow, WSUS commands, 546–547
device drivers. *See also* configuring devices
    and drivers, **88–97**
    causing nonreproducible errors, 88
    compatibility issues, 18
    configuring NICs, 282–283, 921–922
    disabling signature enforcement of, 465
    driver signing, 115
    enabling/disabling, 92–93
    requirements for, 17
    rollback, 91–92, 460, 973
    troubleshooting errors due to, 88
    troubleshooting installation issues, 537
    troubleshooting network adapters, 925
    uninstalling/reinstalling, 93–94
    updating, 88, 91
    vendor's installation recommendations
        for, 94–95
    verifying signed, 97–98, 115
    viewing details of, 90–91
    Windows 10 requirements, 519
device enrollment manager, Intune, 771
Device Enrollment Program (DEP), 780
Device Guard, Windows 10 features,
    393–396, 510
Device Manager
    about, 82–83, 195
    accessing from Control Panel, 721
    configuring devices and drivers, 82–85
    configuring I/O devices, 99–100
    configuring NICs, *919*
    configuring wireless network settings,
        926–927
    enabling/disabling devices, 92–93
    launching and selecting NICs, *280–281*
    right-click menu for, *89*
    rolling back drivers, 91–92
    setting properties from, 86–87

System icon utilities, 728
    troubleshooting network adapters, 925
    uninstalling/reinstalling drivers in, 93–94
    updating drivers, 91
    using, 84–86
    viewing, 85
    viewing driver details, 90–91
Device Settings tab (Properties dialog box),
    108, 108
Device Stage
    about, 82–84
    illustrated, *83*
    selecting printer context window from,
        110
devices. *See also* Devices And Printers;
    specific devices
    configuring. *See* configuring devices and
        drivers
    connectors facilitating communication
        between, 783–784
    creating device groups, 774–776
    enrolling in Intune, 778–783
    health attestation, 397–398
    managing with Intune, 764–766
    redirection with RemoteApp, 360–362,
        822–823
    system utilities, 710
Devices And Printers. *See also* configuring
    devices and drivers
    about, 195
    accessing from Control Panel, 195, 721
    adding printers, *103*, 104
    illustrated, *83*
    printer context menu for, 105, *106*
    Printer window, *110*
    removing printer from, 111–112
DFS (Distributed File System), **642–643**
    advantages of, 642–643
    exam essentials, *657*
    overview of, 642
    review questions and answers, 658–660,
        1008–1009
    types of, 643
DFS Namespaces, 643
DFS Replication, 643
DHCP (Dynamic Host Configuration
    Protocol)
    assigning IP addresses, 943
    configuring dynamic IP addresses,
        953–954

ipconfig switches for, 318
overview of, 917
stateful vs. stateless autoconfiguration,
    306–307
TCP/IP and, 935
using for dynamic IP addresses, 316
DHCP servers, 278, 917
diagnostic loopback address, 301
Dialup group, 876
directory ownership, 254
directory services. *See* AD (Active
    Directory); Azure Active Directory
Disk Cleanup
    cleaning up restore points, 478, 991
    dialog box, *167, 654*
    running, 166–168, 654–655
disk images. *See also* DISM (Deployment
    Image Servicing and Management);
    system images, **51–59**
    adding features to offline disks, 74–75
    applying Windows 10 to VHD, 73
    creating, 55–58, 78
    DISM for, 51, 78
    ICD for, 55–58, 338–339, 575–577
    installing from, 58, 577–578
    manipulating, 58–59
    removing SID numbers, 52–53
    software for, 566
    System Preparation Tool, 50–54, 78,
        565–569, 573–575
    uses of, 51–52
disk maintenance utilities, **165–169,
    652–656**
    Check Disk, 168–169, 655–656
    Disk Cleanup, 166–168, 654–655
    Disk Optimization, 166, *166,* 653, *653*
    exam essentials, 657
    overview of, 652–653
    review questions and answers, 658–660,
        1008–1009
Disk Management, **140–155, 620–639**
    about, 140–142
    adding new disks, 629
    administering hard disk tasks, 622–623
    changing drive letters and paths,
        633–634
    converting basic disk to GPT, 151–153
    creating dynamic from basic disk,
        151–153
    creating extended volumes, 636–637

creating simple, spanned, and striped
    volumes, 635–636
creating volumes or partitions, 629–631
deleting partitions and volumes, 634–635
Disk Management window, *621*
Dispart as alternative to, 621–622
information displayed by, 620–621
managing dynamic storage, 635
managing hard disks, 142–143
managing local disk properties, *144–149*
overview of, 615–616
partitioning disks, 149–151, 523
reassigning drive letters and paths,
    153–154
running out of disk space, 157–158
status codes, 158–159, 638–639
troubleshooting disks, 158–159,
    638–639
upgrading basic disk to dynamic or GPT
    disk, 631–633
viewing disk properties, 623
viewing volume and local disk properties,
    624–629
Volumes tab of Properties dialog, *623*
Disk Optimization
    Optimize Drives window, *166, 653*
    optimizing, defragging disks, 166, 653
disk partitioning, Windows 10, 523–524
disk quotas, NTFS, 606–607
disk setup screen, installing Windows 10, *528*
disk space
    encrypting used space only, 690
    identifying installation problems, *537*
    reserving for offline files, 210
    running out of, 35, 637
    Windows 10 hardware requirements, *518*
disk storage, **607–611**
    basic storage, 607–608
    dynamic storage, 608
    exam essentials, 657
    GPT (GUID Partition Table), 610–611
    overview of, 607
    review questions and answers, 658–660,
        1008–1009
    setting up storage, **127–135**
    simple volumes, 608, *608*
    spanned volumes, *609,* 609
    striped volumes, 609–610
    upgrading basic disk to dynamic or GPT
        disk, 631–633

Disk Usage tab, Manage Offline Folders, 733

Diskpart command-line utility
    as alternative to Disk Management utility, 141, 621–622
    Dispart window, *142, 622*

DISM (Deployment Image Servicing and Management)
    DISM.exe command-line options, *579*
    overview of, 578–579

DISM (Deployment Image Servicing and Management) utility
    applying Windows 10 to VHD, 73
    creating images with, *51, 78*
    manipulating images, *58–59*

Display, Control Panel, 195, 721

Distributed COM Users group, 875

Distributed File System. *See* DFS (Distributed File System)

distribution server, 22

DNS (Domain Name Service)
    overview of, 916
    TCP/IP and, 935

DNS servers
    defining network terminology and roles, 277–278, 916
    TCP/IP and, 298

documents
    printing status for, 108–109
    queueing, 110–111
    signing with smart cards, 694, 903

Documents folder, user tools, 711

domain controllers, 277, 915

domain highlighting, for browser security and privacy, 831

Domain Join, Windows 10 features, 511

Domain Name Service (DNS)
    overview of, 916
    servers. *See* DNS servers
    TCP/IP and, 935

domain selection screen, Windows 10, *530*

domain structure, AD (Active Directory), *913*

domain user accounts, 379, 849

domain-based networks
    Active Directory servers for, 274–276
    member servers of, 277
    Windows Server 2012 R2, 912–914

domains. *See also* domain-based networks

about, 29

Active Directory, 274–276, 379

adding Windows 10 to, 320–321, 957–958

assigning GPOs by, 341

defined, 912

domain user account, 849

gaining access with Workplace Join, 380

joining during installation, 27

structure of, *913*

using GPOs security options for, 415–417

DOS, disk partition configuration utilities, 523

downloading System Center, 335

DRA
    creating on stand-alone Windows 10 computer, 646–648
    recovering encrypted files, 646, 647

Drive Encryption. *See* BitLocker Drive Encryption

drive letters
    assigning, *150*
    showing in Computer folder, 247

Driver Rollback, 91–92, 460, 973

driver signing, 97–98, 115

Driver tab (Network Adapters Properties dialog box), 282–283

drivers. *See* device drivers

drives. *See* hard disks

dual stack operation
    implementations, 308, 312–313
    running IPv4 and IPv6 on same network, 949–950

dual-booting
    configurations, 37–38
    support for, **542–544**

DVD setup screen, *31, 533*

DVD-R/W drive hardware requirements, 14

DVDs
    clean install from, 23–29
    installing hardware drivers from, 94–95, 97
    installing Windows 10 from bootable, 22
    setting up printers from, 102
    upgrades using, 30–34

Dynamic Access Control (DAC), 249, 265, 667

dynamic disks
    about, 128
    creating from basic disk, 151–153

simple volumes, 128, *128*, 156
spanned volumes, *129*, 129, 156
striped volumes, 129–130, 156
uses for, 120
Dynamic Host Configuration Protocol. *See* DHCP (Dynamic Host Configuration Protocol)
dynamic IP addresses, configuring, 953–954
dynamic memory, Hyper-V features, 809
dynamic storage. *See also* dynamic disks
    creating extended volumes, 156–157, 636–637
    creating simple, spanned, and striped volumes, 635–636
    disk storage options, 608
    dynamic disks, 120, 128, 151–152, 153
    GPT (GUID Partition Table), 610–611
    managing, 155, 635
    shrinking volumes, 157
    simple volumes, *128*, 128, 156, 608
    spanned volumes, 129, *129*, 156, 609
    striped volumes, 129–130, 156, 609–610
    upgrading basic disk to dynamic or GPT disk, 631–633

E

early launch of anti-malware protection, 465
Ease of Access Center
    accessibility tools, 709, *709*, 721
    managing Windows 10, 195
Easy Connect (Remote Assistance), 440–444, 745
Edge. *See* Microsoft Edge
Edit Virtual Disk Wizard, 66, *587–588*
editing
    drive letter, 154
    inherited permissions, 253
    Registry, 743–744
editions, Windows 10. *See* versions, Windows 10
EDP (Enterprise Data Protection), 510
Education edition, Windows 10
    business experiences, 508–509
    core experiences, 507–508
    overview of, 11
    version options, 506
EFS (Encrypted File System), **643–645**
    design goals for access control, 668

encrypting files and folders, *606*, 644–645
exam essentials, 657
managing file sharing, 645
NTFS and, 605–606
overview of, 643–644
review questions and answers, 658–660, 1008–1009
elevated privileges, 435–437
email
    Intune, *768*
    signing with smart cards, 694, 903
Encrypted File System. *See* EFS (Encrypted File System)
encryption
    AD RMS, 249
    backing up encrypted files, 470, 983
    Cipher command, 648–649
    configuring folders, 125–126
    configuring user accounts, 853
    of drives, 902
    enabling WPA/WPA2, 291
    of files and folders, 644–645
    of hard drives. *See* BitLocker Drive Encryption
    isolated cryptography, 904
    NTFS and, 605–606
    recovering encrypted, 646–648
    selecting for wireless networks, 294, *295*
    setting up, *606*
    storing passwords, 889
    of used disk space, 690
    verifying offline files are encrypted, 210
Encryption tab, Manage Offline Folders, 734
enrolling devices, in Intune, 778–783
Enterprise Data Protection (EDP), 510
Enterprise edition, Windows 10
    business experiences, 508–509
    core experiences, 507–508
    overview of, 13–14
    preparing to install, 515–518
    version options, 506
enterprise installations. *See also* System Preparation Tool, **49–80**
    activating machines for, 75–77
    disk imaging, 51–59
    exam objectives, 49, 78
    overview, 77–78

review questions and answers, 79–80, 999

video resources, 78

working with virtual machines, **60–75**

environment configuration. *See* configuring Windows 10 environment

environment variables, configuring user accounts, 853

error logs, 36, 538

ETW (Event Tracing for Windows), 340

Event Log Readers group, 875

Event Viewer

  recovery techniques, 973

  using, 493–497

  viewing NIC events, 923, *923*

  when to use, 459

Events tab (Network Adapters Properties dialog box), 283, *284*

Everyone group, 876

exam 70-698 preparation, 4

exam objectives

  access control, 695–696

  App-V (Application Virtualization), 840

  authorization and authentication, 451–452

  automated deployment, 594

  configuring Windows 10 environment, 759

  data security, 237, 265

  desktop applications, 840

  device and driver configuration, 81, 115

  DFS (Distributed File System), 657

  disk maintenance utilities, 657

  disk storage, 657

  EFS (Encrypted File System), 657

  enterprise installations, 49, 78

  file systems, 656

  groups, 905

  hardware security, 695–696

  Hyper-V, 594

  installing applications, 333, 369–370

  installing Windows 10, 3, 44–45, 548

  managing Windows environments, 175, 233

  Microsoft Azure, 840

  Microsoft Intune, 799

  monitoring and recovery, 457, 498–499

  networks, 271, 329, 330

  recovery, 993

  storage configuration, 119, 171–172

  Storage Spaces, 657

  UAC (User Account Control), 905

  user accounts, 905

  Web browsers, 840

Exchange devices, configuring Intune connector for, 783–784

executables, elevated privileges for running, 901–902

Expand utility, 641–642

Export Complete screen, *114*

exporting

  print server settings to file, *113–114*

  virtual machines, 71

express settings screen, Windows 10 installation, *27, 529*

extended volumes

  creating, 635–636

  Extend Volume Wizard, *636*

extension header

  defined, 305

  IPv6, 307, 942

F

failures

  automatic restarts after, 466

  installation, 36–37

  TCP/IP access, 36

  upgrade, 20, 522–523

FAT32

  about, 120, 122

  comparing file system capabilities, *601*

  converting to NTFS, 123–124

  creating new volumes, 630

  features, 121

  managing data compression, 639–640

  overview of, 602

fault tolerance design, 298

faxes, Windows Fax and Scan, 708

FDE (Full Disk Encryption), BitLocker features, 690–691

FDISK, partition configuration, 523

features of Windows 10

  about, 5–6

  deprecated, 10, 512

  modifying for existing Windows disk images, 74–75

  overview of, 5–6, 8–9, 510–512

  review questions and answers, 46–47

  turning on/off, 724, *724*

Fibre Channel, Hyper-V features, 808
File Allocation Table. *See* FAT32
File Explorer
    options, 195, *196*
    system utilities, 710
    using Control Panel, 721
file extensions
    associating apps with, 344
    desktop applications, 805–806
    showing/hiding, 247
File History
    creating system images, 468
    overview of, 196
    using Control Panel, 721
file servers, 249
file systems. *See also* FAT32; NTFS
    about, 120
    cancelling conversions to NTFS, 124
    comparing and selecting, 121–123
    comparing capabilities, *601*
    comparing features, 121
    configuring NTFS, 604–607
    converting, 603–604
    converting FAT32 to NTFS, 123–124
    exam essentials, 656
    FAT32, 602
    NTFS, 602–603
    overview of, 600–601
    review questions and answers, 658–660,
        1008–1009
    selecting, 601–602
files. *See also* file systems
    associating applications with, 344
    backing up and restoring, *192*, *194*, *459*,
        469–472, *984*
    backing up encrypted, 983
    backing up to home folder, 871
    boot log, 464–465
    checking recovery partition for system
        file, 475
    compressing, 159–162
    creating access to data files, *192*, 202
    deploying .msi files, 335–336
    determining permissions for copied or
        moved files, 674
    encrypting with Cipher command,
        648–649
    encrypting with EFS, 644–645
    managing offline files, 209–210
    managing security, 662–663

managing sharing, 645
migrating, 17, 45, *538*
permissions, 249–256
recovering encrypted files, 646–648
recovering from OneDrive, 472–473
refreshing or recycling, 478–479
Registry and File Virtualization, 902
restoring files from Backup and Restore,
    471–472, 985
restoring files from OneDrive, 985–986
restoring from Recycle Bin, 991–992
securing access to, 668
security for, 239
selecting search options, 238
share permissions, 257–260
troubleshooting, 36–37
VHDX, 348
filters
    firewall rules, 327
    InPrivate Filtering, 833–834
    MAC address filter, 291
    SmartScreen Filter, 831
firewalls. *See also* Windows Firewall
    connection security rules for, 328–329
    filtering firewall rules, 327
    monitoring, 329, 966
    need for multiple, 272, 329
    setting LGPO security for, 421
    Windows Firewall with Advanced
        Security, 886
Flash Player, Control Panel, 196, 722
Folder Options, **244–249**
    accessing from Control Panel, *721*
    general options, 245, *245*, 663, *663*
    opening, 244–245
    search options, 248–249, 666–667
    view options, 245–248, 664–666
folders
    access control, 663–666, 668
    accessing local policies, 427, *427*
    Advanced Attributes dialog box, *640*
    compressing/uncompressing, 160–161,
        640–641
    creating/managing shared, 257–258,
        675–676
    encrypting, 125–126, 644–645
    general options, *663*
    home folders, 404–405
    HomeGroup, *322*, *322*
    managing offline folders, 209–210

managing security, 662–663
NTFS permissions, 249–256
OneDrive, 262, *263*
properties, 244–249
refreshing or recycling, 478–479
restoring from Recycle Bin, 991–992
search options, *667*
security, 239
setting up encryption, *606*
share permissions for, 257–260
storing user profiles, 403–404
using compressed (zipped), 161–162
using compressed (zipped) folders, 642
view options, 664–666
Fonts, Control Panel, 196, 722
Full Control permission, NTFS
    applying, 250–251, 669
    share permissions, 259, *259*, 677
    viewing, 254–255, 672–674
Full Disk Encryption (FDE), BitLocker
    features, 690–691
Full Volume Encryption (FVE), BitLocker
    features, 690–691
fully active power state, 736

G

General tab (Folder Options dialog box),
    245, 245, 663, *663*
General tab (IE11 Internet Properties),
    228–229, 835, *835*
General tab (Network Adapters Properties
    dialog box), 281, *281*
General tab (Performance Monitor
    Properties dialog box), 484, *484*
General tab (Properties dialog box)
    disk management properties, 624–625
    service properties, 220
    user properties, 398–399
    volume properties, *144*
Get Skype, Windows applications, 706
Getting Started tasks, *706*
Getting Started, Windows applications,
    705
GHz (gigahertz), CPU speed, 11, 513
Global Catalog, 278–279, 917
global unicast addresses, IPv6, 310–311, 947
gpedit.msc, configuring RemoteApp
    redirection, 823

GPMC (Group Policy Management Console),
    416, 881
GPOs (Group Policy Objects)
    configuring Device Guard, 395
    configuring device redirection, 361–362,
        823
    configuring startup options, 345
    configuring Windows 10 environment,
        702
    creating removable-device policies, 155
    deploying applications, 341–342, 957
    groups vs., 408
    managing/applying local GPOs, 883–885
    security options, 415–417
    understanding, 880–881
    using Group Policy Result Tool, *882*
gpresult (Group Policy Result Tool), 417–418
gpresult (Group Policy Result Tool), 882,
    882
GPT (GUID Partition Table)
    dynamic storage, 610–611
    GPT disks, 151–153
    overview of, 130
    upgrading basic disk to GPT disk,
        631–633
    Windows 10 support, 120
Graph tab (Performance Monitor Properties
    dialog box), 486, *486*
Graph view (Performance Monitor), *482*,
    482
graphics cards. *See* video adapters
Group Policy
    design goals for access control, 668
    remote assistance, 746
    Windows 10 features, 511
Group Policy Management Console
    (GPMC), 416, 881
Group Policy Objects. *See* GPOs (Group
    Policy Objects)
Group Policy Result Tool (gpresult),
    417–418, 882–883
groups, **872–887**
    adding to Intune, 776–777
    adding users, 399–400
    assigning NTFS permissions, 254–256
    assigning user rights, 895–899
    auditing, 894
    built-in, 408–411, 873–876
    configuring local security policies,
        885–886

creating, 412–413, 877–878
creating device groups in Intune, 774–776
deleting, 415, 880
design goals for access control, 668
exam objectives, 905
HomeGroups, *682–687*
managing and creating, 407–415
managing membership, 864–865,
    878–880
managing/applying local policies,
    883–885
membership, *413–415*
overview of, 376, 872–873
review questions and answers, 906–907,
    1013
security descriptors, 253–254, 672
setting account-lockout policies,
    889–891
setting audit policies, 892–894
setting password policies, *887–889*
setting up Intune, 769–770
special, 411–412, 876–877
understanding group policy objects,
    880–881
using account policies, 886–887
using Group Policy Result Tool, 882–883
using local policies, *892, 892*
Guest account, 378, 848
Guests group, 410, 875
GUID Partition Table. *See* GPT (GUID
    Partition Table)

H

hard disks
    adding, 149–151, 629
    administering tasks, 622–623
    changing drive letters and paths, *630,*
        633–634
    converting to dynamic and GPT, 151–153
    disk management for, 120
    disk partitioning, 523–524
    displaying general properties, *144*
    encrypting. *See* BitLocker Drive
        Encryption
    hardware requirements for, 14
    Hyper-V features, 809
    identifying drive or partition for
        installation, 26

identifying installation problems, 537
installing nonsupported, 36
maintaining. *See* disk maintenance
    utilities
managing virtual, 64–66, 585–588
measurement units for space and memory,
    16
partitioning, 20–21
power plans and, 214
RAID, 162–163
reassigning drive letters and paths,
    153–154
recovery drives, 467
running out of space, 157–158
space management options for, 157–158
storage on. *See* disk storage
storage space quotas for, 126–127
troubleshooting, 36, 158–159, 638–639
upgrading basic, *632*
viewing properties, *144–149, 623–629*
virtual. *See* VHDs (virtual hard disks)
Windows 10 hardware requirements,
    517–518
hardware. *See also* Device Manager
    adding hard disks, 149–151
    configuring devices and drivers. *See*
        configuring devices and drivers
    device drivers required, 17
    exam objectives for, 44
    installation requirements for Windows
        10, 14–16, *516–517*
    legacy, *95–97*
    not on HCL, 35
    secure boot for, 397
    selecting from HCL, 16
    Windows-compatible BIOS for, 16
hardware compatibility. *See also* HCL
    (Hardware Compatibility List)
    identifying installation problems, 537
    installing Windows 10, 518–519, 521
Hardware Compatibility List. *See* HCL
    (Hardware Compatibility List)
hardware security
    comparing Windows versions,
        691–692
    exam objectives, 695–696
    features of BitLocker Drive Encryption,
        688, 689–691
    Microsoft BitLocker Administration and
        Monitoring, 693–694

overview of BitLocker Drive Encryption, 687–689

review questions and answers, 697–699, 1009–1010

smart cards, 694–695

using BitLocker in Windows 10, 692, *692*

Hardware tab (Properties dialog box), 145–146

HCL (Hardware Compatibility List)
about, 16
exam objectives for, 44
installing Windows 10, 518–519
NIC not on, 286
troubleshooting network adapters, 925
using hardware not on, 35

HDInsight, Azure applications, 816

headers
IPv4, 305, 307
IPv6, 307, 942, 944

hexadecimal format, IPv6 addresses, 308, 945–946

hibernation
configuring, 738–739
Hibernate mode, 213, 215
managing power states, 736

High Performance power plan, 213–214, 736–737

Histogram view (Performance Monitor), 482, *483*

Home edition, Windows 10
business experiences, 508–509
core experiences, 507–508
features, 12
preparing to install, 514
version options, 506

home folders
backing up files to, 871
setting up, 404–406, 870–871

HomeGroups, **239–244**
accessing, *192*, 196, 722
adding to Start menu, 242, *244*
creating, *240*, 240
defined, 76, 239
joining existing, *240–241*
joining/sharing, 321–323, 682–687, 958–961
passwords, 241–*243*, 323
sharing printers with, 239
using for non Windows 10 OSs, 323

workgroup vs., 272

HomeGroupUser$ account, 378, 848

host requirements, Windows To Go, 218–219, *741*

hot swapping, hard disks, 149, 629

Hyper-V, **60–75**, **806–811**
about, 60, 370
advantages of, 346, 807
configuring virtual machines, 66–75
creating and changing hard disks, 66–67
creating virtual machines, 588–590
desktop applications and, *810*
exam essentials, 594
features, 347–348, 808–809
hard disk types in, *65*
installing, 61–63, 348–350, 582, 809–811
installing in Windows 10, 583
installing in Windows Server 2012 R2, 582
Integration Components (Services), 68–69, 590
managing, 63, *63*
managing virtual hard drives, 585–588
managing virtual machine checkpoints, 591–592
managing virtual switches, 584–585
moving virtual machines, 592–593
overview of, 580–581, 806–807
review questions and answers, 595–597, 1007–1008
using for desktop applications, 345–346
virtual switches, 64
virtualization with, 60–61
what is virtualization, 581

Hyper-V Manager, *63*, 584, *584*

hypervisors. *See also* Hyper-V; VMs (virtual machines), 808

I

ICACLS command, 255–256, 674

ICD (Imaging and Configuration Designer)
creating disk images, 56–58, 575–576
deploying and configuring operating systems and images, 338–339

`icd.exe` switches, *576–577*
overview of, *55–56*, 570
ICMP (Internet Control Message Protocol),
    298
icons
    Control Panel, *192*
    personalization themes, 714
IE. *See* Internet Explorer/Internet Explorer
    11 (IE11)
IECTT (Internet Explorer Compatibility Test
    Tool), 805
IGMP (Internet Group Message Protocol),
    298
IIS_IUSRS groups, 875
IKEv2 (Internet Key Exchange version 2),
    448, *752*
Image Capture Wizard (`Image Capture
    Wizard.exe`), 571, *577–578*
images, disk. *See* disk images
Imaging and Configuration Designer. *See*
    ICD (Imaging and Configuration
    Designer)
inbound rules, firewall, 325, *326*, 328,
    963–965
Indexing Options, Control Panel, 197, 722
Infrastructure mode, wireless connections,
    930
inheritance, controlling permissions
    inheritance, 253, 671
Initial User, built-in accounts, 378, 848
InPrivate Browsing, web browsers, 831,
    833–834
InPrivate Filtering, web browsers,
    833–834
input/output. *See* I/O (input/output)
Install Now button, *24*
install type screen, Windows 10, *528*
installation log files, 36–37
installation status screen, Windows 10,
    529, 535
installing applications. *See also* PnP (Plug
    and Play), **333–373**
    AppLocker, 352–353
    App-V, 362–363
    Azure, 353–363
    configuring UE-V, 350–352
    from Control Panel, 345
    deployment options, 334–342
    exam objectives, 333, 369–370
    filename-extension association, 344

Hyper-V, 61–62, 345–350
review questions and answers, 371–373,
    1004
setting Microsoft account, 367–369
Shims Infrastructure, 343–344, 370
sideloading apps, 366–367
startup options, 345
Upgrade Analytics tool, 343
video resources, 370
installing Hyper-V role, 582
installing Windows 10. *See also* configuring
    devices and drivers; enterprise
    installations, **3–47**
    ADK for, 55–58, 78
    application compatibility, 521
    architecture, 512–513
    BIOS compatibility, 519
    business experiences, 508–509
    clean installs, 17–18, **22–29**, 44
    command-line options, 546–547
    core experiences, *507–508*
    desktop screen, *531, 536*
    from disk image, 58, *577–578*
    disk partitioning, 523–524
    disk setup screen, *528*
    domain selection screen, *530*
    driver requirements, 519
    dual-boot configurations, 37–38
    DVD setup screen, *533*
    exam objectives, 3, 44–45, 548
    express settings screen, *27, 529*
    features, 510–512
    hardware compatibility, 518–519, 521
    hardware requirements, 14–16, *516–517*
    Hyper-V, 61–63, 583, *583*
    identifying installation problems,
        537–538
    install type screen, *528*
    installation status screen, *529, 535*
    installing printers, 102–105
    language and locale settings, 524
    licensing, *527*
    Local user profiles, *542*
    migrating files and settings, **538–541**
    migrating profiles, 541–542
    multiple-boot support, **542–544**
    network installs, 22
    new install vs. upgrade, **519–523**
    overview, 44
    PC account screen, *530*

performing clean install, 524–532
performing upgrade, **532–536**
preparation generally, 513–514
preparing for, 514–518
Ready to Install screen, *535*
review questions and answers, 46–47,
  549–551, 998, 1006–1007
service packs, 42–43, 547
shared network printers, 105
troubleshooting, 35–37, 538
updates, 39–43, **544–546**
upgrades, 17–20, 30–35, 44–45, 343
User Account Control screen, *534*
User Profiles Settings button, *541*
vendor recommendations, 94–95
versions, 506
video resources, 44
Welcome screen, *536*
Windows Activation, 38–39, 544, *545*
instances, monitoring, 480–481
Integration Components (Services), Hyper-V,
  68–69, 590
Interactive groups, 876
Internet browsers. *See* web browsers
Internet Control Message Protocol (ICMP),
  298
Internet Explorer Compatibility Test Tool
  (IECTT), 805
Internet Explorer/Internet Explorer 11
  (IE11). *See also* web browsers
  about, 222
  advanced settings, 839
  Compatibility View, 832–833
  configuring, 834
  connection settings, 838
  content parameters, 837–838
  general parameters, *835*, 835
  InPrivate Browsing and Filtering,
    227–228, 833–834
  privacy parameters, 836–837
  program options, 838–839
  properties, *228–232*
  Protected Mode, 236, 833
  security parameters, 835–836
  understanding web browsers, 830
  Windows 10 features, 511
  Windows accessories, 707
  working with web slices, 831–832
Internet Group Message Protocol (IGMP),
  298

Internet Key Exchange version 2 (IKEv2),
  448, *752*
Internet Options
  configuring IE 11 options, *228–232*
  overview of, 722
Internet Properties dialog box, *197*, 722
Internet Protocol. *See* IP (Internet Protocol)
Internet Protocol security (IPsec), 307, 421
interrupt request (IRQ), 923
Intra-Site Automatic Tunnel Addressing
  Protocol. *See* ISATAP (Intra-Site
  Automatic Tunnel Addressing Protocol)
Intune. *See* Microsoft Intune
Intune App Wrapping tool, 785
I/O (input/output)
  device configuration, 98–101
  network adapter resources, 923
IP (Internet Protocol). *See also* TCP/IP
  (Transmission Control Protocol/Internet
  Protocol)
  IPsec for, 307, 421
  Layer 3 protocols, 941
  TCP/IP services, 298
  testing IP configuration, 317–318, *955*
IP addresses
  APIPA (Automatic Private IP Addressing),
    954
  APIPA for assigning, 316–317
  comparing IPv4 vs. IPv6, 299, 305–306,
    936
  configuring dynamic addresses, 316
  configuring dynamic IP addresses,
    953–954
  configuring static addresses, 315
  configuring static IP addresses, 952–953
  configuring TCP/IP, 952
  connectivity and, 297–298
  diagnostic loopback address, 301
  extension headers, 305, 307
  IP addressing and configuration, 937
  testing IP configuration, 954–955
  version 6. *See* IPv6 addresses
IP Security Policies on Local Computer, 886
`ipconfig` command
  switches, *955*
  testing IP configuration, 317–318, *955*
IPsec (Internet Protocol security), 307, 421
IPv4 addresses
  addressing, 300–304
  classes, 938, *938*

comparing with IPv6, 299, 305–306, 936
headers, 305, 307
overview of, 937–938
subnet masks, *939–941*
subnet masks for unicast addresses,
    302–304
testing configurations for, 317–318
transitions to IPv6, 308
understanding, **937–941**
viewing connection details, 288–289
IPv4-to-IPv6 transmission, 944–945
IPv6 addresses, **304–315**
    address types, 310–312, 947–949
    addressing, 304–308
    assigning, 309–310, 946–947
    comparing IPv4 vs. IPv6, 936
    comparing with IPv4, 299, 305–306, 936
    dual stack, 308, 312–313
    extension header, 305, 307, 942
    format, 308–309, 945
    information commands, 951–952
    integration/migration, 312, 949–951
    overview of, 941–945
    PNRP's use of, 440–441
    prefixes and well-known addresses, 312
    shortcuts, 309, 946
    testing configurations for, 317–318
    transitions from IPv4 to, 308
    tunneling, 312–314
    useful commands for, 314–315
    viewing connection details, 288–289
iris scans, 393
IRQ (interrupt request), 923
ISATAP (Intra-Site Automatic Tunnel
    Addressing Protocol)
    IPv4-to-IPv6 transmission, 308, 945
    IPv6 tunneling, 313, 950–951

K

Kernel Debugger, 465
Keyboard, Control Panel, 197, 723
KMS (Key Management Service), 49, 77–78

L

L2TP (Layer 2 Tunneling Protocol), 448, 753

Language, Control Panel, 197, 723
language settings, installing Windows 10,
    21, 34–35, 524
Laplink utility, 18
laptops. *See also* computers
    hibernation mode, 213
    power plans, 211–214, 735
Large Icons view, Control Panel, 192
Layer 2 Tunneling Protocol (L2TP), 448, 753
layers, OSI model, 287
legacy computers
    HomeGroup for non Windows 10, 323
    using legacy hardware, *95–97*
LGPOs (Local Group Policy Objects)
    accessing, 420
    account policies, 421–422
    account-lockout policies, 424–426
    assigning user rights, 430–434
    audit policies, 427–430
    deploying, 957
    local security policies, 420–421
    managing/applying, 418–420, *884*
    password policies, 422–424
    security options, 415–417
    understanding, 880–881
licensing
    installing Windows 10, *527*
    terms, *25*
Line of Business applications. *See* LOB (Line
    of Business) applications
linear logging, 488
link-local addresses, IPv6, 311, 948
List Folder Contents permission (NTFS),
    251, 252, 254–255
Loadstate.exe, 539, *540–541*
LOB (Line of Business) applications
    building and supporting, 366–367, 826
    CNG and CryptoAPI support, 903
local accounts, user accounts, 849
Local Computer Policy. *See also* Local
    Security Policies
    adding, 419, 884
    applying user-rights policy, 899
    configuring, 885–886
    configuring account-lockout policies,
        891
    configuring audit policies, 894
    configuring password policies, 889
    managing/applying LGPOs, 883
    using local policies, 427, 427, 892

Local Group Policy Objects. *See* LGPOs
    (Local Group Policy Objects)
local groups
    built-in, 408–411
    creating, 412–413
local logon permissions, 407
local policies
    configuring, 886
    using, 427, *427*, 892, *892*
local profiles, migrating, 542, *542*
Local Security Policies. *See also* Local
    Computer Policy
    configuring, 420–421
    using, 646–648
local user accounts
    creating, 387–388, 857–858
    defined, 379, 849
Local Users and Groups
    accessing, 382
    accessing LGPOs, 885
    adding Local Computer Policy, 419, 884
    adding snap-in for, 380–382, *851–852*
    adding users to groups, 865
    assigning home folders, 405, 870
    changing user password, 392, 862
    creating groups, 877–878
    creating user accounts, 387–388, 849,
        857–858
    deleting user accounts, 859–861
    disabling user accounts, 859
    managing group membership, *878–880*
    managing user accounts, *850–852*
    managing user properties, 864
    renaming user accounts, 391–392, 861–862
    setting up user profiles, 867
locale settings, installing Windows 10, 21,
    34–35, 524
Location Aware Printing, 917
Lock Screen feature, personalization
    options, 713–714
log files
    action logs, 36, 538
    counter logs, 488
    debugging apps with ETW, 340
    displaying, 459
    error, 36
    Event Viewer, 459, 495, *496*
    saving and analyzing performance, 487–488
    troubleshooting installation, 36–37, 538
Log On tab (Properties dialog box), 220

logging, circular, 488
logging, enabling boot logging, 464–465,
    977–978
logging, linear, 488
logical drives, 20
log-in/logon
    auditing, 428, 894
    authentication errors, 406–407
    with Microsoft Passport, pictures, or
        biometrics, 863
    OneDrive, 262–264
    with picture, 393, 863
    Smart-Card Domain Logon, 903
    specifying logon account for services, 220
    starting up in Safe Mode, *461–463*
    using logon scripts, 404, 869
log-off, 380, 850
low-resolution video, enabling, 465
LTSB (Long-Term Servicing Branch) service
    option, 40

M

MAC address filter, 291
Mail, Control Panel, 198, 723
MakeAppx.exe, 336
MakeCert.exe, 825
malicious code, 394
malware, 394
Manage Wi-Fi Settings screen, *450*, *451*
mandatory profiles, 403, 542, 868
mandatory updates, 793
Maps, Windows 10 applications, 180, *181*,
    706
Marketplace, Azure applications, 818
MBAM (Microsoft BitLocker
    Administration and Monitoring),
    693–694
MBR (Master Boot Record), 523, 610
MDM (Mobile Device Management), 511,
    779–780
MDOP (Microsoft Desktop Optimization Pack)
    App-V included in, 824
    installing and configuring UE-V, 351–352
    UE-V included in, 812
MDT (Microsoft Deployment Toolkit)
    configuring, 559–561
    downloading and installing, *556–558*
    overview of, *555–557*

media errors, troubleshooting, 35, 537
media services, Azure applications, 816
Member Of tab (Properties dialog box),
    399–400
member servers, 277, 916
memory
    graphics card requirements, 16
    hardware requirements for, 14,
        517–518
    Hyper-V requirements, 810
    identifying installation problems, 537
    insufficient, 35
    measurement units for, 16
    troubleshooting installation, 35
    virtual, 204
memory cards, configuring, 98–101
metering network usage, 789
Microsoft accounts, 368–369
    integrating, 367–369
    Microsoft Passport and, 392–393
    PIN, 369
    settings, 367–369
Microsoft Application Compatibility
    Toolkit. See ACT (Application
    Compatibility Toolkit)
Microsoft Application Virtualization. See
    App-V (Application Virtualization)
Microsoft Azure. See Azure
Microsoft BitLocker Administration and
    Monitoring (MBAM), 693–694
Microsoft Deployment Toolkit. See MDT
    (Microsoft Deployment Toolkit)
Microsoft Desktop Optimization Pack.
    See MDOP (Microsoft Desktop
    Optimization Pack)
Microsoft Edge. See also web browsers, 222
    configuring, 222
    understanding web browsers, 830
    using InPrivate Browsing and Filtering,
        833–834
    Windows 10 features, 511
    Windows accessories, 707
    Windows applications, 706
Microsoft Exchange devices, configuring
    Intune connector for, 783–784
Microsoft Internet Explorer. See Internet
    Explorer/Internet Explorer 11 (IE11)
Microsoft Intune
    adding users, 771–774
    approving/declining updates, 794

automating update approval, 795, *795*
benefits of, 766
Broadband Tethering, 789–790
configuring alerts, 784, *784*
configuring connector site, 783–784
configuring subscriptions, 767–768
creating device groups, 774–776
creating policies, 777–778
creating user groups, 776–777
dashboard, *765*
data synchronization, 790–791
deploying applications, 785–786
deploying software updates, 792–793
deploying third-party updates, 796, *796*
deploying Windows Store apps to all
    users (deep-link), 788
email, *768*
enrolling devices, 778–783
exam objectives, 799
identifying required updates, 793
managing devices, 764–766
metering network usage, 789
overview of, 763–764
provisioning accounts, **769–784**
reports, **796–798**
review questions and answers, 800–802,
    1011–1012
setting up accounts, 768–771
sideloading apps, 786–788
supporting applications, 785–789
updates, **792–796**
Microsoft Intune Software Publisher, 786–788
Microsoft Management Console. See MMC
    (Microsoft Management Console)
Microsoft Office 365
    installing/managing apps, 825–826
    shared computer activation, 823
Microsoft OneDrive. See OneDrive
Microsoft Passport
    for logging in, 392–393, 863
    Windows 10 features, 510
Microsoft Store. See Windows Store
Microsoft System Center
    about, 334–336
    managing Device Guard via, 395
Microsoft System Center 2012 R2
    Configuration Manager
    adding Intune connector for device
        management, 784
    administrative tasks, 766

advantages of, 334–335
setting up device health attestation,
    397–398
Microsoft Windows 10. *See* Windows 10
migration
    benefit of slow migration, 511–512
    DFS simplifying, 643
    files and settings, **538–541**
    files from XP to Windows 10, 17, 45
    Hyper-V features, 808
    IPv6 integration/migration, 949–951
    printers, 113–114
    profiles, 541–542
Mirror Spaces, Storage Spaces, 651
MLGPOs (Multiple Local Group Policy
    Objects), 417, 883
MMC (Microsoft Management Console).
    See also individual snap-ins, **616–620**
    about, 136–137
    adding snap-ins, 138, *139*, *140*, 140,
        618–620
    administrative tools, *616*
    configuring MMC modes, 138, *618*, 618
    customizing console window, 202
    tree, details pane, and action pane, *617*
    using, 616–618
Mobile Device Management (MDM), 511,
    779–780
mobile devices, securing, 688
Mobile Engagement, Azure applications, 817
Mobility edition, Windows 10, 5, 506
Mobility Enterprise edition, Windows 10,
    5, 506
mobility options, **209–219, 732–740**
    about, 209
    configuring advanced power settings, 738
    configuring hibernation, 738–739
    configuring power button, 213–215, 216
    configuring Windows To Go, 217–219
    customizing power policies, 211–212
    improvements in IPv6, 944
    managing power options, 736–738
    managing power settings from command-
        line, 739
    managing power states, 16, 212–213, 736
    metering power consumption, 217, 740
    offline files and synchronization,
        209–210, 732–734
    overview of, 732
    power plans, 737

power policies, *734–735*
    Powercfg.exe, *739*
Modify permission (NTFS)
    applying NTFS permissions, 251–252
    managing files and folders, 669
    viewing, 254–255, 672–674
monitoring
    deciding what to monitor, 480–481
    Event Viewer, 493–497
    exam objectives, 457
    firewalls, 329, 966
    managing performance properties,
        484–487
    performance, 340
    Performance Monitor, 479–480
    Reliability Monitor, 489
    review questions and answers, 500–502
    saving/analyzing data with Performance
        Logs and Alerts, 487–488
    Task Manager, 489–493
    viewing performance information,
        481–483
mounting offline images for maintenance, 74
Mouse, Control Panel, 198, 723
mouse settings, 714
MpCmdRun.exe utility, 202
MSRA command-line switches, 441–442
multicast addresses
    IPv4, 301, 938
    IPv6, 308, 310, 311, 945, 947–948
multifactor authentication, 437, 694–695,
    902–904
Multiple Local Group Policy Objects
    (MLGPOs), 417, 883
multiple-boot
    configurations, 37–38
    support, **542–544**
Music folder, 711

N

names
    configuring user accounts, 853
    rules and conventions, 855–856
Native Boot, 72
Near Field Proximity (NFP), 295, 742–743
near-field communication (NFC), 742–743
NET USER /? command-line utility, 388
NetBT (NetBIOS over TCP/IP), 299, 936

netsh command, 318, *955*
network adapters. *See* NICs (network interface cards)
Network and Sharing Center
    accessing wireless properties, *931–933*
    configuring static IP addresses, *952–953*
    configuring wireless network settings, *926–927*
    configuring wireless NICs, 287–288
    overview of, 198, 723
    viewing wireless connection status and details, *927–929*
network cables, troubleshooting network adapters, *925*
Network Configuration Operators group, 875
network connections. *See also* TCP/IP (Transmission Control Protocol/Internet Protocol)
    Broadband Tethering, 449–451, *754–755*
    broadcasting and, *294*
    checking speed of, 210, 289
    configuring automatic Wi-Fi, *294*
    configuring connection security rules, *965–966*
    connecting and syncing Wi-Fi devices, *295, 296*
    Connections tab (Internet Options dialog box), 231
    firewall security rules, 328–329
    IE 11 settings, 838
    setting up VPN, 448–449
    TCP/IP and, *936*
    troubleshooting network adapters, *925*
    troubleshooting wireless connectivity, *933–934*
    viewing wireless connection details, 288–291
    viewing wireless connection status and details, *927–929*
    wireless connection options, 291–292
network devices, hardware requirements, *517*
network discovery, 277, *916*
Network group, 876
network interface cards. *See* NICs (network interface cards)
Network List Manager Policies, 886
network load balancing (NLB), 808
network protocol. *See* TCP/IP (Transmission Control Protocol/Internet Protocol)

Network tab, Manage Offline Folders, 734
Network Unlock, BitLocker, 690
networks, **271–332**, 675, **910–917**
    about Windows-based, 238–239, 272, 329
    accessing wireless properties, *931–933*
    activating systems with Active Directory, 76–78
    Active Directory domain structure, *912–914*
    adapters. *See* NICs (network interface cards)
    adding Windows 10 to domain, *957–958*
    APIPA (Automatic Private IP Addressing), *954*
    Azure Active Directory, *914–915*
    Azure applications, 817
    checking connection speed of, 210
    clean installs over, 22
    configuring connection security rules, *965–966*
    configuring dynamic IP addresses, *953–954*
    configuring NICs, *918–924*
    configuring share permissions, *676–678*
    configuring static IP addresses, *952–953*
    configuring TCP/IP, *952*
    configuring VPNs, 447–449
    configuring Windows 10 on, *956–957*
    configuring Windows Firewall, 324–329, **961–966**
    configuring wireless NICs, *925–926*
    configuring wireless security, *929–933*
    configuring wireless settings, *926–927*
    creating home folders, 406
    creating/managing shared folders, *675–676*
    device health attestation for, 397–398
    enabling VLAN, 64
    exam objectives, 271, 329–330, *967*
    failure to access TCP/IP resources for, 36
    HomeGroup. *See* HomeGroups
    identifying installation problems, 537
    inbound/outbound firewall rules, 325, *326, 328, 963–965*
    installing shared network printers, 105
    IP addressing and configuration, *937*
    IPv4 addresses, *937–941*
    IPv6 address assignment, *946–947*
    IPv6 address format, *945*

IPv6 address shortcuts, 309, 946
IPv6 address types, 947–949
IPv6 addresses, **941–945**
IPv6 information commands, 951–952
IPv6 integration/migration, 949–951
joining/sharing HomeGroups, 958–961
managing virtual, 63–64
metering usage, 789
monitoring firewalls, 966
overview of, 910
peer-to-peer, 910–912
perimeter firewalls, 272, 329
review questions and answers, 331–332,
    968–970, 1003, 1014–1015
Safe Mode with, 465
sharing for, 256–257
TCP/IP benefits and features, 935–936
terminology and roles, 277–279, 915–917
testing IP configuration, 954–955
troubleshooting cabling, 287
troubleshooting NICs, 925
troubleshooting TCP/IP, 956
troubleshooting wireless connectivity,
    933–934
types of, 76
understanding network printing, 961
video resources, 330
viewing real-time traffic on, 289–290
viewing wireless connection status and
    details, *927–929*
Windows Firewall with Advanced
    Security, 962–963
wireless, **925–934**
New Group dialog box, *412, 877*
New Simple Volume Wizard, *150, 151*
New User dialog box, 384, 387–388,
    853–854, *857*
NFC (near-field communication), 742–743
NFP (Near Field Proximity), 295, 742–743
NICs (network interface cards), **279–297,
    918–926**
    configuring, 86–87, 280–286, 918–924
    configuring wireless settings, 925–926
    drivers for, 88
    hardware requirements, 14
    overview of, 279–280
    selecting from Device Manager, 280–281
    troubleshooting, 286–287, 296–297, 925
    troubleshooting wireless connectivity, 934
    updating, 283, 286
    wireless, 286–291, 296–297

NLB (network load balancing), 808
nodes, peer-to-peer networks, 272
Notepad, Windows accessories, 707
NTFS
    about, 120, 122–123
    cancelling conversions to, 124
    comparing file system capabilities, *601*
    compression support in, 159–160
    configuring, 124–127, 604–607
    converting FAT32 partitions to, 123–124
    creating new volumes, 630
    designing access control goals, 249–250
    encrypting volumes, 648–649
    features supported by, 121
    managing data compression, 639–640
    overview of, 602–603
    security, 605
    security descriptors, 253–254
NTFS permissions
    applying, 668–671
    applying to applications, 260
    assigning, 254–256
    configuring share permissions, 676–678
    creating/managing shared folders,
        675–676
    determining for copied or moved files,
        256, 674
    determining/viewing, 672–674
    inheritance of, *253*
    managing, 252–253
    share vs., 260
    spanned volumes, *609*
    types of, 250–252
NTFS Security tab (Properties dialog box),
    125, 252, 605

O

objects
    auditing access to, 894
    ownership, 672
    performance objects, 480
octets, 301–302
Office Deployment Tool, 362
offline files
    configuring, *733*
    synchronizing, 732–734
offline images, 74–75
OneDrive, 132–135, **260–264**
    Azure vs., 132–133

cloud-based storage, 612–613
configuring, 133–135, 473, 613–615,
    678–681, 986
features, 132–133, 260, *261*
file location screen, *614*
logging into, *262–264*
login screen, *614*
Open My OneDrive folder screen, *615*
restoring files, 472–473, 985–986
subscriptions, *613*
syncing files, 264, *264*
Welcome screen, *612*
Windows applications, 706
Open Systems Interconnection model. *See*
    OSI (Open Systems Interconnection)
    model
operating systems. *See* OSs (operating
    systems)
Optimize Drives window, Computer
    Management MMC, *166*, *653*, 653
organizational units (OUs), 341
OSI (Open Systems Interconnection) model
    benefits and features of TCP/IP, 935
    encapsulation, 279
    layers of, 287
OSs (operating systems). *See also*
    Windows 10
    choosing install vs. upgrade,
        511–512
    Hyper-V requirements, 810
    Hyper-V support, 808
OUs (organizational units), 341
outbound rules, firewalls, 325–328,
    963–965
ownership, permissions, 672

P

packages
    assigning to users, 342
    deploying, 335–336
    making, 336–337
Paint, Windows accessories, 707
Parity Spaces, Storage Spaces, 651
partitions
    adding new disks, 629
    boot, 21
    configuring basic storage, 127–128
    converting FAT32 to NTFS,
        123–124

creating, 149–151, 629–631
deleting, 154–155, 634–635
Format Partition screen, *631–632*
identifying for installation, *26*
recovery partition, 475
security descriptors, 253–254
setting up, 20–21
system, 21
password administrators, Intune, 771
passwords
    Active Directory domain, 274
    authentication errors, 407
    BitLocker recovery password, 689
    changing, 392, 862
    configuring, 853
    entering PIN, 369
    HomeGroup, 241–243, 323, 685–686
    LGPO policies for, 422–424
    managing with BitLocker, 690
    new user options, 384
    password policies, *887–889*
    Power Options settings, 211
    setting on PC account screen, *28*
    troubleshooting authentication, 872
Patch Tuesdays, 39–40
paths
    creating for home folders, 405
    folder display options for, 246
    UNC, 405
pausing printing, 110–111
PC account screen, Windows 10 installation,
    28, *530*
Peer Name Resolution Protocol (PNRP),
    440, 745
peer-to-peer networks
    overview of, 272–274, 910–912
    types of, 76, 272
People, Windows applications, 706
Performance Log Users group, 875
Performance Monitor, **479–488**
    about, 479–480
    choosing what to monitor, 480–481
    data views in, 481–483
    managing properties, 484–487
    saving and analyzing data, 487–488
    uses for, 488
    viewing data, 481–483
Performance Monitor Users group, 875
performance objects, 480
Performance section, Advanced System
    Settings, 728–729

permissions. *See also specific permissions*
  applying NTFS, 668–671
  configuring share permissions, 676–678
  controlling inheritance, 671
  creating/managing shared folders, 675–676
  determining for copied or moved files, 674
  determining/viewing, 672–674
  errors with local logon, 407
  NTFS file and folder, 249–256
  NTFS vs. share, 260
  privileges vs., 430
  share, 257–258, *259*
personal identification number. *See* PIN (personal identification number)
Personal Identity Verification (PIV), smart cards, 437, 694, 902
personalization, **711–717**
  accessing from Control Panel, 723
  background options, 712
  color options, 712–713
  desktop options, 716
  integrating Microsoft accounts and personalization settings with downloaded apps, 827–829
  integrating Microsoft accounts with corporate accounts, 367–369
  overview of, 198, 711–712
  Personalization screen, *186*, 186, *712*
  preferences, 717
  screen saver, 713–714
  start options, *190*, 190, 715–716
  themes, 189, 714–715
Personalization screen, *712*
Phone And Modem, Control Panel, 198, 723
physical smart cards, 438
picture, for logging in, 393
pictures, for logging in, 863
Pictures folder, user tools, 711
PIN (personal identification number)
  entering, 369
  for logging in, 863
  managing with BitLocker, 690
  rules for, 393
ping command, 318
PIV (Personal Identity Verification), smart cards, 437, 694, 902
Plug and Play. *See* PnP (Plug and Play)
PnP (Plug and Play)
  automatic driver installation with, 88–89
  configuring hardware, 82

  configuring NICs, 918
  troubleshooting hardware, 35–36
PNRP (Peer Name Resolution Protocol), 440, 745
Point-to-Point Tunneling Protocol (PPTP), 448, 753
policies. *See also* GPOs (Group Policy Objects), 885–886
  auditing, 894
  creating Intune policies, 777–778
  setting account-lockout policies, 889–891
  setting audit policies, 892–894
  setting password policies, *887–889*
  user rights, *895–899*
  using account policies, 886–887
  using local policies, 892, *892*
Policies tab (Disk Device Properties screen), *100*
port numbers, 279, 327
power button, 214–215, 737
Power Management, network adapters, 285, *286*, 923–924
Power Options, Control Panel, 198, 723
power plans, **734–740**
  advanced settings, 215, 738
  configuring, 736–737
  configuring from command-line, 216, 739
  configuring power policies, *734–735*
  customizing for desktop and laptop, *211–214*
  managing consumption using battery meter, 217, 740
  managing power states, 736
  power button, 214–215, 737
  setting up hibernation, 213, 215, 738–739
Power Saver plan, 213, 214, 736–737
Power Users group, 410, 875
Powercfg.exe switches, 216, *739*
PowerShell commands
  Azure RemoteApp, 822
  configuring storage with, 169–171
  Device Guard, 395–396
  executing remotely, 350
  list of, 207–208, 1018–1023
PPTP (Point-to-Point Tunneling Protocol), 448, 753
preferences, 717
prefix notation, 309
presentation virtualization
  defined, 60, 346, 581
  Hyper-V, 807

Previous Versions tab (Properties dialog box), *148*
Print Management tools, 112–114
printers. *See also* configuring devices and drivers; Devices And Printers, **101–114**
    adding, *103*, 104
    configuring properties, 105–108
    deleting, 111–112
    drivers for, 101
    installation for shared network, 105
    installing, 102–105
    migrating, 113–114
    opening, 84
    pausing, 110–111
    print device vs., 101
    queueing documents, *108*–111
    See What's Printing display for, *109*
    sharing with HomeGroup, 239
    spooling print jobs to, 101–102
    understanding network printing, 961
    viewing printer context window for, *110*
privacy
    defining IE11 options for, *229–230*
    InPrivate Browsing and Filtering, 227–228, 833–834
    Internet browsers, 224
    Protected Mode for IE11, 226
    using Web Slices, 224–225
    web browsers, 830–831
Privacy tab (Internet Options dialog box), 229–230
privileges
    assigning user rights, 430–434
    auditing, 894
    elevating, 435–436, 900–902
    for executables, 436–437
processors. *See* CPUs (central processing units)
product key
    changing, 38, *39*
    identifying installation problems, 537
    managing activation keys and processes, 340–341
    troubleshooting incorrect, 36
Professional edition, Windows 10
    business experiences, 508–509
    core experiences, 507–508
    overview of, 12–13
    preparing to install, 514–515
    version options, 506
Profile tab (Properties dialog box)
    configuring user profiles, 401–404

setting up home folders, 404–406
    using logon scripts, 404
profiles
    configuring user accounts, 853
    copying, 404, 869
    mandatory, 403
    migrating, 541–542
    roaming, 403
    setting up user profiles, 401–402, 866–869
    super-mandatory, 403–404
Programs And Features, Control Panel, 198–199
Programs and Features, Control Panel, 723–724
Programs tab (Internet Options dialog box), 232
properties
    accessing group, *413–414*
    accessing wireless, *931–933*
    configuring advanced device, 87
    configuring NICs, 919–924
    managing user, 398–406, 863–864
    modifying IE11, 228–232
    setting Internet properties, *197*
    viewing disk, *623*, 623
    viewing volume and local disk, *624–629*
Properties dialog box
    accessing group's properties, *413–414*
    configuring advanced device properties, 87
    Driver tab of, *90*
    inbound rule's, 325, *326*
    IPv4, *300*
    logon scripts, 869
    managing group membership, 864–865
    managing local disks, *144–149*
    managing user properties, 398–406, 863–864
    modifying IE11 properties, 228–232
    navigating from Device Manager to, 86–87
    NICs, 86–87, **280–286**
    NTFS Security tab, *125*, 244–249
    printers, 106–108
    services, *220*, 220, *756*
    setting Internet properties, *197*
    setting up user profiles, 866–869
    Sharing tab for folders, 257–258
    tabs of Performance Monitor, 484–487
    Volumes tab, *143*
    wireless network settings from, 292–295

Properties dialog, disk management
   General tab, 624–625
   Hardware tab, 625–626
   Previous version tab, 626, *628*
   Quotas tab, 628–629
   Security tab, 626, *627*
   Sharing tab, 626, *627*, 675–676
   Tools tab, *625*
   Volumes tab, *623*
Protected Mode for IE11, 226, 833
protocols
   defined, 329
   IP. *See* IP (Internet Protocol)
   TCP/IP. *See* TCP/IP (Transmission
      Control Protocol/Internet Protocol)
   tunneling, 312–314, 448
   used for Secure Channel, 386–387
provisioning packages, 338–339
Public Key Policies, 886
publishing applications, 342
Pvk2Pfx.exe, 825

Q

queue, print documents, 108–111
Quick Migration, Hyper-V features, 808
Quota tab (Properties dialog box), 148, *149*
quotas, disk, 606–607

R

radio frequency (RF), troubleshooting
      wireless connectivity, 296–297, 934
RAID (Redundant Array of Independent
      Disks), 162–163, **649–650**
RAID-0 (striped), 162, 649–650
RAID-1 (mirroring), 162, 650
RAID-5 volume, 163, 650
RAM
   Hyper-V requirements, 810
   Windows 10 architecture, 513
   Windows 10 requirements, *516–517*
RDP (Remote Desktop Protocol), 749–750
Read & Execute permission
   applying, 251, 669–670
   determining/viewing effective
      permissions, 254–255, 672–674
Read permission
   applying, 251

determining/viewing effective
      permissions, 254–255
   share permissions, 259, *259*, 677
Ready to Install screen, Windows 10, *32*, *535*
Real-Time Protection mode (Windows
      Defender), 201
recovery. *See also* Performance Monitor
   advanced backup options, **460–469**, 987
   advanced boot options, 973–974
   Backup and Restore utility, 194, 459,
      469–472
   cleaning up restore points, 991
   creating backups, 982–984
   creating restore points, 990
   creating system image, 987–988
   enabling boot logging, 977–978
   exam objectives, 457, 498–499, 993
   launching WinRE, 466
   overview of, 498, 972–973
   Recycle Bin and, 478–479, 991–992
   restoring files from backup, 985
   restoring files from OneDrive, 472–473,
      985–986
   restoring restore points, 990–991
   restoring system image, 988–989
   review questions and answers, 500–502,
      994–996, 1005–1006, 1015
   start up options, 978–979
   starting in Safe Mode, 974–977
   Startup Repair tool, 469, 982
   Startup Settings screen, *975*
   system images, 467–468, 981–982
   System Protection, 476–478, 989–990
   System Restore, 460, 466–468, 979–981
   techniques, 459–460
   Wbadmin.exe command, 473–474,
      986–987
Recovery, Control Panel, 199, 725
Recovery agents, 647
recovery drives, 467
recovery password, BitLocker, 689
Recovery screen, *463*
recovery services, Azure, 817
Recovery tab (Properties dialog box), 221
Recycle Bin
   on desktop, 711
   restoring files and folders, 478–479,
      991–992
redundancy
   RAID for, 649–650
   Storage Spaces for, 650–651

Redundant Array of Independent Disks. *See* RAID (Redundant Array of Independent Disks)
REGEDIT
  configuring system, 192
  editing Registry, 744
  stopping file conversion, 604
REGEDT32
  editing Registry, 744
  stopping file conversion, 604
Region, Control Panel, 200, 725
Registry
  configuring system, 192
  editing, 743–744
  file virtualization and, 437, 902
  registry keys, *744*
  restore points and, 990
  stopping file conversion, 604
  storing configuration information, 191
Registry and File Virtualization, 437, 902
Reliability Monitor, 489
remote account management, 439–447
  about, 439–440
  executing PowerShell commands
    remotely, 350
  Remote Assistance, 440–444
  Remote Desktop, 440, 444–447
Remote Assistance, **745–749**
  command-line switches, 746–747
  defined, 440
  Easy Connect method, 440–444, 745–749
  initial screen, 748
  overview of, 745
  password screen, 749
remote connections. *See also* RemoteApp
    And Desktop Connections, **744–755**
  Broadband Tethering, 449–451, 754–755
  configuring VPN connections, 752–754
  managing Wi-Fi settings, *755*
  overview of, 744–745
  Remote Assistance, 745–749
  Remote Desktop, 445–447, 750–752
  transparent caching, 449, 754
Remote Desktop
  about, 440, 444–445
  configuring, 749–750
  connection options, 445–447, 750–752
  enabling/disabling, 447, *752*
  uses for, 445
Remote Desktop Connection, Windows
    accessories, 708

Remote Desktop Protocol (RDP), 749–750
Remote Desktop Users group, 875
Remote Settings, System utilities, 728
RemoteApp, Azure. *See* Azure RemoteApp
RemoteApp And Desktop Connections
    Control Panel, 725
  device redirection, 360–362, 822–823
  setting up feeds, 359–360, 821
  using, 200, 357–359
RemoteFX, Hyper-V features, 808
removable storage devices. *See also* USB devices
  configuring, 98–101
  policies for, 155
renaming
  computer, 205
  reassigning drive letters and paths,
    153–154
  user accounts, 239, 256, 391–392,
    861–862
Replicators group, 876
Report view (Performance Monitor),
    482, *483*
Reportnow, WSUS commands, 547
reports, Intune, 796–798
Resetauthorization, WSUS commands, 547
resource metering, Hyper-V features, 808
Resources tab (Network Adapters Properties
    dialog box), *285*, 285
restart, user tools, 711
restore points
  creating/using, 466–467, **476–477**, 990
  defined, 989
  deleting/cleaning up, 478, 991
  restoring, 477, 990–991
restoring data. *See also* Backup and Restore;
    recovery; System Restore
  from backup, 471–472
  creating/using restore points, 466, 467
  restoring restore points, 477
  restoring system image, 475
  WBadmin for, 473–474
Resultant Set of Policy (RSoP), 417, 882
reversible encryption, storing passwords,
    889
RF (radio frequency), troubleshooting
    wireless connectivity, 296–297, 934
roaming profiles. *See also* UE-V (User
    Experience Virtualization)
  migrating, 542
  setting up, 868
  using, 403

roles, Hyper-V, 582
rolling back drivers, 91–92, 283
route print command, *956*
routers, 297
RSoP (Resultant Set of Policy), 417, 882
Run, system utilities, 710

S

Safe Mode
    recovery techniques, 973
    starting in, *461–463*, 974–977
    Startup Settings options, 978–979
    when to use, 459
SAM (Security Account Management)
    database, 76
scanner, Windows Fax and Scan, 708
Scanning Option mode (Windows Defender),
    202
Scanstate.exe, 539, *540–541*
Schannel (Secure Channel), 386–387,
    856–857
schema, Active Directory, 275–276,
    913–914
screen saver, personalization options,
    713–714
scripts, logon, 404, 869
Search tab (Folder Options dialog box),
    248–249
searches
    access control options, 666–667
    file, 238
    Folder Options dialog box, 248–249
    Internet, 224
Secure Boot, Windows 10 features, 397,
    510
Secure Channel (Schannel), 386–387,
    856–857
Secure Socket Tunneling Protocol (SSTP),
    448, 753
Secure Sockets Layer (SSL), 856
security. *See also* data security
    account-lockout policies, 424–426
    advantages of AD domain, 274
    authentication. *See* authentication
    connection rules, 965–966
    Credential Guard, 396–397
    DAC policies, 249
    Device Guard, 393–396
    files and folders, **244–256**, 662–663, 668

GPO and LGPO options, 415–417
HomeGroup networks, **239–244**
identifying required updates, 793
IE11 options, *229*, 229
integration using DFS, 643
Internet browsers, 224
IPsec, 307, 421
IPv6 improvements, 944
NTFS, 124–125, 249–256, 605
passwords and usernames, 385–386
peer-to-peer networks, 273–274
removing SID numbers, 52–53
Secure Channel connections,
    386–387
service packs, 547
troubleshooting wireless, 297
web browsers, 830–831
wireless networks, 291–295, 929–933
Security Account Management (SAM)
    database, 76
Security and Maintenance, Control Panel,
    200, 725
security descriptors, 253–254, 672
security fixes, 547
security groups, 776
security identifiers. *See* SID (security
    identifiers)
security policies
    configuring, 885–886
    using, 646–648
Security tab
    displaying volume's disk properties on,
        146, *147*
    Internet Options dialog box,
        229, 229
    NTFS, *605*
See What's Printing display window, *109*
Select Disks screen, Extend Volume
    Wizard, *636*
Select Users dialog box, *414*
server virtualization
    Hyper-V, 807
    overview of, 346, 581
    virtual machines, 910
    what it is, 60
servers. *See also* Windows Server 2012 R2
    applying DAC to, 249
    defined, 277, 915
    DHCP, 278
    DNS, 277–278, 298
    Hyper-V, 61–63, 582

member servers, 277
peer-to-peer network computers as, 272
standalone, 277
Service Administrator role, Intune, 771
service bus, Azure, 816
Service group, 876
service packs
  identifying required updates, 793
  installing, 42–43, 547
service set identifier. *See* SSID (service set
  identifier)
Service Support Administrators, Intune, 771
services
  auditing access, 894
  configuring, 219–222, **756–758**
  options for managing, 219
  setting properties, 220–221
settings, migrating, 538
Settings window
  options, *730–**732***
  overview of, 206–207
  setting up Microsoft account, *368*
  Settings screen, *206*
  Windows accessories, 708, *709*
setup logs, 538
Setup.exe, *571*, *572–573*
shadow copies, 476, 989
Share Permission dialog box, *677*
share permissions
  applying to applications, 260
  configuring, 258–259, 676–678
  creating and managing shared folders,
    257–258
  NTFS vs., 260
shared computer activation
  Azure RemoteApp, 823
  overview of, 362
shared virtual hard disks, 348
sharing applications, Azure RemoteApp,
  820
sharing files and folders
  about network sharing, 256–257
  comparing NTFS with share permissions,
    260
  creating/managing shared folders,
    675–676
  managing file sharing, 645
  with non-Windows 10 computers, 244
  NTFS permissions, 252–256
  share permissions, 257–258, *259*
  using shared resources, 238–239

Sharing tab (Properties dialog box), 146,
  147, 675–676
Sharing Wizard, 248, 257, 675–676
Shims Infrastructure, fixing older
  applications, **343–344**, 370, 805
shutdown
  managing power states, 736
  user tools, 711
SID (security identifiers)
  Active Directory, 662–663
  assigning, 239, 256
  Manage Offline Folders, 734
  removing, 52–53
  user account, 386, 856
side-by-side installation, USMT installation
  options, *540*
sideloading
  apps into online and offline images,
    826–827
  defined, 364, 825
  deploying applications with Microsoft
    Intune, 786–788
  Intune apps, 786–788
  steps for, 366–367
Sigverif.exe, 97, 98
SIM (System Image Manager)
  configuring components, 580
  creating answer files, 579–580
  for unattended deployment, 571
Simple Network Management Protocol
  (SNMP), 936
Simple Spaces, Storage Spaces, 651
simple volumes
  configuring storage, 128, *128*
  creating, 156, 635–636
  types of dynamic storage, *608*, 608
sites. *See* web sites
SkyDrive. *See* OneDrive
Sleep mode
  managing power states, 212, 736
  power plans, 214
smart cards
  for multifactor authentication, 694–695,
    902–904
  overview of, 437–439
  physical and virtual, 903
SmartScreen Filter, for browser security and
  privacy, 831
snap-ins. *See also* MMC (Microsoft
  Management Console)
  adding, 138, *139*, *140*, 140, 618–620

advantages of, 136–137
Disk Management utility, 135, **140–155**
Print Management, 112–114
snapshots, virtual machines, 808
Snipping Tool, Windows accessories, *182*,
    708
SNMP (Simple Network Management
    Protocol), 936
software. *See* applications
software metering, Intune, 789
Software Restriction Policies, 886
Sound, Control Panel, 200
sound settings, personalization, 714
Source tab (Performance Monitor), 484, *485*
spanned volumes
    creating, 156, 635–636
    overview of, *129*, 129
    types of dynamic storage, 609
special groups, 411–412, 876–877
special permissions (NTFS), 250, 252, 670
Speech Recognition, Control Panel, 200, 725
spooling print jobs, 101–102
SQL databases, Azure applications, 816
SSID (service set identifier)
    about, 293
    accessing wireless properties, 932
    configuring wireless security, 929
    connections if not broadcasting, *294*,
        294
    disabling broadcast of, 291
    troubleshooting, 297, 934
    viewing, 288, *289*, 927–928
SSL (Secure Sockets Layer), 856
SSTP (Secure Socket Tunneling Protocol),
    448, 753
standalone servers, 277
standalone serves, 916
standard user accounts. *See* user accounts
Standard User Analyzer (SUA), 805
Start menu
    adding HomeGroup to, 242, *244*
    All Apps section, *178*
    configuring desktop environment,
        703–704
    configuring startup options, 345
    default, 703–704
    personalization, 715–716
    Windows 10 features, *511*
Start screen, *190*, 190
Startup And Recovery, Advanced System
    Settings, 729

Startup Repair tool
    recovery techniques, 459, 973
    troubleshooting boot issues, 982
    using, 469
Startup Settings. *See also* advanced boot
    options
    options, 978–979
    screen, *461*, 465–466, *975*
static IP addresses, configuring TCP/IP, 315,
    952–953
status codes, Disk Management utility,
    158–159
Sticky Notes, Windows accessories, *182*, 708
storage. *See also* Disk Management; Storage
    Spaces
    Azure applications, 816
    basic storage, 127–128
    cloud-based storage, **131–135**
    data compression, 159–162
    disk storage. *See* disk storage
    dynamic storage, *128–130*
    exam objectives, 119, 171, 172
    file-system configuration, **120–127**
    GUID disk-partitioning, 120, 130
    managing, 155–158
    PowerShell, 169–171
    RAID, 162–163
    review questions and answers, 173–174,
        1000–1001
    setting quotas, 126–127
    setting up disk storage, **127–135**
    tools for disk maintenance, 165–169
    troubleshooting Disk Management,
        158–159
    using Disk Management utility, 135,
        140–155
    video resources, 171
Storage Spaces
    about, 163–165, 200–201
    accessing from Control Panel, *164*, 651, 725
    creating storage pools, 164–165, *652*
    exam essentials, 657
    overview of, **650–652**
    review questions and answers, 658–660,
        1008–1009
Store. *See* Windows Store
striped volumes
    creating, 156, 635–636
    overview of, 129–130
    types of dynamic storage, 609–610
SUA (Standard User Analyzer), 805

subnet masks
   defined, 302
   IPv4, 302–304, *939–941*
   IPv6, 309
subscriptions
   event alerts, 497
   Intune, 767–768
super-mandatory profiles, 403–404,
      868–869
switches, managing virtual, 64, 584–585
symmetric multiprocessors, Hyper-V
      support, 808
Sync Center, *210*
   Control Panel, 725
   data synchronization, **790–791**
   offline files and synchronization, 732–734
   overview of, 201
synchronization. *See also* Sync Center
   configuring, 209–210
   connected Wi-Fi devices, 295, *296*
   with devices, *743*
   files from OneDrive, 264, *264*
Sysprep.exe. *See* System Preparation Tool
system events, auditing, 894
System group, 877
System icon
   changing computer name, 729
   changing virtual memory, 729–730
   Control Panel, 726
   features accessed via, 201, 203–206,
      727–729
System Image Manager. *See* SIM (System
      Image Manager)
System Image Recovery tool, 988–989
system images
   backups from, 467–468, 981–982
   creating, 474–475, 987–988
   restoring, 475, 988–989
   system restore and, *981*
system partition, 21, 523
System Preparation Tool, **50–54**
   about, 50–53, 78
   advantages/disadvantages, 54
   command-line options, *574*
   disk imaging, **565–569**, 573–574
   preparing for Windows 10 installation,
      574–575
   preparing system for imaging, 575
   removing SID numbers, 52–53
   switches, 52
   for unattended deployment, 571

System Protection, **989–992**
   cleaning up restore points, 478, 991
   creating/using restore points, 466–467,
      476–477, 990
   enabling/disabling, 466, 979–980
   overview of, 728, 989–990
   restoring restore points, 477, 990–991
System Restore
   enabling System Protection, 466
   opening, 467
   procedures, *466–468*
   recovery techniques, 973
   understanding, 979–981
   when to use, 460
system utilities, 710–711

T

tablets. *See* computers
Task Manager
   about, 185
   accessing, 489
   system utilities, 710–711
   tabs, 489–493
Taskbar
   configuring, *192*, 201
   pinning web sites to, 223, 830
Taskbar And Navigation, Control Panel,
      201, 726
TCP (Transmission Control Protocol), 298
TCP/IP (Transmission Control Protocol/
      Internet Protocol), **297–323, 935–956**
   about, 297–298
   APIPA (Automatic Private IP Addressing),
      316–317, 954
   assigning IPv6 addresses, 946–947
   assigning static addresses, 315
   benefits and features, 298–299, 935–936
   commands, 318–319
   configuring, 952
   configuring dynamic IP addresses,
      953–954
   configuring static IP addresses, 952–953
   DHCP for dynamic IP addresses, 316
   failure to access, 36
   identifying installation problems, 537
   IP addressing and configuration, 937
   IPv4 addresses, 300–304, *937–941*
   IPv6 address format, 945
   IPv6 address shortcuts, 946

IPv6 address types, 947–949
IPv6 addresses, 941–945
IPv6 addressing, 315
IPv6 information commands, 951–952
IPv6 integration/migration, 949–951
testing IP configuration, 317–318,
    954–955
troubleshooting, 319, 956
Telnet
    installing, 724
    using, 199, 724
templates, quota, 126
tenant administrators, Intune accounts,
    770–771
Teredo
    accessing IPv6 address space, 308, 945
    Easy Connect method and, 440, 441
    IPv6 address prefixes, 312
    IPv6 tunneling and, 313–314, 950
Tethering. See Broadband Tethering
themes, personalization options, 714–715
third-party updates, managing with Intune,
    796, 796
This PC, system utilities, 185, 711
threats, Device Guard protection, 394
time synchronization, Control Panel, 720
TLS (Transport Layer Security), 856
Tools tab (Properties dialog box), 145
TPM (Trusted Platform Module)
    changing settings, 688
    smart cards and, 903–904
    storing BitLocker security startup key,
        688–689
    technology, 438–439
tracert command, 318, 955
Transmission Control Protocol (TP), 298
Transmission Control Protocol/Internet
    Protocol. See TCP/IP (Transmission
    Control Protocol/Internet Protocol)
transparent caching, 449, 754
Transport Layer Security (TLS), 856
Troubleshoot screen, Choose An Option, 463
troubleshooting. See also Advanced Boot
    Options; services
    authentication, 871–872
    device installation, 85–86
    disabling Secure Boot, 397
    disk errors, 638–639
    failed upgrades, 20
    following vendor's install
        recommendations, 94–95

identifying installation problems, 537–538
installation, 35–37
network cabling, 287
NICs, 286–287
nonreproducible device driver errors, 88
status codes for Disk Management,
    158–159
TCP/IP, 319, 956
using installation log files, 538
Windows To Go USB drives, 218
wireless networks and cards, 296–297
Troubleshooting, Control Panel, 201, 726
trust relationship, between domains, 913
Trusted Platform Module. See TPM (Trusted
    Platform Module)
trusts, 275
tunneling
    defined, 447, 949–950
    IPv6 tunneling, 312–314
    protocols, 448, 752–753

U

UAC (User Account Control), **899–902**
    about, 435
    Control Panel options for, 383
    elevating user privileges, 435–436,
        900–902
    enabling elevated privileges for
        executables, 436–437
    exam objectives, 905
    managing user accounts, 852–853
    overview of, 899–900
    Registry and File Virtualization, 902
    review questions and answers, 906–907,
        1013
    screen for, 31
UDP (User Datagram Protocol), 298
UE-V (User Experience Virtualization),
    811–813
    components, 811–812
    configuring, 350–352
    installing, 812–813
    overview of, 811
unattended installations. See deploying
    installations; enterprise installations;
    System Preparation Tool
unicast addresses
    defined, 301
    IPv4, 938

IPv6, 308, 310–311, 945, 947
subnet masks and, 302–304
uninstalling/reinstalling device drivers,
    93–94, 283
unsigned drivers, 98, 115
updates, **39–43**
    device driver, 88, 91
    exam objectives, 44, 45
    installing service packs, 42–43
    NIC drivers, 283, 286
    servicing options for, 40
    Windows Store updates, 43, *43*
    Windows Update, 41–42, **544–546**
updates, managing with Intune,
    792–796
    approving/declining, 794
    automating approval, 795, *795*
    deploying third-party, 796, *796*
    identifying required, 793
    overview of, 792–793
upgrade, to Windows 10, **519–523**
    analyzing applications prior to, 343
    checklist for, 19–20, 521–522
    comparing with clean install, 17, 512,
        519–520
    compatibility issues, 521
    desktop screen, *536*
    DVD setup screen, *533*
    exam objectives for, 44, 45
    installation status screen, *535*
    managing failed, 20, 522–523
    performing, **532–536**
    preparing for, 520–521
    Ready to Install screen, *535*
    steps for, **30–35**
    upgrade options, 17–18
    User Account Control screen, *534*
    using USB, 30
    Welcome screen, *536*
    Windows 7 and 8 options, 17–18, 45
Upgrade Analytics tool, 343
USB devices. *See also* configuring devices
    and drivers
    clean install from, 22, 44
    compatible with Windows To Go, 217
    configuring as input/output device,
        98–101
    configuring device redirection, 361–362
    configuring for Windows To Go, 219
    configuring Windows To Go, 740–742
    upgrades from, 30

User Account Control. *See* UAC (User
    Account Control)
User Account, Control Panel, 201, 726
User Account Control screen, *534*
user accounts. *See also* usernames, **375–398,**
    846–871
    account policies, 886–887
    account-lockout policies, 889–891
    adding to groups, 408, 414
    adding users to Intune, 771–774
    assigning packages, 342
    assigning user rights, 430–434, 895–899
    audit policies, 892–894
    auditing account management, 894
    auditing failed resource access, 427–430
    built-in accounts, 847–849
    changing passwords, 392, 862
    creating new local user, 857–858
    creating new users, 383–385, 853–854
    deleting, 389–391, 407, 859–861
    disabling, 388–389, 407, 858–859
    domain accounts, 379, 849
    elevating privileges, 435–436
    exam objectives, 451–452, 905
    features, *377, 377*
    local accounts, 379, 387–388, 849
    local policies, 892, *892*
    Local Users and Groups utility, 850–852
    logging off, 380, 850
    logon scripts, 404, 869
    managing group membership, 864–865
    managing properties, 398–406, 863–864
    options, 383
    overview of, 376–377, 846
    password policies, *887–889*
    permissions, 254–256
    personalizing desktop and screen savers, 191
    Remote Assistance, 440–444
    remote management, 439–447
    renaming, 239, 256, 391–392, 861–862
    restricting hardware removal, 155
    review questions and answers, 906–907,
        1013
    Secure Channel communication, 856–857
    security descriptors, 253–254
    setting up home folders, 870–871
    setting up Intune users and groups,
        769–770
    setting up profile path, 401–402
    SID (Security Identification), 386, 856
    smart cards, 437–439

storage space quotas, 126–127
troubleshooting authentication, 406–407,
   871–872
types of, 377, 847, *847*
User Account Control, 852–853
user profiles, 866–869
username rules and conventions, 855–856
workgroup, 279–280, 379–380, 849
Workplace Join tool, 850
User Datagram Protocol (UDP), 298
User Experience Virtualization. *See* UE-V
   (User Experience Virtualization)
User Profiles
Advanced System Settings, 729
migrating, *541*
user rights
assigning, 895–899
troubleshooting authentication, 872
User State Migration Tool (USMT),
   538–541
usernames. *See also* user accounts
Active Directory domain, 274
rules and conventions, 385–386, 855–856
setting on PC account screen, *28*
troubleshooting authentication, 407, 872
user account options for, 384
users. *See also* user accounts
deploying apps to all users (deep-link),
   788
ownership and security descriptors, 672
PIN and password management with
   BitLocker, 690
tools, 711
Users group, 411, 876
USMT (User State Migration Tool), **538–541**

V

VAMT (Volume Activation Management
   Tool), 340–341
variable length subnet masking (VLSM), 309
versions, Windows 10
business experiences, 6–8
Education, 11
Enterprise, 13–14
feature overview, 5–6, 8–9
Home, 12
list of, 4–5, 506
Professional, 12–13
Windows 7 and 8 upgrade options, 17–18

VGA Mode, Startup Settings options, 978
VHDs (virtual hard disks), **585–588**
about, 64
applying disk image to, 73
booting from, 71–74
changing, 66, 587–588
creating, 65, 586–587
exporting data for, 71
Hyper-V features, 809
managing, 585–586
Native Boot of MBR partitioned, 72–73
shared, 348
types of, *65*, *586*
video
authorization and authentication, 452
configuring devices and drivers, 115
data security, 265
enterprise installations, 78
installation, 44, 370
networks, 330
storage configuration, 171
upgrading drivers, 18
Windows 10 environments, 232–233
video adapters
hardware requirements, 14, *517–518*
memory requirements, 15–16
Videos folder, user tools, 711
View tab (Folder Options dialog box),
   245–248
virtual hard disks. *See* VHDs (virtual hard
   disks)
virtual LANs (VLANs), 64
virtual machines. *See* VMs (virtual
   machines)
virtual memory, 205, 729–730
virtual private networks (VPNs), 447–449,
   752–754
virtual smart cards, 438–439
virtualization. *See also* Hyper-V; VMs
   (virtual machines)
App-V (Application Virtualization), *824*,
   824
Credential Guard protection, 397
managing virtual switches, 584–585
Registry and File Virtualization, 902
types of, 60–61
User Experience Virtualization. *See* UE-V
   (User Experience Virtualization)
what it is, 581
Visual Studio Team Services, Azure
   applications, 817

VLANs (virtual LANs), 64
VLSM (variable length subnet masking), 309
VMs (virtual machines). *See also* Hyper-V,
 66–75
 Azure applications, 816
 creating, 66–68, 588–590
 enabling VLANs, 64
 Hyper-V features, 808–809
 installing Hyper-V Integration
  Components for, 68–69
 managing checkpoints, 69–70, 591–592
 moving, 71, 592–593
 types of virtualization, 60–61, 910
Volume Activation Management Tool
 (VAMT), 340–341
volumes
 adding new disks, 629
 creating, 150–151, 629–631
 creating extended, 636–637
 creating simple, spanned, and striped,
  635–636
 deleting, 154–155, 634–635
 encrypting, 648–649
 extending and shrinking, 156–157
 simple, *128*, 128, 156
 spanned, *129*, 129, 156
 striped, 129–130, 156
 viewing properties of, 143, *143*, *623*,
  624–629
Volumes tab (Properties dialog box), *143*
VPNs (virtual private networks), 447–449,
 752–754

W

Wbadmin.exe command
 backups and restores, 473–474, 986–987
 switches, *987*
WDK (Windows Driver Kit), building apps
 and placing in Windows Store, 825
WDS (Windows Deployment Services)
 advantages/disadvantages, 563–564
 automating deployment, *563–565*
 overview of, **563**
 WDSUTIL command-line options, 563–564
WDSUTIL, 564–565
Web Apps, Azure applications, 816
web browsers. *See also* Internet Explorer/
 Internet Explorer 11 (IE11), **222–232,**
 830–839

about Windows, 222
accessing OneDrive, 260, *261*
Compatibility View, 225, 226, 832–833
configuring IE 11, 834–839
Cortana, 222–223
customizing controls of, 223, 830–831
exam objectives, 840
IE 11 Protected Mode, 833
InPrivate Browsing and Filtering,
 833–834
overview of, 830
pinning sites to Taskbar, 223
review questions and answers, 841–843,
 1012
searchable Address bar, 224
security and privacy, 224
working with web slices, 224–225,
 831–832
web sites
 pinning to Taskbar, 223, 830
 working with Web Slices, 224–225
web slices, working with, 224–225,
 831–832
Welcome screen
 customizing, *52*
 installing Windows 10, *33*
 OneDrive, 132
 upgrade to Windows 10, *536*
WFAS (Windows Firewall with Advanced
 Security). *See also* Windows Firewall
 configuring firewalls, 324–325
 configuring local security policies, 886
 networks and, 962–963
Wi-Fi. *See also* wireless NICs (network
 interface cards)
 configuring Wi-Fi Direct, 742–743
 configuring wireless NICs, 287–288
 connecting if SSID not broadcasting, *294*,
  294
 networks. *See* wireless networks
 setting properties, 292–295
 syncing devices, *295*, *296*
 troubleshooting, 296–297
 viewing Internet connections, 288–291
Wi-Fi Direct, 742–743
Wi-Fi Properties dialog box
 Networking tab, 290
 setting wireless properties, 292–295
Wi-Fi Protected Access. *See* WPA/WPA2
Wi-Fi Status dialog box, *293*
WinAppDeployCmd.exe tool, 336–337

Window Activation
  installing Windows 10, *545*
  reducing software piracy, 544
Windows 7
  AppLocker feature, 813
  Azure data size availability, *612*
  Backup and Restore utility, 720
  BitLocker features, 691–692
  dual-booting, 543
  exam objectives for, 45
  upgrade steps, **30–34**
  upgrade to Windows 10, 17–18, 45,
    519–520, 532–533
Windows 8
  dual-booting, 543
  exam objectives for, 45
  improvements made in Windows 10, 507
  Microsoft Azure data size availability, *611*
  upgrade steps, **30–34**
  upgrade to Windows 10, 17–18, 45,
    519–520, 533–536
Windows 10
  adding to domain, 957–958
  application compatibility with, 19
  Application Deployment tool, 336–337
  architecture for, 10–11
  basic storage for, 127–128
  BitLocker features, 691–693
  business experiences for, 6–8
  checklist for upgrading, 19–20
  configuring on network. *See* configuring
    Windows 10, on networks
  deploying and configuring with ICD,
    55–58, 338–339
  deprecated features, 10
  device drivers required, 17
  Device Guard protection for, 393–396
  DHCP with, 316
  enabling/disabling network discovery,
    277
  environments. *See* configuring Windows
    10 environment
  feature overview, 5–6, 8–9
  installation. *See* installing Windows 10
  IoT Core operating system, 5
  recovery techniques for, 459–460
  returning from Advanced Boot options
    to, 466
  screen after installation, *34*
  screen for, *29*
  static TCP/IP addresses for, 315
  updating, 39–43
  upgrade. *See* upgrade, to Windows 10
  user accounts for, 376–379
  versions, 4–5, 11–14
  XP file migration to, 17, 45
Windows 10 Education edition, 11
Windows 10 Recovery Environment
    (WinRE), 466
Windows Activation, 38–39, 728
Windows Assessment and Deployment Kit.
    See ADK (Assessment and Deployment
    Kit)
Windows Defender, Control Panel, 201–202,
    726
Windows Deployment Services. *See* WDS
    (Windows Deployment Services)
Windows Driver Kit (WDK), building apps
    and placing in Windows Store, 825
Windows Edition, System utilities, 728
Windows Fax and Scan, Windows
    accessories, 708
Windows Firewall, **324–329, 961–966**
  about, 272, 324, *324*
  accessing from Control Panel, 202,
    727
  with advanced security. *See* WFAS
    (Windows Firewall with Advanced
    Security)
  configuring, 961–962
  connection security rules, 328–329,
    965–966
  inbound/outbound rules, 325, *326–328*,
    963–965
  monitoring firewalls, 329, 966
  scenarios using, 329
  UAC permissions for accessing, 901
Windows Hello, 393, 863
Windows Imaging and Configuration
    Designer. *See* ICD (Imaging and
    Configuration Designer)
Windows Performance Analyzer (WPA),
    340
Windows Performance Recorder (WPR),
    340
Windows Performance Toolkit, 340
Windows Phone, enrolling in Intune, 779
Windows Remote Assistance screens. *See*
    Remote Assistance
Windows Server 2012 R2
  Azure data size availability, *611–612*
  BitLocker features, 691–692

connecting to domain, 320–321
DFS (Distributed File System), 642
domain controllers for, 277
domain-based networks, 912–914
GPO deployments using, 341–342
installing Hyper-V in, 61–62, 348–350, 582
RemoteApp connection feeds for, 359–360
setting up Active Directory, 276
Windows Server Update Services. *See* WSUS (Windows Server Update Services)
Windows Store, 363–369, 825–829
  deploying apps to all users (deep-link), 788
  installing applications from, 363–364
  installing applications using Office 365 and, 364–365, 825–826
  integrating Microsoft accounts and personalization settings, 827–829
  overview, 334
  review questions and answers, 841–843, 1012
  settings, *826*
  sideloading applications, 364, 366–367
  sideloading apps into online and offline images, 826–827
  updates, 43, *43*
  Windows accessories, 708
Windows Store for Business, 364, 511
Windows System Image Manager. *See* SIM (System Image Manager)
Windows To Go
  about, 202, 217
  accessing from Control Panel, 727
  configuring, 740–742
  configuring USB drive for, 219
  host requirements, 218–219, *741*
  USB non-compatible error, *740*
Windows Update utility, **39–43**
  about, 39
  Check For Updates, *42*, 42
  configuring, 41
  installing Windows 10, **544–546**
  options, 39–40
  Windows applications, 706
Windows User's tools, 185
Windows Vista migrations, 17
Windows XP migrations, 17, 45
WinRE (Windows 10 Recovery Environment), 466

wipe-and-load installation, 540
wireless networks. *See also* Wi-Fi, **925–934**
  accessing wireless properties, *931–933*
  configuring wireless NICs, 287–288, 925–926
  configuring wireless security, 929–933
  configuring wireless settings, 926–927
  Networking tab, 290
  troubleshooting wireless connectivity, 933–934
  viewing network connection details, 288–291, 927–929
wireless NICs (network interface cards)
  configuring, 287–288, 925–926
  troubleshooting, 296–297
  viewing network connection details, 288–291, 927–929
wireless routers, 297, 934
Work Folders, Control Panel, 202, 727
Workgroup networks
  defined, 76, 239
  as peer-to-peer network, 272–274, 910
workgroup user accounts, 279–280, 379–380, 849
Workplace Join, 380, 850
WPA (Windows Performance Analyzer), 340
WPA/WPA2
  configuring wireless security, 929
  enabling/disabling, 291
  selecting security type for, 294, *295*
WPR (Windows Performance Recorder), 340
Write permission (NTFS), 251, *252*, 254–255
WSUS (Windows Server Update Services)
  command-line options, 546–547
  managing updates with, 41, 792
  receiving updates via, 546
wuapp.exe, 546

X

XPS (XML Paper Specification), document signing, 694
XPS viewer, Windows applications, 707

Z

zipped folders, 161–162

Comprehensive Online Learning Environment

Register on Sybex.com to gain access to the comprehensive online interactive learning environment and test bank to help you study for your MCSA Windows 10 certification.

The online test bank includes:

- **Assessment Test** to help you focus your study to specific objectives
- **Chapter Tests** to reinforce what you've learned
- **Practice Exams** to test your knowledge of the material
- **Digital Flashcards** to reinforce your learning and provide last-minute test prep before the exam
- **Searchable Glossary** to define the key terms you'll need to know for the exam
- **Videos** to guide you through chapter exercises

Go to `http://www.wiley.com/go/sybextestprep` to register and gain access to this comprehensive study tool package.

30% off On-Demand IT Video Training from ITProTV

ITProTV and Sybex have partnered to provide 30% off a premium annual or monthly membership. ITProTV provides a unique, custom learning environment for IT professionals and students alike, looking to validate their skills through vendor certifications. On-demand courses provide over 1,000 hours of video training with new courses being added every month, while labs and practice exams provide additional hands-on experience. For more information on this offer and to start your membership today, visit `http://itpro.tv/sybex30/`.